SECOND EDITION

Physicians' Desk Reference®

For Nonprescription Drugs

1981

Publisher • CHARLES E. BAKER, Jr.

Director of Production
JEROME M. LEVINE

Managing Editor
BARBARA B. HUFF

Medical Consultant
IRVING M. LEVITAS, M.D.

Manager of Production Services
ELIZABETH H. CARUSO

Index Editor
BARBARA R. DePOWEL

Editorial Assistants
SUSAN CVELICH
F. EDYTHE PATERNITI

Contributing Editors
CHARLOTTE ISLER
HARLAND WADE

Business Manager
EDWARD R. BARNHART

Administrative Assistant
DIANE M. WARD

Director of Printing
RALPH G. PELUSO

Art Director
THOMAS DARNSTEADT

Circulation Director
MARC ROSS

Fulfillment Manager
JAMES SCIURBA

Research Director
JAMES D. GLICKMAN

Representatives
K. DOUGLAS CHENEY
JOHN R. MARMERO

Copyright ©1981 by Litton Industries, Inc. Published by Medical Economics Company, a Litton division at Oradell, N.J. 07649.
All rights reserved. None of the content of this publication may be reproduced, stored in a retrieval system, or transmitted in any
form or by any means (electronic, mechanical, photocopying, recording, or otherwise) without the prior written permission of the
publisher.

Officers of Medical Economics Company: President, Carroll V. Dowden; Executive Vice Presidents: H. Mason Fackert, Bartlett R. Rhoades;
Senior Vice Presidents: Charles E. Baker, Jr., Thomas J. McGill; Vice Presidents: Jack E. Angel, Leonard H. Habas, Administration; Kathleen A. Starke, Personnel; Robert T. Smith, Finance; Secretary, Jacob Milkens; Treasurer, Charles O. Bennewitz.

ISBN 0-87489-962-1

Foreword to the Second Edition

PHYSICIANS' DESK REFERENCE For NONPRESCRIPTION DRUGS has been designed to satisfy a growing need for medical information concerning the large number of nonprescription or OTC (over-the-counter) drugs now available.

The PHYSICIANS' DESK REFERENCE For NONPRESCRIPTION DRUGS is published annually by Medical Economics Company, with the cooperation of the manufacturers whose products are described in the Product Information Section. Its purpose is to make available essential information on nonprescription drugs.

The function of the Publisher is the compilation, organization, and distribution of this information. Each product description has been prepared by the manufacturer, and edited and approved by the manufacturer's medical department, medical director, and/or medical consultant. In organizing and presenting the material in PHYSICIANS' DESK REFERENCE For NONPRESCRIPTION DRUGS, the Publisher is providing all the information made available to PHYSICIANS' DESK REFERENCE For NONPRESCRIPTION DRUGS by manufacturers. Besides the information given here, additional information on any product may be obtained from the manufacturer. In making this material available it should be understood that the Publisher is not advocating the use of any product described herein.

CHARLES E. BAKER, JR.
Publisher

HOW TO USE PDR

If you want to find . . .	And you already know . . .	Here's where to look . . .
the brand name of a product	the manufacturer's name	White Section: Manufacturers' Index
	its generic name	Yellow Section: Active Ingredients Index*
the manufacturer's name	the product's brand name	Pink Section: Product Name Index*
	the product's generic name	Yellow Section: Active Ingredients Index*

essential product information, such as:
    active ingredients
    indications
    actions
    warnings
    drug interaction
    precautions
    symptoms & treatment
      of oral overdosage
    dosage & administration
    how supplied
	the product's brand name	Pink Section: Product Name Index*

	the product's generic name	Yellow Section: Active ingredients Index*
a product with a particular chemical action	the chemical action	Yellow Section: Active Ingredients Index*
a product with a particular active ingredient	the active ingredient	Yellow Section: Active Ingredients Index*
a similar acting product	the product classification	Blue Section: Product Category Index*
generic name of a brand name product	the product's brand name	Pink Section: Product Name Index. Generic name will be found under "Active Ingredients" in Product Information Section.

In the Pink, Blue and Yellow Sections, the page numbers following the product name refer to the pages in the Product Identification Section where the product is pictured and the Product Information Section where the drug is comprehensively described.

Contents

INDEX SECTION

Manufacturers' Index (White)—The manufacturers appearing in this index have provided information concerning their products in either the Product Information or Product Identification Sections. Included in this index are the names and addresses of manufacturers, individuals or departments to whom you may address inquiries, a partial list of products as well as emergency telephone numbers, wherever available. 1

Product Name Index (Pink)—Products are listed in alphabetical order by brand name. Page numbers have been included to assist you in locating additional information on described products. **101**

Product Category Index (Blue)—In this section described products are listed according to their appropriate product categories. The headings and sub-headings have been determined by the OTC Review process of the U.S. Food and Drug Administration. **201**

Active Ingredients Index (Yellow)—Products described in the Product Information Section are listed alphabetically in this section. The headings under which specific products are listed have been determined by the OTC Review process of the U.S. Food and Drug Administration. **301**

PRODUCT IDENTIFICATION SECTION **401**
Capsules, tablets and packaging are shown in color as an aid to identification. Products are shown under company headings, and are not necessarily in alphabetical order since some manufacturers prefer to show their products in groups.

PRODUCT INFORMATION SECTION **501**
An alphabetical arrangement, by manufacturer, of nonprescription drugs which are described as to action, uses, administration and dosage, precautions, the form in which supplied and other information concerning their use, including common names and chemical names.

MINOR HEALTH PROBLEMS 667

A guide to self-treatment of minor ailments. Descriptions of symptoms which can generally be relieved by using products obtainable without a prescription.

DIRECTORY OF POISON CONTROL CENTERS 675

A listing of Poison Control Centers compiled from information furnished by the National Clearinghouse of Poison Control Centers. For ease of reference centers are arranged alphabetically by state and city.

FIRST AID FOR POSSIBLE POISONING 676

A quick reference guide to first aid treatment in cases of accidental poisoning.

GLOSSARY 691

Explanation and definitions of terms commonly used in the health field.

PERSONAL HEALTH DIARY 725

Handy forms for maintaining personal health records

Manufacturers' Index

Section 1

The manufacturers whose names appear in this index have provided information concerning their products in either the Product Information or Product Identification Sections. It is through their patronage that PHYSICIANS' DESK REFERENCE For NONPRESCRIPTION DRUGS is made available to you.

Included in this index are the names and addresses of manufacturers, individuals or departments to whom you may address inquiries, a partial list of products as well as emergency telephone numbers wherever available.

The symbol ◆ indicates that the product is shown in the Product Identification Section.

ABBOTT LABORATORIES   405, 502
Consumer Products Division
North Chicago, IL 60064
    (312) 937-7900
OTC Products Available
◆Clear Eyes Eye Drops
Ear Drops by Murine
    (See Murine Ear Wax Removal
    System/Murine Ear Drops)
◆Murine Ear Wax Removal
    System/Murine Ear Drops
◆Murine Plus Eye Drops
◆Murine Regular Formula Eye Drops
◆Selsun Blue Lotion

**ABBOTT LABORATORIES —
ABBOTT PHARMACEUTICALS**   503
North Chicago, IL 60064
    Address inquiries to:
Medical Director   (312) 937-6100
    Distribution Centers
ATLANTA
    Stone Mountain, GA 30302
    P.O. Box 5049   (404) 491-7190
CHICAGO
    Abbott Park
    North Chicago, IL 60064
    P.O. Box 68   (312) 937-5153
DALLAS
    Dallas, TX 75265
    P.O. Box 225295   (214) 398-1350
DENVER
    Denver, CO 80217
    P.O. Box 5466   (303) 399-7576
HONOLULU
    Honolulu, HI 96819
    2815 Kilihau Street (808) 833-1691

LOS ANGELES
    Los Angeles. CA 90060
    60162 Terminal Annex
    (213) 921-0321
MINNEAPOLIS
    Minneapolis, MN 55440
    P.O. Box 271   (612) 599-5666
PHILADELPHIA
    King of Prussia, PA 19406
    920 Eighth Ave., East
    (215) 265-9100
SEATTLE
    Seattle, WA 98124
    P.O. Box 24064   (206) 433-0164
    OTC Products Available
Optilets-500
Optilets-M-500
Surbex-750 with Iron
Surbex-750 with Zinc
Surbex-T

ADRIA LABORATORIES INC.   503
5000 Post Road
Dublin, OH 43017
(includes products formerly marketed
by Warren-Teed Laboratories)
    Mailing Address:
P.O. Box 16529
Columbus, OH 43216
    Address inquiries to:
Medical Department   (614) 764-8100
    OTC Products Available
Modane Bulk
Modane Soft
Modane Tablets & Liquid
Myoflex Creme

ALCON/bp   405, 504
Alcon Laboratories, Inc.
6201 South Freeway
P.O. Box 1959
Fort Worth, TX 76101

    OTC Products Available
◆Adapettes
◆BoilnSoak
◆Clens
◆Flex-Care
◆Preflex
◆Soaclens

**ALLERGAN
PHARMACEUTICALS, INC.**   405, 506
2525 Dupont Drive
Irvine, CA 92713
    Address inquiries to:
Customer Service   (714) 752-4500
    For Medical Emergencies Contact:
Medical Research Dept.
    (714) 752-4500
    OTC Products Available
◆Liquifilm Tears
◆Prefrin Liquifilm
◆Tears Plus

**ALMAY HYPOALLERGENIC
COSMETICS &
TOILETRIES**   406, 506
Almay Inc.
850 Third Avenue
New York, NY 10022
    Address inquiries to:
Professional Service Dept.
Apex, NC 27502   (919) 362-7422
    OTC Products Available
Cheq Antiperspirant/Deodorant Spray
Cheq Extra-Dry Antiperspirant/
    Deodorant Spray (Aerosol)
Cheq Roll-On Antiperspirant/Deodorant
Cheq Soft Powder Extra Dry
    Antiperspirant Spray (Aerosol)
Chip Resistant Top Coat
◆Clean and Gentle Daily Shampoo

(◆ Shown in Product Identification Section)

Clean and Gentle Oil-Free Conditioner
Clear Nail Enamel
Cold Cream
Cold Cream Soap for Normal,
　Combination and Dry Skin
Color Rich Eyeshadow (Wet or Dry)
◆Counter Balance Clear Facial Cleanser
Counter Balance Facial Soap for Oily
　Skin
Counter Balance Fluffy Facial Cleanser
◆Counter Balance Oil-Free Moisturizer
◆Counter Balance Pore Lotion
Cover-up Stick - light, medium, dark
Cuticle Treatment Oil
◆Deep Mist Cleanser
◆Deep Mist Cleansing Lotion
Deep Mist Eye Cream
Deep Mist Gentle Gel Mask
◆Deep Mist Mild Skin Freshener
Deep Mist Moisture Cream
◆Deep Mist Moisture Lotion
Deep Mist Moisture and Replenishing
　Lotion
◆Deep Mist Toning and Refining Lotion
Deep Mist Ultralight Moisture Lotion
Deep Mist Ultralight Night Cream
Deep Mist Ultrarich Night Cream
Deep Pore Cleansing Mask
Enamel Quick Dry
Extra Hold Protein Conditioning Hair
　Spray (Aerosol)
Eye Makeup Remover Pads
Gentle Color Eye Pencils
Gentle Color Lip Color Pencils
Gentle Color Lip Liner Pencils
Gentle Nail Enamel Remover
High Gloss Nail Guard
Lip Gleamer
Lip Polisher
Long on Lashes Lengthening Lashcolor
Nail Enamels: Frosted and Creme
Non-Oily Eye Makeup Remover Pads
Protective Base Coat
◆Protein Conditioning Hair Spray
Pure and Gentle Everyday Conditioning
　Shampoo
Pure Beauty Blotting Powder for Oily
　Skin
Pure Beauty Extra Cover Makeup
Pure Beauty Foundation Lotion for Oily
　Skin
Pure Beauty Fresh Blush
◆Pure Beauty Liquid Makeup
Pure Beauty Moisturizing Makeup
Pure Beauty Richcreme Blush
Pure Beauty Translucent Face Powder
Pure Beauty Translucent Pressed
　Powder
Pure Castile Shampoo
Regular Hold Conditioning Hair Spray
Richcreme Frosted Lipcolor
Richcreme Lipcolor
◆Rich Lash Thickening Lashcolor
Ridge Filling Pre-Coat
Slimliner (Water-Resistant)
◆Softlight Cream Powder Eye Shadow
Twinstick for Lip and Cheek
Under Eye Cover Creme, Ivory, Natural
Waterproof Mascara
Wrinkle Stick

ANABOLIC LABORATORIES, INC.　507
17802 Gillette Avenue
Irvine, CA 92714
　　Address inquiries to:
Georgiana Hennessy　(714) 546-8901
　　OTC Products Available
Ana-Pro (protein products)
Aqua-A
B6-Plus
B12-Plus
Basic Formula
CPA
Cal-M
Calpadon
Cholagest
Chromease
DIU-ERB
Dermagen
Digestaid
Enhance (Vitamin E Topicals)
Ferro-Vite
Flexamide

Hy-C-3000
Hyper-E
I-O-Plexadine
K-Orotate
Lax Special
Lipall-Plus
Nutra-Cal
O-A-Crine
Osatate
Pro-Enz
Prostana
Sedaphan
Selenace
Sofn
Tercopan
Tri-88
Tri-Adrenopan
Tri-B3
Tri-B-Plex
Tri-C-500
Tryptophan-250
Vasotate
Zinotate

ARCO PHARMACEUTICALS, INC.　508
105 Orville Drive
Bohemia, NY 11716
　　Address inquiries to:
Professional Service Dept.
　　　　　　　　(516) 567-9500
　　OTC Products Available
Arco-Cee Tablets
Arco-Lase Tablets
Arcoret Tablets
Arcoret w/Iron Tablets
Arcotinic Tablets
Codexin Extra Strength Capsules
Co-Gel Tablets
Mega-B
Megadose

ASCHER & COMPANY, INC., B.F.　508
P.O. Box 827
Kansas City, MO 64141
　　Address inquiries to:
Joan Bowen Nash　(816) 363-5900
　For Medical Emergencies Contact:
Michael Adams, Pharm D
　　　　　　　　(816) 363-5900
　　OTC Products Available
Ayr Saline Nasal Mist
Mobigesic Analgesic Tablets
Mobisyl Analgesic Creme
Soft 'N Soothe Anti-Itch Creme

**ASTRA PHARMACEUTICAL　509
PRODUCTS, INC.**
7 Neponset Street
Worcester, MA 01606
　　Address inquiries to:
Roy E. Hayward, Jr.　(617) 620-0600
　For Medical Emergencies Contact:
Dr. Michael Young　(617) 620-0600
　　OTC Products Available
Xylocaine Ointment 2.5%

BEACH PHARMACEUTICALS　509
Division of Beach Products, Inc.
　　　Executive Office
5220 S. Manhattan Ave.
Tampa, FL 33611　(813) 839-6565
　Manufacturing and Distribution
Main St. at Perimeter Rd.
Conestee, SC 29605
　　　Toll Free 1-(800) 845-8210
　　Address inquiries to:
Raymond LaForge, Ph.D.
　　　　　　　　(803) 277-7282
Richard Stephen Jenkins
　　　　　　　　(813) 839-6565
　　OTC Products Available
Beelith Tablets
Fer-Bid Improved

**BECTON DICKINSON CONSUMER　510
PRODUCTS**
365 W. Passaic Street
Rochelle Park, NJ 07662
　　Address inquiries to:
Allen C. Foster　(201) 368-7324
　For Medical Emergencies Contact:
Dr. T.J. Medrek　(201) 628-9600
　　OTC Products Available
Cankaid
Mercurochrome II

BEECHAM PRODUCTS　510
P.O. Box 1467
Pittsburgh, PA 15230
　　Address inquiries to:
Professional Services Dept.
　　　　　　　　(412) 928-1050
　　OTC Products Available
B.F.I. Antiseptic First-Aid Powder
Children's Hold
Cuprex
Eno Sparkling Antacid
Hold
Massengill Disposable Douche
Massengill Disposable Medicated
　Douche
Massengill Liquid Concentrate
Massengill Powder
S.T. 37
Scott's Emulsion
Sucrets (Regular, Mentholated &
　Children's Cherry)
Sucrets—Cold Decongestant Formula
Sucrets Cough Control Formula
Thermotabs

BLAIR LABORATORIES, INC.　512
Affiliate, The Purdue Frederick
　Company
50 Washington Street
Norwalk, CT 06856　(203) 853-0123
　　OTC Products Available
Calamatum Lotion, Ointment, Spray
Isodine Antiseptic
Kerid Ear Drops

BLOCK DRUG COMPANY, INC.　513
257 Cornelison Avenue
Jersey City, NJ 07302
　　Address inquiries to:
Barbara Ripianzi　(201) 434-3000
　For Medical Emergencies Contact:
T. Treitler　(201) 434-3000
　　OTC Products Available
Sensodyne Toothpaste
Tegrin for Psoriasis Lotion & Cream
Tegrin Medicated Shampoo

**BOEHRINGER INGELHEIM　406, 514
LTD.**
90 East Ridge
P.O. Box 368
Ridgefield, CT 06877
　　Address inquiries to:
Medical Services Dept.
　　　　　　　　(203) 438-0311
　　OTC Products Available
◆Dulcolax Suppositories
◆Dulcolax Tablets

BREON LABORATORIES INC.　515
90 Park Ave.
New York, NY 10016
　　Address inquiries to:
Medical Department　(212) 972-6316
　　　Main Office
90 Park Avenue
New York, NY 10016 (212) 972-4141
　　　Branch Offices
Atlanta, GA 30336
　5090 MacDougall Drive, S.W.
　　　　　　　　(404) 696-4480
Dallas, TX 75235
　6627 Maple Ave.　(214) 357-4015
Des Plaines, IL 60018
　200 E. Oakton St.　(312) 296-8141
Menlo Park, CA 94025
　160 Scott Drive　(415) 324-4721
　　OTC Products Available
Breonesin Capsules
Fergon Capsules
Fergon Elixir
Fergon Tablets
Measurin Tablets

BRISTOL LABORATORIES　515
(Div. of Bristol-Myers Co.)
Thompson Rd. P.O. Box 657
Syracuse, NY 13201 (315) 432-2000
　　Address medical inquiries to:
Dept. of Medical Service
　(315) 432-2838 or (315) 432-2000
Orders may be placed by calling the
　following toll free numbers:
Within New York State(800) 962-7200

Continental U.S.   1-(800) 448-7700
Alaska - Hawaii   1-(800) 448-1100
Mail orders and all inquiries should be sent to:
Bristol Laboratories
Order Entry Department
P.O. Box 657
Syracuse, NY 13201
OTC Products Available
Naldecon-DX Pediatric Syrup
Naldecon-EX Pediatric Drops

BRISTOL-MYERS PRODUCTS   406, 516
(Div. of Bristol-Myers Co.)
345 Park Avenue
New York, NY 10154
Address inquiries to:
Dr. B. M. Lanman   (212) 644-4287
OTC Products Available
Ammens medicated powder
◆Arthritis Strength Bufferin analgesic
B.Q cold tablets
Ban Basic antiperspirant
Ban Big Ball antiperspirant
Ban cream antiperspirant
Ban roll-on antiperspirant
Ban Super Solid antiperspirant
Body on Tap
◆Bufferin analgesic
◆Comtrex capsules
◆Comtrex liquid
◆Comtrex tablets
Congespirin cold tablets
Congespirin cough syrup
◆Congespirin liquid cold medicine
◆Datril acetaminophen tablets
◆Datril 500 acetaminophen tablets
◆Excedrin analgesic capsules
◆Excedrin analgesic tablets
◆Excedrin P.M. analgesic tablets
◆4-Way cold tablets
4-Way long acting mentholated nasal spray
◆4-Way long acting nasal spray
4-Way mentholated nasal spray
◆4-Way nasal spray
Minit-Rub analgesic balm
Monster vitamins
Monster with Iron vitamins
Multi-Scrub everyday scrubbing lotion with particles
Multi-Scrub medicated cleansing scrub
Mum cream deodorant
◆No Doz keep alert tablets
Pals plus`iron vitamins
Pals vitamins
Pazo hemorrhoid ointment/suppositories
Sal Hepatica laxative
Score hair cream
Tickle antiperspirant
Ultra Ban roll-on
Ultra Ban II antiperspirant
Vitalis Dry Control hair groom
Vitalis Dry Texture hair groom
Vitalis hair groom liquid
Vitalis hair groom tube
Vitalis Regular Hold hair spray
Vitalis Super Hold hair spray

BURTON, PARSONS &   407, 520
COMPANY, INC.
120 Westhampton Avenue
Washington, DC 20027
    (301) 336-5700
Address inquiries to:
Professional Services Dept.
OTC Products Available
◆Konsyl
◆L. A. Formula

CARNATION COMPANY   520
5045 Wilshire Blvd.
Los Angeles, CA 90036
Address inquiries to:
Ron Scott   (213) 932-6535
OTC Products Available
Carnation Evaporated Milk
Carnation Instant Breakfast
Carnation Instant Nonfat Dry Milk
Slender Diet Food For Weight Control (Instant)

Slender Diet Meal Bars For Weight Control
Slender Diet Meal For Weight Control (Canned)

CARTER PRODUCTS   407, 522
Division of Carter-Wallace, Inc.
767 Fifth Avenue
New York, NY 10153 (212) 758-4500
OTC Products Available
◆Answer At-Home Early Pregnancy Test Kit
◆Carter's Little Pills

CETYLITE INDUSTRIES, INC.   523
9051 River Road
Pennsauken, NJ 08110
Address inquiries to:
Mr. S. Wachman   (609) 665-6111
OTC Products Available
Protexin Oral Rinse
Skin Screen

CIBA PHARMACEUTICAL   407, 523
COMPANY
Div. of CIBA-GEIGY Corporation
556 Morris Avenue
Summit, NJ 07901   (201) 277-5000
Shipping Branches
Eastern
14 Henderson Drive
West Caldwell, NJ 07006
    (201) 575-6510
Central
7530 North Natchez Ave.
Niles, IL 60648   (312) 647-9332
Chicago, IL   (312) 763-8700
Western
12850 Moore Street
Cerritos, CA 90701   (213) 404-2651
OTC Products Available
◆Nupercainal Cream
◆Nupercainal Ointment
◆Nupercainal Suppositories
◆Privine Nasal Solution
◆Privine Nasal Spray
Vioform Cream & Ointment

CIRCLE PHARMACEUTICALS,   524
INC.
10377 Hague Road
Indianapolis, IN 46256
Address inquiries to:
Ross A. Deardoff, R.Ph.
    (317) 546-8855
OTC Products Available
Septa Ointment

COLGATE-PALMOLIVE   408, 525
COMPANY
A Delaware Corporation
300 Park Avenue
New York, NY 10022
Address inquiries to:
Consumers:
Consumer Affairs
300 Park Avenue
New York, NY 10022
    (212) 751-1200
Physicians:
Medical Director
909 River Road
Piscataway, NJ 08854
    (201) 463-1212
For Medical Emergencies Contact:
9 AM to 5 PM   (201) 463-1212
5 PM to 9 AM   (201) 547-2500
OTC Products Available
Colgate Dental Cream
Colgate Toothbrushes
Curad Bandages
◆Dermassage Dish Liquid
◆Dermassage Medicated Skin Lotion
◆Fluorigard Anti-Cavity Dental Rinse
◆Mersene Denture Cleanser
Ultra Brite Toothpaste

COMBE INCORPORATED   408, 525
1101 Westchester Avenue
White Plains, NY 10604
Address inquiries to:
Teresa C. Infantino   (914) 694-5454

For Medical Emergencies Contact:
Mark K. Taylor   (914) 694-5454
OTC Products Available
◆Lanacane Medicated Creme
◆Lanacort Creme
◆Vagisil Feminine Itching Medication

COOPER CARE , Inc. (U.S.A.)   408, 526
DERMATOLOGY PRODUCTS
305 Fairfield Avenue
Fairfield, NJ 07006
    (201) 575-3363
OTC Products Available
◆Acnaveen Bar
◆Aveeno Bar
◆Aveeno Colloidal Oatmeal
◆Aveeno Oilated Bath Powder
◆Emulave Bar
Meted Shampoo
Meted 2 Shampoo
Packer's Pine Tar Soap
Pentrax Tar Shampoo

CREIGHTON PRODUCTS   408, 526
CORPORATION
a company of Culbro Corporation
(see also Ex-Lax Pharmaceutical Co., Inc.)
605 Third Avenue
New York NY 10016
Address inquiries to:
M.H. Bedrick   (212) 687-7575
OTC Products Available
◆BiCozene Creme
◆Derma+Soft Creme
◆Gas-X Tablets

DAYWELL LABORATORIES   527
CORPORATION
78 Unquowa Place
Fairfield, CT 06430
Address inquiries to:
Judge J. H. Norton   (203) 255-3154
OTC Products Available
Vergo

DERMAIDE RESEARCH   527
CORPORATION
400 N. Michigan
Chicago, IL 60611
Address inquiries to:
Dermaide Research Corporation
    (312) 467-4040
For Medical Emergencies Contact:
Dermaide Research Corporation
    (312) 467-4040
OTC Products Available
Dermaide Aloe Ointment

DERMIK LABORATORIES, INC.   527
1777 Walton Road, Dublin Hall
Blue Bell, PA 19422
Address inquiries to:
A.M. Packman, V.P. &
Technical Director   (215) 641-1962
Branch Offices
Fort Washington, PA 19034
500 Virginia Drive   (215) 628-6550
Hammond, IN 46320
2500 165th Street   (219) 845-1677
San Leandro, CA 94577
1550 Factor Avenue
P.O. Box 1569   (415) 357-9741
Tucker, GA 30084
4660 Hammermill Road
    (404) 934-3091
OTC Products Available
Fomac Foam
Hytone Cream ½%
Hytone Ointment ½%
Loroxide Acne Lotion (Flesh Tinted)
Shepard's Formulations for Dry Skin Care
Shepard's Cream Lotion
Shepard's Dry Skin Cream
Shepard's Hand Creme
Shepard's Soap
Vanoxide Acne Lotion
Zetar Shampoo

DEWITT INTERNATIONAL   409, 529
CORPORATION
5 N. Watson Road
Taylors, SC 29687
Address inquiries to:
Bud Templeton   (803) 244-8521

(◆ Shown in Product Identification Section)

For Medical Emergencies Contact:
Ron Romano   (803) 244-8521
OTC Products Available
DeWitt's Aspirin
DeWitt's Absorbent Rub
DeWitt's Alertacaps
◆DeWitt's Antacid Powder
DeWitt's B Complex W/Vit. C Capsules
◆DeWitt's Baby Cough Syrup
◆DeWitt's Boric Acid Solution
DeWitt's Calamine Lotion
DeWitt's Camphor Liniment
DeWitt's Camphor Spirits
DeWitt's Carbolized Witch Hazel Salve
DeWitt's Castor Oil
DeWitt's Children's Aspirin
DeWitt's Cold Capsules
DeWitt's Cold Sore Lotion
DeWitt's Creosant Cough Syrup
DeWitt's Feet Treat
DeWitt's Flowaway Tablets
DeWitt's Glycerin
DeWitt's Glycerin & Rosewater
DeWitt's Gumzor
DeWitt's Iodine
DeWitt's Joggers Lotion
DeWitt's Merthiolate
DeWitt's Multi Vitamins
DeWitt's Multi Vit./Iron
◆DeWitt's Oil for Ear Use
DeWitt's Oil of Cloves
DeWitt's Oil of Wintergreen
DeWitt's Olive Oil
◆DeWitt's Pills for Backache & Joint
  Pains
DeWitt's Pyrinyl
DeWitt's Secta Sooth Ampules
DeWitt's Spirit of Peppermint
DeWitt's Sweet Oil
DeWitt's Teething Lotion
DeWitt's Terpin Hydrate w/D.M.
DeWitt's Thera-M Vitamins
DeWitt's Toothache Drops
DeWitt's Turpentine
DeWitt's Vit. C 250 mg. Chewable
  Tablets
DeWitt's Vit. C 250 mg. Tablets
DeWitt's Vit. C 500 mg. Tablets
DeWitt's Vit. E 200 I.U. Capsules
DeWitt's Vit. E 400 I.U. Capsules
DeWitt's Vit. E 1000 I.U. Capsules
DeWitt's Zoo Chews Vitamins
DeWitt's Zoo Chews w/Iron Vitamins
◆HTO Stainless Manzan Hemorrhoidal
  Tissue Ointment

DORSEY LABORATORIES   **409, 530**
Division of Sandoz, Inc.
P.O. Box 83288
Lincoln, NE 68501
    Address inquiries to:
Medical Director   (402) 464-6311
    OTC Products Available
◆Acid Mantle Creme & Lotion
◆Cama Inlay-Tabs
Chexit Tablets
◆Dorcol Pediatric Cough Syrup
Kanulase Tablets
◆Triaminic Expectorant
◆Triaminic Syrup
◆Triaminic-DM Cough Formula
Triaminicin Chewables
◆Triaminicin Tablets
◆Triaminicol Decongestant Cough Syrup
Tussagesic Tablets & Suspension
Ursinus Inlay-Tabs
Uval Sunscreen Lotion

DOW PHARMACEUTICALS   **532**
9550 Zionsville Road
Indianapolis, IN 46268
    Address inquiries to:
Teri S. LeBeau   (317) 873-7394
   For Medical Emergencies Contact:
Dr. Thomas P. Bright (317) 873-7242
Dr. James C. Crane   (317) 873-7344
    Branch Offices
ATLANTA
  Atlanta, GA 30346
  Suite 2005
  20 Perimeter Center, East
        (404) 394-4141

BATON ROUGE
  Baton Rouge, LA 70816
  Suite 101
  4150 S. Sherwood Forest Blvd.
        (504) 293-2222
BOSTON
  Wellesley, MA 02181
  20 William Street   (617) 237-2070
CHARLOTTE
  Charlotte, NC 28210
  Woodlawn Green, Suite 120
  Woodlawn Road   (704) 525-9030
CHICAGO
  Des Plaines, IL 60018
  1400 E. Touhy Avenue
        (312) 391-4700
CINCINNATI
  Cincinnati, OH 45236
  Whitehall Park
  8050 Hosbrook Road
        (513) 793-6200
CLEVELAND
  Strongsville, OH 44136
  P.O. Box 8800   (216) 826-6000
DALLAS
  Dallas, TX 75251
  Suite 600
  12700 Park Central Place
        (214) 387-2211
DALTON (Service Location
  of Atlanta)
  Dalton, GA 30720
  1402 Prosser Dr., S.E.
        (404) 277-3000
DENVER (Service Location
  of Kansas City)
  Denver, CO 80239
  Suite 500
  12075 East 45th St.
        (303) 371-0500
DENVER METAL PRODUCTS
  (Denver Service Location)
        (303) 371-9250
DETROIT
  Southfield, MI 48076
  415 Travelers Tower
  26555 Evergreen Rd.
        (303) 358-1300
GRAND RAPIDS
  Grand Rapids, MI 49506
  611 Cascade
  West Parkway, S.E. (303) 949-9000
HONOLULU (Service Location
  of San Francisco)
  Honolulu, HI 96813
  Suite 801
  677 Ala Moana Blvd.
        (808) 524-3575
HOUSTON
  Houston, TX 77005
  P.O. Box 4269   (713) 626-3170
INDIANAPOLIS
  Indianapolis, IN 46268
  P.O. Box 68511   (317) 873-7000
KANSAS CITY
  Shawnee Mission, KS 66210
  Suite 160
  Corporate Woods
  10890 Benson Dr. (913) 341-2500
LOS ANGELES
  Pasadena, CA 91109
  P.O. Bin 48   (213) 577-1515
MEMPHIS
  Memphis, TN 38137
  Suite 2210
  5100 Poplar Ave.   (901) 767-5000
MINNEAPOLIS
  Minnetonka, MN 55343
  11100 Bren Rd. West
        (612) 938-4300
NEW YORK
  Saddle Brook, NJ 07662
  Park 80 Plaza East (201) 845-5000
PHILADELPHIA
  Moorestown, NJ 08057
  P.O. Box 350   (609) 234-0400
PITTSBURGH
  Pittsburgh, PA 15222
  Room 1313
  Four Gateway Center
        (412) 281-3030

RICHMOND
  Richmond, VA 23288
  1603 Santa Rosa Rd.
        (804) 288-1601
ROCHESTER
  Fairport, NY 14450
  400 Perinton Hills Office Park
        (716) 425-1200
ST. LOUIS
  St. Louis, MO 63105
  800 Pierre Laclede Center
  7733 Forsyth Blvd. (314) 726-5000
SAN FRANCISCO
  Walnut Creek, CA 94596
  P.O. Drawer H.   (415) 944-2000
SEATTLE
  Bellevue, WA 98004
  777 106th N.E.
  Bellevue, WA 98009
  P.O. Box 3547   (206) 455-7250
STAMFORD
  Stamford, CT 06902
  Washington Plaza
  1351 Washington Blvd.
        (203) 359-3300
TAMPA
  Tampa, FL 33609
  Suite 450
  5100 W. Kennedy Blvd.
        (813) 877-8300

    OTC Products Available
Novahistine Cough & Cold Formula
Novahistine Cough Formula
Novahistine DMX
Novahistine Elixir & Cold Tablets
Novahistine Sinus Tablets
Resolve Cold Sore & Fever Blister
  Relief

ENDO LABORATORIES, INC.   **409, 536**
Sub. of the DuPont Company
1000 Stewart Ave.
Garden City, NY 11530
    Address inquiries to:
Director, Professional Services
        (516) 832-2123
Emergency No.   (516) 832-2210
    Branch Offices
Chicago, IL 60641
  4956 W. Belmont Ave.
        (312) 282-0440
Los Angeles, CA 90064
  11400 W. Olympic Blvd.
        (213) 272-7153
    OTC Products Available
◆Percogesic Tablets

EX-LAX PHARMACEUTICAL   **408, 536**
CO., INC.
a company of Culbro Corporation
(see also Creighton Products
  Corporation)
605 Third Avenue
New York, NY 10016
    Address inquiries to:
M.H. Bedrick   (212) 687-7575
    OTC Products Available
◆Ex-Lax Chocolated Laxative
◆Ex-Lax Pills, Unflavored

MAX FACTOR & CO.   **536**
1655 N. McCadden Pl.
Hollywood, CA 90028
    Address inquiries to:
Carol Walters   (213) 856-6280
  For Medical Emergencies Contact:
Joe DiSomma (805) 499-4560 (home)
       (213) 856-6620 (work)
    OTC Products Available
Maxi Unshine Oil Free Make-Up
Maxi Unshine 100% Oil Free Blotting
  Powder
Maxi Unshine 100% Oil Free Blushing
  Powder
Sebb Lotion
Sebb Shampoo

FLEETWOOD COMPANY   **410, 537**
1500 Brook Drive
Downers Grove, IL 60515
    Address inquiries to:
Nelson J. McMahon (312) 495-9300
or Donald R. Kloss   (312) 495-9300

OTC Products Available
Fayd Skin Cream
◆Super Wate-On Emulsion
Tintz Cream Color Shampoo
Wate-Off
◆Wate-On

FLEMING & COMPANY 537
1600 Fenpark Dr.
Fenton, MO 63026
Address inquiries to:
John J. Roth, M.D.   (314) 343-8200
OTC Products Available
Impregon Concentrate
Magonate Tablets
Marblen Suspension Peach/Apricot
Marblen Suspension Unflavored
Marblen Tablets
Nephrox Suspension
Nicotinex Elixir
Obegyn Tablets
Ocean Nasal Mist

FOX PHARMACAL, INC. 538
1750 W. McNab Road
Ft. Lauderdale, FL 33310
Address inquiries to:
Sandra Cook   (305) 971-4100
For Medical Emergencies Contact:
Donald J. Flaster, MD
               (201) 267-3884
OTC Products Available
E-Z Trim
Odrinil
Super Odrinex

G & W LABORATORIES, INC. 538
111 Coolidge Street
South Plainfield, NJ 07080
Address inquiries to:
Customer Service Dept.
               (201) 753-2000
OTC Products Available
Acephen Acetaminophen Rectal
  Suppositories
Aspirin Suppositories
Bisacodyl Suppositories
Hemorrhoidal Rectal Ointment
Hemorrhoidal Suppositories
Hem-Prep Combo
Sani-Supp Foil Wrapped Glycerin
  Suppositories

GEIGY PHARMACEUTICALS 410, 539
Div. of CIBA-GEIGY Corporation
Ardsley, NY 10502   (201) 277-5000
OTC Products Available
◆Otrivin Nasal Spray & Nasal Drops
◆Otrivin Pediatric Nasal Drops
◆PBZ Cream

GERBER PRODUCTS COMPANY 539
Fremont, MI 49412   (616) 928-2000
Address inquiries to:
Professional Communications Dept.
OTC Products Available
Gerber Cereals
  Barley Cereal
  Cereals with Fruit
  High Protein Cereal
  Mixed Cereal
  Oatmeal Cereal
  Rice Cereal
Gerber High Meat Dinners (Strained &
  Junior)
Gerber Junior Cookies
Gerber Junior Foods
Gerber Junior Meats
Gerber Strained Egg Yolks
Gerber Strained Food
Gerber Strained Juices
Gerber Strained Meats
Gerber Teething Biscuits
Gerber Toddler Meals
MBF (Meat Base Formula) Liquid

GLENBROOK 410, 539
  LABORATORIES
Division of Sterling Drug Inc.
90 Park Avenue
New York, NY 10016
Address inquiries to:
Medical Director   (212) 972-4141

OTC Products Available
◆Bayer Aspirin
◆Bayer Children's Chewable Aspirin
  Bayer Children's Cold Tablets
  Bayer Cough Syrup for Children
◆Bayer Timed-Release Aspirin
◆Diaparene Baby Powder
◆Diaparene Baby Wash Cloths
  Jayne's P-W Vermifuge
  Midol
◆Phillip's Milk of Magnesia
  Vanquish

GOODY'S MANUFACTURING 410, 541
CORPORATION
436 Salt Street
Winston-Salem, NC 27108
Address inquiries to:
T.H. Chambers   (919) 723-1831
OTC Products Available
Goody's Extra Strength Tablets
◆Goody's Headache Powders
Sayman Soaps & Salves

HEALTH CARE INDUSTRIES, 410, 541
INC.
4295 S. Ohio Street
Michigan City, IN 46360
Address inquiries to:
Walter Tuman, RPh. PhD. or
Roland C. Zagnoli, RPh.
               (219) 879-8227
OTC Products Available
◆Allimin Filmcoated Tablets
◆Cosanyl Cough Syrup
◆Cosanyl-DM Cough Syrup
◆Oil-O-Sol Liquid

HERBERT LABORATORIES 543
Dermatology Division of Allergan
  Pharmaceuticals, Inc.
2525 DuPont Drive
Irvine, CA 92713   (714) 752-4500
OTC Products Available
Aquacare Dry Skin Cream & Lotion
Aquacare/HP Dry Skin Cream & Lotion
Bluboro Powder Astringent Soaking
  Solution
Clear By Design Acne Gel
Danex Protein Enriched Dandruff
  Shampoo
◆Eclipse After Sun Lotion
◆Eclipse Sunscreen Lip & Face
  Protectant
  Eclipse Sunscreen Lotion & Gel,
  Original
◆Eclipse Sunscreen Lotion, Total (Alcohol
  Base)
◆Eclipse Sunscreen Lotion, Total
  (Moisturizing Base)
◆Eclipse Suntan Lotion, Partial
  Vanseb Cream & Lotion Dandruff
  Shampoo
  Vanseb-T Cream & Lotion Dandruff
  Shampoo

HICKAM, INC., DOW B. 544
P.O. Box 35413
Houston, TX 77035   (713) 723-0690
OTC Products Available
Proderm Topical Dressing

HOECHST-ROUSSEL 411, 544
PHARMACEUTICALS INC.
Routes 202-206 North
Somerville, NJ 08876
Address inquiries to:
Manager, Scientific Services
               (201) 685-2611
For Medical Emergencies Contact:
Medical Department   (201) 685-2000
OTC Products Available
◆Doxidan
◆Festal
◆Surfak

HOLLAND-RANTOS COMPANY, 545
INC.
Post Office Box 385
865 Centennial Avenue
Piscataway, NJ 08854
Address inquiries to:
Mr. Philip L. Frank or
Mr. Murray H. Glantz (201) 885-5777

OTC Products Available
H-R Sterile Lubricating Jelly
Koromex Contraceptive Foam
Koromex Jelly/Cream Applicator
Koromex^{II} Contraceptive Cream
Koromex^{II} Contraceptive Jelly
Koromex^{I}-A Contraceptive Jelly
Nylmerate^{II} Solution Concentrate
Rantex Personal Cloth Wipes
Transi-Lube

HYNSON, WESTCOTT 411, 546
& DUNNING
Division of Becton Dickinson and Co.
Charles & Chase Streets
Baltimore, MD 21201(301) 837-0890
OTC Products Available
◆Lactinex Tablets & Granules
Thantis Lozenges

JAYCO PHARMACEUTICALS 546
890 Poplar Church Road
Camp Hill, PA 17011
Address inquiries to:
Lester J. Lifton, M.D.
               (717) 763-7687
OTC Products Available
F.S.K. (Fecal Staining Kit)
Hydra-Lyte
Lac-Tol
Nuggettes

JOHNSON & JOHNSON 411, 547
BABY PRODUCTS
COMPANY
220 Centennial Avenue
Piscataway, NJ 08854
For Medical Emergencies Contact:
Z. Frann Krajeski, R.N.,B.S.N.
               (201) 524-1456
OTC Products Available
◆Johnson's Baby Bath
◆Sundown Sunscreen, Extra Protection
◆Sundown Sunscreen, Maximal
  Protection
◆Sundown Sunscreen, Moderate
  Protection
◆Sundown Sunscreen, Ultra Protection

JOHNSON & JOHNSON 411, 547
PRODUCTS,
INCORPORATED
501 George Street
New Brunswick, NJ 08903
Address inquiries to:
Information Center
Call Toll Free 10AM-4PM EST Mon-Fri
In Cont. USA   (800) 526-2459
In New Jersey   (800) 352-4845
For Medical Emergencies Contact:
Dr. H.L. Dickstein
  office hours: (201) 524-5125
  after hours: (609) 799-3675
OTC Products Available
◆Johnson & Johnson First Aid Cream

KREMERS-URBAN COMPANY 548
P.O. Box 2038
Milwaukee, WI 53201
Address inquiries to:
Professional Service Dept.
               (414) 354-4300
OTC Products Available
Kudrox Suspension (Double Strength)
Milkinol

LANK LABORATORIES, INC. 548
136 E. 64th St.
New York, NY 10021
Address inquiries to:
Ralph Saunders   (212) 838-2285
For Medical Emergencies Contact:
Ruth Lane   (212) 838-2285
OTC Products Available
Natrasan
Tonel

LANNETT COMPANY, INC., THE 548
9000 State Road
Philadelphia, PA 19136
Address inquiries to:
Medical Service Dept. (215) 333-9000
OTC Products Available
Acetaminophen Tablets & Elixir

(◆ Shown in Product Identification Section)

Acnederm Lotion & Soap
Alphamul
Anulan Suppositories
Bellafedrol AH Tablets
Castaderm
Cebralan MT Tablets
Decavitamin Tablets
Disanthrol Capsules
Disodan Capsules
Disolan Capsules
Disolan Capsules
Disonate Capsules
Disoplex Capsules
Lanamins
Lanatuss Expectorant
Lycolan Elixir
Magnatril Suspension & Tablets
Prelan Tablets
S-A-C Tablets
Salagen Tablets

LASER, INC. 548
2000 N. Main Street
Crown Point, IN 46307
Address inquiries to:
Donald A. Laser   (219) 663-1165
OTC Products Available
D-Sinus Capsules
Fumatinic Tablets
Fumerin Tablets
Lactocal Tablets

LEDERLE LABORATORIES 411, 549
Division of American Cyanamid Co.
Wayne, NJ 07470   (201) 831-1234
Address inquiries on
medical matters to:
Professional Services Dept.
Lederle Laboratories
Pearl River, NY 10965
                  (914) 735-5000
Distribution Centers
ATLANTA
Bulk Address
Chamblee (Atlanta), GA 30341
  5180 Peachtree Industrial Blvd.
Mail Address
Atlanta, GA 30302
  P.O. Box 4272
      (GA Only)   (800) 282-0399
      (All Other) (800) 241-3043
                  (404) 455-0320
BOSTON
Westwood, MA 02090
  201 University Avenue
                  (617) 329-4300
      (MA Only)   (800) 532-9684
      (All Other) (800) 225-6022
CHICAGO
Bulk Address
Rosemont, IL 60018
  10401 W. Touhy Ave.
Mail Address
Chicago, IL 60666
  P.O. Box 66189
      (IL Only)   (800) 942-1493
      (All Other) (800) 323-9744
                  (312) 827-8871
CINCINNATI
Bulk Address
Cincinnati, OH 45241
  10340 Evendale Drive
Mail Address
Cincinnati, OH 45241
  P.O. Box 41316
      (OH Only)   (800) 582-4661
      (All Other) (800) 543-4590
                  (513) 563-6200
DALLAS
Bulk Address
Dallas, TX 75247
  7611 Carpenter Freeway
Mail Address
Dallas, TX 75265
  P.O. Box 225731
      (TX Only)   (800) 442-7510
      (All Other) (800) 527-9770
                  (214) 631-2130
LOS ANGELES
Bulk Address
Los Angeles, CA 90040
  2300 S. Eastern Ave.

Mail Address
Los Angeles, CA 90051
  T.A. Box 2202
      (CA Only)   (800) 372-6325
      (All Other) (800) 423-4120
                  (213) 726-1016
PHILADELPHIA
Fort Washington, PA 19034
  185 Commerce Drive
      (PA Only)   (800) 562-6924
      (NY-NJ-MD-DE) (800) 523-6610
      (CT-VA-WV-DC) (800) 523-6230
      (Phila. Only) (215) 248-3900
      (All Other) (215) 646-7000
OTC Products Available
Acetaminophen Capsules, Tablets, Elixir
Ascorbic Acid Tablets
Aureomycin Ointment 3%
Bisacodyl Tablets
◆Centrum
Dimenhydrinate Tablets
Docusate Sodium (DSS)
Docusate Sodium w/Casanthranol
Ferro-Sequels
Ferrous Fumarate
Ferrous Gluconate Iron Supplement
Ferrous Sulfate
Filibon Prenatal Vitamin Tablets
Gevrabon Liquid
Gevral Protein Powder
Gevral T Tablets
Gevral Tablets
Gevrite Tablets
Guaifenesin
Guaifenesin w/D-Methorphan
  Hydrobromide
Incremin w/Iron Syrup
Lederplex Capsules, Liquid & Tablets
Meclizine HCl
Neoloid Emulsified Castor Oil
Niacin
Peritinic Tablets
Pyridoxine HCl
Rhulicaine
Rhulicort Cream & Lotion
Rhulicream
Rhuligel
Rhulihist Lotion
Rhulispray
Stresscaps Capsules
◆Stresstabs 600 Tablets
◆Stresstabs 600 with Iron
◆Stresstabs 600 with Zinc
Thiamine HCl (Vitamin B-1) Tablets
Vi-Magna Capsules
Vitamin A, Natural
Vitamin C Chewable
Vitamin E, Natural, USP
Vitamin E, USP
Zincon Dandruff Shampoo

LEEMING DIVISION 552
Pfizer Inc.
100 Jefferson Rd.
Parsippany, NJ 07054
Address inquiries to:
Research and Development Dept.
                  (201) 887-2100
OTC Products Available
Ben-Gay External Analgesic Products
Desitin Ointment
Nytilax Tablets
Rheaban Tablets & Liquid
Unisom Nighttime Sleep-Aid
Visine A.C. Eye Drops
Visine Eye Drops

LEHN & FINK PRODUCTS 555
COMPANY
Division of Sterling Drug Inc.
225 Summit Avenue
Montvale, NJ 07645
Address inquiries to:
John Winson   (201) 391-8500
For Medical Emergencies Contact:
Dr. Ernst Zander   (212) 972-4141
OTC Products Available
Medi-Quik
Stri-Dex B.P.
Stri-Dex Medicated Pads

LOMA LINDA FOODS 555
Address inquiries to:
Marketing Office
Riverside, CA 92515 (714) 687-7800

Branch Offices
Atlanta, GA
  P.O. Box 664
  (Calhoun) 30701   (404) 629-4693
Berrien Springs, MI 49103
  140 Sunset Drive   (616) 473-2614
Columbus, OH
  P.O. Box 388
  (Mount Vernon) 43050
                  (614) 397-7077
Dallas, TX
  P.O. Box 246
  (Keene) 76059   (817) 645-8465
Denver, CO
  318 Eugene Way
  (Loveland) 80537   (303) 399-8041
Honolulu, HI 96807
  P.O. Box 1388
                  (808) 848-2051
Newton, NJ 07860
  Box 438, RD 2   (201) 383-7951
Oakland, CA
  1473 Doolittle Drive
  (San Leandro) 94577
                  (415) 562-5133
Portland, OR 97211
  1707 NE Argyle   (503) 283-5983
Riverside, CA 92515
  11503 Pierce St.   (714) 687-7800
OTC Products Available
I-Soyalac: Liquid Concentrate,
  Ready-to-Serve and Powder
Soyalac: Liquid Concentrate,
  Ready-to-Serve and Powder

MACSIL, INC. 556
1326 Frankford Avenue
Philadelphia, PA 19125
                  (215) 423-5566
OTC Products Available
Balmex Baby Powder
Balmex Emollient Lotion
Balmex Ointment

MARION LABORATORIES, INC. 412, 556
10236 Bunker Ridge Road
Kansas City, MO 64137
Address inquiries to:
Steve Wonderly   (816) 761-2500
For Medical Emergencies Contact:
Corporate Medical Director
                  (816) 761-2500
OTC Products Available
◆Ambenyl-D Decongestant Cough
  Formula
◆Debrox Drops
Fumasorb Tablets
◆Gaviscon Antacid Tablets
◆Gaviscon Liquid Antacid
◆Gaviscon-2 Antacid Tablets
◆Gly-Oxide Liquid
Metasep Shampoo
Os-Cal 500 Tablets
Os-Cal Forte Tablets
Os-Cal Plus Tablets
◆Os-Cal Tablets
Os-Cal-Gesic Tablets
◆Pretts Tablets
◆Protect Toothpaste for Sensitive Teeth
◆Throat Discs Throat Lozenges

MAYBELLINE CO. 559
3030 Jackson Ave.
Memphis, TN 38151
Address inquiries to:
Consumer Relations   (901) 320-2386
For Medical Emergencies Contact:
Clinical Affairs Department
                  (901) 320-2011

OTC Products Available
Moisture Whip Lip Balm
Moisture Whip Lipstick
Moisture Whip Liquid Make-up &
  Moisture Whip Cream Make-up
Moisture Whip Protective Facial
  Moisturizer

McNEIL CONSUMER 412, 559
PRODUCTS CO.
McNEILAB, INC.
Fort Washington, PA 19034
Address inquiries to:
Professional Relations Department
Fort Washington, PA 19034

(◆ Shown in Product Identification Section)

Manufacturing Divisions
Fort Washington, PA 19034
Southwest Manufacturing Plant
4001 N. I-35
Round Rock, TX 78664
Distribution Centers
Arlington, TX 76010
3129 Pinewood Drive
(817) 640-1167
Broadview, IL 60153
2122 Roberts Drive (312) 343-1569
Doraville, GA 30360
2801 Bankers Industrial Drive
(404) 448-0200
Glendale, CA 91201
512 Paula Avenue (213) 245-1491
Montgomeryville, PA 18936
2 Progress Drive (215) 699-7081
OTC Products Available
◆Children's CoTylenol Liquid
Cold Formula
◆Children's Tylenol Acetaminophen
Chewable Tablets, Elixir, & Drops
◆CoTylenol Cold Formula Tablets and
Capsules
◆CoTylenol Liquid Cold Formula
◆Extra-Strength Tylenol acetaminophen
Adult Liquid Pain Reliever
◆Extra-Strength Tylenol acetaminophen
Tablets & Capsules
◆Regular Strength Tylenol
acetaminophen Tablets & Capsules
◆Sine-Aid Sinus Headache Tablets

MEAD JOHNSON NUTRITIONAL 562
DIVISION
Mead Johnson & Company
2404 W. Pennsylvania St.
Evansville, IN 47721 (812) 426-6000
Address inquiries to:
Scientific Information Section
Medical Department
OTC Products Available
Casec
Ce-Vi-Sol
Enfamil
Enfamil Nursette
Enfamil Ready-To-Use
Enfamil w/Iron
Enfamil w/Iron Ready-To-Use
Feminins
Fer-In-Sol
Flexical
Isocal
Isocal Tube Feeding Set
Lofenalac
Lonalac
Lytren
MCT Oil
Nutramigen
Poly-Vi-Sol Vitamins, Chewable Tablets
& Drops
Poly-Vi-Sol Vitamins w/Iron, Chewable
Tablets & Drops
Portagen
Pregestimil
Probana
ProSobee
Sustacal
Sustagen
Tempra
Trind
Trind-DM
Tri-Vi-Sol Vitamins, Chewable Tablets &
Drops
Tri-Vi-Sol Vitamin Drops w/Iron

MEDICONE COMPANY 573
225 Varick St.
New York, NY 10014
Address inquiries to:
Professional Service Dept.
(212) 924-5166
OTC Products Available
Derma Medicone
DioMedicone Tablets
Medicone Dressing
Mediconet
Rectal Medicone Suppositories
Rectal Medicone Unguent

MEDIQUE PRODUCTS 574
8050 N. Lawndale
Skokie, IL 60076

Address inquiries to:
Robert E. Musick (312) 674-4903
For Medical Emergencies Contact:
Robert E. Musick, BS R.Ph.
(312) 674-4903
OTC Products Available
Industrials & Prepacks
All Sugar-Free, Alcohol-Free
Formulations
Alamag Fruit-Flavored Antacid Tablets
Alcalak Antacid Tablets
APAP Non-Aspirin Pain Relief Tablets
APAP-Plus Non-Aspirin Extra Strength
Pain Relief Tablets
Aspirin
Aspirin, Buffered
CCP Tablets
Cosyrel Cold Symptom Relief Tablets
Di-Gon Diarrhea Relief Tablets
Femaids Menstrual Relief Capsules
Medidrops Eye Drops
Medi-Koff Sugar-Free Cough
Expectorant/Suppressant
Mediwash Eye Irrigant
Onset Forte Allergy Relief Tablets
Sep-A-Soothe Throat Lozenges
Seracaine Spray For Burns
Sudodrin Decongestant Tablets

MENLEY & JAMES 413, 574
LABORATORIES
a SmithKline Company
One Franklin Plaza
P.O. Box 8082
Philadelphia, PA 19101
Address inquiries to:
Medical Department (215) 854-5000
OTC Products Available
◆A.R.M. Allergy Relief Medicine Tablets
◆Acnomel Cream & Cake
◆Benzedrex Inhaler
◆C3 Cold Cough Capsules
◆Contac Capsules
◆Contac Jr. Childrens' Cold Medicine
◆Dietac Diet Aid Capsules
◆Dietac Diet Aid Drops
◆Dietac Diet Aid Tablets
◆Dietac Once-A-Day Maximum Strength
Diet Aid Capsules
◆Dietac Twice-A-Day Maximum Strength
Diet Aid Capsules
◆Ecotrin Tablets
◆Feosol Elixir
Feosol Plus
◆Feosol Spansule Capsules
◆Feosol Tablets
◆Fortespan Capsules
◆Ornacol Capsules
Ornacol Liquid
◆Ornex Capsules
◆Pragmatar Ointment
◆Quotane Ointment
◆Sine-Off Extra Strength Sinus Medicine
Non-Aspirin Capsules
◆Sine-Off Extra Strength Sinus Medicine
Non-Aspirin Tablets
◆Sine-Off Once-A-Day Sinus Spray
◆Sine-Off Sinus Medicine Tablets
◆Teldrin Spansule Capsules
◆Troph-Iron Liquid & Tablets
◆Trophite Liquid & Tablets

MERICON INDUSTRIES, INC. 580
420-22 S.W. Washington
Peoria, IL 61602
Address inquiries to:
Thomas P. Morrissey (309) 676-0744
OTC Products Available
Delacort
Orazinc
Zinc Tabs

MERRELL-NATIONAL 415, 580
LABORATORIES
Division of Richardson-Merrell Inc.
Cincinnati, OH 45215
Address inquiries to:
Manager Professional Services
(513) 948-9111
MERRELL-NATIONAL LABORATORIES
Inc.
Cayey, Puerto Rico 00633

Address inquiries to:
Manager, Professional Services
MERRELL-NATIONAL LABORATORIES
Division of Richardson-Merrell Inc.
Cincinnati, OH 45215
(513) 948-9111
OTC Products Available
Bacimycin Ointment
Cēpacol Anesthetic Troches
◆Cēpacol Mouthwash/Gargle
◆Cēpacol Throat Lozenges
◆Cēpastat Sore Throat Lozenges
◆Cēpastat Sore Throat Spray/Gargle
◆Children's Cepastat Lozenges
Consotuss Antitussive Syrup
Cotussis Syrup
Decapryn Syrup
Delcid
Diothane Ointment
Ganatrex Elixir
Kolantyl Gel
Kolantyl Wafers
Mercodol Cough Syrup w/Decapryn
Pyridoxine Hydrochloride Tablets
◆Simron Capsules
◆Simron Plus Capsules
Terpin Hydrate & Codeine Elixir

MERRICK MEDICINE 415, 583
COMPANY
501-503 South 8th (76706)
P.O. Box 1489 (76703)
Waco, TX
Address inquiries to:
W.B. Clayton, President
(817) 753-3461
OTC Products Available
◆Percy Medicine

MILES LABORATORIES, INC. 583
1127 Myrtle Street
Elkhart, IN 46514
Address inquiries to:
Medical Department (219) 264-8955
For Medical Emergencies Contact:
Medical Department (219) 262-7886
OTC Products Available
Alka-Seltzer Effervescent Antacid
Alka-Seltzer Effervescent Pain Reliever
& Antacid
Alka-Seltzer Plus Cold Medicine
Alka-2 Chewable Antacid Tablets
Bactine Skin Wound Cleanser
Bugs Bunny With Extra C Multivitamin
Supplement
Chocks Multivitamin Supplement
Chocks Plus Iron Multivitamin
Supplement
Chocks-Bugs Bunny Multivitamin
Supplement
Chocks-Bugs Bunny Plus Iron
Multivitamin Supplement
Flintstones Multivitamin Supplement
Flintstones Plus Iron Multivitamin
Supplement
Flintstones With Extra C Multivitamin
Supplement
Miles Nervine Nighttime Sleep-Aid
One-A-Day Core C 500 Multivitamin
Supplement
One-A-Day Multivitamin Supplement
One-A-Day Multivitamin Supplement
Plus Iron
One-A-Day Multivitamin Supplement
Plus Minerals

MILLER-MORTON COMPANY 415, 586
3800 Cutshaw Avenue
Richmond, VA 23230
Address inquiries to:
DeWitt F. Helm, Jr. (804) 257-2727
For Medical Emergencies Contact:
Dr. Grover D. Cloyd (804) 257-2801
Branch Offices
Dallas, TX 75237
4116 Bronze Way (214) 339-8361
Des Plaines, IL 60018
69 Rawls Road (312) 299-2206

(◆ Shown in Product Identification Section)

Los Angeles, CA 92642
P.O. Box 3040
Garden Grove   (714) 891-3743
Richmond, VA 23231
7500 Darbytown Road
                       (804) 222-1580
OTC Products Available
◆Chap Stick Lip Balm
◆Chap Stick Sunblock 15 Lip Balm

MURO PHARMACEUTICAL, INC.   586
890 East Street
Tewksbury, MA 01876
Address inquiries to:
Professional Service Dept.
                       1-(800) 225-0974
                       (617) 851-5981
OTC Products Available
Duolube Ophthalmic Ointment
Muro Tears
Murocel Ophthalmic Solution
Naso-Mist
Teen 5 & 10 Lotion
Teen 5 Wash

NATURE'S BOUNTY, INC.   415, 587
105 Orville Drive
Bohemia, NY 11716
Address inquiries to:
Professional Service Dept.
                       (516) 567-9500
                       (800) 645-5412
OTC Products Available
Acerola C
Acidophilus Capsules
Alfalfa Tablets
B-1 Tablets
B-2 Tablets
B-6 Tablets
B-12 Tablets
B-50 Tablets
B-100 Tablets
B-100 Time Release Tablets
B-125 Tablets
B Complex & B-12 Tablets
B Complex & C (Time Release)
   Capsules
B & C Liquid
Bee Pollen Tablets
Biotin Tablets
Bone Meal with Vitamin D Tablets
Brewer's Yeast Powder (Debittered)
Brewer's Yeast Tablets
C-250 with Rose Hips Tablets
C-300 with Rose Hips (Chewable)
   Tablets
C-500 with Rose Hips Tablets
C-1000 with Rose Hips Tablets
C-Complex Tablets
C Liquid
C-Time-750 Time Release Tablets
C-Time-1500 Tablets
Calcium Ascorbate Tablets
Calcium Lactate Tablets
Chelated Calcium Tablets
Chelated Chromium Tablets
Chelated Copper Tablets
Chelated Magnesium Tablets
Chelated Manganese Tablets
Chelated Multi-Mineral Tablets
Chelated Potassium Tablets
Chelated Zinc Tablets
Chew-Iron Tablets
Children's Chewables Tablets
Choline Tablets
Claws
Cocoa Butter Soap
Dolomite Tablets
E-200 Capsules
E-200 (Natural Complex) Capsules
E-400 Capsules
E-400 (Natural Complex) Capsules
E-600 (Natural Complex) Capsules
E-1000 (Natural Complex) Capsules
Emulsified E-200 Capsules
Ferrous Sulfate Tablets
Folic Acid Tablets
Garlic Oil Capsules
Garlic & Parsley Capsules
Ginseng, Manchurian Capsules
Glutamic Acid Tablets
l-Glutamine Tablets
Halibut Liver Oil Capsules

Herbal Laxative Tablets
Inositol Tablets
Iron Tablets
Jojoba Shampoo
KLB6 Capsules
KLB6 Complete Tablets
KLB6 Diet Mix
Kelp Tablets
Lecithin Capsules
Lecithin with Vitamin D Capsules
Lecithin Granules
Lecithin, Chewable Tablets
Liver W/B-12 Tablets
l-Lysine Tablets
Magnesium Tablets
Manganese Tablets
Mega V & M Tablets
Mega-B with C Tablets
Multi-Mineral Tablets
Nature's Bounty Hair Booster Tablets
Nature's Bounty Slim
Niacin Tablets
Niacinamide Tablets
Oyster Calcium Tablets
PABA Tablets
Pantothenic Acid Tablets
Papaya Enzyme Tablets
Potassium Tablets
Potassium & B-6 Tablets
Protein For Body Building
Protein Tablets
RNA Tablets
RNA/DNA Tablets
Rutin Tablets
Selenium Tablets
Stress Formula "605" Tablets
Stress Formula "605" w/Iron Tablets
Stress Formula "605" w/Zinc Tablets
Tryptophan Tablets
Ultra "A" Capsules & Tablets
Ultra "A & D" Tablets
Ultra "D" Tablets
Ultra KLB6 Tablets
Ultra Vita-Time Tablets
Vitamin A Capsules & Tablets
Vitamin A & D Tablets
Vitamin C Crystals
Vitamin D Tablets
Vitamin K
Vita-Time Tablets
Water Pill Tablets
Water Pill w/Iron Tablets
Water Pill w/Potassium Capsules
Wheat Germ Oil Capsules
Yeast Plus Tablets
◆Zacne Tablets
Zinc Tablets

NATURSLIM CORPORATION   415, 590
P.O. Box 3609
Santa Rosa, CA 95402
Address inquiries to:
William P. White, Customer
   Relations Director   (707) 528-7311
OTC Products Available
◆NaturSlim II

NORCLIFF THAYER INC.   415, 591
One Scarsdale Road
Tuckahoe, NY 10707 (914) 969-8383
OTC Products Available
◆A-200 Pyrinate Liquid, Gel
◆Co-Salt, Salt Substitute
◆Esotérica Medicated Fade Cream
◆Liquiprin Acetaminophen
Nature's Remedy Natural Vegetable
   Laxative
◆Oxy Wash Antibacterial Skin Wash
◆Oxy-5 Lotion
◆Oxy-10 Lotion
◆Tums Antacid Tablets

NORWICH-EATON   416, 592
PHARMACEUTICALS
Division of MortonNorwich Consumer
   Products Group
17 Eaton Avenue
Norwich, NY 13815

Address inquiries to:
Medical Department (607) 335-2565
Branch Offices
ATLANTA
Avondale Estates, GA 30002
P.O. Box 508   (404) 292-9298
DALLAS
Dallas, TX 75265
Box 225490   (214) 337-4794
ELK GROVE
Elk Grove Village, IL 60007
1350 Greenleaf Avenue
                    (312) 593-0100
GREENVILLE
Greenville, SC 29602
P.O. Box 2468   (803) 277-7110
LOS ANGELES
Los Angeles, CA 90051
Terminal Annex
P.O. Box 2171   (213) 726-0505
WINDSOR LOCKS
Windsor Locks, CT
101 Turnpike Road
Suite #210   (203) 623-5331
OTC Products Available
BPN Ointment
Bacitracin Ointment
Chloraseptic Preparations
          Children's Chloraseptic Lozenges
◆   Chloraseptic Lozenges
◆   Chloraseptic Liquid
◆   Chloraseptic Spray
◆   Chloraseptic Cough Control
          Lozenges
          Chloraseptic Gel
◆Encare
Encare Contraceptive Inserts
Morton Salt Substitute
NP-27 Cream, Liquid, Powder & Spray
   Powder
Necta Sweet
Necta Sweet Saccharin Tablets
◆Norforms
◆Norwich Aspirin
Norwich Bacitracin Ointment
Norwich Glycerin Suppositories
◆Pepto-Bismol Liquid & Tablets
Unguentine Plus
Zinc Oxide Ointment

NUTRITION CONTROL   595
PRODUCTS
Division of Pharmex Inc.
2113 Lincoln Street
P.O. Box 151
Hollywood, FL 33022 (305) 923-2821
OTC Products Available
Bio-Crest Tabseals
Chelated Minerals
Kelex Tabseals

O'CONNOR PRODUCTS   416, 595
COMPANY
24400 Capitol
Redford, MI 48239
Address inquiries to:
Herbert B. Roberts (800) 521-9522
For Medical Emergencies Contact:
Richard B. Seymour (800) 521-9522
OTC Products Available
◆Dex-A-Diet II Capsules
Dex-A-Diet Lite Time Release Capsules
K-Forté Tablets

ORTHO PHARMACEUTICAL   416, 597
CORPORATION
Consumer Products Division
Route #202
Raritan, NJ 08869   (201) 524-0400
For Medical Emergencies Contact:
Dr. B. Malyk   (201) 524-2170
OTC Products Available
◆Conceptrol Birth Control Cream
◆Conceptrol Shields Latex Prophylactics
Conceptrol Supreme Lubricated Thin
   Prophylactics
◆Delfen Contraceptive Foam
Intercept Contraceptive Inserts
◆Masse Breast Cream
◆Ortho Disposable Vaginal Applicators
◆Ortho Personal Lubricant
◆Ortho-Creme Contraceptive Cream
◆Ortho-Gynol Contraceptive Jelly

(◆ **Shown in Product Identification Section**)

ORTHO PHARMACEUTICAL 417, 598
CORPORATION
Dermatological Division
Raritan, NJ 08869
a Johnson & Johnson Company
(201) 524-0400
OTC Products Available
◆Purpose Brand Dry Skin Cream
◆Purpose Brand Shampoo
◆Purpose Brand Soap

PARKE-DAVIS 417, 599
Division of Warner-Lambert Company
201 Tabor Road
Morris Plains, NJ 07950
(201) 540-2000
Regional Sales Offices
Atlanta (Doraville), GA 30340
2935 Northeast Parkway
(404) 449-9691
Baltimore (Hunt Valley), MD 21031
11350 McCormick Road
(301) 666-7810
Dallas, TX 75247
7777 Carpenter Freeway
(214) 631-2323
Detroit (Troy), MI 48207
Suite 412
500 Stephenson Highway
(313) 589-3292
East Hartford, CT 06108
111 Founders Plaza
(203) 528-9601
Memphis, TN 38138
1355 Lynnfield Road
(901) 767-1921
Pittsburgh, PA 15220
Manor Oak Two
1910 Cochran Road
(412) 343-9855
Schaumburg, IL 60195
1111 Plaza Drive (312) 884-6990
Seattle, WA 98188
150 Andover Park, W
(206) 244-7400
Tustin, CA 92680
17822 East 17th St.
(714) 731-3441
OTC Products Available
A.R.D. Anoperineal Dressings
Abdec Baby Vitamin Drops
Abdec Kapseals
Abdol with Minerals Capsules
Acetaminophen (Tapar)
Agoral
Agoral, Marshmallow Flavor
Agoral, Raspberry Flavor
Alcohol, Rubbing (Lavacol)
Alophen Pills
◆Anusol Hemorrhoidal Suppositories
◆Anusol Ointment
Aspirin Compound Tablets
Aspirin Tablets
Benadryl Antihistamine Cream
◆Benadryl Cream
Benylin DM
Caladryl Cream, Lotion
Calcium Lactate Tablets
Capsolin Ointment
Cherry Syrup
Docusate Sodium Capsules (D-S-S
Capsules)
Docusate Sodium with Casanthranol
Capsules (D-S-S Plus Capsules)
Ferrous Sulfate Filmseals
◆Gelusil Liquid & Tablets
Gelusil-M Liquid & Tablets
Gelusil-II Liquid & Tablets
Geriplex Kapseals
Geriplex-FS Kapseals
Geriplex-FS Liquid
Hydrogen Peroxide Solution
Lavacol
Milk of Bismuth
Myadec
Natabec Kapseals
Natabec-FA Kapseals
Niacin Tablets
Paladac
Paladac with Minerals Tablets
Peroxide, Hydrogen
Quinine Sulfate Capsules
Rubbing Alcohol (Lavacol)

Siblin Granules
Terpin Hydrate Elixir, and w/Codeine
Thera-Combex H-P Kapseals
Tucks Cream
Tucks Ointment
Tucks Premoistened Pads
Tucks Take-Alongs
Unibase
Vitamin B Complex, Kapseals
Ziradryl Lotion

PERSON & COVEY, INC. 418, 603
616 Allen Avenue
Glendale, CA 91201
Address inquiries to:
Lorne V. Persōn, President
(213) 240-1030
OTC Products Available
A.C.N.
◆DHS Shampoo
◆DHS Tar Shampoo
◆DHS Zinc Shampoo
Enisyl Tablets
Solbar Plus 15
◆Xerac

PFIPHARMECS DIVISION 418, 603
Pfizer Inc.
235 E. 42nd Street
New York, NY 10017
Address inquiries to:
Pfizer Inc. (212) 573-2323
Branch Offices
Clifton, NJ 07012
230 Brighton Rd. (201) 546-7702
Doraville, GA 30340
4360 Northeast Expressway
(404) 448-6666
Hoffman Estates, IL 60712
2400 W. Central Road
(312) 381-9500
Grand Prairie, TX 75050
502 Fountain Parkway
(817) 261-9131
Irvine, CA 92705
16700 Red Hill Ave.
(714) 540-9180
Portland, OR 97210
3333 N.W. Industrial St.
(503) 222-9281
OTC Products Available
Bacitracin
◆Bonine
Cotril ½% Cream
◆Coryban-D Capsules
◆Coryban-D Cough Syrup
Li-Ban Spray
◆Obron-6 Tablets
◆Rid
◆Roeribec
◆Terramycin Ointment
◆Viterra C
◆Viterra E
◆Viterra High Potency Tablets
◆Viterra Original Formula Tablets
Wart-Off

PHARMACRAFT DIVISION 606
Pennwalt Corporation
755 Jefferson Road
Rochester, NY 14623
Address inquiries to:
Professional Service Dept.
P.O. Box 1212
Rochester, NY 14603
(716) 475-9000
OTC Products Available
Allerest Tablets, Children's Chewable
Tablets, Headache Strength Tablets &
Timed-Release Capsules
CaldeCORT Hydrocortisone Cream
Caldesene Medicated Ointment
Caldesene Medicated Powder
Cruex Medicated Cream
Cruex Medicated Powder
Desenex Foot & Sneaker Spray
Desenex Powders, Foam, Ointment,
Liquid, & Soap
Sinarest Regular & Extra Strength
Tablets

PLOUGH, INC. 418, 607
3030 Jackson Avenue
Memphis, TN 38151

Address inquiries to:
Consumer Relations Dept.
(901) 320-2386
For Medical Emergencies Contact:
Clinical Affairs Dept.
(901) 320-2011
OTC Products Available
◆Aftate for Athlete's Foot
◆Aftate for Jock Itch
◆Aspergum
◆Correctol
◆Cushion Grip
◆Di-Gel
Duration Mentholated Nasal Spray
◆Duration Nasal Spray
◆Duration Nose Drops
◆Regutol
◆St. Joseph Aspirin for Children
◆St. Joseph Cold Tablets for Children
◆St. Joseph Cough Syrup for Children
◆Shade
◆Shade Plus
◆Solarcaine
◆Super Shade

POYTHRESS & CO., INC., WM. P. 610
16 N. 22nd Street
P.O. Box 26946
Richmond, VA 23261 (804) 644-8591
Address inquiries to:
Special Services Department
OTC Products Available
Bensulfoid
Bensulfoid Lotion
Panalgesic

PROCTER & GAMBLE 610
P.O. Box 171
Cincinnati, OH 45201
Address inquiries to:
Arnold P. Austin (513) 977-5547
For Medical Emergencies Contact:
W.S. Lainhart, M.D.
(513) 763-6905
OTC Products Available
Head & Shoulders
Scope

PURDUE FREDERICK 419, 611
COMPANY, THE
50 Washington Street
Norwalk, CT 06856 (203) 853-0123
Address inquiries to:
Medical Department
OTC Products Available
Arthropan Liquid
Betadine Aerosol Spray
◆Betadine Antiseptic Gauze Pad
Betadine Antiseptic Lubricating Gel
◆Betadine Douche
◆Betadine Douche Kit
Betadine Hēlafoam Solution
Betadine Medicated Douche
Betadine Mouthwash/Gargle
◆Betadine Ointment
Betadine Perineal Wash Concentrate
Betadine Shampoo
◆Betadine Skin Cleanser
Betadine Skin Cleanser Foam
◆Betadine Solution
Betadine Solution Swab Aid
Betadine Solution Swabsticks
Betadine Surgical Scrub
Betadine Surgi-Prep Sponge-Brush
◆Betadine Viscous Formula Antiseptic
Gauze Pad
Betadine Whirlpool Concentrate
Parelixir Liquid
Probilagol Liquid
Senokap DSS Capsules
Senokot Suppositories
Senokot Syrup
◆Senokot Tablets/Granules
Senokot Tablets Unit Strip Pack
Senokot w/Psyllium Powder
◆Senokot-S Tablets
Sulfabid Tablets
Supertah Ointment

REQUA MANUFACTURING 420, 612
COMPANY, INC.
1 Seneca Place
Greenwich, CT 06830

Address inquiries to:
John H. Geils   (203) 869-2445
OTC Products Available
◆Charcocaps

RIKER LABORATORIES, INC.   613
Subsidiary of 3M Company
19901 Nordhoff Street
Northridge, CA 91324
Address inquiries to:
Director, Medical Services
     (213) 341-1300, Ext. 421
OTC Products Available
Alu-Cap Capsules
Alu-Tab Tablets
Buf Acne Cleansing Bar
Buf Beauty Bar
Buf Beauty Basics
Buf Beauty Cream
Buf Body Scrub
Buf Foot-Care Kit
Buf Foot-Care Lotion
Buf Foot-Care Soap
Buf Kit for Acne
Buf Lotion
Buf-Ped
Buf-Puf
Buf-Puf Duo
Buf-Puf Nonmedicated Cleansing
   Sponge
Dorbane Tablets
Dorbantyl Capsules
Dorbantyl Forte Capsules
Estomul-M Liquid
Estomul-M Tablets
Medihaler-Epi Aerosol
pHresh 3.5 Cleansing Liquide
Titralac Liquid
Titralac Tablets

ROBINS COMPANY, INC. A. H. 420, 614
1407 Cummings Drive
Richmond, VA 23220
Address inquiries to:
The Medical Department
(804) 257-2000
For Medical Emergencies Contact:
Medical Department   (804) 257-2000
(day or night)
If no answer, call answering service
     (804) 257-7788
OTC Products Available
◆Allbee C-800 Plus Iron Tablets
◆Allbee C-800 Tablets
◆Allbee with C Capsules
◆Dimacol Capsules
◆Dimacol Liquid
◆Dimetane Decongestant Elixir
◆Dimetane Decongestant Tablets
◆Dimetane Elixir
◆Dimetane Tablets
◆Mitrolan Tablets
◆Robitussin
◆Robitussin-CF
◆Robitussin-DM
◆Robitussin-PE
◆Z-Bec Tablets

ROCHE LABORATORIES   420, 618
Division of Hoffmann-La Roche Inc.
340 Kingsland Street
Nutley, NJ 07110
For Medical Information
Write: Professional Services Dept.
Business hours only (8:30 a.m. to
   5:00 p.m. EST), call
     (201) 235-2355
For Medical Emergency Information
   only after hours or on weekends,
   call   (201) 235-2355
Branch Warehouses
Belvidere, NJ 07823
   Water Street   (201) 475-5337
Dallas, TX 75229
   2727 Northaven Rd.
   (P.O. Box 29009)   (214) 241-8573
Decatur, GA 30031
   421 DeKalb Industrial Way
     (404) 296-1241
Des Plaines, IL 60018
   105 E. Oakton St.   (312) 299-0021
   (Chicago)   (312) 775-0733
San Leandro, CA 94577
   1599 Factor Ave.   (415) 352-1660

OTC Products Available
◆Vi-Penta Infant Drops
◆Vi-Penta Multivitamin Drops

RYSTAN COMPANY, INC.   618
470 Mamaroneck Avenue
White Plains, NY 10605
Address inquiries to:
Professional Services Dept.
     (914) 761-0044
Branch Office
Little Falls, NJ 07424
   47 Center Avenue   (201) 256-3737
OTC Products Available
Chloresium Ointment & Solution
Derifil Tablets & Powder

SDA PHARMACEUTICALS, INC.   618
919 Third Avenue
New York, NY 10022
Address inquiries to:
Dr. Edward L. Steinberg
     (212) 688-4420
OTC Products Available
Anorexin Capsules
Anorexin One-Span Capsules

S.S.S. COMPANY   619
71 University Avenue, SW
Atlanta, GA 30315
Address inquiries to:
Lamar Swift   (404) 521-0857
For Medical Emergencies Contact:
Jerry McHan, PhD   (404) 688-6291
OTC Products Available
Mothers Friend Cream
Mothers Friend Liquid
S.S.S. Tonic Liquid
S.S.S. Tonic Tablets
20/20 Contact Lens Wetting Solution
20/20 Eye Drops

SCHERING CORPORATION   421, 619
Galloping Hill Road
Kenilworth, NJ 07033
Address inquiries to:
Professional Services Department
     (201) 931-2000
Branch Offices
Southeast Branch
   5884 Peachtree Rd., NE
   Chamblee, GA 30341
     (404) 457-6315
Midwest Branch
   7500 N. Natchez Avenue
   Niles, IL 60648   (312) 647-9363
Southwest Branch
   1921 Gateway Drive
   Irving, TX 75062   (214) 258-3545
West Coast Branch
   14775 Wicks Blvd.
   San Leandro, CA 94577
     (415) 357-3125
OTC Products Available
A and D Cream
◆A and D Ointment
◆Afrin Menthol Nasal Spray 0.05%
◆Afrin Nasal Spray 0.05%, Nose Drops
   0.05%, Pediatric Nose Drops
   0.025%
◆Afrinol Repetabs Tablets
◆Chlor-Trimeton Allergy Syrup, Tablets &
   Long-Acting Repetabs Tablets
◆Chlor-Trimeton Decongestant Tablets
Chlor-Trimeton Expectorant
◆Cod Liver Oil Concentrate Tablets,
   Capsules
◆Cod Liver Oil Concentrate Tablets
   w/Vitamin C
◆Coricidin Children's Cough Syrup
◆Coricidin Cough Syrup
◆Coricidin 'D' Decongestant Tablets
◆Coricidin Decongestant Nasal Mist
◆Coricidin Demilets Tablets for Children
◆Coricidin Sinus
   Headache Tablets (Extra Strength)
◆Coricidin Medilets Tablets for Children
◆Coricidin Tablets
◆Demazin Decongestant-Antihistamine
   Repetabs Tablets & Syrup
Dermolate Anal-Itch Ointment
Dermolate Anti-Itch Cream & Spray

Dermolate Scalp-Itch Lotion
◆Emko Because Contraceptor Vaginal
   Contraceptive Foam
◆Emko Pre-Fil Vaginal Contraceptive
   Foam
◆Emko Vaginal Contraceptive Foam
◆Mol-Iron Tablets, Liquid & Chronosule
   Capsules
◆Mol-Iron Tablets w/Vitamin C
Sunril Premenstrual Capsules
◆Tinactin Aerosol Powder 1%
◆Tinactin Antifungal 1%, Cream,
   Solution & Powder

**SEARLE CONSUMER   423, 627
PRODUCTS**
Division of Searle Pharmaceuticals Inc.
Box 5110
Chicago, IL 60680
Address inquiries to:
Medical Communications Department
G.D. Searle & Co.   (312) 982-7000
For Medical Emergencies Contact:
Medical Department, G.D. Searle & Co.
(within IL)   (312) 982-7000
(outside IL)   (800) 323-4397
OTC Products Available
◆Dramamine Junior Liquid
◆Dramamine Liquid
◆Dramamine Tablets
◆Icy Hot Balm
◆Icy Hot Rub
◆Metamucil, Instant Mix
◆Metamucil, Instant Mix, Orange Flavor
◆Metamucil Powder
◆Metamucil Powder, Orange Flavor

STAR PHARMACEUTICALS INC.   628
16499 N.E. 19th Ave.
N. Miami Beach, FL 33162
Address inquiries to:
Scott L. Davidson   (305) 949-1612
For Medical Emergencies Contact:
Scott L. Davidson   (305) 949-1612
OTC Products Available
Star-Otic 15 c.c.

**STUART   424, 629
PHARMACEUTICALS**
Div. of ICI Americas, Inc.
Wilmington, DE 19897
Address inquiries to:
John R. Hazlett, Manager
   Professional Services (302) 575-2231
OTC Products Available
ALternaGEL Liquid
Dialose Capsules
Dialose Plus Capsules
Effersyllium Instant Mix
Ferancee Chewable Tablets
Ferancee-HP Tablets
Hibiclens
Hibistat
Hibitane Tincture (Tinted & Non-Tinted)
Kasof Capsules
◆Mylanta Liquid
◆Mylanta Tablets
◆Mylanta-II Liquid
◆Mylanta-II Tablets
◆Mylicon (Tablets & Drops)
◆Mylicon-80 Tablets
Orexin Softab Tablets
Probec-T Tablets
◆Stuart Formula Tablets, The
Stuart Prenatal Tablets
◆Stuartinic Tablets

SUGARLO COMPANY   424, 633
600 Fire Road
P.O. Box 1100
Pleasantville, NJ 08232
Address inquiries to:
Alan E. Kligerman   (609) 645-7500
OTC Products Available
◆LactAid brand lactose enzyme

SYNTEX LABORATORIES, INC.   633
3401 Hillview Avenue
Palo Alto, CA 94304
Address inquiries to:
Medical Affairs   (415) 855-5545
OTC Products Available
Carmol 10, 10% Urea Lotion
Carmol 20, 20% Urea Cream

Methakote Diaper Rash Cream
Topic Benzyl Alcohol Gel

**THOMPSON MEDICAL COMPANY,   634
INC.**
919 Third Avenue
New York, NY 10022
Address inquiries to:
Dr. Edward L. Steinberg
                    (212) 688-4420
OTC Products Available
Appedrine, Maximum Strength
Aspercreme
Control Capsules
Dexatrim
Dexatrim Extra Strength
Prolamine Capsules, Super Strength

THOUGHT TECHNOLOGY, LTD.   635
2193 Clifton Avenue, Suite P.D.R.
Montreal, Canada H4A 2N5
Address inquiries to:
Lawrence Klein, President
                    (514) 484-0305
For Medical Emergencies Contact:
Dr. H.K. Myers   (514) 731-9195
OTC Products Available
GSR 2
GSR/Temp 2

UPJOHN COMPANY, THE   424, 635
7000 Portage Road
Kalamazoo, MI 49001
Address inquiries to:
Medical Services   (616) 323-6615
*Pharmaceutical Sales Areas
and Distribution Centers*
Atlanta (Chamblee),
  GA 30341   (404) 451-4822
Boston (Needham Heights),
  MA 02194   (617) 449-0320
Buffalo (Cheektowaga),
  NY 14240   (716) 681-7160
Chicago (Oak Brook),
  IL 60680   (312) 654-3300
Cincinnati, OH 45214
                    (513) 242-4573
Dallas, TX 75265   (214) 824-3027
Denver, CO 80217   (303) 399-3113
Honolulu, HI 96809 (808) 538-1181
Kalamazoo, MI 49001
                    (616) 323-4000
Kansas City, MO 64141
                    (816) 361-2286
Los Angeles, CA 90051
                    (213) 463-8101
Memphis, TN 38122   (901) 761-4170
Miami, FL 33152   (305) 758-3317
Minneapolis, MN 55440
                    (612) 588-2786
New York
  Long Island, NY 11514
                    (516) 747-1970
Philadelphia (Wayne)
  PA 19087   (215) 265-2100
Pittsburgh (Bridgeville)
  PA 15017
                    (412) 257-0200
Portland, OR 97208 (503) 232-2133
St. Louis, MO 63177
                    (314) 872-8626
San Francisco (Palo Alto)
  CA 94304   (415) 493-8080
Washington, DC 20013
                    (202) 882-6163
OTC Products Available
Alkets Tablets
Aspirin Tablets, USP
Baciguent Antibiotic Ointment
Calcium Gluconate Tablets, USP
Calcium Lactate Tablets, USP
Caripeptic Liquid
Casyllium Granules
Cebefortis
Cebenase Tablets
Cebetinic Tablets
Cheracol Cough Syrup
Cheracol D Cough Syrup
Citrocarbonate Antacid
Clocream Skin Cream
◆Cortaid Cream
◆Cortaid Lotion
◆Cortaid Ointment

Diostate D Tablets
Epinephricaine Rectal Ointment
Ergophene Skin Ointment
Ferrous Sulfate Tablets, USP
Gerizyme Liquid
Hydriodic Acid (Upjohn) Cough Syrup
Hydrolose Syrup
◆Kaopectate Anti-Diarrhea Medicine
◆Kaopectate Concentrate Anti-Diarrhea
  Medicine
Lipomul Oral Liquid
Medicated Foot Powder
Mercresin Tincture
Myciguent Antibiotic Cream
Myciguent Antibiotic Ointment
◆Mycitracin Antibiotic Ointment
Orthoxicol Cough Syrup
P-A-C Compound Capsules & Tablets
Pentacresol Instrument Disinfecting
  Solution
Pentacresol Oral Solution
Phenolax Wafers
Pyrroxate Capsules
Salicresin Fluid
Sigtab Tablets
Super D Perles
Tanicaine Rectal Ointment
Tanicaine Rectal Suppositories
Unicap Capsules & Tablets
Unicap Chewable Tablets
◆Unicap M Tablets
Unicap Plus Iron Tablets
Unicap Senior Tablets
◆Unicap T Tablets
Upjohn Vitamin C Tablets
Upjohn Vitamin E Capsules
Zinc Sulfide Compound Lotion,
  Improved
Zymacap Capsules
Zymalixir Fluid
Zymasyrup Fluid

**VICKS TOILETRY   424, 637
PRODUCTS DIVISION**
Richardson-Merrell Inc.
10 Westport Road
Wilton, CT 06897
Address inquiries to:
Director of Scientific & Regulatory
  Affairs
Vicks Divisions Research &
  Development   (914) 664-5000
For Medical Emergencies Contact
Medical Director
Vicks Divisions Research &
  Development   (914) 664-5000
OTC Products Available
◆Clearasil 5% Benzoyl Peroxide Lotion
  Acne Treatment
Clearasil Medicated Cleanser
Clearasil Soap
Clearasil Stick
◆Clearasil Super Strength Acne
  Treatment Cream
Clearasil Super Strength Acne
  Treatment Cream Vanishing Tinted
Demure Douche
  Liquid
  Packets
Lemon Jelvyn Beauty Cleanser
Lemon Jelvyn Beauty Freshener
◆Topex 10% Benzoyl Peroxide Lotion
  Buffered Acne Medication

ORAL HEALTH PRODUCTS
Benzodent Analgesic Denture Ointment
Complete Denture Cleanser and
  Toothpaste in One
Fasteeth Denture Adhesive Powder
Fixodent Denture Adhesive Cream
Kleenite Denture Cleanser
Lavoris Mouthwash and Gargle

**VICKS HEALTH CARE   424, 638
DIVISION**
Richardson-Merrell Inc.
10 Westport Road
Wilton, CT 06897
Address inquiries to:
Director of Scientific & Regulatory
  Affairs
Vicks Divisions Research &
  Development   (914) 664-5000

For Medical Emergencies Contact
Medical Director
Vicks Divisions Research &
  Development   (914) 664-5000
OTC Products Available
◆Daycare Multi-Symptom Colds Medicine
  Liquid & Capsules
Formula 44 Cough Control Discs
◆Formula 44 Cough Mixture
◆Formula 44D Decongestant Cough
  Mixture
◆Nyquil Nighttime Colds Medicine
Oracin Cherry Flavor Cooling Throat
  Lozenges
Oracin Cooling Throat Lozenges
◆Sinex Decongestant Nasal Spray
◆Sinex Long-Acting Decongestant Nasal
  Spray
Vaposteam
Vatronol Nose Drops
Vicks Blue Cough Drops
Vicks Cough Drops
  Regular Flavor
  Wild Cherry Flavor
  Lemon Flavor
  Blue Mint
Vicks Cough Silencers Cough Drops
Vicks Cough Syrup
Vicks Formula 44 Cough Control Discs
◆Vicks Formula 44 Cough Mixture
◆Vicks Formula 44D Decongestant
  Cough Mixture
Vicks Inhaler
◆Vicks Nyquil Nighttime Colds Medicine
◆Vicks Sinex Decongestant Nasal Spray
◆Vicks Sinex Long-Acting Decongestant
  Nasal Spray
Vicks Throat Lozenges
◆Vicks Vaporub
Vicks Vaposteam
Vicks Vatronol Nose Drops
Victors Menthol-Eucalyptus Vapor
  Cough Drops
  Regular
  Cherry Flavor

WALKER, CORP & CO., INC.   642
20 E. Hampton Place
Syracuse, NY 13206
Address inquiries to:
P.O. Box 1320
Syracuse, NY 13201 (315) 463-4511
For Medical Emergencies Contact:
Robert G. Long   (315) 638-4763
OTC Products Available
Evac-U-Gen

WALLACE LABORATORIES   425, 642
Half Acre Road
Cranbury, NJ 08512
Address inquiries to:
Wallace Laboratories
Div. of Carter-Wallace, Inc.
P.O. Drawer #5
Cranbury, NJ 08512 (609) 655-6000
For Medical Emergencies:
                    (609) 799-1167
OTC Products Available
◆Maltsupex
◆Ryna
◆Ryna-C
◆Ryna-CX
◆Syllact

**WARNER-LAMBERT   425, 644
COMPANY**
201 Tabor Road
Morris Plains, NJ 07950
Address inquiries to:
Robert Kirpitch   (201) 540-3204
For Medical Emergencies Contact:
Dr. Robert Gabrielson
                    (201) 540-2301
OTC Products Available
◆e.p.t. In-Home Early Pregnancy Test
◆Halls Mentho-Lyptus Cough Tablets
◆Listerine Antiseptic
◆Listermint Cinnamon Mouthwash &
  Gargle
◆Listermint Mouthwash & Gargle
◆Lubath Bath Oil
◆Lubriderm Cream
◆Lubriderm Lotion

(◆ Shown in Product Identification Section)

◆Rolaids Antacid Tablets
◆Sinutab Extra Strength Capsule Formula
◆Sinutab Extra Strength Tablets
◆Sinutab Long-Lasting Decongestant Nasal Spray
◆Sinutab Tablets
◆Sinutab II Tablets

WESTWOOD PHARMACEUTICALS INC. 647
468 Dewitt St.
Buffalo, NY 14213
Address inquiries to:
Wilfred J. Larson, President
(716) 887-3400
OTC Products Available
Alpha Keri Bath Oil
Alpha Keri Soap
Alpha Keri Spray
Balnetar
Estar Tar Gel
Fostex BPO 5%
Fostex CM
Fostex Cake
Fostex Cream & Medicated Cleanser
Fostril
Ice Mint
Keri Creme
Keri Facial Cleanser
Keri Facial Soap
Keri Lotion
Lowila Cake
Pernox Lotion
Pernox Scrub
Pernox Shampoo
PreSun 4 Lotion
PreSun 8 Lotion, Creamy Lotion & Gel
PreSun 15 Lotion
PreSun Sunscreen Lip Protection
Sebucare
Sebulex and Sebulex Cream
Sebulex Conditioning Shampoo with Protein
Sebutone & Sebutone Cream
Transact

WHITEHALL LABORATORIES 426, 652
Division of American Home Products Corporation
685 Third Avenue
New York, NY 10017
Address inquiries to:
Medical Department (212) 878-5508
OTC Products Available
◆Anacin Analgesic Capsules
◆Anacin Analgesic Tablets
◆Anacin Maximum Strength Analgesic Capsules
◆Anacin Maximum Strength Analgesic Tablets
◆Anacin-3 Analgesic Tablets
◆Anbesol Antiseptic Anesthetic Gel
◆Anbesol Antiseptic Anesthetic Liquid
◆Arthritis Pain Formula by the Makers of Anacin Analgesic Tablets
Bisodol Antacid Powder
Bisodol Antacid Tablets
Bronitin Asthma Tablets
Bronitin Mist
Cleansing Pads by the Makers of Preparation H Hemorrhoidal Remedies
Compound W Solution
Denalan Denture Cleanser
◆Denorex Medicated Shampoo
◆Denorex Mountain Fresh Scent Medicated Shampoo
Dristan Cough Formula
◆Dristan Decongestant/Antihistamine /Analgesic Tablets
Dristan 12-Hour Nasal Decongestant Capsules
◆Dristan Decongestant/Antihistamine /Analgesic Capsules
Dristan Inhaler
Dristan Long Lasting Menthol Nasal Mist

◆Dristan Long Lasting Nasal Mist
◆Dristan Menthol Nasal Mist
◆Dristan Nasal Mist
Dristan Room Vaporizer
Dristan-AF Decongestant Tablets
Dry and Clear Acne Medication
Dry and Clear Double Strength Cream
Dry and Clear Medicated Acne Cleanser
Freezone Solution
Heather Feminine Deodorant Spray
Heet Analgesic Liniment
Heet Spray Analgesic
InfraRub Analgesic Cream
Momentum Muscular Backache Formula
Neet Aerosol Depilatory
Neet Depilatory Cream
Neet Depilatory Lotion
Outgro Solution
Oxipor VHC Lotion for Psoriasis
Predictor In-Home Early Pregnancy Test
◆Preparation H Hemorrhoidal Ointment
◆Preparation H Hemorrhoidal Suppositories
◆Primatene Mist
Primatene Mist Suspension
◆Primatene Tablets - M Formula
◆Primatene Tablets - P Formula
Quiet World Analgesic/Sleeping Aid
Semicid Vaginal Contraceptive Suppositories
Sleep-Eze Tablets
Sudden Action Breath Freshener
Sudden Beauty Country Air Mask
Sudden Beauty Hair Spray
Trendar Premenstrual Tablets
Viro-Med Liquid
Viro-Med Tablets

J.B. WILLIAMS COMPANY, INC., THE 660
767 Fifth Avenue
New York, NY 10153
Address inquiries to:
R.E. Hansen (212) 752-5700
Branch Offices
Cranford, NJ 07016 (201) 276-8000
OTC Products Available
Acu-Test In-Home Pregnancy Test
Deep-Down Pain Relief Rub
Femlron Multi-Vitamins and Iron
Femlron Tablets
First Sign Nasal Decongestant
Geritol Liquid-High Potency Iron & Vitamin Tonic
Geritol Mega Vitamins
Geritol Tablets - High Potency Iron & Vitamin Tablets
P.V.M. Appetite Control Capsules
P.V.M. Appetite Suppressant Tablets
Serutan Concentrated Powder-Fruit Flavored
Serutan Toasted Granules
Sominex Sleep Aid
Vivarin Stimulant Tablets

Consumer Products Division WINTHROP LABORATORIES 662
Division of Sterling Drug Inc.
90 Park Avenue
New York, NY 10016
Address inquiries to:
Professional Services Dept.
(212) 972-4124
For Medical Emergencies Contact:
Medical Director (212) 972-2640
OTC Products Available
Astring-o-sol
Bronkaid Mist
Bronkaid Mist Suspension
Bronkaid Tablets
Campho-Phenique Liquid & Gel
Caroid Laxative
Caroid Tooth Powder
Creamalin Tablets
Haley's M-O, Regular & Flavored
Mucilose Flakes & Granules
NTZ Drops & Spray
Neocurtasal
Neo-Synephrine Cold Tablets

Neo-Synephrine Jelly
Neo-Synephrine Nasal Sprays (Mentholated)
Neo-Synephrine Nose Drops
Neo-Synephrine II Long Acting Nasal Spray
Neo-Synephrine II Long Acting Nose Drops (Adult & Pediatric Strengths)
Neo-Synephrine II Long Acting Vapor Nasal Spray
pHisoAc
pHisoDan
pHisoDerm
WinGel Liquid & Tablets

WYETH LABORATORIES 427, 665
Division of American Home Products Corporation
P.O. Box 8299
Philadelphia, PA 19101
Address inquiries to:
Professional Service (215) 688-4400
For Medical Emergency Information
Day or night call (215) 688-4400
Wyeth Distribution Centers
Andover, MA 01810
P.O. Box 1776 (617) 475-9075
Boston (617) 423-2644
Atlanta, GA 30302
P.O. Box 4365 (404) 873-1681
Baltimore, MD 21224
101 Kane St. (301) 633-4000
Boston Distribution Center
see under Andover, MA
Buena Park, CA 90620
6530 Altura Blvd. (714) 523-5500
(Los Angeles) (213) 627-5374
Chicago Distribution Center
see under Evanston, IL
Cleveland, OH 44101
Post Office Box 91549
(216) 238-9450
Dallas, TX 75235
P.O. Box 35213 (214) 631-4360
Denver, CO 80201
P.O. Box 2107 (303) 388-3635
Evanston, IL 60204
P.O. Box 1659 (Skokie)
(312) 675-1400
(Chicago) (312) 463-2400
Honolulu, HI 96814
1013 Kawaiahao St.(808) 538-1988
Kansas City Distribution Center,
see under North Kansas City, MO
Kent, WA 98031
Post Office Box 5609
(206) 872-8790
Los Angeles Distribution Center,
see under Buena Park, CA
Memphis, TN 38101
P.O. Box 1698 (901) 353-4680
New York Distribution Center,
see under Secaucus, NJ
North Kansas City, MO 64116
P.O. Box 7588 (816) 842-0680
Philadelphia Distribution Center
Paoli, PA 19301 (215) 644-8000
(215) 878-9500
St. Paul, MN 55164
P.O. Box 43034 (612) 454-6270
Seattle Distribution Center,
see under Kent, WA
Secaucus, NJ 07094
555 Secaucus Rd. (201) 867-0300
(N.Y.C.) (212) 964-0041

OTC Products Available
◆Aludrox Oral Suspension & Tablets
◆Amphojel Suspension & Suspension without Flavor
◆Amphojel Tablets
◆Collyrium Eye Lotion
◆Collyrium with Ephedrine Eye Drops
Nursoy Soy Protein Infant Formula
SMA Iron Fortified Infant Formula
◆Simeco Suspension
◆Wyanoid Ointment
◆Wyanoids Hemorrhoidal Suppositories

(◆ Shown in Product Identification Section)

MEMORANDUM

MEMORANDUM

Section 2

Product Name Index

In this section products are listed in alphabetical sequence by brand name. Page numbers have been included to assist you in locating additional information on described products. The symbol ◆ indicates the product is shown in the Product Identification Section.

A

A.C.N. (Persōn & Covey) p 603
A and D Cream (Schering)
◆ A and D Ointment (Schering) p 421, 619

APAP Non-Aspirin Pain Relief Tablets (Medique)
APAP-Plus Non-Aspirin Extra Strength Pain Relief Tablets (Medique)

A.R.D. Anoperineal Dressings (Parke-Davis)
◆ A.R.M. Allergy Relief Medicine Tablets (Menley & James) p 413, 574
◆ A-200 Pyrinate Liquid, Gel (Norcliff Thayer) p 415, 591
Abdec Baby Vitamin Drops (Parke-Davis)
Abdec Kapseals (Parke-Davis)
Abdol with Minerals Capsules (Parke-Davis)
Acephen Acetaminophen Rectal Suppositories (G & W Laboratories) p 538
Acerola C (Nature's Bounty) p 587
Acetaminophen (Tapar) (Parke-Davis)
◆ Acid Mantle Creme & Lotion (Dorsey) p 409, 530
Acidophilus Capsules (Nature's Bounty) p 587
◆ Acnaveen Bar (CooperCare) p 408, 526
Acnederm Lotion (Lannett) p 548
◆ Acnomel Cream & Cake (Menley & James) p 413, 574
Acu-Test In-Home Pregnancy Test (J.B. Williams) p 660
◆ Adapettes (Alcon/bp) p 405, 505
◆ Afrin Menthol Nasal Spray (Schering) p 421, 619
◆ Afrin Nasal Spray, Nose Drops, Pediatric Nose Drops (Schering) p 421, 619

◆ Afrinol Repetabs Tablets (Schering) p 421, 620
◆ Aftate (Plough) p 418, 607
Agoral, Plain (Parke-Davis) p 599
Agoral Raspberry & Marshmallow Flavors (Parke-Davis) p 599
Alamag Fruit-Flavored Antacid Tablets (Medique)
Alcalak Antacid Tablets (Medique)
Alfalfa Tablets (Nature's Bounty) p 587
Alka-Seltzer Effervescent Antacid (Miles) p 584
Alka-Seltzer Effervescent Pain Reliever Antacid (Miles) p 583
Alka-Seltzer Plus Cold Medicine (Miles) p 584
Alka-2 Chewable Antacid Tablets (Miles) p 584
Alkets Tablets (Upjohn)
◆ Allbee C-800 Plus Iron Tablets (Robins) p 420, 614
◆ Allbee C-800 Tablets (Robins) p 420, 614
◆ Allbee with C Capsules (Robins) p 420, 615
Allerest Headache Strength Tablets (Pharmacraft) p 606
Allerest Tablets & Capsules (Pharmacraft) p 606
◆ Allimin Filmcoated Tablets (Health Care) p 410, 541
Alophen Pills (Parke-Davis)
Alpha Keri Bath Oil (Westwood) p 647
Alpha Keri Soap (Westwood) p 648
Alpha Keri Spray (Westwood)
Alphamul (Lannett)
ALternaGEL Liquid (Stuart) p 629
Alu-Cap Capsules (Riker)
◆ Aludrox Oral Suspension & Tablets (Wyeth) p 417, 665
Alu-Tab Tablets (Riker)
◆ Ambenyl-D Decongestant Cough Formula (Marion) p 412, 556

Ammens medicated powder (Bristol-Myers)
◆ Amphojel Tablets (Wyeth) p 427, 665
◆ Amphojel Suspension & Suspension without Flavor (Wyeth) p 427, 665
◆ Anacin Analgesic Capsules (Whitehall) p 652
Anacin Analgesic Tablets (Whitehall) p 426, 652
◆ Anacin Maximum Strength Analgesic Capsules (Whitehall) p 426, 652
◆ Anacin Maximum Strength Analgesic Tablets (Whitehall) p 426, 652
◆ Anacin-3 Analgesic Tablets (Whitehall) p 426, 652
Ana-Pro (protein products) (Anabolic)
◆ Anbesol Antiseptic Anesthetic Gel (Whitehall) p 426, 652
◆ Anbesol Antiseptic Anesthetic Liquid (Whitehall) p 426, 652
Anorexin Capsules (SDA Pharmaceuticals) p 618
Anorexin One-Span Capsules (SDA Pharmaceuticals) p 618
◆ Answer At-Home Early Pregnancy Test Kit (Carter Products) p 407, 522
Anulan Suppositories (Lannett)
◆ Anusol Ointment (Parke-Davis) p 599
◆ Anusol Suppositories (Parke-Davis) p 599
Appedrine, Maximum Strength (Thompson Medical) p 634
Aqua-A (Anabolic) p 507
Aquacare Dry Skin Cream & Lotion (Herbert) p 543
Aquacare/HP Dry Skin Cream & Lotion (Herbert) p 543
Arco-Cee Tablets (Arco)
Arco-Lase Tablets (Arco)
Arcoret Tablets (Arco)
Arcoret w/Iron Tablets (Arco)
Arcotinic Tablets (Arco)

◆Arthritis Pain Formula by the Makers of Anacin Analgesic Tablets (Whitehall) p 426, 653
◆Arthritis Strength Bufferin (Bristol-Myers) p 406, 516
Arthropan Liquid (Purdue Frederick)
Aspercreme (Thompson Medical) p 634
◆Aspergum (Plough) p 418, 608
Aspirin Suppositories (G & W Laboratories) p 538
Astring-o-sol (Consumer Products Div., Winthrop)
Aureomycin Ointment 3% (Lederle)
◆Aveeno Bar (CooperCare) p 408, 526
◆Aveeno Colloidal Oatmeal (CooperCare) p 408, 526
◆Aveeno Oilated Bath Powder (CooperCare) p 408, 526
Ayr Saline Nasal Mist (Ascher) p 508

B

B-1 Tablets (Nature's Bounty) p 587
B-2 Tablets (Nature's Bounty) p 587
B6-Plus (Anabolic) p 507
B-6 Tablets (Nature's Bounty) p 587
B12-Plus (Anabolic) p 507
B-12 Tablets (Nature's Bounty) p 587
B-50 Tablets (Nature's Bounty) p 587
B-100 Tablets (Nature's Bounty) p 587
B-100 Time Release Tablets (Nature's Bounty) p 587
B-125 Tablets (Nature's Bounty) p 587
B Complex & B-12 Tablets (Nature's Bounty) p 587
B Complex & C (Time Release) Capsules (Nature's Bounty) p 587
B & C Liquid (Nature's Bounty) p 587
B.F.I. (Beecham Products) p 510
BPN Ointment (Norwich-Eaton) p 592
B.Q cold tablets (Bristol-Myers)
Baciguent Antibiotic Ointment (Upjohn) p 635
Bacimycin Ointment (Merrell-National)
Bacitracin Topical Ointment (Pfipharmecs) p 603
Bactine Skin Wound Cleanser (Miles) p 584
Balmex Baby Powder (Macsil) p 556
Balmex Emollient Lotion (Macsil) p 556
Balmex Ointment (Macsil) p 556
Balnetar (Westwood) p 648
Ban Basic antiperspirant (Bristol-Myers)
Ban Big Ball antiperspirant (Bristol-Myers)
Ban cream antiperspirant (Bristol-Myers)
Ban roll-on antiperspirant (Bristol-Myers)
Ban Super Solid antiperspirant (Bristol-Myers)
Basic Formula (Anabolic)
◆Bayer Aspirin & Bayer Children's Chewable Aspirin (Glenbrook) p 410, 539
Bayer Children's Cold Tablets (Glenbrook) p 540
Bayer Cough Syrup for Children (Glenbrook) p 540
◆Bayer Timed-Release Aspirin (Glenbrook) p 410, 540
Bee Pollen Tablets (Nature's Bounty) p 587
Beelith Tablets (Beach) p 509
Bellafedrol AH Tablets (Lannett)
Benadryl Antihistamine Cream (Parke-Davis) p 599
◆Benadryl Cream (Parke-Davis) p 417
Ben-Gay External Analgesic Products (Leeming) p 552
Bensulfoid (Poythress)
Bensulfoid Lotion (Poythress) p 610
Benylin DM (Parke-Davis) p 600
◆Benzedrex Inhaler (Menley & James) p 413, 574
Benzodent Analgesic Denture Ointment (Vicks Toiletry Products)

Betadine Aerosol Spray (Purdue Frederick)
◆Betadine Antiseptic Gauze Pad (Purdue Frederick) p 419
Betadine Antiseptic Lubricating Gel (Purdue Frederick) p 611
◆Betadine Douche (Purdue Frederick) p 419, 611
◆Betadine Douche Kit (Purdue Frederick) p 419
Betadine Hēlafoam Solution (Purdue Frederick)
Betadine Medicated Douche (Purdue Frederick)
Betadine Mouthwash/Gargle (Purdue Frederick)
◆Betadine Ointment (Purdue Frederick) p 419, 612
Betadine Perineal Wash Concentrate (Purdue Frederick)
Betadine Shampoo (Purdue Frederick)
◆Betadine Skin Cleanser (Purdue Frederick) p 419, 611
Betadine Skin Cleanser Foam (Purdue Frederick)
◆Betadine Solution (Purdue Frederick) p 419, 611
Betadine Solution Swab Aid (Purdue Frederick)
Betadine Solution Swabsticks (Purdue Frederick)
Betadine Surgical Scrub (Purdue Frederick)
Betadine Surgi-Prep Sponge-Brush (Purdue Frederick)
◆Betadine Viscous Formula Antiseptic Gauze Pad (Purdue Frederick) p 419
Betadine Whirlpool Concentrate (Purdue Frederick)
◆BiCozene Creme (Creighton Products) p 408, 526
Bio-Crest (Nutrition Control) p 595
Biotin Tablets (Nature's Bounty) p 587
Bisacodyl Suppositories (G & W Laboratories)
Bisacodyl Tablets (Lederle)
Bisodol Antacid Powder (Whitehall) p 653
Bisodol Antacid Tablets (Whitehall) p 653
Bluboro Powder Astringent Soaking Solution (Herbert) p 543
Body on Tap (Bristol-Myers)
◆BoilnSoak (Alcon/bp) p 405, 505
Bone Meal with Vitamin D Tablets (Nature's Bounty) p 587
◆Bonine (Pfipharmecs) p 418, 603
Brewer's Yeast Powder (Debittered) (Nature's Bounty) p 587
Brewer's Yeast Tablets (Nature's Bounty) p 587
Breonesin (Breon) p 515
Bronitin Asthma Tablets (Whitehall)
Bronitin Mist (Whitehall)
Bronkaid Mist (Consumer Products Div., Winthrop) p 662
Bronkaid Mist Suspension (Consumer Products Div., Winthrop) p 662
Bronkaid Tablets (Consumer Products Div., Winthrop) p 663
Buf Acne Cleansing Bar (Riker) p 613
Buf Beauty Bar (Riker)
Buf Beauty Basics (Riker)
Buf Beauty Cream (Riker)
Buf Body Scrub (Riker) p 613
Buf Foot-Care Kit (Riker)
Buf Foot-Care Lotion (Riker)
Buf Foot-Care Soap (Riker)
Buf Kit for Acne (Riker) p 613
Buf Lotion (Riker) p 613
◆Bufferin (Bristol-Myers) p 406, 516
Buf-Ped Foot Cleansing Sponge (Riker)
Buf-Puf Duo (Riker)
Buf-Puf Nonmedicated Cleansing Sponge (Riker) p 613
Bugs Bunny With Extra C Multivitamin Supplement (Miles) p 585

C

◆C3 Cold Cough Capsules (Menley & James) p 413, 574
C-250 with Rose Hips Tablets (Nature's Bounty) p 587
C-300 with Rose Hips (Chewable) Tablets (Nature's Bounty) p 587
C-500 with Rose Hips Tablets (Nature's Bounty) p 587
C-1000 with Rose Hips Tablets (Nature's Bounty) p 587
C-Complex Tablets (Nature's Bounty) p 588
CCP Tablets (Medique) p 574
C Liquid (Nature's Bounty) p 588
CPA (Anabolic)
C-Time-750 Time Release Tablets (Nature's Bounty) p 588
C-Time-1500 Tablets (Nature's Bounty) p 588
Caladryl Lotion & Cream (Parke-Davis) p 600
Calamatum Lotion, Ointment, Spray (Blair) p 512
Calcium Ascorbate Tablets (Nature's Bounty) p 588
Calcium Lactate Tablets (Nature's Bounty) p 588
CaldeCORT Hydrocortisone Cream (Pharmacraft) p 606
Caldesene Medicated Ointment (Pharmacraft) p 606
Caldesene Medicated Powder (Pharmacraft) p 606
Cal-M (Anabolic) p 507
Calpadon (Anabolic)
◆Cama Inlay-Tabs (Dorsey) p 409, 530
Campho-Phenique Liquid (Consumer Products Div., Winthrop) p 663
Cankaid (Becton Dickinson) p 510
Capsolin Ointment (Parke-Davis)
Carmol 10 Lotion (Syntex) p 633
Carmol 20 Cream (Syntex) p 633
Carnation Evaporated Milk (Carnation) p 520
Carnation Instant Breakfast (Carnation) p 521
Carnation Instant Nonfat Dry Milk (Carnation) p 521
Caroid Laxative (Consumer Products Div., Winthrop)
Caroid Tooth Powder (Consumer Products Div., Winthrop)
◆Carter's Little Pills (Carter Products) p 407, 523
Casec (Mead Johnson Nutritional) p 562
Castaderm (Lannett)
Cebēfortis (Upjohn)
Cebenase Tablets (Upjohn)
Cebētinic Tablets (Upjohn)
Cebralan MT Tablets (Lannett)
◆Centrum (Lederle) p 411, 549
Cēpacol Anesthetic Troches (Merrell-National) p 580
◆Cēpacol Mouthwash/Gargle (Merrell-National) p 415, 580
◆Cēpacol Throat Lozenges (Merrell-National) p 415, 580
◆Cēpastat Sore Throat Lozenges (Merrell-National) p 415, 581
◆Cēpastat Sore Throat Spray/Gargle (Merrell-National) p 415, 581
Ce-Vi-Sol (Mead Johnson Nutritional) p 562
◆Chap Stick Lip Balm (Miller-Morton) p 415, 586
◆Chap Stick Sunblock 15 Lip Balm (Miller-Morton) p 415, 586
◆Charcocaps (Requa) p 420, 612
Chelated Calcium Tablets (Nature's Bounty) p 588
Chelated Chromium Tablets (Nature's Bounty) p 588
Chelated Copper Tablets (Nature's Bounty) p 588
Chelated Magnesium Tablets (Nature's Bounty) p 588
Chelated Manganese Tablets (Nature's Bounty) p 588
Chelated Minerals (Nutrition Control)
Chelated Multi-Mineral Tablets (Nature's Bounty) p 588

(◆ Shown in Product Identification Section)

Chelated Potassium Tablets (Nature's Bounty) p 588
Chelated Zinc Tablets (Nature's Bounty) p 588
Cheq Antiperspirant/Deodorant Spray (Almay) p 506
Cheq Extra-Dry Antiperspirant/Deodorant Spray (Aerosol) (Almay) p 506
Cheq Roll-On Antiperspirant/Deodorant (Almay) p 506
Cheq Soft Powder Extra Dry Antiperspirant Spray (Aerosol) (Almay) p 506
Cheracol Cough Syrup (Upjohn)
Cheracol D Cough Syrup (Upjohn) p 635
Chew-Iron Tablets (Nature's Bounty) p 588
Chexit Tablets (Dorsey)
◆Children's Cepastat Sore Throat Lozenges (Merrell-National) p 415, 581
Children's Chewables Tablets (Nature's Bounty) p 588
Children's Hold (Beecham Products) p 510
Chip Resistant Top Coat (Almay) p 506
◆Chloraseptic Cough Control Lozenges (Norwich-Eaton) p 416, 593
Chloraseptic Gel (Norwich-Eaton) p 593
◆Chloraseptic Liquid & Spray (Norwich-Eaton) p 416, 593
◆Chloraseptic Lozenges (Norwich-Eaton) p 416, 593
Chloraseptic Lozenges, Children's (Norwich-Eaton) p 592
Chloresium Ointment & Solution (Rystan) p 618
◆Chlor-Trimeton Allergy Syrup, Tablets & Long-Acting Repetabs Tablets (Schering) p 421, 620
◆Chlor-Trimeton Decongestant Tablets (Schering) p 421, 620
Chlor-Trimeton Expectorant (Schering) p 620
Chocks Multivitamin Supplement (Miles) p 584
Chocks Plus Iron Multivitamin Supplement (Miles) p 584
Chocks-Bugs Bunny Multivitamin Supplement (Miles) p 584
Chocks-Bugs Bunny Plus Iron Multivitamin Supplement (Miles) p 584
Cholagest (Anabolic) p 507
Choline Tablets (Nature's Bounty) p 588
Chromease (Anabolic)
Citrocarbonate Antacid (Upjohn) p 635
Claws (Nature's Bounty)
◆Clean and Gentle Daily Shampoo (Almay) p 406, 506
Clean and Gentle Oil-Free Conditioner (Almay) p 506
Cleansing Pads by the Makers of Preparation H Hemorrhoidal Remedies (Whitehall) p 653
Clear By Design Invisible Greaseless Acne Gel (Herbert) p 543
◆Clear Eyes Eye Drops (Abbott Consumer Products) p 405, 502
Clear Nail Enamel (Almay) p 506
◆Clearasil 5% Benzoyl Peroxide Lotion (Vicks Toiletry Products) p 424, 637
Clearasil Medicated Cleanser (Vicks Toiletry Products)
Clearasil Soap (Vicks Toiletry Products)
Clearasil Stick (Vicks Toiletry Products)
◆Clearasil Super Strength Acne Treatment Cream (Vicks Toiletry Products) p 424, 637
Clearasil Super Strength Acne Treatment Cream Vanishing Tinted (Vicks Toiletry Products)
◆Clens (Alcon/bp) p 405, 505
Clocream Skin Cream (Upjohn)
◆Cod Liver Oil Concentrate Tablets, Capsules (Schering) p 421, 621
◆Cod Liver Oil Concentrate Tablets w/Vitamin C (Schering) p 421, 621
Codexin Extra Strength Capsules (Arco) p 508
Co-Gel Tablets (Arco)
Cold Cream (Almay) p 506
Cold Cream Soap for Normal, Combination and Dry Skin (Almay) p 506

Colgate Dental Cream (Colgate-Palmolive)
Colgate Toothbrushes (Colgate-Palmolive)
◆Collyrium Eye Lotion (Wyeth) p 417, 665
◆Collyrium with Ephedrine Eye Drops (Wyeth) p 417, 665
Color Rich Eyeshadow (Wet or Dry) (Almay) p 506
Complete Denture Cleanser and Toothpaste in One (Vicks Toiletry Products)
Compound W Solution (Whitehall) p 653
◆Comtrex (Bristol-Myers) p 406, 516
◆Conceptrol Birth Control Cream (Ortho Consumer Products) p 416, 597
◆Conceptrol Shields Latex Prophylactics (Ortho Consumer Products) p 416, 597
Conceptrol Supreme Lubricated Thin Prophylactics (Ortho Consumer Products) p 597
◆Congespirin (Bristol-Myers) p 406, 516
Congespirin cough syrup (Bristol-Myers)
◆Congespirin Liquid Cold Medicine (Bristol-Myers) p 406, 517
Consotuss Antitussive Syrup (Merrell-National)
◆Contac Capsules (Menley & James) p 413, 575
◆Contac Jr. Childrens' Cold Medicine (Menley & James) p 413, 575
Control Capsules (Thompson Medical) p 634
◆Coricidin Children's Cough Syrup (Schering) p 421, 622
◆Coricidin Cough Syrup (Schering) p 421, 621
◆Coricidin 'D' Decongestant Tablets (Schering) p 421, 621
◆Coricidin Decongestant Nasal Mist (Schering) p 421, 621
◆Coricidin Demilets Tablets for Children (Schering) p 421, 622
◆Coricidin Extra Strength Sinus Headache Tablets (Schering) p 421, 623
◆Coricidin Medilets Tablets for Children (Schering) p 421, 622
◆Coricidin Tablets (Schering) p 421, 621
◆Correctol Laxative Tablets (Plough) p 418, 608
◆Cortaid Cream (Upjohn) p 424, 635
◆Cortaid Lotion (Upjohn) p 424, 635
◆Cortaid Ointment (Upjohn) p 424, 635
Cotril ½% (Pfipharmecs) p 603
◆Coryban-D Capsules (Pfipharmecs) p 418, 604
◆Coryban-D Cough Syrup (Pfipharmecs) p 418, 604
◆Co-Salt (Norcliff Thayer) p 415, 591
◆Cosanyl Cough Syrup (Health Care) p 410, 542
◆Cosanyl-DM Cough Syrup (Health Care) p 410, 542
Cosyrel Cold Symptom Relief Tablets (Medique)
Cotussis Syrup (Merrell-National)
◆CoTylenol Children's Liquid Cold Formula (McNeil Consumer Products) p 412, 560
◆CoTylenol Cold Formula Tablets and Capsules (McNeil Consumer Products) p 412, 559
◆CoTylenol Liquid Cold Formula (McNeil Consumer Products) p 412, 559
◆Counter Balance Clear Facial Cleanser (Almay) p 406, 506
Counter Balance Facial Soap for Oily Skin (Almay) p 506
Counter Balance Fluffy Facial Cleanser (Almay) p 506
◆Counter Balance Oil-Free Moisturizer (Almay) p 406, 506
◆Counter Balance Pore Lotion (Almay) p 406, 506
Cover-up Stick - light, medium, dark (Almay) p 506
Creamalin Tablets (Consumer Products Div., Winthrop)
Cruex Medicated Cream (Pharmacraft) p 606
Cruex Medicated Powder (Pharmacraft) p 606
Cuprex (Beecham Products) p 510

Curad Bandages (Colgate-Palmolive)
◆Cushion Grip (Plough) p 418, 608
Cuticle Treatment Oil (Almay) p 506

D

◆DHS Shampoo (Persōn & Covey) p 418, 603
◆DHS Tar Shampoo (Persōn & Covey) p 418, 603
◆DHS Zinc Shampoo (Persōn & Covey) p 418, 603
DIU-ERB (Anabolic)
D-Sinus Capsules (Laser) p 548
Danex Protein Enriched Dandruff Shampoo (Herbert) p 543
◆Datril (Bristol-Myers) p 406, 517
◆Datril 500 (Bristol-Myers) p 406, 517
◆Daycare Multi-Symptom Colds Medicine Capsules (Vicks Health Care) p 424, 638
◆Daycare Multi-Symptom Colds Medicine (Vicks Health Care) p 424, 638
◆Debrox Drops (Marion) p 412, 556
Decapryn Syrup (Merrell-National)
Decavitamin Tablets (Lannett)
◆Deep Mist Cleanser (Almay) p 406, 506
◆Deep Mist Cleansing Lotion (Almay) p 406, 506
Deep Mist Eye Cream (Almay) p 506
Deep Mist Gentle Gel Mask (Almay) p 506
◆Deep Mist Mild Skin Freshener (Almay) p 406, 506
Deep Mist Moisture Cream (Almay) p 506
◆Deep Mist Moisture Lotion (Almay) p 406, 506
Deep Mist Moisture and Replenishing Lotion (Almay) p 506
◆Deep Mist Toning and Refining Lotion (Almay) p 406, 506
Deep Mist Ultralight Moisture Lotion (Almay) p 506
Deep Mist Ultralight Night Cream (Almay) p 506
Deep Mist Ultrarich Night Cream (Almay) p 506
Deep Pore Cleansing Mask (Almay) p 506
Deep-Down (J.B. Williams) p 660
Delacort (Mericon) p 580
Delcid (Merrell-National) p 581
◆Delfen Contraceptive Foam (Ortho Consumer Products) p 416, 597
◆Demazin Decongestant-Antihistamine Repetabs Tablets & Syrup (Schering) p 421, 623
Demure Douche (Vicks Toiletry Products)
Denalan Denture Cleanser (Whitehall)
◆Denorex Medicated Shampoo, Regular & Mountain Fresh Herbal (Whitehall) p 426, 653
Derifil Tablets & Powder (Rystan) p 618
Derma Medicone Ointment (Medicone) p 573
Dermagen (Anabolic)
Dermaide Aloe Ointment (Dermaide) p 527
◆Derma+Soft Creme (Creighton Products) p 408, 527
◆Dermassage Dish Liquid (Colgate-Palmolive) p 408, 525
◆Dermassage Medicated Skin Lotion (Colgate-Palmolive) p 408, 525
Dermolate Anti-Itch Cream & Spray (Schering) p 623
Dermolate Anal-Itch Ointment (Schering) p 623
Dermolate Scalp-Itch Lotion (Schering) p 623
Desenex Foam (Pharmacraft) p 607
Desenex Foot & Sneaker Spray (Pharmacraft) p 607
Desenex Ointment & Liquid (Pharmacraft) p 607
Desenex Powders (Pharmacraft) p 607
Desenex Soap (Pharmacraft) p 607
Desitin Ointment (Leeming) p 553
DeWitt's Absorbent Rub (DeWitt)
DeWitt's Alertacaps (DeWitt)
◆DeWitt's Antacid Powder (DeWitt) p 409, 529
DeWitt's Aspirin (DeWitt)

(◆ Shown in Product Identification Section)

DeWitt's B Complex W/Vit. C Capsules (DeWitt)
◆DeWitt's Baby Cough Syrup (DeWitt) p 409, 529
DeWitt's Boric Acid Solution (DeWitt)
DeWitt's Calamine Lotion (DeWitt)
DeWitt's Camphor Liniment (DeWitt)
DeWitt's Camphor Spirits (DeWitt)
DeWitt's Carbolized Witch Hazel Salve (DeWitt)
DeWitt's Castor Oil (DeWitt)
DeWitt's Children's Aspirin (DeWitt)
DeWitt's Cold Capsules (DeWitt)
DeWitt's Cold Sore Lotion (DeWitt)
DeWitt's Creosant Cough Syrup (DeWitt)
DeWitt's Feet Treat (DeWitt)
DeWitt's Flowaway Tablets (DeWitt)
DeWitt's Glycerin (DeWitt)
DeWitt's Glycerin & Rosewater (DeWitt)
DeWitt's Gumzor (DeWitt)
DeWitt's Iodine (DeWitt)
DeWitt's Joggers Lotion (DeWitt)
DeWitt's Merthiolate (DeWitt)
DeWitt's Multi Vitamins (DeWitt)
DeWitt's Multi Vit./Iron (DeWitt)
◆DeWitt's Oil for Ear Use (DeWitt) p 409, 529
DeWitt's Oil of Cloves (DeWitt)
DeWitt's Oil of Wintergreen (DeWitt)
DeWitt's Olive Oil (DeWitt)
◆DeWitt's Pills for Backache & Joint Pains (DeWitt) p 409, 529
DeWitt's Pyrinyl (DeWitt)
DeWitt's Secta Sooth Ampules (DeWitt)
DeWitt's Spirit of Peppermint (DeWitt)
DeWitt's Sweet Oil (DeWitt)
DeWitt's Teething Lotion (DeWitt)
DeWitt's Terpin Hydrate w/D.M. (DeWitt)
DeWitt's Thera-M Vitamins (DeWitt)
DeWitt's Toothache Drops (DeWitt)
DeWitt's Turpentine (DeWitt)
DeWitt's Vit. C 250 mg. Chewable Tablets (DeWitt)
DeWitt's Vit. C 250 mg. Tablets (DeWitt)
DeWitt's Vit. C 500 mg. Tablets (DeWitt)
DeWitt's Vit. E 200 I.U. Capsules
DeWitt's Vit. E 400 I.U. Capsules
DeWitt's Vit. E 1000 I.U. Capsules
DeWitt's Zoo Chews Vitamins (DeWitt)
DeWitt's Zoo Chews w/Iron Vitamins
Dex-A-Diet Lite Time Release Capsules (O'Connor) p 595
◆Dex-A-Diet II Time Release Capsules (O'Connor) p 416, 596
Dexatrim & Dexatrim Extra Strength (Thompson Medical) p 634
Dialose Capsules (Stuart) p 629
Dialose Plus Capsules (Stuart) p 629
◆Diaparene Baby Powder (Glenbrook) p 410, 541
◆Diaparene Baby Wash Cloths (Glenbrook) p 410, 541
◆Dietac Diet Aid Capsules (Menley & James) p 413, 575
◆Dietac Diet Aid Drops (Menley & James) p 413, 575
◆Dietac Diet Aid Tablets (Menley & James) p 413, 576
◆Dietac Maximum Strength Once-A-Day Diet Aid Capsules (Menley & James) p 413, 576
◆Dietac Maximum Strength Twice-A-Day Diet Aid Capsules (Menley & James) p 413, 576
◆Di-Gel (Plough) p 418, 608
Digestaid (Anabolic)
Di-Gon Diarrhea Relief Tablets (Medique)
◆Dimacol Capsules (Robins) p 420, 615
◆Dimacol Liquid (Robins) p 420, 615
◆Dimetane Decongestant Elixir (Robins) p 420, 616
◆Dimetane Decongestant Tablets (Robins) p 420, 616
◆Dimetane Elixir (Robins) p 420, 615
◆Dimetane Tablets (Robins) p 420, 615
DioMedicone Tablets (Medicone) p 573
Diostate D Tablets (Upjohn)
Diothane Ointment (Merrell-National)
Disanthrol Capsules (Lannett)
Disodan Capsules (Lannett)

Disolan Capsules (Lannett)
Disonate Capsules (Lannett)
Disoplex Capsules (Lannett)
Docusate Sodium (DSS) (Lederle)
Docusate Sodium w/Casanthranol (Lederle)
Dolomite Tablets (Nature's Bounty) p 588
Dorbane Tablets (Riker) p 613
Dorbantyl Capsules (Riker) p 613
Dorbantyl Forte Capsules (Riker) p 614
◆Dorcol Pediatric Cough Syrup (Dorsey) p 409, 530
◆Doxidan (Hoechst-Roussel) p 411, 544
◆Dramamine Junior Liquid (Searle Consumer Products) p 423, 627
◆Dramamine Liquid (Searle Consumer Products) p 423, 627
◆Dramamine Tablets (Searle Consumer Products) p 423, 627
Dristan Cough Formula (Whitehall)
◆Dristan Decongestant/Antihistamine/Analgesic Capsules (Whitehall) p 426, 654
◆Dristan Decongestant/Antihistamine/Analgesic (Whitehall) p 426, 654
◆Dristan 12-Hour Nasal Decongestant Capsules (Whitehall) p 426, 654
Dristan Inhaler (Whitehall)
◆Dristan Long Lasting Nasal Mist, Regular & Menthol (Whitehall) p 426, 655
◆Dristan Nasal Mist, Regular & Menthol (Whitehall) p 426, 655
Dristan Room Vaporizer (Whitehall)
◆Dristan-AF Decongestant/Antihistamine/Analgesic (Whitehall) p 426, 655
Dry and Clear, Acne Medication, Lotion & Double Strength Cream (Whitehall) p 656
Dry and Clear Medicated Acne Cleanser (Whitehall) p 656
◆Dulcolax Tablets & Suppositories (Boehringer Ingelheim) p 406, 514
Duolube Ophthalmic Ointment (Muro) p 586
◆Duration (Plough) p 418, 608
Duration Mentholated Nasal Spray (Plough)

E

E-200 Capsules (Nature's Bounty) p 588
E-200 (Natural Complex) Capsules (Nature's Bounty) p 588
E-400 Capsules (Nature's Bounty) p 588
E-400 (Natural Complex) Capsules (Nature's Bounty) p 588
E-600 (Natural Complex) Capsules (Nature's Bounty) p 588
E-1000 (Natural Complex) Capsules (Nature's Bounty) p 588
◆e.p.t. In-Home Early Pregnancy Test (Warner-Lambert) p 425, 644
E-Z Trim (Fox) p 538
Ear Drops by Murine (See Murine Ear Wax Removal System/Murine Ear Drops) (Abbott Consumer Products) p 502
◆Eclipse After Sun Lotion (Herbert) p 411, 543
◆Eclipse Sunscreen Lip & Face Protectant (Herbert) p 411, 543
Eclipse Sunscreen Lotion & Gel, Original (Herbert) p 543
◆Eclipse Sunscreen Lotion, Total (Alcohol Base) (Herbert) p 411, 543
◆Eclipse Sunscreen Lotion, Total (Moisturizing Base) (Herbert) p 411
◆Eclipse Suntan Lotion, Partial (Herbert) p 411, 543
◆Ecotrin Tablets (Menley & James) p 413, 576
Effersyllium Instant Mix (Stuart) p 629
◆Emko Because Contraceptor Vaginal Contraceptive Foam (Schering) p 421, 624
◆Emko Pre-Fil Vaginal Contraceptive Foam (Schering) p 421, 625
◆Emko Vaginal Contraceptive Foam (Schering) p 421, 624
◆Emulave Bar (CooperCare) p 408, 526

Emulsified E-200 Capsules (Nature's Bounty) p 588
Enamel Quick Dry (Almay) p 506
◆Encare (Norwich-Eaton) p 416, 593
Encare Contraceptive Inserts (Norwich-Eaton)
Enfamil Concentrated Liquid & Powder (Mead Johnson Nutritional) p 562
Enfamil Nursette (Mead Johnson Nutritional) p 562
Enfamil Ready-To-Use (Mead Johnson Nutritional) p 563
Enfamil w/Iron Concentrated Liquid & Powder (Mead Johnson Nutritional) p 562
Enfamil w/Iron Ready-To-Use (Mead Johnson Nutritional) p 563
Enhance (Vitamin E Topicals) (Anabolic)
Enisyl (Persòn & Covey) p 603
Eno (Beecham Products) p 511
Epinephricaine Rectal Ointment (Upjohn)
Ergophene Skin Ointment (Upjohn)
◆Esotérica Medicated Cream (Norcliff Thayer) p 415, 591
Estar Tar Gel (Westwood) p 648
Estomul-M Liquid (Riker)
Estomul-M Tablets (Riker)
Evac-U-Gen (Walker, Corp) p 642
◆Excedrin (Bristol-Myers) p 406, 517
◆Excedrin P.M. (Bristol-Myers) p 406, 518
◆Ex-Lax Chocolated Laxative (Ex-Lax Pharm.) p 408, 536
◆Ex-Lax Pills, Unflavored (Ex-Lax Pharm.) p 408, 536
Extra Hold Protein Conditioning Hair Spray (Aerosol) (Almay) p 506
Eye Makeup Remover Pads (Almay) p 506

F

◆4-Way Cold Tablets (Bristol-Myers) p 406, 518
4-Way long acting mentholated nasal spray (Bristol-Myers)
◆4-Way Long Acting Nasal Spray (Bristol-Myers) p 406, 518
4-Way mentholated nasal spray (Bristol-Myers)
◆4-Way Nasal Spray (Bristol-Myers) p 406, 518
F.S.K. (Fecal Staining Kit) (Jayco) p 546
Fasteeth Denture Adhesive Powder (Vicks Toiletry Products)
Fayd Skin Cream (Fleetwood)
Femaids Menstrual Relief Capsules (Medique)
Feminins Tablets (Mead Johnson Nutritional) p 563
FemIron Tablets (J.B. Williams) p 660
FemIron Multi-Vitamins and Iron (J.B. Williams) p 660
Fer-Bid Improved (Beach)
Fergon Capsules (Breon) p 515
Fergon Tablets & Elixir (Breon) p 515
Fer-In-Sol Iron Drops, Syrup & Capsules (Mead Johnson Nutritional) p 563
Ferro-Sequels (Lederle) p 549
Ferrous Sulfate Tablets (Nature's Bounty) p 588
Ferro-Vite (Anabolic)
◆Festal (Hoechst-Roussel) p 411, 544
Filibon (Lederle) p 550
First Sign (J.B. Williams)
Fixodent Denture Adhesive Cream (Vicks Toiletry Products)
Flexamide (Anabolic)
◆Flex-Care (Alcon/bp) p 405, 505
Flexical Elemental Diet (Mead Johnson Nutritional) p 564
Flintstones Multivitamin Supplement (Miles) p 584
Flintstones Plus Iron Multivitamin Supplement (Miles) p 584
Flintstones With Extra C Multivitamin Supplement (Miles) p 585

(◆ Shown in Product Identification Section)

◆Fluorigard Anti-Cavity Dental Rinse (Colgate-Palmolive) p 408, 525
Folic Acid Tablets (Nature's Bounty) p 588
Fomac Foam (Dermik) p 527
Formula 44 Cough Control Discs (Vicks Health Care) p 638
◆Formula 44 Cough Mixture (Vicks Health Care) p 424, 639
◆Formula 44D Decongestant Cough Mixture (Vicks Health Care) p 424, 639
◆Fortespan Capsules (Menley & James) p 413, 577
Fostex BPO 5% (Westwood) p 648
Fostex CM (Westwood) p 649
Fostex Cake (Westwood) p 649
Fostex Cream & Medicated Cleanser (Westwood) p 649
Fostril (Westwood) p 649
Freezone Solution (Whitehall) p 656
Fumasorb Tablets (Marion) p 557
Fumatinic Tablets (Laser) p 549
Fumerin Tablets (Laser) p 549

G

GSR 2 (Thought Technology) p 635
GSR/Temp 2 (Thought Technology)
Ganatrex Elixir (Merrell-National)
Garlic Oil Capsules (Nature's Bounty) p 588
Garlic & Parsley Capsules (Nature's Bounty) p 588
◆Gas-X Tablets (Creighton Products) p 408, 527
◆Gaviscon Antacid Tablets (Marion) p 412, 557
◆Gaviscon Liquid Antacid (Marion) p 412, 557
◆Gaviscon-2 Antacid Tablets (Marion) p 412, 557
Gelusil (Parke-Davis) p 600
Gelusil-M (Parke-Davis) p 600
Gelusil-II Liquid & Tablets (Parke-Davis) p 601
Gentle Color Eye Pencils (Almay) p 506
Gentle Color Lip Color Pencils (Almay) p 506
Gentle Color Lip Liner Pencils (Almay) p 506
Gentle Nail Enamel Remover (Almay) p 506
Gerber Cereals (Gerber)
Gerber High Meat Dinners (Strained & Junior) (Gerber)
Gerber Junior Cookies (Gerber)
Gerber Junior Foods (Gerber)
Gerber Junior Meats (Gerber)
Gerber Strained Egg Yolks (Gerber)
Gerber Strained Food (Gerber)
Gerber Strained Juices (Gerber)
Gerber Strained Meats (Gerber)
Gerber Teething Biscuits (Gerber)
Gerber Toddler Meals (Gerber)
Geriplex Kapseals (Parke-Davis)
Geriplex-FS Kapseals (Parke-Davis) p 601
Geriplex-FS Liquid (Parke-Davis) p 601
Geritol Liquid-High Potency Iron & Vitamin Tonic (J.B. Williams) p 661
Geritol Mega Vitamins (J.B. Williams) p 661
Geritol Tablets - High Potency Iron & Vitamin Tablets (J.B. Williams) p 661
Gerizyme Liquid (Upjohn)
Gevrabon Liquid (Lederle) p 550
Gevral Protein Powder (Lederle)
Gevral T Tablets (Lederle) p 550
Gevral Tablets (Lederle) p 550
Gevrite Tablets (Lederle)
Ginseng, Manchurian Capsules (Nature's Bounty) p 588
Glutamic Acid Tablets (Nature's Bounty) p 588
◆Gly-Oxide Liquid (Marion) p 412, 557
Goody's Extra Strength Tablets (Goody's)
◆Goody's Headache Powders (Goody's) p 410, 541

H

H-R Sterile Lubricating Jelly (Holland-Rantos)

◆HTO Stainless Manzan Hemorrhoidal Tissue Ointment (DeWitt) p 409, 530
Haley's M-O (Consumer Products Div., Winthrop) p 663
Halibut Liver Oil Capsules (Nature's Bounty) p 588
◆Halls Mentho-Lyptus Cough Tablets (Warner-Lambert) p 425, 645
Head & Shoulders (Procter & Gamble) p 610
Heather Feminine Deodorant Spray (Whitehall)
Heet Analgesic Liniment (Whitehall) p 656
Heet Spray Analgesic (Whitehall) p 656
Hem-Prep Combo (G & W Laboratories)
Herbal Laxative Tablets (Nature's Bounty) p 588
Hibiclens Antimicrobial Skin Cleanser (Stuart) p 630
Hibistat Germicidal Hand Rinse (Stuart) p 630
Hibitane Tincture (Tinted & Non-Tinted) (Stuart) p 630
High Gloss Nail Guard (Almay) p 506
Hold (Beecham Products) p 511
Hy-C-3000 (Anabolic)
Hydra-Lyte (Jayco) p 546
Hydrolose Syrup (Upjohn)
Hyper-E (Anabolic)
Hytone Cream ½% (Dermik) p 527
Hytone Ointment ½% (Dermik) p 528

I

I-O-Plexadine (Anabolic)
Ice Mint (Westwood) p 649
◆Icy Hot Balm (Searle Consumer Products) p 423, 627
◆Icy Hot Rub (Searle Consumer Products) p 423, 627
Impregon Concentrate (Fleming)
Incremin w/Iron Syrup (Lederle) p 550
InfraRub Analgesic Cream (Whitehall) p 657
Inositol Tablets (Nature's Bounty) p 588
Intercept Contraceptive Inserts (Ortho Consumer Products) p 597
Iron Tablets (Nature's Bounty) p 588
Isocal Complete Liquid Diet (Mead Johnson Nutritional) p 564
Isocal Tube Feeding Set (Mead Johnson Nutritional)
Isodine Antiseptic (Blair) p 513
I-Soyalac (Loma Linda) p 555

J

Jayne's P-W Vermifuge (Glenbrook)
◆Johnson's Baby Bath (Johnson & Johnson Baby Products Company) p 411, 547
◆Johnson & Johnson First Aid Cream (Johnson & Johnson) p 411, 547
Jojoba Shampoo (Nature's Bounty)

K

K-Forté Tablets (O'Connor) p 596
KLB6 Capsules (Nature's Bounty) p 588
KLB6 Complete Tablets (Nature's Bounty) p 589
KLB6 Diet Mix (Nature's Bounty) p 589
K-Orotate (Anabolic)
Kanulase Tablets (Dorsey)
◆Kaopectate (Upjohn) p 424, 636
◆Kaopectate Concentrate (Upjohn) p 424, 636
Kasof Capsules (Stuart) p 631
Kelex Tabseals (Nutrition Control)
Kelp Tablets (Nature's Bounty) p 588
Keri Creme (Westwood) p 649
Keri Facial Cleanser (Westwood) p 649
Keri Facial Soap (Westwood) p 649
Keri Lotion (Westwood) p 649
Kerid Ear Drops (Blair) p 513
Kleenite Denture Cleanser (Vicks Toiletry Products)
Kolantyl (Merrell-National) p 582
◆Konsyl (Burton, Parsons) p 407, 520
Koromex Contraceptive Foam (Holland-Rantos) p 545
Koromex Jelly/Cream Applicator (Holland-Rantos)

Koromex" Contraceptive Cream (Holland-Rantos) p 545
Koromex" Contraceptive Jelly (Holland-Rantos) p 545
Koromex"-A Contraceptive Jelly (Holland-Rantos) p 545
Kudrox Suspension (Double Strength) (Kremers-Urban) p 548

L

◆L. A. Formula (Burton, Parsons) p 407, 520
l-Glutamine Tablets (Nature's Bounty) p 589
l-Lysine Tablets (Nature's Bounty) p 589
◆LactAid (SugarLo) p 424, 633
◆Lactinex Tablets & Granules (Hynson, Westcott & Dunning) p 411, 546
Lactocal Tablets (Laser) p 549
Lac-Tol (Jayco) p 546
◆Lanacane Medicated Creme (Combe) 'p 408, 525
◆Lanacort Creme (Combe) p 408, 526
Lanamins (Lannett)
Lanatuss Expectorant (Lannett)
Lavacol (Parke-Davis)
Lavoris Mouthwash and Gargle (Vicks Toiletry Products)
Lax Special (Anabolic)
Lecithin Capsules (Nature's Bounty) p 589
Lecithin, Chewable Tablets (Nature's Bounty) p 589
Lecithin with Vitamin D Capsules (Nature's Bounty) p 589
Lecithin Granules (Nature's Bounty) p 589
Lederplex Capsules, Liquid & Tablets (Lederle) p 551
Lemon Jelvyn Beauty Cleanser (Vicks Toiletry Products)
Lemon Jelvyn Beauty Freshener (Vicks Toiletry Products)
Li-Ban Spray (Pfipharmecs) p 604
Lip Gleamer (Almay) p 506
Lip Polishers (Almay) p 506
Lipall-Plus (Anabolic)
Lipomul Oral Liquid (Upjohn)
◆Liquifilm Tears (Allergan) p 406, 506
◆Liquiprin (Norcliff Thayer) p 415, 591
◆Listerine Antiseptic (Warner-Lambert) p 425, 645
◆Listermint Cinnamon Mouthwash & Gargle (Warner-Lambert) p 425, 645
◆Listermint Mouthwash & Gargle (Warner-Lambert) p 425, 645
Liver W/B-12 Tablets (Nature's Bounty) p 589
Lofenalac (Mead Johnson Nutritional) p 565
Lonalac (Mead Johnson Nutritional) p 566
Long on Lashes Lengthening Lashcolor (Almay) p 506
Loroxide Acne Lotion (Dermik) p 528
Lowila Cake (Westwood) p 650
◆Lubath Bath Oil (Warner-Lambert) p 425. 645
◆Lubriderm Cream (Warner-Lambert) p 425, 645
◆Lubriderm Lotion (Warner-Lambert) p 425, 646
Lycolan Elixir (Lannett)
Lytren (Mead Johnson Nutritional) p 566

M

MBF (Meat Base Formula) Liquid (Gerber) p 539
MCT Oil (Mead Johnson Nutritional) p 567
Magnatril Suspension & Tablets (Lannett) p 548
Magnesium Tablets (Nature's Bounty) p 589
Magonate Tablets (Fleming)
◆Maltsupex (Wallace) p 425, 642
Manganese Tablets (Nature's Bounty) p 589
Marblen Suspensions & Tablets (Fleming) p 537
◆Masse Breast Cream (Ortho Consumer Products) p 416, 597

(◆ Shown in Product Identification Section)

Massengill Disposable Douche (Beecham Products) p 511
Massengill Disposable Medicated Douche (Beecham Products) p 511
Massengill Liquid Concentrate (Beecham Products) p 511
Massengill Powder (Beecham Products) p 511
Maxi Unshine Oil Free Make-Up (Max Factor) p 536
Maxi Unshine 100% Oil Free Blotting Powder (Max Factor) p 536
Maxi Unshine 100% Oil Free Blushing Powder (Max Factor) p 537
Measurin Tablets (Breon)
Meclizine HCl (Lederle)
Medicone Dressing Cream (Medicone) p 573
Mediconet (Medicone) p 573
Medidrops Eye Drops (Medique)
Medihaler-Epi Aerosol (Riker)
Medikoff Sugar-Free Cough Expectorant/Suppressant (Medique)
Medi-Quik (Lehn & Fink) p 555
Mediwash Eye Irrigant (Medique)
Mega V & M Tablets (Nature's Bounty) p 589
Mega-B (Arco) p 508
Mega-B with C Tablets (Nature's Bounty) p 589
Megadose (Arco) p 508
Mercodol Cough Syrup w/Decapryn (Merrell-National)
Mercresin Tincture (Upjohn)
Mercurochrome II (Becton Dickinson) p 510
◆ Mersene Denture Cleanser (Colgate-Palmolive) p 408, 525
◆ Metamucil (Searle Consumer Products) p 423, 627
◆ Metamucil, Instant Mix (Searle Consumer Products) p 423, 628
◆ Metamucil, Instant Mix, Orange Flavor (Searle Consumer Products) p 423, 628
◆ Metamucil Powder, Orange Flavor (Searle Consumer Products) p 423, 628
Metasep Shampoo (Marion) p 557
Meted Shampoo (CooperCare)
Meted 2 Shampoo (CooperCare)
Methakote Diaper Rash Cream (Syntex) p 633
Midol (Glenbrook) p 410, 541
Miles Nervine Nighttime Sleep-Aid (Miles) p 585
Milkinol (Kremers-Urban) p 548
Minit-Rub analgesic balm (Bristol-Myers)
◆ Mitrolan Tablets (Robins) p 420, 616
Mobigesic Analgesic Tablets (Ascher) p 509
Mobisyl Analgesic Creme (Ascher) p 509
Modane Bulk (Adria) p 503
Modane Soft (Adria) p 504
Modane Tablets & Liquid (Adria) p 504
Moisture Whip Lip Conditioner (Maybelline) p 559
Moisture Whip Lipstick (Maybelline) p 559
Moisture Whip Liquid Make-up & Moisture Whip Cream Make-up (Maybelline) p 559
Moisture Whip Protective Facial Moisturizer (Maybelline) p 559
◆ Mol-Iron Tablets, Liquid & Chronosule Capsules (Schering) p 421, 626
◆ Mol-Iron Tablets w/Vitamin C (Schering) p 421, 626
Momentum Muscular Backache Formula (Whitehall) p 657
Monster (Bristol-Myers) p 518
Monster with Iron (Bristol-Myers) p 519
Morton Salt Substitute (Norwich-Eaton)
Mothers Friend Cream (S.S.S. Company)
Mothers Friend Liquid (S.S.S. Company)
Mucilose Flakes & Granules (Consumer Products Div., Winthrop)
Multi-Mineral Tablets (Nature's Bounty) p 589
Multi-Scrub everyday scrubbing lotion with particles (Bristol-Myers)

Multi-Scrub medicated cleansing scrub (Bristol-Myers)
Mum cream deodorant (Bristol-Myers)
◆ Murine Ear Wax Removal System/Murine Ear Drops (Abbott Consumer Products) p 405, 502
◆ Murine Plus Eye Drops (Abbott Consumer Products) p 405, 502
◆ Murine Regular Formula Eye Drops (Abbott Consumer Products) p 405, 502
Muro Tears (Muro) p 586
Murocel Ophthalmic Solution (Muro) p 586
Myadec (Parke-Davis) p 602
Myciguent Antibiotic Ointment (Upjohn) p 636
◆ Mycitracin Antibiotic Ointment (Upjohn) p 424, 636
◆ Mylanta Liquid (Stuart) p 424, 631
◆ Mylanta Tablets (Stuart) p 424, 631
◆ Mylanta-II Liquid (Stuart) p 424, 631
◆ Mylanta-II Tablets (Stuart) p 424, 631
◆ Mylicon (Tablets & Drops) (Stuart) p 424, 631
◆ Mylicon-80 Tablets (Stuart) p 424, 632
Myoflex Creme (Adria) p 504

N

NP-27 Cream (Norwich-Eaton) p 595
NP-27 Liquid (Norwich-Eaton) p 595
NP-27 Powder (Norwich-Eaton) p 595
NP-27 Spray Powder (Norwich-Eaton) p 595
NTZ (Consumer Products Div., Winthrop) p 664
Nail Enamels: Frosted and Creme (Almay) p 506
Naldecon-DX Pediatric Syrup (Bristol) p 515
Naldecon-EX Pediatric Drops (Bristol) p 515
Naso-Mist (Muro)
Natabec Kapseals (Parke-Davis) p 602
Natabec-FA Kapseals (Parke-Davis)
Natrasan (Lank) p 548
Nature's Bounty Hair Booster Tablets (Nature's Bounty)
Nature's Bounty Slim (Nature's Bounty)
Nature's Remedy (Norcliff Thayer) p 592
◆ NaturSlim II (NaturSlim) p 415, 590
Necta Sweet Non-Caloric Sweetener (Norwich-Eaton) p 594
Necta Sweet Saccharin Tablets (Norwich-Eaton)
Neet Aerosol Depilatory (Whitehall)
Neet Depilatory Cream (Whitehall)
Neet Depilatory Lotion (Whitehall)
Neocurtasal (Consumer Products Div., Winthrop)
Neoloid (Lederle) p 551
Neo-Synephrine Cold Tablets (Consumer Products Div., Winthrop)
Neo-Synephrine Hydrochloride (Consumer Products Div., Winthrop) p 664
Neo-Synephrine Jelly (Consumer Products Div., Winthrop)
Neo-Synephrine Nose Drops (Consumer Products Div., Winthrop)
Neo-Synephrine II Long Acting Nasal Spray (Consumer Products Div., Winthrop) p 663
Neo-Synephrine II Long Acting Nose Drops (Adult & Pediatric Strengths) (Consumer Products Div., Winthrop)
Neo-Synephrine II Long Acting Vapor Nasal Spray (Consumer Products Div., Winthrop)
Nephrox Suspension (Fleming) p 537
Niacin Tablets (Nature's Bounty) p 589
Niacinamide Tablets (Nature's Bounty) p 589
Nicotinex Elixir (Fleming) p 537
◆ No Doz (Bristol-Myers) p 406, 519
Non-Oily Eye Makeup Remover Pads (Almay) p 506
Norforms Feminine Deodorants (Norwich-Eaton) p 416, 594

◆ Norwich Aspirin (Norwich-Eaton) p 417, 594
Norwich Bacitracin Ointment (Norwich-Eaton) p 594
Norwich Glycerin Suppositories (Norwich-Eaton) p 594
Novahistine Cold Tablets (Dow Pharmaceuticals) p 534
Novahistine Cough & Cold Formula (Dow Pharmaceuticals) p 532
Novahistine Cough Formula (Dow Pharmaceuticals) p 532
Novahistine DMX (Dow Pharmaceuticals) p 533
Novahistine Elixir (Dow Pharmaceuticals) p 534
Novahistine Sinus Tablets (Dow Pharmaceuticals) p 534
Nuggettes (Jayco)
◆ Nupercainal Cream, Ointment, Suppositories (Ciba) p 407, 523
Nursoy Soy Protein Infant Formula (Wyeth) p 666
Nutra-Cal (Anabolic)
Nutramigen (Mead Johnson Nutritional) p 567
Nylmerate II Solution Concentrate (Holland-Rantos) p 545
◆ Nyquil Nighttime Colds Medicine (Vicks Health Care) p 424, 639
Nytilax Tablets (Leeming) p 553

O

O-A-Crine (Anabolic)
Obegyn Tablets (Fleming)
◆ Obron-6 Tablets (Pfipharmecs) p 418, 604
Ocean Mist (Fleming) p 538
Odrinil (Fox) p 538
◆ Oil-O-Sol Liquid (Health Care) p 410, 542
One-A-Day Core C 500 Multivitamin Supplement (Miles) p 585
One-A-Day Multivitamin Supplement (Miles) p 585
One-A-Day Multivitamin Supplement Plus Iron (Miles) p 585
One-A-Day Multivitamin Supplement Plus Minerals (Miles) p 585
Onset Forte Allergy Relief Tablets (Medique)
Optilets-500 (Abbott) p 503
Optilets-M-500 (Abbott) p 503
Oracin Cherry Flavor Cooling Throat Lozenges (Vicks Health Care) p 640
Oracin Cooling Throat Lozenges (Vicks Health Care) p 639
Orazinc (Mericon) p 580
Orexin Softab Tablets (Stuart) p 632
◆ Ornacol Capsules (Menley & James) p 413, 577
Ornacol Liquid (Menley & James)
◆ Ornex Capsules (Menley & James) p 413, 578
◆ Ortho Disposable Vaginal Applicators (Ortho Consumer Products) p 416, 598
◆ Ortho Personal Lubricant (Ortho Consumer Products) p 416, 598
◆ Ortho-Creme Contraceptive Cream (Ortho Consumer Products) p 416, 598
◆ Ortho-Gynol Contraceptive Jelly (Ortho Consumer Products) p 416, 598
Orthoxicol Cough Syrup (Upjohn)
Osatate (Anabolic)
Os-Cal 500 Tablets (Marion) p 558
Os-Cal Forte Tablets (Marion) p 558
Os-Cal Plus Tablets (Marion) p 558
◆ Os-Cal Tablets (Marion) p 412, 558
Os-Cal-Gesic Tablets (Marion) p 558
◆ Otrivin (Geigy) p 410, 539
Outgro Solution (Whitehall) p 657
Oxipor VHC Lotion for Psoriasis (Whitehall) p 657
◆ Oxy Wash (Norcliff Thayer) p 415, 592
◆ Oxy-5 Lotion (Norcliff Thayer) p 415, 592
◆ Oxy-10 Lotion (Norcliff Thayer) p 415, 592
Oyster Calcium Tablets (Nature's Bounty) p 589

P

PABA Tablets (Nature's Bounty) p 589
P-A-C Compound Capsules & Tablets (Upjohn)

(◆ **Shown in Product Identification Section**)

◆PBZ Cream (Geigy) p 410, 539
P.V.M. Appetite Control Capsules (J.B. Williams) p 661
P.V.M. Appetite Suppressant Tablets (J.B. Williams) p 661
Packer's Pine Tar Soap (CooperCare)
Paladac (Parke-Davis)
Paladac with Minerals Tablets (Parke-Davis)
Pals (Bristol-Myers) p 519
Pals Plus Iron (Bristol-Myers) p 519
Panalgesic (Poythress) p 610
Pantothenic Acid Tablets (Nature's Bounty) p 589
Papaya Enzyme Tablets (Nature's Bounty) p 589
Parelixir Liquid (Purdue Frederick)
Pazo Hemorrhoid Ointment/ Suppositories (Bristol-Myers) p 519
Pentacresol Oral Solution (Upjohn)
Pentrax Tar Shampoo (CooperCare)
◆Pepto-Bismol Liquid & Tablets (Norwich-Eaton) p 416, 595
◆Percogesic Tablets (Endo) p 409, 536
◆Percy Medicine (Merrick) p 415, 583
Peritinic Tablets (Lederle) p 551
Pernox (Westwood) p 650
Pernox Lotion (Westwood) p 650
Pernox Shampoo (Westwood) p 650
Phenolax (Upjohn)
◆Phillip's Milk of Magnesia (Glenbrook) p 410, 541
pHisoAc (Consumer Products Div., Winthrop)
pHisoDan (Consumer Products Div., Winthrop)
pHisoDerm (Consumer Products Div., Winthrop) p 664
pHresh 3.5 Cleansing Liquid (Riker) p 614
Poly-Vi-Sol (Mead Johnson Nutritional) p 568
Poly-Vi-Sol Chewable Vitamin Tablets with Iron (Mead Johnson Nutritional) p 568
Poly-Vi-Sol Vitamin Drops with Iron (Mead Johnson Nutritional) p 568
Portagen (Mead Johnson Nutritional) p 568
Potassium Tablets (Nature's Bounty) p 589
Potassium & B-6 Tablets (Nature's Bounty) p 589
◆Pragmatar Ointment (Menley & James) p 413, 578
Predictor In-Home Early Pregnancy Test (Whitehall) p 657
◆Preflex (Alcon/bp) p 405, 505
◆Prefrin Liquifilm (Allergan) p 405, 506
Pregestimil (Mead Johnson Nutritional) p 569
Prelan Tablets (Lannett)
◆Preparation H Hemorrhoidal Ointment & Suppositories (Whitehall) p 426, 658
PreSun 4 Lotion (Westwood) p 650
PreSun 8 Lotion, Creamy Lotion & Gel (Westwood) p 650
PreSun 15 Lotion (Westwood) p 651
PreSun Sunscreen Lip Protection (Westwood) p 651
◆Pretts Tablets (Marion) p 412, 558
◆Primatene Mist (Whitehall) p 426, 658
◆Primatene Mist Suspension (Whitehall) p 426, 658
◆Primatene Tablets - M Formula (Whitehall) p 426, 658
◆Primatene Tablets - P Formula (Whitehall) p 426, 658
◆Privine Nasal Spray & Solution 0.05% (Ciba) p 407, 524
Probana (Mead Johnson Nutritional) p 569
Probec-T Tablets (Stuart) p 632
Probilagol Liquid (Purdue Frederick)
Proderm Topical Dressing (Hickam) p 544
Pro-Enz (Anabolic)
Prolamine Capsules, Super Strength (Thompson Medical) p 635
ProSobee (Mead Johnson Nutritional) p 570
Prostana (Anabolic)
Protective Base Coat (Almay) p 506

◆Protect Toothpaste (Marion) p 412, 558
◆Protein Conditioning Hair Spray (Almay) p 406, 506
Protein For Body Building (Nature's Bounty)
Protein Tablets (Nature's Bounty) p 589
Protexin Oral Rinse (Cetylite) p 523
Pure and Gentle Everyday Conditioning Shampoo (Almay) p 506
Pure Beauty Blotting Powder for Oily Skin (Almay) p 506
Pure Beauty Extra Cover Makeup (Almay) p 506
Pure Beauty Foundation Lotion for Oily Skin (Almay) p 506
Pure Beauty Fresh Blush (Almay) p 506
◆Pure Beauty Liquid Makeup (Almay) p 406, 506
Pure Beauty Moisturizing Makeup (Almay) p 506
Pure Beauty Richcreme Blush (Almay) p 506
Pure Beauty Translucent Face Powder (Almay) p 506
Pure Beauty Translucent Pressed Powder (Almay) p 506
Pure Castile Shampoo (Almay) p 506
◆Purpose Brand Dry Skin Cream (Ortho Dermatological) p 417, 598
◆Purpose Brand Shampoo (Ortho Dermatological) p 417, 598
◆Purpose Brand Soap (Ortho Dermatological) p 417, 598
Pyrroxate Capsules (Upjohn)

Q - R - S

Quiet World Analgesic/Sleeping Aid (Whitehall) p 659
◆Quotane Ointment (Menley & James) p 413, 578
RNA Tablets (Nature's Bounty) p 589
RNA/DNA Tablets (Nature's Bounty) p 589
Rantex Personal Cloth Wipes (Holland-Rantos)
Rectal Medicone Suppositories (Medicone) p 573
Rectal Medicone Unguent (Medicone) p 574
Regular Hold Conditioning Hair Spray (Almay) p 506
◆Regutol (Plough) p 418, 608
Resolve Cold Sore & Fever Blister Relief (Dow Pharmaceuticals) p 535
Rheaban Tablets & Liquid (Leeming) p 553
Rhulicaine (Lederle) p 551
Rhulicort Cream & Lotion (Lederle) p 552
Rhulicream (Lederle) p 551
Rhuligel (Lederle) p 551
Rhulihist (Lederle) p 551
Rhulispray (Lederle) p 551
◆Rich Lash Thickening Lashcolor (Almay) p 406, 506
Richcreme Frosted Lipcolor (Almay) p 506
Richcreme Lipcolor (Almay) p 506
◆Rid (Pfipharmecs) p 418, 604
Ridge Filling Pre-Coat (Almay) p 506
◆Robitussin (Robins) p 420, 617
◆Robitussin-CF (Robins) p 420, 617
◆Robitussin-DM (Robins) p 420, 617
◆Robitussin-PE (Robins) p 420, 617
◆Roeribec Tablets (Pfipharmecs) p 418, 605
◆Rolaids Antacid Tablets (Warner-Lambert) p 425, 646
Rutin Tablets (Nature's Bounty) p 589
◆Ryna Liquid (Wallace) p 425, 643
◆Ryna-C Liquid (Wallace) p 425, 643
◆Ryna-CX Liquid (Wallace) p 425, 643
S-A-C Tablets (Lannett)
SMA Iron Fortified Infant Formula (Wyeth) p 666
S.S.S. Tonic Liquid (S.S.S. Company)
S.S.S. Tonic Tablets (S.S.S. Company)
S.T. 37 (Beecham Products) p 511
◆St. Joseph Aspirin for Children (Plough) p 418, 609
◆St. Joseph Cold Tablets for Children (Plough) p 418, 609

◆St. Joseph Cough Syrup for Children (Plough) p 418, 609
Sal Hepatica laxative (Bristol-Myers)
Salagen Tablets (Lannett)
Salicresin Fluid (Upjohn)
Sani-Supp Foil Wrapped Glycerin Suppositories (G & W Laboratories)
Sayman Soaps & Salves (Goody's)
Scope (Procter & Gamble) p 611
Score hair cream (Bristol-Myers)
Scott's Emulsion (Beecham Products) p 511
Sebb Lotion (Max Factor) p 537
Sebb Shampoo (Max Factor) p 537
Sebucare (Westwood) p 651
Sebulex and Sebulex Cream (Westwood) p 651
Sebulex with Protein (Westwood) p 651
Sebutone & Sebutone Cream (Westwood) p 651
Sedaphan (Anabolic)
Selenace (Anabolic)
Selenium Tablets (Nature's Bounty) p 589
◆Selsun Blue Lotion (Abbott Consumer Products) p 405, 502
Semicid Vaginal Contraceptive Suppositories (Whitehall) p 659
Senokap DSS Capsules (Purdue Frederick)
Senokot Suppositories (Purdue Frederick)
Senokot Syrup (Purdue Frederick)
◆Senokot Tablets/Granules (Purdue Frederick) p 419, 612
Senokot Tablets Unit Strip Pack (Purdue Frederick)
Senokot w/Psyllium Powder (Purdue Frederick)
◆Senokot-S Tablets (Purdue Frederick) p 419, 612
Sensodyne Toothpaste (Block) p 513
Sep-A-Soothe Throat Lozenges (Medique)
Septa Ointment (Circle) p 524
Seracaine Spray For Burns (Medique)
Serutan Concentrated Powder (J.B. Williams) p 661
Serutan Concentrated Powder-Fruit Flavored (J.B. Williams) p 661
Serutan Toasted Granules (J.B. Williams) p 662
◆Shade Plus Sunscreen Lotion (SPF-8) (Plough) p 418, 609
◆Shade Sunscreen Lotion (SPF-6) (Plough) p 418, 609
Shepard's Cream Lotion (Dermik) p 528
Shepard's Dry Skin Cream (Dermik) p 528
Shepard's Hand Cream (Dermik) p 528
Shepard's Soap (Dermik) p 528
Siblin Granules (Parke-Davis)
Sigtab Tablets (Upjohn)
◆Simeco Suspension (Wyeth) p 427, 666
◆Simron (Merrell-National) p 415, 582
◆Simron Plus (Merrell-National) p 415, 582
Sinarest Tablets (Pharmacraft) p 607
◆Sine-Aid Sinus Headache Tablets (McNeil Consumer Products) p 412, 560
◆Sine-Off Extra Strength Sinus Medicine Non-Aspirin Capsules (Menley & James) p 413, 578
◆Sine-Off Extra Strength Sinus Medicine Non-Aspirin Tablets (Menley & James) p 413, 578
◆Sine-Off Once-A-Day Sinus Spray (Menley & James) p 413, 579
◆Sine-Off Sinus Medicine-Aspirin Formula (Menley & James) p 413, 579
◆Sinex Decongestant Nasal Spray (Vicks Health Care) p 424, 640
◆Sinex Long-Acting Decongestant Nasal Spray (Vicks Health Care) p 424, 640
◆Sinutab Extra Strength Capsule Formula (Warner-Lambert) p 425, 646
◆Sinutab Extra Strength Tablets (Warner-Lambert) p 425, 647
◆Sinutab Long-Lasting Decongestant Nasal Spray (Warner-Lambert) p 425, 647
◆Sinutab Tablets (Warner-Lambert) p 425, 646

(◆ Shown in Product Identification Section)

◆Sinutab II Tablets (Warner-Lambert) p 425, 646
Skin Screen (Cetylite) p 523
Sleep-Eze Tablets (Whitehall) p 659
Slender Diet Food For Weight Control (Instant) (Carnation) p 521
Slender Diet Meal Bars For Weight Control (Carnation) p 521
Slender Diet Meal For Weight Control (Canned) (Carnation) p 521
Slimliner (Water-Resistant) (Almay)
◆Soaclens (Alcon/bp) p 405, 505
Sofn (Anabolic)
Soft 'N Soothe Anti-Itch Creme (Ascher) p 509
◆Softlight Cream Powder Eye Shadow (Almay) p 406, 506
◆Solarcaine (Plough) p 418, 609
Solbar Plus 15 (Persōn & Covey) p 603
Sominex (J.B. Williams) p 662
Soyalac: Liquid Concentrate, Ready-to-Serve and Powder (Loma Linda) p 555
Star-Otic (Star) p 628
Stress Formula "605" Tablets (Nature's Bounty) p 589
Stress Formula "605" w/Iron Tablets (Nature's Bounty) p 589
Stress Formula "605" w/Zinc Tablets (Nature's Bounty) p 589
Stresscaps (Lederle) p 552
◆Stresstabs 600 (Lederle) p 411, 552
◆Stresstabs 600 with Iron (Lederle) p 411, 552
◆Stresstabs 600 with Zinc (Lederle) p 411, 552
Stri-Dex B.P. (Lehn & Fink) p 555
Stri-Dex Medicated Pads (Lehn & Fink) p 555
◆Stuart Formula Tablets, The (Stuart) p 424, 632
Stuart Prenatal Tablets (Stuart) p 632
◆Stuartinic Tablets (Stuart) p 424, 632
Sucrets (Regular, Mentholated & Children's Cherry) (Beecham Products) p 512
Sucrets—Cold Decongestant Formula (Beecham Products) p 512
Sucrets Cough Control Formula (Beecham Products) p 512
Sudden Action Breath Freshener (Whitehall)
Sudden Beauty Country Air Mask (Whitehall)
Sudden Beauty Hair Spray (Whitehall)
Sudodrin Decongestant Tablets (Medique)
Sulfabid Tablets (Purdue Frederick)
◆Sundown Sunscreen, Extra Protection (Johnson & Johnson Baby Products Company) p 411, 547
◆Sundown Sunscreen, Maximal Protection (Johnson & Johnson Baby Products Company) p 411, 547
◆Sundown Sunscreen, Moderate Protection (Johnson & Johnson Baby Products Company) p 411, 547
◆Sundown Sunscreen, Ultra Protection (Johnson & Johnson Baby Products Company) p 411, 547
Sunril Premenstrual Caps(Schering) p 626
Super D Perles (Upjohn)
Super Odrinex (Fox) p 538
◆Super Shade (SPF-15) (Plough) p 418, 610
◆Super Wate-On Emulsion (Fleetwood) p 410, 537
Supertah Ointment (Purdue Frederick)
Surbex-750 with Iron (Abbott) p 503
Surbex-750 with Zinc (Abbott) p 503
Surbex-T (Abbott) p 503
◆Surfak (Hoechst-Roussel) p 411, 544
Sustacal (Mead Johnson Nutritional) p 570
Sustagen (Mead Johnson Nutritional) p 571
◆Syllact (Wallace) p 425, 643

T
20/20 Contact Lens Wetting Solution (S.S.S. Company)
20/20 Eye Drops (S.S.S. Company) p 619
Tanicaine Rectal Ointment (Upjohn)
Tanicaine Rectal Suppositories (Upjohn)

◆Tears Plus (Allergan) p 405, 506
Teen 5 & 10 Lotion (Muro) p 587
Teen 5 Wash (Muro) p 587
Tegrin for Psoriasis Lotion & Cream (Block) p 513
Tegrin Medicated Shampoo (Block) p 513
◆Teldrin Spansule Capsules, 8 mg., 12 mg. (Menley & James) p 413, 579
Tempra (Mead Johnson Nutritional) p 572
Tercopan (Anabolic)
◆Terramycin Ointment (Pfipharmecs) p 418, 605
Thantis Lozenges (Hynson, Westcott & Dunning)
Thera-Combex H-P (Parke-Davis) p 602
Thermotabs (Beecham Products) p 512
◆Throat Discs Throat Lozenges (Marion) p 412, 558
Tickle antiperspirant (Bristol-Myers)
◆Tinactin Aerosol Powder 1% (Schering) p 422, 626
◆Tinactin 1% Cream, Solution & Powder (Schering) p 421, 626
Tintz Cream Color Shampoo (Fleetwood)
Titralac Tablets & Liquid (Riker) p 614
Tonel (Lank)
◆Topex 10% Benzoyl Peroxide Lotion Buffered Acne Medication (Vicks Toiletry Products) p 424, 637
Topic Benzyl Alcohol Gel (Syntex) p 633
Transact (Westwood) p 651
Transi-Lube (Holland-Rantos) p 545
Trendar Premenstrual Tablets (Whitehall) p 659
Tri-88 (Anabolic) p 507
Tri-Adrenopan (Anabolic) p 507
◆Triaminic Expectorant (Dorsey) p 409, 530
◆Triaminic Syrup (Dorsey) p 409, 531
◆Triaminic-DM Cough Formula (Dorsey) p 409, 531
◆Triaminicin Chewables (Dorsey) p 531
◆Triaminicin Tablets (Dorsey) p 409, 531
◆Triaminicol Decongestant Cough Syrup (Dorsey) p 409, 531
Tri-B3 (Anabolic) p 508
Tri-B-Plex (Anabolic) p 508
Tri-C-500 (Anabolic) p 508
Trind (Mead Johnson Nutritional) p 572
Trind-DM (Mead Johnson Nutritional) p 572
Tri-Vi-Sol (Mead Johnson Nutritional) p 572
Tri-Vi-Sol Vitamin Drops w/Iron (Mead Johnson Nutritional) p 573
◆Troph-Iron Liquid & Tablets (Menley & James) p 413, 579
◆Trophite Liquid & Tablets (Menley & James) p 413, 579
Tryptophan Tablets (Nature's Bounty) p 589
Tryptophan-250 (Anabolic)
Tucks Cream & Ointment (Parke-Davis) p 602
Tucks Premoistened Pads (Parke-Davis) p 602
Tucks Take-Alongs (Parke-Davis)
◆Tums (Norcliff Thayer) p 415, 592
Tussagesic Tablets & Suspension (Dorsey) p 531
Twinstick for Lip and Cheek (Almay) p 506
◆Tylenol acetaminophen Children's Chewable Tablets, Elixir, Drops (McNeil Consumer Products) p 412, 560
◆Tylenol, Extra-Strength, acetaminophen Adult Liquid Pain Reliever (McNeil Consumer Products) p 412, 561
◆Tylenol, Extra-Strength, acetaminophen Capsules & Tablets (McNeil Consumer Products) p 412, 561
◆Tylenol, Regular Strength, acetaminophen Tablets (McNeil Consumer Products) p 412, 561

U
Ultra "A" Capsules & Tablets (Nature's Bounty) p 589
Ultra "A & D" Tablets (Nature's Bounty) p 589
Ultra Ban roll-on (Bristol-Myers)
Ultra Ban II antiperspirant (Bristol-Myers)

Ultra Brite Toothpaste (Colgate-Palmolive)
Ultra "D" Tablets (Nature's Bounty) p 589
Ultra KLB6 Tablets (Nature's Bounty) p 589
Ultra Vita-Time Tablets (Nature's Bounty) p 589
Under Eye Cover Creme, Ivory, Natural (Almay) p 506
Unguentine Plus (Norwich-Eaton) p 595
Unibase (Parke-Davis)
Unicap Capsules & Tablets (Upjohn) p 636
Unicap Chewable Tablets (Upjohn) p 636
◆Unicap M Tablets (Upjohn) p 424, 636
Unicap Plus Iron Tablets (Upjohn) p 636
Unicap Senior Tablets (Upjohn) p 636
◆Unicap T Tablets (Upjohn) p 424, 637
Unisom Nighttime Sleep-Aid (Leeming) p 554
Upjohn Vitamin C Tablets (Upjohn)
Upjohn Vitamin E Capsules (Upjohn)
Ursinus Inlay-Tabs (Dorsey) p 532
Uval Moisturizing Sunscreen Lotion (Dorsey) p 532

V
◆Vagisil Feminine Itching Medication (Combe) p 408, 526
Vanoxide Acne Lotion (Dermik) p 528
Vanquish (Glenbrook) p 541
Vanseb Cream & Lotion Dandruff Shampoo (Herbert) p 544
Vanseb-T Cream & Lotion Dandruff Shampoo (Herbert) p 544
◆Vaposteam (Vicks Health Care) p 640
Vasotate (Anabolic)
Vatronol Nose Drops (Vicks Health Care) p 641
Vergo (Daywell) p 527
Vicks Blue Cough Drops (Vicks Health Care)
Vicks Cough Drops (Vicks Health Care)
Vicks Cough Silencers Cough Drops (Vicks Health Care) p 641
Vicks Cough Syrup (Vicks Health Care) p 641
Vicks Formula 44 Cough Control Discs (Vicks Health Care) p 638
◆Vicks Formula 44 Cough Mixture (Vicks Health Care) p 424, 639
◆Vicks Formula 44D Decongestant Cough Mixture (Vicks Health Care) p 422, 639
Vicks Inhaler (Vicks Health Care) p 641
◆Vicks Nyquil Nighttime Colds Medicine (Vicks Health Care) p 424, 639
◆Vicks Sinex Decongestant Nasal Spray (Vicks Health Care) p 424, 640
◆Vicks Sinex Long-Acting Decongestant Nasal Spray (Vicks Health Care) p 424, 640
Vicks Throat Lozenges (Vicks Health Care) p 641
◆Vicks Vaporub (Vicks Health Care) p 424, 642
Vicks Vaposteam (Vicks Health Care) p 640
Vicks Vatronol Nose Drops (Vicks Health Care) p 641
Victors Menthol-Eucalyptus Vapor Cough Drops (Vicks Health Care)
Vi-Magna Capsules (Lederle)
Vioform Cream & Ointment (Ciba) p 524
◆Vi-Penta Infant Drops (Roche) p 421, 618
◆Vi-Penta Multivitamin Drops (Roche) p 421, 618
Viro-Med Liquid (Whitehall) p 659
Viro-Med Tablets (Whitehall) p 660
Visine A.C. Eye Drops (Leeming) p 554
Visine Eye Drops (Leeming) p 554
Vitalis Dry Control hair groom (Bristol-Myers)
Vitalis Dry Texture hair groom (Bristol-Myers)
Vitalis hair groom liquid (Bristol-Myers)
Vitalis hair groom tube (Bristol-Myers)
Vitalis Regular Hold hair spray (Bristol-Myers)
Vitalis Super Hold hair spray (Bristol-Myers)

(◆ Shown in Product Identification Section)

Vitamin A Capsules & Tablets (Nature's Bounty) p 589
Vitamin A & D Tablets (Nature's Bounty) p 589
Vitamin C Crystals (Nature's Bounty) p 588
Vitamin D Tablets (Nature's Bounty) p 590
Vita-Time Tablets (Nature's Bounty) p 590
◆**Viterra C** (Pfipharmecs) p 418, 605
◆**Viterra E** (Pfipharmecs) p 418, 605
◆**Viterra High Potency** (Pfipharmecs) p 418, 605
◆**Viterra Original Formula** (Pfipharmecs) p 418, 605
Vivarin (J.B. Williams) p 662

W

Wart-Off (Pfipharmecs) p 605
Wate-Off (Fleetwood)

◆**Wate-On** (Fleetwood) p 410, 537
Water Pill Tablets (Nature's Bounty) p 590
Water Pill w/Iron Tablets (Nature's Bounty) p 590
Waterproof Mascara (Almay) p 506
Wheat Germ Oil Capsules (Nature's Bounty) p 590
WinGel (Consumer Products Div., Winthrop) p 665
Wrinkle Stick (Almay) p 506
◆**Wyanoids Hemorrhoidal Suppositories** (Wyeth) p 427, 666
◆**Wyanoid Ointment** (Wyeth) p 427, 666

X

◆**Xerac** (Persōn & Covey) p 418, 603
Xylocaine 2.5% Ointment (Astra) p 509

Y

Yeast Plus Tablets (Nature's Bounty) p 590

Z

◆**Z-Bec Tablets** (Robins) p 420, 617
◆**Zacne Tablets** (Nature's Bounty) p 415, 590
Zetar Shampoo (Dermik) p 529
Zinc Oxide Ointment (Norwich-Eaton) p 595
Zinc Tabs (Mericon) p 580
Zinc Tablets (Nature's Bounty) p 590
Zincon Dandruff Shampoo (Lederle) p 552
Zinotate (Anabolic)
Ziradryl Lotion (Parke-Davis) p 602
Zymacap Capsules (Upjohn)
Zymalixir Fluid (Upjohn)
Zymasyrup Fluid (Upjohn)

(◆ Shown in Product Identification Section)

MEMORANDUM

Product Category Index

Products described in the Product Information (White) Section are listed according to their classifications. The headings and sub-headings have been determined by the OTC Review process of the U.S. Food and Drug Administration. Classification of products have been determined by the Publisher with the cooperation of individual manufacturers. In cases where there were differences of opinion or where the manufacturer had no opinion, the Publisher made the final decision.

A

ACNE PRODUCTS
(see under DERMATOLOGICALS)

AEROSOLS
Tinactin Aerosol Powder 1% (Schering) p 422, 626

ALLERGY RELIEF PRODUCTS
A.R.M. Allergy Relief Medicine Tablets (Menley & James) p 413, 574
Afrinol Repetabs Tablets (Schering) p 421, 620
Allerest Headache Strength Tablets (Pharmacraft) p 606
Allerest Tablets & Capsules (Pharmacraft) p 606
Bluboro Powder Astringent Soaking Solution (Herbert) p 543
Caladryl Lotion & Cream (Parke-Davis) p 600
Chlor-Trimeton Allergy Syrup, Tablets & Long-Acting Repetabs Tablets (Schering) p 421, 620
Chlor-Trimeton Decongestant Tablets (Schering) p 421, 620
Chlor-Trimeton Expectorant (Schering) p 620
Congespirin Liquid Cold Medicine (Bristol-Myers) p 406, 517
Contac Capsules (Menley & James) p 413, 575
Coricidin Decongestant Nasal Mist (Schering) p 421, 621
Coricidin Medilets Tablets for Children (Schering) p 421, 622
Delacort (Mericon) p 580
Demazin Decongestant-Antihistamine Repetabs Tablets & Syrup (Schering) p 421, 623
Dimetane Decongestant Elixir (Robins) p 420, 616
Dimetane Decongestant Tablets (Robins) p 420, 616
Dimetane Elixir (Robins) p 420, 615
Dimetane Tablets (Robins) p 420, 615

Dristan Decongestant/Antihistamine /Analgesic Tablets (Whitehall) p 426, 654
Dristan Decongestant/Antihistamine /Analgesic Capsules (Whitehall) p 426, 654
Dristan 12-Hour Nasal Decongestant Capsules (Whitehall) p 426, 654
Dristan Long Lasting Nasal Mist, Regular & Menthol (Whitehall) p 426, 655
Dristan Nasal Mist, Regular & Menthol (Whitehall) p 426, 655
Dristan-AF Decongestant/Antihistamine /Analgesic Tablets (Whitehall) p 426, 655
4-Way Long Acting Nasal Spray (Bristol-Myers) p 406, 518
4-Way Nasal Spray (Bristol-Myers) p 406, 518
First Sign (J.B. Williams)
Novahistine Cold Tablets (Dow Pharmaceuticals) p 534
Novahistine Elixir (Dow Pharmaceuticals) p 534
Sinarest Tablets (Pharmacraft) p 607
Sinex Decongestant Nasal Spray (Vicks Health Care) p 424, 640
Sinex Long-Acting Decongestant Nasal Spray (Vicks Health Care) p 424, 640
Teldrin Spansule Capsules, 8 mg., 12 mg. (Menley & James) p 413, 579
Topic Benzyl Alcohol Gel (Syntex) p 633
Triaminic Syrup (Dorsey) p 409, 531
Triaminicin Chewables (Dorsey) p 531
Triaminicin Tablets (Dorsey) p 409, 531
Vatronol Nose Drops (Vicks Health Care) p 641
Vicks Sinex Decongestant Nasal Spray (Vicks Health Care) p 424, 640
Vicks Sinex Long-Acting Decongestant Nasal Spray (Vicks Health Care) p 424, 640
Vicks Vatronol Nose Drops (Vicks Health Care) p 641

Visine A.C. Eye Drops (Leeming) p 554

ANALGESICS
Internal
Acetaminophen & Combinations
Acephen Acetaminophen Rectal Suppositories (G & W Laboratories) p 538
Allerest Headache Strength Tablets (Pharmacraft) p 606
Anacin-3 Analgesic Tablets (Whitehall) p 426, 652
Comtrex (Bristol-Myers) p 406, 516
Congespirin Liquid Cold Medicine (Bristol-Myers) p 406, 517
Coricidin Extra Strength Sinus Headache Tablets (Schering) p 421, 623
Datril (Bristol-Myers) p 406, 517
Datril 500 (Bristol-Myers) p 406, 517
Daycare Multi-Symptom Colds Medicine (Vicks Health Care) p 424, 638
Dristan-AF Decongestant/Antihistamine /Analgesic (Whitehall) p 426, 655
D-Sinus Capsules (Laser) p 548
Excedrin (Bristol-Myers) p 406, 517
Excedrin P.M. (Bristol-Myers) p 406, 518
Liquiprin (Norcliff Thayer) p 415, 591
Novahistine Sinus Tablets (Dow Pharmaceuticals) p 534
Nyquil Nighttime Colds Medicine (Vicks Health Care) p 424, 639
Ornex Capsules (Menley & James) p 413, 578
Percogesic Tablets (Endo) p 409, 536
Quiet World Analgesic/Sleeping Aid (Whitehall) p 659
Sinarest Tablets (Pharmacraft) p 607
Sine-Aid Sinus Headache Tablets (McNeil Consumer Products) p 412, 560
Sine-Off Extra Strength Sinus Medicine Non-Aspirin Capsules (Menley & James) p 413, 578

Sinutab Extra Strength Capsule Formula (Warner-Lambert) p 425, 646
Sinutab Extra Strength Tablets (Warner-Lambert) p 425, 647
Sinutab Tablets (Warner-Lambert) p 425, 646
Sinutab II Tablets (Warner-Lambert) p 425, 646
Sunril Premenstrual Capsules (Schering) p 626
Tempra (Mead Johnson Nutritional) p 572
Tylenol acetaminophen Children's Chewable Tablets, Elixir, Drops (McNeil Consumer Products) p 412, 560
Tylenol, Extra-Strength, acetaminophen Adult Liquid Pain Reliever (McNeil Consumer Products) p 412, 561
Tylenol, Extra-Strength, acetaminophen Capsules & Tablets (McNeil Consumer Products) p 412, 561
Tylenol, Regular Strength, acetaminophen Tablets (McNeil Consumer Products) p 412, 561
Vicks Nyquil Nighttime Colds Medicine (Vicks Health Care) p 424, 639
Viro-Med Liquid (Whitehall) p 659

Aspirin & Combinations
Alka-Seltzer Effervescent Pain Reliever Antacid (Miles) p 583
Anacin Analgesic Capsules (Whitehall) p 652
Anacin Analgesic Tablets (Whitehall) p 426, 652
Anacin Maximum Strength Analgesic Capsules (Whitehall) p 426, 652
Anacin Maximum Strength Analgesic Tablets (Whitehall) p 426, 652
Arthritis Pain Formula by the Makers of Anacin Analgesic Tablets (Whitehall) p 426, 653
Arthritis Strength Bufferin (Bristol-Myers) p 406, 516
Aspergum (Plough) p 418, 608
Aspirin Suppositories (G & W Laboratories) p 538
Bayer Aspirin & Bayer Children's Chewable Aspirin (Glenbrook) p 410, 539
Bayer Children's Cold Tablets (Glenbrook) p 540
Bayer Timed-Release Aspirin (Glenbrook) p 410, 540
Bufferin (Bristol-Myers) p 406, 516
Cama Inlay-Tabs (Dorsey) p 409, 530
Congespirin (Bristol-Myers) p 406, 516
Coricidin 'D' Decongestant Tablets (Schering) p 421, 621
Coricidin Demilets Tablets for Children (Schering) p 421, 622
Coricidin Medilets Tablets for Children (Schering) p 421, 622
Coricidin Tablets (Schering) p 421, 621
Dristan Decongestant/Antihistamine/Analgesic Tablets (Whitehall) p 426, 654
Dristan Decongestant/Antihistamine/Analgesic Capsules (Whitehall) p 426, 654
Ecotrin Tablets (Menley & James) p 413, 576
Excedrin (Bristol-Myers) p 406, 517
4-Way Cold Tablets (Bristol-Myers) p 406, 518
Goody's Headache Powders (Goody's) p 410, 541
Midol (Glenbrook) p 410, 541
Momentum Muscular Backache Formula (Whitehall) p 657
Norwich Aspirin (Norwich-Eaton) p 417, 594
Quiet World Analgesic/Sleeping Aid (Whitehall) p 659
St. Joseph Aspirin for Children (Plough) p 418, 609
St. Joseph Cold Tablets for Children (Plough) p 418, 609
Ursinus Inlay-Tabs (Dorsey) p 532
Vanquish (Glenbrook) p 541
Viro-Med Tablets (Whitehall) p 660

Others
DeWitt's Pills for Backache & Joint Pains (DeWitt) p 409, 529
Mobigesic Analgesic Tablets (Ascher) p 509
Momentum Muscular Backache Formula (Whitehall) p 657
Os-Cal-Gesic Tablets (Marion) p 558

Topical

Anesthetics
Anbesol Antiseptic Anesthetic Gel (Whitehall) p 426, 652
Anbesol Antiseptic Anesthetic Liquid (Whitehall) p 426, 652
BiCozene Creme (Creighton Products) p 408, 376
Campho-Phenique Liquid (Consumer Products Div., Winthrop) p 663
Cēpacol Anesthetic Troches (Merrell-National) p 580
Cēpastat Sore Throat Lozenges (Merrell-National) p 415, 581
Cēpastat Sore Throat Spray/Gargle (Merrell-National) p 415, 581
Chloraseptic Cough Control Lozenges (Norwich-Eaton) p 416, 593
Chloraseptic Gel (Norwich-Eaton) p 593
Chloraseptic Liquid & Spray (Norwich-Eaton) p 416, 593
Chloraseptic Lozenges (Norwich-Eaton) p 416, 593
Formula 44 Cough Control Discs (Vicks Health Care) p 638
Medicone Dressing Cream (Medicone) p 573
Medi-Quik (Lehn & Fink) p 555
Nupercainal Cream, Ointment, Suppositories (Ciba) p 407, 523
Oracin Cherry Flavor Cooling Throat Lozenges (Vicks Health Care) p 640
Oracin Cooling Throat Lozenges (Vicks Health Care) p 639
Panalgesic (Poythress) p 610
Rectal Medicone Suppositories (Medicone) p 573
Rectal Medicone Unguent (Medicone) p 574
Rhulicaine (Lederle) p 551
Solarcaine (Plough) p 418, 609
Unguentine Plus (Norwich-Eaton) p 595
Vicks Cough Silencers Cough Drops (Vicks Health Care) p 641
Vicks Formula 44 Cough Control Discs (Vicks Health Care) p 638
Vicks Throat Lozenges (Vicks Health Care) p 641
Xylocaine 2.5% Ointment (Astra) p 509

Counterirritants
Ben-Gay External Analgesic Products (Leeming) p 552
Deep-Down (J.B. Williams) p 660
Heet Analgesic Liniment (Whitehall) p 656
Heet Spray Analgesic (Whitehall) p 656
Icy Hot Balm (Searle Consumer Products) p 423, 627
Icy Hot Rub (Searle Consumer Products) p 423, 627
InfraRub Analgesic Cream (Whitehall) p 657
Panalgesic (Poythress) p 610
Vicks Vaporub (Vicks Health Care) p 424, 642

Salicylates & Combinations
Aspercreme (Thompson Medical) p 634
Ben-Gay External Analgesic Products (Leeming) p 552
Deep-Down (J.B. Williams) p 660
Heet Analgesic Liniment (Whitehall) p 656
Heet Spray Analgesic (Whitehall) p 656
Icy Hot Balm (Searle Consumer Products) p 423, 627
Icy Hot Rub (Searle Consumer Products) p 423, 627
InfraRub Analgesic Cream (Whitehall) p 657
Mobisyl Analgesic Creme (Ascher) p 509
Myoflex Creme (Adria) p 504

Panalgesic (Poythress) p 610

ANESTHETICS, Topical
(see under ANALGESICS, Topical)

ANORECTAL PRODUCTS
Creams, Foams, Lotions, Ointments
Anusol Ointment (Parke-Davis) p 599
CaldeCORT Hydrocortisone Cream (Pharmacraft) p 606
Dermolate Anal-Itch Ointment (Schering) p 623
HTO Stainless Manzan Hemorrhoidal Tissue Ointment (DeWitt) p 409, 530
Hytone Cream ½% (Dermik) p 527
Hytone Ointment ½% (Dermik) p 528
Lanacane Medicated Creme (Combe) p 408, 525
Lanacort Creme (Combe) p 408, 526
Nupercainal Cream, Ointment, Suppositories (Ciba) p 407, 523
Pazo Hemorrhoid Ointment/Suppositories (Bristol-Myers) p 519
Preparation H Hemorrhoidal Ointment (Whitehall) p 426, 658
Rectal Medicone Unguent (Medicone) p 574
Wyanoid Ointment (Wyeth) p 427, 666

Suppositories
Acephen Acetaminophen Rectal Suppositories (G & W Laboratories) p 538
Anusol Suppositories (Parke-Davis) p 599
Aspirin Suppositories (G & W Laboratories) p 538
Norwich Glycerin Suppositories (Norwich-Eaton) p 594
Nupercainal Cream, Ointment, Suppositories (Ciba) p 407, 523
Pazo Hemorrhoid Ointment/Suppositories (Bristol-Myers) p 519
Preparation H Hemorrhoidal Suppositories (Whitehall) p 426, 658
Rectal Medicone Suppositories (Medicone) p 573
Wyanoids Hemorrhoidal Suppositories (Wyeth) p 427, 666

Other
Cleansing Pads by the Makers of Preparation H Hemorrhoidal Remedies (Whitehall) p 653
Mediconet (Medicone) p 573
Tucks Premoistened Pads (Parke-Davis) p 602

ANOREXICS
(see under APPETITE SUPPRESSANTS)

ANTACIDS

Antacids
Alka-Seltzer Effervescent Pain Reliever Antacid (Miles) p 583
Alka-2 Chewable Antacid Tablets (Miles) p 584
ALternaGEL Liquid (Stuart) p 629
Amphojel Suspension & Suspension without Flavor (Wyeth) p 427, 665
Amphojel Tablets (Wyeth) p 427, 665
Nephrox Suspension (Fleming) p 537
Phillip's Milk of Magnesia (Glenbrook) p 410, 541
Rolaids Antacid Tablets (Warner-Lambert) p 425, 646
Titralac Tablets & Liquid (Riker) p 614
Tums (Norcliff Thayer) p 415, 592

Antacids Combinations
Alka-Seltzer Effervescent Antacid (Miles) p 584
Aludrox Oral Suspension & Tablets (Wyeth) p 417, 665
Bisodol Antacid Powder (Whitehall) p 653
Bisodol Antacid Tablets (Whitehall) p 653
Citrocarbonate Antacid (Upjohn) p 635
Delcid (Merrell-National) p 581
DeWitt's Antacid Powder (DeWitt) p 409, 529
Di-Gel (Plough) p 418, 608
Eno (Beecham Products) p 511

Gaviscon Antacid Tablets (Marion)
p 412, 557
Gaviscon Liquid Antacid (Marion)
p 412, 557
Gaviscon-2 Antacid Tablets (Marion)
p 412, 557
Gelusil (Parke-Davis) p 600
Kolantyl (Merrell-National) p 582
Kudrox Suspension (Double Strength)
(Kremers-Urban) p 548
Magnatril Suspension & Tablets
(Lannett) p 548
Marblen Suspensions & Tablets
(Fleming) p 537
Percy Medicine (Merrick) p 415, 583
Simeco Suspension (Wyeth) p 427,
666
WinGel (Consumer Products Div.,
Winthrop) p 665

Antacids with Antiflatulents
Di-Gel (Plough) p 418, 608
Gelusil-M (Parke-Davis) p 600
Gelusil-II Liquid & Tablets (Parke-Davis)
p 601
Mylanta Liquid (Stuart) p 424, 631
Mylanta Tablets (Stuart) p 424, 631
Mylanta-II Liquid (Stuart) p 424, 631
Mylanta-II Tablets (Stuart) p 424, 631
Simeco Suspension (Wyeth) p 427,
666

ANTIANEMIA
(see under HEMATINICS)

ANTIARTHRITICS
(see under ANALGESICS)

ANTIASTHMATICS
(see under BRONCHODILATORS)

ANTIBIOTICS, Topical
BPN Ointment (Norwich-Eaton) p 592
Baciguent Antibiotic Ointment (Upjohn)
p 635
Bacitracin Topical Ointment
(Pfipharmecs) p 603
Myciguent Antibiotic Ointment (Upjohn)
p 636
Mycitracin Antibiotic Ointment (Upjohn)
p 424, 636
Terramycin Ointment (Pfipharmecs)
p 418, 605

ANTICONSTIPATION
(see under LAXATIVES)

ANTIDIARRHEALS
Charcocaps (Requa) p 420, 612
Kaopectate (Upjohn) p 424, 636
Kaopectate Concentrate (Upjohn)
p 424, 636
Lactinex Tablets & Granules (Hynson,
Westcott & Dunning) p 411, 546
Mitrolan Tablets (Robins) p 420, 616
Pepto-Bismol Liquid & Tablets
(Norwich-Eaton) p 416, 595
Percy Medicine (Merrick) p 415, 583
Rheaban Tablets & Liquid (Leeming)
p 553

ANTIEMETICS
Pepto-Bismol Liquid & Tablets
(Norwich-Eaton) p 416, 595

ANTIFLATULENTS
(see also under ANTACIDS)
Allimin Filmcoated Tablets (Health
Care) p 410, 541
Charcocaps (Requa) p 420, 612
Gas-X Tablets (Creighton Products)
p 408, 527
Mylicon (Tablets & Drops) (Stuart)
p 424, 631
Mylicon-80 Tablets (Stuart) p 424,
632

ANTIFUNGALS
(see under DERMATOLOGICALS)

ANTIHISTAMINES
(see under ALLERGY RELIEF
PRODUCTS or under COLD
PREPARATIONS)

ANTILICE
(see under PEDICULICIDES)

ANTIMICROBIALS, Topical
Anbesol Antiseptic Anesthetic Gel
(Whitehall) p 426, 652
Anbesol Antiseptic Anesthetic Liquid
(Whitehall) p 426, 652
BPN Ointment (Norwich-Eaton) p 592
Bactine Skin Wound Cleanser (Miles)
p 584
Betadine Antiseptic Lubricating Gel
(Purdue Frederick) p 611
Betadine Solution (Purdue Frederick)
p 419, 611
Listerine Antiseptic (Warner-Lambert)
p 425, 645
Medi-Quik (Lehn & Fink) p 555
Mercurochrome II (Becton Dickinson)
p 510
Norwich Bacitracin Ointment
(Norwich-Eaton) p 594
S.T. 37 (Beecham Products) p 511

ANTIMOTION SICKNESS
Bonine (Pfipharmecs) p 418, 603
Dramamine Junior Liquid (Searle
Consumer Products) p 423, 627
Dramamine Liquid (Searle Consumer
Products) p 423, 627
Dramamine Tablets (Searle Consumer
Products) p 423, 627

ANTINAUSEANTS
Dramamine Junior Liquid (Searle
Consumer Products) p 423, 627
Dramamine Liquid (Searle Consumer
Products) p 423, 627
Dramamine Tablets (Searle Consumer
Products) p 423, 627
Pepto-Bismol Liquid & Tablets
(Norwich-Eaton) p 416, 595

ANTIOBESITY PREPARATIONS
(see under APPETITE
SUPPRESSANTS)

ANTIPERSPIRANTS
(see under DERMATOLOGICALS)

ANTIPRURITICS
(see under DERMATOLOGICALS)

ANTIPYRETICS
(see under ANALGESICS)

ANTISEPTICS
(see under ANTIMICROBIALS,
Topical)

ANTITUSSIVES
(see under COUGH PREPARATIONS)

ANTIVERTIGO AGENTS
Nicotinex Elixir (Fleming) p 537

APPETITE SUPPRESSANTS
Anorexin Capsules (SDA
Pharmaceuticals) p 618
Anorexin One-Span Capsules (SDA
Pharmaceuticals) p 618
Appedrine, Maximum Strength
(Thompson Medical) p 634
Codexin Extra Strength Capsules (Arco)
p 508
Control Capsules (Thompson Medical)
p 634
Dex-A-Diet Lite Time Release Capsules
(O'Connor) p 595
Dex-A-Diet II Time Release Capsules
(O'Connor) p 416, 596
Dexatrim & Dexatrim Extra Strength
(Thompson Medical) p 634
Dietac Diet Aid Capsules (Menley &
James) p 413, 575

Dietac Diet Aid Drops (Menley &
James) p 413, 575
Dietac Diet Aid Tablets (Menley &
James) p 413, 576
Dietac Once-A-Day Maximum Strength
Diet Aid Capsules (Menley & James)
p 413, 576
Dietac Twice-A-Day Maximum Strength
Diet Aid Capsules (Menley & James)
p 413, 576
E-Z Trim (Fox) p 538
P.V.M. Appetite Control Capsules (J.B.
Williams) p 661
P.V.M. Appetite Suppressant Tablets
(J.B. Williams) p 661
Pretts Tablets (Marion) p 412, 558
Prolamine Capsules, Super Strength
(Thompson Medical) p 635
Super Odrinex (Fox) p 538

ASTRINGENTS
(see under DERMATOLOGICALS)

B

BATH PREPARATIONS
Alpha Keri Bath Oil (Westwood) p 647
Balnetar (Westwood) p 648

BIOFEEDBACK SYSTEMS
GSR 2 (Thought Technology) p 635

BRONCHODILATORS
Bronkaid Mist (Consumer Products
Div., Winthrop) p 662
Bronkaid Mist Suspension (Consumer
Products Div., Winthrop) p 662
Bronkaid Tablets (Consumer Products
Div., Winthrop) p 663
Primatene Mist (Whitehall) p 426, 658
Primatene Mist Suspension (Whitehall)
p 426, 658
Primatene Tablets - M Formula
(Whitehall) p 426, 658
Primatene Tablets - P Formula
(Whitehall) p 426, 658

C

CANKER SORE PREPARATIONS
External
Campho-Phenique Liquid (Consumer
Products Div., Winthrop) p 663
Cankaid (Becton Dickinson) p 510
Gly-Oxide Liquid (Marion) p 412, 557

COLD PREPARATIONS
Antihistamines & Combinations
A.R.M. Allergy Relief Medicine Tablets
(Menley & James) p 413, 574
Alka-Seltzer Plus Cold Medicine (Miles)
p 584
Allerest Headache Strength Tablets
(Pharmacraft) p 606
Allerest Tablets & Capsules
(Pharmacraft) p 606
C3 Cold Cough Capsules (Menley &
James) p 413, 574
Chlor-Trimeton Decongestant Tablets
(Schering) p 421, 620
Comtrex (Bristol-Myers) p 406, 516
Contac Capsules (Menley & James)
p 413, 575
Coricidin 'D' Decongestant Tablets
(Schering) p 421, 621
Coricidin Demilets Tablets for Children
(Schering) p 421, 622
Coricidin Extra Strength Sinus
Headache Tablets (Schering) p 421,
623
Coricidin Medilets Tablets for Children
(Schering) p 421, 622
Coricidin Tablets (Schering) p 421,
621
Demazin Decongestant-Antihistamine
Repetabs Tablets & Syrup (Schering)
p 421, 623
Dimetane Decongestant Elixir (Robins)
p 420, 616
Dimetane Decongestant Tablets
(Robins) p 420, 616
Dimetane Elixir (Robins) p 420, 615
Dimetane Tablets (Robins) p 420, 615

Dristan Decongestant/Antihistamine/Analgesic Capsules (Whitehall) p 426, 654

Dristan Decongestant/Antihistamine/Analgesic Tablets (Whitehall) p 426, 654

Dristan 12-Hour Nasal Decongestant Capsules (Whitehall) p 426, 654

Dristan Nasal Mist, Regular & Menthol (Whitehall) p 426, 655

Dristan-AF Decongestant/Antihistamine/Analgesic Tablets (Whitehall) p 426, 655

4-Way Long Acting Nasal Spray (Bristol-Myers) p 406, 518

4-Way Nasal Spray (Bristol-Myers) p 406, 518

Formula 44 Cough Mixture (Vicks Health Care) p 424, 639

Naldecon-DX Pediatric Syrup (Bristol) p 515

Novahistine Cold Tablets (Dow Pharmaceuticals) p 534

Novahistine Cough & Cold Formula (Dow Pharmaceuticals) p 532

Novahistine Elixir (Dow Pharmaceuticals) p 534

Novahistine Sinus Tablets (Dow Pharmaceuticals) p 534

Nyquil Nighttime Colds Medicine (Vicks Health Care) p 424, 639

Ryna Liquid (Wallace) p 425, 643

Sinarest Tablets (Pharmacraft) p 607

Sine-Off Extra Strength Sinus Medicine Non-Aspirin Tablets (Menley & James) p 413, 579

Sine-Off Sinus Medicine Tablets -Aspirin Formula (Menley & James) p 413, 579

Sinutab Extra Strength Capsule Formula (Warner-Lambert) p 425, 646

Sinutab Extra Strength Tablets (Warner-Lambert) p 425, 647

Sinutab Tablets (Warner-Lambert) p 425, 646

Teldrin Spansule Capsules, 8 mg., 12 mg. (Menley & James) p 413, 579

Triaminic Syrup (Dorsey) p 409, 531

Triaminicin Tablets (Dorsey) p 409, 531

Tussagesic Tablets & Suspension (Dorsey) p 531

Vicks Formula 44 Cough Mixture (Vicks Health Care) p 424, 639

Vicks Nyquil Nighttime Colds Medicine (Vicks Health Care) p 424, 639

Viro-Med Tablets (Whitehall) p 660

Decongestants

Oral & Combinations

Afrinol Repetabs Tablets (Schering) p 421, 620

Alka-Seltzer Plus Cold Medicine (Miles) p 584

Bayer Children's Cold Tablets (Glenbrook) p 540

CCP Tablets (Medique) p 574

Children's Hold (Beecham Products) p 510

Chlor-Trimeton Decongestant Tablets (Schering) p 421, 620

Comtrex (Bristol-Myers) p 406, 516

Congespirin (Bristol-Myers) p 406, 516

Congespirin Liquid Cold Medicine (Bristol-Myers) p 406, 517

Contac Capsules (Menley & James) p 413, 575

Contac Jr. Childrens' Cold Medicine (Menley & James) p 413, 575

Coricidin Cough Syrup (Schering) p 421, 621

Coricidin 'D' Decongestant Tablets (Schering) p 421, 621

Coricidin Demilets Tablets for Children (Schering) p 421, 622

Coricidin Extra Strength Sinus Headache Tablets (Schering) p 421, 623

Coryban-D Capsules (Pfipharmecs) p 418, 604

CoTylenol Children's Liquid Cold Formula (McNeil Consumer Products) p 412, 560

CoTylenol Cold Formula Tablets and Capsules (McNeil Consumer Products) p 412, 559

CoTylenol Liquid Cold Formula (McNeil Consumer Products) p 412, 559

Daycare Multi-Symptom Colds Medicine Capsules (Vicks Health Care) p 424, 638

Daycare Multi-Symptom Colds Medicine (Vicks Health Care) p 424, 638

Demazin Decongestant-Antihistamine Repetabs Tablets & Syrup (Schering) p 421, 623

Dimacol Capsules (Robins) p 420, 615

Dimacol Liquid (Robins) p 420, 615

Dimetane Decongestant Elixir (Robins) p 420, 616

Dimetane Decongestant Tablets (Robins) p 420, 616

Dristan Decongestant/Antihistamine/Analgesic Capsules (Whitehall) p 426, 654

Dristan Decongestant/Antihistamine/Analgesic Tablets (Whitehall) p 426, 654

Dristan 12-Hour Nasal Decongestant Capsules (Whitehall) p 426, 654

Dristan-AF Decongestant/Antihistamine/Analgesic Tablets (Whitehall) p 426, 655

D-Sinus Capsules (Laser) p 548

4-Way Cold Tablets (Bristol-Myers) p 406, 518

First Sign (J.B. Williams)

Naldecon-DX Pediatric Syrup (Bristol) p 515

Naldecon-EX Pediatric Drops (Bristol) p 515

Novahistine Cold Tablets (Dow Pharmaceuticals) p 534

Novahistine Cough & Cold Formula (Dow Pharmaceuticals) p 532

Novahistine Elixir (Dow Pharmaceuticals) p 534

Novahistine Sinus Tablets (Dow Pharmaceuticals) p 534

Nyquil Nighttime Colds Medicine (Vicks Health Care) p 424, 639

Ornex Capsules (Menley & James) p 413, 578

Robitussin-CF (Robins) p 420, 617

Robitussin-PE (Robins) p 420, 617

St. Joseph Cold Tablets for Children (Plough) p 418, 609

Sine-Off Extra Strength Sinus Medicine Non-Aspirin Tablets (Menley & James) p 413, 579

Sine-Off Sinus Medicine Tablets -Aspirin Formula (Menley & James) p 413, 579

Sinutab Extra Strength Capsule Formula (Warner-Lambert) p 425, 646

Sinutab Extra Strength Tablets (Warner-Lambert) p 425, 647

Sinutab Tablets (Warner-Lambert) p 425, 646

Sinutab II Tablets (Warner-Lambert) p 425, 646

Sucrets—Cold Decongestant Formula (Beecham Products) p 512

Triaminic Syrup (Dorsey) p 409, 531

Triaminicin Chewables (Dorsey) p 531

Triaminicin Tablets (Dorsey) p 409, 531

Trind (Mead Johnson Nutritional) p 572

Tussagesic Tablets & Suspension (Dorsey) p 531

Vicks Nyquil Nighttime Colds Medicine (Vicks Health Care) p 424, 639

Viro-Med Liquid (Whitehall) p 659

Viro-Med Tablets (Whitehall) p 660

Topical & Combinations

Afrin Menthol Nasal Spray (Schering) p 421, 619

Afrin Nasal Spray, Nose Drops, Pediatric Nose Drops (Schering) p 421, 619

Benzedrex Inhaler (Menley & James) p 413, 574

Coricidin Decongestant Nasal Mist (Schering) p 421, 621

Dristan Long Lasting Nasal Mist, Regular & Menthol (Whitehall) p 426, 655

Dristan Nasal Mist, Regular & Menthol (Whitehall) p 426, 655

Duration (Plough) p 418, 608

4-Way Long Acting Nasal Spray (Bristol-Myers) p 406, 518

4-Way Nasal Spray (Bristol-Myers) p 406, 518

NTZ (Consumer Products Div., Winthrop) p 664

Neo-Synephrine Hydrochloride (Consumer Products Div., Winthrop) p 664

Neo-Synephrine II Long Acting Nasal Spray (Consumer Products Div., Winthrop) p 663

Otrivin (Geigy) p 410, 539

Privine Nasal Spray & Solution 0.05% (Ciba) p 407, 524

Sine-Off Once-A-Day Sinus Spray (Menley & James) p 413, 579

Sinex Decongestant Nasal Spray (Vicks Health Care) p 424, 640

Sinex Long-Acting Decongestant Nasal Spray (Vicks Health Care) p 424, 640

Sinutab Long-Lasting Decongestant Nasal Spray (Warner-Lambert) p 425, 647

Vaposteam (Vicks Health Care) p 640

Vatronol Nose Drops (Vicks Health Care) p 641

Vicks Inhaler (Vicks Health Care) p 641

Vicks Sinex Decongestant Nasal Spray (Vicks Health Care) p 424, 640

Vicks Sinex Long-Acting Decongestant Nasal Spray (Vicks Health Care) p 424, 640

Vicks Vaporub (Vicks Health Care) p 424, 642

Vicks Vaposteam (Vicks Health Care) p 640

Vicks Vatronol Nose Drops (Vicks Health Care) p 641

Long-Acting

Afrinol Repetabs Tablets (Schering) p 421, 620

C3 Cold Cough Capsules (Menley & James) p 413, 574

Contac Capsules (Menley & James) p 413, 575

Dristan 12-Hour Nasal Decongestant Capsules (Whitehall) p 426, 654

Dristan Long Lasting Nasal Mist, Regular & Menthol (Whitehall) p 426, 655

Duration (Plough) p 418, 608

Neo-Synephrine II Long Acting Nasal Spray (Consumer Products Div., Winthrop) p 663

Sinex Long-Acting Decongestant Nasal Spray (Vicks Health Care) p 424, 640

Sinutab Long-Lasting Decongestant Nasal Spray (Warner-Lambert) p 425, 647

Teldrin Spansule Capsules, 8 mg., 12 mg. (Menley & James) p 413, 579

Vicks Sinex Long-Acting Decongestant Nasal Spray (Vicks Health Care) p 424, 640

Lozenges

Chloraseptic Cough Control Lozenges (Norwich-Eaton) p 416, 593

Chloraseptic Lozenges (Norwich-Eaton) p 416, 593

Chloraseptic Lozenges, Children's (Norwich-Eaton) p 592

Formula 44 Cough Control Discs (Vicks Health Care) p 638

Sucrets (Regular, Mentholated & Children's Cherry) (Beecham Products) p 512

Sucrets—Cold Decongestant Formula (Beecham Products) p 512

Vicks Formula 44 Cough Control Discs (Vicks Health Care) p 638
Vicks Throat Lozenges (Vicks Health Care) p 641

Other
Aspergum (Plough) p 418, 608
Ayr Saline Nasal Mist (Ascher) p 508
Ocean Mist (Fleming) p 538

COLD SORE PREPARATIONS
Internal
Lactinex Tablets & Granules (Hynson, Westcott & Dunning) p 411, 546
Topical
Anbesol Antiseptic Anesthetic Gel (Whitehall) p 426, 652
Anbesol Antiseptic Anesthetic Liquid (Whitehall) p 426, 652
Campho-Phenique Liquid (Consumer Products Div., Winthrop) p 663
Resolve Cold Sore & Fever Blister Relief (Dow Pharmaceuticals) p 535

COLOSTOMY DEODORIZERS
Derifil Tablets & Powder (Rystan) p 618

CONTACT LENS CARE PRODUCTS
Hard Lens
Cleaning Solution
Clens (Alcon/bp) p 405, 505
Rewetting & Lubricating
Adapettes (Alcon/bp) p 405, 504
Soaking
Soaclens (Alcon/bp) p 405, 505
Wetting
Soaclens (Alcon/bp) p 405, 505
Soft Lens
Cleaners
Preflex (Alcon/bp) p 405, 505
Rewetting & Lubricating
Adapettes (Alcon/bp) p 405, 505
Rinsing
BoilnSoak (Alcon/bp) p 405, 505
Flex-Care (Alcon/bp) p 405, 505
Storage & Disinfection
BoilnSoak (Alcon/bp) p 405, 505
Flex-Care (Alcon/bp) p 405, 505

CONTRACEPTIVES-Female
(see under VAGINAL PREPARATIONS)

CONTRACEPTIVES-Male
Conceptrol Shields Latex Prophylactics (Ortho Consumer Products) p 416, 597
Conceptrol Supreme Lubricated Thin Prophylactics (Ortho Consumer Products) p 597

CORN PADS & PREPARATIONS
Freezone Solution (Whitehall) p 656

COSMETICS
Chip Resistant Top Coat (Almay) p 506
Clear Nail Enamel (Almay) p 506
Color Rich Eyeshadow (Wet or Dry) (Almay) p 506
Enamel Quick Dry (Almay) p 506
Gentle Color Eye Pencils (Almay) p 506
Gentle Color Lip Color Pencils (Almay) p 506
Gentle Color Lip Liner Pencils (Almay) p 506
Gentle Nail Enamel Remover (Almay) p 506
High Gloss Nail Guard (Almay) p 506
Lip Gleamer (Almay) p 506
Lip Polishers (Almay) p 506
Long on Lashes Lengthening Lashcolor (Almay) p 506
Maxi Unshine Oil Free Make-Up (Max Factor) p 536
Maxi Unshine 100% Oil Free Blotting Powder (Max Factor) p 536
Maxi Unshine 100% Oil Free Blushing Powder (Max Factor) p 537
Moisture Whip Lipstick (Maybelline) p 559

Moisture Whip Liquid Make-up & Moisture Whip Cream Make-up (Maybelline) p 559
Nail Enamels: Frosted and Creme (Almay) p 506
Protective Base Coat (Almay) p 506
Rich Lash Thickening Lashcolor (Almay) p 406, 506
Richcreme Frosted Lipcolor (Almay) p 506
Richcreme Lipcolor (Almay) p 506
Ridge Filling Pre-Coat (Almay) p 506
Softlight Cream Powder Eye Shadow (Almay) p 406, 506
Twinstick for Lip and Cheek (Almay) p 506
Waterproof Mascara (Almay) p 506

COUGH PREPARATIONS
Antitussives & Combinations
Ambenyl-D Decongestant Cough Formula (Marion) p 412, 556
Bayer Cough Syrup for Children (Glenbrook) p 540
Benylin DM (Parke-Davis) p 600
C3 Cold Cough Capsules (Menley & James) p 413, 574
Children's Hold (Beecham Products) p 510
Contac Jr. Childrens' Cold Medicine (Menley & James) p 413, 575
Coricidin Children's Cough Syrup (Schering) p 421, 622
Coricidin Cough Syrup (Schering) p 421, 621
Coryban-D Cough Syrup (Pfipharmecs) p 418, 604
Cosanyl Cough Syrup (Health Care) p 410, 542
Cosanyl-DM Cough Syrup (Health Care) p 410, 542
CoTylenol Cold Formula Tablets and Capsules (McNeil Consumer Products) p 412, 559
CoTylenol Liquid Cold Formula (McNeil Consumer Products) p 412, 559
Daycare Multi-Symptom Colds Medicine Capsules (Vicks Health Care) p 424, 638
Daycare Multi-Symptom Colds Medicine (Vicks Health Care) p 424, 638
Dimacol Capsules (Robins) p 420, 615
Dimacol Liquid (Robins) p 420, 615
Dorcol Pediatric Cough Syrup (Dorsey) p 409, 530
Formula 44 Cough Control Discs (Vicks Health Care) p 638
Formula 44 Cough Mixture (Vicks Health Care) p 424, 639
Formula 44D Decongestant Cough Mixture (Vicks Health Care) p 424, 639
Halls Mentho-Lyptus Cough Tablets (Warner-Lambert) p 425, 645
Hold (Beecham Products) p 511
Naldecon-DX Pediatric Syrup (Bristol) p 515
Novahistine Cough & Cold Formula (Dow Pharmaceuticals) p 532
Novahistine Cough Formula (Dow Pharmaceuticals) p 532
Novahistine DMX (Dow Pharmaceuticals) p 533
Nyquil Nighttime Colds Medicine (Vicks Health Care) p 424, 639
Ornacol Capsules (Menley & James) p 413, 577
Robitussin-CF (Robins) p 420, 617
Robitussin-DM (Robins) p 420, 617
Ryna-C Liquid (Wallace) p 425, 643
St. Joseph Cough Syrup for Children (Plough) p 418, 609
Sucrets Cough Control Formula (Beecham Products) p 512
Triaminic-DM Cough Formula (Dorsey) p 409, 531
Triaminicol Decongestant Cough Syrup (Dorsey) p 409, 531
Trind-DM (Mead Johnson Nutritional) p 572
Tussagesic Tablets & Suspension (Dorsey) p 531
Vaposteam (Vicks Health Care) p 640

Vicks Cough Syrup (Vicks Health Care) p 641
Vicks Formula 44 Cough Control Discs (Vicks Health Care) p 638
Vicks Formula 44 Cough Mixture (Vicks Health Care) p 424, 639
Vicks Formula 44D Decongestant Cough Mixture (Vicks Health Care) p 422, 639
Vicks Nyquil Nighttime Colds Medicine (Vicks Health Care) p 424, 639
Vicks Vaporub (Vicks Health Care) p 424, 642
Vicks Vaposteam (Vicks Health Care) p 640
Viro-Med Liquid (Whitehall) p 659
Viro-Med Tablets (Whitehall) p 660
Expectorants & Combinations
Breonesin (Breon) p 515
CCP Tablets (Medique) p 574
Cheracol D Cough Syrup (Upjohn) p 635
Coricidin Children's Cough Syrup (Schering) p 421, 622
Coricidin Cough Syrup (Schering) p 421, 621
DeWitt's Baby Cough Syrup (DeWitt) p 409, 529
Dimacol Capsules (Robins) p 420, 615
Dimacol Liquid (Robins) p 420, 615
Dorcol Pediatric Cough Syrup (Dorsey) p 409, 530
Formula 44 Cough Mixture (Vicks Health Care) p 424, 639
Formula 44D Decongestant Cough Mixture (Vicks Health Care) p 424, 639
Naldecon-DX Pediatric Syrup (Bristol) p 515
Naldecon-EX Pediatric Drops (Bristol) p 515
Novahistine Cough Formula (Dow Pharmaceuticals) p 532
Novahistine DMX (Dow Pharmaceuticals) p 533
Robitussin (Robins) p 420, 617
Robitussin-CF (Robins) p 420, 617
Robitussin-DM (Robins) p 420, 617
Robitussin-PE (Robins) p 420, 617
Ryna-CX Liquid (Wallace) p 425, 643
Triaminic Expectorant (Dorsey) p 409, 530
Tussagesic Tablets & Suspension (Dorsey) p 531
Vaposteam (Vicks Health Care) p 640
Vicks Cough Syrup (Vicks Health Care) p 641
Vicks Formula 44 Cough Mixture (Vicks Health Care) p 424, 639
Vicks Formula 44D Decongestant Cough Mixture (Vicks Health Care) p 422, 639
Vicks Vaporub (Vicks Health Care) p 424, 642
Vicks Vaposteam (Vicks Health Care) p 640
Viro-Med Liquid (Whitehall) p 659
Viro-Med Tablets (Whitehall) p 660
Lozenges
Chloraseptic Cough Control Lozenges (Norwich-Eaton) p 416, 593
Formula 44 Cough Control Discs (Vicks Health Care) p 638
Vicks Cough Silencers Cough Drops (Vicks Health Care) p 641
Vicks Throat Lozenges (Vicks Health Care) p 641

D

DANDRUFF & SEBORRHEA PREPARATIONS
(see under DERMATOLOGICALS)

DECONGESTANTS
(see under COLD PREPARATIONS)

DENTAL PREPARATIONS
Anbesol Antiseptic Anesthetic Gel (Whitehall) p 426, 652
Anbesol Antiseptic Anesthetic Liquid (Whitehall) p 426, 652
Cankaid (Becton Dickinson) p 510

Fluorigard Anti-Cavity Dental Rinse (Colgate-Palmolive) p 408, 525
Gly-Oxide Liquid (Marion) p 412, 557
Mersene Denture Cleanser (Colgate-Palmolive) p 408, 525
Protect Toothpaste (Marion) p 412, 558
Sensodyne Toothpaste (Block) p 513

DENTURE PREPARATIONS
Anbesol Antiseptic Anesthetic Gel (Whitehall) p 426, 652
Anbesol Antiseptic Anesthetic Liquid (Whitehall) p 426, 652
Cushion Grip (Plough) p 418, 608

DEODORANTS
Cheq Antiperspirant/Deodorant Spray (Almay) p 506
Cheq Extra-Dry Antiperspirant/Deodorant Spray (Aerosol) (Almay) p 506
Cheq Roll-On Antiperspirant/Deodorant (Almay) p 506
Cheq Soft Powder Extra Dry Antiperspirant Spray (Aerosol) (Almay) p 506
Chloresium Ointment & Solution (Rystan) p 618
Derifil Tablets & Powder (Rystan) p 618
Listerine Antiseptic (Warner-Lambert) p 425, 645
NP-27 Powder (Norwich-Eaton) p 595
Norforms Feminine Deodorants (Norwich-Eaton) p 416, 594

DERMATOLOGICALS
Abradant
Buf Body Scrub (Riker) p 613
Buf-Puf Nonmedicated Cleansing Sponge (Riker) p 613
Pernox (Westwood) p 650
Pernox Lotion (Westwood) p 650
Analgesic
Calamatum Lotion, Ointment, Spray (Blair) p 512
Vicks Vaporub (Vicks Health Care) p 424, 642
Anesthetics, Topical
Rhulicaine (Lederle) p 551
Antiacne Preparations
Acnaveen Bar (CooperCare) p 408, 526
Acnederm Lotion (Lannett) p 548
Acnomel Cream & Cake (Menley & James) p 413, 574
Bensulfoid Lotion (Poythress) p 610
Buf Acne Cleansing Bar (Riker) p 613
Buf Body Scrub (Riker) p 613
Buf Kit for Acne (Riker) p 613
Clear By Design Invisible Greaseless Acne Gel (Herbert) p 543
Clearasil 5% Benzoyl Peroxide Lotion (Vicks Toiletry Products) p 424, 637
Clearasil Super Strength Acne Treatment Cream (Vicks Toiletry Products) p 424, 637
Dry and Clear, Acne Medication, Lotion & Double Strength Cream (Whitehall) p 656
Dry and Clear Medicated Acne Cleanser (Whitehall) p 656
Fomac Foam (Dermik) p 527
Fostex BPO 5% (Westwood) p 648
Fostex CM (Westwood) p 649
Fostex Cake (Westwood) p 649
Fostex Cream & Medicated Cleanser (Westwood) p 649
Fostril (Westwood) p 649
Loroxide Acne Lotion (Dermik) p 528
Oxy Wash (Norcliff Thayer) p 415, 592
Oxy-5 Lotion (Norcliff Thayer) p 415, 592
Oxy-10 Lotion (Norcliff Thayer) p 415, 592
Pernox (Westwood) p 650
Pernox Lotion (Westwood) p 650
Stri-Dex B.P. (Lehn & Fink) p 555
Stri-Dex Medicated Pads (Lehn & Fink) p 555
Teen 5 & 10 Lotion (Muro) p 587

Topex 10% Benzoyl Peroxide Lotion Buffered Acne Medication (Vicks Toiletry Products) p 424, 637
Transact (Westwood) p 651
Vanoxide Acne Lotion (Dermik) p 528
Xerac (Persōn & Covey) p 418, 603
Zacne Tablets (Nature's Bounty) p 415, 590
Antibacterial
B.F.I. (Beecham Products) p 510
BPN Ointment (Norwich-Eaton) p 592
Betadine Antiseptic Lubricating Gel (Purdue Frederick) p 611
Betadine Ointment (Purdue Frederick) p 419, 612
Betadine Skin Cleanser (Purdue Frederick) p 419, 611
Betadine Solution (Purdue Frederick) p 419, 611
Campho-Phenique Liquid (Consumer Products Div., Winthrop) p 663
Dermaide Aloe Ointment (Dermaide) p 527
Hibiclens Antimicrobial Skin Cleanser (Stuart) p 630
Hibistat Germicidal Hand Rinse (Stuart) p 630
Hibitane Tincture (Tinted & Non-Tinted) (Stuart) p 630
Isodine Antiseptic (Blair) p 513
Listerine Antiseptic (Warner-Lambert) p 425, 645
Loroxide Acne Lotion (Dermik) p 528
NP-27 Powder (Norwich-Eaton) p 595
Norwich Bacitracin Ointment (Norwich-Eaton) p 594
Oxy Wash (Norcliff Thayer) p 415, 592
Rhulicaine (Lederle) p 551
Septa Ointment (Circle) p 524
Vanoxide Acne Lotion (Dermik) p 528
Antibacterial, Antifungal & Combinations
Caldesene Medicated Ointment (Pharmacraft) p 606
Caldesene Medicated Powder (Pharmacraft) p 606
Hibiclens Antimicrobial Skin Cleanser (Stuart) p 630
Hibistat Germicidal Hand Rinse (Stuart) p 630
Hibitane Tincture (Tinted & Non-Tinted) (Stuart) p 630
Vioform Cream & Ointment (Ciba) p 524
Antiburn
Balmex Ointment (Macsil) p 556
Betadine Ointment (Purdue Frederick) p 419, 612
BiCozene Creme (Creighton Products) p 408, 526
Dermaide Aloe Ointment (Dermaide) p 527
Desitin Ointment (Leeming) p 553
Rhulicaine (Lederle) p 551
Unguentine Plus (Norwich-Eaton) p 595
Antidandruff
DHS Tar Shampoo (Persōn & Covey) p 418, 603
DHS Zinc Shampoo (Persōn & Covey) p 418, 603
Danex Protein Enriched Dandruff Shampoo (Herbert) p 543
Denorex Medicated Shampoo, Regular & Mountain Fresh Herbal (Whitehall) p 426, 653
Head & Shoulders (Procter & Gamble) p 610
Listerine Antiseptic (Warner-Lambert) p 425, 645
Sebb Lotion (Max Factor) p 537
Tegrin Medicated Shampoo (Block) p 513
Vanseb Cream & Lotion Dandruff Shampoo (Herbert) p 544
Vanseb-T Cream & Lotion Dandruff Shampoo (Herbert) p 544
Zetar Shampoo (Dermik) p 529
Antidermatitis
BiCozene Creme (Creighton Products) p 408, 526
Caladryl Lotion & Cream (Parke-Davis) p 600

Calamatum Lotion, Ointment, Spray (Blair) p 512
Cortaid Cream (Upjohn) p 424, 635
Cortaid Lotion (Upjohn) p 424, 635
Cortaid Ointment (Upjohn) p 424, 635
Cortril ½% (Pfipharmecs) p 603
Delacort (Mericon) p 580
Dermolate Anti-Itch Cream & Spray (Schering) p 623
Dermolate Scalp-Itch Lotion (Schering) p 623
Estar Tar Gel (Westwood) p 648
Hytone Cream ½% (Dermik) p 527
Hytone Ointment ½% (Dermik) p 528
Lanacort Creme (Combe) p 408, 526
Methakote Diaper Rash Cream (Syntex) p 633
Pragmatar Ointment (Menley & James) p 413, 578
Quotane Ointment (Menley & James) p 413, 578
Rhulicort Cream & Lotion (Lederle) p 552
Solarcaine (Plough) p 418, 609
Ziradryl Lotion (Parke-Davis) p 602
Antifungal & Combinations
Aftate (Plough) p 418, 607
B.F.I. (Beecham Products) p 510
Betadine Antiseptic Lubricating Gel (Purdue Frederick) p 611
Betadine Ointment (Purdue Frederick) p 419, 612
Betadine Skin Cleanser (Purdue Frederick) p 419, 611
Betadine Solution (Purdue Frederick) p 419, 611
Cruex Medicated Cream (Pharmacraft) p 606
Cruex Medicated Powder (Pharmacraft) p 606
Desenex Foam (Pharmacraft) p 607
Desenex Ointment & Liquid (Pharmacraft) p 607
Desenex Powders (Pharmacraft) p 607
Desenex Soap (Pharmacraft) p 607
Hibiclens Antimicrobial Skin Cleanser (Stuart) p 630
Hibistat Germicidal Hand Rinse (Stuart) p 630
Hibitane Tincture (Tinted & Non-Tinted) (Stuart) p 630
NP-27 Cream (Norwich-Eaton) p 595
NP-27 Liquid (Norwich-Eaton) p 595
NP-27 Powder (Norwich-Eaton) p 595
NP-27 Spray Powder (Norwich-Eaton) p 595
Tinactin Aerosol Powder 1% (Schering) p 422, 626
Tinactin 1% Cream, Solution & Powder (Schering) p 421, 626
Antiperspirants
Cheq Antiperspirant/Deodorant Spray (Almay) p 506
Cheq Extra-Dry Antiperspirant/Deodorant Spray (Aerosol) (Almay) p 506
Cheq Roll-On Antiperspirant/Deodorant (Almay) p 506
Cheq Soft Powder Extra Dry Antiperspirant Spray (Aerosol) (Almay) p 506
Antipruritics, Topical
Alpha Keri Bath Oil (Westwood) p 647
Balnetar (Westwood) p 648
Benadryl Antihistamine Cream (Parke-Davis) p 599
BiCozene Creme (Creighton Products) p 408, 526
Caladryl Lotion & Cream (Parke-Davis) p 600
Calamatum Lotion, Ointment, Spray (Blair) p 512
CaldeCORT Hydrocortisone Cream (Pharmacraft) p 606
Campho-Phenique Liquid (Consumer Products Div., Winthrop) p 663
Carmol 10 Lotion (Syntex) p 633
Cortaid Cream (Upjohn) p 424, 635
Cortaid Lotion (Upjohn) p 424, 635
Cortaid Ointment (Upjohn) p 424, 635
Denorex Medicated Shampoo, Regular & Mountain Fresh Herbal (Whitehall) p 426, 653

Derma Medicone Ointment (Medicone) p 573
Dermolate Anal-Itch Ointment (Schering) p 623
Dermolate Anti-Itch Cream & Spray (Schering) p 623
Dermolate Scalp-Itch Lotion (Schering) p 623
Estar Tar Gel (Westwood) p 648
Hytone Cream ½% (Dermik) p 527
Hytone Ointment ½% (Dermik) p 528
Keri Lotion (Westwood) p 649
Lanacane Medicated Creme (Combe) p 408, 525
Lanacort Creme (Combe) p 408, 526
PBZ Cream (Geigy) p 410, 539
Quotane Ointment (Menley & James) p 413, 578
Rhulicort Cream & Lotion (Lederle) p 552
Rhulicream (Lederle) p 551
Rhuligel (Lederle) p 551
Rhulihist (Lederle) p 551
Rhulispray (Lederle) p 551
Sebucare (Westwood) p 651
Sebutone & Sebutone Cream (Westwood) p 651
Shepard's Cream Lotion (Dermik) p 528
Shepard's Dry Skin Cream (Dermik) p 528
Shepard's Hand Cream (Dermik) p 528
Shepard's Soap (Dermik) p 528
Soft 'N Soothe Anti-Itch Creme (Ascher) p 509
Topic Benzyl Alcohol Gel (Syntex) p 633
Tucks Cream & Ointment (Parke-Davis) p 602
Tucks Premoistened Pads (Parke-Davis) p 602
Vagisil Feminine Itching Medication (Combe) p 408, 526
Xylocaine 2.5% Ointment (Astra) p 509
Zetar Shampoo (Dermik) p 529
Ziradryl Lotion (Parke-Davis) p 602

Antipsoriasis Agents
Balnetar (Westwood) p 648
DHS Tar Shampoo (Persōn & Covey) p 418, 603
Denorex Medicated Shampoo, Regular & Mountain Fresh Herbal (Whitehall) p 426, 653
Estar Tar Gel (Westwood) p 648
Oxipor VHC Lotion for Psoriasis (Whitehall) p 657
Quotane Ointment (Menley & James) p 413, 578
Sebutone & Sebutone Cream (Westwood) p 651
Tegrin for Psoriasis Lotion & Cream (Block) p 513
Zetar Shampoo (Dermik) p 529

Antiseborrhea
Denorex Medicated Shampoo, Regular & Mountain Fresh Herbal (Whitehall) p 426, 653
Fostex Cake (Westwood) p 649
Fostex Cream & Medicated Cleanser (Westwood) p 649
Methakote Diaper Rash Cream (Syntex) p 633
Pragmatar Ointment (Menley & James) p 413, 578
Sebucare (Westwood) p 651
Sebulex and Sebulex Cream (Westwood) p 651
Sebulex with Protein (Westwood) p 651
Sebutone & Sebutone Cream (Westwood) p 651
Tegrin Medicated Shampoo (Block) p 513
Zetar Shampoo (Dermik) p 529
Zincon Dandruff Shampoo (Lederle) p 552

Astringents
Bluboro Powder Astringent Soaking Solution (Herbert) p 543

Calamatum Lotion, Ointment, Spray (Blair) p 512
Counter Balance Pore Lotion (Almay) p 406, 506
Deep Mist Mild Skin Freshener (Almay) p 406, 506
Deep Mist Toning and Refining Lotion (Almay) p 406, 506
Mediconet (Medicone) p 573
Tucks Premoistened Pads (Parke-Davis) p 602

Breast Creams
Masse Breast Cream (Ortho Consumer Products) p 416, 597

Coal Tar
Balnetar (Westwood) p 648
Denorex Medicated Shampoo, Regular & Mountain Fresh Herbal (Whitehall) p 426, 653
Estar Tar Gel (Westwood) p 648
Oxipor VHC Lotion for Psoriasis (Whitehall) p 657
Tegrin for Psoriasis Lotion & Cream (Block) p 513
Tegrin Medicated Shampoo (Block) p 513
Zetar Shampoo (Dermik) p 529

Coal Tar & Sulfur
Pragmatar Ointment (Menley & James) p 413, 578
Sebutone & Sebutone Cream (Westwood) p 651
Vanseb-T Cream & Lotion Dandruff Shampoo (Herbert) p 544

Detergents
Danex Protein Enriched Dandruff Shampoo (Herbert) p 543
Fostex Cake (Westwood) p 649
Fostex Cream & Medicated Cleanser (Westwood) p 649
Lowila Cake (Westwood) p 650
Metasep Shampoo (Marion) p 557
Pernox Lotion (Westwood) p 650
pHisoDerm (Consumer Products Div., Winthrop) p 664
Vanseb Cream & Lotion Dandruff Shampoo (Herbert) p 544
Vanseb-T Cream & Lotion Dandruff Shampoo (Herbert) p 544
Zetar Shampoo (Dermik) p 529
Zincon Dandruff Shampoo (Lederle) p 552

Emollients
A and D Ointment (Schering) p 421, 619
Alpha Keri Bath Oil (Westwood) p 647
Aquacare Dry Skin Cream & Lotion (Herbert) p 543
Aquacare/HP Dry Skin Cream & Lotion (Herbert) p 543
Aveeno Oilated Bath Powder (CooperCare) p 408, 526
Balmex Baby Powder (Macsil) p 556
Balmex Emollient Lotion (Macsil) p 556
Balmex Ointment (Macsil) p 556
Balnetar (Westwood) p 648
Buf Lotion (Riker) p 613
Carmol 10 Lotion (Syntex) p 633
Carmol 20 Cream (Syntex) p 633
Chap Stick Lip Balm (Miller-Morton) p 415, 586
Chap Stick Sunblock 15 Lip Balm (Miller-Morton) p 415, 586
Cold Cream (Almay) p 506
Deep Mist Eye Cream (Almay) p 506
Deep Mist Moisture Cream (Almay) p 506
Deep Mist Moisture Lotion (Almay) p 406, 506
Deep Mist Moisture and Replenishing Lotion (Almay) p 506
Deep Mist Ultralight Moisture Lotion (Almay) p 506
Deep Mist Ultralight Night Cream (Almay) p 506
Deep Mist Ultrarich Night Cream (Almay) p 506
Dermassage Medicated Skin Lotion (Colgate-Palmolive) p 408, 525
Desitin Ointment (Leeming) p 553

Eclipse After Sun Lotion (Herbert) p 411, 543
Emulave Bar (CooperCare) p 408, 526
Ice Mint (Westwood) p 649
Keri Creme (Westwood) p 649
Keri Lotion (Westwood) p 649
Lubath Bath Oil (Warner-Lambert) p 425, 645
Lubriderm Cream (Warner-Lambert) p 425, 645
Lubriderm Lotion (Warner-Lambert) p 425, 646
Moisture Whip Lip Conditioner (Maybelline) p 559
Moisture Whip Lipstick (Maybelline) p 559
Moisture Whip Liquid Make-up & Moisture Whip Cream Make-up (Maybelline) p 559
Moisture Whip Protective Facial Moisturizer (Maybelline) p 559
pHisoDerm (Consumer Products Div., Winthrop) p 664
Purpose Brand Dry Skin Cream (Ortho Dermatological) p 417, 598
Shepard's Cream Lotion (Dermik) p 528
Shepard's Dry Skin Cream (Dermik) p 528
Shepard's Hand Cream (Dermik) p 528
Shepard's Soap (Dermik) p 528
Wrinkle Stick (Almay) p 506
Zinc Oxide Ointment (Norwich-Eaton) p 595

Foot Care
Desenex Foot & Sneaker Spray (Pharmacraft) p 607

Fungicides
Betadine Ointment (Purdue Frederick) p 419, 612
Betadine Skin Cleanser (Purdue Frederick) p 419, 611
Betadine Solution (Purdue Frederick) p 419, 611
Caldesene Medicated Powder (Pharmacraft) p 606
Cruex Medicated Cream (Pharmacraft) p 606
Cruex Medicated Powder (Pharmacraft) p 606
Desenex Foam (Pharmacraft) p 607
Desenex Ointment & Liquid (Pharmacraft) p 607
Desenex Powders (Pharmacraft) p 607
Desenex Soap (Pharmacraft) p 607
Tinactin Aerosol Powder 1% (Schering) p 422, 626
Tinactin 1% Cream, Solution & Powder (Schering) p 421, 626

General
A and D Ointment (Schering) p 421, 619
Acid Mantle Creme & Lotion (Dorsey) p 409, 530
Acnederm Lotion (Lannett) p 548
Alpha Keri Bath Oil (Westwood) p 647
Alpha Keri Soap (Westwood) p 648
Aquacare Dry Skin Cream & Lotion (Herbert) p 543
Aquacare/HP Dry Skin Cream & Lotion (Herbert) p 543
Balmex Ointment (Macsil) p 556
Chloresium Ointment & Solution (Rystan) p 618
Cortaid Cream (Upjohn) p 424, 635
Cortaid Lotion (Upjohn) p 424, 635
Cortaid Ointment (Upjohn) p 424, 635
Dermaide Aloe Ointment (Dermaide) p 527
Desitin Ointment (Leeming) p 553
Fostex CM (Westwood) p 649
Keri Facial Cleanser (Westwood) p 649
Lubriderm Lotion (Warner-Lambert) p 425, 646
Purpose Brand Dry Skin Cream (Ortho Dermatological) p 417, 598
Quotane Ointment (Menley & James) p 413, 578
Sebulex and Sebulex Cream (Westwood) p 651
Sebulex with Protein (Westwood) p 651

Shepard's Cream Lotion (Dermik) p 528

Shepard's Dry Skin Cream (Dermik) p 528

Shepard's Hand Cream (Dermik) p 528

Shepard's Soap (Dermik) p 528

Keratolytics

Acnederm Lotion (Lannett) p 548

Bensulfoid Lotion (Poythress) p 610

Buf Acne Cleansing Bar (Riker) p 613

Buf Body Scrub (Riker) p 613

Carmol 10 Lotion (Syntex) p 633

Carmol 20 Cream (Syntex) p 633

Compound W Solution (Whitehall) p 653

Derma+Soft Creme (Creighton Products) p 408, 527

Freezone Solution (Whitehall) p 656

Stri-Dex Medicated Pads (Lehn & Fink) p 555

Powders

Aftate (Plough) p 418, 607

Balmex Baby Powder (Macsil) p 556

Caldesene Medicated Ointment (Pharmacraft) p 606

Caldesene Medicated Powder (Pharmacraft) p 606

Cruex Medicated Powder (Pharmacraft) p 606

Desenex Powders (Pharmacraft) p 607

Diaparene Baby Powder (Glenbrook) p 410, 541

NP-27 Powder (Norwich-Eaton) p 595

NP-27 Spray Powder (Norwich-Eaton) p 595

Pure Beauty Blotting Powder for Oily Skin (Almay) p 506

Pure Beauty Translucent Face Powder (Almay) p 506

Pure Beauty Translucent Pressed Powder (Almay) p 506

Tinactin Aerosol Powder 1% (Schering) p 422, 626

Shampoos

Clean and Gentle Daily Shampoo (Almay) p 406, 506

DHS Shampoo (Persŏn & Covey) p 418, 603

Danex Protein Enriched Dandruff Shampoo (Herbert) p 543

Denorex Medicated Shampoo, Regular. & Mountain Fresh Herbal (Whitehall) p 426, 653

Fostex Cream & Medicated Cleanser (Westwood) p 649

Head & Shoulders (Procter & Gamble) p 610

Metasep Shampoo (Marion) p 557

Pernox Shampoo (Westwood) p 650

Pure and Gentle Everyday Conditioning Shampoo (Almay) p 506

Pure Castile Shampoo (Almay) p 506

Purpose Brand Shampoo (Ortho Dermatological) p 417, 598

Sebb Shampoo (Max Factor) p 537

Sebulex and Sebulex Cream (Westwood) p 651

Sebulex with Protein (Westwood) p 651

Sebutone & Sebutone Cream (Westwood) p 651

Selsun Blue Lotion (Abbott Consumer Products) p 405, 502

Tegrin Medicated Shampoo (Block) p 513

Vanseb Cream & Lotion Dandruff Shampoo (Herbert) p 544

Vanseb-T Cream & Lotion Dandruff Shampoo (Herbert) p 544

Zetar Shampoo (Dermik) p 529

Zincon Dandruff Shampoo (Lederle) p 552

Skin Bleaches

Esotérica Medicated Fade Cream (Norcliff Thayer) p 415, 591

Soaps & Cleansers

Alpha Keri Soap (Westwood) p 648

Aveeno Bar (CooperCare) p 408, 526

Aveeno Colloidal Oatmeal (CooperCare) p 408, 526

Aveeno Oilated Bath Powder (CooperCare) p 408, 526

Betadine Skin Cleanser (Purdue Frederick) p 419, 611

Buf Acne Cleansing Bar (Riker) p 613

Cold Cream Soap for Normal, Combination and Dry Skin (Almay) p 506

Counter Balance Clear Facial Cleanser (Almay) p 406, 506

Counter Balance Facial Soap for Oily Skin (Almay) p 506

Counter Balance Fluffy Facial Cleanser (Almay) p 506

Deep Mist Cleanser (Almay) p 406, 506

Deep Mist Cleansing Lotion (Almay) p 406, 506

Deep Pore Cleansing Mask (Almay) p 506

Desenex Soap (Pharmacraft) p 607

Dry and Clear Medicated Acne Cleanser (Whitehall) p 656

Emulave Bar (CooperCare) p 408, 526

Fomac Foam (Dermik) p 527

Johnson's Baby Bath (Johnson & Johnson Baby Products Company) p 411, 547

Keri Facial Cleanser (Westwood) p 649

Keri Facial Soap (Westwood) p 649

Non-Oily Eye Makeup Remover Pads (Almay) p 506

Oxy Wash (Norcliff Thayer) p 415, 592

Pernox (Westwood) p 650

pHresh 3.5 Cleansing Liquid (Riker) p 614

Purpose Brand Soap (Ortho Dermatological) p 417, 598

Shepard's Soap (Dermik) p 528

Teen 5 Wash (Muro) p 587

Sulfur & Salicylic Acid

Buf Acne Cleansing Bar (Riker) p 613

Fomac Foam (Dermik) p 527

Fostex Cake (Westwood) p 649

Fostex Cream & Medicated Cleanser (Westwood) p 649

Pernox (Westwood) p 650

Pernox Lotion (Westwood) p 650

Pragmatar Ointment (Menley & James) p 413, 578

Sebulex and Sebulex Cream (Westwood) p 651

Sebulex with Protein (Westwood) p 651

Sebutone & Sebutone Cream (Westwood) p 651

Sunburn Preparations

Balmex Ointment (Macsil) p 556

BiCozene Creme (Creighton Products) p 408, 526

Dermaide Aloe Ointment (Dermaide) p 527

Eclipse After Sun Lotion (Herbert) p 411, 543

Medi-Quik (Lehn & Fink) p 555

Rhulicaine (Lederle) p 551

Solarcaine (Plough) p 418, 609

Unguentine Plus (Norwich-Eaton) p 595

Sun Screens

Chap Stick Lip Balm (Miller-Morton) p 415, 586

Chap Stick Sunblock 15 Lip Balm (Miller-Morton) p 415, 586

Eclipse Sunscreen Lip & Face Protectant (Herbert) p 411, 543

Eclipse Sunscreen Lotion & Gel, Original (Herbert) p 543

Eclipse Sunscreen Lotion, Total (Alcohol Base) (Herbert) p 411, 543

Eclipse Suntan Lotion, Partial (Herbert) p 411, 543

Moisture Whip Lip Conditioner (Maybelline) p 559

Moisture Whip Lipstick (Maybelline) p 559

Moisture Whip Liquid Make-up & Moisture Whip Cream Make-up (Maybelline) p 559

Moisture Whip Protective Facial Moisturizer (Maybelline) p 559

PreSun 4 Lotion (Westwood) p 650

PreSun 8 Lotion, Creamy Lotion & Gel (Westwood) p 650

PreSun 15 Lotion (Westwood) p 651

PreSun Sunscreen Lip Protection (Westwood) p 651

Shade Plus Sunscreen Lotion (SPF-8) (Plough) p 418, 609

Shade Sunscreen Lotion (SPF-6) (Plough) p 418, 609

Solbar Plus 15 (Persŏn & Covey) p 603

Sundown Sunscreen, Extra Protection (Johnson & Johnson Baby Products Company) p 411, 547

Sundown Sunscreen, Maximal Protection (Johnson & Johnson Baby Products Company) p 411, 547

Sundown Sunscreen, Moderate Protection (Johnson & Johnson Baby Products Company) p 411, 547

Sundown Sunscreen, Ultra Protection (Johnson & Johnson Baby Products Company) p 411, 547

Super Shade (SPF-15) (Plough) p 418, 610

Uval Moisturizing Sunscreen Lotion (Dorsey) p 532

Wart Removers

Compound W Solution (Whitehall) p 653

Vergo (Daywell) p 527

Wart-Off (Pfipharmecs) p 605

Wet Dressings

Tucks Premoistened Pads (Parke-Davis) p 602

Other

Clean and Gentle Oil-Free Conditioner (Almay) p 506

Cortaid Cream (Upjohn) p 424, 635

Cortaid Lotion (Upjohn) p 424, 635

Cortaid Ointment (Upjohn) p 424, 635

Counter Balance Oil-Free Moisturizer (Almay) p 406, 506

Cover-up Stick - light, medium, dark (Almay) p 506

Cuticle Treatment Oil (Almay) p 506

Deep Mist Gentle Gel Mask (Almay) p 506

Derma Medicone Ointment (Medicone) p 573

Dermassage Dish Liquid (Colgate-Palmolive) p 408, 525

Diaparene Baby Wash Cloths (Glenbrook) p 410, 541

Extra Hold Protein Conditioning Hair Spray (Aerosol) (Almay) p 506

Eye Makeup Remover Pads (Almay) p 506

Ice Mint (Westwood) p 649

Medicone Dressing Cream (Medicone) p 573

Proderm Topical Dressing (Hickam) p 544

Protein Conditioning Hair Spray (Almay) p 406, 506

Pure Beauty Extra Cover Makeup (Almay) p 506

Pure Beauty Foundation Lotion for Oily Skin (Almay) p 506

Pure Beauty Fresh Blush (Almay) p 506

Pure Beauty Liquid Makeup (Almay) p 406, 506

Pure Beauty Moisturizing Makeup (Almay) p 506

Pure Beauty Richcreme Blush (Almay) p 506

Regular Hold Conditioning Hair Spray (Almay) p 506

Sebucare (Westwood) p 651

Shepard's Cream Lotion (Dermik) p 528

Shepard's Dry Skin Cream (Dermik) p 528

Shepard's Hand Cream (Dermik) p 528

Shepard's Soap (Dermik) p 528

Under Eye Cover Creme, Ivory, Natural (Almay) p 506

DIAGNOSTICS

Acu-Test In-Home Pregnancy Test (J.B. Williams) p 660

F.S.K. (Fecal Staining Kit) (Jayco) p 546

Lac-Tol (Jayco) p 546

Predictor In-Home Early Pregnancy Test (Whitehall) p 657

DIETARY SUPPLEMENTS

Acidophilus Capsules (Nature's Bounty) p 587
Alfalfa Tablets (Nature's Bounty) p 587
Allbee C-800 Plus Iron Tablets (Robins) p 420, 614
Allbee C-800 Tablets (Robins) p 420, 614
Allbee with C Capsules (Robins) p 420, 615
Bee Pollen Tablets (Nature's Bounty) p 587
Brewer's Yeast Powder (Debittered) (Nature's Bounty) p 587
Brewer's Yeast Tablets (Nature's Bounty) p 587
Carnation Instant Breakfast (Carnation) p 521
Casec (Mead Johnson Nutritional) p 562
Chew-Iron Tablets (Nature's Bounty) p 588
Choline Tablets (Nature's Bounty) p 588
Enisyl (Persōn & Covey) p 603
FemIron Multi-Vitamins and Iron (J.B. Williams) p 660
FemIron Tablets (J.B. Williams) p 660
Flexical Elemental Diet (Mead Johnson Nutritional) p 564
Garlic Oil Capsules (Nature's Bounty) p 588
Garlic & Parsley Capsules (Nature's Bounty) p 588
Geritol Liquid-High Potency Iron & Vitamin Tonic (J.B. Williams) p 661
Geritol Mega Vitamins (J.B. Williams) p 661
Geritol Tablets - High Potency Iron & Vitamin Tablets (J.B. Williams) p 661
Ginseng, Manchurian Capsules (Nature's Bounty) p 588
Glutamic Acid Tablets (Nature's Bounty) p 588
Incremin w/Iron Syrup (Lederle) p 550
Inositol Tablets (Nature's Bounty) p 588
Isocal Complete Liquid Diet (Mead Johnson Nutritional) p 564
K-Forté Tablets (O'Connor) p 596
KLB6 Capsules (Nature's Bounty) p 588
Kelp Tablets (Nature's Bounty) p 588
l-Glutamine Tablets (Nature's Bounty) p 589
l-Lysine Tablets (Nature's Bounty) p 589
Lecithin Capsules (Nature's Bounty) p 589
Lecithin, Chewable Tablets (Nature's Bounty) p 589
Lecithin Granules (Nature's Bounty) p 589
Mega-B (Arco) p 508
NaturSlim II (NaturSlim) p 415, 590
Optilets-500 (Abbott) p 503
Orazinc (Mericon) p 580
PABA Tablets (Nature's Bounty) p 589
Pantothenic Acid Tablets (Nature's Bounty) p 589
Protein Tablets (Nature's Bounty) p 589
RNA Tablets (Nature's Bounty) p 589
RNA/DNA Tablets (Nature's Bounty) p 589
Rutin Tablets (Nature's Bounty) p 589
Super Wate-On Emulsion (Fleetwood) p 410, 537
Tryptophan Tablets (Nature's Bounty) p 589
Ultra KLB6 Tablets (Nature's Bounty) p 589
Ultra Vita-Time Tablets (Nature's Bounty) p 589
Yeast Plus Tablets (Nature's Bounty) p 590
Z-Bec Tablets (Robins) p 420, 617
Zinc Tabs (Mericon) p 580

DIGESTIVE AIDS

Cholagest (Anabolic) p 507
Festal (Hoechst-Roussel) p 411, 544
Pepto-Bismol Liquid & Tablets (Norwich-Eaton) p 416, 595

DIURETICS

DeWitt's Pills for Backache & Joint Pains (DeWitt) p 409, 529
Odrinil (Fox) p 538
Sunril Premenstrual Capsules (Schering) p 626
Water Pill Tablets (Nature's Bounty) p 590
Water Pill w/Iron Tablets (Nature's Bounty) p 590

DRY SKIN PREPARATIONS
(see under DERMATOLOGICALS, Emollients)

E

EAR PREPARATIONS

Cerumenolytics
(see under EARWAX CONTROL AGENTS)

Other
Star-Otic (Star) p 628

EARWAX CONTROL AGENTS

Debrox Drops (Marion) p 412, 556
DeWitt's Oil for Ear Use (DeWitt) p 409, 529
Ear Drops by Murine (See Murine Ear Wax Removal System/Murine Ear Drops) (Abbott Consumer Products) p 502
Kerid Ear Drops (Blair) p 513
Murine Ear Wax Removal System/Murine Ear Drops (Abbott Consumer Products) p 405, 502

ELECTROLYTE REPLACEMENT, ORAL

K-Forté Tablets (O'Connor) p 596
Lytren (Mead Johnson Nutritional) p 566

ENZYMES & DIGESTANTS

Cholagest (Anabolic) p 507
LactAid (SugarLo) p 424, 633
Papaya Enzyme Tablets (Nature's Bounty) p 589

EXPECTORANTS
(see under COUGH PREPARATIONS)

EYE PREPARATIONS
(see under OPHTHALMICS)

F

FOODS

Allergy Diet
MBF (Meat Base Formula) Liquid (Gerber) p 539
ProSobee (Mead Johnson Nutritional) p 570

Carbohydrate
Hydra-Lyte (Jayco) p 546

Complete Therapeutic
Carnation Instant Breakfast (Carnation) p 521
Flexical Elemental Diet (Mead Johnson Nutritional) p 564
Isocal Complete Liquid Diet (Mead Johnson Nutritional) p 564
Slender Diet Food For Weight Control (Instant) (Carnation) p 521
Slender Diet Meal Bars For Weight Control (Carnation) p 521
Slender Diet Meal For Weight Control (Canned) (Carnation) p 521
Sustacal (Mead Johnson Nutritional) p 570
Sustagen (Mead Johnson Nutritional) p 571

Dietetic
NaturSlim II (NaturSlim) p 415, 590
Slender Diet Food For Weight Control (Instant) (Carnation) p 521
Slender Diet Meal Bars For Weight Control (Carnation) p 521

Slender Diet Meal For Weight Control (Canned) (Carnation) p 521

Infant
(see under INFANT FORMULAS)

Lactose Free
Portagen (Mead Johnson Nutritional) p 568

Low Fat
Slender Diet Meal For Weight Control (Canned) (Carnation) p 521

Low Residue
Hydra-Lyte (Jayco) p 546

Low Sodium
Lonalac (Mead Johnson Nutritional) p 566

Medium Chain Triglycerides
MCT Oil (Mead Johnson Nutritional) p 567
Portagen (Mead Johnson Nutritional) p 568

Nonfat
Carnation Instant Nonfat Dry Milk (Carnation) p 521
Slender Diet Food For Weight Control (Instant) (Carnation) p 521

FOOT CARE PRODUCTS
(see under DERMATOLOGICALS)

FORMULAS
(see under INFANT FORMULAS)

G

GERMICIDES
(see under ANTIMICROBIALS, Topical)

H

HEMATINICS

FemIron Multivitamin & Iron (Williams) p 660
FemIron Tablets (J.B. Williams) p 660
Feosol Elixir (Menley & James) p 413, 576
Feosol Plus (Menley & James) p 577
Feosol Spansule Capsules (Menley & James) p 413, 577
Feosol Tablets (Menley & James) p 413, 577
Ferancee Chewable Tablets (Stuart) p 629
Ferancee-HP Tablets (Stuart) p 629
Fergon Capsules (Breon) p 515
Fergon Tablets & Elixir (Breon) p 515
Fer-In-Sol Iron Drops, Syrup & Capsules (Mead Johnson Nutritional) p 563
Ferro-Sequels (Lederle) p 549
Ferrous Sulfate Tablets (Nature's Bounty) p 588
Fortespan Capsules (Menley & James) p 413, 577
Fumasorb Tablets (Marion) p 557
Fumerin Tablets (Laser) p 549
Geritol Liquid-High Potency Iron & Vitamin Tonic (J.B. Williams) p 661
Geritol Mega Vitamins (J.B. Williams) p 661
Geritol Tablets - High Potency Iron & Vitamin Tablets (J.B. Williams) p 661
Incremin w/Iron Syrup (Lederle) p 550
Iron Tablets (Nature's Bounty) p 588
Mol-Iron Tablets, Liquid & Chronosule Capsules (Schering) p 421, 626
Mol-Iron Tablets w/Vitamin C (Schering) p 421, 626
Peritinic Tablets (Lederle) p 551
Simron (Merrell-National) p 415, 582
Simron Plus (Merrell-National) p 415, 582
Stuartinic Tablets (Stuart) p 424, 632
Tri-88 (Anabolic) p 507
Troph-Iron Liquid & Tablets (Menley & James) p 413, 579

HEMORRHOIDAL PREPARATIONS
(see under ANORECTAL PRODUCTS)

HERPES PREPARATIONS
(see under COLD SORE PREPARATIONS)

I

INFANT FORMULAS

Carbohydrate Supplement
Hydra-Lyte (Jayco) p 546

Concentrate
Carnation Evaporated Milk (Carnation) p 520
Enfamil Concentrated Liquid & Powder (Mead Johnson Nutritional) p 562
Enfamil w/Iron Concentrated Liquid & Powder (Mead Johnson Nutritional) p 562
I-Soyalac (Loma Linda) p 555
Nursoy Soy Protein Infant Formula (Wyeth) p 666
ProSobee (Mead Johnson Nutritional) p 570
SMA Iron Fortified Infant Formula (Wyeth) p 666
Soyalac: Liquid Concentrate, Ready-to-Serve and Powder (Loma Linda) p 555

High Protein
Casec (Mead Johnson Nutritional) p 562
Probana (Mead Johnson Nutritional) p 569

Hypo-Allergenic
MBF (Meat Base Formula) Liquid (Gerber) p 539
Nursoy Soy Protein Infant Formula (Wyeth) p 666
Nutramigen (Mead Johnson Nutritional) p 567
Pregestimil (Mead Johnson Nutritional) p 569
ProSobee (Mead Johnson Nutritional) p 570

Iron Supplement
Enfamil w/Iron Concentrated Liquid & Powder (Mead Johnson Nutritional) p 562
Enfamil w/Iron Ready-To-Use (Mead Johnson Nutritional) p 563
Nursoy Soy Protein Infant Formula (Wyeth) p 666
SMA Iron Fortified Infant Formula (Wyeth) p 666

Lactose Free
Nursoy Soy Protein Infant Formula (Wyeth) p 666
Portagen (Mead Johnson Nutritional) p 568
ProSobee (Mead Johnson Nutritional) p 570

Low Phenylalanine
Lofenalac (Mead Johnson Nutritional) p 565

Medium Chain Triglycerides
Portagen (Mead Johnson Nutritional) p 568
Pregestimil (Mead Johnson Nutritional) p 569

Protein Hydrolysate
Pregestimil (Mead Johnson Nutritional) p 569

Ready-to-feed
Enfamil Nursette (Mead Johnson Nutritional) p 563
Enfamil Ready-To-Use (Mead Johnson Nutritional) p 563
Enfamil w/Iron Ready-To-Use (Mead Johnson Nutritional) p 563
I-Soyalac (Loma Linda) p 555
Nursoy Soy Protein Infant Formula (Wyeth) p 666
SMA Iron Fortified Infant Formula (Wyeth) p 666
Soyalac: Liquid Concentrate, Ready-to-Serve and Powder (Loma Linda) p 555

Sucrose Free
ProSobee (Mead Johnson Nutritional) p 570

INGROWN TOENAIL PREPARATIONS
Outgro Solution (Whitehall) p 657

INSECT BITE & STING PREPARATIONS
Anbesol Antiseptic Anesthetic Gel (Whitehall) p 426, 652
Anbesol Antiseptic Anesthetic Liquid (Whitehall) p 426, 652
B.F.I. (Beecham Products) p 510
BiCozene Creme (Creighton Products) p 408, 526
Bluboro Powder Astringent Soaking Solution (Herbert) p 543
Lanacort Creme (Combe) p 408, 526
Medi-Quik (Lehn & Fink) p 555
Topic Benzyl Alcohol Gel (Syntex) p 633
Unguentine Plus (Norwich-Eaton) p 595

L

LACTOSE TOLERANCE TEST AIDS
Lac-Tol (Jayco) p 546

LAXATIVES

Bulk
Effersyllium Instant Mix (Stuart) p 629
Konsyl (Burton, Parsons) p 407, 520
L. A. Formula (Burton, Parsons) p 407, 520
Metamucil (Searle Consumer Products) p 423, 627
Metamucil, Instant Mix (Searle Consumer Products) p 423, 628
Metamucil, Instant Mix, Orange Flavor (Searle Consumer Products) p 423, 628
Metamucil Powder, Orange Flavor (Searle Consumer Products) p 423, 628
Mitrolan Tablets (Robins) p 420, 616
Modane Bulk (Adria) p 503
Natrasan (Lank) p 548
Serutan Concentrated Powder (J.B. Williams) p 661
Serutan Concentrated Powder-Fruit Flavored (J.B. Williams) p 661
Serutan Toasted Granules (J.B. Williams) p 662
Syllact (Wallace) p 425, 643

Combinations
Correctol Laxative Tablets (Plough) p 418, 608
Dialose Plus Capsules (Stuart) p 629
Doxidan (Hoechst-Roussel) p 411, 544
Haley's M-0 (Consumer Products Div., Winthrop) p 663
Milkinol (Kremers-Urban) p 548
Nature's Remedy (Norcliff Thayer) p 592

Fecal Softeners
Correctol Laxative Tablets (Plough) p 418, 608
Dialose Capsules (Stuart) p 629
Dialose Plus Capsules (Stuart) p 629
DioMedicone Tablets (Medicone) p 573
Dorbantyl Capsules (Riker) p 613
Dorbantyl Forte Capsules (Riker) p 614
Geriplex-FS Kapseals (Parke-Davis) p 601
Geriplex-FS Liquid (Parke-Davis) p 601
Kasof Capsules (Stuart) p 631
Milkinol (Kremers-Urban) p 548
Modane Soft (Adria) p 504
Natrasan (Lank) p 548
Regutol (Plough) p 418, 608
Senokot-S Tablets (Purdue Frederick) p 419, 612
Surfak (Hoechst-Roussel) p 411, 544

Mineral Oil
Agoral, Plain (Parke-Davis) p 599
Haley's M-0 (Consumer Products Div., Winthrop) p 663

Stimulant
Agoral Raspberry & Marshmallow Flavors (Parke-Davis) p 599
Carter's Little Pills (Carter Products) p 407, 523
Correctol Laxative Tablets (Plough) p 418, 608
Dialose Plus Capsules (Stuart) p 629
Dorbane Tablets (Riker) p 613
Dulcolax Tablets & Suppositories (Boehringer Ingelheim) p 406, 514

Evac-U-Gen (Walker, Corp) p 642
Ex-Lax Chocolated Laxative (Ex-Lax Pharm.) p 408, 536
Ex-Lax Pills, Unflavored (Ex-Lax Pharm.) p 408, 536
Herbal Laxative Tablets (Nature's Bounty) p 588
Maltsupex (Wallace) p 425, 642
Modane Tablets & Liquid (Adria) p 504
Nature's Remedy (Norcliff Thayer) p 592
Neoloid (Lederle) p 551
Norwich Glycerin Suppositories (Norwich-Eaton) p 594
Nytilax Tablets (Leeming) p 553
Phillip's Milk of Magnesia (Glenbrook) p 410, 541
Senokot Tablets/Granules (Purdue Frederick) p 419, 612
Senokot-S Tablets (Purdue Frederick) p 419, 612

LIP BALMS
Chap Stick Lip Balm (Miller-Morton) p 415, 586
Chap Stick Sunblock 15 Lip Balm (Miller-Morton) p 415, 586
Moisture Whip Lip Conditioner (Maybelline) p 559
Moisture Whip Lipstick (Maybelline) p 559
PreSun Sunscreen Lip Protection (Westwood) p 651

M

MENSTRUAL PREPARATIONS
Midol (Glenbrook) p 410, 541
Odrinil (Fox) p 538
Sunril Premenstrual Capsules (Schering) p 626
Trendar Premenstrual Tablets (Whitehall) p 659

MINERALS
Bone Meal with Vitamin D Tablets (Nature's Bounty) p 587
Calcium Lactate Tablets (Nature's Bounty) p 588
Cal-M (Anabolic) p 507
Chelated Calcium Tablets (Nature's Bounty) p 588
Chelated Chromium Tablets (Nature's Bounty) p 588
Chelated Copper Tablets (Nature's Bounty) p 588
Chelated Magnesium Tablets (Nature's Bounty) p 588
Chelated Manganese Tablets (Nature's Bounty) p 588
Chelated Multi-Mineral Tablets (Nature's Bounty) p 588
Chelated Potassium Tablets (Nature's Bounty) p 588
Chelated Zinc Tablets (Nature's Bounty) p 588
Chew-Iron Tablets (Nature's Bounty) p 588
Dolomite Tablets (Nature's Bounty) p 588
Ferrous Sulfate Tablets (Nature's Bounty) p 588
Iron Tablets (Nature's Bounty) p 588
Magnesium Tablets (Nature's Bounty) p 589
Manganese Tablets (Nature's Bounty) p 589
Megadose (Arco) p 508
Multi-Mineral Tablets (Nature's Bounty) p 589
One-A-Day Multivitamin Supplement Plus Minerals (Miles) p 585
Orazinc (Mericon) p 580
Os-Cal 500 Tablets (Marion) p 558
Os-Cal Forte Tablets (Marion) p 558
Os-Cal Plus Tablets (Marion) p 558
Os-Cal Tablets (Marion) p 412, 558
Os-Cal-Gesic Tablets (Marion) p 558
Oyster Calcium Tablets (Nature's Bounty) p 589
Potassium Tablets (Nature's Bounty) p 589

ge

Selenium Tablets (Nature's Bounty) p 589
Simron (Merrell-National) p 415, 582
Simron Plus (Merrell-National) p 415, 582
Ultra Vita-Time Tablets (Nature's Bounty) p 589
Vita-Time Tablets (Nature's Bounty) p 590
Zinc Tablets (Nature's Bounty) p 590
Zinc Tabs (Mericon) p 580

MOUTHWASHES

Antibacterial
Cēpastat Sore Throat Spray/Gargle (Merrell-National) p 415, 581
Chloraseptic Liquid & Spray (Norwich-Eaton) p 416, 593
S.T. 37 (Beecham Products) p 511
Scope (Procter & Gamble) p 611

Deodorant
Cēpacol Mouthwash/Gargle (Merrell-National) p 415, 580
Chloresium Ointment & Solution (Rystan) p 618
Protexin Oral Rinse (Cetylite) p 523

N

NASAL DECONGESTANTS
(see under COLD PREPARATIONS)

O

OPHTHALMICS
Clear Eyes Eye Drops (Abbott Consumer Products) p 405, 502
Collyrium Eye Lotion (Wyeth) p 417, 665
Collyrium with Ephedrine Eye Drops (Wyeth) p 427, 665
Duolube Ophthalmic Ointment (Muro) p 586
Liquifilm Tears (Allergan) p 406, 506
Murine Plus Eye Drops (Abbott Consumer Products) p 405, 502
Murine Regular Formula Eye Drops (Abbott Consumer Products) p 405, 502
Muro Tears (Muro) p 586
Murocel Ophthalmic Solution (Muro) p 586
Prefrin Liquifilm (Allergan) p 405, 506
20/20 Eye Drops (S.S.S. Company) p 619
Tears Plus (Allergan) p 405, 506
Visine A.C. Eye Drops (Leeming) p 554
Visine Eye Drops (Leeming) p 554

ORAL HYGIENE AID
Chloraseptic Gel (Norwich-Eaton) p 593
Chloraseptic Lozenges (Norwich-Eaton) p 416, 593
Listerine Antiseptic (Warner-Lambert) p 425, 645
Listermint Cinnamon Mouthwash & Gargle (Warner-Lambert) p 425, 645
Listermint Mouthwash & Gargle (Warner-Lambert) p 425, 645
S.T. 37 (Beecham Products) p 511

P

PEDICULICIDES
A-200 Pyrinate Liquid, Gel (Norcliff Thayer) p 415, 591
Cuprex (Beecham Products) p 510
Li-Ban Spray (Pfipharmecs) p 604
Rid (Pfipharmecs) p 418, 604

POISON IVY & OAK PREPARATIONS
Caladryl Lotion & Cream (Parke-Davis) p 600
Calamatum Lotion, Ointment, Spray (Blair) p 512
CaldeCORT Hydrocortisone Cream (Pharmacraft) p 606
Cortril ½% (Pfipharmecs) p 603
Delacort (Mericon) p 580
Dermolate Anti-Itch Cream & Spray (Schering) p 623
Hytone Cream ½% (Dermik) p 527
Hytone Ointment ½% (Dermik) p 528

Lanacort Creme (Combe) p 408, 526
Medi-Quik (Lehn & Fink) p 555
Rhulihist (Lederle) p 551
Ziradryl Lotion (Parke-Davis) p 602

PREGNANCY TESTS
Acu-Test In-Home Pregnancy Test (J.B. Williams) p 660
Answer At-Home Early Pregnancy Test Kit (Carter Products) p 407, 522
e.p.t. In-Home Early Pregnancy Test (Warner-Lambert) p 425, 644
Predictor In-Home Early Pregnancy Test (Whitehall) p 657

PREMENSTRUAL THERAPEUTICS
(see under MENSTRUAL PREPARATIONS)

S

SALT SUBSTITUTES
Co-Salt (Norcliff Thayer) p 415, 591

SALT TABLETS
Thermotabs (Beecham Products) p 512

SCABICIDES
(see under DERMATOLOGICALS)

SKIN BLEACHES
(see under DERMATOLOGICALS)

SKIN PROTECTANTS
Caldesene Medicated Ointment (Pharmacraft) p 606
Caldesene Medicated Powder (Pharmacraft) p 606
Chap Stick Lip Balm (Miller-Morton) p 415, 586
Chap Stick Sunblock 15 Lip Balm (Miller-Morton) p 415, 586
Skin Screen (Cetylite) p 523

SKIN REMEDIES
(see under DERMATOLOGICALS)

SKIN WOUND PREPARATIONS

Cleansers
Bactine Skin Wound Cleanser (Miles) p 584
Betadine Solution (Purdue Frederick) p 419, 611
Oil-O-Sol Liquid (Health Care) p 410, 542
S.T. 37 (Beecham Products) p 511

Healing Agents
Chloresium Ointment & Solution (Rystan) p 618
Medicone Dressing Cream (Medicone) p 573
Proderm Topical Dressing (Hickam) p 544

Protectants
Johnson & Johnson First Aid Cream (Johnson & Johnson) p 411, 547
Medicone Dressing Cream (Medicone) p 573
Medi-Quik (Lehn & Fink) p 555
Mercurochrome II (Becton Dickinson) p 510
Rhulicaine (Lederle) p 551
S.T. 37 (Beecham Products) p 511
Zinc Oxide Ointment (Norwich-Eaton) p 595

SLEEP AIDS
Miles Nervine Nighttime Sleep-Aid (Miles) p 585
Quiet World Analgesic/Sleeping Aid (Whitehall) p 659
Sleep-Eze Tablets (Whitehall) p 659
Sominex (J.B. Williams) p 662
Unisom Nighttime Sleep-Aid (Leeming) p 554

STIMULANTS
No Doz (Bristol-Myers) p 406, 519
Vivarin (J.B. Williams) p 662

SUGAR SUBSTITUTES
Necta Sweet Non-Caloric Sweetener (Norwich-Eaton) p 594

SUN SCREENS
(see under DERMATOLOGICALS)

SUPPLEMENTS
(see under DIETARY SUPPLEMENTS)

T

TEETHING LOTIONS
Anbesol Antiseptic Anesthetic Gel (Whitehall) p 426, 652
Anbesol Antiseptic Anesthetic Liquid (Whitehall) p 426, 652

THROAT LOZENGES
Aspergum (Plough) p 418, 608
Cēpacol Anesthetic Troches (Merrell-National) p 580
Cēpacol Throat Lozenges (Merrell-National) p 415, 580
Cēpastat Sore Throat Lozenges (Merrell-National) p 415, 581
Children's Cepastat Sore Throat Lozenges (Merrell-National) p 415, 581
Children's Hold (Beecham Products) p 510
Chloraseptic Cough Control Lozenges (Norwich-Eaton) p 416, 593
Chloraseptic Lozenges (Norwich-Eaton) p 416, 593
Chloraseptic Lozenges, Children's (Norwich-Eaton) p 592
Formula 44 Cough Control Discs (Vicks Health Care) p 638
Hold (Beecham Products) p 511
Oracin Cherry Flavor Cooling Throat Lozenges (Vicks Health Care) p 640
Oracin Cooling Throat Lozenges (Vicks Health Care) p 639
Sucrets (Regular, Mentholated & Children's Cherry) (Beecham Products) p 512
Sucrets—Cold Decongestant Formula (Beecham Products) p 512
Sucrets Cough Control Formula (Beecham Products) p 512
Throat Discs Throat Lozenges (Marion) p 412, 558
Vicks Formula 44 Cough Control Discs (Vicks Health Care) p 638
Vicks Throat Lozenges (Vicks Health Care) p 641

TOOTH DESENSITIZERS
Protect Toothpaste (Marion) p 412, 558
Sensodyne Toothpaste (Block) p 513

V

VAGINAL PREPARATIONS

Contraceptives

Creams
Koromex" Contraceptive Cream (Holland-Rantos) p 545

Foams
Emko Because Contraceptor Vaginal Contraceptive Foam (Schering) p 421, 624
Emko Pre-Fil Vaginal Contraceptive Foam (Schering) p 421, 625
Emko Vaginal Contraceptive Foam (Schering) p 421, 624
Koromex Contraceptive Foam (Holland-Rantos) p 545

Inserts, Suppositories
Encare (Norwich-Eaton) p 416, 593
Semicid Vaginal Contraceptive Suppositories (Whitehall) p 659

Jellies, Ointments
Koromex" Contraceptive Jelly (Holland-Rantos) p 545
Koromex"-A Contraceptive Jelly (Holland-Rantos) p 545

Spermicides

Conceptrol Birth Control Cream (Ortho Consumer Products) p 416, 597

Delfen Contraceptive Foam (Ortho Consumer Products) p 416, 597

Intercept Contraceptive Inserts (Ortho Consumer Products) p 597

Ortho-Creme Contraceptive Cream (Ortho Consumer Products) p 416, 598

Ortho-Gynol Contraceptive Jelly (Ortho Consumer Products) p 416, 598

Douches, Cleansing

Betadine Douche (Purdue Frederick) p 419, 611

Massengill Disposable Douche (Beecham Products) p 511

Massengill Disposable Medicated Douche (Beecham Products) p 511

Massengill Liquid Concentrate (Beecham Products) p 511

Massengill Powder (Beecham Products) p 511

Nylmerate" Solution Concentrate (Holland-Rantos) p 545

Other

Betadine Solution (Purdue Frederick) p 419, 611

Norforms Feminine Deodorants (Norwich-Eaton) p 416, 594

Ortho Disposable Vaginal Applicators (Ortho Consumer Products) p 416, 598

Ortho Personal Lubricant (Ortho Consumer Products) p 416, 598

Transi-Lube (Holland-Rantos) p 545

VITAMINS

Vitamins

Aqua-A (Anabolic) p 507

B12-Plus (Anabolic) p 507

KLB6 Capsules (Nature's Bounty) p 588

Tri-B3 (Anabolic) p 508

Tri-C-500 (Anabolic) n 508

Vitamin C Crystals (Nature's Bounty) p 588

Multivitamins

A.C.N. (Persǒn & Covey) p 603

Acerola C (Nature's Bounty) p 587

Allbee C-800 Tablets (Robins) p 420, 614

Allbee with C Capsules (Robins) p 420, 615

B-50 Tablets (Nature's Bounty) p 587

B-100 Tablets (Nature's Bounty) p 587

B-100 Time Release Tablets (Nature's Bounty) p 587

B-125 Tablets (Nature's Bounty) p 587

B Complex & B-12 Tablets (Nature's Bounty) p 587

B Complex & C (Time Release) Capsules (Nature's Bounty) p 587

B & C Liquid (Nature's Bounty) p 587

Brewer's Yeast Powder (Debittered) (Nature's Bounty) p 587

Brewer's Yeast Tablets (Nature's Bounty) p 587

Bugs Bunny With Extra C Multivitamin Supplement (Miles) p 585

C-Complex Tablets (Nature's Bounty) p 588

Children's Chewables Tablets (Nature's Bounty) p 588

Chocks Multivitamin Supplement (Miles) p 584

Chocks-Bugs Bunny Multivitamin Supplement (Miles) p 584

Cod Liver Oil Concentrate Tablets w/Vitamin C (Schering) p 421, 621

Flintstones Multivitamin Supplement (Miles) p 584

Flintstones With Extra C Multivitamin Supplement (Miles) p 585

Geriplex-FS Kapseals (Parke-Davis) p 601

Geriplex-FS Liquid (Parke-Davis) p 601

Geritol Tablets - High Potency Iron & Vitamin Tablets (J.B. Williams) p 661

Halibut Liver Oil Capsules (Nature's Bounty) p 588

KLB6 Complete Tablets (Nature's Bounty) p 589

KLB6 Diet Mix (Nature's Bounty) p 589

Lederplex Capsules, Liquid & Tablets (Lederle) p 551

Mega-B (Arco) p 508

Mega-B with C Tablets (Nature's Bounty) p 589

Megadose (Arco) p 508

Monster (Bristol-Myers) p 518

One-A-Day Core C 500 Multivitamin Supplement (Miles) p 585

One-A-Day Multivitamin Supplement (Miles) p 585

Optilets-500 (Abbott) p 503

Probec-T Tablets (Stuart) p 632

Roeribec Tablets (Pfipharmecs) p 418, 605

Scott's Emulsion (Beecham Products) p 511

Stress Formula "605" Tablets (Nature's Bounty) p 589

Stresscaps (Lederle) p 552

Stresstabs 600 (Lederle) p 411, 552

Surbex-750 with Iron (Abbott) p 503

Surbex-T (Abbott) p 503

Thera-Combex H-P (Parke-Davis) p 602

Tri-Adrenopan (Anabolic) p 507

Tri-B-Plex (Anabolic) p 508

Trophite Liquid & Tablets (Menley & James) p 413, 579

Ultra "A & D" Tablets (Nature's Bounty) p 589

Ultra KLB6 Tablets (Nature's Bounty) p 589

Ultra Vita-Time Tablets (Nature's Bounty) p 589

Unicap Capsules & Tablets (Upjohn) p 636

Unicap Chewable Tablets (Upjohn) p 636

Vi-Penta Multivitamin Drops (Roche) p 421, 618

Vitamin A & D Tablets (Nature's Bounty) p 589

Vita-Time Tablets (Nature's Bounty) p 590

Multivitamins with Minerals

Allbee C-800 Plus Iron Tablets (Robins) p 420, 614

B6-Plus (Anabolic) p 507

Centrum (Lederle) p 411, 549

Chew-Iron Tablets (Nature's Bounty) p 588

Chocks Plus Iron Multivitamin Supplement (Miles) p 584

Chocks-Bugs Bunny Plus Iron Multivitamin Supplement (Miles) p 584

Feminins Tablets (Mead Johnson Nutritional) p 563

Femlron Multi-Vitamins and Iron (J.B. Williams) p 660

Feosol Plus (Menley & James) p 577

Flintstones Plus Iron Multivitamin Supplement (Miles) p 584

Fortespan Capsules (Menley & James) p 413, 577

Fumatinic Tablets (Laser) p 549

Geriplex-FS Kapseals (Parke-Davis) p 601

Geriplex-FS Liquid (Parke-Davis) p 601

Geritol Liquid-High Potency Iron & Vitamin Tonic (J.B. Williams) p 661

Geritol Mega Vitamins (J.B. Williams) p 661

Gevrabon Liquid (Lederle) p 550

Gevral Tablets (Lederle) p 550

Gevral T Tablets (Lederle) p 550

Mega V & M Tablets (Nature's Bounty) p 589

Megadose (Arco) p 508

Monster with Iron (Bristol-Myers) p 519

Myadec (Parke-Davis) p 602

Natabec Kapseals (Parke-Davis) p 602

NaturSlim II (NaturSlim) p 415, 590

One-A-Day Multivitamin Supplement Plus Iron (Miles) p 585

One-A-Day Multivitamin Supplement Plus Minerals (Miles) p 585

Optilets-M-500 (Abbott) p 503

Os-Cal Forte Tablets (Marion) p 558

Os-Cal Plus Tablets (Marion) p 558

Pals (Bristol-Myers) p 519

Pals Plus Iron (Bristol-Myers) p 519

Poly-Vi-Sol Chewable Vitamin Tablets with Iron (Mead Johnson Nutritional) p 568

Poly-Vi-Sol Vitamin Drops with Iron (Mead Johnson Nutritional) p 568

Stress Formula "605" w/Iron Tablets (Nature's Bounty) p 589

Stress Formula "605" w/Zinc Tablets (Nature's Bounty) p 589

Stresstabs 600 with Iron (Lederle) p 411, 552

Stresstabs 600 with Zinc (Lederle) p 411, 552

Stuart Formula Tablets, The (Stuart) p 424, 632

Stuart Prenatal Tablets (Stuart) p 632

Surbex-750 with Zinc (Abbott) p 503

Tri-Vi-Sol Vitamin Drops w/Iron (Mead Johnson Nutritional) p 573

Troph-Iron Liquid & Tablets (Menley & James) p 413, 579

Unicap M Tablets (Upjohn) p 424, 636

Unicap Plus Iron Tablets (Upjohn) p 636

Unicap Senior Tablets (Upjohn) p 636

Unicap T Tablets (Upjohn) p 424, 637

Viterra High Potency (Pfipharmecs) p 418, 605

Viterra Original Formula (Pfipharmecs) p 418, 605

Zacne Tablets (Nature's Bounty) p 415, 590

Z-Bec Tablets (Robins) p 420, 617

Pediatric

Bugs Bunny With Extra C Multivitamin Supplement (Miles) p 585

Ce-Vi-Sol (Mead Johnson Nutritional) p 562

Chocks Multivitamin Supplement (Miles) p 584

Chocks-Bugs Bunny Multivitamin Supplement (Miles) p 584

Flintstones Multivitamin Supplement (Miles) p 584

Flintstones With Extra C Multivitamin Supplement (Miles) p 585

Monster (Bristol-Myers) p 518

Monster with Iron (Bristol-Myers) p 519

Pals (Bristol-Myers) p 519

Pals Plus Iron (Bristol-Myers) p 519

Poly-Vi-Sol (Mead Johnson Nutritional) p 568

Poly-Vi-Sol Vitamin Drops with Iron (Mead Johnson Nutritional) p 568

Tri-Vi-Sol (Mead Johnson Nutritional) p 572

Tri-Vi-Sol Vitamin Drops w/Iron (Mead Johnson Nutritional) p 573

Unicap Chewable Tablets (Upjohn) p 636

Vi-Penta Infant Drops (Roche) p 421, 618

Vi-Penta Multivitamin Drops (Roche) p 421, 618

Prenatal

Filibon (Lederle) p 550

Lactocal Tablets (Laser) p 549

Natabec Kapseals (Parke-Davis) p 602

Obron-6 Tablets (Pfipharmecs) p 418, 604

Stuart Prenatal Tablets (Stuart) p 632

Therapeutic

Fortespan Capsules (Menley & James) p 413, 577

Gevral T Tablets (Lederle) p 550

Mega-B (Arco) p 508

Megadose (Arco) p 508

Stresstabs 600 (Lederle) p 411, 552

Stresstabs 600 with Iron (Lederle) p 411, 552

Stresstabs 600 with Zinc (Lederle) p 411, 552

Other

B-1 Tablets (Nature's Bounty) p 587

B-2 Tablets (Nature's Bounty) p 587

B-6 Tablets (Nature's Bounty) p 587

B-12 Tablets (Nature's Bounty) p 587

Beelith Tablets (Beach) p 509

Bio-Crest (Nutrition Control) p 595
Biotin Tablets (Nature's Bounty) p 587
Bone Meal with Vitamin D Tablets
  (Nature's Bounty) p 587
C-250 with Rose Hips Tablets
  (Nature's Bounty) p 587
C-300 with Rose Hips (Chewable)
  Tablets (Nature's Bounty) p 587
C-500 with Rose Hips Tablets
  (Nature's Bounty) p 587
C-1000 with Rose Hips Tablets
  (Nature's Bounty) p 587
C Liquid (Nature's Bounty) p 588
C-Time-750 Time Release Tablets
  (Nature's Bounty) p 588
C-Time-1500 Tablets (Nature's Bounty)
  p 588
Calcium Ascorbate Tablets (Nature's
  Bounty) p 588
Cod Liver Oil Concentrate Tablets,
  Capsules (Schering) p 421, 621
E-200 Capsules (Nature's Bounty)
  p 588
E-200 (Natural Complex) Capsules
  (Nature's Bounty) p 588

E-400 Capsules (Nature's Bounty)
  p 588
E-400 (Natural Complex) Capsules
  (Nature's Bounty) p 588
E-600 (Natural Complex) Capsules
  (Nature's Bounty) p 588
E-1000 (Natural Complex) Capsules
  (Nature's Bounty) p 588
Emulsified E-200 Capsules (Nature's
  Bounty) p 588
Folic Acid Tablets (Nature's Bounty)
  p 588
Lecithin with Vitamin D Capsules
  (Nature's Bounty) p 589
Mol-Iron Tablets w/Vitamin C
  (Schering) p 421, 626
Niacin Tablets (Nature's Bounty) p 589
Niacinamide Tablets (Nature's Bounty)
  p 589
Nicotinex Elixir (Fleming) p 537
Orexin Softab Tablets (Stuart) p 632
Potassium & B-6 Tablets (Nature's
  Bounty) p 589
Ultra "A" Capsules & Tablets (Nature's
  Bounty) p 589

Ultra "D" Tablets (Nature's Bounty)
  p 589
Vitamin A Capsules & Tablets (Nature's
  Bounty) p 589
Vitamin D Tablets (Nature's Bounty)
  p 590
Viterra C (Pfipharmecs) p 418, 605
Viterra E (Pfipharmecs) p 418, 605
Wheat Germ Oil Capsules (Nature's
  Bounty) p 590

W

WART REMOVERS
  (see under DERMATOLOGICALS)

WEIGHT CONTROL PREPARATIONS
  **(see under APPETITE
  SUPPRESSANTS)**

WET DRESSINGS
  (see under DERMATOLOGICALS)

MEMORANDUM

Active Ingredients Index

In this section the products described in the Product Information (White) Section are listed under their chemical (generic) name according to their principal ingredient(s). Products have been included under specific headings by the Publisher with the cooperation of individual manufacturers.

A

Acerola
C-Complex Tablets (Nature's Bounty) p 588

Acetaminophen
Acephen Acetaminophen Rectal Suppositories (G & W Laboratories) p 538
Allerest Headache Strength Tablets (Pharmacraft) p 606
Anacin-3 Analgesic Tablets (Whitehall) p 426, 652
CCP Tablets (Medique) p 574
Comtrex (Bristol-Myers) p 406, 516
Congespirin Liquid Cold Medicine (Bristol-Myers) p 406, 517
Contac Jr. Childrens' Cold Medicine (Menley & James) p 413, 575
Coricidin Extra Strength Sinus Headache Tablets (Schering) p 421, 623
Coryban-D Cough Syrup (Pfipharmecs) p 418, 604
CoTylenol Children's Liquid Cold Formula (McNeil Consumer Products) p 412, 560
CoTylenol Cold Formula Tablets and Capsules (McNeil Consumer Products) p 412, 559
CoTylenol Liquid Cold Formula (McNeil Consumer Products) p 412, 559
Datril (Bristol-Myers) p 406, 517
Datril 500 (Bristol-Myers) p 406, 517
Daycare Multi-Symptom Colds Medicine Capsules (Vicks Health Care) p 424, 638
Daycare Multi-Symptom Colds Medicine (Vicks Health Care) p 424, 638
Dristan-AF Decongestant/Antihistamine/ Analgesic Tablets (Whitehall) p 426, 655
D-Sinus Capsules (Laser) p 548
Excedrin (Bristol-Myers) p 406, 517
Excedrin P.M. (Bristol-Myers) p 406, 518

Goody's Headache Powders (Goody's) p 410, 541
Liquiprin (Norcliff Thayer) p 415, 591
Novahistine Sinus Tablets (Dow Pharmaceuticals) p 534
Nyquil Nighttime Colds Medicine (Vicks Health Care) p 424, 639
Ornex Capsules (Menley & James) p 413, 578
Percogesic Tablets (Endo) p 409, 536
Quiet World Analgesic/Sleeping Aid (Whitehall) p 659
Sinarest Tablets (Pharmacraft) p 607
Sine-Aid Sinus Headache Tablets (McNeil Consumer Products) p 412, 560
Sine-Off Extra Strength Sinus Medicine Non-Aspirin Capsules (Menley & James) p 413, 578
Sine-Off Extra Strength Sinus Medicine Non-Aspirin Tablets (Menley & James) p 413, 579
Sinutab Extra Strength Capsule Formula (Warner-Lambert) p 425, 646
Sinutab Extra Strength Tablets (Warner-Lambert) p 425, 647
Sinutab Tablets (Warner-Lambert) p 425, 646
Sinutab II Tablets (Warner-Lambert) p 425, 646
Sunril Premenstrual Capsules (Schering) p 626
Tempra (Mead Johnson Nutritional) p 572
Trendar Premenstrual Tablets (Whitehall) p 659
Trind (Mead Johnson Nutritional) p 572
Trind-DM (Mead Johnson Nutritional) p 572
Tylenol acetaminophen Children's Chewable Tablets, Elixir, Drops (McNeil Consumer Products) p 412, 560
Tylenol, Extra-Strength, acetaminophen Adult Liquid Pain Reliever (McNeil Consumer Products) p 412, 561

Tylenol, Extra-Strength, acetaminophen Capsules & Tablets (McNeil Consumer Products) p 412, 561
Tylenol, Regular Strength, acetaminophen Tablets (McNeil Consumer Products) p 412, 561
Vanquish (Glenbrook) p 541
Vicks Nyquil Nighttime Colds Medicine (Vicks Health Care) p 424, 639
Viro-Med Liquid (Whitehall) p 659

Acetic Acid
Star-Otic (Star) p 628

Acetylsalicylic Acid
(see under Aspirin)

Alcohol
Anbesol Antiseptic Anesthetic Gel (Whitehall) p 426, 652
Anbesol Antiseptic Anesthetic Liquid (Whitehall) p 426, 652
Coryban-D Cough Syrup (Pfipharmecs) p 418, 604
Desenex Foot & Sneaker Spray (Pharmacraft) p 607
Diaparene Baby Wash Cloths (Glenbrook) p 410, 541
Dry and Clear Medicated Acne Cleanser (Whitehall) p 656
Freezone Solution (Whitehall) p 656
Heet Analgesic Liniment (Whitehall) p 656
Novahistine Cough Formula (Dow Pharmaceuticals) p 532
Novahistine DMX (Dow Pharmaceuticals) p 533
Oxipor VHC Lotion for Psoriasis (Whitehall) p 657
Protexin Oral Rinse (Cetylite) p 523
Rhulicaine (Lederle) p 551
Skin Screen (Cetylite) p 523
Viro-Med Liquid (Whitehall) p 659

Alfalfa
Alfalfa Tablets (Nature's Bounty) p 587

Alginic Acid
Pretts Tablets (Marion) p 412, 558

Allantoin

HTO Stainless Manzan Hemorrhoidal
  Tissue Ointment (DeWitt) p 409, 530
Tegrin for Psoriasis Lotion & Cream
  (Block) p 513

Aloe

Dermaide Aloe Ointment (Dermaide)
  p 527
Nature's Remedy (Norcliff Thayer)
  p 592

Alpha Tocopheral Acetate *

Viterra E (Pfipharmecs) p 418, 605

Aluminum Acetate

Acid Mantle Creme & Lotion (Dorsey)
  p 409, 530

Aluminum Chlorohydrate

Cheq Antiperspirant/Deodorant Spray
  (Almay) p 506
Cheq Extra-Dry
  Antiperspirant/Deodorant Spray
  (Aerosol) (Almay) p 506
Cheq Roll-On Antiperspirant/Deodorant
  (Almay) p 506
Cheq Soft Powder Extra Dry
  Antiperspirant Spray (Aerosol)
  (Almay) p 506
Desenex Foot & Sneaker Spray
  (Pharmacraft) p 607

Aluminum Glycinate

Bufferin (Bristol-Myers) p 406, 516

Aluminum Hydroxide

Delcid (Merrell-National) p 581
DeWitt's Antacid Powder (DeWitt)
  p 409, 529
Di-Gel (Plough) p 418, 608
Gaviscon Liquid Antacid (Marion)
  p 412, 557
Gelusil-M (Parke-Davis) p 600
Gelusil-II Liquid & Tablets (Parke-Davis)
  p 601
Marblen Suspensions & Tablets
  (Fleming) p 537
Nephrox Suspension (Fleming) p 537
WinGel (Consumer Products Div.,
  Winthrop) p 665

Aluminum Hydroxide Gel

ALternaGEL Liquid (Stuart) p 629
Aludrox Oral Suspension & Tablets
  (Wyeth) p 417, 665
Amphojel Suspension & Suspension
  without Flavor (Wyeth) p 427, 665
Amphojel Tablets (Wyeth) p 427, 665
Di-Gel (Plough) p 418, 608
Gelusil (Parke-Davis) p 600
Kudrox Suspension (Double Strength)
  (Kremers-Urban) p 548
Mylanta Liquid (Stuart) p 424, 631
Mylanta-II Liquid (Stuart) p 424, 631
Simeco Suspension (Wyeth) p 427,
  666

Aluminum Hydroxide Gel, Dried

Aludrox Oral Suspension & Tablets
  (Wyeth) p 417, 665
Amphojel Suspension & Suspension
  without Flavor (Wyeth) p 427, 665
Amphojel Tablets (Wyeth) p 427, 665
Gaviscon Antacid Tablets (Marion)
  p 412, 557
Gaviscon-2 Antacid Tablets (Marion)
  p 412, 557
Mylanta Tablets (Stuart) p 424, 631
Mylanta-II Tablets (Stuart) p 424, 631

Aluminum Hydroxide Preparations

Kolantyl (Merrell-National) p 582
Kudrox Suspension (Double Strength)
  (Kremers-Urban) p 548
Magnatril Suspension & Tablets
  (Lannett) p 548

Aluminum Sulfate

Bluboro Powder Astringent Soaking
  Solution (Herbert) p 543

Amino Acid Preparations

Yeast Plus Tablets (Nature's Bounty)
  p 590

Ammonium Alum

Massengill Powder (Beecham Products)
  p 511

Ammonium Chloride

Chlor-Trimeton Expectorant (Schering)
  p 620
DeWitt's Baby Cough Syrup (DeWitt)
  p 409, 529

Amylase

Festal (Hoechst-Roussel) p 411, 544
Papaya Enzyme Tablets (Nature's
  Bounty) p 589

Anethole

Vicks Cough Silencers Cough Drops
  (Vicks Health Care) p 641

Antipyrine

Collyrium Eye Lotion (Wyeth) p 417,
  665
Collyrium with Ephedrine Eye Drops
  (Wyeth) p 427, 665

Ascorbic Acid
(see under Vitamin C)

Aspirin

Alka-Seltzer Effervescent Pain Reliever
  Antacid (Miles) p 583
Alka-Seltzer Plus Cold Medicine (Miles)
  p 584
Anacin Analgesic Capsules (Whitehall)
  p 652
Anacin Analgesic Tablets (Whitehall)
  p 426, 652
Anacin Maximum Strength Analgesic
  Capsules (Whitehall) p 426, 652
Anacin Maximum Strength Analgesic
  Tablets (Whitehall) p 426, 652
Arthritis Pain Formula by the Makers of
  Anacin Analgesic Tablets (Whitehall)
  p 426, 653
Arthritis Strength Bufferin
  (Bristol-Myers) p 406, 516
Aspergum (Plough) p 418, 608
Aspirin Suppositories (G & W
  Laboratories) p 538
Bayer Aspirin & Bayer Children's
  Chewable Aspirin (Glenbrook) p 410,
  539
Bayer Children's Cold Tablets
  (Glenbrook) p 540
Bayer Timed-Release Aspirin
  (Glenbrook) p 410, 540
Bufferin (Bristol-Myers) p 406, 516
Cama Inlay-Tabs (Dorsey) p 409, 530
Congespirin (Bristol-Myers) p 406, 516
Coricidin 'D' Decongestant Tablets
  (Schering) p 421, 621
Coricidin Demilets Tablets for Children
  (Schering) p 421, 622
Coricidin Medilets Tablets for Children
  (Schering) p 421, 622
Coricidin Tablets (Schering) p 421,
  621
Dristan Decongestant/Antihistamine/
  Analgesic Capsules (Whitehall)
  p 426, 654
Dristan Decongestant/Antihistamine/
  Analgesic Tablets (Whitehall)
  p 426, 654
Ecotrin Tablets (Menley & James)
  p 413, 576
Excedrin (Bristol-Myers) p 406, 517
4-Way Cold Tablets (Bristol-Myers)
  p 406, 518
Goody's Headache Powders (Goody's)
  p 410, 541
Midol (Glenbrook) p 410, 541
Norwich Aspirin (Norwich-Eaton)
  p 417, 594
Panalgesic (Poythress) p 610
Quiet World Analgesic/Sleeping Aid
  (Whitehall) p 659
St. Joseph Aspirin for Children (Plough)
  p 418, 609

St. Joseph Cold Tablets for Children
  (Plough) p 418, 609
Sine-Off Sinus Medicine Tablets-Aspirin
  Formula (Menley & James) p 413,
  579
Triaminicin Tablets (Dorsey) p 409,
  531
Vanquish (Glenbrook) p 541
Viro-Med Tablets (Whitehall) p 660

Aspirin Buffered

Arthritis Pain Formula by the Makers of
  Anacin Analgesic Tablets (Whitehall)
  p 426, 653
Bufferin (Bristol-Myers) p 406, 516

Aspirin Micronized

Arthritis Pain Formula by the Makers of
  Anacin Analgesic Tablets (Whitehall)
  p 426, 653
Momentum Muscular Backache
  Formula (Whitehall) p 657

Attapulgite, Activated

Rheaban Tablets & Liquid (Leeming)
  p 553

B

Bacitracin

BPN Ointment (Norwich-Eaton) p 592
Baciguent Antibiotic Ointment (Upjohn)
  p 635
Bacitracin Topical Ointment
  (Pfipharmecs) p 603
Mycitracin Antibiotic Ointment (Upjohn)
  p 424, 636
Norwich Bacitracin Ointment
  (Norwich-Eaton) p 594
Septa Ointment (Circle) p 524

Balsam Peru

Anusol Ointment (Parke-Davis) p 599
Anusol Suppositories (Parke-Davis)
  p 599
Balmex Baby Powder (Macsil) p 556
Balmex Ointment (Macsil) p 556
Proderm Topical Dressing (Hickam)
  p 544
Rectal Medicone Suppositories
  (Medicone) p 573
Rectal Medicone Unguent (Medicone)
  p 574
Wyanoid Ointment (Wyeth) p 427, 666
Wyanoids Hemorrhoidal Suppositories
  (Wyeth) p 427, 666

Bee Pollen

Bee Pollen Tablets (Nature's Bounty)
  p 587

Beeswax

Wyanoids Hemorrhoidal Suppositories
  (Wyeth) p 427, 666

Beeswax, Synthetic

Johnson & Johnson First Aid Cream
  (Johnson & Johnson) p 411, 547

Belladonna

Contac Capsules (Menley & James)
  p 413, 575

Belladonna Extract

Wyanoids Hemorrhoidal Suppositories
  (Wyeth) p 427, 666

Benzalkonium Chloride

Bactine Skin Wound Cleanser (Miles)
  p 584
Clens (Alcon/bp) p 405, 505
Mediconet (Medicone) p 573
Medi-Quik (Lehn & Fink) p 555
Mercurochrome II (Becton Dickinson)
  p 510
NTZ (Consumer Products Div.,
  Winthrop) p 664
Prefrin Liquifilm (Allergan) p 405, 506

Benzethonium Chloride

Dry and Clear Medicated Acne Cleanser
  (Whitehall) p 656

Emko Because Contraceptor Vaginal Contraceptive Foam (Schering) p 421, 624
Emko Pre-Fil Vaginal Contraceptive Foam (Schering) p 421, 625
Emko Vaginal Contraceptive Foam (Schering) p 421, 624
Methakote Diaper Rash Cream (Syntex) p 633
Sebb Lotion (Max Factor) p 537

Benzocaine
Anbesol Antiseptic Anesthetic Gel (Whitehall) p 426, 652
Anbesol Antiseptic Anesthetic Liquid (Whitehall) p 426, 652
BiCozene Creme (Creighton Products) p 408, 526
Calamatum Lotion, Ointment, Spray (Blair) p 512
Cepacol Anesthetic Troches (Merrell-National) p 580
Chloraseptic Lozenges, Children's (Norwich-Eaton) p 592
Derma Medicone Ointment (Medicone) p 573
Formula 44 Cough Control Discs (Vicks Health Care) p 638
HTO Stainless Manzan Hemorrhoidal Tissue Ointment (DeWitt) p 409, 530
Lanacane Medicated Creme (Combe) p 408, 525
Medicone Dressing Cream (Medicone) p 573
Oracin Cherry Flavor Cooling Throat Lozenges (Vicks Health Care) p 640
Oracin Cooling Throat Lozenges (Vicks Health Care) p 639
Oxipor VHC Lotion for Psoriasis (Whitehall) p 657
Pazo Hemorrhoid Ointment/ Suppositories (Bristol-Myers) p 519
Rectal Medicone Suppositories (Medicone) p 573
Rectal Medicone Unguent (Medicone) p 574
Rhulicaine (Lederle) p 551
Rhulicream (Lederle) p 551
Rhulihist (Lederle) p 551
Rhulispray (Lederle) p 551
Soft 'N Soothe Anti-Itch Creme (Ascher) p 509
Solarcaine (Plough) p 418, 609
Sucrets—Cold Decongestant Formula (Beecham Products) p 512
Vagisil Feminine Itching Medication (Combe) p 408, 526
Vicks Cough Silencers Cough Drops (Vicks Health Care) p 641
Vicks Formula 44 Cough Control Discs (Vicks Health Care) p 638
Vicks Throat Lozenges (Vicks Health Care) p 641
Wyanoid Ointment (Wyeth) p 427, 666

Benzoic Acid
Dry and Clear Medicated Acne Cleanser (Whitehall) p 656

Benzoyl Peroxide
Clear By Design Invisible Greaseless Acne Gel (Herbert) p 543
Clearasil 5% Benzoyl Peroxide Lotion (Vicks Toiletry Products) p 424, 637
Clearasil Super Strength Acne Treatment Cream (Vicks Toiletry Products) p 424, 637
Dry and Clear, Acne Medication, Lotion & Double Strength Cream (Whitehall) p 656
Fostex BPO 5% (Westwood) p 648
Loroxide Acne Lotion (Dermik) p 528
Oxy Wash (Norcliff Thayer) p 415, 592
Oxy-5 Lotion (Norcliff Thayer) p 415, 592
Oxy-10 Lotion (Norcliff Thayer) p 415, 592
Stri-Dex B.P. (Lehn & Fink) p 555
Teen 5 & 10 Lotion (Muro) p 587
Topex 10% Benzoyl Peroxide Lotion Buffered Acne Medication (Vicks Toiletry Products) p 424, 637
Vanoxide Acne Lotion (Dermik) p 528

Benzyl Alcohol
Teen 5 Wash (Muro) p 587
Topic Benzyl Alcohol Gel (Syntex) p 633

Bile Salts
Festal (Hoechst-Roussel) p 411, 544

Bioflavonoids
Acerola C (Nature's Bounty) p 587
Bio-Crest (Nutrition Control) p 595
C-Complex Tablets (Nature's Bounty) p 588

Biotin
B-100 Tablets (Nature's Bounty) p 587
Biotin Tablets (Nature's Bounty) p 587
Brewer's Yeast Powder (Debittered) (Nature's Bounty) p 587
Brewer's Yeast Tablets (Nature's Bounty) p 587
Mega-B (Arco) p 508
Megadose (Arco) p 508
Tri-B-Plex (Anabolic) p 508

Bisacodyl
Carter's Little Pills (Carter Products) p 407, 523
Dulcolax Tablets & Suppositories (Boehringer Ingelheim) p 406, 514

Bismuth Oxyiodide
Wyanoids Hemorrhoidal Suppositories (Wyeth) p 427, 666

Bismuth Subcarbonate
Wyanoids Hemorrhoidal Suppositories (Wyeth) p 427, 666

Bismuth Subgallate
Anusol Suppositories (Parke-Davis) p 599

Bismuth Subnitrate
Balmex Ointment (Macsil) p 556
Percy Medicine (Merrick) p 415, 583

Bismuth Subsalicylate
Pepto-Bismol Liquid & Tablets (Norwich-Eaton) p 416, 595

Bismuth-Formic-Iodine
B.F.I. (Beecham Products) p 510

Bone Meal
Bone Meal with Vitamin D Tablets (Nature's Bounty) p 587

Boric Acid
BoilnSoak (Alcon/bp) p 405, 505
Clear Eyes Eye Drops (Abbott Consumer Products) p 405, 502
Collyrium Eye Lotion (Wyeth) p 417, 665
Collyrium with Ephedrine Eye Drops (Wyeth) p 427, 665
Flex-Care (Alcon/bp) p 405, 505
Massengill Powder (Beecham Products) p 511
Murine Plus Eye Drops (Abbott Consumer Products) p 405, 502
Star-Otic (Star) p 628
Wyanoid Ointment (Wyeth) p 427, 666
Wyanoids Hemorrhoidal Suppositories (Wyeth) p 427, 666

Bornyl Acetate
Vicks Inhaler (Vicks Health Care) p 641

Brompheniramine Maleate
Dimetane Decongestant Elixir (Robins) p 420, 616
Dimetane Decongestant Tablets (Robins) p 420, 616
Dimetane Elixir (Robins) p 420, 615
Dimetane Tablets (Robins) p 420, 615

Buchu Extract
DeWitt's Pills for Backache & Joint Pains (DeWitt) p 409, 529
Odrinil (Fox) p 538
Water Pill Tablets (Nature's Bounty) p 590

Water Pill w/Iron Tablets (Nature's Bounty) p 590

Burow's Solution
Star-Otic (Star) p 628

C

Caffeine
Anacin Analgesic Capsules (Whitehall) p 652
Anacin Analgesic Tablets (Whitehall) p 426, 652
Anacin Maximum Strength Analgesic Capsules (Whitehall) p 426, 652
Anacin Maximum Strength Analgesic Tablets (Whitehall) p 426, 652
Anacin-3 Analgesic Tablets (Whitehall) p 426, 652
CCP Tablets (Medique) p 574
Codexin Extra Strength Capsules (Arco) p 508
Coryban-D Capsules (Pfipharmecs) p 418, 604
DeWitt's Pills for Backache & Joint Pains (DeWitt) p 409, 529
Dex-A-Diet II Time Release Capsules (O'Connor) p 416, 596
Dexatrim & Dexatrim Extra Strength (Thompson Medical) p 634
Dietac Diet Aid Capsules (Menley & James) p 413, 575
Dietac Once-A-Day Maximum Strength Diet Aid Capsules (Menley & James) p 413, 576
Dietac Twice-A-Day Maximum Strength Diet Aid Capsules (Menley & James) p 413, 576
Dristan-AF Decongestant/Antihistamine/ Analgesic (Whitehall) p 426, 655
Dristan Decongestant/Antihistamine/ Analgesic Tablets (Whitehall) p 426, 654
Dristan Decongestant/Antihistamine/ Analgesic Capsules (Whitehall) p 426, 654
Excedrin (Bristol-Myers) p 406, 517
Goody's Headache Powders (Goody's) p 410, 541
No Doz (Bristol-Myers) p 406, 519
Odrinil (Fox) p 538
Prolamine Capsules, Super Strength (Thompson Medical) p 635
Vanquish (Glenbrook) p 541
Vivarin (J.B. Williams) p 662

Cajeput Oil
DeWitt's Oil for Ear Use (DeWitt) p 409, 529

Calamine
Caladryl Lotion & Cream (Parke-Davis) p 600
Calamatum Lotion, Ointment, Spray (Blair) p 512
Rhulihist (Lederle) p 551
Rhulispray (Lederle) p 551

Calcium
Chelated Multi-Mineral Tablets (Nature's Bounty) p 588
Dolomite Tablets (Nature's Bounty) p 588
One-A-Day Multivitamin Supplement Plus Minerals (Miles) p 585

Calcium Acetate
Bluboro Powder Astringent Soaking Solution (Herbert) p 543

Calcium Amino Acid Chelate
Chelated Calcium Tablets (Nature's Bounty) p 588

Calcium Ascorbate
Calcium Ascorbate Tablets (Nature's Bounty) p 588

Calcium Carbaspirin
Ursinus Inlay-Tabs (Dorsey) p 532

Calcium Carbonate
Alka-2 Chewable Antacid Tablets
(Miles) p 584
Balmex Baby Powder (Macsil) p 556
Bisodol Antacid Powder (Whitehall)
p 653
Marblen Suspensions & Tablets
(Fleming) p 537
Obron-6 Tablets (Pfipharmecs) p 418,
604
Os-Cal 500 Tablets (Marion) p 558
Os-Cal Tablets (Marion) p 412, 558
Thermotabs (Beecham Products) p 512
Titralac Tablets & Liquid (Riker) p 614

Calcium Carbonate, Precipitated
Tums (Norcliff Thayer) p 415, 592

Calcium Caseinate
NaturSlim II (NaturSlim) p 415, 590
Slender Diet Meal Bars For Weight
Control (Carnation) p 521

Calcium Docusate
Doxidan (Hoechst-Roussel) p 411, 544
Surfak (Hoechst-Roussel) p 411, 544

Calcium Hydroxide
Percy Medicine (Merrick) p 415, 583

Calcium Lactate
Calcium Lactate Tablets (Nature's
Bounty) p 588
Cal-M (Anabolic) p 507

Calcium (Oyster Shell)
Os-Cal 500 Tablets (Marion) p 558
Os-Cal Forte Tablets (Marion) p 558
Os-Cal Plus Tablets (Marion) p 558
Os-Cal Tablets (Marion) p 412, 558
Os-Cal-Gesic Tablets (Marion) p 558
Oyster Calcium Tablets (Nature's
Bounty) p 589

Calcium Pantothenate
(see also under Pantothenic Acid)
B Complex & C (Time Release)
Capsules (Nature's Bounty) p 587
Megadose (Arco) p 508
Obron-6 Tablets (Pfipharmecs) p 418,
604
Pantothenic Acid Tablets (Nature's
Bounty) p 589
Vergo (Daywell) p 527

Calcium Polycarbophil
Mitrolan Tablets (Robins) p 420, 616

Calcium Undecylenate
Caldesene Medicated Ointment
(Pharmacraft) p 606
Caldesene Medicated Powder
(Pharmacraft) p 606
Cruex Medicated Cream (Pharmacraft)
p 606
Cruex Medicated Powder (Pharmacraft)
p 606

Camphor
Afrin Menthol Nasal Spray (Schering)
p 421, 619
Caladryl Lotion & Cream (Parke-Davis)
p 600
Calamatum Lotion, Ointment, Spray
(Blair) p 512
Campho-Phenique Liquid (Consumer
Products Div., Winthrop) p 663
Deep-Down (J.B. Williams) p 660
DeWitt's Oil for Ear Use (DeWitt)
p 409, 529
Heet Analgesic Liniment (Whitehall)
p 656
Heet Spray Analgesic (Whitehall) p 656
Panalgesic (Poythress) p 610
Rhulicream (Lederle) p 551
Rhuligel (Lederle) p 551
Rhulihist (Lederle) p 551
Rhulispray (Lederle) p 551
Sinex Decongestant Nasal Spray (Vicks
Health Care) p 424, 640
Vaposteam (Vicks Health Care) p 640
Vatronol Nose Drops (Vicks Health
Care) p 641

Vicks Inhaler (Vicks Health Care) p 641
Vicks Sinex Decongestant Nasal Spray
(Vicks Health Care) p 424, 640
Vicks Throat Lozenges (Vicks Health
Care) p 641
Vicks Vaporub (Vicks Health Care)
p 424, 642
Vicks Vaposteam (Vicks Health Care)
p 640
Vicks Vatronol Nose Drops (Vicks
Health Care) p 641

Camphorated Oil
Oil-O-Sol Liquid (Health Care) p 410,
542

Capsicum
Heet Analgesic Liniment (Whitehall)
p 656
InfraRub Analgesic Cream (Whitehall)
p 657

Captan
Sebb Lotion (Max Factor) p 537

Carbamide Peroxide
Cankaid (Becton Dickinson) p 510
Gly-Oxide Liquid (Marion) p 412, 557

Carbamide Preparations
Debrox Drops (Marion) p 412, 556
Ear Drops by Murine
(See Murine Ear Wax Removal
System/Murine Ear Drops) (Abbott
Consumer Products) p 502
Murine Ear Wax Removal
System/Murine Ear Drops (Abbott
Consumer Products) p 405, 502

**Carbolic Acid
(see under Phenol)**

Carboxymethylcellulose Sodium
Pretts Tablets (Marion) p 412, 558

Casanthranol
Dialose Plus Capsules (Stuart) p 629

Cascara Sagrada
Herbal Laxative Tablets (Nature's
Bounty) p 588
Nature's Remedy (Norcliff Thayer)
p 592

Castor Oil
Neoloid (Lederle) p 551
Oil-O-Sol Liquid (Health Care) p 410,
542
Proderm Topical Dressing (Hickam)
p 544

Cedar Leaf Oil
Vicks Vaporub (Vicks Health Care)
p 424, 642

Cellulose
Cholagest (Anabolic) p 507

Cetyl Alcohol
Chap Stick Lip Balm (Miller-Morton)
p 415, 586
Chap Stick Sunblock 15 Lip Balm
(Miller-Morton) p 415, 586
Johnson & Johnson First Aid Cream
(Johnson & Johnson) p 411, 547

Cetylpyridinium Chloride
Cēpacol Anesthetic Troches
(Merrell-National) p 580
Cēpacol Mouthwash/Gargle
(Merrell-National) p 415, 580
Cēpacol Throat Lozenges
(Merrell-National) p 415, 580
Massengill Disposable Douche
(Beecham Products) p 511
Scope (Procter & Gamble) p 611
Sinex Decongestant Nasal Spray (Vicks
Health Care) p 424, 640
Vicks Sinex Decongestant Nasal Spray
(Vicks Health Care) p 424, 640
Vicks Throat Lozenges (Vicks Health
Care) p 641

Charcoal
Activated
Charcocaps (Requa) p 420, 612

Chlorhexidine
Flex-Care (Alcon/bp) p 405, 505

Chlorhexidine Gluconate
Hibiclens Antimicrobial Skin Cleanser
(Stuart) p 630
Hibistat Germicidal Hand Rinse (Stuart)
p 630
Hibitane Tincture (Tinted & Non-Tinted)
(Stuart) p 630

Chlorhydroxyquinoline
Loroxide Acne Lotion (Dermik) p 528
Vanoxide Acne Lotion (Dermik) p 528

Chlorobutanol
Liquifilm Tears (Allergan) p 406, 506
Outgro Solution (Whitehall) p 657

Chlorophyll Preparations
Chloresium Ointment & Solution
(Rystan) p 618
Derifil Tablets & Powder (Rystan)
p 618

Chlorpheniramine Maleate
A.R.M. Allergy Relief Medicine Tablets
(Menley & James) p 413, 574
Alka-Seltzer Plus Cold Medicine (Miles)
p 584
Allerest Headache Strength Tablets
(Pharmacraft) p 606
Allerest Tablets & Capsules
(Pharmacraft) p 606
C3 Cold Cough Capsules (Menley &
James) p 413, 574
Chlor-Trimeton Allergy Syrup, Tablets &
Long-Acting Repetabs Tablets
(Schering) p 421, 620
Chlor-Trimeton Decongestant Tablets
(Schering) p 421, 620
Chlor-Trimeton Expectorant (Schering)
p 620
Comtrex (Bristol-Myers) p 406, 516
Contac Capsules (Menley & James)
p 413, 575
Coricidin 'D' Decongestant Tablets
(Schering) p 421, 621
Coricidin Demilets Tablets for Children
(Schering) p 421, 622
Coricidin Extra Strength Sinus
Headache Tablets (Schering) p 421,
623
Coricidin Medilets Tablets for Children
(Schering) p 421, 622
Coricidin Tablets (Schering) p 421,
621
Coryban-D Capsules (Pfipharmecs)
p 418, 604
CoTylenol Children's Liquid Cold
Formula (McNeil Consumer Products)
p 412, 560
CoTylenol Cold Formula Tablets and
Capsules (McNeil Consumer
Products) p 412, 559
CoTylenol Liquid Cold Formula (McNeil
Consumer Products) p 412, 559
Demazin Decongestant-Antihistamine
Repetabs Tablets & Syrup (Schering)
p 421, 623
Dristan Decongestant/Antihistamine/
Analgesic Capsules (Whitehall)
p 426, 654
Dristan Decongestant/Antihistamine/
Analgesic Tablets (Whitehall)
p 426, 654
Dristan 12-Hour Nasal Decongestant
Capsules (Whitehall) p 426, 654
Dristan-AF Decongestant/Antihistamine/
Analgesic Tablets
(Whitehall) p 426, 655
4-Way Cold Tablets (Bristol-Myers)
p 406, 518
Novahistine Cold Tablets (Dow
Pharmaceuticals) p 534
Novahistine Cough & Cold Formula
(Dow Pharmaceuticals) p 532
Novahistine Elixir (Dow
Pharmaceuticals) p 534
Novahistine Sinus Tablets (Dow
Pharmaceuticals) p 534
Ryna Liquid (Wallace) p 425, 643
Ryna-C Liquid (Wallace) p 425, 643

Sinarest Tablets (Pharmacraft) p 607
Sine-Off Extra Strength Sinus Medicine Non-Aspirin Capsules (Menley & James) p 413, 578
Sine-Off Extra Strength Sinus Medicine Non-Aspirin Tablets (Menley & James) p 413, 579
Sine-Off Sinus Medicine-Aspirin Formula Tablets (Menley & James) p 413, 579
Sinutab Extra Strength Capsule Formula (Warner-Lambert) p 425, 646
Teldrin Spansule Capsules, 8 mg., 12 mg. (Menley & James) p 413, 579
Triaminic Syrup (Dorsey) p 409, 531
Triaminicin Chewables (Dorsey) p 531
Triaminicin Tablets (Dorsey) p 409, 531
Viro-Med Tablets (Whitehall) p 660

Choline
Brewer's Yeast Powder (Debittered) (Nature's Bounty) p 587
Brewer's Yeast Tablets (Nature's Bounty) p 587
Lecithin Granules (Nature's Bounty) p 589

Choline Bitartrate
B-100 Tablets (Nature's Bounty) p 587
Choline Tablets (Nature's Bounty) p 588
Geritol Liquid-High Potency Iron & Vitamin Tonic (J.B. Williams) p 661
Mega-B (Arco) p 508
Megadose (Arco) p 508

Chromium Amino Acid Chelate
Chelated Chromium Tablets (Nature's Bounty) p 588
Chelated Multi-Mineral Tablets (Nature's Bounty) p 588

Cinnamedrine Hydrochloride
Midol (Glenbrook) p 410, 541

Citric Acid
Alka-Seltzer Effervescent Antacid (Miles) p 584
Alka-Seltzer Effervescent Pain Reliever Antacid (Miles) p 583
Listermint Mouthwash & Gargle (Warner-Lambert) p 425, 645
Protect Toothpaste (Marion) p 412, 558

Coal Tar
Balnetar (Westwood) p 648
DHS Tar Shampoo (Persön & Covey) p 418, 603
Denorex Medicated Shampoo, Regular & Mountain Fresh Herbal (Whitehall) p 426, 653
Estar Tar Gel (Westwood) p 648
Oxipor VHC Lotion for Psoriasis (Whitehall) p 657
Pragmatar Ointment (Menley & James) p 413, 578
Sebutone & Sebutone Cream (Westwood) p 651
Tegrin for Psoriasis Lotion & Cream (Block) p 513
Tegrin Medicated Shampoo (Block) p 513
Zetar Shampoo (Dermik) p 529

Cobalamin
B-12 Tablets (Nature's Bounty) p 587
B Complex & C (Time Release) Capsules (Nature's Bounty) p 587
B & C Liquid (Nature's Bounty) p 587
Chew-Iron Tablets (Nature's Bounty) p 588

Cocoa Butter
Wyanoids Hemorrhoidal Suppositories (Wyeth) p 427, 666

Cod Liver Oil
Medicone Dressing Cream (Medicone) p 573
Scott's Emulsion (Beecham Products) p 511

Cod Liver Oil Concentrate
Cod Liver Oil Concentrate Tablets, Capsules (Schering) p 421, 621
Cod Liver Oil Concentrate Tablets w/Vitamin C (Schering) p 421, 621
Desitin Ointment (Leeming) p 553

Codeine
Ryna-C Liquid (Wallace) p 425, 643
Ryna-CX Liquid (Wallace) p 425, 643

Codeine Phosphate
Cosanyl Cough Syrup (Health Care) p 410, 542

Copper
Chelated Multi-Mineral Tablets (Nature's Bounty) p 588
One-A-Day Multivitamin Supplement Plus Minerals (Miles) p 585

Copper Amino Acid Chelate
Chelated Copper Tablets (Nature's Bounty) p 588

Copper Oleate
Cuprex (Beecham Products) p 510

Corn Oil
DeWitt's Oil for Ear Use (DeWitt) p 409, 529
Oil-O-Sol Liquid (Health Care) p 410, 542

Corn Silk Extract
Odrinil (Fox) p 538

Corn Starch
Diaparene Baby Powder (Glenbrook) p 410, 541

Cyanocobalamin
Bugs Bunny With Extra C Multivitamin Supplement (Miles) p 585
Chocks Multivitamin Supplement (Miles) p 584
Chocks Plus Iron Multivitamin Supplement (Miles) p 584
Chocks-Bugs Bunny Multivitamin Supplement (Miles) p 584
Chocks-Bugs Bunny Plus Iron Multivitamin Supplement (Miles) p 584
Flintstones Multivitamin Supplement (Miles) p 584
Flintstones Plus Iron Multivitamin Supplement (Miles) p 584
Flintstones With Extra C Multivitamin Supplement (Miles) p 585
Fortespan Capsules (Menley & James) p 413, 577
Geritol Liquid-High Potency Iron & Vitamin Tonic (J.B. Williams) p 661
One-A-Day Core C 500 Multivitamin Supplement (Miles) p 585
One-A-Day Multivitamin Supplement (Miles) p 585
One-A-Day Multivitamin Supplement Plus Iron (Miles) p 585
One-A-Day Multivitamin Supplement Plus Minerals (Miles) p 585

D

DNA
Brewer's Yeast Powder (Debittered) (Nature's Bounty) p 587
Brewer's Yeast Tablets (Nature's Bounty) p 587

RNA/DNA Tablets (Nature's Bounty) p 589

Danthron
Dorbane Tablets (Riker) p 613
Dorbantyl Capsules (Riker) p 613
Dorbantyl Forte Capsules (Riker) p 614
Doxidan (Hoechst-Roussel) p 411, 544
Modane Tablets & Liquid (Adria) p 504

Dehydrocholic Acid
Cholagest (Anabolic) p 507

Desoxyephedrine-Levo
Vicks Inhaler (Vicks Health Care) p 641

Dextromethorphan Hydrobromide
Ambenyl-D Decongestant Cough Formula (Marion) p 412, 556
Bayer Cough Syrup for Children (Glenbrook) p 540
Benylin DM (Parke-Davis) p 600
C3 Cold Cough Capsules (Menley & James) p 413, 574
Cheracol D Cough Syrup (Upjohn) p 635
Children's Hold (Beecham Products) p 510
Chloraseptic Cough Control Lozenges (Norwich-Eaton) p 416, 593
Comtrex (Bristol-Myers) p 406, 516
Contac Jr. Childrens' Cold Medicine (Menley & James) p 413, 575
Coricidin Children's Cough Syrup (Schering) p 421, 622
Coricidin Cough Syrup (Schering) p 421, 621
Coryban-D Cough Syrup (Pfipharmecs) p 418, 604
Cosanyl-DM Cough Syrup (Health Care) p 410, 542
CoTylenol Cold Formula Tablets and Capsules (McNeil Consumer Products) p 412, 559
CoTylenol Liquid Cold Formula (McNeil Consumer Products) p 412, 559
Daycare Multi-Symptom Colds Medicine Capsules (Vicks Health Care) p 424, 638
Daycare Multi-Symptom Colds Medicine (Vicks Health Care) p 424, 638
Dimacol Capsules (Robins) p 420, 615
Dimacol Liquid (Robins) p 420, 615
Dorcol Pediatric Cough Syrup (Dorsey) p 409, 530
Formula 44 Cough Control Discs (Vicks Health Care) p 638
Formula 44 Cough Mixture (Vicks Health Care) p 424, 639
Formula 44D Decongestant Cough Mixture (Vicks Health Care) p 424, 639
Hold (Beecham Products) p 511
Naldecon-DX Pediatric Syrup (Bristol) p 515
Novahistine Cough & Cold Formula (Dow Pharmaceuticals) p 532
Novahistine Cough Formula (Dow Pharmaceuticals) p 532
Novahistine DMX (Dow Pharmaceuticals) p 533
Nyquil Nighttime Colds Medicine (Vicks Health Care) p 424, 639
Ornacol Capsules (Menley & James) p 413, 577
Robitussin-CF (Robins) p 420, 617
Robitussin-DM (Robins) p 420, 617
St. Joseph Cough Syrup for Children (Plough) p 418, 609
Sucrets Cough Control Formula (Beecham Products) p 512
Triaminic-DM Cough Formula (Dorsey) p 409, 531
Triaminicol Decongestant Cough Syrup (Dorsey) p 409, 531
Trind-DM (Mead Johnson Nutritional) p 572
Tussagesic Tablets & Suspension (Dorsey) p 531
Vicks Cough Silencers Cough Drops (Vicks Health Care) p 641
Vicks Cough Syrup (Vicks Health Care) p 641

Vicks Formula 44 Cough Control Discs
(Vicks Health Care) p 638
Vicks Formula 44 Cough Mixture (Vicks
Health Care) p 424, 639
Vicks Formula 44D Decongestant
Cough Mixture (Vicks Health Care)
p 422, 639
Vicks Nyquil Nighttime Colds Medicine
(Vicks Health Care) p 424, 639
Viro-Med Liquid (Whitehall) p 659
Viro-Med Tablets (Whitehall) p 660

Dextrose

Thermotabs (Beecham Products) p 512

Dibucaine

Nupercainal Cream, Ointment,
Suppositories (Ciba) p 407, 523

Dihydroxyalumium Sodium Carbonate

Rolaids Antacid Tablets
(Warner-Lambert) p 425, 646

p-Diisobutylphenoxypolyethoxyethanol

Ortho-Gynol Contraceptive Jelly (Ortho
Consumer Products) p 416, 598

Dimenhydrinate

Dramamine Junior Liquid (Searle
Consumer Products) p 423, 627
Dramamine Liquid (Searle Consumer
Products) p 423, 627
Dramamine Tablets (Searle Consumer
Products) p 423, 627

Dimethisoquin Hydrochloride

Quotane Ointment (Menley & James)
p 413, 578

Diphenhydramine Hydrochloride

Benadryl Antihistamine Cream
(Parke-Davis) p 599
Caladryl Lotion & Cream (Parke-Davis)
p 600

Disodium EDTA

Massengill Disposable Douche
(Beecham Products) p 511

Docusate Potassium

Dialose Capsules (Stuart) p 629
Dialose Plus Capsules (Stuart) p 629
Kasof Capsules (Stuart) p 631

Docusate Sodium

Correctol Laxative Tablets (Plough)
p 418, 608
DioMedicone Tablets (Medicone) p 573
Dorbantyl Capsules (Riker) p 613
Dorbantyl Forte Capsules (Riker) p 614
Ferro-Sequels (Lederle) p 549
Geriplex-FS Kapseals (Parke-Davis)
p 601
Geriplex-FS Liquid (Parke-Davis) p 601
Milkinol (Kremers-Urban) p 548
Modane Soft (Adria) p 504
Peritinic Tablets (Lederle) p 551
Regutol (Plough) p 418, 608

Dolomite

Dolomite Tablets (Nature's Bounty)
p 588

Domiphen Bromide

Scope (Procter & Gamble) p 611

Doxylamine Succinate

Formula 44 Cough Mixture (Vicks
Health Care) p 424, 639
Nyquil Nighttime Colds Medicine (Vicks
Health Care) p 424, 639
Unisom Nighttime Sleep-Aid (Leeming)
p 554
Vicks Formula 44 Cough Mixture (Vicks
Health Care) p 424, 639
Vicks Nyquil Nighttime Colds Medicine
(Vicks Health Care) p 424, 639

Dyclonine Hydrochloride

Resolve Cold Sore & Fever Blister
Relief (Dow Pharmaceuticals) p 535

E

Edetate Disodium

Adapettes (Alcon/bp) p 405, 504, 505
BoilnSoak (Alcon/bp) p 405, 505
Clens (Alcon/bp) p 405, 505
Flex-Care (Alcon/bp) p 405, 505
Preflex (Alcon/bp) p 405, 505
Soaclens (Alcon/bp) p 405, 505

Ephedrine

Bronkaid Tablets (Consumer Products
Div., Winthrop) p 663
Collyrium with Ephedrine Eye Drops
(Wyeth) p 427, 665

Ephedrine Hydrochloride

HTO Stainless Manzan Hemorrhoidal
Tissue Ointment (DeWitt) p 409, 530

Ephedrine Sulfate

Nyquil Nighttime Colds Medicine (Vicks
Health Care) p 424, 639
Pazo Hemorrhoid Ointment/
Suppositories (Bristol-Myers) p 519
Vatronol Nose Drops (Vicks Health
Care) p 641
Vicks Nyquil Nighttime Colds Medicine
(Vicks Health Care) p 424, 639
Vicks Vatronol Nose Drops (Vicks
Health Care) p 641
Wyanoid Ointment (Wyeth) p 427, 666
Wyanoids Hemorrhoidal Suppositories
(Wyeth) p 427, 666

Epinephrine

Bronkaid Mist (Consumer Products
Div., Winthrop) p 662
Primatene Mist (Whitehall) p 426, 658

Epinephrine Bitartrate

Bronkaid Mist Suspension (Consumer
Products Div., Winthrop) p 662
Primatene Mist Suspension (Whitehall)
p 426, 658

Epinephrine Hydrocholoride

Primatene Tablets - M Formula
(Whitehall) p 426, 658
Primatene Tablets - P Formula
(Whitehall) p 426, 658

Ether

Compound W Solution (Whitehall)
p 653
Freezone Solution (Whitehall) p 656

Ethyl Dihydroxypropyl PABA

Solbar Plus 15 (Persōn & Covey)
p 603

Eucalyptol

(see also under Eucalyptus, Oil of)
Afrin Menthol Nasal Spray (Schering)
p 421, 619
Sinex Decongestant Nasal Spray (Vicks
Health Care) p 424, 640
Vatronol Nose Drops (Vicks Health
Care) p 641
Vicks Sinex Decongestant Nasal Spray
(Vicks Health Care) p 424, 640
Vicks Vatronol Nose Drops (Vicks
Health Care) p 641

Eucalyptus, Oil of

Halls Mentho-Lyptus Cough Tablets
(Warner-Lambert) p 425, 645
Listerine Antiseptic (Warner-Lambert)
p 425, 645
Vaposteam (Vicks Health Care) p 640
Vicks Throat Lozenges (Vicks Health
Care) p 641
Vicks Vaporub (Vicks Health Care)
p 424, 642

Vicks Vaposteam (Vicks Health Care)
p 640

F

Ferric Pyrophosphate

Troph-Iron Liquid & Tablets (Menley &
James) p 413, 579

Ferrous Fumarate

Chew-Iron Tablets (Nature's Bounty)
p 588
Chocks Plus Iron Multivitamin
Supplement (Miles) p 584
Chocks-Bugs Bunny Plus Iron
Multivitamin Supplement (Miles)
p 584
FemIron Tablets (J.B. Williams) p 660
Ferancee Chewable Tablets (Stuart)
p 629
Ferancee-HP Tablets (Stuart) p 629
Ferro-Sequels (Lederle) p 549
Flintstones Plus Iron Multivitamin
Supplement (Miles) p 584
Fumasorb Tablets (Marion) p 557
Fumatinic Tablets (Laser) p 549
Fumerin Tablets (Laser) p 549
Geritol Mega Vitamins (J.B. Williams)
p 661
Monster with Iron (Bristol-Myers)
p 519
One-A-Day Multivitamin Supplement
Plus Iron (Miles) p 585
One-A-Day Multivitamin Supplement
Plus Minerals (Miles) p 585
Pals Plus Iron (Bristol-Myers) p 519
Poly-Vi-Sol Vitamin Drops with Iron
(Mead Johnson Nutritional) p 568
Stresstabs 600 with Iron (Lederle)
p 411, 552
Stuartinic Tablets (Stuart) p 424, 632
Tri-88 (Anabolic) p 507

Ferrous Gluconate

Fergon Capsules (Breon) p 515
Fergon Tablets & Elixir (Breon) p 515
Iron Tablets (Nature's Bounty) p 588
Megadose (Arco) p 508
Simron (Merrell-National) p 415, 582
Simron Plus (Merrell-National) p 415,
582
Water Pill w/Iron Tablets (Nature's
Bounty) p 590

Ferrous Sulfate

Feosol Elixir (Menley & James) p 413,
576
Feosol Plus (Menley & James) p 577
Feosol Spansule Capsules (Menley &
James) p 413, 577
Feosol Tablets (Menley & James)
p 413, 577
Fer-In-Sol Iron Drops, Syrup & Capsules
(Mead Johnson Nutritional) p 563
Ferrous Sulfate Tablets (Nature's
Bounty) p 588
Geritol Tablets - High Potency Iron &
Vitamin Tablets (J.B. Williams) p 661
Mol-Iron Tablets, Liquid & Chronosule
Capsules (Schering) p 421, 626
Mol-Iron Tablets w/Vitamin C
(Schering) p 421, 626
Obron-6 Tablets (Pfipharmecs) p 418,
604
Tri-Vi-Sol Vitamin Drops w/Iron (Mead
Johnson Nutritional) p 573

Folic Acid

Allbee C-800 Plus Iron Tablets
(Robins) p 420, 614
B-100 Tablets (Nature's Bounty) p 587
Brewer's Yeast Powder (Debittered)
(Nature's Bounty) p 587
Brewer's Yeast Tablets (Nature's
Bounty) p 587
Bugs Bunny With Extra C Multivitamin
Supplement (Miles) p 585
Chocks Multivitamin Supplement
(Miles) p 584
Chocks Plus Iron Multivitamin
Supplement (Miles) p 584
Chocks-Bugs Bunny Multivitamin
Supplement (Miles) p 584

Chocks-Bugs Bunny Plus Iron
Multivitamin Supplement (Miles)
p 584
Flintstones Multivitamin Supplement
(Miles) p 584
Flintstones Plus Iron Multivitamin
Supplement (Miles) p 584
Flintstones With Extra C Multivitamin
Supplement (Miles) p 585
Folic Acid Tablets (Nature's Bounty)
p 588
Mega-B (Arco) p 508
Megadose (Arco) p 508
Monster (Bristol-Myers) p 518
Monster with Iron (Bristol-Myers)
p 519
One-A-Day Core C 500 Multivitamin
Supplement (Miles) p 585
One-A-Day Multivitamin Supplement
(Miles) p 585
One-A-Day Multivitamin Supplement
Plus Iron (Miles) p 585
One-A-Day Multivitamin Supplement
Plus Minerals (Miles) p 585
Pals (Bristol-Myers) p 519
Pals Plus Iron (Bristol-Myers) p 519
Simron Plus (Merrell-National) p 415,
582
Stuart Formula Tablets, The (Stuart)
p 424, 632
Stuart Prenatal Tablets (Stuart) p 632
Tri-B-Plex (Anabolic) p 508

Frangula
Herbal Laxative Tablets (Nature's
Bounty) p 588

G

Garlic, Dehydrated
Allimin Filmcoated Tablets (Health
Care) p 410, 541

Garlic Oil
Garlic Oil Capsules (Nature's Bounty)
p 588
Garlic & Parsley Capsules (Nature's
Bounty) p 588

Gingseng
Ginseng, Manchurian Capsules
(Nature's Bounty) p 588

Glacial Acetic Acid
Compound W Solution (Whitehall)
p 653

Glutamic Acid
Glutamic Acid Tablets (Nature's
Bounty) p 588

L-Glutamine
l-Glutamine Tablets (Nature's Bounty)
p 589

Glycerin
Cleansing Pads by the Makers of
Preparation H Hemorrhoidal
Remedies (Whitehall) p 653
Debrox Drops (Marion) p 412, 556
DeWitt's Baby Cough Syrup (DeWitt)
p 409, 529
Gly-Oxide Liquid (Marion) p 412, 557
Kerid Ear Drops (Blair) p 513
Mediconet (Medicone) p 573
Norwich Glycerin Suppositories
(Norwich-Eaton) p 594
S.T. 37 (Beecham Products) p 511

**Glyceryl Guaiacolate
(see under Guaifenesin)**

Glyceryl Monosterate
Buf Lotion (Riker) p 613

Glyceryl PABA
Eclipse Sunscreen Lotion & Gel,
Original (Herbert) p 543
Eclipse Sunscreen Lotion, Total (Alcohol
Base) (Herbert) p 411, 543

Glyceryl Stearate
Johnson & Johnson First Aid Cream
(Johnson & Johnson) p 411, 547

Glycine
Titralac Tablets & Liquid (Riker) p 614

Guaifenesin
Ambenyl-D Decongestant Cough
Formula (Marion) p 412, 556
Breonesin (Breon) p 515
Bronkaid Tablets (Consumer Products
Div., Winthrop) p 663
CCP Tablets (Medique) p 574
Cheracol D Cough Syrup (Upjohn)
p 635
Chlor-Trimeton Expectorant (Schering)
p 620
Coricidin Children's Cough Syrup
(Schering) p 421, 622
Coricidin Cough Syrup (Schering)
p 421, 621
Coryban-D Cough Syrup (Pfipharmecs)
p 418, 604
Dimacol Capsules (Robins) p 420, 615
Dimacol Liquid (Robins) p 420, 615
Dorcol Pediatric Cough Syrup (Dorsey)
p 409, 530
Formula 44D Decongestant Cough
Mixture (Vicks Health Care) p 424,
639
Naldecon-DX Pediatric Syrup (Bristol)
p 515
Naldecon-EX Pediatric Drops (Bristol)
p 515
Novahistine Cough Formula (Dow
Pharmaceuticals) p 532
Novahistine DMX (Dow
Pharmaceuticals) p 533
Robitussin (Robins) p 420, 617
Robitussin-CF (Robins) p 420, 617
Robitussin-DM (Robins) p 420, 617
Robitussin-PE (Robins) p 420, 617
Ryna-CX Liquid (Wallace) p 425, 643
Triaminic Expectorant (Dorsey) p 409,
530
Trind (Mead Johnson Nutritional)
p 572
Trind-DM (Mead Johnson Nutritional)
p 572
Vicks Cough Syrup (Vicks Health Care)
p 641
Vicks Formula 44D Decongestant
Cough Mixture (Vicks Health Care)
p 422, 639
Viro-Med Tablets (Whitehall) p 660

H

HCG Antiserum (rabbitt)
Acu-Test In-Home Pregnancy Test (J.B.
Williams) p 660
Answer At-Home Early Pregnancy Test
Kit (Carter Products) p 407, 522
e.p.t. In-Home Early Pregnancy Test
(Warner-Lambert) p 425, 644
Predictor In-Home Early Pregnancy
Test (Whitehall) p 657

Halibut Liver Oil
Halibut Liver Oil Capsules (Nature's
Bounty) p 588

Hemicellulase
Festal (Hoechst-Roussel) p 411, 544

Hemicellulose
Serutan Concentrated Powder (J.B.
Williams) p 661
Serutan Concentrated Powder-Fruit
Flavored (J.B. Williams) p 661
Serutan Toasted Granules (J.B.
Williams) p 662

Hesperidin Complex
C-Complex Tablets (Nature's Bounty)
p 588

Hexylresorcinol
Oil-O-Sol Liquid (Health Care) p 410,
542
S.T. 37 (Beecham Products) p 511

Sucrets (Regular, Mentholated &
Children's Cherry) (Beecham
Products) p 512

Histamine Dihydrochloride
InfraRub Analgesic Cream (Whitehall)
p 657

Homosalate
Shade Sunscreen Lotion (SPF-6)
(Plough) p 418, 609

Human Chorionic Gonadotropin (HCG)
Answer At-Home Early Pregnancy Test
Kit (Carter Products) p 407, 522
e.p.t. In-Home Early Pregnancy Test
(Warner-Lambert) p 425, 644
Predictor In-Home Early Pregnancy
Test (Whitehall) p 657

Hydrocortisone
CaldeCORT Hydrocortisone Cream
(Pharmacraft) p 606
Cortril ½% (Pfipharmecs) p 603
Delacort (Mericon) p 580
Dermolate Anal-Itch Ointment
(Schering) p 623
Dermolate Anti-Itch Cream & Spray
(Schering) p 623
Dermolate Scalp-Itch Lotion (Schering)
p 623
Hytone Cream ½% (Dermik) p 527
Hytone Ointment ½% (Dermik) p 528

Hydrocortisone Acetate
Cortaid Cream (Upjohn) p 424, 635
Cortaid Lotion (Upjohn) p 424, 635
Cortaid Ointment (Upjohn) p 424, 635
Lanacort Creme (Combe) p 408, 526
Rhulicort Cream & Lotion (Lederle)
p 552

Hydroquinone
Esotérica Medicated Fade Cream (Norcliff
Thayer) p 415, 591

Hydroxyethylcellulose
Preflex (Alcon/bp) p 405, 505

Hydroxypropyl Methylcellulose
Muro Tears (Muro) p 586

8-Hydroxyquinoline Benzoate
NP-27 Cream (Norwich-Eaton) p 595

8-Hydroxyquinoline Sulfate
Medicone Dressing Cream (Medicone)
p 573
Rectal Medicone Suppositories
(Medicone) p 573
Rectal Medicone Unguent (Medicone)
p 574

I

Ichthammol
Derma Medicone Ointment (Medicone)
p 573

Inositol
B-100 Tablets (Nature's Bounty) p 587
Brewer's Yeast Powder (Debittered)
(Nature's Bounty) p 587
Brewer's Yeast Tablets (Nature's
Bounty) p 587
Inositol Tablets (Nature's Bounty)
p 588
Lecithin Granules (Nature's Bounty)
p 589
Mega-B (Arco) p 508
Megadose (Arco) p 508

Iodine
Chelated Multi-Mineral Tablets
(Nature's Bounty) p 588
One-A-Day Multivitamin Supplement
Plus Minerals (Miles) p 585

Iodine Preparations
Anbesol Antiseptic Anesthetic Liquid
(Whitehall) p 426, 652
Kelp Tablets (Nature's Bounty) p 588

Iodochlorhydroxyquin
Vioform Cream & Ointment (Ciba)
p 524

Iron Preparations
Allbee C-800 Plus Iron Tablets
(Robins) p 420, 614
Chelated Multi-Mineral Tablets
(Nature's Bounty) p 588
Chew-Iron Tablets (Nature's Bounty)
p 588
Chocks Plus Iron Multivitamin
Supplement (Miles) p 584
Chocks-Bugs Bunny Plus Iron
Multivitamin Supplement (Miles)
p 584
Enfamil w/Iron Ready-To-Use (Mead
Johnson Nutritional) p 563
FemIron Multi-Vitamins and Iron (J.B.
Williams) p 660
FemIron Tablets (J.B. Williams) p 660
Ferancee Chewable Tablets (Stuart)
p 629
Ferancee-HP Tablets (Stuart) p 629
Ferro-Sequels (Lederle) p 549
Flintstones Plus Iron Multivitamin
Supplement (Miles) p 584
Geritol Liquid-High Potency Iron &
Vitamin Tonic (J.B. Williams) p 661
Geritol Mega Vitamins (J.B. Williams)
p 661
Geritol Tablets - High Potency Iron &
Vitamin Tablets (J.B. Williams) p 661
Incremin w/Iron Syrup (Lederle) p 550
Mol-Iron Tablets, Liquid & Chronosule
Capsules (Schering) p 421, 626
Mol-Iron Tablets w/Vitamin C
(Schering) p 421, 626
Monster with Iron (Bristol-Myers)
p 519
Obron-6 Tablets (Pfipharmecs) p 418,
604
One-A-Day Multivitamin Supplement
Plus Iron (Miles) p 585
One-A-Day Multivitamin Supplement
Plus Minerals (Miles) p 585
Pals Plus Iron (Bristol-Myers) p 519
Peritinic Tablets (Lederle) p 551
Poly-Vi-Sol Chewable Vitamin Tablets
with Iron (Mead Johnson Nutritional)
p 568
Simron (Merrell-National) p 415, 582
Simron Plus (Merrell-National) p 415,
582
Stuartinic Tablets (Stuart) p 424, 632
Super Wate-On Emulsion (Fleetwood)
p 410, 537
Surbex-750 with Iron (Abbott) p 503

Isobutane Propane
Transi-Lube (Holland-Rantos) p 545

**Isopropanol
(see under Isopropyl Alcohol)**

Isopropyl Alcohol
Desenex Foam (Pharmacraft) p 607
Desenex Ointment & Liquid
(Pharmacraft) p 607
Desenex Powders (Pharmacraft) p 607
Desenex Soap (Pharmacraft) p 607
Outgro Solution (Whitehall) p 657
Rhulicaine (Lederle) p 551
Xerac (Persōn & Covey) p 418, 603

Isopropyl Myristate
Chap Stick Lip Balm (Miller-Morton)
p 415, 586
Chap Stick Sunblock 15 Lip Balm
(Miller-Morton) p 415, 586
Shepard's Hand Cream (Dermik) p 528

Isopropyl Palmitate
Johnson & Johnson First Aid Cream
(Johnson & Johnson) p 411, 547

J

Juniper Extract
Odrinil (Fox) p 538
Water Pill Tablets (Nature's Bounty)
p 590
Water Pill w/Iron Tablets (Nature's
Bounty) p 590

K

Kaolin
Kaopectate (Upjohn) p 424, 636
Kaopectate Concentrate (Upjohn)
p 424, 636

Kelp
KLB6 Capsules (Nature's Bounty)
p 588
Ultra KLB6 Tablets (Nature's Bounty)
p 589

L

Lactase (Beta-D-galactosidase)
LactAid (SugarLo) p 424, 633

Lactic Acid
Massengill Liquid Concentrate
(Beecham Products) p 511

Lactobacillus Acidophilus
Acidophilus Capsules (Nature's Bounty)
p 587
Lactinex Tablets & Granules (Hynson,
Westcott & Dunning) p 411, 546

Lactobacillus Bulgaricus
Lactinex Tablets & Granules (Hynson,
Westcott & Dunning) p 411, 546

Lactose
Lac-Tol (Jayco) p 546

Lanolin
A and D Ointment (Schering) p 421,
619
Alpha Keri Bath Oil (Westwood) p 647
Balmex Emollient Lotion (Macsil) p 556
Chap Stick Lip Balm (Miller-Morton)
p 415, 586
Chap Stick Sunblock 15 Lip Balm
(Miller-Morton) p 415, 586
Derma Medicone Ointment (Medicone)
p 573
Diaparene Baby Wash Cloths
(Glenbrook) p 410, 541
Medicone Dressing Cream (Medicone)
p 573
Mediconet (Medicone) p 573
pHisoDerm (Consumer Products Div.,
Winthrop) p 664
Rectal Medicone Unguent (Medicone)
p 574
Shepard's Dry Skin Cream (Dermik)
p 528
Shepard's Soap (Dermik) p 528

Lanolin Alcohol
pHisoDerm (Consumer Products Div.,
Winthrop) p 664
Skin Screen (Cetylite) p 523

Laureth-4
Fostril (Westwood) p 649 ·
Transact (Westwood) p 651

Lecithin
KLB6 Capsules (Nature's Bounty)
p 588
Lecithin Capsules (Nature's Bounty)
p 589
Lecithin, Chewable Tablets (Nature's
Bounty) p 589
Lecithin with Vitamin D Capsules
(Nature's Bounty) p 589
Ultra KLB6 Tablets (Nature's Bounty)
p 589

Licorice
DeWitt's Baby Cough Syrup (DeWitt)
p 409, 529

Lidocaine
Medi-Quik (Lehn & Fink) p 555

Lidocaine Base
Xylocaine 2.5% Ointment (Astra)
p 509

Lidocaine Hydrochloride
Unguentine Plus (Norwich-Eaton) p 595

Lipase
Festal (Hoechst-Roussel) p 411, 544

Live Yeast Cell Derivative
Preparation H Hemorrhoidal Ointment
& Suppositories (Whitehall) p 426,
658

Liver, Desiccated
Liver W/B-12 Tablets (Nature's
Bounty) p 589

Liver Preparations
Tri-88 (Anabolic) p 507

Loeffler's Methylene Blue
F.S.K. (Fecal Staining Kit) (Jayco)
p 546

l-Lysine
l-Lysine Tablets (Nature's Bounty)
p 589

Lysine Hydrochloride
Enisyl (Persōn & Covey) p 603

M

Magnesium
Beelith Tablets (Beach) p 509
Chelated Multi-Mineral Tablets
(Nature's Bounty) p 588
Dolomite Tablets (Nature's Bounty)
p 588
One-A-Day Multivitamin Supplement
Plus Minerals (Miles) p 585

Magnesium Amino Acid Chelate
Chelated Magnesium Tablets (Nature's
Bounty) p 588

Magnesium Carbonate
Bisodol Antacid Tablets (Whitehall)
p 653
DeWitt's Antacid Powder (DeWitt)
p 409, 529
Gaviscon Liquid Antacid (Marion)
p 412, 557
Marblen Suspensions & Tablets
(Fleming) p 537

Magnesium Carbonate Gel
Di-Gel (Plough) p 418, 608

Magnesium Gluconate
Magnesium Tablets (Nature's Bounty)
p 589

Magnesium Glycinate
Bufferin (Bristol-Myers) p 406, 516

Magnesium Hydroxide
Aludrox Oral Suspension & Tablets
(Wyeth) p 417, 665
Bisodol Antacid Powder (Whitehall)
p 653
Delcid (Merrell-National) p 581
Di-Gel (Plough) p 418, 608
Gelusil-M (Parke-Davis) p 600
Gelusil-II Liquid & Tablets (Parke-Davis)
p 601
Kolantyl (Merrell-National) p 582
Kudrox Suspension (Double Strength)
(Kremers-Urban) p 548
Magnatril Suspension & Tablets
(Lannett) p 548
Mylanta Liquid (Stuart) p 424, 631
Mylanta Tablets (Stuart) p 424, 631
Mylanta-II Liquid (Stuart) p 424, 631
Mylanta-II Tablets (Stuart) p 424, 631
Phillip's Milk of Magnesia (Glenbrook)
p 410, 541

Magnesium Oxide
B6-Plus (Anabolic) p 507
Beelith Tablets (Beach) p 509
Cal-M (Anabolic) p 507

Magnesium Salicylate
Mobigesic Analgesic Tablets (Ascher) p 509

Magnesium Sulfate
Obron-6 Tablets (Pfipharmecs) p 418, 604

Magnesium Trisilicate
DeWitt's Antacid Powder (DeWitt) p 409, 529
Gaviscon Antacid Tablets (Marion) p 412, 557
Gaviscon-2 Antacid Tablets (Marion) p 412, 557
Gelusil (Parke-Davis) p 600
Magnatril Suspension & Tablets (Lannett) p 548

Malt Soup Extract
Maltsupex (Wallace) p 425, 642

Manganese
Chelated Multi-Mineral Tablets (Nature's Bounty) p 588

Manganese Amino Acid Chelate
Chelated Manganese Tablets (Nature's Bounty) p 588

Manganese Gluconate
Manganese Tablets (Nature's Bounty) p 589

Meclizine Hydrochloride
Bonine (Pfipharmecs) p 418, 603

Medium Chain Triglycerides
MCT Oil (Mead Johnson Nutritional) p 567
Portagen (Mead Johnson Nutritional) p 568
Pregestimil (Mead Johnson Nutritional) p 569

Menthol
Afrin Menthol Nasal Spray (Schering) p 421, 619
Ben-Gay External Analgesic Products (Leeming) p 552
Deep-Down (J.B. Williams) p 660
Denorex Medicated Shampoo, Regular & Mountain Fresh Herbal (Whitehall) p 426, 653
Derma Medicone Ointment (Medicone) p 573
Dermassage Medicated Skin Lotion (Colgate-Palmolive) p 408, 525
DeWitt's Oil for Ear Use (DeWitt) p 409, 529
Formula 44 Cough Control Discs (Vicks Health Care) p 638
Halls Mentho-Lyptus Cough Tablets (Warner-Lambert) p 425, 645
Heet Spray Analgesic (Whitehall) p 656
Icy Hot Balm (Searle Consumer Products) p 423, 627
Icy Hot Rub (Searle Consumer Products) p 423, 627
Listerine Antiseptic (Warner-Lambert) p 425, 645
Medicone Dressing Cream (Medicone) p 573
Oracin Cherry Flavor Cooling Throat Lozenges (Vicks Health Care) p 640
Oracin Cooling Throat Lozenges (Vicks Health Care) p 639
Panalgesic (Poythress) p 610
Protexin Oral Rinse (Cetylite) p 523
Rectal Medicone Suppositories (Medicone) p 573
Rectal Medicone Unguent (Medicone) p 574

Rhulicaine (Lederle) p 551
Rhulicream (Lederle) p 551
Rhuligel (Lederle) p 551
Rhulihist (Lederle) p 551
Rhulispray (Lederle) p 551
Sinex Decongestant Nasal Spray (Vicks Health Care) p 424, 640
Soft 'N Soothe Anti-Itch Creme (Ascher) p 509
Vaposteam (Vicks Health Care) p 640
Vatronol Nose Drops (Vicks Health Care) p 641
Vicks Cough Silencers Cough Drops (Vicks Health Care) p 641
Vicks Formula 44 Cough Control Discs (Vicks Health Care) p 638
Vicks Inhaler (Vicks Health Care) p 641
Vicks Sinex Decongestant Nasal Spray (Vicks Health Care) p 424, 640
Vicks Throat Lozenges (Vicks Health Care) p 641
Vicks Vaporub (Vicks Health Care) p 424, 642
Vicks Vaposteam (Vicks Health Care) p 640
Vicks Vatronol Nose Drops (Vicks Health Care) p 641

Methionine
Geritol Liquid-High Potency Iron & Vitamin Tonic (J.B. Williams) p 661

Methyl Nicotinate
Deep-Down (J.B. Williams) p 660
Heet Spray Analgesic (Whitehall) p 656

Methyl Salicylate
Ben-Gay External Analgesic Products (Leeming) p 552
Deep-Down (J.B. Williams) p 660
Heet Analgesic Liniment (Whitehall) p 656
Heet Spray Analgesic (Whitehall) p 656
Icy Hot Balm (Searle Consumer Products) p 423, 627
Icy Hot Rub (Searle Consumer Products) p 423, 627
Listerine Antiseptic (Warner-Lambert) p 425, 645
Panalgesic (Poythress) p 610
Sinex Decongestant Nasal Spray (Vicks Health Care) p 424, 640
Vatronol Nose Drops (Vicks Health Care) p 641
Vicks Inhaler (Vicks Health Care) p 641
Vicks Sinex Decongestant Nasal Spray (Vicks Health Care) p 424, 640
Vicks Vatronol Nose Drops (Vicks Health Care) p 641

Methylbenzethonium Chloride
Diaparene Baby Powder (Glenbrook) p 410, 541

Methylcellulose
Clear Eyes Eye Drops (Abbott Consumer Products) p 405, 502
Murine Plus Eye Drops (Abbott Consumer Products) p 405, 502
Murine Regular Formula Eye Drops (Abbott Consumer Products) p 405, 502
Murocel Ophthalmic Solution (Muro) p 586

Methylparaben
Transi-Lube (Holland-Rantos) p 545

Milk Of Magnesia
Haley's M-O (Consumer Products Div., Winthrop) p 663

Mineral Oil
Agoral, Plain (Parke-Davis) p 599
Agoral Raspberry & Marshmallow Flavors (Parke-Davis) p 599
Alpha Keri Bath Oil (Westwood) p 647
DeWitt's Oil for Ear Use (DeWitt) p 409, 529
Haley's M-O (Consumer Products Div., Winthrop) p 663
Keri Lotion (Westwood) p 649
Milkinol (Kremers-Urban) p 548

Nephrox Suspension (Fleming) p 537
Shepard's Dry Skin Cream (Dermik) p 528

Multivitamins
Fortespan Capsules (Menley & James) p 413, 577
KLB6 Complete Tablets (Nature's Bounty) p 589
KLB6 Diet Mix (Nature's Bounty) p 589
Stress Formula "605" Tablets (Nature's Bounty) p 589

Multivitamins with Minerals
Carnation Instant Breakfast (Carnation) p 521
Mega V & M Tablets (Nature's Bounty) p 589
Multi-Mineral Tablets (Nature's Bounty) p 589
NaturSlim II (NaturSlim) p 415, 590
Slender Diet Food For Weight Control (Instant) (Carnation) p 521
Slender Diet Meal Bars For Weight Control (Carnation) p 521
Slender Diet Meal For Weight Control (Canned) (Carnation) p 521
Stress Formula "605" w/Iron Tablets (Nature's Bounty) p 589
Stress Formula "605" w/Zinc Tablets (Nature's Bounty) p 589
Ultra Vita-Time Tablets (Nature's Bounty) p 589
Vita-Time Tablets (Nature's Bounty) p 590

N

Naphazoline Hydrochloride
Clear Eyes Eye Drops (Abbott Consumer Products) p 405, 502
4-Way Nasal Spray (Bristol-Myers) p 406, 518
Privine Nasal Spray & Solution 0.05% (Ciba) p 407, 524
20/20 Eye Drops (S.S.S. Company) p 619

Neomycin Sulfate
BPN Ointment (Norwich-Eaton) p 592
Myciguent Antibiotic Ointment (Upjohn) p 636
Mycitracin Antibiotic Ointment (Upjohn) p 424, 636
Septa Ointment (Circle) p 524

Niacin
Allbee C-800 Plus Iron Tablets (Robins) p 420, 614
Allbee C-800 Tablets (Robins) p 420, 614
Allbee with C Capsules (Robins) p 420, 615
B Complex & B-12 Tablets (Nature's Bounty) p 587
Brewer's Yeast Powder (Debittered) (Nature's Bounty) p 587
Brewer's Yeast Tablets (Nature's Bounty) p 587
Bugs Bunny With Extra C Multivitamin Supplement (Miles) p 585
Chocks Multivitamin Supplement (Miles) p 584
Chocks Plus Iron Multivitamin Supplement (Miles) p 584
Chocks-Bugs Bunny Multivitamin Supplement (Miles) p 584
Chocks-Bugs Bunny Plus Iron Multivitamin Supplement (Miles) p 584
Flintstones Multivitamin Supplement (Miles) p 584
Flintstones Plus Iron Multivitamin Supplement (Miles) p 584
Flintstones With Extra C Multivitamin Supplement (Miles) p 585
Monster (Bristol-Myers) p 518
Monster with Iron (Bristol-Myers) p 519
Niacin Tablets (Nature's Bounty) p 589
One-A-Day Core C 500 Multivitamin Supplement (Miles) p 585

Simeco Suspension (Wyeth) p 427, 666
WinGel (Consumer Products Div., Winthrop) p 665

One-A-Day Multivitamin Supplement (Miles) p 585
One-A-Day Multivitamin Supplement Plus Iron (Miles) p 585
One-A-Day Multivitamin Supplement Plus Minerals (Miles) p 585
Pals (Bristol-Myers) p 519
Pals Plus Iron (Bristol-Myers) p 519
Tri-B3 (Anabolic) p 508
Z-Bec Tablets (Robins) p 420, 617

Niacinamide
A.C.N. (Persōn & Covey) p 603
B-100 Tablets (Nature's Bounty) p 587
B Complex & C (Time Release) Capsules (Nature's Bounty) p 587
B & C Liquid (Nature's Bounty) p 587
Geritol Liquid-High Potency Iron & Vitamin Tonic (J.B. Williams) p 661
Mega-B (Arco) p 508
Megadose (Arco) p 508
Niacinamide Tablets (Nature's Bounty) p 589
Obron-6 Tablets (Pfipharmecs) p 418, 604
Tri-B-Plex (Anabolic) p 508

Nicotinamide
Fortespan Capsules (Menley & James) p 413, 577

Nicotinic Acid
(see also under Niacin)
Nicotinex Elixir (Fleming) p 537

Nonfat Dry Milk
Carnation Instant Breakfast (Carnation) p 521
Carnation Instant Nonfat Dry Milk (Carnation) p 521
Slender Diet Food For Weight Control (Instant) (Carnation) p 521

Nonoxynol-9
Conceptrol Birth Control Cream (Ortho Consumer Products) p 416, 597
Delfen Contraceptive Foam (Ortho Consumer Products) p 416, 597
Emko Because Contraceptor Vaginal Contraceptive Foam (Schering) p 421, 624
Emko Pre-Fil Vaginal Contraceptive Foam (Schering) p 421, 625
Emko Vaginal Contraceptive Foam (Schering) p 421, 624
Encare (Norwich-Eaton) p 416, 593
Intercept Contraceptive Inserts (Ortho Consumer Products) p 597
Koromex Contraceptive Foam (Holland-Rantos) p 545
Koromex^{II}—A Contraceptive Jelly (Holland-Rantos) p 545
Ortho-Creme Contraceptive Cream (Ortho Consumer Products) p 416, 598
Semicid Vaginal Contraceptive Suppositories (Whitehall) p 659

Nutmeg Oil
Vicks Vaporub (Vicks Health Care) p 424, 642

O

Oatmeal
Acnaveen Bar (CooperCare) p 408, 526
Aveeno Bar (CooperCare) p 408, 526
Aveeno Colloidal Oatmeal (CooperCare) p 408, 526
Aveeno Oilated Bath Powder (CooperCare) p 408, 526
Emulave Bar (CooperCare) p 408, 526

Octoxynol
Koromex^{II} Contraceptive Cream (Holland-Rantos) p 545
Koromex^{II} Contraceptive Jelly (Holland-Rantos) p 545

Octoxynol 9
Massengill Disposable Douche (Beecham Products) p 511

Massengill Liquid Concentrate (Beecham Products) p 511

Octyl dimethyl PABA
Eclipse Sunscreen Lip & Face Protectant (Herbert) p 411, 543
Eclipse Sunscreen Lotion & Gel, Original (Herbert) p 543
Eclipse Sunscreen Lotion, Total (Alcohol Base) (Herbert) p 411, 543
Eclipse Suntan Lotion, Partial (Herbert) p 411, 543
Sundown Sunscreen, Extra Protection (Johnson & Johnson Baby Products Company) p 411, 547
Sundown Sunscreen, Maximal Protection (Johnson & Johnson Baby Products Company) p 411, 547
Sundown Sunscreen, Moderate Protection (Johnson & Johnson Baby Products Company) p 411, 547
Sundown Sunscreen, Ultra Protection (Johnson & Johnson Baby Products Company) p 411, 547

Octyl Salicylate
Sundown Sunscreen, Maximal Protection (Johnson & Johnson Baby Products Company) p 411, 547
Sundown Sunscreen, Ultra Protection (Johnson & Johnson Baby Products Company) p 411, 547

Ox Bile Extract
Cholagest (Anabolic) p 507

Oxybenzone
Chap Stick Sunblock 15 Lip Balm (Miller-Morton) p 415, 586
Eclipse Sunscreen Lotion, Total (Alcohol Base) (Herbert) p 411, 543
PreSun 15 Lotion (Westwood) p 651
Shade Plus Sunscreen Lotion (SPF-8) (Plough) p 418, 609
Shade Sunscreen Lotion (SPF-6) (Plough) p 418, 609
Solbar Plus 15 (Persōn & Covey) p 603
Sundown Sunscreen, Extra Protection (Johnson & Johnson Baby Products Company) p 411, 547
Sundown Sunscreen, Maximal Protection (Johnson & Johnson Baby Products Company) p 411, 547
Sundown Sunscreen, Ultra Protection (Johnson & Johnson Baby Products Company) p 411, 547
Super Shade (SPF-15) (Plough) p 418, 610
Uval Moisturizing Sunscreen Lotion (Dorsey) p 532

Oxymetazoline Hydrochloride
Afrin Menthol Nasal Spray (Schering) p 421, 619
Afrin Nasal Spray, Nose Drops, Pediatric Nose Drops (Schering) p 421, 619
Duration (Plough) p 418, 608

Oxyquinoline Sulfate
Derma Medicone Ointment (Medicone) p 573

Oxytetracycline
Terramycin Ointment (Pfipharmecs) p 418, 605

P

PABA
(see under Para-Aminobenzoic Acid)

Padimate O
Chap Stick Lip Balm (Miller-Morton) p 415, 586
Chap Stick Sunblock 15 Lip Balm (Miller-Morton) p 415, 586
Eclipse Sunscreen Lip & Face Protectant (Herbert) p 411, 543
Eclipse Sunscreen Lotion & Gel, Original (Herbert) p 543

Eclipse Sunscreen Lotion, Total (Alcohol Base) (Herbert) p 411, 543
Eclipse Suntan Lotion, Partial (Herbert) p 411, 543
Moisture Whip Lip Conditioner (Maybelline) p 559
Moisture Whip Lipstick (Maybelline) p 559
Moisture Whip Liquid Make-up & Moisture Whip Cream Make-up (Maybelline) p 559
Moisture Whip Protective Facial Moisturizer (Maybelline) p 559
PreSun 4 Lotion (Westwood) p 650
PreSun 15 Lotion (Westwood) p 651
PreSun Sunscreen Lip Protection (Westwood) p 651
Shade Plus Sunscreen Lotion (SPF-8) (Plough) p 418, 609
Sundown Sunscreen, Extra Protection (Johnson & Johnson Baby Products Company) p 411, 547
Sundown Sunscreen, Maximal Protection (Johnson & Johnson Baby Products Company) p 411, 547
Sundown Sunscreen, Moderate Protection (Johnson & Johnson Baby Products Company) p 411, 547
Sundown Sunscreen, Ultra Protection (Johnson & Johnson Baby Products Company) p 411, 547
Super Shade (SPF-15) (Plough) p 418, 610

Pamabrom
Sunril Premenstrual Capsules (Schering) p 626
Trendar Premenstrual Tablets (Whitehall) p 659

Pancreatic Preparations
Cholagest (Anabolic) p 507

Panthenol
B & C Liquid (Nature's Bounty) p 587
Geritol Liquid-High Potency Iron & Vitamin Tonic (J.B. Williams) p 661

Pantothenate, Calcium
Mega-B (Arco) p 508

Pantothenic Acid
Allbee C-800 Plus Iron Tablets (Robins) p 420, 614
Allbee C-800 Tablets (Robins) p 420, 614
Allbee with C Capsules (Robins) p 420, 615
B-100 Tablets (Nature's Bounty) p 587
Brewer's Yeast Powder (Debittered) (Nature's Bounty) p 587
Brewer's Yeast Tablets (Nature's Bounty) p 587
Fortespan Capsules (Menley & James) p 413, 577
Monster (Bristol-Myers) p 518
Monster with Iron (Bristol-Myers) p 519
One-A-Day Multivitamin Supplement Plus Minerals (Miles) p 585
Pals (Bristol-Myers) p 519
Pals Plus Iron (Bristol-Myers) p 519
Tri-Adrenopan (Anabolic) p 507
Tri-B-Plex (Anabolic) p 508
Z-Bec Tablets (Robins) p 420, 617

Papain
Papaya Enzyme Tablets (Nature's Bounty) p 589

Para-Aminobenzoic Acid
B-100 Tablets (Nature's Bounty) p 587
Brewer's Yeast Powder (Debittered) (Nature's Bounty) p 587
Brewer's Yeast Tablets (Nature's Bounty) p 587
Mega-B (Arco) p 508
PABA Tablets (Nature's Bounty) p 589
PreSun 8 Lotion, Creamy Lotion & Gel (Westwood) p 650
PreSun 15 Lotion (Westwood) p 651

Parachlorometaxylenol
Metasep Shampoo (Marion) p 557
Unguentine Plus (Norwich-Eaton) p 595
Zetar Shampoo (Dermik) p 529

Parsley
Garlic & Parsley Capsules (Nature's Bounty) p 588
Water Pill Tablets (Nature's Bounty) p 590
Water Pill w/Iron Tablets (Nature's Bounty) p 590

P-Chloro-M-Xylenol
Cruex Medicated Cream (Pharmacraft) p 606
Cruex Medicated Powder (Pharmacraft) p 606

Pectin
Kaopectate (Upjohn) p 424, 636
Kaopectate Concentrate (Upjohn) p 424, 636

Peppermint Oil
Vicks Cough Silencers Cough Drops (Vicks Health Care) p 641

Peroxide Preparations
Debrox Drops (Marion) p 412, 556
Gly-Oxide Liquid (Marion) p 412, 557

Petrolatum
A and D Ointment (Schering) p 421, 619
Chap Stick Lip Balm (Miller-Morton) p 415, 586
Chap Stick Sunblock 15 Lip Balm (Miller-Morton) p 415, 586
Duolube Ophthalmic Ointment (Muro) p 586
Shepard's Dry Skin Cream (Dermik) p 528

Petroleum Distillate
Rid (Pfipharmecs) p 418, 604

Pheniramine Maleate
Dristan Nasal Mist, Regular & Menthol (Whitehall) p 426, 655
Triaminicol Decongestant Cough Syrup (Dorsey) p 409, 531
Tussagesic Tablets & Suspension (Dorsey) p 531
Ursinus Inlay-Tabs (Dorsey) p 532

Phenobarbital
Primatene Tablets - P Formula (Whitehall) p 426, 658

Phenol
Anbesol Antiseptic Anesthetic Gel (Whitehall) p 426, 652
Anbesol Antiseptic Anesthetic Liquid (Whitehall) p 426, 652
Calamatum Lotion, Ointment, Spray (Blair) p 512
Campho-Phenique Liquid (Consumer Products Div., Winthrop) p 663
Cēpastat Sore Throat Lozenges (Merrell-National) p 415, 581
Cēpastat Sore Throat Spray/Gargle (Merrell-National) p 415, 581
Children's Cepastat Sore Throat Lozenges (Merrell-National) p 415, 581
Chloraseptic Cough Control Lozenges (Norwich-Eaton) p 416, 593
Chloraseptic Gel (Norwich-Eaton) p 593
Chloraseptic Liquid & Spray (Norwich-Eaton) p 416, 593
Chloraseptic Lozenges (Norwich-Eaton) p 416, 593
HTO Stainless Manzan Hemorrhoidal Tissue Ointment (DeWitt) p 409, 530
Solarcaine (Plough) p 418, 609
Unguentine Plus (Norwich-Eaton) p 595

Phenolphthalein
Agoral Raspberry & Marshmallow Flavors (Parke-Davis) p 599

Phenolphthalein, Yellow
Correctol Laxative Tablets (Plough) p 418, 608
Evac-U-Gen (Walker, Corp) p 642
Ex-Lax Chocolated Laxative (Ex-Lax Pharm.) p 408, 536
Ex-Lax Pills, Unflavored (Ex-Lax Pharm.) p 408, 536

Phenylcarbinol
Rhuligel (Lederle) p 551
Rhulispray (Lederle) p 551

Phenylephrine Hydrochloride
Chlor-Trimeton Expectorant (Schering) p 620
Congespirin (Bristol-Myers) p 406, 516
Coricidin Decongestant Nasal Mist (Schering) p 421, 621
Coricidin Demilets Tablets for Children (Schering) p 421, 622
Coryban-D Cough Syrup (Pfipharmecs) p 418, 604
Demazin Decongestant-Antihistamine Repetabs Tablets & Syrup (Schering) p 421, 623
Dimetane Decongestant Elixir (Robins) p 420, 616
Dimetane Decongestant Tablets (Robins) p 420, 616
Dristan Decongestant/Antihistamine/ Analgesic Tablets (Whitehall) p 426, 654
Dristan 12-Hour Nasal Decongestant Capsules (Whitehall) p 426, 654
Dristan Nasal Mist, Regular & Menthol (Whitehall) p 426, 655
Dristan-AF Decongestant/Antihistamine/ Analgesi-c Tablets (Whitehall) p 426, 655
4-Way Nasal Spray (Bristol-Myers) p 406, 518
NTZ (Consumer Products Div., Winthrop) p 664
Neo-Synephrine Hydrochloride (Consumer Products Div., Winthrop) p 664
Prefrin Liquifilm (Allergan) p 405, 506
Sinex Decongestant Nasal Spray (Vicks Health Care) p 424, 640
Sucrets—Cold Decongestant Formula (Beecham Products) p 512
Trind (Mead Johnson Nutritional) p 572
Trind-DM (Mead Johnson Nutritional) p 572
Vicks Sinex Decongestant Nasal Spray (Vicks Health Care) p 424, 640

Phenylpropanolamine Bitartrate
Alka-Seltzer Plus Cold Medicine (Miles) p 584

Phenylpropanolamine Hydrochloride
A.R.M. Allergy Relief Medicine Tablets (Menley & James) p 413, 574
Allerest Headache Strength Tablets (Pharmacraft) p 606
Allerest Tablets & Capsules (Pharmacraft) p 606
Anorexin Capsules (SDA Pharmaceuticals) p 618
Anorexin One-Span Capsules (SDA Pharmaceuticals) p 618
Appedrine, Maximum Strength (Thompson Medical) p 634
Bayer Children's Cold Tablets (Glenbrook) p 540
Bayer Cough Syrup for Children (Glenbrook) p 540
C3 Cold Cough Capsules (Menley & James) p 413, 574
CCP Tablets (Medique) p 574
Children's Hold (Beecham Products) p 510
Codexin Extra Strength Capsules (Arco) p 508
Comtrex (Bristol-Myers) p 406, 516
Congespirin Liquid Cold Medicine (Bristol-Myers) p 406, 517
Contac Capsules (Menley & James) p 413, 575

Contac Jr. Childrens' Cold Medicine (Menley & James) p 413, 575
Control Capsules (Thompson Medical) p 634
Coricidin Children's Cough Syrup (Schering) p 421, 622
Coricidin Cough Syrup (Schering) p 421, 621
Coricidin 'D' Decongestant Tablets (Schering) p 421, 621
Coricidin Extra Strength Sinus Headache Tablets (Schering) p 421, 623
Coryban-D Capsules (Pfipharmecs) p 418, 604
Daycare Multi-Symptom Colds Medicine Capsules (Vicks Health Care) p 424, 638
Daycare Multi-Symptom Colds Medicine (Vicks Health Care) p 424, 638
Dex-A-Diet Lite Time Release Capsules (O'Connor) p 595
Dex-A-Diet II Time Release Capsules (O'Connor) p 416, 596
Dexatrim & Dexatrim Extra Strength (Thompson Medical) p 634
Dietac Diet Aid Capsules (Menley & James) p 413, 575
Dietac Diet Aid Drops (Menley & James) p 413, 575
Dietac Diet Aid Tablets (Menley & James) p 413, 576
Dietac Once-A-Day Maximum Strength Diet Aid Capsules (Menley & James) p 413, 576
Dietac Twice-A-Day Maximum Strength Diet Aid Capsules (Menley & James) p 413, 576
Dorcol Pediatric Cough Syrup (Dorsey) p 409, 530
Dristan Decongestant/Antihistamine/ Analgesic Capsules (Whitehall) p 426, 654
D-Sinus Capsules (Laser) p 548
E-Z Trim (Fox) p 538
4-Way Cold Tablets (Bristol-Myers) p 406, 518
Formula 44D Decongestant Cough Mixture (Vicks Health Care) p 424, 639
Naldecon-DX Pediatric Syrup (Bristol) p 515
Naldecon-EX Pediatric Drops (Bristol) p 515
Novahistine Cold Tablets (Dow Pharmaceuticals) p 534
Novahistine Elixir (Dow Pharmaceuticals) p 534
Ornacol Capsules (Menley & James) p 413, 577
Ornex Capsules (Menley & James) p 413, 578
P.V.M. Appetite Control Capsules (J.B. Williams) p 661
P.V.M. Appetite Suppressant Tablets (J.B. Williams) p 661
Prolamine Capsules, Super Strength (Thompson Medical) p 635
Robitussin-CF (Robins) p 420, 617
St. Joseph Cold Tablets for Children (Plough) p 418, 609
Sinarest Tablets (Pharmacraft) p 607
Sine-Aid Sinus Headache Tablets (McNeil Consumer Products) p 412, 560
Sine-Off Extra Strength Sinus Medicine Non-Aspirin Capsules (Menley & James) p 413, 578
Sine-Off Extra Strength Sinus Medicine Non-Aspirin Tablets (Menley & James) p 413, 579
Sine-Off Sinus Medicine Tablets-Aspirin Formula (Menley & James) p 413, 579
Sinutab Extra Strength Capsule Formula (Warner-Lambert) p 425, 646
Sinutab Extra Strength Tablets (Warner-Lambert) p 425, 647
Sinutab Tablets (Warner-Lambert) p 425, 646
Sinutab II Tablets (Warner-Lambert) p 425, 646

Sucrets—Cold Decongestant Formula
(Beecham Products) p 512
Super Odrinex (Fox) p 538
Triaminic Expectorant (Dorsey) p 409,
530
Triaminic Syrup (Dorsey) p 409, 531
Triaminic-DM Cough Formula (Dorsey)
p 409, 531
Triaminicin Chewables (Dorsey) p 531
Triaminicin Tablets (Dorsey) p 409,
531
Triaminicol Decongestant Cough Syrup
(Dorsey) p 409, 531
Tussagesic Tablets & Suspension
(Dorsey) p 531
Ursinus Inlay-Tabs (Dorsey) p 532
Vicks Formula 44D Decongestant
Cough Mixture (Vicks Health Care)
p 422, 639

Phenyltoloxamine Citrate
Mobigesic Analgesic Tablets (Ascher)
p 509
Percogesic Tablets (Endo) p 409, 536
Sinutab Extra Strength Tablets
(Warner-Lambert) p 425, 647
Sinutab Tablets (Warner-Lambert)
p 425, 646

Phenyltoloxamine Dihydrogen Citrate
Momentum Muscular Backache
Formula (Whitehall) p 657

Phosphorus
Chelated Multi-Mineral Tablets
(Nature's Bounty) p 588
Lecithin Granules (Nature's Bounty)
p 589
One-A-Day Multivitamin Supplement
Plus Minerals (Miles) p 585

Piperonyl Butoxide
Rid (Pfipharmecs) p 418, 604

Plantago Seed
Konsyl (Burton, Parsons) p 407, 520
L. A. Formula (Burton, Parsons) p 407,
520

Polymyxin B Sulfate
BPN Ointment (Norwich-Eaton) p 592
Mycitracin Antibiotic Ointment (Upjohn)
p 424, 636
Septa Ointment (Circle) p 524
Terramycin Ointment (Pfipharmecs)
p 418, 605

Polyoxyethylene Dodecanol
Vaposteam (Vicks Health Care) p 640
Vicks Vaposteam (Vicks Health Care)
p 640

Polysorbate 80
Protexin Oral Rinse (Cetylite) p 523

Polyvinyl Alcohol
Liquifilm Tears (Allergan) p 406, 506
Preflex (Alcon/bp) p 405, 505
Prefrin Liquifilm (Allergan) p 405, 506
Tears Plus (Allergan) p 405, 506

Polyvinylpyrrolidone
Fomac Foam (Dermik) p 527

Potassium
Chelated Multi-Mineral Tablets
(Nature's Bounty) p 588
K-Forté Tablets (O'Connor) p 596
Potassium Tablets (Nature's Bounty)
p 589

Potassium Amino Acid Complex
Chelated Potassium Tablets (Nature's
Bounty) p 588

Potassium Bicarbonate
Alka-Seltzer Effervescent Antacid
(Miles) p 584

Potassium Chloride
K-Forté Tablets (O'Connor) p 596
Thermotabs (Beecham Products) p 512

Potassium Citrate
Hydra-Lyte (Jayco) p 546
K-Forté Tablets (O'Connor) p 596

Potassium Gluconate
K-Forté Tablets (O'Connor) p 596
Potassium Tablets (Nature's Bounty)
p 589
Potassium & B-6 Tablets (Nature's
Bounty) p 589
Water Pill Tablets (Nature's Bounty)
p 590
Water Pill w/Iron Tablets (Nature's
Bounty) p 590

Potassium Nitrate
DeWitt's Pills for Backache & Joint
Pains (DeWitt) p 409, 529

Potassium Sulfate
Obron-6 Tablets (Pfipharmecs) p 418,
604

Povidone
Adapettes (Alcon/bp) p 405, 504, 505
Tears Plus (Allergan) p 405, 506

Povidone-Iodine
Anbesol Antiseptic Anesthetic Liquid
(Whitehall) p 426, 652
Betadine Antiseptic Lubricating Gel
(Purdue Frederick) p 611
Betadine Douche (Purdue Frederick)
p 419, 611
Betadine Ointment (Purdue Frederick)
p 419, 612
Betadine Skin Cleanser (Purdue
Frederick) p 419, 611
Betadine Solution (Purdue Frederick)
p 419, 611
Isodine Antiseptic (Blair) p 513
Massengill Disposable Medicated
Douche (Beecham Products) p 511

Propylene Glycol
Diaparene Baby Wash Cloths
(Glenbrook) p 410, 541
Kerid Ear Drops (Blair) p 513
Skin Screen (Cetylite) p 523
Transi-Lube (Holland-Rantos) p 545

Propylhexedrine
Benzedrex Inhaler (Menley & James)
p 413, 574

Propylparaben
Buf Lotion (Riker) p 613
Transi-Lube (Holland-Rantos) p 545

Protease
Chew-Iron Tablets (Nature's Bounty)
p 588
Festal (Hoechst-Roussel) p 411, 544

Protein Hydrolysate
Methakote Diaper Rash Cream (Syntex)
p 633

Protein Preparations
NaturSlim II (NaturSlim) p 415, 590
Protein Tablets (Nature's Bounty)
p 589

Pseudoephedrine Hydrochloride
Ambenyl-D Decongestant Cough
Formula (Marion) p 412, 556
Cosanyl Cough Syrup (Health Care)
p 410, 542
Cosanyl-DM Cough Syrup (Health Care)
p 410, 542
CoTylenol Children's Liquid Cold
Formula (McNeil Consumer Products)
p 412, 560
CoTylenol Cold Formula Tablets and
Capsules (McNeil Consumer
Products) p 412, 559
CoTylenol Liquid Cold Formula (McNeil
Consumer Products) p 412, 559
Dimacol Capsules (Robins) p 420, 615

Dimacol Liquid (Robins) p 420, 615
First Sign (J.B. Williams)
Novahistine Cough & Cold Formula
(Dow Pharmaceuticals) p 532
Novahistine DMX (Dow
Pharmaceuticals) p 533
Novahistine Sinus Tablets (Dow
Pharmaceuticals) p 534
Robitussin-PE (Robins) p 420, 617
Ryna Liquid (Wallace) p 425, 643
Ryna-C Liquid (Wallace) p 425, 643
Ryna-CX Liquid (Wallace) p 425, 643
Viro-Med Liquid (Whitehall) p 659
Viro-Med Tablets (Whitehall) p 660

Pseudoephedrine Sulfate
Afrinol Repetabs Tablets (Schering)
p 421, 620
Chlor-Trimeton Decongestant Tablets
(Schering) p 421, 620

Psyllium Preparations
Effersyllium Instant Mix (Stuart) p 629
Konsyl (Burton, Parsons) p 407, 520
L. A. Formula (Burton, Parsons) p 407,
520
Metamucil (Searle Consumer Products)
p 423, 627
Metamucil, Instant Mix (Searle
Consumer Products) p 423, 628
Metamucil, Instant Mix, Orange Flavor
(Searle Consumer Products) p 423,
628
Metamucil Powder, Orange Flavor
(Searle Consumer Products) p 423,
628
Modane Bulk (Adria) p 503
Natrasan (Lank) p 548
Syllact (Wallace) p 425, 643

Pyrethrins
A-200 Pyrinate Liquid, Gel (Norcliff
Thayer) p 415, 591
Rid (Pfipharmecs) p 418, 604

Pyrethroids
Li-Ban Spray (Pfipharmecs) p 604

Pyridoxine
Beelith Tablets (Beach) p 509
Brewer's Yeast Powder (Debittered)
(Nature's Bounty) p 587
Brewer's Yeast Tablets (Nature's
Bounty) p 587
Bugs Bunny With Extra C Multivitamin
Supplement (Miles) p 585
Chocks Multivitamin Supplement
(Miles) p 584
Chocks Plus Iron Multivitamin
Supplement (Miles) p 584
Chocks-Bugs Bunny Multivitamin
Supplement (Miles) p 584
Chocks-Bugs Bunny Plus Iron
Multivitamin Supplement (Miles)
p 584
Flintstones Multivitamin Supplement
(Miles) p 584
Flintstones Plus Iron Multivitamin
Supplement (Miles) p 584
Flintstones With Extra C Multivitamin
Supplement (Miles) p 585
Geritol Liquid-High Potency Iron &
Vitamin Tonic (J.B. Williams) p 661
One-A-Day Core C 500 Multivitamin
Supplement (Miles) p 585
One-A-Day Multivitamin Supplement
(Miles) p 585
One-A-Day Multivitamin Supplement
Plus Iron (Miles) p 585
One-A-Day Multivitamin Supplement
Plus Minerals (Miles) p 585

**Pyridoxine Hydrochloride
(see under Vitamin B₆)**

Pyrilamine Maleate

Excedrin P.M. (Bristol-Myers) p 406, 518
4-Way Nasal Spray (Bristol-Myers) p 406, 518
Miles Nervine Nighttime Sleep-Aid (Miles) p 585
Primatene Tablets - M Formula (Whitehall) p 426, 658
Quiet World Analgesic/Sleeping Aid (Whitehall) p 659
Sleep-Eze Tablets (Whitehall) p 659
Sominex (J.B. Williams) p 662
Sunril Premenstrual Capsules (Schering) p 626
Triaminicol Decongestant Cough Syrup (Dorsey) p 409, 531
Tussagesic Tablets & Suspension (Dorsey) p 531
Ursinus Inlay-Tabs (Dorsey) p 532

Pyrithione Zinc

Danex Protein Enriched Dandruff Shampoo (Herbert) p 543

R

RNA

Brewer's Yeast Powder (Debittered) (Nature's Bounty) p 587
Brewer's Yeast Tablets (Nature's Bounty) p 587
RNA Tablets (Nature's Bounty) p 589
RNA/DNA Tablets (Nature's Bounty) p 589

Resorcinol

Acnomel Cream & Cake (Menley & James) p 413, 574
Bensulfoid Lotion (Poythress) p 610
BiCozene Creme (Creighton Products) p 408, 526
Lanacane Medicated Creme (Combe) p 408, 525
Vagisil Feminine Itching Medication (Combe) p 408, 526

Riboflavin

Allbee C-800 Plus Iron Tablets (Robins) p 420, 614
Allbee C-800 Tablets (Robins) p 420, 614
Allbee with C Capsules (Robins) p 420, 615
B-2 Tablets (Nature's Bounty) p 587
B Complex & B-12 Tablets (Nature's Bounty) p 587
B Complex & C (Time Release) Capsules (Nature's Bounty) p 587
B & C Liquid (Nature's Bounty) p 587
Brewer's Yeast Powder (Debittered) (Nature's Bounty) p 587
Brewer's Yeast Tablets (Nature's Bounty) p 587
Bugs Bunny With Extra C Multivitamin Supplement (Miles) p 585
Chocks Multivitamin Supplement (Miles) p 584
Chocks Plus Iron Multivitamin Supplement (Miles) p 584
Chocks-Bugs Bunny Multivitamin Supplement (Miles) p 584
Chocks-Bugs Bunny Plus Iron Multivitamin Supplement (Miles) p 584
Flintstones Multivitamin Supplement (Miles) p 584
Flintstones Plus Iron Multivitamin Supplement (Miles) p 584
Flintstones With Extra C Multivitamin Supplement (Miles) p 585
Fortespan Capsules (Menley & James) p 413, 577
Geritol Liquid-High Potency Iron & Vitamin Tonic (J.B. Williams) p 661
One-A-Day Core C 500 Multivitamin Supplement (Miles) p 585
One-A-Day Multivitamin Supplement (Miles) p 585
One-A-Day Multivitamin Supplement Plus Iron (Miles) p 585
One-A-Day Multivitamin Supplement Plus Minerals (Miles) p 585
Z-Bec Tablets (Robins) p 420, 617

Rose Hips

B Complex & C (Time Release) Capsules (Nature's Bounty) p 587
C-250 with Rose Hips Tablets (Nature's Bounty) p 587
C-300 with Rose Hips (Chewable) Tablets (Nature's Bounty) p 587
C-Complex Tablets (Nature's Bounty) p 588
C-Time-1500 Tablets (Nature's Bounty) p 588
Zacne Tablets (Nature's Bounty) p 415, 590

Rutin

Bio-Crest (Nutrition Control) p 595
C-Complex Tablets (Nature's Bounty) p 588
Rutin Tablets (Nature's Bounty) p 589

S

Saccharin

Necta Sweet Non-Caloric Sweetener (Norwich-Eaton) p 594

Salicylamide

DeWitt's Pills for Backache & Joint Pains (DeWitt) p 409, 529
Os-Cal-Gesic Tablets (Marion) p 558

Salicylic Acid

Acnaveen Bar (CooperCare) p 408, 526
Buf Acne Cleansing Bar (Riker) p 613
Compound W Solution (Whitehall) p 653
Derma+Soft Creme (Creighton Products) p 408, 527
Dry and Clear Medicated Acne Cleanser (Whitehall) p 656
Fomac Foam (Dermik) p 527
Fostex Cake (Westwood) p 649
Fostex Cream & Medicated Cleanser (Westwood) p 649
Freezone Solution (Whitehall) p 656
NP-27 Powder (Norwich-Eaton) p 595
Oxipor VHC Lotion for Psoriasis (Whitehall) p 657
Pernox (Westwood) p 650
Pernox Lotion (Westwood) p 650
Pragmatar Ointment (Menley & James) p 413, 578
Sebucare (Westwood) p 651
Sebulex and Sebulex Cream (Westwood) p 651
Sebulex with Protein (Westwood) p 651
Sebutone & Sebutone Cream (Westwood) p 651
Stri-Dex Medicated Pads (Lehn & Fink) p 555
Vanseb Cream & Lotion Dandruff Shampoo (Herbert) p 544
Wart-Off (Pfipharmecs) p 605

Salicylsalicylic Acid

Momentum Muscular Backache Formula (Whitehall) p 657
Vanseb-T Cream & Lotion Dandruff Shampoo (Herbert) p 544

Saline

Ocean Mist (Fleming) p 538

Salt Substitutes

Co-Salt (Norcliff Thayer) p 415, 591

Selenium

Selenium Tablets (Nature's Bounty) p 589

Selenium Sulfide

Selsun Blue Lotion (Abbott Consumer Products) p 405, 502

Senna

Herbal Laxative Tablets (Nature's Bounty) p 588

Senna Concentrates

Senokot Tablets/Granules (Purdue Frederick) p 419, 612

Sennosides (A & B)

Nytilax Tablets (Leeming) p 553

Sesame Oil

Shepard's Cream Lotion (Dermik) p 528

Shark Liver Oil

Preparation H Hemorrhoidal Ointment & Suppositories (Whitehall) p 426, 658

Silicone Preparations

Skin Screen (Cetylite) p 523

Simethicone

Di-Gel (Plough) p 418, 608
Gas-X Tablets (Creighton Products) p 408, 527
Gelusil-M (Parke-Davis) p 600
Gelusil-II Liquid & Tablets (Parke-Davis) p 601
Mylanta Liquid (Stuart) p 424, 631
Mylanta Tablets (Stuart) p 424, 631
Mylanta-II Liquid (Stuart) p 424, 631
Mylanta-II Tablets (Stuart) p 424, 631
Mylicon (Tablets & Drops) (Stuart) p 424, 631
Mylicon-80 Tablets (Stuart) p 424, 632
Simeco Suspension (Wyeth) p 427, 666

Sodium Bicarbonate

Alka-Seltzer Effervescent Antacid (Miles) p 584
Alka-Seltzer Effervescent Pain Reliever Antacid (Miles) p 583
Bisodol Antacid Tablets (Whitehall) p 653
Citrocarbonate Antacid (Upjohn) p 635
DeWitt's Antacid Powder (DeWitt) p 409, 529
Hydra-Lyte (Jayco) p 546
Massengill Liquid Concentrate (Beecham Products) p 511

Sodium Biphosphate

Preflex (Alcon/bp) p 405, 505

Sodium Borate

BoilnSoak (Alcon/bp) p 405, 505
Flex-Care (Alcon/bp) p 405, 505

Sodium Carboxymethylcellulose (see under Carboxymethylcellulose Sodium)

Sodium Chloride

Ayr Saline Nasal Mist (Ascher) p 508
Hydra-Lyte (Jayco) p 546
Ocean Mist (Fleming) p 538
Thermotabs (Beecham Products) p 512

Sodium Citrate

Chlor-Trimeton Expectorant (Schering) p 620
Citrocarbonate Antacid (Upjohn) p 635
Eno (Beecham Products) p 511
Formula 44 Cough Mixture (Vicks Health Care) p 424, 639
Hydra-Lyte (Jayco) p 546
Listermint Cinnamon Mouthwash & Gargle (Warner-Lambert) p 425, 645
Listermint Mouthwash & Gargle (Warner-Lambert) p 425, 645
Protect Toothpaste (Marion) p 412, 558
Vicks Cough Syrup (Vicks Health Care) p 641
Vicks Formula 44 Cough Mixture (Vicks Health Care) p 424, 639
Viro-Med Liquid (Whitehall) p 659

Sodium Fluoride
Fluorigard Anti-Cavity Dental Rinse
(Colgate-Palmolive) p 408, 525

Sodium Phenolate
Chloraseptic Cough Control Lozenges
(Norwich-Eaton) p 416, 593
Chloraseptic Gel (Norwich-Eaton) p 593
Chloraseptic Liquid & Spray
(Norwich-Eaton) p 416, 593
Chloraseptic Lozenges (Norwich-Eaton)
p 416, 593

Sodium Tartrate
Eno (Beecham Products) p 511

Sorbitol
Transi-Lube (Holland-Rantos) p 545

Soy Protein Concentrate
Slender Diet Meal Bars For Weight
Control (Carnation) p 521

Soybean Oil
Lecithin with Vitamin D Capsules
(Nature's Bounty) p 589
Super Wate-On Emulsion (Fleetwood)
p 410, 537

Soybean Preparations
I-Soyalac (Loma Linda) p 555
NaturSlim II (NaturSlim) p 415, 590
ProSobee (Mead Johnson Nutritional)
p 570
Soyalac: Liquid Concentrate,
Ready-to-Serve and Powder (Loma
Linda) p 555

Spirits of Turpentine
Vicks Vaporub (Vicks Health Care)
p 424, 642

Starch
Balmex Baby Powder (Macsil) p 556

Stearyl Alcohol
Johnson & Johnson First Aid Cream
(Johnson & Johnson) p 411, 547

Strontium Chloride Hexahydrate
Sensodyne Toothpaste (Block) p 513

Sudan III
F.S.K. (Fecal Staining Kit) (Jayco)
p 546

Sulfur
Acnaveen Bar (CooperCare) p 408,
526
Acnomel Cream & Cake (Menley &
James) p 413, 574
Buf Acne Cleansing Bar (Riker) p 613
Fostex CM (Westwood) p 649
Fostex Cake (Westwood) p 649
Fostex Cream & Medicated Cleanser
(Westwood) p 649
Sebulex and Sebulex Cream
(Westwood) p 651
Sebulex with Protein (Westwood) p 651
Sebutone & Sebutone Cream
(Westwood) p 651
Transact (Westwood) p 651
Vanseb Cream & Lotion Dandruff
Shampoo (Herbert) p 544
Vanseb-T Cream & Lotion Dandruff
Shampoo (Herbert) p 544

Sulfur (Colloidal)
Acnederm Lotion (Lannett) p 548
Bensulfoid Lotion (Poythress) p 610

Sulfur, Precipitated
Pragmatar Ointment (Menley & James)
p 413, 578

Sulfur Preparations
Fostril (Westwood) p 649
Pernox (Westwood) p 650
Pernox Lotion (Westwood) p 650
Xerac (Persōn & Covey) p 418, 603

T

Tannic Acid
Outgro Solution (Whitehall) p 657

Tar Preparations
Vanseb-T Cream & Lotion Dandruff
Shampoo (Herbert) p 544
Zetar Shampoo (Dermik) p 529

Tartaric Acid
Eno (Beecham Products) p 511

Terpin Hydrate
Tussagesic Tablets & Suspension
(Dorsey) p 531

Tetrahydronaphthalene
Cuprex (Beecham Products) p 510

Tetrahydrozoline Hydrochloride
Murine Plus Eye Drops (Abbott
Consumer Products) p 405, 502
Murine Regular Formula Eye Drops
(Abbott Consumer Products) p 405,
502
Visine A.C. Eye Drops (Leeming) p 554
Visine Eye Drops (Leeming) p 554

Thenyldiamine Hydrochloride
NTZ (Consumer Products Div.,
Winthrop) p 664

Theophylline
Bronkaid Tablets (Consumer Products
Div., Winthrop) p 663
Primatene Tablets - M Formula
(Whitehall) p 426, 658
Primatene Tablets - P Formula
(Whitehall) p 426, 658

Thiamine
B Complex & B-12 Tablets (Nature's
Bounty) p 587
B Complex & C (Time Release)
Capsules (Nature's Bounty) p 587
B & C Liquid (Nature's Bounty) p 587
Brewer's Yeast Powder (Debittered)
(Nature's Bounty) p 587
Brewer's Yeast Tablets (Nature's
Bounty) p 587
Bugs Bunny With Extra C Multivitamin
Supplement (Miles) p 585
Chew-Iron Tablets (Nature's Bounty)
p 588
Chocks Multivitamin Supplement
(Miles) p 584
Chocks Plus Iron Multivitamin
Supplement (Miles) p 584
Chocks-Bugs Bunny Multivitamin
Supplement (Miles) p 584
Chocks-Bugs Bunny Plus Iron
Multivitamin Supplement (Miles)
p 584
Flintstones Multivitamin Supplement
(Miles) p 584
Flintstones Plus Iron Multivitamin
Supplement (Miles) p 584
Flintstones With Extra C Multivitamin
Supplement (Miles) p 585
Geritol Liquid-High Potency Iron &
Vitamin Tonic (J.B. Williams) p 661
One-A-Day Core C 500 Multivitamin
Supplement (Miles) p 585
One-A-Day Multivitamin Supplement
(Miles) p 585
One-A-Day Multivitamin Supplement
Plus Iron (Miles) p 585
One-A-Day Multivitamin Supplement
Plus Minerals (Miles) p 585

Thiamine Hydrochloride
B-1 Tablets (Nature's Bounty) p 587
Fortespan Capsules (Menley & James)
p 413, 577

Thiamine Mononitrate
Allbee C-800 Plus Iron Tablets
(Robins) p 420, 614

Allbee C-800 Tablets (Robins) p 420,
614
Allbee with C Capsules (Robins) p 420,
615
Mega-B (Arco) p 508
Megadose (Arco) p 508
Z-Bec Tablets (Robins) p 420, 617

Thimerosal
Adapettes (Alcon/bp) p 405, 504, 505
BoilnSoak (Alcon/bp) p 405, 505
Collyrium Eye Lotion (Wyeth) p 417,
665
Collyrium with Ephedrine Eye Drops
(Wyeth) p 427, 665
Flex-Care (Alcon/bp) p 405, 505
Preflex (Alcon/bp) p 405, 505
Soaclens (Alcon/bp) p 405, 505

Thyme, Oil of
DeWitt's Oil for Ear Use (DeWitt)
p 409, 529

Thymol
Bensulfoid Lotion (Poythress) p 610
Listerine Antiseptic (Warner-Lambert)
p 425, 645
Vicks Vaporub (Vicks Health Care)
p 424, 642

Tincture of Benzoin Compound
Vaposteam (Vicks Health Care) p 640
Vicks Vaposteam (Vicks Health Care)
p 640

Tocopherols
E-200 Capsules (Nature's Bounty)
p 588
E-200 (Natural Complex) Capsules
(Nature's Bounty) p 588
E-400 Capsules (Nature's Bounty)
p 588
E-400 (Natural Complex) Capsules
(Nature's Bounty) p 588
E-600 (Natural Complex) Capsules
(Nature's Bounty) p 588
E-1000 (Natural Complex) Capsules
(Nature's Bounty) p 588
Emulsified E-200 Capsules (Nature's
Bounty) p 588

Tolnaftate
Aftate (Plough) p 418, 607
Tinactin Aerosol Powder 1% (Schering)
p 422, 626
Tinactin 1% Cream, Solution & Powder
(Schering) p 421, 626

Triclosan
Rhulicaine (Lederle) p 551
Solarcaine (Plough) p 418, 609

Triethanolamine
Buf Lotion (Riker) p 613

Triethanolamine Salicylate
Mobisyl Analgesic Creme (Ascher)
p 509
Myoflex Creme (Adria) p 504

Tripelennamine Hydrochloride
PBZ Cream (Geigy) p 410, 539
Rhulihist (Lederle) p 551

Tryptophan
Tryptophan Tablets (Nature's Bounty)
p 589

Tyloxapol
Preflex (Alcon/bp) p 405, 505

U

Undecylenic Acid
Desenex Foam (Pharmacraft) p 607
Desenex Ointment & Liquid
(Pharmacraft) p 607
Desenex Powders (Pharmacraft) p 607
Desenex Soap (Pharmacraft) p 607

NP-27 Liquid (Norwich-Eaton) p 595

Urea
Carmol 10 Lotion (Syntex) p 633
Carmol 20 Cream (Syntex) p 633
Kerid Ear Drops (Blair) p 513

Urea Preparations
Aquacare Dry Skin Cream & Lotion (Herbert) p 543
Aquacare/HP Dry Skin Cream & Lotion (Herbert) p 543
Debrox Drops (Marion) p 412, 556
Gly-Oxide Liquid (Marion) p 412, 557

Uva Ursi Extract
DeWitt's Pills for Backache & Joint Pains (DeWitt) p 409, 529
Odrinil (Fox) p 538
Water Pill Tablets (Nature's Bounty) p 590
Water Pill w/Iron Tablets (Nature's Bounty) p 590

V

Vinegar
Massengill Disposable Douche (Beecham Products) p 511

Vitamin A
Aqua-A (Anabolic) p 507
Bugs Bunny With Extra C Multivitamin Supplement (Miles) p 585
Chocks Multivitamin Supplement (Miles) p 584
Chocks Plus Iron Multivitamin Supplement (Miles) p 584
Chocks-Bugs Bunny Multivitamin Supplement (Miles) p 584
Chocks-Bugs Bunny Plus Iron Multivitamin Supplement (Miles) p 584
Flintstones Multivitamin Supplement (Miles) p 584
Flintstones Plus Iron Multivitamin Supplement (Miles) p 584
Flintstones With Extra C Multivitamin Supplement (Miles) p 585
Fortespan Capsules (Menley & James) p 413, 577
Halibut Liver Oil Capsules (Nature's Bounty) p 588
Megadose (Arco) p 508
Monster (Bristol-Myers) p 518
Monster with Iron (Bristol-Myers) p 519
One-A-Day Core C 500 Multivitamin Supplement (Miles) p 585
One-A-Day Multivitamin Supplement (Miles) p 585
One-A-Day Multivitamin Supplement Plus Iron (Miles) p 585
One-A-Day Multivitamin Supplement Plus Minerals (Miles) p 585
Oyster Calcium Tablets (Nature's Bounty) p 589
Pals (Bristol-Myers) p 519
Pals Plus Iron (Bristol-Myers) p 519
Tri-Vi-Sol (Mead Johnson Nutritional) p 572
Tri-Vi-Sol Vitamin Drops w/Iron (Mead Johnson Nutritional) p 573
Ultra "A" Capsules & Tablets (Nature's Bounty) p 589
Ultra "A & D" Tablets (Nature's Bounty) p 589
Vi-Penta Infant Drops (Roche) p 421, 618
Vi-Penta Multivitamin Drops (Roche) p 421, 618
Vitamin A Capsules & Tablets (Nature's Bounty) p 589
Vitamin A & D Tablets (Nature's Bounty) p 589
Zacne Tablets (Nature's Bounty) p 415, 590

Vitamin A Palmitate
A.C.N. (Persōn & Covey) p 603

Vitamins A & D
Balmex Ointment (Macsil) p 556
Carnation Instant Nonfat Dry Milk (Carnation) p 521

Cod Liver Oil Concentrate Tablets, Capsules (Schering) p 421, 621
Cod Liver Oil Concentrate Tablets w/Vitamin C (Schering) p 421, 621
Megadose (Arco) p 508
Obron-6 Tablets (Pfipharmecs) p 418, 604
Scott's Emulsion (Beecham Products) p 511
Stuart Formula Tablets, The (Stuart) p 424, 632
Stuart Prenatal Tablets (Stuart) p 632

Vitamin B₁
Allbee C-800 Plus Iron Tablets (Robins) p 420, 614
Allbee C-800 Tablets (Robins) p 420, 614
Allbee with C Capsules (Robins) p 420, 615
B-1 Tablets (Nature's Bounty) p 587
B-100 Tablets (Nature's Bounty) p 587
B Complex & B-12 Tablets (Nature's Bounty) p 587
B Complex & C (Time Release) Capsules (Nature's Bounty) p 587
B & C Liquid (Nature's Bounty) p 587
Bugs Bunny With Extra C Multivitamin Supplement (Miles) p 585
Chew-Iron Tablets (Nature's Bounty) p 588
Chocks Multivitamin Supplement (Miles) p 584
Chocks Plus Iron Multivitamin Supplement (Miles) p 584
Chocks-Bugs Bunny Multivitamin Supplement (Miles) p 584
Chocks-Bugs Bunny Plus Iron Multivitamin Supplement (Miles) p 584
Flintstones Multivitamin Supplement (Miles) p 584
Flintstones Plus Iron Multivitamin Supplement (Miles) p 584
Flintstones With Extra C Multivitamin Supplement (Miles) p 585
Mega-B (Arco) p 508
Megadose (Arco) p 508
Monster (Bristol-Myers) p 518
Monster with Iron (Bristol-Myers) p 519
Obron-6 Tablets (Pfipharmecs) p 418, 604
One-A-Day Core C 500 Multivitamin Supplement (Miles) p 585
One-A-Day Multivitamin Supplement (Miles) p 585
One-A-Day Multivitamin Supplement Plus Iron (Miles) p 585
One-A-Day Multivitamin Supplement Plus Minerals (Miles) p 585
Orexin Softab Tablets (Stuart) p 632
Pals (Bristol-Myers) p 519
Pals Plus Iron (Bristol-Myers) p 519
Stuart Formula Tablets, The (Stuart) p 424, 632
Stuart Prenatal Tablets (Stuart) p 632
Super Wate-On Emulsion (Fleetwood) p 410, 537
Tri-88 (Anabolic) p 507
Tri-B-Plex (Anabolic) p 508
Troph-Iron Liquid & Tablets (Menley & James) p 413, 579
Trophite Liquid & Tablets (Menley & James) p 413, 579
Z-Bec Tablets (Robins) p 420, 617

Vitamin B₂
Allbee C-800 Plus Iron Tablets (Robins) p 420, 614
Allbee C-800 Tablets (Robins) p 420, 614
Allbee with C Capsules (Robins) p 420, 615
B-2 Tablets (Nature's Bounty) p 587
B-100 Tablets (Nature's Bounty) p 587
B Complex & B-12 Tablets (Nature's Bounty) p 587
B Complex & C (Time Release) Capsules (Nature's Bounty) p 587
B & C Liquid (Nature's Bounty) p 587
Bugs Bunny With Extra C Multivitamin Supplement (Miles) p 585

Chocks Multivitamin Supplement (Miles) p 584
Chocks Plus Iron Multivitamin Supplement (Miles) p 584
Chocks-Bugs Bunny Multivitamin Supplement (Miles) p 584
Chocks-Bugs Bunny Plus Iron Multivitamin Supplement (Miles) p 584
Flintstones Multivitamin Supplement (Miles) p 584
Flintstones Plus Iron Multivitamin Supplement (Miles) p 584
Flintstones With Extra C Multivitamin Supplement (Miles) p 585
Mega-B (Arco) p 508
Megadose (Arco) p 508
Monster (Bristol-Myers) p 518
Monster with Iron (Bristol-Myers) p 519
Obron-6 Tablets (Pfipharmecs) p 418, 604
One-A-Day Core C 500 Multivitamin Supplement (Miles) p 585
One-A-Day Multivitamin Supplement (Miles) p 585
One-A-Day Multivitamin Supplement Plus Iron (Miles) p 585
One-A-Day Multivitamin Supplement Plus Minerals (Miles) p 585
Pals (Bristol-Myers) p 519
Pals Plus Iron (Bristol-Myers) p 519
Stuart Formula Tablets, The (Stuart) p 424, 632
Stuart Prenatal Tablets (Stuart) p 632
Super Wate-On Emulsion (Fleetwood) p 410, 537
Tri-B-Plex (Anabolic) p 508
Z-Bec Tablets (Robins) p 420, 617

Vitamin B₆
Allbee C-800 Plus Iron Tablets (Robins) p 420, 614
Allbee C-800 Tablets (Robins) p 420, 614
Allbee with C Capsules (Robins) p 420, 615
B6-Plus (Anabolic) p 507
B-6 Tablets (Nature's Bounty) p 587
B-100 Tablets (Nature's Bounty) p 587
B Complex & C (Time Release) Capsules (Nature's Bounty) p 587
B & C Liquid (Nature's Bounty) p 587
Beelith Tablets (Beach) p 509
Bugs Bunny With Extra C Multivitamin Supplement (Miles) p 585
Chocks Multivitamin Supplement (Miles) p 584
Chocks Plus Iron Multivitamin Supplement (Miles) p 584
Chocks-Bugs Bunny Multivitamin Supplement (Miles) p 584
Chocks-Bugs Bunny Plus Iron Multivitamin Supplement (Miles) p 584
Flintstones Multivitamin Supplement (Miles) p 584
Flintstones Plus Iron Multivitamin Supplement (Miles) p 584
Flintstones With Extra C Multivitamin. Supplement (Miles) p 585
Fortespan Capsules (Menley & James) p 413, 577
KLB6 Capsules (Nature's Bounty) p 588
Mega-B (Arco) p 508
Megadose (Arco) p 508
Monster (Bristol-Myers) p 518
Monster with Iron (Bristol-Myers) p 519
Obron-6 Tablets (Pfipharmecs) p 418, 604
One-A-Day Core C 500 Multivitamin Supplement (Miles) p 585
One-A-Day Multivitamin Supplement (Miles) p 585
One-A-Day Multivitamin Supplement Plus Iron (Miles) p 585
One-A-Day Multivitamin Supplement Plus Minerals (Miles) p 585
Orexin Softab Tablets (Stuart) p 632
Pals (Bristol-Myers) p 519
Pals Plus Iron (Bristol-Myers) p 519

Potassium & B-6 Tablets (Nature's Bounty) p 589
Simron Plus (Merrell-National) p 415, 582
Stuart Formula Tablets, The (Stuart) p 424, 632
Stuart Prenatal Tablets (Stuart) p 632
Super Wate-On Emulsion (Fleetwood) p 410, 537
Tri-Adrenopan (Anabolic) p 507
Tri-B-Plex (Anabolic) p 508
Ultra KLB6 Tablets (Nature's Bounty) p 589
Z-Bec Tablets (Robins) p 420, 617

Vitamin B₁₂
Allbee C-800 Plus Iron Tablets (Robins) p 420, 614
Allbee C-800 Tablets (Robins) p 420, 614
B12-Plus (Anabolic) p 507
B-12 Tablets (Nature's Bounty) p 587
B-100 Tablets (Nature's Bounty) p 587
B Complex & B-12 Tablets (Nature's Bounty) p 587
B Complex & C (Time Release) Capsules (Nature's Bounty) p 587
B & C Liquid (Nature's Bounty) p 587
Bugs Bunny With Extra C Multivitamin Supplement (Miles) p 585
Chew-Iron Tablets (Nature's Bounty) p 588
Chocks Multivitamin Supplement (Miles) p 584
Chocks Plus Iron Multivitamin Supplement (Miles) p 584
Chocks-Bugs Bunny Multivitamin Supplement (Miles) p 584
Chocks-Bugs Bunny Plus Iron Multivitamin Supplement (Miles) p 584
Flintstones Multivitamin Supplement (Miles) p 584
Flintstones Plus Iron Multivitamin Supplement (Miles) p 584
Flintstones With Extra C Multivitamin Supplement (Miles) p 585
Liver W/B-12 Tablets (Nature's Bounty) p 589
Mega-B (Arco) p 508
Megadose (Arco) p 508
Monster (Bristol-Myers) p 518
Monster with Iron (Bristol-Myers) p 519
Obron-6 Tablets (Pfipharmecs) p 418, 604
One-A-Day Core C 500 Multivitamin Supplement (Miles) p 585
One-A-Day Multivitamin Supplement (Miles) p 585
One-A-Day Multivitamin Supplement Plus Iron (Miles) p 585
One-A-Day Multivitamin Supplement Plus Minerals (Miles) p 585
Orexin Softab Tablets (Stuart) p 632
Pals (Bristol-Myers) p 519
Pals Plus Iron (Bristol-Myers) p 519
Simron Plus (Merrell-National) p 415, 582
Stuart Formula Tablets, The (Stuart) p 424, 632
Stuart Prenatal Tablets (Stuart) p 632
Super Wate-On Emulsion (Fleetwood) p 410, 537
Tri-88 (Anabolic) p 507
Tri-B-Plex (Anabolic) p 508
Troph-Iron Liquid & Tablets (Menley & James) p 413, 579
Trophite Liquid & Tablets (Menley & James) p 413, 579
Z-Bec Tablets (Robins) p 420, 617

Vitamin B Complex
B-50 Tablets (Nature's Bounty) p 587
B-100 Time Release Tablets (Nature's Bounty) p 587
B-125 Tablets (Nature's Bounty) p 587
Children's Chewables Tablets (Nature's Bounty) p 588
Lederplex Capsules, Liquid & Tablets (Lederle) p 551
Mega-B (Arco) p 508
Megadose (Arco) p 508

Orexin Softab Tablets (Stuart) p 632
Probec-T Tablets (Stuart) p 632
Stuart Formula Tablets, The (Stuart) p 424, 632
Stuart Prenatal Tablets (Stuart) p 632
Vi-Penta Multivitamin Drops (Roche) p 421, 618
Yeast Plus Tablets (Nature's Bounty) p 590

Vitamin B Complex with Vitamin C
Fumatinic Tablets (Laser) p 549
Mega-B with C Tablets (Nature's Bounty) p 589
Probec-T Tablets (Stuart) p 632
Roeribex Tablets (Pfipharmecs) p 418, 605
Stresscaps (Lederle) p 552
Stresstabs 600 (Lederle) p 411, 552
Stresstabs 600 with Iron (Lederle) p 411, 552
Stresstabs 600 with Zinc (Lederle) p 411, 552
Surbex-T (Abbott) p 503
Thera-Combex H-P (Parke-Davis) p 602

Vitamin C
A.C.N. (Persōn & Covey) p 603
Acerola C (Nature's Bounty) p 587
Allbee C-800 Plus Iron Tablets (Robins) p 420, 614
Allbee C-800 Tablets (Robins) p 420, 614
Allbee with C Capsules (Robins) p 420, 615
B Complex & C (Time Release) Capsules (Nature's Bounty) p 587
B & C Liquid (Nature's Bounty) p 587
Bio-Crest (Nutrition Control) p 595
Bugs Bunny With Extra C Multivitamin Supplement (Miles) p 585
C-250 with Rose Hips Tablets (Nature's Bounty) p 587
C-300 with Rose Hips (Chewable) Tablets (Nature's Bounty) p 587
C-500 with Rose Hips Tablets (Nature's Bounty) p 587
C-1000 with Rose Hips Tablets (Nature's Bounty) p 587
C-Complex Tablets (Nature's Bounty) p 588
C Liquid (Nature's Bounty) p 588
C-Time-750 Time Release Tablets (Nature's Bounty) p 588
C-Time-1500 Tablets (Nature's Bounty) p 588
Ce-Vi-Sol (Mead Johnson Nutritional) p 562
Chocks Multivitamin Supplement (Miles) p 584
Chocks Plus Iron Multivitamin Supplement (Miles) p 584
Chocks-Bugs Bunny Multivitamin Supplement (Miles) p 584
Chocks-Bugs Bunny Plus Iron Multivitamin Supplement (Miles) p 584
Cod Liver Oil Concentrate Tablets w/Vitamin C (Schering) p 421, 621
Ferancee Chewable Tablets (Stuart) p 629
Ferancee-HP Tablets (Stuart) p 629
Flintstones Multivitamin Supplement (Miles) p 584
Flintstones Plus Iron Multivitamin Supplement (Miles) p 584
Flintstones With Extra C Multivitamin Supplement (Miles) p 585
Fortespan Capsules (Menley & James) p 413, 577
Fumatinic Tablets (Laser) p 549
K-Forté Tablets (O'Connor) p 596
Mol-Iron Tablets w/Vitamin C (Schering) p 421, 626
Monster (Bristol-Myers) p 518
Monster with Iron (Bristol-Myers) p 519
Obron-6 Tablets (Pfipharmecs) p 418, 604
One-A-Day Core C 500 Multivitamin Supplement (Miles) p 585
One-A-Day Multivitamin Supplement (Miles) p 585

One-A-Day Multivitamin Supplement Plus Iron (Miles) p 585
One-A-Day Multivitamin Supplement Plus Minerals (Miles) p 585
Pals (Bristol-Myers) p 519
Pals Plus Iron (Bristol-Myers) p 519
Probec-T Tablets (Stuart) p 632
Simron Plus (Merrell-National) p 415, 582
Stuart Formula Tablets, The (Stuart) p 424, 632
Stuart Prenatal Tablets (Stuart) p 632
Stuartinic Tablets (Stuart) p 424, 632
Tri-Adrenopan (Anabolic) p 507
Tri-C-500 (Anabolic) p 508
Tri-Vi-Sol (Mead Johnson Nutritional) p 572
Tri-Vi-Sol Vitamin Drops w/Iron (Mead Johnson Nutritional) p 573
Vergo (Daywell) p 527
Vi-Penta Infant Drops (Roche) p 421, 618
Vi-Penta Multivitamin Drops (Roche) p 421, 618
Vitamin C Crystals (Nature's Bounty) p 588
Viterra C (Pfipharmecs) p 418, 605
Zacne Tablets (Nature's Bounty) p 415, 590
Z-Bec Tablets (Robins) p 420, 617

Vitamin D
Bone Meal with Vitamin D Tablets (Nature's Bounty) p 587
Bugs Bunny With Extra C Multivitamin Supplement (Miles) p 585
Chocks Multivitamin Supplement (Miles) p 584
Chocks Plus Iron Multivitamin Supplement (Miles) p 584
Chocks-Bugs Bunny Multivitamin Supplement (Miles) p 584
Chocks-Bugs Bunny Plus Iron Multivitamin Supplement (Miles) p 584
Flintstones Multivitamin Supplement (Miles) p 584
Flintstones Plus Iron Multivitamin Supplement (Miles) p 584
Flintstones With Extra C Multivitamin Supplement (Miles) p 585
Fortespan Capsules (Menley & James) p 413, 577
Halibut Liver Oil Capsules (Nature's Bounty) p 588
Megadose (Arco) p 508
Monster (Bristol-Myers) p 518
Monster with Iron (Bristol-Myers) p 519
One-A-Day Core C 500 Multivitamin Supplement (Miles) p 585
One-A-Day Multivitamin Supplement (Miles) p 585
One-A-Day Multivitamin Supplement Plus Iron (Miles) p 585
One-A-Day Multivitamin Supplement Plus Minerals (Miles) p 585
Os-Cal Forte Tablets (Marion) p 558
Os-Cal Plus Tablets (Marion) p 558
Os-Cal Tablets (Marion) p 412, 558
Os-Cal-Gesic Tablets (Marion) p 558
Pals (Bristol-Myers) p 519
Pals Plus Iron (Bristol-Myers) p 519
Super Wate-On Emulsion (Fleetwood) p 410, 537
Tri-Vi-Sol (Mead Johnson Nutritional) p 572
Tri-Vi-Sol Vitamin Drops w/Iron (Mead Johnson Nutritional) p 573
Ultra "A & D" Tablets (Nature's Bounty) p 589
Ultra "D" Tablets (Nature's Bounty) p 589
Vi-Penta Infant Drops (Roche) p 421, 618
Vi-Penta Multivitamin Drops (Roche) p 421, 618
Vitamin A & D Tablets (Nature's Bounty) p 589
Vitamin D Tablets (Nature's Bounty) p 590

Vitamin D₂

Oyster Calcium Tablets (Nature's Bounty) p 589

Vitamin D₃

Carnation Evaporated Milk (Carnation) p 520

Vitamin E

Allbee C-800 Plus Iron Tablets (Robins) p 420, 614
Allbee C-800 Tablets (Robins) p 420, 614
Bugs Bunny With Extra C Multivitamin Supplement (Miles) p 585
Chocks Multivitamin Supplement (Miles) p 584
Chocks Plus Iron Multivitamin Supplement (Miles) p 584
Chocks-Bugs Bunny Multivitamin Supplement (Miles) p 584
Chocks-Bugs Bunny Plus Iron Multivitamin Supplement (Miles) p 584
E-200 Capsules (Nature's Bounty) p 588
E-200 (Natural Complex) Capsules (Nature's Bounty) p 588
E-400 Capsules (Nature's Bounty) p 588
E-400 (Natural Complex) Capsules (Nature's Bounty) p 588
E-600 (Natural Complex) Capsules (Nature's Bounty) p 588
E-1000 (Natural Complex) Capsules (Nature's Bounty) p 588
Emulsified E-200 Capsules (Nature's Bounty) p 588
Flintstones Multivitamin Supplement (Miles) p 584
Flintstones Plus Iron Multivitamin Supplement (Miles) p 584
Flintstones With Extra C Multivitamin Supplement (Miles) p 585
Megadose (Arco) p 508
One-A-Day Core C 500 Multivitamin Supplement (Miles) p 585
One-A-Day Multivitamin Supplement (Miles) p 585
One-A-Day Multivitamin Supplement Plus Iron (Miles) p 585
One-A-Day Multivitamin Supplement Plus Minerals (Miles) p 585
Stuart Formula Tablets, The (Stuart) p 424, 632
Stuart Prenatal Tablets (Stuart) p 632
Vi-Penta Infant Drops (Roche) p 421, 618
Vi-Penta Multivitamin Drops (Roche) p 421, 618
Viterra E (Pfipharmecs) p 418, 605
Wheat Germ Oil Capsules (Nature's Bounty) p 590
Zacne Tablets (Nature's Bounty) p 415, 590
Z-Bec Tablets (Robins) p 420, 617

Vitamins, Multiple

Optilets-500 (Abbott) p 503
Unicap Capsules & Tablets (Upjohn) p 636
Unicap Chewable Tablets (Upjohn) p 636
Unicap Senior Tablets (Upjohn) p 636

Vitamins, Supplement

Natabec Kapseals (Parke-Davis) p 602
Obron-6 Tablets (Pfipharmecs) p 418, 604

Vitamins with Minerals

Centrum (Lederle) p 411, 549
Feminins Tablets (Mead Johnson) p 563
Filibon (Lederle) p 550

Geritol Tablets - High Potency Iron & Vitamin Tablets (J.B. Williams) p 661
Gevrabon Liquid (Lederle) p 550
Gevral T Tablets (Lederle) p 550
Gevral Tablets (Lederle) p 550
Lactocal Tablets (Laser) p 549
Megadose (Arco) p 508
Myadec (Parke-Davis) p 602
Natabec Kapseals (Parke-Davis) p 602
Optilets-M-500 (Abbott) p 503
Poly-Vi-Sol Chewable Vitamin Tablets with Iron (Mead Johnson Nutritional) p 568
Poly-Vi-Sol Vitamin Drops with Iron (Mead Johnson Nutritional) p 568
Stuart Formula Tablets, The (Stuart) p 424, 632
Stuart Prenatal Tablets (Stuart) p 632
Stuartinic Tablets (Stuart) p 424, 632
Surbex-750 with Iron (Abbott) p 503
Surbex-750 with Zinc (Abbott) p 503
Unicap M Tablets (Upjohn) p 424, 636
Unicap Plus Iron Tablets (Upjohn) p 636
Unicap T Tablets (Upjohn) p 424, 637
Viterra High Potency (Pfipharmecs) p 418, 605
Viterra Original Formula (Pfipharmecs) p 418, 605

W

Wheat Germ Oil

Wheat Germ Oil Capsules (Nature's Bounty) p 590

Witch Hazel

Cleansing Pads by the Makers of Preparation H Hemorrhoidal Remedies (Whitehall) p 653
Mediconet (Medicone) p 573
Tucks Cream & Ointment (Parke-Davis) p 602
Tucks Premoistened Pads (Parke-Davis) p 602

X

Xylometazoline Hydrochloride

Dristan Long Lasting Nasal Mist, Regular & Menthol (Whitehall) p 426, 655
4-Way Long Acting Nasal Spray (Bristol-Myers) p 406, 518
Neo-Synephrine II Long Acting Nasal Spray (Consumer Products Div., Winthrop) p 663
Otrivin (Geigy) p 410, 539
Sine-Off Once-A-Day Sinus Spray (Menley & James) p 413, 579
Sinex Long-Acting Decongestant Nasal Spray (Vicks Health Care) p 424, 640
Sinutab Long-Lasting Decongestant Nasal Spray (Warner-Lambert) p 425, 647
Vicks Sinex Long-Acting Decongestant Nasal Spray (Vicks Health Care) p 424, 640

Y

Yeast

Brewer's Yeast Powder (Debittered) & Tablets (Nature's Bounty) p 587
NaturSlim II (NaturSlim) p 415, 590

Z

Zinc

Chelated Multi-Mineral Tablets (Nature's Bounty) p 588

Megadose (Arco) p 508
Obron-6 Tablets (Pfipharmecs) p 418, 604
One-A-Day Multivitamin Supplement Plus Minerals (Miles) p 585
Z-Bec Tablets (Robins) p 420, 617

Zinc Amino Acid Chelate

Chelated Zinc Tablets (Nature's Bounty) p 588

Zinc Chloride

Freezone Solution (Whitehall) p 656
Listermint Cinnamon Mouthwash & Gargle (Warner-Lambert) p 425, 645
Listermint Mouthwash & Gargle (Warner-Lambert) p 425, 645
Protexin Oral Rinse (Cetylite) p 523

Zinc Gluconate

Megadose (Arco) p 508
Zacne Tablets (Nature's Bounty) p 415, 590
Zinc Tablets (Nature's Bounty) p 590

Zinc Oxide

Anusol Ointment (Parke-Davis) p 599
Anusol Suppositories (Parke-Davis) p 599
Balmex Baby Powder (Macsil) p 556
Balmex Ointment (Macsil) p 556
Bensulfoid Lotion (Poythress) p 610
Caldesene Medicated Ointment (Pharmacraft) p 606
Caldesene Medicated Powder (Pharmacraft) p 606
Calamatum Lotion, Ointment, Spray (Blair) p 512
Derma Medicone Ointment (Medicone) p 573
Desitin Ointment (Leeming) p 553
HTO Stainless Manzan Hemorrhoidal Tissue Ointment (DeWitt) p 409, 530
Medicone Dressing Cream (Medicone) p 573
Rectal Medicone Suppositories (Medicone) p 573
Rectal Medicone Unguent (Medicone) p 574
Wyanoid Ointment (Wyeth) p 427, 666
Wyanoids Hemorrhoidal Suppositories (Wyeth) p 427, 666
Zinc Oxide Ointment (Norwich-Eaton) p 595

Zinc Pyrithione

DHS Zinc Shampoo (Persōn & Covey) p 418, 603
Head & Shoulders (Procter & Gamble) p 610
Zincon Dandruff Shampoo (Lederle) p 552

Zinc Sulfate

Chelated Minerals (Nutrition Control)
Orazinc (Mericon) p 580
Surbex-750 with Zinc (Abbott) p 503
Visine A.C. Eye Drops (Leeming) p 554
Zinc Tabs (Mericon) p 580

Zinc Undecylenate

Cruex Medicated Cream (Pharmacraft) p 606
Cruex Medicated Powder (Pharmacraft) p 606
Desenex Ointment & Liquid (Pharmacraft) p 607
Desenex Powders (Pharmacraft) p 607
Desenex Soap (Pharmacraft) p 607
NP-27 Spray Powder (Norwich-Eaton) p 595

Zirconium Oxide

Rhulicream (Lederle) p 551
Rhulihist (Lederle) p 551

MEMORANDUM

MEMORANDUM

MEMORANDUM

Product Identification Section

This section is designed to help you identify products and their packaging.

Participating manufacturers have included selected products in full color. Where capsules and tablets are included they are shown in actual size. Packages generally are reduced in size.

For more information on products included, refer to the description in the PRODUCT INFORMATION SECTION or check directly with the manufacturer.

While every effort has been made to reproduce products faithfully, this section should be considered only as a quick-reference identification aid.

PRODUCT NAME INDEX

A

A and D Ointment (Schering) 421
A.R.M. Allergy Relief Medicine
  (Menley & James) 413
A-200 Pyrinate Liquid (Norcliff Thayer) 415
Acid Mantle Creme and Lotion (Dorsey) 409
Acnaveen (CooperCare) 408
Acnomel Cake and Acne Cream
  (Menley & James) 413
Adapettes (Alcon/bp) 405
Afrin Menthol Nasal Spray 0.05%
  (Schering) 421
Afrin Nasal Spray 0.05%
  (Schering) 421
Afrin Nose Drops (Schering) 421
Afrinol Repetabs Tablets (Schering) 421
Aftate For Athlete's Foot (Plough) 418
Aftate For Jock Itch (Plough) 419
Allbee C-800 Plus Iron Tablets (Robins) 420
Allbee C-800 Tablets (Robins) 420
Allbee With C Capsules (Robins) 420
Allimin Filmcoated Tablet
  (Health Care Industries) 410
Almay Cleansers (Almay) 406
Almay Hair Care (Almay) 406
Almay Make-Up (Almay) 406
Almay Moisturizers (Almay) 406
Almay Purifiers (Almay) 406
ALternaGEL (Stuart) 423
Aludrox Tablets and Suspension (Wyeth) 427
Ambenyl-D (Marion) 412
Amphojel Tablets and Suspension
  (Wyeth) 427
Anacin Analgesic Capsules
  (Whitehall) 426
Anacin Analgesic Capsules,
  Maximum Strength (Whitehall) 426
Anacin Analgesic Tablets (Whitehall) 426
Anacin Analgesic Tablets, Maximum
  Strength (Whitehall) 426
Anacin-3 (Whitehall) 426
Anbesol (Whitehall) 426
Answer (Carter Products) 407
Antacid Powder (DeWitt) 409
Anusol Suppositories and Ointment
  (Parke-Davis) 417
Arthritis Pain Formula (Whitehall) 426
Arthritis Strength Bufferin (Bristol-Myers) 406
Aspergum (Plough) 419
Aveeno Bar (CooperCare) 408
Aveeno Colloidal Oatmeal (CooperCare) 408
Aveeno Oilated (CooperCare) 408

B

Baby Cough Syrup (DeWitt) 409
Bayer Aspirin (Glenbrook) 410
Bayer Children's Chewable Aspirin
  (Glenbrook) 410
Bayer Timed-Release Aspirin
  (Glenbrook) 410
Because Contraceptor
  (Schering/Emko) 421
Benadryl Antihistamine Cream
  (Parke-Davis) 417
Benylin DM Cough Syrup (Parke-Davis) 417
Benzedrex Inhaler (Menley & James) 413
Betadine Antiseptic Gauze Pad
  (Purdue Frederick) 420
Betadine Douche (Purdue Frederick) 419
Betadine Douche Kit (Purdue Frederick) 419
Betadine Ointment (Purdue Frederick) 419
Betadine Skin Cleanser
  (Purdue Frederick) 420
Betadine Solution (Purdue Frederick) 420
Betadine Viscous Formula Antiseptic
  Gauze Pad (Purdue Frederick) 420
BiCozene Creme (Culbro) 408

BoilnSoak (Alcon/bp) 405
Bonine Tablets (Pfipharmecs) 418
Bufferin (Bristol-Myers) 406
Buf-Puf (Riker) 420

C

C3 Cold-Cough Capsules
  (Menley & James) 413
Caladryl Lotion (Parke-Davis) 417
Cama Inlay-Tabs (Dorsey) 409
Carter's Little Pills (Carter Products) 407
Centrum (Lederle) 411
Cēpacol Anesthetic Troches
  (Merrell-National) 415
Cēpacol Mouthwash/Gargle
  (Merrell-National) 415
Cēpacol Throat Lozenges
  (Merrell-National) 415
Cēpastat Sore Throat Lozenges
  (Merrell-National) 415
Cēpastat Sore Throat Lozenges,
  Children's (Merrell-National) 415
Cēpastat Sore Throat Spray/Gargle
  (Merrell-National) 415
Chap Stick Lip Balm (Miller-Morton) 415
Chap Stick Sunblock 15 Lip Balm
  (Miller-Morton) 415
Charcocaps (Requa) 420
Chloraseptic Cough Control
  Lozenges (Norwich-Eaton) 416
Chloraseptic Liquid (Norwich-Eaton) 416
Chloraseptic Lozenges (Norwich-Eaton) 416
Chlor-Trimeton Allergy Syrup (Schering) 421
Chlor-Trimeton Allergy Tablets
  (Schering) 422
Chlor-Trimeton Decongestant Tablets
  (Schering) 422
Chlor-Trimeton Long-Acting Allergy
  Repetabs Tablets (Schering) 422
Clear Eyes (Abbott) 405
Clearasil Acne Treatment Cream
  (Vicks Toiletry) 424
Clearasil 5% Benzoyl Peroxide Lotion
  Acne Treatment (Vicks Toiletry) 424
Clens (Alcon/bp) 405
Cod Liver Oil Concentrate Capsules
  (Schering/White) 422
Cod Liver Oil Concentrate Tablets
  (Schering/White) 422
Cod Liver Oil Concentrate Tablets
  W/Vitamin C (Schering/White) 422
Collyrium Eye Lotion (Wyeth) 427
Comtrex Capsules (Bristol-Myers) 406
Comtrex Liquid (Bristol-Myers) 406
Comtrex Tablets (Bristol-Myers) 406
Conceptrol Birth Control Cream
  (Ortho—Cons. Prods.) 416
Conceptrol Birth Control Cream
  Disposable (Ortho—Cons. Prods.) 416
Conceptrol Shields (Ortho—Cons. Prods.) 417
Conceptrol Supreme
  (Ortho—Cons. Prods.) 417
Congespirin Cold Tablets (Bristol-Myers) 406
Congespirin Liquid Cold Medicine
  (Bristol-Myers) 406
Contac (Menley & James) 413
Contac Jr. (Menley & James) 413
Coricidin Children's Cough Syrup
  (Schering) 422
Coricidin Cough Syrup (Schering) 422
Coricidin 'D' Decongestant
  Tablets (Schering) 422
Coricidin Decongestant Nasal Mist
  (Schering) 422
Coricidin Demilets Tablets (Schering) 422
Coricidin Medilets Tablets (Schering) 422

Coricidin Sinus Headache Tablets
  (Schering) 422
Coricidin Tablets (Schering) 422
Correctol Laxative (Plough) 419
Cortaid Cream (0.5%) (Upjohn) 424
Cortaid Lotion (0.5%) (Upjohn) 424
Cortaid Ointment (0.5%) (Upjohn) 424
Cortril 1/2% (Pfipharmecs) 418
Coryban-D Cold Capsules & Cough
  Syrup (Pfipharmecs) 418
Co-Salt (Norcliff Thayer) 415
Cosanyl Cough Syrup
  (Health Care Industries) 410
Cosanyl-DM Cough Syrup
  (Health Care Industries) 411
CoTylenol Cold Formula Capsules
  & Tablets (McNeil Consumer) 412
CoTylenol Liquid Cold Formula
  (McNeil Consumer) 412
CoTylenol Liquid Cold Formula,
  Children's (McNeil Consumer) 412
Cushion Grip (Plough) 419

D

DHS Shampoo (Persōn & Covey) 418
DHS Tar Shampoo (Persōn & Covey) 418
DHS Zinc Dandruff Shampoo
  (Persōn & Covey) 418
Datril (Bristol-Myers) 406
Datril 500 (Bristol-Myers) 407
Daycare Multi-Symptom Colds
  Medicine Capsules (Vicks Health Care) 424
Daycare Multi-Symptom Colds
  Medicine Liquid
  (Vicks Health Care) 424
Debrox (Marion) 412
Delfen Contraceptive Foam
  (Ortho—Cons. Prods.) 417
Demazin Decongestant-
  Antihistamine Repetabs Tablets
  and Syrup (Schering) 422
Denorex (Whitehall) 426
Derma + Soft Creme (Culbro) 408
Dermassage (Colgate-Palmolive) 408
Dermolate Anal-Itch Ointment
  (Schering) 422
Dermolate Anti-Itch Cream and Spray
  (Schering) 422
Dermolate Scalp-Itch Lotion (Schering) 422
Dex-A-Diet II Capsules (O'Connor) 416
Dialose (Stuart) 423
Dialose Plus (Stuart) 423
Diaparene Baby Powder (Glenbrook) 410
Diaparene Baby Wash Cloths
  (Glenbrook) 410
Dietac Capsules (Menley & James) 413
Dietac Drops (Menley & James) 413
Dietac Tablets (Menley & James) 413
Di-Gel (Plough) 419
Dimacol Capsules (Robins) 420
Dimetane Decongestant Elixir (Robins) 420
Dimetane Decongestant Tablets
  (Robins) 421
Dimetane Elixir (Robins) 420
Dimetane Tablets (Robins) 420
Dorcol Pediatric Cough Syrup (Dorsey) 409
Doxidan (Hoechst-Roussel) 411
Dramamine (Searle Consumer) 423
Dramamine Junior (Searle Consumer) 423
Dristan Capsules (Whitehall) 427
Dristan Long Lasting Nasal Mist
  (Whitehall) 426
Dristan Nasal Mist (Whitehall) 426
Dristan Tablets (Whitehall) 427
Dulcolax Suppositories
  (Boehringer Ingelheim) 406

D

Dulcolax Tablets (Boehringer Ingelheim) 406
Duration Nasal Spray and Nose Drops (Plough) 419

E

e.p.t. In Home Early Pregnancy Test (Warner-Lambert) 425
Eclipse Sunscreen Products (Herbert) 411
Ecotrin Tablets (Menley & James) 414
Effersyllium Instant Mix (Stuart) 423
Emko Contraceptive Foam (Schering/Emko) 422
Emko Pre-Fil Contraceptive Foam (Schering/Emko) 422
Emulave (CooperCare) 408
Encare (Norwich-Eaton) 416
Esotérica (Norcliff Thayer) 416
Excedrin Capsules (Bristol-Myers) 407
Excedrin P.M. (Bristol-Myers) 407
Excedrin Tablets (Bristol-Myers) 407
Ex-Lax (Culbro) 408

F

Feosol Elixir (Menley & James) 414
Feosol Plus (Menley & James) 414
Feosol Spansule Capsules (Menley & James) 414
Feosol Tablets (Menley & James) 414
Ferancee-HP (Stuart) 423
Festal (Hoechst-Roussel) 411
First Aid Cream (Johnson & Johnson) 411
Flex-Care (Alcon/bp) 405
Fluorigard (Colgate-Palmolive) 408
Formula 44 (Vicks Health Care) 425
Formula 44D (Vicks Health Care) 425
Fortespan Capsules (Menley & James) 414
4-Way Cold Tablets (Bristol-Myers) 407
4-Way Long Acting Nasal Spray (Bristol-Myers) 407
4-Way Nasal Spray (Bristol-Myers) 407

G

Gas-X (Culbro) 408
Gaviscon Antacid Tablets (Marion) 412
Gaviscon Liquid Antacid (Marion) 412
Gaviscon-2 Antacid Tablets (Marion) 412
Gelusil (Parke-Davis) 418
Gly-Oxide Liquid (Marion) 412

H

Halls Mentho-Lyptus Cough Tablets (Warner-Lambert) 425
Headache Powders (Goody's) 410
Hemorrhoidal Tissue Ointment (DeWitt) 409
Hibiclens (Stuart) 423

I

Icy Hot (Searle Consumer) 423
Intercept Contraceptive Inserts (Ortho—Cons. Prods.) 417

J

Johnson's Baby Bath (Johnson & Johnson) 411

K

Kaopectate (Upjohn) 424
Kaopectate Concentrate (Upjohn) 424
Kasof (Stuart) 423
Konsyl (Burton, Parsons) 407

L

L.A. Formula (Burton, Parsons) 407
LactAid (SugarLo) 424
Lactinex Tablets & Granules (Hynson, Westcott & Dunning) 411
Lanacane (Combe) 408
Lanacort (Combe) 408
Li-Ban Spray (Pfipharmecs) 418
Liquifilm Tears (Allergan) 405
Liquiprin (Norcliff Thayer) 416

M

Listermint Mouthwash and Gargle (Warner-Lambert) 425
Listerine Antiseptic (Warner-Lambert) 425
Lubath Bath Oil (Warner-Lambert) 426
Lubriderm Lotion (Warner-Lambert) 426

Maltsupex Liquid (Wallace) 425
Maltsupex Powder (Wallace) 425
Massé Breast Cream (Ortho—Cons. Prods.) 417
Maxi Unshine Oil Free Make-Up (Max Factor) 409
Maxi Unshine 100% Oil Free Blotting Powder (Max Factor) 409
Maxi Unshine 100% Oil Free Blushing Powder (Max Factor) 410
Mersene (Colgate-Palmolive) 408
Metamucil (Searle Consumer) 423
Midol (Glenbrook) 410
Mitrolan Chewable Tablets (Robins) 421
Modane (Adria) 405
Mol-Iron Chronosule Capsules (Schering/White) 423
Mol-Iron Tablets (Schering/White) 423
Mol-Iron with Vitamin C Chronosule Capsules (Schering/White) 423
Mol-Iron with Vitamin C Tablets (Schering/White) 423
Murine Ear Drops (Abbott) 405
Murine Ear Wax Removal System (Abbott) 405
Murine Plus (Abbott) 405
Murine Regular Formula (Abbott) 405
Myadec (Parke-Davis) 418
Mycitracin Antibiotic Ointment (Upjohn) 424
Mylanta Liquid (Stuart) 423
Mylanta Tablets (Stuart) 423
Mylanta-II Liquid and Tablets (Stuart) 424
Mylicon (Stuart) 424
Mylicon-80 (Stuart) 424
Myoflex (Adria) 405

N

NaturSlim II (NaturSlim) 415
No-Doz Tablets (Bristol-Myers) 407
Norforms Feminine Deodorants (Norwich-Eaton) 416
Norwich Aspirin (Norwich-Eaton) 416
Nupercainal Anesthetic Ointment (Ciba) 407
Nupercainal Hemorrhoidal Suppositories (Ciba) 407
Nupercainal Pain-Relief Cream (Ciba) 407
Nyquil Nighttime Colds Medicine (Vicks Health Care) 425

O

Oil For Ear Use (DeWitt) 409
Oil-O-Sol Liquid (Health Care Industries) 411
Ornacol Cough & Cold Capsule & Liquid (Menley & James) 414
Ornex Capsules (Menley & James) 414
Ortho Disposable Vaginal Applicators (Ortho—Cons. Prods.) 417
Ortho Personal Lubricant (Ortho—Cons. Prods.) 417
Ortho-Creme Contraceptive Cream (Ortho—Cons. Prods.) 417
Ortho-Gynol Contraceptive Jelly (Ortho—Cons. Prods.) 417
Os-Cal Tablets (Marion) 412
Otrivin 0.1% Nasal Drops (Geigy) 410
Otrivin 0.1% Nasal Spray (Geigy) 410
Otrivin 0.05% Pediatric Nasal Drops (Geigy) 410
Oxy-5 Lotion (Norcliff Thayer) 416
Oxy-10 Lotion (Norcliff Thayer) 416
Oxy Wash (Norcliff Thayer) 416

P

PBZ Cream (Geigy) 410
Pepto-Bismol Liquid and Tablets (Norwich-Eaton) 416
Percogesic (Endo) 409
Percy Medicine (Merrick) 415
Phillips' Milk of Magnesia (Glenbrook) 410
Pills For Backache & Joint Pains (DeWitt) 409
Pragmatar Ointment (Menley & James) 414
Preflex (Alcon/bp) 405
Prefrin Liquifilm (Allergan) 405
Preparation H Hemorrhoidal Ointment (Whitehall) 427
Preparation H Hemorrhoidal Suppositories (Whitehall) 427
Pretts Tablets (Marion) 412
Primatene Mist (Whitehall) 427
Primatene Tablets (Whitehall) 427
Privine Nasal Solution (Ciba) 408
Privine Nasal Spray (Ciba) 407
Protect (Marion) 412
Purpose Brand Dry Skin Cream (Ortho—Derm. Div.) 417
Purpose Brand Shampoo (Ortho—Derm. Div.) 417
Purpose Brand Soap (Ortho—Derm. Div.) 417

Q

Quotane Ointment (Menley & James) 414

R

Regutol Stool Softener (Plough) 419
Rhulicaine (Lederle) 411
Rhulicream (Lederle) 411
Rhuligel (Lederle) 411
Rhulihist Lotion (Lederle) 411
Rhulispray (Lederle) 411
Rid Pediculicide (Pfipharmecs) 418
Robitussin Syrup (Robins) 421
Robitussin-CF Syrup (Robins) 421
Robitussin-DM Syrup (Robins) 421
Robitussin-PE Syrup (Robins) 421
Rolaids Antacid Tablets (Warner-Lambert) 426
Ryna Liquid (Wallace) 425
Ryna-C Liquid (Wallace) 425
Ryna-CX Liquid (Wallace) 425

S

St. Joseph Aspirin For Children (Plough) 419
St. Joseph Cold Tablets For Children (Plough) 419
St. Joseph Cough Syrup For Children (Plough) 419
Sebb Shampoo and Lotion (Max Factor) 410
Selsun Blue (Abbott) 405
Senokot Granules (Purdue Frederick) 420
Senokot Tablets (Purdue Frederick) 420
Senokot S Tablets (Purdue Frederick) 420
Shade Plus Water Resistant Sunscreen Lotion (Plough) 419
Shade Sunscreen Lotion (Plough) 419
Simeco Antacid/Anti-Gas (Wyeth) 427
Simron (Merrell-National) 415
Simron Plus (Merrell-National) 415
Sine-Aid (McNeil Consumer) 413
Sine-Off AF Extra Strength Non-Aspirin Tablets (Menley & James) 414
Sine-Off Extra Strength Sinus Medicine Non-Aspirin Capsules (Menley & James) 414
Sine-Off Once-A-Day Sinus Spray (Menley & James) 414
Sine-Off Tablets Aspirin Formula (Menley & James) 414
Sinex Decongestant Nasal Spray (Vicks Health Care) 425

Sinex Long-Acting Decongestant Nasal Spray (Vicks Health Care) 425
Sinutab (Warner-Lambert) 426
Sinutab, Extra-Strength (Warner-Lambert) 426
Sinutab Long-Lasting Decongestant Sinus Spray (Warner-Lambert) 426
Sinutab-II (Warner-Lambert) 426
Soaclens (Alcon/bp) 405
Solarcaine First Aid Products (Plough) 419
Stresstabs 600 (Lederle) 412
Stresstabs 600 with Iron (Lederle) 412
Stresstabs 600 with Zinc (Lederle) 412
Stuart Formula Tablets (Stuart) 424
Stuartinic (Stuart) 424
Sundown (Johnson & Johnson) 411
Sunril Premenstrual Capsules (Schering) 423
Super Shade 15 Sunblocking Lotion (Plough) 419
Surfak (Hoechst-Roussel) 411
Syllact (Wallace) 425

T

Tears Plus (Allergan) 405
Teldrin Timed-Release Capsules (Menley & James) 414

Terramycin Ointment with Polymyxin B Sulfate (Pfipharmecs) 418
Throat Discs (Marion) 412
Tinactin Cream and Solution (Schering) 423
Tinactin Powder Aerosol and Powder (Schering) 423
Topex Acne Clearing Medication (Vicks Toiletry) 424
Triaminic Expectorant (Dorsey) 409
Triaminic Syrup (Dorsey) 409
Triaminic-DM Cough Formula (Dorsey) 409
Triaminicin Tablets (Dorsey) 409
Triaminicol Decongestant Cough Syrup (Dorsey) 409
Troph-Iron Liquid and Tablets (Menley & James) 415
Trophite Liquid and Tablets (Menley & James) 415
Tucks (Parke-Davis) 418
Tums (Norcliff Thayer) 416
Tylenol Adult Liquid, Extra-Strength (McNeil Consumer) 413
Tylenol Capsules & Tablets, Extra-Strength (McNeil Consumer) 413
Tylenol Capsules & Tablets, Regular Strength (McNeil Consumer) 413
Tylenol Chewable Tablets, Children's (McNeil Consumer) 413

U

Unicap M Tablets (Upjohn) 424
Unicap T Tablets High Potency (Upjohn) 424

V

Vagisil (Combe) 408
Vicks VapoRub (Vicks Health Care) 425
Vi-Penta Infant Drops (Roche) 421
Vi-Penta Multivitamin Drops (Roche) 421
Viterra C (Pfipharmecs) 418
Viterra E (Pfipharmecs) 418
Viterra Multi-Vitamins With Minerals (Pfipharmecs) 418

W

Wart-Off (Pfipharmecs) 418
Wate-On, Regular (Fleetwood) 410
Wate-On, Super (Fleetwood) 410
Wyanoids Hemorrhoidal Suppositories (Wyeth) 427

Z

Zacne (Nature's Bounty) 415
Z-Bec Tablets (Robins) 421
Ziradryl Lotion (Parke-Davis) 418

INDEX BY MANUFACTURER

Abbott Laboratories 405
Adria Laboratories, Inc. 405
Alcon/bp 405
Allergan Pharmaceuticals, Inc. 405
Almay Hypoallergenic Cosmetics & Toiletries 406

Boehringer Ingelheim Ltd. 406
Bristol-Myers Products 406
Burton, Parsons & Company, Inc. 407

Carter Products 407
Ciba Pharmaceutical Company 407
Colgate-Palmolive Company 408
Combe Incorporated 408
CooperCare, Inc. (U.S.A.) 408
Culbro Corporation 408

DeWitt International Corporation 409
Dorsey Laboratories 409

Endo Laboratories, Inc. 409

Max Factor & Co. 409
Fleetwood Company, The 410

Geigy Pharmaceuticals 410
Glenbrook Laboratories 410
Goody's Manufacturing Corporation 410
Health Care Industries, Inc. 410
Herbert Laboratories 411
Hoechst-Roussel Pharmaceuticals Inc. 411
Hynson, Westcott & Dunning 411

Johnson & Johnson Baby Products Company 411
Johnson & Johnson Products, Inc. 411

Lederle Laboratories 411

Marion Laboratories, Inc. 412
McNeil Consumer Products Company 412

Menley & James Laboratories 413
Merrell-National Laboratories 415
Merrick Medicine Company 415
Miller-Morton Company 415

Nature's Bounty, Inc. 415
NaturSlim Corporation 415
Norcliff Thayer Inc. 415
Norwich-Eaton Pharmaceuticals 416

O'Connor Products Company 416
Ortho Consumer Products Division 416
Ortho Dermatological Division 417

Parke-Davis 417
Person & Covey, Inc. 418
Pfipharmecs Division 418
Plough, Inc. 418
Purdue Frederick Company, The 419

Requa Manufacturing Company, Inc. 420
Riker Laboratories, Inc. 420
Robins Company, A. H. 420
Roche Laboratories 421

Schering Corporation 421
Searle Consumer Products 423
Stuart Pharmaceuticals 423
SugarLo Company 424

Upjohn Company, The 424

Vicks Toiletry Division 424
Vicks Health Care Division 424

Wallace Laboratories 425
Warner-Lambert Company 425
Whitehall Laboratories 426
Wyeth Laboratories 427

ABBOTT

Consumer Products Division

CLEAR EYES®
For Immediate Redness
Removal

0.5 Fl. Oz.

Also available in 1.5 Fl. Oz.

Consumer Products Division

4 Fl. Oz.

For Oily
Hair

For Dry
Hair

For Normal
Hair

SELSUN BLUE®
Dandruff Shampoo

Also available in 7 and 11 Fl. Oz.

Alcon/bp

237 ml
(8 fl. oz.)

Also
available:
355 ml
(12 fl. oz.)

BOILnSOAK®
Soft Lens Rinsing, Storage & Heat
Disinfection Solution

Alcon/bp

120 ml
(4 fl. oz.)

SOACLENS®
Hard Lens Soaking &
Wetting Solution

Consumer Products Division

0.5 Fl. Oz.

MURINE® REGULAR FORMULA
For Irritated Eyes

Also available in 1.5 Fl. Oz.

ADRIA

MODANE®
Laxative
Family

Alcon/bp

60 ml
(2 fl. oz.)

CLENS®
Hard Lens Cleaning Solution

ALLERGAN

½ fl oz

Also available: 1 fl oz

LIQUIFILM® TEARS
Ocular Lubricant

Consumer Products Division

0.5 Fl. Oz.

MURINE® PLUS
For **Faster** Redness Removal

Also available in 1.5 Fl. Oz.

Adria

2 Oz. Tube

1 lb. Jar

MYOFLEX®
Analgesic Creme

Alcon/bp

355 ml
(12 fl. oz.)

FLEX-CARE™
Soft Lens Rinsing, Storage & Cold
Disinfection Solution

Allergan

0.7 fl oz

0.7 fl oz Sterile

PREFRIN™ LIQUIFILM®
Ocular Decongestant
(phenylephrine HCl 0.12%)

Consumer Products Division

**MURINE® EAR
WAX REMOVAL
SYSTEM**
0.5 Fl.Oz.

**MURINE®
EAR DROPS**
0.5 Fl. Oz.

ALCON/bp

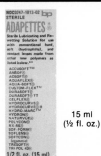

15 ml
(½ fl. oz.)

ADAPETTES®
Hard & Soft Lens Rewetting/
Lubricating Solution

Alcon/bp

45 ml
(1.5 fl. oz.)

PREFLEX®
Soft Lens Cleaning Solution

Allergan

½ fl oz

TEARS PLUS™
Artificial Tears

ALMAY

For Oily Skin   For Normal/ Combination Skin

Almay

ALMAY MAKE-UP

BRISTOL-MYERS

Bottles of 40's &100's

ARTHRITIS STRENGTH BUFFERIN®
(aspirin)

Bristol-Myers

Bottles of 16's & 36's

COMTREX® CAPSULES

Almay

For Dry/ Extra Dry Skin

ALMAY CLEANSERS

Almay

ALMAY HAIR CARE

Bristol-Myers

Bottles of 12's, 36's, 60's, 100's, 165's, 225's, 375's, & 1000's

BUFFERIN®
(aspirin)

Bristol-Myers

Bottles of 36's

CONGESPIRIN® COLD TABLETS

Almay

For Oily Skin   For Normal/ Combination Skin   For Dry/ Extra Dry Skin

ALMAY PURIFIERS

Boehringer Ingelheim Ltd.

Constipation problems?
- Fast Predictable Relief
- Gentle normal movement usually 15 mins. to 1 hour

Dulcolax LAXATIVE

Available in boxes of 2's, 4's, 8's and 50's.

Dulcolax® (bisacodyl USP) Suppository 10 mg

10 mg.

Dulcolax® Suppositories
(bisacodyl USP)

Bristol-Myers

Bottles of 6 and 10 oz.

COMTREX® LIQUID

Bristol-Myers

3 oz. Bottles

CONGESPIRIN® LIQUID COLD MEDICINE

Almay

For Oily Skin   For Normal/ Combination Skin   For Dry/ Extra Dry Skin

ALMAY MOISTURIZERS

Constipation problems?
- Fast Predictable Relief
- Gentle normal movement

Dulcolax LAXATIVE

BI 12

Available in boxes of 24's and bottles of 100's.

5 mg.

Dulcolax® Tablets
(bisacodyl USP)

Bristol-Myers

Bottles of 24's, 60's & 100's

COMTREX® TABLETS

Bristol-Myers

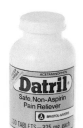

Datril

Bottles of 24's, 100's & 250's

DATRIL®
(acetaminophen)

Bristol-Myers

Bottles of 24's, 50's & 72's

DATRIL 500™
(acetaminophen)

Bristol-Myers

Bottles of 15's, 36's & 60's

4-WAY® COLD TABLETS

12 oz.
Sugar-Free

6 oz.

KONSYL®
(Psyllium Hydrophilic Mucilloid)

Available in 2 oz and 1 oz tubes

NUPERCAINAL®
Anesthetic Ointment

Bristol-Myers

Bottles of 12's, 36's, 100's, 165's, 225's & 375's

EXCEDRIN® TABLETS
Aspirin/Acetaminophen/Caffeine

Bristol-Myers

Atomizers of ½ & 1 oz.

4-WAY® NASAL SPRAY

Burton, Parsons & Company, Inc.

14 oz.
With 50% Dextrose

7 oz.

L.A. FORMULA®
(Psyllium Hydrophilic Mucilloid)

Ciba

Available in boxes of 12 and 24 suppositories
NUPERCAINAL®
Hemorrhoidal Suppositories

Bristol-Myers

Bottles of 24's, 40's & 60's

EXCEDRIN® CAPSULES
Aspirin/Acetaminophen/Caffeine

Bristol-Myers

½ oz.
Atomizers

4-WAY® LONG ACTING NASAL SPRAY
(xylometazoline hydrochloride)

Division of Carter-Wallace Inc.

ANSWER®
At-home early pregnancy test kit

Ciba

1½ oz

NUPERCAINAL®
Pain-Relief Cream

Bristol-Myers

Bottles of 10's, 30's, 50's & 80's

EXCEDRIN P.M.®

Bristol-Myers

Carded 36's
Bottles of 60's

NO-DOZ® TABLETS
(caffeine)

Carter Products

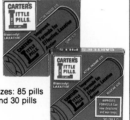
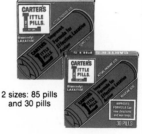

2 sizes: 85 pills and 30 pills

CARTER'S LITTLE PILLS
(5 mg. bisacodyl)

Ciba

½ fl oz

PRIVINE®
Nasal Spray

Ciba

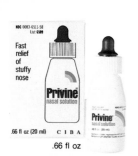

Fast relief of stuffy nose

.66 fl oz (20 ml)

.66 fl oz

PRIVINE®
Nasal Solution

COMBE

4 SECONDS TO RELIEVE ITCHING AND BURNING
• DRY SKIN ITCH
• VAGINAL & RECTAL ITCH
• CRACKED, CHAPPED SKIN • INSECT BITES
• SUNBURN • OTHER SKIN IRRITATIONS

SOOTHES ITCHING AND BURNING

LANACANE
ANESTHETIC COOLING CREME MEDICATION
NET WT. 1 OZ.

LANACANE

1 oz.
Also available in 2.0 oz. tube

LANACANE®
Anesthetic Cooling Creme
Medication

CooperCare

SOAP-FREE
Aveeno bar
for cleansing sensitive skin
NET WT. 3.2 OZ.

3.2 oz and 4.4 oz
(soap free)

AVEENO BAR®
Cleansing Bar for Sensitive Skin

(Aveeno® Colloidal Oatmeal 50%)

CULBRO

Medical Formula for Itching Skin

BiCOZENE
CREME
NET WT. 1 OZ. (28 g.)

Medical Formula for Itching Skin
BiCOZENE
CREME

1 oz. (28 g.)

BICOZENE® CREME

COLGATE-PALMOLIVE

DERMASSAGE
DISHWASHING LIQUID
WITH PROTEIN

dermassage
medicated
skin lotion

DERMASSAGE®
Dishwashing Liquid   Medicated
With Protein   Skin Lotion

Combe

Hydrocortisone Creme, the medication prescribed by doctors for millions

For the temporary relief of minor

SKIN IRRITATIONS RASHES, ITCHING

LANACORT
LANACANE

LANACORT
By the makers of LANACANE

LANACORT
By the makers of LANACANE CREME
NET WT. 1/2 OZ.

½ oz.
Also available in 1 oz. tube

LANACORT™
Hydrocortisone Acetate 0.5% Creme

CooperCare

Aveeno®
Colloidal Oatmeal

bath for sensitive skin

NET WT. 16 OZ.(1 LB.)

1 lb and 4 lb

AVEENO® COLLOIDAL OATMEAL
Bath for Sensitive Skin

(Aveeno® Colloidal Oatmeal)

Culbro

Medical Formula for Hard Callused Skin

DERMA+SOFT
CREME
ACTIVE INGREDIENT: Salicylic Acid 2.5%   NET WT. 1 oz. (28 Grams)

Medical Formula for Hard Callused Skin
DERMA+SOFT
CREME

1 oz. (28 g.)

DERMA + SOFT™ CREME

Colgate-Palmolive

COLGATE
Fluorigard
ANTI-CAVITY
DENTAL RINSE
FLUORIDE
Aids in the Prevention of Cavities

FLUORIGARD™
Anti-Cavity Dental Rinse
With Fluoride

Combe

Doctor-tested Vagisil
medicated creme for prompt soothing relief of
feminine itching, burning & irritation
proven effective, used by over 2.5 million women

Vagisil
Feminine Itching Medication

NOW EXTRA STRENGTH
Vagisil
Feminine Itching Medication
NET WT. 1 OZ.

Vagisil
FEMININE ITCHING MEDICATION

1 oz.
Also available in 2 oz. tube

VAGISIL®
Feminine Itching Medication

CooperCare

Aveeno®
OILATED

Bath for dry, sensitive skin

NET WT. 8 OZ.(½ LB.)

8 oz and 2 lb
(soap free)

AVEENO® OILATED
Bath for Dry, Sensitive Skin

(Aveeno® Colloidal Oatmeal, skin-softening emollients)

Culbro

BIOLOGICALLY TESTED
for effective action

FOR RELIEF OF CONSTIPATION

EX-LAX
PILLS

30 PILLS—UNFLAVORED

FOR RELIEF OF CONSTIPATION

EX-LAX.

THE CHOCOLATED LAXATIVE
18 TABLETS

EX-LAX®

Pill

Chocolated
Tablet

Colgate-Palmolive

NEW FROM COLGATE
mersene
DENTURE CLEANSER

outcleans
the leading tablets
in powering off plaque

40 PACKETS

mersene
denture
cleanser

Cartons of 20, 40,
60 and 96 packets

Individual Packet

MERSENE®
Denture Cleanser

COOPERCARE

dermatology division

SOAP-FREE
Acnaveen®
cleansing bar
for acne
NET WT. 3.5 OZ.

3.5 oz (soap free)

ACNAVEEN®
Cleansing Bar for Acne

(Aveeno® Colloidal Oatmeal 50%,
sulfur 2%, salicylic acid 2%)

CooperCare

SOAP-FREE
Emulave®
cleansing bar
for dry skin
NET WT. 3 OZ.

3 oz (soap free)

EMULAVE®
Cleansing Bar for Dry Skin

(Aveeno® Colloidal Oatmeal 30%,
29% skin-softening emollients)

Culbro

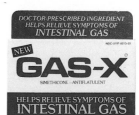

DOCTOR-PRESCRIBED INGREDIENT
HELPS RELIEVE SYMPTOMS OF
INTESTINAL GAS

NEW
GAS-X
SIMETHICONE—ANTIFLATULENT

HELPS RELIEVE SYMPTOMS OF
INTESTINAL GAS

30 Tablets, 80 mg. each

GAS-X®
(simethicone)

DeWITT

ANTACID POWDER

DeWitt

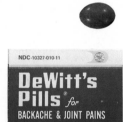

NDC-10327-010-11

DeWitt's Pills *for*
BACKACHE & JOINT PAINS
Analgesic and Mildly Diuretic

CONTENTS 40 PILLS

PILLS FOR BACKACHE & JOINT PAINS

Dorsey

Triaminic-DM
Cough Formula

4 oz, 8 oz

TRIAMINIC-DM™ COUGH FORMULA

Dorsey

NDC 0043-0064-24
Triaminicin Tablets

DECONGESTANT ANALGESIC ANTIHISTAMINIC

For Relief of
Nasal Congestion
and Headache due to
Common Cold/Hay Fever

24 TABLETS

12's, 24's, 48's, 100's

TRIAMINICIN® TABLETS

DeWitt

Baby Cough Syrup
FOR COUGHS DUE TO COLDS

Soothing as Slumber

CONTENTS 3 FL. OZ. (89 ml)

BABY COUGH SYRUP

DORSEY

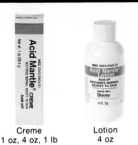

Acid Mantle CREME

Acid Mantle Lotion

Creme
1 oz, 4 oz, 1 lb

Lotion
4 oz

ACID MANTLE® CREME AND LOTION
(aluminum acetate)

Dorsey

Triaminic
Expectorant

4 oz, 8 oz,
Pint

TRIAMINIC® EXPECTORANT

ENDO

Endo 132

Percogesic
for enhanced
relief of pain
contains
no aspirin
child resistant blister pack
24 tablets

PERCOGESIC®
analgesic
Each tablet contains acetaminophen
(APAP) 325 mg. and
phenyltoloxamine citrate 30 mg.

DeWitt

Also available in
Stainless Formulation
in a blue and
yellow tube

MANZAN FORMULA
HTO
hemorrhoidal TISSUE OINTMENT

NET WT. 1 OZ.

Applicator

DeWITT'S MANZAN FORMULA **HTO**
hemorrhoidal TISSUE OINTMENT
NET. WT. 1 OZ.

HEMORRHOIDAL TISSUE OINTMENT

Dorsey

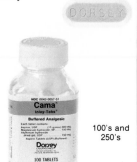

DORSEY

Cama
Inlay-Tabs
Buffered Analgesic

100 TABLETS

100's and
250's

CAMA® INLAY-TABS®

Dorsey

Triaminic
Syrup
Decongestant
Antihistaminic

4 oz, 8 oz,
Pint

TRIAMINIC® SYRUP

MAX FACTOR & CO.

Maxi-Unshine
Oil-Free Make-Up

1¼ Fl. Oz.

Dermatologist tested. Pure, water base
formula. Fragrance free. Available in 10
natural looking shades.
*Contains no natural animal, vegetable
or mineral oils.

MAXI™ UNSHINE™ OIL FREE* MAKE-UP

DeWitt

DeWitt's
NDC 10327-057-50

OIL for EAR USE

CONTENTS ½ FL. OZ.

OIL FOR EAR USE

Dorsey

Dorcol
Pediatric Cough Syrup

4 oz, 8 oz

DORCOL® PEDIATRIC COUGH SYRUP

Dorsey

Triaminicol
Decongestant Cough Syrup

4 oz, 8 oz

TRIAMINICOL® DECONGESTANT COUGH SYRUP

Max Factor & Co.

Dermatologist
tested. Pure
and gentle.
Soaks up oily
shine for hours.
Available in
six trans-
parent shades.

Unshine
100% Oil Free
Blotting Powder

MAX FACTOR

MAXI™ UNSHINE™ 100% OIL FREE BLOTTING POWDER

Max Factor & Co.

Dermatologist tested. Pure and gentle. Available in eight radiant shades.

Won't streak or change color.

MAXI™ UNSHINE™
100% OIL FREE BLUSHING POWDER

Geigy

OTRIVIN® 0.1%
Nasal Drops

OTRIVIN® 0.05%
Pediatric Nasal Drops

Glenbrook

Available in bottles of 30, 72, and 125 tablets

BAYER® TIMED-RELEASE ASPIRIN

Glenbrook

Available in regular and mint flavor 4 oz., 12 oz. and 26 oz.

PHILLIPS'® MILK OF MAGNESIA

Max Factor & Co.

SEBB™
Shampoo and Lotion

Shampoo removes loose or flaking dandruff.
Lotion treats itchy scalp associated with dandruff.

Geigy

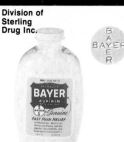

Cream

PBZ®
(tripelennamine hydrochloride)

Glenbrook

Available in 4 oz., 9 oz. and 12½ oz. containers

DIAPARENE® BABY POWDER

GOODY'S

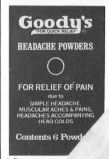

6 Powders

HEADACHE POWDERS

FLEETWOOD

REGULAR WATE-ON®
Tablets 96's

SUPER WATE-ON®
Emulsion 16 oz.

High Calorie Food and Vitamin Supplements for the Gaining of Weight.

GLENBROOK LABORATORIES

Division of Sterling Drug Inc.

Available in packs of 12 tablets and bottles of 24's, 50's, 100's, 200's and 300's

BAYER® ASPIRIN

Glenbrook

Available in 70 cloth and 150 cloth canisters

DIAPARENE® BABY WASH CLOTHS

HEALTH CARE INDUSTRIES

Available in 30, 80, 160, 330 sizes

4¾ grains (308 mg.) per tablet

Dried garlic powder (Allium sativum, dehydrated)

ALLIMIN® FILMCOATED TABLET

GEIGY

OTRIVIN® 0.1%
Nasal Spray

Glenbrook

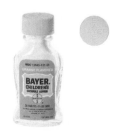

Available in bottle of 36 tablets

BAYER® CHILDREN'S CHEWABLE ASPIRIN

Glenbrook

Available in packages of 12, 30 and 60 Caplets®

MIDOL®

Health Care Industries

Available in 4 fl. oz. 1 pint and 1 gallon sizes

COSANYL® COUGH SYRUP
Each teaspoonful (5 ml.): Codeine phosphate,* 10 mg. d-pseudoephedrine HCl, 30 mg. Peach flavor: Alcohol, 6%
*(Warning: May be habit forming)

Health Care Industries

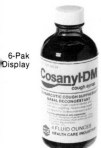

6-Pak
Display

Available in
4 fl. oz. size
Shrink
Wrapped

COSANYL-DM® COUGH SYRUP
Teaspoonful (5 ml.): d-methorphan, 15 mg.
d-pseudoephedrine HCl, 30 mg. Peach
flavor. Alcohol 6%

Hoechst-Roussel

Bottles
of 100
Tablets

Digestive Aid

FESTAL®
(digestive enzymes with bile
constituents)

Johnson & Johnson

1.5 Oz.   .8 Oz.

FIRST AID CREAM

Lederle

1 and 2 oz tubes

RHULICREAM®
Analgesic-Anesthetic Cream

Health Care Industries

Available in
1 oz., 2 oz.,
4 oz., pints
and gallons

2 oz. STREEM-TOP™
OIL-O-SOL® LIQUID

Corn oil 52%, castor oil 40.8%, camphor
oil 6.8%, hexylresorcinol 0.1%

Hoechst-Roussel

50 mg
Bottles of
30 and 100

240 mg
Bottles of
30 and 100

Surfak®
dioctyl calcium sulfosuccinate N.F.
STOOL SOFTENER

30 CAPSULES-240 MG

Stool Softener

SURFAK®
(docusate calcium USP)

Johnson & Johnson

SPF 4   SPF 6   SPF 8   SPF 15

4 Fl. Oz.

SUNDOWN®
Sunscreen and Sunblock Protection

Lederle

2 oz tube

RHULIGEL®
Analgesic-Anesthetic Gel

HERBERT

4 oz.
SPF 5
Moderate
Protection

4 oz.
SPF 10
Maximum
Protection

4 oz.
SPF 15
Ultra
Protection

ECLIPSE® SUNSCREEN PRODUCTS

Hynson, Westcott & Dunning

Product must be refrigerated

Granules: 1 gram packet

Tablets: bottles of 50

LACTINEX®
Tablets & Granules
(Lactobacillus acidophilus and
Lactobacillus bulgaricus)

LEDERLE

Combopack
CENTRUM®
High Potency Multivitamin/
Multimineral Formula

Lederle

4 oz bottle, 75 ml
plastic squeeze bottle

RHULIHIST® Lotion

HOECHST-ROUSSEL

10 capsule
pack and
bottles of
30 and 100

Laxative and Stool Softener

DOXIDAN®
(docusate calcium USP and
danthron USP)

JOHNSON & JOHNSON

1.5 Fl. Oz.

8 Fl. Oz.
Also available:
4 Fl. Oz. & 12 Fl. Oz.
sizes

For hospital nursery
use

**JOHNSON'S
BABY BATH**

Lederle

4 oz can

RHULICAINE™
Anesthetic-Antiseptic
Medicated Spray

Lederle

2 oz and 4 oz can

RHULISPRAY®
Analgesic-Anesthetic Spray

Lederle

Bottles of 30, 60 and 500

STRESSTABS® 600
High Potency Stress Formula
Vitamins

Marion

1 fl. oz.   ½ fl. oz.

DEBROX®
Drops

Marion

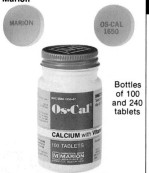

2 fl. oz.   ½ FL. OZ. (15 ml.)

GLY-OXIDE® Liquid

Marion

PARKE-DAVIS
THROAT DISCS

THROAT LOZENGES
Effective for soothing, temporary relief of minor throat irritations from hoarseness and coughs due to colds.
SIXTY DISCS

Box of 60 lozenges

THROAT DISCS®
Throat Lozenges

Lederle

Bottles of 30 & 60

STRESSTABS® 600 with IRON
High Potency Stress Formula
Vitamins

Marion

100-tablet bottle

30-tablet box (foil-wrapped 2's)
GAVISCON®
Antacid Tablets

Marion

Bottles of 100 and 240 tablets

OS-CAL®
Tablets
(calcium with Vitamin D)

Capsules available in blister pack of 20 and bottle of 50.
Tablets available in blister pack of 24 and bottles of 50 and 100.

COTYLENOL® COLD FORMULA
Capsules & Tablets

Lederle

Bottles of 30 & 60

STRESSTABS® 600 with ZINC
High Potency Stress Formula
Vitamins

Marion

12 fl. oz.

GAVISCON®
Liquid Antacid

Marion

Bottle of 60 banana-flavored tablets

PRETTS®
Tablets
(diet control adjunct)

McNeil Consumer

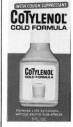

Available in 5 fl. oz. & 10 fl. oz. bottles.

All sizes have child-resistant safety cap and convenient dosage cup.

COTYLENOL® LIQUID COLD FORMULA

4 fl. oz.

AMBENYL®-D
Decongestant Cough Formula

Marion

double-strength
GAVISCON-2
antacid tablets

Box of 48 foil-wrapped tablets

GAVISCON®-2
Antacid Tablets

Marion

3 oz. tube

PROTECT™
Toothpaste for Sensitive Teeth

McNeil Consumer

Available in 4 fl. oz. bottle with child-resistant safety cap and convenient dosage cup.

CHILDREN'S COTYLENOL®
Liquid Cold Formula

McNeil Consumer

No Drowsiness Formula
SINE-AID.®
For sinus headache pain and pressure
50 TABLETS

Available in bottles of
24, 50 & 100.
SINE-AID®
Sinus Headache Tablets

McNeil Consumer

80 mg.

Available in bottles of 30. Elixir available in 2 fl. oz. & 4 fl. oz. bottles. Drops available in ½ fl. oz. bottle.

CHILDREN'S
TYLENOL®
acetaminophen
CHEWABLE TABLETS
Relieves children's fever and pain without aspirin complications
30 Tablets · 80 mg. each   Fruit Flavor

CHILDREN'S TYLENOL®
acetaminophen
Chewable Tablets

All sizes have child-resistant
safety cap.

Menley & James

Packages of 10, 20 and 40
capsules

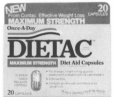

CONTAC®
CONTINUOUS ACTION
DECONGESTANT CAPSULES

Menley & James

Packages of 20 and
40 capsules

NEW
From Contac, Effective Weight Loss
MAXIMUM STRENGTH
Once-A-Day
DIETAC™
MAXIMUM STRENGTH   Diet Aid Capsules

Once-A-Day
DIETAC™ MAXIMUM STRENGTH
Diet Aid Capsules

McNeil Consumer

325 mg.

REGULAR STRENGTH
TYLENOL®
acetaminophen **CAPSULES**
safe, fast pain relief...without aspirin

REGULAR STRENGTH
TYLENOL®
acetaminophen **TABLETS**
safe, fast pain relief...without aspirin

Capsules available in bottles of 24,
50 and 100.
Tablets available in tins and vials of
12, and bottles of 24, 50, 100 and 200.
REGULAR STRENGTH TYLENOL®
acetaminophen
Capsules & Tablets

ACNOMEL
acne cream
For deep-seated treatment of pimples and blemishes due to acne.
Contains resorcinol 2% and sulfur 8%, in a washable, flesh-tinted base.
NET WT. 1 OZ.
(28 GRAMS)

ACNOMEL
acne cream
Contains resorcinol 2%,
sulfur 8%, alcohol 11% (w/w)
NET WT. 1 OZ.
(28 GRAMS)

ACNOMEL® CAKE AND ACNE
CREAM
(resorcinol, sulfate, alcohol)

Menley & James

The Complete Cold Medicine for Children
CONTAC Jr.®

The complete cold medicine for congestion, coughing, aches and fever.
4 FL. OZ.

Includes dose-
by-weight cup

4 oz. and 8 oz. plastic bottles

CONTAC JR.®
COLD MEDICINE FOR CHILDREN

Menley & James

Packages of 24 and
48 capsules

NEW
From Contac, Effective Weight Loss
MAXIMUM STRENGTH
Twice-A-Day
DIETAC™
MAXIMUM STRENGTH   Diet Aid Capsules
24 CAPSULES

Twice-A-Day
DIETAC™ MAXIMUM STRENGTH
Diet Aid Capsules

McNeil Consumer

500 mg.

EXTRA-STRENGTH
TYLENOL®
acetaminophen **CAPSULES**
extra pain relief...contains no aspirin
50 Capsules—500 mg. each

EXTRA-STRENGTH
TYLENOL®
acetaminophen **TABLETS**
extra pain relief...contains no aspirin

Capsules available in bottles of
24, 50 & 100.
Tablets available in vials of 10 and
bottles of 30, 60 and 100.
EXTRA-STRENGTH TYLENOL®
acetaminophen
Capsules & Tablets

Menley & James

20
TABLETS
NEW SPACESAVER PACKAGE
A.R.M.
ALLERGY
RELIEF
MEDICINE
HAY FEVER
ALLERGIES
SINUS CONGESTION
20
TABLETS

Packages of 20 and 40 tablets
A.R.M.® ALLERGY RELIEF
MEDICINE
(chlorpheniramine maleate,
phenylpropanolamine HCl)

Menley & James

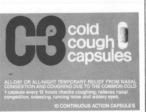

C3 cold cough capsules
ALL-DAY OR ALL-NIGHT TEMPORARY RELIEF FROM NASAL CONGESTION AND COUGHING DUE TO THE COMMON COLD
1 capsule every 12 hours checks coughing; relieves nasal congestion, sneezing, running nose and watery eyes.
10 CONTINUOUS ACTION CAPSULES

C3® COLD-COUGH CAPSULES

Menley & James

Effective weight loss
From the makers of Contac®
Pre-Meal
DIETAC
Diet Aid Drops
· Curbs your appetite at meals
· Helps you lose weight
· Caffeine-free
  can be used in coffee, tea or cola in the evening too
· Clinically proven safe and effective
NEW PRODUCT INFORMATION
SEE BACK PANEL
½ FL. OZ. (15 ml)

PRE-MEAL   ½ Fl. Oz.
DIETAC™
Diet Aid Drops

McNeil Consumer

All sizes have child-resistant safety cap and convenient dosage cup.

EXTRA-STRENGTH
TYLENOL®
acetaminophen
ADULT LIQUID
PAIN RELIEVER
FAST, SAFE PAIN RELIEF without aspirin complications
8 fl. oz.

Available in
8 fl. oz.
& 16 fl. oz.
bottles.

EXTRA-STRENGTH TYLENOL®
acetaminophen
Adult Liquid Pain Reliever

Menley & James

BENZEDREX
INHALER
nasal decongestant

BENZEDREX® INHALER
(propylhexedrine, SK&F)

Menley & James

Packages of 14
and 28 capsules

28
CAPSULES
Effective weight loss
From the makers of Contac®
12 Hour
DIETAC
Diet Aid Capsules
· Timed-release to control your appetite at meals and in between
· Helps you lose weight
· Clinically proven safe and effective
SAFETY SEALED INSIDE
28 CAPSULES

12 Hour
DIETAC™
Diet Aid Capsules

Menley & James

42 Tablets

42
TABLETS
Effective weight loss
From the makers of Contac®
Pre-Meal
DIETAC™
Diet Aid Tablets
· Curbs your appetite at meals
· Helps you lose weight
· Caffeine-free...can be used in the evening
· Clinically proven safe and effective
NEW PRODUCT INFORMATION
SEE BACK PANEL
42 TABLETS

Pre-Meal
DIETAC™
Diet Aid Tablets

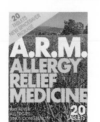

Menley & James

Safely relieves pain and inflammation, protects against stomach upset.

Ecotrin®
DUENTRIC® COATED ASPIRIN for **arthritis**
100 TABLETS 325 MG. (5 GR.) EACH

In 100 and 250
tablet bottles

ECOTRIN® TABLETS
Duentric® coated 5 gr. aspirin

Menley & James

Feosol Plus
Iron plus vitamins
For simple iron
deficiency and iron-
deficiency
anemia
100 CAPSULES

FEOSOL PLUS®
Iron Plus Vitamins

Menley & James

dermatologic ointment
Pragmatar
(with sulfur and salicylic acid)
NET WT. 1 OZ.
(28 GRAMS)

Dermatologic Ointment

1 oz. tube
PRAGMATAR® OINTMENT

Menley & James

20 capsules

Relieves sinus headache and congestion
SINE-OFF
NEW!
Now in Capsules
EXTRA STRENGTH
SINUS
MEDICINE   20
NON-ASPIRIN
CAPSULES

SINE-OFF®
EXTRA STRENGTH SINUS MEDICINE
NON-ASPIRIN CAPSULES

Menley & James

FEOSOL ELIXIR
ferrous sulfate - iron therapy
For iron

12 FL OZ (355 ML.)

12 oz. bottle
FEOSOL® ELIXIR
(ferrous sulfate USP)

Menley & James

FORTESPAN®
brand of therapeutic
multivitamin capsules
for the treatment of
multiple vitamin
deficiencies
30 CAPSULES

FORTESPAN® CAPSULES
Therapeutic multiple vitamins

Menley & James

ointment
Quotane
brand of dimethisoquin hydrochloride
topical anesthetic
NET WT. 1 OZ. (28 grams)

for relief of itching
and mild sunburn

Topical Anesthetic

1 oz. tube
QUOTANE® OINTMENT

Menley & James

**SINE-OFF   ONCE-A-DAY
SINUS SPRAY**
(Xylometazoline HCl
plus cooling
menthol)
Spray once in the morning and once at night for
fast and prolonged relief from sinus and nasal
congestion due to sinusitis,
colds and hay fever.
1/2 FL. OZ.

1/2 fl. oz. and
1 oz. size

SINE-OFF®
ONCE-A-DAY SINUS SPRAY

Menley & James

Feosol
SPANSULE® CAPSULES
ferrous sulfate - iron therapy
For iron
Controlled-release formula
for simple iron deficiency
and iron-deficiency anemia
30 CAPSULES

FEOSOL® SPANSULE® CAPSULES
(ferrous sulfate USP)

Menley & James

For temporary relief from coughing and nasal congestion
associated with common colds and sinusitis
ORNACOL
COUGH
& COLD
CAPSULES
20 CAPSULES   NO SEDATIVES • NO ANTIHISTAMINES

In 30 and 100 capsule packages
and 4 oz. liquid

ORNACOL® COUGH & COLD
CAPSULE & LIQUID

Menley & James

Relieves sinus headache and congestion
SINE-OFF
SINUS
MEDICINE   24
TABLETS

Packages of 24,
48, and 100 tablets

SINE-OFF® TABLETS
ASPIRIN FORMULA

Menley & James

8 mg.

**12-HOUR
ALLERGY RELIEF
Teldrin®**
chlorpheniramine maleate TIMED-RELEASE CAPSULES
Relieves
runny nose,
sneezing and itchy,
watery eyes
12 CAPSULES   8 mg.

TELDRIN®
TIMED-RELEASE CAPSULES
(chlorpheniramine maleate)

Menley & James

Feosol
TABLETS
ferrous sulfate - iron therapy
For iron
Therapy coated tablets
for simple iron deficiency
and iron-deficiency anemia
100 TABLETS

FEOSOL® TABLETS
(ferrous sulfate USP)

Menley & James

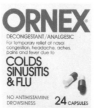

ORNEX
DECONGESTANT/ANALGESIC
For temporary relief of nasal
congestion, headache, aches,
pains and fever due to
COLDS
SINUSITIS
& FLU
NO ANTIHISTAMINE
DROWSINESS   24 CAPSULES

In 24, 48 and 100
capsule packages

ORNEX® CAPSULES
Decongestant/Analgesic

Menley & James

Relieves sinus headache and congestion
SINE-OFF
EXTRA STRENGTH
NON-ASPIRIN
SINUS MEDICINE   20
TABLETS

SINE-OFF® AF
EXTRA STRENGTH NON-ASPIRIN
TABLETS

Menley & James

12 mg.

**12-HOUR
ALLERGY RELIEF
Teldrin®**
chlorpheniramine maleate TIMED-RELEASE CAPSULES
Relieves
runny nose,
sneezing and itchy,
watery eyes
MAXIMUM
STRENGTH
12 CAPSULES   12 mg.

TELDRIN®
TIMED-RELEASE CAPSULES
(chlorpheniramine maleate)

Menley & James

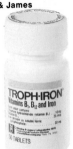

4 oz. liquid and
50 tablet bottle
TROPH-IRON®
LIQUID AND TABLETS
Vitamins B1, B12 and Iron

Merrell-National

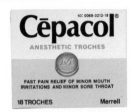

Trade Package: 18 troches in 2 pocket
packs of 9 each

Professional Package: 200 troches
in 100 foil strips of 2 each

CĒPACOL®
ANESTHETIC TROCHES

Merrell-National

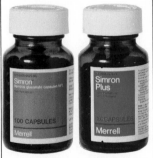

SIMRON™   **SIMRON PLUS®**

Bottles of 100 capsules

NATURE'S BOUNTY

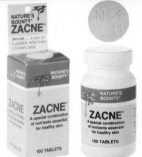

ZACNE®
A special combination of nutrients
essential for healthy skin

Menley & James

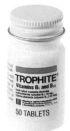

4 oz. liquid and
50 tablet bottle
TROPHITE® LIQUID AND
TABLETS
Vitamins B1, B12

Merrell-National

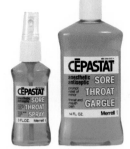

3 oz. w/Spray   14 oz. Gargle

CĒPASTAT®
SORE THROAT SPRAY/GARGLE

MERRICK

PERCY MEDICINE®
(bismuth subnitrate NF & calcium
hydroxide USP)

NaturSlim

1 lb. w/30 time-release
multivitamins with iron
NaturSlim® II

Nutritional Supplement &
Diet Program

MERRELL-NATIONAL

Trade Packages: 6,
12, 18 and 24 oz.

Professional
Package: 4 half
gallons with dis-
pensing pump

CĒPACOL®
MOUTHWASH/GARGLE

Merrell-National

Trade Package: 18 lozenges
in 2 pocket packs of 9 each

Professional Package:
300 lozenges
in 100 foil strips of 3 each

CĒPASTAT® SORE THROAT
LOZENGES

MILLER-MORTON

Ultra sunscreen protection (SPF-15)

Aids prevention and healing of dry,
chapped, sun- and windburned lips.

CHAP STICK®
SUNBLOCK 15 Lip Balm

NORCLIFF THAYER

A-200 PYRINATE® LIQUID

Also available:
A-200 Pyrinate Liquid, 4 fl. oz.
A-200 Pyrinate Gel, 1 oz.

Merrell-National

Trade Package: 27 lozenges in
3 pocket packs of 9 each

Professional Package:
400 lozenges
in 100 foil strips of 4 each

CĒPACOL® THROAT LOZENGES

Merrell-National

Trade Package: 18 lozenges in 2 pocket
packs of 9 each

CHILDREN'S CĒPASTAT®
SORE THROAT LOZENGES

Miller-Morton

CHAP STICK®
Lip Balm

Norcliff Thayer

3 oz.

CO-SALT®
Salt Substitute

Norcliff Thayer

3 oz.
ESOTÉRICA®
Medicated Fade Cream
Fortified Scented with Sunscreen

Also available:
Regular, 3 oz.
Facial, 3 oz.
Fortified Unscented with Sunscreen, 3 oz.

Norcliff Thayer

1 fl. oz.
OXY-10™ LOTION

1 fl. oz.
OXY-5® LOTION

Norwich-Eaton

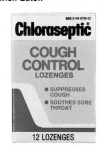

Available: Cartons of 12 lozenges.

**CHLORASEPTIC®
COUGH CONTROL LOZENGES**

Norwich-Eaton

Liquid available in
4 oz., 8 oz., 12 oz.
and 16 oz. bottles

Tablets available
in cartons of
24 and 60.

**PEPTO-BISMOL® LIQUID AND
TABLETS**

Norcliff Thayer

1.16 fl. oz.
35 ml.

LIQUIPRIN®

Norcliff Thayer

4 fl. oz.
OXY WASH™

Norwich-Eaton

Available: Cartons of 12 vaginal
contraceptive inserts.

ENCARE®

O'CONNOR PRODUCTS

Boxes of 10, 24 and 48 capsules. Look for
new package change January, 1981. Also
available Caffeine-Free Dex-A-Diet® Lite
Boxes of 20 and 40.

DEX-A-DIET II® CAPSULES

Norcliff Thayer

Single Roll, Peppermint

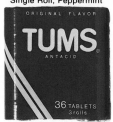

Three Roll Wrap, Peppermint

Bottle 75s, Peppermint
TUMS®

Also available: Tums Single Roll,
Assorted Flavors; Tums Three Roll
Wrap, Assorted Flavors;
Tums Bottle 75s, Assorted Flavors;
Tums Bottle 150s, Peppermint

NORWICH-EATON

Cherry
Menthol
Cherry
Menthol

Available: 6 oz. with sprayer, 12 oz.
refill, 1.5 oz. nitrogen pressurized
pocket spray.

CHLORASEPTIC® LIQUID

Norwich-Eaton

Original
Herbal

Original and Herbal Norforms available
in cartons of 6, 12 and
24 deodorant inserts.

**NORFORMS®
FEMININE DEODORANTS**

ORTHO—CONS. PRODS.

Prefilled Disposable Applicators in
packages of 6's and 10's.

**CONCEPTROL® Birth Control
Cream
Disposable**
(nonoxynol 9, 5%)

Norwich-Eaton

Cherry

Menthol

Available: Cartons of 18 or 45
lozenges.

CHLORASEPTIC® LOZENGES

Norwich-Eaton

5 grains—325 mg.
NORWICH® ASPIRIN

Available in bottles of 100, 250
and 500 tablets.

Ortho—Cons. Prods.

Starter (2.46 oz. tube w/applicator
package)
Refill (2.46 oz. tube only package)

**CONCEPTROL® Birth Control
Cream**
(nonoxynol 9, 5%)

Ortho—Cons. Prods.

Lubricated and Non-Lubricated
packages of 12's and 24's.

CONCEPTROL SHIELDS®
Latex Prophylactics

Ortho—Cons. Prods.

2 oz. tube

MASSÉ® Breast Cream

Ortho—Cons. Prods.

2 oz. and 4 oz. tubes

ORTHO® PERSONAL LUBRICANT

Available in boxes of 12, 24 and 48

1 Oz. Tube

ANUSOL®
Suppositories and Ointment

Ortho—Cons. Prods.

Packages of 12's
Lubricated

CONCEPTROL SUPREME®
Thin Prophylactics

Ortho—Cons. Prods.

Ortho-Creme is intended for use
with a diaphragm

Starter (2.46 oz. tube w/applicator
package). Refill (2.46 oz. and 4.05
oz. tube only packages).

ORTHO-CREME®
Contraceptive Cream
(nonoxynol 9, 2.00%)

**PURPOSE BRAND
DRY SKIN CREAM**

Parke-Davis

Available in 1 Oz. and 2 Oz. Tubes

BENADRYL®
Antihistamine Cream

Ortho—Cons. Prods.

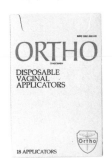

Starter (0.70 oz. vial w/applicator
package)
Refill (0.70 oz. and 1.75 oz. vial
only packages)

DELFEN® Contraceptive Foam
(nonoxynol 9, 12.5%)

Ortho—Cons. Prods.

ORTHO
DISPOSABLE
VAGINAL
APPLICATORS

18 APPLICATORS

Packages of 18 applicators each

ORTHO®
Disposable Vaginal Applicators

Ortho—Derm. Div.

**PURPOSE BRAND
SHAMPOO**

Parke-Davis

4 Fl. Oz.

BENYLIN DM™
Cough Syrup

Ortho—Cons. Prods.

Intercept
CONTRACEPTIVE INSERTS
starter
12 INSERTS WITH APPLICATOR

Starter (12 inserts w/applicator
package)
Refill (12 inserts)

INTERCEPT®
Contraceptive Inserts

(nonoxynol 9, 5.56%)

Ortho—Cons. Prods.

ORTHO-GYNOL is intended for use
with a diaphragm

Starter (2.85 oz. tube w/applicator
package). Refill (2.85 oz. and 4.44
oz. tube only packages).

**ORTHO-GYNOL® Contraceptive
Jelly**
(diisobutylphenoxypolyethoxyethanol,
1.00%)

Ortho—Derm. Div.

**PURPOSE BRAND
SOAP**

Parke-Davis

Available in 2½ and 6 Fl. Oz.

CALADRYL® LOTION

Parke-Davis

100 tablets

50 tablets

Also available:
165 tablets

GELUSIL®
Antacid-Antiflatulent   12 Fl. Oz.

PERSŌN & COVEY

DHS™
Dermato-logical Hair and Scalp Shampoo

DHS™
Tar Shampoo Dermato-logical Hair and Scalp Shampoo

DHS™
Zinc Dandruff Shampoo

Pfipharmecs

LI-BAN™ SPRAY

Net Wt. 5 oz (147.8 ml)

Pfipharmecs

Available in bottles of 100 tablets
250 & 500 mg.

VITERRA® C

Parke-Davis

Available in bottles of 130 and
250 tablets

MYADEC®

High potency vitamin supplement
with minerals

PFIPHARMECS

25 mg.

8 Chewable Tablets
per pack

BONINE® TABLETS
(meclizine HCl)

Pfipharmecs

4 fl. oz.

2 fl. oz.

Kills Lice and Their Eggs on Contact
Head Lice, Body Lice and Crab or Pubic Lice

Special Comb Included

4 fl. oz. (118 ml)

Kills Lice and Their Eggs on Contact
Head Lice, Body Lice and Crab or Pubic Lice

Special Comb Included

2 fl. oz. (59 ml)

RID™ PEDICULICIDE

Pfipharmecs

100 I.U., 200 I.U., 400 I.U.
& 600 I.U.
Available in bottles of 100 capsules
VITERRA® E

Parke-Davis

100 pads

40 pads

TUCKS
Pre-Moistened Pads

Pfipharmecs

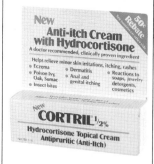

New
Anti-itch Cream with Hydrocortisone
A doctor recommended, clinically proven ingredient

Helps relieve minor skin irritations, itching, rashes
- Eczema
- Poison Ivy, Oak, Sumac
- Insect bites
- Dermatitis
- Anal and genital itching
- Reactions to soaps, jewelry detergents, cosmetics

CORTRIL® ½%
Hydrocortisone Topical Cream
Antipruritic (Anti-Itch)

Pfipharmecs

½ oz. tube

1 oz. tube

TERRAMYCIN® OINTMENT
WITH POLYMYXIN B SULFATE

Pfipharmecs

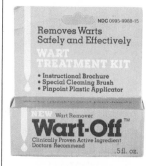

Removes Warts Safely and Effectively
WART TREATMENT KIT
- Instructional Brochure
- Special Cleaning Brush
- Pinpoint Plastic Applicator

Wart-Off™
Wart Remover
Clinically Proven Active Ingredient
Doctors Recommend

.5 fl. oz.

WART-OFF™

Parke-Davis

6 Fl. Oz.

ZIRADRYL® LOTION

Pfipharmecs

4 fl. oz.

Available in 12
& 24 capsules

CORYBAN-D® COLD CAPSULES
& COUGH SYRUP

Pfipharmecs

Original Formula

High Potency Formula

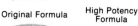

Available in bottles of 100
Sugar Free Tablets
VITERRA®
MULTI-VITAMINS WITH
MINERALS

PLOUGH, INC.

Aerosol Liquid

Gel

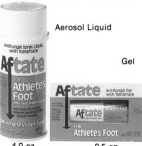

4.0 oz.   0.5 oz.

AFTATE® FOR ATHLETE'S FOOT
(tolnaftate)

Plough, Inc.

Aerosol Powder

Gel

3.5 oz.   0.5 oz.

AFTATE® FOR JOCK ITCH
(tolnaftate)

Plough, Inc.

Liquid   Tablets

Mint and Lemon/Orange flavors,
6 fl. oz. and 12 fl. oz. liquid plus 30,
56 and 100 tablet sizes.
DI-GEL®
(simethicone, aluminum hydroxide,
magnesium hydroxide)

Plough, Inc.

30 tablets per bottle

**ST. JOSEPH® COLD TABLETS
FOR CHILDREN**
(1¼ grs. aspirin and 3.125 mg.
phenylpropanolamine HCl per tablet)

Plough, Inc.

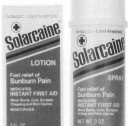

3 fl. oz.   3 oz.
Also available in 6 fl. oz. lotion,
5 oz. spray, 3.5 fl. oz. pump and
1 and 2 oz. First Aid Cream
**SOLARCAINE® FIRST AID
PRODUCTS**
(benzocaine and triclosan)

Plough, Inc.

Cherry
16 Tablet Size

Orange
16 Tablet Size

Also available in Orange and
Cherry flavors, 40 tablet sizes.

ASPERGUM®
(3½ grs. aspirin per tablet)

Plough, Inc.

Also available
in mentholated.

Available in
½ fl. oz. and
1 fl. oz. sizes.   ⅔ fl. oz.

**DURATION®
NASAL SPRAY AND NOSE DROPS**
(oxymetazoline HCl)

Plough, Inc.

Available in 2 fl. oz. and 4 fl. oz.
sizes.

**ST. JOSEPH® COUGH SYRUP
FOR CHILDREN**
(dextromethorphan hydrobromide)

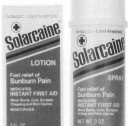

8 oz.

Also available, Disposable Betadine
Medicated Douche. Completely dispos-
able for convenience.
BETADINE® DOUCHE

Plough, Inc.

Available in 15, 30, 60 and
90 tablet sizes.

CORRECTOL® LAXATIVE
(100 mg. docusate sodium and 65 mg.
phenolphthalein per tablet)

Mild Laxative with Stool Softener

Plough, Inc.

Available in 30, 60 and 90
tablet sizes.

**REGUTOL®
STOOL SOFTENER**
(100 mg. docusate sodium per tablet)

Plough, Inc.

4 fl. oz.   4 fl. oz.
SHADE®   **SHADE PLUS™**
Sunscreen   Water Resistant
Lotion   Sunscreen Lotion

Shade® Sunscreen Lotion also
available in 2 and 8 fl. oz. sizes.

Purdue Frederick

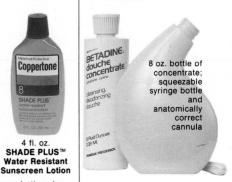

8 oz. bottle of
concentrate;
squeezable
syringe bottle
and
anatomically
correct
cannula

BETADINE® DOUCHE KIT

Plough, Inc.

Available in ¼ oz., ½ oz. and
1 oz. sizes.

**CUSHION GRIP®
Denture Adhesive**

Plough, Inc.

36 tablets per bottle

**ST. JOSEPH® ASPIRIN FOR
CHILDREN**
(1¼ grs. aspirin per tablet)

Plough, Inc.

4 fl. oz.

**SUPER SHADE® 15
Sunblocking Lotion**

Also available in 8 fl. oz.

Purdue Frederick

1 oz. tube; 1 lb. & 5 lb. jars

BETADINE® OINTMENT

Purdue Frederick

4 oz.

1 oz. and 4 oz. plastic bottles;
Also available: Betadine® Skin
Cleanser Foam

BETADINE® SKIN CLEANSER

Purdue Frederick

bottles of
30 and 60
tablets

SENOKOT® S TABLETS

BUF-PUF®
Nonmedicated Cleansing Sponge

A. H. Robins

Available in consumer cartons of 12
and 24 and bottles of 100 and 500

DIMACOL® CAPSULES

Purdue Frederick

8 oz.

BETADINE® SOLUTION

Purdue Frederick

Boxes of 12 and 50

**BETADINE®
ANTISEPTIC GAUZE PAD**

Available in bottles of 60
ALLBEE® C-800 TABLETS

A. H. Robins

4 Fl. Oz.

DIMETANE® ELIXIR
(Brompheniramine maleate elixir, USP)

Purdue Frederick

2 oz., 6 oz.,
and 12 oz.
canisters;
Also
available:
Senokot®
Suppos-
itories and
Senokot®
Syrup

SENOKOT® GRANULES

Purdue Frederick

Boxes of 12 and 50

**BETADINE®
VISCOUS FORMULA
ANTISEPTIC GAUZE PAD**

A. H. Robins

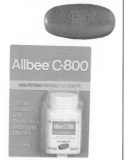

Available in bottles of 60
ALLBEE® C-800 PLUS IRON TABLETS

A. H. Robins

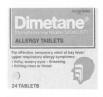

Available in consumer cartons of
24 and bottles of 100 and 500

DIMETANE® TABLETS
(Brompheniramine maleate tablets, USP)

Purdue Frederick

20 tablet pack;
bottles of
50 and 100
tablets; unit
strip pack of
100 tablets

SENOKOT® TABLETS

**CHARCOCAPS®
Intestinal Distress Capsules
for
Diarrhea, Intestinal Gas**

A. H. Robins

Available in bottles of 100 and 1000
ALLBEE® WITH C CAPSULES

A. H. Robins

4 Fl. Oz.

DIMETANE® DECONGESTANT ELIXIR

A. H. Robins

Available in consumer cartons of 24 and 48

DIMETANE® DECONGESTANT TABLETS

A. H. Robins

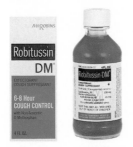

Available in bottles of 4 Fl. Oz., 8 Fl. Oz., 16 Fl. Oz. and 128 Fl. Oz.

ROBITUSSIN-DM® SYRUP

Roche

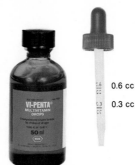

0.6 cc
0.3 cc

VI-PENTA® MULTIVITAMIN DROPS

Schering

Nose Drops 0.05%

Pediatric Nose Drops 0.025%

AFRIN® NOSE DROPS
(oxymetazoline hydrochloride, USP)

A. H. Robins

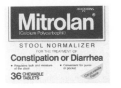

Available in consumer cartons of 36

MITROLAN® CHEWABLE TABLETS
(Calcium Polycarbophil)

A. H. Robins

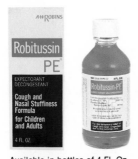

Available in bottles of 4 Fl. Oz., 8 Fl. Oz. and 16 Fl. Oz.

ROBITUSSIN-PE® SYRUP

SCHERING

1 lb jar

WMJ

4 oz tube

A and D Reg. ™ **OINTMENT**

Schering

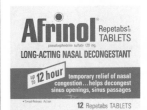

Afrinol® Repetabs® TABLETS

LONG-ACTING NASAL DECONGESTANT

up to 12 hour temporary relief of nasal congestion...helps decongest sinus openings, sinus passages

12 Repetabs TABLETS

AFRINOL® REPETABS® TABLETS
(pseudoephedrine sulfate 120 mg)

A. H. Robins

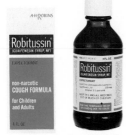

Available in bottles of 4 Fl. Oz., 8 Fl. Oz., 16 Fl. Oz. and 128 Fl. Oz.

ROBITUSSIN® SYRUP
(Guaifenesin syrup, USP)

A. H. Robins

Available in bottles of 60 and 500

Z-BEC® TABLETS

Schering

15 ml

30 ml

AFRIN® NASAL SPRAY 0.05%
(oxymetazoline hydrochloride, USP)

Schering/Emko Product Line

10 g

BECAUSE® CONTRACEPTOR®
(nonoxynol-9)

A. H. Robins

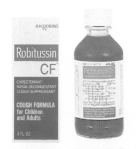

Available in bottles of 4 Fl. Oz., 8 Fl. Oz. and 16 Fl. Oz.

ROBITUSSIN-CF® SYRUP

ROCHE

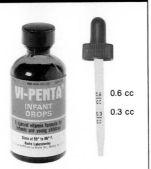

0.6 cc
0.3 cc

VI-PENTA® INFANT DROPS

Schering

15 ml

AFRIN® MENTHOL NASAL SPRAY 0.05%
(oxymetazoline hydrochloride, USP)

Schering

4 oz
(118 ml)

CHLOR-TRIMETON® ALLERGY SYRUP
(chlorpheniramine maleate, USP)

Schering

TW

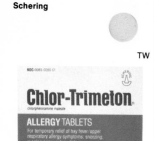

**CHLOR-TRIMETON®
ALLERGY TABLETS**
(chlorpheniramine maleate, USP)

Schering

4 oz
(118 ml)

**CORICIDIN®
COUGH SYRUP**   **CORICIDIN®
CHILDREN'S
COUGH SYRUP**

Schering

**CORICIDIN® MEDILETS®
TABLETS**

Schering

30 g (1.0 oz)   45 ml (1.5 fl. oz)

**DERMOLATE™
ANTI-ITCH CREAM AND SPRAY**
(hydrocortisone 0.5%)

Schering

901

**CHLOR-TRIMETON®
DECONGESTANT TABLETS**
(4 mg chlorpheniramine maleate, USP
and 60 mg pseudoephedrine sulfate)

Schering

20 ml

**CORICIDIN®
DECONGESTANT NASAL MIST**

Schering

**CORICIDIN®
SINUS HEADACHE TABLETS**

Schering

30 g (1.0 oz)   30 ml (1 fl. oz)

**DERMOLATE™
ANAL-ITCH OINTMENT AND
SCALP-ITCH LOTION**
(hydrocortisone 0.5%)

Schering

374

**CHLOR-TRIMETON®
LONG-ACTING ALLERGY
REPETABS® TABLETS**
(chlorpheniramine maleate, USP)

Schering

871
or
524

**CORICIDIN 'D'®
DECONGESTANT TABLETS**

Schering

PKD
or
SN
or
171

**CORICIDIN®
TABLETS**

Schering/Emko Product Line

40 g

**EMKO®
CONTRACEPTIVE FOAM**
(nonoxynol-9)

Schering/White Product Line

**COD LIVER OIL CONCENTRATE
CAPSULES**

**COD LIVER OIL CONCENTRATE
TABLETS**

**COD LIVER OIL CONCENTRATE
TABLETS W/VITAMIN C**

Schering

**CORICIDIN® DEMILETS®
TABLETS**

Schering

ADD
or
133

4 oz (118 ml)

**DEMAZIN® DECONGESTANT-
ANTIHISTAMINE REPETABS®
TABLETS AND SYRUP**

Schering/Emko Product Line

30 g

**EMKO® PRE-FIL®
CONTRACEPTIVE FOAM**
(nonoxynol-9)

Schering/White Product Line

Chronosule®
Capsules

Tablets

with Vitamin C
Chronosule®
Capsules

with Vitamin C
Tablets

MOL-IRON®

SEARLE

DRAMAMINE®
(dimenhydrinate)

Tablets, packets
of 12 (as shown)
and bottles of 36

DRAMAMINE JUNIOR®
(dimenhydrinate)
Liquid, 3 fl oz

Stuart

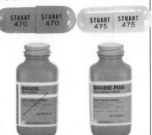

Bottles of 36, 100 and 500 capsules

DIALOSE™
(docusate potassium,
100 mg.)

DIALOSE™ PLUS
(docusate potassium,
100 mg. and casan-
thranol, 30 mg.)

Stool Softeners

Stuart

4 oz.   8 oz.

HIBICLENS®
(chlorhexidine gluconate)

Antimicrobial Skin Cleanser

Schering

SUNRIL®
PREMENSTRUAL CAPSULES

Searle Consumer Products

Powder

Balm, 3½-oz and
7-oz jars

Rub, greaseless,
1¼-oz and
3-oz tubes

ICY HOT®
Analgesic Rub for Muscle
Aches and Arthritis

Stuart

Available in
bottles of
9 and 16 oz.

Convenience
Packet

Stuart

Bottle of 60s
Available in bottles of 36 and 60 capsules

KASOF®
(docusate potassium, 240 mg.)

High Strength Stool Softener

Schering

NK

15 g   10 ml

TINACTIN®
CREAM AND SOLUTION
(tolnaftate 1%)

Searle Consumer Products

Instant Mix
Orange Flavor   Regular

METAMUCIL®
A Natural Fiber Laxative

Stuart

EFFERSYLLIUM®
INSTANT MIX
BULK LAXATIVE

Available in boxes of 12 and 24
Convenience Packets

EFFERSYLLIUM® INSTANT MIX
Bulk Laxative containing
Natural Dietary Fiber

Stuart

5 oz.   12 oz.

MYLANTA® LIQUID
Antacid/Anti-Gas

(magnesium and aluminum hydroxides
with simethicone)

Schering

100 g   **TINACTIN®**   45 g
POWDER AEROSOL AND
POWDER

STUART

5 oz.   12 oz.

ALternaGEL®
High-Potency Aluminum Hydroxide
Antacid

Stuart

Bottles
of
60 tablets

FERANCEE®-HP
Hematinic

Stuart

Available in boxes of 40 (not shown) and
100, bottles of 180, and flip-top Convenience Packs of 48

MYLANTA® TABLETS
Antacid/Anti-Gas

Stuart

Boxes of 60 tablets

12 oz.

MYLANTA®-II LIQUID and TABLETS
High Potency Antacid/Antiflatulent

Stuart

Bottles of 60 tablets

STUARTINIC®
Hematinic

Upjohn

Kaopectate®
diarrhea medicine

for relief of diarrhea

8 FL OZ

Kaopectate® Concentrate
diarrhea medicine

for relief of diarrhea

8 FL OZ

3, 8, 12 oz
&
1 gallon

2, 8, 12 oz

KAOPECTATE®

KAOPECTATE CONCENTRATE™

Anti-Diarrhea Medicine

Vicks Toiletry Div.

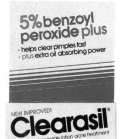

5% benzoyl peroxide plus
- helps clear pimples fast
- plus extra oil absorbing power

NEW IMPROVED!
Clearasil
5% benzoyl peroxide lotion acne treatment
1 FL OZ

1 oz.

CLEARASIL®
5% Benzoyl Peroxide Lotion
Acne Treatment

Stuart

MYLICON DROPS
Antiflatulent

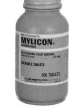

MYLICON

500 TABLETS

Bottles of 100 and 500 tablets

MYLICON DROPS

MYLICON®
Antiflatulent

1 fl. oz.

SugarLo

for milk lovers who can't digest the lactose in milk

30 QUART SUPPLY
Reduces 70% of the lactose in milk. Just add 5 drops to a quart

LactAid®
lactase enzyme

LactAid
lactase enzyme

4 qt. size, 12 qt. size, 30 qt. size

LactAid®
(lactase enzyme)

Upjohn

TRIPLE ANTIBIOTIC
First Aid Ointment
Soothing... Does Not Sting

BURNS
NICKS
CUTS
SCRAPES
SCRATCHES
SCUFFS
ABRASIONS

Mycitracin®
First Aid Ointment

Mycitracin®
First Aid Ointment

½ oz & 1 oz tubes

MYCITRACIN® Antibiotic Ointment

(bacitracin-polymyxin-neomycin topical ointment)

Vicks Toiletry Div.

TOPEX
ACNE CLEARING MEDICATION

HELPS CLEAR AND PREVENT PIMPLES

TOPEX
10% BENZOYL PEROXIDE LOTION 1 FL OZ
ACNE CLEARING MEDICATION

1 oz.

TOPEX®
Acne Clearing Medication
(10% benzoyl peroxide)

Stuart

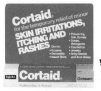

MYLICON-80

STUART 858

100 tablets

GAS
MYLICON-80
SIMETHICONE

Convenience Package of 12s

Convenience Package of 48s

GAS
MYLICON-80
FOR GAS DISTRESS   12 CHEWABLE TABLETS

MYLICON®-80
Antiflatulent

UPJOHN

Cortaid
for the temporary relief of minor SKIN IRRITATIONS, ITCHING AND RASHES

Cortaid

Cortaid

½ oz & 1 oz

CORTAID® Cream

Cortaid
SKIN IRRITATIONS, ITCHING AND RASHES

Cortaid

1 oz & 2 oz

CORTAID® Lotion

Cortaid
for the temporary relief of minor SKIN IRRITATIONS, ITCHING AND RASHES

Cortaid

½ oz & 1 oz

CORTAID® Ointment
hydrocortisone acetate
(equivalent to hydrocortisone 0.5%)

Upjohn

Available in:
Bottles of 30, 60, 90, 180, 500

Bottles of 30, 90, 500

Unicap M
SPECIAL OFFER
30 FREE

Unicap T HIGH POTENCY
SPECIAL OFFER
30 FREE

Unicap T HIGH POTENCY

UNICAP M®
Tablets

UNICAP T®
Tablets
High Potency

Vitamin-mineral supplement

VICKS TOILETRY DIV.

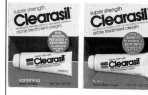

super strength
Clearasil
acne treatment cream

super strength
Clearasil
acne treatment cream

.65 and 1.0 oz. sizes available

CLEARASIL®
Acne Treatment Cream
(10% benzoyl peroxide)

VICKS HEALTH CARE DIV.

NEW
VICKS®
DayCare®
MULTI-SYMPTOM COLDS MEDICINE
Decongestant, Pain Reliever, Cough Suppressant
Relieves Colds Symptoms Without Antihistamine Which Can Cause Drowsy Side Effects.
20 CAPSULES

Blister Packs of 20s, 36s and 60s

DAYCARE®
Multi-Symptom Colds Medicine

(acetaminophen, phenylpropanolamine hydrochloride, dextromethorphan hydrobromide)

Stuart

For relief of painful symptoms of excess

GAS
MYLICON-80

Convenience Package of 12s

Convenience Package of 48s

GAS

MYLICON®-80
Antiflatulent

Vicks Health Care Div.
Bottles of 6 oz. and 10 oz.

VALUABLE COUPON INSIDE

VICKS®
DayCare®
MULTI-SYMPTOM COLDS MEDICINE
Decongestant, Pain Reliever, Cough Suppressant

Relieves Colds Symptoms Without Antihistamines Which Can Cause Drowsy Side Effects.

6 FL OZ

VICKS®
DayCare®
MULTI-SYMPTOM COLDS MEDICINE

6 FL OZ

DAYCARE®
Multi-Symptom Colds Medicine

(acetaminophen, phenylpropanolamine hydrochloride, dextromethorphan hydrobromide)

Stuart

STUART FORMULA

Bottles of 100 tablets

STUART FORMULA® TABLETS
Multivitamin/Multimineral Supplement

Vicks Health Care Div.

Available in 3 oz., 6 oz., 8 oz.

FORMULA 44®
Cough Mixture
(dextromethorphan hydrobromide,
doxylamine succinate, sodium citrate)

Vicks Health Care Div.

Available in ½ oz. and
1 oz. atomizers

SINEX™
Decongestant Nasal Spray
Special Vicks Blend of Aromatics
(menthol, eucalyptol, camphor, methyl
salicylate)

Wallace

1 pint
(473 ml)

4 fl. oz.
(118 ml)

RYNA™ LIQUID
(antihistamine-decongestant)

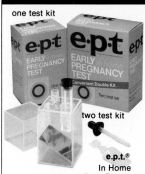

one test kit

two test kit

e.p.t.®
In Home
Early Pregnancy
Test

Vicks Health Care Div.

Available in 3 oz., 6 oz., 8 oz.

FORMULA 44D®
Decongestant Cough Mixture
(dextromethorphan hydrobromide,
phenylpropanolamine hydrochloride,
guaifenesin)

Vicks Health Care Div.

Available in ½ oz.
and 1 oz. atomizers

SINEX™ LONG-ACTING
Decongestant Nasal Spray
(xylometazoline hydrochloride)

Wallace   ℂ

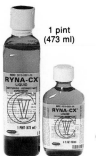

1 pint
(473 ml)

4 fl oz
(118 ml)

RYNA-C® LIQUID
(antitussive-antihistamine-decongestant)

Warner-Lambert

HALLS®
Mentho-Lyptus®
Cough Tablets

Vicks Health Care Div.

6 oz. and 10 oz.

NYQUIL® NIGHTTIME COLDS
MEDICINE
(acetaminophen, doxylamine succinate,
ephedrine sulfate, dextromethorphan
hydrobromide)

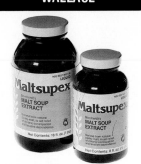

16 fl oz (1 pt)   8 fl oz (½ pt)
MALTSUPEX® LIQUID
(malt soup extract)

Wallace   ℂ

1 pint
(473 ml)

4 fl oz
(118 ml)

RYNA-CX® LIQUID
(antitussive-decongestant-expectorant)

Warner-Lambert

24 OZ. SIZE
LISTERINE
ANTISEPTIC
KILLS GERMS
BY MILLIONS
ON CONTACT

LISTERINE®
Antiseptic

Vicks Health Care Div.

1.5 oz., 3.0 oz.,
6 oz.

VICKS® VapoRub®
Decongestant Vaporizing Ointment

Special Vicks Medication
(camphor, menthol, spirits of turpentine,
eucalyptus oil, cedar leaf oil, nutmeg oil,
thymol)

Wallace

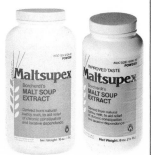

16 oz (1 lb)   8 oz (½ lb)
MALTSUPEX® POWDER
(malt soup extract)

Wallace

SYLLACT™
(powdered psyllium seed husks)

Warner-Lambert

LISTERMINT®
Mouthwash and Gargle

Warner-Lambert

LUBRIDERM®
Lotion

LUBATH®
Bath Oil

For Dry Skin Care

Warner-Lambert

Capsules

Tablets

**EXTRA-STRENGTH
SINUTAB®**

Whitehall

Available in Tins of 12 and Bottles of
20, 40, 75 and 150 Tablets

MAXIMUM STRENGTH ANACIN®
Analgesic Tablets

Whitehall

Liquid
Available in Bottles of
.31 oz. and .74 oz.

Gel
Available in
.24 oz. Tube

ANBESOL®
Antiseptic—Anesthetic

Warner-Lambert

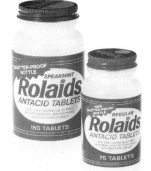

150 tablets

75 tablets

3-roll package

single roll

Available in different flavors

**ROLAIDS®
Antacid Tablets**

Warner-Lambert

**SINUTAB®
Long-Lasting Decongestant Sinus
Spray**

Whitehall

Available in Bottles of 36 and
72 Capsules

MAXIMUM STRENGTH ANACIN®
Analgesic Capsules

Whitehall

Regular Scent
Lotion: 4 oz. and
8 oz. Bottles
Gel: 2 oz. and
4 oz. Tubes

Mountain Fresh
Herbal Scent
Lotion: 4 oz. and
8 oz. Bottles

DENOREX®
Medicated Shampoo

Available in Tins of 12 and Bottles of
30, 50, 100, 200 and 300 Tablets

ANACIN®
Analgesic Tablets

Whitehall

Available in Bottles of 30, 60 and
100 Tablets

ANACIN-3®
Analgesic Tablets
100% ASPIRIN-FREE

Whitehall

Both Available in Bottles of
15 ml. and 30 ml.

DRISTAN®
Nasal Mist

Warner-Lambert

Sinutab®
Temporary relief of
Sinus Headache
and Congestion

SINUTAB®

Sinutab-II
without antihistamines
Temporary relief of
Sinus Headache
and Congestion

SINUTAB-II®
(without antihistamine)

Whitehall

Available in Bottles of 20,
40, 75 and 125 Capsules

ANACIN®
Analgesic Capsules

Whitehall

Available in Packets of 10 and Bottles
of 40, 100 and 175 Tablets

ARTHRITIS PAIN FORMULA
by the makers of ANACIN®

Analgesic Tablets

Whitehall

Available in Bottles of 15 ml. and 30 ml.

Available in 15 ml. Bottle

DRISTAN®
Long Lasting Nasal Mist

Whitehall

Available in Bottles of 24, 50 and
100 Tablets

DRISTAN® TABLETS
Decongestant/Antihistamine/Analgesic

Whitehall

Available in Boxes
of 12, 24 and 48 Suppositories

PREPARATION H®
Hemorrhoidal Suppositories

100 tablets

**ALUDROX®
TABLETS and
SUSPENSION**

Antacid

12 Fl. Oz.

Wyeth

12 Fl. Oz.

**SIMECO®
Antacid/Anti-Gas**

Whitehall

Available in Bottles of 16 and
36 Capsules

DRISTAN® CAPSULES
Decongestant/Antihistamine/Analgesic

Whitehall

Available in 10 cc.
and 15 cc. Inhaler
Units and 15 cc.
and 22.5 cc. Refills.

PRIMATENE® MIST

Wyeth

100 tablets

**AMPHOJEL®
TABLETS and
SUSPENSION**

Antacid

12 Fl. Oz.

Wyeth

**WYANOIDS®
Hemorrhoidal Suppositories**

Whitehall

Available in 1 oz. and 2 oz. Tubes

PREPARATION H®
Hemorrhoidal Ointment

Whitehall

P Formula

M Formula

Both Available in Bottles of 24 and
60 Tablets

PRIMATENE® TABLETS

Wyeth

Lotion 6 Fl. Oz. with separate
eyecup bottle cap

**COLLYRIUM
Eye Lotion
and Eyedrops**

½ Fl. Oz.

For more detailed in-
formation on products
illustrated in this sec-
tion, consult the Prod-
uct Information Sec-
tion or manufacturers
may be contacted di-
rectly.

Section 6

Product Information

This section is made possible through the courtesy of the manufacturers whose products appear on the following pages. The information concerning each product has been prepared, edited and approved by the manufacturer.

Products described in PHYSICIANS' DESK REFERENCE For NONPRESCRIPTION DRUGS comply with labeling regulations. PDR copy may include all the essential information necessary for informed usage such as active ingredients, indications, actions, warnings, drug interactions, precautions, symptoms and treatment of oral overdosage, dosage and administration, professional labeling, and how supplied. In some cases additional information has been supplied to complement the foregoing. The Publisher has emphasized to manufacturers the necessity of describing products comprehensively so that all information essential for intelligent and informed use is available. In organizing and presenting the material in PHYSICIANS' DESK REFERENCE For NONPRESCRIPTION DRUGS, the Publisher is providing all the information made available to PDR by manufacturers.

In presenting the following material to the medical profession, the Publisher is not necessarily advocating the use of any product herein listed.

Abbott Laboratories
Consumer Products Division
NORTH CHICAGO, IL 60064

CLEAR EYES®
Eye Drops

Description: Clear Eyes® is a sterile isotonic buffered solution containing naphazoline hydrochloride 0.012%, boric acid, sodium borate and water. Edetate disodium 0.1% and benzalkonium chloride 0.01% are added as preservatives.

Indications: Clear Eyes is a decongestant ophthalmic solution specially designed to moisturize as it removes redness from eyes irritated due to plant allergies (pollen), overindulgence, fatigue, swimming, colds, wearing contact lenses, and use of eyes in reading, driving, TV and close work. Clear Eyes contains laboratory tested, and scientifically blended ingredients including an effective vasoconstrictor which narrows swollen blood vessels and rapidly whitens reddened eyes in a moisturizing formulation which produces a refreshing, soothing effect. Clear Eyes is a sterile, isotonic solution compatible with the natural fluids of the eye.

Warning: Clear Eyes should only be used for minor eye irritations.

Clear Eyes should not be used by individuals with glaucoma and serious eye diseases. In some instances redness or inflammation may be due to serious eye conditions such as acute iritis, acute glaucoma, or corneal trauma. When redness, pain, or blurring persist, discontinue use. A physician should be consulted at once. Remove contact lenses before using.

Dosage and Administration: One or two drops in eye(s) two or three times daily or as directed by physician. Do not touch bottle tip to any surface, since this may contaminate the solution. Keep container tightly closed. Keep this and all other medicines out of reach of children.

How Supplied: In 0.5 fl. oz. and 1.5 fl. oz. plastic dropper bottle.

[*Shown in Product Identification Section*]

EAR DROPS BY MURINE
See Murine Ear Wax Removal
System/Murine Ear Drops

MURINE EAR WAX REMOVAL SYSTEM/MURINE EAR DROPS

Description: Carbamide peroxide 6.5% in anhydrous glycerin and a 1.0 fl. oz. soft rubber ear syringe. The MURINE EAR WAX REMOVAL SYSTEM is the only self-treatment method on the market for complete ear wax removal. Application of carbamide peroxide drops followed by warm water irrigation is the only effective, medically recommended way to remove hardened ear wax.

Actions: The carbamide peroxide formula in MURINE EAR DROPS is an aid in the removal of hardened cerumen from the ear canal. Anhydrous glycerin penetrates and softens wax while the release of oxygen from carbamide peroxide provides a mechanical action resulting in

the loosening of the softened wax accumulation. It is usually necessary to remove the loosened wax by gentle irrigation with warm water using the soft rubber ear syringe provided.

Indications: The MURINE EAR WAX REMOVAL SYSTEM is indicated as an aid in the removal of hardened or tightly packed cerumen from the ear canal or as an aid in the prevention of ceruminosis.

Caution: If redness, tenderness, pain, dizziness or ear drainage are present or develop, the medication should not be used or continued until a physician is seen. Do not use if ear drum is known to be perforated.

Dosage and Administration: For wax removal, place five drops into affected ear twice daily for three or four days. Tip of bottle should not enter ear canal. Remove softened wax after each application by gently flushing ear with warm (body temperature) water using the soft rubber ear syringe provided. Tip of syringe should be at the edge of the ear canal.

The ear canal can be kept free from accumulated hardened cerumen by regular usage of the MURINE EAR WAX REMOVAL SYSTEM.

How Supplied: The MURINE EAR WAX REMOVAL SYSTEM contains 0.5 fl. oz. drops and a 1.0 fl. oz. soft rubber ear syringe.

Also available in 0.5 fl. oz. drops only, MURINE EAR DROPS

[*Shown in Product Identification Section*]

MURINE® REGULAR FORMULA
Eye Drops

Description: Murine® Regular Formula is a sterile isotonic buffered solution containing glycerin, potassium chloride, sodium chloride, sodium phosphate (monobasic and dibasic), and water. Edetate disodium 0.05% and benzalkonium chloride 0.01% are added as preservatives.

Indications: Murine is non-staining, clear solution formulated to closely match the natural fluid of the eye for gentle, soothing relief from minor eye irritation. Use whenever desired to cleanse or refresh the eyes and to relieve minor irritation due to smog, sun glare, wind, dust, wearing contact lenses and overuse of the eyes in reading, driving, TV and close work.

Warning: Murine Regular Formula should only be used for minor eye irritations. If irritation persists or increases, discontinue use and consult your physician.

Dosage and Administration: Two or three drops into each eye several times a day or as directed by a physician. Do not touch bottle tip to any surface since this may contaminate solution. Remove contact lenses before using. Keep container tightly closed. Keep this and all medications out of reach of children.

How Supplied: In 0.5 fl. oz. and 1.5 fl. oz. plastic dropper bottle.

[*Shown in Product Identification Section*]

MURINE® PLUS
Eye Drops

Description: Murine® Plus is a sterile isotonic buffered solution containing tetrahydrozoline hydrochloride 0.05%, boric acid, sodium borate and water. Edetate disodium, 0.1% and benzalkonium chloride 0.01% are added as preservatives.

Indications: Murine Plus is a decongestant ophthalmic solution designed to refresh and soothe as it removes redness from eyes irritated due to swimming, plant allergies (pollen), overindulgence, colds, smog, sunglare, wind, dust, wearing contact lenses, and overuse of the eyes in reading, driving, TV and close work. Murine Plus contains laboratory tested, and scientifically blended ingredients including an effective vasoconstrictor which narrows swollen blood vessels and rapidly whitens reddened eyes in a formulation which produces a refreshing, soothing effect. Murine Plus is a sterile, isotonic solution compatible with the natural fluids of the eye.

Warning: Murine Plus should only be used for minor eye irritations.

Murine Plus should not be used by individuals with glaucoma and serious eye diseases. In some instances redness or inflammation may be due to serious eye conditions such as acute iritis, acute glaucoma, or corneal trauma. When redness, pain, or blurring persist, discontinue use. A physician should be consulted at once. Remove contact lenses before using.

Dosage and Administration: One or two drops in eye(s) two or three times daily or as directed by physician. Do not touch bottle tip to any surface, since this may contaminate the solution. Keep container tightly closed. Keep this and all other medicines out of reach of children.

How Supplied: In 0.5 fl. oz. and 1.5 fl. oz. plastic dropper bottle.

[*Shown in Product Identification Section*]

SELSUN BLUE®
(selenium sulfide)
Lotion

Selsun Blue is a non-prescription antidandruff shampoo containing a 1% concentration of selenium sulfide in a freshly scented, pH balanced formula to leave hair clean and manageable. Available in formulations for dry, oily or normal hair types.

Clinical testing has shown it to be safe and more effective than other leading shampoos in helping control dandruff symptoms with regular use.

Directions: Shake lotion well before using. Use just enough to lather, rinse thoroughly, and repeat. Use once or twice weekly for effective dandruff control.

Caution: For external use only. Keep this and all shampoos out of children's reach. Avoid getting shampoo in eyes—if this happens, rinse thoroughly with water. When used before or after bleaching, tinting or permanent waving, rinse hair for at least five minutes in cool running water. If irritation occurs, discontinue use. Protect from heat.

How Supplied: 4, 7 and 11 fl. oz. plastic bottles.
[*Shown in Product Identification Section*]

If desired, additional information on any Abbott Product will be provided upon request to Abbott Laboratories.

Abbott Laboratories— Abbott Pharmaceuticals, Inc.
Pharmaceutical Products Division
NORTH CHICAGO, IL 60064

OPTILETS®–500
High Potency Multivitamin for use in treatment of multivitamin deficiency.*

OPTILETS–M–500®
High Potency Multivitamin for use in treatment of multivitamin deficiency.*
Mineral supplementation added.**

Description: A therapeutic formula of ten important vitamins, with and without minerals, in a small tablet with the Abbott Filmtab® coating. Each Optilets-500 tablet provides:

Vitamin C
  (as sodium ascorbate) ....500 mg
Niacinamide ....100 mg
Calcium Pantothenate ....20 mg
Vitamin B$_1$
  (thiamine mononitrate) ....15 mg
Vitamin B$_2$ (riboflavin) ....10 mg
Vitamin B$_6$
  (pyridoxine hydrochloride) ....5 mg
Vitamin A (as palmitate
  1.5 mg, as acetate 1.5 mg—
  total 3 mg) ....10,000 IU
Vitamin B$_{12}$
  (cyanocobalamin) ....12 mcg
Vitamin D
  (ergocalciferol) ....(10 mcg) 400 IU
Vitamin E (as dl-alpha
  tocopheryl acetate) ....30 IU

Each Optilets-M-500 Filmtab contains all the vitamins in the same quantities provided in Optilets-500, plus the following minerals:
Magnesium (as oxide) ....80 mg**
Iron (as dried ferrous sulfate) ..20 mg
Copper (as sulfate) ....2 mg
Zinc (as sulfate) ....1.5 mg**
Manganese (as sulfate) ....1 mg
Iodine (as calcium iodate) ......0.15 mg
* These products contain no folic acid and only dietary supplement levels of vitamins D and E.
** Below USRDA levels.
These products do not contain FD&C Yellow No. 5 (tartrazine).
Dosage and Administration: Usual adult dosage is one Filmtab tablet daily, or as directed by physician.
How Supplied: Optilets-500 tablets are supplied in bottles of 30 (NDC 0074-4287-30) and 100 (NDC 0074-4287-13). Optilets-M-500 tablets are supplied in bottles of 30 (NDC 0074-4286-30) and 100 (NDC 0074-4286-13).

Abbott Laboratories
North Chicago, IL 60064
Ref. 02-5861-4/R8, 02-5551-4/R8

SURBEX–T®
High-Potency Vitamin B-Complex* with 500 mg of Vitamin C

Description: Each Filmtab® tablet provides:
Vitamin C (as sodium
  ascorbate) ....500 mg
Niacinamide ....100 mg
Calcium Pantothenate ....20 mg
Vitamin B$_1$ (thiamine
  mononitrate) ....15 mg
Vitamin B$_2$ (riboflavin) ....10 mg
Vitamin B$_6$ (pyridoxine
  hydrochloride ....5 mg
Vitamin B$_{12}$ (cyanocobalamin) ...10 mcg
Surbex-T does not contain FD&C Yellow No. 5 (tartrazine).
Indications: For use in treatment of Vitamin B-Complex* with Vitamin C deficiency.
* Contains no folic acid; not for treatment of folate deficiency.
Dosage and Administration: Usual adult dosage is one Filmtab tablet daily, or as directed by physician.
How Supplied: Orange-colored tablets in bottles of 50 (NDC 0074-4878-50), 100 (NDC 0074-4878-13), and 500 (NDC 0074-4878-53). Also supplied in Abbo-Pac® unit dose packages of 100 tablets in strips of 10 tablets per strip (NDC 0074-4878-11). Filmtab—Film-sealed Tablets, Abbott.
Abbott Pharmaceuticals, Inc.
North Chicago, IL 60064
Ref. 03-0783-3/R4

SURBEX®–750 with IRON
High-Potency B-Complex with Iron, Vitamin E and 750 mg Vitamin C

Description: Each Filmtab® tablet provides:
VITAMINS
Vitamin C (as sodium ascorbate) 750 mg
Niacinamide .... 100 mg
Vitamin B$_6$ (pyridoxine
  hydrochloride) .... 25 mg
Calcium Pantothenate .... 20 mg
Vitamin B$_1$ (thiamine
  mononitrate) .... 15 mg
Vitamin B$_2$ (riboflavin) .... 15 mg
Vitamin B$_{12}$ (cyanocobalamin) 12 mcg
Folic Acid ....400 mcg
Vitamin E (as dl-alpha tocopheryl
  acetate) .... 30 IU
MINERAL
Elemental Iron (as dried
  ferrous sulfate) .... 27 mg
  equivalent to 135 mg ferrous sulfate
Indications: For the treatment of vitamin C and B-Complex deficiencies and to supplement the daily intake of iron and vitamin E.
Dosage and Administration: Usual adult dosage is one tablet daily or as directed by physician.
How Supplied: Bottles of 50 tablets (NDC 0074-8029-50)
Abbott Pharmaceuticals, Inc.
North Chicago, IL 60064
Ref. 03-0723-2/R2

SURBEX®–750 with ZINC
Zinc, Vitamin B-Complex and Vitamins C and E for persons 12 years of age or older

Description: Daily dose (one Filmtab® tablet) provides:

		%U.S.
VITAMINS		**R.D.A.***
Vitamin E	30 IU	100%
Vitamin C	750 mg	1250%
Folic Acid	0.4 mg	100%
Thiamine (B$_1$)	15 mg	1000%
Riboflavin (B$_2$)	15 mg	882%
Niacin	100 mg	500%
Vitamin B$_6$	20 mg	1000%
Vitamin B$_{12}$	12 mcg	200%
Pantothenic Acid	20 mg	200%
MINERAL		
Zinc**	22.5 mg	150%

* % U.S. Recommended Daily Allowance for Adults.
** Equivalent to 100 mg of Zinc Sulfate.
Ingredients: Sodium ascorbate, niacinamide, zinc sulfate, dl-alpha tocopheryl acetate, povidone, cellulose, pyridoxine hydrochloride, calcium pantothenate, thiamine mononitrate, riboflavin, cyanocobalamin, magnesium stearate, colloidal silicon dioxide, folic acid, in a film-coated tablet with vanillin flavoring and artificial coloring added.
Usual Adult Dose: One tablet daily.
How Supplied: Bottles of 50 tablets (NDC 0074-8152-50).
Abbott Pharmaceuticals, Inc.
North Chicago, IL 60064
Ref. 03-0724-2/R3

If desired, additional information on any Abbott Product will be provided upon request to Abbott Laboratories.

Adria Laboratories Inc.
5000 POST ROAD
DUBLIN, OH 43017

(includes products formerly marketed by Warren-Teed Laboratories)

MODANE® Bulk

Description: Modane Bulk is a powdered mixture consisting of: Psyllium and dextrose in equal parts.
Actions: Modane Bulk acts to increase the frequency of bowel movements by adding bulk and softens the fecal mass by retaining water.
Indications: Modane Bulk is useful in the treatment of constipation resulting from an inadequate or low residue diet. It is also useful as adjunctive therapy in treating the constipation of diverticular disease and in spastic or irritable colon, as well as in the bowel management of hemorrhoids, pregnancy, convalescence and senility.
Contraindications: Intestinal obstruction, fecal impaction.
Adverse Reactions: Esophageal, gastric, small intestinal and rectal obstruction due to the accumulation of mucil-

Continued on next page

Adria—Cont.

aginous components of psyllium have been reported. Most frequently this results from inadequate water intake or underlying organic disease. The dosage and administration schedule and fluid requirements should be carefully observed, as with other preparations.

Precaution: This product may combine with certain other drugs. Do not take this product if you are presently taking salicylates or a prescription drug.

Dosage and Administration: Adults (over 12 years): one rounded teaspoonful taken 1–3 times a day stirred into an 8 ounce glass of water, juice or other suitable liquids and preferably followed by an equal amount of liquid. Children (6 to 12 years): One-half the adult dosage in 8 ounces of liquid.

The laxative effect usually occurs in 12–24 hours, but up to three days of medication may be necessary to achieve full effect.

This product information is for professional use only.

How Supplied:
NDC 0013-5025-72 14 oz. container.
[*Shown in Product Identification Section*]

MODANE® Soft
(Docusate Sodium Capsules)

Description: Each Modane Soft capsule contains docusate sodium, 120 mg, in a soft-gelatin capsule and color additives including FD&C Yellow No. 5 (Tartrazine).

Actions: Modane Soft is a stool softener which has surface active properties believed to permit water and lipid to penetrate the fecal mass and soften the stool for easier passage.

Indications: Functional constipation caused by dry, hard stools. Modane Soft is useful when painful rectal conditions or other patient conditions require a soft, easily passed stool.

Contraindications: Mineral oil administration, or when abdominal pain, nausea, or vomiting are present.

Dosage and Administration: Adults (over 12 years)—1 to 3 capsules daily. Children (6 to 12 years)—1 capsule daily. Usually require 1–2 days for full effect.

How Supplied:
NDC 0013-5031-13 Package of 30 capsules.
[*Shown in Product Identification Section*]

MODANE® TABLETS AND LIQUID
(Danthron)

Description: Modane Tablets (yellow) —Each tablet contains danthron 75 mg and color additives including FD&C Yellow No. 5 (tartrazine). Modane Mild Tablets (half-strength, pink)—Each tablet contains danthron 37.5 mg and color additives including FD&C Yellow No. 5 (tartrazine). Modane Liquid—Each 5 ml (teaspoonful) contains danthron 37.5 mg and alcohol 5%.

Actions: Laxative.

Indications: A laxative designed for gentle overnight relief of constipation without straining, griping or cramping at optimal dosage. There is usually no tolerance build-up or need for increasing dosage with danthron, the laxative component of MODANE having a selective action on the large bowel. MODANE may be useful in the management of constipation in geriatric, cardiac, surgical, pregnant, post partum and pediatric patients. MODANE has been found useful in the management of constipation which may occur with or during the concomitant use of ganglionic blocking agents, antihistamines, tranquilizers, sympathomimetics and anticholingergics.

Contraindications: Should not be used when abdominal pain, nausea, vomiting or other signs and/or symptoms of appendicitis are present.

Precautions: Frequent or prolonged use of this preparation may result in dependence on laxatives. Pink coloration of urine is harmless and usually signals an alkaline urine (frequently a diagnostic aid). If excessive bowel activity due to excessive dosage causes perianal irritation, discontinue MODANE temporarily and/or decrease dosage. Hypokalemia may impair the effectiveness of Modane. MODANE TABLETS and MODANE MILD TABLETS contain FD&C Yellow No. 5 (tartrazine) which may cause allergic-type reactions (including bronchial asthma) in certain susceptible individuals. Although the overall incidence of FD&C Yellow No. 5 (tartrazine) sensitivity in the general population is low, it is frequently seen in patients who also have aspirin hypersensitivity.

Dosage and Administration: Modane Tablet (yellow)—Adults—1 tablet with the evening meal. Modane Mild Tablet (half-strength, pink)—Adults—1 or 2 tablets with the evening meal. For hypersensitive, diet-restricted and bedfast patients; also children (6 to 12 years of age)—1 tablet with the evening meal. Modane Liquid—Adults—1 to 2 teaspoonfuls with the evening meal. For hypersensitive, diet-restricted and bedfast patients; also children (6 to 12 years of age)—1 teaspoonful with the evening meal. Children (1 to 6 years of age)—¼ to 1 teaspoonful, according to age, with the evening meal. Infants (6 to 12 months of age)—⅕ to ¼ teaspoonful (20 to 25 drops), according to age, with the evening meal.

How Supplied:
Modane Tablets
NDC 0013-5011-17 Bottle of 100 Tablets
NDC 0013-5011-23 Bottle of 1000 Tablets
NDC 0013-5011-18 Stat-Pak® (Unit Dose of one tablet) 100's only
NDC 0013-5011-07 Package of 10
NDC 0013-5011-13 Package of 30
Modane Mild Tablets
NDC 0013-5021-17 Bottle of 100 Tablets
NDC 0013-5021-23 Bottle of 1000 Tablets
Modane Liquid
NDC 0013-5033-51 Pint
A.H.F.S. 56:12
[*Shown in Product Identification Section*]

MYOFLEX® CREME
(Triethanolamine Salicylate)

Description: Triethanolamine salicylate 10% in a non-greasy base. Nonirritating, nonburning, odorless, stainless, readily absorbed.

Actions: Topical Analgesic. Penetration assured with maximal salicylate appearing in urine 5 hours after application.

Indications: An effective analgesic rub for sore muscles, joint attachments, stiffness and strains; a helpful topical adjunct in arthritis and rheumatism. Excellent as a hand cream for patients with minor rheumatic stiffness and soreness of the hands. Excellent for sore feet.

Contraindications: Do not use in patient's manifesting idiosyncrasy to salicylates.

Warnings: For external use only. Avoid getting into eyes or on mucous membranes. To be used only according to directions. Keep out of the reach of children.

Precautions: Apply to affected parts only. Do not apply to irritated skin or if excessive irritation develops, consult physician. A 2 oz. tube contains the salicylate equivalent of about 56 grains of aspirin.

Adverse Reactions: None reported, but if applied to large skin areas may cause typical salicylate side effects such as tinnitus, nausea, or vomiting.

Dosage and Administration: Adults — Rub into area of soreness two or three times daily. Wrists, elbows, knees and ankles may be wrapped loosely with 2″ or 3″ elastic bandage after liberal application.

How Supplied:
NDC 0013-5404-61 Tubes, 2 oz.
NDC 0013-5404-74 Jars, 1 lb.
[*Shown in Product Identification Section*]

Alcon/bp
Alcon Laboratories, Inc.
6201 SOUTH FREEWAY
FORT WORTH, TX 76101

HARD CONTACT LENS PRODUCTS

ADAPETTES®
Sterile lubricating and rewetting solution for use with conventional hard contact lenses, soft (hydrophilic) contact lenses, and contact lenses made from other new polymers.[7]

Description: A sterile, buffered, isotonic, aqueous solution containing Adsorbobase®* (povidone with other water soluble polymers) with thimerosal 0.004% and edetate disodium 0.1% added as preservatives. ADAPETTES is designed for use, while the contact lens is on the eye, as a rewetting and/or lubricating solution. ADAPETTES may also help remove particulate material.

Administration: Place one drop of ADAPETTES on each lens 3 or 4 times a day or as needed. If minor irritation, discomfort or blurring occur while wearing

the lenses, place a drop of ADAPETTES on the eye and blink 2 or 3 times.
Warning: If discomfort persists after using ADAPETTES, the patient should remove lenses and see an eye care practitioner.
Supplied: ½ fl. oz. (15 ml) plastic dropper vials.
*Patented
[*Shown in Product Identification Section*]

CLENS®
A Concentrated Cleansing Solution for Hard Contact Lenses

Description: CLENS is a concentrated solution specially formulated for the effective cleansing of hard contact lenses. Routine use of CLENS helps prevent mucus, oil and other troublesome deposits from accumulating on the lens surfaces.
Warning: Should not be used as a soaking or wetting solution.
Contains: Active Ingredients: benzalkonium chloride 0.02%, edetate disodium 0.1%.
Supplied: 2 fl. oz plastic containers.
[*Shown in Product Identification Section*]

SOACLENS®
Dual-Purpose Soaking and Wetting Solution for Hard Contact Lenses

Description: SOACLENS is a carefully balanced, tear-like solution, buffered to closely approximate the pH and tonicity of the eye. Thimerosal 0.004% and edetate disodium 0.1% are added as preservatives.
The routine use of SOACLENS, for overnight storage of the lenses, facilitates maximum hydration and wettability. The convenient one-step soaking and wetting procedure helps assure prolonged comfort and wearing time.
Directions: Fill kit with sufficient SOACLENS to cover lens. Insert lens onto eye directly from SOACLENS bath or lens may be rinsed with water or a few drops of SOACLENS before reinsertion.
Supplied: 4 fl. oz. (120ml) plastic containers. A complimentary disposable storage case is supplied with each carton of SOACLENS.
[*Shown in Product Identification Section*]

SOFT CONTACT LENS PRODUCTS
(or lenses made from other new polymers)

ADAPETTES®
Sterile lubricating and rewetting solution for use with conventional hard contact lenses, soft (hydrophilic) contact lenses, and contact lenses made from other new polymers.[7]

Description: A sterile, buffered, isotonic, aqueous solution containing Adsorbobase®* (povidone with other water soluble polymers) with thimerosal 0.004% and edetate disodium 0.1% added as preservatives. ADAPETTES is designed for use, while the contact lens is on the eye, as a rewetting and/or lubricating solution. ADAPETTES may also help remove particulate material.

Administration: Place one drop of ADAPETTES on each lens 3 or 4 times a day or as needed. If minor irritation, discomfort or blurring occur while wearing the lenses, place a drop of ADAPETTES on the eye and blink 2 or 3 times.
Warning: If discomfort persists after using ADAPETTES, the patient should remove lenses and see an eye care practitioner.
Supplied: ½ fl. oz. (15 ml) plastic dropper vials.
*Patented
[*Shown in Product Identification Section*]

BOILnSOAK®
Sterile, preserved, saline solution for rinsing, storage and heat disinfection of soft (hydrophilic) contact lenses.[1]

Description: A sterile, buffered, isotonic, aqueous solution containing boric acid, sodium borate and sodium chloride 0.7%, preserved with thimerosal 0.001% and edetate disodium 0.1%.
Administration: After lenses have been cleaned with PREFLEX®, BOILnSOAK is used to rinse lenses free of loosened debris and traces of the cleaner. Disinfection of lenses is accomplished by immersing lenses in BOILnSOAK, in the carrying case, and heating them in a thermal unit designed for this procedure. If no thermal unit is available, lenses may be disinfected by immersing them in BOILnSOAK, in the carrying case, and dropping the sealed case into a pan of already boiling water. Remove the pan from heat after ten minutes and allow the water to cool before handling lenses.
Warnings: Fresh BOILnSOAK must be used daily for disinfection and storage. NEVER REUSE BOILnSOAK. DO NOT ALTERNATE THE HEAT AND CHEMICAL DISINFECTING REGIMENS. DO NOT ALTERNATE USE OF BOILnSOAK WITH COLD (CHEMICAL) DISINFECTING PRODUCTS. Do not touch tip of bottle to any surface since this may contaminate solution. If irritation occurs and persists or increases, discontinue use and consult your eye care practitioner.
Supplied: 8 fl. oz. (237 ml) and 12 fl. oz. (355 ml) plastic containers.
[*Shown in Product Identification Section*]

FLEX–CARE®
Sterile solution for rinsing, storage and cold (chemical) disinfection of soft (hydrophilic) contact lenses or lenses made from other new polymers.[6]

Description: A sterile, buffered, isotonic, aqueous solution containing sodium chloride, sodium borate and boric acid, having a tonicity of approximately 289 mOsm. Thimerosal 0.001%, edetate disodium 0.1% and chlorhexidine 0.005% are added as preservatives. FLEX-CARE is used as the rinsing, storage and disinfection solution in conjunction with the PREFLEX® and FLEX-CARE cold (chemical) disinfection system.
Administration: After cleaning with PREFLEX, each lens should be thor-

oughly rinsed with FLEX-CARE (for approximately 10 seconds) to remove loosened debris and traces of the cleaner, prior to storage and disinfection of lenses in FLEX-CARE. Lenses should be completely submerged, in their storage case, and stored in FLEX-CARE for a minimum of 4 hours to assure disinfection. Prior to reinsertion of lenses, they should be rinsed with fresh FLEX-CARE.
Warnings: Fresh FLEX-CARE must be used daily for storage. NEVER REUSE FLEX-CARE. NEVER HEAT LENSES IN FLEX-CARE. DO NOT ALTERNATE USE OF FLEX-CARE WITH HEAT DISINFECTING PRODUCTS OR OTHER COLD (CHEMICAL) DISINFECTING PRODUCTS.
WHEN THE ENZYMATIC CONTACT LENS CLEANER (PAPAIN) IS USED IN CONJUNCTION WITH THIS PRODUCT, CARE MUST BE TAKEN TO EFFECTIVELY CLEAN AND THOROUGHLY RINSE THE LENS AFTER ENZYME TREATMENT AND BEFORE LENS DISINFECTION. Do not touch the dropper tip of bottle to any surface since this may contaminate the solution
Supplied: 12 fl. oz (355 ml) plastic containers.
[*Shown in Product Identification Section*]

PREFLEX®
Sterile cleaning solution for use with soft (hydrophilic) contact lenses or lenses made from other new polymers.[3]

Description: A sterile, buffered, isotonic, aqueous solution consisting of sodium phosphates, sodium chloride, tyloxapol, hydroxyethylcellulose and polyvinyl alcohol, with thimerosal 0.004% and edetate disodium 0.2% added as preservatives. Daily cleaning with PREFLEX helps prevent oil, mucus and other troublesome deposits from accumulating on the lens surfaces.
Administration: Before handling lenses, hands should be cleaned with non-cosmetic soap, rinsed thoroughly, and dried with a lint-free towel. Apply 3 drops of PREFLEX to each lens surface and thoroughly clean by rubbing between thumb and forefinger for at least 20 seconds. Lenses should be rinsed, disinfected and stored in accordance with the lens care procedures recommended by the eye care practitioner.
Warning: PREFLEX is not intended for use directly in the eye.
Supplied: 1.5 fl. oz. (45 ml) plastic containers.
[*Shown in Product Identification Section*]

1-7:

ACCUGEL™ (droxifilcon)
Strieter Laboratories

AMSOF® (deltafilcon A)
Lombart Lenses, Ltd.
Div. of American Sterilizer Co.

Continued on next page

Alcon/bp—Cont.

AOSOFT® (tetrafilcon A)
American Optical Corp.
Soft Contact Lens Division

AQUAFLEX® (tetrafilcon A)
UCO Optics, Inc.

AQUA-SOFT® (deltafilcon A)
Aquarius Soft Lens, Inc.

CUSTOM-FLEX™ (deltafilcon A)
Custom Contact Lens Lab., Inc.

DURASOFT® (phemfilcon A)
Wesley-Jessen, Inc.

DURASOFT® TT (phemfilcon A)
Wesley-Jessen, Inc.

FLEXLENS™ (hefilcon A) PHP
PHP (U.S. Pat. 3,721,657)
Trademark of Automated Optics, Inc.
Manufactured by Flexlens™, Inc.

GELFLEX® (dimefilcon A)
Dow Corning Ophthalmics, Inc.

HYDROCURVE® (hefilcon A) PHP
PHP (U.S. Pat. 3,721,657)
Trademark of Automated Optics, Inc.
Manufactured by Soft Lenses, Inc.

HYDROCURVE® II (bufilcon A)
Soft Lenses, Inc.

HYDRO-MARC® (etafilcon A)
Frontier Contact Lenses, Inc.

HYDRON® (polymacon)
National Patent Development Corp.

MIRACON™ (hefilcon B)
Bausch & Lomb Soflens Division
Bausch & Lomb, Inc.

NATURVUE® (hefilcon A) PHP
PHP (U.S. Pat. 3,721,657)
Trademark of Automated Optics, Inc.
Manufactured by Milton Roy Co.

NU-SOFT® (deltafilcon A)
Vent-Air Optics, Inc.

PERMALENS® (perfilcon A)
Cooper Laboratories

SOF-FORM® (deltafilcon A)
Sof-Form, Inc.
Div. of Salvatori Ophthalmics, Inc.

SOFLENS® (polymacon)
Bausch & Lomb Soflens Division
Bausch & Lomb, Inc.

SOFT-FLOW™ (deltafilcon A)
Medicornea, Inc.

SOFTICS™ (deltafilcon A)
Advanced Soft Optics, Inc.

SOFTSITE® (hefilcon A) PHP
PHP (U.S. Pat. 3,721,657)
Trademark of Automated Optics, Inc.
Manufactured by
Paris Contact Lens Laboratory

TRÈSOFT® (ocufilcon A)
Alcon Optic Division
Alcon Laboratories, Inc.

TRI POL 43® (deltafilcon A)
Comfortflex Hydrophilics, Inc.
Div. of Capitol Contact Lenses, Inc.

3-7:

CABCURVE™ (porofocon B)
Soft Lenses, Inc.

RX-56® (porofocon A)
Rynco Scientific Corp.

SOFTCON® (vifilcon A, cosmetic)
American Optical Corp.
Soft Contact Lens Division

1-3:

SOFTCON® (vifilcon A, therapeutic)
American Optical Corp.
Soft Contact Lens Division

3, 6, 7:

POLYCON® (silafocon A)
Syntex Ophthalmics, Inc.

3-6:

MESO® (cabufocon A)
Danker Laboratories, Inc.

Allergan Pharmaceuticals, Inc.
**2525 DUPONT DRIVE
IRVINE, CA 92713**

LIQUIFILM® TEARS
Artificial Tears

Active Ingredient: Polyvinyl alcohol 1.4% with chlorobutanol 0.5% as a preservative and sodium chloride.
Indications: Dry eye conditions and hard contact lens wear discomfort.
Actions: Soothes and lubricates dry eyes and promotes comfort and longer wearing of hard contact lenses.
Warnings: If irritation persists or increases, discontinue use. Keep container tightly closed. Do not touch dropper tip to any surface to prevent contamination. Not for use with soft contact lenses. Keep out of reach of children.
Precaution: (See Warnings).
Dosage and Administration: 1 drop in the eye as needed, or as directed by physician.
Professional Labeling: Same as outlined under Indications.
How Supplied: 15 ml and 30 ml plastic bottles.
[*Shown in Product Identification Section*]

PREFRIN™ LIQUIFILM®
decongestant ophthalmic solution

Active Ingredient: Phenylephrine HCl 0.12%, polyvinyl alcohol 1.4%, and benzalkonium chloride 1:25,000.
Indications: Minor eye irritations.
Actions: Lubricates and whitens the eye; relieves and soothes minor eye irritations.
Warnings: Do not use in presence of narrow-angle glaucoma. If irritation persists or increases, discontinue use. Keep container tightly closed; do not touch dropper tip to any surface to avoid contamination. Not for use with soft contact lenses. Pupillary dilation may occur in some individuals.
Precaution: (See Warnings).
Dosage and Administration: 1 or 2 drops in each eye; repeat in 3 to 4 hours as needed.
Professional Labeling: Same as outlined under Indications.
How Supplied: 20 ml plastic bottle.
[*Shown in Product Identification Section*]

TEARS PLUS™
Artificial Tears

Active Ingredient: Polyvinyl alcohol 1.4% and povidone, with chlorobutanol 0.5% as a preservative and sodium chloride.
Indications: Dry eye conditions.
Actions: Soothes and lubricates dry eyes.
Warnings: If irritation persists or increases, discontinue use. Keep container tightly closed. Do not touch dropper tip to any surface to prevent contamination. Not for use with soft contact lenses. Keep out of reach of children.
Precaution: (See Warnings).
Dosage and Administration: 1 drop in the eye as needed or directed.
Professional Labeling: Same as outlined under Indications.
How Supplied: 15 ml plastic bottles.
[*Shown in Product Identification Section*]

Almay Hypoallergenic Cosmetics and Toiletries
Almay, Inc.
**850 THIRD AVENUE
NEW YORK, NY 10022**

Almay Hypoallergenic Cosmetics and Toiletries
Almay, Inc.
**PROFESSIONAL SERVICE DEPT.
APEX, NC 27502**

ALMAY HYPOALLERGENIC COSMETICS, SKIN CARE PRODUCTS AND TOILETRIES manufacture a complete line of high fashion cosmetics and skin care (treatment-aid) products including antiperspirant/deodorants; astringents; bath products; cleansers; conditioners; covering agents; moisturizers and emollients; hair and nail care products.
Cosmetics as well as skin care products are prepared for three skin types: normal/combination skin; dry skin and oily skin. ALL ALMAY PRODUCTS ARE FRAGRANCE-FREE AND FREE OF MASKING ODORS. All products are formulated in accordance with Almay's Cosmetic Control System to assure hypoallergenicity. The Rabbit Ear Assay for comedogenicity has been added to the roster of safety testing. All of the Almay foundation lotions, moisture lotions and blushers have been shown to be non-comedogenic.
Almay manufactures two lines of skin care (treatment-aid) products, a Deep Mist collection for the care of normal/combination and dry skin and a Counter Balance collection for the care of oily skin. Our Pure Beauty line of makeup, blushers and face powder is comprised of formulations for all skin types. For normal/combination skin Almay recommends cleansing with Almay Cold Cream Soap, Deep Mist Cleansing Lotion or Deep Mist Cleanser (Cream) for soap-sensitive individuals; Deep Mist Toning and Refining Lotion, a stimulating purifier;

Deep Mist Ultralight Moisture Lotion to alleviate dryness and Pure Beauty Liquid Makeup. Combination skin refers to T-Zone oiliness limited to the forehead, nose and chin with normal or somewhat dry cheeks and temples.

For dry to very dry skin Almay recommends Deep Mist Cleanser which protects the skin by the deposition of a fine oily film; Deep Mist Mild Skin Freshener for toning, Deep Mist Moisture Lotion or Cream to alleviate excessive dryness and Pure Beauty Moisturizing Makeup.

For oily skin Almay recommends cleansing with Counter Balance Facial Soap, Counter Balance Pore Lotion, a potent lipid (skin oil) remover, Counter Balance Oil-Free Moisturizer for dry, scaly areas and Pure Beauty Foundation Lotion, an oil-free, water-based makeup.

Pure Beauty Extra Cover Makeup may be used for all skin types, if heavier coverage is required because of blemishes or other minor skin defects.

Pure and Gentle Everyday Conditioning Shampoo, Clean and Gentle Oil-Free Conditioner and Protein Conditioning Hair Spray may be used as often as needed for all types of hair to enhance, luster, sheen and combability. These products are particularly helpful in the care of hair that has been chemically, mechanically or environmentally damaged, e.g. excessive sun exposure.

Almay's hypoallergenic cosmetics are high fashioned, and are obtainable in a wide variety of shades.

Literature: Almay's Product Formulary and Cosmetic Guide lists products, ingredient disclosures and the action and uses of all products. A detailed description of the Almay Cosmetic Control System is likewise available as well as lay literature dealing with cosmetics.

[*Shown in Product Identification Section*]

Anabolic Laboratories, Inc.
17802 GILLETTE AVENUE
IRVINE, CA 92714

AQUA-A
Chewable, emulsified "water solublized" vitamin A tablets

Description: AQUA-A is a pleasant tasting emulsified vitamin A formula (from non-fish oil sources), providing excellent absorption. It is in a soft tablet form which may be chewed, dissolved in the mouth or swallowed providing 25,000 I.U. of vitamin A (palmitate) per tablet.
Indication: For use as a vitamin A supplement.
Warning: Keep out of the reach of children.
Dosage and Administration: One tablet daily to be chewed or allowed to dissolve in the mouth for faster and better absorption.
How Supplied: Bottle of 90 tablets.

B6-PLUS
Vitamin B6 supplement with Magnesium

Description: B6-PLUS combines vitamin B6 and magnesium which function together as coenzyme and cofactor in many reactions throughout the body, along with other supportive factors. Each tablet provides:

		% U.S. RDA*
Vitamin B6 (pyridoxine HCl)	50 mg	2500
Vitamin B1 (thiamine HCl)	10 mg	667
Vitamin B2 (riboflavin)	2.4 mg	141
Niacin	20 mg	100
Potassium (as potassium citrate)	50 mg	**
Magnesium (as magnesium oxide)	50 mg	12.5

In a base containing concentrate of adrenal substance.
Percentage of U.S. Recommended Daily Allowance for adults and children four or more years of age.
**RDA has not been established.
Indication: Vitamin B6 supplement.
Dosage and Administration: Usual adult dosage one or two tablets daily or as directed by physician.
How Supplied: Bottle of 100 tablets.

B12-PLUS
Vitamin B12 supplement

Description: Each tablet provides 250 mcg of vitamin B12 on an ion exchange resin designed to release the vitamin in the intestine insuring maximum absorption. Provides 4167% of the U.S. Recommended Daily Allowance for adults and children four or more years of age.
Indication: Vitamin B12 supplement.
Dosage and Administration: Usual adult dosage one or two tablets daily or as directed by physician.
How Supplied: Bottle of 120 or 60 tablets.

CAL-M
Calcium-Magnesium supplement

Description: Three tablets provide:

		% U.S. RDA*
Calcium (from calcium lactate)	250 mg	25
Magnesium (from magnesium oxide)	200 mg	50
Vitamin B1 (thiamine)	45 mg	3000
Vitamin B6 (pyridoxine HCl)	45 mg	2250
Niacin	90 mg	450
Vitamin D (from yeast)	400 I.U.	100

*Percentage of U.S. Recommended Daily Allowance for adults and children four or more years of age.
Indication: CAL-M is a source of calcium and magnesium when it is desired to increase dietary intake of these minerals. CAL-M also contains other supportive factors including vitamin D which aids in the absorption of calcium.
Dosage and Administration: Usual adult dosage three tablets daily or as directed by physician.
How Supplied: Bottle of 90 tablets.

CHOLAGEST
Digestive aid

Description: CHOLAGEST is a complete formula containing digestive enzymes to aid in absorption of protein, fats and carbohydrates, and bile extract to aid in emulsifying fats. In addition, CHOLAGEST contains dehydrocholic acid which thins out thickened bile allowing for much smoother flow. Each tablet provides:

Pancreatic concentrate*	100 mg
Cellulase	2.5 mg
Ox bile extract	65 mg
Dehydrocholic acid	20 mg

* Standardized to supply 10,000 Wilson Units of amylase, 9,000 Wilson Units of protease and 240 Wilson Units of lipase.
Indication: For use as a comprehensive formulation of natural enzymes to assist in the digestion of protein fats and carbohydrates.
Warning: Keep out of the reach of children.
Dosage and Administration: One or two tablets before each meal.
How Supplied: Bottle of 90 tablets.

TRI-88
Sustained release iron capsules

Description: TRI-88 is a sustained release formula containing iron, vitamins B_{12} and B_1, and whole liver. Because the iron is slowly released over several hours and is present as the fumarate, intestinal disturbances and other uncomfortable side effects often associated with the administration of iron are minimized. Each capsule provides:

Iron (ferrous fumarate)	110 mg
Vitamin B_1 (thiamine hydrochloride)	5 mg
Vitamin B_{12} (cyanocobalamin)	30 mcg
Whole liver	100 mg

Indication: For use as an iron supplement.
Warnings: Keep out of the reach of children. Not for pernicious anemia.
Dosage and Administration: One capsule daily after breakfast.
How Supplied: Bottles of 60 and 30 capsules. Available with child-resistant cap.

TRI-ADRENOPAN
Sustained release pantothenic acid capsules

Description: TRI-ADRENOPAN is a sustained release, high-potency pantothenic acid formula with vitamins C and B6, and other supportive factors. Two capsules provide:

Pantothenic acid (calcium pantothenate)	250 mg
Vitamin C (ascorbic acid)	100 mg
Vitamin B6 (pyridoxine hydrochloride)	25 mg

In a base containing whole adrenal substance, whole pituitary and liver.
Indication: For use as a pantothenic acid supplement.

Continued on next page

Anabolic—Cont.

Dosage and Administration: One or two capsules after breakfast and dinner.
How Supplied: Bottle of 60 capsules.

TRI–B3
Sustained release niacin capsules

Description: TRI-B3 is a sustained release niacin product supplied in specially coated pellets designed to release over several hours. This feature reduces or eliminates the flushing and skin irritation often present when administering straight niacin. Each capsule provides 300 mg of niacin.
Indications: For use as vitamin B_3 (niacin) supplement.
Administration and Dosage: One capsule daily after breakfast.
How Supplied: Bottle of 90 capsules.

TRI–B–PLEX
Sustained release B-complex capsules

Description: TRI-B-PLEX is a complete, balanced, high-potency B-complex formula in sustained release form designed to release over an eight hour period ensuring maximum and efficient utilization and effectiveness. Two capsules provide:

Vitamin B_1
(thiamine hydrochloride) ....100 mg
Vitamin B_2
(riboflavin) ....40 mg
Niacinamide ....200 mg
Vitamin B_6
(pyridoxine hydrochloride) ......50 mg
Folic acid ....400 mcg
Vitamin B_{12}
(cyanocobalamin) ....25 mcg
Biotin ....300 mcg
Pantothenic acid
(calcium pantothenate) ....100 mg

Indication: For use as a complete B-complex supplement.
Dosage and Administration: One capsule after breakfast and one after dinner.
How Supplied: Bottle of 60 capsules.

TRI–C–500
Sustained release vitamin C capsules

Description: TRI-C-500 is a high-potency, sustained release vitamin C product designed to maintain high blood and tissue levels of vitamin C throughout the day. TRI-C-500 provides 500 mg of vitamin C (ascorbic acid) per capsule.
Indication: For use as a vitamin C supplement.
Dosage and Administration: One capsule after breakfast and dinner.
How Supplied: Bottles of 120 and 60 capsules.

Products are cross-indexed by

generic and chemical names in the

YELLOW SECTION

Arco Pharmaceuticals, Inc.
105 ORVILLE DRIVE
BOHEMIA, NY 11716

CODEXIN™ Extra Strength Capsules
Time Release Appetite suppressant and diuretic

Active Ingredients: Each continuous action capsule contains:
Phenylpropanolamine HCl ....75 mg.
Caffeine...200 mg.
Indication: For continuous all day appetite control.
Caution: For adult use only. Do not give this product to children under 12 years of age. Do not exceed recommended dose. If nervousness, dizziness, sleeplessness, rapid pulse, palpitations, or other symptoms occur discontinue medication and consult your physician. If you have, or are being treated for high blood pressure, heart diabetes, thyroid or other disease, or while pregnant, or nursing under the age of 18 do not take this drug except under the advice of a physician or pharmacist.
Precaution: If you are taking any prescription drugs or another medication containing Phenylpropanolamine do not take this drug except under the advice and supervision of a physician.
Dosage and Administration: One capsule in the morning between 10 and 11 o'clock with a full glass of water.
How Supplied: Continuous action capsules. Package of 21 and 42 with 1200 calorie diet plan.

MEGA–B®
(super potency vitamin B complex, sugar & starch free)

Composition: Each Mega-B Tablet contains the following Mega Vitamins:

B_1 (Thiamine Mononitrate)	100 mg.
B_2 (Riboflavin)	100 mg.
B_6 (Pyridoxine Hydrochloride)	100 mg.
B_{12} (Cyanocobalamin)	100 mcg.
Choline Bitartrate	100 mg.
Inositol	100 mg.
Niacinamide	100 mg.
Folic Acid	100 mcg.
Pantothenic Acid	100 mg.
d-Biotin	100 mcg.
Para-Aminobenzoic Acid (PABA)	100 mg.

In a base of yeast to provide the identified and unidentified B-Complex Factors.
Advantages: Each Mega-B capsule-shaped tablet provides the highest vitamin B complex available in a single dose. Mega-B was designed for those patients who require truly Mega vitamin potencies with the convenience of minimum dosage.
Indications: Mega-B is indicated in conditions characterized by depletions or increased demand of the water-soluble B-complex vitamins. It may be useful in the nutritional management of patients during prolonged convalescence associated with major surgery. It is also indicated for stress conditions, as an adjunct to antibiotics and diuretic therapy, pre and post operative cases, liver conditions, gastro-intestinal disorders interfering with intake or absorbtion of water-soluble vitamins, prolonged or wasting diseases, diabetes, burns, fractures, severe infections, and some psychological disorders.
Warning: NOT INTENDED FOR TREATMENT OF PERNICIOUS ANEMIA, OR OTHER PRIMARY OR SECONDARY ANEMIAS.
Dosage: Usual dosage is one Mega-B tablet daily, or varied, depending on clinical needs.
Supplied: Yellow capsule shaped tablets in bottles of 30, 100 and 500.

MEGADOSE™
(multiple mega-vitamin formula with minerals, sugar and starch free)

Composition:

Vitamin A	25,000 USP Units
Vitamin D	1,000 USP Units
Vitamin C w/Rose Hips	250 mg.
Vitamin E	100 IU
Folic Acid	400 mcg.
Vitamin B_1	80 mg.
Vitamin B_2	80 mg.
Niacinamide	80 mg.
Vitamin B_6	80 mg.
Vitamin B_{12}	80 mcg.
Biotin	80 mcg.
Pantothenic Acid	80 mg.
Choline Bitartrate	80 mg.
Inositol	80 mg.
Para-Aminobenzoic Acid	80 mg.
Rutin	30 mg.
Citrus Bioflavonoids	30 mg.
Betaine Hydrochloride	30 mg.
Glutamic Acid	30 mg.
Hesperidin Complex	5 mg.
Iodine (from Kelp)	0.15 mg.
Calcium Gluconate*	50 mg.
Zinc Gluconate*	25 mg.
Potassium Gluconate*	10 mg.
Ferrous Gluconate*	10 mg.
Magnesium Gluconate*	7 mg.
Manganese Gluconate*	6 mg.
Copper Gluconate*	0.5 mg.

---

*Natural mineral chelates in a base containing natural ingredients.
Dosage: One tablet daily.
Supplied: Capsule shaped tablets in bottles of 30, 100 and 250.

Ascher & Company, Inc., B.F.
P.O. BOX 827
KANSAS CITY, MO 64141

AYR® Saline Nasal Mist

Active Ingredient: Sodium chloride 0.65% with benzalkonium chloride and versene as antibacterial and antifungal preservatives, in a soothing, isotonic saline mist buffered to neutral pH and physiologically compatible with nasal membranes.
Indications: AYR Saline Nasal Mist is indicated for dry, inflamed and swollen nasal membranes due to colds, overuse of decongestant nasal sprays and inhalers, and low humidity.

Actions: AYR Saline Nasal Mist alleviates symptoms of rebound phenomena (rhinitis medicamentosa) following overuse (due to tachyphylaxis) of topical decongestants containing sympathomimetic amines. Restores vital moisture to nasal tissues. Washes thick secretions from nose and sinuses.

Dosage and Administration: Squeeze twice in each nostril as often as needed.

How Supplied:
NDC 0225-0380-80   50 ml spray bottle
Manufactured for B.F. Ascher & Company, Inc.

MOBIGESIC® Analgesic Tablets

Active Ingredients: 300 mg magnesium salicylate and 30 mg phenyltoloxamine citrate

Indications: MOBIGESIC is indicated for headaches, menstrual cramps, low back pain, muscular aches, toothaches, joint pain, discomfort of colds, flu, and sinusitis.

Actions: MOBIGESIC is a unique, analgesic formulation which provides relief from pain and inflammation, relaxes muscles and reduces fever.

Warnings: Keep this and all drugs out of reach of children. In case of accidental overdose, seek professional assistance or contact a Poison Control Center immediately. Store at room temperature.

Precaution: When used for the temporary symptomatic relief of colds, if relief does not occur within 3 days, discontinue use and consult physician. This preparation may cause drowsiness. Do not drive or operate machinery while taking this medication. Do not administer to children under 6 years of age or exceed recommended dosage unless directed by physician.

Dosage and Administration: Adults: 1 or 2 tablets every four hours, maximum daily dose 8 tablets. Children (6 to 12 years): One half of the adult dose, maximum daily dose 4 tablets. Do not use more than 10 days unless directed by physician.

How Supplied:
NDC 0225-0355-12 Package of 18 tablets
NDC 0225-0355-10 Bottle of 50 tablets
NDC 0225-0355-15 Bottle of 100 tablets
Manufactured for B.F. Ascher & Company, Inc.

MOBISYL® Analgesic Creme

Active Ingredient: Triethanolamine salicylate

Description: MOBISYL is a greaseless, odorless, penetrating, analgesic creme.

Indications: For adults and children, 12 years of age and older, MOBISYL is indicated for the temporary relief of minor aches and pains of muscles and joints, such as simple backache, lumbago, arthritis, neuralgia, strains, bruises and sprains.

Actions: MOBISYL penetrates fast into sore, tender joints and muscles where pain originates. It works to reduce inflammation. Helps soothe stiff joints and muscles and gets you going again.

There is no burning sensation when you apply MOBISYL, only soothing relief, and MOBISYL doesn't irritate normal skin. MOBISYL won't stain clothing and has no tell-tale medicine smell.

Warnings: For external use only. Avoid contact with the eyes. Discontinue use if condition worsens or if symptoms persist for more than 7 days, and consult a physician. Do not use on children under 12 years of age except under the advice and supervision of a physician. In case of accidental ingestion, seek professional assistance or contact a Poison Control Center immediately. Close cap tightly. Keep this and all drugs out of the reach of children.

Dosage and Administration: Place a liberal amount of MOBISYL Creme in your palm and massage into the area of pain and soreness three or four times a day and at bedtime. MOBISYL may be worn under makeup or bandages.

How Supplied:
NDC 0225-0360-11   100 gram tubes
NDC 0225-0360-35   8 oz jars
Manufactured for B.F. Ascher & Co., Inc.

SOFT 'N SOOTHE® Creme

Active Ingredients: Benzocaine and menthol. Soft 'N Soothe also contains natural oat protein, lanolin oil, light weight mineral oil, and lanolin alcohol, to help give you soft, luxurious-feeling skin.

Indications: Soft 'N Soothe is medicated for the relief of itching and pain associated with dryness of skin, poison ivy, and non-poisonous insect bites. Soft 'N Soothe may also be used to relieve itching and pain in external anal and external vaginal areas.

Actions: Soft 'N Soothe is a greaseless, moisturizing creme for the relief of itching and pain. The vanishing, moisturizing creme penetrates the skin to aid in natural healing.

Warning: For external use only. Avoid contact with the eyes. Keep this and all medication out of reach of children. In case of accidental ingestion, seek professional assistance or contact a Poison Control Center immediately. Close cap tightly. Store at room temperature.

Precaution: If condition worsens, or if symptoms persist for more than 7 days, discontinue use of the product and consult a physician.

For use on children under 12, consult your physician.

Dosage and Administration: Apply Soft 'N Soothe liberally to affected areas. Repeat as needed 3 to 4 times daily and before retiring.

How Supplied:
NDC 0225-0370-09   50 gram tubes
Manufactured for B.F. Ascher & Company, Inc.

Products are cross-indexed by

generic and chemical names in the

YELLOW SECTION

Astra Pharmaceutical Products, Inc.
7 NEPONSET ST.
WORCESTER, MA 01606

XYLOCAINE® (lidocaine) 2.5% OINTMENT

Composition: Diethylaminoacet-2, 6-xylidide 2.5% in a water miscible ointment vehicle consisting of polyethylene glycols and propylene glycol.

Action and Uses: A topical anesthetic ointment for fast, temporary relief of pain and itching due to minor burns, sunburn, minor cuts, abrasions, insect bites and minor skin irritations. The ointment can be easily removed with water. It is ineffective when applied to intact skin.

Administration and Dosage: Apply topically in liberal amounts for adequate control of symptoms. When the anesthetic effect wears off additional ointment may be applied as needed.

Important Warning: *In persistent, severe or extensive skin disorders, advise patient to use only as directed. In case of accidental ingestion advise patient to seek professional assistance or to contact a poison control center immediately. Keep out of the reach of children.*

Caution: *Do not use in the eyes. Not for prolonged use. If the condition for which this preparation is used persists or if a rash or irritation develops, advise patient to discontinue use and consult a physician.*

How Supplied: Available in tube of 35 grams (approximately 1.25 ounces).

Beach Pharmaceuticals
Division of BEACH PRODUCTS, INC.
5220 SOUTH MANHATTAN AVE.
TAMPA, FL 33611

BEELITH Tablets
Magnesium Oxide with Vitamin B6

Each tablet contains: Magnesium oxide 600 mg and pyridoxine hydrochloride (Vitamin B_6) 25 mg equivalent to B_6 20 mg.

Dosage: The usual adult dose is one or two tablets daily.

Actions and Uses: BEELITH is a dietary supplement for patients deficient in magnesium and/or pyridoxine. Each tablet yields approximately 362 mg of elemental magnesium & supplies 1000% of the Adult U.S. Recommended Daily Allowance (RDA) for vitamin B_6 & 90% of the RDA for magnesium.

Precaution: Excessive dosage might cause laxation.

Caution: If you are presently taking any prescription drug, consult your physician before taking this product.

Drug Interaction Precautions: Do not take this product if you are presently taking a prescription antibiotic drug containing any form of tetracycline.

Warning: Keep this and all drugs out of the reach of children. In case of acci-

Continued on next page

Beach—Cont.

dental overdose, seek professional assistance or contact a Poison Control Center immediately.

Becton Dickinson Consumer Products
365 W. PASSAIC STREET
ROCHELLE PARK, NJ 07662

CANKAID®
(carbamide peroxide 10%)
Antiseptic Treatment for the Mouth

Active Ingredient: Carbamide peroxide 10% in specially prepared anhydrous glycerol. Artificial flavor added.
Indications and Actions: CANKAID gives quick, temporary relief from minor mouth irritations such as canker sores, sore or injured gums, and inflammation caused by dentures, mouth appliances (orthodontics), or dental procedures. Carbamide peroxide cleanses oral wounds and inflammation gently but thoroughly with its antiseptic, microfoaming action. CANKAID coats and clings to tissue, prolonging its soothing, protective effects.
Precaution: If severe or persistent symptoms occur in the mouth or throat, consult physician or dentist promptly. Do not administer to children under three years of age unless directed by physician or dentist. Keep out of reach of children.
Dosage and Administration: Do not dilute. Use four times daily, or as directed by physician or dentist. Apply directly onto affected area with painless, no touch tip. To treat widespread inflammation or hard to reach areas, apply 10 drops onto tongue; mix with saliva; swish thoroughly; expectorate.
How Supplied: CANKAID comes in liquid form, in ¾ fl. oz. plastic bottles.

MERCUROCHROME II™
Clear First Aid Liquid

Active Ingredient: Benzalkonium chloride 0.13%, ethyl alcohol 3.2%.
Indications and Actions: MERCUROCHROME II is a topical first aid product used to cleanse minor skin wounds. It inhibits microbial invasion and growth in and around the wounded area. It does not sting or irritate injured skin. MERCUROCHROME II is colorless; it will not stain clothes or skin.
Precaution: In case of deep or puncture wounds, or serious burns, consult physician. If redness, irritation, or swelling develops or persists, or if infection occurs, discontinue use and consult physician. Keep out of reach of children. Do not use near the eyes. In case of accidental ingestion seek professional assistance. Benzalkonium chloride is inactivated by contact with soap.
Dosage and Administration: For external use only. Apply to minor cuts, scratches and skin abrasions one to three times daily.

How Supplied: MERCUROCHROME II comes in liquid form, in 1 fl. oz. plastic bottles.

Beecham Products
DIVISION OF BEECHAM INC.
POST OFFICE BOX 1467
PITTSBURGH, PA 15230

B.F.I.®
Antiseptic First-Aid Powder

Active Ingredient: Bismuth-Formic-Iodide 16.0%. Other ingredients—Boric Acid, Bismuth Subgallate, Zinc Phenolsulfonate, Potassium Alum, Thymol, Amol (mono-n-amyl hydroquinone ether), Menthol, Eucalyptol, and inert diluents.
Indications: For cuts, abrasions, minor burns, skin irritations, athlete's foot and dermatitis due to poison ivy and poison oak.
Actions: B.F.I. First-Aid Powder promotes healing of cuts, scratches, abrasions and minor burns. Relieves itching, chafing and irritations from prickly heat, sunburn, mosquito bites, athlete's foot and poison ivy and oak.
Warnings: Keep out of reach of children. If redness, irritation, swelling or pain persists or increases or if infection occurs, discontinue use and consult physician. For deep or puncture wounds or serious burns, consult physician.
Symptoms and Treatment of Oral Overdosage: In the event of ingestion of large quantities, consult a physician, local poison control center, or the Rocky Mt. Poison Control Center at (303)-629-1123, 24 hours a day.
Dosage and Administration: Freely sprinkle B.F.I. on the injured area to completely cover the area. Avoid use on extensive denuded (raw) areas particularly on infants and children.
How Supplied: ¼ oz., 1¼ oz. and 8 oz. shaker top container.

CHILDREN'S HOLD®
4 Hour Cough Suppressant and Decongestant Lozenge

Active Ingredient: 3.75 mg. dextromethorphan HBr and 6.25 mg. phenylpropanolamine HCl per lozenge.
Indications: Suppresses coughs for up to 4 hours and helps provide relief of nasal congestion up to 4 hours.
Actions: Dextromethorphan is the most widely-used, non-narcotic/non-habit forming antitussive. Taken in a 5-10 mg. dose, it has been recognized as being effective for children (3-12 years) in relieving the discomfort of coughs up to 4 hours by reducing coughing intensity and frequency. Phenylpropanolamine is also non-narcotic and non-habit forming, and works as a decongestant.
Warnings: Persons with diabetes, high blood pressure, heart or thyroid disease should use only as directed by a physician. If symptoms persist or are accompanied by high fever, consult physician promptly. Do not administer to children under 3. Do not exceed recommended

dosage. Keep this and all other medications out of the reach of children.
Drug Interaction: Avoid the use of medications containing phenylpropanolamine when under treatment with monoamine oxidase inhibitors unless under the advice and supervision of a physician.
Symptoms and Treatment of Oral Overdosage: The principal symptoms of overdose are restlessness, dizziness, anxiety. Should these symptoms appear or a large overdose be suspected, seek professional advice by contacting your physician, the local poison control center, or The Rocky Mt. Poison Control Center at (303)-629-1123, 24 hrs. a day.
Dosage and Administration: Children over 6 years: Take 2 suppressants one after the other, every 4 hours. Children 3-6 years: One suppressant every 4 hours. Let dissolve fully.
How Supplied: 10 individually wrapped lozenges come packaged in a plastic tube container.

CUPREX®
Pediculicide

Active Ingredient: Tetrahydronaphthalene—30.97%; Copper Oleate—.03%
Indications: For the elimination of head lice, crab lice, body lice and their nits.
Actions: Cuprex provides an effective treatment for the elimination of lice and nits in the forms indicated above.
Warnings: Keep out of reach of children. Flammable—keep away from heat and open flame. Harmful if swallowed. Keep away from eyes. Store out of direct sunlight. Do not use more than twice in 48 hour period. Where skin is raw, broken or infected, consult a physician.
Precaution: Excessive or prolonged contact with the skin may produce erythema, edema, itching, and burning. In the event of excessive contact with skin or eyes, flush with copious amounts of clear water.
Symptoms and Treatment of Oral Overdosage: If ingestion is suspected, consult your physician, your local poison control center, or the Rocky Mt. Poison Control Center at (303)-629-1123, 24 hours a day.
Dosage and Administration: For Head Lice and Nits: Apply gently but thoroughly to scalp and hair using small quantities at a time. After 15 minutes, wash hair and scalp thoroughly with soap and warm water. While still damp, comb hair with a fine comb. For Crab Lice and Nits: Apply thoroughly on effected hairy areas. After 15 minutes, wash thoroughly with soap and warm water; while still damp, comb hair with fine comb. It is not necessary to shave the hair in uncomplicated cases. Body Lice and Nits: Treat skin and hair as for crab lice. General Instructions: If repeat application is required, apply a bland ointment or oil between treatments to avoid drying of skin. All infested clothing should be deloused to prevent reinfestation.
How Supplied: 3 and 16 fl. oz. bottles.

ENO®
Sparkling Antacid

Active Ingredient: When mixed with water, one level teaspoon of Eno produces 2,160 mg. of sodium tartrate and 495 mg. of sodium citrate. Contains 780 mg. of sodium per teaspoonful.

Indications: For relief from the symptoms of sour stomach, acid indigestion, and heartburn.

Actions: Eno is a good tasting, fast acting and effective antacid. It is free of aspirin or sugar and is 100% antacid.

Warnings: If under 60 years of age, don't take more than 6 teaspoonfuls in a 24 hour period. If over 60, don't take over 3 teaspoonfuls. Don't use maximum dosage for over 2 weeks, or use the product if on a sodium restricted diet, except under the advice of a physician. May have a laxative effect. Keep out of reach of children.

Symptoms and Treatment of Oral Overdosage: In case of a large overdose, consult your physician, your local poison control center, or the Rocky Mt. Poison Control Center at (303)-629-1123, 24 hours a day.

Dosage and Administration: Adults —1 level teaspoonful in 6 ozs. of water. May be repeated every 4 hours. Children 4–6—¼ level teaspoonful; children 7–15—½ level teaspoonful.

How Supplied: 3⅞ and 7¾ oz. bottles.

HOLD®
4 Hour Cough Suppressant Lozenge

Active Ingredient: 7.5 mg. dextromethorphan HBr per lozenge.

Indications: Suppresses coughs for up to 4 hours.

Actions: Dextromethorphan is the most widely used, non-narcotic/non-habit forming antitussive. A 10-20 mg. dose has been recognized as being effective in relieving the discomfort of coughs up to 4 hours by reducing cough intensity and frequency.

Warnings: If cough persists or is accompanied by high fever, consult a physician promptly. Do not administer to children under 6. Keep this and all other medications out of the reach of children. DO NOT EXCEED RECOMMENDED DOSE.

Drug Interaction: No known drug interaction.

Symptoms and Treatment of Oral Overdosage: The principal symptom of over dosage with dextromethorphan HBr is slowing of respiration. Should a large overdose be suspected seek professional assistance by contacting your physician, the local poison control center, or The Rocky Mt. Poison Control Center at (303)-629-1123, 24 hrs. a day.

Dosage and Administration: Adults (12 years and older): Take 2 suppressants one after the other, every 4 hours as needed. Children (6-12 years): One suppressant every 4 hours as needed. Let dissolve fully.

How Supplied: 10 individually wrapped suppressants come packaged in a plastic tube container.

MASSENGILL®
Disposable Douches
MASSENGILL®
Liquid Concentrate
MASSENGILL® Powder

Ingredients:

DISPOSABLES: Vinegar and Water— Water, Vinegar, Methyl Paraben, Sodium Benzoate, Citric Acid, Propyl Paraben

Country Flowers—Water, SD Alcohol 40, Lactic Acid, Sorbic Acid, Sodium Bicarbonate, Cetylpyridinium Chloride, Octoxynol-9, Disodium EDTA, Fragrance, D&C Red #19

Mountain Herbs—Water, Octoxynol-9, SD Alcohol 40, Lactic Acid, Fragrance, Sorbic Acid, Sodium Bicarbonate, Cetylpyridinium Chloride, Disodium EDTA, D&C Yellow #10, FD&C Blue #1

LIQUID CONCENTRATE: Water, SD Alcohol 40, Lactic Acid, Sodium Bicarbonate, Octoxynol-9, Fragrance, D&C Yellow #10, FD&C Yellow #6. (Alcohol 19.6%)

POWDER: Boric Acid, Ammonium Alum., Fragrance, Berberine.

Indications: Recommended for routine cleansing at the end of menstruation, after use of contraceptive creams or jellies (check the contraceptive package instructions first) or to rinse out the residue of prescribed vaginal medication (as directed by physician).

Actions: The buffered acid solutions of Massengill Douches are valuable adjuncts to specific vaginal therapy following the prescribed use of vaginal medication or contraceptives and in feminine hygiene.

Directions:

DISPOSABLES: Twist off wing-shaped tab cap from bottle containing premixed solution, attach nozzle supplied and use. Unit is completely disposable.

LIQUID CONCENTRATE: Fill cap ¾ full, to measuring line, and pour contents into douche bag containing 1 quart of warm water. Mix thoroughly.

POWDER: Dissolve two rounded teaspoonfuls in a douche bag containing 1 quart of warm water. Mix thoroughly.

Warning: Vaginal cleansing douches should not be used more than twice weekly except on the advice of a physician. If irritation occurs, discontinue use.

How Supplied: Disposable—6 oz. disposable plastic bottle.

Liquid Concentrate—4 oz., 8 oz., plastic bottles. Packettes—12's.

Powder—3 oz., 6 oz., 12 oz., 16 oz., jars. Packettes—6's, 10's, 12's.

MASSENGILL® Disposable
Medicated Douche

Active Ingredient: 0.23% povidone-iodine.

Indications: For temporary relief of minor irritation and itching associated with vaginitis due to monilia, Trichomonas vaginalis and Haemophilus vaginalis.

Action: Povidone-iodine is widely recognized as an effective broad spectrum microbicide against both gram negative and gram positive bacteria, fungi, yeasts and protozoa. While remaining active in the presence of blood, serum or bodily secretions, it possesses none of the irritating properties of iodine.

Warnings: If symptoms persist after seven days of use, or if redness, swelling or pain develop during treatment, consult a physician. Women with iodine-sensitivity should not use this product. You may douche during menstruation if you douche gently. Do not douche during pregnancy unless directed by a physician. Douching does not prevent pregnancy. Keep out of the reach of children.

Dosage and Administration: Dosage is provided as a single unit concentrate to be added to 6 oz. of sanitized water supplied in a disposable bottle. A specially designed nozzle is provided. After use the unit is discarded. Use once daily for up to 7 days.

How Supplied: 6 oz. bottle of sanitized water with 0.17 oz. vial of povidone-iodine and nozzle.

SCOTT'S EMULSION®
Vitamin A and D Food Supplement

Active Ingredient: Cod Liver Oil which provides 5,000 International Units of Vitamin A per 4 teaspoons of Scott's Emulsion (100% of RDA) and 400 International Units of Vitamin D per 4 teaspoons (100% of RDA).

Indications: Provides daily requirements of Vitamin A and D.

Actions: Scott's Emulsion supplies natural Vitamins A and D from cod liver oil. The product is in a highly emulsified form for more rapid absorption by the body. Flavoring agents are included to help mask the flavor of cod liver oil.

Dosage and Administration: 4 teaspoons per day provides 100% of the adult RDA for Vitamins A and D.

How Supplied: 6¼ and 12½ fl. oz. bottles.

S.T.37®
Antiseptic Solution

Active Ingredient: .1% hexylresorcinol in a glycerin-aqueous solution

Indications: For use on cuts, abrasions, burns, scalds, sunburn and the hygienic care of the mouth.

Actions: S.T.37 is a non-stinging, non-staining antiseptic solution that provides soothing protection and helps relieve pain of burns, cuts, abrasions and mouth irritations.

Warnings: If redness, irritation, swelling or pain persists or increases or if infection occurs, discontinue use and consult physician. In case of deep or puncture wounds or serious burns, consult physician. Keep out of reach of children.

Symptoms and Treatment of Oral Overdosage: In case of a large overdose of S.T. 37, seek professional assistance. Contact a physician, the local poison control center, or call the Rocky Mt. Poison Control Center at (303)-629-1123, 24 hours a day.

Dosage and Administration: For cuts, burns, scalds and abrasions apply undiluted, bandage lightly keeping ban-

Continued on next page

Beecham—Cont.

dage wet with S.T.37 antiseptic solution. For hygienic care of the mouth, dilute with 1 or 2 parts of warm water.
How Supplied: 5 and 12 fl. oz. bottles.

SUCRETS® (Regular, Mentholated, and Children's Cherry-Flavored)
Sore Throat Lozenges

Active Ingredient: Hexylresorcinol, 2.4 mg. per lozenge
Indications: Temporary relief of minor sore throat pain and mouth irritations.
Actions: Hexylresorcinol's soothing demulcent/anesthetic action quickly relieves minor throat irritations.
Warnings: Do not administer to children under 3 years of age unless directed by a physician. Keep all medications out of the reach of children. Persistent sore throat or sore throat accompanied by high fever, headache, nausea or vomiting usually indicates a severe infection and may be serious. Consult a physician promptly in such case, or if sore throat persists more than 2 days.
Drug Interaction: No known drug interaction
Symptoms and Treatment of Oral Overdosage: Should a large overdose of Sucrets (Regular, Mentholated or Children's Cherry-Flavored) be suspected, with symptoms of profuse sweating, nausea, vomiting and diarrhea, seek professional assistance. Call your physician, local poison control center or the Rocky Mountain Poison Control Center at (303)-629-1123, 24 hrs. a day.
Dosage and Administration: Use as needed. For best results dissolve slowly—do not chew.
Professional Labeling: Same as those outlined under Indications.
How Supplied: Sucrets-Regular: Available in tins of 24, jars of 55, or rolls of 7 individually wrapped lozenges. Sucrets-Mentholated and Sucrets-Children's Cherry Flavored are available in tins of 24 lozenges.

SUCRETS®–Cold Decongestant Formula
Decongestant Lozenges

Active Ingredient: Benzocaine, 5 mg., phenylephrine hydrochloride, 5 mg., phenylpropanolamine hydrochloride, 10 mg./per lozenge
Indications: For fast temporary relief of nasal congestion and minor throat irritation.
Warnings: Severe or persistent sore throat, sore throat accompanied by high fever, headache, nausea or vomiting may be serious. In such cases consult a physician promptly. Individuals with high blood pressure, heart disease, diabetes or thyroid disease should use only as directed by a physician. Do not use more than 2 days or administer to children under 12 years of age unless directed by a physician. Keep out of reach of children.
Drug Interaction: Avoid the use of medications containing phenylpropanolamine when under treatment with mon-

amine oxidase inhibitors unless under the advice and supervision of a physician.
Symptoms and Treatment of Oral Overdosage: The principal symptoms of an overdose are restlessness, dizziness, anxiety. Should these symptoms appear or a large overdose be suspected, seek professional assistance. Call your physician, the local poison control center or the Rocky Mt. Poison Control Center at (303)-629-1123, 24 hours a day.
Dosage and Administration: Adults (12 years and over): Slowly dissolve one lozenge in the mouth. One additional lozenge every 3 hours, but do not exceed 6 lozenges in 24 hours. Do not exceed recommended dosage. Children (under 12 years): Only as directed by a physician.
Professional Labeling: Same as those outlined under Indications.
How Supplied: Available in plastic boxes of 12 lozenges.

SUCRETS® COUGH CONTROL FORMULA
Cough Control Lozenges

Active Ingredient: Dextromethorphan hydrobromide, 7.5 mg./lozenge.
Indications: For temporary suppression of cough and relief of minor throat irritation.
Actions: Dextromethorphan is the most widely used non-narcotic/non-habit forming antitussive. A 15 mg. dose in adults (7.5 mg in children over 6) has been recognized as being effective in relieving the frequency and intensity of cough for up to 4 hours.
Warnings: If cough persists or is accompanied by high fever, consult a physician promptly. Do not use more than two days or administer to children under 6 unless directed by a physician. Keep out of the reach of children.
Drug Interaction: No known drug interaction.
Symptoms and Treatment of Oral Overdosage: Slowing of respiration is the principal symptom of dextromethorphan HBr overdose. Should a large overdose be suspected, seek professional assistance. Call your physician, the local poison control center or the Rocky Mt. Poison Control Center at (303)-629-1123, 24 hours a day.
Dosage and Administration: Adults (12 years and over): Take 2 lozenges every 4 hours as needed. Let dissolve fully in mouth. Children (6–12 years): One lozenge every 4 hours as needed. Let dissolve fully in mouth. Do not exceed recommended dosage.
Professional Labeling: Same as those outlined under Indications.
How Supplied: Available in tins of 24 lozenges.

THERMOTABS®
Buffered Salt Tablets

Active Ingredient: Per tablet—sodium chloride—450 mg.; potassium chloride—30 mg.; calcium carbonate—18 mg.; dextrose—200 mg.

Indications: To minimize fatigue and prevent muscle cramps and heat prostration due to excessive perspiration.
Actions: Thermotabs are designed for tennis players, joggers, golfers and other athletes who experience excessive perspiration. Also for use in steel mills, industrial plants, kitchens, stores, or other locations where high temperatures cause heat fatigue, cramps or heat prostration.
Warnings: Keep out of reach of children.
Precaution: Individuals on a salt-restricted diet should use THERMOTABS only under the advice and supervision of a physician.
Symptoms and Treatment of Oral Overdosage: Signs of salt overdose include diarrhea and muscular twitching. If an overdose is suspected, contact a physician, the local poison control center, or call the Rocky Mt. Poison Control Center at (303)-629-1123, 24 hours a day.
Dosage and Administration: One tablet with a full glass of water, 5 to 10 times a day depending on temperature and conditions.
How Supplied: 100 and 1,000 tablet bottles; 500 tablet wall dispenser.

Blair Laboratories, Inc.
Affiliate, The Purdue Frederick Company
50 WASHINGTON STREET
NORWALK, CT 06856

CALAMATUM® LOTION
(Calamine, zinc oxide, phenol, camphor and benzocaine 3%)
Antipruritic/Anesthetic/Analgesic

Description: CALAMATUM Lotion is a soothing, greaseless lotion containing astringent, anesthetic, analgesic and antipruritic ingredients.
Composition: CALAMATUM Lotion contains calamine, zinc oxide, phenol, camphor and benzocaine 3% in a non-greasy base.
Indications: CALAMATUM Lotion helps relieve itching and minor pain of poison ivy, oak and sumac; of insect and chigger bites; of rashes, prickly heat and minor skin irritations.
Action: CALAMATUM Lotion provides prompt medicated relief of itching and helps prevent scratching that might spread infection or cause scarring. It soothes and dries skin irritations. CALAMATUM Lotion dries to form its own "bandage" that stays on until washed off.
Caution: Do not bandage. Do not use in the eye. When symptoms are severe, recurrent, or persistent, or if sensitivity arises, consult a physician. Keep out of reach of children. Keep from freezing.
Administration: Shake well. Spread in a thin film over the affected area three or four times a day until relieved. Wash off once daily with warm water.
How Supplied: 3¾ fluid ounces (111 ml) in plastic bottles.
Also Available: CALAMATUM® Ointment (1½ oz.) providing the same ingredients as CALAMATUM Lotion in a soothing greaseless ointment.

CALAMATUM® Spray (3 oz.—85 g) is a cooling, soothing spray containing benzocaine 1.05%, calamine, zinc oxide, menthol, camphor, and isopropanol 19.9% by weight.

ISODINE® ANTISEPTIC
(povidone–iodine)
Antiseptic/Germicide

Description: ISODINE Antiseptic is a topical antiseptic microbicide which essentially retains the broad-range, nonselective microbicidal activity of iodine, yet is virtually free of the undesirable features associated with tincture of iodine. Unlike tincture of iodine, topically applied ISODINE Antiseptic can be bandaged or taped.

Composition: ISODINE Antiseptic is an aqueous solution of povidone-iodine. ISODINE Antiseptic is a film-forming, water-soluble iodine complex, virtually nonstinging and nonirritating to skin, wounds and mucous membranes.

Actions: ISODINE Antiseptic kills bacteria (including antibiotic-resistant strains), fungi, viruses, protozoa and yeasts. It maintains germicidal activity in the presence of blood, pus and serum. The golden-brown film formed by topically applied ISODINE Antiseptic can be easily washed off skin and natural fabrics.

Indications: ISODINE Antiseptic helps prevent infection in minor cuts, scratches, abrasions and minor burns. This potent, yet gentle, antiseptic kills germs promptly.

Caution: In case of deep or puncture wounds or serious burns, or if redness, irritation, swelling or pain persists or increases, or if infection occurs, consult physician. Keep out of reach of children.

Administration: Apply full strength to injured area. Cover with gauze or adhesive bandage if desired.

Supplied: 1 oz. plastic bottles.

KERID® EAR DROPS
(Urea and glycerin in propylene glycol)
Earwax Removal Aid

Description: KERID Ear Drops are an improved preparation to help loosen and remove excess earwax easily and effectively.

Composition: Active ingredients are urea and glycerine in propylene glycol. Preservatives are methyl paraben and propyl paraben.

Action and Uses: KERID Ear Drops help soften and loosen earwax so that it may simply wash out when gently flushed with water. Helps prevent "swimmer's ear." When used routinely (once or twice a month), KERID Ear Drops help prevent earwax buildup.

Caution: Do not use in presence of inflammation, pain or fever. If irritation develops, consult a physician.

Administration: Fill ear canal with KERID Ear Drops. Insert cotton plug in ear and allow drops to remain for 30 to 60 minutes. Gently wash ear canal with warm water. In stubborn cases where a second application is necessary, repeat procedure, allow to remain overnight,

gently wash out in morning. As with all medication, keep out of reach of children.

How Supplied: 8 cc. bottle with cellophane-wrapped blunt-end dropper.

Block Drug Company, Inc.
257 CORNELISON AVENUE
JERSEY CITY, NJ 07302

SENSODYNE® TOOTHPASTE
Desensitizing dentifrice

Description: Each tube contains strontium chloride hexahydrate (10%) in a pleasantly flavored cleansing/polishing dentifrice.

Actions/Indications: Tooth hypersensitivity is a dentally recognized condition in which individuals experience pain from exposure to hot, cold, sweet or sour stimuli, from chewing fibrous foods, or from tactile stimuli (e.g. toothbrushing.) Hypersensitivity usually occurs when the protective enamel covering on teeth wears away (which happens most often at the gum line) and exposes the dentin underneath.

Running through the dentin are microscopic small "tubules" which, according to many authorities, carry the pain impulses to the nerve of the tooth.

Sensodyne provides a unique ingredient—strontium chloride which is believed to be deposited in the tubules where it blocks the pain. The longer Sensodyne is used, the more of a barrier it helps build against pain.

The effect of Sensodyne may not be manifested immediately and may require a few weeks or longer of use for relief to be obtained. A number of clinical studies in the U.S. and other countries have provided substantial evidence of Sensodyne's performance attributes. Complete relief of hypersensitivity has been reported in approximately 65% of users and measurable relief or reduction in hypersensitivity in approximately 90%. Sensodyne has been commercially available for over 17 years and has received wide dental endorsement.

Contraindications: Subjects with severe dental erosion should brush properly and lightly with any dentifrice to avoid further removal of tooth structure. Subjects with identified idiosyncracies to dentifrice flavorants may also react to those in Sensodyne.

Dosage: Use twice a day as in regular dental care.

NOTE: Individuals should be instructed to use SENSODYNE frequently and in place of their reqular dentifrice since relief from pain tends to be cumulative. If relief does not occur after 3 months, a dentist should be consulted.

How Supplied: SENSODYNE Toothpaste is supplied as a paste in tubes of 4 oz. and 2.1 oz.

(U.S. Patent No. 3,122,483)

TEGRIN® MEDICATED SHAMPOO

Highly effective shampoo for moderate-to-severe dandruff and the relief of flaking, itching, and scaling associated with eczema, seborrhea, and psoriasis. Two

commercial product versions are available: a cream shampoo and a lotion shampoo, each in two scents.

Description: Each tube of cream shampoo or bottle of lotion shampoo contains 5% special alcohol extract of coal tar in a pleasantly scented, high-foaming, cleansing shampoo base with emollients, conditioners and other formula components.

Actions/Indications: Coal Tar is obtained in the destructive distillation of bituminous coal and is a highly effective agent for the local therapy of a number of dermatological disorders. The action of tar is believed to be keratoplastic, antiseptic, antipruritic and astringent. The special extract of coal tar used in the Tegrin products is prepared in such a way as to reduce the pitch and other irritant components found in crude coal tar without reduction in therapeutic potency. Coal tar extract has been used clinically for many years as a remedy for dandruff and for scaling associated with scalp disorders such as eczema, seborrhea, and psoriasis. Its mechanism of action has not been fully established, but it is believed to retard the rate of turnover of epidermal cells with regular use. A number of clinical studies have demonstrated the performance attributes of Tegrin Shampoo against dandruff and seborrheic dermatitis. In addition to relieving the above symptoms, Tegrin shampoo used regularly, maintains scalp and hair cleanliness and leaves the hair lustrous and manageable.

Contraindications: For External Use Only—Should irritation develop, discontinue use. Avoid contact with eyes. Keep out of reach of children.

Dosage: Use regularly as a shampoo. Wet hair thoroughly. Rub Tegrin liberally into hair and scalp. Rinse thoroughly. Briskly massage a second application of the shampoo into a rich lather. Rinse thoroughly.

How Supplied:
Tegrin Cream Shampoo is supplied in 2 oz., 3.2 oz., and 5 oz. collapsible tubes. Tegrin Lotion Shampoo is supplied in 3.75 and 6.6 oz. plastic bottles.

TEGRIN® for Psoriasis Lotion and Cream

Description: Each tube of cream or bottle of lotion contains special crude coal tar extract (5%) and allantoin (1.7%) in a greaseless, stainless vehicle.

Actions/Indications: Crude coal tar is obtained in the destructive distillation of bituminous coal and is a highly effective agent for the local therapy of a number of dermatological disorders. The action of tar is believed to be keratoplastic, antiseptic, antipruritic and astringent. The special coal tar extract used in the Tegrin products is prepared in such a way as to reduce the pitch and other irritant components found in crude coal tar. Allantoin (5-Ureidohydantoin) is a debriding and dispersing agent for psoriatic scales and is believed to accelerate proliferation of normal skin cells. The combination of coal tar extract and allantoin

Continued on next page

Block—Cont.

used in Tegrin has been demonstrated in a number of controlled clinical studies to have a high level of efficacy in controlling the itching and scaling of psoriasis.

Contraindications: Discontinue medication should irritation or allergic reactions occur. Avoid contact with eyes and mucous membranes. Keep out of reach of children.

Dosage and Administration: Apply 2 to 4 times daily as needed, massaging thoroughly into affected areas. A hot bath before application will help to soften heavy scales. Once condition is under control, maintenance therapy should be individually adjusted. Occlusive dressings are not required.

How Supplied: Tegrin Lotion 6 fl. oz., Tegrin Cream 2 oz. and 4.4 oz. tubes.

Boehringer Ingelheim Ltd.
90 EAST RIDGE
POST OFFICE BOX 368
RIDGEFIELD, CT 06877

DULCOLAX®
brand of bisacodyl USP
Tablets of 5 mg.................BI-CODE 12
Suppositories of 10 mg..BI-CODE 52
Laxative

Description: Dulcolax is a contact laxative acting directly on the colonic mucosa to produce normal peristalsis throughout the large intestine. Its unique mode of action permits either oral or rectal administration, according to the requirements of the patient. Because of its gentleness and reliability of action without side effects, Dulcolax may be used whenever constipation is a problem. In preparation for surgery, proctoscopy, or radiologic examination, Dulcolax provides satisfactory cleansing of the bowel, obviating the need for an enema.

Dulcolax is a colorless, tasteless compound that is practically insoluble in water and alkaline solution. It is designated chemically bis(p-acetoxyphenyl)-2-pyridylmethane.

Actions: Dulcolax differs markedly from other laxatives in its mode of action: it is virtually nontoxic, and its laxative effect occurs on contact with the colonic mucosa, where it stimulates sensory nerve endings to produce parasympathetic reflexes resulting in increased peristaltic contractions of the colon. Administered orally, Dulcolax is absorbed to a variable degree from the small bowel but such absorption is not related to the mode of action of the compound. Dulcolax administered rectally in the form of suppositories is negligibly absorbed. The contact action of the drug is restricted to the colon, and motility of the small intestine is not appreciably influenced. Local axon reflexes, as well as segmental reflexes, are initiated in the region of contact and contribute to the widespread peristaltic activity producing evacuation. For this reason, Dulcolax may often be employed satisfactorily in patients with ganglionic blockage or spinal cord damage (paraplegia, poliomyelitis, etc.).

Indications: *Acute Constipation:* Taken at bedtime, Dulcolax tablets are almost invariably effective the following morning. When taken before breakfast, they usually produce an effect within six hours. For a prompter response and to replace enemas, the suppositories, which are usually effective in 15 minutes to one hour, can be used.

Chronic Constipation and Bowel Retraining: Dulcolax is extremely effective in the management of chronic constipation, particularly in older patients. By gradually lengthening the interval between doses as colonic tone improves, the drug has been found to be effective in redeveloping proper bowel hygiene. There is no tendency to "rebound".

Preparation for Radiography: Dulcolax tablets are excellent in eliminating fecal and gas shadows from x-rays taken of the abdominal area. For barium enemas, no food should be given following the administration of the tablets, to prevent reaccumulation of material in the cecum, and a suppository should be given one to two hours prior to examination.

Preoperative Preparation: Dulcolax tablets have been shown to be an ideal laxative in emptying the G.I. tract prior to abdominal surgery or to other surgery under general anesthesia. They may be supplemented by suppositories to replace the usual enema preparation. Dulcolax will not replace the colonic irrigations usually given patients before intracolonic surgery, but is useful in the preliminary emptying of the colon prior to these procedures.

Postoperative Care: Suppositories can be used to replace enemas, or tablets given as an oral laxative, to restore normal bowel hygiene after surgery.

Antepartum Care: Either tablets or suppositories can be used for constipation in pregnancy without danger of stimulating the uterus.

Preparation for Delivery: Suppositories can be used to replace enemas in the first stage of labor provided that they are given at least two hours before the onset of the second stage.

Postpartum Care: The same indications apply as in postoperative care, with no contraindication in nursing mothers.

Preparation for Sigmoidoscopy or Proctoscopy: For unscheduled office examinations, adequate preparation is usually obtained with a single suppository. For sigmoidoscopy scheduled in advance, however, administration of tablets the night before in addition will result in adequate preparation almost invariably.

Colostomies: Tablets the night before or a suppository inserted into the colostomy opening in the morning will frequently make irrigations unnecessary, and in other cases will expedite the procedure.

Contraindication: There is no contraindication to the use of Dulcolax, other than an acute surgical abdomen.

Precaution: Dulcolax tablets contain FD&C Yellow No. 5 (tartrazine) which may cause allergic-type reactions (including bronchial asthma) in certain susceptible individuals. Although the overall incidence of FD&C Yellow No. 5 (tartrazine) sensitivity in the general population is low, it is frequently seen in patients who also have aspirin hypersensitivity.

Adverse Reactions: As with any laxative, abdominal cramps are occasionally noted, particularly in severely constipated individuals.

Dosage:
Tablets
Tablets must be swallowed whole, not chewed or crushed, and should not be taken within one hour of antacids or milk.

Adults: Two or three (usually two) tablets suffice when an ordinary laxative effect is desired. This usually results in one or two soft, formed stools.

Up to six tablets may be safely given in preparation for special procedures when greater assurance of complete evacuation of the colon is desired. In producing such thorough emptying, these higher doses may result in several loose, unformed stools.

Children: One or two tablets, depending on age and severity of constipation, administered as above. Tablets should not be given to a child too young to swallow them whole.

Suppositories
Adults: One suppository at the time a bowel movement is required. Usually effective in 15 minutes to one hour.

Children: Half a suppository is generally effective for infants and children under two years of age. Above this age, a whole suppository is usually advisable.

Combined
In preparation for surgery, radiography and sigmoidoscopy, a combination of tablets the night before and a suppository in the morning is recommended (see Indications).

How Supplied: Dulcolax, brand of bisacodyl: Yellow, enteric-coated tablets of 5 mg in boxes of 24, bottles of 100, 1000 and unit strip packages of 100; suppositories of 10 mg in boxes of 2, 4, 8, 50 and 500.

Note: Dulcolax suppositories and tablets should be stored at temperatures not above 86°F (30°C).

Also Available: Dulcolax® Bowel Prep Kit. Each kit contains:
1 Dulcolax suppository of 10 mg bisacodyl;
4 Dulcolax tablets of 5 mg bisacodyl;
Complete patient instructions.

Clinical Applications: Dulcolax can be used in virtually any patient in whom a laxative or enema is indicated. It has no effect on the blood picture, erythrocyte sedimentation rate, urinary findings, or hepatic or renal function. It may be safely given to infants and the aged, pregnant or nursing women, debilitated patients, and may be prescribed in the presence of such conditions as cardiovascular, renal, or hepatic diseases.

026-D (11/80)
[Shown in Product Identification Section]

Breon Laboratories Inc.
90 PARK AVE.
NEW YORK, NY 10016

BREONESIN®
brand of guaifenesin capsules, USP

Description: Each red, oval-shaped BREONESIN capsule contains 200 mg of guaifenesin in an easy to swallow, soft gelatin capsule.

Indications: BREONESIN is indicated for the temporary relief of coughs. BREONESIN is an expectorant which helps to loosen phlegm (sputum) and bronchial secretions, and acts to thin mucus. Coughs due to minor throat and bronchial irritation that occur with the common cold are temporarily relieved.

Warnings: Persistent cough may indicate a serious condition. Consult your physician if cough persists for more than 1 week, recurs, or is accompanied by high fever, rash or persistent headache. Do not take this product for persistent coughs due to smoking, asthma or emphysema, or coughs accompanied by excessive secretions, except under the advice and supervision of your physician.

Dosage: Adults and Children 12 years of age and over: 1 or 2 capsules in a 24-hour period. Children under 12 years: as directed by your physician.

Store at controlled room temperature, between 15°C and 30°C (59°F and 86°F).

Supplied by:
BREON LABORATORIES INC.
New York, N.Y. 10016
Mfg. by R.P. Scherer Corp.
Monroe, N.C. 28110

FERGON®
brand of ferrous gluconate
FERGON ELIXIR

Composition: FERGON (brand of pure ferrous gluconate) is stabilized to maintain a minimum of ferric ions. It contains not less than 11.5 per cent iron. Each FERGON tablet contains 320 mg. FERGON Elixir 6% contains 300 mg per teaspoon.

Action and Uses: FERGON preparations produce rapid hemoglobin regeneration in patients with iron deficiency anemias. FERGON is better utilized and better tolerated than other forms of iron because of its low ionization constant and solubility in the entire pH range of the gastrointestinal tract. It does not precipitate proteins or have the astringency of more ionizable forms of iron, does not interfere with peristaltic or diastatic activities of the digestive system, and will not produce nausea, abdominal cramps, constipation or diarrhea in the great majority of patients.

FERGON preparations are indicated in anemias amenable to iron therapy: (1) hypochromic anemia of infancy and childhood; (2) idiopathic hypochromic anemia; (3) hypochromic anemia of pregnancy; and (4) anemia associated with chronic blood loss.

Administration and Dosage: Adults—one or two FERGON tablets or one or two teaspoons of FERGON Elixir three times daily. Children 6–12 years—one FERGON tablet or one teaspoon of FERGON Elixir one to three times daily, as directed by the physician. Infants—30 drops of FERGON Elixir, gradually increasing to 1 teaspoon daily.

How Supplied: FERGON, tablets of 320 mg (5 grains), bottles of 100, 500 and 1,000. FERGON Elixir 6% (5 grains per teaspoon), bottles of 1 pint.

FERGON registered trademark of Sterling Drug Inc.

FERGON® CAPSULES

Composition: Each FERGON Capsule contains 435 mg of ferrous gluconate, yielding 50 mg of elemental iron.

Action and Uses: FERGON preparations produce rapid hemoglobin regeneration in patients with iron deficiency anemias. FERGON is better utilized and better tolerated than other forms of iron because of its low ionization constant and solubility in the entire pH range of the gastrointestinal tract. It does not precipitate proteins or have the astringency of more ionizable forms of iron, does not interfere with peristaltic or diastatic activities of the digestive system, and will not produce nausea, abdominal cramps, constipation or diarrhea in the great majority of patients. The pellets of ferrous gluconate contained in FERGON Capsules are coated to permit maximum availability of iron in the upper small bowel, the site of maximum absorption. FERGON preparations are indicated in anemias amenable to iron therapy: (1) hypochromic anemia of infancy and childhood; (2) idiopathic hypochromic anemia; (3) hypochromic anemia of pregnancy; and (4) anemia associated with chronic blood loss.

Administration and Dosage: 1 FERGON Capsule daily for mild to moderate iron deficiency anemia. For more severe anemia the dosage may be increased.

How Supplied: FERGON Capsules, bottles of 30.

Bristol Laboratories
(Division of Bristol-Myers Co.)
SYRACUSE, NY 13201

NALDECON–DX™
Pediatric Syrup

Description: Each teaspoonful (5 ml.) of Naldecon-DX Syrup contains:
dextromethorphan
    hydrobromide ....7.5 mg
phenylpropanolamine
    hydrochloride ....9 mg
guaifenesin ....100 mg
alcohol 5%

Indications: Provide prompt relief from cough and nasal congestion due to the common cold, bronchitis, nasopharyngitis and recurrent bronchial coughing. Dextromethorphan temporarily quiets non-productive coughing by its antitussive action while guaifenesin's expectorant action helps loosen phlegm and bronchial secretions. Phenylpropanolamine reduces swelling of nasal passages; shrinks swollen membranes. This combination product is antihistamine-free.

Contraindications: Hypersensitivity to guaifenesin, dextromethorphan or sympathomimetic amines.

Warnings: Nervousness, dizziness or sleeplessness may occur if recommended dosage is exceeded. Do not give this product to a child with high blood pressure, heart disease, diabetes or thyroid disease except under the advice and supervision of a physician. Do not give this product to a child presently taking a prescription drug containing a monamine oxidase inhibitor except under the advice and supervision of a physician. Do not administer this product for persistent or chronic cough such as occurs with asthma or emphysema or when cough is accompanied by excessive secretions except under the care and advice of a physician. A persistent cough may be a sign of a serious condition. If cough persists for more than 1 week, tends to recur, or is accompanied by high fever, rash or persistent headaches, consult a physician.

Dosage and Administration: Children 2 to 6 years—1 teaspoonful 4 times daily. Over 6 years—2 teaspoons 4 times daily.

How Supplied: Naldecon-DX Syrup in 4 oz. and pint bottles.

(1) 8/80

NALDECON–EX™
Pediatric Drops

Description: Each 1 ml. drop of Naldecon-EX contains:
phenylpropanolamine
    hydrochloride ....9 mg
guaifenesin ....30 mg
alcohol 0.6%

Indications: Combined decongestant/expectorant designed specifically to promptly reduce the swelling of nasal membranes and to help loosen phlegm and bronchial secretions through productive coughing. This dual action is of particular value in infants with common cold, acute bronchitis, bronchiolitis, tracheobronchitis, nasopharyngitis and croup. This combination product is antihistamine-free.

Contraindications: Hypersensitivity to guaifenesin or sympathomimetic amines.

Warnings: Nervousness, dizziness or sleeplessness may occur if recommended dosage is exceeded. Do not give this product to a child with high blood pressure, heart disease, diabetes or thyroid disease except under the advice and supervision of a physician. Do not give this product to a child presently taking a prescription drug containing a monamine oxidase inhibitor except under the advice and supervision of a physician. Do not administer this product for persistent or chronic cough such as occurs with asthma or emphysema or when cough is accompanied by excessive secretions except under the care and advice of a physician. A persistent cough may be a sign of a serious condition. If cough persists for more than 1 week, tends to recur, or is accompanied

Continued on next page

Bristol—Cont.

by high fever, rash or persistent headaches, consult a physician.

Dosage and Administration: Dose should be adjusted to age or weight and be given 4 times a day (see calibrations on dropper). Administer by mouth only.

1–3 Months: (8–12 lbs.)	¼ ml
4–6 Months: (13–17 lbs.)	½ ml
7–9 Months: (18–20 lbs.)	¾ ml
10 Months or over (21 lbs. or more)	1 ml

Bottle label dosage reads as follows: children under 2 years of age: use only as directed by a physician.

How Supplied: Naldecon-EX Pediatric Drops in 20 ml. bottles with calibrated dropper.

(1) 8/80

Bristol-Myers Products
(Div. of Bristol-Myers Co.)
345 PARK AVENUE
NEW YORK, NY 10154

ARTHRITIS STRENGTH BUFFERIN®
Analgesic

Composition: Aspirin 7½ gr. (486 mg.) in a formulation buffered with Di-Alminate,® Bristol-Myers' brand of Aluminum Glycinate 1.125 gr. (72.9 mg.) and Magnesium Carbonate 2.25 gr. (145.8 mg.).

Action and Uses: ARTHRITIS STRENGTH BUFFERIN is specially formulated to give temporary relief from the minor aches and pains, stiffness, swelling and inflammation of arthritis and rheumatism. ARTHRITIS STRENGTH BUFFERIN also reduces pain and fever of colds and "flu" and provides fast, effective pain relief for: simple headache, lower back muscular aches from fatigue, sinusitis, neuralgia, neuritis, tooth extraction, muscle strain, athletic soreness, painful distress associated with normal menstrual periods. The leading aspirin substitute acetaminophen cannot provide relief from inflammation.
ARTHRITIS STRENGTH BUFFERIN PROVIDES INGREDIENTS FOR STOMACH PROTECTION JUST LIKE REGULAR BUFFERIN WHICH HELP PREVENT THE STOMACH UPSET ASPIRIN OFTEN CAUSES.

Contraindications: Hypersensitivity to salicylates.

Caution: If pain persists for more than 10 days or redness is present or in Arthritic or Rheumatic conditions affecting children under 12, consult physician immediately. Do not take without consulting physician if under medical care.
WARNING: Keep this and all medicines out of children's reach. In case of accidental overdose, contact a physician immediately.

Administration and Dosage: Two tablets with water. Repeat after four hours if necessary. Do not exceed 8 tablets in any 24 hour period. If dizziness, impaired hearing or ringing in ear occurs, discontinue use. Not recommended for children.

Overdose: (Symptoms and Treatment) Typical of aspirin.

How Supplied: Tablets in bottles of 40 and 100. Samples available upon request.

Product Identification: White elongated tablet.

Literature Available: Upon request. [*Shown in Product Identification Section*]

BUFFERIN® Analgesic

Composition: Aspirin 5 gr. (324 mg.) in a formulation buffered with Di-Alminate®, Bristol-Myers's brand of Aluminum Glycinate ¾ gr. (48.6 mg.), and Magnesium Carbonate 1½ gr. (97.2 mg.).

Action and Uses: Bufferin® is for relief of simple headache; and for temporary relief of: minor arthritic pain, the painful discomforts and fever of colds and "flu", menstrual cramps, muscular aches from fatigue and toothache. Bufferin® helps prevent the stomach upset often caused by plain aspirin.

Contraindications: Hypersensitivity to salicylates.

Caution: If pain persists for more than 10 days or redness is present or, in Arthritic or Rheumatic conditions affecting children under 12, consult physician immediately. Do not take without consulting physician if under medical care. Consult a dentist for toothache promptly.

Warning: Keep this and all medicines out of children's reach. In case of accidental overdose, consult a physician immediately.

Dosage: 2 tablets every four hours as needed. Do not exceed 12 tablets in 24 hours, unless directed by a physician. For children 6-12, one-half dose. Under 6, consult physician.

Overdose: (Symptoms and treatment) Typical of aspirin.

How Supplied: Tablets in bottles of 12, 36, 60, 100, 165, 225, and 375. For hospital and clinical use: bottle—1,000; boxed 200x2 tablet foil packets. Samples available on request.

Product Identification Mark: White tablet with letter "B" on one surface.

Literature Available: Upon request. [*Shown in Product Identification Section*]

COMTREX®
Multi-Symptom Cold Reliever

Composition: Each tablet, fluid ounce (30 ml.), and capsule contains: [See table below].

Actions and Uses: COMTREX® contains safe and effective fast acting ingredients including a non-aspirin analgesic, a decongestant, an antihistamine and a cough reliever. COMTREX relieves these major cold symptoms: nasal and sinus congestion, runny nose, sneezing post nasal drip, watery eyes, coughing, fever, minor sore throat pain (systemically), headache, body aches and pain.

Contraindications: Hypersensitivity to acetaminophen or antihistamines.

Caution: Do not take without consulting a physician if under medical care. Do not drive a car or operate machinery while taking this cold remedy as it may cause drowsiness.

Warning: Keep this and all medicine out of children's reach. In case of accidental overdose, consult a physician immediately. Persistent cough may indicate the presence of a serious condition. Persons with a high fever or persistent cough, or with high blood pressure, diabetes, heart or thyroid disease should not use this preparation unless directed by a physician. Do not use for more than 10 days unless directed by a physician.

Administration and Dosage:
Tablets—Adults: 2 tablets every 4 hours as needed not to exceed 12 tablets in 24 hours. Children 6-12 years: ½ the adult dose. Under 6, consult a physician.
Liquid—Adults: 1 fluid ounce (30 ml.) every 4 hours as needed, not to exceed 6 fluid ounces (180 ml.) in 24 hours. Children 6-12 years: ½ the adult dose. Under 6, consult a physician.
Capsules—Adults: 2 capsules every 4 hours as needed not to exceed 12 capsules in 24 hours. Children 6–12 years: ½ the adult dose. Under 6, consult a physician.

Overdose: The signs and symptoms observed would be those produced by the acetaminophen, which may cause hepatotoxicity in some patients. Since clinical and laboratory evidence may be delayed up to 1 week, close clinical monitoring and serial hepatic enzyme determinations are recommended.

How Supplied: Tablets in bottles of 24's, 50's. Capsules in bottles of 16's and 36's, 100's. Liquid in 6 oz. and 10 oz. plastic bottles. Samples available on request.

Product Identification Mark: Yellow tablet with letter "C" on one surface. Orange and Yellor capsules with "Bristol-Myers" and "Comtrex" on one side.

Literature Available: Upon request. [*Shown in Product Identification Section*]

CONGESPIRIN®
Chewable Cold Tablets for Children

Composition: Each tablet contains aspirin 81 mg. (1¼ grains) phenylephrine hydrochloride (1¼ mg.).

Action and Uses: For the temporary relief of nasal congestion, fever, aches

	COMTREX Tablets	COMTREX Liquid	COMTREX Capsules
Acetaminophen	325 mg.	650 mg.	325 mg.
Phenylpropanolamine HCl:	12 ½ mg.	25 mg.	12 ½ mg.
Chlorpheniramine Maleate:	1 mg.	2 mg.	1 mg.
Dextromethorphan HBr	10 mg.	20 mg.	10 mg.
Alcohol:	—	20% by Volume	—

and pains of the common cold or "flu". Plus an effective nasal decongestant to help relieve stuffiness, runny nose and sneezing from colds.

Dosage and Administration:
Under Age 2 consult your physician

2–3 YRS.	2 TABLETS
4–5 YRS.	3 TABLETS
6–8 YRS.	4 TABLETS
9–10 YRS.	5 TABLETS
11 YRS	6 TABLETS
12+ YRS.	8 TABLETS

Repeat dose in four hours if necessary. Do not give more than four doses per day unless prescribed by your physician.

Contraindications: Hypersensitivity to acetaminophen.

Caution: If child is under medical care, do not administer without consulting physician. Do not exceed recommended dosage. Consult your physician if symptoms persist or if high fever, high blood pressure, heart disease, diabetes or thyroid disease is present. Do not administer for more than 10 days unless directed by your physician.

Warning: KEEP THIS AND ALL MEDICINES OUT OF CHILDREN'S REACH. IN CASE OF ACCIDENTAL OVERDOSAGE, CONTACT A PHYSICIAN IMMEDIATELY.

How Supplied: Tablets in bottles of 36.
Product Identification Mark: Two layer (orange/white) circular tablet with letter "C" imprinted on the orange side.

CONGESPRIN®
Liquid Cold Medicine

Composition: Each 5 ml. teaspoon contains Acetaminophen 130 mg., Phenylpropanolamine Hydrochloride 6 ¼ mg., Alcohol 10% by volume.

Action and Uses: Reduces fever and relieves aches and pains associated with colds and "flu". Contains an effective decongestant for the temporary relief of nasal congestion due to the common cold, hay fever or other respiratory allergies. Reduces swelling of nasal passages, shrinks swollen membranes, restores freer breathing.

Dosage and Administration:
Children 3–5, 1 teaspoon every 3–4 hours.
Children 6–12, 2 teaspoons every 3–4 hours.
Children under 3 years use only as directed by your physician.
Do not give more than 4 doses a day unless directed by your physician.

Contraindications: Hypersensitivity to acetaminophen.

Caution: If child is under medical care, do not administer without consulting physician. Do not exceed recommended dosage. Consult your physician if symptoms persist or if high fever, high blood pressure, heart disease, diabetes or thyroid disease is present. Do not administer for more than 10 days unless directed by your physician.

Warning: KEEP THIS AND ALL MEDICINES OUT OF CHILDREN'S REACH. IN CASE OF ACCIDENTAL OVERDOSAGE, CONTACT A PHYSICIAN IMMEDIATELY.

How Supplied: In 3 oz. plastic, unbreakable bottles.
[*Shown in Product Identification Section*]

DATRIL® Analgesic

Composition: Each tablet contains acetaminophen 5 gr. (325 mg.)

Actions and Uses: The **DATRIL** formula contains a safe, effective, non-aspirin analgesic that relieves pain fast, without causing the gastric bleeding that aspirin tablets can cause. DATRIL is also less likely to cause the nausea and stomach upset that plain aspirin tablets can cause. DATRIL provides relief from the pain of: ● Headache ● Colds or "flu" ● Bursitis ● Menstrual discomfort ● Sinusitis ● Muscular aches due to fatigue or overexertion ● Muscular backache ● Neuralgia. **DATRIL** also helps reduce fever of colds or "flu" and provides temporary relief from toothache and minor arthritic or rheumatic aches and pain. For most persons with peptic ulcer **DATRIL** may be used safely and comfortably when taken as directed for recommended conditions.

Contraindications: Hypersensitivity to acetaminophen.

Caution: If pain persists for more than 10 days or redness is present or in arthritic or rheumatic conditions affecting children under 12, consult physician immediately. Do not take without consulting a physician if under medical care. Consult a dentist for toothache promptly.

Warning: Do not give to children under 6 or use for more than 10 days unless directed by a physician. Keep this and all medicines out of reach of children. In case of accidental overdose contact a physician promptly.

Dosage: 2 tablets every four hours, 1 to 4 times daily as needed, or as directed by a physician. For children 6–12 years of age use half the adult dose.

Overdose: A massive overdose of acetaminophen may cause hepatotoxicity in some patients. Since clinical and laboratory evidence may be delayed up to 1 week, close clinical monitoring and serial hepatic enzyme determinations are recommended.

How Supplied: Tablets in bottles of 24, 100 and 250. Samples available on request.

Product Identification Mark: White tablet with name "Datril" on one surface.

Literature Available: Upon request.
[*Shown in Product Identification Section*]

DATRIL 500™

Composition: Each tablet contains acetaminophen, 7.5 gr. (500 mg.)

Actions and Uses: DATRIL 500 has been specially developed to provide fast, extra-strength pain relief. It contains a non-aspirin ingredient (acetaminophen) which is less likely to irritate the stomach than plain aspirin. DATRIL 500 is fast-acting. DATRIL 500 Extra-Strength tablets are for the temporary relief of minor aches, pains, headaches and fever. For most persons with peptic ulcer DA-

TRIL 500 may be used when taken as directed for recommended conditions.

Contraindictions: Hypersensitivity to acetaminophen.

Caution: Severe or recurrent pain or high or continued fever may be indicative of serious illness. Under these conditions consult a physician.

Warning: Do not give to children 12 and under or use for more than 10 days unless directed by a physician. Keep this and all medicines out of reach of children. In case of accidental overdose contact a physician immediately.

Dosage: Adults: Two tablets. May be repeated in 4 hours if needed. Do not exceed 8 tablets in any 24 hour period.

Overdose: A massive overdose of acetaminophen may cause hepatotoxicity in some patients. Since clinical and laboratory evidence may be delayed up to 1 week, close clinical monitoring and serial hepatic enzyme determinations are recommended.

How Supplied: Tablets in bottles of 24's, 50's and 72's. Samples available on request.

Product Identification Mark: White tablet with DATRIL 500 on one surface.

Literature Available: Upon request.
[*Shown in Product Identification Section*]

EXCEDRIN® Analgesic

Composition: Each tablet and capsule contains Acetaminophen 250 mg.; Aspirin 250 mg.; and Caffeine 65 mg.

Action and Uses: Extra-Strength Excedrin formula provides fast, effective relief from pain of: headache, sinusitis, colds or 'flu', muscular aches and menstrual discomfort. Also recommended for temporary relief of toothaches and minor arthritic pains.

Contraindications: Hypersensitivity to salicylates or acetaminophen.

Caution: Do not give to children under 6 or use for more than 10 days unless directed by physician. If sinus or arthritis pain persists (say for a week) or if skin redness is present, or in arthritic conditions affecting children under 12 consult physician immediately. Consult dentist for toothache promptly. Do not take without consulting physician if under medical care.

Warning: Keep this and all medicines out of children's reach. In case of accidental overdose, contact a physician immediately.

Administration and Dosage: *Tablets* —Adults, 2 tablets every 4 hours as needed. Do not exceed 8 tablets in 24 hours unless directed by a physician. *Capsules*—Adults, 2 capsules every 4 hours as needed. Do not exceed 8 capsules in 24 hours unless directed by a physician. For children 6–12, one-half adult dose.

How Supplied: Bottles of 12, 36, 60, 100, 165, 225, and 375 tablets. Capsules in bottles of 24's, 40's and 60's. A metal tin of 12 tablets. All sizes packaged in child resistant safety closure except 100's (for tablets); 60's (for capsules) which is a size

Continued on next page

Bristol-Myers—Cont.

not recommended for households with young children.

Product Identification Mark: White, circular tablet with letter "E" imprinted on both sides. Red capsules with "EXCE-DRIN" printed on 2 sides.

Literature Available: Upon request.

EXCEDRIN P.M.® Nighttime Analgesic

Composition: Each tablet contains Acetaminophen 500 mg. and Pyrilamine Maleate 25 mg.

Action and Uses: Excedrin P.M. has a special formula that provides prompt relief of nighttime pain and aids sleep for people with headache, bursitis, colds or "flu", sinusitis, muscle aches and menstrual discomfort. Also recommended for temporary relief of toothaches and minor arthritic pain.

Contraindications: Hypersensitivity to acetaminophen.

Caution: Do not exceed 2 tablets in 24 hours. Do not give to children under 12 or use for more than 10 days unless directed by physician. If sinus or arthritis pain persists (say for a week) or if skin redness is present, or in arthritic conditions affecting children under 12, consult physician immediately. Do not drive a car or operate machinery after use. Consult dentist promptly for toothache. Do not take without consulting physician if under medical care.

Warning: If sleeplessness persists for more than two weeks, consult your physician. Insomnia may be a symptom of serious underlying medical ailments. Take this product with caution if alcohol is being consumed. **Do not take this product if you have asthma, glaucoma or enlargement of the prostate gland except under the advice and supervision of a physician.** Keep this and all medicines out of children's reach. In case of accidental overdose, contact a physician immediately.

Administration and Dosage: Adults take two tablets at bedtime to help relieve pain and aid sleep.

How Supplied: Bottles of 10, 30, 50, and 80 tablets. All sizes packaged in child resistant safety closure except 50's, which is a size not recommended for households with young children.

Product Identification Mark: Blue/green circular tablet with letters "PM" imprinted on one side.

[*Shown in Product Identification Section*]

4-WAY® Cold Tablets

Composition: Each tablet contains aspirin 324 mg., phenylpropanolamine HCl 12½ mg., and chlorpheniramine maleate 2 mg.

Action and Uses: For temporary relief of minor aches and pains, fever, nasal congestion and runny nose as may occur in the common cold.

Dosage and Administration: Adults—2 tablets every 4 hours, if needed. Do not exceed 6 tablets in 24 hours. Children 6–12 years—1 tablet every 4 hours. Do not exceed 4 tablets in 24 hours. Under age 6, consult a physician.

Warning: Do not take without consulting a physician if under medical care.

Contraindications: Hypersensitivity to aspirin or antihistamines.

Caution: This preparation may cause drowsiness. Do not drive or operate machinery while taking this medication. Individuals with high blood pressure, heart disease, diabetes, or thyroid disease should use only as directed by physician. Do not exceed recommended dosage.

KEEP THIS AND ALL MEDICINES OUT OF CHILDREN'S REACH. IN CASE OF ACCIDENTAL OVERDOSE, CONTACT PHYSICIAN IMMEDIATELY.

How Supplied: Carded 15's and bottles of 36's and 60's.

Product Identification Mark: Pink and White tablet with number "4" on one surface.

[*Shown in Product Identification Section*]

4-WAY® Nasal Spray

Composition: Phenylephrine hydrochloride 0.5%, naphazoline hydrochloride 0.05%, pyrilamine maleate 0.2%, in a buffered isotonic aqueous solution with thimerosal 0.005% added as a preservative. Also available in a mentholated formula.

Action and Uses: For relief of nasal congestion, runny nose, sneezing, and itching nose, which may be symptoms of common cold, sinusitis, nasal allergies, or hay fever.

Dosage and Administration: With head in a normal upright position, put atomizer tip into nostril. Squeeze atomizer with firm, quick pressure while inhaling. Adults-spray twice into each nostril. Children 6-12-spray once. Under 6-consult physician. Repeat in three hours, if needed.

Warning: Overdosage in young children may cause marked sedation. Do not exceed recommended dosage. Follow directions carefully. If symptoms persist, con-

Each MONSTER Multiple Vitamin Supplement Tablet supplies:

		Percentage of Recommended Dietary Allowances set by the National Research Council:	
		2–6	6–12
Vitamin A, U.S.P. units	3500	140%	106%
Vitamin D, U.S.P. units	400	100%	100%
Vitamin C (ascorbic acid), mg.	40	100%	100%
Vitamin B₁ (thiamin), mg.	1.1	122%	92%
Vitamin B₂ (riboflavin), mg.	1.2	109%	100%
Vitamin B₆ (pyridoxine), mg.	1.2	133%	100%
Vitamin B₁₂, mcg.	5	333%	250%
Niacin, mg.	15	125%	94%
Folic acid, mcg.	100	50%	33%
Pantothenic acid, mg.	5	*	*

*Recommended Daily Allowance (RDA) has not been established.

Each MONSTER with Iron Multiple Vitamin Supplement Tablet supplies:

		Percentage of Recommended Dietary Allowances set by the National Research Council:	
		2–6	6—12
Vitamin A, U.S.P. units	3500	140%	106%
Vitamin D, U.S.P. units	400	100%	100%
Vitamin C (ascorbic acid), mg.	40	100%	100%
Vitamin B₁ (thiamin), mg.	1.1	122%	92%
Vitamin B₂ (riboflavin), mg.	1.2	109%	100%
Vitamin B₆ (pyridoxine), mg.	1.2	133%	100%
Vitamin B₁₂, mcg.	5	333%	250%
Niacin, mg.	15	125%	94%
Folic acid, mcg.	100	50%	33%
Pantothenic acid, mg.	5	*	*
Iron (ferrous fumarate), mg	10	100%	100%

*Recommended Daily Allowance (RDA) has not been established.

sult physician. Keep out of children's reach.

How Supplied: Atomizers of ½ fluid ounce and 1 fluid ounce.

[*Shown in Product Identification Section*]

4–WAY® Long Acting Nasal Spray

Composition: Xylometazoline Hydrochloride 0.1% in a buffered isotonic aqueous solution. Thimerosal, 0.005% added as a preservative. Also available in a mentholated formula.

Action and Uses: Provides temporary relief of nasal congestion due to the common cold, sinusitis, hayfever or other upper respiratory allergies.

Dosage and Administration: With head in a normal upright position, put atomizer tip into nostril. Squeeze atomizer with firm, quick pressure while inhaling. Adults: Spray 2 or 3 times in each nostril every 8 to 10 hours. For children under 12, consult physician.

Warning: For adult use only. Do not give this product to children under 12 years except under the advice and supervision of a physician. Do not exceed recommended dosage because symptoms may occur such as burning, stinging, sneezing, or an increase of nasal discharge. Do not use this product for more than 3 days. If symptoms persist, consult a physician.

KEEP OUT OF CHILDREN'S REACH

How Supplied: Atomizers of ½ fluid ounce.

[*Shown in Product Identification Section*]

MONSTER®
(Brand)
Monster shaped chewable multiple vitamins

Dosage: One tablet daily for children over two years of age. May be chewed or dissolved in the mouth.

(See table on preceding page)

Made with NATURAL SWEETENERS, artificial coloring and flavoring.

Action and Uses: MONSTER shaped multiple vitamins, especially made for children, are a dietary supplement to assure necessary vitamin intake. MONSTER contains ten important vitamins.

Administration and Dosage: MONSTER may be chewed, dissolved orally, or crushed and added to foods, either liquid or solid.

Daily: one tablet.

Supplied: MONSTER vitamins are supplied in delicious fruit flavors in bottles of 60's and 100's.

MONSTER (Brand) with Iron
Monster shaped chewable vitamins with iron

Dosage: One tablet daily for children over two years of age. May be chewed or dissolved in the mouth.

(See table on preceding page)

Made with NATURAL SWEETENERS, artificial coloring and flavoring.

KEEP OUT OF REACH OF CHILDREN.

Action and Uses: MONSTER with iron is a specially formulated dietary

TABLE I
Each PALS Multiple Vitamin Supplement Tablet contains:

Daily Dose: 1 PALS® Vitamin Tablet.	Percentages of Recommended Dietary Allowances set by the National Research Council: 2–6* 6–10*		Percentages of Recommended Dietary Allowances set by the National Research Council: 2–6* 6–10*	
Vitamin A 3500 USP Units	140%	106%	Vitamin B$_6$ (pyridoxine) .... 1 mg. 111% 83%	
Vitamin D 400 USP Units	100%	100%	Vitamin B$_{12}$ (cyanocobalamin) .... 2.5 mcg. 62% 50%	
Vitamin C 60 mg.	150%	150%	Niacin .... 14 mg. 127% 93%	
Vitamin B$_1$ (thiamine) .... 0.8 mg.	100%	73%	Folic Acid .... 50 mcg. 100% 66%	
Vitamin B$_2$ (riboflavin) ...... 1.3 mg.	145%	108%	Pantothenic Acid .... 5 mg. ** **	

*Figures based on values for 6 and 10 year olds respectively. **RDA not established.
Made with NATURAL SWEETENERS, artificial colors & flavors.

TABLE II
Each PALS Plus iron Multiple Vitamin Supplement Tablet contains:

Daily Dose: 1 PALS® Vitamin Tablet.	Percentages of Recommended Dietary Allowances set by the National Research Council: 2–6* 6–10*		Percentages of Recommended Dietary Allowances set by the National Research Council: 2–6* 6–10*	
Vitamin A 3500 USP Units	140%	106%	Vitamin B$_{12}$ (cyanocobalamin) .... 2.5 mcg. 62% 50%	
Vitamin D 400 USP Units	100%	100%	Niacin .... 14 mg. 127% 93%	
Vitamin C 60 mg.	150%	150%	Folic Acid .... 50 mcg. 100% 66%	
Vitamin B$_1$ (thiamine) .... 0.8 mg.	100%	73%	Pantothenic Acid .... 5 mg. ** **	
Vitamin B$_2$ (riboflavin) ...... 1.3 mg.	145%	108%	Iron (ferrous fumarate) .... 12 mg. 120% 120%	
Vitamin B$_6$ (pyridoxine) ..... 1 mg.	111%	83%		

*Figures based on values for 6 and 10 year olds respectively. **RDA not established.
Made with NATURAL SWEETENERS, artificial colors & flavors. KEEP OUT OF REACH OF CHILDREN.

supplement containing needed vitamins plus iron for children. Each tablet provides ten important vitamins plus iron.

Administration and Dosage: MONSTER with iron may be chewed, dissolved orally, or crushed and added to solid or liquid foods. One tablet daily.

Supplied: MONSTER with iron are supplied in delicious fruit flavors in bottles of 60's and 100's.

NO DOZ® TABLETS

Composition: Each tablet contains 100 mg. Caffeine. No Doz is non-habit forming.

Action and Uses: Helps restore mental alertness.

Dosage and Administration:
For Adults: 2 tablets initially, thereafter, 1 tablet every three hours should be sufficient.

Caution: Do not take without consulting physician if under medical care. No stimulant should be substituted for normal sleep in activities requiring physical alertness.

KEEP THIS AND ALL MEDICINES OUT OF THE REACH OF CHILDREN.

How Supplied: Carded 15's and 36's and bottles of 60's.

Product Identification Mark: A white tablet with No Doz on one side.

[*Shown in Product Identification Section*]

PALS® (Brand)
Animal shaped chewable multiple vitamins

[See table above].

Actions and Uses: PALS animal shaped multiple vitamins, especially made for children, are a dietary supplement to assure necessary vitamin intake. PALS contain ten important vitamins.

Administration and Dosage: PALS may be chewed, dissolved orally, or crushed and added to foods, either liquid or solid. Daily: one tablet.

Supplied: PALS are supplied in delicious fruit flavors—grape, lemon, orange, lime and cherry—and in five colors. Bottles of 21, 60, 100.

Bristol-Myers—Cont.

PALS® (Brand) Plus Iron
Multiple vitamins plus iron

(See table on preceding page)

Action and Uses: PALS Plus iron is a specially formulated dietary supplement containing needed vitamins plus iron for growing children. Each tablet provides ten important vitamins plus iron.

Administration and Dosage: PALS Plus iron may be chewed, dissolved orally, or crushed and added to solid or liquid foods. One tablet daily.

Supplied: PALS Plus iron are supplied in delicious fruit flavors—grape, lemon, orange, lime and cherry—and in five colors. Bottles of 60 and 100.

PAZO® HEMORRHOID OINTMENT/SUPPOSITORIES

Composition: Triolyte®, Bristol-Myers brand of the combination of benzocaine (0.8%) and ephedrine sulphate (0.24%); zinc oxide (4.0%); camphor (2.18%), in an emollient base.

Action and Uses: Pazo helps shrink swelling of inflamed hemorrhoid tissue. Provides prompt, temporary relief of burning itch and pain in many cases.

Administration:

Ointment—Apply stainless Pazo well up in rectum night and morning, and after each bowel movement. Repeat as often during the day as may be necessary to maintain comfort. Continue for one week after symptoms subside. When applicator is used, lubricate applicator first with Pazo. Insert slowly, then simply press tube.

Suppositories—Remove foil and insert one Pazo suppository night and morning, and after each bowel movement. Repeat as often during the day as may be necessary to maintain comfort. Continue for one week after symptoms subside.

Warning: If the underlying condition persists or recurs frequently, despite treatment, or if any bleeding or hard irreducible swelling is present, consult your physician.

Keep out of children's reach. Keep in a cool place.

How Supplied:

Ointment—1-ounce and 2-ounce tubes with plastic applicator.

Suppositories—Boxes of 12 and 24 wrapped in silver foil.

Literature Available: Yes.

Burton, Parsons & Company, Inc.
120 WESTHAMPTON AVE.
WASHINGTON, DC 20027

KONSYL®
Plantago Ovata Coating
Brand of Psyllium Hydrophilic Mucilloid

Composition: Konsyl contains 100% highly refined mucilloid of the blond psyllium seed. It forms moist, smooth bulk which disperses intimately with the contents of the intestine to promote natural elimination.

Action and Uses: Konsyl provides nonirritating bulk for the treatment of chronic constipation, spastic constipation, nonspecific diarrhea, irritable colon, following anorectal surgery, rectal disorders, obesity, and wherever intensive bulk producing therapy is indicated. If reducing the patient's diet is desired, the bulk of Konsyl helps to prevent overeating when taken before meals.

Administration and Dosage: A rounded teaspoonful one to three times each day. In cases of constipation, each dose should be taken with a full glass of fluid. In cases of diarrhea, each dose should be taken in one-third of a glass of fluid. The patient should be instructed to stir Konsyl into a glass of water, fruit juice, or milk, and drink promptly. Dosage and/or its frequency can be reduced as symptoms disappear.

Side Effects: None.
Precautions: None.
Contraindications: Where obstruction of the bowel exists as the result of growths, adhesions or other causes, Konsyl may, by its bulk, cause difficulty.
How Supplied: Powder, containers of 6 and 12 ounces.
[*Shown in Product Identification Section*]

L. A. FORMULA®
Plantago Ovata Coating
Brand of Psyllium Hydrophilic Mucilloid

Composition: L. A. Formula contains 50% Plantago Ovata Coating (blond psyllium) dispersed in an equal amount of dextrose. It forms moist, smooth bulk which disperses intimately with the contents of the intestine to provide natural elimination. Each dose contains approximately 22 calories and a negligible amount of sodium.

Action and Uses: L. A. Formula is prepared by an ultra-fine pulverization process which permits quick dispersion, yet delays gel formation. Its high degree of palatability provides good patient acceptance.

L. A. Formula provides nonirritating bulk for the treatment of chronic constipation, spastic constipation, nonspecific diarrhea, irritable colon, following anorectal surgery, rectal disorders, obesity, and wherever intensive bulk producing therapy is indicated. If reducing the patient's diet is desired, the bulk of L. A. Formula helps to prevent overeating when taken before meals.

Administration and Dosage: A rounded teaspoonful one to three times each day. In cases of constipation, each dose should be taken with a full glass of fluid. In cases of diarrhea, each dose should be taken in one-third glass of fluid. If reducing the patient's appetite is desirable, the dose should be prescribed before meals, since the bulk frequently helps to prevent overeating. The patient should be instructed to stir L. A. Formula into a glass of water, fruit juice, or milk, and drink promptly. Dosage and/or its frequency can be reduced as the symptoms disappear.

Side Effects: None.
Precautions: None.
Contraindications: Where obstruction of the bowel exists as the result of growths, adhesions or other causes, L. A. Formula may, by its bulk, cause difficulty.
How Supplied: Powder, containers of 7 and 14 ounces.
[*Shown in Product Identification Section*]

Carnation Company
5045 WILSHIRE BLVD.
LOS ANGELES, CA 90036

CARNATION® EVAPORATED MILK

Active Ingredients: Milk, vitamin D_3.
Indications: Formulas based on Carnation evaporated milk are indicated for any normal, healthy infant who is being bottle-fed.

Precautions: Follow formula mixing instructions carefully. Use clean equipment and clean bottles during preparation. Use water containing a minimum of impurities, or which has been previously boiled. Do not save the contents of partially-consumed bottles. Store prepared formula in the refrigerator until ready to use, but do not store longer than 48 hours. Because of the formulas' protein contents (range 2.1–2.8%), pediatricians occasionally advise temporary discontinuance of the use of evaporated milk-based formulas for premature babies and for infants who develop severe diarrhea or vomiting (extrarenal water loss).

Symptoms and Treatment of Oral Overdosage: No adverse effects have been noted for properly-prepared evaporated milk-based formula. Prolonged feeding of undiluted evaporated milk (141 kcal per 100 ml) to an infant might lead to dehydration; a physician should be contacted to rehydrate the infant properly.

Dosage and Administration: The 24-hour Carnation evaporated milk-based formulas recommended for the average infant are indicated below. A pediatrician should be contacted for advice or approval on the exact formula appropriate for a given infant. Abbreviations used: evap for evaporated milk, oz for fluid ounces, Tb for tablespoons, and syrup for corn syrup or other carbohydrate syrup.

Birth–2 weeks: 5 oz evap, 11 oz water, 2 Tb syrup. **2–4 wks:** 7 oz evap. 14 oz water, 2½ Tb syrup. **1–2 mos:** 10 oz evap, 16 oz water, 2½ Tb syrup. **2–3 mos:** 12 oz evap, 18 oz water, 2½ Tb syrup. **3–5 mos:** 13 oz evap, 17 oz water, 1½ Tb syrup. **After 5 mos:** 14 oz evap, 14 oz water, no syrup. Added vitamins and iron should be prescribed by the pediatrician.

Professional Labeling: Instructions for using Carnation evaporated milk as a base for infant formula are not given on the product label; however, the label does indicate that "Additional vitamin C and iron should be supplied from other sources." Instructions may be obtained from a doctor, nurse, or by writing to Carnation Company.

How Supplied: The formula base, Carnation evaporated milk, is available in 5.33-fl-oz (170-g) or 13-fl-oz (411-g) cans at most grocery stores.

CARNATION® INSTANT BREAKFAST

Active Ingredients: Protein sources (nonfat dry milk, whey, caseinate); multivitamins and minerals.

Indications: When one envelope of Carnation instant breakfast is mixed with 8 fl. oz. (237 ml) vitamin D milk as directed, it is to be used as a meal replacement or as a supplement to the regular diet by children ages 4 years and over and adults. As such, it is indicated for low fiber/roughage diets, for burn patients, for those who temporarily cannot chew solid food, and for certain high-protein diets when a supplement is needed. When prepared with 8 fl. oz. nonfat milk, the product is also indicated for low-fat, low-cholesterol, and low-calorie diets.

Actions: When mixed with vitamin D whole milk as directed, one serving provides 280 kilocalories, 35% U.S. RDA for protein, and at least 25% U.S. RDA for all vitamins and minerals for which a U.S. RDA has been established, except for biotin. When mixed with 8 fl. oz. nonfat milk, one serving provides 220 kilocalories.

Drug Interaction: No known drug interaction.

Symptoms and Treatment of Oral Overdosage: No known symptoms of overdosage. Overconsumption might lead to excessive kilocalorie intake. Based on medical judgment, not on actual clinical experience, persons with lactose intolerance might develop temporary G.I. gas or diarrhea, depending on degree of overdosage.

Dosage and Administration: One envelope is to be mixed with 8 fl. oz. vitamin D milk. May be taken orally or by stomach tube.

Professional Labeling: Same as those described under Indications and Actions.

How Supplied: Available in either 6- or 10-envelope cartons, each envelope containing 1.21 to 1.26 oz (34.3 to 35.7 g), depending on flavor variety: Vanilla, Chocolate, Strawberry, Eggnog, Chocolate Malt, and Coffee.

CARNATION® INSTANT NONFAT DRY MILK

Active Ingredients: Nonfat dry milk, 2203 I.U. % vitamin A palmitate, 440 I.U. % vitamin D₂.

Indications: For use by individuals wishing to reduce fat and caloric intakes by replacing nonfat milk for regular full-fat milk in the diet.

Actions: When mixed according to package directions, one 8-fl-oz. (237-ml) serving provides 80 kilocalories and 0.16 g fat.

Warnings: Not recommended for use as a base for formula preparation for infants less than 6 months old.

Drug Interaction: No known drug interaction.

Dosage and Administration: After reconstituting Carnation instant nonfat dry milk with the appropriate amount of water (100 g by weight mixed with 950 ml water, or 350 ml by volume mixed with 950 ml water equals 1 litre), to be consumed orally, as an alternative to fresh whole milk in the diet.

How Supplied: Available either in 3.2 oz. (90.7 g) envelopes which reconstitute to one quart (in either 5- or 10-envelope cartons), or in boxes containing bulk powder in amounts which reconstitute to the following volumes of fluid milk: 3 qt, 8 qt, 14 qt, 20 qt, and 50 qt.

SLENDER® DIET FOOD FOR WEIGHT CONTROL (INSTANT)

Active Ingredients: Nonfat dry milk, multivitamins and minerals; 0.0009% BHA added to strawberry flavor as a preservative.

Indications: One envelope of Slender instant is to be mixed with 6 fl. oz. (178 ml) vitamin D milk. It is to be used as a meal replacement to maintain or slowly lose weight, or as a complete dietary replacement for more rapid weight loss when at least four servings are consumed daily as the total diet. Slender instant is intended for children ages 4 years and older and adults.

Actions: When consumed as directed, one serving of Slender instant supplies 225 kilocalories, 25% of the U.S. RDA for protein, and 25% of U.S. RDA of all vitamins and minerals for which a U.S. RDA has been established. Safety, and efficacy for weight loss, for patients consuming four servings per day have been clinically demonstrated for a period of three weeks.

Drug Interaction: No known drug interaction.

Symptoms and Treatment of Oral Overdosage: No known symptoms exist. Overconsumption might lead to excessive kilocalorie intake. Based on medical judgment, not on actual clinical experience, persons with lactose intolerance might develop temporary G.I. gas or diarrhea, depending on degree of overdosage.

Dosage and Administration: Taken orally, one or more daily servings (up to four per day), each mixed with 6 fl. oz. vitamin D milk.

Professional Labeling: Same information as outlined under Indications and Actions.

How Supplied: Available in 1.05 to 1.07 oz. envelopes (depending on flavor variety), which come in cartons containing 4 envelopes. Available flavors are Dutch Chocolate, Chocolate, Vanilla, Strawberry, and Variety Pack.

SLENDER® DIET MEAL FOR WEIGHT CONTROL (CANNED)

Active Ingredients: Skim milk, multivitamins, and minerals.

Indications: For use as a meal replacement to maintain or slowly lose weight, or as a complete dietary replacement for more rapid weight loss when at least four servings are consumed daily. Slender liquid is intended for children ages 4 years and older and adults.

Actions: One serving of Slender liquid (one 10-fl.-oz. can) supplies 225 kilocalories, 25% of the U.S. RDA for protein, and 25% of U.S. RDA of all vitamins and minerals for which a U.S. RDA has been established. Safety, and efficacy for weight loss, for patients consuming four servings per day have been clinically demonstrated for a period of three weeks.

Drug Interactions: No known drug interaction.

Symptoms and Treatment of Oral Overdosage: No known symptoms exist. Overconsumption might lead to excessive kilocalorie intake. Based on medical judgment, not on actual clinical experience, persons with lactose intolerance might develop temporary G.I. gas or diarrhea, depending on degree of overdosage.

Dosage and Administration: Taken orally, one or more daily servings up to four servings per day.

Professional Labeling: Same information as outlined under Indications and Actions.

How Supplied: Available in 10-fl.-oz. (296-ml; 313-g) cans in the following varieties: Chocolate, Chocolate Fudge, Milk Chocolate, Chocolate Malt, Vanilla, Strawberry, Banana, Peach.

SLENDER® DIET MEAL BARS FOR WEIGHT CONTROL

Active Ingredients: Protein sources, including peanuts, whey, calcium caseinate, egg white, and soy; multivitamins and minerals.

Indications: For use as a meal replacement to maintain or slowly lose weight, or as a complete dietary replacement for more rapid weight loss when at least four servings are consumed daily. Slender bars are intended for children ages 4 years and older and adults.

Actions: One serving of two Slender diet meal bars supplies 275 kilocalories, 25% of the U.S. RDA for protein, and 25% of U.S. RDA of all vitamins and minerals for which a U.S. RDA has been established. Safety, and efficacy for weight loss, for patients consuming four servings per day have been clinically demonstrated for a period of three weeks.

Drug Interaction: No known drug interaction.

Symptoms and Treatment of Oral Overdosage: No known symptoms exist. Overconsumption might lead to excessive kilocalorie intake.

Dosage and Administration: Taken orally, one or more daily servings (of two bars), up to four servings per day.

Professional Labeling: Same information as outlined under Indications and Actions.

Continued on next page

Carnation—Cont.

How Supplied: Available in two-bar pouches, four pouches per carton. Each bar weighs 0.98 to 1.00 oz. (27.6 to 28.6 g), depending on flavor variety. Available flavors are Chocolate, Chocolate Peanut Butter, Cinnamon, Vanilla, Chocolate Chip, Chocolate Fudge, Chocolate Caramel Nut.

Carter Products
Division of Carter-Wallace, Inc.
767 FIFTH AVENUE
NEW YORK, NY 10153

ANSWER®
At–Home Early Pregnancy
Test Kit

Active Ingredients: Each kit contains: HCG antiserum (rabbit) and HCG on sheep red blood cells, dried (test tube with chemical material) and a Buffer solution (plastic vial with test liquid).

Indications: A diagnostic aid for early determination of pregnancy, based on the presence of Human Chorionic Gonadotropin (HCG) in the urine. The sensitivity of ANSWER is such that pregnancy can often be determined as early as the 9th day after an expected menstrual period.

Actions: ANSWER is a rapid, specific test. Based on its sensitivity, most urine specimens contain an adequate concentration of HCG to be detected nine days after the day the period was expected. In studies conducted with untrained people, 96% of the time the test was performed correctly. This number is based on reports which include a population of normal pregnant and non-pregnant females comparing results to results obtained by trained laboratory personnel.

Directions for Use:

A. Urine Collection—Before you start the test.

Collect a small amount of your first morning urine in a clean, well-rinsed glass container. The container must be washed and rinsed absolutely clean since any trace of detergent could give a false reading.

The test should be performed immediately. However, if you cannot do this, keep the urine sample covered in the refrigerator until you are ready to do the test. Sediment may form, but do not shake the container of urine. Only the clear urine at the top of the container should be used. Be sure to test your urine the same day it is collected. Be sure to bring urine to room temperature before testing.

Note: If urine is cloudy, pink, or red in color or has a strong odor, do not perform the test, as certain substances can cause false test results.

B. Performance of the test.

1. Remove test tube from stand and tap it gently to make sure the chemical material is at the bottom of the test tube. Remove stopper from the test tube and replace tube in stand. Keep

the stopper because you will use it later.

2. Fill dropper with urine by squeezing the rubber bulb.

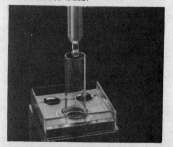

3. Empty 2 drops of urine from dropper into test tube.

4. Remove plastic vial and hold with tip pointing up making sure no liquid is in the neck of the vial. Snap off tip of vial and squeeze all contents of the vial into the test tube.

5. Replace stopper in test tube. Remove

test tube from stand and turn over several times until chemical material is completely mixed with liquid.

6. Replace test tube in the stand. Place the stand (with the mirror facing you) on a solid surface away from vibration, such as on a heavy chest or bookcase where it will not be hit or bumped or otherwise disturbed, and where the mirror can be easily seen. Allow to remain UNDISTURBED at room temperature for 2 hours.
Keep stand away from heat, vibration, and direct sunlight. Do not place stand on the refrigerator or on the same table or kitchen counter as a mixer or blender since these can cause vibrations when they are running. Do not place it on the stove, next to a heater, or in the window because heat or direct sunlight can disturb the test. Make sure stand is not moved during this 2-hour period. Note: If stand is moved or jarred during the initial 2-hour waiting period, take tube from stand, shake several times and return it to stand for another 2 hours undisturbed. This reshaking procedure can be done only once and only within the first 2 hours.

C. How to read the test (results).
The test is to be read no sooner than 2 hours and no later than 4 hours after the tube is placed in the stand above the mirror.

PREGNANCY HORMONE
NOT DETECTED

No Ring

PREGNANCY HORMONE DETECTED

Ring

Ring

Do not pick up or touch stand or tube. Read results by looking at the bottom of the tube in the mirror at base of stand. If the image you see in the mirror shows no ring as in illustration 1, pregnancy hormone is not detected.

If the image you see in the mirror shows a well-formed ring or doughnut-like ring, as in illustrations 2 and 3, pregnancy hormone is detected.

Important: This test is not intended to replace your doctor's diagnosis: If your test result shows pregnancy hormone detected, this should be confirmed by your doctor. If your result shows pregnancy hormone not detected, you may want to retest in one week. If you miss a second period, see your doctor.

Warnings: DO NOT REUSE, USE ONLY ONCE AND DISCARD.

Sometimes, around the time of "change of life" or in the case of certain diseases, ANSWER will show the presence of a hormone resembling the pregnancy hormone in your urine, even though you may not be pregnant. If your test result shows pregnancy hormone is detected, you should see your doctor. If you have missed a period or for any reason you think that you may be pregnant no matter what the result of the test, you should see your doctor. Don't guess; if you are not sure of your test result, consult your doctor.

ANSWER is not meant to replace an examination by your doctor. If you have been taking medication, the test may not work. In this case, you should have a test performed by your doctor or a professional laboratory. No test is perfect. Laboratory test results and a doctor's examination go hand in hand. Although the ANSWER method of detecting pregnancy is reliable, it is not 100% accurate. False results (pregnancy hormone detected when there is no pregnancy or pregnancy hormone not detected when the woman is pregnant) can occur in about 5% of women tested.

Precaution:
- Store the whole kit in a cool, dry place, not more than 30°C (86°F). Do not put in the freezer.
- ANSWER is not for internal use (it is for in vitro diagnostic use). Keep it out of the reach of children.
- Use only as directed. Do not use earlier than 9 days after the day you expected your period.
- Do not use after the expiration date stamped on the box.
- If the liquid in the plastic vial is cloudy, do not use the kit. Return to place of purchase for a new kit.

How Supplied: Available in kits of one test each. Each kit includes a test tube containing Human Chorionic Gonadotropin antiserum (rabbit) and Human Chorionic Gonadotropin on sheep red blood cells, dried; a plastic vial containing a buffer solution; a dropper for transferring urine; and a stand for conducting the test. The stand includes a mirror for convenient reading without disturbing the test.
[*Shown in Product Identification Section*]

CARTER'S LITTLE PILLS®
A Stimulant Laxative

Active Ingredient: 5 mg bisacodyl, U.S.P. in each enteric coated pill.
Indications: For effective short-term relief of simple constipation (infrequent or difficult bowel movement).
Actions: Bisacodyl is a stimulant laxative that promotes bowel movement by one or more direct actions on the intestine.
Directions for Use: Adult dosage is 1 to 3 pills (usually 2) at bedtime. Children over 3 years of age, 1 pill at bedtime.
Warnings: Do not chew. Do not give to children under 3 years of age or to persons who cannot swallow without chewing. Do not use this product when abdominal pain, nausea, or vomiting are present. Do not take this product within one hour before or after taking an antacid and/or milk. This product may cause abdominal discomfort, faintness, rectal burning or mild cramps. Store in a cool place at temperatures not above 86°F (30°C).

Prolonged or continued use of this product can lead to laxative dependence and loss of normal bowel function. Serious side effects from prolonged use or overdose can occur.

If you have noticed a sudden change in bowel habits that persists over a period of two weeks, consult a physician before using a laxative. This product should be used only occasionally, but in any event, no longer than daily for one week, except on the advice of a physician.
Drug Interaction Precaution: No known drug interaction.
Treatment of Overdosage: In case of accidental overdose seek professional assistance or contact a Poison Control Center immediately.
Professional Labeling: For effective short-term relief of simple constipation. For use in preparation of the patient for surgery or for preparation of the colon for x-ray and endoscopic examination.
How Supplied: Available in packages of 30 pills and 85 pills.
[*Shown in Product Identification Section*]

Cetylite Industries, Inc.
9051 RIVER ROAD
P.O. BOX CN6
PENNSAUKEN, NJ 08110

PROTEXIN ORAL RINSE
Deodorant Mouthwash

Active Ingredient: SDA 38-B; Polysorbate 80; Water; Flavoring; Zinc Chloride.
Indications: Oral debris, ropy saliva, offensive oral odors, unpleasant aftertaste.
Actions: Clears the mouth of debris and ropy saliva and leaves a pleasant, freshening, long-lasting taste.
Warnings: To be used only as directed.
Precaution: None needed.
Dosage and Administration: As per label.
Professional Labeling: None needed.
How Supplied: 3 two ounce bottles per package.

SKIN SCREEN
Skin Protectant

Active Ingredients: Lanolin derivative, silicone, oil of mink.
Indications: For use on technicians' hands as well as the lip areas and facial hair of patients to reduce the sticking of cements or other dental and laboratory adhesive materials.
Actions: The specially formulated ingredients provide long lasting protection against the repeated use of soaps and detergents.
Warnings: For external use only.
Drug Interaction: None known.
Precaution: None needed.
Symptoms and Treatment of Oral Overdosage: Not applicable.
Dosage and Administration: Externally, freely as needed.
Professional Labeling: None.
How Supplied: Three 4 ounce bottles per package.

CIBA Pharmaceutical Company
Division of CIBA-GEIGY Corporation
SUMMIT, NJ 07901

NUPERCAINAL®
Anesthetic Ointment
Suppositories
Pain-Relief Cream

Caution:
Nupercainal products are not for prolonged or extensive use and should never be applied in or near the eyes.
Consult labels before using.
Keep this and all medications out of reach of children.
NUPERCAINAL SHOULD NOT BE SWALLOWED. SWALLOWING OR USE OF A LARGE QUANTITY IS HAZARDOUS, PARTICULARLY TO CHILDREN. CONSULT A PHYSICIAN OR POISON CONTROL CENTER IMMEDIATELY.

Nupercainal is a fast-acting, long-lasting pain reliever that you can use for a number of painful skin conditions. It comes in 3 different forms: (1) **Nupercainal Anesthetic Ointment** is for hemorrhoids and for general use; (2) **Nupercainal Suppositories** are for hemorrhoids only; (3) **Nupercainal Pain-Relief Cream** is for general use only. The **Cream** is half as strong as the **Ointment.**
How to use Nupercainal Anesthetic Ointment (for general use). This soothing Ointment helps lubricate dry, inflamed skin and gives fast, temporary relief of pain and itching. It is recom-

Continued on next page

The full prescribing information for each CIBA drug is contained herein and is that in effect as of December 1, 1980.

CIBA—Cont.

mended for sunburn, nonpoisonous insect bites, minor burns, cuts, and scratches. **DO NOT USE THIS PRODUCT IN OR NEAR YOUR EYES.**

Apply to affected areas gently. If necessary, cover with a light dressing for protection. Do not use more than 1 ounce of Ointment in a 24-hour period for an adult; do not use more than one-quarter of an ounce in a 24-hour period for a child. If irritation develops, discontinue use and consult your doctor.

How to use Nupercainal Anesthetic Ointment for fast, temporary relief of pain and itching due to hemorrhoids (also known as piles).

Remove cap from tube and set it aside. Attach the white plastic applicator to the tube. Squeeze the tube until you see the Ointment begin to come through the little holes in the applicator. Using your finger, lubricate the applicator with the Ointment. Now insert the entire applicator gently into the rectum. Give the tube a good squeeze to get enough ointment into the rectum for comfort and lubrication. Remove applicator from rectum and wipe it clean. Apply additional Ointment to anal tissues to help relieve pain, burning, and itching. For best results use Ointment morning and night and after each bowel movement. After each use detach applicator, and wash it off with soap and water. Put cap back on tube before storing. In case of rectal bleeding, discontinue use and consult your doctor.

How to use Suppositories for hemorrhoids (also known as piles).

Tear off one suppository along the perforated line.

Remove foil wrapper. Insert the suppository, rounded end first, well into the anus until you can feel it moving into your rectum. For best results, use one suppository after each bowel movement. Each suppository is sealed in its own foil packet to reduce danger of leakage when carried in pocket or purse. **To prevent melting, do not store above 86°F (30°C).**

Pain-Relief Cream for general use. This Cream is particularly effective for fast, temporary relief of pain and itching associated with sunburn, cuts, scratches, minor burns and nonpoisonous insect bites. **DO NOT USE THIS PRODUCT IN OR NEAR YOUR EYES.** Apply liberally to affected area and rub in gently. This Cream is water-washable, so be sure to reapply after bathing, swimming or sweating. If irritation develops, discontinue use and consult your doctor.

Nupercainal Anesthetic Ointment contains 1% (one percent) dibucaine USP in a lubricant base. Available in tubes of 1 and 2 ounces.

Nupercainal Suppositories contain 2.5 mg dibucaine USP. Available in boxes of 12 and 24.

Nupercainal Pain-Relief Cream contains 0.5% (one-half of one percent) dibucaine USP in a water-soluble base. Available in 1½ ounce tubes.

Dibucaine USP is officially classified as a "topical anesthetic" and is one of the strongest and longest lasting of all pain relievers. It is not a narcotic.

     C80-43   (9/80)

[Shown in Product Identification Section]

PRIVINE®
0.05% Nasal Solution
0.05% Nasal Spray

Caution: Do not use Privine if you have glaucoma. Privine is an effective nasal decongestant **when you use it in the recommended dosage.** If you use too much, too long, or too often, Privine may be harmful to your nasal mucous membranes and cause burning, stinging, sneezing or an increased runny nose. Do not use Privine by mouth.

Keep this and all medications out of the reach of children. Do not use Privine with children under 6 years of age, except with the advice and supervision of a doctor. OVERDOSAGE IN YOUNG CHILDREN MAY CAUSE MARKED SEDATION AND IF SEVERE, EMERGENCY TREATMENT MAY BE NECESSARY. IF NASAL STUFFINESS PERSISTS AFTER 3 DAYS OF TREATMENT, DISCONTINUE USE AND CONSULT A DOCTOR.

Privine is a nasal decongestant that comes in two forms: Nasal Solution (in a bottle with a dropper) and Nasal Spray (in a plastic squeeze bottle). Both are for prompt, and prolonged relief of nasal congestion due to common colds, sinusitis, hay fever, etc.

How to use Nasal Solution. Squeeze rubber bulb to fill dropper with proper amount of medication. For best results, tilt head as far back as possible and put two drops of solution into your right nostril. Then lean head forward, inhaling and turning your head to the left. Refill dropper by squeezing bulb. Now tilt head as far back as possible and put two drops of solution into your left nostril. Then lean head forward, inhaling, and turning your head to the right.

Use only 2 drops in each nostril. Do not repeat this dosage more than every 3 hours.

The Privine dropper bottle is designed to make administration of the proper dosage easy and to prevent accidental overdosage. Privine will not cause sleeplessness, so you may use it before going to bed.

Important: After use, be sure to rinse the dropper with very hot water. This helps prevent contamination of the bottle with bacteria from nasal secretions. Use of the dispenser by more than one person may spread infection.

Note: Privine Nasal Solution may be used on contact with glass, plastic, stainless steel and specially treated metals used in atomizers. Do not let the solution come in contact with reactive metals, especially aluminum. If solution becomes discolored, it should be discarded.

How to use Nasal Spray. For best results do **not** shake the plastic squeeze bottle.

Remove cap. With head held upright, spray twice into each nostril. Squeeze the bottle sharply and firmly while sniffing through the nose.

For best results use every 4 to 6 hours. Do not use more often than every 3 hours. Avoid overdosage. Follow directions for use carefully.

Privine Nasal Solution contains 0.05% naphazoline hydrochloride USP with benzalkonium chloride as a preservative. Available in bottles of .66 fl. oz. (20 ml) with dropper, and bottles of 16 fl. oz. (473 ml). Privine Nasal Spray contains 0.05% naphazoline hydrochloride USP with benzalkonium chloride as a preservative. Available in plastic squeeze bottles of ½ fl. oz. (15 ml).

     C80-5   (1/80)

[Shown in Product Identification Section]

VIOFORM®
(iodochlorhydroxyquin USP)

Listed in USP, a Medicare designated compendium.

Indications and Directions For Use: A soothing antifungal and antibacterial preparation for the treatment of inflamed conditions of the skin, such as eczema, athlete's foot and other fungal infections.

Apply to the affected area 2 or 3 times a day or use as directed by physician.

Caution: May prove irritating to sensitized skin in rare cases. If this should occur, discontinue treatment and consult physician. May stain.

KEEP OUT OF REACH OF CHILDREN.

How Supplied:

Ointment, 3% iodochlorhydroxyquin in a petrolatum base; tubes of 1 ounce.

Cream, 3% iodochlorhydroxyquin in a water-washable base; tubes of 1 ounce.

     (7/80)

Circle
Pharmaceuticals, Inc.
10377 HAGUE ROAD
INDIANAPOLIS, IN 46256

SEPTA OINTMENT
Triple Antibiotic Ointment

Description: Each gram contains *Polymyxin B Sulfate 5,000 units, Bacitracin 400 units, Neomycin Sulfate 5 mg. (Equiv. to 3.5 mg. Neomycin Base).

Indications: Help prevent & treat infections in minor cuts, burns and abrasions, as an aid to healing.

Precautions: For external use only.

Dosage and Administration: Apply directly to affected area and cover with sterile gauze if necessary. May be applied 2 to 5 times daily as the condition indicates.

How Supplied: 1 oz. tube

Products are cross-indexed by

generic and chemical names in the

YELLOW SECTION

Colgate-Palmolive Company
A Delaware Corporation
300 PARK AVENUE
NEW YORK, NY 10022

DERMASSAGE DISH LIQUID

Composition: DERMASSAGE DISH LIQUID is a mild light duty liquid detergent. This product contains a combination of surfactant ingredients that provide good cleaning performance. In addition DERMASSAGE DISH LIQUID is the only light duty liquid that contains protein. Ingredients in order of predominance: sodium dodecyl benzene sulfonate, ammonium tridecyl ethoxylated (3) alcohol sulfate, ethyl alcohol, lauric/myristic monoethanol amide, sodium xylene sulfonate, sodium cumene sulfonate, magnesium sulfate, polypeptide solids, N-Hydroxyethyl ethylene, diamine triacedic acid, trisodium sodium salt, almond perfume, formaldehyde.

Indications: DERMASSAGE DISH LIQUID can actually improve dry, irritated detergent hands—hands that are red, chapped and dry. These effects were confirmed in clinical tests conducted during severe adverse cold weather conditions.

Actions: DERMASSAGE DISH LIQUID combines surfactant ingredients that provide good cleaning performance and protein to help minimize irritation and drying.

Contraindications: Hypersensitivity to any ingredient in this preparation.

Precautions: Although rare, irritation or sensitization may occur. In this event, discontinue use.

Directions: Use in place of regular dish detergent or as a light duty liquid for hand laundering, etc.

How Supplied:
12 oz.
22 oz.
32 oz.
48 oz. (limited distribution)
DERMASSAGE DISH LIQUID supplied in opaque plastic containers
[*Shown in Product Identification Section*]

DERMASSAGE MEDICATED SKIN LOTION

Active Ingredient: 0.11% Menthol
Other Ingredients: Water, mineral oil, TEA-stearate, propylene glycol, stearic acid, diammonium phosphate, methylparaben, lanolin, triclosan, fragrance, urea, propylparaben.

Indications: Dermassage Medicated Skin Lotion is a rich, creamy formula that replaces lost moisture and helps soothe and smooth away rough, dry, chapped skin.

Actions: Dermassage Medicated Skin Lotion contains moisturizers and emollients that work deep into pores to soften the skin and prevent dryness from becoming soreness. The active ingredient (menthol) works as an anti-pruritic and a mild analgesic.

Contraindications: Sensitivity to any ingredient in this product.

Warnings: For External Use Only. Not for use on mucous membranes.

Dosage and Administration: Used daily Dermassage helps keep skin feeling soft and moist. Apply as desired to relieve the itching and irritation of dry, sore skin.

How Supplied:
6 oz.
10 oz.
15 oz.
Dermassage Medicated Skin Lotion is supplied in white opaque plastic bottles.
[*Shown in Product Identification Section*]

FLUORIGARD ANTI–CAVITY DENTAL RINSE

Fluorigard is accepted by the American Dental Association.

Active Ingredient: Sodium Fluoride (0.05%) in a neutral solution.

Other Ingredients: Water, Glycerin, SD Alcohol 38-B (6%), Poloxamer 338, Poloxamer 407, Sodium Benzoate, Sodium Saccharin, Benzoic Acid, Flavor, FD & C Blue No. 1, FD & C Yellow No. 5.

Indications: Good tasting Fluorigard Anti-Cavity Dental Rinse is fluoride in liquid form. It helps get cavity-fighting fluoride to back teeth, as well as front teeth; even floods those dangerous spaces between teeth where brushing might miss. 70% of all cavities happen in back teeth and between teeth.

Actions: Fluorigard Anti-Cavity Dental Rinse is a 0.05% Sodium Fluoride solution which has been proven effective in reducing cavities.

Contraindications: Sensitivity to any ingredient in this product.

Warnings: Do not swallow. For rinsing only. Not to be used by children under 6 years of age unless recommended by a dentist. Keep out of reach of young children. If an amount considerably larger than recommended for rinsing is swallowed, give as much milk as possible and contact a physician immediately.

Directions: Use once daily after thoroughly brushing teeth. For persons 6 years of age and over, fill measuring cap to 10 ml. level (2 teaspoons), rinse around and between teeth for one minute, then spit out. For maximum benefit, use every day and do not eat or drink for at least 30 minutes afterward. Rinsing may be most convenient at bedtime. This product may be used in addition to a fluoride toothpaste.

How Supplied:
6 oz.
10 oz.
16 oz.
1 Gallon Professional Size for use in dentists offices only.
[*Shown in Product Identification Section*]

MERSENE DENTURE CLEANSER

Composition: Mersene is a premeasured denture cleanser in crystalline form. The product utilizes an active chlorine system for plaque removal and stain prevention, active oxygen and a detergent system for effervescent cleaning. Major ingredients in order of predominance: Trisodium Phosphate, Potassium Troclosene and Sodium Perborate.

Indications: Mersene Denture Cleanser is more effective at removing plaque than the leading tablets. This effectiveness has been confirmed through clinical testing.

The product has a color timed indicator that turns from deep blue to clear when the cleaning is complete and a pleasant peppermint flavor.

Actions: Mersene Denture Cleanser has the ingredients and effervescent action to remove and disperse most of the complex organic matrix and microbial mass of which plaque is composed. Thus, calculus has less chance to form.

Contraindications: There have been isolated instances where use of Mersene has been identified with the darkening of certain dentures. This can be easily corrected by professional cleaning.

Precautions: Eye and skin irritant. Harmful if swallowed. In case of eye or skin contact, flush thoroughly with water. If swallowed, feed milk, or water. Call a physician.

Directions:
1) Empty pre-measured packet into container and add very warm water to cover denture.
2) Place denture into effervescing blue solution. Allow to soak until blue color clears—about 15 minutes
3) Rinse denture thoroughly. Denture is now clean, fresh, and ready for use.

How Supplied: Mersene is available in 20, 40, 60, and 96 packet cartons.
[*Shown in Product Identification Section*]

Combe Incorporated
1101 WESTCHESTER AVENUE
WHITE PLAINS, NY 10604

LANACANE® Medicated Creme

Active Ingredients: 6.0% Benzocaine; 2.0% Resorcinol.

Indications: LANACANE Creme Medication is specially formulated to give prompt, temporary relief from dry skin itching, vaginal and rectal itching, rashes, insect bites, sunburn, chafing, poison ivy, poison oak, chapping, sore detergent hands, minor burns and other irritated skin conditions. LANACANE checks bacteria to help speed natural healing.

Actions: Benzocaine is a local anesthetic of low toxicity considered to be one of the safest and most widely used of the over-the-counter topical anesthetics. Temporary anesthesia is elicited by penetrating the cutaneous barriers and blocking sensory receptors for the perception of pain and itching. Resorcinol activity is both antimicrobial and mildly keratolytic.

Warnings: Read enclosed circular carefully before using. Not for prolonged use. Do not get into the eyes. Some skin and membrane irritations may be caused by internal systemic disorders. If condi-

Continued on next page

Combe—Cont.

tion persists for more than seven days or worsens, discontinue use and consult your physician. Keep out of reach of children.

Drug Interaction Precaution: Benzocaine has been known to occasionally cause allergic dermatitis. Cross-reactions have been reported with para-phenylenediamine, a hair dye, sulfonamide and sun screens containing para-aminobenzoic acid esters.

Dosage and Administration: Apply LANACANE Creme Medication liberally to the affected area. Repeat as needed three or four times daily.

How Supplied: Available in 1.0 and 2.0 oz. tubes.
[*Shown in Product Identification Section*]

LANACORT™ HYDROCORTISONE ACETATE 0.5% CREME

Active Ingredient: 0.5% Hydrocortisone Acetate.

Indication: Lanacort™ Creme is specially formulated to provide relief from minor skin irritation, rashes, itching due to eczema (symptoms are redness, itching, and flaking), dermatitis (an irritated condition of the skin including inflammation and redness)... also due to soaps, detergents, cosmetics, jewelry, poison ivy, oak, sumac; insect bites; and for genital and rectal itching.

Action: Hydrocortisone Acetate is an anti-inflammatory corticosteroid[1,2], whose mechanism of action is still being elucidated. Current thinking suggests the following modes of action: (1) controlling the rate of protein synthesis; (2) reducing the amounts of prostaglandin substrate available for the enzyme.[3] Corticosteroids are also known to reduce immune hypersensitivity by reducing the inflammatory response.[1]

Warning: For external use only. Avoid contact with the eyes. If conditions worsen or if symptoms persist for more than 7 days, discontinue use and consult a physician. Do not use on children under 2 years of age except under the advice and supervision of a physician. Keep out of reach of children.

Dosage and Administration: Apply to affected area 3 or 4 times daily.

How Supplied: Available in 0.5 and 1.0 oz. tubes.

References:
1. Goodman and Gilman, The Pharmacological Basis of Therapeutics, Page 1487, 5th Ed., MacMillan, 1975.
2. Su-Chen L. Hong, Lawrence Levine, J. Bio. Chem., Vol. 251, No. 18, pp. 5814–5816, 1976.
3. Ryszard J. Gryglewski, et al., Prostoglandins, Vol. 10, No. 2, pp. 343–35 August 1975.

[*Shown in Product Identification Section*]

VAGISIL® Feminine Itching Medication

Active Ingredients: 5.0% Benzocaine; 2.0% Resorcinol.

Indications: VAGISIL Medication has been formulated to give prompt, effective relief from the discomfort of minor itching, burning, and other irritations in the external vaginal area. VAGISIL forms a cooling, protective film over irritated tissues. Helps check bacteria to speed natural healing. Lightly scented, stainless, greaseless.

Actions: Benzocaine is a local anesthetic of low toxicity considered to be one of the safest and most widely used of the over-the-counter topical anesthetics. Temporary anesthesia is elicited by penetrating the cutaneous barriers and blocking sensory receptors for the perception of pain and itching. Resorcinol activity is both antimicrobial and mildly keratolytic.

Warnings: Read enclosed circular carefully before using. Not for prolonged use. Do not get into eyes. Some skin and membrane irritations may be caused by internal systemic disorders. If condition persists for more than seven days or worsens, discontinue use and consult physician. Keep out of reach of children.

Drug Interaction Precaution: Benzocaine has been known to occasionally cause allergic dermatitis. Cross-reactions have been reported with para-phenylenediamine, a hair dye, sulfonamide and sun screens containing para-aminobenzoic acid esters.

Dosage and Administration: Apply VAGISIL Creme Medication liberally to the affected area. Repeat as needed three or four times daily.

How Supplied: Available in 1.0 and 2.0 oz. tubes.
[*Shown in Product Identification Section*]

CooperCare, Inc. (U.S.A.)
DERMATOLOGY PRODUCTS
305 FAIRFIELD AVENUE
FAIRFIELD, NJ 07006

ACNAVEEN® BAR
Cleansing Bar For Acne

Acnaveen Bar is a special soap-free cleansing bar for acne. It contains colloidal oatmeal, 2% sulfur, and 2% salicylic acid, to help cleanse and soothe irritated skin.

Ingredients: Aveeno® Colloidal Oatmeal, 50%; sulfur, 2%; salicylic acid, 2%; in a sudsing soap-free base containing a mild surfactant.
[*Shown in Product Identification Section*]

AVEENO®
Colloidal Oatmeal-Bath for sensitive skin

AVEENO® Colloidal Oatmeal is a natural cereal derivative developed specially for soothing and cleansing sensitive skin. AVEENO® Colloidal Oatmeal contains no soaps or synthetic detergents that may be harmful to the skin. It cleanses naturally because of its unique adsorptive action.

Infants and children with sensitive skin will also benefit from soothing, calming AVEENO® Colloidal Oatmeal baths.
[*Shown in Product Identification Section*]

AVEENO BAR®
For cleansing sensitive skin

Aveenobar is made especially for sensitive skin that is irritated by ordinary soaps.

More than 50% of this mild skin cleanser is colloidal oatmeal, noted for its soothing and protective qualities.

Aveenobar is completely soap-free. It leaves no harsh alkaline film to irritate delicate skin... it leaves it feeling soft and comfortable.

Ingredients: Aveeno® Colloidal Oatmeal, 50%; specially selected lanolin derivative; in a sudsing soapfree base containing a mild surfactant.
[*Shown in Product Identification Section*]

AVEENO® OILATED

AVEENO® Oilated contains AVEENO® Colloidal Oatmeal, a natural cereal derivative developed specially for soothing and cleansing sensitive skin... and a combination of emollients to make dry skin feel soft, supple, and smooth. AVEENO® Oilated contains no soaps or synthetic detergents that may be harmful to the skin. It *cleanses naturally* because of its unique adsorptive action.

Contents: AVEENO® Colloidal Oatmeal, liquid petrolatum and a specially selected emollient.
[*Shown in Product Identification Section*]

EMULAVE® BAR
Cleansing Bar for Dry Skin

Emulave is a unique, soap-free cleanser for dry, sensitive skin that is irritated by ordinary soaps. Emulave contains over 29% skin-softening emollients to help replace natural skin oils and 30% colloidal oatmeal, recommended for its soothing and protective qualities.

Ingredients: A combination of vegetable oils, specially selected lanolin derivative and glycerine 29%, Aveeno® Colloidal Oatmeal, 30%; in a sudsing soap-free base containing a mild surfactant.
[*Shown in Product Identification Section*]

Creighton Products Corporation
a company of Culbro Corporation
(see also Ex-Lax Pharmaceutical Co., Inc.)
605 THIRD AVENUE
NEW YORK, NY 10016

BiCOZENE® Creme External Analgesic

Active Ingredients: Benzocaine 6%, resorcinol 1.67% in a specially prepared cream base.

Indications: For the temporary relief of pain and itching due to minor burns, sunburn, minor cuts, abrasions, insect bites, and minor skin irritations. For all kinds of external itching skin conditions; vaginal, rectal, poison ivy, heat rash, chafing, eczema, and common itching of the skin.

Actions: Benzocaine is a topical anesthetic and resorcinol is a topical antipruritic, at the concentrations used in BiCo-

zene Creme. Both exert their actions by depressing cutaneous sensory receptors. **Warnings: Caution:** Use only as directed. Keep away from the eyes. Not for prolonged use. If the condition for which this preparation is used persists, or if a rash or irritation develops, discontinue use and consult a physician. For external use only. **Warning**—Keep out of the reach of children.
Drug Interaction Precautions: No known drug interaction.
Dosage and Administration: Apply to affected area morning, night, and as needed.
How Supplied: BiCozene Creme is available in 1-ounce tubes.
[*Shown in Product Identification Section*]

DERMA+SOFT® Creme

Active Ingredient: Salicylic acid 2.5% in a specially prepared cream base.
Actions: The unique stainless, greaseless creme formula of Derma-Soft softens and removes corns and calluses.
Warnings: Do not apply Derma-Soft to moles, birthmarks, or warts. **Caution:** Derma-Soft should not be used by diabetics or persons with poor circulation. For external use only. Store in a cool, dry place. KEEP ALL MEDICINES OUT OF THE REACH OF CHILDREN.
Drug Interaction Precautions: No known drug interactions.
Dosage and Administration: Thoroughly wash area to be treated. Dry with a rough, clean towel, rubbing off any loose dead skin. Apply Derma-Soft directly on corns and calluses. Avoid applying to healthy skin. Use treatment daily for two weeks. In stubborn cases, continue use for another two weeks. If condition persists, see your physician.
How Supplied: Derma-Soft Creme is available in 1-oz. tubes.
[*Shown in Product Identification Section*]

GAS-X® Antiflatulent

Active Ingredient: Simethicone, 80 mg per tablet.
Indications: Helps relieve symptoms of intestinal gas.
Actions: Simethicone is a surface-active agent, having pronounced antifoaming action. Small bubbles (foam) are broken up through reduction in surface tension.
Warning: Keep this and all medicines out of the reach of children.
Drug Interaction Precautions: No known drug interaction.
Dosage and Administration: Adults: Chew one tablet as needed after meals and at bedtime. Do not exceed six tablets in 24 hours, except under the advice and supervision of a physician.
Professional Labeling: Gas-X may be useful in the alleviation of postoperative gas pain, and for use in endoscopic examination.
How Supplied: Gas-X is available in boxes of 30 tablets and convenience packages of 12 tablets.
[*Shown in Product Identification Section*]

Daywell Laboratories Corporation
78 UNQUOWA PLACE
FAIRFIELD, CT 06430

VERGO®

Composition: Vergo contains Pancin®, a special formulation of calcium pantothenate, ascorbic acid and starch.
Action and Uses: It is believed that warts are caused by a virus, and that the widespread occurrence of warts among children is due to the infectious nature of the wart virus. The child with warts is three times more likely to develop new warts as a child who has not been infected previously. For this reason the early treatment of warts is recommended. Above all, treatment should be conservative and should not affect or injure the surrounding tissues. Vergo gives the same relief and results in the treatment of warts of the adult. Vergo is a conservative, painless and safe treatment of warts. It is convenient, easy to apply, and will not burn, blister or leave scars. The ingredients are essential to the soundness of tissues and skin and will relieve the pain of warts and promote healing. Vergo is not irritating and there are no contraindications to its use. The average treatment time is from 2 to 8 weeks depending on the size of the wart and the response of the patient. It is important that the directions be carefully followed and that treatment be continued without interruption as long as necessary. Mosaic-type warts are more resistant and usually require longer treatment for relief.
Administration and Dosage: Cleanse area with soap and water; rinse thoroughly. Apply Vergo liberally to wart or corn. Do not massage or rub in. Cover with plain Band-Aid® or gauze and adhesive tape. Change dressing and apply Vergo twice a day, morning and evening.
Side Effects: None known.
How Supplied: In one-half ounce tubes.
Product Identification Mark: Vergo®.
Literature Available: Yes.

Dermaide Research Corporation
400 N. MICHIGAN AVENUE
CHICAGO, IL 60611

DERMAIDE® Aloe Ointment

Active Ingredient: 70% gel of the Aloe vera plant in a special white, homogenous base of mineral oil, steric acid, petroleum, triethanolamine, beeswax, synthetic spermaceti, propylparaben, methyl paraben, and fragrance. It contains no anesthetic drug.
Indications: Topical application for minor burns, cold injuries, irradiation injuries, cuts, abrasions, and skin irritations. It is non-toxic, non-staining, and non-greasy.
Warnings: May cause occasional skin sensitivity in which case it should be immediately washed off and further use discontinued. It has not been studied for

safety in or around the eyes or in pregnant women.
Dosage and Administration: Wash and rinse the affected area thoroughly with lukewarm water, apply DERM-AIDE ALOE OINTMENT generously over the area. Continue to apply as often as necessary to keep the injured area covered. If the affected area needs a dressing, attach a sterile non-adherent bandage. If relief is not obtained within 24 hours, consult a physician.
How Supplied: 2 ounce and 4 ounce jars

Dermik Laboratories, Inc.
1777 WALTON ROAD, DUBLIN HALL
BLUE BELL, PA 19422

FOMAC® FOAM
(medicated foam cleanser)

Description: Salicylic acid 2% in a soap-free, mild detergent system. Patent No. 4147782.
Indications: Acne and oily skin.
Directions: DO NOT SHAKE. Invert container and squeeze a puff of Fomac Foam into palm of hand and massage, gently but thoroughly, into affected area until foam disappears. For best results, do not wet skin. Leave on skin 3 - 5 minutes, then rinse well with lukewarm water and pat dry. Use once or twice daily, or as recommended by physician. Discontinue use of all soaps or other skin cleansers.
Precautions: If redness or irritation occurs or increases, reduce frequency of applications. If irritation persists, discontinue use and consult your physician. Keep away from eyes. For external use only. Keep out of the reach of children. Keep tightly closed. Store at room temperature.
How Supplied: 3 fl. oz. non-aerosol bottle.

HYTONE® CREAM ½%
(hydrocortisone ½%)

Active Ingredient: Hydrocortisone 0.5%.
Indications: For the temporary relief of minor skin irritations, itching, and rashes due to eczema, dermatitis, insect bites, poison ivy, poison oak, poison sumac, soaps, detergents, cosmetics, and jewelry, and for itchy genital and anal areas.
Actions: Provides temporary relief of itching and minor skin irritations.
Warnings: For External Use Only. Avoid contact with eyes. If condition worsens, or if symptoms persist for more than 7 days, discontinue use of this product and consult a physician. Do not use on children under 2 years of age except under the advice and supervision of a physician. KEEP OUT OF THE REACH OF CHILDREN.
Dosage and Administration: For adults and children 2 years of age and

Continued on next page

Dermik—Cont.

older: Apply to affected area not more than 3 or 4 times daily, or as directed by physician.

How Supplied: Tube, 1 ounce.

HYTONE® OINTMENT ½%
(hydrocortisone ½%)

Active Ingredient: Hydrocortisone 0.5%.

Indications: For the temporary relief of minor skin irritations, itching, and rashes due to eczema, dermatitis, insect bites, poison ivy, poison oak, poison sumac, soaps, detergents, cosmetics, and jewelry, and for itchy genital and anal areas.

Actions: Provides temporary relief of itching and minor skin irritations.

Warnings: For External Use Only. Avoid contact with eyes. If condition worsens, or if symptoms persist for more than 7 days, discontinue use of this product and consult a physician. Do not use on children under 2 years of age except under the advice and supervision of a physician. KEEP OUT OF THE REACH OF CHILDREN.

Dosage and Administration: For adults and children 2 years of age and older: Apply to affected area not more than 3 or 4 times daily, or as directed by physician.

How Supplied: Tube, 1 ounce.

LOROXIDE® ACNE LOTION (Flesh Tinted)

Description: Loroxide® Lotion contains (as dispensed) benzoyl peroxide 5.5%, and chlorhydroxyquinoline 0.25% incorporated in a flesh-tinted lotion of propylene glycol, cetyl alcohol, hydroxyethylcellulose, kaolin, caramel, talc, cholesterol and related sterols, propylene glycol stearate, polysorbate 20, lanolin alcohol, propylparaben, methylparaben, tetrasodium EDTA, pH buffers, antioxidants, silicone emulsion, silica, decyl oleate, vegetable oil, purcelline oil syn., titanium dioxide, cyclohexanediamine tetraacetic acid, calcium phosphate, and purified water.

Actions: Provides keratolytic, peeling and drying action.

Indications: An aid in the treatment of acne and oily skin.

Contraindications: This product is contraindicated for use by patients having known hypersensitivity to benzoyl peroxide, chlorhydroxyquinoline or any other component of this preparation.

Precautions: For external use only. Keep away from eyes. Do not add any other medicaments or substances to this lotion unless specifically directed by physician to do so. Patients should be observed carefully for possible local irritation or sensitivity during long-term topical therapy. If any irritation or sensitivity is observed, discontinue use and consult physician. Apply with caution on neck and/or other sensitive areas. There may be a slight, transitory stinging or burning sensation on initial application

which invariably disappears on continued use. Ultraviolet and cold quartz light should be employed in lesser amounts as this lotion is keratolytic and drying. Harsh, abrasive cleansers should not be used simultaneously with this lotion. Colored or dyed garments may be bleached by the oxidizing action of benzoyl peroxide. Chlorhydroxyquinoline may cause temporary light-yellowish skin staining in rare cases. Occurrence of excessive redness or peeling indicates that the amount and frequency of application should be reduced. Keep out of the reach of children.

Adverse Reactions: The sensitizing potential of benzoyl peroxide and chlorhydroxyquinoline are low; but they can, on occasion, produce allergic reaction.

Directions: Shake well before using. Apply a thin film to affected areas with light massaging to blend in each application 1 or 2 times daily or in accordance with the physician's directions.

How Supplied: Bottles, 25 grams (0.88 oz.) net weight as dispensed. A "Dermik Color Blender™" is provided which enables the patient to alter the basic shade of the lotion to match the skin color.

SHEPARD'S CREAM LOTION
Skin Lubricant—Moisturizer

Composition: Water, sesame oil, SD alcohol 40-B, stearic acid, propylene glycol, ethoxydiglycol, glycerin, triethanolamine, glyceryl stearate, letyl alcohol, may contain fragrance ("scented" only), simethicone, methylparaben, propylparaben, vegetable oil, monoglyceride citrate, BHT and citric acid.

Indications: For generalized dryness and itching, sunburn, "winter-itch"; dry skin; heat rash.

Actions and Uses: Shepard's Cream Lotion is a rich lotion containing soothing Oil of Sesame.

Dosage and Administration: Apply as often as needed. Use particularly after bathing and exposure to sun, water, soaps and detergents.

How Supplied: Scented and Unscented 8 oz. bottle and 16 oz. pump bottle.

SHEPARD'S DRY SKIN CREAM
Concentrated Moisturizer

Composition: Lanolin, mineral oil, petrolatum and ceresin.

Indications: For day or night lubrication of severe and persistent dry skin.

Actions: Rich in lanolin, contains no water, helps retain moisture that makes skin feel soft, smooth, supple; for problem dry skin particularly on hands, elbows, feet and legs.

Dosage and Administration: A small amount is rubbed into dry skin areas as needed.

How Supplied: Unscented, 3 ¼ oz. jars.

SHEPARD'S HAND CREAM
Concentrated
Moisturizer—Non-greasy Emollient

Composition: Water, glyceryl stearate, ethoxydiglycol, propylene glycol, glycerin, stearic acid, isopropyl myris-

tate, cetyl alcohol, urea, lecithin, may contain fragrance ("scented" only) methylparaben and propylparaben.

Indications: For problem dry skin of the hands, face, elbows, feet, legs. Helps resist effects of soaps, detergents and chemicals.

Actions: Soothing, rich lubricant containing isopropyl myristate in a non-greasy or sticky base containing no lanolin or mineral oil. Shepard's Hand Cream helps retain moisture that makes skin feel soft, smooth, supple.

Dosage and Administration: A small amount is rubbed into dry skin areas as needed.

How Supplied: Scented and Unscented, 4 oz. jars.

SHEPARD'S MOISTURIZING SOAP
Cleanser for Dry Skin

Composition: Soap (Sodium Tallowate & Cocoate Types), Water, Glycerin, Fragrance, Coconut Acid, Sodium Chloride, Lanolin, Titanium Dioxide, o-Tolyl Biguanide

Indications: As a daily cleanser of dry skin of the face, hands, or in the bath or shower. Shepard's Soap helps to give the skin an all over smoothness.

Actions: A lightly scented, non-detergent moisturizing soap containing lanolin that cleanses the skin while helping to minimize the excessive drying inherent in most detergent-type soaps.

Dosage and Administration: Use regularly to cleanse face and hands as well as in the bath or shower.

How Supplied: 4 oz. bars.

VANOXIDE® ACNE LOTION
(Dries on Clear)

Description: Vanoxide® Acne Lotion contains (as dispensed) benzoyl peroxide 5% and chlorhydroxyquinoline 0.25% incorporated in a water washable, vanishing lotion consisting of purified water, propylene glycol, hydroxy- ethylcellulose, FD&C color, cholesterol-sterol, cetyl alcohol, propylene glycol stearate, polysorbate 20, lanolin alcohol, propylparaben, decyl oleate, purcelline oil syn., antioxidants, vegetable oil, methylparaben, tetrasodium EDTA, buffers, cyclohexanediamine tetra- acetic acid, calcium phosphate, silicone emulsion, and silica.

Actions: Provides keratolytic, peeling and drying action.

Indications: An aid in the treatment of acne and oily skin

Contraindications: This product is contraindicated for use by patients having known hypersensitivity to benzoyl peroxide, chlorhydroxyquinoline or any other component of this preparation.

Precautions: For external use only. Keep away from eyes. Do not add any other medicaments or substances to this lotion unless specifically directed by physician to do so. Patients should be observed carefully for possible local irritation or sensitization during long-term topical therapy. If any irritation or sensitivity is observed, discontinue use and consult physician. Apply with caution on neck and/or other sensitive areas. There may be a slight, transitory stinging or burning sensation on initial application which invariably disappears on continued use. Ultraviolet and cold quartz light should be employed in lesser amounts as this lotion is keratolytic and drying. Harsh, abrasive cleansers should not be used simultaneously with lotion. Colored or dyed garments may be bleached by the oxidizing action of benzoyl peroxide. Chlorhydroxyquinoline may cause temporary light-yellowish skin staining in rare cases. Occurrence of excessive redness or peeling indicates that the amount and frequency of application should be reduced. Keep out of the reach of children.

Adverse Reactions: The sensitizing potential of benzoyl peroxide and chlorhydroxyquinoline are low but they can, on occasion, produce allergic reaction.

Directions: Shake well before using. Apply a small quantity to affected areas with light massaging 1 or 2 times daily or in accordance with the physician's directions.

How Supplied: Bottles, 25 grams (0.88 oz.) as dispensed and 50 grams (1.76 oz.) as dispensed.

ZETAR® SHAMPOO

Active Ingredients: WHOLE Coal Tar (as Zetar®) 1.0%, and parachlorometaxylenol 0.5% in a golden foam shampoo which produces soft, fluffy abundant lather.

Actions and Indications: Antiseptic, antibacterial, antiseborrheic. Loosens and softens scales and crusts. Indicated in psoriasis, seborrhea, dandruff, cradle-cap and other oily, itchy conditions of the body and scalp.

Contraindications: Acute inflammation, open or infected lesions.

Precautions: If undue skin irritation develops or increases, discontinue use and consult physician. In rare instances, temporary discoloration of blond, bleached, or tinted hair may occur. Avoid contact with eyes.

Dosage and Administration: Massage into moistened scalp. Rinse. Repeat; leave on 5 minutes. Rinse thoroughly.

How Supplied: 6 oz. plastic bottles.

DeWitt International Corporation
5 N. WATSON ROAD
TAYLORS, SC 29687

DEWITT'S ANTACID POWDER

Active Ingredients: (1) Magnesium Trisilicate (2) Sodium Bicarbonate (275 mg. Sodium/teaspoonful) (3) Aluminum Hydroxide (4) Magnesium Carbonate

Indications: To alleviate symptoms of Heartburn, Sour Stomach and Acid Indigestion.

Actions: A combination of rapid-acting aluminum carbonate and long-acting magnesium trisilicate powder which renders a palatable, pleasantly flavored suspension when stirred in water.

Warnings: Do not use this product except under the advice and supervision of a physician if you have a kidney disease or if you are on a sodium restricted diet. Do not take more than 8 teaspoonfuls in a 24 hour period, or use the maximum dosage for more than 2 weeks except under the advice and supervision of a physician. In case of accidental overdose, seek professional assistance or contact a Poison Control Center immediately.

Drug Interaction: Do not take this product if presently taking a prescription antibiotic drug containing any form of tetracycline.

Symptoms and Treatment of Oral Overdosage: Severe uncompensated alkalosis, may occur. Discontinue use of antacids.

Dosage and Administration: One teaspoonful in a glass of water, up to 8 times per day or as directed by a physician.

Professional Labeling: Same as under indications.

How Supplied: In 4 ounce clear polystyrene plastic bottles.
[*Shown in Product Identification Section*]

DEWITT'S BABY COUGH SYRUP

Active Ingredients: Glycerin, Ammonium Chloride, Licorice—flavored with Anise Oil.

Indications: For coughs due to colds.

Actions: This pleasant tasting Anise flavored cough syrup gives an effective demulcent effect provided by the glycerin and licorice ingredients. Ammonium Chloride provides a gentle expectorant effect.

Warnings: Shake well before using. If cough has persisted for 10 days or if there is a high fever, consult your physician. Persistent cough may indicate a serious condition. In case of accidental overdose, seek professional assistance or contact a poison control center immediately. Keep all medicine out of children's reach.

Drug Interaction: No known drug interactions.

Dosage and Administration: For infants under one year of age: ten drops in water if desired. For children one to five years of age: one-half ($\frac{1}{2}$) teaspoonful. For children over five years of age: one teaspoonful. Any of the above dosages may be repeated at two hour intervals if necessary.

Professional Labeling: Same as those outlined under indications.

How Supplied: Available in clear 3 oz. glass bottles.
[*Shown in Product Identification Section*]

DEWITT'S OIL FOR EAR USE

Active Ingredients: Cajeput Oil, Thyme Oil, Camphor, Menthol in base of Corn Oil and Mineral Oil.

Indications: For use as an aid in loosening and removing wax accumulations.

Actions: A combination of oils and camphor formulated to soften excess or impacted ear wax, which can be removed from the ear easily without the use of instruments which may be painful.

Warnings: Keep this and all medicine out of children's reach. In case of accidental ingestion, seek professional assistance or contact a Poison Control Center immediately. If wax has not been removed and hearing or ear noises have not improved, consult your doctor. Earache may be a sign of a serious condition.

Drug Interaction: No known drug interaction.

Dosage and Administration: Warm the drops before using by placing the bottle in warm water. Put into the ear 5 to 10 drops of the oil using the combination dropper cap. Place a small amount of cotton at ear opening. May be repeated in 2 hours, or morning and evening for a few days. Thoroughly cleanse the ear with warm water or a solution of Boric Acid and warm water.

Professional Labeling: Same as outlined under indications.

How Supplied: In $\frac{1}{2}$ ounce glass bottles with a combination dropper-cap.
[*Shown in Product Identification Section*]

DEWITT'S PILLS FOR BACKACHE AND JOINT PAINS

Active Ingredients: Salicylamide, Potassium Nitrate, Uva Ursi, Buchu and Caffeine.

Indications: For backache and joint pains, muscular aches, headaches and mild urinary irritations caused by non-organic disturbances of a minor nature.

Actions: Analgesic ingredients help in relief of minor pains. Mild diuretic action helps eliminate retained fluids, flushes out bladder wastes and irritations that often cause physical distress including too frequent or difficult passage of urine.

Warnings: Keep this and all medicines out of the reach of children. In case of accidental overdose, seek professional assistance or contact a Poison Control Center immediately.

Drug Interaction: No known drug interactions.

Precaution: A few pills will turn the urine blue or green because of the presence of Methylene Blue as a coloring agent.

Symptoms and Treatment of Oral Overdosage:

Symptoms: Vomiting; epigastric pain; profuse perspiration; headache; dizziness; tinnitus; visual disturbances; delirium; restlessness, excitement, convulsions; pulse rapid, feeble; BP low; pallor; skin eruptions; dyspnea. Urine shows salicylate reaction: ferric chloride produces port-wine color (not affected by prior boiling).

Treatment: Lavage or emetics; saline cathartic. I.V. fluids containing sodium bicarbonate or lactate 40 to 60 mEq/L and potassium 30 to 40 mEq/L at a rate of 3 to 5 L/sq.M of BSA to correct acid-base disturbances (acidosis common in young children) and to promote excretion. Treatment otherwise supportive. Dialysis in extreme cases (for peritoneal dialysis, 5% normal serum albumin [human] should be used).

Continued on next page

DeWitt—Cont.

Dosage and Administration: For adult use only. Take 3 pills before meals and 3 pills at bedtime, up to a maximum of 12 pills per day. Swallow with a glass of water. Drink plenty of water between meals.

Professional Labeling: Same as those outlined under indications.

How Supplied: Individual blistering of pills packaged in cartons of 20, 40 and 80 pills.

[*Shown in Product Identification Section*]

HTO STAINLESS MANZAN HEMORRHOIDAL TISSUE OINTMENT

Active Ingredients: Zinc Oxide, Benzocaine, Phenol ½%, Allantoin, Ephedrine HCl.

Indications: For temporary relief of many cases of pain and itching from swollen, inflamed hemorrhoidal tissue caused by edema, infection or inflammation.

Actions: The base of petrolatum and lanolin provides an emollient preparation which provides a more comfortable bowel movement due to its lubricating properties. The active ingredients provide an anesthetic action and help to relieve irritations due to itching, inflamed hemorrhoidal tissue caused by edema, infection or inflammation.

Warnings: In case of accidental ingestion, seek professional assistance or contact a Poison Control Center immediately.

Drug Interaction: No known drug interaction.

Precaution: Not for prolonged use. If rash or rectal bleeding occurs, discontinue use and consult a physician.

Dosage and Administration: Cleanse the external affected parts with warm water and toilet soap; dry with a soft towel. After gently inserting the applicator as far as possible into the rectum, squeeze tube to apply a liberal amount of HTO. Use night and morning and after bowel movements when convenient.

Professional Labeling: Same as listed under indications.

How Supplied: In 1 ounce metal tubes with a rectal applicator.

[*Shown in Product Identification Section*]

IDENTIFICATION PROBLEM?

Consult the

Product Identification Section

where you'll find

products pictured

in full color.

Dorsey Laboratories
Division of Sandoz, Inc.
LINCOLN, NE 68501

ACID MANTLE® CREME AND ACID MANTLE® LOTION

Description: A greaseless, water-miscible preparation containing buffered aluminum acetate.

Indications: Provides relief from mild skin irritation due to exposure to soaps, detergents, chemicals, alkalis. Aids in the treatment of diaper rash, acne, eczema and dry, rough, scaly skin from varied causes.

Application: Apply several times daily, especially after wet work.

Caution: Limited compatibility and stability with Vitamin A, neomycin and water-soluble antibiotics. For external use only. Not for ophthalmic use.

How Supplied: Creme: 1 oz tubes; 4 oz and 1 lb jars. Lotion: 4 oz.

[*Shown in Product Identification Section*]

CAMA® INLAY-TABS®

Description: Each CAMA INLAY-TAB contains: aspirin USP 600 mg (10 grains); magnesium hydroxide, USP 150 mg; aluminum hydroxide dried gel USP 150 mg.

Indications: An analgesic in arthritis and rheumatism.

Contraindications: Hypersensitivity to salicylates.

Warnings: The antipyretic effect of salicylates may mask the diagnostic importance of persistent fever.

Precautions: The occasional occurrence of mild salicylism may require adjustment of dosage.

Adverse Reactions: Overdosage of salicylates will cause tinnitus, nausea, vomiting and gastrointestinal upsets and bleeding.

Dosage and Administration: Adults —one tablet every four hours. Physicians may increase the dosage as required to provide satisfactory relief of symptoms. Usually, a dose of one to two tablets four times daily is adequate.

How Supplied: Cama Inlay-Tabs (white with salmon inlay) in bottles of 100 and 250.

[*Shown in Product Identification Section*]

DORCOL® PEDIATRIC COUGH SYRUP

Description: Each teaspoonful (5 ml) of DORCOL Pediatric Cough Syrup contains: phenylpropanolamine hydrochloride 6.25 mg, guaifenesin 50 mg, dextromethorphan hydrobromide 5 mg, alcohol 5%.

Indications: Provides prompt relief of cough and nasal congestion due to the common cold. The expectorant component helps loosen bronchial secretions. The decongestant, expectorant and antitussive are provided in an antihistamine-free formula.

Contraindications: DORCOL Pediatric Cough Syrup is contraindicated in the presence of hypersensitivity to any of the ingredients. The use of pressor amines such as phenylpropanolamine hydrochloride is contraindicated in those patients taking monamine oxidase inhibitors for antihypertensive or antidepressant indications.

Precautions: Exercise prescribing caution in patients with persistent or chronic cough such as occurs with chronic bronchitis, bronchial asthma, or emphysema. Use with caution in patients with hypertension, hyperthyroidism cardiovascular disease or diabetes mellitus.

Adverse Reactions: Occasional blurred vision, cardiac palpitations, flushing, gastrointestinal upsets, nervousness, dizziness, or sleeplessness may occur.

Dosage and Administration: Children 6–12 years—2 teaspoonfuls every 4 hours. Children 2–6 years—1 teaspoonful every 4 hours. The suggested dosage in pediatric patients 3 months to 2 years of age is 3 drops per kilogram of body weight administered every four hours. For nighttime cough relief, give the last dose at bedtime.

How Supplied: DORCOL Pediatric Cough Syrup (grape-colored) in 4 fl oz and 8 fl oz bottles.

[*Shown in Product Identification Section*]

TRIAMINIC® EXPECTORANT

Description: Each teaspoonful (5 ml) of TRIAMINIC Expectorant contains: phenylpropanolamine hydrochloride 12.5 mg, guaifenesin 100 mg, alcohol 5%.

Indications: Provides prompt relief of cough and nasal congestion due to the common cold. The expectorant component helps loosen bronchial secretions. The decongestant and expectorant are provided in an antihistamine-free formula.

Contraindications: TRIAMINIC Expectorant is contraindicated in the presence of hypersensitivity to any of the ingredients. The use of pressor amines such as phenylpropanolamine hydrochloride is contraindicated in those patients taking monamine oxidase inhibitors for antihypertensive or antidepressant indications.

Precautions: Exercise prescribing caution in patients with persistent or chronic cough such as occurs with chronic bronchitis, bronchial asthma, or emphysema. Use with caution in patients with hypertension, hyperthyroidism cardiovascular disease or diabetes mellitus.

Adverse Reactions: Occasional blurred vision, cardiac palpitations, flushing, gastrointestinal upsets, nervousness, dizziness, or sleeplessness may occur.

Dosage and Administration: Adults —2 teaspoonfuls every 4 hours. Children 6–12 years—1 teaspoonful every 4 hours. Children 2–6—½ teaspoonful every 4 hours. The suggested dosage in pediatric patients 3 months to 2 years of age is 4 to 5 drops per kilogram of body weight administered every four hours.

How Supplied: TRIAMINIC Expectorant (yellow) in 4 fl oz, 8 fl oz and pint bottles.

[*Shown in Product Identification Section*]

TRIAMINIC® SYRUP

Description: Each teaspoonful (5 ml) of TRIAMINIC Syrup contains: phenylpropanolamine hydrochloride 12.5 mg and chlorpheniramine maleate 2 mg in a nonalcoholic vehicle.

Indications: For the temporary relief of nasal congestion, sneezing, and itchy watery eyes that may occur in hay fever or other upper respiratory allergies, the common cold and sinusitis.

Contraindications: TRIAMINIC Syrup is contraindicated in the presence of hypersensitivity to any of the ingredients. The use of pressor amines such as phenylpropanolamine hydrochloride is contraindicated in those patients taking monamine oxidase inhibitors for antihypertensive or antidepressant indications.

Precautions: Caution should be observed in operating a motor vehicle or performing potentially hazardous tasks requiring mental alertness. Alcoholic beverages and other CNS depressants may potentiate the sedative effects of antihistamines. Caution should be observed in the presence of hypertension, hyperthyroidism, cardiovascular disease or diabetes mellitus. Because of anticholinergic action of antihistamines they should be administered with caution to patients with bronchial asthma, narrow angle glaucoma, stenosing peptic ulcer, pyloroduodenal obstruction, prostatic hypertrophy or other bladder neck obstruction.

Adverse Reactions: Drowsiness, blurred vision, palpitations, flushing, gastrointestinal upsets, nervousness, dizziness, or sleeplessness may occur. May cause excitability especially in children.

Dosage and Administration: Adults —two teaspoonfuls every 4 hours. Children 6–12 years—1 teaspoonful every 4 hours, children 2–6—½ teaspoonful every 4 hours. The suggested dosage in pediatric patients 3 months to 2 years of age is 4 to 5 drops per kilogram of body weight administered every four hours.

How Supplied: TRIAMINIC Syrup (orange), in 4 fl oz, 8 fl oz and pint bottles.

[*Shown in Product Identification Section*]

TRIAMINIC–DM™ COUGH FORMULA

Description: Each teaspoonful (5 ml) of TRIAMINIC-DM Cough Formula contains: phenylpropanolamine hydrochloride 12.5 mg and dextromethorphan hydrobromide 10 mg in a nonalcoholic vehicle.

Indications: Provides prompt, temporary relief of cough and nasal congestion due to the common cold. The decongestant and antitussive are provided in an antihistamine free formula.

Contraindications: TRIAMINIC-DM Cough Formula is contraindicated in the presence of hypersensitivity to any of the ingredients. The use of pressor amines such as phenylpropanolamine hydrochloride is contraindicated in those patients taking monamine oxidase inhibitors for antihypertensive or antidepressant indications.

Precautions: Exercise prescribing caution in patients with persistent or chronic cough such as occurs with chronic bronchitis, bronchial asthma, or emphysema. Use with caution in patients with hypertension, hyperthyroidism cardiovascular disease or diabetes mellitus.

Adverse Reactions: Occasional blurred vision, cardiac palpitations, flushing, gastrointestinal upsets, nervousness, dizziness, or sleeplessness may occur.

Dosage and Administration: Adults —2 teaspoonfuls every 4 hours. Children 6–12—1 teaspoonful every 4 hours. Children 2–6 years—½ teaspoonful every 4 hours. The suggested dosage in pediatric patients 3 months to 2 years of age is 1½ drops per kilogram of body weight administered every 4 hours.

How Supplied: TRIAMINIC-DM Cough Formula (dark red) in 4 fl oz and 8 fl oz bottles.

[*Shown in Product Identification Section*]

TRIAMINICIN® CHEWABLES

Description: Each TRIAMINICIN Chewable contains: phenylpropanolamine hydrochloride 6.25 mg, chlorpheniramine maleate 0.5 mg.

Indications: For relief of children's nasal congestion due to the common cold or nasal allergies.

Precautions: Patients should be advised not to drive a car or operate dangerous machinery if drowsiness occurs. Use with caution in the presence of hypertension, hyperthyroidism, cardiovascular disease or diabetes.

Adverse Reactions: Occasional drowsiness, blurred vision, cardiac palpitations, flushing, dizziness, nervousness or gastrointestinal upsets.

Dosage: Children 2 to 6—1 chewable tablet 4 times a day; children 6 to 12—2 chewable tablets 4 times a day.

How Supplied: TRIAMINICIN Chewables (hexagonal, yellow) in blister packs of 24.

TRIAMINICIN® TABLETS

Description: Each TRIAMINICIN TABLET contains: phenylpropanolamine hydrochloride 25 mg, chlorpheniramine maleate 2 mg, aspirin 450 mg, caffeine 30 mg.

Indications: For prompt, temporary relief of nasal congestion, simple headache, and minor aches and pains due to the common cold, hay fever and similar conditions.

Contraindications: Sensitivity to salicylates.

Precautions: Patients should be advised not to drive a car or operate dangerous machinery if drowsiness occurs. Use with caution in the presence of hypertension, hyperthyroidism, cardiovascular disease or diabetes.

Adverse Reactions: Occasional drowsiness, blurred vision, cardiac palpitations, flushing, dizziness, nervousness or gastrointestinal upsets.

Dosage: Adults—One tablet four times a day.

How Supplied: Triaminicin Tablets (yellow) in blister packs of 12, 24, 48 and bottles of 100.

[*Shown in Product Identification Section*]

TRIAMINICOL® DECONGESTANT COUGH SYRUP

Description: Each teaspoonful (5 ml) of TRIAMINICOL Decongestant Cough Syrup contains: phenylpropanolamine hydrochloride 12.5 mg, pheniramine maleate 6.25 mg, pyrilamine maleate 6.25 mg, dextromethorphan hydrobromide 15 mg, ammonium chloride 90 mg, in a palatable nonalcoholic vehicle.

Indications: For relief of coughs, especially when accompanied by stuffed and runny noses, due to the common cold. It combines the effective, nonnarcotic, antitussive action of dextromethorphan hydrobromide with a proven nasal decongestant.

Contraindications: TRIAMINICOL Decongestant Cough Syrup is contraindicated in the presence of hypersensitivity to any of the ingredients. The use of pressor amines such as phenylpropanolamine hydrochloride is contraindicated in those patients taking monamine oxidase inhibitors for antihypertensive or antidepressant indications.

Precautions: Exercise prescribing caution in patients with persistent or chronic cough such as occurs with chronic bronchitis, bronchial asthma, or emphysema. Patients should be advised not to drive a car or operate dangerous machinery if drowsiness occurs. Use with caution in the presence of hypertension, hyperthyroidism, cardiovascular disease or diabetes.

Adverse Reactions: Occasional drowsiness, blurred vision, cardiac palpitations, flushing, dizziness, nervousness or gastrointestinal upsets.

Dosage and Administration: Adults —2 teaspoonfuls every 4 hours; children 6 to 12—1 teaspoonful every 4 hours; children 2 to 6—½ teaspoonful every 4 to 6 hours. For nighttime cough relief, give the last dose at bedtime.

How Supplied: TRIAMINICOL Decongestant Cough Syrup (dark red) in 4 fl oz and 8 fl oz.

[*Shown in Product Identification Section*]

TUSSAGESIC® TABLETS and TUSSAGESIC® SUSPENSION

Description: Each Tussagesic Timed Release Tablet contains: phenylpropanolamine hydrochloride 25 mg, pheniramine maleate 12.5 mg, pyrilamine maleate 12.5 mg, dextromethorphan hydrobromide 30 mg, terpin hydrate 180 mg, acetaminophen 325 mg.

Each teaspoonful (5 ml) of Tussagesic Suspension contains: phenylpropanolamine hydrochloride 12.5 mg, pheniramine maleate 6.25 mg, pyrilamine maleate 6.25 mg, dextromethorphan hydrobromide 15 mg, terpin hydrate 90 mg, acetaminophen 120 mg.

Indications: For prompt relief of symptoms associated with the common

Continued on next page

Dorsey—Cont.

cold such as cough, nasal congestion, simple headache and minor muscular aches and pains. Tussagesic contains the effective, nonnarcotic antitussive, dextromethorphan hydrobromide; a proven decongestant; an expectorant; and the well-tolerated analgesic, acetaminophen.

Precautions: Patients should be advised not to drive a car or operate dangerous machinery if drowsiness occurs. Use with caution in the presence of hypertension, hyperthyroidism, cardiovascular disease or diabetes.

Adverse Reactions: Occasional drowsiness, blurred vision, cardiac palpitations, flushing, dizziness, nervousness or gastrointestinal upsets.

Dosage and Administration: Tablets: Adults—1 tablet, swallowed whole, in morning, midafternoon and before retiring. Suspension: Children 1 to 6—½ teaspoonful every 4 hours; children 6 to 12—1 teaspoonful every 4 hours; adults—2 teaspoonfuls every 4 hours.

How Supplied: Tussagesic Tablets (orange) in bottles of 100. Tussagesic Suspension (orange) in pint bottles.

URSINUS® INLAY–TABS®

Description: Each URSINUS INLAY-TAB contains: Calurin® (calcium carbaspirin) equivalent to 300 mg aspirin; phenylpropanolamine hydrochloride 25 mg; pheniramine maleate 12.5 mg; pyrilamine maleate 12.5 mg.

Indications: For prompt, temporary relief of nasal congestion, simple headache and minor aches and pains associated with sinusitis and the common cold. Ursinus contains Calurin, the freely-soluble aspirin complex, to provide prompt analgesic action. Orally effective phenylpropanolamine hydrochloride with two antihistamines decongests and promotes drainage of nasal passages.

Contraindications: Sensitivity to salicylates.

Precautions: Patients should be advised not to drive a car or operate dangerous machinery if drowsiness occurs. Use with caution in the presence of hypertension, hyperthyroidism, cardiovascular disease, or diabetes.

Adverse Reactions: Drowsiness, blurred vision, cardiac palpitations, flushing, dizziness, nervousness or gastrointestinal upsets may occur occasionally.

Dosage and Administration: Adults —One tablet four times daily.

How Supplied: Ursinus Inlay-Tabs (white with yellow inlay) in bottles of 24 and 100.

UVAL® MOISTURIZING SUNSCREEN LOTION

Description: Contains: oxybenzone 6% and 2-Ethylhexyl p-methoxycinnamate 5%.

Action: UVAL absorbs a broad spectrum of ultraviolet solar radiation in the wavelength range most damaging to human skin (260 nm to 350 nm). UVAL is not oily or greasy. Contains no dyes, fragrances or drying alcohols. UVAL rubs in transparent and doesn't interfere with make-up color. When properly applied, UVAL protects the skin from sunburning and tanning and aids in the prevention of visible changes in the skin such as wrinkling, drying and freckling due to overexposure to the sun. UVAL permits you to stay in the sun ten times longer than without a sun protectant. UVAL contains two UV light absorbing ingredients, skin moisturizers and a natural protein to protect your skin and help keep it soft. Overexposure to the sun may lead to premature aging of the skin and skin cancer. Regular and liberal use of UVAL Moisturizing Sunscreen Lotion over the years may help reduce the incidence of these harmful effects.

Directions: Shake well before using. Apply evenly to exposed skin, rub in well and allow to dry. To maintain protection, reapply after swimming or excessive perspiring.

Caution: Avoid getting lotion into eyes. If skin sensitivity develops, discontinue use and consult a physician. For external use only. Keep this preparation out of the reach of children.

How Supplied: In plastic squeeze bottles of 4 oz.

Dow Pharmaceuticals
THE DOW CHEMICAL COMPANY
P. O. BOX 68511
9550 ZIONSVILLE ROAD
INDIANAPOLIS, IN 46268

NOVAHISTINE® COUGH FORMULA
Antitussive–Expectorant
Liquid

Description: Each 5 ml teaspoonful contains: dextromethorphan hydrobromide, 10 mg. and guaifenesin (glyceryl guaiacolate), 100 mg. The formulation also contains alcohol, 7.5%.

Actions: Dextromethorphan suppresses the cough reflex by a direct effect on the cough center in the medulla of the brain. Although it is chemically related to morphine, it produces no analgesia or addiction. Its antitussive activity is about equal to that of codeine.

Guaifenesin (glyceryl guaiacolate) acts as an expectorant by increasing respiratory tract fluid which reduces the viscosity of tenacious secretions, thus making expectoration easier.

Indications: For the control of exhausting cough spasms and to convert a dry, nonproductive cough to a productive one. Generally, such coughs include those associated with colds, influenza and pertussis. It may also be used to provide symptomatic cough relief in some chronic respiratory disorders, such as tuberculosis or bronchitis, especially when these are associated with dry, nonproductive coughing.

Contraindications: NOVAHISTINE COUGH FORMULA is contraindicated in persistent or chronic cough such as occurs with smoking, asthma, or emphysema, or when cough is accompanied by excessive secretions, except on advice of a physician.

This drug is contraindicated in patients with hypersensitivity or idiosyncrasy to the formula ingredients.

Warnings: Patients taking MAO inhibitors should not be given drug preparations containing dextromethorphan.

If cough persists for more than 1 week, tends to recur, or is accompanied by high fever, rash or persistent headache, consult a physician.

Precautions: Dextromethorphan is incompatible with penicillins, tetracyclines, salicylates, phenobarbital and high concentrations of iodides.

  Note: Guaifenesin interferes with the colorimetric determination of 5-hydroxyindoleacetic acid (5-HIAA) and vanilmandelic acid (VMA).

Adverse Reactions: These occur infrequently with usual doses. When they occur, adverse reactions may include nausea and dizziness, gastrointestinal upset or vomiting.

Dosage and Administration: Adults and children 12 years or older, 2 teaspoonfuls every 4 hours. Children 6 to under 12 years, 1 teaspoonful every 4 hours. Children 2 to under 6 years, ½ teaspoonful every 4 hours. Not more than 4 doses in 24 hours. For children under 2 years of age give only as directed by a physician.

How Supplied: In 4 fluid ounce bottles (NDC 0183-1020-58) and 8 fluid ounce bottles (NDC 0183-1020-88).

NOVAHISTINE® COUGH & COLD FORMULA
Antitussive-Decongestant-
Antihistamine
Liquid

Description: Each 5 ml. teaspoonful of NOVAHISTINE COUGH & COLD FORMULA contains dextromethorphan hydrobromide, 10 mg., pseudoephedrine hydrochloride, 30 mg., and chlorpheniramine maleate, 2 mg. The formulation also contains alcohol, 5%.

Actions: Dextromethorphan suppresses the cough reflex by a direct effect on the cough center in the medulla of the brain. Although it is chemically related to morphine, it produces no analgesia or addiction. Its antitussive activity is about equal to that of codeine.

Pseudoephedrine is an orally effective nasal decongestant. Pseudoephedrine is a sympathomimetic amine with peripheral effects similar to epinephrine and central effects similar to, but less intense than, amphetamines. It has the potential for excitatory side-effects. At the recommended oral dosage, pseudoephedrine has little or no pressor effect in normotensive adults. Patients have not been reported to experience the rebound congestion sometimes experienced with frequent, repeated use of topical decongestants.

Chlorpheniramine is an antihistaminic drug which possesses anticholinergic and sedative effects. It is considered one of the most effective and least toxic of the histamine antagonists. Chlorpheniramine antagonizes many of the pharmacologic actions of histamine. It prevents released histamine from dilating capillaries and causing edema of the respiratory mucosa.

Indications: For the relief of exhausting, nonproductive cough and nasal congestion associated, for example, with the common cold, acute upper respiratory infections, sinusitis, and hay fever or upper respiratory allergies.

Contraindications: NOVAHISTINE COUGH & COLD FORMULA is contraindicated in persistent or chronic cough such as occurs with smoking, asthma, or emphysema, or when cough is accompanied by excessive secretions, except on advice of a physician. It is also contraindicated in patients with narrow-angle glaucoma, urinary retention, peptic ulcer, or during an asthmatic attack, patients with severe hypertension, severe coronary artery disease, and patients on MAO inhibitor therapy.

Nursing Mothers: Pseudoephedrine is contraindicated in nursing mothers because of the higher than usual risk for infants from sympathomimetic amines.

Hypersensitivity: This drug is contraindicated in patients with hypersensitivity or idiosyncrasy to antitussives, sympathomimetic amines or antihistamines. Patient idiosyncrasy to adrenergic agents may be manifested by insomnia, dizziness, weakness, tremor or arrhythmias.

Warnings: Use judiciously and sparingly in patients with hypertension, diabetes mellitus, ischemic heart disease, increased intraocular pressure, hyperthyroidism, or prostatic hypertrophy. Sympathomimetics may produce central nervous system stimulation and convulsions or cardiovascular collapse with accompanying hypotension.

Do not exceed recommended dosage.

Use in Pregnancy: The safety of pseudoephedrine for use during pregnancy has not been established.

Use in Elderly: The elderly (60 years and older) are more likely to have adverse reactions to sympathomimetics. Overdosage of sympathomimetics in this age group may cause hallucinations, convulsions, CNS depression, and death. Antihistamines may cause excitability, especially in children. If cough persists for more than 1 week, tends to recur, or is accompanied by high fever, rash or persistent headache, consult a physician.

Precautions: Drugs containing pseudoephedrine should be used with caution in patients with diabetes, hypertension, cardiovascular disease and hyperreactivity to ephedrine. The antihistaminic agent may cause drowsiness and ambulatory patients who operate machinery or motor vehicles should be cautioned accordingly.

Adverse Reactions: These occur infrequently with usual doses. When they occur, adverse reactions may include nausea and dizziness, gastrointestinal upset or vomiting.

Because of the pseudoephedrine in NOVAHISTINE COUGH & COLD FOR-MULA, hyperreactive individuals may display ephedrine-like reactions such as tachycardia, palpitations, headache, dizziness or nausea. Sympathomimetic drugs have been associated with certain untoward reactions including fear, anxiety, tenseness, restlessness, tremor, weakness, pallor, respiratory difficulty, dysuria, insomnia, hallucinations, convulsions, CNS depression, arrhythmias and cardiovascular collapse with hypotension.

Patients may experience mild sedation. Possible side effects from the antihistamine may include dry mouth, dizziness, weakness, anorexia, nausea, vomiting, headache, nervousness, polyuria, heartburn, diplopia, dysuria and, very rarely, dermatitis.

Drug Interactions: MAO inhibitors and beta adrenergic blockers increase the effects of pseudoephedrine (sympathomimetics). Sympathomimetics may reduce the antihypertensive effects of methyldopa, mecamylamine, reserpine and veratrum alkaloids.

Antihistamines have been shown to enhance one or more of the effects of tricyclic antidepressants, barbiturates, alcohol and other central nervous system depressants.

Dosage and Administration: Adults and children 12 years or older, 2 teaspoonfuls every 4 hours. Children 6 to under 12 years, 1 teaspoonful every 4 hours. Children 2 to under 6 years, ½ teaspoonful every 4 hours. Not more than 4 doses in 24 hours. For children under 2 years of age, at the discretion of the physician.

Note: NOVAHISTINE COUGH & COLD FORMULA does not require a prescription. The package label has dosage instructions as follows: Adults and children 12 years or older, 2 teaspoonfuls every 4 hours. Children 6 to under 12 years, 1 teaspoonful every 4 hours. Not more than 4 doses in 24 hours. For children under 6 years of age give only as directed by a physician.

How Supplied: In 4 fluid ounce bottles (NDC 0183-1025-58) and 8 fluid ounce bottles (NDC 0183-1025-88).

NOVAHISTINE® DMX
Antitussive-Decongestant
Liquid

Description: Each 5 ml. teaspoonful of NOVAHISTINE DMX contains: dextromethorphan hydrobromide, 10 mg., pseudoephedrine hydrochloride, 30 mg., and guaifenesin (glyceryl guaiacolate), 100 mg. Dextromethorphan, a synthetic nonnarcotic antitussive, is the dextrorotatory isomer of 3-methoxy-N- methylmorphinan. Pseudoephedrine hydrochloride is the salt of a pharmacologically active stereoisomer of ephedrine (1-phenyl-2-methylamino propanol). The formulation also contains alcohol, 10%.

Actions: Dextromethorphan suppresses the cough reflex by a direct effect on the cough center in the medulla of the brain. Although it is chemically related to morphine, it produces no analgesia or addiction. Its antitussive activity is about equal to that of codeine.

Pseudoephedrine hydrochloride is an orally effective nasal decongestant. Pseudoephedrine is a sympathomimetic amine with peripheral effects similar to epinephrine and central effects similar to, but less intense than, amphetamines. Therefore, it has the potential for excitatory side effects. Pseudoephedrine at the recommended oral dosage has little or no pressor effect in normotensive adults. Patients taking pseudoephedrine orally have not been reported to experience the rebound congestion sometimes experienced with frequent, repeated use of topical decongestants. Pseudoephedrine is not known to produce drowsiness.

Guaifenesin (glyceryl guaiacolate) acts as an expectorant by increasing respiratory tract fluid which reduces the viscosity of tenacious secretions, thus making expectoration easier.

Indications: NOVAHISTINE DMX is indicated when exhausting, nonproductive cough accompanies respiratory tract congestion. It is useful in the symptomatic relief of upper respiratory congestion associated with the common cold, influenza, bronchitis, and sinusitis.

Contraindications: Sympathomimetic amines are contraindicated in patients with severe hypertension, severe coronary artery disease, and in patients on MAO inhibitor therapy. Patient idiosyncrasy to adrenergic agents may be manifested by insomnia, dizziness, weakness, tremor or arrhythmias.

Nursing mothers: Pseudoephedrine is contraindicated in nursing mothers because of the higher than usual risk for infants from sympathomimetic amines.

Hypersensitivity: This drug is contraindicated in patients with hypersensitivity or idiosyncrasy to sympathomimetic amines, dextromethorphan, or to other formula ingredients.

Warnings: Sympathomimetic amines should be used judiciously and sparingly in patients with hypertension, diabetes mellitus, ischemic heart disease, increased intraocular pressure, hyperthyroidism and prostatic hypertrophy. Sympathomimetics may produce central nervous system stimulation with convulsions or cardiovascular collapse with accompanying hypotension. See, however, Contraindications.

Use in pregnancy: The safety of pseudoephedrine for use during pregnancy has not been established.

Use in elderly: The elderly (60 years and older) are more likely to have adverse reactions to sympathomimetics. Overdosage of sympathomimetics in this age group may cause hallucinations, convulsions, CNS depression, and death.

Precautions: Pseudoephedrine should be used with caution in patients with diabetes, hypertension, cardiovascular dis-

Continued on next page

Information on Dow products is based on labeling in effect in December, 1980.

Dow—Cont.

ease and hyperreactivity to ephedrine. See, however, Contraindications.

Adverse Reactions: Adverse reactions occur infrequently with usual oral doses of NOVAHISTINE DMX. When they occur, adverse reactions may include gastrointestinal upset and nausea. Because of the pseudoephedrine in NOVAHISTINE DMX, hyperreactive individuals may display ephedrine-like reactions such as tachycardia, palpitations, headache, dizziness or nausea. Sympathomimetic drugs have been associated with certain untoward reactions including fear, anxiety, tenseness, restlessness, tremor, weakness, pallor, respiratory difficulty, dysuria, insomnia, hallucinations, convulsions, CNS depression, arrhythmias, and cardiovascular collapse with hypotension.

Note: Guaifenesin interferes with the colorimetric determination of 5-hydroxyindoleacetic acid (5-HIAA) and vanilmandelic acid (VMA).

Drug Interactions: MAO inhibitors and beta adrenergic blockers increase the effects of pseudoephedrine (sympathomimetics). Sympathomimetics may reduce the antihypertensive effects of methyldopa, mecamylamine, reserpine, and veratrum alkaloids.

Dosage: Adults and older children, two teaspoonfuls, 3 to 4 times a day. Children 6 to 12 years of age, one teaspoonful, 3 to 4 times a day. Children 2 to 5 years of age, one-half teaspoonful, 3 to 4 times a day. May be given to children under 2 at the discretion of the physician.

Note: NOVAHISTINE DMX does not require a prescription. The package label has dosage instructions as follows:

Adults, and children over 12 years of age, two teaspoonfuls, every four hours. Children 6 to 12 years of age, one teaspoonful, every four hours. Children 2 to 5 years of age, one-half teaspoonful, every four hours. Not more than four doses every 24 hours. For children under 2 years of age, give only as directed by a physician.

How Supplied: As a red syrup in 4 fluid ounce bottles (NDC 0183-1015-58) and 8 fluid ounce bottles (NDC 0183-1015-88).

NOVAHISTINE® ELIXIR
NOVAHISTINE® COLD TABLETS
Decongestant—Antihistaminic

Description: Each 5 ml. teaspoonful of elixir or each tablet contains: phenylpropanolamine hydrochloride, 18.75 mg., chlorpheniramine maleate, 2 mg. The elixir also contains alcohol, 5%.

Actions: NOVAHISTINE, Elixir or Cold Tablets, has decongestant and antihistaminic actions. Phenylpropanolamine hydrochloride, an orally effective nasal decongestant, is a sympathomimetic amine similar in action to ephedrine but with less central nervous system stimulation. Phenylpropanolamine, at the recommended oral dosage, has no significant effect on blood pressure and pulse rate in normotensive adults. Patients taking phenylpropanolamine orally have not been reported to experience the rebound congestion sometimes experienced with frequent, repeated use of topical decongestants.

Chlorpheniramine maleate, an antihistaminic effective for the symptomatic relief of allergic rhinitis, possesses mild anticholinergic and sedative effects. Chlorpheniramine antagonizes many of the pharmacologic actions of histamine. It prevents released histamine from dilating capillaries and causing edema of the respiratory mucosa.

Indications: NOVAHISTINE Elixir or Cold Tablets are indicated for the temporary relief of nasal congestion and eustachian tube congestion associated with the common cold, sinusitis, and hay fever (allergic rhinitis). They also provide temporary relief of runny nose, sneezing, itching of nose or throat and itchy and watery eyes as may occur in hay fever (allergic rhinitis). May be given concomitantly, when indicated, with analgesics and antibiotics.

Contraindications: Sympathomimetic amines are contraindicated in patients with severe hypertension, severe coronary artery disease, in patients on MAO inhibitor therapy, and in nursing mothers.

Antihistamines are contraindicated in patients with narrow-angle glaucoma, urinary retention, peptic ulcer, during an asthmatic attack, and in patients receiving MAO inhibitors.

NOVAHISTINE Elixir or Cold Tablets are contraindicated in patients with hyersensitivity or idiosyncrasy to sympathomimetic amines or antihistamines.

Warnings: If sympathomimetic amines are used in patients with hypertension, diabetes mellitus, ischemic heart disease, increased intraocular pressure, hyperthyroidism, or prostatic hypertrophy, judicious caution should be exercised. The elderly (60 years and older) are more likely to have adverse reactions to sympathomimetics. Safety for use during pregnancy has not been established. Antihistamines may cause excitability, especially in children.

At dosages higher than the recommended dose, nervousness, dizziness, or sleeplessness may occur.

Precautions: Caution should be exercised if used in patients with high blood pressure, heart disease, diabetes or thyroid disease. The antihistamine may cause drowsiness, and ambulatory patients who operate machinery or motor vehicles should be cautioned accordingly.

Adverse Reactions: Drugs containing sympathomimetic amines have been associated with certain untoward reactions including fear, anxiety, tenseness, restlessness, tremor, weakness, pallor, respiratory difficulty, dysuria, insomnia, hallucinations, convulsions, CNS depression, arrhythmias, and cardiovascular collapse with hypotension. Phenylpropanolamine is considered safe and relatively free of unpleasant side-effects, when taken at recommended dosage. However, there have been isolated reports of individuals experiencing an acute hypertensive episode after taking therapeutic doses of phenylpropanolamine-containing preparations.

Patients sensitive to antihistamine drugs may experience mild sedation. Other side-effects from antihistamines may include dry mouth, dizziness, weakness, anorexia, nausea, vomiting, headache, nervousness, polyuria, heartburn, diplopia, dysuria, and, very rarely, dermatitis.

Drug Interactions: MAO inhibitors and beta adrenergic blockers increase the effects of sympathomimetics. Sympathomimetics may reduce the antihypertensive effects of methyldopa, mecamylamine, reserpine and veratrum alkaloids. Antihistamines have been shown to enhance one or more of the effects of tricyclic antidepressants, barbiturates, alcohol, and other central nervous system depressants.

Dosage: Adults, 2 teaspoonfuls or tablets every 4 hours; children 6 to 12 years, 1 teaspoonful or tablet every 4 hours; children 2 to 5 years, ½ teaspoonful every 4 hours. *Do not exceed 4 doses in a 24-hour period.* For children under 2 years, at the discretion of the physician.

Note: NOVAHISTINE Elixir or Cold Tablets do not require a prescription. The package label has dosage instructions as follows:

Adults, 2 teaspoonfuls or tablets every 4 hours; children 6 to 12 years, 1 teaspoonful or tablet every 4 hours. Not more than 4 doses in 24 hours. For children under 6 years, consult a physician.

How Supplied: NOVAHISTINE Elixir, as a green liquid in 4 fluid ounce bottles (NDC 0183-1021-58) and 8 fluid ounce bottles (NDC 0183-1021-88). NOVAHISTINE Cold Tablets in unit dose packages of 24 tablets (NDC 0183-0022-24) and 48 tablets (NDC 0183-0022-48).

NOVAHISTINE®
SINUS TABLETS
Analgesic-Decongestant-Antihistamine

Description: Each NOVAHISTINE SINUS TABLET contains acetaminophen, 325 mg., pseudoephedrine hydrochloride, 30 mg., and chlorpheniramine maleate, 2 mg.

Actions: Combines the actions of a nasal decongestant, pseudoephedrine; an antihistamine, chlorpheniramine; and an analgesic, acetaminophen.

Acetaminophen is a synthetic non-narcotic derivative of paraminophenol with an analgesic effect similar to that of aspirin. Unlike aspirin, acetaminophen has no anti-inflammatory or uricosuric activity. It produces less gastric irritation than salicylates, does not appear to depress prothrombin levels at recommended doses and usually can be taken by persons sensitive to aspirin.

Pseudoephedrine hydrochloride, an orally effective nasal decongestant, is a sympathomimetic amine with peripheral and central effects. It has the potential for excitatory side-effects. Pseudoephedrine at the recommended oral dosage has little or no pressor effect in normotensive adults. Patients taking pseudoephedrine orally have not been reported to experience the rebound congestion sometimes experienced with frequent, repeated use of topical decongestants.

Chlorpheniramine maleate is one of the most effective and least toxic of the histamine antagonists. The antihistaminic action of chlorpheniramine prevents released histamine from dilating capillaries and causing edema of the respiratory mucosa. It also possesses anticholinergic and sedative effects.

Indications: NOVAHISTINE SINUS TABLETS provide temporary relief of nasal and upper respiratory tract congestion, sneezing, runny nose, watery eyes, myalgia, and headache associated with colds and other viral infections, sinusitis, influenza, and seasonal and perennial nasal allergies.

May be given concomitantly, when indicated, with antibiotics.

Contraindications: Patients with severe hypertension, severe coronary artery disease, on MAO inhibitor therapy, narrow angle glaucoma, urinary retention, peptic ulcer, during an asthmatic attack, seriously impaired liver and kidney function, gastrointestinal bleeding, severe or recurrent pain, in nursing mothers and hypersensitivity to its ingredients.

Repeated administration of acetaminophen-containing products is contraindicated in patients with anemia or cardiac, pulmonary, renal and hepatic disease.

Warnings: Drugs containing sympathomimetics should be used judiciously and sparingly in patients with hypertension, diabetes mellitus, ischemic heart disease, increased intraocular pressure, hyperthyroidism, or prostatic hypertrophy. Sympathomimetics may produce central nervous system stimulation and convulsions or cardiovascular collapse with accompanying hypotension. Antihistamines may impair mental and physical abilities required for the performance of potentially hazardous tasks, such as driving a vehicle or operating machinery, and mental alertness in children. Acetaminophen should be used judiciously in patients with pre-existing anemias, peptic ulcer and diminished hepatic or renal function.

Safety in pregnancy has not been established. The elderly (60 years and older) are more likely to have adverse reactions to sympathomimetics and antihistamines.

Precautions: Patients with hypertension, cardiovascular, liver and kidney disease, anemia, hyperreactivity to ephedrine, or a history of bronchial asthma, (see Contraindications) should not exceed recommended dose.

Adverse Reactions: Sympathomimetics have been associated with certain untoward reactions including fear, anxiety, tenseness, restlessness, tremor, weakness, pallor, respiratory difficulty, dysuria, insomnia, hallucinations, convulsions, CNS depression, arrhythmias, and

cardiovascular collapse with hypotension.

Possible side-effects of antihistamines are drowsiness, restlessness, dizziness, weakness, dry mouth, anorexia, nausea, headache and nervousness, blurring of vision, heartburn, dysuria and very rarely, dermatitis.

Side-effects of acetaminophen associated with higher than recommended doses include anorexia, nausea, vomiting, excitement (CNS stimulation) and abdominal pain. Chronic ingestion has in rare occasions caused methemoglobinemia, agranulocytosis, thrombocytopenia, hemolytic anemia and renal necrosis.

Drug Interactions: MAO inhibitors and beta adrenergic blockers increase the effect of sympathomimetics and the anticholinergic (drying) effects of antihistamines. Sympathomimetics may reduce the antihypertensive effects of methyldopa, mecamylamine, reserpine and veratrum alkaloids. Concomitant use of antihistamines with alcohol, tricyclic antidepressants, barbiturates and other central nervous system depressants may have an additive effect.

Dosage and Administration: Adults, 2 tablets every 4 hours; children 6 to 12 years, 1 tablet every 4 hours. Not more than 4 doses in 24 hours. For children under 6 years, at the discretion of a physician.

Overdosage: Acetaminophen in massive overdosage has caused liver damage and fatal hepatic necrosis.

How Supplied: Boxes of 24 tablets (NDC 0183-0071-24) and 48 tablets (NDC 0183-0071-48). Tablets are white with the Dow diamond on one side and number 71 on the other.

RESOLVE™ COLD SORE & FEVER BLISTER RELIEF
1% dyclonine hydrochloride U.S.P.
Topical Anesthetic Gel
FOR EXTERNAL USE

Description: Each gram of RESOLVE contains dyclonine hydrochloride (4'-butoxy-3-piperidinopropiophenone hydrochloride) 10 mg.

Actions: RESOLVE produces surface anesthesia when applied topically to inflamed or abraded skin or to mucous membranes. Effective anesthesia varies with the individual and the area, but usually begins within 2 to 10 minutes after application and may persist for an hour or longer. Relief of local symptoms may continue after tactile sensibility has returned.

Indications: RESOLVE is useful for the relief of local discomfort due to cold sores (fever blisters). For best results the gel should be applied within the first few hours after the appearance of local symptoms of tingling, itching, burning or pain.

Contraindications: RESOLVE is contraindicated in patients known to be hypersensitive (allergic) to the anesthetic or other ingredients of the formulation. Do not use in the eyes.

Warnings: RESOLVE is for external use only. Skin irritation may occur but it is usually slight.

As with other topical anesthetics, RESOLVE should not be used repeatedly or to cover extensive areas because of the possibility of systemic absorption. Discontinue use if bacterial infection develops.

Precautions: RESOLVE should be used with caution in areas from which rapid or significant systemic absorption could occur, such as broken or abraded skin or oral mucosa. The drug should also be used cautiously in patients sensitive to various allergens including drugs or those with a strong family history of allergy.

Development of secondary or delayed cutaneous hypersensitivity on repeated usage is possible. Since this reaction may resemble an exacerbation or progression of the cold sore, it could lead to an increased number of applications when, in fact, further applications should be stopped. Thus, if local irritation or sensitivity occurs, the use of RESOLVE should be discontinued.

Usage in Pregnancy. Safe use during pregnancy has not been established.

Adverse Reactions: Systemic reactions could result from high plasma levels of dyclonine due to extensive application or rapid absorption. Cardiovascular and central nervous system reactions have occurred after instillation of 20 to 30 ml. of 1% dyclonine HCl solution into the trachea, esophagus, or bladder preliminary to endoscopy. Because of slow percutaneous absorption, such reactions are unlikely to occur following application of recommended dosages of RESOLVE. However, hypersensitivity or other idiosyncratic systemic reactions cannot be ruled out at any dosage.

Local irritant reactions (primary) have been observed in some laboratory animals. In guinea pigs and in about 15% of human volunteers, repeated applications of 0.5 ml. of a 2% dyclonine HCl solution with occluded dressing produced secondary or delayed skin hypersensitivity. Such hypersensitivity could also be produced by RESOLVE. Continued use on a cold sore which appears worse or spreading is therefore not recommended.

Dosage and Administration:
RESOLVE should be applied sparingly on cold sores and as soon as possible after the first symptoms of tingling, itching, burning, or pain. The area of discomfort and a narrow margin of the surrounding normal skin should be covered by one to two drops of RESOLVE. Running or dripping and spreading of the gel to the other lip should be avoided. Applications may be timed to follow such activities as eating, brushing of teeth, and washing of face to avoid removal of medication.

RESOLVE may be applied approximately every four hours. If the cold sore appears to progress or spread, the use of RESOLVE should be discontinued (see also Precautions and Adverse Reactions).

Continued on next page

Information on Dow products is based on labeling in effect in December, 1980.

Dow—Cont.

How Supplied: In 0.10 oz. (3 gm.) plastic tubes (NDC 0183-3010-10).

Information on Dow products is based on labeling in effect in December, 1980.

Endo Laboratories, Inc.
Subsidiary of the DuPont Company
1000 STEWART AVENUE
GARDEN CITY, NEW YORK 11530

PERCOGESIC®
Analgesic Tablets

Description: Each tablet contains:
Acetaminophen (APAP) ....325 mg
Phenyltoloxamine citrate............. 30 mg
Uses: For relief of mild to moderate pain and discomfort due to simple headache; for temporary relief of such pain associated with muscle and joint soreness, neuralgia, sinusitis, minor menstrual cramps, the common cold or grippe, toothache, and minor aches and pains of rheumatism and arthritis.
Precautions: If arthritic or rheumatic pain persists for more than 10 days; in the presence of redness or swelling; or in arthritic or rheumatic conditions affecting children under 12 years of age, consult a physician immediately. When used for the temporary symptomatic relief of colds, if relief does not occur within three days, discontinue use and consult physician. This preparation may cause drowsiness. Do not drive or operate machinery while taking this medication. Do not administer to children under six years of age or exceed recommended dosage unless directed by physician.
Administration and Dosage: Adults—1 or 2 tablets every 4 hours; maximum daily dose 8 tablets. Children: 6-12 years—one-half adult dose; maximum daily dose 4 tablets. Do not use for more than 10 days unless directed by physician.
How Supplied: PERCOGESIC® tablets are available in blister-strip boxes of 24 tablets and bottles of 100.
PERCOGESIC® is an Endo registered U.S. trademark.
LK
[*Shown in Product Identification Section*]

Products are cross-indexed by

generic and chemical names

in the

YELLOW SECTION

Ex-Lax Pharmaceutical Co., Inc.
a company of Culbro Corporation
(see also Creighton Products Corporation)
605 THIRD AVENUE
NEW YORK, NY 10016

EX–LAX® Chocolated Laxative

Active Ingredient: Yellow phenolphthalein, 90 mg per tablet.
Indications: For short-term relief of constipation.
Actions: Yellow phenolphthalein was previously categorized as a "stimulant" laxative. Recent research appears to indicate that phenolphthalein acts primarily by its effect on intestinal absorption of water and electrolytes, thus causing propulsive activity. The main mode of action appears to be as a noncompetitive inhibitor of the enzymes, sodium and potassium adenosine triphosphatase, resulting in failure of salt and water absorption.
Warnings: Caution: Do not take any laxative when abdominal pain, nausea, or vomiting are present. Frequent or prolonged use of this or any other laxative may result in dependence on laxatives. If skin rash appears, do not use this or any other preparation containing phenolphthalein.
Ex-Lax is a medicine, not a candy. **Warning:** Keep this and all other medicines out of the reach of children.
Drug Interaction Precautions: No known drug interaction.
Dosage and Administration: Adults: 1 to 2 tablets, preferably at bed time. Children over 6 years: ½ to 1 tablet. Adult dosage may be slightly increased or decreased to suit individual requirements. If slightly increased adult dose is necessary, take it the following day.
How Supplied: Available in boxes of 6, 18, 48, and 72 chewable chocolate-flavored tablets.
[*Shown in Product Identification Section*]

EX–LAX® Pills, Unflavored Laxative

Active Ingredient: Yellow phenolphthalein, 90 mg per tablet.
Indications: For short-term relief of constipation.
Actions: Yellow phenolphthalein was previously categorized as a "stimulant" laxative. Recent research appears to indicate that phenolphthalein acts primarily by its effect on intestinal absorption of water and electrolytes, thus causing propulsive activity. The main mode of action appears to be as a noncompetitive inhibitor of the enzymes, sodium and potassium adenosine triphosphatase, resulting in failure of salt and water absorption.
Warnings: Caution: Do not take any laxative when abdominal pain, nausea, or vomiting are present. Frequent or prolonged use of this or any other laxative may result in dependence on laxatives. If skin rash appears, do not use this or any other preparation containing phenolphthalein.

Ex-Lax is a medicine, not a candy. **Warning:** Keep this and all other medicines out of the reach of children.
Drug Interaction Precautions: No known drug interaction.
Dosage and Administration: Adults: 1 to 2 tablets with a glass of water, preferably at bed time. Children over 6 years: 1 tablet. Adult dosage may be increased or decreased to suit individual requirements. If increased adult dose is necessary, take it the following day.
How Supplied: Available in boxes of 8, 30, and 60 unflavored pills.
[*Shown in Product Identification Section*]

Max Factor & Co.
1655 N. McCADDEN PLACE
HOLLYWOOD, CA 90028

MAXI™UNSHINE™
Oil Free* Make-Up

Indications: A waterbased, fragrance free liquid make-up for persons with oily skin or skin which is oily in patches.
Actions: Provides light, even coverage. Facial shine, caused by accumulation of surface skin lipids, is minimized. Product has been dermatologically tested to insure minimum potential for irritation and sensitization. Should be used with the other MAXI™UNSHINE™ products for best effect.
*Contains no natural animal, vegetable or mineral oils.
Available in ten (10) shades: Buff, Bisque, Soft Beige, Warm Honey, Beige Blush, Deep Beige, Natural Tan, Golden Tan, Tawny Bronze and Mahogany.
How Supplied: Available in 1¼ fluid ounce glass bottle. Bottle also available in self-service/blister carded package.
[*Shown in Product Identification Section*]

MAXI™UNSHINE™
100% Oil Free Blotting Powder

Indications: A pure and gentle oil absorbing make-up powder base for persons with oily skin or skin which is oily in patches.
Actions: Oil absorbing action keeps skin looking and feeling fresh by absorbing surface skin lipids. Helps prevent make-up from streaking; maintains matte appearance. Product has been dermatologically tested to insure minimum potential for irritation and sensitization. Should be used with the other MAXI™ UNSHINE™ products for best effect.
Available in a selection of six transparent shades: Transparent Natural*, Transparent Buff, Transparent Beige, Transparent Tan, Transparent Tawny, and Transparent Bronze*.
*Available June, 1981.
How Supplied: Self service/blister carded package contains .33 ounce compact with washable sponge puff applicator.
[*Shown in Product Identification Section*]

MAXI™UNSHINE™
100% Oil Free Blushing Powder

Indications: A pure and gentle blusher for persons with oily skin or skin which is oily in patches.

Actions: Provides light, even coloration to cheeks. Oil absorbing action keeps skin looking fresh, minimizes oily shine caused by accumulation of surface skin lipids.

Product has been dermatologically tested to insure minimum potential for irritation and sensitization. Should be used with other MAXI™UNSHINE™ products for best effect.

Available in a selection of eight shades: Blushing Pink, Warm Cinnamon, Blushing Peach, Fresh Raspberry, Natural Pink*, Blushing Coral*, Tawny Burgundy*, and Rich Plum*.
*Available June, 1981.

How Supplied: Self service/blister carded package contains .15 ounce compact with washable sponge puff applicator.
[*Shown in Product Identification Section*]

SEBB® Dandruff Treatment Lotion

Active Ingredients: Benzethonium Chloride, and N-trichloromethylmercapto-4-cyclohexene -1, 2 - dicarboximide (captan) in a 19% alcoholic lotion.

Indications: For temporary relief of dandruff and itchy scalp associated with dandruff.

Actions: Clinical studies show the active ingredients in SEBB Lotion significantly reduce the degree of flaking in cases of dandruff.

Dosage and Administration: Shake well (settled ingredients are important). For best results start treatment with a clean scalp. So before first SEBB Lotion application, shampoo hair thoroughly, then towel dry. Use SEBB Lotion daily until condition is under control, then only as often as necessary. Shampooing is not necessary each time SEBB Lotion is applied. Just shampoo as often as normal.

Application for Men: Apply SEBB Lotion liberally, moistening entire scalp area well. After applying SEBB Lotion, regular hair grooming aids may be used.

Application for Women: Moisten entire scalp area well with SEBB Lotion by parting hair sectionally and using saturated cotton pad or eye dropper. Allow SEBB Lotion to dry on scalp. SEBB Lotion is odorless and will not discolor hair. No special rinsing or massaging is necessary. SEBB Lotion does not interfere with the use of regular hair beautifying aids.

How Supplied: Available in 8 fluid ounce glass bottle.
[*Shown in Product Identification Section*]

SEBB® Shampoo

Description: SEBB shampoo has been designed especially for oily scalps and to help remove dandruff flakes. Leaves hair shiny and manageable.

Composition: Contains water, TEA-lauryl sulfate, coconut acid, triethanolamine, disodium monooleamidosulfosucci-nate, cocamide DEA, sodium lauryl sulfate, PEG-8 distearate, hydroxypropyl methylcellulose, tetrasodium EDTA, fragrance, sodium o-phenyl phenate, chloroxylenol, FD&C yellow No. 5, FD&C yellow No. 6.

Dosage and Administration: Apply a small amount to wet hair. Lather and rinse. Apply again. Massage scalp gently, yet thoroughly. Leave on hair for 2–3 minutes, then rinse.

How Supplied: Available in an 8 fluid ounce plastic bottle.
[*Shown in Product Identification Section*]

Fleetwood Company
1500 BROOK DRIVE
DOWNERS GROVE, IL 60515

SUPER WATE–ON® EMULSION

Description: A concentrated high-caloric oral liquid emulsion taken to supplement vitamin and food intake so as to provide the extra calories necessary to increase body weight.

Nutritional Information: Daily dose (3 ozs.) containing the following and will supply adults and children 4 or more years of age the indicated percentage of the U.S. Recommended Daily Allowance (R.D.A.)*

	*(R.D.A.)
400 IU Vitamin D	100%
2.25 mg Thiamine (Vitamin B₁)	150%
2.55 mg Riboflavin (Vitamin B₂)	150%
30 mg Niacin	150%
3.0 mg Vitamin B₆	150%
9.0 mcg Vitamin B₁₂	150%
15.0 mg Pantothenic Acid	150%
27.0 mg Iron	150%

3 ounces also provides: Calories-541 Fats-62% w/w, Carbohydrates-10.6% w/w
(Daily dosage of 1 ounce mixed with 8 ounces whole milk, taken 3 times daily, would give total of 991 calories per day).

Ingredients: Soybean Oil, Water, Sugar, Polyoxyethlene 20 Sorbitan Monostearate, Propylene Glycol, Sorbitan Monostearate, Ferric Ammonium Citrate, Artificial Flavor, Exanthan Gum, Sorbic Acid, Methyl Paraben, Propyl Paraben, Panthenol, Niacinamide, L-Lysine Monohydrochloride, Riboflavin 5 Phosphate, Buthlated Hydroxyanisole, Thiamine Hydrochloride, Pyndoxine Hydrochloride, Calciferol, Cyanocobalamin.

Dosage: Adults and Children 4 or more years of age. Take 1 ounce (2 tablespoonfuls) mixed in an 8 ounce glass of milk three times daily AFTER or between meals. Mix thoroughly using spoon, mixer or blender. May be taken direct from spoon.

Availability: Most pharmacies stock WATE-ON or can quickly obtain supply from local wholesalers.

Samples: Available at no cost to physicians that make request to above address.

How Supplied: 16 ounce bottle with weight-gaining plan booklet. Choice of 5 flavors.

OTHER WATE-ON® FORMS AVAILABLE
REGULAR WATE-ON TABLETS 96's
REGULAR WATE-ON EMULSION 16 oz.
SUPER WATE-ON TABLETS 96's
SUPER WATE-ON P-410 SHAKE MIX 16 oz.
FLEETWOOD's RED LABEL IRON & VITAMIN TONIC 16 oz.
(SUPER WATE-ON products contain about 44% more calories than comparable Regular WATE-ON products).
[*Shown in Product Identification Section*]

Fleming & Company
1600 FENPARK DR.
FENTON, MO 63026

MARBLEN Suspensions and Tablet

Composition: A modified 'Sippy Powder' antacid containing magnesium and calcium carbonates;

Action and Uses: The peach/apricot (pink) or unflavored (green) antacid suspensions are sugar-free and neutralize 18 mEq acid per teaspoonful with a low sodium content of 18mg per fl. oz. Each pink tablet consumes 18.0 mEq acid.

Administration and Dosage: One teaspoonful rather than a tablespoonful or one tablet to reduce patient cost by ⅔.

How Supplied: Plastic pints and bottles of 100 and 1000.

NEPHROX SUSPENSION
(aluminum hydroxide)
Antacid Suspension

Composition: A watermelon flavored aluminum hydroxide (320mg as gel)/mineral oil (10% by volume) antacid per teaspoonful.

Action and Uses: A sugar-free/saccharin-free pink suspension containing no magnesium and low sodium (19mg/oz). Extremely palatable and especially indicated in renal patients. Each teaspoon consumes 9 mEq acid.

Administration and Dosage: Two teaspoonfuls or as directed by a physician.

Caution: To be taken only at bedtime. Do not use at any other time or administer to infants, expectant women, and nursing mothers except upon the advice of a physician as this product contains mineral oil.

How Supplied: Plastic pints and gallons.

NICOTINEX Elixir
nicotinic acid

Composition: Contains niacin 50 mg./tsp. in a sherry wine base (amber color).

Action and Uses: Produces flushing when tablets fail. To increase micro-circulation of inner-ear in Meniere's, tinnitus and labyrinthine syndromes. For 'cold hands & feet', and as a vehicle for additives.

Continued on next page

Fleming—Cont.

Administration and Dosage: One or two teaspoonful on fasting stomach.
Side Effects: Patients should be warned of dermal flush. Ulcer and gout patients may be affected by 14% alcoholic content.
Contraindications: Severe hypotension and hemorrhage.
How Supplied: Plastic pints and gallons.

OCEAN MIST
(buffered saline)

Composition: Special isotonic saline, buffered with sodium bicarbonate to proper pH so as not to irritate the nose.
Action and Uses: Rhinitis medicamentosa, rhinitis sicca and atrophic rhinitis. For patients 'hooked on nose drops' and glaucoma patients on diuretics having dry nasal capillaries. OCEAN may be used as a mist or drop.
Administration and Dosage: One or two squeezes in each nostril.
Supplied: Plastic 45cc spray bottles and pints.

Fox Pharmacal, Inc.
1750 W. McNAB ROAD
FT. LAUDERDALE, FL 33310

E–Z TRIM™
Timed-release Diet Aid Capsules

Active Ingredient: Phenylpropanolamine HCl ....75 mg.
Indications: Phenylpropanolamine is a sympathomimetic amine with demonstrated appetite-suppressant effects. For use in programs of weight reduction adjunctively to reduced caloric intake.
Warnings: Do not exceed recommended dosage. Do not take this product for periods exceeding three months. Do not give this product to children under 12 years. Do not take this product if you are taking another medication containing phenylpropanolamine HCl. If you have or are being treated for high blood pressure, heart disease, diabetes, thyroid disease or depression or are pregnant or nursing, do not take this product except under the supervision of a physician. If you become nervous, sleepless or dizzy, stop the medication.
Dosage and Administration: Take one capsule at mid-morning.
How Supplied: Consumer packages of 22 capsules.

ODRINIL™ Natural Diuretic

Active Ingredients: Powdered Extract of Buchu; Powdered Extract of Uva Ursi; Powdered Extract of Corn Silk; Powdered Extract of Juniper; Caffeine.
Indications: To aid in the relief of simple water retention or "bloating" such as experienced in the premenstrual period and not associated with disease conditions.
Actions: Herbal extracts contained in this product have been recommended for

centuries to aid in the excretion of excess sodium and thereby overcome excessive water retention that results from salt retention. Caffeine is widely recognized as having similar diuretic properties.
Warnings: This product is not indicated for water retention that results from kidney, heart or other systemic disease. It should not be used when such diseases or conditions are present except on the advice of a physician.
Drug Interaction Precautions: None.
Dosage and Administration: One tablet with a glass of water after each meal and before retiring when premenstrual bloating is experienced. The product has no value as a preventative, but is only effective when water retention is present.
How Supplied: Packages of 60 tablets.

SUPER ODRINEX™ Reducing Aid

Active Ingredients:
Phenylpropanolamine HCl ....25 mg.
Caffeine ....100 mg.
Indications: For use in short term (8–12 weeks) programs of weight reduction adjunctively to reduced caloric intake.
Actions: Phenylpropanolamine is a sympathomimetic amine with demonstrated appetite-suppressant effects. Clinical trials have shown that individuals on restricted caloric intake lose several times as much weight when taking SUPER ODRINEX adjunctively to the dietary restrictions as patients on the same dietary restrictions but receiving placebo tablets.
Warnings: Individuals known to suffer from heart disease of any kind, sugar diabetes, elevated blood pressure, or thyroid conditions should use this product only after consultation with a physician. Do not exceed recommended dosage. Discontinue use when desired weight is attained. For adult use only. Do not administer this product to children under the age of 12 except on the advice of a physician.
Drug Interaction Precautions: Do not use concurrently with Cough, Cold or Allergy preparations which contain a decongestant.
Precautions: Some sensitive persons may experience nervousness or insomnia, especially if they are prone to excessive intake of coffee, tea, cocoa or soft drinks containing caffeine.
Overdosage: Ingestion of marked overdoses is not usually life-threatening, but marked drowsiness or jitteryness may occur. The persistence of these symptoms is short-lived.
Dosage and Administration: One tablet with a glass of water three times daily, ½ hour before meals. For use by Adults only.
How Supplied: In packages of 50 or 110 tablets, each containing Phenylpropanolamine HCl 25 mg. and Caffeine 100 mg.

G & W Laboratories, Inc.
111 COOLIDGE STREET
SOUTH PLAINFIELD, NJ 07080

ACEPHEN
Acetaminophen Rectal Suppositories

Active Ingredient: Acetaminophen
Indications: For the temporary relief of fever, minor aches, pains, and headaches.
Warning: Adults—do not use consistently for more than 10 days, except on the advice of a physician. Children—do not use more than 5 days, except on the advice of a physician. **Keep this and all drugs out of the reach of children. In case of accidental ingestion, seek professional assistance or contact a poison control center immediately.**
Dosage and Administration: 650 mg.:
Adults: One suppository every 4–6 hours. No more than a total of 4 suppositories in any 24 hour period. Children (6–12 years): One half suppository every 4–6 hours. No more than a total of 4 suppositories in any 24 hour period.
120 mg.:
Children (3–6 years): One suppository every 4–6 hours. No more than 6 suppositories in any 24 hour period. Children (under 3): Consult a physician.
STORE BELOW 80°F. OR REFRIGERATE.
How Supplied: Available in 650 mg. and 120 mg. Packaged in boxes of 12's.

ASPIRIN SUPPOSITORIES

Description: Each suppository contains aspirin 125 mg., 300 mg., or 600 mg., in a specially blended hydrogenated vegetable oil base.
Indications and Use: For the relief of headaches and simple muscular aches and pains. Note: Store in a cool place 8°–15°C. (46°–59°F).
Caution: For children under 4 years of age, consult a physician.
Warning: Keep this and all drugs out of the reach of children. In case of accidental ingestion, seek professional assistance or contact a poison control center immediately.
Dosage and Administration: Remove foil wrapper and insert one suppository well up into rectum 3 or 4 times daily as required.
How Supplied:
125 mg.—Pediatric Suppositories
300 mg. and 600 mg.—Adult Suppositories
Boxes of 12's.

(See Manufacturers' Index for additional products available.)

Products are

indexed alphabetically

in the

PINK SECTION

GEIGY Pharmaceuticals
Division of CIBA-GEIGY
Corporation
ARDSLEY, NY 10502

OTRIVIN®
xylometazoline hydrochloride USP
Adult Nasal Spray and Drops 0.1%
Pediatric Nasal Drops 0.05%

Description: Otrivin, xylometazoline HCl, a sympathomimetic amine, is a white, odorless, crystalline powder which is soluble in water and freely soluble in alcohol. Chemically, it is 2-(4- *tert*-butyl-2, 6-dimethylbenzyl)-2-imidazoline monohydrochloride.

This preparation is available in 0.1% solution for adults and 0.05% solution for children under 12.

Nasal Spray contains 0.1% and *Nasal Drops* contain 0.1% or 0.05% xylometazoline hydrochloride USP, potassium phosphate monobasic, potassium chloride, sodium phosphate dibasic, sodium chloride, and benzalkonium chloride 1:5,000 as preservative in water.

Actions: Its sympathomimetic (adrenergic) action constricts the smaller arterioles of the nasal passages, effecting a decongesting action. This vasoconstriction results from alpha-adrenergic receptor stimulation of vascular smooth muscle.

Indications: For decongestion of the nasal mucosa.

Contraindications: Narrow-angle glaucoma. Concurrent MAO inhibitor therapy. Tricyclic antidepressant therapy. Hypersensitivity to any component of this preparation.

Sensitivity to even small doses of adrenergic substances as manifested by sleeplessness, dizziness, lightheadedness, weakness, tremulousness, or cardiac arrhythmias.

Warnings: Systemic effects from the use of topical decongestants may occur due to rapid absorption through the nasal mucous membrane and from gastrointestinal absorption if given in excess so that the solution is swallowed. Such reactions are most likely to occur in infants and the elderly.

Because of the possibility of generalized vasoconstriction and tachycardia, nose drops (as all sympathomimetic amines) should be used very cautiously in patients with hypertenson, heart disease, including angina, hyperthyroidism and advanced arteriosclerotic conditions.

Overdosage may produce profound CNS depression in children, possibly requiring intensive supportive treatment.

Usage in Pregnancy: Clinical data are inadequate to establish conditions for safe use of nose drops in pregnancy.

Directions:
Nasal Spray 0.1%—Spray 2 or 3 times into each nostril every 8–10 hours. With head upright, squeeze sharply and firmly while inhaling (sniffing) through the nose.

Nasal Drops 0.1%—For adults and children 12 years and older. Put 2 or 3 drops into each nostril every 8 to 10 hours. Tilt head as far back as possible. Immediately bend head forward toward knees, hold a few seconds, then return to upright positon.

Pediatric Nasal Drops 0.05%—For children 2 to 12 years of age. Put 2 or 3 drops into each nostril every 8 to 10 hours. Tilt head as far back as possible. Immediately bend head forward toward knees, hold a few seconds, then return to upright position.

How Supplied: *Otrivin Nasal Spray/ Nasal Drops* are available in unbreakable plastic spray packages of ½ fl oz (15 ml) and in plastic dropper bottles of .66 fl oz (20 ml).

Otrivin Pediatric Nasal Drops Available in plastic dropper bottles of .66 fl oz (20 ml).

(8/80)
[*Shown in Product Identification Section*]

PBZ®
tripelennamine hydrochloride
Antihistamine Cream

Description: PBZ Cream is a topical antihistaminic preparation containing 2% tripelennamine hydrochloride.

Indications: For the temporary relief of itching due to minor skin disorders, ivy and oak poisoning, hives, sunburn, insect bites (nonpoisonous), and stings.

Directions: Apply gently to the affected area 3 or 4 times daily or according to physician's directions.

Caution: If the condition persists or irritation develops, discontinue use and consult physician. Do not use in eyes.
KEEP OUT OF REACH OF CHILDREN.

How Supplied: *Cream,* 2% tripelennamine hydrochloride in a water-washable base; tubes of 1 ounce.

(1/80)
[*Shown in Product Identification Section*]

Gerber Products Company
FREMONT, MI 49412

MBF* (Meat Base Formula) Liquid
Hypoallergenic Infant feeding
Formula, Gerber

Composition: Hypoallergenic liquid formula made from water, beef hearts, cane sugar, sesame oil, modified tapioca starch, tricalcium phosphate, calcium citrate, potassium chloride, iodized salt, sodium ascorbate, ferrous sulfate, tocopheryl acetate, thiamin hydrochloride, vitamin A palmitate, calcium pantothenate, pyridoxine hydrochloride, vitamin D, cupric sulfate, phytonadione (vitamin K_1), folic acid, potassium iodide and biotin.

Nutrient Content: 1:1 dilution contains 20 cal/fl.oz., 12.2% solids, 2.6% protein, 3.2% fat and 6.0% carbohydrate with a Ca/P ratio of 1.5. Vitamin and mineral content per 15 fl. oz. can is:

Vitamin A	1600.0 I.U.
Vitamin D	360.0 I.U.
Vitamin K	24.0 mcg
Vitamin E	6.6 I.U.
Vitamin C	54.0 mg
Vitamin B_1 (Thiamin)	0.54 mg
Vitamin B_2 (Riboflavin)	0.90 mg
Vitamin B_6 (Pyridoxine)	0.78 mg
Vitamin B_{12}	7.8 mcg
Niacin	3.6 mg
Folic Acid	24.0 mcg
Pantothenic Acid	1.8 mg
Biotin	9.0 mcg
Choline	90.0 mg
Inositol	150.0 mg
Calcium	900.0 mg
Phosphorus	600.0 mg
Magnesium	36.0 mg
Iron	12.0 mg
Iodine	30.0 mcg
Zinc	3.0 mg
Copper	0.36 mg
Manganese	30.0 mcg
Sodium	246.0 mg
Potassium	486.0 mg
Chloride	438.0 mg

Action and Uses: A nutritionally adequate formula for infants and children intolerant to cow's and goat's milk whose symptoms may be diarrhea, colic, eczema, upper respiratory, etc. Useful in the management of galactosemia and milk induced steatorrhea.

Administration and Dosage: Provides 20 cal/fl.oz. when diluted 1:1; similar to other milk-based and soy-based infant formulas. Concentrated liquid added to previously boiled (not hot) water is to be divided among prescribed number of bottles, easily fed thru cross-cut nipples.

MBF's content of essential nutrients conforms to the infant formula standard established by the U.S. Food and Drug Administration in 1971 and the 1980 American Academy of Pediatrics infant formula recommendations.

Side Effects: None.
Precautions: None.
Contraindications: None.
How Supplied: Concentrated Liquid, 15 fl. oz. cans.
Literature Available: Yes.
*Trademark

Glenbrook Laboratories
Division of Sterling Drug Inc.
90 PARK AVENUE
NEW YORK, NY 10016

BAYER® ASPIRIN AND BAYER®
CHILDREN'S CHEWABLE ASPIRIN
Aspirin (Acetylsalicylic Acid)

Composition: Bayer Aspirin—Aspirin 5 grains. (325 mg.)
Bayer Children's Chewable Aspirin—Aspirin 1¼ grains (81 mg.) per orange flavored chewable tablet.

Action and Uses: Analgesic, antipyretic, anti-inflammatory. For relief of headache; painful discomfort and fever of colds and flu; muscular aches and pains; temporary relief of minor pains of arthritis, rheumatism, bursitis, lumbago, sciatica; toothache, teething pains, and pain following dental procedures; neuralgia and neuritic pain; functional menstrual pain; sleeplessness when caused by minor painful discomforts; painful discomfort and fever accompanying immunizations.

Continued on next page

Glenbrook—Cont.

Administration and Dosage: The following dosages are those provided in the packaging, as appropriate for self-medication. Larger or more frequent dosage may be necessary as appropriate to the condition or needs of the patient.

Bayer Aspirin—5 grain (325 mg.) tablets

Adult Dose: One or two tablets with water. May be repeated every four hours as necessary up to 12 tablets a day.

Children's Dose: To be administered only under adult supervision.

Under 2 years ....per physician
2 to under 4 years ....½ tablet
4 to under 6 years ....¾ tablet
6 to under 9 years ....1 tablet
9 to under 11 years ....1¼ tablets
11 to under 12 years ....1½ tablets
Over 12 years ....same as adult
Indicated dosage may be repeated every 4 hours, up to but not more than five times a day. Larger dosage may be prescribed per physician.

Bayer Children's Chewable Aspirin— 1¼ grain (81 mg.) tablets

Under 2 years ....per physician
2 to under 4 years.......................2 tablets
4 to under 6 years.......................3 tablets
6 to under 9 years.......................4 tablets
9 to under 11 years...................5 tablets
11 to under 12 years...................6 tablets
Indicated dosage may be repeated every 4 hours, up to but not more than five times a day. Larger dosage may be prescribed per physician.

Contraindications: Hypersensitivity to salicylates. To be used with caution in presence of peptic ulcer, asthma, or with anticoagulant therapy.

How Supplied:
Bayer Aspirin 5 grains (325 mg.)—
NDC-12843-101-10, packs of 12 tablets
NDC-12843-101-11, bottles of 24 tablets
NDC-12843-101-17, bottles of 50 tablets
NDC-12843-101-12, bottles of 100 tablets
NDC-12843-101-20, bottles of 200 tablets
NDC-12843-101-13, bottles of 300 tablets
Child-resistant safety closures on 12s, 24s, 50s, 200s, 300s. Bottle of 100s available without safety closure for households without small children.
Bayer Children's Chewable Aspirin 1¼ grains (81 mg.)—
NDC-12843-131-05, bottle of 36 tablets with child-resistant safety closure.
Samples available on request.
[*Shown in Product Identification Section*]

BAYER® CHILDREN'S COLD TABLETS

Composition: Each tablet contains phenylpropanolamine HCl 3.125 mg., aspirin 1¼ gr. (81 mg.); the tablets are orange flavored and chewable.

Action and Uses: Bayer Children's Cold Tablets combine two effective ingredients: a gentle decongestant to relieve nasal congestion and ease breathing, and genuine Bayer Aspirin to reduce fever and relieve minor aches and pains of colds and flu.

Administration and Dosage: The following dosage is provided in the packaging, as appropriate for self-medication only under adult supervision.

Under 3 years - consult physician
3 years - 1 tablet
4 to 5 years - 2 tablets
6 to 12 years - 4 tablets
Indicated dosage may be repeated every four hours up to but not more than four times a day. Larger or more frequent dosage may be necessary as appropriate to the condition or needs of the patient.

Contraindications: Side effects at higher doses may include nervousness, dizziness, sleeplessness. To be used with caution in presence of high blood pressure, heart disease, diabetes, asthma, or thyroid disease.

How Supplied: NDC-12843-181-01, bottles of 30 tablets with child-resistant safety closure.
Samples available on request.

BAYER® COUGH SYRUP FOR CHILDREN

Composition: Each 5 ml. (1 tsp.) contains phenylpropanolamine HCl 9 mg. and dextromethorphan hydrobromide 7.5 mg., alcohol 5% Cherry flavored.

Action and Uses: Bayer Cough Syrup for Children combines two effective ingredients in a syrup with a very appealing cherry flavor: a gentle nasal decongestant and a cough suppressant.

Administration and Dosage: The following dosage is provided on the packaging, as appropriate for self-medication by an adult:

Under 2 years ....per physician
2–5 years: 1 teaspoon every 4 hours, not to exceed 4 teaspoons every 24 hours.
6–12 years: 2 teaspoons every 4 hours, not to exceed 8 teaspoons every 24 hours.

Contraindications and Precautions: Do not give to children under 2, or exceed recommended dosage, unless directed by a physician. Persistent cough may indicate the presence of a serious condition. Persons with persistent cough, high fever, high blood pressure, heart disease, diabetes or thyroid disease should use only as directed by a physician. Keep out of reach of children.

How Supplied: NDC–12843-401-02, 3.0 oz. bottles. Samples available on request.

BAYER® TIMED–RELEASE ASPIRIN
(aspirin)

Description: Each oblong white scored tablet contains 10 grains (650 mg.) of aspirin in microencapsulation form.

Indications: Bayer Timed-Release Aspirin is indicated for the temporary relief of low grade pain amenable to relief with salicylates, such as in rheumatoid arthritis, osteoarthritis, spondylitis, bursitis and other forms of rheumatism, as well as in many common musculoskeletal disorders. It possesses the same advantages for other types of prolonged aches and pains, such as minor injuries, dental pain and dysmenorrhea. Its long-lasting effectiveness should also make it valuable as an analgesic in simple headache, colds, grippe, flu and other similar conditions in which aspirin is indicated for symptomatic relief, either by itself or as an adjunct to specific therapy.

Dosage: Two Bayer Timed-Release Aspirin tablets q. 8 h. provide effective long-lasting pain relief. This two-tablet (20 grain or 1300 mg.) dose of timed-release aspirin promptly produces salicylate blood levels greater than those achieved by a 10-grain (650 mg.) dose of regular aspirin, and in the second 4 hour period produces a salicylate blood level curve which approximates that of two successive 10-grain (650 mg.) doses of regular aspirin at 4 hour intervals. The 10-grain (650 mg.) scored Bayer Timed-Release Aspirin tablets permit administration of aspirin in multiples of 5 grains (325 mg.), allowing individualization of dosage to meet the specific needs of the patient.

For the convenience of patients on a regular aspirin dosage schedule, two 10-grain (650 mg.) Bayer Timed-Release Aspirin tablets may be administered with water every 8 hours. Whenever possible, two tablets (20 grains or 1300 mg.) should be given before retiring to provide effective analgesic and anti-inflammatory action—for relief of pain throughout the night and lessening of stiffness upon arising. Do not exceed 6 tablets in 24 hours. Bayer Timed-Release Aspirin has been made in a special capsule-shaped tablet to permit easy swallowing. However, for patients who do have difficulty, Bayer Timed-Release Aspirin tablets may be gently crumbled in the mouth and swallowed with water without loss of timed-release effect. There is no bitter "aspirin" taste. For children under 12, per physician.

Side Effects: Side effects encountered with regular aspirin may be encountered with Bayer Timed-Release Aspirin. Tinnitus and dizziness are the ones most frequently encountered.

Contraindications and Precautions: Bayer Timed-Release Aspirin is contraindicated in patients with marked aspirin hypersensitivity, and should be given with extreme caution to any patient with a history of adverse reaction to salicylates. It may cautiously be tried in patients intolerant to aspirin because of gastric irritation, but the usual precautions for any form of aspirin should be observed in patients with gastric ulcers, bleeding tendencies, asthma, or hypoprothrombinemia.

Supplied:
Tablets in Bottle of 30's
NDC-12843-191-72
Tablets in Bottle of 72's
NDC-12843-191-74
Tablets in Bottle of 125's
NDC-12843-191-76
All sizes packaged in child-resistant safety closure except 72's which is a size recommended for households without young children.
Samples available upon request.
[*Shown in Product Identification Section*]

DIAPARENE® BABY POWDER

Description: Powder comprised of corn starch, magnesium carbonate, fragrance, and methylbenzethonium chloride.

Action and Uses: Diaparene Baby Powder has a corn starch base for high absorbency to help keep baby skin dry and for soothing diaper rash, prickly heat, and chafing.

Administration and Dosage: Apply liberally to baby's skin after bath and with each diaper change.

How Supplied: Canister sizes of 4 oz., 9 oz., 12½ oz.

[*Shown in Product Identification Section*]

DIAPARENE™ BABY WASH CLOTHS

Description: Wash cloths are impregnated with a cleansing solution containing water, SD alcohol-40, propylene glycol, lanolin, sodium nonoxynol-9-phosphate, sorbic acid, citric acid, disodium phosphate, oleth-20, and fragrance.

Action and Uses: Diaparene Baby Wash Cloths contain lanolin and a mild cleansing solution to clean and condition baby's skin.

Administration and Dosage: Wipe baby's skin with solution-impregnated wash cloths as required.

How supplied: Canisters in sizes of 70 and 150 wash cloths.

[*Shown in Product Identification Section*]

MIDOL®

Composition: Each Caplet® contains Aspirin 454 mg (7 grains); Cinnamedrine Hydrochloride 14.9 mg; Caffeine 32.4 mg.

Action and Uses: Analgesic, antipyretic, antispasmodic. For fast relief of functional menstrual pain, cramps, irritability; "nervous" headache and the irritability associated with premenstrual tension; headache, neuralgia; low backache due to fatigue, strain or menstruation.

Usage Adult Dosage: Two Caplets with water. Repeat one or two Caplets every four hours as needed, up to eight Caplets per day.

How Supplied: White, capsule-shaped Caplets.

NDC-12843-151-34, strip packs of 12 Caplets

NDC-12843-151-36, bottles of 30 Caplets

NDC-12843-151-38, bottles of 60 Caplets

Child-resistant safety closures on bottles of 30 to 60 Caplets.

Samples Supplied: Available upon request.

[*Shown in Product Identification Section*]

PHILLIPS' MILK OF MAGNESIA

Composition: A suspension of magnesium hydroxide, meeting all USP specifications.

Action and Uses: Phillips' Milk of Magnesia is a mild saline laxative and is indicated for the relief of constipation especially in patients with hemorrhoids, obstetric patients, cardiacs, and in geriatric patients where straining at stool is contraindicated. Phillips' also acts as an antacid, and is effective for the relief of symptoms associated with gastric hyperacidity.

Administration and Dosage: As a laxative, adults 2 to 4 tbsp. followed by a glass of water. Children-infants 1 tsp.; over one year ¼ to ½ adult dose, depending on age. As a antacid, 1 to 3 tsps. with a little water, up to four times a day. Children-1 to 12 years: ¼ to ½ adult dose up to four times a day.

Contraindications: Abdominal pain, nausea, vomiting or other symptoms of appendicitis.

How Supplied: Phillips' Milk of Magnesia is available in regular and mint in bottles of:

Regular

4 fl. oz.	NDC-12843-353-01
12 fl. oz.	NDC-12843-353-02
26 fl. oz.	NDC-12843-353-03

Mint

4 fl oz.	NDC-12843-363-04
12 fl. oz.	NDC-12843-363-05
26 fl. oz.	NDC-12843-363-06

[*Shown in Product Identification Section*]

VANQUISH®

Composition: Each Caplet contains aspirin 227 mg., acetaminophen 194 mg., caffeine 33 mg., dried aluminum hydroxide gel 25 mg.; magnesium hydroxide 50 mg.

Action and Uses: A buffered analgesic, antipyretic for relief of headache; muscular aches and pains; neuralgia and neuritic pain; pain following dental procedures; for painful discomforts and fever of colds and flu; functional menstrual pain, headache and pain due to cramps; temporary relief from minor pains of arthritis, rheumatism, bursitis, lumbago, sciatica.

Usual Adult Dosage: Two caplets with water. May be repeated every four hours if necessary up to 12 tablets per day. Larger or more frequent doses may be prescribed by physician if necessary.

Contraindications: Hypersensitivity to salicylates.

(To be used with caution during anticoagulant therapy or in asthmatic patients.)

How Supplied: White, capsule-shaped Caplets in bottles of:

15 Caplets NDC 12843-17142

30 Caplets NDC 12843-17144

60 Caplets NDC 12843-17146

100 Caplets NDC 12843-17148

IDENTIFICATION PROBLEM?

Consult the

Product Identification Section

where you'll find

products pictured

in full color.

Goody's Manufacturing Corporation
436 SALT STREET
WINSTON-SALEM, NC 27108

GOODY'S HEADACHE POWDERS

Active Ingredient: 520 mg. Aspirin, 260 mg. Acetaminophen 32.5 mg. Caffeine

Indications: For relief of pain due to simple headache, muscular aches and pains, headaches accompanying head colds.

Actions: Combination of active ingredients have analgesic, antipyretic and anti-inflammatory activity.

Warnings: Do not take more than recommended dosage or take regularly for more than 10 days without consulting your physician. Keep out of reach of children. In case of accidental overdose, contact a physician immediately.

Symptoms and Treatment of Oral Overdosage: Symptoms consist of dizziness, ringing in the ears, nausea, diarrhea, incoherent speech, and coma. Treatment varies but drinking two glasses of milk will dilute and slow absorption. Activated charcoal may be given orally in a 5 ml/kg dose. Emptying the stomach is advised.

Dosage and Administration: Adults: one powder with water or other liquid. May be repeated in 3 or 4 hours. Do not take more than 4 powders in any 24 hour period. For children under 12, only as directed by a physician.

How Supplied: Available in 2 dose envelope, 6 dose small box, 24 and 50 dose carton.

[*Shown in Product Identification Section*]

Health Care Industries, Inc.
4295 S. OHIO STREET
MICHIGAN CITY, IN 46360

ALLIMIN® Filmcoated Tablets
Antiflatulent Tablets

Active Ingredient: Dried garlic powder (Allium sativum, dehydrated), 4¾ grains (308 mg.) per tablet. Filmcoated (sugarless) for ease of swallowing.

Indications: For expelling gas from stomach and intestines. Is indicated when entrapped gas is associated with tension of gastrointestinal muscles and/or sphincters.

Actions: Allimin® relaxes the smooth muscle of the tense gastrointestinal tract and sphincters, thus allowing entrapped gas to escape.

Warnings: Keep this and all medications out of reach of children. There is no known case of hypersensitivity, but in such an event, discontinue use and consult a physician. If symptoms persist consult physician.

Drug Interaction: No known drug interaction.

Symptoms and Treatment of Oral Overdosage: These symptoms are based on medical judgment and not on

Continued on next page

Health Care—Cont.

clinical studies: Nausea and vomiting may occur with overdosage. Discontinue use, drink at least 6 to 8 fl. oz. of milk or water for dilution effect and consult physician.

Dosage and Administration: Two (2) tablets after meals when needed. Swallow whole with liquids: water, milk, fruit or vegetable juices.

Professional Labeling: Same as outlined above.

How Supplied: Cartons of 30 pouched tablets and plastic bottles of 80, 160, and 330 tablets. (NDC #036038-)

[*Shown in Product Identification Section*]

COSANYL® Cough Syrup   ©
Cough suppressant/nasal decongestant

Active Ingredients: Each teaspoonful (5 ml.): Codeine phosphate, 10 mg. (Warning: May be habit forming): d-pseudoephedrine HCl, 30 mg. Peach flavor. Alcohol, 6%.

Indications: For the temporary relief of cough, and for temporary relief of nasal congestion due to the common cold or inhaled irritants causing upper respiratory allergies.

Actions: Codeine is a well-known, centrally acting anti-tussive. d-pseudoephedrine reduces congestion of the nasopharyngeal mucosa.

Warnings: May cause or aggravate constipation. Consult a physician or act under his advice for children on other drugs or under 2 years of age, for chronic cough, if one has high blood pressure, heart, thyroid, diabetic, pulmonary diseases, shortness of breath. Do not exceed recommended dosage. If after 7 days, cough persists, or with fever, rash, headache, consult a physician. Keep all drugs out of childrens' reach.

Drug Interaction Precaution: Consult a physician or act under his advice and supervision for concomitant use with a prescription antihypertensive or antidepressant drug containing a monoamine oxidase inhibitor. Avoid use with alcoholic beverages.

Symptoms and Treatment of Oral Overdosage: These symptoms are based on medical judgment and not on clinical studies: Depending on degree of oral overdosage, codeine symptoms may include: depressed respiration in severe cases, and in other cases, somnolence, sedation. Use with alcoholic beverages could cause a comatose state. Although d-pseudoephedrine in recommended doses won't normally cause symptoms of sympathomimetic overstimulation, signs of marked overdose may include hypertension, headache, tachycardia, flushing, etc. Codeine and d-pseudoephedrine effects in overdose, may tend to counteract one another to some degree. But for extreme overdose, prompt gastric evacuation and supportive care is indicated and in this event or in case of accidental ingestion, seek professional assistance or contact a Poison Control Center immediately.

Dosage and Administration: Adults: 2 teaspoonsful every 4 hours. Maximum 12 teaspoonsful in 24 hours. Children (6 to under 12 years): ½ of adult dose above. Children (2 to under 6 years): ¼ of adult dose. Screw safety cap on tightly.

Professional Labeling: Same as outlined above.

How Supplied: 4 fl. oz. with safety cap. Pharmacy dispensing units are pints and gallons. (NDC #11010-001-)

[*Shown in Product Identification Section*]

COSANYL-DM® Cough Syrup
Non-narcotic cough suppressant/nasal decongestant

Active Ingredients: Teaspoonful (5 ml.): d-methorphan, 15 mg; d-pseudoephedrine HCl, 30 mg. Peach flavor. Alcohol 6%.

Indications: For the temporary relief of cough, and for temporary relief of nasal congestion due to the common cold or upper respiratory allergies.

Actions: d-methorphan is a well-known, centrally acting anti-tussive with a 6 to 8 hour duration of action for nighttime relief. d-pseudoephedrine reduces congestion of the naso-pharyngeal mucosa.

Warnings: Consult a physician or act under his advice for children on other drugs or under 2 years of age, for chronic cough, if one has high blood pressure, heart, thyroid, diabetic, pulmonary diseases, shortness of breath. Do not exceed recommended dosage. If after 7 days, cough persists, or with fever, rash, headache, consult a physician. Keep all drugs out of childrens' reach.

Drug Interaction Precaution: Consult a physician or act under his advice and supervision for concomitant use with a prescription antihypertensive or antidepressant drug containing a monoamine oxidase inhibitor. Avoid use with alcoholic beverages.

Symptoms and Treatment of Oral Overdosage: Symptoms are based on medical judgment and not clinical studies: d-pseudoephedrine in recommended doses normally won't cause sympathomimetic side effects but particularly sensitive persons, especially with overdosage, may experience nervousness, restlessness, sleeplessness or other signs of overstimulation of the sympathetic nervous system. In such an event, discontinue use and seek professional assistance to establish a reduced dosage. In case of marked overdosage or accidental ingestion, seek professional assistance or contact a Poison Control Center immediately.

Dosage and Administration: Adults: 2 teaspoonsful every 6 to 8 hours. Maximum 8 teaspoonsful in 24 hours. Children (6 to under 12 years): ½ of adult dose above. Children (2 to under 6 years): ¼ of adult dose. For night time cough relief, give the last dose at bedtime.

Professional Labeling: Same as outlined above.

How Supplied: 4 fl. oz. shrink-wrapped, in 6-Pak Display unit. (NDC #11010-002-04)

[*Shown in Product Identification Section*]

OIL-O-SOL® Liquid
Skin wound cleanser/dressing

Active Ingredients: Corn oil 52%, Castor oil 40.8%, Camphor oil 6.8%, Hexylresorcinol 0.1% (all % are wt. to wt.)

Indications: For minor cuts, scratches, and surface abrasions. For minor burns, non-venomous insect bites. Can be used to treat minor sunburn.

Actions: Corn oil is a natural vegetable oil which provides emollient effects. Castor oil is a quick drying natural oil for a protectant effect. Camphor oil provides mild local analgesic and rubefacient action and topical cooling effect to ease pain. Hexylresorcinal is added for its topical anti-bacterial effects, which helps to prevent infection.

Warnings: For EXTERNAL USE ONLY. Keep out of the eyes and mucous membranes. If burns or wounds are deep or extensive, consult a physician. If redness, irritation, swelling or pain persist, or if infection occurs, discontinue use, see physician.

Drug Interaction Precaution: No known drug interactions.

Symptoms and Treatment of Oral Overdosage: Since Oil-O-Sol® is for EXTERNAL USE ONLY, oral ingestion would be accidental or other mis-use. These symptoms are based on medical judgment and not on clinical studies: Corn oil, Castor oil, and Hexylresorcinol are all edible and have a high order of safety in these concentrations. Accidental ingestion may cause indigestion, nausea, vomiting, or catharsis. In extreme oral misuse, camphor could have CNS toxic effects of an overstimulation type. In such an extreme case, dilute by drinking large amounts of water and immediately seek professional assistance or contact a Poison Control Center. When used EXTERNALLY as recommended, Oil-O-Sol® overdose has never occurred.

Usage and Administration: Clean area thoroughly with mild soap and water. Then clean with Oil-O-Sol.® Saturate a sterile gauze pad with Oil-O-Sol® and apply to injured part. For ready-to-use speed and convenience, use Oil-O-Sol® STREEM-TOP™ with pump applicator or Oil-O-Sol® PAD-ETTE™ pre-saturated gauze pads.

Professional Labeling: Same as outlined above.

How Supplied: 1, 2, 4 fl. oz. liquid, 2 oz. STREEM-TOP™ pump, and 24 PAD-ETTE™ jar. Economy sizes, pint and gallon. (NDC #0543-0001-)

[*Shown in Product Identification Section*]

Products are cross-indexed

by product classifications

in the

BLUE SECTION

Herbert Laboratories
Dermatology Division of Allergan
  Pharmaceuticals, Inc.
2525 DUPONT DRIVE
IRVINE, CA 92713

AQUACARE® (2% urea)
AQUACARE®/HP (10% urea)
Dry Skin Cream and Lotion

Active Ingredient:
Cream: 2% urea in emollient base
HP Cream: 10% urea in emollient base
Lotion: 2% urea in emollient base
HP Lotion: 10% urea in emollient base
Indications: For dry, rough skin
Actions: Moisturizes, softens and smooths dry, rough skin.
Warnings: For external use only. Discontinue use if irritation occurs. Keep out of reach of children.
Drug Interaction: No known drug interaction.
Precaution: (See Warnings)
Symptoms and Treatment of Oral Overdosage: Push fluids
Dosage and Administration: Apply 2 to 3 times daily to affected area, or as physician directs.
Professional Labeling: Same as outlined under Indications.
How Supplied:
Aquacare
Cream: 2.5 oz plastic tube
Lotion: 8 oz plastic bottle
Aquacare/HP
Cream: 2.5 oz plastic tube
Lotion: 8 oz and 16 oz plastic bottle

BLUBORO® POWDER
ASTRINGENT SOAKING SOLUTION

Active Ingredient: Aluminum sulfate and calcium acetate
Indications: Inflammation of the skin due to allergies, poison ivy, insect bites, or athlete's foot and swelling associated with minor bruises.
Actions: Astringent soaking solution for relief of inflammatory conditions of the skin.
Warnings: Do not use plastic or other impervious material to prevent evaporation without consulting physician. If irritation occurs or persists, discontinue use and consult physician. Prepare fresh solution daily. For external use only. Keep out of reach of children. Store at room temperature.
Drug Interaction: No known drug interaction.
Precaution: (See Warnings)
Symptoms and Treatment of Oral Overdosage: Push fluids.
Dosage and Administration: Dissolve one or two packs in a pint (16 oz.) of cool or warm water. The resulting mixture is ready for use—do not strain or filter. One packet per pint of water yields a 1:40 dilution; two packets per pint yield a 1:20 dilution of a modified Burow's solution of buffered aluminum acetate.
If desired, soak a clean dressing or bandage in solution and apply loosely on the inflamed skin. Remove, re-moisten and reapply every 15-30 minutes. Do not let dressings dry out. Keep applying 4 to 8 hours or as directed by a physician.

Professional Labeling: Same as outlined under Indications.
How Supplied: 12 packets box
                                100 packets box

CLEAR BY DESIGN™ ACNE GEL
Invisible, Greaseless Acne Gel

Active Ingredient: 2.5% Benzoyl peroxide
Indications: A topical aid in the treatment of acne vulgaris.
Actions: Benzoyl peroxide provides antibacterial activity against Propionibacterium acne along with drying and peeling action.
Warnings: Avoid contact with eyes, lips and mouth. If excess dryness, flakiness, or irritation occurs, discontinue use and consult your physician. Colored or dyed garments may be bleached by the oxidizing action of benzoyl peroxide.
Precautions: Keep tube tightly closed. Keep out of reach of children. Store at controlled room temperature (59°–86°F). Avoid heat. FOR EXTERNAL USE ONLY.
Dosage and Administration: Wash problem areas with mild soap and dry. Using fingertips, gently spread Clear By Design on all affected areas one to two times a day, or as directed by your physician.
Professional Labeling: Same as outlined above.
How Supplied: 1.5 and 3 oz plastic tubes.

DANEX® PROTEIN ENRICHED
DANDRUFF SHAMPOO

Active Ingredient: Pyrithione zinc 1%
Indications: Dandruff flaking
Actions: Helps control dandruff flaking.
Warnings: For external use only. Keep out of eyes; if contact occurs, rinse with water immediately. Keep out of reach of children.
Drug Interaction: No known drug interaction.
Precaution: (See Warnings)
Symptoms and Treatment of Oral Overdosage: Induce emesis, gastric lavage. Push fluids.
Dosage and Administration: Shake well before using. Apply shampoo, lather, rinse and repeat. Use once or twice weekly, or as physician directs.
Professional Labeling: Same as outlined under Indications.
How Supplied: 4 oz and 8 oz plastic bottles.

ECLIPSE® AFTER SUN LOTION

Indications: Dry, rough skin
Actions: Moisturizes and enhances a tan by helping to prevent peeling and flaking.
Warnings: For external use only. Keep out of reach of children.
Drug Interaction: No known drug interaction.
Precaution: None
Symptoms and Treatment of Oral Overdosage: Push fluids.
Dosage and Administration: Apply liberally after sunning, bathing, showering or when the skin is dry or chapped.

Professional Labeling: Same as outlined under Indications.
How Supplied: 6 oz plastic bottle.

ECLIPSE® SUNSCREEN LIP & FACE PROTECTANT SPF 6

Active Ingredient: Padimate O (octyl dimethyl PABA)
Indications: Drying, chapping and burning from wind and sun.
Actions: Protects lips, ears, face and hands from sunburn and drying.
Warnings: None
Drug Interaction: No known drug interaction.
Precaution: None
Symptoms and Treatment of Oral Overdosage: Push fluids.
Dosage and Administration: Apply as often as needed.
Professional Labeling: Same as outlined under Indications.
How Supplied: .15 oz stick

PARTIAL ECLIPSE®
Suntan Lotion—(SPF 5)
ORIGINAL ECLIPSE®
Sunscreen Lotion and Gel—(SPF 10)
TOTAL ECLIPSE®
Sunscreen Lotion (Moisturizing Base & Alcohol Base)—(SPF 15)

Active Ingredient:
Partial Eclipse (SPF 5): Padimate O (octyl dimethyl PABA)
Eclipse Lotion (SPF 10): Padimate O (octyl dimethyl PABA) & glyceryl PABA
Eclipse Gel (SPF 10): Padimate O (octyl dimethyl PABA), glyceryl PABA with alcohol (55%)
Total Eclipse (SPF 15) (Moisturizing Base): Padimate O (octyl dimethyl PABA) and oxybenzone (benzophenone-3)
Total Eclipse (SPF 15) (Alcohol Base): Oxybenzone (benzophenone-3), padimate O (octyl dimethyl PABA) and glyceryl PABA with alcohol (81%)
Indications: Prevention of harmful effects of sun
Actions: Selectively screens the harmful rays of the sun to help prevent sunburn, premature aging and skin cancer.
Partial Eclipse protects from the burning rays yet permits a rich, healthy tan for skin that sometimes burns.
Original Eclipse Lotion and Gel allow a gradual tan for skin that burns easily.
Total Eclipse (Moisturizing and Alcohol base) screens the burning and tanning rays for the most sun-sensitive skin either dry or oily respectively.
Warnings: For external use only. Do not use if sensitive to benzocaine, sulfonamides, aniline dyes, PABA or related compounds. Avoid contact with eyes or eyelids. If contact occurs, rinse thoroughly with water. If irritation develops, discontinue use. If it persists, consult a physician. Keep out of reach of children. May stain some fabrics. Total Eclipse (alcohol base) & Eclipse Gel—Avoid flame.
Drug Interaction: No known drug interaction.

Continued on next page

Herbert—Cont.

Symptoms and Treatment of Oral Overdosage: Partial Eclipse, Eclipse Lotion & Total Eclipse (Moisturizing Base): Push fluids.

Total Eclipse (Alcohol Base) & Eclipse Gel: Induce emesis by aspiration or gastric lavage. Then push fluids.

Dosage and Administration: Apply liberally & evenly to all exposed skin; Partial Eclipse (every 2-4 hours), Eclipse Lotion (every 4-6 hours), Total Eclipse (Moisturizing Base)—(every 6-8 hours). Apply in thin, even film to all exposed skin; Total Eclipse (alcohol base)—(every 6-8 hours), Eclipse Gel—(every 4-6 hours).

Professional Labeling: Same as outlined under Indications.

How Supplied: Eclipse Lotion: 6 & 4 oz plastic bottles, Partial Eclipse & both Total Eclipses: 4 oz plastic bottles, Eclipse Gel: 3 oz plastic tube.

[*Shown in Product Identification Section*]

VANSEB®
Cream and Lotion Dandruff Shampoos with Protein
VANSEB-T®
Cream and Lotion Dandruff Shampoos with Protein

Active Ingredient:
Vanseb Cream and Lotion Shampoos: 2% sulfur and 1% salicylic acid.
Vanseb-T Cream and Lotion Shampoos: 5% coal tar solution, 1% salicylic acid and 2% sulfur.

Indications: Seborrheic dermatitis and dandruff.

Actions: Helps rid the scalp of flakes and oily debris. The unique blend of surfactants and proteins leaves the hair lustrous and manageable.

Warnings: For external use only. Discontinue use if irritation occurs. Keep out of reach of children. Keep out of eyes; if contact occurs, rinse with water immediately.

Drug Interaction: No known drug interaction.

Precaution: (See Warnings)

Symptoms and Treatment of Oral Overdosage: Induce emesis, gastric lavage. Then push fluids.

Dosage and Administration: Massage into wet hair and scalp. Continue several minutes. Rinse and repeat, or as physician directs. Shake lotion shampoo well before using.

Professional Labeling: Same as outlined under Indications.

How Supplied:
Cream Shampoos: 3 oz plastic tubes
Lotion Shampoos: 4 oz plastic bottles

Products are cross-indexed by

generic and chemical names

in the

YELLOW SECTION

Hickam, Inc., Dow B.
POST OFFICE BOX 35413
HOUSTON, TX 77035

PRODERM TOPICAL DRESSING

Active Ingredients: Each .82 cc delivered to the site contains Castor Oil, USP 650 mg. and Balsam Peru, NF 72.5 mg.

Indications: An aid in the management of decubitus ulcers.

Actions: Proderm Topical Dressings serves as a soothing protective dressing and speeds healing by increasing capillary blood flow into the ulcerated area.

Warnings: Avoid spraying in eyes or nostrils. Flammable, do not expose to fire or open flame. Contents under pressure. Do not puncture or incinerate. Do not store at temperature above 120° F. Keep out of reach of children. Use only as directed. Intentional misuse by deliberately concentrating and inhaling the contents can be harmful or fatal.

Drug Interaction: No known drug interactions.

Dosage and Administration: Apply Proderm three times daily. Shake can well. Hold approximately 12 inches from the area to be treated, press valve and coat rapidly.

Professional Labeling: As above.

How Supplied: Available in 4 oz. aerosol cans.

Hoechst-Roussel Pharmaceuticals Inc.
SOMERVILLE, NJ 08876

DOXIDAN®
Laxative with Stool Softener

Active Ingredients: Doxidan is a combination of 60 mg docusate calcium USP and 50 mg danthron USP.

Actions: Doxidan has a highly effective stool softener and a mild peristaltic stimulant that acts mainly in the lower bowel. Due to the effectiveness of the stool softening component, Doxidan produces soft, formed, easily evacuated stools, with the least possible disturbance of normal body physiology.

Indications: Doxidan is a safe, gentle laxative for the management of constipation. It has proved clinically effective in the management of constipation in geriatric or inactive patients, obstetric patients, and following surgery, particularly anorectal procedures. It may be used as a safe and effective evacuant prior to x-ray examination of the colon in preparing patients for barium enema.

Warnings: Do not use when abdominal pain, nausea, or vomiting is present. Frequent or prolonged use of this preparation may result in dependence on laxatives. A harmless pink or orange discoloration may appear in alkaline urine. In some patients occasional cramping may occur.

Dosage and Administration: Adults and children over 12—one or two capsules daily. Children 6 to 12—one capsule daily. Best given at bedtime, Doxidan will usually provide a gentle evacua-

---

tion in 8 to 12 hours. Dosage should be maintained for 2 to 3 days or until bowel movements return to normal. For use in children under 6, consult a physician.

How Supplied: Packs of 10; bottles of 30, 100 (NSN 6505-00-074-3169) and 1,000 (NSN 6505-00-890-1247) maroon, soft-gelatin capsules; and in Unit Dose 100s (10×10 strips) (NSN 6505-00-118-1700, 6505-00-163-7700A).

[*Shown in Product Identification Section*]

FESTAL®
Digestive Aid

Active Ingredients: Each enteric-coated tablet contains the following: lipase 6,000 NF units; amylase 30,000 NF units; protease 20,000 NF units; hemicellulase 50 mg; and bile constituents 25 mg.

Actions: Festal provides a high degree of protected digestive activity in a formula of standardized enzyme and bile constituents. Enteric coating of the tablet prevents release of ingredients in the stomach, so that high enzymatic activity is delivered to the site in the intestinal tract where digestion normally takes place.

Indications: Festal is indicated in any condition where normal digestion is impaired by insufficiency of natural digestive enzymes, or when additional digestive enzymes may be beneficial. These conditions often manifest complaints of discomfort due to excess intestinal gas, such as bloating, cramps and flatulence. The following are conditions or situations where Festal may be helpful: pancreatic insufficiency, enteritis, postgastrectomy syndrome, chronic pancreatitis, pancreatic necrosis, chronic hepatitis, gallbladder disease, surgical patients following cholecystectomy, subtotal gastrectomy, pancreatectomy and other surgery of the upper gastrointestinal tract, removal of gas prior to x-ray examination; and in the healthy individual who may experience temporary digestive deficiency due to over-indulgence in excessively fatty meals.

Dosage and Administration: Usual adult dose is one or two tablets with each meal, or as directed by a physician.

How Supplied: Bottles of 100 and 500 white, enteric-coated tablets for oral use.
[*Shown in Product Identification Section*]

SURFAK®
Stool Softener

Active Ingredient: Surfak 50 mg and 240 mg capsules contain docusate calcium USP

Actions: Surfak provides homogenization and formation of soft, easily evacuated stools without disturbance of body physiology, discomfort of bowel distention, oily leakage or interference with vitamin absorption. Surfak is non-habit forming.

Indications: Surfak is indicated for the prevention and treatment of constipation in conditions in which hard stools may cause discomfort, or in those conditions where laxative therapy is undesirable or contraindicated. Surfak is useful in patients who require only stool softening without propulsive action to accomplish defecation. Surfak does not cause peristaltic stimulation, and because of its safety it may be effectively used in patients with heart conditions, anorectal conditions, obstetrical patients, following surgical procedures, ulcerative colitis, diverticulitis and bedridden patients.

Warnings: Surfak has no known side effects or disadvantages, except for the unusual occurrence of mild, transitory cramping pains.

Dosage and Administration: Adults —one red 240 mg capsule daily for several days or until bowel movements are normal. Children and adults with minimal needs—one to three orange 50 mg capsules daily. For use in children under 6, consult a physician.

How Supplied: 240 mg red, soft gelatin capsules—bottles of 30 (NSN 6505-00-117-8607), 100 (NSN 6505-00-926-8844), 500 (NSN 6505-00-148-9815) and unit dose 100s (10 x 10 strips) (NSN 6505-00-118-1449); 50 mg orange, soft gelatin capsules—bottles of 30 and 100.
[*Shown in Product Identification Section*]

Holland-Rantos Company, Inc.
P. O. BOX 385
865 CENTENNIAL AVE.
PISCATAWAY, NJ 08854

KOROMEX® CONTRACEPTIVE FOAM

Description: KOROMEX CONTRACEPTIVE FOAM is a pure white delicately fragranced aerosol foam. It is highly spermicidal, non-staining, non-greasy.

Composition: Active ingredient is nonoxynol 9 12.5% in a base of water, propylene glycol, propellant 114, Isopropyl alcohol, Laureth-4, cetyl alcohol, propellant 12, PEG-50 stearate and fragrance.

Action: Spermicidal.

Indication: Contraception.

Side Effects: Should sensitivity to the ingredients or irritation of the vagina or penis develop, the patient should discontinue use and be instructed to consult a physician.

Warning: Contents under pressure. Do not puncture or incinerate container. Do not expose to heat or store at temperatures above 120° F. KEEP OUT OF REACH OF CHILDREN.

Dosage and Administration: One applicatorful of KOROMEX CONTRACEPTIVE FOAM should be inserted prior to each intercourse.

The patient may have intercourse any time up to one hour after the foam has been inserted. If intercourse is repeated, another applicatorful of the KOROMEX FOAM should be inserted.

When KOROMEX CONTRACEPTIVE FOAM is used, a cleansing douche is not essential. However, if a douche is recommended or desired, the patient should be instructed to wait at least 6 hours after intercourse.

How Supplied: KOROMEX CONTRACEPTIVE FOAM 22 gms. (0.78 oz.) can with applicator and purse for storage. Refills are available in 22 gm (0.78 oz.) and 55 gm (1.94 oz.).

KOROMEX[II] CONTRACEPTIVE CREAM

Composition: KOROMEX[II] CONTRACEPTIVE CREAM... Pearly-white in appearance... for those patients whose aesthetic preference is for a preparation with a lesser lubrication factor. Active ingredient is Octoxynol 3.0%—in a base of purified water, propylene glycol, stearic acid, sorbitan stearate, polysorbate 60, boric acid and fragrance. pH buffered and adjusted to 4.5.

Indications: Contraception and vaginal lubrication in conjunction with a vaginal diaphragm.

Warning: Keep this and all medication out of the reach of children.

Administration and Dosage: Approximately ½ teaspoon of KOROMEX[II] CONTRACEPTIVE CREAM is placed on the dome surface of the diaphragm coming in direct contact with the cervix. The cream is then spread over the rubber and around the rim.

How Supplied: #20 KOROMEX[II] C/C CREAM with measured dose applicator (2.65 oz.—75 grams), #25 KOROMEX[II] C/C CREAM refill (2.65 oz.—75 grams), #225 KOROMEX[II] C/C CREAM large refill (4.51 oz.—128 grams).

KOROMEX[II] CONTRACEPTIVE JELLY

Composition: KOROMEX[II] CONTRACEPTIVE JELLY contains the active ingredient Octoxynol 1.0%—in a base of purified water, propylene glycol, cellulose gum, boric acid, sorbitol, starch, simethicone and fragrance. pH buffered and adjusted to 4.5. Pleasantly scented to meet the patient's aesthetic requirements. Homogenized to help eliminate the primary patient complaint of messiness.

Indications: Contraception and vaginal lubrication in conjunction with a vaginal diaphragm.

Warning: Keep this and all medication out of the reach of children.

Administration and Dosage: Approximately ½ teaspoon of KOROMEX[II] CONTRACEPTIVE JELLY is placed on the dome surface of the diaphragm coming in direct contact with the cervix. The jelly is then spread over the rubber and around the rim.

How Supplied: #10 KOROMEX[II] C/C JELLY with measured dose applicator (2.85 oz.—81 grams), #15 KOROMEX[II] C/C JELLY refill (2.85 oz.—81 grams), #115 KOROMEX[II] C/C JELLY—large refill (4.76 oz.—135 grams).

KOROMEX[II]-A CONTRACEPTIVE JELLY

Composition: Active ingredient Nonoxynol-9 2% in a base of propylene glycol, boric acid, sorbitol, cellulose gum, starch, simethicone, purified water, and fragrance. pH 4.5

Indications: Contraception and vaginal lubricant.

Action and Uses: KOROMEX[II]-A CONTRACEPTIVE JELLY provides contraception immediately after insertion. It may, however, be introduced up to one hour before intercourse.

Side Effects: Should sensitivity to the ingredients or irritation of the vagina, or penis develop, discontinue use and consult your physician.

Warning: Keep this and all medication out of the reach of children.

Administration and Dosage: As directed by physician.

How Supplied: In 4.76 oz. (135 grams) tubes with applicator and 4.76 oz. (135 grams) refill tubes.

NYLMERATE[II]® Solution Concentrate

Composition: SD alcohol 23A 50% v/v, purified water, acetic acid, boric acid, polysorbate 20, nonoxynol-9, sodium acetate, FD & C Blue #1, D & C Yellow #10.

Action and Uses: A cleansing acidified buffered vaginal irrigant. In recommended dilution pH is 4.5, thereby aiding in adjusting the vaginal pH. Helps relieve and combats offensive odors and pruritus by removing accumulated discharges.

Useful as an adjunct in specific vaginal therapy or routine vaginal cleansing.

Directions: One tablespoonful or ½ capful (filled to the top line inside of cap) to one quart of warm water. Do not add solution until the water is first added to the douche bag, then mix thoroughly.

Warning: Do not use more than twice weekly unless directed to do so by the physician. Do not use full strength. If irritation occurs, discontinue use.

How Supplied: 16 fluid oz. (473 ml) in a plastic bottle with measuring cap.

TRANSI-LUBE®
The Sexual Foaming Lubricant

Description: TRANSI-LUBE is a sexual lubricant that closely approximates the normal female transudate to enhance sexual pleasure. This medically oriented lubricant has the mild taste and aroma of strawberries. It is non-greasy, non-staining, non-irritating, maintains its lubricity for a long period of time, and is aesthetically acceptable to men and women. TRANSI-LUBE is not a contraceptive.

Indications For Use: To enhance sexual pleasure. For improved sexual communication and response regardless of any physical or psychological disability.

Note: TRANSI-LUBE is not intended as a body lubricant. Genital play or sexual arousal is pleasantly enhanced when both partners use TRANSI-LUBE.

Contains: Purified water, isobutane propane, propylene glycol, sorbitol, PEG 14M, ceteth 10, methyl and propyl parabens, citric acid and flavor.

Side Effects: Should sensitivity to the ingredients or irritation of the vaginal area or penis develop, discontinue use.

Continued on next page

Holland-Rantos—Cont.

Due to the propellant, some coldness or irritation may be felt if placed directly on the penis or vagina. It is preferable to place the product on the hand, waiting 10 to 15 seconds before application.

Caution: Do not insert nozzle into the vagina or any body oriface for direct application.

Warning: FLAMMABLE—do not use near flame or while smoking. Contents under pressure. Do not puncture or incinerate. Do not store above 120° F. Keep out of reach of children. Use only as directed. Intentional misuse by deliberately concentrating and inhaling the contents can be harmful or fatal.

Packaging: Containers of 3¼ oz. (92 grams).

Hynson, Westcott & Dunning
Division of Becton Dickinson and Co.
CHARLES & CHASE STS.
BALTIMORE, MD 21201

LACTINEX® TABLETS AND GRANULES

Composition: A viable mixed culture of *Lactobacillus acidophilus* and *L. bulgaricus* with the naturally occurring metabolic products that are produced by these organisms.

Action and Uses: Lactinex has been found to be useful in the treatment of uncomplicated diarrhea (including that due to antibiotic therapy) and acute fever blisters (cold sores).

Indications and Dosage: (for adults and children):

Gastrointestinal Disturbances—4 tablets or 1 packet of granules added to or taken with cereal, food, milk, fruit juice or water; three or four times a day.

Fever Blisters (Cold Sores)—4 tablets or 1 packet of granules chewed and swallowed three or four times a day. Each dose may be followed by a small amount of milk, fruit juice or water.

Lactinex Must Be Refrigerated
Individuals sensitive to milk products should not use Lactinex.

How Supplied: Tablets—bottles of fifty (NDC 0011-8368-50). Granules, boxes of twelve, 1 gram packets (unit dose dispensing), (NDC 0011-8367-12).

Literature Available: On request.

[*Shown in Product Identification Section*]

Products are cross-indexed

by product classifications

in the

BLUE SECTION

Jayco Pharmaceuticals
890 POPLAR CHURCH DRIVE
SUITE 305
CAMP HILL, PA 17011

F.S.K.
Fecal Staining Kit

Description: A complete set of stains and chemicals to prepare samples of stool to assist in the diagnosis of fat malabsorption and detect fecal leukocytes in diarrheal states. The kit provides stain to examine stools for neutral and split fats and to supra-vital stain leukocytes. Each kit contains 50 cc each of Loeffler's methylene blue, a saturated solution of Sudan Black III, acetic acid (36%) and ethyl alcohol (95%) in dropper fitted plastic bottles.

Usage: Each kit contains easy to follow directions for staining, examination and interpretation of the stool specimens. Interpretation of the different fat globules found in stool is given as well as differential diagnosis of leukocytes in the stool.

In addition, Loeffler's methylene blue can be used as a supra-vital stain for urinary sediments.

How Supplied: Each kit contains four dropper bottles, packing materials used for storage, a stand for the bottles, and complete instructions.

References:
1. Drummey, G. D., Microscopic Examination of the Stool for Steatorrhea *N.E.J.M.*, 264:85–87 1961.
2. Harris, J. C., et. al., Fecal Leukocytes in Diarrheal Illness *Ann Int Med*, 76:697–703 1972.

HYDRA-LYTE™
Oral Glucose Electrolyte Drink Mix

Description: A dietary supplement to replace and maintain electrolytes and water losses during mild and moderate diarrhea in children and adults and to provide nutritional support during parenteral therapy.

Formulated to supply electrolytes and water lost through diarrhea, HYDRA-LYTE enhances the absorption of sodium and water through the addition of sugars.

Usage: Intake of HYDRA-LYTE should be adjusted to individual requirements and should be in small frequent amounts. It should be ingested freely, to quench thirst.

All other food intake, except for water, should be discontinued.

HYDRA-LYTE can be used directly with unflavored gelatin to provide an inexpensive, high electrolyte containing, tasty gelatin dessert. When used to help maintain or replenish fluid and electrolyte losses during diarrheal episodes, HYDRA-LYTE should be used only under medical supervision in conformity with a physician's recommendation.

Ingredients: Dextrose, sucrose, sodium chloride and citrate, potassium citrate, sodium bicarbonate, artificial flavoring and coloring, 0.05% sodium benazoate as preservative.

HYDRA-LYTE provides 84 mEq Sodium, 59 mEq Chloride, 10 mEq Bicarbonate, 10 MEq Potassium, 67 mM Glucose and 35 mM Sucrose.

How Supplied: HYDRA-LYTE is available in convenient foil-lined packets, two packets per box.

References:
1. Sack, R.B., et. al., The current status of oral therapy in the treatment of acute diarrheal illness *American Journal of Clinical Nutrition* 31:2251 1978
2. Pierce, N.F. and Hirschhorn N, Oral fluid—a simple weapon against dehydration in diarrhoea *WHO Chronicle* 31:87 1977
3. Moenginah, P.A., et.al., Oral Sucrose Therapy for diarrhea *Lancet* 1:323 1975

LAC–TOL
Lactose Tolerance Test

Description: The lactose tolerance test is a method of determining lactase deficiency. Lactose, a sugar found in milk and milk products, is digested by the intestinal disaccharidase lactase. Lactase deficiency results in maldigestion of lactose. This may produce clinical symptoms of lactose intolerance.

LAC-TOL contains 50 grams of lactose combined with sodium citrate and flavorings. This enhances solubility of the lactose and provides a pleasant tasting solution for the lactose tolerance test.

Indications: LAC-TOL is indicated as the test solution for the lactose tolerance test.

Directions: See package insert.

Interpretations: Using venous blood samples, a peak maximal rise of 25 mg/100 ml in the blood glucose signifies normal lactase activity. A peak rise below 20 mg/100 ml strongly suggests lactase deficiency. With the use of capillary blood, the glucose determinations will be higher.

In diabetic patients, a subsequent glucose-galactose tolerance test (GGTT) should be performed.

References:
Peternel, W.W., Lactose Tolerance in Relation to Intestinal Lactase Activity, *Gastroenterology*. Vol 48: 299–306, 1965.

Welsh, J.D., Isolated Lactase Deficiency in Humans: Report on 100 patients, *Medicine*. Vol 49: 257–277, 1970.

Welsh, J.D., On the Lactose Tolerance Test, *Gastroenterology*. Vol 51: 445–446, 1966.

Products are

indexed alphabetically

in the

PINK SECTION

Johnson & Johnson
Baby Products Company
220 CENTENNIAL AVENUE
PISCATAWAY, NJ 08854

JOHNSON'S Baby Bath
Infant Bathing Product

Description: JOHNSON'S Baby Bath is an effective, extremely mild, clear liquid surfactant (cleansing) system especially formulated for bathing infants and children. When mixed with water it produces a cleansing lather which is superior in mildness to the skin and eyes.

Indications: JOHNSON'S Baby Bath is indicated for routine bathing of infants, children, and adults when an extremely mild, and effective cleansing action is desired.

Composition: The ingredients in JOHNSON'S Baby Bath and their intended function are as follows: Water (vehicle), Sodium Trideceth Sulfate (Anionic Surfactant), Cocamidopropyl Sultaine (Amphoteric Surfactant), PEG-150 Distearate (Nonionic Thickener & Emollient), PPG-15 Stearyl Ether (Emollient), Benzyl Alcohol (Microbiological Preservative), Sodium Phosphate (Buffer Component), Quaternium-15 (Microbiological Preservative), Fragrance, Disodium Phosphate (Buffer Component), Tetrasodium EDTA (Chelating Agent).

Clinical Studies:
Skin Irritation Potential
Occlusive patch testing of adult volunteers compared the cumulative irritation potential of 50% solutions of JOHNSON'S Baby Bath and another liquid baby bath. This exaggerated exposure technique indicated a significantly lower irritation potential for JOHNSON'S Baby Bath (44% of maximum irritation potential vs 83% for the other liquid baby bath). Pure bar soap, even at 1% concentration, is too irritating to be used in such a test.

MAXIMUM CUMULATIVE IRRITATION

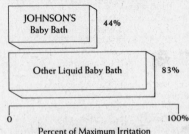

JOHNSON'S Baby Bath 44%

Other Liquid Baby Bath 83%

0   Percent of Maximum Irritation   100%

Arm Immersion Studies
Arm immersion studies assessed the relative irritation potential of soaps and a mild detergent bar versus JOHNSON'S Baby Bath. In one study JOHNSON'S Baby Bath was found to be milder than the leading pure bar soap, the leading deodorant bar, the leading toilet soap bar, and a leading mild detergent complexion bar.

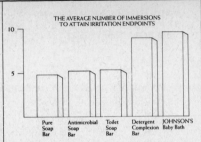

THE AVERAGE NUMBER OF IMMERSIONS TO ATTAIN IRRITATION ENDPOINTS

Pure Soap Bar · Antimicrobial Soap Bar · Toilet Soap Bar · Detergent Complexion Bar · JOHNSON'S Baby Bath

Human Ocular Sting and Irritation Potential
It is particularly important that a skin cleanser used for infants be gentle and non-irritating to human eyes.

After results obtained from preclinical tests showed no significant eye damage, the adult human ocular sting and irritation potential of both a normal use and a three times normal use (~24%) concentration of JOHNSON'S Baby Bath were assessed. A test solution was instilled into the lower cul-de-sac of one eye of volunteer subjects and sterile water into the other. All such clinical studies have shown that JOHNSON'S Baby Bath is as gentle to human eyes as water, even at three times normal use concentration.

Directions for Use: Pour onto wet washcloth or hand, work up lather, apply to body, rinse.

How Supplied: JOHNSON'S Baby Bath is available in three convenient sizes: 4 fluid ounce, 8 fluid ounce, and 12 fluid ounce. The 8 and 12 fluid ounce sizes have dispenser top caps which are easily opened with one hand. A 1.5 fluid ounce size is also available for professional use only, suitable for individual patient bassinets.

SUNDOWN® SUNSCREENS
Moderate Protection (SPF 4)
Extra Protection (SPF 6)
Maximal Protection (SPF 8)
Ultra Protection (SPF 15)

Active Ingredients:
Moderate Protection: Padimate O (Octyl dimethyl PABA)
Extra Protection: Padimate O (Octyl dimethyl PABA) and Oxybenzone
Maximal and Ultra Protection: Padimate O (Octyl dimethyl PABA), Oxybenzone and Octyl salicylate

Indications: Sunscreens to help prevent harmful effects from the sun. SUNDOWN Moderate, Extra, Maximal and Ultra Protection provide 4, 6, 8, and 15 times your natural sunburn protection, respectively. Moderate and Extra Protection permit tanning, Maximal Protection permits minimal tanning and Ultra Protection permits no tanning. Liberal and regular use may help reduce the chance of premature aging and wrinkling of the skin, and skin cancer, due to overexposure to the sun. Moderate, Extra and Maximal Protection are waterproof requiring reapplication after 80 minutes in the water or excessive perspiration. Ultra Protection is water resistant and should be reapplied after 40 minutes in the water or after excessive perspiration.

Actions: Absorption of Ultraviolet light

Warnings: For external use only. Avoid contact with eyes. Discontinue use if signs of irritation or rash appear. Use on children under 6 months of age only with the advice of physician. Keep out of reach of children.

Symptoms and Treatment of Oral Overdose: If ingested, remove material from stomach by gastric lavage or emesis induction. Give demulcent or milk. Observe and treat symptomatically. If appropriate monitor serum electrolytes. Flush eyes with a gentle stream of tepid water or isotonic saline.

Dosage and Administration: Shake well. Apply generously and evenly to all exposed areas. Reapply after prolonged swimming or excessive perspiration.

How Supplied: 4 fluid ounce bottles.

Johnson & Johnson
Products, Inc.
501 GEORGE STREET
NEW BRUNSWICK, NJ 08903

JOHNSON & JOHNSON FIRST AID CREAM
Skin Wound Protectant

Active Ingredient: Contains: Cetyl alcohol, Glyceryl stearate, Isopropyl palmitate, Stearyl alcohol, Synthetic beeswax as the skin wound protectants.

Indications: For minor cuts, scrapes and burns.

Actions: Helps protect minor skin wounds against contamination.

Warnings: Not for use on large, deep, or puncture wounds, serious burns or animal bites. If redness, irritation, swelling, or pain persists or increases, or if infection occurs, discontinue use and consult physician. Should not be used for more than ten days. If condition worsens or persists, see your physician. Not for use in eyes or on chronic skin conditions.

Drug Interaction Precaution: No known drug interaction.

Symptoms and Treatment of Oral Overdosage: There is no known history of any oral ingestion/toxicity case. However, animal studies reveal significant safety with oral ingestion; the lethal dose in both rats and mice exceeds 40 ml/kg of body weight. Therefore, only symptomatic treatment and observation would be required in the case of ingestion.

[*Shown in Product Identification Section*]

IDENTIFICATION PROBLEM?

Consult the

Product Identification Section

where you'll find

products pictured

in full color.

Kremers-Urban Company
BOX 2038
MILWAUKEE, WI 53201

KUDROX® SUSPENSION
(DOUBLE STRENGTH) ANTACID

Composition: A pleasantly flavored SUSPENSION containing a concentrated combination of aluminum hydroxide gel and magnesium hydroxide in d-sorbitol.

One teaspoonful of KUDROX Liquid contains not more than 0.65 mEq (15 mg.) of sodium.

Action and Uses: A palatable antacid to alleviate acid indigestion, heartburn and/or sour stomach, or whenever antacid therapy is the treatment indicated for symptomatic relief of hyperacidity associated with the diagnosis of peptic ulcer, gastritis, peptic esophagitis, gastric hyperacidity, and hiatal hernia. The ratio of aluminum hydroxide to magnesium hydroxide is such that undesirable bowel effects are minimal. Each 5cc dose of SUSPENSION will neutralize approximately 25 mEq of HCl. High concentration of the active ingredients produces prompt, long lasting neutralization without the acid rebound associated with calcium carbonate containing antacids.

Dosage: KUDROX SUSPENSION, half that ordinarily employed with other liquid antacids. Usual dose only 1 teaspoonful 30 minutes after meals and at bedtime. May be taken undiluted or mixed with water or milk. In peptic ulcer, 2 to 4 teaspoonfuls after meals and at bedtime.

Warning: Antacids containing magnesium hydroxide or magnesium salts should be administered cautiously in patients with renal insufficiency.

Drug Interaction Precaution: This product should not be taken if the patient is currently taking a prescription drug containing any form of tetracycline.

Supplied: KUDROX SUSPENSION, 12 oz. plastic bottles (NDC 0091-4475-42).

MILKINOL®

Composition: MILKINOL is a unique formulation containing liquid petrolatum for lubrication with a special mixture of emulsifiers to aid in penetration and softening of fecal mass and to disperse oil in any beverage.

Action and Uses: Pleasant, dependable MILKINOL provides safe, gentle lubrication for the constipation problem. No oily taste, no purgative griping, not habit forming, sugar free.

Dosage: Adults 1 to 2 tablespoonfuls. Children over 6: 1 to 2 teaspoonfuls. Infants, young children, expectant mothers, aged or bedridden patients, use only as directed by physician. Pour MILKINOL in a glass, add ¼ glass fruit juice, soft drink, milk, or even water. Stir and drink.

Precautions: Prolonged usage, without intermission is not advised. Should be given at bedtime ONLY.

Supplied: 8 oz. glass bottles (NDC 0091-7580-08).

Lank Laboratories, Inc.
136 EAST 64 STREET
NEW YORK, NY 10021

NATRASAN®

Description: NATRASAN provides gently-stimulating bulk and smooth stool-softening action to encourage natural, satisfying, and comfortable relief from functional constipation.

All vegetable NATRASAN powder is a highly refined mucilloid of blond psyllium (Plantago Ovata), together with an equal amount of dextrose as a dispersing agent.

Each teaspoonful of NATRASAN contains a negligible amount of sodium and approximately 14 calories.

Indications: Natural vegetable laxative for treatment of constipation.

Warning: Keep this and all medications out of the reach of children.

Dosage and Administration: Usual adult dosage: 1 heaping teaspoonful 1 to 3 times daily (as needed). Children less, according to age.

Directions:
1. Fill ½ glass with water, milk, or juice. Then, sprinkle heaping teaspoonful of "Natrasan" powder into liquid.
2. Stir briskly. Then drink immediately. Be sure to follow with additional glass of water.

Because "Natrasan" contains no chemical drugs or irritating roughage, it may take 2 or 3 days before it starts to become fully effective. But your patience, and continued use, should be well rewarded.

How Supplied: Powder, containers of 8 oz. and 12 oz.

The Lannett Company, Inc.
9000 STATE ROAD
PHILADELPHIA, PA 19136

ACNEDERM™ LOTION

Composition: Grease-free, water-washable, non-staining suspension containing dispersible sulfur 5%, zinc sulfate 1% and zinc oxide 10% in a flesh-tinted powder foundation base. Isopropyl alcohol, 21% by volume.

Action and Uses: Medication of acne lesions. Combats oiliness of skin and excessive keratinization of sebaceous glands; promotes drying and peeling in acne, seborrheic dermatitis, rosacea, tinea corporis and tinea versicolor.

Administration and Dosage: Apply several times daily and at bedtime to affected areas, either with finger tips or sponge. Allow to dry and remove excess with powder puff or cleansing tissue.

Precautions: Discontinue treatment if excessive dryness or skin irritation occurs.

How Supplied: Bottles of 2 fl. oz.
Literature Available: Yes.

MAGNATRIL™ SUSPENSION
AND TABLETS

Composition: Each tablet contains: Aluminum Hydroxide Gel (dried) 4 grs.,

Magnesium Trisilicate 7 grs., Magnesium Hydroxide 2 grs. Each teaspoonful of suspension contains: Colloidal suspension of Magnesium and Aluminum Hydroxides with 4 grs. Magnesium Trisilicate.

Action and Uses: Indicated to alleviate the symptoms of heartburn, sour stomach, and/or acid indigestion.

Drug Interaction Precautions: Do not take this product if you are presently taking a prescription of antibiotic drug containing any form of tetracycline.

Warning: Do not take more than 16 teaspoonsful in a 24 hour period, or use the maximum dosage of this product for more than 2 weeks, except under the advice and supervision of a physician. Do not use this product except under the advice and supervision of a physician if you have kidney disease.

Administration and Dosage: Tablets — Adults: 2 tablets well chewed, 1 or 2 hours following meals, or whenever symptoms are pronounced. Suspension —Adults, 1 to 4 teaspoonsful in water or milk four times a day, twenty minutes after meals and at bedtime, or as directed by a physician.

How Supplied: Tablets—Boxes of 50 and 100 cellophane-stripped tablets. Suspension—Bottles of 12 fl. oz.
Literature Available: Yes.

Laser, Inc.
2000 N. MAIN ST.
CROWN POINT, IN 46307

D-SINUS Capsules
Decongestant—Analgesic

Composition: Each lavender and white capsule contains:
Phenylpropanolamine
  Hydrochloride ..18 mg. (decongestant)
Acetaminophen ....325 mg. (analgesic)

Action: D-SINUS is specifically formulated for the temporary relief of nasal congestion, headache, aches, pains and fever due to sinusitis, colds and influenza. D-SINUS contains no sedatives or antihistamines and, therefore, does not produce drowsiness in most patients. Thus D-SINUS is particularly useful for working patients, students, and others who must remain alert.

D-SINUS contains the vasoconstrictor, phenylpropanolamine, which acts as a "decongestant". D-SINUS contains acetaminophen, a well recognized compound with documented analgesic and antipyretic effects. It produces analgesia as effective as that of aspirin but with less risk of gastric irritation or the liability of kidney damage attributable to certain other analgesics. D-SINUS can be used by patients who are sensitive to aspirin.

Warning: Do not give to children under six years of age or use for more than 10 days, unless directed by a physician.

Caution: Individuals with heart disease, diabetes, thyroid disease or high blood pressure, should use this preparation only as directed by a physician. If stimulation occurs, sleeplessness can be avoided by taking final dose several hours before retiring.

Overdosage: No cases of overdosage with D-SINUS have been reported to date, however, it is likely that symptoms would be those of the individual components. Symptoms of overdosage could include elevated blood pressure, tachycardia, rapid pulse and respiration, dilated pupils, disorientation, nausea, anorexia and excitation of the central nervous system. Treatment is essentially symptomatic. Immediate evacuation of the stomach should be induced through emesis and gastric lavage. If marked excitement is present, one of the short-acting barbiturates or chloral hydrate may be administered.

Dosage: Adults —Two capsules every four hours. Do not exceed eight capsules in 24 hours. **Children,** (6 to 12 years) —One capsule every four hours. Do not exceed four capsules in 24 hours.

How Supplied: Bottles of 24, 100 and 1000 capsules.

FUMATINIC® Tablets

Composition: Each sugar coated tablet contains:

Elemental Iron ....100 mg.
  (as Ferrous Fumarate, 304.2 mg.)
Vitamin C
  (Ascorbic Acid) ....200 mg.
Vitamin B₁₂
  (Oral Concentrate) ....15 mcg.
Folic Acid ....0.1 mg.
Vitamin B₁
  (Thiamine Mononitrate) ....10 mg.
Vitamin B₂
  (Riboflavin) ....10 mg.
Vitamin B₆
  (Pyridoxine Hydrochloride) ....3 mg.
Niacinamide ....20 mg.
Calcium Pantothenate ....10 mg.
Vitamin E
  (d-alpha-tocopherol acetate) .....30 I.U.

Indication: Prevention and treatment of iron deficiency anemia, especially when associated with vitamin C and B complex depletion.

Warning: Keep this and all medications out of the reach of children.

Dosage: Adults, 1 or 2 tablets daily, or as directed by physician.

How Supplied: Bottles of 100 and 1000 tablets.

FUMERIN Tablets

Composition: Each tablet contains:
Ferrous Fumarate ....195 mg.
(Equivalent to 63.9 mg. of elemental iron)

Indications: For use as a source of iron in the treatment of iron deficiency anemia.

Warning: Keep this and all medications out of the reach of children.

Dosage: Adults, 2 or 3 tablets daily, or as directed by physician. Children, consult physician.

How Supplied: Bottles of 100 and 1000.

LACTOCAL Tablets
Prenatal Dietary Supplement

Composition: Each tablet contains:

		% USRDA
Vitamin A (Acetate)	5000 I.U.	62.5
Vitamin D (Calciferol)	400 I.U.	100
Thiamine Mononitrate	3 mg.	176
Riboflavin	2 mg.	100
Pyridoxine Hydrochloride	10 mg.	400
Vitamin B₁₂ (Cobalamin Concentrate)	8 mcg.	100
Niacinamide	20 mg.	100
d-Calcium Pantothenate	10 mg.	92
Vitamin C (Ascorbic Acid)	60 mg.	100
Folic Acid	0.8 mg.	100
Iron (as Ferrous Fumarate 100 mg.)	33 mg.	183
Zinc (as Zinc Sulfate)	15 mg.	100
Copper (as Copper Sulfate)	2 mg.	100
Calcium (as Calcium Carbonate 400 mg.)	160 mg.	12.3
Magnesium (as Magnesium Sulfate)	10 mg.	2.2

% USRDA—Percentage of U.S. Recommended Daily Allowance for pregnant or lactating women.

Warning: Keep this and all medications out of the reach of children.

Indications: As a nutritional supplement in pregnancy and lactation.

Dosage: One tablet daily, or as directed by physician.

How Supplied: Bottles of 100 and 1000 tablets.

Lederle Laboratories
A Division of American Cyanamid Co.
WAYNE, NJ 07470

CENTRUM®
High Potency
Multivitamin-Multimineral Formula

Composition: Each tablet contains:

	For Adults Percentage of U.S. Recommended Daily Allowance (U.S. RDA)
Vitamin A (as Acetate)	5000 I.U. (100%)
Vitamin E (as dl-Alpha Tocopheryl Acetate)	30 I.U. (100%)
Vitamin C (as Ascorbic Acid)	90 mg (150%)
Folic Acid (as Folacin)	400 mcg (100%)
Vitamin B₁ (as Thiamine Mononitrate)	2.25 mg (150%)
Vitamin B₂ (as Riboflavin)	2.6 mg (153%)
Niacinamide	20 mg (100%)
Vitamin B₆ (as Pyridoxine Hydrochloride)	3 mg (150%)
Vitamin B₁₂ (as Cyanocobalamin)	9 mcg (150%)

Vitamin D	400 I.U. (100%)
Biotin	45 mcg (15%)
Pantothenic Acid (as Calcium Pantothenate)	10 mg (100%)
Calcium (as Dibasic Calcium Phosphate)	162 mg (16%)
Phosphorus (as Dibasic Calcium Phosphate)	125 mg (13%)
Iodine (as Potassium Iodide)	150 mcg (100%)
Iron (as Ferrous Fumarate)	27 mg (150%)
Magnesium (as Magnesium Oxide)	100 mg (25%)
Copper (as Cupric Oxide)	3 mg (150%)
Manganese (as Manganese Sulfate)	7.5 mg*
Potassium (as Potassium Sulfate)	7.5 mg*
Zinc (as Zinc Sulfate)	22.5 mg (150%)

*Recognized as essential in human nutrition, but no U.S. RDA established.

Recommended Intake: Adults, 1 tablet daily.

How Supplied:
Capsule-shaped tablets, light peach, engraved LL— bottles of 100 tablets
[*Shown in Product Identification Section*]

FERRO-SEQUELS®
(sustained release iron)
Capsules

Composition: Each capsule contains 150 mg. of ferrous fumarate equivalent to approximately 50 mg. of elemental iron, so prepared that it is released over a 5 to 6 hour period, and 100 mg. of docusate sodium (DSS) to counteract constipating effect of iron.

Indications: For the treatment of iron deficiency anemias.

Dosage: 1 capsule, once or twice daily or as prescribed by the physician.

Precautions: In case of accidental overdose, seek professional assistance or contact a Poison Control Center immediately.

How Supplied: Capsules (hard shell, light green) printed "Lederle" and "Ferro-Sequels"—bottles of 30, 100, and 1,000; unit-dose 10 × 10's.

Military and USPHS Depots:
NSN 6505-00-149-0103, 30's
NSN 6505-00-074-2981, 1000's
NSN 6505-00-131-8870, individually sealed 100's

Continued on next page

The information on each product appearing here is based on labelling effective in November, 1980 and is either the entire official brochure or an accurate condensation therefrom. Official brochures are enclosed in product packages. Information concerning all Lederle products may be obtained from the Professional Services Department, Lederle Laboratories, Pearl River, New York, 10965.

Lederle—Cont.

FILIBON®
(prenatal tablets)

Each tablet contains:

	For Pregnant or Lactating Women Percentage of U.S. Recommended Daily Allowance (U.S. RDA)
Vitamin A (as Acetate)	5000 I.U. (63%)
Vitamin D$_2$	400 I.U. (100%)
Vitamin E (as dl-Alpha Tocopheryl Acetate)	30 I.U. (100%)
Vitamin C (Ascorbic Acid)	60 mg (100%)
Folic Acid (Folacin)	0.4 mg (50%)
Vitamin B$_1$ (as Thiamine Mononitrate)	1.5 mg (88%)
Vitamin B$_2$ (as Riboflavin)	1.7 mg (85%)
Niacinamide	20 mg (100%)
Vitamin B$_6$ (as Pyridoxine Hydrochloride)	2 mg (80%)
Vitamin B$_{12}$ (as Cyanocobalamin)	6 mcg (75%)
Calcium (as Calcium Carbonate)	125 mg (10%)
Iodine (as Potassium Iodide)	150 mcg (100%)
Iron (as Ferrous Fumarate)	18 mg (100%)
Magnesium (as Magnesium Oxide)	100 mg (22%)

A phosphorus-free vitamin and mineral dietary supplement for use in prenatal care and lactation.

Recommended Intake: 1 daily, or as prescribed by the physician.

How Supplied: Capsule-shaped tablets (film-coated, pink) engraved LL—bottles of 100.

GEVRABON®
(vitamin-mineral supplement)

Composition: Each fluid ounce (30 ml.) contains:

	For Adults Percentage of U.S. Recommended Daily Allowance (U.S. RDA)
Vitamin B$_1$ (as Thiamine Hydrochloride)	5 mg (333%)
Vitamin B$_2$ (as Riboflavin-5-Phosphate Sodium)	2.5 mg (147%)
Niacinamide	50 mg (250%)
Vitamin B$_6$ (Pyridoxine Hydrochloride)	1 mg (50%)
Vitamin B$_{12}$ (as Cyanocobalamin)	1 mcg (17%)
Pantothenic Acid (as D-Pantothenyl Alcohol)	10 mg (100%)
Iodine (as Potassium Iodide)	100 mcg (67%)
Iron (as Ferrous Gluconate)	15 mg (83%)
Magnesium (as Magnesium Chloride)	2 mg (0.5%)
Zinc (as Zinc Chloride)	2 mg (13%)
Inositol	100 mg.
Choline (as Tricholine Citrate)	100 mg.
Manganese (as Manganese Chloride)	2 mg.

Alcohol 18%

*Recognized as essential in human nutrition but no U.S. RDA established.

Indications: For use as a nutritional supplement.

Administration and Dosage: Adult: One ounce (30 ml.) daily or as prescribed by the physician as a nutritional supplement.

How Supplied: Liquid (sherry flavor)—decanters of 16 fl. oz. and bottles of 1 gallon.

VA Depots:
NSN 6505-01-091-7541A

GEVRAL®
Multivitamin and Multimineral Supplement for Adults and Children 4 or More Years of Age
TABLETS

Composition: Each tablet contains:

	For Adults Percentage of U.S. Recommended Daily Allowance (U.S. RDA)
Vitamin A (as Acetate)	5000 I.U. (100%)
Vitamin E (as dl-Alpha Tocopheryl Acetate)	30 I.U. (100%)
Vitamin C (as Ascorbic Acid)	60 mg (100%)
Folic Acid (as Folacin)	0.4 mg (100%)
Vitamin B$_1$ (as Thiamine Mononitrate)	1.5 mg (100%)
Vitamin B$_2$ (as Riboflavin)	1.7 mg (100%)
Niacinaminde	20 mg (100%)
Vitamin B$_6$ (as Pyridoxine Hydrochloride)	2 mg (100%)
Vitamin B$_{12}$ (as Cyanocobalamin)	6 mcg (100%)
Calcium (as Dibasic Calcium Phosphate)	162 mg (16%)
Phosphorus (as Dibasic Calcium Phosphate)	125 mg (13%)
Iodine (as Potassium Iodide)	150 mcg (100%)
Iron (as Ferrous Fumarate)	18 mg (100%)
Magnesium (as Magnesium Oxide)	100 mg (25%)

Indications: Supplementation of the diet.

Administration and Dosage: One tablet daily or as prescribed by the physician.

How Supplied: Tablets (film-coated, brown) engraved LL—bottle of 100.

GEVRAL® T
High Potency Multivitamin and Multimineral Supplement for Adults and Children 4 or More Years of Age
TABLETS

Each tablet contains:

	Percentage of U.S. Recommended Daily Allowance (U.S. RDA)
Vitamin A (as Acetate)	5000 I.U. (100%)
Vitamin E (as dl-Alpha Tocopheryl Acetate)	45 I.U. (150%)
Vitamin C (as Ascorbic Acid)	90 mg (150%)
Folic Acid (as Folacin)	0.4 mg (100%)
Vitamin B$_1$ (as Thiamine Mononitrate)	2.25 mg (150%)
Vitamin B$_2$ (as Riboflavin)	2.6 mg (153%)
Niacinamide	30 mg (150%)
Vitamin B$_6$ (as Pyridoxine Hydrochloride)	3 mg (150%)
Vitamin B$_{12}$ (as Cyanocobalamin)	9 mcg (150%)
Vitamin D$_2$	400 I.U. (100%)
Calcium (as Dibasic Calcium Phosphate)	162 mg (16%)
Phosphorus (as Dibasic Calcium Phosphate)	125 mg (13%)
Iodine (as Potassium Iodide)	225 mcg (150%)
Iron (as Ferrous Fumarate)	27 mg (150%)
Magnesium (as Magnesium Oxide)	100 mg (25%)
Copper (as Cupric oxide)	1.5 mg (150%)
Zinc (as Zinc Oxide)	22.5 mg (150%)

Indications: For the treatment of vitamin and mineral deficiencies.

Dosage: 1 tablet daily or as prescribed by physician.

How Supplied: Tablets (film coated, maroon). Printed LL—bottle of 100.

INCREMIN®
WITH IRON • SYRUP
(vitamins plus iron)
Dietary Supplement

Composition: Each teaspoonful (5 ml.) contains:

Elemental Iron (as Ferric Pyrophosphate)	30 mg.
L-Lysine HCl	300 mg.
Thiamine HCl (B$_1$)	10 mg.
Pyridoxine HCl (B$_6$)	5 mg.
Vitamin B$_{12}$ (Cyanocobalamin)	25 mcgm.
Sorbitol	3.50 Gm.
Alcohol	0.75%

Each teaspoonful (5 ml.) supplies the following Minimum Daily Requirements:

	Child under 6	Child over 6	Adults
Vitamin B$_1$	20 MDR	13$\frac{1}{3}$ MDR	10 MDR
Iron	4 MDR	3 MDR	3 MDR

Indications: For the prevention and treatment of iron deficiency anemia in children and adults. Keep this and all medications out of the reach of children.

Administration and Dosage:
Children
One teaspoonful (5 ml.) daily for the prevention of iron deficiency anemia. Three teaspoonfuls (15 ml.) daily in divided doses for treatment.
Adults
One teaspoonful (5 ml.) for prevention. Four teaspoonfuls (20 ml.) daily in divided doses for treatment.

How Supplied: Syrup (cherry flavor)—bottles of 4 and 16 fl. oz.

LEDERPLEX®
Dietary Supplement of B-Complex Vitamins for Adults and Children 4 or More Years of Age
Capsules—Liquid—Tablets

Each Capsule or Tablet Contains:
For Adults-
Percentage of U.S.
Recommended Daily
Allowance (U.S. RDA)

Vitamin B_1 (as Thiamine
  Mononitrate) .... 2.25 mg (150%)
Vitamin B_2 (as
  Riboflavin) .... 2.6 mg (153%)
Niacinamide.................... 30 mg (150%)
Vitamin B_6 (as Pyridoxine
  Hydrochloride)............ 3 mg (150%)
Vitamin B_{12} (as
  Cyanocobalamin)........ 9 mcg (150%)
Pantothenic Acid (as Calcium
  Pantothenate)............. 15 mg (150%)
Indications: For the prevention of Vitamin B complex deficiencies.
Dosage: *Children*—1 capsule or tablet daily.
Adults—1 capsule or tablet daily.

Each 10 ml (2 teaspoonfuls) contains:

Vitamin B_1 (as Thiamine
  Hydrochloride)............ 2.25 mg (150%)
Vitamin B_2 (Riboflavin) 2.6 mg (153%)
Niacinamide.................. 30 mg (150%)
Vitamin B_6 (as Pyridoxine
  Hydrochloride)............ 3 mg (150%)
Vitamin B_{12} (as Cobalamin
  Concentrate NF)......... 9 mcg (150%)
Pantothenic Acid (as
  Panthenol) .... 15 mg (150%)
Preservative:
  Sodium Benzoate .... 0.1% w/w
Indications: For the prevention of Vitamin B complex deficiencies:
Recommended intake:
Adults—10 ml. or 2 teaspoonfuls daily.
How Supplied: Capsules (hard shell, brown)—bottles of 100. Liquid (orange flavor)—bottles of 12 fl. oz. Tablets (coated brown)—bottles of 100.

NEOLOID®
(emulsified castor oil)

Composition: NEOLOID Emulsified Castor Oil U.S.P. 36.4% (w/w) with preservative, emulsifying and flavoring agents in water. NEOLOID is an emulsion with an exceptionally bland, pleasant taste.
Indications: For the treatment of isolated bouts of constipation.
Administration and Dosage:
Infants—½ to 1½ teaspoonfuls.
Children—Adjust between infant and adult dose.
Adult— Average dose, 2 to 4 tablespoonfuls, or as prescribed by the physician.
Precautions: Not to be used when abdominal pain, nausea, vomiting, or other symptoms of appendicitis are present. Frequent or continued use of this preparation may result in dependence on laxatives. Do not use during pregnancy except on competent advice. Keep this and all drugs out of the reach of children. In case of accidental overdosage seek professional assistance or contact a Poison Control Center immediately.

How Supplied: Bottles of 4 fl. oz. (peppermint flavor).

PERITINIC®
(hematinic with vitamins and fecal softener)
Tablets

Each tablet contains:
Elemental Iron
  (as Ferrous Fumarate).............100 mg.
Docusate Sodium U.S.P. (DSS)
  (to counteract the con-
  constipating effect of iron)......100 mg.
Vitamin B_1
  (as Thiamine Mononitrate)......7.5 mg.
  (7 ½ MDR)
Vitamin B_2 (Riboflavin)................7.5 mg.
  (6¼ MDR)
Vitamin B_6
  (Pyridoxine Hydrochloride)......7.5 mg.
Vitamin B_{12}
  (Cyanocobalamin) ....50 mcg.
Vitamin C (Ascorbic Acid)..........200 mg.
  (6⅔ MDR)
Niacinamide (3 MDR)....................30 mg.
Folic Acid ....0.05 mg.
Pantothenic Acid
  (as D-Pantothenyl Alcohol).......15 mg.
MDR—Adult Minimum Daily Requirement
Precaution: In case of accidental overdose, seek professional assistance or contact a Poison Control Center immediately.
Action and Uses: In the prevention of nutritional anemias, certain vitamin deficiencies, and iron-deficiency anemias.
Administration and Dosage:
Adults: 1 or 2 tablets daily.
How Supplied: Tablets (maroon, capsule-shaped, film coated)—bottles of 60.

RHULICAINE™

Active Ingredient: Benzocaine, Triclosan, and Menthol. SD 40 Alcohol 32% w/w, Isopropyl Alcohol 9% w/w.
Indications:
SOOTHES • ANTISEPTIC • AIDS HEALING
Prompt cooling relief of sunburn pain. Antiseptic protection for minor skin irritations: cuts, burns, scrapes and scratches.
FOR EXTERNAL USE ONLY.
Precaution: Not for deep or puncture wounds or serious burns. Not for prolonged use. If condition for which this preparation is used persists, or if infection, rash or irritation develops, discontinue use and consult a physician.
Dosage and Administration: Use several times daily, or as necessary for relief of pain and antiseptic protection.
How Supplied: 4 oz can.
[*Shown in Product Identification Section*]

RHULICREAM®
RHULIGEL®
RHULIHIST®
RHULISPRAY®
(analgesic-anesthetic)

Composition: RHULICREAM: A soothing, bland ointment containing as active ingredients:

Zirconium oxide .... 1 %
Benzocaine .... 1 %
Menthol .... 0.7 %
Camphor.. 0.3 %
Inactive Ingredients:
Isopropyl alcohol .... 8.8 %
Methylparaben .... 0.08 %
Propylparaben .... 0.02 %

RHULIGEL: Active ingredients are:
Phenylcarbinol .... 2 % w/w
Menthol USP .... 0.3 % w/w
Camphor USP..................... 0.3 % w/w
Alcohol................................. 31 % w/w

RHULIHIST: Active ingredients are:
Tripelennamine HCl USP.............. 1 %
Calamine USP................................ 3 %
Zirconium oxide .... 1 %
Benzocaine .... 1 %
Camphor USP .... 0.1 %
Menthol USP.................................. 0.1 %
Preservatives:
Methylparaben .... 0.08 %
Propylparaben .... 0.02 %

RHULISPRAY: A cool, soothing, convenient spray that is nonstaining because it dries instantly.
Active ingredients are: (percent w/w)
Phenylcarbinol 0.674%
Menthol 0.025%
Camphor 0.253%
Calamine 4.710%
Benzocaine 1.153%
Isopropyl Alcohol 28.767%
Inactive Ingredients and
  Propellant 64.418%

All:
Indications: For the temporary relief of itching, pain, and discomfort of ivy and oak poisoning, nonpoisonous insect bites, mild sunburn and other minor skin irritations.
Administration and Dosage: Apply to affected area 2 or 3 times daily and at bedtime.
Precautions: Avoid application around the eyes and genitalia, or on infected wounds. A physician should be consulted if the condition persists.
How Supplied: RHULICREAM: Tubes of 1 oz. and 2 oz. RHULIGEL: Tubes of 2 oz. RHULIHIST: Bottles of 4 fl. oz.; plastic squeeze bottle of 75 ml. RHULISPRAY: (Hydrocarbon Aerosol) 2 and 4 oz. cans.
[*Shown in Product Identification Section*]

Continued on next page

The information on each product appearing here is based on labelling effective in November, 1980 and is either the entire official brochure or an accurate condensation therefrom. Official brochures are enclosed in product packages. Information concerning all Lederle products may be obtained from the Professional Services Department, Lederle Laboratories, Pearl River, New York, 10965.

Lederle—Cont.

RHULICORT™
(Hydrocortisone 0.5% in soothing AQUATAIN™)
Cream and Lotion

Active Ingredient: Hydrocortisone Acetate equivalent to 0.5% Hydrocortisone
Preservative: Benzyl Alcohol 2.0%
Indications: For the temporary relief of minor skin irritations, itching, and rashes due to poison ivy, poison oak, poison sumac, insect bites, eczema, dermatitis, soaps, detergents, cosmetics, and jewelry, and for itchy genital and anal areas.
Directions for Use: *For adults and children 2 years of age and older*—apply to affected area not more than 3 to 4 times daily. For children under 2 years of age there is no recommended dosage except under the advice and supervision of a physician.
Warnings: For external use only. Avoid contact with eyes. If condition worsens, or if symptoms persist for more than 7 days, discontinue use of this product and consult a physician. Do not use on children under 2 years of age except under the advice and supervision of a physician. Keep this and all drugs out of the reach of children. In case of accidental ingestion, seek professional assistance or contact a Poison Control Center immediately.
How Supplied:
Cream - 20 gm tubes
Lotion - 60 ml bottles.

STRESSCAPS®
(Stress formula B+C vitamins)

Each capsule contains:

For Adults-Percentage of U.S. Recommended Daily Allowance (U.S. RDA)

Vitamin B_1 (as Thiamine
  Mononitrate) .... 10 mg (667%)
Vitamin B_2 (as Riboflavin)10 mg (588%)
Vitamin B_6 (as Pyridoxine
  Hydrochloride)............ 2 mg (100%)
Vitamin B_{12}
  (as Cyanocobalamin).. 6 mcg (100%)
Vitamin C (as Ascorbic
  Acid)............................. 300 mg (500%)
Niacinamide.................... 100 mg (500%)
Pantothenic Acid (as Calcium
  Pantothenate).............. 20 mg (200%)
Indications: For the treatment of vitamin deficiencies.
Dosage and Administration: Adults, 1 capsule daily or as directed by the physician.
How Supplied: *Capsules* (hard shell, opaque brown)—bottles of 30, 100, and 500.

STRESSTABS® 600
High Potency
Stress Formula Vitamins

Each tablet contains:

For Adults-Percentage of U.S. Recommended Daily Allowance (U.S. RDA)

Vitamin E (as *dl*-Alpha
  Tocopheryl Acetate)... 30 I.U. (100%)
Vitamin C (L-Ascorbic
  Acid)...........................600 mg (1000%)
B_1 (as Thiamine
  Mononitrate) .... 15 mg (1000%)
Vitamin B_2 (as
  Riboflavin) .... 15 mg (882%)
Niacinamide ....100 mg (500%)
Vitamin B_6 (as Pyridoxine
  Hydrochloride)............ 5 mg (250%)
Vitamin B_{12}
  (as Cyanocobalamin) 12 mcg (200%)
Pantothenic Acid (as Calcium
  Pantothenate USP).... 20 mg (200%)
Recommended Intake: Adults, 1 tablet daily or as directed by physician.
Supplied: Capsule-shaped tablets (film-coated orange)-bottles of 30, 60 and 500; unit-dose 10 x 10's.
VA Depot:
NSN 6505-00-375-4618A
[*Shown in Product Identification Section*]

STRESSTABS® 600 with IRON
High Potency
Stress Formula Vitamins

Each tablet contains:

For Adults-Percentage of U.S. Recommended Daily Allowance (U.S. RDA)

Vitamin E (as *dl*-Alpha
  Tocopheryl Acetate) ..30 I.U. (100%)
Vitamin C (L-Ascorbic
  Acid) ....600 mg (1000%)
Folic Acid (as
  Folacin) .... 400 mcg (100%)
Vitamin B_1 (as Thiamine
  Mononitrate) .... 15 mg (1000%)
Vitamin B_2 (as
  Riboflavin) .... 15 mg (882%)
Niacinamide...................100 mg (500%)
Vitamin B_6 (as Pyridoxine
  Hydrochloride) .... 25 mg (1250%)
Vitamin B_{12}
  (as Cyanocobalamin) 12 mcg (200%)
Pantothenic Acid (as Calcium
  Pantothenate USP) ... 20 mg (200%)
Iron (as Ferrous
  Fumarate) .... 27 mg (150%)
Recommended Intake: Adults, 1 tablet daily or as directed by physician.
Supplied: Capsule-shaped tablets (film-coated, orange-red, scored)—bottles of 30 and 60.
[*Shown in Product Identification Section*]

STRESSTABS® 600 with ZINC
High Potency
Stress Formula Vitamins

Each tablet contains:

For Adults-Percentage of U.S. Recommended Daily Allowance (U.S. RDA)

Vitamin E (as *dl*-Alpha
  Tocopheryl Acetate) 45 I.U. (150%)
Vitamin C
  (L-Ascorbic Acid).....600 mg. (1000%)
Folic Acid (as
  Folacin) ....400 mcg. (100%)
Vitamin B_1 (as Thiamine Mononitrate)....20 mg. (1333%)
Vitamin B_2
  (as Riboflavin)............10 mg. (588%)
Niacinamide................100 mg. (500%)
Vitamin B_6 (as Pyridoxine Hydrochloride)....10 mg. (500%)
Vitamin B_{12} (as Cyano-
  Cobalamin) ....25 mcg. (417%)
Pantothenic Acid (as Calcium
  Pantothenate USP) 25 mg. (250%)
Copper (as Cupric
  Oxide) .... 3 mg. (150%)
Zinc (as Zinc Sulfate)23.9 mg. (159%)
Recommended Intake: Adults, 1 tablet daily or as directed by the physician.
Supplied: Capsule-shaped Tablet (film coated, peach color)—bottles of 30 and 60.
[*Shown in Product Identification Section*]

ZINCON®
Dandruff Shampoo

Contains pyrithione zinc 1%, a clinically proven anti-dandruff compound to help control dandruff flaking. Used regularly, ZINCON leaves hair clean and easy to manage. It is recommended by dermatologists, does not cause dry or oily hair, has a pleasant fragrance and may be used on gray or dyed hair.
How Supplied: 4 fl. oz. and 8 fl. oz. unbreakable plastic bottles.

Leeming Division
Pfizer, Inc.
100 JEFFERSON ROAD
PARSIPPANY, NJ 07054

BEN–GAY® External Analgesic Products

Description: Ben-Gay is a combination of methyl salicylate and menthol in a suitable base for topical application. In addition to the Original Ointment (methyl salicylate, 18.3%; menthol, 16%), Ben-Gay is offered as a Greaseless/Stainless Ointment (methyl salicylate, 15%; menthol, 10%), an Extra Strength Balm (methyl salicylate, 30%; menthol, 8%), a Lotion and a Clear Gel (both of which contain methyl salicylate, 15%; menthol, 7%).
Action and Uses: Methyl salicylate and menthol are external analgesics which stimulate sensory receptors, including receptors of warmth and cold. This produces a counter-irritant response which alleviates the more severe pain in the

joints and muscles where applied to provide transient, temporary symptomatic relief.

Several double blind clinical studies of Ben-Gay products have shown the effectiveness of the menthol-methyl salicylate combination in counteracting minor pain of skeletal muscle stress and arthritis.

Three studies involving a total of 102 normal subjects in which muscle soreness was experimentally induced showed statistically significant beneficial results from use of the active product vs. placebo for lowered Muscle Action Potential (spasms), greater rise in threshold of muscular pain and greater reduction in perceived muscular pain.

Six clinical studies of a total of 207 subjects suffering from minor pain and skeletal muscular spasms due to osteoarthritis and rheumatoid arthritis showed the active product to give statistically significant beneficial results vs. placebo for lowered Muscle Action Potential (spasm), greater relief of perceived pain, increased range of motion of the affected joints and increased digital dexterity.

Directions: Rub generously into painful area, then massage gently until Ben-Gay disappears. Repeat as necessary.

Warning: Use only as directed. Keep away from children to avoid accidental poisoning. Do not swallow. If swallowed, induce vomiting, call a physician. Keep away from eyes, mucous membrane, broken or irritated skin. If skin irritation develops, pain lasts 10 days or more, redness is present, or with arthritis-like conditions in children under 12, call a physician.

DESITIN® OINTMENT

Description: Desitin Ointment is a combination of Zinc Oxide (40%), Cod Liver Oil (high in Vitamins A & D), and Talc in a petrolatum-lanolin base suitable for topical application.

Actions and Uses: Desitin Ointment is designed to provide relief of diaper rash, superficial wounds and burns, and other minor skin irritations. It helps prevent incidence of diaper rash, protects against urine and other irritants, soothes chafed skin and promotes healing.

Relief and protection is afforded by the combination of Zinc Oxide, Cod Liver Oil, Lanolin and Petrolatum. They provide a physical barrier by forming a protective coating over skin or mucous membrane which serves to reduce further effects of irritants on the affected area and relieves burning, pain or itch produced by them. In addition to its protective properties, Zinc Oxide acts as an astringent that helps heal local irritation and inflammation by lessening the flow of mucus and other secretions.

Several studies have shown the effectiveness of Desitin Ointment in the relief and prevention of diaper rash.

Two clinical studies involving 90 infants demonstrated the effectiveness of Desitin Ointment in curing diaper rash. The diaper rash area was treated with Desitin Ointment at each diaper change for a period of 24 hours, while the untreated

site served as controls. A significant reduction was noted in the severity and area of diaper dermatitis on the treated area.

Ninety-seven (97) babies participated in a 12-week study to show that Desitin Ointment helps prevent diaper rash. Approximately half of the infants (49) were treated with Desitin Ointment on a regular daily basis. The other half (48) received the ointment as necessary to treat any diaper rash which occurred. The incidence as well as the severity of diaper rash was significantly less among the babies using the ointment on a regular daily basis.

In a comparative study of the efficacy of Desitin Ointment vs. a baby powder, forty-five babies were observed for a total of eight weeks. Results support the conclusion that Desitin Ointment is a better prophylactic against diaper rash than the baby powder.

Several other studies show that Desitin Ointment helps relieve other skin disorders, such as contact dermatitis.

Directions: To prevent diaper rash, apply Desitin Ointment to the diaper area—especially at bedtime when exposure to wet diapers may be prolonged. If diaper rash is present, or at the first sign of redness, minor skin irritation or chafing, simply apply Desitin Ointment three or four times daily as needed. In superficial noninfected surface wounds and minor burns, apply a thin layer of Desitin Ointment, using a gauze dressing, if necessary. For external use only.

How Supplied: Desitin Ointment is available in 1.25 ounce (35g), 2.25 ounce (63g), 4.25 (120g) 8 ounce (226g) tubes, and 1-lb. (452g) jars.

NYTILAX® TABLETS
(sennosides A and B)

Description: Each blue Nytilax Tablet contains 12 mg. of crystalline Sennosides A and B calcium salts, the most highly purified form available for these glycosides, derived from the *Cassia Acutifolia* plant and standardized by chemical rather than biological assay.

Actions and Uses: Indicated for relief of chronic or occasional functional constipation. Recent additional support has been given to the current theory that upon ingestion, the sugar glycosides Sennosides A and B are transported without chemical change through the alimentary canal to the colon, where they are hydrolyzed to their aglycone derivatives by the colonic flora, leading to localized nerve plexus stimulation and peristalsis-induced defecation. The effect is gentle and predictable, with well-formed stools being produced, usually within 8–10 hours. Contrary to a previously published opinion, the clinical evidence now available strongly indicates that the senna glycosides are not excreted into the milk of lactating mothers and, therefore, have no effect on the bowel function of nursing infants. The high chemical purity of the Sennoside A and B calcium salts facilitates individualized dosage regulation and further minimizes the possibility of rare adverse reactions such as loose

stools or abdominal discomfort. Sennosides A and B, as contained in Nytilax Tablets, have been found in numerous clinical studies to be highly effective for varieties of functional constipation: chronic, geriatric, antepartum and postpartum, drug-induced, pediatric and surgical-related, and in lower bowel x-ray preparative procedures.

Dosage and Administration:
Adults—1 or 2 tablets at bedtime. If you do not readily respond to laxatives, take 3 tablets at bedtime.
Children—Consult a physician.
Warnings: Do not take any laxative when abdominal pain, nausea or vomiting are present. Frequent or prolonged use of laxatives may result in dependence.
Keep out of the reach of children.
How Supplied: Boxes of 12 or 24 tablets.

RHEABAN® TABLETS and LIQUID
(attapulgite)

Description: Rheaban is an anti-diarrheal medication containing activated attapulgite and is offered in liquid and tablet forms.

The liquid is mint-flavored with each fluid ounce containing 4.2 grams of activated attapulgite.

Each white Rheaban tablet contains 600 mg. of collodial activated attapulgite.

Rheaban contains no narcotics, opiates or other habit-forming drugs.

Actions and Uses: Rheaban is indicated for relief of diarrhea and the cramps and pains associated with it. Attapulgite, which has been activated by thermal treatment, is a highly sorptive substance which absorbs nutrients and digestive enzymes as well as noxious gases, irritants, toxins and some bacteria and viruses that are common causes of diarrhea.

In clinical studies to show the effectiveness in relieving diarrhea and its symptoms, 100 subjects suffering from acute gastroenteritis with diarrhea participated in a double-blind comparison of Rheaban to a placebo. Patients treated with the attapulgite product showed significantly improved relief of diarrhea and its symptoms vs. the placebo.

Dosage and Administration:
LIQUID
Adults—2 tablespoons after initial bowel movement, 1 tablespoon after subsequent bowel movements.
Children 6 to 12 years—1 tablespoon after initial bowel movement, ½ tablespoon after each subsequent bowel movement.
Children 3 to 6 years—½ tablespoon after initial bowel movement, ½ tablespoon after each subsequent bowel movement.
Infant and Children under 3 years—Only as directed by physician.
TABLETS
Adults—2 tablets after initial bowel movement, 2 tablets after each subsequent bowel movement.

Continued on next page

Leeming—Cont.

Children 6 to 12 years—1 tablet after initial bowel movement, 1 tablet after each subsequent bowel movement.
Children 3 to 6 years—Use Rheaban Liquid.

Warnings: Do not use for more than two days, or in the presence of high fever, Tablets should not be used for children under 6 years of age, and liquid should not be used for children under 3 years of age, unless directed by physician. If diarrhea persists consult a physician.

How Supplied:
 Liquid—5.5 ounce bottles
 Tablets—Boxes of 12 tablets

UNISOM® NIGHTTIME SLEEP-AID
(doxylamine succinate)

Description: Pale blue oval scored tablets containing 25 mg. of doxylamine succinate, 2-(α-(2-dimethylaminoethoxy)α-methylbenzyl) pyridine succinate.

Action and Uses: Doxylamine succinate is an antihistamine of the ethanolamine class, which characteristically shows a high incidence of sedation. In a comparative clinical study of over 20 antihistamines on more than 3000 subjects, doxylamine succinate 25 mg. was one of the three most sedating antihistamines, producing a significantly reduced latency to end of wakefulness and comparing favorably with established hypnotic drugs such as secobarbital and pentobarbital in sedation activity. It was chosen as the antihistamine, based on dosage, causing the earliest onset of sleep. In another clinical study, doxylamine succinate 25 mg. scored better than secobarbital 100 mg. as a nighttime hypnotic. Two additional, identical clinical studies involving a total of 121 subjects demonstrated that doxylamine succinate 25 mg. reduced the sleep latency period by a third, compared to placebo. Duration of sleep was 26.6% longer with doxylamine succinate, and the quality of sleep was rated higher with the drug than with placebo. An EEG study of 6 subjects confirmed the results of these studies.

Administration and Dosage: One tablet 30 minutes before retiring. Not for children under 12 years of age.

Side Effects: Occasional anticholinergic effects may be seen.

Precautions: Unisom® should be taken only at bedtime.

Contraindications: Asthma, glaucoma, enlargement of the prostate gland. This product should not be taken by pregnant women, or those who are nursing a baby.

Warnings: Should be taken with caution if alcohol is being consumed. Product should not be taken if patient is concurrently on any other drug, without prior consultation with physician. Should not be taken for longer than two weeks unless approved by physician.

How Supplied: Boxes of 8 or 16 tablets.

VISINE® Eye Drops
(tetrahydrozoline HCl)

Description: Visine is a sterile, isotonic, buffered ophthalmic solution containing tetrahydrozoline hydrochloride 0.05%, boric acid, sodium borate, sodium chloride and water. It is preserved with benzalkonium chloride 0.01% and disodium edetate 0.1%.

Indications: Visine is a decongestant ophthalmic solution designed to provide symptomatic relief of conjunctival edema and hyperemia secondary to ocular allergies, minor irritations, and so called non-specific or catarrhal conjunctivitis. Beneficial effects include amelioration of burning, irritation, pruritus, soreness, and excessive lacrimation. Relief is afforded by tetrahydrozoline hydrochloride, a sympathomimetic agent, which brings about decongestion by vasoconstriction. Reddened eyes are rapidly whitened by this effective vasoconstrictor, which limits the local vascular response by constricting the small blood vessels. The onset of vasoconstriction becomes apparent within minutes and the effect is prolonged. While some vasoconstrictors may produce a dilation of the pupil or cause rebound hyperemia, there is no evidence that the use of Visine, with tetrahydrozoline hydrochloride, results in either condition.

The effectiveness of Visine in relieving conjunctival hyperemia and associated symptoms has been demonstrated by numerous clinicals, including several double blind studies, involving more than 2,000 subjects suffering from acute or chornic hyperemia induced by a variety of conditions. Visine was found to be efficacious in providing relief from conjunctival hyperemia and associated symptoms in over 90% of subjects.

Dosage and Administration: Place one or two drops in each eye two or three times a day or as directed by a physician. To avoid contamination of this product, do not touch tip of container to any other surface. Replace cap after using.

Warning: Visine should be used only for minor eye irritations. If relief is not obtained within 72 hours, or if irritation or redness persists or increases, discontinue use and consult your physician. In some instances irritation or redness is due to serious eye conditions such as infection, foreign body in the eye, or chemical corneal trauma requiring the attention of a physician. If you experience severe eye pain, headache, rapid change of vision, sudden appearance of floating spots, acute redness of the eyes, pain on exposure to light, or double vision, consult a physician at once. If you have glaucoma, do not use this product except under the advice and supervision of a physician.

How Supplied: In 0.5 fl. oz., 0.75 fl. oz. and 1.0 fl. oz. plastic dispenser bottle and 0.5 fl. oz. plastic bottle with dropper.

VISINE® A.C. Eye Drops
(tetrahydrozoline hydrochloride and zinc sulfate)

Description: Visine A.C. is a sterile, isotonic, buffered ophthalmic solution containing tetrahydrozoline hydrochloride 0.05%, zinc sulfate 0.25%, boric acid, sodium citrate, sodium chloride, and water. It is preserved with benzalkonium chloride 0.01% and disodium edetate 0.1%.

Indications: Visine A.C. is an ophthalmic solution combining the effects of the decongestant tetrahydrozoline hydrochloride with the astringent effects of zinc sulfate. It is designed to provide symptomatic relief of conjunctival edema and hyperemia secondary to ocular allergies, minor irritation due to colds and other causes, as well as the so called non-specific or catarrhal conjunctivitis. Beneficial effects include amelioration of burning, irritation, pruritus, soreness, excessive lacrimation and removal of mucus from the eye. Relief is afforded by both ingredients, tetrahydrozoline hydrochloride and zinc sulfate.

Tetrahydrozoline hydrochloride is a sympathomimetic agent, which brings about decongestion by vasoconstriction. Reddened eyes are rapidly whitened by this effective vasoconstrictor, which limits the local vascular response by constricting the small blood vessels. The onset of vasoconstriction becomes apparent within minutes and the effect is prolonged. While some vasoconstrictors produce a dilation of the pupil or cause rebound hyperemia, there is no evidence that the use of Visine, with tetrahydrozoline hydrochloride, results in either condition. Zinc sulfate is an ocular astringent which, by precipitating protein, helps to clear mucus from the outer surface of the eye.

The effectiveness of Visine A.C. in relieving conjunctival hyperemia and associated symptoms induced by cold and allergy has been clinically demonstrated. In one double blind study involving cold and allergy sufferers experiencing acute episodes of minor eye irritation, Visine A.C. produced statistically significant beneficial results versus a placebo of normal saline solution in relieving irritation of bulbar conjunctiva, irritation of palpebral conjunctiva, and mucous build-up. Treatment with Visine A.C. also significantly improved burning and itching symptoms.

Dosage and Administration: Place one or two drops in each eye two or three times a day or as directed by a physician. To avoid contamination of this product, do not touch tip of container to any other surface. Replace cap after using

Warning: Visine A.C. should be used only for minor eye irritations. If relief is not obtained within 72 hours, or if irritation or redness persists or increases, discontinue use and consult your physician. In some instances irritation or redness is due to serious eye conditions such as infection, foreign body in the eye, or other mechanical or chemical corneal trauma requiring the attention of a physician. If you experience severe eye pain, headache, rapid change in vision, sudden ap-

pearance of floating spots, acute redness of the eyes, pain on exposure to light, or double-vision consult a physician at once. If you have glaucoma, do not use this product except under the advice and supervision of a physician.
How Supplied: In 0.5 fl. oz. and 1.0 fl. oz. plastic dispenser bottle.

Lehn & Fink Products Company
Division of Sterling Drug Inc.
225 SUMMIT AVENUE
MONTVALE, NJ 07645

MEDI-QUIK®
Antiseptic-Anesthetic First Aid Spray

Description: Lidocaine 2.5%, Benzalkonium Chloride 0.1%, Ethyl alcohol 38% by volume.
Indications: First aid spray for sunburn, minor cuts, scrapes, poison ivy, burns, insect bites.
Action: Antiseptic-Anesthetic First-Aid Spray.
Caution: "Not for deep or puncture wounds or serious burns. Not for prolonged use. If the condition for which Medi-Quik is used persists, or irritation, redness, swelling or pain persists or increases, or a rash or infection develops, discontinue use and consult physician."
Symptoms and Treatment of Oral Overdosage: None from small amounts. Large amounts produce ethyl alcohol effects.
Dosage and Administration: "Hold can 4 to 6 inches from surface. Press button on top of can. Spray only until area is wetted. This will dry quickly to a water-washable, non-staining film. May be repeated as necessary."
How Supplied: Spray can of 3 oz. and Pump Spray of 4 oz.

STRI-DEX®
Medicated Pads for acne vulgaris

Description: Clear, stainless solution containing salicylic acid 0.5%, alcohol 28% by volume in a vehicle consisting of water, sulfonated alkyl benzenes, citric acid, sodium carbonate, fragrance and simethicone.
Indications: Aid in the topical treatment of acne vulgaris.
Action: Comedolytic on microcomedones. Helps prevent development of comedones and papules. Softens blackheads, helps resolve comedones and papules and helps prevent infection. Removes dirt, bacteria and oil.
Precautions: "Keep away from eyes. If skin irritation develops, discontinue use and consult physician."
Symptoms and Treatment of Oral Overdosage: None with ingestion of small amounts. Larger amounts can cause gastrointestinal irritation with nausea and vomiting. Treatment: dilute with milk or water. Empty stomach only if very large quantities ingested.
Dosage and Administration: "1. Wash and dry face. 2. Wipe the Stri-Dex Medicated Pad over your face in the morning and at night. 3. Girls-apply your makeup over the Stri-Dex medication. Boys-apply in place of your regular shaving lotion."
Professional Labeling: Patient should be informed that a certain amount of dryness or peeling is to be expected.
How Supplied: Containers containing 42 pads or 75 pads.

STRI-DEX® B.P.
10% Benzoyl Peroxide Cream for acne vulgaris

Description: 10% Benzoyl Peroxide in a greaseless, colorless, odorless vanishing cream.
Indications: For topical treatment of acne vulgaris.
Action: Effective antibacterial against P. acnes. Also provides peeling and drying action. Helps clear comedones, papules and pustules and prevent formation of new lesions. Reduces skin oiliness.
Caution: "Avoid contact with eyes, lips and mouth. If excessive dryness or undue irritation of the skin develops, discontinue use and consult physician. May bleach dyed fabrics."
Directions: "Wash acne areas thoroughly and apply cream once a day initially, then two or three times a day, or as directed by a physician."
Symptoms and Treatment of Oral Overdosage: Moderately irritating and toxic if swallowed. Dilute with demulcents such as milk or eggwhite.
How Supplied: Tubes of 1 oz.

Loma Linda Foods
RIVERSIDE, CA 92515

I-SOYALAC®   Ⓚ PAREVE
Description: A corn free, milk free nutritionally balanced formula for infants. Liquid products are packed in solderless cans, eliminating lead from this source. i-Soyalac contains a negligible amount of soy carbohydrates and has a high polyunsaturated to saturated fatty acid ratio together with a liberal supply of Vitamin E. (For the significance of this, see Potter and Nestel, "The effects of dietary fatty acids and cholesterol on the milk lipids of lactating women, and the plasma cholesterol of breast-fed infants." Am., J. Clin. Nutr. 29, 54, 1976; Hodgson et al. "Comparison of serum cholesterol in children fed high, moderate, or low cholesterol milk diets during neonatal period." Metabolism 25, 739, 1976; Widdowson et al. "Body fat of British and Dutch infants." Brit. Med. J., March 22, 653, 1975). When prepared as directed, one quart of i-Soyalac daily, contains essential nutrients in balanced combination and sufficient quantities to provide adequate nutrition for infants.
Action and Uses: When breast milk is not available or the supply is inadequate, i-Soyalac provides a highly satisfactory alternative or supplement. It is especially valuable for all—infants, children, and adults—who may be sensitive to animal milk and/or corn products. It may also be prescribed for low cholesterol di-

ets; for pre-operative and post-operative diets; for fortifying any milk free diet; for geriatric cases, etc.
Preparation: Standard dilution is—
Ready to Serve	—as canned
Concentrate	—one part mixed with an equal part water
Powder (can)	—four scoops to one cup water
Powder (pouch)	—contents of one pouch to 8 fl. oz. of water

Typical Analysis: Standard Dilution
%W/V

Protein	2.1
Fat	3.7
Carbohydrates	6.6
Minerals	0.4
Fiber	0.0
Water	90.0
Calories	20 per fluid oz.

One quart of i-Soyalac, standard dilution, provides the following nutrients:

Vitamin A	(I.U.)	2000
Vitamin D	(I.U.)	400
Vitamin E	(I.U.)	15
Vitamin K	(mcg)	50
Vitamin C	(mg)	60
Vitamin B₁	(mcg)	500
Vitamin B₂	(mcg)	600
Niacin	(mg)	8
Vitamin B₆	(mcg)	400
Folic Acid	(mcg)	100
Pantothenic Acid	(mg)	3
Vitamin B₁₂	(mcg)	2
Biotin	(mcg)	50
Choline	(mg)	100
Inositol	(mg)	100
Calcium	(mg)	600
Phosphorus	(mg)	400
Magnesium	(mg)	60
Iron	(mg)	12
Iodine	(mcg)	45
Copper	(mcg)	500
Zinc	(mg)	5
Manganese	(mcg)	500
Potassium	(mg)	750
Sodium	(mg)	350
Chloride	(mg)	500

Supply:
i-Soyalac Ready to Serve liquid:
32 fl. oz. cans, 6 cans per case
i-Soyalac Double Strength Concentrate:
13 fl. oz. cans, 12 cans per case
i-Soyalac Powder—Cans:
1 lb. cans, 12 cans per case
i-Soyalac Powder—Pouches:
34 g. pouches, 18 pouches per case

SOYALAC®   Ⓚ PAREVE
Description: A milk free nutritionally balanced formula for infants. Liquid products are packed in solderless cans, eliminating lead from this source. Soyalac has a high polyunsaturated to saturated fatty acid ratio together with a liberal supply of Vitamin E. (For the significance of this, see Potter and Nestel, "The effects of dietary fatty acids and cholesterol on the milk lipids of lactating women, and the plasma cholesterol of breast-fed infants." Am., J. Clin. Nutr. 29, 54, 1976; Hodgson et al. "Comparison of serum cholesterol in children fed high, moderate, or low cholesterol milk diets during neonatal period." Metabolism 25,

Continued on next page

Loma Linda—Cont.

739, 1976; Widdowson et al. "Body fat of British and Dutch infants." Brit. Med. J., March 22, 653, 1975). When prepared as directed, one quart of Soyalac daily contains essential nutrients in balanced combination and sufficient quantities to provide adequate nutrition for infants.

Action and Uses: Soyalac provides a highly satisfactory alternative or supplement for infants when breast milk is not available or the supply is inadequate. It is especially valuable for all infants, children, and adults - who may be sensitive to dairymilk, or who prefer a vegetarian diet. It may also be prescribed successfully for use in hypocholestrogenic diets; for pre-operative and post-operative diets; for fortifying any milk free diet; for geriatric cases, etc.

Preparation: Standard dilution is—

Ready to Serve—as canned

Concentrate—one part mixed with an equal part of water

Powder (can)—four scoops to one cup of water

Powder (pouch)—contents of one pouch to 8 fl. oz. of water

Typical Analysis: Standard Dilution

	%W/V
Protein	2.1
Fat	3.7
Carbohydrates	6.6
Minerals	0.4
Fiber	0.0
Water	90.0
Calories	20 per fluid oz.

One quart of Soyalac, standard dilution, provides the following nutrients:

Vitamin A	(I.U.)	2000
Vitamin D	(I.U.)	400
Vitamin E	(I.U.)	15
Vitamin K	(mcg)	50
Vitamin C	(mg)	60
Vitamin B_1	(mcg)	500
Vitamin B_2	(mcg)	600
Niacin	(mg)	8
Vitamin B_6	(mcg)	400
Folic Acid	(mcg)	100
Pantothenic Acid	(mg)	3
Vitamin B_{12}	(mg)	2
Biotin	(mcg)	50
Choline	(mg)	100
Inositol	(mg)	100
Calcium	(mg)	600
Phosphorus	(mg)	400
Magnesium	(mg)	70
Iron	(mg)	12
Iodine	(mcg)	45
Copper	(mcg)	500
Zinc	(mg)	5
Manganese	(mg)	1
Potassium	(mg)	700
Sodium	(mg)	330
Chloride	(mg)	370

Supply:

Soyalac Ready to Serve liquid:
32 fl. oz. cans, 6 can per case

Soyalac Double Strength Concentrate:
13 fl. oz. cans, 12 cans per case

Soyalac Powder—Cans:
1 lb. cans, 12 cans per case

Soyalac Powder—Pouches:
34 g. pouches, 18 pouches per case

Macsil, Inc.
1326 FRANKFORD AVENUE
PHILADELPHIA, PA 19125

BALMEX® BABY POWDER

Composition: Contains BALSAN® (specially purified balsam Peru), zinc oxide, talc, starch, calcium carbonate.

Action and Uses: Absorbent, emollient, soothing—for diaper irritation, intertrigo, and other common dermatological conditions. In acute, simple miliaria, itching ceases in minutes and lesions dry promptly. For routine use after bathing and each diaper change.

How Supplied: 4 oz. shaker top cans.

BALMEX® EMOLLIENT LOTION

Gentle and effective scientifically compounded infant's skin conditioner.

Composition: Contains a special lanolin oil (non-sensitizing, dewaxed, moisturizing fraction of lanolin), BALSAN® (specially purified balsam Peru) and silicone.

Action and Uses: The special Lanolin Oil aids nature lubricate baby's skin to keep it smooth and supple. Balmex Emollient Lotion is also highly effective as a physiologic conditioner on adult's skin.

How Supplied: Available in 6 oz. dispenser-top plastic bottles.

BALMEX® OINTMENT

Composition: Contains BALSAN® (specially purified balsam Peru), vitamins A and D, zinc oxide, and bismuth subnitrate in an ointment base containing silicone.

Action and Uses: Emollient, protective, anti-inflammatory, promotes healing—for diaper rash, minor burns, sunburn, and other simple skin conditions; also decubitus ulcers, skin irritations associated with ileostomy and colostomy drainage. Nonstaining, readily washes out of diapers and clothing.

How Supplied: 1, 2, 4 oz. tubes; 1 lb. plastic jars (½ oz. tubes for Hospitals only).

Marion Laboratories, Inc.
Pharmaceutical Division
MARION INDUSTRIAL PARK
10236 BUNKER RIDGE ROAD
KANSAS CITY, MO 64137

AMBENYL®-D Decongestant Cough Formula
Antitussive, Expectorant, Nasal Decongestant

Two teaspoonfuls (10 ml) contain the following active ingredients:

Guaifenesin (glyceryl
guaiacolate) .... 200 mg
Pseudoephedrine
Hydrochloride .... 60 mg
Dextromethorphan
Hydrobromide .... 30 mg
Also contains 9.5% Alcohol.

Indications: Ambenyl®-D is for temporary relief of nasal congestion due to the common cold or associated with sinusitis, helps loosen phlegm, calms cough impulses without narcotics and temporarily helps you cough less.

Directions for Use: Adult Dose (12 years and over)—Two teaspoonfuls every six hours. Child Dose (6–12 years)—One teaspoonful every six hours. (2–6 years)—One-half teaspoonful every six hours. No more than four doses per day.

Warnings: Do not give this product to children under two years except under the advice and supervision of a physician. Do not take this product for persistent or chronic cough such as occurs with smoking, asthma, or emphysema, or where cough is accompanied by excessive secretions except under the advice and supervision of a physician.

Do not exceed recommended dosage because at higher doses nervousness, dizziness, or sleeplessness may occur.

Caution: A persistent cough may be a sign of a serious condition. If cough persists for more than one week, tends to recur, or is accompanied by high fever, rash, or persistent headache, consult a physician.

If symptoms do not improve within seven days or are accompanied by high fever, consult a physician before continuing use. Do not take this product if you have high blood pressure, heart disease, diabetes, or thyroid disease, except under the advice and supervision of a physician.

Drug Interaction Precaution: Do not take this product if you are presently taking a prescription antihypertensive or antidepressant drug containing a monoamine oxidase inhibitor except under the advice and supervision of a physician.

How Supplied: Ambenyl-D Decongestant Cough Formula is supplied in a 4-fluid-ounce bottle.

Revised formula 1981

[*Shown in Product Identification Section*]

DEBROX® Drops

Description: Carbamide peroxide 6.5% in specially prepared anhydrous glycerol.

Actions: Debrox® penetrates, softens and facilitates removal of earwax, without causing the wax to swell. Upon direct contact with earwax, carbamide peroxide releases oxygen to form a dense foam which helps to break up wax accumulations. These actions result in a chemomechanical cleansing, debriding effect. Any remaining wax may be removed by flushing with warm water, using a soft rubber bulb ear syringe. Avoid excessive pressure.

Indications: Debrox provides a safe, nonirritating method of removing earwax. Aids in the prevention of ceruminosis. Used regularly, Debrox Drops helps keep the ear canal free from blockage due to accumulated earwax.

Caution: Consult physician if redness, irritation, swelling or pain persists or increases.

Dosage and Administration: Use directly from bottle. Tilt head sideways and squeeze bottle gently so that 5-10 drops flow into ear. Tip of bottle should not enter ear canal. Keep drops in ear for several minutes while head remains tilted or by inserting cotton. Repeat twice daily for at least 3-4 days or as directed by physician. Any remaining wax may be removed by flushing with warm water, using a soft rubber bulb ear syringe.

How Supplied: Debrox Drops is available in ½- or 1-fl.-oz. plastic squeeze bottles with applicator spouts.

[*Shown in Product Identification Section*]

FUMASORB® Tablets
(iron therapy)

Each tablet contains:
Elemental Iron (as 200 mg of
ferrous fumarate) .... 66 mg
Indications: For prophylaxis treatment of iron deficiencies or anemias due to partial or complete iron deficiency.
Dosage: Prophylaxis—one (1) tablet daily for adults and children over 5 years. Treatment—one (1) tablet three (3) times a day or as directed by a physician. For infants—as directed by a physician. To minimize gastric disturbances, take after meals or with food.
How Supplied: Available in bottle of 100 tablets.

GAVISCON® Antacid Tablets

Composition: Each chewable tablet contains the following active ingredients:
Aluminum hydroxide dried gel... 80 mg
Magnesium trisilicate .... 20 mg
and the following inactive ingredients: sucrose, alginic acid, sodium bicarbonate, starch, calcium stearate and flavoring.
Actions: Unique formulation produces soothing foam which floats on stomach contents. Foam containing antacid precedes stomach contents into the esophagus when reflux occurs to help protect the sensitive mucosa from further irritation. GAVISCON acts locally without neutralizing entire stomach contents to help maintain integrity of the digestive process. Endoscopic studies indicate that GAVISCON® Antacid Tablets are equally as effective in the erect or supine patient.
Indications: For temporary relief of heartburn, sour stomach, and/or acid indigestion.
Directions: Chew two to four tablets four times a day or as directed by a physician. Tablets should be taken after meals and at bedtime or as needed. For best results follow by a half glass of water or other liquid. DO NOT SWALLOW WHOLE.
Warnings: Except under the advice and supervision of a physician: do not take more than 16 tablets in a 24-hour period or 16 tablets daily for more than 2 weeks; do not use this product if you are on a sodium restricted diet. Each GAVISCON Tablet contains approximately 0.8 mEq sodium.
Drug Interaction Precautions: Do not take this product if you are presently taking a prescription antibiotic drug containing any form of tetracycline.

How Supplied: Available in bottle of 100 tablets and in foil-wrapped 2's in box of 30 tablets.
[*Shown in Product Identification Section*]

GAVISCON® Liquid Antacid

Each tablespoonful (15 ml) contains the following active ingredients:
Aluminum hydroxide .... 95 mg
Magnesium carbonate .... 412 mg
And the following inactive ingredients: water, sorbitol solution, glycerin, sodium alginate, xanthan gum, edetate disodium, methylparaben, propylparaben, flavorings and colors.
Indications: For the relief of heartburn, sour stomach, and/or acid indigestion, and upset stomach associated with heartburn, sour stomach, and/or acid indigestion.
Directions: Shake well before using. Take one to two tablespoonfuls four times a day or as directed by a physician. GAVISCON Liquid should be taken after meals and at bedtime, followed by a half glass of water.
Warnings: Except under the advice and supervision of a physician: do not take more than eight tablespoonfuls in a 24-hour period or eight tablespoonfuls daily for more than two weeks. Do not use this product if you have a kidney disease; do not use this product if you are on a sodium restricted diet. Each tablespoonful of GAVISCON Liquid contains approximately 1.7 mEq sodium.
Drug Interaction Precautions: Do not take this product if you are presently taking a prescription antibiotic drug containing any form of tetracycline.
How Supplied: Available in 12-fl.-oz. (355 ml) bottle.
Revised formula 6/80.
[*Shown in Product Identification Section*]

GAVISCON®-2 Antacid Tablets

Each chewable tablet contains the following active ingredients:
Aluminum hydroxide dried gel 160 mg
Magnesium trisilicate .... 40 mg
and the following inactive ingredients: sucrose, alginic acid, sodium bicarbonate, starch, calcium stearate and flavoring.
Indications: For temporary relief of heartburn, sour stomach, and/or acid indigestion.
Directions: Chew one to two tablets four times a day or as directed by a physician. Tablets should be taken after meals and at bedtime or as needed. For best results follow by a half glass of water or other liquid. DO NOT SWALLOW WHOLE.
Warnings: Except under the advice and supervision of a physician: do not take more than 8 tablets in a 24-hour period or 8 tablets daily for more than 2 weeks; do not use this product if you are on a sodium restricted diet. Each GAVISCON®-2 Tablet contains approximately 1.6 mEq sodium.
Drug Interaction Precautions: Do not take this product if you are presently taking a prescription antibiotic drug containing any form of tetracycline.

How Supplied: Box of 48 foil-wrapped tablets.
[*Shown in Product Identification Section*]

GLY-OXIDE® Liquid
(cleansing antiseptic for the mouth)

Description: Carbamide peroxide 10% in specially prepared anhydrous glycerol. Artificial flavor added.
Actions: GLY-OXIDE® is a safe, stabilized oxygenating agent. Specifically formulated for topical oral administration, it provides unique chemomechanical cleansing and debriding action, which allows normal healing to occur.
Indications: Local treatment and hygienic prevention (as an aid to professional care) of minor oral inflammation such as canker sores, denture irritation and post-dental procedure irritation. GLY-OXIDE Liquid provides effective aid to oral hygiene when normal cleansing measures are inadequate or impossible (e.g., total-care geriatric patients). As an adjunct to oral hygiene (orthodontics, dental appliances) after regular brushing.
Precautions: Severe or persistent oral inflammation or denture irritation may be serious. If these or unexpected effects occur, consult physician or dentist promptly.
Dosage and Administration: DO NOT DILUTE—use directly from the bottle. Apply 4 times daily after meals and at bedtime, or as directed by a dentist or physician. Place several drops on affected area; expectorate after 2-3 minutes, or place 10 drops onto tongue, mix with saliva, swish for several minutes, expectorate. Do not rinse. Foams on contact with saliva.
How Supplied: GLY-OXIDE Liquid is available in ½-fl.-oz. and 2-fl.-oz. non-spill plastic squeeze bottles with applicator spouts.
[*Shown in Product Identification Section*]

METASEP® Shampoo
(medicated shampoo concentrate)

Leaves hair soft and manageable... provides long-lasting control.

Active Ingredient: Parachlorometaxylenol 2%
Other Ingredients: Isopropyl alcohol NF 9%, sodium lauryl sulfate, water, lauramide DEA, laneth-10 acetate, citric acid USP, fragrance.
Indications: Use as an aid in relief of dandruff and associated conditions.
Directions: Wet hair thoroughly. Apply Metasep® Medicated Shampoo and massage to foamy lather. Allow lather to remain five minutes. Rinse hair thoroughly and repeat.
Caution: Avoid contact with eyes.
How Supplied: Available in 4-fl.-oz. bottle.

Continued on next page

Marion—Cont.

OS–CAL® Tablets
(calcium with Vitamin D)

Each tablet contains: 625 mg of calcium carbonate from oyster shell which provides:

Elemental calcium............. 250 mg
Ergocalciferol (Vitamin D₂)..... 125 USP Units

Indications: Os-Cal® Tablets provide a source of calcium when it is desired to increase the dietary intake of this mineral. Os-Cal also contains Vitamin D₂ to aid in the absorption of calcium.

Directions: Take one tablet three times a day at mealtime. Three tablets daily provide:

	Quantity	%U.S.RDA* for Adults
Calcium	750 mg	75%
Vitamin D₂	375 units	94%

*Percent U.S. Recommended Daily Allowance

How Supplied: Available in bottles of 100, 240, 500, and 1000 tablets.
[*Shown in Product Identification Section*]

OS–CAL® 500 TABLETS
(calcium supplement)

Each tablet contains: 1,250 mg of calcium carbonate from oyster shell which provides:
Elemental calcium .... 500 mg

Indications: Os-Cal® 500 Tablets provide a source of calcium where it is desired or recommended by a physician to increase the dietary intake of this mineral.

Directions: Take one tablet two or three times a day at mealtime or as directed. Two tablets daily provide:

	Quantity	%U.S.RDA†
Calcium	1,000 mg	100%* 77%**

Three tablets daily provide:

Calcium	1,500 mg	150%* 115%**

†Percent U.S. Recommended Daily Allowance.
*For adults and children 12 or more years of age.
**For pregnant and lactating women.
How Supplied: Available in bottle of 60 tablets.

OS–CAL FORTE®Tablets
(multivitamin and mineral supplement)

Each tablet contains:
Vitamin A (palmitate) 1668 USP Units
Ergocalciferol
(Vitamin D₂)............... 125 USP Units
Thiamine mononitrate
(Vitamin B₁) .... 1.7 mg
Riboflavin (Vitamin B₂)............... 1.7 mg
Pyridoxine hydrochloride
(Vitamin B₆)............................. 2.0 mg
Cyanocobalamin (Vitamin B₁₂) 1.6 mcg
Ascorbic acid (Vitamin C)............ 50 mg
dl-alpha-tocopherol acetate
(Vitamin E)............................. 0.8 IU
Niacinamide .... 15 mg
Calcium (from oyster shell*)....... 250 mg
Iron (as ferrous fumarate)............. 5 mg

Copper (as sulfate)........................ 0.3 mg
Iodine (as potassium iodide)...... 0.05 mg
Magnesium (as oxide)................... 1.6 mg
Manganese (as sulfate)................. 0.3 mg
Zinc (as sulfate)............................. 0.5 mg
*Trace minerals from oyster shell: copper, iron, magnesium, manganese, silica and zinc.
Indication: Multivitamin and mineral supplement.
Dosage: One tablet three times daily or as directed by physician.
How Supplied: Available in bottle of 100 tablets.

OS–CAL–GESIC® Tablets
(anti-arthritic)

Each tablet contains:
Salicylamide .... 400 mg
Calcium (from oyster shell) .... 100 mg
Ergocalciferol
(Vitamin D₂)....................50 USP Units
Indication: For temporary relief of symptoms associated with arthritis.
Dosage: Initially—2 tablets hourly for 3 or 4 doses. Maintenance—1 or 2 tablets 4 times daily.
How Supplied: Available in bottles of 100 tablets.

OS–CAL® Plus Tablets
(multivitamin and multimineral supplement)

Each tablet contains:
Calcium (from oyster shell*)...... 250 mg
Ergocalciferol
(Vitamin D₂)................ 125 USP Units
*Trace minerals from oyster shell: copper, iron, magnesium, manganese, silica and zinc.
Plus:
Vitamin A (palmitate) 1666 USP Units
Vitamin C (ascorbic acid)............. 33 mg
Vitamin B₂ (riboflavin).............. 0.66 mg
Vitamin B₁ (thiamine
mononitrate).......................... 0.5 mg
Vitamin B₆ (pyridoxine HCl)...... 0.5 mg
Vitamin B₁₂ (cyanocobalamin) 0.03 mcg
Niacinamide................................. 3.33 mg
Iron (as ferrous fumarate) .... 16.6 mg
Zinc (as the sulfate).................... 0.75 mg
Manganese (as the sulfate)....... 0.75 mg
Copper (as the sulfate)............. 0.036 mg
Iodine (as potassium iodide) ... 0.036 mg
Indications: As a multivitamin and multimineral supplement.
Dosage: One (1) tablet three times a day before meals or as directed by a physician. For children under four years of age, consult a physician.
How Supplied: Available in bottle of 100 tablets.

PRETTS® Tablets
(diet control adjunct)

Each Pretts® Tablet contains:
Alginic acid.................................... 200 mg
Sodium carboxymethyl-
cellulose .... 100 mg
Sodium bicarbonate .... 70 mg
Contains FD&C Yellow No. 5 (tartrazine) as a color additive.
Indications: For use as an adjunct to diet control. Pretts tablets provide bulk to help satisfy the feeling of hunger caused by emptiness, making it easier for

you to adhere to your specific diet regimen.
Those on a sodium restricted diet should consult their physician.
Actions: Pretts Tablets, when chewed, introduce a bulky foam into the gastrointestinal tract to create a feeling of fullness and to help alleviate hunger pangs; this serves as an aid in helping the patient eat less.
Dosage and Administration: Take two to four tablets with a full glass of water three or four times a day, or as needed. Chew each tablet individually followed by small sips of water. Do not swallow tablets whole!
How Supplied: Available in bottle of 60 tablets. Tablets imprinted with MARION/1177.
[*Shown in Product Identification Section*]

PROTECT™ Toothpaste for Sensitive Teeth

Active Ingredients: Sodium citrate and citric acid in Pluronic* polyol base.
Also Contains: Water, glycerin USP, colloidal silicon dioxide, sodium metaphosphate, flavor, sodium saccharin, potassium sorbate, sodium lauryl sulfate, FD&C green #3.
Directions: Used in regular daily brushing as directed by your dentist, Protect formula steadily builds protection against painful sensitivity such as cold and pressure. Protect works hard to keep your teeth sparkling clean, too, and you'll find its bright, minty taste is a refreshing change from other toothpastes.
How Supplied: Available in 3-oz. tube.
U.S. Patent 4,011,309
*Pluronic is a trademark of BASF Wyandotte Labs for Poloxamer 407.
[*Shown in Product Identification Section*]

THROAT DISCS Throat Lozenges

Description: Each lozenge contains Capsicum, Peppermint, Anise, Cubeb, Glycyrrhiza Extract (Licorice), and Linseed.
Indications: Effective for soothing, temporary relief of minor throat irritations from hoarseness and coughs due to colds.
Precautions: For severe or persistent cough or sore throat, or sore throat accompanied by high fever, headache, nausea, and vomiting, consult physician promptly. Not recommended for children under 3 years of age.
Dosage: Allow lozenge to dissolve slowly in mouth. One or two should give the desired relief. Do not use more than four lozenges per hour.
How Supplied: Available in box of 60.
[*Shown in Product Identification Section*]

Products are cross-indexed by

generic and chemical names

in the

YELLOW SECTION

Maybelline Co.
3030 JACKSON AVENUE
MEMPHIS, TN 38151

MOISTURE WHIP®
LIP CONDITIONER
Lip Balm with Sunscreen

Active Ingredient: Padimate O
Indications: A hypo-allergenic lip balm which moisturizes lips. It will help protect lips from the sun (Sun Protection Factor of 2) and also chapping and drying effects of the wind and cold. Keeps lips feeling soft and moist. It has no taste or color.
Actions: Sunscreen and moisturization.
Dosage and Administration: Use daily and reapply as needed for maximum protection. Can be used under lip color.
How Supplied: .15 oz. tube.

MOISTURE WHIP® LIPSTICK
Lipstick with Sunscreen

Active Ingredient: Padimate O
Indications: A hypo-allergenic, moisturizing lipstick in fashionable shades. It will help protect lips from the sun (Sun Protection Factor of 2) and help prevent dryness and chapping. Keeps lips soft and moist.
Actions: Sunscreen and moisturization.
Dosage and Administration: Use daily and reapply as needed for maximum protection.
How Supplied: .12 oz. tube. Comes in 30 shades.

MOISTURE WHIP®
LIQUID MAKE-UP AND
MOISTURE WHIP®
CREAM MAKE-UP
Foundation Make-up with Sunscreen

Active Ingredient: Padimate O
Indications: A hypo-allergenic foundation make-up which is moisturizing. Used daily it will help protect skin from the premature aging effect of too much sun (Sun Protection Factor of 2). Feels light and sheer.
Actions: Sunscreen and moisturization.
Dosage and Administration: Use daily.
How Supplied: 1 fl. oz. liquid (bottle) and 1 oz. cream (jar). Both come in six shades.

MOISTURE WHIP® PROTECTIVE FACIAL MOISTURIZER
Facial Moisturizer with Sunscreen

Active Ingredient: Padimate O
Indications: A facial moisturizer that does more than just moisturize. Used daily, it will help protect skin from the premature aging effect of too much sun (Sun Protection Factor of 2) and thus help prevent wrinkles from coming along too soon. The product absorbs quickly and is fragrance free. Suitable for use under makeup.
Actions: Sunscreen and moisturization.
Dosage and Administration: Use daily first thing in the morning, the last thing at night.
How Supplied: 4 fl. oz. lotion (bottle) and 2 oz. cream (jar).

McNeil Consumer Products Company
McNEILAB, INC.
FORT WASHINGTON, PA 19034

COTYLENOL® Cold Formula Tablets and Capsules

Description: Each CoTylenol Tablet or Capsule contains acetaminophen 325 mg., chlorpheniramine maleate 2 mg., pseudoephedrine hydrochloride 30 mg. and dextromethorphan hydrobromide 15 mg.
Actions and Indications: CoTylenol Cold Formula Tablets and Capsules combine the non-salicylate analgesic-antipyretic acetaminophen with the decongestant pseudoephedrine hydrochloride, the cough suppressant dextromethorphan hydrobromide and the antihistamine chlorpheniramine maleate to help relieve nasal congestion and coughing as well as the fever, aches, pains and general discomfort associated with colds and other upper respiratory infections.
While the acetaminophen component is equal to aspirin in analgesic and antipyretic effectiveness, it is unlikely to produce many of the side effects associated with aspirin and aspirin-containing products. Thus, CoTylenol Cold Formula Tablets and Capsules are particularly well suited for relief of cold symptoms in patients who should avoid aspirin, such as those with ulcer, gastritis and hiatus hernia; those taking anticoagulants, and those allergic to aspirin.
Usual Dosage: Adults: Two tablets or capsules every six hours, not to exceed 8 tablets or capsules per day. Children (6–12 years): One tablet or capsule every six hours, not to exceed 4 tablets or capsules per day.
Note: Since CoTylenol Cold Formula Tablets and Capsules are available without prescription, the following appears on the package label: "WARNING: Do not exceed the recommended dosage or administer to children under 6. Reduce dosage if nervousness, restlessness, or sleeplessness occurs. If you have asthma, glaucoma, high blood pressure, heart disease, diabetes, thyroid disease, enlargement of the prostate gland, or are presently taking a prescription drug for the treatment of high blood pressure or emotional disorders, do not take except under the advice and supervision of a physician. This preparation may cause drowsiness. Do not drive or operate machinery while taking this medication. If symptoms do not improve within seven days or are accompanied by high fever, consult a physician before continuing use. Keep this and all medication out of the reach of children. In case of accidental overdosage, contact a physician immediately."
Overdosage: Acetaminophen in massive overdosage may cause hepatic toxicity in some patients. In all cases of suspected overdose, immediately call your regional poison center or the Rocky Mountain Poison Center's toll-free number (800-525-6115) for assistance in diagnosis and for directions in the use of N-acetylcysteine as an antidote. Adverse

effects are rare when acetaminophen is used as recommended. However, as with all drugs, overdosage may cause serious toxicity.
How Supplied: Tablets (colored yellow, imprinted "CoTylenol")—blister packs of 24's and bottles of 50 and 100. Capsules (colored dark green and light yellow, imprinted "CoTylenol")—blister packs of 20 and bottles of 50.
[*Shown in Product Identification Section*]

CoTYLENOL® Liquid Cold Formula

Description: Each 30 ml (1 fl. oz.) contains acetaminophen 650 mg, chlorpheniramine maleate 4 mg, pseudoephedrine hydrochloride 60 mg, and dextromethorphan hydrobromide 30 mg (alcohol 7.5%).
Actions and Indications: CoTylenol Liquid Cold Formula combines the non-salicylate analgesic-antipyretic acetaminophen with the decongestant pseudoephedrine hydrochloride, the cough suppressant dextromethorphan hydrobromide and the antihistamine chlorpheniramine maleate to help relieve nasal congestion and coughing, as well as the fever, aches, pains and general discomfort associated with colds and other upper respiratory infections. While the acetaminophen component is equal to aspirin in analgesic and antipyretic effectiveness, it is unlikely to produce many of the side effects associated with aspirin and aspirin-containing products. Thus, CoTylenol Liquid Cold Formula is particularly well suited for relief of cold symptoms in patients who should avoid aspirin, such as those with ulcer, gastritis and hiatus hernia; those taking anticoagulants and those allergic to aspirin.
Usual Dosage: Measuring cup is provided and marked for accurate dosing. Adults: 1 fluid ounce (2 tbsps.) every 6 hours as needed, not to exceed 4 doses in 24 hours. Children (6-12 yrs.): ½ fluid ounce (1 tbsp.) every 6 hours as needed, not to exceed 4 doses in 24 hours.
Note: Since CoTylenol Liquid Cold Formula is available without a prescription, the following appears on the package label: "WARNING: Do not exceed the recommended dosage or administer to children under 6. Reduce dosage if nervousness, restlessness or sleeplessness occurs. Persistent cough may indicate a serious condition. Persons with a high fever, rash or persistent cough or headache or asthma, emphysema or with glaucoma, high blood pressure, heart disease, diabetes, thyroid disease, enlargement of the prostrate gland, or who are presently taking a prescription drug for the treatment of high blood pressure or emotional disorders, do not take, except under the advice and supervision of a physician. This preparation may cause drowsiness. Do not drive or operate machinery while taking this medication. If symptoms do not improve within five days, consult a physician before continuing use. Keep this and all medication out of the reach of children. In case of acci-

Continued on next page

McNeil Consumer—Cont.

dental overdosage, contact a physician immediately."

Overdosage: Acetaminophen in massive overdosage may cause hepatic toxicity in some patients. In all cases of suspected overdose, immediately call your regional poison center or the Rocky Mountain Poison Center's toll-free number (800-525-6115) for assistance in diagnosis and for directions in the use of N-acetylcysteine as an antidote. Adverse effects are rare when acetaminophen is used as recommended. However, as with all drugs, overdosage may cause serious toxicity.

How Supplied: Cherry/mint flavored mentholated (colored amber) bottles of 5 and 10 oz. with child-resistant safety cap and special dosage cup graded in ounces and tablespoons.

[*Shown in Product Identification Section*]

Children's CoTYLENOL®
Liquid Cold Formula

Description: Children's CoTYLENOL Liquid Cold Formula is stable, cherry-flavored, red in color and contains 8.5% alcohol. Each teaspoon (5 ml.) contains acetaminophen 160 mg., chlorpheniramine maleate 1 mg., and pseudoephedrine hydrochloride 15 mg.

Actions and Indications: Children's CoTYLENOL Liquid Cold Formula combines the nonsalicylate analgesic-antipyretic acetaminophen with the decongestant pseudoephedrine hydrochloride and the antihistamine chlorpheniramine maleate to help relieve nasal congestion, dry runny noses and prevent sneezing as well as to relieve the fever, aches, pains and general discomfort due to colds and "flu".

While the acetaminophen component is equal to aspirin in analgesic and antipyretic effectiveness, it is unlikely to produce the following side effects often associated with aspirin or aspirin-containing products: allergic reactions, even in aspirin-sensitive children or those with a history of allergy in general; "therapeutic toxicity" in feverish children, since electrolyte imbalance and acid-base changes are not likely to occur; gastric irritation even in children with an already upset stomach.

Dosage: Children 6–11 years—two teaspoonfuls every 6 hours as needed, not to exceed 4 doses in 24 hours. 12 years and over—four teaspoonfuls every 6 hours, not to exceed 4 doses in 24 hours. Children under 6 only as directed by physician. For accurate measurements, use the convenient measuring cup provided.

Note: Since Children's CoTYLENOL Cold Formula is available without prescription, the following information appears on the package label: "WARNING: Do not exceed the recommended dosage. Reduce dosage if nervousness, restlessness, or sleeplessness occurs. Do not use if high blood pressure, heart disease, diabetes, or thyroid disease is present unless directed by a physician. This preparation may cause drowsiness. Do not drive or operate machinery while taking this medication. Persons with a high fever or persistent cough should not use this preparation unless directed by a physician. Keep this and all medication out of the reach of children. Do not take for longer than 10 days unless directed by a physician. Your physician is the best source of counsel and guidance when cold symptoms are present. In case of accidental overdosage, contact a physician immediately."

Overdosage: Acetaminophen in massive overdosage may cause hepatic toxicity in some patients. In all cases of suspected overdose, immediately call your regional poison center or the Rocky Mountain Poison Center's toll-free number (800-525-6115) for assistance in diagnosis and for directions in the use of N-acetylcysteine as an antidote. Adverse effects are rare when acetaminophen is used as recommended. However, as with all drugs, overdosage may cause serious toxicity.

How Supplied: Bottle of 4 fl. oz. with child-resistant safety cap.

[*Shown in Product Identification Section*]

SINE–AID®
Sinus Headache Tablets

Description: Each SINE-AID Tablet contains acetaminophen 325 mg. and phenylpropanolamine hydrochloride 25 mg.

Actions: Acetaminophen is a clinically proven analgesic-antipyretic. Acetaminophen produces analgesia by elevation of the pain threshold and antipyresis through action on the hypothalamic heat-regulating center. Phenylpropanolamine hydrochloride is a sympathomimetic amine and provides vasoconstriction to the nasopharyngeal mucosa. Although similar in action to ephedrine, phenylpropanolamine HCl is less likely to cause CNS stimulation.

Indications: SINE-AID provides effective symptomatic relief from sinus headache pain and pressure caused by sinusitis. Since it contains no antihistamine, SINE-AID will not produce the drowsiness that may interfere with work, driving an automobile or operating dangerous machinery. SINE-AID is particularly well suited in patients with aspirin allergy, hemostatic disturbances (including anticoagulant therapy), and bleeding diatheses (e.g. ulcer, gastritis, hiatus hernia).

Precautions and Adverse Reactions: Acetaminophen has rarely been found to produce any side effects. It is usually well tolerated by aspirin-sensitive patients. If a rare sensitivity reaction occurs, the drug should be stopped. In patients with high blood pressure, diabetes, or thyroid disease, phenylpropanolamine hydrochloride should be used with caution and only as directed by a physician. Do not use in patients receiving MAO inhibitors.

Usual Dosage: Adult dosage: Two tablets every four hours, no more than 6 tablets in any 24-hour period.

Note: Since SINE-AID tablets are available without a prescription, the following appears on the package labels: "CAUTION: Individuals with high blood pressure, heart disease, diabetes, thyroid disease, and children under 12 should use only as directed by a physician. Do not exceed recommended dosage unless directed by a physician. WARNING: If symptoms of sinusitis or colds persist after 3 days, consult a physician. Keep this and all medications out of the reach of children. In case of accidental overdose, contact a physician immediately."

Overdosage: Acetaminophen in massive overdosage may cause hepatic toxicity in some patients. In all cases of suspected overdose, immediately call your regional poison center or the Rocky Mountain Poison Center's toll-free number (800-525-6115) for assistance in diagnosis and for directions in the use of N-acetylcysteine as an antidote. Adverse effects are rare when acetaminophen is used as recommended. However, as with all drugs, overdosage may cause serious toxicity.

How Supplied: Tablets (colored white, imprinted "SINE-AID")—bottles of 24, 50 and 100.

[*Shown in Product Identification Section*]

Children's TYLENOL®
acetaminophen
Chewable Tablets, Elixir, Drops

Description: Each Children's TYLENOL Chewable Tablet contains 80 mg. acetaminophen in a fruit flavored tablet. Children's TYLENOL acetaminophen Elixir and Drops are stable, cherry flavored, red in color and contain only 7% alcohol.

Children's TYLENOL Elixir: Each 5 ml. contains 120 mg. acetaminophen.

Infant TYLENOL Drops: Each 0.6 ml. (one calibrated dropperful) contains 60 mg. acetaminophen.

Actions: TYLENOL acetaminophen is an antipyretic and analgesic clinically proven in pediatric use. TYLENOL acetaminophen produces antipyresis through action on the hypothalamic heat-regulating center and analgesia by elevation of the pain threshold.

Indications: Children's TYLENOL Chewable Tablets, Elixir and Drops are designed for treatment of infants and children with conditions requiring reduction of fever or relief of pain—such as mild upper respiratory infections (tonsillitis, common cold, "grippe"), headache, myalgia, post-immunization reactions, post-tonsillectomy discomfort and gastroenteritis. In conjunction with antibiotics and sulfonamides, TYLENOL acetaminophen is useful as an analgesic and antipyretic in many bacterial or viral infections, such as bronchitis, pharyngitis, tracheobronchitis, sinusitis, pneumonia, otitis media, and cervical adenitis.

Precautions and Adverse Reactions: If a rare sensitivity reaction occurs, the drug should be stopped. TYLENOL acetaminophen has rarely been found to produce any side effects. It is usually well tolerated by aspirin-sensitive patients.

Usual Dosage: Doses may be repeated 3 or 4 times daily.

Children's TYLENOL Chewable Tablets: 3 years: One and one-half tablets. 4–5 years: Two and one-half tablets. 6–8 years: Three tablets. 9–12 years: Four tablets.

Children's TYLENOL Elixir: Under 1 year: One-half teaspoonful. 1 to 3 years: One-half to one teaspoonful. 3 years: One teaspoonful. 4–5 years: One and one-half teaspoonfuls. 6–8 years: Two teaspoonfuls. 9–12 years: Three teaspoonfuls.

Infant TYLENOL Drops: Under 1 year: 0.6 ml. 1 to 3 years: 0.6 to 1.2 ml. 3 years: 1.2 ml. 4–5 years: 1.8 ml.

Note: Since Children's TYLENOL acetaminophen Chewable Tablets, Elixir and Drops are available without prescription as an analgesic, the following appears on the package labels: "WARNING: Consult a physician for use by children under 3 or for use longer than 10 days. Keep this and all medication out of the reach of children. In cases of accidental overdosage, contact a physician immediately."

Overdosage: Acetaminophen in massive overdosage may cause hepatic toxicity in some patients. In all cases of suspected overdose, immediately call your regional poison center or the Rocky Mountain Poison Center's toll-free number (800-525-6115) for assistance in diagnosis and for directions in the use of N-acetylcysteine as an antidote. Adverse effects are rare when acetaminophen is used as recommended. However, as with all drugs, overdosage may cause serious toxicity.

How Supplied: Chewable Tablets (colored pink, scored, imprinted "TYLENOL")—Bottles of 30. Elixir (colored red)—bottles of 2 and 4 fl. oz. Drops (colored crimson)—bottles of ½ oz. (15 ml.) with calibrated plastic dropper.

All packages listed above have child-resistant safety caps.

[*Shown in Product Identification Section*]

Regular Strength
TYLENOL® acetaminophen
Tablets and Capsules

Description: Each Regular Strength TYLENOL Tablet or Capsule contains acetaminophen 325 mg.

Actions: TYLENOL acetaminophen is a clinically proven analgesic and antipyretic. TYLENOL acetaminophen produces analgesia by elevation of the pain threshold and antipyresis through action on the hypothalamic heat-regulating center.

Indications: TYLENOL acetaminophen provides effective analgesia in a wide variety of arthritic and rheumatic conditions involving musculoskeletal pain, as well as in other painful disorders such as headache, dysmenorrhea, myalgias and neuralgias. In addition, TYLENOL is indicated as an analgesic and antipyretic in diseases accompanied by discomfort and fever, such as the common cold and other viral infections. TYLENOL is particularly well suited as an analgesic-antipyretic in the presence of aspirin allergy, hemostatic disturbances (including anticoagulant therapy), and bleeding diatheses (e.g. hemophilia) and upper gastrointestinal disorders (e.g., ulcer, gastritis, hiatus hernia).

Precautions and Adverse Reactions: If a rare sensitivity reaction occurs, the drug should be stopped. TYLENOL acetaminophen has rarely been found to produce any side effects. It is usually well tolerated by aspirin-sensitive patients.

Usual Dosage: *Adults:* One to two tablets or capsules every 4–6 hours. Not to exceed 12 tablets or capsules per day. *Children* (6 to 12): One-half to one tablet 3 or 4 times daily. (TYLENOL acetaminophen Chewable Tablets, Elixir and Drops are available for greater convenience in younger patients.)

Note: Since TYLENOL acetaminophen tablets and capsules are available without prescription as an analgesic, the following appears on the package labels: "Consult a physician for use by children under 6 or for use longer than 10 days. WARNING: Keep this and all medication out of the reach of children. In case of accidental overdosage, contact a physician immediately." In connection with its use for temporary relief of minor aches and pains of arthritis and rheumatism: "Caution: If pain persists for more than 10 days, or redness is present, or in arthritic or rheumatic conditions affecting children under 12 years, consult a physician immediately."

Overdosage: Acetaminophen in massive overdosage may cause hepatic toxicity in some patients. In all cases of suspected overdose, immediately call your regional poison center or the Rocky Mountain Poison Center's toll-free number (800-525-6115) for assistance in diagnosis and for directions in the use of N-acetylcysteine as an antidote. Adverse effects are rare when acetaminophen is used as recommended. However, as with all drugs, overdosage may cause serious toxicity.

How Supplied: Tablets (colored white, scored, imprinted "TYLENOL")—tins and vials of 12 and bottles of 24, 50, 100 and 200. Capsules (colored gray and white, imprinted "TYLENOL 325 mg")—bottles of 24, 50 and 100.

Also available: For additional pain relief, Extra-Strength TYLENOL® Capsules and Tablets, 500 mg. and Extra-Strength TYLENOL® Adult Liquid Pain Reliever (colored green; 1 fl. oz. = 1000 mg.).

[*Shown in Product Identification Section*]

Extra-Strength
TYLENOL® acetaminophen
Tablets and Capsules

Description: Each Extra-Strength TYLENOL Tablet or Capsule contains acetaminophen 500 mg.

Actions: TYLENOL acetaminophen is a clinically proven analgesic and antipyretic. Acetaminophen produces analgesia by elevation of the pain threshold and antipyresis through action on the hypothalamic heat-regulating center.

Indications: For relief of pain and fever. TYLENOL Extra-Strength Tablets and Capsules provide increased analgesic strength for minor conditions when the usual doses of mild analgesics are insufficient.

Precautions and Adverse Reactions: If a rare sensitivity reaction occurs, the drug should be stopped. TYLENOL acetaminophen has rarely been found to produce any side effects. It is usually well tolerated by aspirin-sensitive patients.

Usual Dosage: Adults: Two tablets or capsules 3 or 4 times daily. No more than a total of eight tablets or capsules in any 24-hour period.

Note: Since TYLENOL Extra-Strength Tablets and Capsules are available without a prescription, the following appears on the package labels: "Severe or recurrent pain or high or continued fever may be indicative of serious illness. Under these conditions, consult a physician. WARNING: Keep this and all medication out of the reach of children. In case of accidental overdosage, contact a physician immediately."

Overdosage: Acetaminophen in massive overdosage may cause hepatic toxicity in some patients. In all cases of suspected overdose, immediately call your regional poison center or the Rocky Mountain Poison Center's toll-free number (800-525-6115) for assistance in diagnosis and for directions in the use of N-acetylcysteine as an antidote. Adverse effects are rare when acetaminophen is used as recommended. However, as with all drugs, overdosage may cause serious toxicity.

How Supplied: Tablets (colored white, imprinted "TYLENOL" and "500")—vials of 10 and bottles of 30, 60 and 100; Capsules (colored red and white, imprinted "TYLENOL 500 mg.")—bottles of 24, 50 and 100.

Also Available: For adults who prefer liquids or can't swallow solid medication, Extra-Strength TYLENOL® Adult Liquid Pain Reliever (1 fl. oz. = 1000 mg.).

[*Shown in Product Identification Section*]

Extra-Strength
TYLENOL® acetaminophen
Adult Liquid Pain Reliever

Description: Each 15 ml. (½ fl. oz. or one tablespoonful) contains 500 mg. acetaminophen (alcohol 8½%).

Actions: TYLENOL acetaminophen is a clinically proven analgesic and antipyretic. Acetaminophen produces analgesia by elevation of the pain threshold and antipyresis through action on the hypothalamic heat-regulating center.

Indications: TYLENOL acetaminophen provides fast, effective relief of pain and/or fever for adults who prefer liquids or can't swallow solid medication, e.g., the aged, patients with easily triggered gag reflexes, extremely sore throats, or those on liquid diets.

Precautions and Adverse Reactions: If a rare sensitivity reaction occurs, the drug should be stopped. TYLENOL acetaminophen has rarely been found to produce any side effects. It is usually well tolerated by aspirin-sensitive patients.

Usual Dosage: Extra-Strength TYLENOL Adult Liquid is an adult preparation. Not for use in children under 12. Measuring cup is marked for accurate dosage.

Continued on next page

McNeil Consumer—Cont.

Extra-Strength Dose—1 fl. oz. (30 ml or 2 tablespoonsful, 1000 mg) which is equivalent to two 500 mg Extra-Strength TYLENOL Tablets or Capsules. Take every 4 to 6 hours, no more than 4 doses in any 24 hour period.

Note: Since TYLENOL Extra-Strength Adult Liquid Pain Reliever is available without a prescription, the following appears on the package labels: "Severe or recurrent pain or high or continued fever may be indicative of serious illness. Under these conditions, consult a physician. WARNING: Keep this and all medication out of the reach of children. In case of accidental overdosage, contact a physician immediately."

Overdosage: Acetaminophen in massive overdosage may cause hepatic toxicity in some patients. In all cases of suspected overdose, immediately call your regional poison center or the Rocky Mountain Poison Center's toll-free number (800-525-6115) for assistance in diagnosis and for directions in the use of N-acetylcysteine as an antidote. Adverse effects are rare when acetaminophen is used as recommended. However, as with all drugs, overdosage may cause serious toxicity.

How Supplied: Mint-flavored liquid (colored green), bottles of 8 and 16 fl. oz. with child resistent safety cap and special dosage cup.

[*Shown in Product Identification Section*]

Mead Johnson Nutritional Division

Mead Johnson & Company
2404 W. PENNSYLVANIA ST.
EVANSVILLE, IN 47721

CASEC® powder
Calcium caseinate
Protein modifier

Composition: Consists of dried, soluble calcium caseinate (88% protein) derived from skim milk curd and lime water (calcium carbonate) by a special process. Contains only 42.6 mg sodium per 6 packed level tbsp. (1 ounce).

Action and Uses: Supplementing infant formulas or breast feeding when extra protein is desired. Supplementing diets of children and adults, including sodium restricted diets and diets low in fat or cholesterol. Modifying infant formulas or supplementing breast feedings in the management of simple, mild diarrheas.

Precautions: Additional water should be given as needed to meet the infant's daily water requirement. This is particularly important for infants with diarrhea. If diarrhea continues unimproved, Casec feedings should be discontinued and specific therapy instituted.

Preparation: *For breast-fed infants:* Use 2 packed level tbsp. powder to 6 fl. oz. water. Feed from dropper, spoon or nursing bottle. For protein supplementation—give as needed. Each ounce of mixture provides about 1.3 g protein. In diar-

rhea—give 1 ounce of this mixture before each feeding. Continue 2 or 3 days after symptoms are relieved. *For bottle-fed infants:* The powder may be added to the regular formula as follows: For protein supplementation—sufficient powder to provide the amount of extra protein desired. In simple diarrheas—Use 2 to 4 packed level tbsp. powder in 24-hour formula. After stools have remained firm for 3 days withdraw modifier gradually.

How Supplied: Casec® powder
    NDC 0087-0390-02 Cans of 3⅓ oz. (94.41 gm)

CE-VI-SOL®
Vitamin C supplement drops
For Infants

Composition: Each 0.6 ml supplies 35 mg ascorbic acid.

Action and Uses: Dietary supplement of vitamin C for infants.

Administration and Dosage: 0.6 ml (35 mg) or as indicated. Dropper calibrated for doses of 0.6 and 0.3 ml (35 and 17.5 mg ascorbic acid).

How Supplied: Ce-Vi-Sol® drops (with calibrated dropper)
    NDC 0087-0400-01 Bottles of 1⅔ fl. oz. (50 ml)

ENFAMIL® concentrated liquid • powder
Infant formula

Composition: Infant formula nearly identical to mother's milk. Caloric distribution: 9% from protein, 50% from fat, 41% from carbohydrate.

Each quart of ENFAMIL formula (20 kcal./fl. oz.) supplies 640 kilocalories and the following vitamins and minerals.

Vitamin A, I.U.	1600
Vitamin D, I.U.	400
Vitamin E, I.U.	12
Vitamin C (Ascorbic acid), mg.	52
Folic acid (Folacin), mg.	0.1
Thiamine (Vitamin B₁), mg.	0.5
Riboflavin (Vitamin B₂), mg.	0.6
Niacin, mg.	8
Vitamin B₆, mg.	0.4
Vitamin B₁₂, mcg.	2
Pantothenic acid, mg.	3
Choline, mg.	45
Calcium, mg.	520
Phosphorus, mg.	440*
Iodine, mcg.	65
Iron, mg.	1.4
(Supply 5 mg iron per quart from other sources)	
Magnesium, mg.	45
Copper, mg.	0.6
Zinc, mg.	4
Manganese, mg.	1
Chloride, mg.	489
Potassium, mg.	616
Sodium, mg.	238

*Enfamil powder contains 400 mg phosphorus

NOTE: FER-IN-SOL® iron supplement drops are a convenient source of added iron.

Action and Uses: For feeding of full term and premature infants and a supplementary formula for relief bottle feeding of breast-fed babies. "When breast-feeding is unsuccessful, inappropriate or

stopped early, infant formulas provide the best alternative for meeting nutritional needs during the first year."[1]

Preparation: For 20 kcal./fl. oz.: With concentrated liquid—1 part to 1 part water. With powder—1 level measure to each 2 fl. oz. water; or 1 level 8 oz. measuring cup to water sufficient to make a quart of formula.

Precautions: Prepared formula not fed immediately and opened cans of liquid should be stored in the refrigerator and used within 48 hours.

How Supplied: Powder, 16-oz. (1-lb.) cans with measuring scoop. Concentrated liquid, 40 kcal./fl. oz., 13-fl. oz. cans.

Also available, Enfamil concentrated liquid or powder with iron; 12 mg iron per quart of 20 kcal./fl. oz. Concentrated liquid, 13-fl. oz. cans. Powder, 16-oz. (1-lb.) cans with scoop.

[1]AAP Committee On Nutrition: Commentary on Breast-Feeding and Infant Formulas, Including Proposed Standards for Formulas. Pediatrics 57:279, 1976.

ENFAMIL® with Iron
concentrated liquid •powder
Infant formula

Composition: Infant formula nearly identical to mother's milk, with added iron (12 mg./qt.). Caloric distribution: 9% from protein, 50% from fat, 41% from carbohydrate. Except for the higher iron content, the normal dilution (20 kcal./fl. oz.) has the same vitamin and mineral content as Enfamil (see Enfamil).

Action and Uses: For feeding of full term and premature infants to supply a daily intake of iron with the formula. Feeding of infants with special needs for exogenous iron, such as: premature infants, offspring of anemic mothers, infants of multiple births, infants with low birth weights and those who grow rapidly, infants who have minor losses of blood at birth or in surgery. As a supplementary formula for relief bottle feeding of breast-fed infants. "When breast-feeding is unsuccessful, inappropriate or stopped early, infant formulas provide the best alternative for meeting nutritional needs during the first year."[1] For older infants the formula provides an easily digestible "beverage milk" plus a supplement of iron. One quart (32 fl. oz.) of formula supplies 12 mg. of iron.

Preparation: For 20 kcal./fl. oz.: With concentrated liquid—1 part to 1 part water. With powder—1 level measure to each 2 fl. oz. water; or 1 level 8 oz. measuring cup to water sufficient to make a quart of formula.

Precautions: If therapeutic or larger supplementary amounts of iron are indicated, the iron content of the formula should be taken into account (12 mg. iron per qt.) in calculating the total iron dosage. Prepared Enfamil with Iron formula not fed immediately and opened cans of Enfamil with Iron liquid should be stored in the refrigerator and used within 48 hours.

How Supplied: Liquid—13-fl. oz. cans. Powder—16-oz. (1-lb.) cans.

[1]AAP Committee on Nutrition: Commentary on Breast-Feeding and Infant Formulas, Including Proposed Standards for Formulas. Pediatrics 57:279, 1976.

ENFAMIL NURSETTE®
Infant formula

Composition: Glass formula bottle filled with ready-to-feed Enfamil® (infant formula) 20 kcal./fl. oz. (See Enfamil concentrated liquid and powder for nutrient values.)

Action and Uses: A very convenient form of Enfamil for routine formula feeding at home or away. Especially useful for first weeks at home, infants of working mothers, infant travel, emergency feedings, or as a supplementary formula for relief bottle feeding of breast-fed babies. "When breast-feeding is unsuccessful, inappropriate or stopped early, infant formulas provide the best alternative for meeting nutritional needs during the first year."[1]

Preparation: Remove cap, attach any standard sterilized nipple unit and feed baby. The Nursette bottle needs no refrigeration until opened and can be fed at room temperature. Interchangeable with Enfamil Ready-To-Use liquid in cans and formulas in normal dilution (20 kcal./fl. oz.) prepared from Enfamil concentrated liquid or powder.

Note: Contents remaining in bottle after feeding should be discarded. Nipples and collar rings should be washed, rinsed and sterilized before reuse.

How Supplied: Available in convenient 4 fl. oz., 6 fl. oz., and 8 fl. oz. Nursette® bottles, packed four bottles to a sealed carton, six 4-packs per case. Enfamil Nursette with Iron also available in 6-fl. oz. bottles.

[1]AAP Committee On Nutrition: Commentary on Breast-Feeding and Infant Formulas, Including Proposed Standards for Formulas. Pediatrics 57:279, 1976.

ENFAMIL® ready-to-use
Infant formula

Composition: Filled cans of ready-to-feed Enfamil infant formula 20 kcal./fl. oz. (see Enfamil concentrated liquid and powder for nutrient values.)

Action and Uses: A very convenient form of Enfamil for routine formula feeding at home. Especially useful for feeding of infants during first weeks at home, infants of working mothers, infant travel, emergency feedings, as a supplementary formula for relief bottle feeding of breast-fed babies. "When breast-feeding is unsuccessful, inappropriate or stopped early, infant formulas provide the best alternative for meeting nutritional needs during the first year."[1]

Preparation: Pour liquid into sterilized nursing bottle without diluting. No refrigeration is necessary for the unopened cans. The formula need not be heated before feeding baby. Interchangeable with formulas in normal dilution (20 kcal./fl. oz.) prepared from Enfamil concentrated liquid or powder and Enfamil Nursette® in filled formula bottles.

Precautions: Opened cans of Enfamil Ready-To-Use formula should be stored in refrigerator and used within 48 hours.

How Supplied: 8-fl. oz. cans, in an easy to carry handy six-can pack, 4 packs per case, and 32-fl. oz. (1-qt.) cans, six cans per case.

[1]AAP Committee on Nutrition: Commentary on Breast-Feeding and Infant Formulas, Including Proposed Standards for Formulas. Pediatrics 57:279, 1976.

ENFAMIL® with Iron ready-to-use
Infant formula

Composition: Filled cans of ready-to-feed Enfamil with Iron infant formula 20 kcal./fl. oz. (see Enfamil with Iron concentrated liquid & powder for nutrient values.)

Action and Uses: A very convenient form of Enfamil with Iron for routine formula feeding at home or away, especially useful for routine feeding of infants during first weeks at home, infants of working mothers, infant travel, emergency feedings, as a supplementary formula for relief bottle feeding of breast-fed babies. "When breast-feeding is unsuccessful, inappropriate or stopped early, infant formulas provide the best alternative for meeting nutritional needs during the first year."[1]

Preparation: Pour desired amount of liquid into sterilized nursing bottle without diluting. No refrigeration is necessary for unopened cans. The formula need not be heated before feeding baby. Interchangeable with formulas in normal dilution (20 kcal./fl. oz.) prepared from Enfamil with Iron concentrated liquid or powder. One quart (32 fl. oz.) of Enfamil with Iron Ready-To-Use infant formula supplies 12 mg of iron.

Precautions: If therapeutic or larger supplementary amounts of iron are indicated, the iron content of the formula should be taken into account (12 mg per qt.) in calculating the total iron dosage. Opened cans of Enfamil with Iron Ready-To-Use formula should be stored in the refrigerator and used within 48 hours.

How Supplied: 8-fl. oz. cans, in an easy to carry handy six-can pack, 4 packs per case, and 32-fl. oz. (1-qt.) cans, six cans per case.

[1]AAP Committee On Nutrition: Commentary on Breast-Feeding and Infant Formulas, Including Proposed Standards for Formulas. Pediatrics 57:279, 1976.

FEMININS® tablets
Multivitamin-mineral supplement for women taking oral contraceptives

Composition: Each tablet supplies:

	% U.S. RDA* Adults	
Vitamin A, I.U.	5000	100
Vitamin D, I.U.	400	100
Vitamin E, I.U.	10	33
Vitamin C (Ascorbic acid), mg.	200	333
Folic acid (Folacin), mg.	0.1	25
Thiamine (Vitamin B₁), mg.	1.5	100
Riboflavin (Vitamin B₂), mg.	3	176
Niacin, mg.	15	75
Vitamin B₆, mg.	25	1250
Vitamin B₁₂, mcg.	10	167
Pantothenic acid, mg.	10	100
Iron, mg.	18	100
Zinc, mg.	10	67

*U.S. Recommended Daily Allowance

Ingredients: Vitamin A acetate, ergocalciferol, dl-alpha-tocopheryl acetate, sodium ascorbate, folic acid, thiamine mononitrate, riboflavin, niacinamide, pyridoxine hydrochloride, cyanocobalamin, calcium pantothenate, ferrous fumarate, zinc oxide, and artificial coloring.

Action and Uses: Daily diet supplementation during use of oral contraceptives. Feminins tablets provide vitamin and mineral supplementation for the special needs of women taking oral contraceptives.

Administration and Dosage: One tablet a day, or as indicated.

How Supplied: Feminins® tablets
NDC 0087-0470-01　　　Bottles of 100
[*Shown in Product Identification Section*]

FER-IN-SOL®
Iron supplement
- drops
- syrup
- capsules
Ferrous sulfate, Mead Johnson

Composition:

	Supplies	
	Ferrous Sulfate	As Elemental Iron
Fer-In-Sol	mg	mg
Drops (per 0.6 ml dose)	75	15
Syrup (per 5 ml teaspoonful)	90	18
Capsule (1 capsule)	190 (dried)	60

Action and Uses: Source of supplemental iron.

Administration and Dosage:
drops
0.6 ml daily supplies 15 mg of elemental iron, 100% of the U.S. RDA for infants and 150% of the U.S. RDA for children under 4 years of age.
Give in water or in fruit or vegetable juice.
Fer-In-Sol should be given immediately after meals. When an infant or child is taking iron, stools may appear darker in color. This is to be expected and should be no cause for concern. When drops containing iron are given to young babies, some darkening of the membrane covering the baby's teeth may occur. This is

Continued on next page

Mead Johnson Nutritional—Cont.

not serious or permanent. The enamel of the teeth is not affected. Should this darkening or staining occur, it may be removed by rubbing the baby's teeth with a little baking soda on a small cloth once a week.

syrup

1 teaspoon (5 ml) daily supplies 18 mg of elemental iron, 100% of the U.S. RDA for adults and children 4 or more years of age.

capsules

One capsule daily supplies 60 mg of elemental iron, 333% of the U.S. RDA for pregnant or lactating women.

How Supplied: Fer-In-Sol® drops (with calibrated 'Safti-Dropper')

NDC 0087-0740-02 Bottles of 1-⅔ fl. oz. (50 ml)

6505-00-664-0856 (1-⅔ fl. oz., 50 ml)

Defense

Fer-In-Sol® syrup

NDC 0087-0741-01 Bottles of 16 fl. oz.

Fer-In-Sol® capsules

NDC 0087-0742-01 Bottles of 100

[*Shown in Product Identification Section*]

FLEXICAL®
Nutritionally balanced elemental diet

Flexical is a nutritionally complete and balanced diet in which protein is present in predigested or elemental form and fat and carbohydrate are present in simple, readily digestible form. (Protein in the form of predigested hydrolyzed casein plus three essential amino acids assures a protein efficiency unsurpassed by other commercially available protein sources. MCT® Oil as a component of the fat source offers extreme ease of digestion and absorption. Carbohydrates in simple, easily-digestible forms supply approximately 60% of calories.)

Composition: Corn syrup solids, enzymatically hydrolyzed casein, partially hydrogenated soy oil, modified tapioca starch, medium chain triglycerides (fractionated coconut oil), lecithin, amino acids (L-methionine, L-tyrosine, L-tryptophan), vitamins (vitamin A palmitate, ergocalciferol, dl-alpha-tocopheryl acetate, sodium ascorbate, folic acid, thiamine hydrochloride, riboflavin, niacinamide, pyridoxine hydrochloride, cyanocobalamin, biotin, calcium pantothenate, phytonadione, choline chloride) and minerals (calcium citrate, potassium chloride, dibasic magnesium phosphate, potassium citrate, dibasic calcium phosphate, ferrous sulfate, cupric sulfate, zinc sulfate, manganese sulfate, and potassium iodide).

Each 454 grams of powder (1-lb. can), when reconstituted with 1,656 ml water (56 fl. oz.) supplies about 2 liters at 1 Cal./ml (30 Cal./fl. oz.). Each 2,000 Calories provides 45 grams protein equivalent, 67.9 g fat, 305 g carbohydrate and the following vitamins and minerals:

	Per 2000 Cal.	% U.S. RDA Adults & Children Over 4 Yrs. of Age
Protein (equivalent), g.	45	100
Fat, g.	67.9	*
Carbohydrate, g.	305	*
Vitamin A, I.U.	5000	100
Vitamin D, I.U.	400	100
Vitamin E, I.U.	45	150
Vitamin C (Ascorbic acid), mg.	300	500
Folic acid (Folacin), mg.	0.4	100
Thiamine (Vitamin B_1), mg.	3.8	250
Riboflavin (Vitamin B_2), mg.	4.3	250
Niacin, mg.	50	250
Vitamin B_6, mg.	5	250
Vitamin B_{12}, mcg.	15	250
Biotin, mg.	0.3	100
Pantothenic acid, mg.	25	250
Vitamin K_1, mcg.	250	*
Choline, mg.	500	*
Calcium, g.	1.2	120
Phosphorus, g.	1	100
Iodine, mcg.	150	100
Iron, mg.	18	100
Magnesium, mg.	400	100
Copper, mg.	2	100
Zinc, mg.	20	133
Manganese, mg.	5	*
Chloride, g.	2	*
Potassium, g.	2.5	*
Sodium, g.	0.7	*

*U.S. Recommended Daily Allowance (U.S.R.D.A.) has not been established.

Actions and Uses: Flexical low-residue, elemental diet is specially formulated to provide for the nutritional needs of critically ill patients who require a diet with minimum digestive activity and low levels of fecal residue. Flexical is valuable in the nutritional management of preoperative bowel preparation, short bowel syndrome and malabsorption problems, G.I. fistulae, chemotherapeutic and radiation therapy, inflammatory bowel disease, post-acute and chronic pancreatitis, enteral nutrition of the critically ill. Flexical may also serve as an alternative to clear fluids which, although low residue, are frequently not nutritionally complete; as an adjunct to, or as a transitional phase in the replacement of parenteral feeding.

Precautions and Adverse Reactions: Under certain circumstances, the following side effects have been noted in patients receiving low residue elemental diets: nausea, vomiting, diarrhea, anorexia, chronic constipation and fecal impaction. Most of these appear to be related primarily to the hyperosmolarity of the diet. It is recommended that initially Flexical be diluted to 0.5 Cal./ml or less and then gradually be increased to 1 Cal./ml Additional water should be encouraged in addition to that used in Flexical.

Preparation: A full day's supply of Flexical is prepared by emptying the contents of the 1-lb. can into 56 fl. oz. (1656 ml) of water and mixing thoroughly in a blender. This will provide about 67 fl. oz.

(2000 ml) and 2000 Cal. at 1 Cal./ml or 30 Cal./fl. oz.

A single serving of Flexical is prepared by emptying the contents of the 2-oz. can into 7 fl. oz. (207 ml) of water and mixing thoroughly in a blender. This will provide about 8.3 fl. oz. (250 ml) and 250 Cal. at 1 Cal./ml or 30 Cal./fl. oz.

Reconstituted Flexical should be refrigerated. Unused portions should be discarded after 24 hours.

Feeding Instructions: Because some patients may be sensitive to the osmolality of Flexical at the 1.0 Cal./ml dilution, it may be advisable to dilute the product to 0.5 Cal./ml or less on the first day/days of use, and as tolerance is established, the caloric density may be increased to full strength. Sufficient extra fluids should be given each patient daily to maintain adequate urinary output.

When fed orally, Flexical should be served well chilled and sipped gradually. Because of the special flavor characteristics of Flexical, it is well to clearly counsel patients that its flavor differs significantly from other liquid diets. As patients understand the very special importance of Flexical, acceptability generally increases. Unflavored Flexical may be mixed with a variety of clear liquids to help improve taste acceptance.

Serving Suggestions: Flexical may be served for oral use very well chilled or with ice cubes; in a covered glass, sipped through a straw; frozen and eaten with a spoon. Flexical may also be fed by nasogastric tube; gastrostomy tube and enterostomy tube.

How Flexical Elemental Diet is Supplied: Flexical is available in a choice of convenient packages. Each 1-lb. can of Flexical provides 2000 Cal. and offers the convenience of a full day's supply. Six 1-lb. cans are provided in each shipping case.

Each 2-oz. can of Flexical provides 250 Cal. and offers the convenience of a single serving per can. Eight 2-oz. cans are included in each carton (thus, 2000 Cal.) and six cartons are provided in each shipping case.

Flexical® Unflavored Powder

NDC 0087-0569-42 Cans of 1 lb.

NDC 0087-0569-41 Cans of 2 oz., 8 cans per carton

ISOCAL®
Complete liquid diet

Composition: Water, glucose oligosaccharides, soy oil, calcium caseinate, sodium caseinate, medium chain triglycerides (fractionated coconut oil), soy protein isolate, potassium citrate, lecithin, calcium citrate, magnesium chloride, calcium chloride, dibasic calcium phosphate, dibasic magnesium phosphate, sodium citrate, carrageenan, potassium chloride, vitamins (vitamin A palmitate, ergocalciferol, dl-alpha-tocopheryl acetate, sodium ascorbate, folic acid, thiamine hydrochloride, riboflavin, niacinamide, pyridoxine hydrochloride, cyanocobalamin, biotin, calcium pantothenate, phytonadione, and choline chloride) and minerals (potassium iodide, ferrous sulfate, cupric sulfate, zinc sulfate and manganese sulfate).

(See table at right)

Actions and Uses: Isocal is a complete liquid diet specifically formulated to provide well-balanced nutrition when used as the sole source of nourishment. The formulation of Isocal is especially designed to meet the special nutritional requirements of tube-fed patients and provide these unique characteristics:

An isotonic osmolality to avoid the problems associated with formulas of high osmotic concentrations: e.g., diarrhea, cramps, vomiting, nausea.

No lactose—to preclude the diarrhea and other side effects associated with lactose intolerance.

MCT® Oil (Medium Chain Triglycerides) as a component of the fat source is easily digestible and well absorbed.

100% of the U.S. RDA's for protein and all known essential vitamins and minerals in 2000 Calories. Also, additional amounts of vitamin C and the B-complex vitamins are of particular value to many tube-fed patients.

Preparation and Administration: Isocal is ready to feed and requires no additional water; shake well before opening. Unopened Isocal should be stored at room temperature. After opening, Isocal should be covered and refrigerated if not used immediately.

Nasogastric tube feedings with Isocal, Complete Liquid Diet, may be given using a standard tube feeding set, or the Isocal Tube Feeding Set. Feedings may be given by continuous drip or at intervals. The rate should be adjusted for the best comfort and needs of the individual patient. When initiating feedings it is recommended that the volume given be no more than 8 fluid ounces. This amount should be administered over a period of about 30 minutes.

Isocal has a bland, unsweetened taste because it is specifically formulated for tube feedings. However, patients on long-term oral diet may prefer the taste of Isocal to the sweet taste of some oral liquid nutritional supplements.

Precautions: Additional water should be given as needed to meet the patient's requirements. Particular attention should be given to water supply for comatose and unconscious patients and others who cannot express the usual sensations of thirst. Additional water is important also when renal-concentrating ability is impaired, when there is extensive breakdown of tissue protein, or when water requirements are high, as in fever. Tube feeding preparations should be at room temperature during administration.

How Supplied: Isocal® Complete Liquid Diet
  NDC 0087-0355-01 Cans of 8 fl. oz.
  NDC 0087-0355-02 Cans of 12 fl. oz.
  NDC 0087-0355-44 Cans of 32 fl. oz. (1 quart)
  NDC 0087-0356-01 Bottles of 8 fl. oz.
  VA 8940-00-624899 (8-oz. cans)

Also Available:
  NDC 0087-0357-01 Isocal Tube Feeding Set

	Per 250 Cal. (8 fl. oz.)	Adults & Children 4 or more yrs. % U.S. RDA	Per 375 Cal. (12 fl. oz.)	Adults & Children 4 or more yrs. % U.S. RDA	Per 2000 Cal. (64 fl. oz.)	Adults & Children 4 or more yrs. % U.S. RDA
Calories	250	*	375	*	2000	*
Protein, g.	8.1	12.5	12.1	19	65	100
Fat, g.	10.5	*	15.7	*	84	*
Carbohydrate, g.	31.2	*	46.8	*	250	*
Vitamin A, I.U.	625	12.5	935	19	5000	100
Vitamin D, I.U.	50	12.5	75	19	400	100
Vitamin E, I.U.	9.4	31	14	46	75	250
Vitamin C (Ascorbic acid), mg.	37.5	63	56	95	300	500
Folic acid (Folacin), mg.	0.05	12.5	0.07	19	0.4	100
Thiamine (Vitamin B_1), mg.	0.48	32	0.72	48	3.8	250
Riboflavin (Vitamin B_2), mg.	0.54	32	0.81	48	4.3	250
Niacin, mg.	6.2	31	9.4	46	50	250
Vitamin B_6, mg.	0.62	31	0.93	46	5	250
Vitamin B_{12}, mcg.	1.9	31	2.8	46	15	250
Biotin, mg.	0.04	12.5	0.06	19	0.3	100
Pantothenic acid, mg.	3.1	31	4.7	46	25	250
Vitamin K_1, mcg.	31	*	47	*	250	*
Choline, mg.	62.5	*	93.7	*	500	*
Calcium, g.	0.15	15	0.225	23	1.2	120
Phosphorus, g.	0.125	12.5	0.188	19	1	100
Iodine, mcg.	19	12.5	28	19	150	100
Iron, mg.	2.25	12.5	3.4	19	18	100
Magnesium, mg.	50	12.5	75	19	400	100
Copper, mg.	0.25	12.5	0.37	19	2	100
Zinc, mg.	2.5	17	3.7	25	20	133
Manganese, mg.	0.6	*	0.9	*	5	*
Chloride, mg.	250	*	375	*	2000	*
Potassium, mg.	312	*	468	*	2500	*
Sodium, mg.	125	*	187	*	1000	*

*U.S. Recommended Daily Allowance (U.S. RDA) has not been established.

LOFENALAC® powder
Low phenylalanine food

Composition: Low phenylalanine formula made from 49.2% corn syrup solids, 18.7% specially processed casein hydrolysate (an enzymic digest of casein containing amino acids and small peptides, processed to remove most of the phenylalanine), 18% corn oil, 9.57% modified tapioca starch, 1.45% calcium citrate, 0.8% L-tyrosine, 0.76% dibasic calcium phosphate, 0.58% dibasic potassium phosphate, 0.2% L-tryptophan, 0.18% L-histidine hydrochloride monohydrate, 0.12% potassium citrate, 0.1% magnesium oxide, 0.1% L-methionine, 0.04% calcium hydroxide, vitamins (vitamin A palmitate, ergocalciferol, dl-alpha-tocopheryl acetate, sodium ascorbate, folic acid, thiamine hydrochloride, riboflavin, niacinamide, pyridoxine hydrochloride, cyanocobalamin, biotin, calcium pantothenate, phytonadione, choline chloride and inositol), and minerals (ferrous sulfate, cupric sulfate, zinc sulfate, manganese sulfate, and sodium iodide). *Proximate analysis* (powder): protein (equivalent) 15%, fat 18%, carbohydrate 59.6%, minerals (ash) 3.6%. Phenylalanine content of Lofenalac powder is approximately 0.08% (not more than 0.1% nor less than 0.06%). Each 100 g of powder supplies about 460 kilocalories and 80 mg phenylalanine. One packed level measure contains 9.5 g Each quart of formula in normal dilution supplies these vitamins and minerals.

	Per Qt.
Protein, g	+
Vitamin A, I.U.	1600
Vitamin D, I.U.	400
Vitamin E, I.U.	10
Vitamin C (Ascorbic acid), mg	52
Folic acid (Folacin), mcg	100
Thiamine (Vitamin B_1), mg	0.5
Riboflavin (Vitamin B_2), mg	0.6
Niacin, mg	8
Vitamin B_6, mg	0.4
Vitamin B_{12}, mcg	2
Biotin, mg	0.05
Pantothenic acid, mg	3
Vitamin K_1, mcg	100
Choline, mg	85
Inositol, mg	30
Calcium, mg	600
Phosphorus, mg	450
Iodine, mcg	45
Iron, mg	12
Magnesium, mg	70
Copper, mg	0.6
Zinc, mg	4
Manganese, mg	1
Chloride, mg	450

Continued on next page

Mead Johnson Nutritional—Cont.

Potassium, mg	650
Sodium, mg	300

+The protein is incomplete since it contains an inadequate amount of the essential amino acid, phenylalanine, for normal growth. With added phenylalanine, the PER is greater than that of casein.

The nutrient levels meet Food and Drug Administration requirements for infant formula, except for protein. Each quart supplies 12 mg iron (from ferrous sulfate).

Action and Uses: For use as basic food in low phenylalanine dietary management of infants and children with phenylketonuria. Provides essential nutrients without the high phenylalanine content (approx. 5%) present in natural food proteins.

Preparation: 20 Kcal./fl.oz. Formula for Infants: To make a quart of formula, add one packed level 8-oz. measuring cup (139 g) of Lofenalac powder to 29 fl. oz. water. For smaller amounts of formula, add 1 packed level measuring scoop (9.5 g) of powder to each 2 fluid ounces of water.

To prepare as a beverage for older children (about 30 kcal./fl.oz.), add an 8-ounce measuring cup of powder to 2½ cups of warm water; mix with beater until smooth, then store in refrigerator. Prescribe a specific amount of this mixture daily, and carefully add specific amounts of other foods to the diet.

When fed at the level of 50 kilocalories per pound of body weight (110 kcal./kg), this product provides about 9 mg. phenylalanine per pound (20 mg./kg). This is within a phenylalanine range (20 to 30 mg./kg) recommended as needed by phenylketonuric patients for growth. Other foods should be given as required to provide needed calories and bring phenylalanine intake to adequate, but not excessive, level. The diet and the phenylalanine intake must be adapted to individual needs.

Store bottled formula in refrigerator and use within 24 hours.

Contraindications: Lofenalac (low phenylalanine food) should not be used for normal infants and children, but should be used only as part of the diet of patients with phenylketonuria. Continued usage must be carefully and frequently supervised by the physician and the diet periodically adjusted on the basis of frequent tests of urine and blood.

How Supplied: Lofenalac®
NDC 0087-0340-01 Cans of 40 oz. (2½ lb.)
Consult Lofenalac® product brochure for details.

LONALAC® powder
Low sodium, high protein beverage mix

Composition: High protein food for use in low sodium diets, containing lactose, casein, coconut oil, monobasic calcium phosphate, potassium carbonate, calcium hydroxide, calcium chloride, potassium chloride, magnesium oxide, calcium carbonate, vitamin A palmitate, thiamine hydrochloride, riboflavin, niacinamide, artificial color and flavoring. One pound of Lonalac powder supplies 122.5 g protein, 172.4 g carbohydrate, and 127.1 g fat.

Each quart (20 Cal./fl. oz.) contains the following vitamins and minerals:

Vitamin A, I.U.	960
Thiamine (Vitamin B$_1$), mg.	0.4
Riboflavin (Vitamin B$_2$), mg.	1.7
Niacin, mg.	0.8
Calcium, g.	1.1
Phosphorus, g.	1
Iron, mg.	1
Magnesium, mg.	90
Potassium, g.	1.2
Sodium, mg.	25

It contains only 25 mg sodium per quart of normal dilution, in contrast to 480 mg per quart of milk.

Action and Uses: A substitute for milk when dietary sodium restriction is prescribed, as in congestive heart failure, hypertension, nephrosis, acute nephritis, toxemia of pregnancy, hepatic cirrhosis with ascites, and therapy with certain drugs.

Preparation: For 20 Cal./fl. oz.: 1 level 8-oz. measuring cup (about 4-½ oz. or 125 g) Lonalac powder to 3½ cups of water. Concentrated preparation: ½ cup Lonalac powder to 1 cup water. Store bottled formula in refrigerator and use within 24 hours.

Precautions: Care should be taken to avoid additional sodium intake from other dietary or non-dietary sources. Subjects receiving low sodium diets must be observed for signs of sodium deprivation such as weakness, exhaustion and abdominal cramps. In long term management (using Lonalac), additional sources of sodium must be given since Lonalac is almost void of the essential nutrient sodium.

How Supplied: Lonalac®
NDC 0087-0391-01 Cans of 16 oz. (1 lb.)
VA 8940-00-191-6565 (1 lb. can)

LYTREN®
Oral electrolyte solution

Lytren provides important electrolytes plus carbohydrate in a balanced formulation. It is designed for oral administration when food intake is discontinued.

Composition:
Ingredients: Water, corn syrup solids, dextrose, sodium citrate, potassium chloride, citric acid, sodium biphosphate, potassium citrate, calcium chloride, and magnesium sulfate.

Concentrations of Electrolytes (9 kcal./fl. oz.):

Electrolyte	mEq/L	Approximate mEq/4 fl. oz. (118 ml)	mOsm/L
Sodium	30	3.5	30
Potassium	25	3	25
Calcium	4	0.5	2
Magnesium	4	0.5	2
Chloride	25	3	25
Citrate	36	4	12
Sulfate	4	0.5	2
Phosphate	5	0.6	5
Total*	133	15.6	103

*NOTE: Lytren oral electrolyte solution is nearly isotonic (compared to extracellular fluid) and has an osmolality of approximately 290 mOsm. per kilogram of water.

Indications: When intake of the usual foods and liquids is discontinued, oral feedings of Lytren solution may be used:
- To supply water and electrolytes for maintenance.
- To replace mild to moderate fluid losses.

Such oral electrolyte feedings have particular application in mild and moderate diarrheas, to forestall dehydration,[1-6] and in postoperative states.

Intake and Administration: Feed by nursing bottle, glass or straw.

Administration of Lytren solution should be begun as soon as intake of usual foods and liquids is discontinued, and before serious fluid losses or deficits develop.

Intake of Lytren solution should approximate the patient's calculated daily water requirements, for maintenance and for replacement of losses. The prescribed quantity may be divided and used throughout the day as desired or appropriate. (Note: No more than this amount of Lytren should be given. Additional liquid to satisfy thirst should be water or other non-electrolyte-containing fluids.)

•For infants and young children. The water requirement should be calculated on the basis of body surface area. Estimated daily water requirements such as the following may be used as a general guide:

For maintenance in illness—1500 ml (50 fl. oz.) per square meter.[7]

For maintenance plus replacement of moderate losses (as in diarrhea or vomiting)—2400 ml (80 fl. oz.) per square meter.[7]

Daily amount of Lytren solution based on these estimated requirements is shown in the Intake Guide table. Intake should be adjusted according to the size of the individual patient and the clinical conditions.

•For older children and adults. When fluid losses are mild to moderate, amounts such as the following may be given daily: Children 5 to 10 years—1 to 2 quarts. Older children and adults—2 to 3 quarts.[7]

Intake should be adjusted on the basis of clinical indications, amount of fluid loss, patient's usual water intake and other relevant factors.

[See table on next page].

•Lytren In conjunction with other fluids. When severe fluid losses or accumulated deficits require parenteral fluid therapy, Lytren solution by mouth may be given simultaneously to supply part of the estimated fluid requirement. After emergency needs have been met, Lytren solution alone may be used.

Contraindications:
Lytren should not be used:
•In the presence of severe, continuing diarrhea or other critical fluid losses requiring parenteral fluid therapy.

- In intractable vomiting, adynamic ileus, intestinal obstruction or perforated bowel.
- When renal function is depressed (anuria, oliguria) or homeostatic mechanisms are impaired.

Precautions: Lytren oral electrolyte solution should only be used in the recommended volume intakes in order to avoid excessive electrolyte ingestion. Do not mix with, or give with, other electrolyte-containing liquids, such as milk or fruit juices.

Urgent needs in severe fluid imbalances must be met parenterally. When Lytren solution by mouth is used in addition to parenteral fluids, do not exceed total water and electrolyte requirements.

Intake of Lytren should be reduced promptly and steadily upon reintroduction of other electrolyte-containing foods into the diet. Should be administered on physician's orders only.

How Supplied:

Lytren—32 fl. oz., Ready to Use.

Lytren is also available in the hospital in an 8-fl. oz. Nursette® Disposable Bottle and Beniflex® Disposable Nurser System.

References:

1. Darrow DC: Pediatrics 9:519–533 (May) 1952. 2. Harrison HE: Pediat Clin North America, May 1954. pp 335–348. 3. Vaughan VC, III, in Nelson WE: Textbook of Pediatrics, ed 7, Philadelphia, WB Saunders Company, 1959, pp 187–189. 4. Brooke CE, Anast CS: JAMA 179:148–153 (March) 1962. 5. Darrow DC, Welsh JS: J Pediat 56:204–210 (Feb) 1960. 6. Cooke RE: JAMA 167:1243–1246 (July 5) 1958. 7. Worthen HG, Raile RB: Minnesota Med 37:558–564 (Aug) 1954. 8. McLester JS, Darby WJ: Nutrition and Diet in Health and Disease, ed 6, Philadelphia, WB Saunders Company, 1952, pp 32–34.

MCT® Oil
Medium chain triglycerides oil

Composition: MCT Oil contains triglycerides of medium chain fatty acids which are more easily digested and absorbed than conventional food fat.

MCT Oil is bland tasting and light yellow in color. It provides 8.3 Cal./g. One tablespoon (15 ml.) weighs 14 g. and contains 115 Cal. It is a lipid fraction of coconut oil and consists primarily of the triglycerides of C_8 and C_{10} saturated fatty acids. Approximate percentages are:

Fatty Acid	%
Shorter than C_8	< 3
C_8 (Octanoic)	68
C_{10} (Decanoic)	24
Longer than C_{10}	< 5

Actions and Uses: MCT Oil is a special dietary supplement for use in the nutritional management of children and adults who cannot efficiently digest and absorb conventional long chain food fats. One tablespoonful 3 to 4 times per day or as recommended by the physician. MCT Oil should be mixed with fruit juices, used on salads and vegetables, incorporated into sauces for use on fish, chicken, or lean meat, or used in cooking or bak-

ing. Recipes or professional literature available upon request.

Precaution: In persons with advanced cirrhosis of the liver, large amounts of medium chain triglycerides in the diet may result in elevated blood and spinal fluid levels of medium chain fatty acids (MCFA), due to impaired hepatic clearance of these fatty acids, which are rapidly absorbed via the portal vein. These elevated levels have been reported to be associated with reversible coma and precoma in certain subjects with advanced cirrhosis, particularly with portacaval shunts. Therefore, diets containing high levels of medium chain triglyceride fat should be used with caution in persons with hepatic cirrhosis and complications thereof, such as portacaval shunts or tendency to encephalopathy.

Use of MCT Oil-containing products in abetalipoproteinemia is not indicated.

How Supplied: MCT® Oil

NDC 0087-0365-03 Bottles of 1 quart

NUTRAMIGEN® powder
Protein hydrolysate formula

Composition: Ingredients: 43.3% sugar (sucrose), 19.2% casein enzymically hydrolyzed and charcoal-treated to reduce allergenicity, 18% corn oil, 16.5% modified tapioca starch, 1.12% dibasic calcium phosphate, 0.91% potassium citrate, 0.34% calcium citrate, 0.3% calcium hydroxide, 0.1% magnesium oxide, 0.057% potassium chloride, vitamins (vitamin A palmitate, ergocalciferol, dl-alpha-tocopheryl acetate, sodium ascorbate, folic acid, thiamine hydrochloride, riboflavin, niacinamide, pyridoxine hydrochloride, cyanocobalamin, biotin, calcium pantothenate, phytonadione, choline chloride and inositol), and minerals (ferrous sulfate, manganese sulfate, cupric sulfate, zinc sulfate, and sodium iodide).

One quart of Nutramigen formula (4.9 oz. Nutramigen Powder) supplies 640 kilocalories and the following vitamins and minerals:

Vitamin A, I.U.	1600
Vitamin D, I.U.	400
Vitamin E, I.U.	10
Vitamin C, mg.	52
Folic acid, mcg.	100
Thiamine, mg.	0.5
Riboflavin, mg.	0.6
Niacin, mg.	8
Vitamin B_6, mg.	0.4
Vitamin B_{12}, mcg.	2
Biotin, mg.	0.05
Pantothenic acid, mg.	3
Vitamin K_1, mcg.	100
Choline, mg.	85
Inositol, mg.	30
Calcium, mg.	600
Phosphorus, mg.	450
Iodine, mcg.	45
Iron, mg.	12
Magnesium, mg.	70
Copper, mg.	0.6
Zinc, mg.	4
Manganese, mg.	1
Chloride, mg.	450
Potassium, mg.	650
Sodium, mg.	300

Action and Uses: Feeding of infants and children allergic or intolerant to ordinary food proteins (intact proteins). Provides a formula with predigested protein for infants with diarrhea or other gastrointestinal disturbances. Provides lactose-free feedings in galactosemia.

Precautions: Initial feedings of Nutramigen should be diluted to 10 kcal./fl. oz. and gradually increased to 20 kcal./fl. oz. over a period of 3 to 5 days. Individuals with lengthy episodes of diarrhea and/or receiving antibiotics may require supplemental vitamin K.

In a few instances, premature infants and infants with long-standing malabsorption problems have been reported to have metabolic acidosis when receiving a casein hydrolysate formula for an extended period of time. The etiology of this acidosis is obscure. The overall incidence is rare and can be satisfactorily controlled by giving the patient 2-3 mEq./kg./day of sodium bicarbonate, which may be conveniently added to the formula.

Preparation: For 10 kcal./fl. oz.: 1 packed level measure to 4 fl. oz. water, or ½ level 8 oz. measuring cup to water sufficient to make a quart of formula. For 20 kcal./fl. oz.: 1 packed level measure powder (9.5 g.) to 2 fl. oz. water, or 1 level 8 oz. measuring cup (139 g.) to water sufficient to make a quart of formula.

Continued on next page

LYTREN INTAKE GUIDE
for infants and young children

(Adjust to meet individual needs)

LYTREN SOLUTION
DAILY INTAKE

*Averages of Benedict-Talbot estimated surface areas for boys and girls.[8]	Body Weight Kg.	Body Weight Lb.	Average Surface Area Sq. Meter*	Maintenance Approx. Fl. Oz.[†]	Maintenance plus Replacement of Moderate Losses Approx. Fl. Oz.[‡]
[†]Based on water requirement	3	6–7	0.2	10	16
of 1500 ml. (50 fl. oz.) per sq.	5	11	0.29	15	23
meter.[7]	7	15	0.38	19	30
[‡]Based on water requirement	10	22	0.49	25	40
of 2400 ml. (80 fl. oz.) per sq.	12	26	0.55	28	44
meter.[7]	15	33	0.64	32	51
	18	40	0.76	38	61

Mead Johnson Nutritional—Cont.

Store bottled formula in refrigerator and use within 24 hours.

How Supplied: Nutramigen®
NDC 0087-0338-01 Cans of 16 oz. (1 lb.), with measure.

POLY-VI-SOL®
Multivitamin supplement
drops • chewable tablets

Composition: Usual daily doses supply:

	Drops 1.0 ml	Chewable Tablet 1 tablet
Vitamin A, I.U.	1500	2500
Vitamin D, I.U.	400	400
Vitamin E, I.U.	5	15
Vitamin C, mg.	35	60
Folic acid, mg.	—	0.3
Thiamine, mg.	0.5	1.05
Riboflavin, mg.	0.6	1.2
Niacin, mg.	8	13.5
Vitamin B_6, mg.	0.4	1.05
Vitamin B_{12}, mcg.	2	4.5

Action and Uses: Daily vitamin supplementation for infants and children. Chewable tablets useful also for adults.
Administration and Dosage: Usual doses as above, or as indicated.
How Supplied: Poly-Vi-Sol® multivitamin supplement drops: (with 'Safti-Dropper' marked to deliver 1.0 ml)
NDC 0087-0402-02 Bottles of 1 fl. oz. (30 ml)
NDC 0087-0402-03 Bottles of 1⅔ fl. oz. (50 ml)
6505-00-104-8433 (50 ml) (Defense)
Poly-Vi-Sol® multivitamin supplement chewable tablets
NDC 0087-0412-02 Bottles of 24
NDC 0087-0412-03 Bottles of 100
NDC 0087-0412-05 Bottles of 1000
Poly-Vi-Sol® multivitamin supplement chewable tablets in Circus Shapes:
NDC 0087-0414-01 Bottles of 24
NDC 0087-0414-02 Bottles of 100

POLY-VI-SOL® with Iron
Multivitamin and Iron supplement
chewable tablets

Composition: Each tablet supplies same vitamins as Poly-Vi-Sol tablets (see above) plus 12 mg iron (from 40 mg ferrous fumarate).
Action and Uses: Daily vitamin and iron supplement for adults and children.
Administration and Dosage: 1 tablet daily.
How Supplied: Poly-Vi-Sol® multivitamin and iron supplement chewable tablets.
NDC 0087-0455-02 Bottles of 100
NDC 0087-0455-04 Bottles of 1000
Poly-Vi-Sol® multivitamin and iron supplement chewable tablets in Circus Shapes.
NDC 0087-0456-02 Bottles of 100

POLY-VI-SOL® with Iron
Multivitamin and Iron supplement
drops

Composition: Each 1.0 ml supplies:
Vitamin A, I.U. 1500
Vitamin D, I.U. 400

Vitamin E, I.U. 5
Vitamin C, mg. 35
Thiamine, mg. 0.5
Riboflavin, mg. 0.6
Niacin, mg. 8
Vitamin B_6, mg. 0.4
Iron, mg. 10
Action and Uses: Daily vitamin and iron supplement for infants.
Administration and Dosage: Drop into mouth with "Safti-Dropper." Dose: 1.0 ml daily, or as indicated.
How Supplied: Poly-Vi-Sol® multivitamin and iron supplement drops (with dropper marked to deliver 1 ml)
NDC 0087-0405-01 Bottles of 1⅔ fl. oz. (50 ml)

PORTAGEN®
Nutritionally complete dietary with Medium Chain Triglycerides and "Lactose-Free" (Less than 0.15% w/w Lactose)
U.S. Patent No. 3,450,819

Composition: Corn syrup solids, medium chain triglycerides (fractionated coconut oil), sodium caseinate, sugar (sucrose), corn oil, calcium citrate, potassium chloride, dibasic magnesium phosphate, dicalcium phosphate, potassium citrate, lecithin, vitamins (vitamin A palmitate, ergocalciferol, dl-alpha-tocopheryl acetate, sodium ascorbate, folic acid, thiamine hydrochloride, riboflavin, niacinamide, pyridoxine hydrochloride, cyanocobalamin, biotin, calcium pantothenate, phytonadione, and choline chloride), and minerals (ferrous sulfate, cupric sulfate, zinc sulfate, manganese sulfate, and sodium iodide).

One packed level 8-oz. measuring cup (136 g) of Portagen powder supplies 640 Calories, 22.4 g protein, 30.5 g fat, 73.6 g carbohydrate, and the following vitamins and minerals:

	One Quart 20 Cal./ fl. oz.	One Quart 30 Cal./ fl. oz.
Vitamin A, I.U.	5000	7500
Vitamin D, I.U.	500	750
Vitamin E, I.U.	20	30
Vitamin C (Ascorbic acid), mg.	52	78
Folic acid (Folacin), mg.	0.1	0.15
Thiamine (Vitamin B_1), mg.	1	1.5
Riboflavin (Vitamin B_2), mg.	1.2	1.8
Niacin, mg.	13	20
Vitamin B_6, mg.	1.3	2
Vitamin B_{12}, mcg.	4	6
Biotin, mg.	0.05	0.075
Pantothenic acid, mg.	6.7	10
Vitamin K_1, mcg.	100	150
Choline, mg.	85	125
Calcium, mg.	600	900
Phosphorus, mg.	450	680
Iodine, mcg.	45	70
Iron, mg.	12	18
Magnesium, mg.	130	200
Copper, mg.	1	1.5
Zinc, mg.	6	9
Manganese, mg.	2	3

Chloride, mg.	550	825
Potassium, mg.	800	1200
Sodium, mg.	300	450

Action and Uses: A nutritionally complete dietary is prepared by adding Portagen powder to water.

This dietary may be used, according to physician recommendation, as the major or sole constituent of the diet. Or, it may be used as a beverage to be consumed with each meal, or it may be incorporated in various recipes. Recipes or professional literature available upon request.

The fat blend of Portagen contains 87% Medium Chain Triglycerides, which are glycerol esters of Octanoic (C_8) and Decanoic (C_{10}) acids; along with corn oil which provides linoleic acid, an essential fatty acid.

When compared to conventional food fat, Medium Chain Triglycerides or medium chain fatty acids are: (1) more rapidly hydrolyzed, (2) not dependent on bile salts for emulsification, (3) carried by the portal circulation, and (4) not dependent on chylomicron formation or lymphatic transport.

Portagen may be used where conventional food fats are not well digested or absorbed. Impaired fat absorption may be a nutritional problem in the following conditions: *Intraluminal defect in hydrolysis of fat*, decreased pancreatic lipase (pancreatic insufficiency and cystic fibrosis of the pancreas) or decreased bile salts (chronic liver disease, biliary atresia, and biliary obstruction); *Mucosal defect in absorption of fat*, decreased permeability (sprue and idiopathic steatorrhea) or decreased surface (intestinal resection and blind loop syndrome) or defective lipoprotein lipase system (hyperchylomicronemia); and *Lymphatic defect in transport of fat* with intestinal lymphatic obstruction (lymphangiectasia, chylothorax, chyluria, chylous ascites and exudative enteropathy).

Preparation: *To Prepare as a Beverage (30 kilocalories per fluid ounce):* Add 1½ packed level 8-oz. measuring cups of Portagen powder (203 g) to 3 cups of water. Mix with electric mixer, egg beater or fork until smooth. Then stir in enough water to make 1 quart of beverage. A measuring scoop is enclosed to simplify the preparation of smaller amounts of the beverage. To prepare 1 cup (8 oz.) of beverage add 5 *firmly packed* scoops (1.8 oz.) of Portagen powder to ⅔ cup of water. Mix as above. Then stir in enough water to make one cup of beverage.
To Prepare as an Infant Formula (in normal dilution of 20 kilocalories per fluid ounce): Add 1 packed level 8-oz. measuring cup (136 g) of Portagen powder to 3 cups of water. Mix with electric mixer, egg beater or fork until smooth. Then stir in enough water to make 1 quart of formula. To prepare 1 cup (8 oz.) of infant formula, add 3 *firmly packed* scoops (1.2 oz.) of Portagen powder to ⅔ cup of water. Mix as above. Then stir in enough water to make 1 cup of formula.
Store bottled formula in refrigerator and use within 24 hours.

Precautions: Recent studies indicate that contrary to earlier recommendations, Portagen should not be used in cases of abetalipoproteinemia (faulty chylomicron formation). The usual intake of water should be maintained when Portagen beverage is used as the sole article or major part of the diet. In persons with advanced cirrhosis of the liver, large amounts of medium chain triglycerides in the diet may result in elevated blood and spinal fluid levels of medium chain fatty acids (MCFA), due to impaired hepatic clearance of these fatty acids, which are rapidly absorbed via the portal vein. These elevated levels have been reported to be associated with reversible coma and pre-coma in certain subjects with advanced cirrhosis, particularly with portacaval shunts. Therefore, diets containing high levels of medium chain triglyceride fat should be used with caution in persons with hepatic cirrhosis and complications thereof, such as portacaval shunts or tendency to encephalopathy.

How Supplied: Portagen® Powder
   NDC 0087-0387-01 Cans of 16 oz. (1 lb.)

PREGESTIMIL®
Protein hydrolysate formula with medium chain triglycerides and added amino acids

Composition: 52.4% corn syrup solids, 15.5% casein enzymically hydrolyzed and charcoal-treated to reduce allergenicity, 10.5% corn oil, 10.3% modified tapioca starch, 7.7% medium chain triglycerides (fractionated coconut oil), 1.1% calcium citrate, 0.88% potassium citrate, 0.79% dibasic calcium phosphate, 0.18% lecithin, 0.15% L-cystine, 0.15% L-tyrosine, 0.08% magnesium oxide, 0.07% potassium chloride, 0.06% L-tryptophan, vitamins (vitamin A palmitate, ergocalciferol, dl-alpha-tocopheryl acetate, sodium ascorbate, folic acid, thiamine hydrochloride, riboflavin, niacinamide, pyridoxine hydrochloride, cyanocobalamin, biotin, calcium pantothenate, phytonadione, choline chloride, and inositol) and minerals (ferrous sulfate, cupric sulfate, zinc sulfate, manganese sulfate and sodium iodide).

One quart of Pregestimil formula (20 Kcal./fl. oz.) supplies 18 g protein equivalent, 25.7 g fat, 86.4 g carbohydrate and the following vitamins and minerals:

		% U. S. RDA Children Under 4 Years of Age
Vitamin A, I.U.	2000	80
Vitamin D, I.U.	400	100
Vitamin E, I.U.	15	150
Vitamin C, mg.	52	130
Folic acid, mcg.	100	50
Thiamine, mg.	0.5	71
Riboflavin, mg.	0.6	75
Niacin, mg.	8	89
Vitamin B₆, mg.	0.4	57
Vitamin B₁₂, mcg.	2	67
Biotin, mg.	0.05	33
Pantothenic acid, mg.	3	60
Vitamin K₁, mcg.	100	*
Choline, mg.	85	*
Inositol, mg.	30	*
Calcium, mg.	600	75
Phosphorus, mg.	400	50

Iodine, mcg.	45	64
Iron, mg.	12	120
Magnesium, mg.	70	35
Copper, mg.	0.6	60
Zinc, mg.	4	50
Manganese, mg.	0.2	*
Chloride, mg.	550	*
Potassium, mg.	700	*
Sodium, mg.	300	*

*U.S. Recommended Daily Allowance (U.S. RDA) has not been established. The nutrient levels meet Food & Drug Administration requirements for infant formula.

Action and Uses: Provides very easily digestible and assimilable fat, carbohydrate, and protein for feeding of infants and children with severe problems of diarrhea, dietary intolerance, disaccharidase deficiency, or malabsorption. For the nutritional management of infants following intestinal resection where temporary deficiency of intestinal enzymes may be found, or in infants with cystic fibrosis. In infants with severe malabsorption problems of non-specific etiologies, such as chronic diarrhea, nutritional maintenance with Pregestimil permits trial of specific disaccharides, milk protein or regular dietary fats to determine if the dietary intolerance is due to a component of conventional feedings.

Precautions: Initial feedings of Pregestimil should be diluted to 10 kcal./fl. oz. or less and gradually increased to 20 kcal./fl. oz. over a period of 3 to 5 days. Individuals with lengthy episodes of diarrhea and/or receiving antibiotics may require supplemental vitamin K. In a few instances, premature infants and infants with long-standing malabsorption problems have been reported to have metabolic acidosis when receiving a casein hydrolysate formula for an extended period of time. The etiology of this acidosis is obscure. The overall incidence is rare and can be satisfactorily controlled by giving the patient 2-3 mEq./kg./day of sodium bicarbonate, which may be conveniently added to the formula.

Preparation: For 10 kcal./fl. oz.: add one packed level scoop (enclosed) (9.7 g.) of Pregestimil powder to each 4 fl. oz. (120 ml.) of water. Always add powder to water. To make a quart of 10 kcal./fl. oz. formula, add 1/2 level 8 oz. measuring cup (71 g.) of powder to 29 fl. oz. (858 ml.) of water. For 20 kcal./fl. oz.: add one packed level scoop (9.7 g.) of Pregestimil powder to each 2 fl. oz. (60 ml.) of water. To make a quart of 20 kcal./fl. oz. formula, add one packed level 8 oz. measuring cup (141 g.) of powder to 29 fl. oz. (858 ml.) of water.

Caution: Store remaining liquid formula in refrigerator in a covered container and use within 24 hours after mixing.

How Supplied: Pregestimil®
   NDC 0087-0367-01 Cans of 16 oz. (1 lb.) with measuring scoop

PROBANA® powder
High protein formula with banana powder

Composition: Special infant formula, containing protein milk powder (whole milk curd and skim milk curd with added lactic acid and calcium chloride), banana powder, dextrose, an enzymic casein hydrolysate, corn oil, vitamins (vitamin A palmitate, ergocalciferol, dl-alpha-tocopheryl acetate, sodium ascorbate, folic acid, thiamine hydrochloride, riboflavin, niacinamide, pyridoxine hydrochloride, cyanocobalamin, calcium pantothenate, phytonadione), and minerals (cupric sulfate, potassium iodide, and manganese sulfate).

One quart of Probana formula (20 kcal./fl. oz.) supplies 640 kilocalories and the following vitamins and minerals:

Vitamin A, I.U.	5000
Vitamin D, I.U.	1000
Vitamin E, I.U.	10
Vitamin C (Ascorbic acid), mg.	52
Folic acid (Folacin), mcg.	50
Thiamine (Vitamin B₁), mg.	0.6
Riboflavin (Vitamin B₂), mg.	1
Niacin, mg.	8
Vitamin B₆, mg.	0.5
Vitamin B₁₂, mcg.	2.5
Pantothenic acid, mg.	3
Vitamin K₁, mcg.	100
Calcium, mg.	1100
Phosphorus, mg.	850
Iodine, mcg.	65
Magnesium, mg.	80
Copper, mg.	0.6
Manganese, mg.	2
Potassium, mg.	1150
Sodium, mg.	580

NOTE: Supply 6.4 mg. iron per quart from other sources. Fer-in-Sol® iron supplement drops are a convenient source of added iron.

Supplies generous protein, part in predigested form; moderately low fat; carbohydrate largely as simple sugars.

Action and Uses: Suitable for feeding of infants and children with celiac syndrome (as associated with cystic fibrosis of the pancreas, gluten-induced enteropathy or "idiopathic" celiac disease), steatorrhea or malabsorption due to various causes, or diarrhea.

Precautions: Initial feedings should be diluted to 10 kcal./fl. oz. and gradually increased to 20 kcal./fl. oz. over a period of 3 to 5 days.

Preparation: For 10 kcal./fl. oz.: use 1 packed level measure to 4 fl. oz. water, or ½ level 8 oz. measuring cup to water sufficient to make a quart of formula. For 20 kcal./fl. oz.: 1 packed level measure powder (9.8 g.) to 2 fl. oz. water or 1 level 8-oz. measuring cup (146 g.) to water sufficient to make a quart of formula. In impaired pancreatic function, more concentrated feedings sometimes used, with extra water given.

Store bottled formula in refrigerator and use within 24 hours.

How Supplied: Probana®
   NDC 0087-0346-01 Cans of 16 oz. (1 lb.), with measure.

Continued on next page

Mead Johnson Nutritional—Cont.

PROSOBEE® concentrated liquid
● ready-to-use
Milk-free formula with soy protein isolate

ProSobee Concentrated Liquid
Ingredients: 74.9% Water, 13.4% corn syrup solids, 5.3% soy oil, 4.1% soy protein isolate, 1.3% coconut oil, 0.3% tribasic calcium phosphate, 0.2% lecithin, 0.16% tribasic potassium citrate, 0.09% salt, 0.09% magnesium chloride, 0.031% L-methionine, 0.022% calcium carbonate, 0.007% carrageenan, vitamins (vitamin A palmitate, ergocalciferol, dl-alpha-tocopheryl acetate, sodium ascorbate, folic acid, thiamine hydrochloride, riboflavin, niacinamide, pyridoxine hydrochloride, cyanocobalamin, biotin, calcium pantothenate, phytonadione, choline chloride and inositol) and minerals (potassium iodide, ferrous sulfate, cupric sulfate, zinc sulfate and manganese sulfate).

ProSobee Ready-To-Use:
Ingredients: 87.1% Water, 6.9% corn syrup solids, 2.7% soy oil, 2.1% soy protein isolate, 0.7% coconut oil, 0.15% tribasic calcium phosphate, 0.1% lecithin, 0.08% tribasic potassium citrate, 0.05% salt, 0.04% magnesium chloride, 0.016% L-methionine, 0.01% carrageenan, 0.004% calcium carbonate, vitamins (vitamin A palmitate, ergocalciferol, dl-alpha-tocopheryl acetate, sodium ascorbate, folic acid, thiamine hydrochloride, riboflavin, niacinamide, pyridoxine hydrochloride, cyanocobalamin, biotin, calcium pantothenate, phytonadione, choline chloride and inositol) and minerals (potassium iodide, ferrous sulfate, cupric sulfate, zinc sulfate and manganese sulfate).

One quart of ProSobee formula, normal dilution (20 kcal./fl. oz.) supplies 640 kilocalories and the following vitamins and minerals:

Vitamin A, I.U.	2000
Vitamin D, I.U.	400
Vitamin E, I.U.	10
Vitamin C (Ascorbic acid), mg...	52
Folic acid (Folacin), mcg.	100
Thiamine (Vitamin B₁), mg.	0.5
Riboflavin (Vitamin B₂), mg.	0.6
Niacin, mg.	8
Vitamin B₆, mg.	0.4
Vitamin B₁₂, mcg.	2
Biotin, mg.	0.05
Pantothenic acid, mg.	3
Vitamin K₁, mcg.	100
Choline, mg.	50
Inositol, mg.	30
Calcium, mg.	600
Phosphorus, mg.	475
Iodine, mcg.	65
Iron, mg.	12
Magnesium, mg.	70
Copper, mg.	0.6
Zinc, mg.	5
Manganese, mg.	0.2
Chloride, mg.	520
Potassium, mg.	780
Sodium, mg.	275

Action and Uses: Formula for infants sensitive to milk, infants potentially allergic to milk on the basis of a family history of allergy and infants with galactosemia. As a milk substitute for children and adults with poor tolerance to milk. As a dietary trial food when milk sensitivity or lactose or sucrose intolerance is suspected.

Preparation: *Concentrated liquid:* For 20 kcal./fl. oz., 1 part ProSobee concentrated liquid to 1 part water. ProSobee may be used to replace milk as a beverage or in cooking. A pleasant-tasting beverage is made with two parts ProSobee concentrated liquid to one part water.

How Supplied: ProSobee®
List 308-01 Cans of 13 fl. oz. Concentrated Liquid (40 kcal./fl. oz.)
List 309-01 Cans of 32 fl. oz. (1 qt.) Ready-To-Use (20 kcal./fl. oz.)
List 309-42 Cans of 8 fl. oz. Ready-To-Use (20 kcal./fl. oz.)

SUSTACAL®
● liquid (ready to use)
● powder (mix with milk)
● pudding (ready-to-eat)
Nutritionally complete food

Composition: Vanilla Liquid—
Ingredients: Water, sugar (sucrose), corn syrup, calcium caseinate, partially hydrogenated soy oil, soy protein isolate, sodium caseinate, potassium citrate, artificial flavor, dibasic magnesium phosphate, salt (sodium chloride), potassium chloride, calcium carbonate, dibasic calcium phosphate, sodium citrate, lecithin, carrageenan, vitamins (vitamin A palmitate, ergocalciferol, dl-alpha-tocopheryl acetate, sodium ascorbate, folic acid, thiamine hydrochloride, riboflavin, niacinamide, pyridoxine hydrochloride, cyanocobalamin, biotin, phytonadione and choline bitartrate) and minerals (sodium iodide, ferric pyrophosphate, ferrous sulfate, cupric sulfate, zinc sulfate and manganese sulfate).

(In addition to the above, Chocolate liquid contains Dutch process cocoa [alkalized], and artificial color.) Eggnog flavored liquid contains artificial color.
Proximate analysis (g/100 ml)

Protein	6.1
Fat	2.3
Carbohydrate	14
Ash	1.1
Water	84.2

Each 12-fl.-oz. can of Sustacal supplies 21.7 g. protein, 8.3 g. fat, 49.6 g. carbohydrate, 360 Calories (1 Calorie per ml.) and the following vitamins and minerals:

		% U.S. RDA Adults and Children 4 or More Years of Age
Vitamin A, I.U.	1670	33
Vitamin D, I.U.	133	33
Vitamin E, I.U.	10	33
Vitamin C (Ascorbic acid), mg.	20	33
Folic acid (Folacin), mg.	0.133	33
Thiamine (Vitamin B₁), mg.	0.5	33
Riboflavin (Vitamin B₂), mg.	0.6	35
Niacin, mg.	7	35
Vitamin B₆, mg.	0.7	35
Vitamin B₁₂, mcg.	2	33
Biotin, mg.	0.1	33
Pantothenic acid, mg.	3.5	35
Vitamin K₁, mcg.	83.3	*
Choline, mg.	83.3	*
Calcium, mg.	360	36
Phosphorus, mg.	360	33
Iodine, mcg.	50	33
Iron, mg.	6	33
Magnesium, mg.	135	33
Copper, mg.	0.7	35
Zinc, mg.	5	33
Manganese, mg.	1	*
Chloride, mg.	560	*
Potassium, mg.	740	*
Sodium, mg.	333	*

*U.S. RDA (Recommended Daily Allowance) not established.

Vanilla Powder—Nonfat dry milk, sugar, corn syrup solids, artificial flavor, dibasic magnesium phosphate, vitamins (vitamin A palmitate, ergocalciferol, dl-alpha-tocopheryl acetate, sodium ascorbate, folic acid, thiamine hydrochloride, niacinamide, pyridoxine hydrochloride, cyanocobalamin, biotin and calcium pantothenate) and minerals (ferrous sulfate, cupric carbonate, zinc sulfate, and manganese sulfate). (In addition to the above, Chocolate Powder contains Dutch process cocoa [alkalized], and lecithin.)

With the exception of lactose, one pouch of Sustacal powder mixed with 8-fl. oz. whole milk provides essentially the same nutritional value as a 12 fl. oz. can of Sustacal.

Vanilla Pudding—Water, nonfat milk, sugar, partially hydrogenated soy oil, modified food starch, artificial flavor, dibasic magnesium phosphate, sodium stearoyl lactylate, dibasic sodium phosphate, carrageenan, artificial color (includes FD&C Yellow No. 5), and vitamins and minerals (vitamin A palmitate, sodium ascorbate, thiamine hydrochloride, riboflavin, niacinamide, ferric pyrophosphate, ergocalciferol, dl-alpha-tocopheryl acetate, pyridoxine hydrochloride, folic acid, cyanocobalamin, zinc sulfate, cupric sulfate, biotin and calcium pantothenate).

In addition to the above, Chocolate contains Dutch process cocoa (alkalized).

Proximate Analysis (% w/w):

Protein	4.8
Fat	6.7
Carbohydrate	22.6
Ash	1.2
Water	64.8

Each 5-oz. tin of Sustacal Pudding supplies the following nutrients:

		% RDA
Calories	240	*
Protein, g.	6.8	15
Fat, g.	9.5	*
Cholesterol, mg. (less than 5 mg. per 100 g.)**	<5	
Carbohydrate, g.	32	*
Caloric Distribution, %		
Protein	11	
Fat	36	
Carbohydrate	53	
Vitamin A, I. U.	750	15
Vitamin D, I. U.	60	15

Vitamin E, I. U.	4.5	15
Vitamin C (Ascorbic Acid), mg.	9	15
Folic acid (Folacin), mg.	0.06	15
Thiamine (Vitamin B$_1$), mg.	0.23	15
Riboflavin (Vitamin B$_2$), mg.	0.26	15
Niacin, mg.	3	15
Vitamin B$_6$, mg.	0.3	15
Vitamin B$_{12}$, mcg.	0.9	15
Biotin, mg.	0.05	15
Pantothenic acid, mg.	1.5	15
Calcium, mg.	225	20
Phosphorus, mg.	225	20
Iodine, mcg.	22.5	15
Iron, mg.	2.7	15
Magnesium, mg.	60.0	15
Copper, mg.	0.3	15
Zinc, mg.	2.25	15
Manganese, mg.	0.07	*
Chloride, mg.	212.0	*
Potassium, mg.	290.0	*
Sodium, mg. (85 mg. per 100 g.)	120***	*

*No established U. S. RDA

**This information on cholesterol content is provided for individuals who, on the advice of a physician, are modifying their dietary intake of cholesterol.

***Chocolate flavor contains 100 mg. sodium per serving (70 mg. per 100 g.)

Action and Uses: Sustacal liquid and powder are ideally formulated to provide for the nutritional needs of the broad range of patients requiring an oral supplement or high protein diet (21.7 g. protein in one 12 fl. oz. serving). Sustacal is of particular value to patients in these situations: **lactose intolerance** (Sustacal liquid is lactose-free); **anorexia and food prejudice** (excellent taste in a choice of vanilla, chocolate, and eggnog flavors); **malnutrition/vitamin and mineral deficiencies** (each 12 fl. oz. can provides between 33–36% of U.S. RDA's for every vitamin and mineral for which U.S. RDA's are established); **ill, injured, surgical and convalescent patients and those with impediments to eating and swallowing.**

Sustacal Pudding is a convenient and well-accepted means of providing supplemental nutrition. Routine usage of Sustacal Pudding is appropriate for the majority of patients requiring nutritional supplementation and is especially appropriate to help avoid taste fatigue and form monotony associated with liquid supplements. Sustacal Pudding's nutritional balance is compatible with most normal complete diets.

Preparation: Liquid: ready to serve in 30 Cal./fl. oz. dilution (one Cal. per milliliter). Powder: mix contents of one packet instantly with 8-fl. oz. whole milk to prepare a 40-calorie-per-fluid-ounce dilution. To prepare powder in 30 Calorie per-fluid-ounce dilution, add 90 ml. (3 fl. oz.) of water to this mixture. Makes approximately 12 fluid ounces. Both forms may be used orally or by tube. Vanilla flavor is recommended for tube feeding if chocolate allergy is suspected.

In initiating tube feeding, particularly for malnourished patients, it may be ad-

visable to start with ⅓ to ½ the desired daily caloric ration and with a half-strength concentration; then increase gradually over next few days.

Precautions: When Sustacal is used as the sole food, give additional water as needed for adequate daily intake. This is particularly important for unconscious or semiconscious patients. Do not begin postoperative tube feedings until peristalsis is reestablished. Electrolyte content of Sustacal should be considered for cardiac patients and others who tend to have edema.

Store bottled formula in refrigerator and use same day or next.

How Supplied: Sustacal® Vanilla liquid and powder.
NDC 0087-0351-42 Cans of 8 fl. oz.
NDC 0087-0351-01 Cans of 12 fl. oz.
NDC 0087-0351-44 Cans of 32 fl. oz. (1 quart)
NDC 0087-0353-01 Packets of 1.9 oz., 4 packets per carton
NDC 0087-0353-43 Cans of 3.8 lb.
VA8940-00-627857 (8 fl. oz., van.)
VA8940-00-876-9044 (12 fl. oz., van.)
Sustacal® Chocolate liquid and powder.
NDC 0087-0350-01 Cans of 12 fl. oz.
NDC 0087-0352-01 Packets of 1.9 oz., 4 packets per carton
VA8940-00-035-6129 (12 fl. oz., choc.)
Sustacal® Eggnog liquid.
NDC 0087-0457-42 Cans of 8 fl. oz., 12 cans per case
NDC 0087-0457-44 Cans of 32 fl. oz., 6 cans per case
Sustacal® Pudding
NDC 0087-0409-41 Vanilla, 5 oz. tins, 4 tins per carton, 12 cartons per case
NDC 0087-0410-41 Chocolate, 5 oz. tins, 4 tins per carton, 12 cartons per case
NDC 0087-0415-41 Butterscotch, 5 oz. tins, 4 tins per carton, 12 cartons per case
VA8940-01-074-3125 (Vanilla, 5 oz. tins)
VA8940-01-074-3124 (Chocolate, 5 oz. tins)
VA8940-01-074-3123 (Butterscotch, 5 oz. tins)

SUSTAGEN® powder
Nutritional supplement

Composition: Contains all essential vitamins and minerals. Made from nonfat milk, corn syrup solids, powdered whole milk, calcium caseinate, dextrose, artificial vanilla flavor, vitamins (vitamin A palmitate, ergocalciferol, dl-alpha-tocopheryl acetate, ascorbic acid, folic acid, thiamine hydrochloride, riboflavin, niacinamide, pyridoxine hydrochloride, cyanocobalamin, biotin, calcium pantothenate, phytonadione, and choline bitartrate), and minerals (ferrous sulfate, dibasic magnesium phosphate, cupric carbonate, zinc sulfate, and manganese sulfate).

Chocolate-flavored Sustagen also contains sugar and cocoa. High in protein, low in fat; generous in vitamins, calcium and iron. Easily mixed with water to make a pleasant-tasting beverage or a feeding via nasogastric tube.

One pound of Sustagen powder supplies 106.7 g protein, 301.6 g carbohydrate, 15.9 g fat and the following vitamins and minerals:

Vitamin A, I.U.	5000
Vitamin D, I.U.	400
Vitamin E, I.U	45
Vitamin C (Ascorbic acid), mg.	300
Folic acid (Folacin), mg.	0.4
Thiamine (Vitamin B$_1$), mg.	3.8
Riboflavin (Vitamin B$_2$), mg.	4.3
Niacin, mg.	50
Vitamin B$_6$, mg.	5
Vitamin B$_{12}$, mcg.	15
Biotin, mg.	0.3
Pantothenic acid, mg.	25
Vitamin K$_1$, mg.	0.25
Choline, mg.	500
Calcium, g.	3.2
Phosphorus, g.	2.4
Iodine, mcg.	150
Iron, mg.	18
Magnesium, mg.	400
Copper, mg.	2
Zinc, mg.	20
Manganese, mg.	5
Potassium, g.	3.2*
Sodium, g.	1.2

*Chocolate powder supplies 3.5 g of potassium

Actions and Uses: Orally or by tube, provides a complete diet or extra nutritional support for ill, injured, surgical, and convalescent patients and those with impediments to eating or swallowing. Useful in peptic ulcer for buffering effect plus nutrition.

Preparation: Oral dilution: Mix equal parts (by volume) of Sustagen powder and water. This yields about 50 Cal./fl. oz. One pound (3 packed level cups) Sustagen powder and 3 cups water make about a quart. ⅔ packed level cup Sustagen powder and ⅔ cup water make a single serving.

Refrigerate reconstituted Sustagen and use within 24 hours.

Tube-feeding dilution: Use 400 g. Sustagen powder to 800 ml. water for 1 liter. This mixture yields about 45 Cal./fl. oz. More dilute mixtures may be utilized if desired. **In initiating tube feeding,** particularly for malnourished patients, it may be advisable to start with ⅓ to ½ the desired daily caloric ration and with a halfstrength concentration; then increased gradually over next few days. Vanilla flavor is recommended for tube feeding if chocolate allergy is suspected.

Precautions: When Sustagen is used as the sole food, give additional water as needed for adequate daily intake. This is particularly important for unconscious or semiconscious patients. Do not begin post-operative tube feedings until peristalsis is reestablished. Electrolyte content of Sustagen should be considered for cardiac patients and others who tend to have edema.

How Supplied: Sustagen® vanilla
NDC 0087-0393-01 Cans of 16 oz. (1 lb.)
NDC 0087-0393-02 Cans of 40 oz. (2-½ lb.)

Continued on next page

Mead Johnson Nutritional—Cont.

NDC 0087-0393-03 Cans of 5 lb.
VA 8940-00-584-2702 (Cans of 5 lb.)
Sustagen chocolate
NDC 0087-0394-01 Cans of 16 oz. (1 lb.)

TEMPRA®
Acetaminophen

DROPS AND SYRUP–for infants and younger children.
Composition: Tempra is acetaminophen, a safe and effective analgesic-antipyretic. It is not a salicylate. It contains no phenacetin or caffeine. It has no effect on prothrombin time. Tempra offers prompt, non-irritating therapy. Because it provides significant freedom from side effects, it is particularly valuable for patients who do not tolerate aspirin well.
Action and Uses: Tempra drops and syrup are useful for reducing fever and for the temporary relief of minor aches, pains and discomfort associated with the common cold or "flu," inoculations or vaccination. Tempra syrup is valuable in reducing pain following tonsillectomy and adenoidectomy.
Administration and Dosage: 3 or 4 times daily or as needed. DROPS (1 gr per 0.6 ml) and SYRUP (2 gr per 5 ml tsp.)—

Age	Drops		Syrup	
Under 1.	0.6	ml	½	tsp.
1 to 3	0.6-1.2	ml	½-1	tsp.
3 to 6	1.2	ml	1	tsp.
6 to 12	2.4	ml	2	tsp.

Drops given with calibrated 'Safti-Dropper' or mixed with water or fruit juices. Syrup given by teaspoon.
Precaution: Acetaminophen has been reported to potentiate the effect of orally administered anticoagulants.
Contraindications: The only known contraindication is possible rare sensitivity to acetaminophen or to one of the ingredients of the drops or syrup. Acetaminophen may be contraindicated in the patient with known glucose-6-phosphate dehydrogenase deficiency.
Side Effects: Infrequent, nonspecific side effects have been reported with the therapeutic use of acetaminophen.
Overdosage: The occurrence of acetaminophen overdose toxicity is uncommon in children. The pediatric age group appears less vulnerable than adults to developing hepatotoxicity, even with large overdoses.
In the event of a child ingesting a large overdose of acetaminophen, **immediately** contact a Poison Control Center or Mead Johnson Medical Affairs Department for information on the antidotes used to treat acetaminophen overdosage. Following the ingestion of a large quantity of acetaminophen, patients may be asymptomatic for several days. Likewise, clinical laboratory evidence of hepatotoxicity may be delayed for up to a week. Parents' estimates of the quantity of a drug ingested are often also unreliable. Therefore, any report of the ingestion of an overdose should be corroborated by assaying for the acetaminophen plasma concentration. Since plasma levels at specific time points following an overdose correlate closely with the potential occurrence and probable severity of hepatotoxicity, it is important to accurately determine the elapsed time from ingestion of an overdose to the time of plasma acetaminophen determination.
Close clinical monitoring and serial hepatic enzyme studies are recommended for patients who delay presentation until several days following a reported acetaminophen overdose.
Note: A prescription is not required for Tempra drops or syrup as an analgesic. To prevent its misuse by the layman, the following information appears on the package label: Do not use for more than 10 days or administer to children under 3 years of age unless so directed by your physician.
How Supplied: Tempra® (acetaminophen) drops: (With calibrated 'Safti-Dropper.')
NDC 0087-0730-01 Bottles of 15 ml
Tempra® (acetaminophen) syrup:
NDC 0087-0733-04 Bottles of 4 fl. oz.
NDC 0087-0733-03 Bottles of 16 fl. oz.
No ℞ required.
Literature Available: Yes.

TRIND® syrup
expectorant • nasal decongestant
• analgesic/antipyretic

Composition:

	per 5 ml teaspoonful
Glyceryl guaiacolate (guaifenesin)	50 mg
Phenylephrine hydrochloride	2.5 mg
Acetaminophen (Tempra®)	120 mg

Syrup contains 15% alcohol
Action and Uses: Treats the 3 most common cold symptoms without risk of adverse codeine, antihistamine or aspirin side effects. Indicated for oral use in the symptomatic treatment of colds. Trind effectively facilitates productive cough, clears stuffy nose and reduces aches and fever.
Administration and Dosage: 3 or 4 times daily.

Children under 3 (only as directed by physician)	½ tsp. per 10 kg. (22 lbs.)
3–6 years	1 tsp.
6–12 years	1 or 2 tsp.
Adults	2–4 tsp.

Side Effects: Infrequent, nonspecific side effects have been reported with the therapeutic use of acetaminophen.
Warning: Do not use more than ten days or administer to children under three unless directed by physician. Persons with high blood pressure, heart disease, diabetes, thyroid disease, or with high fever or persistent cough should use only as directed by a physician.
Contraindications: The only known contraindication is possible rare sensitivity to acetaminophen or to one of the ingredients of the syrup. Acetaminophen may be contraindicated in the patient with known glucose-6-phosphate dehydrogenase deficiency.
How Supplied: Trind® syrup (available without prescription)
NDC 0087-0750-01 Bottles of 4 fl. oz.

TRIND-DM® syrup
decongestant • analgesic/antipyretic
cough suppressant • expectorant

Composition:

	per 5 ml teaspoonful
Phenylephrine hydrochloride	2.5 mg
Acetaminophen (Tempra®)	120 mg
Dextromethorphan hydrobromide	7.5 mg
Glyceryl guaiacolate (guaifenesin)	50 mg

Syrup contains 15% alcohol
Action and Uses: For relief of cough and cold symptoms. Includes the basic formulation of Trind® with the addition of dextromethorphan hydrobromide, which acts as a cough suppressant. Trind-DM was formulated to avoid the unpleasant side effects associated with narcotics (such as codeine), antihistamines, and aspirin that are often the ingredients of many popular cough and cold remedies.
Administration and Dosage: 3 or 4 times daily.

Children under 3 (only as directed by physician)	½ tsp. per 10 kg. (22 lbs.)
3-6 years	1 tsp.
6-12 years	1 or 2 tsp.
Adults	2-4 tsp.

Side Effects: Infrequent, nonspecific side effects have been reported with the therapeutic use of acetaminophen.
Warning: Do not use more than ten days or administer to children under three unless directed by physician. Individuals with high blood pressure, heart disease, diabetes, thyroid disease, or with high fever or persistent cough should use only as directed by a physician. Persistent cough or high fever may indicate the presence of a serious condition.
Contraindications: The only known contraindication is possible rare sensitivity to acetaminophen or to one of the ingredients of the syrup. Acetaminophen may be contraindicated in the patient with known glucose-6-phosphate dehydrogenase deficiency.
How Supplied: Trind-DM® Syrup: (Available without prescription.)
NDC 0087-0753-01 Bottles of 4 fl. oz.

TRI-VI-SOL®
Vitamins A, D and C Supplement
infants' drops • chewable tablets

	Drops 1.0 ml	1 Tablet
Vitamin A, I.U.	1500	2500
Vitamin D, I.U.	400	400
Vitamin C, mg.	35	60

Action and Uses: Tri-Vi-Sol drops and tablets provide vitamins A, D and C.
How Supplied: Tri-Vi-Sol® drops: (with 'Safti-Dropper' marked to deliver 1 ml)
NDC 0087-0403-02 Bottles of 1 fl. oz. (30 ml)

NDC 0087-0403-03 Bottles of 1⅔ fl. oz. (50 ml)

Tri-Vi-Sol® tablets:
NDC 0087-0413-02 Bottles of 100 tablets

TRI-VI-SOL® with Iron
Vitamins A, D, C and Iron
Infants' Drops

Composition: Each 1.0 ml supplies same vitamins as in Tri-Vi-Sol® vitamin drops (see above) plus 10 mg iron.

Action and Uses: Tri-Vi-Sol with Iron vitamins A, D, C and Iron for infants.

Administration and Dosage: Drop into mouth with 'Safti-Dropper'. Dose: 1.0 ml daily, or as indicated.

How Supplied: Tri-Vi-Sol® vitamin drops with Iron (with dropper marked to deliver 1 ml)
NDC 0087-0453-03 Bottles of 1⅔ fl. oz. (50 ml)

Medicone Company
225 VARICK ST.
NEW YORK, NY 10014

DERMA MEDICONE® Ointment

Composition: Each gram contains:
Benzocaine.................................... 20.0 mg.
8-Hydroxyquinoline sulfate...... 10.5 mg.
Menthol.. 4.8 mg.
Ichthammol................................. 10.0 mg.
Zinc oxide..................................137.3 mg.
Petrolatum, Lanolin, perfume.............q.s.

Action and Uses: For prompt, temporary relief of intolerable itching, burning and pain associated with minor skin irritations. A bland, non-toxic, well balanced formula in a non-drying base which will not disintegrate or liquefy at body temperature and is not washed away by urine, perspiration or exudate. Exerts a soothing, cooling influence on irritated skin surfaces by affording mild anesthesia to control the scratch reflex, promotes healing of the affected area and checks the spread of infection. Useful for symptomatic relief in a wide variety of pruritic skin irritations resulting from insect bites, prickly heat, eczema, chafed and raw skin surfaces, sunburn, fungus infections, plant poisoning, pruritus ani and pruritus vulvae—mouth sores, cracked lips, under dentures.

Administration and Dosage: Apply liberally directly to site of irritation and gently rub into affected area for better penetration and absorption. Cover area with gauze if necessary.

Precautions: Do not use in the eyes. If the condition for which this preparation is used persists, or if rash or irritation develops, discontinue use and consult physician.

How Supplied: 1 ounce tubes and one pound jars.

DioMEDICONE® Tablets

Composition: Each tablet contains:
50 mg. dioctyl sodium sulfosuccinate (a surface tension reducing wetting agent) and excipient q.s. to prevent hard stool formation.

Action and Uses: A gentle-acting, non-habit forming stool-softener for effective management of simple constipation due to hard, dry fecal matter. A medically accepted, clinically proven mode of treatment in preventing hard stool formation. Reduces surface tension of intestinal fluids, permitting better infiltration of waste matter, producing a soft pliable fecal mass, making evacuation easy and comfortable. Reduces straining. Does not irritate the intestinal tract or produce peristalsis. Useful in hemorrhoidal and anorectal conditions, during and after pregnancy and whenever smooth, easy bowel evacuation is essential such as in cardiac conditions and before and following surgery. May be safely used as directed, by anyone over 6 years of age.

Administration and Dosage: Children 6 to 12 years: 1 or 2 tablets (50 to 100 mg.) daily with water. Adults and older children: 1 to 4 tablets (50 to 200 mg.) daily with water. Initial dosages may be reduced as normal bowel function is restored. Note: The effect of DioMEDICONE in producing soft, pliable stools usually takes 2 to 3 days.

How Supplied: 50 mg. tablets in vials of 50 tablets.

MEDICONE® DRESSING Cream

Composition: Each gram contains:
Benzocaine................................. 5.0 mg.
8-Hydroxyquinoline sulfate...... 0.5 mg.
Cod liver oil...............................125.0 mg.
Zinc oxide..................................125.0 mg.
Menthol.. 1.8 mg.
Petrolatum, Lanolin, talcum,
paraffin & perfume.........................q.s.

Action and Uses: Meets the first requisite in the treatment of minor burns, wounds and other denuded skin lesions by exerting mild, cooling anesthetic action for the prompt temporary relief of pain, burning and itching. A stable, non-toxic anesthetic dressing which does not liquefy or wash off at body temperature, nor is it decomposed by exudate, urine or perspiration. Promotes granulation and aids epithelization of affected tissue. The anesthetic, antipruritic, antibacterial properties make Medicone Dressing ideal for the treatment of 1st and 2nd degree burns, minor wounds, abrasions, diaper rashes and a wide variety of pruritic skin irritations.

Administration and Dosage: The smooth, specially formulated consistency allows comfortable application directly to the painful, irritated affected area. It may be spread on gauze before application or covered with gauze as desired.

Precautions: Do not use in the eyes. If the condition for which this preparation is used persists or if a rash or irritation develops, discontinue use and consult physician.

How Supplied: Tubes of 1 ounce and 1 lb. jars.

MEDICONET®
(medicated rectal wipes)

Composition: Each cloth wipe medicated with Benzalkonium chloride, 0.02%; Ethoxylated lanolin, 0.5%; Methylparaben, 0.15%; Hamamelis water, 50%; Glycerin, 10%; Purified water, USP and Perfume, q.s.

Action and Uses: Soft disposable cloth wipes which fulfill the important requisite in treating anal discomfort by providing the facility for gently and thoroughly cleansing the affected area. For the temporary relief of intolerable pain, itching and burning in minor external hemorrhoidal, anal and outer vaginal discomfort. Lanolized, delicately scented, durable and delightfully soft. Antiseptic, antipruritic, astringent. Useful as a substitute for harsh, dry toilet tissue. May also be used as a compress in the pre- and post-operative management of anorectal discomfort. The hygienic Mediconet pad is generally useful in relieving pain, burning and itching in diaper rash, sunburn, heat rash, minor burns and insect bites.

How Supplied: Boxes of 20 individually packaged, pre-moistened cleansing cloths.

RECTAL MEDICONE®
SUPPOSITORIES

Composition: Each suppository contains:
Benzocaine.. 2 gr.
8-Hydroxyquinoline sulfate..............¼ gr.
Zinc oxide.. 3 gr.
Menthol...⅟₇ gr.
Balsam Peru.. 1 gr.
Cocoa butter—vegetable & petroleum oil base; Certified color added........q.s.

Action and Uses: A soothing, non-toxic, comprehensive formula carefully designed to meet the therapeutic requirements in adequately treating simple hemorrhoids and minor anorectal disorders. Performs the primary function of promptly alleviating pain, burning and itching temporarily by exerting satisfactory local anesthesia. The muscle spasm, present in many cases of painful anal and rectal conditions, is controlled and together with the emollients provided, helps the patient to evacuate the bowel comfortably and normally. The active ingredients reduce congestion and afford antisepsis, accelerating the normal healing process. Used pre- and post-surgically in hemorrhoidectomy, in prenatal and postpartum care and whenever surgery is contraindicated for the comfort and well-being of the patient during treatment of an underlying cause.

Administration and Dosage: One suppository in the morning and one at night and after each stool, or as directed. Use of the suppositories should be continued for 10 to 15 days after cessation of discomfort to help protect against recurrence of symptoms. See Rectal Medicone Unguent for concurrent internal-external use.

Precautions: If a rash or irritation develops, or bleeding from the rectum occurs, discontinue use and consult physician.

How Supplied: Boxes of 12 and 24 individually foil-wrapped green suppositories.

Continued on next page

Medicone—Cont.

RECTAL MEDICONE® UNGUENT

Composition: Each gram contains:
Benzocaine.................................... 20 mg.
8-Hydroxyquinoline sulfate...... 5 mg.
Menthol.. 4 mg.
Zinc oxide...................................100 mg.
Balsam Peru .... 12.5 mg.
Petrolatum ....625 mg.
Lanolin..210 mg.
Certified color added

Action and Uses: A soothing, effective formulation which affords prompt, temporary relief of pain, burning and itching by exerting surface anesthetic action on the affected area in minor internal-external hemorrhoids and anorectal disorders. The active ingredients promote healing and protect against irritation, aiding inflamed tissue to retrogress to normal. The emollient petrolatum-lanolin base provides lubrication making bowel movements easier and more comfortable. Accelerates the normal healing process. Non-toxic. Rectal Medicone Unguent and Rectal Medicone Suppositories are excellent for concurrent management of internal-external irritations.

Administration and Dosage: For internal use—attach pliable applicator and lubricate tip with a small amount of Unguent to ease insertion. Apply liberally into affected area morning and night and after each stool or as directed. When used externally, cover area with gauze. When used with Rectal Medicone Suppositories, insert a small amount of Unguent into the rectum before inserting suppository.

Precautions: If a rash or irritation develops or rectal bleeding occurs, discontinue use and consult physician.

How Supplied: 1½ ounce tubes with pliable rectal applicator.

Medique Products
8050 N. LAWNDALE
SKOKIE, IL 60076

CCP Cough and Cold Tablets

Active Ingredients: Each tablet contains: Phenylpropanolamine HCl 25 mg., Acetaminophen 325 mg., Caffeine 64.8 mg., Guaifenesin 100 mg.

Will not cause drowsiness.

Indications: For temporary relief of symptoms of the Common Cold; nasal congestion, minor aches and pains, post nasal drip associated with the common cold and sinusitis.

Warning: Do not take this for persistent or chronic cough or where cough is accompanied by excessive secretions, consult a physician. Discontinue use if rapid pulse, dizziness or palpitations occur.

Caution: If cough persists for more than 1 week, tends to recur or is accompanied by high fever, or persistent headache, consult a physician. Do not exceed recommended dosage. Do not take if you have high blood pressure, heart disease, diabetes, or thyroid disease, consult a

physician. Do not take this product if you are presently taking as antihypertensive or antidepressant drug, consult a physician.

Dosage: Adult: One tablet four times a day.

How Supplied:
1000 Bottle—NDC-47682-106-04
500 Industrial Pak—NDC-47682-106-13
100 Industrial Pak—NDC-47682-106-33

Menley & James Laboratories
a SmithKline company
ONE FRANKLIN PLAZA
P. O. BOX 8082
PHILADELPHIA, PA 19101

A.R.M.® Allergy Relief Medicine
Fast and effective relief

Product Information: Allergies are caused by sensitivity to things like grass and tree pollen, dust, pollution—even pet dander. For allergy sufferers, A.R.M. represents a new era in non-prescription allergy care.

Product Benefits: A.R.M. combines two important medicines in one safe, fast-acting tablet:

● The highest level of antihistamine available without prescription-for better relief of sneezing, runny nose and itchy, weepy eyes.

● A clinically-proven sinus decongestant to help ease breathing and drain sinus congestion for hours.

Dosage: One tablet every 4 hours, not to exceed 4 tablets daily. Children (6-12 years): one-half the adult dose (break tablet in half). Children under 6 years use only as directed by physician.

Warning: Do not exceed recommended dosage. If symptoms do not improve within 7 days, or are accompanied by high fever, consult a physician before continuing use. Stop use if dizziness, sleeplessness or nervousness occurs. If you have or are being treated for depression, high blood pressure, glaucoma, diabetes, asthma, difficulty in urination due to enlarged prostate, heart disease or thyroid disease, use only as directed by physician. During pregnancy, use only as directed by a physician since safe use in pregnancy has not been clearly established. Do not take this product if you are taking another medication containing phenylpropanolamine.

Avoid alcoholic beverages while taking this product. Do not drive or operate heavy machinery as this preparation may cause drowsiness.

May cause excitability, especially in children. Keep this and all medicines out of reach of children. In case of accidental overdose, consult physician or poison control center immediately.

Formula: Each A.R.M. tablet contains chlorpheniramine maleate, 4.0 mg., phenylpropanolamine HCl, 37.5 mg.

How Supplied: Consumer packages of 20 and 40 tablets.

[*Shown in Product Identification Section*]

ACNOMEL® CREAM AND CAKE
acne therapy

Description: *Cream*—sulfur, 8%; resorcinol, 2%; alcohol, 11% (w/w); in a stable, grease-free, flesh-tinted vehicle. Standard strength for home application, morning or night. *Cake* (half strength) —sulfur, 4%; resorcinol, 1%; a washable, flesh-tinted cake base; in a handy compact for convenient use away from home.

Action and Uses: Acnomel provides effective acne therapy. Easily applied, flesh-tinted, it conceals as it heals. Because Acnomel is virtually invisible when applied, it is well accepted by even the most self-conscious person.

Directions: Wash and dry affected areas thoroughly. Apply a thin coating with fingertips or a moist sponge two or three times daily. Do not rub in.

Warning: If undue skin irritation develops or increases, discontinue use and consult physician. Do not apply to acutely inflamed area. Keep out of eyes and off eyelids. Keep this and all medicines out of reach of children. In case of accidental ingestion, contact a physician or poison control center immediately.

How Supplied: *Cream*—in specially lined 1 oz. tubes. *Cake*—handy 1 oz. plastic containers.

Remarks: Do not dilute or compound. When prescribing write for original container.

[*Shown in Product Identification Section*]

BENZEDREX® INHALER
nasal decongestant

Composition: Each Benzedrex Inhaler is packed with propylhexedrine, 250 mg.; menthol, 12.5 mg.; and aromatics.

Action and Uses: It relieves—*in a matter of seconds*—the congestion of head colds and hay fever. Also useful for the relief of ear block and pressure pain in air travelers.

Benzedrex rarely causes undesirable stimulation or interferes with sleep.

Directions: Insert in nostril. Close other nostril. Inhale twice. Treat other nostril the same way. Avoid excessive use. Inhaler loses potency after 2 or 3 months' use but some aroma may linger.

Warning: Keep this and all medicines out of reach of children. In the case of accidental overdose or ingestion of contents, seek professional assistance or contact a poison control center immediately.

How Supplied: In single plastic tubes.

[*Shown in Product Identification Section*]

C3®
Cold Cough Capsules

Product Information: All-day or all-night temporary relief from nasal congestion and coughing due to the common cold. C3 acts through your system to check coughing; relieves nasal congestion, sneezing, running nose and watery eyes. Just one capsule taken in the morning and one at bedtime maintain a prolonged, around-the-clock therapeutic action in your system of a highly effective medical formula.

Dosage: 1 capsule every 12 hours.

Caution: Children under 12 years of age and individuals with high blood pressure, heart disease, diabetes, or thyroid disease should use only as directed by physician. Not recommended for children under 6 years of age. If high fever is present or cough persists, see a physician as these symptoms may indicate a serious condition. Do not exceed recommended dosage. Do not take this product for persistent or chronic cough such as occurs with smoking, asthma, or emphysema, or where cough is accompanied by excessive secretions except on the advice of a physician.

Warning: Do not take this product if you are taking another medication containing phenylpropanolamine. Keep this and all medicines out of the reach of children. In case of accidental overdose, get professional aid or call a poison control center immediately. Do not drive or operate machinery as this preparation may cause drowsiness.

Formula: Each capsule contains chlorpheniramine maleate 4 mg., phenylpropanolamine hydrochloride 50 mg., dextromethorphan hydrobromide 30 mg.

How Supplied: Consumer package of 10 capsules.

[Shown in Product Identification Section]

CONTAC®
Continuous Action Decongestant Capsules

Product Information: Contac provides an increased amount of decongestant and antihistamine to give prolonged, round-the-clock relief from nasal congestion due to the common cold, hay fever and sinusitis. With just one capsule in the morning and one at bedtime, you feel better all day, sleep better all night, to awake refreshed, breathing freely without congestion.

Product Benefits: Each Contac continuous action capsule contains over 600 "tiny time pills". Some go to work right away for fast relief. The rest are scientifically timed to dissolve slowly, to give up to 12 hours of prolonged relief. Contac provides increased amounts of:

- A DECONGESTANT to help clear nasal and sinus passages and to reduce swollen nasal and sinus tissues.
- AN ANTIHISTAMINE to help relieve itchy, watery eyes; sneezing, running nose and postnasal drip.

Dosage: One capsule every 12 hours.

Warnings: Children under 12 should use only as directed by physician. Do not exceed recommended dosage. If symptoms do not improve within 7 days, or are accompanied by high fever, consult a physician before continuing use. Stop use if dizziness, sleeplessness or nervousness occurs.

Individuals with high blood pressure, glaucoma, diabetes, asthma, difficulty in urination due to enlarged prostate, heart disease or thyroid disease should use only as directed by physician. Do not take this product if you are taking another medication containing phenylpropanolamine.

Avoid alcoholic beverages while taking this product. Do not drive or operate heavy machinery as this preparation may cause drowsiness.

May cause excitability, especially in children. Keep this and all medicines out of reach of children. In case of accidental overdose, consult physician or poison control center immediately. Store at controlled room temperature (59°–86°F.).

Drug Interaction Precaution: Do not take if you are presently taking a prescription antihypertensive or antidepressant drug containing a monoamine oxidase inhibitor except under the advice and supervision of a physician.

Formula: Each capsule contains phenylpropanolamine hydrochloride 75.0 mg.; chlorpheniramine maleate 8.0 mg.

How Supplied: Consumer packages of 10, 20 and 40 capsules. Also, Industrial Dispensary Package of 200 capsules (2's in strip dispenser) for industrial dispensaries only.

[Shown in Product Identification Section]

CONTAC JR.®
The Complete Cold Medicine For Children

Product Information: For congestion, coughing, body aches and fever due to colds. Relieves symptoms with these reliable medicines:

A gentle decongestant. For temporary relief of nasal congestion. Helps your child breathe more freely. A safe, sensible, non-narcotic cough quieter. Calms worrisome coughs due to colds.

A trusted, non-aspirin pain reliever and fever reducer. Provides temporary relief of muscular aches and pains, headaches, discomforts of fever due to colds and "flu."

Product Benefits: The good medicines in Contac Jr. were specially chosen to help relieve your child's congestion, coughing, body aches and fever due to colds-without harsh drugs. Medical authorities know that for children, dose by weight-not age-means the dose you give is right for consistent controlled relief. Use the enclosed Contac Jr. Accu-Measure® Cup to select the right dose for your child's body weight.

Dosage: One dose every four hours, not to exceed 6 times daily. Use the enclosed Contac Jr. Accu-Measure Cup to measure the right dose for your child. You control the proper dose according to your child's body weight so the strength is always right. For dose by teaspoon see bottle label.

Caution: Do not exceed recommended dosage for your child's body weight. For children under 31 lbs. or under 3 years of age, consult a physician.

Warning: If symptoms persist for 7 days or are accompanied by high fever, severe or recurrent pain, or if child has diabetes or heart disease, consult your physician. Keep this and all medicines out of children's reach. In case of accidental overdose, contact a physician immediately. Do not take this product if you are taking another medication containing phenylpropanolamine.

Formula: Each 5 cc (average teaspoon) contains: phenylpropanolamine HCl 9.375 mg.; acetaminophen 162.5 mg.; dextromethorphan hydrobromide 5.0 mg.; alcohol 10% by volume.

How Supplied: A clear red liquid in 4 oz. and 8 oz. Family Size bottles.

[Shown in Product Identification Section]

DIETAC™
Once-A-Day Diet Aid Capsules

Product Benefits:
- Timed-release-just one capsule controls your appetite for 12 hours.
- Helps you lose weight.
- Contains a mild stimulant to help relieve fatigue often caused by dieting.

Dosage: Take one capsule each morning.

Warning: Do not exceed recommended dosage. Do not take this product for periods exceeding three months. Do not give this product to children under 12 years. Do not take this product if you are taking another medication containing phenylpropanolamine. If you have or are being treated for high blood pressure, heart disease, diabetes, thyroid disease or depression, take this product only under the supervision of a physician. If you become nervous, sleepless or dizzy, stop the medication. The recommended dose of this product contains about as much caffeine as a cup of coffee so take with caution while taking caffeine-containing beverages such as coffee, tea or cola drinks.

Keep this and all medicines out of reach of children. In case of accidental overdose, contact a physician or poison control center immediately.

Formula: Each capsule contains phenylpropanolamine HCl 50 mg. (appetite suppressant), caffeine 200 mg. (mild stimulant)

How Supplied: Consumer packages of 14 and 28 capsules

Also Available:
Once-A-Day Dietac Maximum Strength Capsules 20's & 40's.
Twice-A-Day Dietac Maximum Strength Capsules 24's & 48's.
Pre-Meal Dietac Diet Aid Tablets 42's.
Pre-Meal Dietac Diet Aid Drops ½ oz.

[Shown in Product Identification Section]

DIETAC™
Diet Aid Drops

Product Benefits:
- Provides a clinically proven safe and effective appetite suppressant.
- Effectively curbs your appetite at meals.
- Helps you lose weight.
- Caffeine-free-can be used in coffee, tea or cola—in the evening, too.

Dosage: Add five drops to your hot or cold beverage 30 minutes before each meal.

Continued on next page

Menley & James—Cont.

DO NOT EXCEED 5 DROPS PER DOSE. DO NOT EXCEED 3 DOSES PER DAY.

Warning: Do not exceed recommended dosage. Do not take this product for periods exceeding three months.

Do not give this product to children under 12 years. Do not take this product if you are taking another medication containing phenylpropanolamine. If you have or are being treated for high blood pressure, heart disease, diabetes, thyroid disease or depression, take this product only under the supervision of a physician. If you become nervous, sleepless, or dizzy, stop the medication.

Keep this and all medicines out of reach of children. In case of accidental overdose, contact a physician or poison control center immediately.

Formula: Each 0.2 ml. (approximately 5 drops) contains phenylpropanolamine HCl 25 mg. (appetite suppressant).

How Supplied: In consumer packages with ½ oz. bottle.

Also Available:

Once-A-Day Dietac Maximum Strength Diet Aid Capsules 20's & 40's.
Twice-A-Day Dietac Maximum Strength Diet Aid Capsules 24's & 48's.
Once-A-Day Dietac Diet Aid Capsules 14's & 28's.
Pre-Meal Dietac Diet Aid Tablets 42's.

[*Shown in Product Identification Section*]

DIETAC™
Pre–Meal Diet Aid Tablets

Product Benefits:
- Provides a clinically proven safe and effective appetite suppressant.
- Curbs your appetite at meals.
- Helps you lose weight.
- Caffeine-free-can be used in the evening.

Dosage: Take one tablet 30 minutes before each meal. Do not exceed 3 tablets per day.

Warning: Do not exceed recommended dosage. Do not take this product for periods exceeding three months. Do not give this product to children under 12 years. Do not take this product if you are taking another medication containing phenylpropanolamine. If you have or are being treated for high blood pressure, heart disease, diabetes, thyroid disease or depression, take this product only under the supervision of a physician. If you become nervous, sleepless or dizzy, stop the medication.

Keep this and all medicines out of reach of children. In case of accidental overdose, contact a physician or poison control center immediately.

Formula: Each tablet contains phenylpropanolamine HCl 25 mg. (appetite suppressant).

How Supplied: In consumer packages of 42 tablets.

Also Available:

Once-A-Day Dietac Maximum Strength Diet Aid Capsules 20's & 40's.
Twice-A-Day Dietac Maximum Strength Diet Aid Capsules 24's & 48's.
Once-A-Day Dietac Diet Aid Capsules 14's & 28's.
Pre-Meal Dietac Diet Aid Drops ½ oz.

[*Shown in Product Identification Section*]

DIETAC®
Maximum Strength
Once-A-Day Diet Aid
Capsules

Product Benefits:
- No stronger, longer-lasting appetite suppressant available without a prescription
- Timed-release—Just one capsule controls your appetite for 12 hours
- Helps you lose weight
- Caffeine-free
- Provides clinically-proven safe and effective appetite suppressant.

Dosage: Take one capsule each morning.

Warning: Do not exceed recommended dosage. Do not take this product for periods exceeding three months. Do not give this product to children under 12 years. Do not take this product if you are taking another medication containing phenylpropanolamine. If you have or are being treated for high blood pressure, heart disease, diabetes, thyroid disease or depression, take this product only under the supervision of a physician. If you become nervous, sleepless or dizzy, stop the medication.

Keep this and all medicines out of reach of children. In case of accidental overdose, contact a physician or poison control center immediately.

Formula: Each capsule contains phenylpropanolamine HCl 75 mg. (appetite suppressant).

How Supplied: In consumer packages of 20's & 40's.

Also Available:

Once-A-Day Dietac Diet Aid Capsules 14's & 28's.
Twice-A-Day Dietac Maximum Strength Diet Aid Capsules 24's & 48's.
Pre-Meal Dietac Diet Aid Tablets 42's.
Pre-Meal Dietac Diet Aid Drops ½ oz.

[*Shown in Product Identification Section*]

DIETAC®
Maximum Strength
Twice-A-Day Diet Aid
Capsules

Product Benefits:
- No stronger appetite suppressant available without a prescription.
- Caffeine-free.
- Provides clinically-proven safe and effective appetite suppressant.

Dosage: Take two capsules daily, one at 10 A.M. another at 4 P.M.

Warning: Do not exceed recommended dosage. Do not take this product for periods exceeding three months. Do not give this product to children under 12 years. Do not take this product if you are taking another medication containing phenylpropanolamine. If you have or are being treated for high blood pressure, heart disease, diabetes, thyroid disease or depression, take this product only under the supervision of a physician. If you

become nervous, sleepless or dizzy, stop the medication.

Keep this and all medicines out of reach of children. In case of accidental overdose, contact a physician or poison control center immediately.

Formula: Each capsule contains phenylpropanolamine HCl 37.5 mg. (appetite suppressant).

How Supplied: In consumer packages of 24's and 48's.

Also Available:

Once-A-Day Dietac Maximum Strength Diet Aid Capsules 20's & 40's.
Once-A-Day Dietac Diet Aid Capsuls 14's & 28's.
Pre-Meal Dietac Diet Aid Tablets 42's.
Pre-Meal Dietac Diet Aid Drops ½ oz.

[*Shown in Product Identification Section*]

ECOTRIN®
Enteric-coated Aspirin

When aspirin is needed and gastric discomfort makes therapy with uncoated aspirin tablets impractical—particularly for temporary relief of minor aches and pains of arthritis and rheumatism.

Each Ecotrin tablet contains aspirin, specially processed with Duentric® coating to protect against the possibility of stomach discomfort and upset often associated with aspirin therapy. Technical advances allow these Ecotrin tablets to be smaller and easier to swallow than before, yet have precisely the same strength.

Formula: Each tablet contains 325 mg. (5 gr.) aspirin.

Usual Dosage: 1 or 2 tablets every 4 hours, as necessary. Do not exceed 12 tablets in 24 hours unless directed by a physician.

High aspirin dosage is recommended in arthritis and rheumatic conditions (40–80 gr. daily) and in acute rheumatic fever (up to 120 gr. daily), in divided doses. In arthritic and rheumatic conditions, concomitant use of Ecotrin often permits a reduction in steroid dosage.

Warning: If under medical care, do not use without physician's approval. If pain persists more than 10 days or redness is present, or in arthritic or rheumatic conditions affecting children under 12, consult a physician immediately. Discontinue use if dizziness, ringing in ears or impaired hearing occurs.

Keep this and all medicines out of reach of children. In case of accidental overdose, contact a physician or poison control center immediately.

EASY-OPENING CAP available on 250 tablet bottle—intended for households without children.

How Supplied: 5 grain tablets, in bottles of 100, 250 and 1000.

[*Shown in Product Identification Section*]

FEOSOL® ELIXIR
Hematinic

Description: Feosol Elixir, an unusually palatable iron elixir, provides the body with ferrous sulfate—iron in its most efficient form. The standard elixir for simple iron deficiency and iron-deficiency

anemia when the need for such therapy has been determined by a physician.
Each 5 ml. (1 teaspoonful) contains ferrous sulfate USP, 220 mg. (44 mg. of elemental iron); alcohol, 5%.
Usual Dosage: *Adults*—1 to 2 teaspoonfuls three times daily. *Children*—½ to 1 teaspoonful three times daily preferably between meals. *Infants*—as directed by physician. Mix with water or fruit juice to avoid temporary staining of teeth; do not mix with milk or wine-based vehicles.
Warning: The treatment of any anemic condition should be under the advice and supervision of a physician. Since oral iron products interfere with absorption of oral tetracycline antibiotics, these products should not be taken within two hours of each other. Occasional gastrointestinal discomfort (such as nausea) may be minimized by taking with meals and by beginning with one teaspoonful the first day, two the second, etc. until the recommended dosage is reached. Iron-containing medication may occasionally cause constipation or diarrhea, and liquids may cause temporary staining of the teeth (this is less likely when diluted). Keep this and all medicines out of reach of children. In case of accidental overdose, contact a physician or poison control center immediately.
How Supplied: A clear orange liquid in 12 fl. oz. bottles.
Also Available: Feosol® Tablets, Feosol® Spansule® capsules.
[*Shown in Product Identification Section*]

FEOSOL® SPANSULE® CAPSULES
Hematinic

Description: Feosol *Spansule* capsules provide the body with ferrous sulfate—iron in its most efficient form—for simple iron deficiency and iron-deficiency anemia, when the need for such therapy has been determined by a physician.
The special *Spansule* capsule formulation—ferrous sulfate in pellets—reduces stomach upset, a common problem with iron.
Formula: Each capsule contains 167 mg. of dried ferrous sulfate USP (50 mg. of elemental iron), equivalent to 250 mg. of ferrous sulfate USP.
Usual Dosage: *Adults and Children* —One to two Feosol *Spansule* capsules daily, depending on severity of iron deficiency. Children too young to swallow the capsule can be given the contents in a spoonful of soft, cool food (applesauce, custard, etc.). *Children under 6*—Use Feosol® Elixir.
Warnings: The treatment of any anemic condition should be under the advice and supervision of a physician. Since oral iron products interfere with absorption of oral tetracycline antibiotics, these products should not be taken within two hours of each other. Keep this and all medicines out of reach of children. In case of accidental overdose, contact a physician or poison control center immediately. Iron-containing medicine may occasionally cause constipation or diarrhea.

How Supplied: Bottles of 30 and 500 capsules; in Single Unit Packages of 100 capsules (intended for institutional use only).
Also available in Tablets and Elixir.
[*Shown in Product Identification Section*]

FEOSOL® TABLETS
Hematinic

Description: Feosol Tablets provide the body with ferrous sulfate, iron in its most efficient form, for iron deficiency and iron-deficiency anemia when the need for such therapy has been determined by a physician. The distinctive triangular-shaped tablet has a special coating to prevent oxidation and improve palatability.
Formula: Each tablet contains 200 mg. of dried ferrous sulfate USP (65 mg. of elemental iron), equivalent to 325 mg. (5 grains) of ferrous sulfate USP.
Usual Dosage: *Adults*—one tablet 3 to 4 times daily, after meals and upon retiring. *Children 6 to 12 years*—one tablet three times a day after meals. *Children under 6 years and infants*—use Feosol® Elixir.
Warning: The treatment of any anemic condition should be under the advice and supervision of a physician. Since oral iron products interfere with absorption of oral tetracycline antibiotics, these products should not be taken within two hours of each other.
Occasional gastrointestinal discomfort (such as nausea) may be minimized by taking with meals and by beginning with one tablet the first day, two the second, etc. until the recommended dosage is reached. Iron-containing medication may occasionally cause constipation or diarrhea.
Keep this and all medicines out of reach of children. In case of accidental overdose, contact a physician or poison control center immediately.
How Supplied: Bottles of 100 and 1000 tablets; in Single Unit Packages of 100 tablets (intended for institutional use only).
Also available in Spansule® capsules and Elixir.
[*Shown in Product Identification Section*]

FEOSOL PLUS®
Iron plus vitamins

Description: For use in iron deficiency and iron-deficiency anemia where additional vitamins are indicated.
Modified Formula (No prescription required):
Formula: Each Feosol Plus capsule contains:
Dried ferrous sulfate ....200 mg.
(equivalent to 325 mg. ferrous sulfate USP; 65 mg. of elemental iron)
Folic acid ....0.2 mg.
Ascorbic acid
(Vitamin C) ....50 mg.
Thiamine HCl
(Vitamin B₁) ....2 mg.
Riboflavin
(Vitamin B₂) ....2 mg.
Pyridoxine HCl
(Vitamin B₆) ....2 mg.

Vitamin B₁₂
(activity equivalent) ....5 mcg.
(derived from streptomyces fermentation)
Nicotinic acid (niacin) ....20 mg.
Usual Dosage: *Adults and Children (over 3 yrs.)* One capsule twice daily or as directed by physician.
Warning: The treatment of any anemic condition should be under the advice and supervision of a physician.
Since oral iron products tend to interfere with absorption of oral tetracycline antibiotics, these products should not be taken within two hours of each other. Keep this and all medicines out of reach of children. In case of accidental overdose, contact a physician or poison control center immediately. Iron-containing medication may occasionally cause constipation or diarrhea.
How Supplied: Bottles of 100 capsules.
[*Shown in Product Identification Section*]

FORTESPAN®
Therapeutic Multivitamins

Description: For the treatment of multiple vitamin deficiencies.
Formula: Each Fortespan capsule contains:
Ascorbic acid (Vitamin C) .... 150 mg.
Thiamine mononitrate
(Vitamin B₁) .... 6 mg.
Riboflavin (Vitamin B₂ as
the phosphate) .... 6 mg.
Nicotinamide .... 60 mg.
Pyridoxine HCl (Vitamin B₆) .... 6 mg.
Vitamin A ...10,000 International Units
Vitamin D ....400 International Units
Vitamin B₁₂
(cyanocobalamin) .... 15 mcg.
Pantothenic acid (as
dl-panthenol) .... 6 mg.
FD&C Yellow #5 (tartrazine) as a color additive.
Usual Dosage: One Fortespan capsule at breakfast or as directed by physician.
Warning: Keep this and all medicines out of reach of children. In case of accidental overdose, contact a physician or poison control center immediately.
How Supplied: Bottles of 30 and 100 capsules.
[*Shown in Product Identification Section*]

ORNACOL®
Relieves coughing and nasal congestion.

Description: Ornacol is specifically formulated for temporary relief from coughing and nasal congestion due to the common cold and sinusitis.
Ornacol contains no sedatives or antihistamines and, therefore, does not produce drowsiness in most people. This makes it especially suited for working people and others who must remain alert.
Composition: Each red and gray Ornacol Cough & Cold Capsule contains: 30 mg. dextromethorphan hydrobromide; 25 mg. phenylpropanolamine hydrochloride.

Continued on next page

Menley & James—Cont.

Each teaspoonful (5 ml.) of Ornacol Cough & Cold Liquid contains: dextromethorphan HBr 15 mg; phenylpropanolamine HCl 12.5 mg.; alcohol 8%.

Dosage: Ornacol Capsules: *Adults and children over 12*—one capsule four times a day.

Children—use Ornacol Liquid.

Ornacol Liquid: *Adults and children over 12*—two teaspoonfuls four times a day. *Children (4-12)*—one teaspoonful four times a day. *Children under 4*—consult your physician.

Warning: Persistent cough may indicate the presence of a serious condition. Persons with a high fever or persistent cough should not use this preparation unless directed by a physician. Do not take this product if you are taking another medication containing phenylpropanolamine.

Individuals with high blood pressure, heart disease, diabetes or thyroid disease should use only as directed by a physician. If relief does not occur within three days, discontinue use and consult a physician.

Keep this and all medicines out of reach of children. In case of accidental overdose, contact a physician or a poison control center immediately.

Supplied: Ornacol Cough & Cold Capsules in packages of 20 and bottles of 100. Ornacol Cough & Cold Liquid in 4 fl. oz. bottles.

[*Shown in Product Identification Section*]

ORNEX®
decongestant/analgesic

Composition: Each blue and white Ornex capsule contains: 18 mg. phenylpropanolamine hydrochloride; 325 mg. acetaminophen.

Action: For temporary relief of nasal congestion, headache, aches, pains and fever due to colds, sinusitis and flu. No antihistamine drowsiness.

Dosage: Adults—Two capsules every 4 hours. Do not exceed 8 capsules in 24 hours. Children (6 to 12 years)—One capsule every 4 hours. Do not exceed 4 capsules in 24 hours.

Warning: Do not give to children under 6 years or use for more than 10 days, unless directed by physician. Individuals with high blood pressure, heart disease, diabetes or thyroid disease should use only as directed by physician. Do not take this product if you are taking another medication containing phenylpropanolamine.

This package is child-safe; however, keep this and all medicines out of reach of children. In case of accidental overdose, contact a physician or poison control center immediately.

Supplied: In consumer packages of 24 and 48 capsules, in bottles of 100 capsules. Also, Dispensary Packages of 800 capsules for industrial dispensaries and student health clinics only.

[*Shown in Product Identification Section*]

PRAGMATAR® OINTMENT

Description: Cetyl alcohol-coal tar distillate, 4%; precipitated sulfur, 3%; salicylic acid, 3%—in an oil-in-water emulsion base.

Action and Uses: Pragmatar is highly effective in a wide range of common skin disorders both in adults and in children: seborrheic affections, especially of the scalp, including dandruff and "cradle cap"; subacute and chronic dermatitis; eczematous eruptions; fungous infections, including "athlete's foot", etc. *Note:* For use in infants and when otherwise desired, Pragmatar may be diluted by mixing a few drops of water with a small quantity of the ointment in the palm of the hand.

Precautions: Keep out of eyes and off eyelids. Use with care near the groin or on acutely inflamed areas. Do not use on blistered surfaces. If rash or irritation develops, discontinue use.

Administration and Dosage: *On the scalp:* Part hair and massage into small areas before retiring. Apply sparingly but thoroughly to entire scalp. Remove with a light shampoo the following morning. Use no more often than once daily. *On other areas:* Use small quantities, confining application to affected surfaces. Apply no more often than once daily.

Warning: Keep this and all medicines out of reach of children. In case of accidental ingestion, contact a physician or poison control center immediately.

How Supplied: 1 oz. tubes.

[*Shown in Product Identification Section*]

QUOTANE® OINTMENT
topical anesthetic

Description: Quotane Ointment contains dimethisoquin hydrochloride, 0.5%; preserved with thimerosal 1:50,000; in a white, water-miscible emulsion base.

Action and Uses: For prompt, prolonged relief of itching, pain and burning due to: poison ivy, hemorrhoids, prickly heat, poison oak, hives, mild sunburn, athlete's foot, abrasions, minor burns, eczema, and insect bites. Not chemically related to the various "-caine" type preparations.

Directions: Apply a light coating when necessary, not more than 4 times daily, or as directed by physician.

Use special applicator for itching hemorrhoids (do not apply to bleeding hemorrhoids).

If the condition for which the preparation is used persists, or if a rash or irritation develops, discontinue use and consult physician.

Warning: Quotane Ointment should not be used in the eyes or on eyelids. Do not apply to bleeding hemorrhoids or to extensive areas. Not for prolonged use. Keep this and all drugs out of reach of children. In case of accidental ingestion, contact a physician or poison control center immediately.

Keep tube tightly closed to prevent drying.

How Supplied: In 1 oz. tubes (with rectal applicator).

Remarks: Not compatible with tannic acid.

[*Shown in Product Identification Section*]

SINE–OFF® Extra Strength
Sinus Medicine
Non-Aspirin Capsules
Relieves headache and congestion

Product Information: Sine-Off Extra Strength Sinus Medicine Non-Aspirin Capsule provides extra strength relief from headache, pain, pressure and congestion due to sinusitis, allergic sinusitis or the common cold. This formula contains **acetaminophen,** a pain reliever that is unlikely to cause gastric irritation or allergic reactions often associated with aspirin-containing products.

Product Benefits: Eases headache pain and pressure • promotes sinus drainage • shrinks swollen membranes to relieve congestion • relieves postnasal drip.

Dosage: Adults and children over 12 years of age: 2 capsules every 6 hours, not to exceed 8 capsules in any 24-hour period. Children under 12 should use only as directed by physician.

Warnings: Do not exceed recommended dosage. If symptoms do not improve within 7 days, consult a physician before continuing use. Individuals being treated for depression, high blood pressure, asthma, heart disease, diabetes, thyroid disease, glaucoma or enlarged prostate should use only as directed by a physician.

Avoid alcoholic beverages while taking this product. Do not drive or operate heavy machinery as this preparation may cause drowsiness.

Stop use if dizziness, sleeplessness or nervousness occurs. Safe use in pregnancy has not been established. Therefore, product should be used during pregnancy only as directed by a physician. Do not take this medication if you are taking another product containing phenylpropanolamine.

May cause excitability, especially in children. This package is child-safe; however, keep this and all medicines out of reach of children. In case of accidental overdose, contact a physician immediately.

Formula: Each capsule contains: Chlorpheniramine maleate, 2.0 mg.; phenylpropanolamine HCl, 18.75 mg.; acetaminophen, 500 mg. **(500 mg. is a non-standard dosage of acetaminophen, as compared to the standard of 325 mg.).**

How Supplied: Consumer packages of 20 capsules.

Also Available: Sine-Off® Extra Strength Sinus Medicine Non-Aspirin Tablets 20's. Sine-Off® Sinus Medicine Tablets with Aspirin in 24's, 48's, 100's. Sine-Off® Once-A-Day Sinus Spray.

[*Shown in Product Identification Section*]

SINE–OFF® Extra Strength Sinus Medicine Non-Aspirin Tablets
Relieves sinus headache and congestion

Product Information: Sine-Off provides extra strength relief from headache, pain, pressure and congestion due to sinusitis, allergic sinusitis, or the common cold. This formula contains acetaminophen, a pain reliever that is unlikely to cause gastric irritation or allergic reactions often associated with aspirin-containing products.

Product Benefits: Eases headache, pain and pressure; promotes sinus drainage; shrinks swollen membranes to relieve congestion; relieves drip.

Dosage: Adults and children over 12 years of age, 2 tablets per dose. Allow at least 6 hours between doses. Do not exceed 8 tablets in any 24 hour period.

Warning: Individuals with high blood pressure, heart disease, diabetes, thyroid disease, high fever, or glaucoma should use only as directed by physician. Do not drive or operate heavy machinery as this preparation may cause drowsiness. Consult your physician if symptoms persist or before exceeding the recommended dosage. Do not take this medication if you are taking another product containing phenylpropanolamine. Keep this and all medicines out of reach of children. In case of accidental overdose, contact a physician immediately.

Formula: Each tablet contains chlorpheniramine, 2.0 mg.; phenylpropanolamine HCl, 18.75 mg.; acetaminophen 500 mg. (500 mg. is a non-standard extra strength dosage of acetaminophen, as compared to the standard of 325 mg.).

How Supplied: Consumer packages of 20 tablets.

Also Available: Sine-Off® Tablets with Aspirin in 24's, 48's, 100's. Sine-Off® Once-A-Day Sinus Spray ½ oz., 1 oz. Sine-Off® Extra Strength Non-Aspirin Tablets 20's.

[*Shown in Product Identification Section*]

SINE–OFF® Once-A-Day Sinus Spray
Fast and prolonged relief from sinus and nasal congestion

Product Information: Sine-Off Once-A-Day Sinus Spray promotes fast (5–10 minutes) sinus and nasal drainage, shrinks swollen membranes, helps decongest sinus openings and clear nasal passages. Lasts hours longer (up to 10 hours) than regular spray for temporary relief from sinus and nasal congestion due to sinusitis, colds and hay fever.

Dosage: Hold head upright. Squeeze bottle firmly and quickly 2 or 3 times in each nostril. Repeat morning and night.

Warning: This product is for temporary relief; do not exceed recommended dosage because symptoms may occur such as burning, stinging, sneezing, or increase of nasal discharge. Do not use this product for more than 3 days. If symptoms persist, consult a physician. For adult use only. Do not use for children under 12 years except under the advice of a physician. Use by more than one person

may spread infection. Keep out of children's reach.

Active Ingredient: Xylometazoline HCl, NF, 0.1%. Also contains thimerosal 0.001% and aromatics (menthol, eucalyptol, camphor, methyl salicylate).

How Supplied: In consumer package spray bottle ½ and 1 fl. oz.

Also Available: Sine-Off® Tablets with Aspirin in 24's, 48's, 100's. Sine-Off® Extra Strength Non-Aspirin Tablets 20's and Extra Strength Non-Aspirin Capsules 20's.

[*Shown in Product Identification Section*]

SINE–OFF® Sinus Medicine Tablets–Aspirin Formula
Relieves sinus headache and congestion

Product Information: Sine-Off relieves headache, pain, pressure and congestion due to sinusitis, allergic sinusitis, or the common cold.

Product Benefits: Eases headache, pain and pressure; promotes sinus drainage; shrinks swollen membranes to relieve congestion; relieves postnasal drip.

Dosage: Adults: 2 tablets every 4 hours, not to exceed 8 tablets daily. Children (6–12) one-half the adult dosage. Children under 6 years use only as directed by physician.

Warning: Individuals with high blood pressure, heart disease, diabetes, thyroid disease, high fever, or glaucoma should use only as directed by physician. Do not drive or operate heavy machinery as this preparation may cause drowsiness. Consult your physician if symptoms persist or before exceeding the recommended dosage. Do not take this medication if you are taking another product containing phenylpropanolamine. This package is child-safe; however, keep this and all medicines out of reach of children. In case of accidental overdose, contact a physician immediately.

Formula: Chlorpheniramine maleate 2.0 mg.; phenylpropanolamine HCl 18.75 mg. aspirin 325.0 mg.

How Supplied: Consumer packages of 24, 48 and 100 tablets.

Also Available: Sine-off® Extra Strength Non-Aspirin Capsules 20's, and Extra Strength Non-Aspirin Tablets 20's. Sine-Off® Once-A-Day Sinus Spray ½ and 1 oz.

[*Shown in Product Identification Section*]

TELDRIN®
Chlorpheniramine maleate Timed-Release Allergy Capsules, 8 mg. and Maximum Strength 12 mg.

Description: Each Teldrin Timed-Release capsule contains chlorpheniramine maleate, 8 mg. or Maximum Strength 12 mg., so formulated that a portion of the antihistamine dose is released initially, and the remaining medication is released gradually over a prolonged period.

Indications: Teldrin provides up to 12 hours of relief from hay fever/upper respiratory allergy symptoms: sneezing; runny nose; itchy, watery eyes.

Dosage: DOSAGE SHOULD BE INDIVIDUALIZED ACCORDING TO THE

NEEDS AND THE RESPONSE OF THE USER.

Adults and children over 12 years of age: Just one capsule in the morning, and one in the evening. Do not give to children under 12 without the advice and consent of a physician. Not to exceed 24 mg. (2 capsules) in 24 hours.

Warning: Do not take this product if you have asthma, glaucoma, or difficulty in urination due to enlargement of the prostate gland, except under the advice and supervision of a physician.

Do not drive or operate heavy machinery as this preparation may cause drowsiness. Avoid alcoholic beverages while taking this product. May cause excitability, especially in children. Keep this and all medicines out of the reach of children. In case of accidental overdose, contact a physician or poison control center immediately.

How Supplied: 8 mg. and Maximum Strength 12 mg. Timed-Release capsules in packages of 12 and 24 capsules, in bottles of 50 and 500; in Single Unit Packages of 100 (intended for institutional use only).

[*Shown in Product Identification Section*]

TROPH–IRON®
Vitamins B_1, B_{12} and Iron

Description: Each 5 ml. (1 teaspoonful) and each tablet contains thiamine hydrochloride (vitamin B_1), 10 mg.; cyanocobalamin (vitamin B_{12}), 25 mcg.; elemental iron, 30 mg., present as soluble ferric pyrophosphate.

Indications: For deficiencies of vitamins B_1, B_{12} and iron.

Dosage and Administration: Adults and children 4 years of age and over. One 5 ml. teaspoonful or one tablet daily—or as directed by physician.

The treatment of any anemic condition should be under the advice and supervision of a physician. Since oral iron products interfere with absorption of oral tetracycline antibiotics, these products should not be taken within two hours of each other.

Iron-containing medications may occasionally cause gastrointestinal discomfort, such as nausea, constipation or diarrhea.

Warning: Keep this and all medicines out of reach of children. In case of accidental overdose, contact a physician or poison control center immediately.

How Supplied: Liquid—a clear red liquid in 4 fl. oz. (118 ml) bottles; Tablets—bottles of 50. (While its effectiveness is in no way affected, Troph-Iron liquid may darken as it ages.)

[*Shown in Product Identification Section*]

TROPHITE®
Vitamins B_1 and B_{12}

Description: Each 5 ml (1 teaspoonful) and each tablet contains thiamine hydrochloride (vitamin B_1), 10 mg.; and cyanocobalamin (vitamin B_{12}), 25 mcg.

Indications: For deficiencies of vitamins B_1 and B_{12}.

Continued on next page

Menley & James—Cont.

Dosage and Administration: Adults and children 4 years of age and over: One 5 ml. teaspoonful or one tablet daily—or as directed by physician. Children under 4 years: ½ teaspoonful daily.

Trophite Liquid may be mixed with water, milk, or fruit or vegetable juices immediately before taking.

Warning: Keep this and all medicines out of reach of children. In case of accidental overdose, contact a physician or poison control center immediately.

How Supplied: Liquid—4 fl. oz. (118 ml.) bottles. Tablets—bottles of 50.

[Shown in Product Identification Section]

Mericon Industries, Inc.
420-22 S.W. WASHINGTON STREET
PEORIA, IL 61602

DELACORT
(hydrocortisone USP ½%)

Active Ingredient: Hydrocortisone USP ½%.

Indications: For the temporary relief of minor skin irritations, itching and rashes due to eczema, dermatitis, insect bites, poison ivy, poison oak, poison sumac, soaps; detergents, cosmetics, and jewelry, and for itchy genital and anal areas.

Warnings: For external use only. Avoid contact with the eyes. If condition worsens, or if symptoms persist for more than 7 days discontinue use (of this product) and consult a physician. Do not use on children 2 years of age except under the advice and supervision of a physician.

Precaution: KEEP OUT OF REACH OF CHILDREN.

Dosage and Administration: For adults and children 2 years of age and older: Apply to affected area 3 or 4 times daily.

How Supplied: 2 oz. and 4 oz. squeeze bottle.

ORAZINC®
(zinc sulfate)

Active Ingredient: Zinc Sulfate U.S.P. 220 mg. and 110 mg. Capsules.

Indications: A Dietary Supplement containing Zinc.

Warnings: Should be taken with milk or meals to alleviate possible gastric distress.

Symptoms and Treatment of Oral Overdosage: Nausea, mild diarrhea or rash—to control, reduce dosage or discontinue.

Dosage and Administration: One capsule daily or as recommended by Physician.

How Supplied: Bottles of 100 and 1000 Capsules each.

ZINC TABS
(zinc sulfate U.S.P.)

Active Ingredient: Zinc (As Zinc Sulfate U.S.P.) 15 mg. and 25 mg. Tablets.

Indications: A Dietary Supplement containing Zinc.

Warnings: Should be taken with milk or meals to alleviate possible gastric distress.

Symptoms and Treatment of Oral Overdosage: Nausea, mild diarrhea or rash—to control, reduce dosage or discontinue.

Dosage and Administration: One capsule daily or as recommended by Physician.

How Supplied: Bottles of 100 and 1000 Capsules each.

MERRELL-NATIONAL LABORATORIES
Division of Richardson-Merrell Inc.
CINCINNATI, OH 45215

MERRELL-NATIONAL LABORATORIES Inc.
CAYEY, PUERTO RICO 00633

CĒPACOL® Mouthwash/Gargle

Description:

Ceepryn® (cetylpyridinium chloride)............................ 1:2000

Alcohol 14%

Phosphate buffers and aromatics

Cēpacol is a soothing, pleasant tasting mouthwash/gargle. It has a low surface tension, approximately ½ that of water. This property is the basis of the spreading action in the oral cavity as well as its foaming action. Cēpacol leaves the mouth feeling fresh and clean and helps provide soothing, temporary relief of dryness and minor irritations.

Uses: Recommended as a mouthwash and gargle for daily oral care; as an aromatic mouth freshener to provide a clean feeling in the mouth; as a soothing, foaming rinse to freshen the mouth.

Used routinely before dental procedures, helps give patient confidence of not offending with mouth odor. Often employed as a foaming and refreshing rinse before, during, and after instrumentation and dental prophylaxis. Convenient as a mouth-freshening agent after taking dental impressions. Helpful in reducing the unpleasant taste and odor in the mouth following gingivectomy.

Used in hospitals as a mouthwash and gargle for daily oral care. Also used to refresh and soothe the mouth following emesis; inhalation therapy, and intubations, and for swabbing the mouths of patients incapable of personal care.

Warning: Keep out of reach of children.

Instructions For Use: Rinse vigorously after brushing or any time to freshen the mouth. Particularly useful after meals or before social engagements. Aromatic Cēpacol leaves the mouth feeling refreshingly clean.

Use full strength every two or three hours as a soothing, foaming gargle, or as directed by a physician or dentist. May also be mixed with warm water.

How Supplied:

6 oz., 12 oz., 18 oz., 24 oz., and a unit package of 4/2-quart bottles

3 oz. Hospital Bedside Bottles (not for retail sale)

3 oz. Dental Chairside Bottles (not for retail sale)

5 oz. Hospital Bedside Bottle (not for retail sale)

14 oz. Direct Stream Dispenser (not for retail sale)

Professional Unit of 4/2-quart bottles with dispensing pump (not for retail sale)

Product Information as of October, 1971 (Package Information amended April, 1977)

[Shown in Product Identification Section]

CĒPACOL® Throat Lozenges

Description:

Ceepryn® (cetylpyridinium chloride)..........................1:1500

Benzyl alcohol 0.3%

Aromatics

Yellow mint-flavored hard candy base

Cetylpyridinium chloride (Ceepryn) is a cationic quaternary ammonium compound. This is a surface-active agent, which in aqueous solution, has a surface tension lower than that of water.

Cetylpyridinium chloride in the concentration used in Cēpacol is non-irritating to tissues.

Indications: Cēpacol Lozenges stimulate salivation to help provide soothing temporary relief of dryness and minor irritation of mouth and throat and resulting cough.

Warning: Severe sore throat or sore throat accompanied by high fever or headache or nausea and vomiting, or any sore throat persisting more than two days may be serious. Consult a physician promptly. Persons with a high fever or persistent cough should not use this preparation unless directed by physician. Do not administer to children under 3 years of age unless directed by physician. Keep this and all medication out of children's reach.

Instructions For Use: May be used as needed. Allow to dissolve slowly in the mouth.

How Supplied:

Trade Package: 27 lozenges in 3 pocket packs of 9 each.

Professional Package: 400 lozenges in 100 foil strips of 4 each.

Product Information as of October, 1971 (Package Information amended October, 1980)

[Shown in Product Identification Section]

CĒPACOL® Anesthetic Troches

Description:

Ceepryn® (cetylpyridinium chloride)................................... 1:1500

Benzocaine

Aromatics

Green citrus-flavored hard candy base

Cetylpyridinium chloride (Ceepryn) is a cationic quaternary ammonium compound, which is a surface-active agent. Aqueous solutions of cetylpyridinium chloride have a surface tension lower than that of water.

Cetylpyridinium chloride in the concentration used in Cēpacol is non-irritating to tissues.

Actions:
Anesthetic effect for pain relief
Stimulates salivation—Relieves dryness
Indications: *Sore Throat:* For fast, temporary relief of pain and discomfort due to minor sore throat. For temporary relief of pain and discomfort associated with tonsillitis and pharyngitis. *Mouth Irritations:* For fast, temporary relief of pain and discomfort due to minor mouth irritations. For temporary relief of discomfort associated with stomatitis. For adjunctive, temporary relief of pain and discomfort following periodontal procedures and minor surgery of the mouth.
Warning: Severe sore throat or sore throat accompanied by high fever or headache or nausea and vomiting, or any sore throat persisting more than two days may be serious. Consult a physician promptly. Do not administer to children under 3 years of age unless directed by physician. Keep this and all medication out of children's reach.
Instructions For Use: May be used as needed. Allow to dissolve slowly in the mouth.
How Supplied:
Trade Package: 18 troches in 2 pocket packs of 9 each.
Professional Package: 200 troches in 100 foil strips of 2 each.
Product Information as of July, 1972 (Package Information amended October, 1980)

CEPASTAT®
sore throat spray/gargle and lozenges

Description:
Sore Throat Spray/Gargle
A liquid available as a spray or gargle containing phenol (1.4%) and glycerin in a pleasant, soothing, aqueous solution.
Lozenges
Cooling sugar-free lozenges containing phenol (1.45%) and menthol (0.12%) in a sorbitol base flavored with eucalyptus oil.
Indications:
Sore Throat Spray/Gargle and Lozenges
1. Sore throat:
   For prompt temporary relief of minor pain or discomfort associated with pharyngitis or tonsillitis or following tonsillectomy.
2. Sore mouth or gums:
   For prompt temporary relief of minor pain or discomfort associated with pericoronitis or periodontitis or with dental procedures such as extractions, gingivectomies, and other minor oral surgery.
Action:
Sore Throat Spray/Gargle
Phenol is a recognized topical anesthetic. Glycerin provides a soothing effect.
Lozenge
Phenol is a recognized topical anesthetic. Menthol provides a cooling sensation to aid in symptomatic relief and adds to the lozenge effect in stimulating salivary flow.

Warning*:
Sore Throat Spray/Gargle and Lozenges
Do not exceed recommended dosage. If soreness is severe, persists for more than 2 days, or is accompanied by high fever, headache, nausea or vomiting, consult your physician or dentist promptly. Do not give to children under 6 years unless directed by physician and dentist. Do not use for more than 10 days at a time.
KEEP OUT OF REACH OF CHILDREN.
Note To Diabetics*: Each lozenge contains approximately 2 grams of carbohydrate as sorbitol.
Instructions For Use:
Sore Throat Spray/Gargle
  For minor sore throat pain:
    As gargle, use full strength. Limit gargling to 15 seconds and expel.
    As spray, spray 5 times (children 6 to 12 years, spray 3 times) and expel. Repeat either gargle or spray every 2 hours, if necessary.
  For discomforts of mouth or gums:
    As gargle, use full strength. Swish around sore or painful areas for 15 seconds and expel. Repeat every 2 hours, if necessary.
Lozenges
  Adults
    Dissolve 1 lozenge in mouth every 2 hours. Do not exceed 9 lozenges per day.
  Children (6 to 12 years of age)
    Dissolve 1 lozenge in mouth every 3 hours. Do not exceed 4 lozenges per day.
How Supplied:
Sore Throat Spray
  3-ounce bottles with sprayer
Gargle
  14-ounce bottles without sprayer
All bottles are shatterproof plastic.
Lozenges
  300 lozenges in 100 strips of 3 each
  Boxes of 18 lozenges as 2 pocket packs of 9 lozenges each
Product Information as of July, 1980

*This section appears on the label for the consumer.
[*Shown in Product Identification Section*]

Children's
CEPASTAT®
sore throat lozenges

Description: Cherry-flavored, sugar-free lozenges containing phenol 0.73% and menthol 0.12% in a sorbitol base. Specially formulated for children 6 years of age and older.
Indications:
1. Sore throat:
   For prompt temporary relief of minor pain or discomfort associated with pharyngitis or tonsillitis or following tonsillectomy.
2. Sore mouth or gums:
   For prompt temporary relief of minor pain or discomfort associated with pericoronitis or periodontitis or with dental procedures such as extractions, gingivectomies, and other minor oral surgery.
Action: Phenol is a recognized topical anesthetic. Menthol provides a cooling

sensation to aid in symptomatic relief and adds to the lozenge effect in stimulating salivary flow.
Warnings*: Do not exceed recommended dosage. If soreness is severe, persists for more than 2 days, or is accompanied by high fever, headache, nausea, or vomiting, consult your physician or dentist promptly. Do not give to children under 6 years unless directed by physician or dentist. Do not use for more than 10 days at a time.
KEEP OUT OF REACH OF CHILDREN.
Note To Diabetics*: Each lozenge contains approximately 2 grams of carbohydrate as sorbitol.
Directions*: DO NOT CHEW. 6 to 12 years: 1 lozenge every 3 hours, followed by another after the first one dissolves, if needed during the 3-hour period; do not use more than 2 in 3 hours or more than 10 daily. Over 12 years: 1 lozenge every 2 hours, followed by another after the first dissolves, if needed during the 2-hour period; do not use more than 2 in 2 hours or more than 18 daily. Under 6 years: consult your physician or dentist.
How Supplied: Boxes of 18 lozenges as 2 pocket packs of 9 lozenges each

*This section appears on the label for the consumer.
Product Information as of July, 1980
[*Shown in Product Identification Section*]

DELCID®

Description: Each teaspoonful (5 ml.) contains a balanced combination of 600 mg. aluminum hydroxide [$Al(OH)_3$] and 665 mg. magnesium hydroxide [$Mg.(OH)_2$]. The sodium content is not more than 15 mg. per teaspoonful.
Actions: The balanced ratio of antacids provides reduction of gastric acidity and gives symptomatic comfort to the patient. The acid neutralizing capacity is 42 mEq. for each 5 ml.
Indications: Delcid is used to relieve the symptoms of hyperacidity associated with peptic ulcer, gastritis, peptic esophagitis, gastric hyperacidity, and hiatal hernia, and to relieve the following symptoms: heartburn, sour stomach, or acid indigestion.
Warnings*: Do not take more than 6 teaspoonfuls in a 24-hour period or use the maximum dosage of this product for more than 2 weeks, except under the advice and supervision of a physician. May have laxative effect. Do not use this product except under the advice and supervision of a physician if you have kidney disease. Keep this and all drugs out of the reach of children. In case of accidental overdose, seek professional assistance or contact a poison control center immediately.
Drug Interaction Precautions*: Do not take this product if you are presently taking a prescription antibiotic drug containing any form of tetracycline.
Adverse Reactions: Miscellaneous reports include diarrhea, nausea, and vomiting.

Continued on next page

Merrell-National—Cont.

Dosage and Administration: 1 teaspoonful, ½ to 1 hour after meals and at bedtime or as directed.

Directions:* Take as needed to alleviate symptoms: 1 teaspoonful every 4 hours, or as directed by a physician.

How Supplied: 8 fl. oz. plastic bottles

---

*This section appears on the label for the consumer.

Product Information as of April, 1977

KOLANTYL®

Description: Each teaspoonful (5 ml.) of Kolantyl Gel contains:

Aluminum hydroxide
[Al (OH)$_3$] ....150 mg.

Magnesium hydroxide
[Mg.(OH)$_2$] ....150 mg.

Each Kolantyl Wafer contains:

Aluminum hydroxide ....180 mg.
(supplied as dried aluminum hydroxide gel)

Magnesium hydroxide ....170 mg.

Actions: The balanced ratio of antacids provides reduction of gastric acidity and gives symptomatic comfort to the patient. The acid neutralizing capacity is 10.5 mEq. for each 5 ml. of gel and 10.8 mEq. for each wafer.

Indications: Kolantyl is used to relieve the symptoms of hyperacidity associated with peptic ulcer, gastritis, peptic esophagitis, gastric hyperacidity, and hiatal hernia, and to relieve the following symptons: heartburn, sour stomach, or acid indigestion.

Warnings*: Do not take more than 12 teaspoonfuls of gel or 12 wafers in a 24-hour period or use the maximum dosage of this product for more than 2 weeks, except under the advice and supervision of a physician. May have laxative effect. Do not use this product except under the advice and supervision of a physician if you have kidney disease. Keep this and all drugs out of the reach of children. In case of accidental overdose, seek professional assistance or contact a poison control center immediately.

Drug Interaction Precautions*: Do not take this product if you are presently taking a prescription antibiotic drug containing any form of tetracycline.

Adverse Reactions: Miscellaneous reports include nausea and vomiting, abdominal discomfort, stomatitis, rash, dizziness, and diarrhea.

Dosage and Administration:
Kolantyl Gel: 1 to 4 teaspoonfuls ½ to 1 hour after meals and at bedtime or as directed. May be taken undiluted or mixed with milk or water, particularly if the patient is on a regular milk regimen.
Kolantyl Wafers: 1 to 4 wafers ½ to 1 hour after meals and at bedtime or as directed. Wafers may be chewed or allowed to dissolve in the mouth.

Directions:*
Kolantyl Gel—Take as needed to alleviate symptoms: 1 to 4 teaspoonfuls every 4 hours, or as directed by a physician.

Kolantyl Wafers—Take as needed to alleviate symptoms: 1 to 4 wafers every 4 hours, or as directed by a physician. Wafers may be chewed or allowed to dissolve in the mouth.

How Supplied:
Kolantyl Gel: 6 oz. and 12 oz. bottles
Kolantyl Wafers: boxes of 32 wafers, boxes of 96 wafers, and boxes of 400 wafers in sealed strips of 4 wafers each

---

*This section appears on the label for the consumer.

Product Information as of November, 1976

SIMRON™

Description:
Each maroon, soft-gelatin Simron capsule contains:

Elemental iron ....10 mg.
(supplied as ferrous gluconate)

Sacagen™ (polysorbate 20).....400 mg.

Actions: Ferrous gluconate provides a source of elemental iron that will prevent and correct iron deficiency and iron-deficiency anemia. Sacagen (polysorbate 20) is polyoxyethylene 20 sorbitan monolaurate. It is an amber-colored liquid intended to enhance iron absorption and, as a surfactant, aids in the prevention of constipation.

Indications: For the prevention and treatment of iron deficiency and iron-deficiency anemia.

Simron is unusually well tolerated in patients who cannot tolerate other oral iron preparations and in patients with gastrointestinal disease, including peptic ulcer and ulcerative colitis.

Simron is indicated in the treatment of iron-deficiency anemia of patients with a potential for upper gastrointestinal bleeding because it rarely produces black stools, which could mask evidence of bleeding. Simron is indicated in the treatment of iron-deficiency anemia of patients with ulcerative colitis because only small amounts of unabsorbed irritant iron salts are present in the stool. Simron is indicated in the prevention and treatment of iron deficiency and iron-deficiency anemia of pregnancy.

Contraindications: Simron is contraindicated in the treatment of patients with disease associated with increased iron storage (hemochromatosis).

Warnings: Simron should be stored out of the reach of children because of the possibility of iron intoxication from accidental overdosage. Individuals with normal iron balance should not chronically take iron.

Precautions: When anemia is diagnosed, the type of anemia should be established. When iron-deficiency anemia is diagnosed, the cause of the iron deficiency should be established.

Ferrous iron compounds taken by mouth can impair the absorption of tetracycline and tetracycline derivatives. Antacids given concomitantly with iron compounds will decrease the absorption of iron.

Adverse Reactions: The incidence of adverse gastrointestinal reactions is re-

duced with Simron. Gastric irritation, nausea, constipation, and diarrhea are rarely observed.

Dosage and Administration: For the prevention and treatment of iron deficiency and iron-deficiency anemia the recommended dose is 1 Simron capsule three times a day *between meals*. This supplies 30 mg. elemental iron. It should be noted that in patients with continued blood loss it may be necessary to exceed the recommended dose of Simron to obtain optimum therapeutic effect.

Overdosage: As little as 1 gram of elemental iron ingested orally may be toxic. Onset of symptoms usually occurs approximately 30 minutes after ingestion. Initially, gastrointestinal symptoms predominate (vomiting, diarrhea, melena). Shock, dyspnea, lethargy, and coma may follow. Metabolic acidosis may then occur.

Standard measures used to treat acute iron intoxication may include the following: 1) induced vomiting, 2) gastric lavage with 1% sodium bicarbonate, 3) general supportive measures for the treatment of shock and acidosis. Deferoxamine mesylate (Desferal®) should be given intramuscularly for patients not in shock, and intravenously for patients in shock. The manufacturer's recommendations should be consulted for details of administration. Some authors recommend 8000 mg. deferoxamine in 50 ml. of water via nasogastric tube.

How Supplied: Bottles of 100 soft-gelatin capsules

Product Information as of November, 1974
[Shown in Product Identification Section]

SIMRON PLUS®

Description: Each maroon, soft-gelatin capsule contains:

Elemental iron ....10 mg.
(supplied as ferrous gluconate)

Sacagen™ (polysorbate 20) ....400 mg.

Ascorbic acid.....................................50 mg.
(supplied as sodium ascorbate)

Pyridoxine hydrochloride..............1.0 mg.

Folic acid ....0.1 mg.

Vitamin B$_{12}$..................................3.33 mcg.
(supplied as cyanocobalamin)

Actions: Ferrous gluconate provides a source of elemental iron that will prevent and correct iron deficiency and iron-deficiency anemia. Sacagen (polysorbate 20) is polyoxyethylene 20 sorbitan monolaurate. It is an amber-colored liquid intended to enhance iron absorption and, as a surfactant, aids in the prevention of constipation.

In addition, factors necessary for normal hematopoiesis are supplied: ascorbic acid (as sodium ascorbate), pyridoxine hydrochloride, folic acid, and vitamin B$_{12}$ (as cyanocobalamin).

Indications: For the prevention and treatment of iron deficiency and iron-deficiency anemia or anemia due to decreased erythrocyte formation except pernicious anemia or anemias due to bone marrow deficiencies. Simron Plus is indicated in the prevention and treatment of iron deficiency and iron-deficiency anemia of pregnancy.

Contraindications: Simron Plus is contraindicated in the treatment of patients with disease associated with increased iron storage (hemochromatosis).
Warnings: Simron Plus should be stored out of the reach of children because of the possibility of iron intoxication from accidental overdosage. Individuals with normal iron balance should not chronically take iron. Folic acid alone is improper therapy in the treatment of pernicious anemia and other megaloblastic anemias where vitamin B_{12} is deficient.
Precautions: When anemia is diagnosed, the type of anemia should be established. When iron-deficiency anemia is diagnosed, the cause of the iron deficiency should be established.
Ferrous iron compounds taken by mouth can impair the absorption of tetracycline and tetracycline derivatives. Antacids given concomitantly with iron compounds will decrease the absorption of iron. This preparation is not a reliable substitute for parenterally administered cyanocobalamin (vitamin B_{12}) in the management of pernicious anemia.
Parenteral cyanocobalamin should be used in patients receiving folic acid unless pernicious anemia has been ruled out, since folic acid may correct blood disorders of pernicious anemia while nervous system changes progress. Periodic examinations and laboratory studies of pernicious anemia patients are essential.
Adverse Reactions: The incidence of adverse gastrointestinal reactions is reduced with Simron Plus. Gastric irritations, nausea, constipation, and diarrhea are rarely observed. Allergic sensitization has been reported following both oral and parenteral administration of folic acid.
Dosage and Administration: The recommended dose of Simron Plus is 1 capsule three times a day between meals.
Overdosage: As little as 1 gram of elemental iron ingested orally may be toxic. Onset of symptoms usually occurs approximately 30 minutes after ingestion. Initially, gastrointestinal symptoms predominate (vomiting, diarrhea, melena). Shock, dyspnea, lethargy, and coma may follow. Metabolic acidosis may then occur.
Standard measures used to treat acute iron intoxication may include the following: 1) induced vomiting, 2) gastric lavage with 1% sodium bicarbonate, 3) general supportive measures for the treatment of shock and acidosis. Deferoxamine mesylate (Desferal®) should be given intramuscularly for patients not in shock, and intravenously for patients in shock. The manufacturer's recommendation should be consulted for details of administration. Some authors recommend 8000 mg. deferoxamine in 50 ml. of water via nasogastric tube.
How Supplied: Bottles of 100 soft-gelatin capsules
Product Information as of November, 1974
[*Shown in Product Identification Section*]

Merrick Medicine Company
P. O. BOX 1489 (76703)
501-503 S. 8TH STREET (76706)
WACO, TX

PERCY® MEDICINE
For relief of simple diarrhea and excess acid conditions of the stomach.

Active Ingredients: The active ingredients in an aqueous solution of 10 ml adult dose are as follows:
Bismuth Subnitrate NF .... 959.0 mg.
Calcium Hydroxide USP .... 21.9 mg.
The solution contains 5% alcohol, used as a preservative.
Indications: An antacid-astringent for simple diarrhea and for temporary relief of gastric discomfort due to overeating or other dietary indiscretions.
Drug Interaction Precautions: No known drug interaction.
Dosage and Directions For Use: Shake well before using. Administer orally 3 or 4 times daily as required. Vary dosage according to age. For use in infants and children under 6 years of age, consult your physician:

AGE BY YEARS	DOSAGE
6 to 12	1 to 1½ teaspoonfuls
12 to 18	1 to 2 teaspoonfuls
Over 18 and adults	2 teaspoonfuls

Normally, the clear liquid portion of this product (before shaking) is a light lemon color with a sweet palatable flavor. After a long period of time, the color may darken and flavor change. If the product is found to have lost its sweet agreeable flavor and light color, use is not recommended. PERCY MEDICINE may cause stool to darken temporarily.
Warning: Do not use for more than 2 days or in the presence of high fever or in infants or children under 6 years of age unless directed by a physician.
Professional Labeling: Same as those outlined under indications.
How Supplied: Available only in 3 fl. oz. glass bottle encased in an outer carton (NDC 0322-2222-03), (UPC 0322-2222-03).
[*Shown in Product Identification Section*]

Miles Laboratories, Inc.
P. O. BOX 340
ELKHART, IN 46515

ALKA–SELTZER® Effervescent Pain Reliever & Antacid

Active Ingredient: Each tablet contains: aspirin 324 mg., heat treated sodium bicarbonate 1904 mg., citric acid 1000 mg. ALKA-SELTZER® in water contains principally the antacid sodium citrate and the analgesic sodium acetylsalicylate. Buffered pH is between 6 and 7.
Indications: ALKA-SELTZER® Effervescent Pain Reliever & Antacid is an analgesic and an antacid and is indicated for relief of sour stomach, acid indigestion or heartburn with headache or body aches and pains. Also for fast relief of upset stomach with headache from overindulgence in food and drink—especially recommended for taking before bed and again on arising. Effective for pain relief alone: headache or body and muscular aches and pains.
Actions: When the ALKA-SELTZER® Effervescent Pain Reliever & Antacid tablet is dissolved in water, the acetylsalicylate ion differs from acetylsalicylic acid chemically, physically and pharmacologically. Being fat insoluble, it is not absorbed by the gastric mucosal cells. Studies and observations in animals and man including radiochrome determinations of fecal blood loss, measurement of ion fluxes and direct visualization with gastrocamera, have shown that, as contrasted with acetylsalicylic acid, the acetylsalicylate ion delivered in the solution does not alter gastric mucosal permeability to permit back-diffusion of hydrogen ion, and gastric damage and acute gastric mucosal lesions are therefore not seen after administration of the product. ALKA-SELTZER® Effervescent Pain Reliever & Antacid has the capacity to neutralize gastric hydrochloric acid quickly and effectively. In-vitro, 154 ml. of 0.1 N hydrochloric acid are required to decrease the pH of one tablet of ALKA-SELTZER® Effervescent Pain Reliever & Antacid in solution to 4.0. Measured against the in vitro standard established by the Food and Drug Administration one tablet neutralizes 17.2 mEq of acid. In vivo, the antacid activity of two ALKA-SELTZER® Effervescent Pain Reliever & Antacid tablets is comparable to that of 10 ml. of milk of magnesia. ALKA-SELTZER® Effervescent Pain Reliever & Antacid is able to resist pH changes caused by the continuing secretion of acid in the normal individual and to maintain an elevated pH until emptying occurs.
ALKA-SELTZER® Effervescent Pain Reliever & Antacid provides highly water soluable acetylsalicylate ions which are fat insoluble. Acetylsalicylate ions are not absorbed from the stomach. They empty from the stomach and thereby become available for absorption from the duodenum. Thus, fast drug absorption and high plasma acetylsalicylate levels are achieved. Plasma levels of salicylate following the administration of ALKA-SELTZER® Effervescent Pain Reliever & Antacid solution (acetylsalicylate ion equivalent to 640 mg. acetylsaliylic acid) can reach 29 mg./liter in 10 minutes and rise to peak levels as high as 55 mg./liter within 30 minutes.
Warnings: Except under the advice and supervision of a physician, do not take more than, Adults: 8 tablets in a 24 hour period. (60 years of age or older: 4 tablets in a 24 hour period), Children (6–12), 4 tablets in a 24 hour period, (3–5), 2 tablets in a 24 hour period, or use the maximum dosage for more than 10 days (5 days for children). Do not use if you are allergic to aspirin or have asthma, if you have a coagulation (bleeding) disease, or

Continued on next page

Miles—Cont.

if you are on a sodium restricted diet. Each tablet contains 551 mg. of sodium. Keep this and all drugs out of the reach of children.

Dosage and Administration: ALKA-SELTZER® Effervescent Pain Reliever and Antacid is taken in solution, approximately three ounces of water per tablet is sufficient.

Adults: 2 tablets every 4 hours. Children: (6–12) 1 tablet, (3–5) ½ tablet, every 4–6 hours; children under 3, as directed by a physician. CAUTION: If symptoms persist or recur frequently, or if you are under treatment for ulcer, consult your physician.

How Supplied: Tablets: in bottles of 8 and 25; individually foil sealed; box of 12; dispenser boxes of 36 tablets in 18 foil twin packs; 100 tablets in 50 foil twin packs; carton of 72 tablets in 36 foil twin packs. Product Identification Mark: "Alka-Seltzer" embossed on each tablet.

ALKA-SELTZER® Effervescent Antacid

Active Ingredient: Each tablet contains heat treated sodium bicarbonate 958 mg., citric acid 832 mg., potassium bicarbonate 312 mg. ALKA-SELTZER® Effervescent Antacid in water contains principally the antacids sodium citrate and potassium citrate.

Indications: ALKA-SELTZER® Effervescent Antacid is indicated for relief of acid indigestion, sour stomach or heartburn.

Actions: The ALKA-SELTZER® Effervescent Antacid solution provides quick and effective neutralization of gastric acid. Measured by the in vitro standard established by the Food and Drug Administration one tablet will neutralize 10.6 mEq of acid.

Warnings: Except under the advice and supervision of a physician, do not take more than: Adults: 8 tablets in a 24 hour period (60 years of age or older: 7 tablets in a 24 hour period), Children 4 tablets in a 24 hour period; or use the maximum dosage of this product for more than 2 weeks.

Do not use this product if you are on a sodium restricted diet. Each tablet contains 296 mg. of sodium.

Keep this and all drugs out of the reach of children.

Dosage and Administration: ALKA-SELTZER® Effervescent Antacid is taken in solution; approximately 3 oz. of water per tablet is sufficient. Adults: one or two tablets every 4 hours as needed. Children: ½ the adult dosage.

How Supplied: Tablets: individually foil sealed, box of 12; dispenser boxes of 20 tablets in 10 foil twin packs; 36 tablets in 18 foil twin packs.

ALKA-2® Chewable Antacid Tablets

Active Ingredient: Each ALKA-2 chewable antacid tablet contains calcium carbonate 500 mg.

Indications: ALKA-2 is an antacid for occasional use to obtain relief from transient symptoms of acid indigestion, heartburn, and sour stomach.

Actions: ALKA-2 provides quick and effective neutralization of gastric acidity. Measured by the in vitro standard established by the Food and Drug Administration, each tablet will neutralize 10/mEq of acid.

Warnings: Do not take more than 16 tablets in a 24-hour period or use the maximum dosage of this product for more than 2 weeks, except under the advice and supervision of a physician. May cause constipation. Keep this and all drugs out of the reach of children.

Dosage and Administration: Chew 1 or 2 tablets every two hours or as directed by a physician. Not to exceed 16 tablets in a 24 hour period.

How Supplied: Tablets: rolls of 10, triple roll, 10 tablets per roll; bottle of 85

Product Identification Mark: "Alka 2" embossed on each tablet.

ALKA-SELTZER PLUS® Cold Medicine

Active Ingredient:

Each dry ALKA-SELTZER PLUS® Cold Tablet contains the following active ingredients: phenylpropanolamine bitartrate 24.08 mg., chlorpheniramine maleate 2.0 mg., aspirin 324.0 mg. The product is dissolved in water prior to ingestion and the aspirin is converted into its soluble ionic form, sodium acetylsalicylate.

Indications: For relief of the symptoms of head colds, common flu, sinus congestion and hay fever.

Actions: Each tablet contains: A decongestant which helps restore free breathing, shrink swollen nasal tissue and relieve sinus congestion due to head colds or hay fever. An antihistamine which helps relieve the runny nose, sneezing, sniffles, itchy watering eyes that accompany colds or hay fever. Specially buffered aspirin which relieves headache, scratchy sore throat, general body aches and the feverish feeling of a cold and common flu.

Warnings: Do not use if you are allergic to aspirin or have asthma, or if you have a coagulation (bleeding) disease. Individuals with high blood pressure, diabetes, heart or thyroid disease or on a sodium restricted diet should use only as directed by a physician. Each tablet con-

tains 482 mg. of sodium. If drowsiness occurs, do not drive a car or operate machinery.

Dosage and Administration: ALKA-SELTZER PLUS® is taken in solution; approximately 3 ounces of water per tablet is sufficient. Adults: two tablets every 4 hours up to 8 tablets in 24 hours. Children (6–12): Half of adult dosage. Children under 6 years: Consult your physician.

How Supplied: Tablets: carton of 20 tablets in 10 foil twin packs; carton of 36 tablets in 18 foil twin packs. **Product Identification Mark:** "Alka-Seltzer Plus" embossed on each tablet.

BACTINE® Skin Wound Cleanser

Active Ingredient: Benzalkonium Chloride 0.13% w/w

Indications: First aid product to clean superficial skin wounds.

Actions: Contains a safe and effective non-irritating antimicrobial (germ killing) ingredient. Does not delay wound healing.

Warnings: (Aerosol Spray and Liquid Spray)

For external use only. Avoid spraying in eyes, mouth, ears or on sensitive areas of the body. This product is not for use on wild or domestic animal bites. If you have an animal bite or puncture wound, consult your physician immediately. Do not use this product for more than 10 days. If condition worsens or persists, see your physician. Do not bandage tightly. Keep this and all drugs out of reach of children. In case of accidental ingestion, seek professional assistance or contact a Poison Control Center immediately.

(Aerosol Only): Contents under pressure. Do not puncture or incinerate. Do not store at temperature above 120° F. Use only as directed. Intentional misuse by deliberately concentrating and inhaling the contents can be harmful or fatal.

Dosage and Administration: (Liquid First Aid Spray)

To spray, hold bottle upright 2 to 3 inches from wound and squeeze repeatedly to direct spray across wound. To flush, invert bottle and squeeze firmly to direct stream across wound. Apply to affected area until excess drains freely and wound is thoroughly clean. To aid in removing foreign particles, dab wound with clean gauze saturated with product. (Aerosol First Aid Spray)

Shake well. Hold can 2 to 3 inches from

One Tablet Provides		% of U.S. RDA	
		For Children 2 To 4	For Adults and Children Over 4 Years
Vitamins	Quantity	Years of Age	of Age
Vitamin A	2500 I.U.	100	50
Vitamin D	400 I.U.	100	100
Vitamin E	15 I.U.	150	50
Vitamin C	250 mg.	625	417
Folic Acid	0.3 mg.	150	75
Thiamine	1.05 mg.	150	70
Riboflavin	1.20 mg.	150	70
Niacin	13.50 mg.	150	67
Vitamin B_6	1.05 mg.	150	52
Vitamin B_{12}	4.5 mcg.	150	75

| | One Tablet Provides | | % of U.S. RDA | |
Vitamins		Quantity	For Children 2 to 4 Years of Age	For Adults and Children over 4 Years of Age
Vitamin A		2500 I. U.	100	50
Vitamin D		400 I. U.	100	100
Vitamin E		15 I. U.	150	50
Vitamin C		60 mg.	150	100
Folic Acid		0.3 mg.	150	75
Thiamine		1.05 mg.	150	70
Riboflavin		1.20 mg.	150	70
Niacin		13.50 mg.	150	67
Vitamin B_6		1.05 mg.	150	52
Vitamin B_{12}		4.5 mcg.	150	75
Mineral:				
Iron (Elemental)		15 mg.	150	83

wound. Apply to affected area until excess drains freely and wound is thoroughly clean. To aid in removing foreign particles, dab wound with clean gauze saturated with product.
How Supplied: 2 oz., 4 oz. liquid spray, 16 oz. liquid, 3 oz. aerosol.

CHOCKS® Plus Iron Multivitamin Supplement
(Multivitamin Supplement with Iron)

CHOCKS® Multivitamin Supplement
(Multivitamin Supplement)

CHOCKS®–BUGS BUNNY® Multivitamin Supplement
(Multivitamin Supplement)

CHOCKS®–BUGS BUNNY® Plus Iron Multivitamin Supplement
(Multivitamin Supplement with Iron)

FLINTSTONES® Plus Iron Multivitamin Supplement
(Multivitamin Supplement with Iron)

FLINTSTONES® Multivitamin Supplement
(Multivitamin Supplement)

Vitamin Ingredients: Each multivitamin supplement with iron contains the ingredients listed in the chart above.

FLINTSTONES®, CHOCKS® BUGS BUNNY®, and CHOCKS® Multivitamin Supplement provide the same quantities of vitamins, but do not provide iron.
Indication: Dietary supplementation
Dosage and Administration: One chewable tablet daily. For adults and children two years and older; tablet must be chewed.
Precaution:
IRON SUPPLEMENTS ONLY.
Contains iron, which can be harmful in large doses. Close tightly and keep out of reach of children. In case of overdose con-

tact a Poison Control Center immediately.
How Supplied: All six preparations are supplied in bottles of 60 and 100.

FLINTSTONES® With Extra C Multivitamin Supplement
BUGS BUNNY® With Extra C Multivitamin Supplement

Vitamin Ingredients: Each multivitamin supplement contains the ingredients listed in the chart on preceding page.
Indication: Dietary supplementation
Dosage and Administration: One chewable tablet daily for adults and children two years and older; tablet must be chewed.
How Supplied: Bottles of 60's

MILES® Nervine Nighttime Sleep–Aid

Active Ingredient: Each capsule-shaped tablet contains pyrilamine maleate 25 mg.
Indications: Nighttime sleep-aid. Helps you fall asleep and relieves occasional sleeplessness.
Actions: Antihistamines act on the central nervous system and produce drowsiness.
Warnings: Use only as directed. Do not give to children under 12 years of age. Do not take this product when: pregnant or nursing a baby; alcohol is being consumed. NOT FOR PROLONGED USE. If sleeplessness persists continuously for more than 2 weeks, consult your physician. Insomnia may be a symptom of serious underlying medical illness. Keep this and all drugs out of the reach of children. In case of accidental overdose, seek professional assistance or contact a Poison Control Center immediately. DO NOT TAKE THIS PRODUCT IF YOU HAVE ASTHMA, GLAUCOMA OR ENLARGEMENT OF THE PROSTATE GLAND EXCEPT UNDER THE ADVICE AND SUPERVISION OF A PHYSICIAN.
Dosage and Administration: Two tab-

lets at bedtime or as directed by a physician. Maximum during 24 hours—4 tablets.
How Supplied: Bottles of 12's, 30's, and 50's capsule-shaped tablets.

ONE–A–DAY® Vitamins
(Multivitamin Supplement)
ONE–A–DAY® Vitamins Plus Iron
(Multivitamin Supplement with Iron)
ONE–A–DAY® Vitamins Plus Minerals
(Multivitamin/Multimineral Supplement)
Supplements for adults and children 4 or more years of age.

Vitamin Ingredients:
One tablet daily of ONE–A–DAY® Vitamins Plus Minerals provides:

Vitamins	Quantity	% of U.S. RDA
Vitamin A	5,000 I. U.	100
Vitamin E	15 I. U.	50*
Vitamin C	60 mg.	100
Folic Acid	0.4 mg.	100
Thiamine	1.5 mg.	100
Riboflavin	1.7 mg.	100
Niacin	20 mg.	100
Vitamin B_6	2 mg.	100
Vitamin B_{12}	6 mcg.	100
Vitamin D	400 I. U.	100
Pantothenic Acid	10 mg.	100

Minerals	Quantity	% of U.S. RDA
Iron	18 mg.	100
Calcium	100 mg.	10
Phosphorus	100 mg.	10
Iodine	150 mcg.	100
Magnesium	100 mg.	25
Copper	2 mg.	100
Zinc	15 mg.	100

* 15 I.U. meets the recommended dietary allowances established by the National Academy of Sciences.
ONE–A–DAY® Vitamins Plus Iron provides the same quantities of vitamins, except pantothenic acid, plus 18 mg. iron. ONE–A–DAY® Vitamins provides the same quantities of vitamins, except pantothenic acid, with no minerals.
Indication: Dietary supplementation
Dosage and Administration: One tablet daily.
Precaution:
IRON SUPPLEMENTS ONLY.
Contains iron, which can be harmful in large doses. Close tightly and keep out of reach of children. In case of overdose contact a Poison Control Center immediately.
How Supplied: ONE–A–DAY® Vitamins Plus Minerals, bottles of 30, 60 and 100. ONE–A–DAY® Vitamins Plus Iron, bottles of 60, 100, 240 and 365. ONE–A–DAY® Vitamins, bottles of 25, 60, 100, 250 and 365.

Continued on next page

Miles—Cont.

ONE-A-DAY CORE C 500™
Multivitamin Supplement
Supplement for adults and children 12 or more years of age.

Vitamin Ingredients:
One tablet daily of
ONE-A-DAY Core C 500™ provides:

Vitamins	Quantity	% of U.S. RDA
Vitamin A	5,000 I.U.	100
Vitamin E	15 I.U.	50
Vitamin C	500 mg.	833
Folic Acid	0.4 mg.	100
Thiamine	1.5 mg.	100
Riboflavin	1.7 mg.	100
Niacin	20 mg.	100
Vitamin B$_6$	2 mg.	100
Vitamin B$_{12}$	6 mcg.	100
Vitamin D	400 I.U.	100

Indication: Dietary supplementation
Dosage and Administration: One tablet daily.
How Supplied: Bottles of 60's.

Miller-Morton Company
3800 CUTSHAW AVENUE
RICHMOND, VA 23230

CHAP STICK® Lip Balm

Active Ingredients: 44% Petrolatums, 1.5% Padimate O (2-ethyl-hexyl p-dimethylaminobenzoate, 1% Lanolin, 1% Isopropyl Myristate, .5% Cetyl Alcohol.
Indications: Aids prevention and healing of dry, chapped, sun and windburned lips.
Actions: A specially designed lipid complex hydrophobic base containing Padimate O which forms a barrier to prevent moisture loss and protect lips from the drying effects of cold weather, wind and sun which cause chapping. The special emollients soften the skin by forming an occlusive film thus inducing hydration, restoring suppleness to the lips, and preventing drying from evaporation of water that diffuses to the surface from the underlying layers of tissue. Chap Stick also protects the skin from the external environment and its sunscreen offers protection from exposure to the sun.
Warning: Discontinue use if signs of irritation appear.
Symptoms and Treatment of Oral Ingestion: The oral LD50 in rats is greater than 5 gm/kg. There have been no reported overdoses in humans. There are no known symptoms of overdosage.
Dosage and Treatment: For dry, chapped lips apply as needed. To help prevent dry, chapped sun or windburned lips, apply to lips as needed before, during and following exposure to sun, wind, water and cold weather.
Professional Labeling: None.
How Supplied: Available in 4.25 gm tubes in Regular, Mint, Cherry, Orange, Grape, Lemon-Lime, and Strawberry flavors.
[*Shown in Product Identification Section*]

CHAP STICK® SUNBLOCK 15
Lip Balm

Active Ingredients: 44% Petrolatums, 7% Padimate O, 3% Oxybenzone, 0.5% Lanolin, 0.5% Isopropyl Myristate, 0.5% Cetyl Alcohol.
Indications: Ultra Sunscreen Protection (SPF-15). Aids prevention and healing of dry, chapped, sun and windburned lips. Overexposure to sun may lead to premature aging of skin and lip cancer. Liberal and regular use may help reduce the sun's harmful effects.
Actions: Ultra sunscreen protection for the lips, plus the attributes of Chap Stick® Lip Balm. The emollients in the specially-designed lipid complex hydrophobic base soften the lips by forming an occlusive film while the two sunscreens have specific ultraviolet absorption ranges which overlap to offer ultra sunscreen protection (SPF-15).
Warning: Discontinue use if signs of irritation appear.
Symptoms and Treatment of Oral Ingestion: Toxicity studies indicate this product to be extremely safe. The oral LD$_{50}$ in rats is greater than 5 gm./kg. There are no known symptoms of overdosage.
Dosage and Treatment: For ultra sunscreen protection, apply evenly and liberally to lips before exposure to sun. Reapply as needed. For dry, chapped lips, apply as needed. To help prevent dry, chapped, sun, and windburned lips, apply to lips as needed before, during, and following exposure to sun, wind, water, and cold weather.
How Supplied: 4.25 gm. tube.
[*Shown in Product Identification Section*]

Muro Pharmaceutical, Inc.
890 EAST STREET
TEWKSBURY, MA 01876

DUOLUBE™

Contains: White petrolatum and liquid petrolatum.
Dosage: Adults and children: Pull down the lower lid of the affected eye and apply a small ribbon (one-fourth inch) to the inside of the eyelid.
Indications: (1) For the temporary relief of discomfort due to minor irritations of the eye or to exposure to wind or sun. (2) For use as a protectant against further irritation or to relieve dryness of the eye. (3) For use as a lubricant to prevent further irritation or to relieve dryness of the eye.
Warnings: For all OTC ophthalmic emollient drug products. (i) Do not use for more than 72 hours except under the advice and supervision of a physician. If symptoms persist or worsen, discontinue use of this product and consult a physician. (ii) If you experience severe eye pain, headache, rapid change in vision (side or straight ahead), sudden appearance of floating spots, acute redness of the eyes, pain on exposure to light, or double vision, consult a physician at once. (iii) To avoid contamination of this

---

product, do not touch tip to any other surface. Replace cap after using.
Supplied: 3.5 g tubes.

MURO TEARS™
Artificial Tears

Ingredients: Hydroxypropyl methylcellulose, dextran 40, sodium and potassium chloride (total chlorides 0.85%). Also contains benzalkonium chloride 0.01% as a preservative, disodium EDTA and purified water. Buffered with sodium borate and boric acid.
Indications: For the temporary relief of burning and irritation due to dryness of the eye.
Directions: Adults and Children: Instill 1 or 2 drops in the affected eye(s) as needed.
Warnings: Do not use this product for more than 72 hours except under the advice and supervision of a physician. If symptoms persist or worsen, discontinue use of this product and consult a physician.
If you experience severe eye pain, headache, rapid change in vision (side or straight ahead), sudden appearance of floating spots, acute redness of the eye, pain on exposure to light, or double vision, consult a physician at once.
To avoid contamination of the product, do not touch tip of container to any surface. Replace cap after using.
If solution changes color or becomes cloudy, do not use.
How Supplied: 15 ml plastic dropper bottles NDC 0451-3515-85. Store at room temperature.

MUROCEL
(methylcellulose)

Description: A sterile ophthalmic solution containing methylcellulose 1%. Also contains methylparaben and propylparaben as preservatives, with sodium chloride and purified water.
Dosage: Adults and Children: Instill 1 or 2 drops in the affected eye(s).
Indications: (1) For the temporary relief of burning and irritation due to dryness of the eye. (2) For the temporary relief of discomfort due to minor irritations of the eye or to exposure to wind or sun. (3) For use as a protectant against further irritation or to relieve dryness of the eye. (4) For use as a lubricant to prevent further irritation or relieve dryness of the eye.
Warnings: For all OTC ophthalmic demulcent drug products. (i) Do not use this product more than 72 hours except under the advice and supervision of a physician. If symptoms persist or worsen, discontinue use of this product and consult a physician. (ii) To avoid contamination of this product, do not touch tip of container to any other surface. Replace cap after using. (iii) If you experience severe eye pain, headache, rapid change in vision (side or straight ahead), sudden appearance of floating spots, acute redness of the eyes, pain on exposure to light or double vision, consult a physician at once.

How Supplied
15 and 30 ml plastic dropper bottles. Keep tightly closed—Store at room temperature. (Formerly #35).

TEEN™ 5 LOTION
TEEN™ 10 LOTION
TEEN™ 5 WASH
(Benzoyl Peroxide)

Contents: Benzoyl Peroxide 5% or 10% in a washable, grease-free, vanishing lotion base.

Indications: Antibacterial, antiseptic acne lotion medication for use as an aid in the treatment of the blemishes and pimples associated with acne. May also be used to dry up oily skin.

Directions: Shake well before use. Wash affected areas with a mild soap before using. Using the fingertips, apply one to three times a day or as directed by physician.

Caution: EXTERNAL USE ONLY. Avoid contact with eyes, lips, mouth and sensitive areas of the neck. Colored clothing or hair may become bleached. Keep tightly closed and avoid excessive heat. Keep out of the reach of children. KEEP FROM HEAT.

How Supplied: Teen 5 and Teen 10 Lotion in one ounce plastic bottles. Also, Teen 5 Wash in 6 fl. ounce plastic bottle.

Teen 5 Lotion	NDC 0451-1450-05
Teen 10 Lotion	NDC 0451-1460-05
Teen 5 Wash	NDC 0451-1600-03

Nature's Bounty, Inc.
105 ORVILLE DRIVE
BOHEMIA, NY 11716

ACEROLA "C"
Each chewable tablet contains:
Vitamin C with
  rose hips and acerola ....100 mg.
Citrus Bioflavonoids
  Complex .... 5 mg.
Supplied: Tablets, bottles of 100, 500.

ACIDOPHILUS
Aid in maintaining healthy balance of intestinal flora.
Each capsule contains live lactobacillus acidophilus
Supplied: Capsules, bottles of 100.

ALFALFA (500 mg.)
Supplied: Tablets, bottles of 100, 500, 1000.

B–1 (100 mg.)
Tablets, Bottles of 100
B–1 (250 mg.)
Tablets, Bottles of 100
B–1 (500 mg.)
Tablets, Bottles of 100, 500

B–2 (100 mg.)
Tablets, Bottles of 100

B–100® Ultra B—Complex Vitamin
Each tablet contains:

			MDR*
Vitamin B-1	100 mg.		10,000 %
Vitamin B-2	100 mg.		8,200 %
Vitamin B-6	100 mg.		**
Vitamin B-12	100 mcg.		**
Niacinamide	100 mg.		1,000 %
Folic Acid	100 mcg.		**
Pantothenic Acid	100 mg.		**
d-Biotin	100 mcg.		***
Para Aminobenzoic Acid (PABA)	100 mg.		***
Chlorine Bitartrate	100 mg.		***
Inositol	100 mg.		***

*MDR, Minimum Daily Requirement
**Need in human nutrition established but no MDR established
***Need in human nutrition has not been established.

B–6 (50 mg.)
Tablets, Bottles of 100, 250
B–6 (100 mg.)
Tablets, Bottles of 100, 250, 500
B–6 (500 mg.)
Tablets, Bottles of 100, 500

B–12 (25 mcg.)
Tablets, 100, 500
B–12 (50 mcg.)
Tablets, Bottles of 100, 500
B–12 (100 mcg.)
Tablets, Bottles of 100, 250
B–12 (250 mcg.)
Tablets, Bottles of 100, 250, 500
B–12 (500 mcg.)
Tablets, Bottles of 100, 250
B–12 (1000 mcg.)
Tablets, Bottles of 100, 250

B–50®
(Vitamin B Complex)
Tablets, Bottles of 50, 100, 250, 500

B–100®
Ultra B—Complex Vitamin
Sugar and Starch Free
[See table above].

Recommended Intake: Adults, 1 tablet daily or as directed by physician.
Supplied: Capsule-shaped tablets (protein-coated)—bottles of 50, 100 and 250.

B–100® (TIME RELEASE)
(Vitamin B Complex)
Tablets, Bottles of 50, 100, 250

B–125®
(Vitamin B Complex)
Tablets, Bottles of 50, 100, 500

B & C LIQUID
Each teaspoon (5cc.) contains:
Vitamin C ....300 mg.
Vitamin B-1
  (thiamine hydrochloride) ...... 15 mg.
Vitamin B-2
  (riboflavin) .... 10 mg.
Vitamin B-6
  (pyridoxine hydrochloride) ... 5 mg.
Vitamin B-12
  (cobalamin concentrate) .... 5 mcg.
Niacinamide ....100 mg.
d-Panthenol .... 20 mg.
Supplied: 4 oz. bottle.

B–COMPLEX AND B–12
Each tablet contains:
Protease (from natural
  Carica Papaya) .... 10 mg.
Vitamins:
B–12 (from Cobalamin) .... 25 mcg.
B–1 (Thiamine) .... 7 mg.
B–2 (Riboflavin) .... 14 mg.
Niacin .... 4.5 mg.
Supplied: Tablets, bottles of 90.

B–COMPLEX & C
(TIME RELEASE)
Each time release capsule contains vitamins:
C (with rose hips) ....200 mg.
B–1 (Thiamine) .... 10 mg.
B–2 (Riboflavin) .... 10 mg.
B–6 (Pyridoxine HCl) .... 5 mg.
B–12 (Cobalamin) .... 10 mcg.
Niacinamide .... 50 mg.
Calcium Pantothenate .... 10 mg.
Supplied: Capsules, bottles of 100, 250.

BEE POLLEN (500 mg.)
Tablets, Bottles of 100, 250
BEE POLLEN "1000" ™
Tablets, Bottles of 100

BIOTIN (0.3 mg.)
Tablets, Bottles of 100, 500

BONE MEAL W/VIT. D
Tablets, Bottles of 100, 250, 500, 1000

BREWER'S YEAST POWDER
(DEBITTERED)
A specially cultivated brewer's yeast containing B complex vitamins in natural high potency.
Supplied: 16 oz. can.

BREWER'S YEAST
Tablets, Bottles of 250, 500, 1000

C–250 W/ROSE HIPS
Tablets, Bottles of 100, 500
C–300 W/ROSE HIPS (CHEWABLE)
Tablets, Bottles of 100, 250, 500
C–500 W/ROSE HIPS
Tablets, Bottles of 100, 250, 500
C–1000 W/ROSE HIPS
Tablets, Bottles of 100, 250, 500

Continued on next page

Nature's Bounty—Cont.

C–COMPLEX

Each tablet contains:
Vitamin C with rose hips ......500 mg.
Bioflavonoids ....100 mg.
Rutin (Buckwheat) .... 50 mg.
Hesperidin Complex .... 25 mg.
Acerola .... 1.0 mg.
Supplied: Tablets, bottles of 100, 250.

VITAMIN C CRYSTALS

One teaspoonful provides:
Vitamin C ....5000 mg.
Supplied: 6 oz. bottle.

C–LIQUID

One teaspoon supplies:
Vitamin C with Rose Hips ...... 300 mg.
Supplied: 4 oz. bottles.

C–TIME 750™ (TIME RELEASE)
Tablets, Bottles of 100, 250

C–TIME 1500™
with Rose Hips
Sustained Release Tablets
Sugar and Starch Free

Each tablet contains: (U.S.R.D.A.)
Vitamin C
  with Rose Hips .... 1500 mg. (2500%)

Recommended Intake: Adults, 1 tablet daily or as directed by physician.
Supplied: Capsule-shaped tablets (protein-coated to provide gradual release of Vitamin C over a prolonged period of time). Bottles of 30, 100 and 250.

CALCIUM ASCORBATE (500 mg.)
Tablets, Bottles of 100, 250, 500

CALCIUM LACTATE (10 gr.)
Tablets, Bottles of 100, 250, 500, 1000

CHELATED CALCIUM

Each tablet contains:
Calcium Amino Acid
  Chelate .... 750 mg.
  (equivalent to 150 mg. elemental Calcium)
Supplied: Tablets, bottles of 100, 500.

CHELATED CHROMIUM

Each tablet contains:
Chromium Amino Acid
  Chelate .... 50 mg.
  (equivalent to 1000 mcg. of elemental Chromium)
Supplied: Tablets, bottles of 100, 500.

CHELATED COPPER

Each tablet contains:
Copper Amino Acid Chelate ...... 20 mg.
  (equivalent to 2 mg. of elemental Copper)
Supplied: Tablets, bottles of 100.

CHELATED MAGNESIUM

Each tablet contains:
Magnesium Amino Acid
  Chelate .... 500 mg.
  (equivalent to 100 mg. of elemental Magnesium)
Supplied: Tablets, bottles of 100.

CHELATED MANGANESE

Each tablet contains:
Manganese Amino Acid
  Chelate .... 50 mg.
  (equivalent to 5 mg. of elemental Manganese)
Supplied: Tablets, bottles of 100.

CHELATED MULTI–MINERALS

A multiple mineral amino acid chelate of 10 minerals.
Supplied: Tablets, bottles of 100, 250.

CHELATED POTASSIUM

Each tablet contains:
Potassium Amino Acid
  Complex .... 495 mg.
  (equivalent to 99 mg. of elemental Potassium)
Supplied: Tablets, bottles of 100, 250.

CHELATED ZINC

Each tablet contains:
Zinc Amino Acid Chelate .... 150 mg.
  (equivalent to 15 mg. of elemental Zinc)
Supplied: Tablets, bottles of 100, 250.

CHEW–IRON

Each chewable tablet contains:
Ferrous Fumarate .... 150 mg.
  (elemental iron 50 mg)
B–12 (Cobalamin) .... 33 mcg.
B–1 (Thiamine) .... 10 mg.
Protease (from natural
  Papaya) .... 10 mg.
Supplied: Tablets, bottles of 100, 250.

CHILDREN'S CHEWABLE VITAMINS

A popular chewable vitamin formula containing 10 essential vitamins.
Supplied: Tablets, bottles of 100, 250, 500.

CHOLINE (650 mg.)
Tablets, Bottles of 100, 500

DOLOMITE
Tablets, Bottles of 100, 250, 500, 1000

E–200 (d–ALPHA TOCOPHEROL ACETATE)
Capsules, Bottles of 100, 250, 500, 1000
E–400 (d–ALPHA TOCOPHEROL ACETATE)
Capsules, Bottles of 100, 250, 500, 1000

E–200 (NATURAL COMPLEX)
Capsules, Bottles of 100, 250, 500, 1000
E–400 (NATURAL COMPLEX)
Capsules, Bottles of 100, 250
E–600 (NATURAL COMPLEX)
Capsules, Bottles of 50, 100, 250
E–1000 (NATURAL COMPLEX)
Capsules, Bottles of 50, 100, 250

EMULSIFIED E–200
Capsules, Bottles of 100
2 oz. Jar
2 oz. Bottle
3 oz. Bar

FERROUS SULFATE (5 gr.)
Tablets, Bottles of 250, 500

FOLIC ACID (0.4 mg.)
Tablets, Bottles of 250, 500
FOLIC ACID (0.8 mg.)
Tablets, Bottles of 250, 500

GARLIC OIL (15 gr.)
Capsules, Bottles of 100, 500
GARLIC OIL (77 gr.)
Capsules, Bottles of 100, 500

GARLIC & PARSLEY (7½ minim)

Each capsule contains:
Concentrated garlic oil ....10 mg.
Concentrated parsley .... 1 mg.
Supplied: Capsules, bottles of 100, 250, 500.

GINSENG, MANCHURIAN
Capsules, Bottles of 50, 100, 250, 500

GLUTAMIC ACID (500 mg.)
Tablets, Bottles of 100, 500

HALIBUT LIVER OIL

Each capsule contains:
Vitamin A (from halibut
  liver oil) .... 5000 USP Units
Vitamin D (from halibut
  liver oil) .... 85 USP Units
Supplied: Capsules, bottles of 100.

HERBAL LAXATIVE

A gentle vegetable and herb laxative.
Supplied: Tablets, bottles of 100.

INOSITOL (650 mg.)
Tablets, Bottles of 100, 500

IRON
(Ferrous Gluconate, 5 gr.)
Tablets, Bottles of 100, 250, 500

KELP
Tablets, Bottles of 250, 500, 1000

KLB6®
Natural Diet Aid

Six capsules contain:
Vitamin B-6
  (Pyridoxine HCl) .... 21 mg.

Cider Vinegar ....240 mg.
Soya Lecithin ....600 mg.
Kelp ....150 mg.
Supplied: Capsules, bottles of 100, 250, 500.

KLB6 COMPLETE®

The famous KLB6® formula with wheat bran (500 mg) and 100% of RDA of 10 essential vitamins.
Supplied: Capsules, bottles of 100, 250, 500.

KLB6 DIET MIX®

Balanced low-calorie meal replacement fortified with kelp, lecithin and Vitamin B6.
Supplied: 14 oz. can.

L–GLUTAMINE (500 mg.)
Tablets, Bottles of 50, 100, 500

L–LYSINE (500 mg.)
Tablets, Bottles of 100, 500

LECITHIN (1200 mg.)
Capsules, Bottles of 100, 250

LECITHIN, CHEWABLE (1200 mg)

Supplied: Tablets, bottles of 100, 250.

LECITHIN W/VIT. D

Each capsule contains:
Soya Lecithin ....259.2 mg.
Soy Bean Oil ....170.2 mg.
Vitamin D ....150 USP units
Supplied: Capsules, bottles of 100.

LECITHIN GRANULES

Each tablespoon contains 7.5 gms of lecithin.
Supplied: 14 oz. can.

LIVER W/B–12
Tablets, Bottles of 100, 250

MAGNESIUM
(Magnesium Gluconate, 30 mg.)
Supplied: Tablets, bottles of 100.

MANGANESE
(Manganese Gluconate, 50 mg.)
Supplied: Tablets, bottles of 100.

MEGA B® W/C

High B-Complex formula with Vitamin C (500 mg).
Supplied: Tablets, bottles of 60, 180.

MEGA V & M™

Mega potency multiple vitamin and mineral formula.
Supplied: Tablets, bottles of 30, 60, 100, 250.

MULTI–MINERALS

A multiple mineral formula containing nine essential minerals.
Supplied: Tablets, bottles of 100, 250.

NATURE'S BOUNTY HAIR BOOSTER™

Vitamin-Mineral Complex for the hair.
Supplied: Tablets, bottles of 100.

NATURE'S BOUNTY SLIM®

100% Natural High Protein Powder plus Vitamins.
Supplied: 16 oz. can.

NIACIN (100 mg.)
Tablets, Bottles of 100, 500
NIACIN (250 mg.)
Tablets, Bottles of 100, 500

NIACINAMIDE (500 mg.)
Tablets, Bottles of 100, 250

OYSTER CALCIUM

Each tablet contains:
Calcium ....375 mg.
Vitamin A ....800 I.U.
Vitamin D-2 ....200 I.U.
Supplied: Tablets, bottles of 100, 500.

PABA
(Para-Aminobenzoic Acid, 100 mg.)
Tablets, Bottles of 250, 500, 1000
PABA
(Para-Aminobenzoic Acid, 500 mg.)
Tablets, Bottles of 100, 500

PANTOTHENIC ACID (100 mg.)
Tablets, Bottles of 100, 250
PANTOTHENIC ACID (200 mg.)
Tablets, Bottles of 100, 250

PAPAYA ENZYME (1 gr.)

Aid to starch and protein digestion.
Supplied: Tablets, bottles of 100, 250.

POTASSIUM & B–6

Each tablet contains:
Potassium ....30 mg.
Vitamin B-6
 (pyridoxine HCl) ....50 mg.
Supplied: Tablets, bottles of 90, 250.

POTASSIUM
(Potassium Gluconate, 83.5 mg.)
Tablets, Bottles of 100, 250

PROTEIN (250 mg.)

A food supplement from soya, dried malt extract and dry milk powder.
Supplied: Tablets, bottles of 100, 250, 500.

RNA
(100 mg from brewer's yeast)
Supplied: Tablets, bottles of 100, 250.

RNA/DNA
(100 mg of each from brewer's yeast)
Supplied: Tablets, bottles of 100, 250.

RUTIN (50 mg.)
Tablets, Bottles of 250, 500

SELENIUM (50 mcg.)
Tablets, Bottles of 100, 250

STRESS FORMULA "605" ™

Hi-potency stress formula vitamins.
Supplied: Tablets, bottles of 60, 250.

STRESS FORMULA "605" ™ W/IRON

Hi-potency stress formula vitamins with iron (27 mg).
Supplied: Tablets, bottles of 60, 250.

STRESS FORMULA "605" ™ W/ZINC

Hi-potency stress formula with zinc (23.9 mg.).
Supplied: Tablets, bottles of 60, 250.

TRYPTOPHAN (200 mg.)
Tablets, Bottles of 30, 100
TRYPTOPHAN (667 mg.)
Tablets, Bottles of 30, 100

ULTRA "A"
(Vitamin A, 25,000 USP Units)
Capsules, Bottles of 100, 250, 500
ULTRA "A"
(Vitamin A, 25,000 USP Units)
Tablets, Bottles of 100, 500, 1000

ULTRA "A & D"
(25,000 UNITS OF VIT. A & 1,000 UNITS OF VIT. D)
Tablets, Bottles of 100, 500, 1000

ULTRA "D"
(1000 USP units Vit. D)
Supplied: Tablets, bottles of 100, 500, 1000.

ULTRA KLB6™

Three tablets contain:
Lecithin ....1200 mg.
Vitamin B-6 .... 350 mg.
Kelp .... 100 mg.
Cider Vinegar .... 240 mg.
Supplied: Tablets, bottles of 100, 250, 500.

ULTRA VITA–TIME™

Ultra potency vitamins, minerals, amino acids and lipotropic formula.
Supplied: Tablets, bottles of 50, 100, 250, 500.

VITAMIN A (10,000 USP UNITS)
Capsules, Bottles of 100, 250, 500
VITAMIN A (10,000 USP UNITS)
Tablets, Bottles of 100, 250, 500, 1000

VITAMIN A & D
(10,000 UNITS VIT. A & 400 UNITS VIT. D)
Tablets, Bottles of 100, 250, 500, 1000

Continued on next page

Nature's Bounty—Cont.

VITAMIN D (400 USP UNITS)
Tablets, Bottles of 100, 250, 500, 1000

VITA–TIME™
High potency vitamins, minerals and amino acids.
Supplied: Tablets, bottles of 100, 250, 500, 1000.

WATER PILL (NATURAL DIURETIC)
Each tablet contains:
Buchu Leaves Powder ....50 mg.
Uva Ursi Leaves Powder ....50 mg.
Parsley Leaves Powder ....50 mg.
Juniper Berries Powder ....10 mg.
Potassium ....20 mg.
Supplied: Tablets, bottles of 50, 100, 250.

WATER PILL WITH IRON (NATURAL DIURETIC)
Each tablet contains:
Same as above plus:
Iron (ferrous gluconate) ....6 mg.
Supplied: Tablets, bottles of 50, 100, 250.

WATER PILL W/POTASSIUM
Capsules, Bottles of 50, 100, 250

WHEAT GERM OIL (6 minim)
Capsules, Bottles of 100, 250
WHEAT GERM OIL (14 minim)
Capsules, Bottles of 100, 250
WHEAT GERM OIL (20 minim)
Capsules, Bottles of 100, 250

YEAST PLUS VITAMIN
B12, B-Complex with minerals and amino acids.
Supplied: Tablets, bottles of 100, 250.

ZACNE®
Each tablet contains:
Zinc Gluconate .... 25 mg.
Vitamin C
with Rose Hips .... 75 mg.
B–6 (Pyridoxine HCl) .... 10 mg.
Vitamin A
(fish liver oils) .... 500 I.U.
Vitamin E .... 25 I.U.
Directions: As a dietary supplement, two tablets three times daily before meals.
Supplied: Tablets, bottles of 100, 500.
[*Shown in Product Identification Section*]

ZINC (10 mg.)
(Zinc Gluconate)
Tablets, Bottles of 100, 250, 500, 1000
ZINC (25 mg.)
Tablets, Bottles of 100, 500
ZINC (50 mg.)
Tablets, Bottles of 100, 500
ZINC (100 mg.)
Tablets, Bottles of 100, 500

NaturSlim Corporation
P.O. BOX 3609
SANTA ROSA, CA 95402

NATURSLIM® II
Active Ingredients: NaturSlim II diet program consists of a high potency sustained release vitamin-mineral tablet and a specially formulated whole protein powder with vegetable fiber. Time-release "Twice-a-Day" multivitamin-mineral tablet contains: Folic Acid, Thiamine, Riboflavin, Vitamin B-6, Calcium, Phosphorus, Iodine, Iron, Magnesium and Potassium. Soya and casein based protein powder contains: Protein, Vitamin A, Vitamin D, Vitamin E, Vitamin C, Thiamine, Niacin, Pantothenic Acid, Vitamin B-12, Biotin, Calcium, Phosphorus, Iron, Magnesium, Copper and Zinc. [See table below].

AMINO ACID PROFILE

	%	Mgs
** Isoleucine	4.70	560
** Leucine	7.88	940
** Lysine	6.24	750
** Methionine	2.10	250
Cystine	1.32	160
** Phenylalanine	5.26	630
** Threonine	3.62	435
** Tryptophan	1.42	170
** Valine	4.60	550
Histidine	2.30	280
Arginine	6.90	830
Aspartic Acid	9.88	1180
Serine	4.93	590
Glutamic Acid	20.43	2450
Proline	5.98	720
Glycine	3.94	470
Alanine	3.94	470
Tyrosine	4.16	500

**Essential Amino Acids.
Directions: Simply stir or blend two rounded Tbsp. (15 gm) of *NaturSlim II* powder into 8 oz. of lowfat protein fortified Milk or other juices. See the *NaturSlim* Reducing Program information booklet enclosed for additional information.

The accompanying "twice-a-day" sustained-release tablets have been specifically designed as an integral part of the NaturSlim II reducing program. Selected nutrients are released over a prolonged period through the day.

Contains No Sugar or Artificial Sweeteners

The accompanying "Twice-a-day" sustained-release tablets have been specifically designed as an integral part of the NaturSlim II reducing program. Selected nutrients are released over a prolonged period throughout the day.

Two Tablets

Provide the Following:		% U.S. RDA
Folic Acid	400 mcg	100%
Riboflavin (Vitamin B₂)	20 mgs	1180%
Pyridoxine (Vitamin B₆)	75 mgs	3750%
Calcium	140 mgs	15%
Phosphorus	70 mgs	8%
Iodine (Potassium Iodide)	225 mcg	150%

NUTRITIONAL INFORMATION

Serving Size
2 Tbsp. (15 grams)

2 Tbsp. (15 grams) with 8 oz. lowfat protein fortified milk fortified with Vitamins A & D

	Serving	With milk
Servings per container	30	
Calories	50	190
Protein	12 grams	22 grams
Carbohydrates	0 grams	13 grams
Fat	0 grams	5 grams

Percentage of U.S. Recommended Daily Allowance (U.S. RDA) for Adults and Children Over 12 Years Old

	Serving	With milk
Protein	25	50
Vitamin A	50	60
Vitamin C	50	50
Thiamine	50	60
Riboflavin	*	30
Niacin	50	50
Calcium	8	40
Iron	15	15
Vitamin D	50	70
Vitamin E	50	50
Vitamin B₆	*	6
Folic Acid	*	*
Vitamin B₁₂	50	60
Phosphorus	15	40
Iodine	*	*
Magnesium	2	8
Zinc	50	50
Copper	50	50
Biotin	50	50
Pantothenic Acid	50	50

*Contains less than 2% of the U.S. RDA. However, these nutrients are furnished at 100% (or higher) of the U.S. RDA in the NaturSlim II sustained-release tablets furnished in the NaturSlim reducing program.

Iron (Ferrous
  Sulfate) ....18 mgs 100%
Magnesium (Magnesium
  Oxide) ....160 mgs 40%
Potassium (Potassium
  Chloride) ....99 mgs ***
***U.S. RDA has not been established.
Indications: NaturSlim II is indicated
for those seeking a nutritionally balanced diet plan providing 800 or more
calories per day including one regular
meal.
Actions: A safe, effective aid to health-
ful weight reduction and diet control.
The pure whole protein containing bulk
dietary fiber accompanying the "once a
day" sustained release tablet which has
been specifically designed to compliment
a low caloric diet.
Warnings: Use only as directed in the
accompanying diet plan. Do not use as
the sole or primary source of calories for
weight reduction.
Dosage and Administration: Two
tablespoons of the protein supplement
taken in liquid of choice morning and
noon. Twice a day vitamin-mineral tablet and a balanced evening meal.
Professional Labeling: Same as those
listed under Indications.
How Supplied: Available in display
box with literature, 30 twice a day tablets in plastic bottle, and 1 lb. can of protein.
[*Shown in Product Identification Section*]

Norcliff Thayer Inc.
**ONE SCARSDALE ROAD
TUCKAHOE, NY 10707**

A–200 Pyrinate® Liquid, Gel

A-200 Pyrinate® Liquid
Description: Active Ingredients: pyrethrins 0.165%, piperonyl butoxide technical 2.00% (equivalent to 1.60% (butylcarbityl) (6-propylpiperonyl) ether and
0.40% related compounds), deodorized
kerosene 5.00%. Inert ingredients
92.835%.
A-200 Pyrinate® Gel
Description: Active Ingredients: pyrethrins 0.333%, piperonyl butoxide technical 4.00% (equivalent to 3.2% (butylcarbityl) (6-propylpiperonyl) ether and
0.8% related compounds), deodorized
kerosene 5.333%. Inert ingredients
90.334%.
Actions: A-200 Pyrinate is an effective
pediculicide for control of head lice (Pediculus humanus capitis), pubic lice
(Phthirus pubis) and body lice (Pediculus
humanus corporis), and their nits.
Indications: A-200 Pyrinate Liquid and
Gel are indicated for the treatment of
human pediculosis—head lice, body lice
and pubic lice, and their eggs. A-200
Pyrinate Gel is specially formulated for
pubic lice and head lice in children,
where control of application is desirable.
Contraindications: A-200 Pyrinate is
contraindicated in individuals hypersensitive to any of its ingredients or allergic
to ragweed.
Precautions: A-200 Pyrinate is for external use only. It is harmful if swal-

lowed or inhaled. It may be irritating to
the eyes and mucous membranes. In case
of accidental contact with eyes, they
should be immediately flushed with water. If skin irritation or signs of infection
are present, a physician should be consulted.
Administration and Dosage: Apply
sufficient A-200 Pyrinate to completely
"wet" the hair and scalp or skin of any
infested area. Allow application to remain no longer than 10 minutes. Wash
and rinse with plenty of warm water. Remove dead lice and eggs from hair with
fine comb. To restore body and luster to
hair following scalp applications, follow
with a good shampoo. If necessary, this
treatment may be repeated, but should
not exceed two applications within 24
hours.
In order to prevent reinfestation with
lice, all clothing and bedding must be
sterilized or treated concurrent with the
application of this preparation.
How Supplied: A-200 Pyrinate Liquid
in 2 and 4 fl. oz. bottles. A-200 Pyrinate
Gel in 1 oz. tubes.
Literature Available: Patient literature available upon request.
[*Shown in Product Identification Section*]

CO–SALT®
Salt Substitute
Composition: Substitute for table salt;
contains potassium chloride, ammonium
chloride, choline bitartrate, silica and
lactose. Looks, sprinkles, tastes like salt.
Contains less than 10 mg sodium per
100 g which is considered dietetically sodium free.
Action and Uses: Sprinkled on food or
in cooking, gives food salt flavor while
helping to reduce sodium intake. Appropriate for persons on low salt diets, as for
example those with the following conditions: congestive heart failure, hypertension, edema of pregnancy, obesity, cirrhosis of the liver, renal disease, corticosteroid therapy.
Caution: Excessive sodium depletion
may give rise to symptoms such as weakness, nausea, muscle cramps; and in severe cases uremia may supervene. On
the appearance of early symptoms, the
sodium intake must be liberalized.
Contraindications: Oliguria and severe
kidney disease.
How Supplied: 3 oz. container with
shaker top.
[*Shown in Product Identification Section*]

ESOTERICA® MEDICATED FADE
CREAM
Regular
Facial
Fortified Scented with Sunscreen
Fortified Unscented with Sunscreen
Composition: Regular and Facial:
Active Ingredient: Hydroquinone 2%.
Other Ingredients: Water, glyceryl stea-
rate, isopropyl palmitate, propylene gly-
col, ceresin, mineral oil, stearyl alcohol,
propylene glycol stearate, PEG-6-32 stea-
rate, poloxamer 188, steareth-20,
laureth-23, dimethicone, sodium lauryl
sulfate, citric acid, sodium bisulfite,

methylparaben, propylparaben, trisodium EDTA, BHA.
Fortified Scented and Unscented with
Sunscreen:
Active Ingredients: Hydroquinone 2%,
padimate O 3.3%, oxybenzone 2.5%.
Other Ingredients: Water, glyceryl stearate, isopropyl palmitate, ceresin, propylene glycol, stearyl alcohol, PEG-6-32
stearate, poloxamer 188, mineral oil,
steareth-20, laureth-23, steareth-10, allantoin ascorbate, dimethicone, sodium
lauryl sulfate, methylparaben, propylparaben, sodium bisulfite, BHA, trisodium EDTA.
Fragrance in all except Fortified Unscented with Sunscreen.
Indications: Regular and Fortified
Scented and Unscented with Sunscreen:
Indicated for helping fade darkened skin
areas including age spots, liver spots,
freckles and melasma on the face, hands,
legs and body and when used as directed
helps prevent their recurrence. Facial:
Specially designed to help fade darkened
skin areas including age spots, liver
spots, freckles and melasma on the face
and when used as directed helps prevent
their recurrence. It has emollients to
help moisturize while it lightens, so it
makes an excellent night cream as well.
Actions: Esotérica Medicated helps
bleach and lighten hyperpigmented skin.
Contraindications: Should not be used
by persons with known sensitivity to hydroquinone.
Warnings: Do not use if skin is irritated.
Some individuals may be sensitive to the
active ingredient(s) in this cream. Discontinue use if irritation appears. Avoid
contact with eyes. Excessive exposure to
the sun should be avoided. For external
use only.
Fortified Scented and Unscented with
Sunscreen: Not for use in the prevention
of sunburn.
Directions: Apply Esotérica to areas you
wish to lighten and rub in well. Use
cream in the morning and at bedtime for
at least six weeks for maximum results.
Esotérica is greaseless and may be used
under makeup.
How Supplied: 3 oz. glass jars.
[*Shown in Product Identification Section*]

LIQUIPRIN®
(acetaminophen)
Description: Liquiprin is a nonsalicylate analgesic and antipyretic particularly suitable for children. Each 2.5 ml
(one calibrated dropperful) contains 120
mg (2 gr.) of acetaminophen. Liquiprin is
raspberry flavored, reddish pink solution, and does not contain alcohol.
Actions: Liquiprin safely and effectively reduces fever and pain at any age
without the hazards of salicylate therapy
(e.g., gastric mucosal irritation).
Indications: Liquiprin is indicated as
treatment of infants and children with
conditions requiring reduction of fever
and/or relief of pain such as mild upper
respiratory infections (tonsillitis, common cold, flu), teething, headache, myalgia, postimmunization reactions, post-

Continued on next page

Norcliff Thayer—Cont.

tonsillectomy discomfort and gastroenteritis. As adjunctive therapy with antibiotics or sulfonamides, Liquiprin may be useful as an analgesic and antipyretic in bacterial or viral infections, such as bronchitis, pharyngitis, tracheobronchitis, sinusitis, pneumonia, otitis media and cervical adenitis.

Precautions and Adverse Reactions: If a sensitivity reaction occurs, the drug should be discontinued. Liquiprin Drops has rarely been found to produce side effects. It is usually well tolerated by patients who are sensitive to products containing aspirin.

Usual Dosage: Liquiprin should be administered 3 or 4 times daily in the following dosages:
Under 1 year: Up to 1.25 ml
1 to 3 years: 1.25 ml–2.5 ml
3 to 6 years: 2.5 ml
6 to 12 years: 5 ml

How Supplied: Liquiprin is available in a 1.16 fl. oz. (35 ml) plastic bottle with a calibrated dropper.
[*Shown in Product Identification Section*]

NATURE'S REMEDY®
Natural Vegetable Laxative

Active Ingredients: Cascara sagrada 150 mg, aloe 100 mg.

Indications: For gentle, overnight relief of constipation.

Actions: Nature's Remedy has two natural active ingredients that give gentle, overnight relief of constipation. These ingredients, cascara sagrada and aloe, gently stimulate the body's natural function.

Warnings: Do not take any laxative when nausea, vomiting, abdominal pain, or other symptoms of appendicitis are present. Frequent or prolonged use of laxatives may result in dependence on them.

Dosage and Administration: Adults, swallow two tablets daily along with a full glass of water; children (8–15 yrs.), one tablet daily; or as directed by a physician.

How Supplied: Beige, film-coated tablets with foil-backed blister packaging in boxes of 12s, 30s and 60s.

OXY-5® LOTION
OXY-10™ LOTION
Benzoyl Peroxide Lotion 5% and 10%

Description: 5% or 10% benzoyl peroxide in a colorless, odorless, greaseless lotion base.

Indications: A topical aid in the treatment of acne vulgaris.

Action: Provides antibacterial activity against Propionibacterium acnes plus the drying and desquamation necessary in the topical treatment of acne.

Dosage and Administration: Shake well before using. Wash affected area with soap and water. Dry well. Dab lotion on existing pimples and smooth into oily acne-prone areas. Apply one to three times daily or as required.

Contraindications: Should not be used by patients with known sensitivity to benzoyl peroxide.

Caution: Avoid contact with eyes, lips and mucous membranes. For external use only. Discontinue use if excessive irritation or dryness develops. May bleach hair and colored fabrics.

How Supplied: 1 fl. oz. plastic bottles.
[*Shown in Product Identification Section*]

OXY WASH™ Antibacterial Skin Wash

Active Ingredient: Benzoyl peroxide 10%

Indications: Kills acne bacteria. Thoroughly cleanses acne-prone skin. Removes excess oils.

Actions: Antibacterial skin wash. Helps remove the cause of pimples to aid in keeping skin clean, clear and healthy looking.

For a complete anti-acne program, follow Oxy Wash with Oxy-5® acne-pimple medication. Or for stubborn and adult acne, use Oxy-10™ extra strength acne-pimple medication.

Contraindications: Should not be used by patients with known sensitivity to benzoyl peroxide.

Warnings: Avoid contact with eyes, lips and mucous membranes. If excessive dryness or undue irritation of the skin develops, discontinue use and consult physician. Colored or dyed garments may be bleached by the oxidizing action of benzoyl peroxide. To prevent bleaching, avoid contact with hair. For external use only. Keep out of reach of children.

Dosage and Administration: Shake well. Wet area to be washed. Apply Oxy Wash massaging gently for 1 to 2 minutes. Rinse thoroughly. Use 2 to 3 times daily or as directed by physician.

How supplied: 4 fl. oz. plastic bottles.
[*Shown in Product Identification Section*]

TUMS® Antacid Tablets

Active Ingredient: Calcium carbonate, Precipitated U.S.P. 500 mg

Indications: For fast relief of acid indigestion, heartburn and sour stomach.

Actions: A novel antacid composition providing liquid effectiveness in a low cost, pleasant-tasting tablet. TUMS tablets are free of the chalky aftertaste usually associated with calcium carbonate therapy and remain pleasant-tasting even during long-term therapy. TUMS lowers the upper limit of the pH range without affecting the innate antacid efficiency of calcium carbonate. One tablet, when tested *in vitro* according to the *Federal Register* procedure (*Fed. Reg.* 39:19862, June 4, 1974), neutralizes 10 mEq of 0.1 N HCl. This high neutralization capacity combined with a rapid rate of reaction makes TUMS an ideal antacid for management of conditions associated with hyperacidity. The mild, water-insoluble active ingredient of TUMS is non-systemic. It effectively neutralizes free acid yet does not cause systemic alkalosis in the presence of normal renal function. A double-blind placebo controlled clinical study demonstrated that

calcium carbonate taken at a dosage of 16 TUMS tablets daily for a two-week period was non-constipating/non-laxative.

Contraindications: Renal disease, hypercalcemia, concurrent administration with large amounts of milk.

Warnings: TUMS should not be used by patients who are severely debilitated or suffering from kidney failure. For Self-Medication: Do not take more than 16 tablets in a 24-hour period or use the maximum dosage of this product for more than 2 weeks, except under the advice and supervision of a physician.

Dosage and Administration: Chew 1 or 2 TUMS tablets as symptoms occur. Repeat hourly if symptoms return, or as directed by a physician. No water is required. Simulated Drip Method: The pleasant-tasting TUMS tablet may be kept between the gum and cheek and allowed to dissolve gradually by continuous sucking to prolong the effective relief time.

Professional Labeling: Indicated in the management of peptic ulcer, gastritis, gastric hyperacidity, hiatal hernia and peptic esophagitis.

How Supplied: Peppermint and Assorted Flavors of Cherry, Lemon, Orange and Wintergreen are available in 12-tablet rolls, 3-roll wraps, and bottles of 75 tablets. Peppermint flavor is also available in bottles of 150 tablets.
[*Shown in Product Identification Section*]

Norwich-Eaton Pharmaceuticals
Division of MortonNorwich
Consumer Products Group
17 EATON AVENUE
NORWICH, NY 13815

BPN TRIPLE ANTIBIOTIC OINTMENT

Active Ingredient: A triple antibiotic ointment in an inert petrolatum base. Each gram contains: Bacitracin 500 units, Polymixin B 5,000 units, (as Sulfate), Neomycin base (as Sulfate) 3.5 mg.

Indications: A topical antibiotic ointment to help prevent infection in minor cuts and abrasions; an aid to healing.

Warnings: In case of deep or puncture wounds or serious burns consult physician. If redness, irritation, swelling or pain persists, or increases or if infection occurs, discontinue use and consult physician. Do not use in the eyes.

Dosage and Administration: Spread liberally over affected area once or twice daily; cover with a dry, sterile dressing. For external use only.

How Supplied: Tubes of ½ ounce.

CHILDREN'S CHLORASEPTIC® LOZENGES

Active Ingredient: Each Children's Chloraseptic Lozenge contains 5 mg. benzocaine in a grape flavored base of sugar and corn syrup solids.

Actions: Children's Chloraseptic Lozenges provide prompt, temporary relief of minor sore throat pain which may accompany conditions such as tonsillitis, pharyngitis and in post-tonsillectomy soreness, and discomfort of minor mouth and gum irritations.

Dosage and Administration: Allow one lozenge to dissolve slowly in the mouth. Repeat hourly if needed. Do not take more than 12 lozenges per day. Not for children under 3 unless directed by a physician.

How Supplied: Carton of 18 lozenges.

MENTHOL CHLORASEPTIC®
LIQUID
CHERRY CHLORASEPTIC®
LIQUID
MENTHOL CHLORASEPTIC®
SPRAY
CHERRY CHLORASEPTIC®
SPRAY

Active Ingredient: An alkaline solution containing phenol and sodium phenolate (total phenol 1.4%). In addition, Menthol and Cherry Chloraseptic 1.5 oz Spray contain compressed nitrogen as a propellant.

Indications: Pleasant-tasting Chloraseptic is an antiseptic, anesthetic, deodorizing mouthwash and gargle. It is an alkaline solution designed specifically to maintain oral hygiene and to relieve local soreness and irritation without "caines." Chloraseptic may be used as a topical anesthetic while antibacterials are used systemically in the treatment of infection. Chloraseptic acts promptly, often providing effective surface anesthesia in minutes. It is a valuable adjunct for temporary relief of pain and discomfort and will reduce oral bacterial flora temporarily to improve oral hygiene. Chloraseptic is indicated for prompt temporary relief of discomfort due to the following conditions: *Medical* —oropharyngitis and throat infections; acute tonsillitis; posttonsillectomy soreness; peritonsillar abscess; oropharyngeal manifestations of postnasal drip; throat and mouth dryness (smoker's cough); and before intubation (anti-gag) and after (for soreness); *Dental*—after oral surgery or extractions; aphthous ulcers and infectious stomatitis; Vincent's infection; gingivitis; preinjection topical anesthesia; insertion of immediate denture; pericoronitis; and x-rays and impressions (anti-gag).

Dosage and Administration: Chloraseptic Mouthwash and Gargle—*Irritated throat:* Advise patient to spray 5 times (children 6-12 years of age, 3 times) and swallow. May be used as a gargle. Repeat every 2 hours if necessary. *After oral surgery:* Advise patient to allow full-strength solution to run over affected areas for 15 seconds without swishing, then expel remainder. Repeat every 2 hours if necessary. Not for children under 6 years of age unless directed by a physician or dentist. *Adjunctive gingival therapy:* Rinse vigorously with full-strength solution for 15 seconds, working between teeth, then expel remainder. Repeat every 2 hours if necessary. *Daily deodorizing mouthwash and gargle:* Dilute with equal parts of water and rinse

thoroughly, or spray full strength, then expel remainder.

Chloraseptic Spray: *Irritated throat:* Advise patient to spray throat about 2 seconds (children 6 to 12 years about 1 second) and swallow. Repeat every 2 hours if necessary. After oral surgery: Advise patient to spray affected area for 1 to 2 seconds, allow solution to remain for 15 seconds, without swishing, then expel remainder. Repeat every 2 hours if necessary. *Adjunctive gingival therapy:* Spray affected area for about 2 seconds, swish for 15 seconds working between teeth, then expel remainder. Repeat every 2 hours if necessary. *Daily deodorizing spray:* Spray, rinse thoroughly, and expel remainder. Not for children under 6 years of age unless directed by a physician or dentist.

Packaging: Menthol Chloraseptic—6 oz. bottle with sprayer, 8 and 12 oz. bottles without sprayer, and 1.5 oz. spray can. Cherry Chloraseptic—6 oz. bottle with sprayer, 12 oz. bottle without sprayer, and 1.5 oz. spray can. No prescription necessary.

[*Shown in Product Identification Section*]

MENTHOL CHLORASEPTIC®
LOZENGES
CHERRY CHLORASEPTIC®
LOZENGES

Description: Each Chloraseptic Lozenge contains phenol, sodium phenolate (total phenol 32.5 mg).

Action and Uses: Chloraseptic Lozenges provide prompt temporary relief of discomfort due to mouth and gum irritations and of minor sore throat due to colds. They are anesthetic and antiseptic —and also may be used as a topical adjunct to systemic antibacterial therapy for severe cases. For prompt temporary relief of pain and discomfort associated with the following conditions: *Medical* —oropharyngitis and throat infections; acute tonsillitis; posttonsillectomy soreness; peritonsillar abscess; oropharyngeal manifestations of postnasal drip; and throat and mouth dryness (smoker's cough); *Dental*—after oral surgery; aphthous ulcers and infectious stomatitis; Vincent's infection; gingivitis; and pericoronitis.

Administration and Dosage: Adults: Dissolve 1 lozenge in the mouth every 2 hours; do not exceed 8 lozenges per day. Children 6-12 years: Dissolve 1 lozenge in the mouth every 3 hours; do not exceed 4 lozenges per day. Not for children under 6 unless directed by a physician or dentist.

Packaging: Menthol and Cherry Chloraseptic Lozenges—packages of 18, and 45 lozenges.

No prescription necessary.

[*Shown in Product Identification Section*]

CHLORASEPTIC® COUGH
CONTROL LOZENGES

Description: Each CHLORASEPTIC Cough Control Lozenge contains phenol and sodium phenolate (total phenol 32.5 mg.), and a 10 mg. therapeutic dose of dextromethorphan hydrobromide.

Action and Uses: CHLORASEPTIC Cough Control Lozenges provide fast relief of minor sore throat pain and control coughs due to colds. Each lozenge contains two active ingredients. One is the same agent contained in CHLORASEPTIC, a widely used medication for relief of minor sore throat pain. This ingredient acts as a local anesthetic stopping sore throat pain by temporarily blocking the nerve impulse transmission to the ninth cranial nerve. The second agent, dextromethorphan hydrobromide, a nonnarcotic antitussive, acts by selective suppression of the central cough mechanism. Dual-active CHLORASEPTIC Cough Control Lozenges provide temporary symptomatic relief of coughs and minor sore throat pain.

Administration and Dosage: Adults: Dissolve one lozenge slowly in mouth every two hours; do not exceed eight lozenges per day. Children 6 to 12 years: Dissolve one lozenge slowly in mouth every four hours; do not exceed four lozenges per day. Do not administer to children under 6 years of age unless directed by a physician.

Caution: Persistent cough may indicate the presence of a serious condition. Persons with a high fever or persistent cough should not use this preparation unless directed by physician. Consult physician promptly if sore throat is severe or lasts more than two days, or if accompanied by high fever, headache, nausea or vomiting.

Warning: Do not take this product for persistent cough such as occurs with smoking, asthma, emphysema, or where cough is accompanied by excessive secretions except with the advice and supervision of a physician.

Packaging: Pocket-size box of 12 lozenges.

[*Shown in Product Identification Section*]

CHLORASEPTIC® GEL

Description: Chloraseptic Gel contains phenol, sodium phenolate (total phenol 1.4%) in a special adherent base.

Indications: For prompt, temporary relief of discomfort from minor mouth and gum irritations.

Warnings: If irritation or pain persists, discontinue use and consult physician or dentist. Do not administer to children under 6 years of age unless directed by a physician.

Administration: Apply directly to the affected areas. Repeat as necessary.

How Supplied: Chloraseptic Gel is available in 1/4-oz. tubes.

ENCARE®
Vaginal Contraceptive Inserts

Description: ENCARE is an effervescent vaginal contraceptive insert containing a premeasured dose of the spermicide nonoxynol 9 (2.27%).

Action: When used as directed, EN-CARE dissolves and effervesces into a spermicidal barrier that immobilizes and kills sperm on contact.

Continued on next page

Norwich-Eaton—Cont.

Indications: Prevention of pregnancy. ENCARE is useful in managing a broad-spectrum of contraceptive indications. **Primary contraception:** when oral contraceptives or the IUD are contraindicated; for patients concerned about the risk of hormonal or mechanical side-effects; when sexual activity is infrequent or intermittent. **Transitional contraception:** during the initial cycle of oral contraception, or in the three months following IUD insertion, when O.C. users desire pregnancy and unprotected intercourse should not occur immediately; prior to surgical procedures if hormones are contraindicated. **Adjunctive contraception:** for O.C. users to keep on hand for use when consecutive tablets are missed; with the IUD, for extra midcycle protection; with condoms for additional contraceptive and prophylactic effectiveness.

Effectiveness: ENCARE is not as effective as the pill or IUD in actual use, but is approximately as effective as vaginal foam contraceptives. Use-effectiveness will depend on how correctly and consistently patients follow package instructions.

Precautions: When pregnancy is medically contraindicated, the contraceptive program should be determined by a physician. If allergic reactions to cream, foam, jelly, or suppository-type contraceptives have been experienced, a physician should be consulted before use.

Adverse Reactions: In some instances, irritation of the vagina or penis accompanies use of the product. If this occurs, use should be discontinued. As ENCARE effervesces, there may be some sensation of warmth; however, this should not be cause for concern. Some users report that this sensation diminishes through repeated use.

Dosage and Administration: ENCARE must be inserted according to instructions and at least **ten minutes** before intercourse. Best protection will occur when inserted deep in the vagina, close to the cervix.

Contraceptive protection lasts during the period from ten minutes to one hour following insertion. A new ENCARE must be inserted each time intercourse is repeated. The patient should wait at least six hours after intercourse before douching, if a douche is desired.

How Supplied: Boxes of 12 inserts. ENCARE should be stored at a temperature below 86°F (30°C). Should the product inadvertently be exposed to higher temperatures, hold under cold water for two minutes before removing protective wrap.

Eaton-Merz Laboratories, Inc.
Distributed by Eaton-Merz Laboratories, Inc.
Manufactured by Norwich-Eaton Pharmaceuticals
Norwich, New York 13815
Division of Morton-Norwich Products, Inc.
[*Shown in Product Identification Section*]

NECTA SWEET® NON-CALORIC SWEETENER

Active Ingredient:
12.3 mg. sodium saccharin per ¼ grain tablet
24.6 mg. sodium saccharin per ½ grain tablet
49.2 mg. sodium saccharin per 1 grain tablet

Indications: A non-nutritive, artificial sweetener for persons who must restrict their intake of sugar.

Actions: Instant dissolving tablets containing no proteins, fat, available carbohydrates or calories.

Warning: Use of this product may be hazardous to your health. This product contains saccharin which has been determined to cause cancer in laboratory animals.

How Supplied: Available in ¼ grain, ½ grain and 1 grain tablets packaged 500 and 1000 per bottle.

NORFORMS® FEMININE DEODORANTS

Norforms Unscented Ingredients: PEG-20, PEG-6, PEG-20 Palmitate, Methylbenzethonium Chloride, Methylparaben, Lactic Acid.
Norforms Herbal Ingredients: PEG-20, PEG-6, PEG-20 Palmitate, Fragrance, Methylbenzethonium Chloride, Methylparaben, Lactic Acid.
Usage: Feminine Deodorant
Actions: Norforms' deodorant action effectively controls feminine odor in most women for over 8 full hours. They begin working internally the minute they are inserted, spreading a film over the walls of the vagina.

Warnings: If one wishes to become pregnant, Norforms or any internal personal hygiene product should not be used for 6 hours prior to or following intercourse. **Norforms are not recommended for contraception,** but any product introduced into the vaginal area during that time may sometimes interfere with conception.

Most obstetricians advise against the use of products such as douches, sprays or vaginal deodorants during pregnancy. The subject of vaginal hygiene during this time should be discussed with a physician before using Norforms.

Several symptoms may signal **unrelated** medical problems during Norforms use: 1. A discharge which is unusual in color, consistency or amount. 2. A burning or itching sensation in the vaginal area. 3. An abnormal or stronger than usual odor. A physician should be consulted immediately if any of these symptoms occur—especially if they are accompanied by unusual swelling or tenderness, fever, or by pains or cramps in the lower abdomen.

Dosage and Administration: One deodorant a day. Each deodorant can be easily inserted into the vagina with a finger, or the inserter which is available in the package.

Professional Labeling: Same as those outlined under Usage.

How Supplied: Available in both unscented and herbal fragranced forms. Package sizes include 6, 12 and 24 deodorants.
[*Shown in Product Identification Section*]

NORWICH® ASPIRIN

Active Ingredient: Aspirin (5 Grain)
Indications: For pain relief of simple headache and the fever of colds and flu.
Actions: Analgesic, antipyretic
Warnings: Keep all medicines out of reach of children. In case of accidental overdose, contact a physician immediately. Do not take if asthmatic, or during last 3 months of pregnancy except under advice and supervision of physician.
Caution: Do not take if you have ulcers, ulcer symptoms or bleeding problems. If taking medicines for anticoagulation (thinning the blood), diabetes, gout or arthritis, consult physician. Discontinue use if ringing in the ears occurs.
Dosage and Administration: Adults: 1 or 2 tablets every 3-4 hours up to 6 times a day. Children: under 3 years, consult physician; 3-6 years, ½-1 tablet; over 6 years, 1 tablet. May be taken every 3-4 hours up to 3 times a day.
Professional Labeling: Same as outlined under Indications.
How Supplied: In bottles of 100, 250 and 500 tablets.
[*Shown in Product Identification Section*]

NORWICH BACITRACIN ANTIBIOTIC OINTMENT

Active Ingredient: Bacitracin Ointment U.S.P. (500 units Bacitracin per gram in an ointment base)
Indications: An antibiotic ointment to help prevent infection in minor cuts, burns, abrasions.
Warnings: In case of deep or puncture wounds or serious burns, consult physician. If redness, irritation, swelling or pain persists or increases or if infection occurs, discontinue use and consult physician. Do not use in the eyes.
Dosage and Administration: Apply once or twice a day to injured area and cover with a sterile gauze bandage.
How Supplied: Tubes of ½ oz. and 1 oz.

NORWICH® GLYCERIN SUPPOSITORIES

Active Ingredient: Glycerin
Indications: A convenient aid for prompt yet gentle relief of simple constipation.
Action: Laxative
Warning: Do not use when abdominal pain, nausea, or vomiting are present. Frequent or prolonged use of this preparation may result in dependence on laxatives.
Dosage and Administration: Insert one suppository into the rectum. Keep in place five minutes or longer. Repeat as needed. For infants and small children: hold larger end of infants size suppository, insert tapered end well up into the rectum; keep in place five minutes or longer. The suppository need not melt completely to produce laxative action.

Professional Labeling: Same as those outlined under Indications.
How Supplied: Adult formula available in shatterproof jars containing 12, 24 and 50 suppositories. Infant formula available in shatterproof jars containing 12, and 24 suppositories.

NORWICH-EATON ZINC OXIDE OINTMENT

Active Ingredient: 20% Zinc Oxide in a white ointment base with mineral oil.
Indications: A protective ointment for external use to relieve the discomfort of minor skin irritations.
Dosage and Administration: Apply freely on gauze or directly to affected parts. Bandage lightly, if necessary.
How Supplied: Tubes of 1 oz. and 2¼ oz.

NP–27® CREAM

Active Ingredient: 8-Hydroxyquinoline Benzoate 2.5%
Indications: For Athlete's Foot and Ringworm
Actions: Antifungal/anti-itch. Deep acting antifungal NP-27 quickly relieves itching and discomfort of Athlete's Foot and Ringworm. Combats and controls infection causing fungi; helps skin even in severe or persistent cases.
Warnings: In case of fungal infections of nails, or if symptoms persist, consult a physician. Diabetics should not use this or any topical foot medication without first consulting a physician.
Dosage and Administration: After vigorously washing affected area, rub NP-27 Cream gently into skin until cream disappears, then apply a generous second coating of cream over area. Repeat treatment morning and night. After symptoms have disappeared, continue treatment once a day for another week.
How Supplied: 1½ oz. tubes.

NP–27® LIQUID

Active Ingredient: Undecylenic Acid 10% w/w.
Indications: For Athlete's Foot & Ringworm
Action: Antifungal
Warnings: Temporary smarting may occur. Avoid getting into eyes. In case of ringworm of nails or scalp, or if symptoms persist, see physician. Persons with impaired circulation, including diabetics, should not use this or any topical foot medication, without first consulting a physician. Keep all medicines out of reach of children. In case of accidental ingestion, seek professional assistance or contact a Poison Control Center.
Dosage and Administration: Cleanse affected and adjacent areas night and morning with soap and water. Spray NP-27 Liquid liberally on the affected area. Continue for a week after symptoms disappear to help prevent recurrence.
How Supplied: Available in 2 oz. and 4 oz. bottles.

NP–27® POWDER

Active Ingredient: Salicylic Acid 1.5%
Indications: For Athlete's Foot
Actions: Antifungal/anti-itch. Guards against fungus growth; protects broken skin from infection; helps prevent odor.
Warnings: Diabetics should not use this or any topical foot medication without consulting a physician.
Dosage and Administration: Sprinkle a generous quantity of NP-27 Powder on feet, especially between toes, daily.
How Supplied: Available in 1¾ oz. bottles.

NP–27® SPRAY POWDER

Active Ingredient: Zinc Undecylenate 20%
Indications: For effective relief of Athlete's Foot discomfort.
Actions: antifungal/anti-itch
Warnings: For external use only. Use only as directed. Diabetics should not use this or any topical foot medication without first consulting a physician. Avoid spraying in eyes. Contents under pressure. Do not puncture or incinerate. Do not store at temperature above 120°F. Keep out of reach of children. Use only as directed. Intentional misuse by deliberately concentrating and inhaling the contents can be harmful or fatal.
Dosage and Administration: Shake well before using. Hold NP-27 spray about 5 inches from affected area. Spray area completely, especially between toes.
How Supplied: 4 oz. and 8 oz. cans.

PEPTO–BISMOL® Liquid and Tablets
For upset stomach, indigestion and nausea.
Controls common diarrhea.

Active Ingredient: Bismuth subsalicylate. Contains no sugar.
Indications: For indigestion—soothes irritated stomach with a protective coating action. For nausea brings fast, sure relief from distress of that queasy, nauseated feeling. For diarrhea, controls common diarrhea within 24 hours, without constipating, relieving gas pains and abdominal cramps.
Keep all medicines out of reach of children.
Caution: This product contains salicylates. If taken with aspirin and ringing of the ears occur, discontinue use. If taking medicines for anticoagulation (thinning the blood), diabetes, or gout, consult physician before taking this product. If diarrhea is accompanied by high fever or continues more than 2 days, consult a physician.
Note: The beneficial medication may cause a temporary darkening of the stool and tongue.
Dosage Directions: LIQUID
Adults—2 tablespoonfuls.
Children—according to age:
10 to 14 years—4 teaspoonfuls
 6 to 10 years—2 teaspoonfuls
 3 to 6 years—1 teaspoonful
Repeat above dosage every ½ to 1 hour, if needed until 8 doses are taken.

TABLETS
Adults   —2 Tablets
Children—(6 to 10 years)   1 Tablet
Children—(3 to 6 years)   ½ Tablet
Chew or dissolve in mouth. Repeat every ½ to one hour as needed to maximum of 8 doses.
[*Shown in Product Identification Section*]

UNGUENTINE PLUS FIRST AID & BURN CREAM

Active Ingredients: An antiseptic, anesthetic moisturizing cream containing lidocaine hydrochloride 2%, parachlorometaxylenol 2%, phenol 0.5% in a moisturizing cream base.
Indications: An anesthetic/antiseptic moisturizing cream to help stop pain, prevent infection and promote healing in sunburn, minor burns, windburn, chapping, cuts and minor itch due to insect bites.
Warnings: Consult physician in cases of deep or puncture wounds, serious burns, infection or persistent pain or if irritation or swelling develops.
Dosage and Administration: Apply to affected parts and protect with gauze if necessary.
How Supplied: Tubes of ½ oz., 1 oz. and 2 oz.

Nutrition Control Products
Division of Pharmex Inc.
2113 LINCOLN STREET
P.O. BOX 151
HOLLYWOOD, FL 33022

BIO-CREST Double Strength Bioflavonoid Complex with Rutin and Vitamin C.

Composition: Each Tabseal provides 200 mg. NCP Citrus Bioflavonoid Complex, 250 mg. Ascorbic Acid, 50 mg. Rutin.
Action and Uses: Dietary supplement.
How Supplied: Bottle of 100 Tabseals.

O'Connor Products Company
24400 CAPITOL
REDFORD, MI 48239

DEX–A–DIET® LITE
Time Release Capsules

Active Ingredient: Each capsule contains 75 mg. of Phenylpropanolamine HCl.
Indications: Caffeine free appetite suppressant in conjunction with a diet plan.
Actions: Phenylpropanolamine HCl is a sympathomimetic amine similar in chemical structure to other drugs used in obesity, the amphetamines. Actions include central nervous system stimulation and elevation of blood pressure. Such drugs used in obesity are commonly known as "anorectics" or "anorexigenics". Clinical studies have shown that in adult obese subjects a reduction in appetite has been achieved.

Continued on next page

O'Connor—Cont.

Because Dex-A-Diet Lite Time Release Capsules may be purchased without a prescription, the following caution and information appear on the package labeling.

Caution: Do not exceed recommended dosage. Do not use if high blood pressure, heart disease, diabetes, kidney, thyroid or other disease is present. Not to be used during pregnancy or by anyone under the age of 18 except on physician's advice.

Drug Interaction Caution: While taking any medication do not take this or any other drug without consulting a pharmacist or physician. Keep this and all drugs out of the reach of children. In case of accidental overdose, seek professional assistance or contact a poison control center immediately. For the prescribing physician, the following information is provided below.

Precaution: Use with caution in persons with hypertension, heart disease, diabetes, kidney or thyroid disease. As with any product containing a sympathomimetic, this product should not be used in patients taking MAO inhibitors.

Symptoms and Treatment of Oral Overdosage: Symptoms may include rapid pulse and respiration, disorientation, elevated blood pressure, tachycardia, dilated pupils, headache, excitation of the central nervous system, nausea and anorexia. **Treatment** is essentially symptomatic. Immediate evacuation of the stomach should be induced through emesis and gastric lavage. If marked excitement is present, one of the short-acting barbiturates or chloral hydrate may be used.

Dosage and Administration: (Adults) take one Dex-A-Diet Lite at mid-morning with a full glass of water. Read and follow the Dex-A-Diet Lite diet plan.

Professional Labeling: Same as those outlined under Indication.

How Supplied: Available in a box of 20 capsules and a box of 40 capsules, each individually stripped.

DEX–A–DIET II®
Weight Reduction Plan with dx275 Time Release Capsules

Active Ingredient: Each capsule contains 75 mg. of Phenylpropanolamine HCl and 200 mg. of Caffeine.

Indications: As an appetite suppressant in conjunction with a diet plan.

Actions: Phenylpropanolamine HCl is a sympathomimetic amine similar in chemical structure to other drugs used in obesity, the amphetamines. Actions include central nervous system stimulation and elevation of blood pressure. Such drugs used in obesity are commonly known as "anorectics" or "anorexigenics". Clinical studies have shown that in adult obese subjects a reduction in appetite has been achieved. Dex-A-Diet II combines dx275 (the action of an appetite suppressant, mild diuretic and effective stimulant) with a complete diet plan for a total reduction regimen that is safe and effective.

Because Dex-A-Diet II Weight Reduction Plan may be purchased without a prescription, the following caution and information appear on the package labeling.

Caution: Do not exceed recommended dosage. Discontinue use if rapid pulse, dizziness or palpitations occur. Do not use if high blood pressure, heart disease, diabetes, kidney, thyroid or other disease is present. Not to be used during pregnancy or by anyone under the age of 18 except on physician's advice.

Drug Interaction Caution: While taking any medication do not take this or any other medication without consulting a pharmacist or physician. Keep this and all drugs out of the reach of children. In case of accidental overdose, seek professional assistance or contact a poison control center immediately.

For the prescribing physician, the following information is provided below.

Precaution: Use with caution in persons with hypertension, heart disease, diabetes, kidney or thyroid disease. As with any product containing a sympathomimetic, this product should not be used in patients taking MAO inhibitors.

Symptoms and Treatment of Oral Overdosage: Symptoms may include rapid pulse and respiration, disorientation, elevated blood pressure, tachycardia, dilated pupils, headache, excitation of the central nervous system, nausea and anorexia. **Treatment** is essentially symptomatic. Immediate evacuation of the stomach should be induced through emesis and gastric lavage. If marked excitement is present, one of the short-acting barbiturates or chloral hydrate may be used.

Dosage and Administration: (Adults) Take one Dex-A-Diet II Capsule at mid-morning with a full glass of water. Read and follow the Dex-A-Diet II diet plan.

Professional Labeling: Same as those outlined under Indications.

How Supplied: Available in a box of 24 capsules and a box of 48 capsules each individually stripped.

[*Shown in Product Identification Section*]

K–FORTE™ Dietary Plan

Active Ingredient: Each six orange-flavored chewable tablets contain:
Potassium (from Potassium Gluconate, Potassium Citrate and Potassium Chloride) ....234 mg. (6 mEq)
and Vitamin C (Ascorbic Acid) ....60 mg. (100% USRDA*)
*United States Recommended Daily Allowance for adults and children 4 or more years of age.

Indications: Suggested usage is as a convenient source of potassium.

Actions: Potassium is supplied from the gluconate, citrate and chloride forms in a good-tasting chewable tablet.

Because K-Forté Dietary Plan Tablets may be purchased without a prescription, the following information appears on the label.

Keep this and all medicine out of the reach of children and the package insert states:

Potassium is one of your body's most important elements. Though it is contained in many of the foods you eat, sometimes a supplement is needed, especially if you're taking diuretics, laxatives or certain blood pressure lowering drugs. Depletion of potassium in your system may result in nausea, muscle fatigue, or leg cramps. O'Connor Products has developed a good-tasting, chewable potassium supplement in a safe, convenient form that is compounded from three important potassium salts to aid absorption into the system. K-Forté helps you get the potassium you need to stay healthy. So, if your diet lacks important potassium, ask your doctor, or your pharmacist, about K-Forté.

A list of foods high in potassium is also given in the package insert.

For the prescribing physician, the following information is provided below.

Contraindications: Potassium supplements are contraindicated in patients with hyperkalemia since a further increase in serum potassium concentration in such patients can produce cardiac arrest. Hyperkalemia may complicate any of the following conditions; chronic renal failure, systemic acidosis such as diabetic acidosis, acute dehydration, extensive tissue breakdown as in severe burns, adrenal insufficiency, or the administration of a potassium-sparing diuretic.

Precaution: The treatment of potassium depletion, particularly in the presence of cardiac disease, renal disease or acidosis requires careful attention to acid-base balance and appropriate monitoring of serum electrolytes, the electrocardiogram and the clinical status of the patient.

Symptoms and Treatment of Oral Overdosage: The administration of oral potassium salts to persons with normal excretory mechanisms for potassium rarely causes serious hyperkalemia. It is important to recognize that hyperkalemia is usually asymptomatic and may be manifested only by an increased serum potassium concentration and characteristic electrocardiographic changes. Late manifestations include muscle-paralysis and cardiovascular collapse from cardiac arrest.

Treatment includes elimination of foods and medicines containing potassium-sparing diuretics and intravenous administration of dextrose and insulin and if acidosis is present with intravenous sodium bicarbonate.

The following information is provided in the labeling.

Dosage and Administration: Chew one or two tablets three times daily (or as directed by a physician), before meals, with a full glass of water, as a convenient source of potassium supplementation.

Professional Labeling: Same as those outlined under Indications.

How Supplied: Available in bottles of 90 tablets with a child-resistant cap.

Ortho Pharmaceutical Corporation
Consumer Products Division
RARITAN, NJ 08869

CONCEPTROL®
Birth Control Cream

Description: A contraceptive cream containing the active ingredient Nonoxynol-9, 5% in an oil-in-water emulsion at pH 4.5.
Indication: Contraception.
Action and Uses: A spermicidal cream for intravaginal contraception.
Warning: Burning and/or irritation of the vagina or penis have been reported. In such cases, the medication should be discontinued and a physician consulted. Not effective if taken orally. Keep out of reach of children. When pregnancy is contraindicated, the contraceptive program should be discussed with a physician.
Dosage and Administration: CONCEPTROL should be inserted prior to each intercourse. One applicatorful of CONCEPTROL inserted just before intercourse is adequate for only one time. An additional applicatorful is required each time intercourse is repeated. If intercourse has not occurred within one hour after application of CONCEPTROL, repeat the application before intercourse. If a douche is desired for cleansing purposes, wait at least six hours following intercourse. Refer to directions and diagrams for detailed instructions. CONCEPTROL is an easy to use, pleasant and reliable method of birth control. While no method of contraception can provide an absolute guarantee against becoming pregnant, for maximum protection, CONCEPTROL Cream must be used according to directions.
How Supplied: CONCEPTROL Cream in packages of 6 and 10 Disposable Applicators per package, Premeasured-Prefilled-Prewrapped. Also available in packages containing a 2.46 oz. Starter tube with applicator and 2.46 oz. Refill tube only.
[*Shown in Product Identification Section*]

CONCEPTROL SHIELDS®
Latex Prophylactics

Advantages: Advanced Design—Each prophylactic is specially contoured for greater comfort and sensitivity. Sensitive—All CONCEPTROL SHIELDS are made from a premium quality, thin latex. Lubrication — CONCEPTROL SHIELDS are available with a special "dry" lubricant that is less messy; they are also available non-lubricated. Reservoir—CONCEPTROL SHIELDS have a reservoir tip to aid in the prevention of spillage.
How Supplied: CONCEPTROL SHIELDS are available lubricated and non-lubricated, in packages of 12's and 24's.
[*Shown in Product Identification Section*]

CONCEPTROL SUPREME®
Thin Prophylactics

Advantages: Advanced Design—Each prophylactic is designed to be extra light for a more natural feeling. Sensitive—ALL CONCEPTROL SUPREME prophylactics are made from a premium quality, very thin latex. Lubrication—ALL CONCEPTROL SUPREME prophylactics are lubricated with a special "dry" lubricant that's less messy. Reservoir—Each CONCEPTROL SUPREME prophylactic has a reservoir tip to aid in the prevention of spillage.
How Supplied: CONCEPTROL SUPREME prophylactics are available lubricated in packages of 12.
[*Shown in Product Identification Section*]

DELFEN®
Contraceptive Foam

Description: A contraceptive foam in an aerosol dosage formulation containing 12.5% Nonoxynol-9 and buffered to normal vaginal pH 4.5.
Indication: Contraception.
Action and Uses: A spermicidal foam for intravaginal contraception.
Warning: Burning and/or irritation of the vagina or penis have been reported. In such cases, the medication should be discontinued and a physician consulted. Not effective if taken orally. Do not burn or puncture container. Keep out of reach of children.
When pregnancy is contraindicated, the contraceptive program should be discussed with a physician.
Dosage and Administration: Insert DELFEN Contraceptive Foam just prior to each intercourse. You may have intercourse any time up to one hour after you have inserted the foam. If you repeat intercourse, insert another applicatorful of DELFEN Foam. After shaking the vial, place the measured-dose (5cc) applicator over the top of the vial, then press applicator down very gently. Fill to the top of the barrel threads. Remove applicator to stop flow of foam. Insert the filled applicator well into the vagina and depress the plunger. Remove the applicator with the plunger in depressed position. If a douche is desired for cleansing purposes, wait at least six hours after intercourse. Refer to directions and diagrams for detailed instructions. DELFEN Foam is a reliable method of birth control. While no method of birth control can provide an absolute guarantee against becoming pregnant, for maximum protection, DELFEN Foam must be used according to directions.
How Supplied: DELFEN Contraceptive Foam 0.70 oz. Starter vial with applicator. Also available in 0.70 oz. and 1.75 oz. Refill vial only.
[*Shown in Product Identification Section*]

INTERCEPT®
Contraceptive Inserts

Description: A single dose vaginal contraceptive insert containing the active ingredient nonoxynol-9, 5.56% at pH 4.5.
Indication: Contraception
Action: A spermicidal insert for intravaginal contraception.
Warning: Should sensitivity to the ingredients or irritation of the vagina or penis develop, discontinue use and consult a physician. Not effective if taken orally. Keep out of reach of children. When pregnancy is contraindicated, the contraceptive program should be discussed with a physician.
Dosage and Administration: INTERCEPT should be inserted into the vagina at least ten minutes prior to male penetration to insure proper dispersion. INTERCEPT provides protection from ten minutes to one hour after product insertion. Insert a new INTERCEPT Contraceptive Insert each time intercourse is repeated. If a douche is desired for cleansing purposes, wait at least six hours following intercourse.
INTERCEPT is an effective method of contraception. No product, however, can provide an absolute guarantee against becoming pregnant.
How Supplied: INTERCEPT Contraceptive Inserts are available in a starter package containing 12 inserts with applicator and in a 12 insert refill package.
[*Shown in Product Identification Section*]

MASSE®
Breast Cream

Composition: MASSE Breast Cream.
Action and Uses: MASSE Breast Cream is especially designed for care of the nipples of pregnant and nursing women.
Administration and Dosage:
BEFORE BIRTH
During the last two or three months of pregnancy, it is often desirable to prepare the nipple and the nipple area of the breast for eventual nursing. In these cases, MASSE is used once or twice daily in the following manner: Carefully cleanse the breast with a soft, clean cloth and plain water and dry. Squeeze a ribbon of MASSE, approximately an inch long, and lightly massage into the nipple and immediate surrounding area. Do so until the cream has completely disappeared. The massage motion should be gentle and outward.
AFTER BABY IS BORN
During the nursing period MASSE is used as follows: BEFORE AND AFTER EACH NURSING cleanse the breasts with a clean cloth and water. After drying squeeze a ribbon of MASSE, approximately an inch long, and gently massage into the nipple and the immediate surrounding area.
Contraindications: MASSE should not be used in cases of acute mastitis or breast abscess.
Caution: In cases of excessive tenderness or irritation of any kind, consult your physician.
How Supplied: MASSE Breast Cream is available in a 2 oz. tube.
[*Shown in Product Identification Section*]

Continued on next page

Ortho Pharm.—Cont.

ORTHO–CREME®
Contraceptive Cream

Description: ORTHO-CREME Contraceptive Cream is a pure white and pleasantly scented cream of cosmetic consistency. ORTHO-CREME is a greaseless, non-staining and non-irritating spermicidal cream which contains the active ingredient Nonoxynol-9.

Action and Uses: A spermicidal vaginal cream for use with a vaginal diaphragm when control of conception is desirable. Esthetically pleasing.

Dosage and Administration: Used in conjunction with a vaginal diaphragm. Prior to insertion, put an applicatorful (about a teaspoonful) of ORTHO-CREME Contraceptive Cream into the cup of the dome of the diaphragm and spread a small amount around the edge with the fingertip. This will aid in insertion and provide protection.

Some doctors recommend that the diaphragm be inserted every night to afford maximum protection.

It is also important to remember that if intercourse occurs more than six hours after insertion, or if repeated intercourse takes place, an additional application of ORTHO-CREME is necessary. DO NOT REMOVE THE DIAPHRAGM—simply add more ORTHO-CREME with the applicator provided in the applicator package, being careful not to dislodge the diaphragm.

Remember, another application of OR-THO-CREME is required each time intercourse is repeated, regardless of how little time has transpired since the diaphragm has been in place.

In addition, it is essential that the diaphragm remain in place for at least six hours after intercourse. Removal of the diaphragm before this time may increase the risk of becoming pregnant. There is no urgency in removing the diaphragm—it may remain in position for up to 24 hours. If a douche is desired for cleansing purposes, wait at least 6 hours after intercourse. Refer to directions and diagrams for detailed instructions. While no method of contraception can provide an absolute guarantee against becoming pregnant, for maximum protection, OR-THO-CREME must be used according to directions.

How Supplied: 2.46 oz. Starter tube with measured-dose applicator. Regular size 2.46 oz. Refill tube only. Large size 4.05 oz. Refill tube only.
[*Shown in Product Identification Section*]

ORTHO® Disposable
Vaginal Applicators

Action and Uses: ORTHO Disposable applicators are made of paperboard and are designed to provide a simple, clean, accurate method for inserting tubed vaginal jellies and creams into the vagina. The applicator may be readily filled directly from the tube used and then discarded.

How Supplied: Packages of 18 applicators each.
[*Shown in Product Identification Section*]

ORTHO–GYNOL®
Contraceptive Jelly

Description: ORTHO-GYNOL Contraceptive Jelly is a water dispersible spermicidal jelly having a pH of 4.5 which contains the active ingredient p-diisobutylphenoxypolyethoxyethanol.

Action and Uses: A spermicidal vaginal jelly for use with a vaginal diaphragm whenever the control of conception is desirable. Esthetically acceptable.

Dosage and Administration: Used in conjunction with a vaginal diaphragm. Prior to insertion, put an applicatorful (about a teaspoonful) of ORTHO-GYNOL Contraceptive Jelly into the cup of the dome of the diaphragm and spread a small amount around the edge with the fingertip. This will aid in insertion and provide protection.

Some doctors recommend that the diaphragm be inserted every night to afford maximum protection.

It is also important to remember that if intercourse occurs more than six hours after insertion, or if repeated intercourse takes place, an additional application of ORTHO-GYNOL is necessary. DO NOT REMOVE THE DIAPHRAGM—simply add more ORTHO-GYNOL with the applicator provided in the applicator package, being careful not to dislodge the diaphragm.

Remember, another application of OR-THO-GYNOL is required each time intercourse is repeated, regardless of how little time has transpired since the diaphragm has been in place.

In addition, it is essential that the diaphragm remain in place for at least six hours after intercourse. Removal of the diaphragm before this time may increase the risk of becoming pregnant. There is no urgency in removing the diaphragm—it may remain in position for up to 24 hours. If a douche is desired for cleansing purposes, wait at least 6 hours after intercourse. Refer to directions and diagrams for complete instructions. While no method of contraception can provide an absolute guarantee against becoming pregnant, for maximum protection OR-THO-GYNOL must be used according to directions.

How Supplied: 2.85 oz. Starter tube with measured-dose applicator. Regular size 2.85 oz. Refill tube only. Large size 4.44 oz. Refill tube only.
[*Shown in Product Identification Section*]

ORTHO® PERSONAL LUBRICANT

Description: ORTHO PERSONAL LUBRICANT is especially formulated as a sexual lubricant that is designed to be gentle and non-irritating for both women and men. It is a non-staining, water soluble jelly that is safe for delicate tissue.

Dosage and Administration: Apply a one (1″) to two (2″) inch ribbon of product, or desired amount, to external vaginal area and/or penis. Repeat applications may be used by one or both partners. If desired, this product may be used inside the vagina.

For easy insertion of rectal thermometers, tampons, douche nozzles and enema nozzles, use desired amount.

How Supplied: ORTHO PERSONAL LUBRICANT is available in 2 oz. and 4 oz. tubes.
[*Shown in Product Identification Section*]

Ortho Pharmaceutical Corporation
DERMATOLOGICAL DIVISION
RARITAN, NJ 08869
a Johnson & Johnson Company

PURPOSE Brand Dry Skin Cream

Composition: Contains purified water, petrolatum, propylene glycol, glyceryl stearate, sodium lactate, almond oil, steareth-20, cetyl alcohol, cetyl esters wax, mineral oil, steareth-2, xanthan gum, sorbic acid, lactic acid and fragrance.

Action and Uses: PURPOSE Dry Skin Cream is formulated especially to meet the need for an effective dry skin cream that dermatologists can recommend. PURPOSE Dry Skin Cream moisturizes dry, chapped and irritated skin and provides effective, lasting relief from drying and scaling. PURPOSE Dry Skin Cream smoothes easily into skin for all-over body care.

Administration and Dosage: Instruct patients to use PURPOSE Dry Skin Cream as any other dry skin cream.

How Supplied: 3 oz. tube.
[*Shown in Product Identification Section*]

PURPOSE Brand Shampoo

Composition: Contains water, amphoteric 19, PEG-44 sorbitan laurate, PEG-150 distearate, sorbitan laurate, boric acid, fragrance, and benzyl alcohol.

Action and Uses: PURPOSE shampoo is formulated especially to meet the need for a mild shampoo that Dermatologists can recommend. PURPOSE shampoo helps control oily scalp and hair and helps remove the scales of dandruff leaving hair clean and manageable. Safe for color-treated hair. PURPOSE shampoo works into a rich, pleasant lather. It may be used daily.

Administration and Dosage: Instruct patients to use PURPOSE Shampoo as any other shampoo.

How Supplied: 7 fluid oz. plastic bottle.
[*Shown in Product Identification Section*]

PURPOSE Brand Soap

Composition: Contains sodium and potassium salts of fatty acids, glycerin, water and mild fragrance.

Action and Uses: Extraordinary mild PURPOSE Soap was created to wash tender, sensitive skin. Formulated especially to meet the need for a mild soap that Dermatologists can recommend. This translucent washing bar is non-medicated and completely free of harsh detergents or other ingredients that might dry or irritate skin.

Administration and Dosage: Wash face with PURPOSE soap two or three times a day or as directed by your physician. Rinse with warm water. For complete skin care, use it also for bath and shower.

How Supplied: 3.6 oz. bar in plastic soap dish.

[*Shown in Product Identification Section*]

Parke-Davis
Division of Warner-Lambert
   Company
**201 TABOR ROAD
MORRIS PLAINS, NJ 07950**

AGORAL® Plain
AGORAL® Raspberry
AGORAL® Marshmallow

Description: Each tablespoonful (15 ml) contains 4.2 grams mineral oil and 0.2 grams phenolphthalein in a thoroughly homogenized emulsion with agar, tragacanth, acacia, egg albumin, glycerin and water. Agoral is pleasantly flavored marshmallow (white) or raspberry (pink).

Agoral is also available without phenolphthalein as Agoral Plain (white). Because of Agoral's palatability, patient acceptance usually remains high.

Actions: Agoral, containing mineral oil, facilitates defecation by lubricating the fecal mass and softening the stool. More effective than nonemulsified oil in penetrating the feces, Agoral thereby greatly reduces the possibility of oil leakage at the anal sphincter. Phenolphthalein gently stimulates motor activity of the lower intestinal tract. Agoral's combined lubricating-softening and peristaltic actions can help to restore a normal pattern of evacuation.

Indications: Relief of constipation. Agoral may be especially required when straining at stool is a hazard, as in hernia, cardiac, or hypertensive patients; during convalescence from surgery; before and after surgery for hemorrhoids or other painful anorectal disorders; for patients confined to bed.

The management of chronic constipation should also include attention to fluid intake, diet and bowel habits.

Contraindication: Sensitivity to phenolphthalein.

Warning: In case of nausea, vomiting, or abdominal pain, do not take laxatives. To avoid dependence on laxatives, do not use continuously. **Caution:** If skin rash appears do not use this or any other preparation containing phenolphthalein.

Dosage and Management:

	Adults	Children over 6 years
Agoral Plain (without phenolphthalein)	½ to 1 tblsp.	1 to 2 tsp.
Agoral Raspberry	½ to 1 tblsp.	1 to 2 tsp.
Agoral Marshmallow	½ to 1 tblsp.	1 to 2 tsp.

Take at bedtime only, unless other time is advised by physician.

Agoral may be taken alone or in milk, water, or any miscible food.

Expectant or nursing mothers, bedridden or aged patients, young children or infants: use only on advice of physician.

Supplied: Agoral Plain (without phenolphthalein), plastic bottles of 16 fl oz (N 0047-0071-16). Agoral (raspberry flavor), plastic bottles of 16 fl oz (N 0047-0072-16). Agoral (marshmallow flavor), plastic bottles of 8 fl oz (N 0047-0070-08) and 16 fl oz (N 0047-0070-16).

STORE BETWEEN 59 and 86 F (15 and 30 C).

ANUSOL®
Suppositories/Ointment

Description:

	Anusol Suppositories each contains	Anusol Ointment each gram
Bismuth subgallate	2.25%	—
Bismuth Resorcin Compound	1.75%	—
Benzyl Benzoate	1.2 %	12 mg
Peruvian Balsam	1.8 %	18 mg
Zinc Oxide	11.0 %	110 mg
Analgine™ (pramoxine hydrochloride)	—	10 mg

Anusol Suppositories also contain the following inactive ingredients: bismuth subiodide, calcium phosphate and certified coloring in a bland hydrogenated vegetable oil base.

Anusol Ointment also contains the following inactive ingredients: calcium phosphate and kaolin in a liquid petrolatum-cocoa butter-polyethylene wax base containing glyceryl mono-oleate and glyceryl stearate.

Actions: Anusol Suppositories and Anusol Ointment help to relieve pain, itching and discomfort arising from irritated anorectal tissues. They have a soothing, lubricant action on mucous membranes. Analgine (pramoxine hydrochloride) in Anusol Ointment is a rapidly acting local anesthetic for the skin and mucous membranes of the anus and rectum. Analgine is also chemically distinct from procaine, cocaine, and dibucaine and can often be used in the patient previously sensitized to other surface anesthetics. Surface analgesia lasts for several hours.

Indications: Anusol Suppositories and Anusol Ointment are adjunctive therapy for the symptomatic relief of pain and discomfort in: external and internal hemorrhoids, proctitis, papillitis, cryptitis, anal fissures, incomplete fistulas, and relief of local pain and discomfort following anorectal surgery.

Anusol Ointment is also indicated for pruritus ani.

Contraindications: Anusol Suppositories and Anusol Ointment are contraindicated in those patients with a history of hypersensitivity to any of the components of the preparations.

Precautions: Symptomatic relief should not delay definitive diagnoses or treatment.

If irritation develops, these preparations should be discontinued. These preparations are not for ophthalmic use.

Adverse Reactions: Upon application of Anusol Ointment, which contains Analgine (pramoxine HCl), a patient may occasionally experience burning, especially if the anoderm is not intact. Sensitivity reactions have been rare; discontinue medication if suspected.

Dosage and Administration: Anusol Suppositories—Adults: Remove foil wrapper and insert suppository into the anus. One suppository in the morning and one at bedtime, and one immediately following each evacuation.

Anusol Ointment—Adults: After gentle bathing and drying of the anal area, apply freely to the exterior surface and gently rub in. For internal use, attach the plastic applicator and insert into the anus part way by applying gentle continuous pressure. Then squeeze the tube to deliver medication. Ointment should be applied every 3 or 4 hours, or, when necessary, every 2 hours.

NOTE: If staining from either of the above products occurs, the stain may be removed from fabric by hand or machine washing with household detergent.

How Supplied: Anusol Suppositories—boxes of 12(N 0047-0088-12), 24 (N 0047-0088-24) and 48 (N 0047-0088-48); in silver foil strips with Anusol W/C printed in red.

Anusol Ointment—1-oz tubes (N 0047-0075-01) with plastic applicator.

Store between 59° and 86°F (15° and 30°C).

[*Shown in Product Identification Section*]

BENADRYL® Antihistamine Cream

Description: Greaseless disappearing cream contains 2% Benadryl (diphenhydramine hydrochloride) in a water-miscible ointment base.

Indications: For relief of itching due to insect bites and other minor skin irritations (rashes, inflammation). FOR EXTERNAL USE ONLY.

Warning: Should not be applied to blistered, raw or oozing areas of the skin. If burning sensation results, discontinue use. In case of accidental ingestion, seek professional assistance or contact a Poison Control Center immediately.

Caution: Do not use in eyes. If condition persists or a rash or irritation devel-

Continued on next page

This product information was prepared in December, 1980. On these and other Parke-Davis Products, detailed information may be obtained by addressing PARKE-DAVIS, Division of Warner-Lambert Company, Morris Plains, NJ 07950.

Parke-Davis—Cont.

ops, discontinue use and consult a physician.

Directions: Apply locally for itching three or four times daily or as directed by the physician.

How Supplied:
1-oz tubes (N 0071-3058-13)
2-oz tubes (N 0071-3058-15)
[*Shown in Product Identification Section*]

BENYLIN DM®

Description: Each teaspoonful (5 ml) contains 10 mg dextromethorphan hydrobromide and 5% alcohol; also contains, as inactive ingredients, sugar; water; glucose liquid; glycerin; ammonium chloride; sodium citrate; raspberry imitation flavor; citric acid; caramel; menthol; and D&C Red 33.

Nonnarcotic; Contains No Antihistamine

Indications: Antitussive—For the temporary relief of coughs due to minor throat and bronchial irritation as may occur with the common cold or with inhaled irritants

Warnings: An antitussive product taken in combination with an antihistamine product may cause marked drowsiness. Do not give this product to children under 2 years of age, except under the advice and supervision of a physician. Do not take this product for persistent or chronic cough such as occurs with smoking, asthma, or emphysema, or where cough is accompanied by excessive secretions, except under the advice and supervision of a physician.

Caution: A persistent cough may be a sign of a serious condition. If cough persists for more than 1 week, tends to recur, or is accompanied by high fever, rash, or persistent headache, consult a physician.

Dosage: For the temporary relief of cough—

Adults—1 to 2 teaspoonfuls every 4 hours, or 3 teaspoonfuls every 6 to 8 hours, not to exceed 12 teaspoonfuls in 24 hours

Children 6 to under 12 years—½ to 1 teaspoonful every 4 hours, or 1½ teaspoonfuls every 6 to 8 hours, not to exceed 6 teaspoonfuls in 24 hours

Children 2 to under 6 years—¼ to ½ teaspoonful every 4 hours, or ¾ teaspoonful every 6 to 8 hours, not to exceed 3 teaspoonfuls in 24 hours

Children under 2 years—there is no recommended dosage, except under the advice and supervision of a physician

How Supplied: N 0071-2401-17 (Stock No. 22-2401-621): 4-oz bottles in cartons of 12.

[*Shown in Product Identification Section*]

CALADRYL® Lotion
CALADRYL Cream

Description: Caladryl Lotion—A drying, antihistaminic, calamine-Benadryl® lotion containing calamine, 1% Benadryl (diphenhydramine hydrochloride), camphor, and 2% alcohol

Caladryl Cream—a drying, antihistaminic, calamine-Benadryl cream containing 1% Benadryl (diphenhydramine hydrochloride) calamine, and camphor.

Indications: For relief of itching due to mild poison ivy or oak, insect bites, or other minor skin irritations, and soothing relief of mild sunburn

Warnings: Should not be applied to blistered, raw, or oozing areas of the skin. Discontinue use if burning sensation or rash develops or condition persists. Remove by washing with soap and water.

Caution: *FOR EXTERNAL USE ONLY* Keep away from eyes or other mucous membranes.

Directions: Caladryl Lotion—*SHAKE WELL*

Apply topically three or four times a day. Cleanse skin with soap and water and dry area before each application.

Caladryl Cream—Apply topically three or four times a day. Cleanse skin with soap and water and dry area before each application. Use on extensive areas of the skin or for longer than seven days only as directed by a physician.

How Supplied: Caladryl Lotion—N 0071-3181-16 (Stock No. 22-181-378) 2½-oz (75 ml) squeeze bottles and 6-oz bottles Caladryl Cream—N 0071-3226-14 (Stock No. 21-226-77) 1½-oz tubes.

[*Shown in Product Identification Section*]

GELUSIL®
Antacid–Antiflatulent
Liquid/Tablets

Each teaspoonful (5 ml) or tablet contains:

200 mg aluminum hydroxide
200 mg magnesium hydroxide
25 mg simethicone

Advantages:
- High acid-neutralizing capacity
- Low sodium content
- Simethicone for antiflatulent activity
- Good taste for better patient compliance
- Fast dissolution of chewed tablets for prompt relief

Indications: Gelusil, a carefully balanced combination of two widely used antacids and the antiflatulent simethicone, is effective for the relief of symptoms associated with heartburn, sour stomach, and acid indigestion. Gelusil also provides symptomatic relief of hyperacidity associated with the diagnosis of peptic ulcer, gastritis, peptic esophagitis, gastric hyperacidity, and hiatal hernia. Gelusil is also indicated to alleviate or relieve the symptoms of gas, postoperative gas pain, or for use in endoscopic examination.

Actions and Uses: The proven neutralizing powers of aluminum hydroxide and of magnesium hydroxide combine to give Gelusil dependable antacid action without the acid rebound sometimes associated with calcium carbonate.

The pleasant peppermint-flavored taste of Gelusil Liquid and Tablets encourages patient acceptance of, and compliance with, recommended antacid regimens. Gelusil Tablets are easy to chew and are specifically formulated to dissolve

readily, providing prompt onset of action and reliable relief of symptoms.

Gelusil is appropriate whenever there is a need for well-accepted, effective antacid-antiflatulent therapy.

Dosage and Administration: Two or more teaspoonfuls or tablets one hour after meals and at bedtime, or as directed by a physician.

Tablets should be chewed.

The following information is provided to facilitate treatment:

Gelusil	LIQUID	TABLETS
Acid-neutralizing capacity	24 mEq/ 10 ml	22 mEq/ 2 tabs
Sodium	0.7 mg/ 5 ml	0.8 mg/ tab
Lactose	0	0

Warnings: Do not take more than 12 tablets or teaspoonfuls in a 24-hour period, or use this maximum dosage for more than two weeks, or use this product if you have kidney disease, except under the advice and supervision of a physician.

Keep this and all drugs out of the reach of children.

Drug Interaction Precaution: Do not take this product if you are presently taking a prescription antibiotic drug containing any form of tetracycline. As with all aluminum-containing antacids, Gelusil may prevent proper absorption of the tetracycline.

How Supplied:

Liquid—In plastic bottles of 6 fl oz (N 0047-0036-06) and 12 fl oz (N 0047-0036-12).

Tablets—White, embossed W/C Gelusil 034—individual strips of 10 in boxes of 50 (N 0047-0034-50), 100 (N 0047-0034-51) and 1000 (N 0047-0034-60); 165 tablets loose-packed in plastic bottles (N 0047-0034-32).

Store between 59° and 86°F (15° and 30°C).

[*Shown in Product Identification Section*]

GELUSIL-M®
Antacid–Antiflatulent
Liquid/Tablets

Each teaspoonful (5 ml) or tablet contains:

300 mg aluminum hydroxide
200 mg magnesium hydroxide
25 mg simethicone

Advantages:
- High acid-neutralizing capacity
- Low sodium content
- Simethicone for antiflatulent activity
- Good taste for better patient compliance
- Fast dissolution of chewed tablets for prompt relief
- Especially useful for those whose bowel functions are adversely affected by magnesium hydroxide.

Indications: Gelusil-M, a carefully balanced combination of two widely used antacids and the antiflatulent simethicone, is effective for the relief of symptoms associated with heartburn, sour stomach, and acid indigestion. Gelusil-M also provides symptomatic relief of hyperacidity associated with the diagnosis of peptic ulcer, gastritis, peptic esophagitis, gastric hyperacidity, and hiatal hernia. Gelusil-M is also indicated to alleviate or relieve the symptoms of gas, postoperative gas pain, or for use in endoscopic examination.

Actions and Uses: The proven neutralizing power of aluminum hydroxide and magnesium hydroxide combine to give Gelusil-M dependable antacid action without the acid rebound sometimes associated with calcium carbonate. The pleasant spearmint-flavored taste .of Gelusil-M Liquid and Tablets encourages patient acceptance of, and compliance with, recommended antacid regimens.

Gelusil-M Tablets are easy to chew and are specifically formulated to dissolve readily, providing prompt onset of action and reliable relief of symptoms.

Gelusil-M is appropriate whenever there is a need for well-accepted, effective antacid-antiflatulent therapy.

Dosage and Administration: Two or more teaspoonfuls or tablets one hour after meals and at bedtime, or as directed by a physician.

Tablets should be chewed.

The following information is provided to facilitate treatment:

Gelusil-M	LIQUID	Tablets
Acid-neutral-izing capacity	30 mEq/ 10 ml	25 mEq/ 2 tabs
Sodium	1.2 mg/ 5 ml	1.3 mg/ tab
Lactose	0	0

Warnings: Do not take more than 10 teaspoonfuls or tablets in a 24-hour period, or use this maximum dosage for more than two weeks, or use this product if you have kidney disease, except under the advice and supervision of a physician. Keep this and all drugs out of the reach of children.

Drug Interaction Precaution: Do not take this product if you are presently taking a prescription antibiotic drug containing any form of tetracycline. As with all aluminum-containing antacids, Gelusil-M may prevent proper absorption of the tetracycline.

How Supplied:
Liquid—In plastic bottles of 12 fl oz (N 0071-2044-22).
Tablets—White, embossed W/C 045—individual strips of 10 in boxes of 100 (N 0071-0045-24).
Store between 59° and 86°F (15° and 30°C).

GELUSIL–II®
Antacid-Antiflatulent
Liquid/Tablets
High Potency

Each teaspoonful (5 ml) or tablet contains:
400 mg aluminum hydroxide
400 mg magnesium hydroxide
30 mg simethicone
Advantages:
● High acid-neutralizing capacity

● Low sodium content
● Simethicone for antiflatulent activity
● Good taste for better patient compliance
● Fast dissolution of chewed tablets for prompt relief
● Double strength antacid

Indications: Gelusil-II, a carefully balanced high-potency combination of two widely used antacids and the antiflatulent simethicone, is effective for the relief of symptoms associated with heartburn, sour stomach, and acid indigestion. Gelusil-II also provides symptomatic relief of hyperacidity associated with the diagnosis of peptic ulcer, gastritis, peptic esophagitis, gastric hyperacidity, and hiatal hernia. Gelusil-II may be used concomitantly for relief of pain. Gelusil-II is also indicated to alleviate or relieve the symptoms of gas, postoperative gas pain, or for use in endoscopic examination.

Actions and Uses: The proven neutralizing powers of aluminum hydroxide and magnesium hydroxide combine to give Gelusil-II dependable antacid action without the acid rebound sometimes associated with calcium carbonate. The higher potency of Gelusil-II is achieved by greater concentration of antacid ingredients per dosage unit.

The pleasant taste of Gelusil-II Liquid (citrus-flavored) and Tablets (orange-flavored) encourages patient acceptance of, and compliance with, recommended antacid regimens.

Gelusil-II Tablets are easy to chew and are specifically formulated to dissolve readily, providing prompt onset of action and reliable relief of symptoms.

Gelusil-II is appropriate whenever there is a need for well-accepted, effective antacid-antiflatulent therapy.

Dosage and Administration: Two or more teaspoonfuls or tablets one hour after meals and at bedtime, or as directed by a physician. Tablets should be chewed.

The following information is provided to facilitate treatment:

Gelusil-II	LIQUID	TABLETS
Acid-neutral-izing capacity	48 mEq/ 10 ml	42 mEq/ 2 tabs
Sodium	1.3 mg/ 5 ml	2.1 mg/ tab
Lactose	0	0

Warnings: Do not take more than 8 tablets or teaspoonfuls in a 24-hour period, or use this maximum dosage for more than two weeks, or use this product if you have kidney disease, except under the advice and supervision of a physician. Keep this and all drugs out of the reach of children.

Drug Interaction Precaution: Do not take this product if you are presently taking a prescription antibiotic drug containing any form of tetracycline. As with all aluminum-containing antacids, Gelusil-II may prevent proper absorption of the tetracycline.

How Supplied:
Liquid—In plastic bottles of 12 fl oz (N-0071-2042-22).

Tablets—Double-layered white/orange, embossed W/C 043—individual strips of 10 in boxes of 80 (N 0071-0043-22).
Store between 59° and 86°F (15° and 30°C).

GERIPLEX-FS® KAPSEALS®

Composition: Each Kapseal represents:
Vitamin A ....(1.5 mg) 5,000 IU* (acetate)
Vitamin C.. 50 mg (ascorbic acid)†
Vitamin B_1.. 5 mg (thiamine mononitrate)
Vitamin B_2.. 5 mg (riboflavin)
Vitamin B_{12}, crystalline (cyanocobalamin)......................... 2 mcg
Choline dihydrogen citrate.. 20 mg
Nicotinamide .... 15 mg (niacinamide)
Vitamin E (dl-alpha tocopheryl acetate) .... (5 mg) 5 IU*
Ferrous sulfate‡ .... 30 mg
Copper sulfate.................................... 4 mg
Manganese sulfate (monohydrate)................................ 4 mg
Zinc sulfate .... 2 mg
Calcium phosphate, dibasic (anhydrous)................................. 200 mg
Taka-Diastase® (aspergillus oryzae enzymes)...........................2½ gr.
Docusate sodium .... 100 mg

* International Units
†Supplied as sodium ascorbate
‡Supplied as dried ferrous sulfate equivalent to the labeled amount of ferrous sulfate

Action and Uses: A preparation containing vitamins, minerals, and a fecal softener for middle-aged and older individuals. The fecal softening agent, docusate sodium, acts to soften stools and make bowel movements easier.

Administration and Dosage: USUAL DOSAGE —One Kapseal daily, with or immediately after a meal.

How Supplied: N 0071-0544—Bottles of 100 and in unit-dose packages of 100 (10 strips of 10). Parcode® No. 544.

GERIPLEX-FS®
LIQUID
Geriatric Vitamin Formula with Iron and a Fecal Softener

Composition: Each 30 ml represents vitamin B_1 (thiamine hydrochloride), 1.2 mg; vitamin B_2 (as riboflavin-5'-phosphate sodium), 1.7 mg; vitamin B_6 (pyridoxine hydrochloride), 1 mg; vitamin B_{12} (cyanocobalamin) crystalline, 5 mcg; niacinamide, 15 mg; iron (as ferric

Continued on next page

This product information was prepared in December, 1980. On these and other Parke-Davis Products, detailed information may be obtained by addressing PARKE-DAVIS, Division of Warner-Lambert Company, Morris Plains, NJ 07950.

Parke-Davis—Cont.

ammonium citrate, green), 15 mg; Pluronic® F-68,* 200 mg; alcohol, 18%.

Administration and Dosage: USUAL ADULT DOSAGE—Two tablespoonfuls (30 ml) daily or as recommended by the physician.

How Supplied: N 0071-2454-23—Bottles of 16 fl oz (1 pt).

*Pluronic is a registered trademark of BASF Wyandotte Corporation for polymers of ethylene oxide and propylene oxide.

MYADEC®

Each tablet represents:		% of US Recommended Daily Allowances (US RDA)
Vitamins		
Vitamin A	10,000 IU*	200%
Vitamin D	400 IU	100%
Vitamin E	30 IU	100%
Vitamin C	250 mg	417%
Folic Acid	0.4 mg	100%
Thiamine	10 mg	667%
Riboflavin	10 mg	588%
Niacin†	100 mg	500%
Vitamin B$_6$	5 mg	250%
Vitamin B$_{12}$	6 mcg	100%
Pantothenic Acid	20 mg	200%
Minerals		
Iodine	150 mcg	100%
Iron	20 mg	111%
Magnesium	100 mg	25%
Copper	2 mg	100%
Zinc	20 mg	133%
Manganese	1.25 mg	‡

Ingredients: Sodium ascorbate, magnesium oxide, microcrystalline cellulose, niacinamide, ferrous fumarate, ascorbic acid, zinc sulfate monohydrate, gelatin, vitamin E acetate, polyvinylpyrrolidone, calcium pantothenate, hydroxypropyl methylcellulose, silicon dioxide, riboflavin, thiamine mononitrate, magnesium stearate, pyridoxine hydrochloride, propylene glycol, cupric sulfate anhydrous, sugar, manganese sulfate monohydrate, vitamin A acetate, ethylcellulose, citric acid anhydrous, polysorbate 80, folic acid, wax, potassium iodide, vitamin D$_2$, titanium dioxide, vanillin, FD&C Yellow No. 6, FD&C Blue No. 2, FD&C Red No. 3, and vitamin B$_{12}$.

* International Units
† Supplied as niacinamide
‡ No US Recommended Daily Allowance (US RDA) has been established for this nutrient.

Actions and Uses: For prevention of certain vitamin deficiencies. Also supplies various minerals normally present in body tissues.
Dosage: One tablet daily
How Supplied: N 0071-0335. In bottles of 130 and 250.
[*Shown in Product Identification Section*]

NATABEC® KAPSEALS®

Each capsule represents:

Vitamins	
Vitamin A	4,000 IU*
Vitamin D	400 IU
Vitamin C (ascorbic acid)	50 mg
Thiamine (vitamin B$_1$)	3 mg
Riboflavin (vitamin B$_2$)	2.0 mg
Nicotinamide (niacinamide)	10 mg
Vitamin B$_6$	3 mg
Vitamin B$_{12}$	5 mcg
Minerals	
Calcium carbonate	600 mg
Ferrous Sulfate**	150 mg

*IU = International Units
**Supplied as dried ferrous sulfate equivalent to the labeled amount of ferrous sulfate.
Action and Uses: A multivitamin and multimineral supplement for use during pregnancy and lactation.
Dosage: One Kapseal daily, or as directed by physician.
How Supplied: N 0071-0390. In bottles of 100. Parcode® 390.
The color combination of the banded capsule is a Parke-Davis trademark registered in the US Patent Office.

THERA-COMBEX H-P®
High-Potency Vitamin B Complex with 500 mg Vitamin C

Composition: Each Kapseal contains:

Ascorbic acid (vitamin C)	500 mg
Thiamine (vitamin B$_1$) mononitrate	25 mg
Riboflavin (vitamin B$_2$)	15 mg
Pyridoxine hydrochloride (vitamin B$_6$)	10 mg
Vitamin B$_{12}$ (cyanocobalamin)	5 mcg
Nicotinamide (niacinamide)	100 mg
dl-Panthenol	20 mg

Uses: For the prevention or treatment of vitamin B complex and vitamin C deficiencies.
Dosage: One or two capsules daily
How Supplied: N 0071-0550—Bottles of 30. Also unit-dose packages of ten 10s; Parcode® No. 550

TUCKS®
Premoistened Pads

Composition: Premoistened pads saturated with a solution containing witch hazel, 50%; glycerin, USP, 10%; purified water, USP, de-ionized, qs; buffered to approximately pH 4.6; methylparaben, USP, 0.1%, and benzalkonium chloride, USP, 0.003%, added as preservatives
Action and Uses: *Prophylactically,* as an after-stool wipe to remove most causes of local irritation; temporarily helps prevent pruritus ani and vulvae, and similar perianal or perineal irritations
As soothing, *cleansing* pad during menstruation, and in the temporary management of vulvitis, pruritus ani and vulvae.

As a *compress,* to temporarily help relieve the discomfort of simple hemorrhoids, anorectal surgical wounds, episiotomies
Warning: In case of continued irritation or rectal bleeding, discontinue use and consult physician promptly.
Dosage and Administration: Use in addition to toilet tissue. For further temporary relief, apply Tucks to affected areas for 15 to 30 minutes as needed.
How Supplied: Jars of 40 and 100. Also available as Tucks Take-Alongs®, individual, foil-wrapped, nonwoven wipes, 12 per box
Tucks—N 0071-1703
Tucks Take-Alongs—N 0071-1704-01
[*Shown in Product Identification Section*]

TUCKS® OINTMENT, CREAM

Composition: Tucks Ointment and Cream contain a specially formulated aqueous phase of 50% witch hazel (hamamelis water). Both have an acid pH, pleasant odor, and are nonstaining.
Action and Uses: Tucks Ointment and Tucks Cream exert a temporary, soothing, mildly astringent effect on such superficial irritations as hemorrhoids, pruritus ani and vulvae, postpartum discomfort, anorectal wounds. Tucks Cream is excellent for nipple care by nursing mothers.
Warning: If itching or irritation continue, discontinue use and consult your physician. In case of rectal bleeding, consult your physician promptly.
Dosage and Administration: Apply locally three or four times daily. Applicator provided for rectal instillation.
How Supplied: Tucks Ointment and Tucks Cream (water-washable) in 40-g tubes with rectal applicators
Tucks Ointment—N 0071-3021-14
Tucks Cream—N 0071-3022-14

ZIRADRYL® Lotion

Description: A green-tinted, pleasantly perfumed aqueous suspension of 2% Benadryl® (diphenhydramine hydrochloride) and 2% zinc oxide; contains 2% alcohol.
Indications: Antipruritic—zinc oxide-Benadryl lotion for relief of itching in ivy or oak poisoning.
Warning: *FOR EXTERNAL USE ONLY* Should not be applied to extensive, or raw, oozing areas, or for a prolonged time, except as directed by a physician. Hypersensitivity to any of the components may occur.
Caution: Do not use in the eyes. If the condition for which this preparation is used persists or if a rash or irritation develops, discontinue use and consult physician.
Directions: *SHAKE WELL*
For relief of itching, cleanse affected area and apply generously three or four times daily. Temporary stinging sensation may follow application. Discontinue use if stinging persists. Easily removed with water.
How Supplied: N 0071-3224-19 (Stock No. 22-3224-39) 6-oz bottles
[*Shown in Product Identification Section*]

Person & Covey, Inc.
616 ALLEN AVENUE
GLENDALE, CA 91201

A.C.N.®
Water-miscible Vitamin A,C, and Niacinamide Tablets

Description:
Each tablet contains: % of U.S. RDA*
Vitamin A ....25,000 I.U. 500
Ascorbic Acid ....250 mg 417
Niacinamide ....25 mg 125
*Percentage of U.S. Recommended Daily Allowance.
Indication: For use as a dietary supplement.
Dosage: One tablet daily as a dietary supplement. For adults and children 4 or more years of age.
Warnings: Keep all medication out of the reach of children. Store in a dry place at room temperature. Avoid heat.
How Supplied: In bottles of 100 tablets.
NDC 0096-0014-11

DHS™ Shampoo
Dermatological Hair and Scalp Shampoo

DHS™ contains a unique blend of special cleansing agents that provide a luxurious lather which cleans the hair and scalp.
DHS™ conditioners reduce the need for after rinses and leave the hair lustrously clean.
DHS™ is especially formulated for pH balance. DHS may be used daily.
Directions: (1) Wet hair thoroughly; apply DHS, lather and rinse. Reapply DHS, lather and rinse again. Repeat as necessary or as directed by your physician.
Caution: For external use only. Keep out of the reach of children. Avoid contact with the eyes.
Contents: purified water, TEA-lauryl sulfate, sodium-chloride, PEG-8 distearate, cocamide DEA, cocamide MEA, fragrance and FD&C yellow #6.
How Supplied: 8 fluid and 16 fluid ounce plastic bottles with easy to use dispenser.
NDC 0096-0727-08
NDC 0096-0727-16
[*Shown in Product Identification Section*]

DHS™ Tar Shampoo
Dermatological Hair and Scalp Shampoo

DHS™ Tar Shampoo aids in the control of the scaling of seborrhea (dandruff) and psoriasis of the scalp.
Directions: (1) Wet hair thoroughly; apply a liberal quantity of DHS™ Tar Shampoo and massage into a lather. (2) Rinse thoroughly and repeat application. (3) Allow lather to remain on scalp for about 5 minutes. (4) Use DHS Tar Shampoo once or twice weekly or as directed by your physician.
Caution: Avoid contact with the eyes. In case of contact, wash out with water. If irritation occurs, discontinue use and consult physician.

Warning: Keep out of the reach of children. For external use only.
DHS™ Tar Shampoo contains: Tar, equivalent to 0.5% Coal Tar U.S.P., TEA-lauryl sulfate, purified water, sodium chloride, PEG-8 disterate, cocamide DEA, cocamide MEA.
How Supplied: 4 and 8 fluid ounce plastic bottles with easy to use dispenser.
NDC 0096-0728-04
NDC 0096-0728-08
[*Shown in Product Identification Section*]

DHS™ Zinc Dandruff Shampoo
2% Zinc Pyrithione

DHS™ Zinc Shampoo aids in the control of dandruff/seborrheic dermatitis of the scalp.
Directions: Shake well before using. (1) Wet hair thoroughly; apply a liberal quantity of DHS™ Zinc and massage into a lather. (2) Rinse thoroughly and repeat application. (3) Allow lather to remain on scalp for about 5 minutes. (4) Use DHS Zinc at least twice weekly for the first two weeks then regularly thereafter, or as directed by physician.
Caution: Avoid contact with eyes. In case of contact, wash out with water. If irritation occurs, discontinue use and consult physician.
Warning: Keep out of the reach of children. For external use only.
DHS™ Zinc contains: 2% zinc pyrithione, purified water, TEA-lauryl sulfate, PEG-8 distearate, sodium chloride, cocamide DEA, cocamide MEA, magnesium aluminum silicate, hydroxypropyl methylcellulose, fragrance, and FD&C yellow #6.
How Supplied: 6 fluid ounce plastic bottles.
NDC 0096-0729-06.
[*Shown in Product Identification Section*]

ENISYL™ Tablets
Lysine Hydrochloride

Composition: Each tablet contains Lysine 334 mg and 500 mg respectively (from the hydrochloride).
Indication: For use as a dietary supplement.
Dosage: Adults: one to three tablets daily as a dietary supplement.
Actions: Improves utilization of vegetable proteins such as rice, wheat, corn, etc.
Warnings: Keep out of the reach of children. Store in a dry place at room temperature. Avoid heat.
How Supplied: In bottles of 100 and 250 tablets. 334 and 500 mg.
NDC 0096-0777-11   NDC 0096-0777-52
NDC 0096-0778-11   NDC 0096-0778-52

SOLBAR® Plus 15

Solbar® Plus 15: Specially formulated to provide ultra protection from the sun's burning and tanning rays. Provides a high degree of sunburn protection for sun sensitive skin and fair skinned persons, blondes, brunettes and redheads. Fragrant-free formula ... contains no drying alcohol.

Directions: Smooth evenly on all exposed skin. To ensure maximum protection reapply after swimming or exercise.
Caution: For external use only. If irritation or sensitization occurs discontinue use and consult a physician. Avoid contact with the eyes. Keep this and all drugs out of the reach of children. Solbar® Plus 15 contains: Oxybenzone USP 5%, Ethyl Dihydroxypropyl PABA 5%, Purified Water, Isopropyl Palmitate, PPG-20 Lanolin Ether, PPG-2 Lanolin Ether, Glyceryl Stearate, PEG-100 Stearate, Carbomer 934, PEG-15 Cocamine, Sodium Hydroxide, Methylparaben, Propylparaben.
How Supplied: 4 ounce plastic tube.
NDC 0096-0681-04

XERAC®
(alcohol gel)

Composition:
Isopropyl Alcohol 44%
Microcrystalline Sulfur 4%
Effects: A medicated antiseptic gel to promote drying and peeling of the skin. An aid in the management of acne. Invisible when applied to the skin.
Directions: Apply a thin film to affected areas one to three times daily, or as directed by physician.
Precautions: Avoid overuse. If undue skin irritation develops or becomes excessive, discontinue use and consult physician. Avoid contact with eyes. Keep this and all medication out of the reach of children. For external use only.
How Supplied: 45 g (1-½ oz.) plastic tube.
NDC 0096-0787-45

Pfipharmecs Division
PFIZER INC.
235 EAST 42ND STREET
NEW YORK, NY 10017

BACITRACIN TOPICAL OINTMENT

How Supplied: Each gram contains 500 units of Bacitracin. Available in ½ oz tubes sold in cartons of twelve. A prescription is not required.

BONINE
(meclizine HCl)

For motion sickness. Available in convenient OTC packet of 8 chewable tablets of 25 mg meclizine HCl. No prescription required.
[*Shown in Product Identification Section*]

CORTRIL® 1/2% CREAM
(hydrocortisone 1/2%)

Active Ingredient: Hydrocortisone ½%
Indications: For the temporary relief of minor skin irritations, itching, and rashes due to poison ivy, poison oak or poison sumac, eczema, dermititis, insect bites, soaps, detergents, cosmetics, and jewelry, and for itchy genital and anal areas.

Continued on next page

Pfipharmecs—Cont.

Actions: Antipruritic (anti-itch)
Warnings: For external use only. Avoid contact with eyes. If condition worsens, or if symptoms persist for more than 7 days, discontinue use of this product and consult a physician. Do not use on children under 2 years of age except under the advice and supervision of a physician.
Dosage and Administration: For adults and children 2 years of age or older. Apply to affected area not more than 3 to 4 times daily. For children under 2 years of age, there is no recommended dosage except under the advice and supervision of a physician.
How Supplied: 1 ounce tube.
[*Shown in Product Identification Section*]

CORYBAN®-D CAPSULES
Decongestant Cold Capsules

Composition: Each capsule contains:
Caffeine U.S.P. ....30 mg.
Chlorpheniramine maleate
  U.S.P..2 mg.
Phenylpropanolamine HCl ....25 mg.
Indications: Coryban-D is a combination of ingredients designed to relieve nasal/sinus congestion, runny nose and watery eyes.
Administration and Dosage: Adults — two capsules three times a day, not to exceed six capsules in 24 hours. Children 6 to 12—one capsule three times a day, not to exceed three capsules in 24 hours. A physician should be consulted if symptoms persist. For children under 6 years, as directed by a physician.
Warning: Drowsiness may appear in some cases. If this occurs, the operation of vehicles or machinery should be avoided. Individuals with high blood pressure, heart disease, diabetes or thyroid disease should use only as directed by a physician. Coryban-D should be kept out of the reach of children.
How Supplied: In bottles of 24 or packs of 12, light and dark blue capsules.
[*Shown in Product Identification Section*]

CORYBAN®-D COUGH SYRUP
With Decongestant

Composition: Each 5 ml (1 teaspoonful) contains:
Dextromethorphan HBr U.S.P....7.5 mg.
Guaifenesin ....50 mg.
Phenylephrine HCl..........................5 mg.
Acetaminophen ....120 mg.
Alcohol*...7.5%
* Small loss unavoidable
Description: Coryban-D cough syrup is a non-narcotic, cough suppressant containing a combination of ingredients which act to provide relief of common symptoms associated with coughs due to colds or allergy.
Indications:
Coryban-D provides effective relief from
• irritating coughs due to colds, flu or allergy yet non-narcotic.
• stuffy nose due to the common cold, hay fever and other allergies.

• chest congestion by liquefying and loosening bronchial mucus.
• aches and pains accompanying a cold.
Administration and Dosage: Adults — two teaspoonfuls every four hours not to exceed 12 teaspoonfuls in a 24 hour period. Children 6 to 12 years—one-half adult dosage. Children 3 to 6 years—one-half teaspoonful every four hours not to exceed 3 teaspoonfuls in a 24 hour period. Under 3 years—as directed by physician.
Warning: Unless directed by a physician, the recommended dosage should not be exceeded. Coryban-D Cough Syrup should not be used longer than ten days, or given to children under 6 years of age. Because drowsiness may occur, patients should not drive or operate machinery. If high fever or persistent coughs are observed, a serious condition may be present and Coryban-D Cough Syrup should be used only with the physician's approval. Individuals with high blood pressure, heart disease, diabetes, or thyroid disease should use only as directed by the physician. Keep out of the reach of children.
How Supplied: Coryban-D Cough Syrup is available in 4-ounce dripless spout bottles. Sorbitol, which is contained in this product, is a nutritive, carbohydrate sweetening agent which is metabolized more slowly than sugar.
**Recommended Storage: Store below 77°F. (25°C.)
Do not refrigerate.**
[*Shown in Product Identification Section*]

LI-BAN™ SPRAY
Lice Control Spray
not for use on humans

Active Ingredient:
(5-Benzyl-3-furyl) methyl 2.2-
  dimethyl-3-(2-methylpropenyl)
  cyclopropanecarboxylate   0.500%
Related Compounds   0.068%
Aromatic petroleum
  hydrocarbons   0.664%
Inert Ingredients   98.768%
                  100.000%
Indications: A highly active synthetic pyrethroid for the control of lice and louse eggs on garments, bedding, furniture and other inanimate objects.
Precaution: PRECAUTIONARY STATEMENTS: HAZARDS TO HUMANS AND DOMESTIC ANIMALS CAUTION: Avoid contamination of feed and foodstuffs. Cover or remove fishbowls. **This product is not for use on humans or animals.** If lice infestations should occur on humans, consult either your physician or pharmacist for a product for use on humans.
PHYSICAL OR CHEMICAL HAZARDS: Contents under pressure. Do not use or store near heat or open flame. Do not puncture or incinerate container. Exposure to temperatures above 130°F may cause bursting.
Dosage and Administration: DIRECTIONS FOR USE: It is a violation of Federal law to use this product in a manner inconsistent with its labeling.

Shake well before each use. Remove protective cap. Aim spray opening away from person. Push button to spray.
To kill lice and louse eggs: Spray in an inconspicuous area to test for possible staining or discoloration. Inspect again after drying, then proceed to spray entire area to be treated.
Hold container upright with nozzle away from you. Depress valve and spray from a distance of 8 to 10 inches.
Spray each square foot for 3 seconds.
Spray only those garments, parts of bedding, including mattresses and furniture that cannot be either laundered or dry cleaned.
Allow all sprayed articles to dry thoroughly before use.
Repeat treatment as necessary.
Buyer assumes all risks of use, storage or handling of this material not in strict accordance with directions given herewith.
DISPOSAL OF CONTAINER
Wrap container and dispose of in trash. Do not incinerate.
How Supplied: 5 ounce aerosol can with instruction brochure.
[*Shown in Product Identification Section*]

OBRON-6® Tablets   OTC
Prenatal Vitamins

Each tablet provides the listed vitamins and minerals:

VITAMINS	AMOUNT	% US RDA*
Vitamin A	5,000 IU	62.5
Vitamin D	400 IU	100
Vitamin C	50 mg	83
Vitamin B_1	3 mg	176
Vitamin B_2	2 mg	100
Niacin	20 mg	100
Vitamin B_6	8.2 mg	328
Vitamin B_{12}	2 mcg	25
Pantothenic Acid	0.92 mg	9
MINERALS		
Calcium	243 mg	18.7
Iron	33 mg	183
Magnesium	1 mg	0.2
Zinc	0.4 mg	2.7
Manganese	0.33 mg	**
Potassium	1.7 mg	**

Recommended Dosage: One tablet daily, or as directed by physician.
How Supplied: In bottles of 100 pink sugar free tablets.
*Percentage of U.S. Recommended Daily Allowance (RDA) for pregnant or lactating women.
**Manganese and potassium are recognized as essential in human nutrition, but no U.S. RDA has been established.

RID™
Liquid Pediculicide

Description: Rid is a liquid pediculicide whose active ingredients are: pyrethrins 0.3%, piperonyl butoxide, technical 3.00%, equivalent to 2.4% (butylcarbityl) (6-propylpiperonyl) ether and to 0.6% related compounds, petroleum distillate 1.20% and benzyl alcohol 2.4%. Inert ingredients 93.1%.
Actions: RID kills head lice (Pediculus humanus capitis), body lice (Pediculus humanus humanus), and pubic or crab

lice (Phthirus pubis), and their eggs on contact.

The pyrethrins act as a contact poison and affect the parasite's nervous system, resulting in paralysis and death. The efficacy of the pyrethrins is enhanced by the synergist, piperonyl butoxide.

Indications: RID is indicated for the treatment of infestations of head lice, body lice and pubic (crab) lice and their eggs.

Warning: RID should not be used by ragweed sensitized persons.

Precautions: This product is for external use only. It is harmful if swallowed. It should not be inhaled. It should be kept out of the eyes and contact with mucous membranes should be avoided. If accidental contact with eyes occurs, flush immediately with water. In case of infection or skin irritation, discontinue use and consult a physician. Consult a physician if infestation of eyebrows or eyelashes occurs. Avoid contamination of feed or foodstuffs. Do not reuse container. Destroy when empty.

Do not transport or store below 32°F (0°C).

Dosage and Administration: (1) Apply RID undiluted to hair and scalp or to any other infested area until entirely wet. Do not use on eyelashes or eyebrows. (2) Allow RID to remain on area for 10 minutes but no longer. (3) Wash thoroughly with warm water and soap or shampoo. (4) Dead lice and eggs may require removal with fine-toothed comb provided. A second application is seldom needed. If necessary, treatment may be repeated but do not exceed two consecutive applications within 24 hours.

Since lice infestations are spread by contact, each family member should be examined carefully. If infested, he or she should be treated promptly to avoid spread or reinfestation of previously treated individuals. Contaminated clothing and other articles, such as hats, etc. should be dry cleaned, boiled or otherwise treated until decontaminated to prevent reinfestation or spread.

How Supplied: In 2 and 4 fl. oz. bottles. Fine-toothed comb to aid in removal of dead lice and nits and patient instruction booklet are included in each package of RID.

[*Shown in Product Identification Section*]

ROERIBEC® TABLETS
High Potency B Complex with 500 mg. of Vitamin C

Composition: Each tablet contains:

		%RDA
Vitamin C		
(L-Ascorbic Acid)	500 mg	833
Vitamin B₁		
(Thiamine Mononitrate)	10 mg	666
Vitamin B₂		
(Riboflavin)	10 mg	590
Niacin (Niacinamide)	100 mg	500
Vitamin B₆		
(Pyridoxine Hydrochloride)	8.2 mg	410
Vitamin B₁₂		
(Cyanocobalamin)	4 mcg	67

Pantothenic Acid

(Calcium
Pantothenate) .... 18 mg 180

Dosage: One tablet daily or as directed by a physician.

How Supplied: RoeriBeC is supplied in bottles of 100 red, easy-to-swallow film coated (sugar free) tablets.

TERRAMYCIN® OINTMENT
(oxytetracycline hydrochloride topical ointment with polymyxin B sulfate)

How Supplied: Each gram contains oxytetracycline hydrochloride equivalent to 30 mg. of oxytetracycline; and also 10,000 units of polymyxin B sulfate. Available in ½ ounce and one ounce tubes, both sizes sold in cartons of twelve. A prescription is *not* required.
[*Shown in Product Identification Section*]

VITERRA C

How Supplied: Available as 250 mg & 500 mg tablets, in bottles of 100.
[*Shown in Product Identification Section*]

VITERRA E

How Supplied: Available as capsules of 100 I.U., 200 I.U., 400 I.U. and 600 I.U., in bottles of 100.
[*Shown in Product Identification Section*]

VITERRA® ORIGINAL FORMULA TABLETS
Vitamins and Minerals

Composition: Each tablet contains:

		% U.S.
Vitamins	**Amount**	**RDA***
Vitamin A		
(Vitamin A Acetate)	5,000 IU	100
Vitamin D		
(Ergocalciferol)	400 IU	100
Vitamin E		
(dl-Alpha Tocopheryl Acetate)	3.7 IU	12
Vitamin C		
(L-Ascorbic Acid)	50 mg	83
Vitamin B₁		
(Thiamine Mononitrate)	3 mg	200
Vitamin B₂ (Riboflavin)	3 mg	176
Niacin (Niacinamide)	25 mg	125
Vitamin B₆		
(Pyridoxine Hydrochloride)	0.82 mg	41
Vitamin B₁₂		
(Cyanocobalamin)	2 mcg	33
Pantothenic Acid		
(D-Calcium Pantothenate)	4.6 mg	46
Minerals		
Calcium (Calcium Carbonate and Dibasic Calcium Phosphate)	140 mg	14
Phosphorous (Dibasic Calcium Phosphate)	70 mg	7
Iodine (Potassium Iodide)	150 mcg	100
Iron (Ferrous Fumarate)	10 mg	55
Magnesium (Magnesium Sulfate)	5 mg	1.25
Copper (Cupric Sulfate)	1 mg	50
Zinc (Zinc Sulfate)	1.2 mg	8

Manganese
(Manganese Sulfate)   1 mg   **

* Percentage of U.S. Recommended Daily Allowance (RDA) for adults and children 4 or more years of age.
** Manganese is recognized as essential in human nutrition but no U.S. RDA has been established.

Description: An original formula containing vitamins plus minerals.
Administration and Dosage: One tablet daily, or as directed by a physician.
How Supplied: In bottles of 100 yellow film coated (sugar free) tablets.
[*Shown in Product Identification Section*]

VITERRA® HIGH POTENCY TABLETS
Vitamins and Minerals

Composition: Each tablet contains:

		% U.S.
Vitamins	**Amount**	**RDA***
Vitamin A		
(Vitamin A Acetate)	10,000 IU	200
Vitamin D		
(Ergocalciferol)	400 IU	100
Vitamin E (dl Alpha Tocopheryl Acetate)	5 IU	16.7
Vitamin C		
(L-Ascorbic Acid)	150 mg	250
Vitamin B₁		
(Thiamine Mononitrate)	10 mg	666
Vitamin B₂ (Riboflavin)	10 mg	590
Niacin (Niacinamide)	100 mg	500
Vitamin B₆		
(Pyridoxine Hydrochloride)	1.6 mg	80
Vitamin B₁₂		
(Cyanocobalamin)	5 mcg	83
Pantothenic Acid		
(Calcium Pantothenate)	4.6 mg	46
Minerals		
Calcium (Calcium Carbonate)	0.05 g	5
Iodine (Potassium Iodide)	150 mcg	100
Iron (Ferrous Fumarate)	10 mg	55
Magnesium (Magnesium Sulfate)	5 mg	1.25
Copper (Cupric Sulfate)	1 mg	50
Zinc (Zinc Sulfate)	1.2 mg	8
Manganese (Manganese Sulfate)	1 mg	**

* Percentage of U.S. Recommended Daily Allowance (RDA) for adults and children 4 or more years of age.
** Manganese is recognized as essential in human nutrition but no U.S. RDA has been established.

Description: A higher potency formula containing vitamins plus minerals.
Administration and Dosage: One tablet daily, or as directed by a physician.
How Supplied: In bottles of 100 salmon-red film coated (sugar free) tablets.
[*Shown in Product Identification Section*]

WART–OFF™

Active Ingredient: Salicylic Acid, U.S.P., 17%, in Flexible Collodion, U.S.P.
Indications: Removal of Warts
Warnings: Keep this and all medications out of reach of children to avoid accidental poisoning.
Flammable—Do not use near fire or flame. For external use only. In case of

Continued on next page

Pfipharmecs—Cont.

accidental ingestion, contact a physician or a Poison Control Center immediately. Do not use near eyes or on mucous membranes. Diabetics or other people with impaired circulation should not use Wart-Off™. Do not use on moles, birthmarks or unusual warts with hair growing from them. If wart persists, see your physician. If pain should develop, consult your physician. **Do not apply to surrounding skin.**

Dosage and Administration: Instructions For Use: Read warning and enclosed instructional brochure. Apply Wart-Off™ to warts only. Before applying, soak affected area in hot water for several minutes. If any tissue has been loosened, remove by rubbing surface of wart gently with special brush enclosed in Wart-Off™ package. Dry thoroughly. Warts are contagious, so don't share your towel. Apply once or twice daily. Using plastic applicator attached to cap, apply one drop at a time until entire wart is covered. Lightly cover with small adhesive bandage. Replace cap tightly. This treatment may be used daily for three to four weeks if necessary.

How Supplied: 0.5 fluid ounce bottle with pinpoint plastic applicator, special cleaning brush and instructional brochure.

[*Shown in Product Identification Section*]

Pharmacraft Division
**PENNWALT CORPORATION
755 JEFFERSON ROAD
ROCHESTER, NY 14623**

ALLEREST® TABLETS, CHILDREN'S CHEWABLE TABLETS, HEADACHE STRENGTH TABLETS, TIMED RELEASE CAPSULES

Active Ingredients:
acetaminophen
　Headache Strength, 325 mg.
chlorpheniramine maleate
　Tablets, 2 mg.
　Children's Chewables, 1 mg.
　Timed Release, 4 mg.
phenylpropanolamine HCl
　Tablets, 18.7 mg.
　Children's Chewables, 9.4 mg.
　Headache Strength, 18.7 mg.
　Timed Release, 50 mg.

Indications: Allerest is indicated for symptomatic relief of hay fever, pollen allergies, upper respiratory allergies (perennial allergic rhinitis), allergic colds, sinusitis and nasal passage congestion. Those symptoms include headache pain, sneezing, runny nose, itching or watery eyes and itching nose and throat.

Actions: Allerest contains the antihistamine chlorpheniramine maleate which acts to suppress the symptoms of allergic rhinitis. In addition, it contains the decongestant phenylpropanolamine which acts to reduce swelling of the upper respiratory tract mucosa. Headache Strength also contains acetaminophen to relieve headache pain.

Contraindications: Known hypersensitivity to the ingredients in this drug.

Warnings: Allerest should be used with caution in patients with cardiac disorders, hypertension, hyperthyroidism or diabetes. Since drowsiness may occur, patients should be instructed not to operate a car or machinery.

Adverse Reactions: Drowsiness; excitability, especially in children; nervousness; and dizziness.

Dosage and Administration: TABLETS AND HEADACHE STRENGTH —Adult, 2 tablets every 4 hours. Not to exceed 8 tablets in 24 hours. Children (6–12)—half the adult dose. Dosage for children under 6 should be individualized under the supervision of a physician. CHILDREN'S CHEWABLE TABLETS—Children (6–12) 2 tablets every 4 hours. Not to exceed 8 tablets in 24 hours. Children under 6 consult a physician. Adults double the children's dose. TIMED RELEASE CAPSULES—Adults, 1 capsule in the morning and one capsule in the evening. If symptoms are especially severe, one capsule every 8 hours may be taken. Not to exceed 3 capsules in 24 hours. Do not give to children under 12 years without physician's approval.

Overdosage: Acetaminophen in massive overdosage may cause hepatotoxicity.

Drug Interaction Precautions: Not to be taken by patients currently taking a prescription antihypertensive or antidepressant drug containing a monoamine oxidase inhibitor except under the advice and supervision of a physician.
Antihistamines and oral nasal decongestants have additive effects with alcohol and other CNS depressants.

How Supplied: TABLETS packaged on blister cards in 24 and 48 count cartons, and in 75 count glass bottles. CHILDREN'S CHEWABLE TABLETS packaged on blister cards in 24 count cartons. HEADACHE STRENGTH TABLETS packaged on blister cards in 24 and 48 count cartons. CAPSULES supplied in bottles of 10 and 20 count.

CaldeCORT®

Active Ingredient: hydrocortisone acetate (equivalent to hydrocortisone 0.5%)

Indications: Provides temporary relief from itching, minor skin irritations and rashes due to eczema, dermatitis, insect bites, poison ivy, poison oak, poison sumac, soaps, detergents, cosmetics and jewelry, and for itchy genital and anal areas.

Actions: An anti-dermatitis cream for the temporary relief from itching and minior skin irritations.

Warnings: For external use only. Avoid contact with the eyes. If condition worsens, or if symptoms persist for more than 7 days, discontinue use of this product and consult a physician. Do not use on children under 2 years of age except under the advice and supervision of a physician.

Dosage and Administration: For adults and children 2 years of age and older: Apply to affected area not more than 3 or 4 times daily. For children un-der 2 years of age: There is no recommended dosage except under the advice and supervision of a physician.

How Supplied: Anti-Itch Cream, ½ and 1 oz. tubes.

CALDESENE® MEDICATED POWDER AND OINTMENT

Active Ingredients:
calcium
undecylenate
　Powder, 10%
zinc oxide
　Cream

Indications: Caldesene Medicated Powder is indicated to help heal, relieve and prevent diaper rash, prickly heat and chafing. Medicated Ointment helps prevent diaper rash and sooth minor skin irritations.

Actions: Antifungal and antibacterial Medicated Powder inhibits the growth of bacteria and fungi which cause diaper rash. Also, forms a protective coating to repel moisture, sooth and comfort minor skin irritations, helps heal and prevent chafing and prickly heat. Medicated Ointment forms a protective skin coating to repel moisture and promote healing of diaper rash, while its natural ingredients protect irritated skin against wetness. Sooths minor skin irritations, superficial wounds and burns.

Warnings: Keep this and all drugs out of the reach of children. In case of accidental ingestion, seek professional assistance or contact a Poison Control Center immediately.

Dosage and Administration: Cleanse and dry affected area. Smooth on Caldesene 3–4 times daily, or after each diaper change, or as directed by a physician.

How Supplied: Medicated Powder, 2.0 oz. and 5.0 oz. shaker containers. Medicated Ointment; 1.25 oz. and 4.0 oz. collapsible tubes.

CRUEX® MEDICATED POWDER AND CREAM

Active Ingredients:
calcium
undecylenate
　Powder, 10%
zinc undecylenate
　Cream, 20%
p-chlor-m-xylenol
　Cream, 3%

Indications: Recommended for the relief and prevention of Jock Itch (Tinea cruris) and relief of excessive perspiration, itching, chafing, rash and irritation in the groin area. Cruex relieves odor too.

Actions: Antifungal Medicated Powder is effective in the treatment of superficial fungous infections of the skin. Antifungal and antibacterial Medicated Cream is effective in the treatment and prevention of superficial infections of the skin.

Warnings: For external use only. Keep away from eyes and other mucous membranes. Use only as directed. Do not use if skin is pustular or severely broken—consult your physician. Keep this and all drugs out of the reach of children. In case of accidental ingestion, seek professional assistance or contact a Poison Control Center immediately. For aerosol container only; contents under pressure. Do not puncture or incinerate. Flammable mixture, do not use near a fire or flame. Do not store at temperature above 120° F. Use only as directed. Intentional misuse by deliberately concentrating and inhaling the contents can be harmful or fatal.

Dosage and Administration: Cleanse and dry the affected area. Apply Cruex Medicated Powder to affected area once or twice a day or as directed by a physician. Apply Cruex Medicated Cream liberally as often as needed or as directed by a physician. For the best results rub cream into the skin.

How Supplied: Medicated Powder, 1.8 oz., 3.5 oz. and 5.5 oz. aerosol containers; 1.5 oz. and 3.0 oz. plastic squeeze bottles. Medicated Cream, 15 gm. tube.

DESENEX® ANTIFUNGAL POWDER, PENETRATING FOAM, OINTMENT, FOOT & SNEAKER SPRAY, LIQUID AND SOAP

Active Ingredients:
undecylenic acid
Powder, 2%
Ointment, 5%
Penetrating Foam, 10%
Liquid, 10%
Soap, 2%
zinc undecylenate
Powder, 20%
Ointment, 20%
isopropyl alcohol
Penetrating Foam, 35.2%
Liquid, 47%
aluminum chlorhydrex PG
Foot & Sneaker Spray
alcohol
Foot & Sneaker Spray, 89.3%,v/v
Indications: Desenex is indicated for the topical treatment of Athlete's Foot (T. rubrum, T. mentagrophytes, T. floccosum) and ringworm of the body exclusive of the nails and scalp.
Action: Medicated Powders Ointment and Penetrating Foam are effective antifungal treatment of superficial fungous infections of the skin. Penetrating Foam quickly dissolves into a highly concentrated liquid. Foot & Sneaker Spray is a formulated liquid that dries to a fine powder to protect feet from odor causing perspiration wetness. Powder also helps keep feet dry and comfortable. Medicated Liquid is effective antifungal and antibacterial treatment of superficial infections of the skin.
Warnings: For external use only. If symptoms do not improve in 4 weeks, discontinue use and consult your physician. Desenex is not recommended for nail or scalp infections. Keep this and all drugs out of the reach of children. In case of accidental ingestion, seek professional assistance or contact a Poison Control Center immediately. For Liquid and Foam; Do not use near eyes. For Spray-On Powder, Foot & Sneaker Spray and Penetrating Foam only; Contents under pressure. Do not puncture or incinerate. Flammable mixture, do not use near fire or flame. Do not store at temperature above 120° F. Use only as directed. Intentional misuse

by deliberately concentrating and inhaling the contents can be harmful or fatal.
Dosage and Administration: Cleanse affected and adjacent areas morning and evening with soap (such as Desenex Soap) and water. Powder-dust powder gently on the skin. To assure continued prophylaxis against fungous infections, dust powder freely between the toes and over the feet. Ointment—apply liberally every night before retiring. If condition persists, a physician or foot specialist should be contacted. Soap—work up into rich lather using hot or warm water. Rinse and dry thoroughly. Use at least twice daily or as recommended by a physician or foot specialist. Frequent use is recommended to obtain maximum effectiveness. Liquid and Spray—hold the bottle or can at a convenient angle and press down on the valve, aiming spray at affected areas from a distance of 4 to 6 inches. Spray liberally in between and around toes for Athlete's Foot. Foot & Sneaker Spray—shake can well, hold 6 inches from area and spray onto the soles of your feet, and between toes daily. To curtail foot, shoe and sneaker odor, spray liberally over entire inside area of shoes and sneakers. After spraying, allow sneakers to dry one minute before wearing. Penetrating Foam—Shake well. INVERT CONTAINER and direct Penetrating Foam between toes and other infected foot areas. Apply twice daily or as needed.
How Supplied: Spray-On Powder; 2.7 oz. and 5.5 oz. aerosol containers. Powder, 1.5 oz. and 3.0 oz. shaker containers. Ointment; 0.9 oz. and 1.8 oz. tubes. Liquid; 1.5 oz. pump spray bottle. Foot & Sneaker Spray; 2.7 oz. aerosol container. Penetrating Foam; 1.5 oz. aerosol container. Soap; 3.25 oz. bar.

SINAREST® TABLETS

Active Ingredients:
acetaminophen:
Tablets, 325 mg.
Extra Strength, 500 mg.
chlorpheniramine maleate
Tablets 2 mg.
Extra Strength, 2 mg.
phenylpropanolamine HCl
Tablets, 18.7 mg.
Extra Strength, 18.7 mg.
Indications: Sinarest is indicated for symptomatic relief from the headache pain, pressure and congestion associated with sinusitis, allergic rhinitis or the common cold.
Actions: Sinarest contains an antihistamine (chlorpheniramine maleate) and a decongestant (phenylpropanolamine) for the relief of sinus and nasal passage congestion as well as an analgesic (acetaminophen) to relieve pain and discomfort.
Contraindications: Known hypersensitivity to any of the ingredients in this compound.
Warnings: Sinarest should be used with caution in patients with high blood pressure, heart disease, diabetes or thyroid disease. Since drowsiness may occur, patients should be instructed not to operate a car or machinery. This product

should not be taken for more than 10 consecutive days.
Adverse Reactions: Drowsiness; excitability, especially in children; nervousness; and dizziness.
Dosage and Administration: SINAREST TABLETS—Adult—take 2 tablets every 4 hours. Not to exceed 8 tablets in 24 hours. Children (6–12 years)—One half of adult dosage. Dosage for children under 6 should be individualized under the supervision of a physician. EXTRA STRENGTH TABLETS—Adults and Children over 12—take 2 tablets every 6 hours. Not to exceed 8 tablets in 24 hours. Not recommended for children 12 and under.
Overdosage: Acetaminophen in massive overdosage may cause hepatotoxicity.
Drug Interaction Precaution: Not to be taken by patients currently taking a prescription antihypertensive or antidepressant drug containing a monoamine oxidase inhibitor except under the advice and supervision of a physician. Antihistamines and oral nasal decongestants have additive effects with alcohol and other CNS depressants.
How Supplied: Blister packages of 20 and 40 tablets and 80 tablet bottle. Extra Strength tablets: packages of 24 and 48 tablets.

Plough, Inc.
3030 JACKSON AVENUE
MEMPHIS, TN 38151

AFTATE®
Antifungal
Sprinkle Powder/Aerosol Spray Powder
Aerosol Spray Liquid/Pump Spray Liquid/Gel

Active Ingredients: Tolnaftate 1% (Also contains: Aerosol Spray Liquid—36% alcohol; Pump Spray Liquid—83% alcohol; Aerosol Spray Powder—14% alcohol.)
Indications: AFTATE affords excellent topical treatment and prophylaxis of tinea pedis, tinea cruris, tinea corporis, and tinea manuum due to infection with *Trichophyton rubrum, Trichophyton mentagrophytes and Epidermophyton floccosum.*
Actions: AFTATE is a highly active synthetic fungicidal agent that is effective in the treatment of superficial fungus infections of the skin. It is inactive systemically, virtually nonsensitizing, and does not ordinarily sting or irritate intact or broken skin, even in the presence of acute inflammatory reactions.
Warnings: For external use only. Keep out of eyes. Not recommended for nail and scalp infections. If symptoms do not improve in ten (10) days or if irritation occurs, discontinue use unless directed otherwise by a physician.
Dosage and Administration: Liberal use, twice daily.

Continued on next page

Plough—Cont.

How Supplied:
AFTATE for Athlete's Foot
Sprinkle Powder—2.25 oz. bottle.
Aerosol Spray Powder—3.5 oz. can
Gel—.5 oz. tube.
Aerosol Spray Liquid—4 oz. can.
Pump Spray Liquid—1.5 fl. oz. bottle.
AFTATE for Jock Itch
Aerosol Spray Powder—3.5 oz. can.
Sprinkle Powder—1.5 oz. bottle.
Gel—.5 oz. tube.
[*Shown in Product Identification Section*]

ASPERGUM®
Analgesic
Gum Tablet

Active Ingredients: Each gum tablet contains aspirin 3½ gr.
Indications: For temporary relief of minor sore throat pain, simple headache, aches and pains of colds and flu, and muscular aches and pains.
Actions: ASPERGUM is a convenient way to administer aspirin to children and adults who cannot or will not gargle properly or who cannot readily swallow tablets.
Warnings: Do not use more than 2 days or administer to children under 3 years of age unless directed by a physician.
Do not exceed maximum dosage (in adults) of 16 tablets in 24 hours; (in children 6–12 years) of 8 tablets in 24 hours, unless directed by physician; (in children 3–6 years) of 3 tablets in 24 hours.
Precaution: ASPERGUM is not intended for treatment of severe or persistent sore throat pain, high fever, headache, nausea or vomiting.
Dosage and Administration: Adults—chew 2 tablets; repeat as required up to a maximum of 16 in any 24 hour period, or as directed by physician. Children—6 to 12 years—chew 1 to 2 tablets as required up to 8 daily, or as directed by physician. Children—3 to 6 years—chew 1 tablet as required up to 3 daily. Children under 3 years of age, consult physician.
How Supplied:
ASPERGUM tablets in chewing gum form. Individual blister packaging.
Orange flavored: boxes of 16 and 40 tablets.
Cherry flavored: boxes of 16 and 40 tablets.
[*Shown in Product Identification Section*]

CORRECTOL®
Laxative
Tablets

Active Ingredients: Yellow phenolphthalein, 65 mg. and docusate sodium, 100 mg. per tablet.
Indications: For temporary relief of constipation.
Actions: Yellow phenolphthalein—stimulant laxative; docusate sodium—fecal softener.
Warnings: Not to be taken in case of nausea, vomiting, abdominal pain, or signs of appendicitis. Take only as needed —as frequent or continued use of laxatives may result in dependence on them. If skin rash appears, do not use this or any other preparation containing phenolphthalein.
Dosage and Administration
Dosage: Adults—1 or 2 tablets daily as needed, at bedtime or on arising.
Children over 6 years—1 tablet daily as needed.
How Supplied: Individual foil-backed blister packaging in boxes of 15, 30, 60 and 90 tablets.
[*Shown in Product Identification Section*]

CUSHION GRIP®
Thermoplastic Denture Adhesive

Indications: A soft pliable thermoplastic adhesive which creates a secure seal to help reduce looseness, shifting, clicking of dentures.
Actions: Securely holds dentures comfortably for up to 4 days. Won't wash off in water. Even after repeated cleaning. CUSHION GRIP remains in place, remains soft and pliable. . . recreates a secure seal each time dentures are reinserted. CUSHION GRIP is safe for plastic and porcelain plates.
Caution: Intended for use only on nondefective dentures. Ill-fitting, broken or irritating dentures may impair health of patient. Periodic dental examination is recommended at least every six months.
Directions for Use: Refer patient to detailed instructions supplied with each package.
How Supplied: In tubes of ¼, ½ and 1 oz.
[*Shown in Product Identification Section*]

DI–GEL®
Antacid · Anti-Gas
Tablets/Liquid

Active Ingredients: DI-GEL Tablets: Each tablet contains: Simethicone 25 mg., aluminum hydroxide-magnesium carbonate codried gel 282 mg., magnesium hydroxide 85 mg.
Sodium Content: 10.6 mg. per tablet.
DI-GEL Liquid: Each teaspoonful contains: Simethicone 25 mg., aluminum hydroxide (equivalent to aluminum hydroxide dried gel, U.S.P.) 282 mg., magnesium hydroxide 87 mg.
Sodium Content: 8.5 mg. per teaspoonful.
Indications: For fast, temporary relief of acid indigestion, heartburn, sour stomach and accompanying painful gas symptoms.
Actions: The antacid system in DI-GEL relieves and soothes acid indigestion, heartburn and sour stomach. At the same time, the simethicone "defoamers" eliminate gas.
When air becomes entrapped in the stomach, heartburn and acid indigestion can result, along with sensations of fullness, pressure and bloating.
Warnings: Do not take more than 20 teaspoonfuls or tablets in a 24 hour period, or use the maximum dosage of this product for more than 2 weeks, except under the advice and supervision of a physician. If you have kidney disease or if you are on a sodium restricted diet, do not use this product except under the advice and supervision of a physician. May cause constipation or have a laxative effect.
Drug Interaction: This product should not be taken if patient is presently taking a prescription antibiotic drug containing any form of tetracycline.
Dosage and Administration: Two teaspoonfuls or tablets every 2 hours, or after or between meals and at bedtime, not to exceed 20 teaspoonfuls or tablets per day, or as directed by a physician.
How Supplied:
DI-GEL Liquid in Mint and Lemon/Orange Flavors - 6 and 12 fl. oz. bottles.
DI-GEL Tablets in Mint and Lemon/Orange Flavors - In boxes of 30, 56 and 100 individual strip packaging.
[*Shown in Product Identification Section*]

DURATION® Long Lasting Topical
Nasal Decongestant
Nasal Spray/Nose Drops/
Mentholated Nasal Spray

Active Ingredients: Oxymetazoline HCl 0.05%
Preservative: Phenylmercuric Acetate 0.002% (Mentholated Nasal Spray also contains the following aromatics: menthol, camphor, eucalyptol.)
Indications: Temporary relief, for up to 12 hours, of nasal congestion due to colds, hay fever and sinusitis.
Actions: The sympathomimetic action of DURATION constricts the smaller arterioles of the nasal passages, producing a prolonged, gentle and predictable decongesting effect up to 12 hours.
Warnings: Do not exceed recommended dosage because symptoms may occur such as burning, stinging, sneezing, or increase of nasal discharge. Do not use this product for more than 3 days. If symptoms persist, consult a physician. The use of dispenser by more than one person may spread infection.
Dosage and Administration:
DURATION Nasal Spray—With head upright, spray 2 or 3 times in each nostril twice daily—morning and evening. To spray, squeeze bottle quickly and firmly. Not recommended for children under 6.
DURATION Nose Drops—Tilt head back, apply 2 or 3 drops into each nostril twice daily—morning and evening. Not recommended for children under 6.
Used at bedtime, DURATION helps restore freer nasal breathing throughout the night.
How Supplied:
DURATION Nasal Spray—½ & 1 fl. oz. Plastic Squeeze Bottle
DURATION Mentholated Nasal Spray—½ fl. oz. Plastic Squeeze Bottle
DURATION Nose Drops—⅔ fl. oz. Bottle.
[*Shown in Product Identification Section*]

REGUTOL®
Stool Softener
Tablets

Active Ingredients: Each tablet contains 100 mg. docusate sodium.
Indications: For relief of constipation.
Actions: REGUTOL contains docusate sodium which aids natural regularity

and promotes easier elimination by moistening and softening dry, hard, constipating waste. REGUTOL does not cause cramps or spasms.

Dosage and Administration: Adults and children over six years old—1 tablet twice a day until regularity is restored.

How Supplied: REGUTOL tablets in boxes of 30, 60 and 90 individual blister packaging.

[*Shown in Product Identification Section*]

ST. JOSEPH® Aspirin for Children
Pediatric Analgesic/Antipyretic Chewable Tablets

Active Ingredient: Aspirin 81 mg. (1¼ grain) per tablet.

Indications: For temporary reduction of fever, relief of minor aches and pains of cold and flu.

Actions: Analgesic/Antipyretic

Precaution: Do not administer this product for more than 5 days. If symptoms persist or new ones occur, consult physician. If fever persists for more than three days, or recurs, consult physician. Severe or persistent sore throat with high fever, headaches, nausea or vomiting may be serious. Consult physician if not relieved in two days.

Dosage and Administration:
Dosage by Age and Weight
To be administered only under adult supervision.
[See table above].
May be repeated in 4 hours but not more than 5 times a day unless prescribed by physician.
ST. JOSEPH Aspirin for Children may be given one of five ways. Always follow with ½ glass of water, milk, or fruit juice.
1. CHEWED, followed by liquid.
2. SWALLOWED whole, followed by liquid.
3. DISSOLVED on tongue, followed by liquid.
4. CRUSHED or dissolved in a teaspoon of liquid.
5. POWDERED for infant use, when so directed by physician.
How Supplied: Chewable orange flavored tablets in plastic bottles of 36 tablets. Child-resistant packaging.
[*Shown in Product Identification Section*]

ST. JOSEPH® Cold Tablets for Children
Pediatric Analgesic/Antipyretic/ Nasal Decongestant

Active Ingredients: Aspirin, 81 mg. (1¼ grain) and phenylpropanolamine hydrochloride 3.125 mg. per tablet.
Indications: Temporary reduction of fever, relief of minor aches and pains, nasal congestion, runny nose, difficult

Age (Years)	Weight (lbs.)	Dosage
Under 2	Below 27	As directed by physician.
2 through 3	27 to 35	2 tablets
4 through 5	36 to 45	3 tablets
6 through 8	46 to 65	4 tablets
9 through 10	66 to 76	5 tablets
11 years	77 to 83	6 tablets
12 years and older	84 and over	8 tablets

Age (Years)	Weight (lbs.)	Dosage
Under 2	Below 27	As directed by physician.
2 through 3	27 to 35	2 tablets
4 through 5	36 to 45	3 tablets
6 through 8	46 to 65	4 tablets
9 through 10	66 to 76	5 tablets
11 years	77 to 83	6 tablets
12 and over	84 and over	8 tablets

nasal breathing accompanying colds and flu.

Actions: Aspirin provides analgesia and antipyresis. Phenylpropanolamine hydrochloride restricts the smaller arterioles of nasal passages resulting in a nasal decongestant effect. Helps decongest sinus openings and sinus passages, thus promoting sinus drainage.

Precaution: Do not administer this product for more than 5 days. If symptoms persist or new ones occur, consult physician. If fever persists for more than three days, or recurs, consult physician. Severe or persistent sore throat with high fever, headaches, nausea or vomiting may be serious. Consult physician if not relieved in two days.

Dosage and Administration:
Dosage by Age and Weight
To be administered only under adult supervision.
[See table below].
May be repeated in 4 hours if necessary, but not more than 4 times a day unless prescribed by physician.
How Supplied: Chewable orange flavored tablets in plastic bottles of 36 tablets. Child-resistant packaging.
[*Shown in Product Identification Section*]

ST. JOSEPH® Cough Syrup for Children
Pediatric
Antitussive Syrup

Active Ingredient: Dextromethorphan hydrobromide 7.5 mg. per 5 cc.
Indications: For relief of coughing of colds and flu for up to 8 hours.
Actions: Antitussive
Warning: Should not be administered to children for persistent or chronic cough such as occurs with asthma or emphysema or where cough is accompanied by excessive secretions except under physician's advice.
Dosage and Administration:
Dosage:
[See table on next page].
How Supplied: Cherry tasting syrup in plastic bottle of 2 and 4 fl. ozs.
[*Shown in Product Identification Section*]

SHADE®
Sun Protection Factor 6
Sunscreen Lotion

Active Ingredient: Homosalate 8% and oxybenzone 3%.
Indications: Sunscreen to help prevent sunburn. SHADE Sunscreen Lotion 6 provides 6 times your natural sunburn protection. For allover application or for spot use on unprotected areas. Liberal and regular use may help reduce chances of premature aging and wrinkling of the skin, and skin cancer, due to long-term overexposure to sun.
Actions: Sunscreen.
Warnings: Avoid contact with eyes or mouth. Discontinue use if signs of irritation or rash appear.
Dosage and Administration: Apply evenly and liberally to exposed skin. Reapply after swimming or exercise.
How Supplied: In plastic bottles of 4- and 8-fl. ozs.
[*Shown in Product Identification Section*]

SHADE PLUS™
Sun Protection Factor 8
Water Resistant Sunscreen Lotion

Active Ingredients: 7% Padimate 0 and 3% oxybenzone.
Indications: For maximal protection in and out of the water. SHADE PLUS provides 8 times your natural sunburn protection. Provides maximal sunburn protection for people with sun-sensitive skin. Excellent for use on children. Liberal and regular use may help reduce chances of premature aging and wrinkling of skin, and skin cancer, due to long-term overexposure to sun.
Actions: Sunscreen.
Dosage and Administration: Apply evenly and liberally to exposed skin. To insure maximum protection, reapply after swimming or exercise.
How Supplied: 4 fl. oz. plastic bottles.
[*Shown in Product Identification Section*]

SOLARCAINE®
Antiseptic· Topical Anesthetic
Pump Spray Liquid/Lotion/Cream/ Aerosol Spray Liquid

Active Ingredients:
SOLARCAINE Aerosol Spray—to deliver benzocaine 9.4% (w/w), triclosan 0.18% (w/w). Also contains isopropyl alcohol 24% (w/w) in total contents.
SOLARCAINE Pump Spray—Benzocaine 2% (w/w), triclosan 0.1% (w/w), phenol 0.3% (w/w). Also contains isopropyl alcohol 31% (w/w).
SOLARCAINE Lotion—Benzocaine and triclosan.

Continued on next page

Plough—Cont.

SOLARCAINE Cream—Benzocaine and triclosan.

Indications: Medicated first aid to provide fast temporary relief of sunburn pain, minor burns, cuts, scrapes, chapping and skin injuries, poison ivy, detergent hands, insect bites (non-venomous).

Actions: Benzocaine provides local anesthetic action to relieve itching and pain. Triclosan provides antimicrobial activity. Phenol (which is contained in the pump spray) also provides antimicrobial, local anesthetic and counterirritant activity.

Caution: Not for use in eyes. Not for deep or puncture wounds or serious burns, nor for prolonged use. If condition persists, or infection, rash or irritation develops, discontinue use.

Warnings: For Aerosol Spray—Flammable—Do not spray while smoking or near fire. Do not spray into eyes or mouth. Avoid inhalation. Contents under pressure. For external use only.

Dosage and Administration: Lotion and Cream—Apply freely as needed. Spray—Hold 3 to 5 inches from injured area. Spray until wet. To apply to face, spray on palm of hand. Use often for antiseptic protection.

How Supplied:
SOLARCAINE Aerosol Spray—3- and 5-oz. cans.
SOLARCAINE Pump Spray—3.5 fl. oz. bottles.
SOLARCAINE Lotion—3- and 6-fl oz. bottles.
SOLARCAINE Cream—1- and 2-oz. tubes.
[*Shown in Product Identification Section*]

SUPER SHADE®
Sun Protection Factor 15
Sunblocking Sunscreen Lotion

Active Ingredients: 7% Padimate 0 and 3% oxybenzone.

Indications: Sunscreen to help prevent sunburn. SUPER SHADE Sunblocking Lotion 15 provides 15 times your natural sunburn protection. Provides the highest degree of sunburn protection for allover application or spot use on face, shoulders, etc. Liberal and regular use may help reduce chances of premature aging and wrinkling of skin, and skin cancer, due to long-term overexposure to sun. Contains no drying alcohol, no parabens. Virtually non-staining, does not sting skin.

Actions: Sunscreen.

Warnings: Avoid contact with eyes or mouth. Discontinue use if signs of irritation or rash appear.

Age	Weight	Dosage
Under 2 years	below 27 lbs.	As directed by Physician.
2 to under 6 yrs.	27 to 45 lbs.	1 teaspoonful every 6 to 8 hours. (Not to exceed 4 teaspoonfuls daily.)
6 to under 12 yrs.	46 to 83 lbs.	2 teaspoonfuls every 6 to 8 hours. (Not to exceed 8 teaspoonfuls daily.)
12 years and older	84 and greater	4 teaspoonfuls every 6 to 8 hours. (Not to exceed 16 teaspoonfuls daily.)

Dosage and Administration: Apply evenly and liberally to exposed skin. Resists removal by perspiration and water, but to insure maximum protection, reapply after swimming or exercise.

How Supplied: 4 fl. oz. and 8 fl. oz. Squeeze Bottle.
[*Shown in Product Identification Section*]

Poythress & Co., Wm. P., Incorporated
16 N. 22nd ST.
POST OFFICE BOX 26946
RICHMOND, VA 23261

BENSULFOID® LOTION

Composition: A greaseless, cosmetic lotion containing Bensulfoid, 6% (a fusion of finely divided sulfur, 33% by weight, onto colloidal bentonite); resorcinol, 2%; thymol, 0.5%; zinc oxide, 6%; alcohol, 12% by volume. Preservative: hexachlorophene, 0.1%.

Action and Uses: For the topical treatment of acne. Bensulfoid Lotion massages into the skin, penetrating the epidermal layer and exerting keratolytic, germicidal and fungicidal actions on the acne lesions. The effectiveness of the lotion is greatly enhanced by this penetration into the pores and therefore it need not be applied but once a day. When used as directed there is no evidence of medication on the skin. Bensulfoid Lotion may be used as a cosmetic base.

Method of Application: Before retiring wash affected area vigorously with soap and hot water using a washcloth or complexion brush. Keep skin free of lotion until morning. Wash gently each morning with soap and warm water, and after drying skin apply the lotion. With a finger tip gently massage Bensulfoid Lotion into the skin a little at a time until completely absorbed, using the smallest amount that will cover the acne area. Conspicuous blemishes may be retouched for the sake of appearance. Bensulfoid Lotion can be used regularly or intermittently as needed.

Precautions: If chapping occurs, discontinue for a few days. If undue skin irritation develops or increases, discontinue use and consult physician. Avoid getting into the eyes. Contact with blond, white or red hair may cause temporary discoloration. Persons with sensitive skins may experience a transient warming or smarting sensation.

How Supplied: In 2-ounce bottles.
Literature Available: Yes.

PANALGESIC

Composition: Methyl salicylate, 50%; aspirin, 8%; menthol and camphor, 4%; emollient oils, 20%; alcohol, 18% by weight.

Action and Uses: Panalgesic, an external application for relief of superficial aches and pains, supplies salicylates in the proper environment for maximum skin absorption, producing counterirritation, analgesia, local anesthesia, and asepsis. Panalgesic lessens the discomfort of muscular fatigue, and of trauma, and increases the blood level of salicylate by dermal absorption.

Method of Application: Apply externally to affected area with a gentle massage 3 or 4 times daily.

Warning: Do not use otherwise than as directed. Keep out of reach of children to avoid accidental poisoning. Discontinue use if excessive irritation of the skin develops. Avoid getting into eyes or on mucous membrane.

How Supplied: 4-ounce; 1-pint; one-half gallon bottles.

Procter & Gamble
P. O. BOX 171
CINCINNATI, OH 45201

HEAD & SHOULDERS®
Antidandruff Shampoo

Description: Head & Shoulders (lotion and cream form) is an antidandruff shampoo containing 2.0% zinc pyrithione suspended in an anionic detergent system with cosmetic excipients.

Composition: LOTION: Zinc pyrithione in a shampoo base of water, TEA-lauryl sulfate, cocamide MEA, triethanolamine, magnesium aluminum silicate, hydroxypropyl methylcellulose, fragrance, FD&C Green No. 3, and D&C Green No. 5.
CREAM: Zinc pyrithione in a shampoo base of water, sodium cocoglyceryl ether sulfonate, sodium chloride, sodium lauroyl sarcosinate, cocamide DEA, cocoyl sarcosine, fragrance, FD&C Green No. 3, and D&C Green No. 5.

Indications: Clinical testing has indicated that use of Head & Shoulders shampoo on a regular basis effectively controls dandruff and seborrheic dermatitis of the scalp.

Precautions: Not to be taken internally. Keep out of children's reach. Avoid getting shampoo in eyes—if this happens, rinse eyes with water.

Dosage and Administration: For treatment of dandruff/seborrheic dermatitis of the scalp, use Head & Shoulders regularly. It is gentle enough to use every time you shampoo. A minimum of four shampooings are recommended before antidandruff/antiseborrheic effectiveness should be expected. The active compound, zinc pyrithione, is substantive to the scalp and remains, allowing for therapeutic action until subsequent shampooing.

How Supplied: Head & Shoulders lotion form is supplied in 4.0 fl. oz., 7.0 fl. oz., 11.0 fl. oz., and 15.0 fl. oz. unbreakable plastic bottles. Head & Shoulders cream form is supplied in 2.5 oz. and 4.0

oz. jars or 1.7 oz., 2.5 oz., 4.0 oz., and 7.0 oz. tubes.
Literature available on request.

SCOPE®
Oral Rinse

Description: Scope is an oral rinse, green in color, with a pleasant tasting, fresh wintergreen flavor. It has a low surface tension, approximately ½ that of water. Scope refreshes the mouth and leaves it feeling clean.
Composition: Cetylpyridinium chloride (.045%), domiphen bromide (.005%) and SD alcohol 38F (18.5%) in a mouthwash base of water, glycerin, polysorbate 80, flavor, sodium saccharin, FD&C Blue No. 1 and FD&C Yellow No. 5.
Consumer Use: For mouth refreshment and as an aid to daily oral care. Scope also helps provide soothing, temporary relief of dryness and minor irritations of the mouth and throat.
Dental Office Use: Scope is used before, during and after instrumentation and dental prophylaxis in the interest of enhancing patient comfort, as well as to provide dentists with a more pleasant working environment. Scope's low surface tension also makes it ideal for preparing oral surfaces for impressions. A pre-impression rinse with Scope helps remove debris and ropy saliva from the oral cavity. It is also used for mouth freshening after taking impressions. Scope is guaranteed not to clog dental spray units (it contains no sugar).
Consumer Usage Instructions: Rinse or gargle for 20 seconds with one ounce of Scope first thing in the morning, after meals or when needed for mouth refreshment.
Consumer Precautions: Keep out of reach of children. Do not administer to any child under six years of age. Any sore throat may be serious; consult your doctor promptly.
Dental Office Precautions: Keep out of reach of children. Not to be used undiluted. Because of high alcohol content, avoid contact with eyes and ingestion of the undiluted concentrate.
How Supplied: Scope is supplied to consumers in 6, 12, 18, 24 and 40 fl. oz. bottles and is available to the dental profession in a one gallon concentrate (each gallon makes 3.5 gallons of regular Scope). A pump attachment for the gallon container, 18 oz. operatory decanters and a spray attachment for the decanter are available for office use.

Products are

indexed alphabetically

in the

PINK SECTION

Purdue Frederick Company, The
50 WASHINGTON STREET
NORWALK, CT 06856

BETADINE®
ANTISEPTIC LUBRICATING GEL
(povidone-iodine)

Broad-spectrum microbicidal lubricant to help protect delicate mucosal tissues. It is water-soluble and greaseless, packaged in a convenient, single-use packette.
Uses: To help protect delicate mucosal tissues from urinary catheters, douche cannulas, gloved fingers, specula and other instruments in gynecologic examinations. It is particularly suited for use with urinary catheters. It is compatible with rubber appliances and surgical instruments.
Directions: Apply gel along length of catheter or speculum, or apply with gloved finger.
Supplied: ⅙ oz. (5 g) single-use, disposable packette.

BETADINE® SOLUTION
(povidone-iodine)
Antiseptic, germicide

Action and Uses: For preoperative prepping of operative site, including the vagina, and as a general topical microbicide for: disinfection of wounds; emergency treatment of lacerations and abrasions; second– and third–degree burns; as a prophylactic anti-infective agent in hospital and office procedures, including postoperative application to incisions to help prevent infection; trichomonal, monilial, and nonspecific infectious vaginitis; oral moniliasis (thrush); bacterial and mycotic skin infections; decubitus and stasis ulcers; preoperatively, in the mouth and throat, as a swab. BETADINE Solution is microbicidal, and not merely bacteriostatic. It *kills* gram-positive and gram-negative bacteria (including antibiotic-resistant strains), fungi, viruses, protozoa and yeasts.
Administration: Apply full strength as often as needed as a paint, spray, or wet soak. May be bandaged. In preoperative prepping, avoid "pooling" beneath the patient.
How Supplied: ½ oz., 8 oz., 16 oz. (1 pt.), 32 oz. (1 qt.) and 1 gal. plastic bottles and 1 oz. packettes.
Also Available: BETADINE SOLUTION SWAB AIDS for degerming small areas of skin or mucous membranes prior to injections, aspirations, catheterization and surgery; boxes of 100 packettes. Also: disposable BETADINE SOLUTION SWABSTICKS, in packettes of 1's and 3's.
[*Shown in Product Identification Section*]

BETADINE® DOUCHE
(povidone-iodine)

A pleasantly scented solution, clinically effective in nonspecific infectious vaginitis and against vaginal moniliasis and *Trichomonas vaginalis* vaginitis. Also effective as a cleansing douche.

Advantages: Low surface tension, with uniform wetting action to assist penetration into vaginal crypts and crevices. Active in the presence of blood, pus, or vaginal secretions. Virtually nonirritating to vaginal mucosa. Will not stain skin or natural fabrics.
Directions for Use: As a Therapeutic Douche: Two (2) tablespoonfuls to a quart of lukewarm water once daily. As a Routine Cleansing Douche: One (1) tablespoonful to a quart of lukewarm water once or twice per week.
How Supplied: 1 oz., 8 oz., 1 gallon plastic bottles. Disposable ½ oz. (1 tablespoonful) packettes.
Also Available: BETADINE Douche Kit is supplied as individual units, each containing:
(1) 8 oz. plastic bottle of BETADINE Douche concentrate;
(2) 14 oz., squeezable, plastic syringe bottle;
(3) anatomically-correct cannula;
(4) instruction booklet.
The 8 oz. bottle of BETADINE Douche concentrate is sufficient for up to 40 cleansing douches.
Directions for Use:
As a Therapeutic Douche: Add one (1) tablespoonful of BETADINE Douche concentrate to the 14 oz. syringe bottle which is then filled to the top with lukewarm water. Douche, then repeat the procedure. For daily use.
As a Routine Cleansing Douche: Add BETADINE Douche concentrate to FIRST FILL-LINE on syringe bottle. Add lukewarm water up to WATER FILL-LINE. For use once or twice a week.
Also Available: BETADINE® Medicated Douche is a hygienic, **disposable,** convenient method to provide symptomatic relief of minor vaginal soreness, irritation, itching.
BETADINE Medicated Douche is supplied as individual units, each containing:
(1) 0.18 fl. oz. (5.2 ml) BETADINE Douche Concentrate;
(2) 6 fl. oz. (177 ml) of sanitized water in a squeezable, plastic syringe bottle with nozzle (when mixed, a 0.25% solution of povidone-iodine is formed);
(3) instruction booklet.
The syringe bottle and nozzle are completely disposable to avoid contamination from previously used douche accessories. Also supplied in a "Twin Pack."
[*Shown in Product Identification Section*]

BETADINE® SKIN CLEANSER
(povidone-iodine)

BETADINE Skin Cleanser is a sudsing antiseptic liquid cleanser. It essentially retains the nonselective microbicidal action of iodine, yet virtually without the undesirable features associated with iodine. BETADINE Skin Cleanser kills gram-positive and gram-negative bacteria (including antibiotic-resistant strains), fungi, viruses, protozoa and yeasts. It forms rich golden lather, virtu-

Continued on next page

Purdue Frederick—Cont.

ally nonirritating; nonstaining to skin and natural fabrics.

Indications: BETADINE Skin Cleanser aids in degerming the skin of patients with common pathogens, including Staphylococcus aureus. To help prevent the recurrence of acute inflammatory skin infections caused by iodine-susceptible pyogenic bacteria. In pyodermas, as a topical adjunct to systemic antimicrobial therapy. To help prevent spread of infection in acne pimples.

Directions for Use: Wet the skin and apply a sufficient amount of Skin Cleanser to work up a rich golden lather. Allow lather to remain about 3 minutes. Then rinse. Repeat 2-3 times a day or as needed.

Caution: In rare instances of local sensitivity, discontinue use by the individual.

How Supplied: 1 fl. oz. and 4 fl. oz. plastic bottles.

Note: Blue stains on starched linen will wash off with soap and water.

[*Shown in Product Identification Section*]

BETADINE® OINTMENT
(povidone-iodine)

Action and Uses: To help prevent infection in burns, lacerations and abrasions. Infected stasis ulcers. Common skin infections. For degerming skin in hyperalimentation, catheter care, the umbilical area or circumcision.

BETADINE Ointment, in a water-soluble base, is a topical agent active against organisms commonly encountered in skin and wound infections. The active ingredient substantially retains the broad-spectrum germicidal activity of iodine without the undesirable features or disadvantages of iodine. BETADINE Ointment is virtually nonirritating, does not block air from reaching the site of application, and washes easily off skin and natural fabrics. The site to which BETADINE Ointment is applied can be bandaged.

Administration: Apply directly to affected area as needed. May be bandaged.

Supplied: $\frac{1}{32}$ oz. and $\frac{1}{8}$ oz. packettes; 1 oz. tubes; 16 oz. (1 lb.) (av.) jars .

[*Shown in Product Identification Section*]

SENOKOT® TABLETS/GRANULES
(standardized senna concentrate)

Action and Uses: Indicated for relief of functional constipation (chronic or occasional). SENOKOT Tablets/Granules contain a natural vegetable derivative, purified and standardized for uniform action. The current theory of the mechanism of action is that glycosides are transported to the colon, where they are changed to aglycones that stimulate Auerbach's plexus to induce peristalsis. This virtually colon-specific action is gentle, effective and predictable, usually inducing comfortable evacuation of well-formed stool within 8-10 hours. Found effective even in many previously intractable cases of functional constipation, SENOKOT preparations may aid in re-

habilitation of the constipated patient by facilitating regular elimination. At proper dosage levels, SENOKOT preparations are virtually free of adverse reactions (such as loose stools or abdominal discomfort) and enjoy high patient acceptance. Numerous and extensive clinical studies show their high degree of effectiveness in varieties of functional constipation: chronic, geriatric, antepartum and postpartum, drug-induced, and pediatric, as well as in functional constipation concurrent with heart disease or anorectal surgery.

Contraindications: Acute surgical abdomen.

Administration and Dosage: Preferably at bedtime. GRANULES (deliciously cocoa-flavored): Adults: 1 level tsp. (maximum—2 level tsp. b.i.d.). For older, debilitated, and OB/GYN patients, the physician may consider prescribing $\frac{1}{2}$ the initial adult dose. Children above 60 lb.: $\frac{1}{2}$ level tsp. (maximum—1 level tsp. b.i.d.). TABLETS: Adults: 2 tablets (maximum—4 tablets b.i.d.). For older, debilitated, and OB/GYN patients, the physician may consider prescribing $\frac{1}{2}$ the initial dose. Children above 60 lb.: 1 tablet (maximum—2 tablets b.i.d.). To meet individual requirements, if comfortable bowel movement is not achieved by the second day, decrease or increase dosage daily by $\frac{1}{2}$ level tsp. or 1 tablet (up to maximum) until optimal dose for evacuation is established.

How Supplied: Granules: 2, 6, and 12 oz. plastic canisters. Tablets: Box of 20, bottles of 50 and 100.

SENOKOT Tablets Unit Strip Packs in boxes of 100 tablets; each tablet individually sealed in see-through pockets.

[*Shown in Product Identification Section*]

SENOKOT®-S
(docusate sodium and standardized senna concentrate)
Stool Softener/Natural Laxative Combination

Action and Uses: SENOKOT-S Tablets are designed to relieve both aspects of functional constipation—dry, hard stools and bowel inertia. They provide a classic stool softener combined with a natural neuroperistaltic stimulant: docusate sodium softens the stool for smoother and easier evacuation, while standardized senna concentrate gently stimulates Auerbach's plexus in the colonic wall. This coordinated dual action of the two ingredients results in colon-specific, predictable laxative effect, usually in 8–10 hours. Administering the tablets at bedtime allows the patient an uninterrupted night's sleep, with a comfortable evacuation in the morning. Flexibility of dosage permits fine adjustment to individual requirements. At proper dosage levels, SENOKOT-S Tablets are virtually free from side effects. SENOKOT-S Tablets are highly suitable for relief of postsurgical and postpartum constipation, and effectively counteract drug-induced constipation. They facilitate regular elimination in impaction-prone and elderly patients, and are indi-

cated in the presence of cardiovascular disease where straining must be avoided, as well as in the presence of hemorrhoids and anorectal disease.

Contraindications: Acute surgical abdomen.

Administration and Dosage: (preferably at bedtime) Recommended Initial Dosage: ADULTS—2 tablets (maximum dosage—4 tablets b.i.d.); CHILDREN (above 60 lbs.)—1 tablet (maximum dosage—2 tablets b.i.d.). For older or debilitated patients, the physician may consider prescribing half the initial adult dose. To meet individual requirements, if comfortable bowel movement is not achieved by the second day, dosage may be decreased or increased by 1 tablet, up to maximum, until the most effective dose is established.

Supplied: Bottles of 30 and 60 Tablets.

[*Shown in Product Identification Section*]

Requa Manufacturing Company, Inc.
1 SENECA PLACE
GREENWICH, CT 06830

CHARCOCAPS®
Activated Vegetable Charcoal

Active Ingredient: Each capsule contains 260 mg. (4 gr.) activated vegetable charcoal USP.

Indications: For the prevention and relief of intestinal gas, and of diarrhea and gastrointestinal distress associated with ingestion.

Actions: Adsorbent and detoxicant. Adsorbs many toxic and nontoxic irritants which cause diarrhea and gastrointestinal distress. Adsorbs intestinal gas and allays related discomfort.

Warnings: Although studies have reported use for much longer periods without antinutritional or other untoward effects, general use is best limited to a period of one week. Prolonged use in infants and children under 3 years of age may possibly interfere with nutrition.

Drug Interaction Precaution: Activated charcoal can adsorb and inactivate a wide range of ingested substances, including drugs, and is an effective antidote for many drugs while they are in the digestive tract. Therefore, CHARCOCAPS should be taken either one or more hours before, or one or more hours after a drug.

Symptoms and Treatment of Oral Overdosage: Overdosage has not been encountered.

Dosage and Administration: 2 capsules repeated every $\frac{1}{2}$ to 1 hour as needed up to 8 doses (16 capsules) per day.

How Supplied: Bottles of 36 capsules.

[*Shown in Product Identification Section*]

Products are cross-indexed by

generic and chemical names in the

YELLOW SECTION

Riker Laboratories, Inc.
NORTHRIDGE, CA 91324

BUF™ ACNE CLEANSING BAR

Description: BUF™ ACNE CLEANSING BAR is an unscented, non-irritating cleanser for use as a drying adjunct to acne skin care. The addition of salicylic acid 1% and sulfur 1% in the formulation provides a mild drying effect on the skin.
Actions and Uses: For best results, use with BUF-PUF® NONMEDICATED CLEANSING SPONGE to provide gently abrasive and drying actions to assist in the management of acne.
Administration: Wet face with warm water. Work up a creamy lather in BUF-PUF (or your washcloth) with BUF ACNE CLEANSING BAR, and lightly massage the skin. Rinse thoroughly and pat dry. If undue irritation or dryness occurs, discontinue use and consult your physician.
How Supplied: Available as 3.5 oz. bars.

BUF™ BODY SCRUB

Description: BUF BODY SCRUB includes one BUF-PUF® brand non-medicated polyester cleansing sponge mounted on a custom reusable handle.
Actions and Uses: BUF BODY SCRUB is a stimulating new way to bathe and shower. The product's unique polyester sponge cleans and refreshes your skin . . . and the contoured handle is designed to put your back and shoulders within easy reach. This unique feature makes BUF BODY SCRUB particularly suitable for individuals with acne on back and shoulders. For general skin care, BUF BODY SCRUB "buffs away" surface dullness and roughness, and helps to create a satiny-smooth skin. And, it successfully smooths thick, roughened skin on areas such as feet, knees, and elbows. These difficult-to-reach areas can now be easily accessible with the BUF BODY SCRUB.
Administration: After moistening BUF BODY SCRUB, work up a foamy lather with your favorite soap or cleanser. (If you have oily skin or skin with acne, use BUF™ Acne Cleansing Bar, specially formulated to thoroughly clean your skin and remove excess oil). Next, test it on your arm and adjust the speed and pressure to your liking. Then glide BUF BODY SCRUB all over your skin, moving it up and down, back and forth, or in a circular motion . . . whichever feels most comfortable for you. The BUF-PUF® SPONGE On the BUF BODY SCRUB is **replaceable** when wet or dry. The plastic handle should be retained as it is reusable and should last for many uses.

BUF™ KIT FOR ACNE

Description: BUF-PUF® NONMEDICATED CLEANSING SPONGE and BUF™ ACNE CLEANSING BAR were designed to work together as a skin cleansing system for adjunctive care of acne. The contents of the KIT are:
  1 BUF-PUF CLEANSING SPONGE
  1 BUF ACNE CLEANSING BAR
  1 Reusable tray for storing the components of the KIT.
Actions and Uses: Used together Buf-Puf and Buf Acne Cleansing Bar form a system that provides the gently abrasive, thorough cleansing that acne patients need. See individual product descriptions.

BUF™ LOTION

Description: Buf Lotion is a fresh-scented moisturizing lotion which softens, smoothes and lubricates rough, dry skin. Ingredients: water, sterol extract, propylene glycol, sesame, oil, glyceryl monostearate, stearic acid, triethanolamine, methyl paraben, propylparaben and fragrance.
Actions and Uses: Buf Lotion complements the cleansing action of Buf-Puf® Nonmedicated Cleansing Sponge by restoring the natural moisture and body oils to the skin. It penetrates quickly and leaves no greasy film. Clinical testing has shown Buf Lotion to be non-sensitizing and non-comedogenic.
Administration: After bathing or washing, apply Buf Lotion and rub into the skin until the lotion vanishes.
How Supplied: Available in 6 oz plastic bottles.

BUF-PUF® Nonmedicated Cleansing Sponge

Description: BUF-PUF is a unique skin care product that helps clean, smooth and refresh the skin. Made of polyester fibers, BUF-PUF contains no chemicals or medications. Its mild abrasive action buffs away dirt, oil and dead skin cells as you wash.
Actions and Uses: BUF-PUF is designed to help make your skin smoother, cleaner, and more translucent. It does this by:
1. Helping to remove the top outer layer of dead skin cells.
2. Removing the dirt and debris trapped in this layer.
3. Uncovering the fresher, moister, more translucent cell layers underneath.
The above process is called epidermabrasion (epiderm = outer skin; abrasion = a wearing away). Epidermabrasion with BUF-PUF® can help a dull, muddy facial complexion become clearer and more translucent. With BUF-PUF, you control how much or now little surface buffing takes place for improved skin appearance and feel.
Administration:
For your FIRST USE
1. Develop a good lather with BUF-PUF with warm water and the soap best suited to your skin type. If you have acne or problem skin, use BUF™ Acne Cleansing Bar in place of soap. It is a specially formulated cleanser that effectively cleans and reduces the oiliness of your skin.

2. Test it on the back of your hand before using it on your face. Practice changing the (a) speed and (b) pressure with which you move it.
3. Now *gently* and *slowly* glide the lathered sponge over your face. Start with the forehead, then the temples, cheeks, chin and nose.
4. Use no more than 5 seconds on each area. You can move the sponge up and down, back and forth, or in a circle—whatever is easiest for you.
5. Rinse face and dry.
6. Continue to use BUF-PUF® very gently for several days. After this initial period, usage and pressure may be increased to best fit your skin sensitivity.
7. Apply a moisturizer such as BUF™ LOTION to areas more prone to dryness. *If you have very oily skin or acne you should not use a moisturizer.*
For SUBSEQUENT uses
Follow the same basic instructions, but gradually increase the: (a) pressure, (b) speed, and (c) duration of use. Reduce any of these three variables if your skin feels too dry or tender.
1. If you have dry or sensitive skin, use BUF-PUF *very lightly* for the first week or two—and no more than once a day.
2. If you have oily or hardy skin, still use it very lightly for the first week or two—but you may use it twice a day.
How Supplied: One round cleansing sponge.
[*Shown in Product Identification Section*]

DORBANE®
(brand of danthron)
Laxative

Composition: Each tablet contains: Danthron 75 mg.
Dorbane promotes colonic peristalsis and is a superior laxative in the management and treatment of constipation.
Dosage: 1 or 2 tablets once daily, 1 hour after the evening meal. As treatment progresses, dosage may be gradually decreased. May cause harmless discoloration of the urine.
Warning: Do not use when abdominal pain, nausea, or vomiting are present. Frequent or prolonged use of this preparation may result in dependence on laxatives.
Keep this and all medications out of the reach of children.
Note: Variation in color may occur from lot to lot, but this has no effect on the laxative action of the tablets.
Availability: Bottles of 100 (NDC **0089-0173-10**), 500 (NDC **0089-0173-50**) and 1000 (NDC **0089-0173-80**) orange, scored tablets.

DORBANTYL® Laxative
Stool Softener

For relief of occasional constipation. May cause harmless discoloration of urine.
Composition: Each capsule contains: Danthron, 25 mg.; docusate sodium, 50 mg.

Continued on next page

Riker—Cont.

Dosage: ADULTS: 2 capsules at bedtime; repeat if needed to cause bowel movement. CHILDREN: 6 to 12 years of age: 1 capsule taken as above. Under 6 years of age: use only on advice of physician.

Warning: Do not use when abdominal pain, nausea, or vomiting are present. Frequent or prolonged use of this preparation may result in dependence on laxatives.

Keep this and all medications out of the reach of children. Professional literature available to physicians on request.

Availability: Bottles of 30 NDC **0089-0174-03** 100 NDC **0089-0174-10** and 250 orange NDC **0089-0174-25** and black capsules.

DORBANTYL® FORTE Laxative Stool Softener

For relief of occasional constipation. May cause harmless discoloration of urine.

Composition: Each capsule contains: Danthron, 50 mg.; docusate sodium, 100 mg.

Dosage: ADULTS: 1 capsule at bedtime; repeat if needed to cause bowel movement. CHILDREN: Use regular Dorbantyl.

Warning: Do not use when abdominal pain, nausea, or vomiting are present. Frequent or prolonged use of this preparation may result in dependence on laxatives.

Keep this and all medication out of the reach of children.

Note: 1 Dorbantyl **Forte** capsule is equivalent to 2 regular Dorbantyl capsules.

Professional literature available to physicians on request.

Availability: Bottles of 30 (NDC **0089-0178-03**), 100 (NDC **0089-0178-10**) and 250 (NDC **0089-0178-25**) orange and grey capsules.

pHresh 3.5™ Cleansing Liquid

Description: pHresh 3.5 is a special skin cleansing formula which, due to its low pH, is designed to be gentle, non-irritating, and non-drying even when used on the most sensitive skin. It can be used by people with all skin types, and is even compatible with baby's tender skin.

Actions and Uses: pHresh 3.5 cleans thoroughly yet leaves the skin feeling moist, smooth, and fresh ... pH balanced. Use pHresh 3.5:
—to replace soap
—to help reverse skin irritations caused by alkaline soaps or detergents
—to cleanse oily skin
—for intimate hygiene
—for gentle cleansing of skin fold and heat rash areas
—for washing and bathing infants especially those with diaper rash
—as a soothing bath additive

Administration: pHresh 3.5 may be used regularly for washing face, hands, or the entire body. Use as you would soap. Pour a generous amount from the bottle and apply to wet skin.

How Supplied: Available in 6 fl. oz. plastic bottles.

TITRALAC®
Tablets and Liquid

Description:

Liquid: Each teaspoonful (5 ml.) of white, spearmint-flavored liquid contains calcium carbonate 1.00 gm. and glycine for a smooth, pleasant taste. One teaspoonful of liquid approximates two tablets. *Tablets:* Each white, spearmint-flavored tablet contains calcium carbonate 0.42 gm. and glycine for a smooth, pleasant taste.

Indications: As an antacid for the relief of heartburn, sour stomach and/or acid indigestion and symptomatic relief of hyperacidity associated with the diagnosis of peptic ulcer, gastritis, peptic esophagitis, gastric hyperacidity, and hiatal hernia.

Dosage: One teaspoonful, or two tablets, taken one hour after meals or as directed by a physician. Tablets can be chewed, swallowed, or allowed to melt in the mouth.

Warnings: Do not take more than 19 tablets or 8 teaspoons in a 24 hour period, or use the maximum dose of this product for more than two weeks except under the advice and supervision of a physician.

Neutralizing Capacity:
Titralic Liquid: 19 milliequivalents per 5 ml. Titralac Tablets: 15 milliequivalents per 2 tablets.

These neutralization equivalents are expressed as milliequivalents of acid neutralized in 15 minutes when tested in accordance with USP antacid effectiveness test as prescribed in the code of Federal Regulations for OTC antacid products.

Availability: *Tablets:* bottles of 40 (NDC **0089-0355-04**), 100 (NDC **0089-0355-10**), 500 (NDC **0089-0355-50**) and 1000 (NDC **0089-0355-80**) white, spearmint-flavored tablets and boxes containing 60 individually sealed tablets. *Liquid,* bottles of 12 fl. oz. (NDC **0089-0355-12**), spearmint-flavored Liquid. No prescription required.

Robins Company, A. H.
1407 CUMMINGS DRIVE
RICHMOND, VA 23220

ALLBEE® C–800 TABLETS
ALLBEE® C–800
plus IRON TABLETS
Allbee C-800

One tablet daily provides:	Percentage of U.S. Recommended Daily Allowances (U.S. RDA)	
Vitamin E	150	45 I.U.
Vitamin C	1333	800 mg
Thiamine (Vitamin B$_1$)	1000	15 mg
Riboflavin (Vitamin B$_2$)	1000	17 mg
Niacin	500	100 mg
Vitamin B$_6$	1250	25 mg
Vitamin B$_{12}$	200	12 mcg
Pantothenic Acid	250	25 mg

Ingredients: Ascorbic Acid, Niacinamide, Starch, Vitamin E Acetate, Hydrolyzed Protein, Calcium Pantothenate, Artificial Color, Pyridoxine Hydrochloride, Hydroxypropyl Methylcellulose, Riboflavin, Stearic Acid, Povidone, Thiamine Mononitrate, Ethylcellulose, Propylene Glycol, Lactose, Magnesium Stearate, Silicon Dioxide, Polysorbate 20, Vanillin, Gelatin, Sodium Lauryl Sulfate, Sorbic Acid, Sodium Benzoate, Cyanocobalamin.

Allbee C-800 plus Iron

One tablet daily provides: Vitamin Composition	Percentage of U.S. Recommended Daily Allowances (U.S. RDA)	
Vitamin E	150	45.0 I.U.
Vitamin C	1333	800.0 mg
Folic Acid	100	0.4 mg
Thiamine (Vitamin B$_1$)	1000	15.0 mg
Riboflavin (Vitamin B$_2$)	1000	17.0 mg
Niacin	500	100.0 mg
Vitamin B$_6$	1250	25.0 mg
Vitamin B$_{12}$	200	12.0 mcg
Pantothenic Acid	250	25.0 mg
Mineral Composition		
Iron	150	27.0 mg

Ingredients: Ascorbic Acid, Niacinamide, Ferrous Fumarate, Starch, Vitamin E Acetate, Hydrolyzed Protein, Calcium Pantothenate, Artificial Color, Pyridoxine Hydrochloride, Hydroxypropyl Methylcellulose, Povidone, Riboflavin, Stearic Acid, Thiamine Mononitrate, Ethylcellulose, Propylene Glycol, Lactose, Magnesium Stearate, Silicon Dioxide, Polysorbate 20, Vanillin, Gelatin, Folic Acid, Sodium Lauryl Sulfate, Sorbic Acid, Sodium Benzoate, Cyanocobalamin.

Actions and Uses: The components of Allbee C-800 have important roles in general nutrition, healing of wounds, and prevention of hemorrhage. Allbee C-800 is recommended for nutritional supplementation of these components in conditions such as febrile diseases, chronic or acute infections, burns, fractures, surgery, physiologic stress, alcoholism, prolonged exposure to high temperature, geriatrics, gastritis, peptic ulcer, and colitis; and in weight-reduction and other special diets.

In dentistry, Allbee C-800 is recommended for nutritional supplementation of its components in conditions such as herpetic stomatitis, aphthous stomatitis, cheilosis, herpangina and gingivitis.

In addition, Allbee C-800 Plus Iron is recommended as a nutritional source of iron. The iron is present as ferrous fumarate, a well-tolerated salt. The ascorbic acid in the formulation enhances the absorption of iron.

Precautions: Do not take Allbee C-800 Plus Iron within two hours of oral tetracycline antibiotics, since oral iron products interfere with absorption of tetracycline. Not intended for treatment of iron-deficiency anemia.

Adverse Reactions: Iron-containing medications may occasionally cause gastrointestinal discomfort, nausea, constipation or diarrhea.

Dosage: The recommended OTC dosage for adults and children twelve or more years of age is one tablet daily. Under the direction and supervision of a physician, the dose and frequency of administration may be increased in accordance with the patient's requirements.

How Supplied: Allbee C-800—orange, film-coated, elliptically-shaped tablets in bottles of 60 (NDC 0031-0677-62). Allbee C-800 Plus Iron—red, film-coated, elliptically-shaped tablets in bottles of 60 (NDC 0031-0678-62).

[*Shown in Product Identification Section*]

ALLBEE® WITH C CAPSULES

One capsule daily provides:

	Percentage of U.S. Recommended Daily Allowance (U.S. RDA)	
Vitamin C	500	300.0 mg
Thiamine (Vitamin B$_1$)	1000	15.0 mg
Riboflavin (Vitamin B$_2$)	600	10.2 mg
Niacin	250	50.0 mg
Vitamin B$_6$	250	5.0 mg
Pantothenic Acid	100	10.0 mg

Ingredients: Ascorbic Acid; Gelatin; Niacinamide; Lactose; Corn Starch; Thiamine Mononitrate; Calcium Pantothenate; Riboflavin; Magnesium Stearate; Pyridoxine Hydrochloride; Light Mineral Oil; FD&C Yellow No. 5; Vanillin; Artificial Color.

Action and Uses: Allbee with C is a high potency formulation of B and C vitamins. Its components have important roles in general nutrition, healing of wounds, and prevention of hemorrhage. It is recommended for deficiencies of B-vitamins and ascorbic acid in conditions such as febrile diseases, chronic or acute infections, burns, fractures, surgery, toxic conditions, physiologic stress, alcoholism, prolonged exposure to high temperature, geriatrics, gastritis, peptic ulcer, and colitis; and in conditions involving special diets and weight-reduction diets.

In dentistry, Allbee with C is recommended for deficiencies of B-vitamins and ascorbic acid in conditions such as herpetic stomatitis, aphthous stomatitis, cheilosis, herpangina, gingivitis.

Precaution: This product contains FD&C Yellow No. 5 (tartrazine) which may cause allergic-type reactions (including bronchial asthma) in certain susceptible individuals. Although the overall incidence of FD&C Yellow No. 5 (tartrazine) sensitivity in the general population is low, it is frequently seen in patients who have aspirin hypersensitivity.

Dosage: The recommended OTC dosage for adults and children twelve or more years of age, other than pregnant or lactating women, is one capsule daily. Under the direction and supervision of a physician, the dose and frequency of ad-

ministration may be increased in accordance with the patient's requirements.

How Supplied: Yellow and green capsules, monogrammed AHR and 0674, in bottles of 30 (NDC 0031-0674-56), 100 (NDC 0031-0674-63), 1,000 capsules (NDC 0031-0674-74) and in Dis-Co® Unit Dose Packs of 100 (NDC 0031-0674-64).

[*Shown in Product Identification Section*]

DIMACOL® CAPSULES
DIMACOL® LIQUID

Composition: Each capsule or 5 ml (one teaspoonful) contains:

Guaifenesin, USP ....100 mg
Pseudoephedrine
   Hydrochloride, USP ....30 mg
Dextromethorphan
   Hydrobromide, USP ....15 mg
Liquid: Alcohol 4.75%

Actions: Dimacol helps reduce nasal congestion and suppresses cough associated with the common cold and other upper respiratory disorders.

Guaifenesin enhances the output of lower respiratory tract fluid. The enhanced flow of less viscid secretions promotes ciliary action, and facilitates the removal of inspissated mucus. As a result, dry unproductive coughs become more productive and less frequent. *Pseudoephedrine hydrochloride* is an orally effective nasal decongestant. Through its vasoconstrictor action, pseudoephedrine gently but promptly reduces edema and congestion of nasal passages. *Dextromethorphan hydrobromide* is a synthetic, non-narcotic cough suppressant. The antitussive effectiveness of dextromethorphan has been demonstrated in both animal and clinical studies, and the incidence of toxic effects has been remarkably low.

Indications: Dimacol is indicated for the management of cough accompanied by nasal mucosal congestion and edema, and nasal hypersecretion, associated with the common cold, upper respiratory infection and sinusitis.

Contraindications: Hypersensitivity to any of the ingredients. Dimacol should not be administered to patients receiving MAO inhibitors.

Precautions: Administer with caution in the presence of hypertension, heart disease, peripheral vascular disease, diabetes or hyperthyroidism. As with all products containing sympathomimetic amines, use with caution in patients with prostatic hypertrophy or glaucoma.

Note: Guaifenesin has been shown to produce a color interference with certain clinical laboratory determinations of 5-hydroxyindoleacetic acid (5-HIAA) and vanilmandelic acid (VMA).

Adverse Reactions: The following adverse reactions may possibly occur: nausea, vomiting, dry mouth, nervousness, insomnia.

Dosage and Administration: Adults and children over 12 years of age, one capsule or one teaspoonful (5 ml) three times a day.

Children 6 to 12 years, ½ teaspoonful 3 times a day. Children under 6 years of age, as directed by a physician.

How Supplied: Orange and green capsules in bottles of 100 (NDC 0031-1650-63), and 500 (NDC 0031-1650-70) and consumer packages of 12 (NDC 0031-1650-46) and 24 (NDC 0031-1650-54) (individually packaged).

Orange colored, chocolate flavored liquid in bottles of one pint (NDC 0031-1660-25).

[*Shown in Product Identification Section*]

DIMETANE®
brand of Brompheniramine Maleate, USP
Tablets—4 mg
Elixir—2 mg/5 ml
   Alcohol, 3%

Actions: Brompheniramine maleate is an antihistamine, with anticholinergic (drying) and sedative side effects. Antihistamines appear to compete with histamine for cell receptor sites on effector cells.

Indications: For effective, temporary relief of hay fever/upper respiratory allergy symptoms: itchy, watery eyes; sneezing; itching nose or throat.

Contraindications: *Use in Newborn or Premature Infants.* This drug should not be used in newborn or premature infants.

Use in Nursing Mothers. Because of the higher risk of antihistamines for infants generally and for newborns and prematures in particular, antihistamine therapy is contraindicated in nursing mothers.

Use in Lower Respiratory Disease. Antihistamines **should NOT** be used to treat lower respiratory tract symptoms including asthma.

This drug is also contraindicated in the following conditions: hypersensitivity to brompheniramine maleate and other antihistamines of similar chemical structure; monoamine oxidase inhibitor therapy (see Drug Interaction section).

Warnings: Antihistamines should be used with considerable caution in patients with: narrow angle glaucoma; stenosing peptic ulcer; pyloroduodenal obstruction; symptomatic prostatic hypertrophy; bladder neck obstruction.

Use in Children. In infants and children, especially, antihistamines in **overdosage** may cause hallucinations, convulsions, or death.

As in adults, antihistamines may diminish mental alertness in children. In the young child, particularly, they may produce excitation.

Use in Pregnancy. Experience with this drug in pregnant women is inadequate to determine whether there exists a potential for harm to the developing fetus.

Continued on next page

Robins—Cont.

Use with CNS Depressants. Dimetane has additive effects with alcohol and other CNS depressants (hypnotics, sedatives, tranquilizers, etc.)

Use in Activities Requiring Mental Alertness. Patients should be warned about engaging in activities requiring mental alertness, such as driving a car or operating appliances, machinery, etc.

Use in the Elderly (approximately 60 years or older). Antihistamines are more likely to cause dizziness, sedation, and hypotension in elderly patients.

Precautions: As with other antihistamines, Dimetane has an atropine-like action and, therefore, should be used with caution in patients with: history of bronchial asthma; increased intraocular pressure; hyperthyroidism; cardiovascular disease; hypertension.

Drug Interactions: MAO inhibitors prolong and intensify the anticholinergic (drying) effects of antihistamines.

Adverse Reactions: The most frequent adverse reactions are italicized:
General: Urticaria, drug rash, anaphylactic shock, photosensitivity, excessive perspiration, chills, dryness of mouth, nose, and throat.
Cardiovascular System: Hypotension, headache, palpitations, tachycardia, extrasystoles.
Hematologic System: Hemolytic anemia, thrombocytopenia, agranulocytosis.
Nervous System: Sedation, sleepiness, dizziness, disturbed coordination, fatigue, confusion, restlessness, excitation, nervousness, tremor, irritability, insomnia, euphoria, paresthesias, blurred vision, diplopia, vertigo, tinnitus, acute labyrinthitis, hysteria, neuritis, convulsions.
G.I. System: Epigastric distress, anorexia, nausea, vomiting, diarrhea, constipation.
G.U. System: Urinary frequency, difficult urination, urinary retention, early menses.
Respiratory System: Thickening of bronchial secretions, tightness of chest and wheezing, nasal stuffiness.
Overdosage: Antihistamine overdosage reactions may vary from central nervous system depression to stimulation. Stimulation is particularly likely in children. Atropine-like signs and symptoms—dry mouth; fixed, dilated pupils; flushing; and gastrointestinal symptoms may also occur.
If vomiting has not occurred spontaneously, the patient should be induced to vomit. This is best done by having him drink a glass of water or milk after which he should be made to gag. Precautions against aspiration must be taken, especially in infants and children.
If vomiting is unsuccessful, gastric lavage is indicated within 3 hours after ingestion and even later if large amounts of milk or cream were given beforehand. Isotonic and ½ isotonic saline is the lavage solution of choice.
Saline cathartics, such as milk of magnesia, by osmosis draw water into the bowel and therefore, are valuable for their action in rapid dilution of bowel content.
Stimulants should not be used.
Vasopressors may be used to treat hypotension.
Dosage and Administration: The recommended OTC dosage is:
Adults and children 12 years of age and over: 1 tablet or 2 teaspoonfuls every four to six hours, not to exceed 6 tablets or 12 teaspoonfuls in 24 hours.
Children 6 to under 12 years: ½ tablet or 1 teaspoonful every four to six hours, not to exceed 3 tablets or 6 teaspoonfuls in 24 hours.
Children under 6 years: use as directed by a physician.
Under physician supervision, children 2 to under 6 years: ½ teaspoonful every four to six hours, not to exceed 3 teaspoonfuls in 24 hours.
How Supplied: 4 mg tablets are available as peach-colored, compressed, scored tablets in cartons of 24 individually packaged blister units (NDC 0031-1857-54), and in bottles of 100 (NDC 0031-1857-63) and 500 (NDC 0031-1857-70). 2 mg per 5 ml peach-colored liquid is available in bottles of 4 fl. oz. (NDC 0031-1807-12), 1 pint (NDC 0031-1807-25) and 1 gallon (NDC 0031-1807-29).
[*Shown in Product Identification Section*]

DIMETANE® DECONGESTANT ELIXIR
DIMETANE® DECONGESTANT TABLETS

Elixir:
Each 5 ml (1 teaspoonful) contains:
Phenylephrine
    Hydrochloride, USP ....5 mg
Brompheniramine
    Maleate, USP ....2 mg
Alcohol 2.3 percent
Tablet:
Each tablet contains:
Phenylephrine
    Hydrochloride, USP ....10 mg
Brompheniramine
    Maleate, USP ....4 mg
Indications: For temporary relief of nasal congestion due to the common cold, sinusitis, hay fever or other upper respiratory allergies; runny nose, sneezing, itching of the nose or throat and itchy and watery eyes as may occur in allergic rhinitis (such as hay fever). Temporarily restores freer breathing through the nose.
Contraindications: Hypersensitivity to any of the ingredients; marked hypertension.
Warnings: May cause excitability, especially in children. Use with caution in children under 2 years. Prescribe cautiously for patients with asthma, glaucoma, difficulty in urination due to enlargement of the prostate gland, high blood pressure, heart disease, diabetes or thyroid disease and for patients who are receiving MAO inhibitors or antihypertensive medication. May cause drowsiness. Doses in excess of the recommended dosage may cause nervousness, dizziness or sleeplessness.

Cautions: Patients should be warned about driving a motor vehicle, operating heavy machinery, or consuming alcoholic beverages while taking this product.
Recommended Dosage: *Elixir:* Adults and children 12 years of age and over: 2 teaspoonfuls every 4 hours, not to exceed 12 teaspoonfuls in a 24-hour period; children 6 to under 12 years: 1 teaspoonful every 4 hours, not to exceed 6 teaspoonfuls in a 24-hour period; children 2 to under 6 years: ½ teaspoonful every 4 hours, not to exceed 3 teaspoonfuls in a 24-hour period.
Tablets: Adults and children 12 years of age and over: 1 tablet every 4 hours, not to exceed 6 tablets in a 24-hour period; children 6 to under 12 years: ½ tablet every 4 hours, not to exceed 3 tablets in a 24-hour period.
How Supplied: *Tablets*—light blue, capsule shaped tablets in cartons of 24 (NDC 0031-2117-54) and 48 (NDC 0031-2117-59) individually packaged blister units.
Elixir—red colored, grape flavored liquid in 4 fl. oz. bottle (NDC 0031-2127-12).
[*Shown in Product Identification Section*]

MITROLAN® Tablets
brand of Calcium Polycarbophil

Each chewable tablet contains:
Calcium Polycarbophil (equivalent to 500 mg Polycarbophil, USP)
Actions: Mitrolan (calcium polycarbophil) is a hydrophilic agent. As a bulk laxative, Mitrolan retains free water within the lumen of the intestine, and indirectly opposes dehydrating forces of the bowel, promoting well-formed stools. In diarrhea, when the intestinal mucosa is incapable of absorbing water at normal rates, Mitrolan absorbs free fecal water, forming a gel and producing formed stools. Thus, in both diarrhea and constipation, the drug works by restoring a more normal moisture level and providing bulk in the patient's intestinal tract.
Indications: For the treatment of constipation or diarrhea, associated with conditions such as irritable bowel syndrome and diverticulosis. Also for the treatment of acute non-specific diarrhea. Restores normal stool consistency by regulating its water and bulk content.
Contraindications: As with all hydrophilic bulking agents, calcium polycarbophil should not be used in patients with signs of gastrointestinal obstruction.
Adverse Reactions: Abdominal fullness may be noted occasionally. An adjustment of the dosage schedule with smaller doses given more frequently but spaced evenly throughout the day may provide relief of this symptom during continued use of Mitrolan.
Directions of Use:
CHEW TABLETS BEFORE SWALLOWING.
Recommended dosage for OTC use: Adults—Chew and swallow 2 tablets 4 times a day, or as needed. Do not exceed 12 tablets in a 24-hour period. Children (6 to under 12 years)—Chew and swallow 1 tablet 3 times a day, or as needed. Do

not exceed 6 tablets in a 24-hour period. Children (3 to under 6 years)—Chew and swallow 1 tablet 2 times a day, or as needed. Do not exceed 3 tablets in a 24-hour period.

For episodes of severe diarrhea, the dose may be repeated every ½ hour, but do not exceed the maximum daily dosage. Dosage may be adjusted according to individual response.

When using as a laxative, patient should drink a full glass (8 fl. oz.) of water or other liquid with each dose.

Sodium Content: Less than 0.02 mEq (0.46 mg) per tablet.

How Supplied: *Chewable Tablets* —cartons of 36 individually packaged blister units (NDC 0031-1535-57).
[*Shown in Product Identification Section*]

ROBITUSSIN®
ROBITUSSIN–CF®
ROBITUSSIN–DM®
ROBITUSSIN–PE®

Composition: *Robitussin* contains Guaifenesin, USP 100 mg in 5 ml (1 teaspoonful) of palatable aromatic syrup; alcohol 3.5%. *Robitussin-CF* contains in each 5 ml (1 teaspoonful): Guaifenesin, USP 100 mg, Phenylpropanolamine Hydrochloride, USP 12.5 mg, Dextromethorphan Hydrobromide, USP 10 mg; alcohol 4.75%. *Robitussin-DM* contains in each 5 ml (1 teaspoonful): Guaifenesin, USP 100 mg and Dextromethorphan Hydrobromide, USP 15 mg; alcohol 1.4%. *Robitussin-PE* contains in each 5 ml (1 teaspoonful): Guaifenesin, USP 100 mg and Pseudoephedrine Hydrochloride, USP 30 mg; alcohol 1.4%.

Action and Uses: All four preparations employ the expectorant action of guaifenesin which enhances the output of respiratory tract fluid (RTF). The enhanced flow of less viscid secretions promotes ciliary action, and facilitates the removal of inspissated mucus. As a result, unproductive coughs become more productive and less frequent. *Robitussin* is therefore, useful in combatting coughs associated with the common cold, bronchitis, laryngitis, tracheitis, pharyngitis, pertussis, influenza and measles, and for coughs provoked by chronic paranasal sinusitis. In *Robitussin-CF* the guaifenesin is supplemented with phenylpropanolamine which provides mild vasoconstrictor action resulting in a nasal decongestant effect and dextromethorphan, a synthetic, non-narcotic, centrally-acting cough suppressant. In *Robitussin-DM*, the guaifenesin is supplemented by dextromethorphan. In *Robitussin-PE*, the expectorant action of guaifenesin is supplemented by a sympathomimetic amine, pseudoephedrine, which helps reduce mucosal congestion and edema in the nasal passages.

Contraindications: Hypersensitivity to any of the components. *Robitussin-DM* is also contraindicated in patients who are receiving MAO inhibitors. *Robitussin-CF* and *Robitussin-PE* are also contraindicated in marked hypertension, hyperthyroidism or in patients who are receiving MAO inhibitors or antihypertensive medication.

Precautions: *Robitussin-CF* and *Robitussin-PE* should be administered with caution to patients with hypertension, cardiac disorders, diabetes or peripheral vascular disease. As with all products containing sympathomimetic amines, these products should be used with caution in patients with prostatic hypertrophy or glaucoma.

Note: Guaifenesin has been shown to produce a color interference with certain clinical laboratory determinations of 5-hydroxyindoleacetic acid (5-HIAA) and vanillylmandelic acid (VMA).

Adverse Reactions: No serious side effects have been reported from guaifenesin or dextromethorphan. Possible adverse reactions of *Robitussin-CF* and *Robitussin-PE* include nausea, vomiting, dry mouth, nervousness, insomnia, restlessness or headache.

Dosage: The following dosages are recommended for *Robitussin* and *Robitussin-CF*: Adults and children 12 years of age and over: 2 teaspoonfuls every four hours, not to exceed 12 teaspoonfuls in a 24-hour period; children 6 to under 12 years: 1 teaspoonful every four hours, not to exceed 6 teaspoonfuls in a 24-hour period; children 2 to under 6 years: ½ teaspoonful every four hours, not to exceed 3 teaspoonfuls in a 24-hour period; children under 2 years: use only as directed by physician. *Robitussin-DM*: Adults and children 12 years of age and over: 2 teaspoonfuls every six to eight hours, not to exceed 8 teaspoonfuls in a 24-hour period; children 6 to under 12 years: 1 teaspoonful every six to eight hours, not to exceed 4 teaspoonfuls in a 24-hour period; children 2 to under 6 years: ½ teaspoonful every six to eight hours, not to exceed 2 teaspoonfuls in a 24-hour period; children under 2 years: use only as directed by physician. *Robitussin-PE*: Adults and children 12 years of age and over: 2 teaspoonfuls every six hours, not to exceed 8 teaspoonfuls in a 24-hour period; children 6 to under 12 years: 1 teaspoonful every six hours, not to exceed 4 teaspoonfuls in a 24-hour period; children 2 to under 6 years: ½ teaspoonful every six hours, not to exceed 2 teaspoonfuls in a 24-hour period; children under 2 years: use as directed by physician.

How Supplied: *Robitussin* (wine-colored) in bottles of 4 fl. oz. (NDC 0031-8624-12), 8 fl. oz. (NDC 0031-8624-18), pint (NDC 0031-8624-25) and gallon (NDC 0031-8624-29). *Robitussin-DM* (cherry-colored) in bottles of 4 fl. oz. (NDC 0031-8684-12), 8 fl. oz. (NDC 0031-8684-18), pint (NDC 0031-8684-25), and gallon (NDC 0031-8684-29). *Robitussin-CF* (red-colored) in bottles of 4 fl. oz. (NDC 0031-8677-12), 8 fl. oz. (NDC 0031-8677-18), and pint (NDC 0031-8677-25). *Robitussin-PE* (orange-red) in bottles of 4 fl. oz. (NDC 0031-8695-12), 8 fl. oz. (NDC 0031-8695-18) and pint (NDC 0031-8695-25). *Robitussin* also available in 1 fl. oz. bottles (4 x 25's-NDC 0031-8624-02) and Dis-Co® Unit Dose Packs of 10 x 10's in 5 ml (NDC 0031-8624-23), 10 ml (NDC 0031-8624-26) and 15 ml (NDC 0031-8624-28). *Robitussin-DM* also available in Dis-

Co® Unit Dose Packs of 10 x 10's in 5 ml (NDC 0031-8684-23) and 10 ml (NDC 0031-8684-26).
[*Shown in Product Identification Section*]

Z–BEC® Tablets

One tablet daily provides:

Vitamin Composition	Percentage of U.S. Recommended Daily Allowance (U.S. RDA)	
Vitamin E	150	45.0 I.U.
Vitamin C	1000	600.0 mg
Thiamine (Vitamin B$_1$)	1000	15.0 mg
Riboflavin (Vitamin B$_2$)	600	10.2 mg
Niacin	500	100.0 mg
Vitamin B$_6$	500	10.0 mg
Vitamin B$_{12}$	100	6.0 mcg
Pantothenic Acid	250	25.0 mg
Mineral Composition		
Zinc	150	22.5 mg*

*22.5 mg zinc (equivalent to zinc content in 100 mg Zinc Sulfate, USP)

Ingredients: Sodium Ascorbate; Niacinamide; Zinc Sulfate; Vitamin E; Lactose; Calcium Pantothenate; Gelatin; Hydroxypropyl Methylcellulose; Povidone; Stearic Acid; Modified Starch; Thiamine Mononitrate; Artificial Color; Pyridoxine Hydrochloride; Riboflavin; Silica; Propylene Glycol; Vanillin; Cyanocobalamin.

Actions and Uses: Z-BEC is a high potency formulation. Its components have important roles in general nutrition, healing of wounds, and prevention of hemorrhage. It is recommended for deficiencies of these components in conditions such as febrile diseases, chronic or acute infections, burns, fractures, surgery, leg ulcers, toxic conditions, physiologic stress, alcoholism, prolonged exposure to high temperature, geriatrics, gastritis, peptic ulcer, and colitis; and in conditions involving special diets and weight-reduction diets.

In dentistry, Z-BEC is recommended for deficiencies of its components in conditions such as herpetic stomatitis, aphthous stomatitis, cheilosis herpangina and gingivitis.

Precaution: Not intended for the treatment of pernicious anemia.

Dosage: The recommended OTC dosage for adults and children twelve or more years of age, other than pregnant or lactating women, is one tablet daily with food or after meals. Under the direction and supervision of a physician, the dose and frequency of administration may be increased in accordance with the patient's requirements.

Continued on next page

Prescribing information on A. H. Robins products listed here is based on official labeling in effect December 1, 1980, with Indications, Contraindications, Warnings, Precautions, Adverse Reactions, and Dosage stated in full.

Robins—Cont.

How Supplied: Green film-coated, capsule shaped tablets in bottles of 60 (NDC 0031-0689-62) and 500 (NDC 0031-0689-70).
[*Shown in Product Identification Section*]

Roche Laboratories
Division of Hoffmann-La Roche Inc.
340 KINGSLAND STREET
NUTLEY, NJ 07110

VI–PENTA® INFANT DROPS
VI–PENTA® MULTIVITAMIN DROPS

The following text is complete prescribing information based on official labeling in effect December 1, 1980.
Composition: Vi-Penta Infant Drops and Vi-Penta Multivitamin Drops are designed to fill the vitamin needs of specific age groups. (See Composition Table below.)
[See table below].
Action and Uses: Vi-Penta Drops are water miscible and can be mixed with food or infant formula, or placed directly on the tongue.
Vi-Penta Infant Drops—a selective formula for prevention of vitamin deficiencies in infants and young children. *Vi-Penta Multivitamin Drops*—a comprehensive formula for daily nutritional support in adults as well as children of all ages. It is an especially convenient dosage form when a small volume liquid vitamin supplement is desired, such as to supplement the diets of those patients with conditions which permanently or temporarily impair their ability to swallow, chew or consume normal amounts and/or kinds of food.
Dosage: The average daily dose is 0.6 cc; therapeutic doses should be given according to the needs of the patient.
How Supplied: Vi-Penta Infant Drops and Vi-Penta Multivitamin Drops—fruit flavored, 50-cc bottles packaged with calibrated dropper.
[*Shown in Product Identification Section*]

Rystan Company, Inc.
470 MAMARONECK AVE.
WHITE PLAINS, NY 10605

CHLORESIUM® Ointment and Solution
Healing and Deodorizing Agent

Composition: Ointment: 0.5% water-soluble chlorophyll derivatives (Rystan brand, 100% concentration) in a hydrophilic base. Solution: 0.2% chlorophyll derivatives in isotonic saline solution.
Action and Uses: To promote normal healing, relieve pain and inflammation and reduce malodors in wounds, burns, surface ulcers, cuts, abrasions and skin irritations.
Administration and Dosage: Ointment: Apply generously and cover with gauze, linen or other appropriate dressing. Dressings preferably changed no more often than every 48 to 72 hours. Solution: Apply full strength as continuous wet dressing, or instill directly into sinus tracts, fistulae, deep ulcers or cavities. As a mouthwash, use half strength.
Side Effects: CHLORESIUM Ointment and Solution are soothing and nontoxic. Sensitivity reactions are extremely rare, and only a few instances of slight itching or irritation have been reported.
How Supplied: Ointment: 1 oz. and 4 oz. tubes, 1 lb. jars. Solution: 2 oz., 8 oz. and 32 oz. bottles.

DERIFIL® Tablets and Powder
Fecal and Urinary Deodorizer

Composition: 100 mg. water-soluble chlorophyll derivatives (Rystan brand, 100% concentration) per tablet or per teaspoonful of prepared solution.
Action and Uses: Oral tablet or solution for control of fecal and urinary odors in colostomy, ileostomy or incontinence; also to deodorize certain necrotic, ulcerative lesions such as decubitus ulcers; also urinary and fecal fistulas and certain breath and body odors not related to faulty hygiene.
Administration and Dosage: In incontinence, one tablet by mouth (or one teaspoonful of solution prepared by dissolving 1 oz. of powder in 1 pint of water) daily at mealtime or any other convenient time. For other conditions, the effective dosage varies with the severity of the odor problem (ordinarily within the range of one to three tablets daily) and is best determined by trial and error. NOTE: Deodorizing effect is cumulative, may require up to seven days to reach maximum. If preferred, tablets may be placed directly in the ostomy appliance.
Side Effects: No toxic effects have been reported from use of DERIFIL, even at high dosage levels for extended periods. A temporary, mild laxative effect may be noted, and the stool is commonly stained dark green. Isolated instances of stomach discomfort or cramps have been reported on high dosages of DERIFIL.
How Supplied: Bottles of 30, 100 and 1000 tablets; 1 oz. and 10 oz. bottles of powder.

SDA Pharmaceuticals, Inc.
919 THIRD AVENUE
NEW YORK, NY 10022

ANOREXIN™
Capsules
Anorectic for simple exogenous obesity contains:
phenylpropanolamine HCl 25 mg
caffeine 100 mg

One-Span™
Sustained Release Capsules contains:
phenylpropanolamine HCl 50 mg
caffeine 200 mg

Description: Each capsule contains phenylpropanolamine HCl, an anorexiant, and caffeine, a mild stimulant.
Indication: ANOREXIN is indicated as adjunctive therapy in a regimen of weight reduction based on caloric restriction in the management and control of simple exogenous obesity.
Caution: Do not exceed recommended dosage. Discontinue use if rapid pulse, dizziness or palpitations occur. Do not use if high blood pressure, heart, kidney, diabetes, thyroid or other disease is pre-

Vi-Penta Composition Table

Each 0.6 cc of Vi-Penta Infant Drops provides:	% minimum daily requirements (MDR)	
	Infants (under 1 year)	Young Children (1–6 years)
Vitamin A (as the palmitate) 5000 U.S.P. Units	333%	166%
Vitamin D₂ 400 U.S.P. Units	100%	100%
Vitamin C 50 mg	500%	250%
Vitamin E (as *dl-α*-tocopheryl acetate) 2 Int. Units	*	*

Each 0.6 cc of Vi-Penta Multivitamin Drops provides:	% minimum daily requirements (MDR)		
	Infants (under 1 year)	Children (1-6 years)	(6-12 years)
Vitamin A (as the palmitate) 5000 U.S.P. Units	333%	166%	166%
Vitamin D₂ 400 U.S.P. Units	100%	100%	100%
Vitamin C 50 mg	500%	250%	250%
Vitamin B₁ (as hydrochloride) 1 mg	400%	200%	133%
Vitamin B₂ (as riboflavin-5'-phosphate sodium) 1 mg	166%	111%	111%
Vitamin B₆ 1 mg	*	*	*
Vitamin E (as *dl-α*-tocopheryl acetate) 2 Int. Units	*	*	*
d-Biotin 30 mcg	†	†	†
Niacinamide 10 mg	*	200%	133%
D-Panthenol (equiv. to 11.6 mg Calcium pantothenate) 10 mg	†	†	†

*MDR for these vitamins has not been determined.
†The need for these vitamins in human nutrition has not been established.

sent, or if pregnant or lactating, nor to be used by anyone under the age of 18, except on physician's advice. Keep this and all drugs out of the reach of children. In case of accidental overdose seek professional assistance or contact a Poison Control Center immediately.

Precaution: Avoid use if taking prescription, anti-hypertensive or anti-depressive drugs containing monoamine oxidase inhibitors or other medication containing sympathomimetic amines. Avoid continuous use longer than 3 months.

Adverse Reactions: Side effects are rare when taken as directed. Nausea or nasal dryness may occasionally occur.

Dosage and Administration:
ANOREXIN™ Capsules: One capsule 30–60 minutes before each meal three times a day with one or two full glasses of water.

ANOREXIN™ One-Span™ Sustained Release Capsules: One capsule with a full glass of water once a day mid-morning (10:00 A.M.)

How Supplied:
ANOREXIN™ Capsules: Bottles of 50, packaged with 1200 calorie ANOREXIN Diet Plan.

ANOREXIN™ One-Span™ Sustained Release Capsules: Bottles of 21, packaged with 1200 calorie ANOREXIN Diet Plan.

A U.S. Government advisory panel of medical and scientific experts has determined the combination of active ingredients in this product as safe and effective when taken as directed for appetite control to aid in weight reduction by caloric restriction.

Reference: Griboff, Solomon, I., M.D., F.A.C.P. et al., A Double-Blind Clinical Evaluation of a Phenylpropanolamine-Caffeine Combination and a Placebo in the Treatment of Exogenous Obesity, Current Therapeutic Research 17, 6:535, 1975 (June).

S.S.S. Company
71 UNIVERSITY AVENUE, S.W.
POST OFFICE BOX 4447
ATLANTA, GA 30302

20/20 Eye Drops
(naphazoline hydrochloride 0.012%)

Active Ingredients: Naphazoline Hydrochloride 0.012%, buffered with Sodium Carbonate, preserved with Thimerosal, 0.0050%.

Indications: For the temporary relief of minor eye irritation due to smoke, wind blown pollen, dust, smog and hayfever.

Actions: Naphazoline, an occular decongestant, constricts the small arterioles on the surface of the eye and thus helps remove the redness. Eyes are soothed and cleared in a few minutes.

Warnings: If irritation persists or increases, discontinue use and consult a physician. Do not touch the dispenser tip

or allow it to be exposed longer than necessary. Keep the container tightly closed.

Drug Interaction Precaution: No known drug interaction.

Dosage and Administration: Use two drops in each eye for the relief of minor eye irritation. May be repeated.

How Supplied: Available in a 0.5 fl. oz. plastic bottle.

Schering Corporation
GALLOPING HILL ROAD
KENILWORTH, NJ 07033

A and D Ointment
REG. T.M.

Description: An ointment containing the emollients anhydrous lanolin and petrolatum.

Indications: *Diaper rash*—**A and D Ointment** provides prompt, soothing relief for diaper rash and helps heal baby's tender skin; forms a moisture-proof shield that helps protect against urine and detergent irritants; comforts baby's skin and helps prevent chafing.

Chafed Skin—**A and D Ointment** helps skin retain its vital natural moisture; quickly soothes chafed skin in adults and children and helps prevent abnormal dryness.

Abrasions and Minor Burns—**A and D Ointment** soothes and helps relieve the smarting and pain of abrasions and minor burns, encourages healing and prevents dressings from sticking to the injured area.

Warning: Keep this and all drugs out of the reach of children.

Overdosage: In case of accidental ingestion, seek professional assistance or contact a poison control center immediately.

Dosage and Administration: *Diaper Rash*—Simply apply a thin coating of **A and D Ointment** at each diaper change. A modest amount is all that is needed to provide protective and healing action.

Chafed Skin—Gently smooth a small quantity of **A and D Ointment** over the area to be treated.

Abrasions, Minor Burns—Wash with lukewarm water and mild soap. When dry apply **A and D Ointment** liberally. When a sterile dressing is used, change the dressing daily and apply fresh **A and D Ointment**. If no improvement occurs after 48 to 72 hours or if condition worsens, consult your physician.

How Supplied: A and D Ointment is available in 1½-ounce (42.5 g) and 4-ounce (113 g) tubes and 1-pound (454 g) jars.

Store away from heat.

Copyright© 1973, 1977, Schering Corporation. All rights reserved.

[*Shown in Product Identification Section*]

AFRIN®
Nasal Spray 0.05%
Menthol Nasal Spray 0.05%
Nose Drops 0.05%
Pediatric Nose Drops 0.025%

Description: AFRIN products contain oxymetazoline hydrochloride, the lon-

gest acting topical nasal decongestant available. Each ml of AFRIN Nasal Spray and Nose Drops contains oxymetazoline hydrochloride, USP 0.5 mg (0.05%); aminoacetic acid 3.8 mg; sorbitol solution, USP 57.1 mg; phenylmercuric acetate 0.02 mg; benzalkonium chloride 0.2 mg; sodium hydroxide to adjust the pH to a weak acid solution (5.5-6.5); and purified water, q.s. 1 ml.

Each ml of AFRIN Pediatric Nose Drops contains oxymetazoline hydrochloride, USP 0.25 mg (0.025%); aminoacetic acid 3.8 mg; sorbitol solution, USP 57.1 mg; phenylmercuric acetate 0.02 mg; benzalkonium chloride 0.2 mg; hydrochloric acid to adjust the pH to a weak acid solution (4.0-5.0); and purified water, q.s. 1 ml.

AFRIN Menthol Nasal Spray contains cooling aromatic vapors of menthol, eucalyptol and camphor in addition to the ingredients of AFRIN Nasal Spray.

Indications: For temporary relief of nasal congestion due to the common cold, sinusitus, hay fever or other upper respiratory allergies.

Actions: The sympathomimetic action of AFRIN products constrict the smaller arterioles of the nasal passages, producing a prolonged, gentle and predictable decongesting effect. In just a few minutes a single dose, as directed, provides prompt, temporary relief of nasal congestion that lasts up to 12 hours. AFRIN products last up to 3 or 4 times longer than most ordinary nasal sprays.

AFRIN products used at bedtime help restore free nasal breathing through the night.

Warnings: Do not exceed recommended dosage because symptoms may occur, such as burning, stinging, sneezing or increase of nasal discharge. Do not use these products for more than 3 days. If symptoms persist, consult a physician. The use of the dispensers by more than one person may spread infection. Keep these and all medicines out of the reach of children.

Overdosage: In case of accidental ingestion, seek professional assistance or contact a Poison Control Center immediately.

Dosage and Administration: Because AFRIN has a long duration of action, twice-a-day administration—in the morning and at bedtime—is usually adequate.

AFRIN Nasal Spray and Menthol Nasal Spray, 0.05%—For adults and children 6 years of age and over: With head upright, spray 2 or 3 times into each nostril twice daily—morning and evening. To spray, squeeze bottle quickly and firmly and sniff briskly. Not recommended for children under six.

AFRIN Nose Drops—For adults and children 6 years of age and over: Tilt head back, apply 2 or 3 drops into each nostril twice daily—morning and evening. Im-

Continued on next page

Information on Schering products appearing on these pages is effective as of March 1, 1981.

Schering—Cont.

mediately bend head forward toward knees. Hold a few seconds, then return to upright position. Not recommended for children under six.

AFRIN Pediatric Nose Drops—Children 2 through 5 years of age: Tilt head back, apply 2 or 3 drops into each nostril twice daily—morning and evening. Promptly move head forward toward knees. Hold a few seconds, then return child to upright position. For children under 2 years, use only as directed by a physician.

How Supplied: AFRIN Nasal Spray 0.05% (1:2000), 15 ml and 30 ml plastic squeeze bottles.

AFRIN Menthol Nasal Spray 0.05% (1:2000), 15 ml plastic squeeze bottle.

AFRIN Nose Drops, 0.05% (1:2000), 20 ml dropper bottle.

AFRIN Pediatric Nose Drops, 0.025% (1:4000), 20 ml dropper bottle.

[*Shown in Product Identification Section*]

AFRINOL®
Repetabs® Tablets
Long-Acting Nasal Decongestant

Active Ingredients: Each Repetabs Tablet contains: 120 mg pseudoephedrine sulfate. Half the dose (60 mg) is released after the tablet is swallowed and the other half is released hours later; continuous relief is provided for up to 12 hours.

Indications: For temporary relief of nasal congestion due to the common cold, hay fever or other upper respiratory allergies, and nasal congestion associated with sinusitis.

Actions: Promotes nasal and/or sinus drainage, helps decongest sinus openings, sinus passages.

Warnings: Do not exceed recommended dosage because at higher doses nervousness, dizziness or sleeplessness may occur. Do not take this preparation if you have high blood pressure, heart disease, diabetes, or thyroid disease, except under the advice and supervision of a physician. If symptoms do not improve within 7 days or are accompanied by high fever, consult a physician before continuing use. Keep this and all drugs out of the reach of children.

Drug Interactions: Do not take this product if you are presently taking a prescription antihypertensive or antidepressant drug containing a monoamine oxidase inhibitor, except under the advice and supervision of a physician.

Overdosage: In case of accidental overdose, seek professional assistance or contact a poison control center immediately.

Dosage and Administration: Adults and children 12 years and over—One tablet every 12 hours. AFRINOL is not recommended for children under 12 years of age.

How Supplied: AFRINOL Repetabs Tablets—Boxes of 12 and bottles of 100. Store between 2° and 30°C (36° and 86° F) Protect from excessive moisture.

[*Shown in Product Identification Section*]

CHLOR–TRIMETON®
Allergy Syrup
Allergy Tablets
Long Acting Allergy REPETABS® Tablets

Active Ingredients: Each Allergy Tablet contains: 4 mg CHLOR-TRIMETON (brand of chlorpheniramine maleate, USP); Each REPETABS® Tablet contains: 8 mg CHLOR-TRIMETON (brand of chlorpheniramine maleate). Half the dose (4 mg) is released after the tablet is swallowed, and the other half is released hours later; continuous relief is provided for up to 12 hours.

Each teaspoonful (5 ml) of Allergy Syrup contains: 2 mg CHLOR-TRIMETON (brand of chlorpheniramine maleate) in a pleasant-tasting syrup containing approximately 7% alcohol.

Indications: For temporary relief of hay fever/upper respiratory allergy symptoms: sneezing; running nose; watery, itchy eyes.

Actions: The active ingredient in CHLOR-TRIMETON is an antihistamine with anticholinergic (drying) and sedative side effects. Antihistamines appear to compete with histamine for cell receptor sites on effector cells.

Warnings: May cause drowsiness. May cause excitability especially in children. Do not take these products if you have asthma, glaucoma or difficulty in urination due to enlargement of the prostate gland, or give the REPETABS Tablets to children under 12 years, or the Allergy Syrup and Tablets to children under 6 years, except under the advice and supervision of a physician. Keep these and all drugs out of the reach of children.

Precautions: Avoid driving a motor vehicle or operating heavy machinery. Avoid alcoholic beverages while taking these products.

Overdosage: In case of accidental overdose, seek professional assistance or contact a Poison Control Center immediately.

Dosage and Administration: Allergy Syrup—Adults and Children 12 years and over: Two teaspoonfuls (4 mg) every 4 to 6 hours, not to exceed 12 teaspoonfuls in 24 hours; Children 6 through 11 years: one teaspoonful (2 mg) every 4 to 6 hours, not to exceed 6 teaspoonfuls in 24 hours; For children under 6 years, consult a physician.

Allergy Tablets—Adults and Children 12 years and over: One tablet (4 mg) every 4 to 6 hours, not to exceed 6 tablets in 24 hours. Children 6 through 11 years: One half the adult dose (break tablet in half) every 4 to 6 hours, not to exceed 3 whole tablets in 24 hours. For children under 6 years, consult a physician.

Allergy REPETABS Tablets—Adults and Children 12 years and over: One tablet (8 mg) in the morning and one tablet in the evening, not to exceed 3 tablets in 24 hours. For children under 12 years, consult a physician.

Professional Labeling: Dosage—Allergy Syrup: Children 2 through 5 years: ½ teaspoonful (1 mg) every 4 to 6 hours; Allergy Tablets: Children 2 through 5

years: one-quarter tablet (1 mg) every 4 to 6 hours.

Allergy REPETABS Tablets—Children 6 to 12 years: One tablet (8 mg) at bedtime or during the day, as indicated.

How Supplied: CHLOR-TRIMETON Allergy Tablets, 4 mg, yellow compressed, scored tablets impressed with the Schering trademark and product identification letters, TW or numbers, 080; box of 24, bottles of 100 and 1000, canisters of 5000.

CHLOR-TRIMETON Allergy Syrup: 2 mg per 5 ml, blue-green-colored liquid; 4-fluid ounce (118 ml) and 128-fluid ounce (3.2 liters) bottles. Protect from light; however, if color fades potency will not be affected.

[*Shown in Product Identification Section*]

CHLOR-TRIMETON Allergy REPETABS Tablets, 8 mg, sugar-coated, yellow tablets branded in red with the Schering trademark and product identification letters, CC or numbers, 374; boxes of 24, 48, bottles of 100 and 1000, canister of 5000.

[*Shown in Product Identification Section*]

Note: also available—CHLOR-TRIMETON Expectorant (brand of antihistamine-decongestant expectorant-antitussive); each 5 ml (1 teaspoonful) contains 2 mg chlorpheniramine maleate, USP; 10 mg phenylephrine hydrochloride, USP; 100 mg ammonium chloride, NF; 50 mg sodium citrate; 50 mg guiafenesin, NF, and alcohol 1 per cent or less, in a cherry-flavored demulcent syrup.

CHLOR–TRIMETON® Decongestant Tablets

Active Ingredients: Each Tablet contains: 4 mg. CHLOR-TRIMETON (brand of chlorpheniramine maleate, USP) and 60 mg. pseudoephedrine sulfate.

Indications: For temporary relief of nasal/sinus passage congestion due to hay fever and sinusitis.

Actions: The antihistamine, chlorpheniramine maleate, provides temporary relief of sneezing; watery, itchy eyes; running nose due to hay fever and other upper respiratory allergies. The decongestant, pseudoephedrine sulfate, temporarily restores freer breathing through the nose and promotes sinus drainage.

Warnings: Consult your physician before continuing use if symptoms do not improve within 7 days or are accompanied by high fever. May cause drowsiness. May cause excitability especially in children. Do not exceed recommended dosage because at higher doses nervousness, dizziness or sleeplessness are more likely to occur. Except under the advice and supervision of a physician, this product should not be used in children under 6 years or by persons with asthma, glaucoma, difficulty in urination due to enlargement of the prostate gland, high blood pressure, heart disease, diabetes or thyroid disease. Keep this and all drugs out of the reach of children.

Drug Interaction: Do not take this product if you are presently taking a prescription antihypertensive or antidepressant medication containing a monoamine oxidase inhibitor, except under the advice and supervision of a physician.

Precautions: Avoid driving a motor vehicle or operating heavy machinery. Also avoid alcoholic beverages while taking this product.

Overdosage: In case of accidental overdose, seek professional assistance or contact a Poison Control Center immediately.

Dosage and Administration: Adults and children 12 years and over—One tablet **every 4 hours,** not to exceed 4 tablets in 24 hours. Children 6 through 11 years—One half the adult dose (break tablet in half) **every 4 hours,** not to exceed 2 whole tablets in 24 hours. For children under 6 years, consult a physician.

Professional Labeling: Dosage—Children 2-5 years—one-quarter the adult dose every 4 hours, not to exceed 1 tablet in 24 hours.

How Supplied: CHLOR-TRIMETON Decongestant Tablets—boxes of 24's and 48's.

[*Shown in Product Identification Section*]

COD LIVER OIL CONCENTRATE
Tablets
Capsules
Tablets with Vitamin C

Active Ingredients: Tablets—A pleasantly flavored concentrate of cod liver oil with Vitamins A & D added. Each chewable tablet provides: 4000 IU of vitamin A and 200 IU of vitamin D.
Capsules—A concentrate of cod liver oil with Vitamin A, with Vitamin D added. Each capsule provides: 10,000 IU of vitamin A and 400 IU of vitamin D.
Tablets with Vitamin C—A pleasantly-flavored concentrate of cod liver oil with Vitamins A, D and C added. Each tablet provides, 4000 IU of Vitamin A, 200 IU of Vitamin D and 50 mg of Vitamin C. Tablets may be chewed or swallowed.
Cod Liver Oil Concentrate Tablets and Tablets with Vitamin C contain FD&C Yellow No. 5 (tartrazine) as a color additive.

Indications: Cod Liver Oil Concentrate Tablets and Capsules are recommended for prevention and treatment of diseases due to deficiencies in Vitamins A and D. The tablets with Vitamin C are recommended for prevention and treatment of diseases due to deficiencies of Vitamins A, D and C.

Warnings: Keep this and all drugs out of the reach of children.

Overdosage: In case of accidental overdose, seek professional assistance or contact a Poison Control Center immediately.

Dosage and Administration: Tablets: Two tablets daily, or as prescribed by a physician, taken preferably before meals.
Capsules: One capsule daily, or as prescribed by a physician, taken preferably before meals.
Tablets with Vitamin C: Two tablets daily, taken preferably before meals.

How Supplied: Cod Liver Oil Concentrate Tablets: bottles of 100 and 240. Cod Liver Oil Concentrate Capsules: bot-

tles of 40 and 100. Cod Liver Oil Concentrate Tablets with Vitamin C: bottles of 100 tablets.

[*Shown in Product Identification Section*]

CORICIDIN® Tablets
CORICIDIN 'D'® Decongestant Tablets
CORICIDIN® Cough Syrup
CORICIDIN® Decongestant Nasal Mist

Active Ingredients: CORICIDIN Tablets—2 mg CHLOR-TRIMETON® (brand of chlorpheniramine maleate, USP); 325 mg (5gr) aspirin, USP.
CORICIDIN 'D' Decongestant Tablets—2 mg chlorpheniramine maleate, USP; 12.5 mg phenylpropanolamine hydrochloride, NF; 325 mg (5 gr) aspirin, USP.
CORICIDIN Cough Syrup—Each teaspoonful (5 ml) of fruit-flavored syrup contains 10 mg dextromethorphan hydrobromide; 12.5 mg phenylpropanolamine hydrochloride; 100 mg guaifenesin and less than 0.5% alcohol.
CORICIDIN Decongestant Nasal Mist—0.5% phenylephrine hydrochloride, USP.

Indications: CORICIDIN Tablets—For effective, temporary relief of cold symptoms.
CORICIDIN 'D' Decongestant Tablets—For congested cold and sinus symptoms.
CORICIDIN Cough Syrup—For temporary relief of coughs and stuffy noses.
CORICIDIN Decongestant Nasal Mist—For temporary relief of congested nasal passages due to the common cold, hay fever or sinusitis.

Actions: CORICIDIN Tablets relieve annoying cold symptoms such as minor aches and pains, fever, sneezing, running nose and watery/itchy eyes.
CORICIDIN 'D' Tablets relieve the same annoying cold symptoms as well as stuffy nose, nasal membrane swelling and sinus headache.
CORICIDIN Cough Syrup helps loosen the phlegm in a non-productive cough, temporarily soothes irritated throat membranes, suppresses annoying coughs and helps relieve stuffy noses.
CORICIDIN Decongestant Nasal Mist is "symptom specific" and designed to shrink swollen nasal membranes promptly and help restore freer breathing through the nose.

Warnings: CORICIDIN Tablets—Drink a full glass of water with each dose. Adults should not take this product for more than 10 days; children 6 through 11 not more than 5 days. If fever persists or recurs, neither adults nor children should use for more than 3 days. If symptoms persist or new ones occur, consult your physician. May cause drowsiness. May cause excitability, especially in children. This product contains aspirin. Do not take this product if you are allergic to aspirin or if you have asthma, glaucoma, difficulty in urination due to enlargement of the prostate gland, stomach distress, ulcers or bleeding problems, or give this product to children under 6 years, except under the advice and supervision of a physician. Stop taking this product if ringing in the ears or other symptoms

occur. Use during pregnancy ONLY under your doctor's direction. Keep this and all drugs out of the reach of children.
CORICIDIN 'D' Decongestant Tablets—Drink a full glass of water with each dose. Adults should not take this product for more than 7 days; children 6 through 11 not more than 5 days. If fever persists or recurs, neither adults nor children should use for more than 3 days. If symptoms persist or new ones occur, consult your physician. May cause drowsiness. May cause excitability especially in children. Do not exceed recommended dosage because at higher doses nervousness, dizziness or sleeplessness may occur. This product contains aspirin. Do not take this product if you are allergic to aspirin or if you have asthma, glaucoma, difficulty in urination due to enlargement of the prostate gland, stomach distress, ulcers or bleeding problems, high blood pressure, heart disease, diabetes or thyroid disease, or give this product to children under 6 years, except under the advice and supervision of a physician. Stop taking this product if ringing in the ears or other symptoms occur. Use during pregnancy ONLY under your doctor's direction. Keep this and all drugs out of the reach of children.
CORICIDIN Cough Syrup—Do not exceed recommended dosage because at higher doses nervousness, dizziness or sleeplessness are more likely to occur. This product should not, except under the direction of a physician, be used for persistent or chronic cough such as occurs with smoking, asthma or emphysema or where cough is accompanied by excessive secretions. CORICIDIN Cough Syrup should not be used in children under 2 years of age or by persons with high blood pressure, heart disease, diabetes or thyroid disease, except under the advice and supervision of a physician. Keep this and all drugs out of the reach of children.
CORICIDIN Decongestant Nasal Mist —Do not exceed recommended dosage because symptoms may occur such as burning, stinging, sneezing, or increase of nasal discharge. Do not use this product for more than 3 days. If symptoms persist, consult a physician. The use of this dispenser by more than one person may spread infection. For adult use only. Do not give this product to children under 12 years of age except under the advice and supervision of a physician. Keep this and all medicines out of the reach of children.

Drug Interactions: CORICIDIN Tablets—Do not take this product if you are presently taking a prescription drug for anticoagulation (thinning of the blood), diabetes, gout or arthritis, except under the advice and supervision of a physician.
CORICIDIN 'D' Decongestant Tablets—Do not take this product if you are presently taking a prescription antihy-

Continued on next page

Information on Schering products appearing on these pages is effective as of March 1, 1981.

Schering—Cont.

pertensive or antidepressant drug containing a monoamine oxidase inhibitor or a prescription drug for anticoagulation (thinning of the blood), diabetes, gout or arthritis, except under the advice and supervision of a physician.

CORICIDIN Cough Syrup—Do not take this product if you are presently taking a prescription antihypertensive or antidepressant drug containing a monoamine oxidase inhibitor, except under the advice and supervision of a physician.

Precautions: CORICIDIN Tablets and CORICIDIN 'D' Decongestant Tablets —Avoid alcoholic beverages while taking these products. Also avoid driving a motor vehicle or operating heavy machinery.

CORICIDIN Cough Syrup—A persistent cough may be a sign of a serious condition. If cough or other symptoms persist for more than one week, tend to recur or are accompanied by high fever, rash or persistent headache, consult a physician before continuing use.

CORICIDIN Decongestant Nasal Mist— The use of this dispenser by more than one person may spread infection. Do not exceed recommended dosage. If symptoms are not relieved after three days, consult your physician as continuing use may cause increasing nasal obstruction.

Overdosage: In case of accidental overdose of the tablets or syrup or accidental ingestion of the nasal mist, seek professional assistance or contact a Poison Control Center immediately.

Dosage and Administration: CORICIDIN Tablets—Adults and children 12 years and over—2 tablets every 4 hours not to exceed 12 tablets in 24 hours. Children 6 through 11 years: 1 tablet every 4 hours not to exceed 5 tablets in 24 hours.

CORICIDIN 'D' Decongestant Tablets —Adults and children 12 years and over: 2 tablets every 4 hours not to exceed 12 tablets in 24 hours. Children 6 through 11 years: 1 tablet every 4 hours not to exceed 5 tablets in 24 hours.

CORICIDIN Cough Syrup—NEW DOSAGE: Read carefully. Adults and chldren 12 years and over: 2 teaspoonfuls every 4 hours. Children 6–11 years: 1 teaspoonful every 4 hours. Children 2–5 years: ½ teaspoonful every 4 hours. Do not exceed 6 doses per day.

CORICIDIN Decongestant Nasal Mist— For adults and children 12 years of age and over: With head upright spray two or three times in each nostril, not more frequently than every four hours.

How Supplied: CORICIDIN Tablets— bottles of 12, 24, 60, 100 and 1000. Dispensing Package, box of 100 packets, 4 tablets in each packet.

CORICIDIN 'D' Decongestant Tablets— bottles of 12, 24, 50, and 100. Dispensing Package, box of 100 packets, 4 tablets in each packet.

CORICIDIN Cough Syrup—bottles of 4 oz. (118 ml).

CORICIDIN Decongestant Nasal Mist— Plastic squeeze bottles of ⅔ fl. oz. (20 ml).
[*Shown in Product Identification Section*]

CORICIDIN® MEDILETS® Tablets for Children
CORICIDIN® DEMILETS® Tablets for Children
CORICIDIN® Children's Cough Syrup

Active Ingredients: CORICIDIN MEDILETS Tablets—1.0 mg CHLOR-TRIMETON® (brand of chlorpheniramine maleate, USP); 80 mg (1¼ gr) aspirin.

CORICIDIN DEMILETS Tablets—1.0 mg chlorpheniramine maleate, USP; 80 mg (1¼ gr) aspirin; 6.25 mg phenylpropanolamine hydrochloride.

CORICIDIN Children's Cough Syrup —Each teaspoonful (5 ml) contains: 5 mg dextromethorphan hydrobromide; 6.25 mg phenylpropanolamine hydrochloride; 100 mg guaifenesin and less than 0.5% alcohol.

Indications: CORICIDIN MEDILETS Tablets—For temporary relief of cold symptoms in children. CORICIDIN DEMILETS Tablets—For temporary relief of children's congested cold and sinus symptoms.

CORICIDIN Children's Cough Syrup— For temporary relief of children's cough symptoms and stuffy nose.

Actions: CORICIDIN MEDILETS Tablets provide relief of minor aches, pains, fever, running nose, sneezing and watery/itchy eyes that may accompany colds.

CORICIDIN DEMILETS Tablets provide relief of annoying cold symptoms: running nose, stuffy nose, sneezing, watery/ itchy eyes, minor aches, pains and fever.

CORICIDIN Children's Cough Syrup provides temporary relief of cough symptoms, decongests stuffy noses, helps loosen the phlegm in a non-productive cough and temporarily soothes irritated throat membranes.

Warnings: CORICIDIN MEDILETS Tablets—Give water with each dose. Do not give this product for more than 5 days, but if fever is present, persists or recurs limit use to 3 days; if symptoms persist or new ones occur, consult your physician. This product may cause drowsiness; therefore, driving a motor vehicle or operating heavy machinery must be avoided while taking it. Alcoholic beverages must also be avoided while taking this product. It may cause excitability, especially in children. This product contains aspirin. Do not give this product to persons who are allergic to aspirin or to those who have asthma, glaucoma, difficulty in urination due to enlargement of the prostate gland, stomach distress, ulcers or bleeding problems, or to children less than 6 years old, except under the advice and supervision of a physician. If ringing in the ears or other symptoms occur, stop giving this product. Use during pregnancy ONLY under a doctor's direction. Keep this and all drugs out of the reach of children.

CORICIDIN DEMILETS Tablets—Give water with each dose. Do not give this product for more than 5 days, but if fever is present, persists or recurs, limit dosage to 3 days; if symptoms persist or new ones occur, consult a physician. This product may cause drowsiness, therefore, driving a motor vehicle or operating heavy machinery must be avoided while taking it. Alcoholic beverages must also be avoided while taking this product. It may cause excitability, especially in children. Do not exceed recommended dosage because at higher doses nervousness, dizziness or sleeplessness are more likely to occur. This product contains aspirin. Do not administer this product to persons who are allergic to aspirin or to those who have asthma, glaucoma, difficulty in urination due to enlargement of the prostate gland, stomach distress, ulcers or bleeding problems, high blood pressure, heart disease, diabetes or thyroid disease, or give this product to children less than 6 years old, except under the advice and supervision of a physician. Use during pregnancy ONLY under a doctor's direction. If ringing in the ears or other symptoms occur, stop giving this product. Keep this and all drugs out of the reach of children.

CORICIDIN Children's Cough Syrup—Do not exceed recommended dosage because at higher doses nervousness, dizziness or sleeplessness are more likely to occur. This product should not, except under the direction of a physician, be used for persistent or chronic cough such as occurs with smoking, asthma or emphysema or where cough is accompanied by excessive secretions. CORICIDIN Children's Cough Syrup should not be used in children under 2 years of age or in persons with high blood pressure, heart disease, diabetes or thyroid disease, except under the advice and supervision of a physician. A persistent cough may be a sign of a serious condition. If cough or other symptoms persist for more than one week, tend to recur or are accompanied by high fever, rash or persistent headache, consult a physician before continuing use. Keep this and all drugs out of the reach of children.

Drug Interactions: CORICIDIN MEDILETS Tablets—Do not give this product to persons who are presently taking a prescription drug for anticoagulation (thinning of the blood), diabetes, gout or arthritis, except under the advice and supervision of a physician.

CORICIDIN DEMILETS Tablets—Do not give this product to persons who are presently taking a prescription antihypertensive or antidepressant drug containing a monoamine oxidase inhibitor or a prescription drug for anticoagulation (thinning of the blood), diabetes, gout or arthritis, except under the advice and supervision of a physician. CORICIDIN Children's Cough Syrup—Do not give this product to persons who are presently taking a prescription antihypertensive or antidepressant drug containing a monoamine oxidase inhibitor, except under the advice and supervision of a physician.

Overdosage: In case of accidental overdose, seek professional assistance or contact a Poison Control Center immediately.

Dosage and Administration: CORICIDIN MEDILETS Tablets—Under 6 years: As directed by physician. 6 to 12 years: Two MEDILETS Tablets every 4 hours not to exceed 12 tablets in a 24-hour period, or as directed by physician. CORICIDIN DEMILETS Tablets—Under 6 years: As directed by physician. 6 to 12 years: Two DEMILETS Tablets every 4 hours not to exceed 12 tablets in a 24-hour period, or as directed by physician. Limit dosage to three days; if symptoms persist, a physician should be consulted. CORICIDIN Children's Cough Syrup—Children 2 through 5 years: 1 teaspoonful every 4 hours not to exceed 6 teaspoonfuls in a 24-hour period. Children 6 through 11 years: 2 teaspoonfuls every 4 hours not to exceed 12 teaspoonfuls in a 24-hour period.

How Supplied: CORICIDIN MEDILETS Tablets—boxes of 24 and 36, individually wrapped in a child's protective pack.
CORICIDIN DEMILETS Tablets—boxes of 24 and 36, individually wrapped in a child's protective pack.
CORICIDIN Children's Cough Syrup—bottles of 4 fl. oz. (118 ml).
[*Shown in Product Identification Section*]

CORICIDIN® Extra Strength Sinus Headache Tablets

Active Ingredients: Each tablet contains: acetaminophen 500 mg (500 mg is a non-standard extra strength tablet of acetaminophen, as compared to the standard of 325 mg); CHLOR-TRIMETON (brand of chlorpheniramine maleate) 2 mg; phenylpropanolamine hydrochloride 12.5 mg.

Indications: For temporary relief of sinus headache and congestion.

Actions: CORICIDIN Sinus Headache Tablets have been formulated with an antihistamine for temporary relief of the running nose that often accompanies upper respiratory allergies and sinusitis; a non-aspirin pain reliever for temporary relief of sinus headache pain and a decongestant for temporary relief of nasal membrane swelling, thus promoting freer breathing.

Warnings: Consult your physician: if symptoms persist, do not improve within 7 days, if new symptoms occur, or if fever persists for more than 3 days (72 hours) or recurs. May cause drowsiness. May cause excitability, especially in children. Do not exceed recommended dosage because severe liver damage may occur and at higher doses nervousness, dizziness or sleeplessness are more likely to occur. Except under the advice and supervision of a physician, this product should not be used in children less than 12 years old or by persons with high blood pressure, heart disease, diabetes or thyroid disease, asthma, glaucoma or difficulty in urination due to enlargement of the prostate gland. Keep this and all drugs out of the reach of children.

Drug Interactions: Do not take this product if you are presently taking a prescription antihypertensive or, antidepressant medication containing a monoamine oxidase inhibitor, except under the advice and supervision of a physician.

Precautions: Avoid alcoholic beverages while taking this product. Also, avoid driving a motor vehicle or operating heavy machinery.

Overdosage: In case of accidental overdose, seek professional assistance or contact a poison control center immediately.

Dosage and Administration: Adults and children 12 years and older: 2 tablets every 6 hours not to exceed 8 tablets in a 24-hour period, or as directed by a physician. Swallow one tablet at a time.

How Supplied: Box of 24.
[*Shown in Product Identification Section*]

DEMAZIN®
Decongestant-Antihistamine
REPETABS® Tablets
Syrup

Active Ingredients: Each REPETABS® Tablet contains: 20 mg. phenylephrine and 4 mg CHLOR-TRIMETON® (brand of chlorpheniramine maleate, USP). Half the dose is in the outside coating for rapid absorption and prompt effect. The other half is in the inner core coated for repeat action.
Each teaspoonful (5 ml.) of syrup contains 2.5 mg. phenylephrine hydrochloride, USP and 1 mg. CHLOR-TRIMETON® (brand of chlorpheniramine maleate, USP) in a pleasant-tasting syrup containing approximately 7.5% alcohol. DEMAZIN Syrup contains FD&C Yellow No. 5 (tartrazine) as a color additive.

Indications: For temporary relief of nasal congestion, watery eyes, running nose, and sneezing associated with hay fever, sinus congestion and the common cold.

Actions: Phenylephrine hydrochloride is a sympathomimetic agent which acts as an upper respiratory and pulmonary decongestant and mild bronchodilator. It exerts desirable sympathomimetic action with relatively little central nervous system excitation, so that wakefulness and nervousness are reduced to a minimum. Chlorpheniramine maleate antagonizes many of the characteristic effects of histamine. It is of value clinically in the prevention and relief of many allergic manifestations.
The oral administration of phenylephrine hydrochloride with chlorpheniramine maleate produces a complementary action on congestive conditions of the upper respiratory tract, thus often obviating the need for topical nasal therapy.

Warnings: If symptoms do not improve within 7 days or are accompanied by high fever consult a physician before continuing use. May cause drowsiness. May cause excitability especially in children. Do not exceed recommended dosage because at higher doses nervousness, dizziness or sleeplessness are more likely to occur. Except under the advice and supervision of a physician, this product should not be used in children under 6 years of age or by persons with high blood pressure, heart disease, diabetes,

thyroid disease, asthma, glaucoma or difficulty in urination due to enlargement of the prostate gland.
Keep this and all drugs out of the reach of children.

Drug Interaction: Do not take this product if you are presently taking a prescription antihypertensive or antidepressant drug containing a monoamine oxidase inhibitor, except under the advice and supervision of a physician.

Precautions: Avoid alcoholic beverages while taking this product. Also avoid driving a motor vehicle or operating heavy machinery.

Overdosage: In case of accidental overdose, seek professional assistance or contact a Poison Control Center immediately.

Dosage and Administration: Tablets—Adults and children 12 years and over: One tablet morning and evening. Children under 12 years, consult a physician. Syrup—Adults: Two teaspoonfuls four times daily or as directed by a physician. Children 6 to 12 years: One teaspoonful four times daily or as directed by a physician. For children under 6 years, consult a physician. Not more than 4 doses every 24 hours.

Professional Labeling: Dosage: Syrup—Children 2 to 5 years: 1 teaspoonful, four times daily.

How Supplied: DEMAZIN REPETABS Tablets, blue, sugar-coated tablets branded in red with the Schering trademark and either product identification letters, ADD or numbers, 133; box of 24 tablets and bottles of 100 and 1000.
DEMAZIN Syrup, blue-colored liquid, bottles of 4 fluid ounces (118 ml) and 128 fluid ounces (1 gallon). Store the syrup between 2° and 25°C (36° and 77°F).
[*Shown in Product Identification Section*]

DERMOLATE™ Anti-Itch Cream
DERMOLATE™ Anti-Itch Spray
DERMOLATE™ Anal-Itch Ointment
DERMOLATE™ Scalp-Itch Lotion

Active Ingredients: DERMOLATE Anti-Itch Cream contains hydrocortisone 0.5% in a greaseless, vanishing cream. DERMOLATE Anti-Itch Spray contains hydrocortisone 0.5% in a clear, cooling, fast-drying spray. Alcohol content 24%. DERMOLATE Anal-Itch Ointment contains hydrocortisone 0.5% in a soothing, lubricating ointment. DERMOLATE Scalp-Itch Lotion contains hydrocortisone 0.5% in a clear, non-greasy liquid that dries in minutes. Isopropyl alcohol content 47%.

Indications: DERMOLATE Anti-Itch Cream and Spray—For the temporary relief of minor skin irritations, itching and rashes due to eczema, dermatitis, insect bites, poison ivy, poison oak, poison sumac, soaps, detergents, cosmetics and jewelry.

Continued on next page

Schering—Cont.

DERMOLATE Anal-Itch Ointment—For the temporary relief of itchy anal areas.
DERMOLATE Scalp-Itch Lotion—For temporary relief of itching and minor scalp irritation due to scalp dermatitis.

Actions: DERMOLATE Anti-Itch Cream and Spray provide temporary relief of itching and minor skin irritations. DERMOLATE Anal-Itch Ointment provides temporary relief of anal itching. DERMOLATE Scalp-Itch Lotion provides temporary relief of itching and minor scalp irritation due to scalp dermatitis.

Warnings: All DERMOLATE forms are for external use only. Avoid contact with the eyes. Discontinue use and consult a physician if condition worsens or if symptoms persist for more than seven days. Do not use on children under 2 years of age except under the advice and supervision of physician. Keep these and all drugs out of the reach of children.

Overdosage: In case of accidental ingestion, seek professional assistance or contact a Poison Control Center immediately.

Dosage and Administration: DERMOLATE Anti-Itch Cream—For adults and children 2 years of age and older: Gently massage into affected skin area not more than 3 or 4 times daily. For children under 2 years of age, there is no recommended dosage except under the advice and supervision of a physician.

DERMOLATE Anti-Itch Spray—For adults and children 2 years of age and older: Spray on affected skin area not more than 3 or 4 times daily. For chilren under 2 years of age, there is no recommended dosage except under the advice and supervision of a physician.

DERMOLATE Anal-Itch Ointment—Adults and children 2 years of age and older: Apply to affected area not more than 3 to 4 times daily. For children under 2 years of age, there is no recommended dosage except under the advice and supervision of a physician.

DERMOLATE Scalp-Itch Lotion—For adults and children 2 years of age and older: Part the hair and apply directly to the scalp by squeezing a small amount onto affected areas. Massage into the scalp and repeat this process until desired coverage is achieved. Maintain normal hair care but do not wash out DERMOLATE Lotion immediately after application. Apply to affected scalp areas not more than 3 to 4 times daily. For children under 2 years of age, there is no recommended dosage except under the advice and supervision of a physician.

How Supplied: DERMOLATE Anti-Itch Cream—30 g (1.0 oz.) tube, and 15 g (½ oz) tubes and institutional package, 50 × 2g (¹/₁₅ oz) tubes.
DERMOLATE Anti-Itch Spray—45 ml (1.5 fl. oz.) pump spray bottle.
DERMOLATE Anal-Itch Ointment—30 g (1.0 fl. oz.) tube.
DERMOLATE Scalp-Itch Lotion—30 ml (1 fl. oz.) plastic squeeze bottle.

Store all forms between 2° and 30°C (36° and 86°F).
Protect the spray from freezing.
[*Shown in Product Identification Section*]

EMKO® BECAUSE® CONTRACEPTOR®
Vaginal Contraceptive Foam

Description: A non-hormonal, non-scented aerosol foam contraceptive in a self-contained, tampon-size unit providing six applications of an 8.0% concentration of the spermicide nonoxynol-9.

Indications: Vaginal contraceptive intended for the prevention of pregnancy. BECAUSE Foam provides effective protection alone or it may be used instead of spermicidal jelly or cream to give added protection with a diaphragm.
BECAUSE Foam also may be used to give added protection to other methods of contraception: with a condom; as a backup to the IUD or oral contraceptives during the first month of use; in the event more than one oral contraceptive pill is forgotten and extra protection is needed during the menstrual cycle.

Actions: Each applicatorful of BECAUSE Foam provides the correct amount of nonoxynol-9, the most widely used spermicide, to prevent pregnancy effectively. The foam covers the inside of the vagina and forms a layer of spermicidal material between the sperm and the cervix. The powerful spermicide prevents pregnancy by killing sperm after contact. BECAUSE Foam is effective immediately upon insertion. No waiting period is needed for effervescing or melting to take place since BECAUSE is introduced into the vagina as a foam.

Warnings: If vaginal or penile irritation occurs and continues, a physician should be consulted. Not effective orally. Where pregnancy is contraindicated, further individualization of the contraceptive program may be needed. Do not burn or puncture container. Keep this and all drugs out of the reach of children and in case of accidental ingestion, call a Poison Control Center, emergency medical facility, or a doctor.

Dosage and Administration: One applicatorful of BECAUSE Contraceptive Foam must be inserted before each act of sexual intercourse. BECAUSE Foam can be inserted immediately or up to one hour before intercourse. If more than one hour has passed before intercourse or if intercourse is repeated, another applicatorful of BECAUSE Foam must be inserted.

Directions for Use: Although no contraceptive can guarantee 100% effectiveness, for reliable protection against pregnancy read and follow directions carefully.
With the container pushed all the way into the barrel, shake well. Pull container upward until it stops. Tilt container to side to release foam into barrel. Allow foam to fill barrel to about one inch from end and return container to straight position. Foam will expand to fill remainder of barrel.
Gently insert applicator barrel deep into the vagina (close to the cervix). Push con-

tainer all the way into the barrel. This deposits the foam properly. Remove the Contraceptor with the container still pushed all the way in the applicator barrel to avoid withdrawing any of the foam. As with other vaginal contraceptive products, douching is *not* recommended after using BECAUSE Foam. However, if douching is desired for cleansing purposes, you *must* wait at least six hours following your last act of sexual intercourse to allow BECAUSE Foam's full spermicidal activity to take place. Refer to package insert directions and diagrams for further details and applicator cleansing instructions.

How to Use the BECAUSE CONTRACEPTOR with a Diaphragm.
Insert one applicatorful of BECAUSE Foam directly into the vagina according to above directions and then insert diaphragm. After insertion, BECAUSE Foam is effective immediately and remains effective up to one hour before intercourse. If more than one hour has passed or you are going to repeat intercourse, insert another applicatorful of BECAUSE Foam *without removing your diaphragm.*

Storage: Contents under pressure. Do not burn, incinerate, or puncture the applicator. Store at normal room temperature. Do not expose to extreme heat or open flame or store at temperatures above 120°F. If stored at temperatures below 60°F, warm to room temperature before using.

How Supplied: Disposable 10 gm CONTRACEPTOR containing six applications of BECAUSE Contraceptive Foam. This foam is also available in two other forms, PRE-FIL® Foam with the "fill-in-advance" applicator and EMKO® Foam with the regular applicator.
[*Shown in Product Identification Section*]

EMKO®
Vaginal Contraceptive Foam

Description: A non-hormonal, non-scented aerosol foam contraceptive containing an 8.0% concentration of the spermicide nonoxynol-9.

Indications: Vaginal contraceptive intended for the prevention of pregnancy. EMKO Foam provides effective protection alone or it may be used instead of spermicidal jelly or cream to give added protection with a diaphragm.
EMKO Foam also may be used to give added protection to other methods of contraception: with a condom; as a backup to the IUD or oral contraceptives during the first month of use; in the event more than one oral contraceptive pill is forgotten and extra protection is needed during the menstrual cycle.

Actions: Each applicatorful of EMKO Foam provides the correct amount of nonoxynol-9, the most widely used spermicide, to prevent pregnancy effectively. The foam covers the inside of the vagina and forms a layer of spermicidal material between the sperm and the cervix. The powerful spermicide prevents pregnancy by killing sperm after contact. EMKO Foam is effective immediately upon insertion. No waiting period is needed for effervescing or melting to take place since EMKO is introduced into the vagina as a foam.

Warnings: If vaginal or penile irritation occurs and continues, a physician should be consulted. Not effective orally. Where pregnancy is contraindicated, further individualization of the contraceptive program may be needed. Do not burn or puncture can. Keep this and all drugs out of the reach of children and in case of accidental ingestion, call a Poison Control Center, emergency medical facility, or a doctor.

Dosage and Administration: One applicatorful of EMKO Contraceptive Foam must be inserted before each act of sexual intercourse. EMKO Foam can be inserted immediately or up to one hour before intercourse. If more than one hour has passed before intercourse or if intercourse is repeated, another applicatorful of EMKO Foam must be inserted.

Directions for Use: Although no contraceptive can guarantee 100% effectiveness, for reliable protection against pregnancy read and follow directions carefully.

Check Foam Supply with Weigh Cap.
With the cap on the can, hold the can in midair by the white button. As long as the black is showing, a full dose of foam is available. Use only if black is showing to assure a full application. SHAKE CAN WELL before filling applicator. Remove cap and place the can in an upright position on a level surface. Place the EMKO regular applicator in an upright position over valve on top of can. Press down on the applicator gently. Allow foam to fill to the ridge in applicator barrel. The plunger will rise up as the foam fills the applicator. Remove the filled applicator from the can to stop flow. Gently insert deep into the vagina (close to the cervix). Push plunger into applicator until it stops. This deposits the foam properly. Remove the applicator with the plunger still pushed all the way in to avoid withdrawing any of the foam. As with other vaginal contraceptive products, douching is *not* recommended after using EMKO Foam. However, if douching is desired for cleansing purposes, you *must* wait at least six hours following your last act of sexual intercourse to allow EMKO Foam's full spermicidal activity to take place. Refer to package insert directions and diagrams for further details and applicator cleansing instructions.

How to Use EMKO with a Diaphragm.
Insert one applicatorful of EMKO Foam directly into the vagina according to above directions and then insert your diaphragm. After insertion, EMKO Foam is effective immediately and remains effective up to one hour before intercourse. If more than one hour has passed or you are going to repeat intercourse, insert another applicatorful of EMKO Foam *without removing your diaphragm.*

Storage: Contents under pressure. Do not burn, incinerate or puncture can. Store at normal room temperature. Do not expose to extreme heat or open flame or store at temperatures above 120°F. If

stored at temperatures below 60°F, warm to room temperature before using.

How Supplied: EMKO Contraceptive Foam, 40 gm can with applicator and storage purse. Refill cans without applicator and purse available in 40 gm and 90 gm sizes. All sizes feature a unique weighing cap that indicates when a new foam supply is needed. EMKO Foam also comes in two other forms, PRE-FIL® with the "fill-in-advance" applicator and BECAUSE® CONTRACEPTOR®, the portable six-use, combination foam/applicator unit.
[*Shown in Product Identification Section*]

EMKO® PRE-FIL®
Vaginal Contraceptive Foam

Description: A non-hormonal, non-scented aerosol foam contraceptive, for use with the "fill-in-advance" applicator, containing 8.0% concentration of the spermicide nonoxynol-9.

Indications: Vaginal contraceptive intended for the prevention of pregnancy. PRE-FIL Foam provides effective protection alone or it may be used instead of spermicidal jelly or cream to give added protection with a diaphragm.
PRE-FIL Foam also may be used to give added protection to other methods of contraception: with a condom; as a backup to the IUD or oral contraceptives during the first month of use; in the event more than one oral contraceptive pill is forgotten and extra protection is needed during the menstrual cycle.

Actions: Each applicatorful of PRE-FIL Foam provides the correct amount of nonoxynol-9, the most widely used spermicide, to prevent pregnancy effectively. The foam covers the inside of the vagina and forms a layer of spermicidal material between the sperm and the cervix. The powerful spermicide prevents pregnancy by killing sperm after contact.
PRE-FIL Foam is effective immediately upon insertion. No waiting period is needed for effervescing or melting to take place since PRE-FIL is introduced into the vagina as a foam.

Warnings: If vaginal or penile irritation occurs and continues, a physician should be consulted. Not effective orally. Where pregnancy is contraindicated, further individualization of the contraceptive program may be needed. Do not burn or puncture can. Keep this and all drugs out of the reach of children and in case of accidental ingestion, call a Poison Control Center, emergency medical facility, or a doctor.

Dosage and Administration: One applicatorful of PRE-FIL Contraceptive Foam must be inserted before each act of sexual intercourse. PRE-FIL Foam can be inserted immediately or up to one hour before intercourse. If more than one hour has passed before intercourse or if intercourse is repeated, another applicatorful of PRE-FIL Foam must be inserted.

Directions for Use: Although no contraceptive can guarantee 100% effectiveness, for reliable protection against pregnancy read and follow directions carefully.

Check Foam Supply with Weigh Cap.
With the cap on the can, hold the can in midair by the white button. As long as the black is showing, a full dose of foam is available. Use only if black is showing to assure a full application. SHAKE CAN GENTLY before filling applicator. Remove cap and place the can in an upright position on a level surface.
PRE-FIL Foam can only be used with the special "fill-in-advance" applicator. The PRE-FIL applicator has two parts: an inner tube and an outer barrel. Remove inner tube from outer barrel. Place *inner* tube in upright position over valve on top of can and press down until pink plunger stops rising. Continue to press for a few seconds before removing inner tube from can. To be sure inner tube is completely filled, press pink plunger. If it can be depressed, inner tube is not full—repeat filling procedure.
Place inner tube into outer barrel. *The foam can only be released when the inner tube is inside the outer barrel.* Gently insert applicator deep into the vagina (close to the cervix). Push pink plunger back into applicator until it stops. This deposits the foam properly. Remove the applicator with the plunger still pushed all the way in to avoid withdrawing any of the foam.
PRE-FIL's "fill-in-advance" applicator can be filled and stored, ready for use either immediately or up to seven days.
As with other vaginal contraceptive products, douching is *not* recommended after using PRE-FIL Foam. However, if douching is desired for cleansing purposes, you *must* wait at least six hours following your last act of sexual intercourse to allow PRE-FIL Foam's full spermicidal activity to take place. Refer to package insert directions and diagrams for further details and applicator cleansing instructions.
How to Use PRE-FIL with a Diaphragm
Insert one applicatorful of PRE-FIL Foam directly into the vagina according to above directions and then insert diaphragm. After insertion, PRE-FIL Foam is effective immediately and remains effective up to one hour before intercourse. If more than one hour has passed or you are going to repeat intercourse, insert another applicatorful of PRE-FIL Foam *without removing your diaphragm.*

Storage: Contents under pressure. Do not burn, incinerate, or puncture can or filled applicator. Store at normal room temperature. Do not expose to extreme heat or open flame or store at temperatures above 120°F. If stored at temperatures below 60°F, warm to room temperature before using. Prefilled applicator may be stored up to seven days.

How Supplied: EMKO PRE-FIL Contraceptive Foam, 30 gm can with applicator and purse. Refill can without applicator and purse in 60 gm size. Both sizes feature a unique weighing cap that indi-

Continued on next page

Information on Schering products appearing on these pages is effective as of March 1, 1981.

Schering—Cont.

cates when a new supply of foam is needed. This foam also comes in two other forms, EMKO® Foam with the regular applicator and BECAUSE® CONTRACEPTOR®, the portable six-use, combination foam/applicator unit.
[*Shown in Product Identification Section*]

MOL–IRON®
Tablets
Liquid
CHRONOSULE® Capsules
Tablets with Vitamin C
CHRONOSULE® Capsules with
  Vitamin C

Active Ingredients: MOL-IRON products contain a specially processed preparation of ferrous sulfate. They are highly effective and unusually well tolerated even by children and pregnant women. Tablets: Each tablet contains 195 mg. ferrous sulfate, USP (39 mg. elemental iron).
Liquid: Each 4 ml teaspoonful of loganberry-flavored liquid contains 195 mg. ferrous sulfate, USP (39 mg. elemental iron) and alcohol 4.75%.
CHRONOSULE Capsules: Each capsule contains 390 mg. ferrous sulfate, USP (78 mg. elemental iron) in sustained release form.
Tablets with Vitamin C: Each tablet contains 195 mg. ferrous sulfate (39 mg. elemental iron) and ascorbic acid 75 mg.
MOL-IRON Tablets, Tablets with Vitamin C, and CHRONOSULE capsules contain FD&C Yellow No. 5 (tartrazine) as a color additive.
Indications: For the prevention and treatment of iron-deficiency anemias. The CHRONOSULE capsules supply adequate amounts of iron in the form of specially coated beadlets, fabricated to disintegrate gradually over a 6 to 8 hour period, effecting a continued release of absorbable ferrous iron while traversing the stomach and small intestine.
Unpleasant side effects are minimized.
Warnings: Keep these and all drugs out of the reach of children. In case of accidental overdose, seek professional assistance or contact a Poison Control Center immediately.
Dosage and Administration: Tablets—(Taken preferably after meals): Adults and Children 12 years and older—1 or 2 tablets 3 times daily; Children 6 through 11 years—1 tablet 3 times daily; or as prescribed by a physician.
Liquid—(Taken preferably after meals): Adults and Children 12 years and older—1 or 2 teaspoonfuls 3 times daily; Children 6 through 11 years—1 teaspoonful 3 times daily; Children 2 through 5 years—1 teaspoonful 2 times daily; Children less than 2 years old—½ teaspoonful 3 times daily; or as prescribed by a physician. The liquid should be administered in a small quantity of water or fruit juice (not milk).
CHRONOSULE Capsules—(Taken preferably after meals): Adults and Children 12 years and older—1 CHRONOSULE capsule once or twice daily; Children 6

through 11 years—1 capsule daily; or as prescribed by a physician.
Tablets with Vitamin C—(Taken preferably after meals): Adults and Children 12 years and older—1 or 2 tablets 3 times daily; Children 6 through 11 years—1 tablet 3 times daily; or as prescribed by a physician.
How Supplied: MOL-IRON Tablets—maroon colored tablets, bottles of 100 and 1000; MOL-IRON Liquid—bottles of 16 fl. oz.; MOL-IRON CHRONOSULE Capsules—bottles of 30 and 250; MOL-IRON Tablets with Vitamin C—bottles of 100.
Store the tablet and capsule forms between 2° and 30°C (36° and 86°F) and the liquid between 15° and 30°C (59° and 86°F).
[*Shown in Product Identification Section*]

SUNRIL® Premenstrual Capsules

Active Ingredients: Acetaminophen 300 mg, an effective analgesic. Pamabrom 50 mg (2- amino- 2-methyl- 1-propanol- 8-bromo- theophyllinate), a mild, effective diuretic. Pyrilamine maleate 25 mg, a mild antihistamine.
Indications: For relief of premenstrual tension, edema and related pain.
Warning: Keep out of reach of children.
Precautions: Do not drive or operate machinery while taking this medication as this preparation may cause drowsiness. Limit dosage to no more than 10 consecutive days unless recommended by your physician. Should not be used by anyone with a known sensitivity to any one of the ingredients.
Overdosage: In case of accidental overdose, seek professional assistance or contact a Poison Control Center immediately.
Dosage and Administration: 1 capsule every 3 to 4 hours. Do not exceed 4 capsules within a 24 hour period. Start using at first sign of discomfort, usually 4 to 7 days before onset of menstruation.
How Supplied: SUNRIL® Premenstrual Capsules are pink and lavender capsules; available in bottles of 100.
[*Shown in Product Identification Section*]

TINACTIN® Antifungal
Cream 1%
Solution 1%
Powder 1%
Powder (1%) Aerosol

Description: TINACTIN Cream 1% is a white homogeneous, nonaqueous preparation containing the highly active synthetic fungicidal agent, tolnaftate. Each gram contains 10 mg. tolnaftate solubilized in polyethylene glycol-400 and propylene glycol with carboxypolymethylene, monoamylamine, titanium dioxide, and butylated hydroxytoluene.
TINACTIN Solution 1% contains in each ml. tolnaftate, 10 mg. and butylated hydroxytoluene, 1 mg. in a nonaqueous, homogeneous vehicle of polyethylene glycol-400. The solution solidifies at low temperatures but liquefies readily when warmed, retaining its potency.

Each gram of TINACTIN Powder 1% contains tolnaftate 10 mg. in a vehicle of corn starch and talc.
TINACTIN Powder Aerosol contains 91 mg. tolnaftate in a vehicle of butylated hydroxytoluene, talc, and polyethylene-polypropylene glycol monobutyl ether. It also contains 14% denatured alcohol and sufficient inert propellant of isobutane to make 100 grams. The spray deposits a white clinging powder containing a concentration of 1% tolnaftate.
Indications: TINACTIN Cream and Solution are highly active antifungal agents that are effective in killing superficial fungi of the skin which cause tinea pedis (athlete's foot), tinea cruris (jock itch) and tinea corporis (body ringworm). TINACTIN Powder and Powder Aerosol are effective in killing superficial fungi of the skin which cause tinea cruris (jock itch) and tinea pedis (athlete's foot). All forms begin to relieve burning, itching and soreness within 24 hours. Symptoms are usually cleared in 2 to 3 weeks. Where skin is thickened, treatment may take 4 to 6 weeks. The powder and powder aerosol forms aid the drying of naturally moist areas and begin to relieve burning and itching within 24 hours.
Actions: The active ingredient in TINACTIN is a highly active synthetic fungicidal agent that is effective in the treatment of superficial fungus infections of the skin. It is inactive systemically, virtually nonsensitizing, and does not ordinarily sting or irritate intact or broken skin, even in the presence of acute inflammatory reactions.
TINACTIN products are odorless, greaseless, and do not stain or discolor the skin, hair, or nails.
Warnings: Keep these and all drugs out of the reach of children.
TINACTIN Powder Aerosol: Avoid spraying in eyes. Contents under pressure. Do not puncture or incinerate. Flammable mixture, do not use or store near heat or open flame. Exposure to temperatures above 120°F. may cause bursting. Use only as directed. Intentional misuse by deliberately concentrating and inhaling the contents can be harmful or fatal.
Precautions: If burning or itching do not improve within 10 days, become worse, or if irritation occurs, discontinue use and consult your physician or podiatrist.
TINACTIN products are for external use only. Keep out of eyes.
TINACTIN Cream and Solution are not recommended for nail or scalp infections. TINACTIN Powder and Powder Aerosol are not recommended for use on scalp.
Overdosage: In case of accidental ingestion, seek professional assistance or contact a Poison Control Center immediately.
Dosage and Administration: TINACTIN Cream—Wash and dry infected area morning and evening. Then apply one-half inch ribbon of cream and rub gently on infected area. Spread evenly. To help prevent recurrence, continue treatment for two weeks after disappearance of all symptoms.

TINACTIN Solution—Wash and dry infected area morning and evening. Then apply two or three drops and massage gently to cover the infected area. To help prevent recurrence, continue treatment for two weeks after disappearance of all symptoms.

TINACTIN Powder—Sprinkle powder liberally on all areas of infection and in shoes or socks. To help prevent recurrence of athlete's foot or jock itch, bathe daily, dry carefully and apply TINACTIN Powder.

TINACTIN Powder Aerosol—Shake well before using. Spray from a distance of 6 to 10 inches. Spray powder liberally on all areas of infection and in shoes or socks. To help prevent recurrence of jock itch or athlete's foot, bathe daily, dry carefully and apply TINACTIN Powder Aerosol.

How Supplied: TINACTIN Antifungal Cream 1%, 15 g (½ oz.) collapsible tube with dispensing tip. TINACTIN Antifungal Solution 1%, 10 ml (⅓ oz.) plastic squeeze bottle. TINACTIN Antifungal Powder 1%, 45 g (1.5 oz.) plastic container. TINACTIN Antifungal Powder (1%) Aerosol, 100 g (3.5 oz.) spray can. Store the aerosol between 35° and 86°F (2° and 30°C).

[*Shown in Product Identification Section*]

Information on Schering products appearing on these pages is effective as of March 1, 1981.

Searle Consumer Products
Division of Searle
Pharmaceuticals Inc.
BOX 5110
CHICAGO, IL 60680

DRAMAMINE® Liquid
(dimenhydrinate syrup USP)
DRAMAMINE® Tablets
(dimenhydrinate USP)
DRAMAMINE JUNIOR® Liquid
(dimenhydrinate syrup USP)

Active Ingredient: Dimenhydrinate is the chlorotheophylline salt of the antihistaminic agent diphenhydramine. Dimenhydrinate contains not less than 53% and not more than 56% of diphenhydramine, and not less than 44% and not more than 47% of 8-chlorotheophylline, calculated on the dried basis.

Indications: Dramamine is indicated for the prevention and treatment of the nausea, vomiting or vertigo of motion sickness. Such an illness may arise from the motion of ships, planes, trains, automobiles, buses, swings, or even amusement park rides. Regardless of the cause of motion sickness, Dramamine has been found to be effective in its prevention or treatment.

Actions: While the precise mode of action of dimenhydrinate is not known, it has a depressant action on hyperstimulated labyrinthine function.

Warning: Caution should be used when Dramamine is given in conjunction with certain antibiotics which may cause oto-

toxicity, since Dramamine is capable of masking ototoxic symptoms and an irreversible state may be reached.

Precautions: Drowsiness may be experienced by some patients, especially on high dosage, although this action frequently is not undesirable in some conditions for which the drug is used. However, because of possible drowsiness, patients taking Dramamine should be cautioned against operating automobiles or dangerous machinery. Patients should also avoid alcoholic beverages while taking medication. Dramamine should not be used in the presence of asthma, glaucoma, or enlargement of the prostate gland, except on advice of a physician.

Dosage and Administration

Dramamine Tablets: To prevent motion sickness, the first dose should be taken one-half to one hour before starting your activity. Additional medication depends on travel conditions. *Adults*—Nausea or vomiting may be expected to be controlled for approximately four hours with 50 mg of Dramamine, and prevented by a similar dose every four hours. Its administration may be attended by some degree of drowsiness in some patients, and 100 mg every four hours may be given in conditions in which drowsiness is not objectionable or is even desirable. The usual adult dosage is 1 to 2 tablets every four to six hours, not to exceed 8 tablets in 24 hours. *Children 6 to 12 years:* ½ to 1 tablet every six to eight hours, not to exceed 3 tablets in 24 hours. *Children 2 to 6 years:* Up to ½ tablet every six to eight hours, not to exceed 1½ tablets in 24 hours. Children may also be given Dramamine Junior cherry-flavored liquid in accordance with directions for use. Not for frequent or prolonged use except on advice of a physician. Do not exceed recommended dosage.

Dramamine Junior Liquid and Dramamine Liquid: To prevent motion sickness, the first dose should be taken one-half to one hour before starting your activity. Additional medication depends on travel conditions. *Dosage: Children 6 to 12 years:* 2 to 4 teaspoonfuls (4 ml per teaspoonful) every six to eight hours, not to exceed 12 teaspoonfuls in 24 hours. *Children 2 to 6 years:* 1 to 2 teaspoonfuls every six to eight hours, not to exceed 6 teaspoonfuls in 24 hours. *Children under 2 years:* only on advice of a physician. *Adults:* 4 to 8 teaspoonfuls every four to six hours, not to exceed 32 teaspoonfuls in 24 hours. Not for frequent or prolonged use except on advice of a physician. Do not exceed recommended dosage. Use of a measuring device is recommended for all liquid medication.

How Supplied: *Tablets*—scored, white tablets of 50 mg, with SEARLE debossed on one side and 1701 on the other side, in packages of 12 and bottles of 36 (OTC). Also available in unit-dose packets of 100, and in bottles of 100, 500, 1,000, and 2,500. *Liquid*—12.5 mg per 4 ml, bottles of 3 oz (Dramamine Junior) (OTC). Also available in pint bottles.

[*Shown in Product Identification Section*]

ICY HOT® BALM
(topical analgesic balm)
ICY HOT® RUB
(topical analgesic cream)

Active Ingredients:
ICY HOT BALM—methyl salicylate 29%, menthol 8%.
ICY HOT RUB—methyl salicylate 12%, menthol 9%.

Description: Icy Hot Balm and Icy Hot Rub are topically applied analgesics containing two active ingredients, methyl salicylate and menthol. It is the particular concentration of these ingredients, in combination with inert ingredients, that results in the distinct combined heating/cooling sensation of Icy Hot.

Actions: Icy Hot is classified as a counterirritant which, when rubbed into the intact skin, provides relief of deep-seated pain through a counterirritant action rather than through a direct analgesic effect. In acting as a counterirritant, Icy Hot replaces the patient's perception of pain with another sensation that blocks deep pain temporarily by its action on or near the skin surface.

Warnings: Use only as directed. Keep away from children to avoid accidental poisoning. Keep away from eyes, mouth, genitalia, mucous membranes, and broken, irritated, or very sensitive skin. Do not swallow. If swallowed, induce vomiting and call a physician. If skin irritation develops, discontinue use. Consult a physician if pain lasts 10 days or more, if redness is present, or before using on children under 12 years of age.

Adverse Reactions: The most common adverse reactions that may occur with Icy Hot use are skin irritation and blistering. The most serious adverse reaction is severe toxicity that occurs if the product is ingested.

Directions for Use: Apply to painful area; massage until Icy Hot is completely absorbed. Repeat as necessary.

How Supplied:
ICY HOT BALM is available in jars in two sizes—3½ oz and 7 oz.
ICY HOT RUB is available in tubes in two sizes—1¼ oz and 3 oz.
[*Shown in Product Identification Section*]

METAMUCIL®
(psyllium hydrophilic mucilloid)

Description: Metamucil is a bulk laxative that provides a bland, nonirritating bulk and promotes normal elimination. It contains refined hydrophilic mucilloid, a highly efficient dietary fiber, derived from the husk of the psyllium seed (*Plantago ovata*). An equal amount of dextrose, a carbohydrate, is added as a dispersing agent. Each dose contains about 1 mg of sodium, 31 mg of potassium, and 14 calories. Carbohydrate content is approximately 3.6 g; psyllium mucilloid content is 3.4 g.

Indications: Metamucil is indicated in the management of chronic constipation, in irritable bowel syndrome, as adjunctive therapy in constipation of duodenal ulcer and diverticular disease, in the

Continued on next page

Searle Consumer—Cont.

bowel management of patients with hemorrhoids, and for constipation during pregnancy, convalescence, and senility.

Actions: Metamucil is uniform, instantly miscible, palatable, and nonirritative in the gastrointestinal tract.

Dosage and Administration: The usual adult dosage is one rounded teaspoonful (7 g) stirred into a standard 8-oz glass of cool water or other suitable liquid and taken orally one to three times a day, depending on the need and response. It may require continuing use for 2 or 3 days to provide optimal benefit. Best results are observed if each dose is followed by an additional glass of liquid.

Contraindications: Intestinal obstruction, fecal impaction.

How Supplied: Powder, containers of 7 oz, 14 oz, and 21 oz.

[*Shown in Product Identification Section*]

INSTANT MIX METAMUCIL®
(psyllium hydrophilic mucilloid)

Description: Instant Mix Metamucil is provided in premeasured single-dose packets for oral use. Each packet contains about 3.6 g of refined hydrophilic mucilloid, a highly efficient dietary fiber, derived from the husk of the psyllium seed (*Plantago ovata*), together with citric acid, sucrose (a carbohydrate), potassium bicarbonate, calcium carbonate, flavoring, and sodium bicarbonate. Each dose contains approximately 7 mg of sodium, 60 mg of calcium, 280 mg of potassium, and less than 4 calories. Carbohydrate content is about 0.9 g: psyllium mucilloid content is 3.6 g.

Indications: Instant Mix Metamucil is indicated for its smoothage effect in the management of chronic constipation, in irritable bowel syndrome, as adjunctive therapy in constipation of duodenal ulcer and diverticular disease, in the bowel management of patients with hemorrhoids, and for constipation during pregnancy, convalescence, and senility.

Actions: Instant Mix Metamucil, effervescent and requiring no stirring, is uniform, instantly miscible, palatable, and nonirritative in the gastrointestinal tract.

Contraindications: Intestinal obstruction, fecal impaction.

Dosage and Administration: The usual adult dosage is the contents of one packet, taken one to three times daily as follows: 1. Entire contents of a packet are poured into a standard 8-oz water glass. 2. The glass is slowly filled with cool water. 3. Entire contents are drunk immediately. (An additional glass of water may be taken for best results.)

How Supplied: Cartons of 16 and of 30 single-dose packets.

[*Shown in Product Identification Section*]

Orange Flavor METAMUCIL®
Powder
(psyllium hydrophilic mucilloid)

Description: Metamucil is a bulk laxative that provides a bland, nonirritating bulk and promotes normal elimination. It contains refined hydrophilic mucilloid, a highly efficient dietary fiber, derived from the husk of the psyllium seed (*Plantago ovata*), with sucrose (a carbohydrate) as a dispersing agent, citric acid, flavoring and coloring. Each dose contains about 1 mg of sodium, 31 mg of potassium, and 28 calories. Carbohydrate content is approximately 7.1 g; psyllium mucilloid content is 3.4 g.

Indications: Metamucil is indicated in the management of chronic constipation, in irritable bowel syndrome, as adjunctive therapy in constipation of duodenal ulcer and diverticular disease, in the bowel management of patients with hemorrhoids, and for constipation during pregnancy, convalescence, and senility.

Actions: Metamucil is uniform, instantly miscible, palatable, and nonirritative in the gastrointestinal tract.

Contraindications: Intestinal obstruction, fecal impaction.

Dosage and Administration: The usual adult dosage is one rounded tablespoonful (11 g) stirred into a standard 8-oz glass of cool water and taken orally one to three times a day, depending on the need and response. It may require continuing use for 2 or 3 days to provide optimal benefit. Best results are observed if each dose is followed by an additional glass of liquid.

How Supplied: Powder, containers of 7 oz, 14 oz, and 21 oz.

[*Shown in Product Identification Section*]

Orange Flavor
INSTANT MIX METAMUCIL®
(psyllium hydrophilic mucilloid)

Description: Orange Flavor Instant Mix Metamucil is provided in premeasured, single-dose packets for oral use. Each packet contains about 3.6 g of refined hydrophilic mucilloid, a highly efficient dietary fiber derived from the husk of the psyllium seed (*plantago ovata)*, together with sucrose (a carbohydrate), citric acid, potassium bicarbonate, flavoring, coloring, and sodium bicarbonate. Each dose contains approximately 6 mg of sodium, 307 mg of potassium, and $4\frac{1}{2}$ calories. Carbohydrate content is about 1.1 g; psyllium mucilloid content is 3.6 g.

Indications: Instant Mix Metamucil is indicated in the management of chronic constipation, in irritable bowel syndrome, as adjunctive therapy in constipation of duodenal ulcer and diverticular disease, in the bowel management of patients with hemorrhoids, and for constipation during pregnancy, convalescence, and senility.

Actions: Instant Mix Metamucil, effervescent and requiring no stirring, is uniform, instantly miscible, palatable, and nonirritative in the gastrointestinal tract.

Contraindications: Intestinal obstruction, fecal impaction.

Dosage and Administration: The usual adult dosage is the contents of one packet, taken one to three times daily as follows: 1. Entire contents of a packet are poured into a standard 8-oz water glass. 2. The glass is slowly filled with cool water. 3. Entire contents are drunk immediately. (An additional glass of water may be taken for best results.)

How Supplied: Cartons of 16 and of 30 single-dose packets.

[*Shown in Product Identification Section*]

The preceding prescribing information for Searle Consumer Products was current as of February 1, 1981.

Star Pharmaceuticals, Inc.
16499 N.E. 19TH AVE.
N. MIAMI BEACH, FL 33160

STAR–OTIC®
Antibacterial, Antifungal,
Nonaqueous Ear Solution
For Prevention of "Swimmer's Ear"

Active Ingredients: Acetic acid 1.0% nonaqueous, Burow's solution 10%, Boric acid 1.0%, in a propylene glycol vehicle, with an acid pH and a low surface tension.

Indications: For the prevention of otitis externa, commonly called "Swimmer's Ear".

Actions: Star-Otic is antibacterial, antifungal, hydrophilic, has an acid pH and a low surface tension. Acetic acid and boric acid inhibit the rapid multiplication of microorganisms and help maintain the lining mantle of the ear canal in its normal acid state. Burow's solution (aluminum acetate) is a mild astringent. Propylene glycol reduces moisture in the ear canal.

Warning: Do not use in ear if tympanic membrane (ear drum) is perforated or punctured.

Drug Interaction Precaution: No known drug interaction. Virtually non-sensitizing and safe to use as directed.

Symptoms and Treatment of Overdosage: Discontinue use if undue irritation or sensitivity occurs.

Dosage and Administration: Adults and Children: For the prevention of otitis externa (Swimmer's Ear) instill 2–3 drops of Star-Otic in each ear before and after swimming or bathing in susceptible persons, or as directed by physician.

Professional Labeling: Same as those outlined under Indications.

How Supplied: Available in 15 cc measured drop, safety tip, plastic bottle.

Products are cross-indexed by

generic and chemical names in the

YELLOW SECTION

Stuart Pharmaceuticals
Div. of ICI Americas Inc.
WILMINGTON, DE 19897

ALternaGEL®
Liquid
High-Potency Aluminum Hydroxide
Antacid

Composition: ALternaGEL is available as a white, pleasant-tasting, low sodium, high-potency aluminum hydroxide liquid antacid.

Each 5 ml. teaspoonful contains 600 mg. aluminum hydroxide (equivalent to dried gel, USP) providing 12 milliequivalents (mEq) of acid-neutralizing capacity (ANC), and less than 2 mg. (.087 mEq) of sodium per teaspoonful.

Indications: ALternaGEL is indicated for the symptomatic relief of hyperacidity associated with peptic ulcer, gastritis, peptic esophagitis, gastric hyperacidity, hiatal hernia, and heartburn.

ALternaGEL will be of special value to those patients for whom magnesium-containing antacids are undesirable, such as patients with renal insufficiency, patients requiring control of attendant G.I. complications resulting from steroid or other drug therapy, and patients experiencing the laxation which may result from magnesium or combination antacid regimens.

Directions for Use: One or two teaspoonfuls, as needed, between meals and at bedtime, or as directed by a physician. May be followed by a sip of water if desired.

Patient Warnings: As with all medications, ALternaGEL should be kept out of the reach of children.

ALternaGEL may cause constipation.

Except under the advice and supervision of a physician, more than 18 teaspoonfuls should not be taken in a 24-hour period, or the maximum recommended dosage taken for more than two weeks.

Drug Interaction Precaution: ALternaGEL should not be taken concurrently with an antibiotic containing any form of tetracycline.

How Supplied: ALternaGEL is available in bottles of 12 fluid ounces and 5 fluid ounces.
NDC 0038-0860.

DIALOSE™ Capsules
Stool Softener

Composition: Each capsule contains docusate potassium, 100 mg.

Action and Uses: DIALOSE is indicated for treating constipation due to hardness, or lack of moisture in the intestinal contents. DIALOSE is an effective stool softener, whose gentle action will help to restore normal bowel function gradually, without griping or acute discomfort.

Dosage and Administration:
Adults: Initially, one capsule three times a day.
Children, 6 years and over: One capsule at bedtime, or as directed by physician.
Children, under 6 years: As directed by physician.

It is helpful to increase the daily intake of fluids by taking a glass of water with each dose. When adequate laxation is obtained, the dose may be adjusted to meet individual needs.

How Supplied: Bottles of 36, 100, and 500 pink capsules, printed "STUART 470". Also available in 100 capsule unit dose boxes (10 strips of 10 capsules each).
NDC 0038-0470.

DIALOSE™ PLUS Capsules
Stool Softener
plus Peristaltic Activator

Composition: Each capsule contains: docusate potassium, 100 mg. and casanthranol, 30 mg.

Action and Uses: DIALOSE PLUS is indicated for the treatment of constipation generally associated with any of the following: hardness, or lack of moisture in the intestinal contents, or decreased intestinal motility.

DIALOSE PLUS combines the advantages of the stool softener, docusate potassium, with the peristaltic activating effect of casanthranol.

Warning: As with any laxative, DIALOSE PLUS should not be used when abdominal pain, nausea, or vomiting are present. Frequent or prolonged use may result in dependence on laxatives.

Dosage and Administration:
Adults: Initially, one capsule two times a day.
Children: As directed by physician.
When adequate laxation is obtained the dose may be adjusted to meet individual needs.

It is helpful to increase the daily intake of fluids by taking a glass of water with each dose.

How Supplied: Bottles of 36, 100, and 500 yellow capsules, printed "STUART 475". Also available in 100 capsule unit dose boxes (10 strips of 10 capsules each).
NDC 0038-0475.

EFFERSYLLIUM® Instant Mix
Bulk Laxative

Composition: Each rounded teaspoonful, or individual packet (7 g.) contains psyllium hydrocolloid, 3 g.

Actions and Uses: EFFERSYLLIUM produces a soft, lubricating bulk which promotes natural elimination.

EFFERSYLLIUM is not a one-dose, fast-acting purgative or cathartic. Administration for several days may be needed to establish regularity.

Effersyllium contains less than 7 mg. sodium per rounded teaspoonful.

Dosage and Administration:
Adults: One rounded teaspoonful, or one packet, in a glass of water one to three times a day, or as directed by physician.
Children, 6 years and over: One level teaspoonful, or one-half packet (3.5 g.) in one-half glass of water at bedtime, or as directed by physician. *Children, under 6 years:* As directed by physician.

Note: To avoid caking, always use a dry spoon to remove EFFERSYLLIUM from its container. Dosage should be placed in a dry glass. Add water, stir and drink im-

mediately. REPLACE CAP TIGHTLY. KEEP IN A DRY PLACE.

Warning: As with all medication, keep out of the reach of children.

How Supplied: Bottles of 9 oz. and 16 oz. of tan, granular powder. Convenient pouch package 7 g. per packet in boxes of 12 or 24.
NDC 0038-0440.

FERANCEE®
Chewable Tablets

Composition: Each tablet contains: iron (from 200 mg. ferrous fumarate), 67 mg. and Vitamin C (as ascorbic acid, 49 mg. and sodium ascorbate, 114 mg.), 150 mg. Contains FD&C Yellow #5 (tartrazine) as a color additive.

Action and Uses: A pleasant tasting hematinic for iron-deficiency anemias, FERANCEE is particularly useful when chronic blood loss, onset of menses, or pregnancy create additional demands for iron supplementation. Because ferrous fumarate is unusually well-tolerated, FERANCEE can be administered between meals when iron absorption is maximal. The peach-cherry flavored chewable tablets dissolve quickly in the mouth and may be either chewed or swallowed.

Dosage and Administration:
Adults: Two tablets daily, or as directed by physician.
Children over 6 years of age: One tablet daily, or as directed by physician.
Children under 6 years of age: As directed by physician.

How Supplied: Bottles of 100 brown and yellow, two-layer tablets embossed "STUART 650" on brown layer. A childproof cap is standard on each bottle as a safeguard against accidental ingestion by children.
NDC 0038-0650.

FERANCEE®–HP Tablets

Composition: Each tablet contains: iron (from 330 mg. ferrous fumarate), 110 mg.; Vitamin C (as ascorbic acid, 350 mg. and sodium ascorbate, 281 mg.), 600 mg. Contains FD&C Yellow #5 (tartrazine) as a color additive.

Action and Uses: FERANCEE-HP is a high potency formulation of iron and Vitamin C and is intended for use as either:

(1) intensive therapy for the acute and/or severe iron deficiency anemia where a high intake of elemental iron is required, or

(2) a maintenance hematinic for those patients needing a daily iron supplement to maintain normal hemoglobin levels.

The use of well-tolerated ferrous fumarate provides high levels of elemental iron with a low incidence of gastric distress. The inclusion of 600 mg. of Vitamin C per tablet serves to maintain more of the iron in the absorbable ferrous state.

Precautions: Because FERANCEE-HP contains 110 mg. of elemental iron per tablet, it is recommended that its use be

Continued on next page

Stuart—Cont.

limited to adults, i.e. over age 12 years. As with all medication, FERANCEE-HP should be kept out of the reach of children.

Dosage and Administration:
For acute and/or severe iron deficiency anemia, two or three tablets per day taken one tablet per dose after meals. (Each tablet provides 110 mg. elemental iron.)

For maintenance of normal hemoglobin levels in most patients with a history of recurring iron deficiency anemia, one tablet per day taken after a meal should be sufficient.

How Supplied: FERANCEE-HP is supplied in bottles of 60 red, film coated, oval shaped tablets.

NDC 0038-0863.

Note: A childproof safety cap is standard on each bottle of 60 tablets as a safeguard against accidental ingestion by children.

HIBICLENS® Antiseptic Antimicrobial Skin Cleanser (chlorhexidine gluconate)

Description: HIBICLENS is an antimicrobial skin cleanser possessing bactericidal activities. HIBICLENS contains 4% chlorhexidine gluconate, chemically unique hexamethylenebis (biguanide), in a mild, sudsing base adjusted to pH 5.0–6.5 for optimal activity and stability as well as compatability with the normal pH of the skin.

Action: HIBICLENS is bactericidal on contact and has a persistent antimicrobial effect against a wide range of microorganisms, including gram-positive bacteria, and gram-negative bacteria such as *Pseudomonas aeruginosa.* The effectiveness of HIBICLENS is not significantly reduced by the presence of organic matter, such as pus or blood.[1]

In a study[2] simulating surgical use, the immediate bactericidal effect of HIBICLENS after a single six-minute scrub resulted in a 99.9% reduction in resident bacterial flora, with a reduction of 99.98% after the eleventh scrub. Reductions on surgically gloved hands were maintained over the six-hour test period.

HIBICLENS displays persistent antimicrobial action. In one study[2], 93% of a radiolabeled formulation of HIBICLENS remained present on uncovered skin after five hours.

Indications: HIBICLENS is indicated for use as a surgical scrub, as a health-care personnel handwash, and as a skin wound cleanser.

Safety: The extensive use of chlorhexidine gluconate for over 20 years outside the United States has produced no evidence of absorption of the compound through intact skin. The potential for producing skin reactions is extremely low. HIBICLENS can be used many times a day without causing irritation, dryness, or discomfort. When used for cleaning superficial wounds, HIBICLENS will neither cause additional tissue injury nor delay healing.

Precautions: HIBICLENS is for topical use only. The sudsing formulation may be irritating to the eyes. If HIBICLENS should get into the eyes, rinse out promptly and thoroughly with water.

Keep out of ears. Chlorhexidine gluconate, like various other antimicrobial agents, has been reported to cause deafness when instilled in the middle ear. In the presence of a perforated eardrum particular care should be taken to prevent exposure of inner ear tissues to HIBICLENS.

HIBICLENS should not be used by persons with sensitivity to any of its components. Adverse reactions, including dermatitis and photosensitivity, are rare, but if they do occur, discontinue use. Keep this and all other drugs out of the reach of children. AVOID EXCESSIVE HEAT (104°F).

Directions for Use:

As a surgical scrub: Wet hands and forearms to the elbows with warm water. (Avoid using very cold or very hot water.) Dispense about 5 ml. of HIBICLENS into cupped hands. Spread over both hands. Scrub hands and forearms for 3 minutes without adding water . . . using a brush or sponge. (Avoid using extremely hard-bristled brushes.) While scrubbing, pay particular attention to fingernails, cuticles, and interdigital spaces. (Do not use pressure to produce additional lather.) Rinse thoroughly with warm water. Dispense about 5 ml. of HIBICLENS into cupped hands. Wash for an additional 3 minutes. (No need to use brush or sponge.) Then rinse thoroughly. Dry thoroughly.

As a health-care personnel handwash: Wet hands with warm water. (Avoid using very cold or very hot water.) Dispense about 5 ml. of HIBICLENS into cupped hands. Wash for 15 seconds. (Do not use excessive pressure to produce additional lather.) Rinse thoroughly with warm water. Dry thoroughly.

As a skin wound cleanser: Rinse the wound area with water. Apply a small amount of HIBICLENS to the wound and wash gently to remove dirt and debris. Rinse again thoroughly.

How Supplied: In plastic disposable bottles: for general handwashing locations, 4 oz. and 8 oz. with dispenser caps, and 16 oz. filled globes; for surgical scrub areas, 32 oz. and 1 gal. The 32 oz. bottle is designed for a special foot-operated wall dispenser. A hand-operated wall dispenser is available for the 16 oz. globe. Hand pumps are available for 16 oz., 32 oz., and 1 gal. sizes. NDC 0038-0575.

References:
1. Lowbury, EJL, and Lilly, HA: The effect of blood on disinfection of surgeons' hands, Brit. J. Surg. 61:19–21 (Jan.) 1974.
2. Peterson AF, Rosenberg A, Alatary SD: Comparative evaluation of surgical scrub preparations, Surg. Gynecol. Obstet. 146:63–65 (Jan.) 1978.

HIBISTAT™ (chlorhexidine gluconate) Germicidal Hand Rinse

Description: HIBISTAT is a germicidal hand rinse effective against a wide range of microorganisms. HIBISTAT is a clear, colorless liquid containing 0.5% w/w chlorhexidine gluconate in 70% isopropyl alcohol with emollients.

Actions and Uses: HIBISTAT is indicated for health-care personnel use as a germicidal hand rinse. HIBISTAT is for hand hygiene on physically clean hands. It is used in those situations where hands are physically clean, but in need of degerming, when routine handwashing is not convenient or desirable. HIBISTAT provides rapid germicidal action and has a persistent effect.

HIBISTAT should be used in-between patients and procedures where there are no sinks available or continued return to the sink area is inconvenient or time-consuming. HIBISTAT can be used as an alternative to detergent-based products when hands are physically clean. Also, HIBISTAT is an effective germicidal hand rinse following a soap and water handwash.

Cautions: Keep out of eyes and ears. If HIBISTAT should get into eyes or ears, rinse out promptly and thoroughly with water. Chlorhexidine gluconate has been reported to cause deafness when instilled in the middle ear through perforated ear drums. Irritation or other adverse reactions, such as dermatitis or photosensitivity are rare; but if they do occur, discontinue use. Keep this and all other drugs out of the reach of children.
AVOID EXCESSIVE HEAT (104°).

Directions for Use: Dispense about 5 ml. of HIBISTAT into cupped hands and rub vigorously until dry (about 15 seconds), paying particular attention to nails and interdigital spaces. HIBISTAT dries rapidly in use. No water or toweling are necessary.

How Supplied: In plastic disposable bottles of 4 oz. and 8 oz. with flip-top cap. NDC 0038-0585.

HIBITANE® Tincture (Tinted) HIBITANE® Tincture (Non-Tinted) (chlorhexidine gluconate) Patient Preoperative Skin Preparation

Description: HIBITANE Tincture is a patient preoperative skin preparation possessing both a rapid and persistent antimicrobial effect against a wide range of microorganisms. It contains 0.5% chlorhexidine gluconate in 70% isopropyl alcohol.

Actions and Uses: HIBITANE Tincture offers wide-range bactericidal activity for the preparation of the skin at the surgical site and prior to skin puncture or vessel puncture. It provides rapid action on contact and maintains persistent antimicrobial effect, not being significantly affected by pus or blood. HIBITANE Tincture (Tinted) contains a skin colorant to provide visible demarcation of the skin. HIBITANE Tincture (Non-Tinted) is slightly colored, but will not tint the skin. Both products are nondetergent and ready to use without dilution.

Cautions: Keep out of eyes and ears. If HIBITANE Tincture should get into eyes or ears, rinse immediately and thoroughly with water. Chlorhexidine gluconate has been reported to cause deafness when instilled in the middle ear through perforated ear drums. Irritation or other adverse reactions such as dermatitis or photosensitivity are rare, but if they do occur, discontinue use. HIBITANE Tincture may be irritating if used on mucosal tissue. Keep this and all other drugs out of the reach of children. AVOID EXCESSIVE HEAT (104°F).

Directions for Use: Apply HIBITANE Tincture liberally to surgical site and swab for at least 2 minutes. Dry with a sterile towel. Repeat this procedure for an additional 2 minutes, and allow skin to air dry.

How Supplied: HIBITANE Tincture is supplied in plastic disposable bottles of 4 oz. and 1 gal. pour package bottles.
HIBITANE® Tincture (Tinted) NDC 0038-0580.
HIBITANE® Tincture (Non-Tinted) NDC 0038-0583.

KASOF® Capsules
High Strength Stool Softener

Composition: Each KASOF capsule contains docusate potassium, 240 mg.

Action and Uses: KASOF provides a highly efficient wetting action to restore moisture to the bowel, thus softening the stool to prevent straining. KASOF is especially valuable for the severely constipated, as well as patients with anorectal disorders, such as hemorrhoids and anal fissures. KASOF is ideal for patients with any condition that can be complicated by straining at stool, for example, cardiac patients. The action of KASOF does not interfere with normal peristalsis and generally does not cause griping or extreme sensation of urgency. KASOF is sodium-free, containing a unique potassium formulation, without the problems associated with sodium intake. The simple, one-a-day dosage helps assure patient compliance in maintaining normal bowel function.

Dosage and Administration: Adults: 1 KASOF capsule daily for several days, or until bowel movements are normal and gentle. It is helpful to increase the daily intake of fluids by drinking a glass of water with each dose.

How Supplied: KASOF is available in bottles of 30 and 60 brown, gelatin capsules, printed "Stuart 380".
NDC 0038-0380.

MYLANTA®
Liquid and Tablets
Antacid/Antiflatulent

Composition: Each chewable tablet or each 5 ml. (one teaspoonful) of liquid contains:
Aluminum hydroxide
  (Dried Gel, USP in tablet and equiv. to Dried Gel, USP in liquid)........200 mg.
Magnesium hydroxide ....200 mg.
Simethicone......................................20 mg.
Sodium Content: 0.68 mg. (0.03 mEq) sodium per 5 ml. teaspoonful of liquid; 0.77 mg. (0.03 mEq) per tablet.

Acid Neutralizing Capacity: Each teaspoonful of MYLANTA liquid will neutralize 12.7 mEq of acid. Each MYLANTA tablet will neutralize 11.5 mEq.

Indications: MYLANTA, a well-balanced combination of two antacids and simethicone, is effective for the relief of symptoms associated with gastric hyperacidity, and mucus-entrapped air or "gas". These indications include:
  Common heartburn (pyrosis)
  Hiatal hernia
  Peptic esophagitis
  Gastritis
  Peptic ulcer
The soft, easy-to-chew tablets and exceptionally pleasant tasting liquid encourage patients' acceptance, thereby minimizing the skipping of prescribed doses. MYLANTA is appropriate whenever there is a need for consistently effective relief of temporary gastric hyperacidity and mucus-entrapped gas.

Directions for Use: One or two teaspoonfuls of liquid or one or two tablets, well-chewed, every two to four hours between meals and at bedtime, or as directed by physician.

Patient Warnings: Keep this and all drugs out of the reach of children.
Except under the advice and supervision of a physician: Do not take more than 24 teaspoonfuls or 24 tablets in a 24 hour period or use the maximum dose for more than two weeks. Do not use this product if you have kidney disease.

Drug Interaction Precaution: Do not use with patients who are presently taking a prescription antibiotic containing any form of tetracycline.

How Supplied: MYLANTA is available as a white, pleasant tasting liquid suspension, and as a two-layer yellow and white chewable tablet, embossed on yellow layer "STUART 620". Liquid supplied in bottles of 5 oz. and 12 oz. Tablets supplied in boxes of individually wrapped 40's and 100's, economy size bottles of 180, and consumer convenience packs of 48. Also available for hospital use in liquid unit dose cups of 1 oz., and bottles of 5 oz.
NDC 0038-0610 (liquid). NDC 0038-0620 (tablets).

MYLANTA®-II
Liquid and Tablets
High Potency Antacid/Antiflatulent

Composition: Each chewable tablet or each 5 ml. (one teaspoonful) of liquid contains:
Aluminum hydroxide
  (Dried Gel, USP in tablet and equiv. to Dried Gel, USP in liquid)   400 mg.
Magnesium hydroxide   400 mg.
Simethicone   30 mg.
Sodium Content: 1.14 mg. (0.05 mEq) sodium per 5 ml. teaspoonful of liquid; 1.3 mg. (0.06 mEq) per tablet.

Acid Neutralizing Capacity: Each teaspoonful of MYLANTA-II liquid will neutralize 25.4 mEq of acid. Each MYLANTA-II tablet will neutralize 23.0 mEq.

Indications: MYLANTA-II is a high-potency antacid with an antiflatulent. The soft, easy-to-chew tablets and exceptionally pleasant tasting liquid encourage patient acceptance, thereby minimizing the skipping of prescribed doses. MYLANTA-II is effective in relieving the symptoms of gastric hyperacidity, and mucus-entrapped gas associated with peptic ulcer, and other conditions involving a high output of gastric acid. The high potency of MYLANTA-II is achieved through its concentration of noncalcium antacid ingredients. Thus MYLANTA-II can produce both rapid and long lasting neutralization without the acid rebound associated with calcium carbonate. The balanced formula of aluminum and magnesium hydroxides minimizes undesirable bowel effects. Simethicone is effective for the relief of concomitant distress caused by mucus-entrapped gas and swallowed air.

Directions for Use: One or two teaspoonfuls of liquid, or one or two tablets, well-chewed, between meals and at bedtime, or as directed by physician.
Because patients with peptic ulcer vary greatly in both acid output and gastric emptying time, the amount and schedule of dosages should be varied accordingly.

Patient Warnings: Keep this and all drugs out of the reach of children.
Except under the advice and supervision of a physician: Do not take more than 12 teaspoonfuls or 12 tablets in a 24 hour period or use the maximum dose for more than two weeks. Do not use this product if you have kidney disease.

Drug Interaction Precaution: Do not use with patients who are presently taking a prescription antibiotic containing any form of tetracycline.

How Supplied: MYLANTA-II is available as a white, pleasant tasting liquid suspension, and a two-layer green and white chewable tablet, embossed on green layer "STUART 851". Liquid supplied in 12 oz. bottles. Tablets supplied in boxes of 60 individually wrapped chewable tablets. Also available for hospital use in liquid unit dose cups of 1 oz., and bottles of 5 oz.
NDC 0038-0852 (liquid). NDC 0038-0851 (tablets).

MYLICON® Tablets and Drops
Antiflatulent

Composition: Each tablet or 0.6 ml. of drops contains simethicone, 40 mg.

Action and Uses: For relief of the painful symptoms of excess gas in the digestive tract. MYLICON is a valuable adjunct in the treatment of many conditions in which the retention of gas may be a problem, such as: postoperative gaseous distention, air swallowing, functional dyspepsia, peptic ulcer, spastic or irritable colon, diverticulitis.
The defoaming action of MYLICON relieves flatulence by dispersing and preventing the formation of mucus-sur-

Continued on next page

Stuart—Cont.

rounded gas pockets in the gastrointestinal tract. MYLICON acts in the stomach and intestines to change the surface tension of gas bubbles enabling them to coalesce; thus the gas is freed and is eliminated more easily by belching or passing flatus.

Dosage and Administration:
Tablets—One or two tablets four times daily after meals and at bedtime. May also be taken as needed or as directed by a physician. TABLETS SHOULD BE CHEWED THOROUGHLY.
Drops—0.6 ml. four times daily after meals and at bedtime. May also be taken as needed or as directed by a physician. Shake well before using.
How Supplied: Bottles of 100 and 500 white, scored, chewable tablets, embossed front "STUART", reverse "450," and dropper bottles of 30 ml. pink, pleasant tasting liquid. Also available in 100 tablet unit dose boxes (10 strips of 10 tablets each).
NDC 0038-0450 (tablets).
NDC 0038-0630 (drops).

MYLICON®–80 Tablets
High-Capacity Antiflatulent

Composition: Each tablet contains simethicone, 80 mg.
Action and Uses: For relief of the painful symptoms of excess gas in the digestive tract. MYLICON-80 is a high capacity antiflatulent for adjunctive treatment of many conditions in which the retention of gas may be a problem, such as the following: air swallowing, functional dyspepsia, postoperative gaseous distension, peptic ulcer, spastic or irritable colon, diverticulitis.
MYLICON-80 has a defoaming action that relieves flatulence by dispersing and preventing the formation of mucus-surrounded gas pockets in the gastrointestinal tract. MYLICON-80 acts in the stomach and intestines to change the surface tension of gas bubbles enabling them to coalesce; thus, the gas is freed and is eliminated more easily by belching or passing flatus.
Dosage and Administration: One tablet four times daily after meals and at bedtime. May also be taken as needed or as directed by a physician. TABLETS SHOULD BE CHEWED THOROUGHLY.
How Supplied: Economical bottles of 100 and convenience packages of individually wrapped 12 and 48 pink, scored, chewable tablets embossed "STUART 858". Also available in 100 tablet unit dose boxes (10 strips of 10 tablets each).
NDC 0038-0858.

OREXIN® SOFTAB® Tablets

Composition: Each tablet contains: thiamine mononitrate, 10 mg.; Vitamin B_6 (as pyridoxine hydrochloride), 5 mg.; and Vitamin B_{12} (cyanocobalamin), 25 mcg.
Action and Uses: OREXIN is a high-potency vitamin supplement providing thiamine mononitrate and Vitamins B_6 and B_{12}.
OREXIN SOFTAB tablets are specially formulated to dissolve quickly in the mouth. They may be chewed or swallowed. Dissolve tablet in a teaspoonful of water or fruit juice if liquid is preferred.
Dosage and Administration: One tablet daily, or as directed by physician.
How Supplied: Bottles of 100 pale pink SOFTAB tablets, embossed "STUART". NDC 0038-0280.

PROBEC®–T Tablets

Composition: Each tablet contains: Vitamin C (as ascorbic acid, 67 mg. and sodium ascorbate, 600 mg.), 600 mg.; thiamine mononitrate, 15 mg.; riboflavin, 10 mg.; Vitamin B_6 (as pyridoxine hydrochloride), 5 mg.; Vitamin B_{12} (cyanocobalamin), 5 mcg.; niacinamide, 100 mg.; calcium pantothenate, 20 mg. Contains FD&C yellow #5 (tartrazine) as a color additive.
Actions and Uses: PROBEC-T is a high-potency B complex supplement with 600 mg. of Vitamin C in easy to swallow odorless tablets.
Dosage and Administration: One tablet a day with a meal, or as directed by physician.
How Supplied: Bottles of 60, salmon colored, capsule-shaped tablets. NDC 0038-0840.

THE STUART FORMULA® Tablets

Composition: Each tablet contains:
Vitamins: Vitamin A (as palmitate), 5000 I.U.; Vitamin D (ergocalciferol), 400 I.U.; Vitamin E (as dl-alpha tocopheryl acetate), 15 I.U.; Vitamin C (as ascorbic acid), 60 mg.; folic acid, 0.4 mg.; thiamine (as thiamine mononitrate), 1.5 mg.; riboflavin, 1.7 mg.; niacin (as niacinamide), 20 mg.; Vitamin B_6 (as pyridoxine hydrochloride), 2 mg.; Vitamin B_{12} (cyanocobalamin), 6 mcg.
Minerals: calcium 160 mg.; phosphorus, 125 mg.; iodine, 150 mcg.; iron (from 54 mg. ferrous fumarate) 18 mg.; magnesium, 100 mg.
Actions and Uses: The STUART FORMULA tablet provides a well-balanced multivitamin/multimineral formula intended for use as a daily dietary supplement for adults and children over age four.
Dosage and Administration: One tablet daily or as directed by a physician.
How Supplied: Bottles of 100, 250 and 500 white round tablets. Childproof safety caps are standard on the 100 and 250 tablet bottles as a safeguard against accidental ingestion by children. NDC 0038-0866.

STUART PRENATAL® Tablets

Composition: Each tablet contains:

Vitamins:	% U.S. RDA*	
A (as acetate)	100%	8,000 I.U.
D (ergocalciferol)	100%	400 I.U.
E (as dl-alpha tocopheryl acetate)	100%	30 I.U.
C (ascorbic acid)	100%	60 mg.
Folic Acid	100%	0.8 mg.
Thiamine (as thiamine mononitrate)	100%	1.7 mg.
Riboflavin	100%	2 mg.
Niacin (as niacinamide)	100%	20 mg.
B_6 (as pyridoxine hydrochloride)	160%	4 mg.
B_{12} (cyanocobalamin)	100%	8 mcg.
Minerals:		
Calcium (from 679 mg. calcium sulfate anhydrous)	15%	200 mg.
Iodine (from potassium iodide)	100%	150 mcg.
Iron (from 182 mg. ferrous fumarate)	333%	60 mg.
Magnesium (from magnesium oxide)	22%	100 mg.

* Recommended Daily Allowance
Action and Uses: STUART PRENATAL is a multivitamin/multimineral supplement for pregnant and lactating women. It provides vitamins equal to 100% or more of the U.S. RDA for pregnant and lactating women, plus essential minerals, including 60 mg. of elemental iron as well-tolerated ferrous fumarate, and 200 mg. of elemental calcium (non-alkalizing and phosphorus-free). Stuart Prenatal also contains .8 mg. folic acid.
Dosage and Administration: During and after pregnancy, one tablet daily after a meal, or as directed by a physician.
How Supplied: Bottles of 100 and 500 pink capsule-shaped tablets. A childproof safety cap is standard on 100 tablet bottles as a safeguard against accidental ingestion by children. NDC 0038-0270.

STUARTINIC® Tablets

Composition: Each tablet contains: iron (from 300 mg. ferrous fumarate), 100 mg.; Vitamin C (as ascorbic acid, 300 mg. and sodium ascorbate, 225 mg.), 500 mg.; Vitamin B_{12} (cyanocobalamin), 25 mcg.; thiamine mononitrate, 6 mg.; riboflavin, 6 mg.; Vitamin B_6 (as pyridoxine hydrochloride), 1 mg.; niacinamide, 20 mg.; calcium pantothenate, 10 mg. Contains FD&C yellow #5 (tartrazine) as a color additive.
Action and Uses: STUARTINIC is a complete hematinic for patients with history of iron deficiency anemia who also lack adequate amounts of B-complex vitamins due to poor diet.
The use of well-tolerated ferrous fumarate in STUARTINIC provides a high level of elemental iron with a low incidence of gastric distress. The inclusion of 500 mg. of Vitamin C per tablet serves to maintain more of the iron in the absorbable ferrous state. The B-complex vitamins improve nutrition where B-complex deficient diets contribute to the anemia.
Precautions: Because STUARTINIC contains 100 mg. of elemental iron per tablet, use should be confined to adults, i.e. over age 12 years. As with all medications, STUARTINIC should be kept out of the reach of children.
Dosage and Administration: One tablet daily taken after a meal to maintain normal hemoglobin levels in most patients with chronic iron deficiency

anemia resulting from inadequate diet. Higher doses of STUARTINIC can be taken as directed by the physician.

How Supplied: STUARTINIC is supplied in bottles of 60 and 500 yellow, film coated, oval shaped tablets. NDC 0038-0862.

Note: A childproof safety cap is standard on each bottle of 60 tablets. The physician should prescribe or recommend the bottle of 60 tablets, where appropriate, to provide that additional safeguard against accidental ingestion by children.

SugarLo Company
POST OFFICE BOX 1100
PLEASANTVILLE, NJ 08232

LACTAID®
(lactase enzyme)

Description: Each 5 drop dosage contains not less than 1000 NLU (Neutral Lactase Units) of Beta-D-galactosidase derived from Kluyveromyces lactis yeast. The enzyme is in a liquid carrier of glycerol (50%), water (30%), and inert yeast dry matter (20%) 4–5 drops hydrolyzes approximately 70% of the lactose in 1 quart of milk at refrigerator temperature, @ 42°F–6°C in 24 hours, or will do the same in 2 hours @ 85°F–30°C. Additional time and/or enzyme required for 100% lactose conversion. 1 U.S. quart of milk will contain approximately 50 gm lactose prior to lactose hydrolysis and will contain 15 gm or less, after. Hydrolysis converts the lactose into its simple sugar components, glucose and galactose.

Actions: Converts the disaccharide lactose into its monosugar components, glucose and galactose.

Indications: Lactase insufficiency in the patient, suspected from g.i. disturbances after consumption of milk or milk content products: e.g., bloat, distension, flatulence, diarrhea; or identified by a lactose tolerance test.

Precautions: Diabetics should be aware that the milk sugar will now be metabolically available and must be taken into account (25 gm glucose and 25 gm galactose per quart). No reports received of any diabetics' reactions. Galactosemics may not have milk in any form, lactase enzyme modified or not. No drug interactions. Overdose impossible.

Usage: Added to milk. 4–5 drops per quart depending on level of lactose conversion desired.

Toxicity: None. LactAid is not a drug but a food which modifies another food to make it more digestible.

Other Uses: Veterinary indications: treatment of milk for animals with gastric surgery; sick young animals; sick or healthy older animals.

How Supplied: Retail sale units of 4, 12 or 30 dosages at 5 drops per dose. Bulk institutional size also available. Sample and full product information to doctors, dietitians and institutions, on request. Also from dairies in some locations in U.S. as ready to drink hydrolyzed LactAid milk, with the enzyme modification having been done at the dairy to a 70% conversion level. Persons who find this 70% level to be inadequate can further modify the milk at home by utilizing the LactAid liquid drops covered in this description. Any store unable to purchase from its wholesaler can order direct from SugarLo Company.

[*Shown in Product Identification Section*]

Syntex Laboratories, Inc
STANFORD INDUSTRIAL PARK
PALO ALTO, CA 94304

CARMOL® 10
10% urea lotion
for total body
dry skin care.

Active Ingredient: Urea 10% in a blend of purified water, stearic acid, isopropyl palmitate, propylene glycol dipelargonate, PEG-8 dioleate, propylene glycol, PEG-8 distearate, cetyl alcohol, sodium laureth sulfate, triethanolamine, carbomer 940, xanthan gum; scented with hypoallergenic fragrance.

Indications: For total body dry skin care.

Actions: Keratolytic and antipruritic. CARMOL 10 is non-occlusive, contains no mineral oil or petrolatum. CARMOL 10 is hypoallergenic; contains no lanolin, parabens or other preservatives.

Precautions: For external use only. Discontinue use if irritation occurs. Keep out of the reach of children. In case of accidental ingestion, seek professional assistance or contact a poison control center immediately.

Dosage and Administration: Rub in gently on hands, face or body. Repeat as necessary.

How Supplied: 6 fl. oz. bottle.

CARMOL® 20
20% Urea Cream
Extra strength for
rough, dry skin

Active Ingredients: Urea 20% in a nonlipid vanishing cream containing purified water, isopropyl myristate, isopropyl palmitate, stearic acid, propylene glycol, triethanolamine, sodium laureth sulfate, carbomer 940, hypoallergenic fragrance, xanthan gum.

Indications: Especially useful on rough, dry skin of hands, elbows, knees and feet.

Actions: Keratolytic. Contains no parabens, lanolin or mineral oil.

Precautions: For external use only. Keep away from eyes. Use with caution on face or broken or inflamed skin; transient stinging may occur. Discontinue use if irritation occurs. Keep out of the reach of children. In case of accidental ingestion, seek professional assistance or contact a poison control center immediately.

Dosage and Administration: Apply once or twice daily or as directed. Rub in well.

How Supplied: 3 oz. tubes, 1 lb. jars.

METHAKOTE® Diaper Rash Cream

A product of Syntex Laboratories, Inc.

Composition: METHAKOTE is a unique topical amino acid/antiseptic formulation of a protein hydrolysate fortified with methionine and cysteine, and benzethonium chloride in an emollient, water-washable cream.

Action and Uses: For topical treatment and prevention of diaper rash. Valuable in seborrhea capitis, intertrigo and chafing.

The amino acids help assure more rapid healing and tissue regeneration. Benzethonium chloride aids in preventing ammoniacal diaper rash by inhibiting *Bacillus ammoniagenes.* METHAKOTE is *non-staining, greaseless, and washable.*

Administration and Dosage: *For diaper rash,* at every diaper change gently sponge diaper area with lukewarm water, dry and apply METHAKOTE freely to the area including skin folds. *For cradle cap,* wash infant's scalp with mild soap three to five consecutive days. Dry hair by patting gently with towel. Air-dry the head for a half-hour. Then rub in METHAKOTE for two or three minutes, working from forehead to back of head. *For chafing and intertrigo,* apply METHAKOTE several times daily to affected areas.

Precautions: For external use only. Keep out of reach of children. In case of accidental ingestion, seek professional assistance or contact a poison control center immediately.

How Supplied: 1½ oz. and 3 oz. tubes.

TOPIC®
Benzyl alcohol gel
Relieves itching

Active Ingredients: 5% benzyl alcohol in a cooling, mildly drying gel base that contains camphor, menthol, 30% isopropyl alcohol, purified water, hectorite, propylene glycol, sodium laureth sulfate, perfume and color. The unique gel base is greaseless, non-occlusive and water-washable.

Indications: For temporary relief of itching caused by contact dermatitis (such as poison oak and ivy), insect bites, miliaria (heat rash), allergic dermatitis and localized neurodermatitis.

Actions: Antipruritic. TOPIC combines the antipruritic action of benzyl alcohol with the cooling effect of its alcohol gel base.

Precautions: For external use only. Keep away from eyes. Not for use on acutely inflamed skin. May sting temporarily on broken skin. Discontinue use if irritation develops. Keep out of the reach of children. In case of accidental ingestion, seek professional assistance or contact a poison control center immediately.

Dosage and Administration: Shake tube before using. Apply a thin film of TOPIC. Repeat as needed.

How Supplied: 2 oz. tubes.

Thompson Medical Company, Inc.
919 THIRD AVENUE
NEW YORK, NY 10022

MAXIMUM STRENGTH APPEDRINE®
Anorectic for Weight Control

Each tablet contains:

phenylpropanolamine HCl	25 mg
caffeine	100 mg

Each three tablets contain:

Vitamin A	5000 IU
Vitamin D	400 IU
Vitamin E	30 IU
Vitamin C (Ascorbic Acid)	60 mg
Folic Acid	0.4 mg
Vitamin B_1 (Thiamine HCl)	1.5 mg
Vitamin B_2 (Riboflavin)	1.7 mg
Niacinamide	20 mg
Vitamin B_6 (Pyridoxine HCl)	2 mg
Vitamin B_{12} (Cyanocobalamin)	6 mcg
d-Calcium Pantothenate	10 mg

Description: Each tablet contains phenylpropanolamine HCl, an anorexiant and caffeine, a mild stimulant and one third of the recommended daily adult requirement of major vitamins.

Indications: Maximum Strength APPEDRINE is indicated as adjunctive therapy in the management of simple exogenous obesity in a regimen of weight reduction and control based on caloric restriction.

Caution: Do not exceed recommended dosage. Discontinue use if rapid pulse, dizziness or palpitations occur. Do not use, if high blood pressure, heart, diabetes, kidney, thyroid or other disease is present or if pregnant, nursing or by anyone under the age of 18 except on the advice of a physician. Keep this and all drugs out of the reach of children. In case of accidental overdose, seek professional assistance or contact a Poison Control Center immediately.

Precaution: Avoid use if taking prescription, anti-hypertensive and anti-depressive drugs containing monoamine oxidase inhibitors or other medication containing sympathomimetic amines. Avoid continuous use longer than 3 months.

Adverse Reactions: Side effects are rare when taken as directed. Nausea or nasal dryness may occasionally occur.

Dosage and Administration: Adults: One tablet 30–60 minutes before each meal three times a day with one or two full glasses of water.

How Supplied: Maximum Strength APPEDRINE® packages of 30 and 60 tablets packaged with 1200 Calorie Maximum Strength Appedrine Diet Plan.

Reference: Griboff, Solomon, I., M.D., F.A.C.P. et al., A Double-Blind Clinical Evaluation of a Phenylpropanolamine-Caffeine Combination and a Placebo in the Treatment of Exogenous Obesity, Current Therapeutic Research 17, 6:535, 1975 (June).

ASPERCREME™

Description: 10% Triethanolamine Salicylate in a pleasantly scented lotion and cream.

Actions: External analgesic with rapid penetration and absorption.

Indications: An effective salicylate analgesic for temporary relief from minor pains of arthritis, rheumatism and muscular aches. Moderately effective in relieving the sensation of burning and tingling, frequently occurring in the hands and feet of elderly patients.

Contraindications: Do not use in patients manifesting idiosyncrasy to salicylates.

Warning: Use only as directed. If pain persists for more than ten days or in arthritic or rheumatic conditions affecting children under twelve years of age, consult a physician immediately. Keep out of reach of children.

Precautions: For external use only. Occasionally where this product has been used extensively, moderate peeling of the skin may occur. This is a normal reaction to salicylates on the skin, and should not warrant discontinuance of the use of the product.

Dosage and Administration: Apply to painful areas with gentle massage until absorbed into skin, three or four times daily, especially before retiring. Relief lasts for hours.

How Supplied: Lotion; 6 oz plastic bottle. Cream; 3 oz, 5 oz and 1 ¼ oz. plastic tubes.

References: Golden, Emanuel L., M.D., A Double-Blind Comparison of Orally Ingested Aspirin and a Topically Applied Salicylate Cream in the Relief of Rheumatic Pain, Current Therapeutic Research, 24, 5:524, 1978 (Sept.).

CONTROL™ Capsules
Prolonged action anorectic for weight control containing phenylpropanolamine HCl 75 mg

Description: Phenylpropanolamine HCl is a sympathomimetic, related to ephedrine but with less CNS stimulation. Useful as an anorexiant.

Indication: CONTROL is indicated as adjunctive therapy in a regimen of weight reduction based on caloric restriction in the management and control of simple exogenous obesity.

Caution: For Adults use only.
Do not exceed recommended dose. If nervousness, dizziness, sleeplessness, rapid pulse, palpitations or other symptoms occur discontinue medication and consult your physician. If you have or are being treated for high blood pressure, heart, diabetes, thyroid or other disease, or while pregnant, or nursing or under the age of 18 do not take this drug except under the advice of a physician. Keep this and all drugs out of the reach of children. In case of accidental overdose seek professional assistance or contact a Poison Control Center immediately.

Precaution: Avoid use if taking prescription, anti-hypertensive and anti-depressive drugs containing monoamine oxidase inhibitors or other medication containing sympathomimetic amines. Avoid continuous use for longer than 3 months.

Adverse Reactions: Side effects are rare when taken as directed. Nausea or nasal dryness may occasionally occur.

Dosage and Administration: One capsule with a full glass of water once a day at mid-morning (10:00 A.M.).

How Supplied: CONTROL™ Capsules—Packages of 14, 28 and 56 capsules, packaged with 1200 Calorie CONTROL Diet Plan.

DEXATRIM™ Capsules
Prolonged action anorectic for weight control contains

phenylpropanolamine HCl	50 mg
caffeine	200 mg

DEXATRIM™ Extra Strength Capsules

phenylpropanolamine	75 mg
caffeine	200 mg

Description: Phenylpropanolamine hydrochloride is a sympathomimetic, related to ephedrine but with less CNS stimulation. Useful as an anorexiant. Caffeine is a mild stimulant.

Indication: DEXATRIM and Extra Strength DEXATRIM Capsules are indicated as adjunctive therapy in a regimen of weight reduction based on caloric restriction in the management and control of simple exogenous obesity.

Studies comparing DEXATRIM to prescription anorexiants have shown DEXATRIM to be equally effective in helping to suppress appetite and in resultant weight loss. DEXATRIM, however, unlike prescription products, has been shown to induce little to no untoward CNS effects. When DEXATRIM was compared to mazindol in a six-week, double-blind study employing 67 outpatients[1] similar weight losses were reported for all subjects. DEXATRIM patients reported no significant adverse effects, while 18% of the mazindol patients reported side effects which included nervousness, nausea and insomnia.

In a six week double-blind parallel study comparing phenylpropanolamine HCl to diethylpropion similar weight losses occurred in 62 clinically obese patients. Ninety-six percent of the patients receiving phenylpropanolamine HCl and 87% of the patients receiving diethylpropion lost weight.[2]

Caution: Do not exceed recommended dosage. Discontinue use if rapid pulse, dizziness or palpitations occur. Do not use if high blood pressure, heart, diabetes, kidney, thyroid or other disease is present or if pregnant, nursing or by anyone under the age of 18 except on the advice of a physician. Keep this and all drugs out of the reach of children. In case of accidental overdose seek professional assistance or contact a Poison Control Center immediately.

Precaution: Avoid use if taking prescription, anti-hypertensive and anti-depressive drugs containing monoamine oxidase inhibitors or other medication containing sympathomimetic amines. Avoid continuous use for longer than 3 months.

Adverse Reactions: Side effects are rare when taken as directed. Nausea or nasal dryness may occasionally occur.

Dosage and Administration:
DEXATRIM™ Capsules: One capsule with a full glass of water mid-morning (10:00 AM)
Extra Strength DEXATRIM™ Capsules: One capsule with a full glass of water mid-morning (10:00 AM)

How Supplied:
DEXATRIM™ Capsules: Packages of 28 or 56 with 1200 calorie DEXATRIM Diet Plan
Extra Strength DEXATRIM™ Capsules: Packages of 20 and 40 with 1200 calorie DEXATRIM Diet Plan.

A U.S. Government advisory panel of medical and scientific experts has determined the combination of active ingredients in this product is safe and effective when taken as directed for appetite control to aid in weight reduction by caloric restriction.

---

1. Report on file, Professional Services, Thompson Medical Company, Inc. 919 Third Avenue, New York, New York 10022.
2. Report on file, Professional Services, Thompson Medical Company, Inc. 919 Third Avenue, New York, New York 10022.

**Super Strength
PROLAMINE™ Capsules
Continuous Action Anorectic for Weight Control**

Each capsule contains:

phenylpropanolamine HCl	37.5 mg
caffeine	140 mg

Description: Each capsule contains phenylpropanolamine hydrochloride an anorexiant and caffeine, a mild stimulant.

Indication: Super Strength PROLAMINE is indicated as adjunctive therapy in the regimen of weight reduction based on caloric restriction in the management and control of simple exogenous obesity. In a six-week double-blind study of 70 obese patients comparing phenylpropanolamine HCl to a placebo, 35% of the subjects taking phenylpropanolamine HCl experienced a weight loss of 8 pounds or more. Only 9% of the subjects taking placebo lost that amount of weight. Results were statistically significant at the 0.05 probability level.[1]

Caution: Do not exceed recommended dosage. Discontinue use if rapid pulse, dizziness, or palpitations occur. Do not take if you have high blood pressure, heart disease, diabetes, kidney, thyroid, or other disease or if pregnant or lactating. Keep this and all drugs out of the reach of children. In case of accidental overdose seek professional assistance or contact a Poison Control Center immediately.

Precaution: Avoid use if taking prescription, anti-hypertensive and antidepressive drugs containing monoamine oxidase inhibitors or other medication containing sympathomimetic amines.

Avoid continuous use for longer than 3 months.

Adverse Reactions: Side effects are rare when taken as directed. Nausea or nasal dryness may occasionally occur.

Dosage and Administration: one capsule at 10 A.M. and 1 capsule at 4 P.M.

How Supplied: Super Strength PROLAMINE™ Capsules: Packages of 20 and 50 packaged with 1200 Calorie PROLAMINE Diet Plan.

A U.S. Government advisory panel of medical and scientific experts has determined the combination of active ingredients in this product as safe and effective when taken as directed for appetite control to aid in weight reduction by caloric restriction.

---

1. Report on file, Professional Services, Thompson Medical Company, Inc. 919 Third Avenue, New York, New York 10022

Thought Technology Ltd.
2193 CLIFTON AVENUE
SUITE P.D.R.
MONTREAL, CANADA H4A 2N5

GSR 2™
Biofeedback Relaxation System

Description: Each kit contains a handheld, battery-operated GSR unit, 30-minute learning system on tape cassette or record, instruction booklet, and earphone for private listening.

Indications: A behavioral tool, designed for both clinical and home use, the GSR 2 helps develop the relaxation strategies necessary for the control of stress by making patients aware of their own changing stress levels.

Actions: The GSR 2 monitors fluctuations in skin resistance caused by alterations in sympathetic nervous system activity and translates them into an audible tone which increases in pitch with rising stress, and decreases with relaxation. By learning to lower the tone patients learn to lower stress levels.
The GSR 2 is inexpensive and portable, so it can be used virtually anywhere, anytime your patient wants to practice stress control. The monitor is activated automatically by resting fingers on built-in sensor plates.

Warnings: None

Also Available: The GSR/Temp 2 system which monitors peripheral vascular constriction resulting in skin tempera-

ture fluctuations, in addition to skin resistance.

How Supplied: All U.S. orders are sent from Thought Technology's N.Y. warehouse, via U.P.S.

Upjohn Company, The
KALAMAZOO, MI 49001

BACIGUENT® Antibiotic Ointment

Active Ingredient: Each gram contains 500 units of bacitracin.

Indications: *Baciguent* is a first aid ointment to help prevent infection and aid in the healing of minor cuts, burns and abrasions.

How Supplied: Available in ½ oz, 1 oz and 4 oz tubes.

CHERACOL D® Cough Syrup

Active Ingredients: Each teaspoonful (5 ml) contains dextromethorphan hydrobromide, 10 mg, and guaifenesin, 100 mg, in a pleasant-tasting vehicle. Contains 4.75% alcohol.

Indications: *Cheracol D* Cough Syrup helps quiet dry, hacking coughs, and helps loosen phlegm and mucus. Recommended for adults and children 2 years of age and older.

Dosage and Administration: Adults: 2 teaspoonfuls. Children 2 to 6 years: ½ teaspoonful. These doses may be repeated every four hours if necessary.

How Supplied: Available in 2 oz, 4 oz and 6 oz bottles.

CITROCARBONATE® Antacid

Active Ingredients: When dissolved, each 3.9 grams (1 teaspoonful) contains sodium bicarbonate, 0.78 gram and sodium citrate, 1.82 grams. Each teaspoonful contains 30.46 mEq (700.6 mg) of sodium.

Indications: For the temporary relief of heartburn, acid indigestion, and sour stomach.

Dosage and Administration: Adults: 1 to 2 teaspoonfuls (not to exceed 5 teaspoonfuls per day) in a glass of cold water after meals. Children 6 to 12 years: ¼ to ½ adult dose. For children under 6 years: Consult physician. Persons 60 years or older: ½ to 1 teaspoonful after meals.

How Supplied: Available in 4 oz and 8 oz bottles.

CORTAID® Cream
CORTAID® Ointment
CORTAID® Lotion
(hydrocortisone acetate)

Antipruritic

Description: *Cortaid* Cream contains hydrocortisone acetate (equivalent to 0.5% hydrocortisone) in a greaseless, odorless, vanishing cream that leaves no residue. *Cortaid* Ointment contains hydrocortisone acetate (equivalent to 0.5% hydrocortisone) in a soothing, lubricating ointment. *Cortaid* Lotion contains hydrocortisone acetate (equivalent to

Continued on next page

Upjohn—Cont.

0.5% hydrocortisone) in a greaseless, odorless, vanishing lotion.

Indications: All *Cortaid* forms are indicated for the temporary relief of minor skin irritations, itching and rashes due to eczema, dermatitis, insect bites, poison ivy, poison oak, poison sumac, soaps, detergents, cosmetics, and jewelry, and for itchy genital and anal areas.

Uses: The vanishing action of *Cortaid* Cream makes it cosmetically acceptable when the skin rash treated is on an exposed part of the body such as the hands or arms. *Cortaid* Ointment is best used where protection, lubrication and soothing of dry and scaly lesions is required; the ointment is also preferred for treating itchy genital and anal areas. *Cortaid* Lotion is thinner than the cream and is especially suitable for hairy body areas such as the scalp or arms.

Warnings: All *Cortaid* formulations are for external use only. Avoid contact with the eyes. If condition worsens or if symptoms persist for more than seven days, discontinue use of this product and consult a physician. Do not use on children under two years of age except under the advice and supervision of a physician. Keep this and all drugs out of the reach of children. In case of accidental ingestion, seek professional assistance or contact a poison control center immediately.

Dosage and Administration: For adults and children two years of age and older. Apply the cream, ointment, or lotion by gently massaging *Cortaid* into the affected area not more than three to four times daily.

How Supplied: *Cortaid* (hydrocortisone acetate) is available in: Cream ½ oz and 1 oz tubes; Ointment ½ oz and 1 oz tubes; Lotion 1 oz and 2 oz bottles.
[*Shown in Product Identification Section*]

KAOPECTATE®
Anti-Diarrhea Medicine

Active Ingredients: Each fluid ounce (2 tablespoonfuls) contains kaolin, 90 grains; pectin, 2 grains, in a pleasant-tasting liquid. Contains no alcohol.

Indications: For the relief of diarrhea.

Dosage and Administration: Adults: 4 to 8 tablespoonfuls. Children over 12 years: 4 tablespoonfuls. Children 6 to 12 years: 2 to 4 tablespoonfuls. Children 3 to 6 years: 1 to 2 tablespoonfuls. Infants and children under 3 years old: only as directed by a physician. For best results, take full recommended dose after each bowel movement.

How Supplied: Available in 3 oz unit-dose, 8 oz, 12 oz, and gallon bottles; bilingual labeling in Spanish and English available for 8 oz and 12 oz bottles.
[*Shown in Product Identification Section*]

KAOPECTATE CONCENTRATE™
Anti-Diarrhea Medicine

Active Ingredients: Each fluid ounce (2 tablespoonfuls) contains kaolin, 135

grains; pectin, 3 grains, in a mint-flavored liquid. Contains no alcohol.

Indications: For the relief of diarrhea.

Dosage and Administration: Adults: 3 to 6 tablespoonfuls. Children over 12 years: 3 tablespoonfuls. Children 6 to 12 years: 2 tablespoonfuls. Children 3 to 6 years: 1 tablespoonful. Infants and children under 3 years: only as directed by a physician. For best results, take full recommended dose after each bowel movement.

How Supplied: Available in 2 oz unit-dose, 8 oz and 12 oz bottles.
[*Shown in Product Identification Section*]

MYCIGUENT® Antibiotic Ointment

Active Ingredient: Each gram contains 5 mg of neomycin sulfate (equivalent to 3.5 mg neomycin).

Indications: *Myciguent* is a first aid ointment to help prevent infection and aid in the healing of minor cuts, burns and abrasions.

How Supplied: Available in ½ oz, 1 oz and 4 oz tubes.

MYCITRACIN® Antibiotic Ointment

Active Ingredients: Each gram contains 500 units of bacitracin, 5 mg of neomycin sulfate (equivalent to 3.5 mg neomycin) and 5000 units of polymyxin B sulfate.

Indications: *Mycitracin* is a first aid ointment to help prevent infection and aid in the healing of minor cuts, burns and abrasions.

How Supplied: Available in 1/32 oz unit-dose, ½ oz and 1 oz tubes.
[*Shown in Product Identification Section*]

UNICAP® Capsules/Tablets
Multivitamin Supplement

Indications: Dietary multivitamin supplement of ten essential vitamins in capsule or tablet form for adults and children 4 or more years of age.

Ingredients:	Each capsule (or tablet) contains:	% U.S. RDA*
Vitamin A	5000 Int. Units	100
Vitamin D	400 Int. Units	100
Vitamin E	15 Int. Units	50
Vitamin C	60 mg	100
Folic Acid	400 mcg	100
Thiamine	1.5 mg	100
Riboflavin	1.7 mg	100
Niacin	20 mg	100
Vitamin B6	2 mg	100
Vitamin B12	6 mcg	100

*Percentage of U.S. Recommended Daily Allowance

How Supplied: Available in bottles of 90, 240 and 1000 capsules; bottles of 60 and 90 tablets.

UNICAP CHEWABLE® Tablets

Indications: Dietary multivitamin supplement with ten essential vitamins in an orange-flavored chewable tablet for children 4 or more years of age.

Ingredients:	Each tablet contains:	% U.S. RDA*
Vitamin A	5000 Int. Units	100
Vitamin D	400 Int. Units	100
Vitamin E	15 Int. Units	50
Vitamin C	60 mg	100
Folic Acid	400 mcg	100
Thiamine	1.5 mg	100
Riboflavin	1.7 mg	100
Niacin	20 mg	100
Vitamin B6	2 mg	100
Vitamin B12	6 mcg	100

* Percentage of U.S. Recommended Daily Allowance

How Supplied: Available in bottle of 90 tablets.

UNICAP M® Tablets

Indications: Dietary supplement of 11 essential vitamins plus iron and five more minerals for persons 12 or more years of age.

Ingredients:	Each tablet contains:	% U.S. RDA*
Vitamin A	5000 Int. Units	100
Vitamin D	400 Int. Units	100
Vitamin E	15 Int. Units	50
Vitamin C	60 mg	100
Folic Acid	400 mcg	100
Thiamine	1.5 mg	100
Riboflavin	1.7 mg	100
Niacin	20 mg	100
Vitamin B6	2 mg	100
Vitamin B12	6 mcg	100
Pantothenic Acid	10 mg	100
Iodine	150 mcg	100
Iron	18 mg	100
Copper	2 mg	100
Zinc	15 mg	100
Manganese	1 mg	+
Potassium	5 mg	+

* Percentage of U.S. Recommended Daily Allowance.
+ No U.S. RDA has been established for this nutrient.

How Supplied: Available in bottles of 30, 60, 90, 180 and 500 tablets.
[*Shown in Product Identification Section*]

UNICAP PLUS IRON™ Tablets

Indications: Dietary multivitamin supplement with 11 essential vitamins and iron for persons 12 or more years of age.

Ingredients:	Each tablet contains:	% U.S. RDA*
Vitamin A	5000 Int. Units	100
Vitamin D	400 Int. Units	100
Vitamin E	15 Int. Units	50
Vitamin C	60 mg	100
Folic Acid	400 mcg	100
Thiamine	1.5 mg	100
Riboflavin	1.7 mg	100
Niacin	20 mg	100
Vitamin B6	2 mg	100
Vitamin B12	6 mcg	100
Pantothenic Acid	10 mg	100
Iron	18 mg	100

* Percentage of U.S. Recommended Daily Allowance.

How Supplied: Available in bottles of 60 and 90 tablets.

UNICAP SENIOR® Tablets

Indications: Dietary supplement of ten essential vitamins plus six minerals for adults. Especially formulated for adults 51 years and older who need only 10 mg of iron.

Ingredients:	Each tablet contains:	% U.S. RDA*
Vitamin A	5000 Int. Units	100
Vitamin E	15 Int. Units	50
Vitamin C	60 mg	100
Folic Acid	400 mcg	100
Thiamine	1.2 mg	80
Riboflavin	1.7 mg	100
Niacin	14 mg	70
Vitamin B$_6$	2 mg	100
Vitamin B$_{12}$	6 mcg	100
Pantothenic Acid	10 mg	100
Iodine	150 mcg	100
Iron	10 mg	56
Copper	2 mg	100
Zinc	15 mg	100
Manganese	1 mg	+
Potassium	5 mg	+

* Percentage of U.S. Recommended Daily Allowance
+ No U.S. RDA has been established for this nutrient.
How Supplied: Available in bottle of 90 tablets.

UNICAP T® Tablets
High Potency
Vitamin-Mineral Supplement

Indications: High potency dietary supplement of 11 essential vitamins and six minerals for persons 12 or more years of age.

Ingredients:	Each tablet contains:	% U.S. RDA*
Vitamin A	5000 Int. Units	100
Vitamin D	400 Int. Units	100
Vitamin E	15 Int. Units	50
Vitamin C	300 mg	500
Folic Acid	400 mcg	100
Thiamine	10 mg	667
Riboflavin	10 mg	588
Niacin	100 mg	500
Vitamin B$_6$	6 mg	300
Vitamin B$_{12}$	18 mcg	300
Pantothenic Acid	10 mg	100
Iodine	150 mcg	100
Iron	18 mg	100
Copper	2 mg	100
Zinc	15 mg	100
Manganese	1 mg	+
Potassium	5 mg	+

* Percentage of U.S. Recommended Daily Allowance
+ No U.S. RDA has been established for this nutrient.
How Supplied: Available in bottles of 30, 90 and 500 tablets.
[*Shown in Product Identification Section*]

IDENTIFICATION PROBLEM?

Consult the

Product Identification Section

where you'll find

products pictured

in full color.

Vicks Toiletry Products Division
RICHARDSON-MERRELL INC.
TEN WESTPORT ROAD
WILTON, CT 06897

CLEARASIL® Super Strength Acne Treatment Cream Vanishing and Tinted

Active Ingredients: Benzoyl Peroxide 10% in an odorless, greaseless cream base, containing water, propylene glycol, bentonite, glyceryl stearate SE, isopropyl myristate, cellulose gum, dimethicone, methylparaben, and propylparaben. The tinted formula also contains titanium dioxide and iron oxides.
Indications: For the topical treatment of acne vulgaris.
Actions: CLEARASIL Super Strength Acne Treatment Cream contains benzoyl peroxide, an antibacterial and keratolytic as well as bentonite as an oil absorbant. The product 1) helps heal and prevent acne pimples, 2) helps absorb excess skin oil often associated with acne blemishes, 3) helps your skin look fresh. The Vanishing formula works invisibly. The Tinted formula hides pimples while its works.
Warnings: Persons with a known sensitivity to benzoyl peroxide should not use this medication. Excessive dryness may occur especially when used by persons with unusually dry, sensitive, or maturing skin. If itching, redness, burning, swelling or undue dryness occurs, discontinue use. If symptoms persist, consult a physician promptly. For external use only. Keep from eyes, lips, mouth and sensitive areas of the neck. Colored or dyed fabrics may be bleached by the oxidizing action of this product. Keep this and all medicine out of the reach of children.
Symptoms and Treatment of Ingestion: These symptoms are based upon medical judgement, not on actual experience. Theoretically, ingestion of very large amounts may cause nausea, vomiting, abdominal discomfort and diarrhea. Treatment is symptomatic, with bedrest and observation.
Directions For Use: 1. Wash thoroughly. (Clearasil® Antibacterial Soap and Clearasil® Pore Deep Cleanser are excellent products to use in your cleansing regimen.) **2.** Try this sensitivity test. Apply cream sparingly with fingertips to one or two small affected areas during the first three days. If no discomfort or reaction occurs, apply up to two times daily, wherever pimples and oil are a problem. **3.** If bothersome dryness or peeling occurs, reduce dosage to one application per day or every other day.
How Supplied: Available in both Vanishing and Tinted formulas in 1 oz. and .65 oz. squeeze tubes.
[*Shown in Product Identification Section*]

CLEARASIL®
5% Benzoyl Peroxide Lotion
Acne Treatment

Active Ingredients: Benzoyl Peroxide 5% in a colorless, greaseless lotion which

contains water, propylene glycol, glyceryl stearate SE, bentonite, cellulose gum, isopropyl myristate, sodium citrate, dimethicone, methylparaben, propylparaben.
Indications: For the topical treatment of acne vulgaris.
Actions: CLEARASIL 5% Benzoyl Peroxide Lotion contains benzoyl peroxide, an antibacterial and keratolytic. The product **1. Helps heal and prevent acne pimples.** Benzoyl peroxide dries up existing pimples and kills acne causing bacteria to help prevent new ones. In fact, benzoyl peroxide is the strongest acne pimple medicine you can buy without a prescription.
2. Helps absorb excess skin oil often associated with acne blemishes. Contains bentonite which is a unique oil absorbing ingredient that allows Clearasil Lotion to absorb **more** excess skin oil than 5% benzoyl peroxide alone.
3. Helps your skin look fresh. Extra oil absorption helps your skin look less oily, more natural.
4. Works invisibly. A colorless, odorless, and greaseless lotion.
Warnings: Persons with a known sensitivity to benzoyl peroxide should not use this medication. Excessive dryness may occur especially when used by persons with unusually dry, sensitive, or maturing skin. If itching, redness, burning, swelling or undue dryness occurs, discontinue use. If symptoms persist, consult a physician promptly. For external use only. Keep from eyes, lips, mouth and sensitive areas of the neck. Colored or dyed fabrics may be bleached by the oxidizing action of this product. Keep this and all medicine out of the reach of children.
Symptoms and Treatment of Ingestion: These symptoms are based upon medical judgement, not on actual experience. Theoretically, ingestion of very large amounts may cause nausea, vomiting, abdominal discomfort and diarrhea. Treatment is symptomatic, with bedrest and observation.
Directions For Use:
SHAKE WELL BEFORE USING.
1. Wash thoroughly. (Clearasil® Antibacterial Soap and Clearasil® Pore Deep Cleanser are excellent products to use in your cleansing regimen) **2.** Try this sensitivity test. Apply lotion sparingly with fingertips to one or two small affected areas during the first three days. If no discomfort or reaction occurs, apply up to two times daily, wherever pimples and oil are a problem **3.** If bothersome dryness or peeling occurs, reduce dosage to one application per day or every other day.
How Supplied: Available in a 1 fl. oz. squeeze bottle.
[*Shown in Product Identification Section*]

TOPEX®
10% Benzoyl Peroxide Lotion
Buffered Acne Medication

Active Ingredient: 10% Benzoyl Peroxide in a colorless, greaseless lotion

Continued on next page

Vicks Toiletry—Cont.

which is fragrance-free and contains water, propylene glycol, stearic acid, PEG-20 stearate, glyceryl stearate, isopropyl palmitate, zinc laurate, benzoic acid.

Indications: For the topical treatment of acne vulgaris.

Actions: TOPEX 10% Benzoyl Peroxide Lotion contains benzoyl peroxide, an antibacterial and keratolytic. The product 1) dries and helps heal acne lesions (pimples), 2) reduces comedones (blackheads and whiteheads), 3) kills bacteria associated with acne lesions, and 4) helps prevent acne lesions from forming.

Warnings: Persons with a known sensitivity to benzoyl peroxide should not use this medication. Persons with unusually dry, sensitive, or maturing skin may experience excessive dryness. If itching, redness, burning, swelling or undue dryness occurs, discontinue use. If symptoms persist, consult a physician promptly. For external use only. Keep from eyes, lips, mouth and sensitive areas of the neck. Colored or dyed fabrics may be bleached by the oxidizing action of this product. Keep this and all medicine out of the reach of children.

Symptoms and Treatment of Ingestion: These symptoms are based upon medical judgement, not on actual experience. Theoretically, ingestion of very large amounts may cause nausea, vomiting, abdominal discomfort and diarrhea. Treatment is symptomatic, with bedrest and observation.

Directions For Use: Follow your normal cleansing routine. Shake bottle well. Some people are sensitive to the active ingredients of acne medications, so for the first three days apply lotion sparingly with fingertips to one or two small affected areas. If no discomfort or reaction occurs, apply one to three times daily to areas where pimples normally appear to help prevent breakouts and to existing pimples to clear them fast. Gently rub in lotion until it disappears. Although Topex has been specially formulated to address the problem of the overdrying effects of benzoyl peroxide, some people may still experience bothersome dryness or flaking; if so, reduce number of daily applications.

How Supplied: Available in a 1 fl. oz. squeeze bottle.

[*Shown in Product Identification Section*]

IDENTIFICATION PROBLEM?

Consult the

Product Identification Section

where you'll find

products pictured

in full color.

Vicks Health Care Division
RICHARDSON-MERRELL INC.
TEN WESTPORT ROAD
WILTON, CT 06897

DAYCARE®
Multi-Symptom Colds Medicine in oral liquid form

Active Ingredients: Each fluid ounce (2 tbs.) contains Acetaminophen 650 mg., Dextromethorphan Hydrobromide 20 mg., Phenylpropanolamine Hydrochloride 25 mg. in an orange, apricot-flavored, cooling liquid base. Also contains Alcohol 10%.

Indications: For the temporary relief of major colds symptoms, as follows: nasal congestion, sinus congestion, coughing, headaches, body aches and fever without antihistamines which can cause drowsy side effects.

Actions: VICKS DAYCARE liquid is an antitussive, antipyretic, decongestant and analgesic. It helps clear stuffy nose, congested sinus openings. Calms, quiets coughing. Eases headache pain and the ache-all-over feeling. Reduces fever due to colds and flu. By relieving these symptoms without antihistamines which can cause drowsy side effects, helps patients get through an active day.

Warning: Do not administer to children under 6 years of age unless directed by a physician. Persistent cough may indicate the presence of a serious condition. Persons with a high fever or persistent cough or with high blood pressure, diabetes, heart or thyroid disease should not use this preparation unless directed by a physician. Do not use more than ten days unless directed by a physician. Do not exceed recommended dosage unless directed by a physician. As with all medication, keep out of reach of children.

Symptoms and Treatment of Overdosage: These symptoms are based upon medical judgement, not on actual experience, since no significant incidence of overdose has been brought to our attention in clinical or consumer experience. Ingestion of very large amounts may cause dizziness, drowsiness, nausea, diarrhea, insomnia, nervousness, anxiety, tremors, tachycardia, extrasystoles, headache, sweating, confusion and delerium. Treatment is symptomatic, with bedrest and observation.

Dosage: A plastic measuring cup with 1 and 2 tablespoonful gradations is supplied.

Adults (12 and over): one fluid ounce (2 tablespoonfuls)

Children: (6-12): one-half fluid ounce (1 tablespoonful)

May be repeated every four hours as needed.

Maximum 4 doses per day.

How Supplied: Available in 6 fl. oz. and 10 fl. oz. bottles.

[*Shown in Product Identification Section*]

DAYCARE®
Multi-Symptom Colds Medicine capsules

Active Ingredients: Each orange and white capsule contains Acetaminophen

325mg., Phenylpropanolamine Hydrochloride 12.5mg, Dextromethorphan Hydrobromide 10mg.

Indications: Relieves colds symptoms without antihistamines which can cause drowsy side effects.

Actions: VICKS DAYCARE capsules are analgesic, antipyretic, decongestant and antitussive multi-symptom colds medicine. They relieve stuffy nose, sinus congestion, headache, body aches, coughing and fever.

Warning: Do not administer to children under 6 years of age unless directed by a physician. Persistent cough may indicate the presence of a serious condition. Persons with a high fever or persistent cough or with high blood pressure, diabetes, heart or thyroid disease should not use this preparation unless directed by a physician. Do not use more than 10 days unless directed by a physician. Do not exceed recommended dose unless directed by a physician. As with all medicine, keep out of reach of children.

Symptoms and Treatment of Overdosage: These symptoms are based upon medical judgment, not on actual experience. No significant incidence of overdosage with DAYCARE capsules has been brought to our attention in clinical or consumer experience. Ingestion of very large amounts may cause dizziness, nausea, insomnia, nervousness, anxiety, tremors tachycardia, extrasystoles, headache, sweating, confusion and delerium. Treatment is symptomatic, with bedrest and observation.

Dosage: Adults (12 and over): 2 capsules every 4 hours.

Children (6 to 12): 1 capsule every 4 hours.

Maximum 4 doses per day.

How Supplied: Available in 8's (trial size), 20's, 36's, and 60's child-resistant blister packs.

Expiration date is noted on package.

[*Shown in Product Identification Section*]

FORMULA 44® COUGH CONTROL DISCS

Active Ingredients per disc: Dextromethorphan (equivalent to Dextromethorphan Hydrobromide) 5 mg., Benzocaine 1.25 mg., Special Vicks Medication (menthol, anethole, peppermint oil) 0.35% in a dark brown sugar base.

Indications: Provides temporary relief from coughs and relieves throat irritation caused by colds, flu, bronchitis.

Actions: VICKS FORMULA 44 COUGH CONTROL DISCS are antitussive, local anesthetic and demulcent cough drops. They calm, quiet coughs and help coat and soothe irritated throats.

Warning: Do not exceed recommended dosage. Do not administer to children under 4 unless directed by physician. Persistent cough may indicate presence of a serious condition. Persons with high fever or persistent cough should not use this preparation unless directed by physician. As with all medication, keep out of reach of children.

Symptoms and Treatment of Overdosage: These symptoms are based upon medical judgement, not on actual experience, since no significant incidence of overdose has been brought to our attention in clinical or consumer experience. Though unlikely, ingestion of large amounts may cause dizziness, drowsiness, nausea, vomiting, diarrhea, central excitement and a possibility of cyanosis in young children. Treatment is symptomatic, with bedrest and observation.

Dosage:

ADULTS (12 years and over) 2 discs. Dissolve in mouth. Two additional discs every three hours as needed.

CHILDREN (4 to 12 years) 1 disc. Dissolve in mouth. One additional disc every three hours as needed.

How Supplied: Available as individual foil wrapped portable packets in boxes of 24.

FORMULA 44® COUGH MIXTURE

Active Ingredients per 2 tsp. (10 ml.): Dextromethorphan Hydrobromide 15 mg., Doxylamine Succinate 7.5 mg., Sodium Citrate 500 mg. in a pleasant tasting, dark brown syrup base. Also contains Alcohol 10%.

Indications: For the temporary relief of coughs due to colds, flu, bronchitis.

Actions: VICKS FORMULA 44 COUGH MIXTURE is an antitussive, antihistamine, demulcent and expectorant. Calms and quiets coughs. Reduces sneezing and sniffling. Coats, soothes irritated throat.

Warning: Do not exceed recommended dosage unless directed by a physician. Do not administer to children under 6 years of age unless directed by a physician. Persistent cough may indicate the presence of a serious condition. Persons with a high fever or persistent cough should not use the product unless directed by a physician. FORMULA 44 may cause drowsiness. Do not drive or operate machinery while taking the product. If relief does not occur within three days, discontinue use and consult a physician. As with all medication, keep out of reach of children.

Symptoms and Treatment of Overdosage: These symptoms are based on medical judgement and not on clinical experience, since no significant incidence of overdose has been brought to our attention in clinical or consumer experience. Presenting symptom is drowsiness. Nausea, vomiting, dizziness, ataxia, mydriasis and headache may ensue with ingestion of excessive amounts. Treatment is symptomatic, with bedrest and observation.

Dosage:

Adults: 12 years and over—2 teaspoonfuls

Children: 6 to 12 years: 1 teaspoonful Repeat every 4 hours as needed.

No more than 6 doses per day.

How Supplied: Available in 3 fl. oz., 6 fl. oz. and 8 fl. oz. bottles.

[*Shown in Product Identification Section*]

FORMULA 44D® DECONGESTANT COUGH MIXTURE

Active Ingredients per 2 tsp. (10 ml): Dextromethorphan Hydrobromide 20 mg., Phenylpropanolamine Hydrochloride 25 mg., Guaifenesin 100 mg. in a red, cherry-flavored, cooling syrup. Also contains Alcohol 10%.

Indications: Relieves coughs, decongests nasal passages and loosens upper chest congestion due to colds, flu, bronchitis.

Actions: VICKS FORMULA 44D is an antitussive, nasal decongestant, expectorant and demulcent. It calms, quiets coughs; relieves nasal congestion; loosens phlegm, mucus; and coats, soothes an irritated throat.

Warning: Do not exceed recommended dosage unless directed by physician. Do not administer to children under 2 years of age unless directed by physician. Persistent cough may indicate the presence of a serious condition. Persons with a high fever or persistent cough or with high blood pressure, diabetes, heart or thyroid disease should not use this preparation unless directed by physician. As with all medication, keep out of reach of children.

Symptoms and Treatment of Overdosage: These symptoms are based upon medical judgement, not on actual experience, since no significant incidence of overdose has been brought to our attention in clinical or consumer experience. Ingestion of large amounts may cause drowsiness, dizziness, nausea, vomiting, diarrhea, central excitement, restlessness, anxiety, sweating, tremor, extrasystoles, confusion and delerium. Treatment is symptomatic, with bedrest and observation.

Dosage:

ADULTS (12 years and over): 2 teaspoonfuls

CHILDREN (6–12 years): 1 teaspoonful

(2–6 years): ½ teaspoonful

No more than 6 doses per day. Repeat every 4 hours as needed.

How Supplied: Available in 3 fl. oz., 6 fl. oz. and 8 fl. oz. bottles.

[*Shown in Product Identification Section*]

NYQUIL®
Nighttime Colds Medicine in oral liquid form.

Active Ingredients per fluid oz. (2 tbs.): Acetaminophen 600 mg., Doxylamine Succinate 7.5 mg., Ephedrine Sulfate 8.0 mg., and Dextromethorphan Hydrobromide 15.0 mg. Also contains Alcohol 25%, and FD&C Yellow No. 5 (tartrazine).

Indications: For the temporary relief of major cold and flu symptoms, as follows: nasal & sinus congestion, coughing, sneezing, minor sorethroat pain, aches and pains, runny nose, headache, fever.

Actions: Decongestant, antipyretic, antihistaminic, antitussive, analgesic. Helps decongest nasal passages and sinus openings, relieves sniffles and sneezing, eases aches and pains, reduces fever, soothes headache, minor sore throat pain, and quiets coughing due to a cold. By relieving these symptoms, also helps patient get to sleep to get the rest he needs.

Warning: This preparation may cause drowsiness. Do not drive or operate machinery while taking this medication. Do not give to children under ten, unless directed by physician. If relief does not occur within three days, discontinue use and consult physician. Reduce dosage if nervousness, restlessness or sleeplessness occurs. Do not use if high blood pressure, heart disease, diabetes or thyroid disease is present unless directed by physician.

Persistent cough may indicate a serious condition. Persons with a high fever or persistent cough should not use this preparation unless directed by a physician. Do not exceed recommended dosage. As with all medication, keep out of reach of children.

Symptoms and Treatment of Overdosage: These symptoms are based on medical judgement and not on actual clinical experience, since no significant incidence of overdose has been brought to our attention in clinical or consumer experience. Presenting symptom of overdosage is drowsiness. Large overdoses may cause emesis, ataxia, nausea, vomiting, restlessness, vertigo, dysuria, palpitations, tinnitus, diaphoresis, insomnia. Treatment is symptomatic, with bedrest and observation.

Dosage and Dosage Form: A green, anise-flavored oral liquid (syrup). A plastic measuring cup with 1 and 2 tablespoonful gradations is supplied.

ADULTS (12 and over): One fluid ounce (2 tablespoonfuls) at bedtime.

CHILDREN 10 to 12: One half ounce (1 tablespoonful) at bedtime.

If confined to bed or at home, a total of 4 doses may be taken per day, each 4 hours apart.

How Supplied: Available in 6 fl. oz. and 10 fl. oz. bottles.

[*Shown in Product Identification Section*]

ORACIN®
Cooling Throat Lozenges

Active Ingredients per lozenge: Benzocaine 6.25 mg., Menthol 0.1% in a green, cooling (sugarless) sorbitol base. FD&C Yellow No. 5 (tartrazine) is a color additive.

Indications: Provides temporary relief of minor sore throat pain.

Actions: VICKS ORACIN is a local anesthetic, demulcent throat lozenge. It soothes and cools to temporarily relieve minor throat irritations and ease pain.

Warning: Do not exceed recommended dosage. Severe or persistent sore throat, or sore throat accompanied by high fever, headache, nausea and vomiting may be serious. Consult physician promptly. Do not use more than 2 days or administer to children under 6 years of age unless directed by a physician. As with all medication, keep out of reach of children.

Continued on next page

Vicks Health Care—Cont.

VICKS ORACIN is not a product for diabetics.

Symptoms and Treatment of Overdosage: These symptoms are based upon medical judgement, not on actual experience, since no significant incidence of overdose has been brought to our attention in clinical or consumer experience. Presenting symptom after ingesting large amounts would be diarrhea. Theoretically, ingestion of very large amounts may cause nausea, vomiting, gastrointestinal upset, central excitement, and a possibility of cyanosis in young children. Treatment is symptomatic, with bedrest and observation.

Dosage: ADULTS AND CHILDREN (6 years and over): allow one lozenge to dissolve slowly in the mouth. Repeat hourly as needed. Do not take more than 12 lozenges per day.

How Supplied: Available in boxes of 18.

ORACIN®
Cherry Flavor
Cooling Throat Lozenges

Active Ingredients per lozenge: Benzocaine 6.25 mg., Menthol 0.08% in a red, cherry flavored, cooling (sugarless) sorbitol base.

Indications: Provides temporary relief of minor sore throat pain.

Actions: VICKS ORACIN is a local anesthetic, demulcent throat lozenge. It soothes and cools to temporarily relieve minor throat irritations and ease pain.

Warning: Do not exceed recommended dosage. Severe or persistent sore throat, or sore throat accompanied by high fever, headache, nausea and vomiting may be serious. Consult physician promptly. Do not use more than 2 days or administer to children under 6 years of age unless directed by a physician. As with all medication, keep out of reach of children. VICKS ORACIN is not a product for diabetics.

Symptoms and Treatment of Overdosage: These symptoms are based upon medical judgement, not on actual experience, since no significant incidence of overdose has been brought to our attention in clinical or consumer experience. Presenting symptom after ingesting large amounts would be diarrhea. Theoretically, ingestion of very large amounts may cause nausea, vomiting, gastrointestinal upset, central excitement, and a possibility of cyanosis in young children. Treatment is symptomatic, with bedrest and observation.

Dosage: ADULTS AND CHILDREN (6 years and over): allow one lozenge to dissolve slowly in the mouth. Repeat hourly as needed. Do not take more than 12 lozenges per day.

How Supplied: Available in boxes of 18.

SINEX™
Decongestant Nasal Spray

Active Ingredients: Phenylephrine Hydrochloride 0.5%, Cetylpyridinium Chloride 0.04%, Special Vicks Blend of Aromatics (menthol, eucalyptol, camphor, methyl salicylate). Also contains Thimerosol 0.001% as a preservative.

Indications: To provide temporary relief of nasal and sinus congestion of head colds and hay fever.

Actions: VICKS SINEX is a decongestant nasal spray. The product shrinks swollen membranes to restore freer breathing; gives fast relief of nasal stuffiness and congested sinus openings; allows congested sinuses to drain; and instantly cools irritated nasal passages.

Warning: Do not exceed recommended dosage. Follow directions for use carefully. For children under 6 years, consult your physician. If condition persists consult physician. As with all medication, keep out of reach of children.

Symptoms and Treatment of Ingestion: These symptoms are based upon medical judgement, not on actual experience, since no significant incidence of overdose or ingestion has been brought to our attention in clinical or consumer experience. Though unlikely, ingestion of very large amounts may cause restlessness, anxiety, ventricular arrhythmias, nausea and gastrointestinal upset. Treatment is symptomatic, with bedrest and observation.

Directions For Use: Keep head and dispenser upright. May be used every 3 hours as needed.

ADULTS: Spray quickly, firmly 2 times up each nostril, sniffing the spray upward.

CHILDREN 6 to 12 years: Spray 1 time up each nostril.

How Supplied: Available in ½ fl. oz. and 1 fl. oz. plastic spray bottles.
[*Shown in Product Identification Section*]

SINEX™ LONG-ACTING
Decongestant Nasal Spray

Active Ingredient: Xylometazoline Hydrochloride 0.1% in an aqueous solution containing mentholated vapors. Also contains thimerosal 0.001% as a preservative.

Indications: For temporary relief of nasal congestion due to the common cold, hay fever or other upper respiratory allergies or nasal congestion associated with sinusitis.

Actions: Xylometazoline constricts the arterioles of the nasal passages—resulting in a nasal decongestant effect which lasts up to ten hours, restoring freer breathing through the nose. SINEX LONG-ACTING helps decongest sinus openings and sinus passages thus promoting sinus drainage.

Warning: For adult use only. Do not administer the product to children under 12 years except under the advice and supervision of a physician. Do not exceed recommended dosage because symptoms may occur such as burning, stinging, sneezing or increse of nasal discharge. Do not use the product for more than three

days. If symptoms persist, consult a physician. The use of this dispenser by more than one person may spread infection. In case of accidental ingestion, seek professional assistance or contact a Poison Control Center immediately. As with all medication, keep out of reach of children.

Symptoms and Treatment of Oral Ingestion: These symptoms are based upon medical judgement, not on actual experience, since no significant incidence of overdose or ingestion has been brought to our attention in clinical or consumer experience. Depending upon the amount of oral ingestion, somnolence, sedation, or deep coma may occur. With excessive ingestion, profound CNS depression may be accompanied by hypertension, bradycardia, and decreased cardiac output, which may be followed by rebound hypotension and cardiovascular collapse. Prompt gastric evacuation and intensive supportive care is indicated following marked overdosage.

Dosage and Administration: Adults: 2 sprays in each nostril every 8 to 10 hours or as directed by a physician. Spray quickly, firmly, sniffing the spray upward. Keep head and dispenser upright.

How Supplied: Available in ½ fl. oz. and 1 fl. oz. plastic spray bottles.
[*Shown in Product Identification Section*]

VAPOSTEAM®
Liquid Medication for
Hot Steam Vaporizers.

Active Ingredients: Polyoxyethylene Dodecanol 1.8%, Aromatics (eucalyptus oil, camphor, menthol) 12.4%, Tincture of Benzoin 5%, in a liquid vehicle. Also contains Alcohol 55%.

Indications: For the symptomatic relief of colds, coughs, chest congestion.

Actions: VAPOSTEAM increases the action of steam to help relieve colds symptoms in the following ways: relieves coughs of colds, even croupy coughs, eases stuffy nasal congestion, loosens phlegmy chest congestion, and moistens dry, irritated breathing passages.

Warning: VAPOSTEAM is for hot steam medication only. Do not ingest. Persistent coughing may indicate the presence of a serious condition. If symptoms persist, discontinue use and consult physician. Persons with high fever or persistent cough should not use this preparation except as directed by a physician. Keep away from open flame or extreme heat. Do not direct steam from vaporizer towards face. As with all medication, keep out of reach of children.

Symptoms and Treatment of Ingestion: Based on the medical literature and clinical judgement, ingestion of large amounts may cause nausea, vomiting, epigastric pain, discomfort and weakness, coma and death. Treatment should consist of cautious gastric lavage, barbiturates for convulsions, Metrazol for coma and supportive therapy as indicated.

Dosage and Administration: In a hot steam vaporizer: Use one tablespoonful of VAPOSTEAM with each quart of water added to the vaporizer. In an open bowl: Simply add VAPOSTEAM to any ordinary bowl of hot water—2 teaspoonfuls for each pint of water—and breathe in the medicated vapors.

How Supplied: Available in 4 fl. oz. and 6 fl. oz. bottles.

VATRONOL®
Nose Drops

Active Ingredients: Ephedrine Sulfate 0.5%, Special Vicks Aromatic Blend (menthol, eucalyptol, camphor, methyl salicylate) 0.06% in an aqueous base. Also contains Thimerosal 0.001% as a preservative.

Indications: Relieves nasal congestion caused by head colds and hay fever.

Actions: VICKS VATRONOL is a decongestant nose drop. It helps restore freer breathing by relieving nasal stuffiness and congested sinus openings. VATRONOL also cools irritated nasal passages.

Warning: Do not exceed recommended dosage. Overdosage may cause nervousness, restlessness, or sleeplessness. Do not use for more than 4 consecutive days or administer to children under 6, unless directed by a physician. As with all medication, keep out of reach of children.

Symptoms and Treatment of Ingestion: These symptoms are based upon medical judgement, not on actual experience, since no significant incidence of overdose or ingestion has been brought to our attention in clinical or consumer experience. Ingestion of very large quantities may cause restlessness, anxiety, sweating, tremor, rapid pulse, extrasystoles, confusion, delirium, nausea and gastrointestinal upset. Treatment is symptomatic, with bedrest and observation.

Dosage:
  ADULTS: Fill dropper to upper mark.
  CHILDREN (6–12 years): Fill dropper to lower mark.
Apply up one nostril, repeat in other nostril.
Repeat every 4 hours as needed.

How Supplied: Available in ½ fl. oz. and 1 fl. oz. dropper bottles.

VICKS® COUGH SILENCERS
Cough Drops

Active Ingredients per lozenge: Dextromethorphan (expressed as Dextromethorphan Hydrobromide) 2.5 mg., Benzocaine 1 mg., Special Vicks Medication (menthol, anethole, peppermint oil) 0.35% in a cooling green, sugar base.

Indications: Provides all-day relief from coughs of colds, excessive smoking, dry or irritated throats when used as directed.

Actions: VICKS COUGH SILENCERS are antitussive, local anesthetic and demulcent throat lozenges.

Warning: Do not administer to children under 4 years of age unless directed by a physician. Severe or persistent cough, sore throat, or sore throat accompanied by fever, headache, nausea and vomiting may be serious. Consult physician promptly. Persons with a high fever

or persistent cough should not use this preparation unless directed by a physician. As with all medication, keep out of reach of children.

Symptoms and Treatment of Overdosage: These symptoms are based upon medical judgement, not on actual experience, since no significant incidence of overdose has been brought to our attention in clinical or consumer experience. Though unlikely, ingestion of large quantities may cause dizziness, drowsiness, nausea, vomiting, gastrointestinal upset, diarrhea, central excitement, and a possibility of cyanosis in young children. Treatment is symptomatic, with bedrest and observation.

Dosage: Age 12 and over, 2 drops, dissolve in mouth one at a time, then 1 or 2 each hour as needed. Ages 4 to 12, 1 drop, dissolve in mouth then 1 drop each hour as needed. Do not exceed recommended dosage.

How Supplied: Available in boxes of 15's.

VICKS® COUGH SYRUP
Expectorant, Antitussive Cough Syrup

Active Ingredients per tsp. (5 ml.): Dextromethorphan Hydrobromide 3.5 mg., Guaifenesin 25 mg., Sodium Citrate 200 mg. in a red, cherry-flavored, syrup base. Also contains Alcohol 5%.

Indications: Provides temporary relief of coughs due to colds, helps loosen phlegm and rid passageways of bothersome mucus, and soothes a cough-irritated throat.

Actions: VICKS COUGH SYRUP is an antitussive, expectorant and demulcent. It calms, quiets coughs of colds, flu and bronchitis; loosens phlegm, promotes drainage of bronchial tubes; and coats and soothes a cough irritated throat.

Warning: Do not exceed recommended dosage. Do not administer to children under 2 years of age unless directed by a physician. Persistent cough may indicate the presence of a serious condition. Persons with a high fever or persistent cough should not use this preparation unless directed by a physician. As with all medication, keep out of reach of children.

Symptoms and Treatment of Overdosage: These symptoms are based upon medical judgement, not on actual experience, since no significant incidence of overdose has been brought to our attention in clinical or consumer experience. Ingestion of large amounts may cause drowsiness, dizziness, nausea, vomiting, diarrhea, central excitement and alkalosis. Treatment is gastric lavage and symptomatic treatment with bedrest and observation.

Dosage:
  ADULTS (12 years and over): 3 teaspoonfuls
  CHILDREN (6–12 years): 2 teaspoonfuls
     (2–6 years): 1 teaspoonful
Repeat every 4 hours as needed.

How Supplied: Available in 3 fl. oz. and 6 fl. oz. bottles.

VICKS® INHALER
with decongestant action

Active Ingredients per inhaler: l-Desoxyephedrine 50 mg., Special Vicks Medication (menthol, camphor, methyl salicylate, bornyl acetate) 150 mg.

Indications: Provides temporary relief of nasal congestion of colds and hay fever. Decongests sinus openings.

Actions: VICKS INHALER is an intranasal inhaled decongestant. It shrinks swollen membranes and provides fast relief from a stuffy nose.

Warning: As with all medication, keep out of reach of children.

Symptoms and Treatment of Ingestion: These symptoms are based upon medical judgement, not on actual experience, since no significant incidence of overdose or ingestion has been brought to our attention in clinical or consumer experience. Though VICKS INHALER is unlikely to be ingested, consumption of large quantities of its active ingredients may cause dizziness, nervousness, headache, tachycardia, nausea and vomiting. Treatment is symptomatic, with bedrest and observation.

Directions For Use: Inhale medicated vapor through each nostril while blocking off other nostril. Use as often as needed.
VICKS INHALER is medically effective for 3 months after first use.

How Supplied: Available as a cylindrical plastic nasal inhaler (net wt. 0.007 oz.).

VICKS® THROAT LOZENGES

Active Ingredients per lozenge: Benzocaine 5 mg., Cetylpyridinium Chloride 1.66 mg., Special Vicks Medication (menthol, camphor, eucalyptus oil) in a red cooling sugar base.

Indications: For fast-acting temporary relief of minor sore throat pain, and minor coughs due to colds.

Actions: VICKS THROAT LOZENGES are local anesthetic and demulcent cough drops. They temporarily soothe minor sore throat irritations —ease pain —and relieve irritation and dryness of mouth and throat.

Warning: Do not exceed recommended dosage. Severe or persistent cough, sore throat, or sore throat accompanied by high fever, headache, nausea, and vomiting may be serious. Consult physician promptly. Do not use more than 2 days or administer to children under 3 years of age unless directed by physician. As with all medication, keep out of reach of children.

Symptoms and Treatment of Overdosage: These symptoms are based upon medical judgement, not on actual experience, since no significant incidence of overdose has been brought to our attention in clinical or consumer experience. Though unlikely, ingestion of large amounts may cause nausea, vomiting, gastrointestinal upset, central excitement, and a possibility of cyanosis in

Continued on next page

Vicks Health Care—Cont.

young children. Treatment is symptomatic, with bedrest and observation.
Dosage: ADULTS AND CHILDREN 3 years and over: allow one lozenge to dissolve slowly in mouth. Repeat hourly as needed.
How Supplied: Box of 12's.

VICKS® VAPORUB®
Decongestant Vaporizing Ointment

For use as a rub or in steam.

Active Ingredients: Special Vicks Medication (menthol, spirits of turpentine, eucalyptus oil, camphor, cedar leaf oil, nutmeg oil, thymol) 14% in a petrolatum base.
Indications: For the symptomatic relief of nasal congestion (up to 8 hours), bronchial mucous congestion, coughs, laryngitis and huskiness, muscular tightness and muscular aches and pains due to colds. Also for chapped hands.
Actions: The inhaled vapors of VICKS VAPORUB have a decongestant, and antitussive effect. Applied externally, the medication acts as a local analgesic. The ointment is soothing to chapped hands and skin.
Warning: For external application and use in steam only. Do not swallow or place in nostrils. If fever is present or cough or other symptoms persist, see your doctor. In case of illness in very young children, it is wise to consult your physician. To avoid possibility of fire, never expose VAPORUB to flame or place VAPORUB in any container in which you are heating water. Do not direct steam from vaporizer toward face. As with all medication, keep out of reach of children.
Symptoms and Treatment of Ingestion: These symptoms are based upon medical judgement, not on actual experience, since no significant incidence of overdose or ingestion has been brought to our attention in clinical or consumer experience. Ingestion of large quantities may cause nausea, vomiting, abdominal discomfort, diarrhea. Theoretically, very large quantities could cause weakness, vertigo, convulsions and drowsiness. If the extent of accidental ingestion is not known, treatment should consist of cautious gastric lavage. Otherwise, supportive and symptomatic treatment as necessary. If indicated, saline cathartics, demulcents and barbiturates for convulsions. Do not induce emesis.
Dosage:
AS A RUB: For relief of head and chest cold symptoms and coughs due to colds. Rub on throat, chest and back. Cover with a dry warm cloth if desired. Repeat as needed, especially at bedtime for continuous breathing relief.
For relief of muscle tightness, apply hot, moist towel to affected area. Remove towel, then massage well with VAPORUB. Cover with a dry, warm cloth if desired.
For chapped hands and skin, apply liberally as a dressing.

IN STEAM: Fill medicine cup of vaporizer with VICKS VAPORUB and follow directions of vaporizer manufacturer. VAPORUB may also be used in a steam bowl. Fill a bowl ¾ full with steaming water and add 2 teaspoonfuls of VAPORUB (after removing from heat). Then inhale steaming vapors. Add extra steaming water as steam decreases.
How Supplied: Available in 1.5 oz., 3.0 oz. and 6.0 oz. plastic jars.
[*Shown in Product Identification Section*]

Walker, Corp & Co., Inc.
P.O. BOX 1320
EASTHAMPTON PL. &
N. COLLINGWOOD AVE.
SYRACUSE, NY 13201

EVAC-U-GEN®

Description: Evac-U-Gen® is available as purple scored tablets, each containing 97.2 mg. of yellow phenolphthalein.
Action and Uses: For temporary relief of occasional constipation and to help restore a normal pattern of evacuation. A mild, non-griping, stimulant laxative in chewable, anise-flavored form, Evac-U-Gen provides softening of the feces through selective action on the intramural nerve plexus of intestinal smooth muscle, and increases the propulsive peristaltic activity of the colon.
Indications: Because of its gentle action and non-toxic nature, Evac-U-Gen is a particularly suitable laxative in pregnancy, in the presence of hemorrhoids, for children and the elderly. It is especially useful when straining at the stool is a hazard, as in hernia, cardiac or hypertensive patients.
Contraindications: Contraindicated in patients with a history of sensitivity to phenolphthalein. Evac-U-Gen should not be used when abdominal pain, nausea, vomiting, or other symptoms of appendicitis are present.
Side Effects: If skin rash appears, use of Evac-U-Gen or other preparations containing phenolphthalein should be discontinued. May cause coloration of feces or urine if they are sufficiently alkaline.
Warning: Frequent or prolonged use may result in dependence on laxatives.
Administration and Dosage: Adults: chew one or two tablets night or morning. **Children:** 3 to 10 years, chew ½ tablet daily. Intensity of action is proportional to dosage, but individually effective doses vary. Evac-U-Gen is usually active 6 to 8 hours after administration, but residual action may last 3 to 4 days.
How Supplied: Evac-U-Gen is available in bottles of 35, 100, 500, 1000, 2000 and 6000 tablets.

Products are cross-indexed by
generic and chemical names in the
YELLOW SECTION

Wallace Laboratories
HALF ACRE ROAD
CRANBURY, NJ 08512

MALTSUPEX®
(malt soup extract)
Powder, Liquid, Tablets

Composition: 'Maltsupex' is a nondiastatic extract from barley malt, which is available in powder, liquid, and tablet form. 'Maltsupex' has a gentle laxative action and promotes soft, easily passed stools. Each **Tablet** contains 750 mg of 'Maltsupex' and approximately 0.15 to 0.25 mEq of potassium. Each tablespoonful (0.5 fl oz) of **Liquid** and each heaping tablespoonful of **Powder** contains approximately 16 grams of Malt Soup Extract and 3.1 to 5.5 mEq of potassium.
Indications: 'Maltsupex' is indicated for the dietary management and treatment of functional constipation in infants and children. It is also useful in treating constipation in adults, including those with laxative dependence.
Warnings: Do not use when abdominal pain, nausea or vomiting are present. If constipation persists, consult a physician. Keep this and all medications out of the reach of children.
'Maltsupex' Powder and Liquid only—Do not use these products except under the advice and supervision of a physician if you have kidney disease.
Precautions: In patients with diabetes, allow for carbohydrate content of approximately 14 grams per tablespoonful of **Liquid** (56 calories), 13 grams per tablespoonful of **Powder** (52 calories), and 0.6 grams per **Tablet** (3 calories).
Tablets only: This product contains FD&C Yellow No. 5 (tartrazine) which may cause allergic-type reactions (including bronchial asthma) in certain susceptible individuals. Although the overall incidence of FD&C Yellow No. 5 (tartrazine) sensitivity in the general population is low, it is frequently seen in patients who also have aspirin hypersensitivity.
Dosage and Administration: General—The recommended daily dosage of 'Maltsupex' may vary from 6 to 32 grams for infants (2 years or less) and 12 to 64 grams for children and adults, accompanied by adequate fluid intake with each dose. Use the smallest dose that is effective and lower dosage as improvement occurs. Use heaping measures of the **Powder**. 'Maltsupex' **Liquid** mixes more easily if stirred first in one or two ounces of warm water.
Powder and Liquid (Usual Dosage)—
Adults: 2 tablespoonfuls (32 g) twice daily for 3 or 4 days, or until relief is noted, then 1 to 2 tablespoonfuls at bedtime for maintenance, as needed. Drink a full glass (8 oz) of liquid with each dose. **Children:** 1 or 2 tablespoonfuls in 8 ounces of liquid once or twice daily (with cereal, milk or preferred beverage). **Bottle-Fed Infants (over 1 month):** ½ to 2 tablespoonfuls in the day's total formula, or 1 to 2 teaspoonfuls in a single feeding to correct constipation. To prevent constipation (as when switching to whole

milk) add 1 to 2 teaspoonfuls to the day's formula or 1 teaspoonful to every second feeding. **Breast-Fed Infants (over one month):** 1 to 2 teaspoonfuls in 2 to 4 ounces of water or fruit juice once or twice daily.

Tablets—**Adults:** Start with 4 tablets (3 g) four times daily (with meals and bedtime) and adjust dosage according to response. Drink a full glass (8 oz) of liquid with each dose.

How Supplied: 'Maltsupex' is supplied in 8 ounce (NDC 0037-9101-12) and 16 ounce (NDC 0037-9101-08) jars of 'Maltsupex' Powder; 8 fluid ounce (NDC 0037-9001-12) and 1 pint (NDC 0037-9001-08) bottles of 'Maltsupex' Liquid; and in bottles of 100 'Maltsupex' Tablets (NDC 0037-9201-01).

'Maltsupex' **Powder** and **Liquid** are Distributed by

WALLACE LABORATORIES
Division of
CARTER-WALLACE, INC.
Cranbury, New Jersey 08512

'Maltsupex' **Tablets** are Manufactured by

WALLACE LABORATORIES
Division of
CARTER-WALLACE, INC.
Cranbury, New Jersey 08512

[*Shown in Product Identification Section*]

RYNA™
(Liquid)
RYNA–C®
(Liquid)
RYNA–CX®
(Liquid)

Description:
Each 5 ml (one teaspoonful) of **RYNA Liquid** contains:
Chlorpheniramine maleate..............2 mg
Pseudoephedrine hydrochloride....30 mg
in a clear, slightly yellow colored, lemon-vanilla flavored demulcent base containing no sugar, dyes, or alcohol.
Each 5 ml (one teaspoonful) of **RYNA-C Liquid** contains, in addition:
Codeine phosphate..........................10 mg
(WARNING: May be habit-forming)
in a colorless, cinnamon-flavored, demulcent base containing no sugar, dyes, or alcohol.
Each 5 ml (one teaspoonful) of **RYNA-CX Liquid** contains:
Codeine phosphate..........................10 mg
(WARNING: May be habit-forming)
Pseudoephedrine hydrochloride....30 mg
Guaifenesin....................................100 mg
in a clear, colorless, cherry-vanilla-menthol flavored demulcent base containing no sugar, dyes, or alcohol.

Actions:
Chlorpheniramine maleate in RYNA and RYNA-C is an antihistamine that antagonizes the effects of histamine.
Codeine Phosphate in RYNA-C and RYNA-CX is a centrally-acting antitussive that relieves cough.
Pseudoephedrine hydrochloride in RYNA, RYNA-C and RYNA-CX is a sympathomimetic nasal decongestant that acts to shrink swollen mucosa of the respiratory tract.
Guaifenesin in RYNA-CX is an expectorant that increases mucus flow to help

prevent dryness and relieve irritated respiratory tract membranes.

Indications:
RYNA is indicated for the temporary relief of the concurrent symptoms of nasal congestion, sneezing, itchy and watery eyes, and running nose as occurs with the common cold or allergic rhinitis.
RYNA-C is indicated for the above when cough is also a concurrent symptom.
RYNA-CX is indicated for the temporary relief of the concurrent symptoms of dry, nonproductive cough and nasal congestion.

Directions:
Adults: 2 teaspoonfuls every 6 hours.
Children 6–under 12 years: 1 teaspoonful every 6 hours.
Children 2–under 6 years: ½ teaspoonful every 6 hours (see WARNINGS).
Do not exceed 4 doses in 24 hours.

Warnings:
Do not give these products to children taking other medications. Do not give RYNA or RYNA-C to children under 6 years, nor RYNA-CX to children under 2 years except under the advice and supervision of a physician. Do not exceed recommended dosage unless directed by a physician because nervousness, dizziness, or sleeplessness may occur at higher doses. If symptoms do not improve within 3 days or are accompanied by high fever, discontinue use and consult a physician.

For RYNA-C and RYNA-CX only: Codeine may cause or aggravate constipation. A persistent cough may be a sign of a serious condition.

Do not take these products except under the advice and supervision of a physician if you have any of the following symptoms or conditions: cough that persists more than 3 days or tends to recur; chronic cough, such as occurs with smoking, asthma, or emphysema; cough accompanied by excessive secretions, high-fever, rash, or persistent headache; chronic pulmonary disease or shortness of breath; high blood pressure; thyroid disease or diabetes.

For RYNA and RYNA-C only: Do not take these products except under the advice and supervision of a physician if you have asthma, glaucoma, or difficulty in urination due to enlargement of the prostate. Both products contain an antihistamine which may cause excitability, especially in children, or drowsiness or which may impair mental alertness. Combined with alcohol, sedatives, or other depressants may have an additive effect. Do not drive motor vehicles, operate machinery, or drink alcoholic beverages while taking these products.

KEEP THIS AND ALL DRUGS OUT OF THE REACH OF CHILDREN. IN CASE OF ACCIDENTAL OVERDOSE, SEEK PROFESSIONAL ASSISTANCE OR CONTACT A POISON CONTROL CENTER IMMEDIATELY.

Drug Interaction Precaution: Do not take these products if you are presently taking a prescription antihypertensive or antidepressant drug containing a monoamine oxidase inhibitor, except un-

der the advice and supervision of a physician.

How Supplied:
RYNA: bottles of 4 fl oz (NDC 0037-0638-66), one pint (NDC 0037-0638-68), and one gallon (NDC 0037-0638-69).

RYNA-C: bottles of 4 fl oz (NDC 0037-0522-66), one pint (NDC 0037-0522-68), and one gallon (NDC 0037-0522-69).

RYNA-CX: bottles of 4 fl oz (NDC 0037-0801-66), one pint (NDC 0037-0801-68), and one gallon (NDC 0037-0801-69).

[*Shown in Product Identification Section*]

SYLLACT®
(Powdered Psyllium Seed Husks)

Description: Each rounded teaspoonful of fruit-flavored **'Syllact'** contains approximately 3.3 g of powdered psyllium seed husks and an equal amount of dextrose as a dispersing agent, and provides about 14 calories. Potassium sorbate, methyl- and propylparaben are added as preservatives.

Actions: The active ingredient in 'Syllact' is hydrophilic mucilloid, nonabsorbable dietary fiber derived from the powdered husks of natural psyllium seed, which acts by increasing the water content and bulk volume of stools. It gives 'Syllact' a bland, non-irritating, laxative action and promotes physiologic evacuation of the bowel.

Indications: 'Syllact' is indicated for the treatment of constipation and, when recommended by a physician, in other disorders where the effect of additional bulk and fiber is desired.

Warnings: Do not swallow dry. Drink a full glass (8 oz) of water or other liquid with each dose. If constipation persists, consult a physician. Do not use if fecal impaction, intestinal obstruction, or abdominal pain, nausea or vomiting are present. Keep this and all medications out of the reach of children.

Dosage and Administration: The actual daily dosage depends on the need and response of the patient. Adults may take up to 9 teaspoonfuls daily, in divided doses, for several days to provide optimum benefit when constipation is chronic or severe. Lower the dosage as improvement occurs. Use a dry spoon to measure powder. Tighten lid to keep out moisture.

Usual Adult Dosage—One rounded teaspoonful of 'Syllact' in a full glass (8 oz) of cool water or other beverage taken orally one to three times daily. If desired, an additional glass of liquid may be taken after each dose.

Children's Dosage—**6 years and older**—Half the adult dosage with the same fluid intake requirement.

Continued on next page

Wallace—Cont.

How Supplied: 'Syllact' Powder—in 10 oz jars (NDC 0037-9501-13).

Rev. 6/80

[*Shown in Product Identification Section*]
WALLACE LABORATORIES
Division of
CARTER-WALLACE, INC.
Cranbury, New Jersey 08512

Warner-Lambert Company
201 TABOR ROAD
MORRIS PLAINS, NJ 07950

e.p.t.®
In-Home Early Pregnancy Test
For *In-Vitro* Diagnostic Use

Reagents: HCG (Human Chorionic Gonadotropin) on Sheep Red Blood Cells, HCG Antiserum (Rabbit)

Indications: For use in detecting HCG hormone in the urine to detect pregnancy.

Actions: E.P.T. is a urine test. E.P.T. is a fast, highly accurate, easy, completely safe and completely private way for a woman to determine whether she is pregnant. E.P.T. is a simple urine test, designed to be done by a woman herself in her own home.

E.P.T. will answer the question "Am I pregnant?" in two hours. E.P.T. is for external use only—it is for *In Vitro* Diagnostic Use.

How E.P.T. works and when you'll want to use it.
When you become pregnant you begin to produce a hormone called HCG—Human Chorionic Gonadotropin. This hormone appears in your urine. When the HCG level is high enough, E.P.T. will detect the presence of the HCG in the urine. This HCG level occurs at about the *ninth day* after the day on which you expected your period. It is possible to get a positive result before the ninth day (indicating you may be pregnant) although in many cases the level of HCG will not be sufficient to give an accurate, clear reading before that time. We advise that you wait until at least your ninth "late day" so that you can test with greater confidence.

If you should obtain a negative result with E.P.T. and yet your period still does not begin, repeat the test one week later. (You may have miscalculated your dates). If you get a second negative reading, and your period has still not begun, check with your doctor. If E.P.T. indicates that you are pregnant, of course you will want to see your doctor at once for advice on health measures for proper fetal development.

Directions:
Read all the following information carefully
IT IS IMPORTANT THAT YOU FOLLOW THESE INSTRUCTIONS WITH CARE TO ACHIEVE AN ACCURATE RESULT. When instructions are followed, no other in-home use test is more accurate than E.P.T.

Urine collection: For maximum accuracy test from the ninth day after you have missed an expected period. Wash kit lid with soap or detergent. Rinse it absolutely clean. Traces of soap or detergent could cause a false reading. You need two hours for the test, so if you haven't this much time in the morning, cover and store your urine specimen in the refrigerator. Sediment may form but do not shake the specimen. Use the urine at the top of the container. Be sure to do the test the day the urine was collected. *Use only first morning urine.* Use first morning urine because if you are pregnant, this urine contains more HCG than urine collected at any other time of day. Accurate results may depend on your using *first morning urine.*

1. Remove the glass test tube from the support. Take off the rubber stopper and put the tube back into the support. Keep the stopper—you will need it later.
2. Fill the dropper with first morning urine.
3. Hold the dropper vertically above the test tube. Do not touch test tube with the dropper tip. Place three free-falling drops of the urine into the test tube (try to use just three drops but remember that a tiny bit more or less will not hurt the test.)
4. Twist off the top of the plastic vial and squeeze all the contents into the test tube.
5. Take the test tube from the support and press the rubber stopper back into place. SHAKE VIGOROUSLY FOR AT LEAST 10 SECONDS to mix contents adequately.
6. Replace the test tube in the support.
7. IMPORTANT: Put the support holding the test tube on a flat, solid surface free from vibrations. *Put it where it will not be disturbed or jiggled,* but where there is good light for reading the result. Do not put it on a windowsill or radiator where it will be subject to sunlight or heat. A bookshelf, the top of a heavy chest, desk or table are good choices. Be sure though, that you put the suppport where you will be able to read the results in the mirror without having to disturb it.
8. LET THE TEST TUBE AND STAND REMAIN UNDISTURBED FOR TWO HOURS BEFORE READING THE RESULTS. DO NOT RISK A FALSE READING BY MOVING OR OTHERWISE INTERFERING WITH THE TEST TUBE AND STAND. Although you may be able to read your result from about 1 to 2½ hours after you started the test, the most reliable time to read it is at 2 hours.
9. READING E.P.T. RESULTS
When two hours have passed, E.P.T. is ready to give you the results of your test. *Do not touch the support, but look into the mirror* under the test tube.
POSTIVE: A DONUT-SHAPED RING (MUST HAVE A HOLE IN THE CENTER.)
This ring can vary in clarity, thickness and color. Any ring indicates that your urine does contain pregnancy hormone; and you can assume you are pregnant.

You should now plan to consult your physician, who is best able to advise you.
NEGATIVE: NO RING, JUST A DEPOSIT—NO RING.
This means that no pregnancy hormone has been detected, and you probably are not pregnant. Your overdue period should begin soon. In the unlikely event that a week passes and you still have not menstruated, you should perform another test, using a new E.P.T. kit; because 1) you may have miscalculated your period; 2) there may not yet have been sufficient HCG in your urine at the time of the first test; or 3) the test might have been performed incorrectly. If a second test still gives a negative result, there is little chance that you are pregnant. However, there could be other important reasons why your period has not begun and you should see your physician.
REMEMBER: Do not touch the test tube and support until you have read the result in the mirror. The pattern reflected in the mirror from the bottom of the test tube is the only reading that counts. Read the result two hours after you started the test.
Limits of the Test: If you allow the test to stand for much longer than two hours, a false or confusing ring may develop. The result you see at two hours is the result by which you should be guided. Each E.P.T. test tube of reagents, vial of special purified water and dropper are not reuseable. Although E.P.T. is highly accurate in detecting pregnancy, a low incidence of false results (positive when no pregnancy exists, or negative when pregnancy is present) can occur (see Table 1 and Table 2 on next page).

What the results mean
A positive result indicates that your urine contains HCG and you can assume you are pregnant. When tested by consumers, E.P.T. was 97% accurate when a positive result was obtained. You should now consult with your physician who is best able to guide you.

A negative result means that no HCG has been detected. When tested by consumers, E.P.T. was 84% accurate when a negative result was obtained. There is the possibility that your urine gave a false negative result because of miscalculating your menstrual cycle and as a result there may not have been enough HCG in the urine. If a week passes and you still have not started menstruating you should do the test again. If it is still negative in this later test there is little chance that you are pregnant, but because there could be other important reasons why you have not started menstruating you should see your doctor without delay.

Storage: Store below 86° Fahrenheit (30° Centigrade).
Do not freeze.

How Supplied: One E.P.T. kit including test tube of reagents, vial of special purified water, dropper, lid, mirror and support in carton with package insert.
An E.P.T. 2-test kit including two test tubes of reagents, two vials of special purified water, two droppers, one lid, mir-

ror and plastic support in carton with package insert.

E.P.T. is an *In Vitro* diagnostic test; not for internal use.

[*Shown in Product Identification Section*]

HALLS® MENTHO–LYPTUS®
Cough Tablets

Active Ingredients: Each tablet contains eucalyptus oil and menthol.

Indications: For temporary relief of minor throat irritation and cough due to colds and to allergies. Makes nasal passages feel clearer.

Warning: Persistent cough may indicate presence of a serious condition. Persons with high fever or persistent cough should use this preparation only as directed by a physician.

Dosage: Allow to dissolve slowly in mouth. Repeat as often as necessary.

How Supplied: Halls Mentho-Lyptus Cough Tablets are available in single sticks of 9 tablets each, in 3-stick packs, and in bags of 30 tablets. They are available in four flavors: Regular, Cherry, Honey-Lemon and Ice Blue.

[*Shown in Product Identification Section*]

LISTERINE® Antiseptic

Active Ingredients: Thymol, Eucalyptol, Methyl Salicylate and Menthol. Also contains: Water, Alcohol 26.9%, Benzoic Acid, Poloxamer 407 and Caramel.

Indications: For general oral hygiene, bad breath, minor cuts, scratches, insect bites, infectious dandruff.

Actions: Listerine Antiseptic, a unique combination of aromatic oils in a hydroalcoholic vehicle, provides long lasting oral deodorant activity. Its antibacterial action against odor causing bacteria, its odor-masking properties, and its low surface tension which aids in the removal of oral debris, account for its efficacy as an oral mouthwash and gargle.

Warnings: Do not administer to children under three years of age. Keep this and all drugs out of the reach of children. Not for ingestion.

Directions: For bad breath and general oral hygiene—Rinse full strength for 30 seconds with ⅔ ounce (4 teaspoonfuls) morning and night.

For minor cuts, scratches and insect bites—apply directly to injury.

For infectious dandruff symptoms—massage on scalp.

Storage: Cold weather may cloud Listerine. Its antiseptic properties are not affected.

How Supplied: Listerine Antiseptic is supplied in 3, 6, 12, 18, 24, 36 and 48 Fl. Oz. bottles.

[*Shown in Product Identification Section*]

LISTERMINT®
Mouthwash and Gargle

Ingredients: Water, SD Alcohol 38-B, Glycerin, Poloxamer 407, Sodium Lauryl Sulfate, Sodium Citrate, Sodium Saccharin, Flavoring, Zinc Chloride, Citric Acid, D&C Yellow No. 10, FD&C Green No. 3.

Indications: Listermint is a green, mint flavored, pleasant tasting mouthwash and gargle which is recommended

Table 1
Laboratory Evaluation of e.p.t.
(Single Test Results)

# of Urine Samples Tested	e.p.t. result	Clinical Diagnosis	e.p.t. Accuracy
200	197 Positive*	198 Pregnant	99.5%
	3 Negative**	2 Not Pregnant	

*Positive indicates pregnancy
**Negative indicates no pregnancy

Table 2
Consumer Use Tests
(Single Test Performed at Home by Individuals)

Actual Clinical State	Test Readings	
	Positive	Negative
Pregnant	451 (Accurate)	36 (Inaccurate)
Not Pregnant	15 (Inaccurate)	183 (Accurate)
Total Tests	466	219

Conclusion
1. First test is 97% accurate if positive reading is obtained.
2. First test is 84% accurate if negative reading is obtained; however, a repeat test one week later improves the accuracy to 96%.

for daily oral care and provides a refreshing mouth feeling and long lasting breath protection.

Directions: Rinse and gargle for 30 seconds with a half mouthful of Listermint first thing in the morning, after meals or when needed for mouth refreshment and clean breath.

How Supplied: Listermint is supplied to consumers in 6, 12, 18, 24 and 32 Fl. Oz. bottles.

[*Shown in Product Identification Section*]

LISTERMINT®
Cinnamon Mouthwash and Gargle

Ingredients: Water, SD Alcohol 38-B, Glycerin, Poloxamer 407, Sodium Lauryl Sulfate, Flavoring, Sodium Citrate, Sodium Saccharin, Zinc Chloride, Citric Acid, FD&C Red No. 40.

Indications: Listermint Cinnamon is a red, cinnamon flavored, zesty tasting mouthwash and gargle which is recommended for daily oral care and provides a refreshing mouth feeling and long lasting breath protection.

Directions: Rinse and gargle for 30 seconds with half a mouthful of Listermint Cinnamon first thing in the morning, after meals or when needed for mouth refreshment and clean breath.

How Supplied: Listermint Cinnamon is supplied to consumers in 6, 12, 18 and 24 Fl. Oz. bottles.

[*Shown in Product Identification Section*]

LUBATH® BATH OIL

Composition: Contains mineral oil, PPG-15 Stearyl Ether, Oleth-2, Nonoxynol-5, Fragrance, D&C Green No. 6.

Actions and Uses: Lubath is a lanolin-free, mineral oil based, bath oil designed for softening and soothing dry skin during the bath. The formula disperses into countless droplets of oil that coat the skin and help lubricate and soften. It is equally effective in hard or soft water and provides an excellent way to moisturize the skin.

Administration and Dosage: One to two capfuls (16 oz. size) or two to four capfuls (8 oz. and 4 oz. size) in bath, or apply with moistened cloth in shower and rinse. For use as a skin cleanser, rub into wet skin and rinse.

Precautions: Avoid getting in eyes, if this occurs, flush with clear water. When using any bath oil, take precautions against slipping. For external use only.

How Supplied: Available in 4, 8 and 16 fl. oz. plastic bottles.

[*Shown in Product Identification Section*]

LUBRIDERM® CREAM
Dry Skin Cream

Composition:
Scented: Contains Water, Mineral Oil, Petrolatum, Glycerin, Glyceryl Stearate, PEG-100 Stearate, Squalane, Lanolin, Lanolin Alcohol, Lanolin Oil, Cetyl Alcohol, Sorbitan Laurate, Fragrance, Methylparaben, Butylparaben, Propylparaben, Quaternium-15.
Unscented: Contains Water, Mineral Oil, Petrolatum, Glycerin, Glyceryl Stearate, PEG-100 Stearate, Squalane, Lanolin, Lanolin Alcohol, Lanolin Oil, Cetyl Alcohol, Sorbitan Laurate, Methylparaben, Butylparaben, Propylparaben, Quaternium-15.

Actions and Uses: Lubriderm Cream is an emollient cream indicated for relieving extremely dry, chapped skin. The formula contains emollients which help restore and maintain the skin's normal suppleness while smoothing, soothing and softening.

Administration and Dosage: Apply several times daily.

Continued on next page

Warner-Lambert—Cont.

Precautions: For external use only.
How Supplied: Available in 4 oz. tubes. Scented also available in 1.5 oz. tubes.

LUBRIDERM® LOTION
Skin Lubricant Moisturizer

Composition:
Scented—Contains Water, Mineral Oil, Petrolatum, Sorbitol, Lanolin, Lanolin Alcohol, Stearic Acid, Triethanolamine, Cetyl Alcohol, Fragrance, Butylparaben, Methylparaben, Propylparaben, Sodium Chloride.
Unscented—Contains Water, Mineral Oil, Petrolatum, Sorbitol, Lanolin, Lanolin Alcohol, Stearic Acid, Triethanolamine, Cetyl Alcohol, Butylparaben, Methylparaben, Propylparaben, Sodium Chloride.
Actions and Uses: Lubriderm Lotion is an oil-in-water emulsion indicated for use in softening, soothing and moisturizing dry chapped skin. Lubriderm relieves the roughness, tightness, and discomfort associated with dry or chapped skin and helps protect the skin from further drying.
Lubriderm's extra rich formula smoothes easily into skin without leaving a sticky film.
Administration and Dosage: Apply as often as needed to hands, face and body for skin protection.
Precautions: For external use only.
How Supplied:
Scented: Available in 4, 8 and 16 fl. oz. plastic bottles.
Unscented: Available in 8 and 16 fl. oz. plastic bottles.
[*Shown in Product Identification Section*]

ROLAIDS® Antacid Tablets

Active Ingredient: Each chewable tablet contains:
Dihydroxyaluminum sodium
     carbonate......................................334 mg.
Indications: For the relief of any or all of the following: heartburn, sour stomach, acid indigestion. For the relief of upset stomach associated with any or all of the following: heartburn, sour stomach, acid indigestion.
Actions: Rolaids® provides rapid neutralization of stomach acid accompanied by the release of carbon dioxide. Each tablet has acid neutralizing capacity of 75-80 ml of 0.1N hydrochloric acid and the ability to maintain the pH of the stomach contents close to 3.5 for a significant period of time - the pH never reaching into the alkaline region.
Due to the relatively low solubility and other physical and chemical properties of dihydroxyaluminum sodium carbonate (DASC), it is for the most part nonabsorbed.
Although sodium is present in DASC, the sodium is available for absorption only when the antacid reacts with stomach acid. When Rolaids are consumed in excess of the amount of acid present in the stomach, this sodium is unavailable for

absorption and the active ingredient is passed through the digestive system unchanged, with no sodium released.
Warnings: Keep this and all drugs out of the reach of children. Do not take more than 24 tablets in a 24 hour period, nor use the maximum dosage of this product for more than two weeks, nor use this product if you are on a sodium restricted diet, except under the advice and supervision of a physician.
Each Rolaids® Antacid Tablet contains 53 mg. sodium.
Drug Interaction Precaution: Do not take this product if you are presently taking a prescription antibiotic drug containing any form of tetracycline.
Dosage and Administration: Chew 1 or 2 tablets as symptoms occur; repeat hourly if symptoms return, or as directed by a physician.
Professional Labeling: The following information is provided to facilitate treatment:
Acid neutralizing
     capacity......................7.5-8 mEq/tablet
     (equivalent to 75-80 ml 0.1N HCl)
How Supplied: Rolaids® Antacid Tablets are available in regular, spearmint and wintergreen flavors, in rolls of 12 tablets, and bottles of 75 and 150 tablets.
[*Shown in Product Identification Section*]

SINUTAB® Tablets

Active Ingredients: Each tablet contains:
Acetaminophen ....325 mg.
Phenylpropanolamine HCl .... 25 mg.
Phenyltoloxamine Citrate .... 22 mg.
Indications: For temporary relief of sinus headache and congestion.
Actions: Sinutab® contains: an analgesic (acetaminophen) to relieve pain, a decongestant (phenylpropanolamine hydrochloride) to reduce congestion of the nasopharyngeal mucosa, and an antihistamine (phenyltoloxamine citrate) to help control allergic symptoms.
Acetaminophen is both analgesic and antipyretic. Because acetaminophen is not a salicylate, Sinutab® can be used by patients who are allergic to aspirin.
Phenylpropanolamine hydrochloride, a sympathomimetic amine, provides vasoconstriction of the nasopharyngeal mucosa resulting in a nasal decongestant effect.
Phenyltoloxamine citrate is an antihistamine to provide relief of running nose, sneezing, itching of the nose or throat, and itchy and watery eyes as may occur in allergic rhinitis.
Warnings: Do not give to children under 6 years of age or use for more than 10 days unless directed by a physician. Keep this and all drugs out of the reach of children.
Caution: Do not exceed recommended dosage. Individuals with high blood pressure, heart disease, diabetes, thyroid disease, or those using monoamine oxidase inhibitors, should use only as directed by physician. This preparation may cause drowsiness. Do not drive or operate machinery while taking this medication.

Dosage: Adults: 2 tablets initially, followed by 1 tablet every 4 hours. Do not exceed 6 tablets in 24 hours. Otherwise, as directed by a physician. Children (6-12 years): one-half the adult dosage.
Storage: Store at room temperature.
How Supplied: Sinutab® tablets are pink, uncoated and scored so that tablets may be split in half. They are supplied in safety-capped bottles of 100 tablets and in child-resistant blister packs in boxes of 12 and 30 tablets.

SINUTAB–II® Tablets

Active Ingredients: Each tablet contains:
Acetaminophen ....325 mg.
Phenylpropanolamine HCl .... 25 mg.
Indications: For temporary relief of sinus headache and congestion.
Actions: Sinutab-II® contains: an analgesic (acetaminophen) to relieve pain, and a decongestant (phenylpropanolamine hydrochloride) to reduce congestion of the nasopharyngeal mucosa. It contains no antihistamine which can cause drowsiness, and thus there is no interference with driving or the operation of machinery.
Acetaminophen is both analgesic and antipyretic. Because acetaminophen is not a salicylate, Sinutab-II® can be used by patients who are allergic to aspirin.
Phenylpropanolamine hydrochloride, a sympathomimetic amine, provides vasoconstriction of the nasopharyngeal mucosa, resulting in a nasal decongestant effect.
Warnings: Do not give to children under 6 years of age or use for more than 10 days unless directed by a physician. Keep this and all drugs out of the reach of children.
Caution: Do not exceed recommended dosage. Individuals with high blood pressure, heart disease, diabetes, thyroid disease, or those using monoamine oxidase inhibitors, should use only as directed by a physician.
Dosage: Adults: 2 tablets initially, followed by 1 tablet every 4 hours. Do not exceed 6 tablets in 24 hours. Otherwise, as directed by a physician. Children (6-12 years): one-half the adult dosage.
Storage: Store at room temperature.
How Supplied: Sinutab-II® tablets are green, uncoated and scored so that tablets may be split in half. They are supplied in child-resistant blister packs in boxes of 12 and 30 tablets.

SINUTAB® Extra Strength Capsule Formula

Active Ingredients: Each capsule contains:
Acetaminophen ....500 mg.
Phenylpropanolamine HCl .....18.75 mg.
Chlorpheniramine Maleate ....2 mg.
Indications: For temporary relief of sinus headache and congestion, to promote nasal and sinus drainage, and to alleviate running nose as may occur in allergic rhinitis (such as hay fever).
Actions: Sinutab® Extra Strength Capsule Formula contains an analgesic (acetaminophen) to relieve pain, a deconges-

tant (phenylpropanolamine hydrochloride) to reduce congestion of the nasopharyngeal mucosa, and an antihistamine (chlorpheniramine maleate) to help control allergic symptoms.

Acetaminophen is both analgesic and antipyretic. Because acetaminophen is not a salicylate, Sinutab® Extra Strength Capsule Formula can be used by patients who are allergic to aspirin. Phenylpropanolamine hydrochloride, a sympathomimetic amine, provides vasoconstriction of the nasopharyngeal mucosa resulting in a nasal decongestant effect.

Chlorpheniramine maleate is an antihistamine incorporated to provide relief of running nose, sneezing, itching of the nose or throat, and itchy and watery eyes as may occur in allergic rhinitis.

Warnings: Do not give this product to children under 12 years of age except under the advice and supervision of a physician. May cause drowsiness. May cause excitability especially in children. Except under the advice and supervision of a physician, do not take this product if you have asthma, glaucoma, difficulty in urination due to enlargement of the prostate gland, high blood pressure, heart disease, diabetes, or thyroid disease. Do not exceed recommended dosage because at higher dosage nervousness, dizziness, sleeplessness, or severe liver damage may occur. If symptoms persist, do not improve within 7 days, or are accompanied by high fever, or if new symptoms occur, consult a physician before continuing use. Do not take this product for more than 10 days.

Keep this and all drugs out of the reach of children. In case of accidental overdose, seek professional assistance or contact a Poison Control Center immediately.

Drug Interaction Precaution: Do not take this product if you are presently taking a prescription antihypertensive or antidepressant drug containing a monoamine oxidase inhibitor except under the advice and supervision of a physician.

Caution: Avoid driving a motor vehicle or operating heavy machinery, and avoid alcoholic beverages while taking this product.

Dosage: Adults: 2 capsules every 6 hours, not to exceed 8 capsules in 24 hours. Otherwise, as directed by a physician.

Storage: Store at room temperature.

How Supplied: Sinutab® Extra Strength Capsule Formula capsules are red and yellow. They are supplied in child-resistant blister packs in boxes of 24 capsules.

SINUTAB® Extra Strength Tablets

Active Ingredients: Each tablet contains:
Acetaminophen ....500 mg.
Phenylpropanolamine HCl .... 25 mg.
Phenyltoloxamine Citrate .... 22 mg.
Indications: For temporary relief of sinus headache and congestion, to promote nasal and sinus drainage, and to allevi-

ate running nose as may occur in allergic rhinitis (such as hay fever).

Actions: Sinutab® Extra Strength Tablets contain: an analgesic (acetaminophen) to relieve pain, a decongestant (phenylpropanolamine hydrochloride) to reduce congestion of the nasopharyngeal mucosa, and an antihistamine (phenyltoloxamine citrate) to help control allergic symptoms.

Acetaminophen is both analgesic and antipyretic. Because acetaminophen is not a salicylate, Sinutab® Extra Strength Tablets can be used by patients who are allergic to aspirin.

Phenylpropanolamine hydrochloride, a sympathomimetic amine, provides vasoconstriction of the nasopharyngeal mucosa, resulting in a nasal decongestant effect.

Phenyltoloxamine citrate is an antihistamine to provide relief of running nose, sneezing, itching of the nose or throat, and itchy and watery eyes as may occur in allergic rhinitis.

Warnings: Do not give this product to children under 12 years of age except under the advice and supervision of a physician. May cause drowsiness. May cause excitability especially in children. Except under the advice and supervision of a physician do not take this product if you have asthma, glaucoma, difficulty in urination due to enlargement of the prostate gland, high blood pressure, heart disease, diabetes, or thyroid disease. Do not exceed recommended dosage because at higher doses nervousness, dizziness, sleeplessness or severe liver damage may occur. If symptoms persist, do not improve within 7 days, or are accompanied by high fever, or if new symptoms occur, consult a physician before continuing use. Do not take this product for more than 10 days.

Keep this and all drugs out of the reach of children. In case of accidental overdose, seek professional assistance or contact a Poison Control Center immediately.

Drug Interaction Precaution: Do not take this product if you are presently taking a prescription antihypertensive or antidepressant drug containing a monoamine oxidase inhibitor except under the advice and supervision of a physician.

Caution: Avoid driving a motor vehicle or operating heavy machinery and avoid alcoholic beverages while taking this product.

Dosage: Adults: 2 tablets every 6 hours, or 2 tablets 3 times a day, not to exceed 6 tablets in 24 hours. Otherwise as directed by a physician.

Storage: Store at room temperature.

How Supplied: Sinutab® Extra Strength Tablets are yellow and uncoated. They are supplied in child-resistant blister packs in boxes of 24 tablets.

SINUTAB® Long-Lasting Decongestant Nasal Spray

Active Ingredient: An isotonic aqueous buffered solution of xylometazoline hydrochloride 0.1%. Preserved with benzalkonium chloride.

Indications: For temporary relief of nasal congestion and to promote sinus drainage. Relief lasts for 8 to 10 hours.

Actions: Xylometazoline hydrochloride possesses sympathomimetic properties resulting in a decongestant effect on nasal mucosa.

Warnings: Follow directions for use carefully. For adult use only. Do not give this product to children under 12 years except under the advice and supervision of a physician. Do not exceed recommended dosage because symptoms may occur such as burning, stinging, sneezing, or increase of nasal discharge. Do not use this product for more than 3 days. If symptoms persist, consult a physician. The use of this dispenser by more than one person may spread infection.

KEEP THIS AND ALL DRUGS OUT OF THE REACH OF CHILDREN. In case of accidental ingestion, seek professional assistance or contact a Poison Control Center immediately.

Directions: Hold head in normal upright position. Hold bottle upright and place tip loosely in the nostril. Squeeze quickly and firmly. Sniff with each spray.

Dosage: Adults: 2 to 3 sprays in each nostril every 8 to 10 hours, not to exceed 3 times in 24 hours, or use as directed by physician.

Storage: Store at room temperature.

How Supplied: Sinutab® Long-Lasting Decongestant Nasal Spray is supplied in ½ Fl. Oz. (15 ml.) plastic squeeze-spray bottles.

Warren-Teed Laboratories

Warren-Teed products are now marketed by Adria Laboratories Inc.
Please see the Adria product monographs.

Westwood Pharmaceuticals Inc.
468 DEWITT ST.
BUFFALO, NY 14213

ALPHA KERI®
Therapeutic bath oil

Composition: Contains mineral oil, lanolin oil, PEG-4 dilaurate, benzophenone-3, D&C green 6, fragrance.

Action and Uses: ALPHA KERI is a water-dispersible, antipruritic oil for care of dry skin. ALPHA KERI effectively deposits a thin, uniform, emulsified film of oil over the skin. This film helps relieve itching, lubricates and softens the skin. ALPHA KERI is valuable as an aid in the treatment of dry, pruritic skin and mild skin irritations such as chronic atopic dermatitis; pruritus senilis and hiemalis; contact dermatitis; "bath-itch"; xerosis or asteatosis; ichthyosis; soap dermatitis; psoriasis.

Administration and Dosage: ALPHA KERI *should always be used with water,*

Continued on next page

Westwood—Cont.

either added to water or rubbed on to wet skin. Because of its inherent cleansing properties it is not necessary to use soap when ALPHA KERI is being used.

For exact dosage, label directions should be followed.

BATH: Added as directed to bathtub of water. For optimum relief: 10 to 20 minute soak.

SHOWER: Small amount is poured into wet washcloth and rubbed on to wet skin. Rinse follows.

SPONGE BATH: Added as directed to a basin of warm water then rubbed over entire body with washcloth.

SITZ BATH: Added as directed to tub water. Soak should last for 10 to 20 minutes.

INFANT BATH: Added as directed to basin or bathinette of water.

SKIN CLEANSING OTHER THAN BATH OR SHOWER: A small amount is rubbed on to wet skin, which is then patted dry.

Precaution: The patient should be warned to guard against slipping in tub or shower.

How Supplied: 4 fl. oz. (NDC 0072-3600-04), 8 fl. oz. (NDC 0072-3600-08) and 16 fl. oz. (NDC 0072-3600-16) plastic bottles. Also available for patients who prefer to shower—ALPHA KERI SPRAY—5 oz. (NDC 0072-3600-05) aerosol container, ALPHA KERI SOAP—4 oz. (NDC 0072-3500-04) bar.

ALPHA KERI® SOAP

Composition: Contains therapeutic ALPHA KERI® bath oil in a non-detergent soap.

Action and Uses: ALPHA KERI SOAP, rich in emollient oils, thoroughly cleanses as it soothes and softens the skin.

Indications: Adjunctive use in dry skin care.

Administration and Dosage: To be used as any other soap.

How Supplied: 4 oz. (NDC 0072-3500-04) bar.

BALNETAR®
Water-dispersible Emollient Tar

Composition: Contains WESTWOOD® TAR (equivalent to 2.5% Coal Tar USP).

Action and Uses: For temporary relief of itching and scaling due to psoriasis, eczema, and other tar-responsive dermatoses. Tar ingredient is chemically and biologically standardized to insure uniform therapeutic activity. BALNETAR exerts keratoplastic, antieczematous, antipruritic, and emollient actions. It deposits microfine particles of tar over the skin in a lubricant-moisturizing film that helps soften and remove scales and crusts, making the skin smoother and more supple. BALNETAR is an important adjunct in a wide range of dermatoses, including: atopic dermatitis; chronic eczematoid dermatitis; seborrheic dermatitis.

Contraindications: Not indicated when acute inflammation is present.

Administration and Dosage: BALNETAR *should always be used with water. . . either added to water or rubbed into wet skin.*

IN THE TUB—Add as directed to a bathtub of water (3–6 capfuls). Soap is not used. The patient soaks for 10 to 20 minutes and then pats dry.

FOR DIRECT APPLICATION—A small amount is rubbed into the wet skin. Excess is wiped off with tissue to help prevent staining of clothes or linens.

FOR SCALP APPLICATION —A small amount is rubbed into the wet scalp with fingertips.

Caution: If irritation persists, discontinue use. In rare instances temporary discoloration of blond, bleached or tinted hair may occur. In rare cases BALNETAR may cause allergic sensitization attributable to coal tar.

Precaution: After use of BALNETAR, patient should avoid exposure to direct sunlight unless sunlight is being used therapeutically in a supervised, modified Goeckerman regimen. Contact with the eyes should be avoided. Patient should be cautioned against slipping when BALNETAR is used in bathtub. Also advise patient that use in a plastic or fiberglass tub may cause staining of the tub.

How Supplied: 8 fl. oz. (NDC 0072-4200-08) plastic shatter-proof bottle.

ESTAR®
Therapeutic Tar Gel

Composition: WESTWOOD® TAR (biologically equivalent to 5% Coal Tar USP) in a hydroalcoholic gel (29% alcohol).

Actions and Uses: A therapeutic aid in the treatment of eczema, psoriasis, and other tar-responsive dermatoses such as atopic dermatitis, lichen simplex chronicus, and nummular eczema. ESTAR exerts keratoplastic, antieczematous, and antipruritic actions. It is equivalent in its photodynamic activity to 5% crude coal tar in either hydrophilic ointment or petrolatum. ESTAR provides the characteristic benefits of tar therapy in a form that is readily accepted by patients and nursing staff, due to its negligible tar odor and staining potential, and the superior cosmetic qualities of its gel base. ESTAR is suitable for use in a modified Goeckerman regimen, either in the hospital or on an outpatient basis; it also can be used in follow-up treatment to help maintain remissions. Substantivity to the skin can be demonstrated by examination with a Wood's light, which shows residual microfine particles of tar on the skin several days after application.

Contraindications: ESTAR should not be applied to acutely inflamed skin or used by individuals who are known to be sensitive to coal tar.

Administration and Dosage:

Psoriasis: ESTAR can be applied at bedtime in the following manner: the patient should massage ESTAR into affected areas, allowing the gel to remain for five minutes, and then remove excess by patting with tissues. This procedure minimizes staining of skin and clothing, leaving behind an almost invisible layer of the active tar. If any staining of fabric should occur, it can be removed easily by standard laundry procedures.

The same technique of application may be used the following morning. If dryness occurs, an emollient may be applied one hour after ESTAR.

Because of ESTAR's superior substantivity and cosmetic qualities, patients who might otherwise be hospitalized for tar/UV therapy can now be treated as outpatients. The patient can easily apply ESTAR at bedtime and the following morning, then report for UV treatment that day. Laboratory tests and clinical experience to date suggest that it may be advisable to carefully regulate the length of UV exposure.

Chronic atopic dermatitis, Lichen simplex chronicus, Nummular eczema, and Seborrheic dermatitis: One or two applications per day, as described above, are suggested. If dryness occurs, an emollient may be applied one hour after ESTAR and between applications as needed.

Caution: AFTER USING, TREATED AREAS SHOULD BE PROTECTED FROM SUNLIGHT, ESPECIALLY IF ESTAR HAS BEEN USED ON THE FACE. THIS PRECAUTION SHOULD BE TAKEN FOR AT LEAST 24 HOURS AFTER APPLICATION, UNLESS OTHERWISE DIRECTED. ESTAR SHOULD NOT BE USED ON HIGHLY INFLAMED OR BROKEN SKIN. If used on the scalp, temporary discoloration of blond, bleached, or tinted hair may occur. If undue irritation develops or increases, the usage schedule should be changed or ESTAR discontinued. Contact with the eyes should be avoided. In case of contact, flush eyes with water.

Slight staining of clothing may occur. Standard laundry procedures will usually remove stains. For external use only.

How Supplied: 3 oz. (NDC 0072-7600-03) plastic tube.

FOSTEX® BPO 5%
Anti-Bacterial
Acne Gel

Composition: Contains benzoyl peroxide 5% in a disappearing gel base.

Action and Uses: FOSTEX BPO 5% is a penetrating, disappearing gel which helps unclog pores, kill bacteria, promote rapid drying of oily skin, and gently desquamates.

Indications: A topical aid for the control of acne vulgaris.

Administration and Dosage: After washing, rub FOSTEX BPO 5% into affected areas twice daily. In fair-skinned individuals or in excessively dry climates it is suggested that therapy be initiated with one application daily. The desired degree of drying and peeling can be obtained by increasing or decreasing frequency of use.

Caution: Avoid contact with eyes, lips and mouth. If undue skin irritation develops or increases, discontinue use and consult physician. For external use only. May bleach colored fabric. Keep this and all drugs out of the reach of children.

Store at controlled room temperature (59°–86°F).
How Supplied: .65 oz. (NDC 0072-3300-01) tube.

FOSTEX® CAKE
Acne Skin Cleanser

Composition: Contains sulfur 2%, salicylic acid 2%, plus a combination of soapless cleansers and wetting agents.
Action and Uses: FOSTEX CAKE is a surface-active, penetrating anti-seborrheic cleanser for therapeutic washing of the skin in the local treatment of acne and other skin conditions characterized by excessive oiliness. Degreases, dries and mildly desquamates.
Administration and Dosage: FOSTEX CAKE is used instead of soap to wash the face and other affected areas, followed by thorough rinse. FOSTEX CAKE is used two to three times a day, or as directed. Frequency of use determines degree of drying.
Caution: If undue skin irritation develops or increases, adjust usage schedule or discontinue use. If necessary, treat with anti-inflammatory measures. For external use only. Contact with the eyes should be avoided. In case of contact, flush eyes thoroughly with water.
How Supplied: 3¾ oz. (NDC 0072-3000-01) bar.

FOSTEX® CM
Medicated Acne
Cover-up

Active Ingredient: 2% sulfur, in a flesh-tinted greaseless base.
Indications: FOSTEX CM is a medicated cover-up acne cream to help heal and conceal acne blemishes, pimples, and blackheads.
Actions: Degreases, dries and mildly desquamates skin in the local treatment of acne and other skin conditions characterized by excessive oiliness.
Warnings: For external use only. Keep this and all drugs out of reach of children. Avoid contact with eyes. In case of contact, flush eyes with water.
Precaution: If undue skin irritation develops or increases, discontinue use and consult physician.
Dosage and Administration: After removing excess oil by washing affected areas, smooth FOSTEX CM on skin to conceal blemishes. Use up to 2 or 3 times a day.
How Supplied: 1 oz. (NDC 0072-4100-01) tube.

FOSTEX® CREAM and
MEDICATED CLEANSER
Acne Skin Cleanser and Dandruff Shampoo

Composition: Contains 2% sulfur, 2% salicylic acid, plus a combination of soapless cleansers and wetting agents.
Action and Uses: A penetrating antiseborrheic cleanser for the local treatment of acne, dandruff and other seborrheic skin conditions, characterized by excessive oiliness. Degreases, dries and mildly desquamates.

Administration and Dosage: WASHING THE SKIN—Instead of using soap, the face and other affected areas are washed with FOSTEX, followed by a thorough rinse. FOSTEX is usually used two to three times a day or as directed. Frequency of use determines degree of drying. SHAMPOO—After wetting the hair and scalp a liberal amount of FOSTEX is massaged into the scalp for a thorough shampoo followed by a rinse. The shampoo is then repeated, and the scalp rinsed thoroughly. No other shampoos are required. FOSTEX is used as often as necessary to keep the scalp free from excessive oiliness or scaling, or as often as directed.
Caution: If undue skin irritation develops or increases, adjust the usage schedule or discontinue use. If necessary, after discontinuance anti-inflammatory measures may be used. For external use only. Avoid contact with eyes. In case of contact, flush eyes thoroughly with water.
How Supplied: FOSTEX CREAM in 4 oz. (NDC 0072-3200-01) tube and FOSTEX MEDICATED CLEANSER in 5 oz. (NDC 0072-3400-05) bottle.

FOSTRIL®
Drying Lotion for Acne

Composition: Contains 6% laureth-4, 2% sulfur, in a greaseless base.
Action and Uses: Promotes drying and peeling of the skin in the treatment of acne. Daily use of FOSTRIL should result in a desirable degree of dryness and peeling in about 7 days. FOSTRIL removes excess oil and follicular obstruction, helping to remove comedones. It also helps prevent epithelial closure of pores and formation of new lesions.
Administration and Dosage: A thin film is applied to affected areas once or twice daily, or as directed.
Caution: If undue skin irritation develops or increases, adjust usage schedule or discontinue use. Anti-inflammatory measures may be used if necessary. For external use only. Contact with eyes should be avoided. In case of contact, flush eyes thoroughly with water.
How Supplied: 1 oz. (NDC 0072-3800-01) tube.

ICE MINT® FOOT CREME

Composition: Water, stearic acid, syn. cocoa butter, lanolin oil, camphor, menthol, beeswax, mineral oil, sodium borate, triethanolamine, camphor oil, dioctyl sodium sulfosuccinate, eucalyptus oil, peppermint oil, white thyme oil.
Indications: ICE MINT, with lanolin, cools and refreshes tired feet as it softens corns and calluses. It soothes, cools and softens dry and chapped skin.
Warnings: Keep out of reach of children. For external use only.
Dosage and Administration: Rub ICE MINT on feet with fingertips. Wash hands after application.
How Supplied: 4 oz. (NDC 0072-1100-4) jar.

KERI® CREME
Concentrated Moisturizer—
Nongreasy Emollient

Composition: Contains water, mineral oil, talc, sorbitol, ceresin, lanolin alcohol/mineral oil, magnesium stearate, glyceryl oleate/propylene glycol, isopropyl myristate, methylparaben, propylparaben, fragrance, quaternium-15.
Actions and Uses: KERI CREME is a concentrated moisturizer and nongreasy emollient for problem dry skin—hands, face, elbows, feet, legs. KERI CREME helps retain moisture that makes skin feel soft, smooth, supple. Helps resist the drying effects of soaps, detergents and chemicals.
Administration and Dosage: A small amount is rubbed into dry skin areas as needed.
How Supplied: 2.25 oz. (NDC 0072-5800-01) tube.

KERI® FACIAL CLEANSER

Composition: Water, glycerine, squalane, propylene glycol, glyceryl stearate (and) PEG-100 stearate, stearic acid, steareth-20, lanolin alcohol, magnesium aluminum silicate, cetyl alcohol, beeswax, PEG-20-sorbitan beeswax, methylparaben, propylparaben, quaternium-15, fragrance.
Indications: KERI FACIAL CLEANSER is a gentle, soapless moisturizing cleanser.
Precaution: Avoid contact with eyes.
Dosage and Administration: Use KERI FACIAL CLEANSER in place of soap. Apply a sufficient amount to facial area, massaging the area to be cleansed. Rinse thoroughly with water and pat dry. To remove make-up, apply generously and wipe off with a facial tissue.
How Supplied: 4 oz. (NDC 0072-8600-04) plastic bottle.

KERI® FACIAL SOAP

Composition: KERI® LOTION concentrate in a gentle, non-detergent soap.
Action and Uses: KERI FACIAL SOAP helps keep skin soft while thoroughly cleansing.
Administration and Dosage: To be used as facial soap.
How Supplied: 3.25 oz. (NDC 0072-4900-03) bar.

KERI® LOTION and
KERI LOTION, FRESHLY SCENTED
Skin Lubricant—Moisturizer

Composition: Contains mineral oil, water, propylene glycol, glyceryl stearate/PEG-100 stearate, PEG-40 stearate, PEG-4 dilaurate, laureth-4, lanolin oil, methylparaben, propylparaben, fragrance, carbomer-934, triethanolamine, dioctyl sodium sulfosuccinate, quaternium-15. FRESHLY SCENTED: FD&C blue 1, D&C yellow 10.
Action and Uses: KERI LOTION lubricates and helps hydrate the skin, making it soft and smooth. It relieves itching, helps maintain a normal moisture bal-

Continued on next page

Westwood—Cont.

ance and supplements the protective action of skin lipids. Indicated for generalized dryness and itching; detergent hands; chapped or chafed skin; sunburn; "winter-itch"; aging, dry skin; diaper rash; heat rash.

Administration and Dosage: Apply as often as needed. Use particularly after bathing and exposure to sun, water, soaps and detergents.

How Supplied: 6½ oz. (NDC 0072-4600-56), 13 oz. (NDC 0072-4600-63) and 20 oz. (NDC 0072-4600-70) plastic bottles. Also available as KERI LOTION FRESHLY SCENTED—6½ oz. (NDC 0072-4500-56), 13 oz. (NDC 0072-4500-63), and 20 oz. (NDC 0072-4500-70) plastic bottles.

LOWILA® CAKE
Soap-free Skin Cleanser

Composition: Contains dextrin, sodium lauryl sulfoacetate, water, boric acid, urea, sorbitol, mineral oil, PEG-14 M, lactic acid, dioctyl sodium sulfosuccinate, cellulose gum, fragrance.

Action and Uses: LOWILA CAKE is indicated when soap should not be used, for cleansing skin that is sensitive or irritated, or in dermatitic and eczematous conditions. Used for general bathing, infant bathing, routine washing of hands and face and shampooing. The pH of LOWILA CAKE helps protect the skin's normal acid mantle and create an environment favorable to therapy and healing.

Administration and Dosage: LOWILA CAKE is used in place of soap. Lathers well in both hard and soft water.

How Supplied: 3¾ oz. (NDC 0072-2300-01) bar.

PERNOX®
Medicated Lathering Scrub Cleanser for Acne

Composition: Contains 2% sulfur, 1.5% salicylic acid, in a combination of soapless cleansers, wetting agents, and abradant polyethylene granules.

Actions and Uses: A lathering scrub cleanser for acne, oily skin. PERNOX provides microfine, uniform-size scrub particles with a rounded surface area to enable patients to achieve effective and gentle desquamation as they wash their skin. PERNOX helps loosen and remove comedones, dries, peels and degreases acne skin. It lathers abundantly and leaves the skin feeling smooth.

Contraindications: Not indicated when acute inflammation is present or in nodular or cystic acne.

Administration and Dosage: After wetting the skin, PERNOX is applied with the fingertips and massaged into the skin for about one-half to one minute. The skin is then thoroughly rinsed. May be used instead of soap one to two times daily, or as directed.

Caution: If undue skin irritation develops or increases, adjust usage schedule or discontinue use. If necessary, anti-inflammatory measures may be used after

discontinuance. For external use only. Contact with eyes should be avoided. In case of contact, flush eyes thoroughly with water.

How Supplied: 2 oz (NDC 0072-5200-02) and 4 oz. (NDC 0072-5200-04) tubes; lemon scented: 2 oz. (NDC 0072-5300-02) and 4 oz. (NDC 0072-5300-04) tubes.

PERNOX® LOTION
Lathering Abradant Scrub Cleanser for Acne

Composition: Contains 2% sulfur, 1.5% salicylic acid, in a combination of soapless cleansers, wetting agents, and abradant polyethylene granules.

Actions and Uses: PERNOX LOTION is a therapeutic abradant scrub cleanser in lotion form that is to be used routinely instead of soap. It gently desquamates or peels acne or oily skin. PERNOX LOTION also removes excessive oil from the skin surface and will produce mild drying of the affected skin areas when used regularly. It helps skin feel fresher and smoother with each wash.

Contraindications: Not indicated when acute inflammation is present or in nodular or cystic acne.

Administration and Dosage: To be shaken well before using.

PERNOX may be used instead of soap one or two times daily or as directed. The skin should be wet first and PERNOX applied with the fingertips. The lather should be massaged into skin for one-half to one minute. The patient then rinses thoroughly and pats dry.

Caution: If undue skin irritation develops or increases, adjust usage schedule or discontinue use. For external use only. Contact with eyes should be avoided. In case of contact, flush eyes with water.

How Supplied: 5 oz. (NDC 0072-7900-05) plastic bottle.

PERNOX® SHAMPOO
For Oily Hair

Composition: A blend of biodegradable cleansers and hair conditioners, containing: sodium laureth sulfate, water, lauramide DEA, quaternium 22, PEG-75 lanolin/hydrolyzed animal protein, sodium chloride, fragrance, lactic acid, sorbic acid, disodium EDTA, FD&C yellow 6, FD&C blue 1.

Actions and Uses: A gentle but thorough shampoo especially formulated to cleanse, control and condition oily hair. Especially suitable for adjunctive use with acne patients. PERNOX SHAMPOO works into a rich, pleasant lather, leaves the hair lustrous and manageable. Its special conditioners help prevent tangles and fly away hair. Gentle enough to be used every day. It contains a refreshing natural scent.

Administration and Dosage: A liberal amount is massaged into wet hair and scalp. A good lather is worked up, massaging thoroughly. This is followed by a rinse and repeat application. A final rinse is used. No other shampoos or hair conditioners are necessary. May be used as needed.

Caution: For external use only. Contact with the eyes should be avoided. In case of contact, flush eyes with water.

How Supplied: 8 fl. oz. (NDC 0072-5500-08) shatter-proof plastic bottles.

PRESUN® 4 SUNSCREEN LOTION
Moderate Sunscreen Protection

Composition: Contains 4% Padimate O, 10% SD alcohol 40, water, mineral oil, PPG-15 stearyl ether, stearyl alcohol, mono- and diglycerides, benzyl alcohol, laureth-23, carbomer 934, ceteth-10, sodium hydroxide.

Action and Uses: PRESUN 4 provides 4 times an individual's natural protection. Liberal and regular use may help reduce the chance of premature aging of the skin and skin cancer from overexposure to the sun. PRESUN 4 provides moderate protection, permits tanning, and reduces the chance of sunburn.

Administration and Dosage: Apply liberally and evenly 30 minutes before exposure. Reapply after swimming or excessive sweating. If used, cosmetics or emollients may be applied after PRESUN.

Caution: For external use only. Keep out of the reach of children. Discontinue use if irritation or rash appears. AVOID CONTACT WITH EYES.

How Supplied: 4 oz. (NDC 0072-5900-04) plastic bottle.

PRESUN® 8
LOTION, CREAMY LOTION, AND GEL
Maximal Sunscreen Protection

Composition: LOTION: Contains 5% (w/w) aminobenzoic acid (PABA), 55% (w/w) SD alcohol 40, water, glycerin, choleth-24, hydroxypropyl cellulose. CREAMY LOTION: Contains 5% aminobenzoic acid (PABA), 15% SD alcohol 40, water, PEG-8, PPG-15 stearyl ether, glyceryl stearate/PEG-100 stearate, glycerin, mineral oil, magnesium aluminum silicate, titanium dioxide, DEA-cetyl phosphate, benzyl alcohol, mono- and diglycerides, fragrance, cetyl alcohol, cellulose gum, simethicone. GEL: Contains 5% (w/w) aminobenzoic acid (PABA), 55% (w/w) SD alcohol 40, water, animal protein derivative, hydroxyethyl cellulose.

Action and Uses: PRESUN 8 provides 8 times an individual's natural protection. Liberal and regular use may reduce the chance of premature aging of the skin and skin cancer from overexposure to the sun. PRESUN 8 permits limited tanning and reduces the chance of sunburn. It gives maximum protection in the erythemogenic range, screening out the burning rays of the sun.

Contraindications: Do not use if sensitive to aminobenzoic acid, benzocaine, sulfonamides or aniline dyes.

Administration and Dosage: Apply liberally and evenly one hour before exposure. Let dry before dressing. Reapply after swimming or excessive sweating. If used, cosmetics or emollients may be applied after PRESUN.

Caution: For external use only. Keep out of the reach of children. Avoid contact with light-colored fabric, as staining may result. Avoid flame. Discontinue use if irritation or rash appears. AVOID CONTACT WITH EYES.

How Supplied: Lotion: 4 fl. oz. (NDC 0072-5400-04) and 7 fl. oz. (NDC 0072-5400-07) plastic bottles. Creamy Lotion: 4 oz. (NDC 0072-8502-04) plastic bottle. Gel: 3 oz. (NDC 0072-7700-03) plastic tube.

PRESUN® 15 SUNSCREEN LOTION
Ultra Sunscreen Protection

Composition: 5% Aminobenzoic acid (PABA), 5% Padimate O, 3% oxybenzone, 58% SD alcohol 40, water, PPG-15 stearyl ether, hydroxypropyl cellulose.

Actions and Uses: PRESUN 15 provides 15 times an individual's natural protection. Liberal and regular use may reduce the chance of premature aging of the skin and skin cancer from overexposure to the sun. PRESUN 15 permits no tanning and provides the highest degree of sunburn protection.

Contraindications: Do not use if sensitive to aminobenzoic acid, benzocaine, sulfonamides or aniline dyes.

Administration and Dosage: Apply liberally and evenly one hour before exposure. Let dry before dressing. Reapply after swimming or excessive sweating. If used, cosmetics or emollients may be applied after PRESUN.

Caution: For external use only. Keep out of the reach of children. Avoid contact with light-colored fabric, as staining may result. Avoid flame. Discontinue use if irritation or rash appears. AVOID CONTACT WITH EYES.

How Supplied: 4 oz. (NDC 0072-8800-04) plastic bottle.

PRESUN® SUNSCREEN LIP PROTECTION

Active Ingredient: 4% Padimate 0.

Indications: For dry, chapped, cracked lips associated with sun and wind exposure.

Dosage and Administration: Apply PRESUN LIP PROTECTION to lips as required.

How Supplied: ⅙ (.16) oz. (NDC 0072-8700-01) tube.

SEBUCARE®
Antiseborrheic Scalp Lotion

Contains: 1.8% Salicylic acid, 61% alcohol, water, PPG-40 butyl ether, laureth-4, dihydroabietyl alcohol, fragrance.

Action and Uses: An aid in the treatment of dandruff, seborrhea capitis and other scaling conditions of the scalp. SEBUCARE helps control scaling, oiliness and itching. The unique base helps soften brittle hair and grooms the hair, thus eliminating the need for hair dressing which often impedes antiseborrheic treatment. SEBUCARE should be used every day in conjunction with therapeutic shampoos such as SEBULEX® or FOSTEX® CREAM.

Administration and Dosage: SEBUCARE is applied directly to scalp and massaged thoroughly with fingertips. Comb or brush as usual. Grooms as it medicates. Use once or twice daily or as directed.

Precaution: Volatile—Flame should be avoided. Contact with eyes should be avoided. In case of contact, flush eyes thoroughly with water. For external use only.

How Supplied: 4 fl. oz. (NDC 0072-4800-04) plastic bottle.

SEBULEX® and SEBULEX CREAM
Antiseborrheic Treatment Shampoo

Composition: Contains 2% sulfur and 2% salicylic acid in SEBULYTIC® brand of surface-active cleansers and wetting agents.

Action and Uses: A penetrating therapeutic shampoo for the temporary relief of itchy scalp and the scaling of dandruff, SEBULEX helps relieve itching, remove dandruff, excess oil. It penetrates and softens the crusty, matted layers of scales adhering to the scalp, and leaves the hair soft and manageable.

Administration and Dosage: SEBULEX LIQUID should be shaken before being used. SEBULEX or SEBULEX CREAM is massaged into wet scalp. Lather should be allowed to remain on scalp for about 5 minutes and then rinsed. Application is repeated, followed by a thorough rinse. Initially, SEBULEX or SEBULEX CREAM can be used daily, or every other day, or as directed, depending on the condition. Once symptoms are under control, one or two treatments a week usually will maintain control of itching, oiliness and scaling.

Caution: If undue skin irritation develops or increases, discontinue use. Contact with eyes should be avoided. In case of contact, flush eyes thoroughly with water.

How Supplied: SEBULEX in 4 oz. (NDC 0072-2700-04) and 8 oz. (NDC 0072-2700-08) plastic bottles; SEBULEX CREAM in 4 oz. (NDC 0072-2800-04) tube.

SEBULEX® CONDITIONING SHAMPOO WITH PROTEIN
Antiseborrheic Treatment and Conditioning Shampoo

Composition: Contains 2% sulfur, 2% salicylic acid, water, sodium octoxynol-3 sulfonate, sodium lauryl sulfate, lauramide DEA, acetamide MEA, amphoteric-2, hydrolyzed animal protein, magnesium aluminum silicate, propylene glycol, methylcellulose, PEG-14 M, fragrance, disodium EDTA, dioctyl sodium sulfosuccinate, FD & C blue 1, D & C yellow 10.

Action and Uses: SEBULEX CONDITIONING SHAMPOO provides effective temporary control of the scaling and itching of dandruff and seborrheic dermatitis, while adding protein to the hair shaft to increase its manageability.

Administration and Dosage: SEBULEX CONDITIONING SHAMPOO should be shaken before use. It is to be massaged into the wet scalp. For optimum dandruff control and conditioning,

lather should be allowed to remain on scalp for about 5 minutes and then rinsed off. Application is repeated, followed by a thorough rinse. Initially, SEBULEX CONDITIONING SHAMPOO may be used daily, or as directed, to achieve control of symptoms. Two or three treatments per week usually will maintain control of oiliness, itching, and scaling.

Caution: If undue skin irritation develops or increases, use should be discontinued. Contact with eyes should be avoided. In cases of contact, eyes should be flushed thoroughly with water.

How Supplied: 4 oz. (NDC 0072-2600-04) and 8 oz. (NDC 0072-2600-08) plastic bottles.

SEBUTONE® and SEBUTONE CREAM
Antiseborrheic Tar Shampoo

Composition: WESTWOOD® TAR (equivalent to 0.5% Coal Tar USP), 2% sulfur and 2% salicylic acid in SEBULYTIC® brand of surface-active cleansers and wetting agents.

Action and Uses: A surface-active, penetrating therapeutic shampoo for the temporary relief of itchy scalp and the scaling of stubborn dandruff and psoriasis. Provides prompt and prolonged relief of itching, helps control oiliness and rid the scalp of scales and crust. Tar ingredient is chemically and biologically standardized to produce uniform therapeutic activity. Wood's light demonstrates residual microfine particles of tar on the scalp several days after a course of SEBUTONE shampoo. In addition to its antipruritic and antiseborrheic actions, SEBUTONE also helps offset excessive scalp dryness with a special moisturizing emollient.

Administration and Dosage: SEBUTONE liquid should be shaken before being used. A liberal amount of SEBUTONE or SEBUTONE CREAM is massaged into the wet scalp for 5 minutes and the scalp is then rinsed. Application is repeated, followed by a thorough rinse. Use as often as necessary to keep the scalp free from itching and scaling or as directed. No other shampoo or soap washings are required.

Caution: If undue skin irritation develops or increases, discontinue use. In rare instances, temporary discoloration of white, blond, bleached or tinted hair may occur. Contact with the eyes is to be avoided. In case of contact flush eyes with water.

How Supplied: SEBUTONE in 4 oz. (NDC 0072-5000-04) and 8 oz. (NDC 0072-5000-08) plastic bottles; SEBUTONE CREAM in 4 oz. (NDC 0072-5100-01) tube.

TRANSACT®
Transparent Medicated Acne Gel

Composition: Contains 6% laureth-4, 2% sulfur and 37% alcohol in a greaseless gel base.

Action and Uses: TRANSACT is a transparent, nonstaining and greaseless

Continued on next page

Westwood—Cont.

gel, which leaves a fresh, clean fragrance on the skin. It dries, peels and degreases the skin of acne patients. Its effect is controlled by frequency of application and climatic conditions.

Administration and Dosage: After washing acne skin thoroughly, a thin film is applied to affected areas once daily or as directed. A brief tingling sensation may be expected upon application. Patient should anticipate beneficial drying and peeling in 5 to 7 days. Since TRANSACT is a highly active drying agent it should be used sparingly when initiating therapy, particularly for patients with sensitive skin. 1. Patients with tender skin may best be started on one application every other day. 2. Most other patients can be started on one daily application. 3. When patients develop tolerance, applications may be increased to two and then three times daily to maintain an adequate therapeutic effect. 4. TRANSACT is also for use on the shoulders and back. In dry or cold climates skin is more reactive to TRANSACT and frequency of use should be reduced. During warm, humid months, frequency of use may be increased.

Caution: If undue skin irritation develops, usage schedule should be adjusted or TRANSACT discontinued. For external use only. Contact with the eyes should be avoided. In case of contact, flush eyes with water. Avoid flame.

How Supplied: 1 oz. (NDC 0072-5600-01) plastic tube.

Whitehall Laboratories
Division of American Home Products Corporation
685 THIRD AVENUE
NEW YORK, NY 10017

ANACIN®
Analgesic Tablets and Capsules

Active Ingredients: Aspirin 400 mg., Caffeine 32 mg., per tablet or capsule.

Indications and Actions: Anacin relieves pain of headache, neuralgia, neuritis, sprains, muscular aches, discomforts and fever of colds, pain caused by tooth extraction and toothache, menstrual discomfort. Anacin also temporarily relieves the minor aches and pains of arthritis and rheumatism.

Warnings: Keep this and all medicines out of children's reach. In case of accidental overdose, contact a physician immediately.

Precautions: If pain persists for more than 10 days, or redness is present, or in arthritic or rheumatic conditions affecting children under 12 years of age, consult a physician immediately.

Dosage: Two tablets or capsules with water every 4 hours, as needed. Do not exceed 10 tablets or 10 capsules daily. For children 6–12, half the adult dosage.

Professional Labeling: Same as those outlined under Indications.

How Supplied: Tablets: In tins of 12's and bottles of 30's, 50's, 100's, 200's and 300's. Capsules: In bottles of 20's, 40's, 75's and 125's.

[*Shown in Product Identification Section*]

MAXIMUM STRENGTH ANACIN®
Analgesic Tablets and Capsules

Active Ingredients: Aspirin 500 mg. and Caffeine 32 mg. per tablet and capsule.

Indications and Actions: Maximum Strength Anacin provides fast, effective, temporary relief of headaches, minor aches, pains and fever ... temporary relief of minor aches and pains of arthritis and rheumatism ... discomforts and fever of colds or "flu" ... pain caused by tooth extraction and discomfort associated with normal menstrual periods.

Precautions: If pain persists for more than 10 days, or redness is present, or in arthritic or rheumatic conditions affecting children under 12 years of age, consult a physician immediately.

Warning: Keep this and all medicines out of the reach of children.

Dosage: Adults: Initial dose 2 tablets or capsules with water, may be followed by 1 tablet or capsule after 3 hours or 2 tablets or capsules after 6 hours. Do not exceed 8 tablets or capsules in any 24 hour period. Not recommended for children under 12 years of age.

How Supplied: Tablets: Tins of 12's and bottles of 20's, 40's, 75's, and 150's. Capsules: bottles of 36's and 72's.

[*Shown in Product Identification Section*]

ANACIN-3®
Analgesic Tablets

Active Ingredients: Each tablet contains acetaminophen 500 mg. and caffeine 32 mg.

Indications: Anacin-3 acts fast to provide relief from pain of headache, colds or "flu", sinusitis, muscle strain, backache and menstrual discomfort. It is recommended for temporary relief of minor arthritis pain, toothaches and to reduce fever.

Actions: Anacin-3 is a safe and effective analgesic.

Warnings: Do not give to children under 12 or use for more than 10 days unless directed by a physician. Keep this and all medicines out of reach of children. In case of accidental overdose, contact a physician immediately.

Caution: If pain persists for more than 10 days or redness is present or in arthritic or rheumatic conditions affecting children under 12, consult physician immediately. Do not take without consulting a physician if under medical care. Promptly consult a dentist for toothache.

Dosage and Administration: Adults: Two tablets, 3 or 4 times a day. Do not exceed 8 tablets in any 24-hour period.

Professional Labeling: Same as those outlined under Indications.

How Supplied: Tablets in bottles of 30's, 60's, and 100's.

[*Shown in Product Identification Section*]

ANBESOL®
Antiseptic Anesthetic
Gel

Description: Anbesol Gel is a safe and effective antiseptic-anesthetic that can be used by all family members for the temporary relief of minor mouth pain, especially for cold sores and fever blisters.

Active Ingredients: Benzocaine (6.3%), Phenol (0.5%), Alcohol (70%).

Indications: For fast temporary pain relief of cold sores, fever blisters, toothache, denture irritation, sore gums and teething.

Actions: Helps dry and relieve the pain of cold sores, fever blisters. Temporarily deadens sensations of nerve endings to provide relief of pain and discomfort; reduces oral bacterial flora temporarily as an aid in oral hygiene.

Warnings: Do not use near eyes. Keep all medicine out of the reach of children.

Precautions: Not for prolonged use. If the condition persists or irritation develops, discontinue use and consult your physician or dentist.

Dosage and Administration: For topical application to the affected area on the lips or within the mouth.

Professional Labeling: Same as outlined under Indications.

How Supplied: Clear gel—.25 oz. tube.

[*Shown in Product Identification Section*]

ANBESOL®
Antiseptic Anesthetic
Liquid

Description: Anbesol Liquid is a safe and effective antiseptic-anesthetic solution that can be used by all family members for temporary relief of minor mouth pain and for first aid needs.

Active Ingredients: Benzocaine (6.3%), Phenol (0.5%), Povidone-Iodine (Yields 0.04% available Iodine), Alcohol (70%).

Indications: For temporary relief of pain due to denture irritation, toothache, teething, cold sores/fever blisters as well as minor cuts, scrapes and burns.

Actions: Temporarily deadens sensations of nerve endings to provide relief of pain and discomfort; reduces oral bacterial flora temporarily as an aid in oral hygiene.

Warnings: Do not use near eyes. Keep this and all medicines out of the reach of children.

Precautions: Not for prolonged use. If pain, redness, rash, irritation or swelling persists, or if infection occurs, discontinue use and see your physician or dentist. In case of deep or puncture wounds or serious burns, consult your doctor.

Dosage and Administration: For topical application to the skin and mucous membranes. Apply freely, locally to affected area.

Professional Labeling: Same as outlined under Indications.

How Supplied: Amber liquid. Two sizes—.31 and .74 fluid ounce bottles.

[*Shown in Product Identification Section*]

ARTHRITIS PAIN FORMULA
By the Makers of Anacin® Analgesic Tablets

Active Ingredients: Each tablet contains 7½ grains microfined aspirin. Also contains two buffers, 20 mg. dried Aluminum Hydroxide Gel and 60 mg. Magnesium Hydroxide.

Indications: Fast, temporary relief from minor aches and pain of arthritis and rheumatism and low back pain. Also relieves the pain of headache, neuralgia, neuritis, sprains, muscular aches, discomforts and fever of colds, pain caused by tooth extraction and toothache and menstrual discomfort.

Actions: Arthritis Pain Formula contains 50% more pain relief medicine than ordinary aspirin or regular buffered aspirin. APF® also provides extra stomach protection because, in addition to containing two buffers, the pain reliever is microfined. This means the pain-relieving particles are so fine they dissolve rapidly and so are less apt to cause stomach upset.

Warnings: Keep this and all medications out of children's reach. In case of accidental overdose, contact a physician immediately. In arthritic or rheumatic conditions, if pain persists for more than 10 days, or redness is present, consult a physician immediately.

Dosage and Administration: Convenient daily schedule for adults: Initial dose: Two tablets with water, thereafter, 1 tablet every 3 hours. Do not exceed 8 tablets in any 24-hour period. Not recommended for children under 12 years of age.

Professional Labeling: Same as stated under "Indications".

How Supplied: In plastic bottles of 40, 100 and 175 tablets. Also available in pocket-size 10's with five envelopes each containing 2 tablets.

[*Shown in Product Identification Section*]

BISODOL®
Antacid Powder

Active Ingredients: Per teaspoonful: Sodium Bicarbonate 644 mg., Magnesium Carbonate 475 mg.

Indications: Antacid to relieve the symptoms of acid indigestion, heartburn, and sour stomach.

Actions: Bisodol Powder is a combination of two well-established antacids, Magnesium Carbonate and Sodium Bicarbonate.

Warnings: Do not take more than four teaspoonfuls in a 24-hour period, or use the maximum dosage for more than two weeks, except under the advice and supervision of a physician. Do not use this product except under advice and supervision of a physician if you have kidney disease. May cause constipation or have laxative effect. Do not use this product except under the advice and supervision of a physician if you are on a sodium restricted diet. Each teaspoonful contains 6.8 mEq. (157 mg.) of sodium.

Keep this and all medicines out of the reach of children. In case of accidental overdose, seek professional assistance or contact a poison control center immediately.

Dosage and Administration: Adults: Take one teaspoonful of Bisodol in a glass of water after meals and at bedtime, or as directed by a physician.

Children under 12 years: As directed by a physician.

Professional Labeling: Same as those outlined under Indications.

How Supplied: White powder in 3 oz. and 5 oz. cans.

BISODOL®
Antacid Tablets

Active Ingredients: Calcium Carbonate 194 mg., Magnesium Hydroxide 178 mg. per tablet.

Indications: Antacid to relieve the symptoms of acid indigestion, heartburn, and sour stomach.

Actions: Bisodol Tablets are a combination of two well-established antacids, Calcium Carbonate and Magnesium Hydroxide. Bisodol Tablets contain virtually no sodium (0.036 mg./tablet).

Warnings: Do not take more than 16 tablets in a 24-hour period, or use the maximum dosage for more than two weeks, except under the advice and supervision of a physician.

Do not use this product, except under the advice and supervision of a physician, if you have kidney disease. May cause constipation or have laxative effect.

Keep out of reach of children. In case of accidental overdose, seek professional assistance or contact a poison control center immediately.

Dosage and Administration: Adults: One to two tablets every two hours, or as directed by a physician. Chew thoroughly or, if preferred, swallow with a glass of water or milk.

Children under 12 years: As directed by a physician.

Professional Labeling: Same as those outlined under Indications.

How Supplied: White uncoated tablets in tins of 30 and bottles of 100.

CLEANSING PADS
By The Makers of Preparation H® Hemorrhoidal Remedies

Active Ingredients: Witch hazel (50% w/v) and Glycerin (10% w/v).

Indications: Hemorrhoidal tissue irritation, anal cleansing wipe; everyday hygiene of the outer vaginal area, final cleansing step at diaper changing time.

Actions: Cleansing Pads are scientifically developed, soft cloth pads which are impregnated with a solution specially designed to gently soothe, freshen and clean the anal or genital area. Cleansing Pads are superior for a multitude of types of personal hygiene uses and are especially recommended for hemorrhoid sufferers.

Warnings: In case of rectal bleeding, consult physician promptly. In case of continued irritation, discontinue use and consult a physician.

Precaution: Keep this and all medicines out of the reach of children.

Dosage and Administration: As a personal wipe—use as a final cleansing step after regular toilet tissue or instead of tissue, in cases of special sensitivity. As a compress—hemorrhoid sufferers will get additional relief by using Cleansing Pads as a compress. Fold pad and hold in contact with inflamed anal tissue for 15 to 30 minutes. Repeat several times daily while inflammation lasts.

How Supplied: Jars of 40's and 100's.

COMPOUND W®
Solution

Active Ingredients: Each drop of Compound W Solution contains Salicylic Acid 14.2% w/w and Glacial Acetic Acid 9% w/w in a flexible collodion vehicle; Ether 57%.

Indications: Removes common warts quickly—painlessly.

Actions: Warts are common benign skin lesions caused by an infectious virus which stimulates mitosis in the prickle layer resulting in the production of elevated epithelial growths. The keratolytic action of Salicylic and Acetic Acids in a flexible collodion vehicle causes the cornified epithelium to swell, soften, macerate and then desquamate.

Warnings: Flammable—do not use near fire or flame. For external use only. In case of accidental ingestion, seek professional assistance or contact a poison control center immediately. Do not use on face or on mucous membranes. If you are a diabetic, or have impaired circulation, do not use as it may cause serious complications. Do not use on moles, birthmarks, or on areas that do not have the typical appearance of the common wart. To avoid irritating skin surrounding the wart, confine the product to the wart itself. If condition persists, see your physician. Keep this and all medicines out of the reach of children.

Dosage and Administration: Soak the affected area in hot water for five minutes. If any tissue has been loosened, remove by rubbing with a washcloth or soft brush. Dry thoroughly. Using glass rod provided, completely cover the wart only with solution. To avoid irritating the skin surrounding the wart, confine the solution to the wart only. Allow the liquid to dry, then re-apply. Repeat procedure for six to seven days. If wart still remains, repeat for up to another seven days. Follow directions carefully. Replace cap tightly.

Professional Labeling: Same as those outlined under Indications.

How Supplied: Compound W is available in .31 fluid oz. clear bottles with glass applicators.

DENOREX®
Medicated Shampoo
DENOREX®
Mountain Fresh Herbal Scent
Medicated Shampoo

Active Ingredients:
Lotion: Coal Tar Solution 9.0%, Menthol 1.5%. Also contains TEA-

Continued on next page

Whitehall—Cont.

Lauryl Sulfate, Water, Lauramide DEA, Stearic Acid, Chloroxylenol.

Gel: Coal Tar Solution 9.0%, Menthol 1.5%. Also contains TEA-Lauryl Sulfate, Water, Hydroxypropyl Methylcellulose, Chloroxylenol.

Indications: Helps relieve scaling —itching—flaking of dandruff, seborrhea and psoriasis. Regular use promotes cleaner, healthier hair and scalp.

Actions: Denorex Shampoo is antiseborrheic and antipruritic. Loosens and softens scales and crusts. Coal tar helps correct abnormalities of keratinization by decreasing epidermal proliferation and dermal infiltration. Denorex also contains the antipruritic agent, menthol, which is "one of the most widely used antipruritics in dermatologic therapy of various diseases accompanied by itching". (The United States Dispensatory—26th Edition.)

Warnings: For external use only. Discontinue treatment if irritation develops. Avoid contact with eyes. Keep this and all medicines out of children's reach.

Directions: For best results, shampoo every other day during first 10 days of treatment, and two or three times a week thereafter. For severe scalp problems use daily. Wet hair thoroughly and briskly massage until a rich lather is obtained. Rinse and repeat. Scalp may tingle slightly during treatment.

Professional Labeling: Same as stated under Indications.

How Supplied:
Lotion: 4 oz. and 8 oz. Bottles in Regular and Mountain Fresh Herbal Scents
Gel: 2 oz. Tube in Regular Scent
4 oz. Tube in Regular Scent
[Shown in Product Identification Section]

DRISTAN®
12-Hour Nasal Decongestant Capsules

Active Ingredients: Each Dristan 12-Hour Nasal Decongestant Capsule contains: Chlorpheniramine Maleate 4 mg., Phenylephrine Hydrochloride 20 mg.

Indications: Dristan 12-Hour Nasal Decongestant Capsules provide 12 hour relief from nasal congestion, runny nose, watery, itchy eyes and sneezing due to the common cold and hay fever/allergies.

Actions: Dristan 12-Hour Capsules are specially formulated capsule containing a decongestant to help restore free breathing by reducing the swollen nasal membranes and by draining the nasal passages, and an antihistamine to help control sneezing, excessive nasal discharge and watery, itchy eyes due to the common cold and hay fever/allergies.

Chlorpheniramine Maleate is an antihistamine effective in the control of rhinorrhea, sneezing and lacrimation in allergic and infectious disorders of the respiratory tract.

Phenylephrine HCl is an oral nasal decongestant (Sympathomimetic Amine) effective as a vasoconstrictor to help reduce nasal/sinus congestion.

Warnings: Do not exceed recommended dosage or give to children under 12 years of age unless directed by a physician. Not to be used by individuals with high blood pressure, heart disease, diabetes, or thyroid disease without consulting a physician. Do not drive or operate machinery while taking this medication, as this preparation may cause drowsiness in some persons.

Precaution: Keep this and all medicines out of the reach of children.

Dosage and Administration: Usual dose of 1 capsule provides 12 hours of prolonged action, after which the dosage may be repeated. Do not exceed 1 capsule every 12 hours.

Professional Labeling: Same as those outlined under Indications.

How Supplied: Timed-release capsules in packages of 6's, 10's and 15's.

DRISTAN®
Decongestant/Antihistamine/Analgesic Capsules

Active Ingredients: Each Dristan Capsule contains: Phenylpropanolamine HCl 12.5 mg., Chlorpheniramine Maleate 2 mg., Aspirin 325 mg., and Caffeine 16.2 mg. to counteract possible drowsiness from the antihistamine.

Indications: Dristan Decongestant/Antihistamine/Analgesic Capsules are indicated for temporary relief of concurrent symptoms of colds, sinusitis, hay fever, or other upper respiratory allergies: nasal congestion, sneezing, runny nose, fever, headache and minor aches and pains.

Actions: Each ingredient in Dristan Capsules is selected for temporary relief of symptoms of colds, sinusitis, hay fever, or other upper respiratory allergies. Each capsule contains aspirin as an analgesic and antipyretic, an oral nasal decongestant to reduce swollen mucosa of the upper respiratory tract, and an antihistamine as a rhinitis suppressant.

Aspirin is both analgesic and antipyretic. Therapeutic doses of aspirin will effectively reduce an elevated body temperature. Also, aspirin is effective in reducing the discomfort of pain associated with headache.

Phenylpropanolamine HCl is an oral nasal decongestant (Sympathomimetic Amine), effective as a vasoconstrictor to help reduce nasal/sinus congestion.

Chlorpheniramine Maleate is an antihistamine effective in the control of rhinorrhea, sneezing, and lacrimation in allergic and infectious disorders of the respiratory tract.

Warnings: May cause drowsiness. May cause excitability especially in children. Do not take this product if you have asthma, glaucoma, difficulty in urination due to enlargement of prostate gland, high blood pressure, heart disease, diabetes, or thyroid disease except under advice and supervision of a physician. Do not exceed recommended dosage because at higher doses nervousness, dizziness, or sleeplessness may occur. If symptoms do not improve within seven days or are accompanied by a high fever, consult a physician before continuing use. This product contains aspirin. Do not take this product if you are allergic to aspirin.

Drug Interaction: Do not take this product if you are presently taking a prescription antihypertensive or antidepressant drug containing a monoamine oxidase inhibitor except under the advice and supervision of a physician.

Precautions: Do not give to children under six except under advice and supervision of physician. Avoid alcoholic beverages and driving a motor vehicle or operating heavy machinery while taking this product.

Dosage and Administration: Adults: Two capsules every four hours not to exceed 12 capsules in 24 hours. Children 6–12: One capsule every four hours not to exceed six capsules in 24 hours.

Professional Labeling: Same as those outlined under Indications.

How Supplied: Red/White capsules in bottles of 16 and 36.
[Shown in Product Identification Section]

DRISTAN®
Decongestant/Antihistamine/Analgesic Tablets

Active Ingredients: Each Dristan Tablet contains: Phenylephrine HCl 5 mg., Chlorpheniramine Maleate 2 mg., Aspirin 325 mg. and Caffeine 16.2 mg. to counteract possible drowsiness from the antihistamine.

Indications: Dristan Decongestant/Antihistamine/Analgesic Tablets are indicated for temporary relief of concurrent symptoms of colds, sinusitis, hay fever, or other upper respiratory allergies: nasal congestion, sneezing, runny nose, fever, headache and minor aches and pains.

Actions: Each ingredient in Dristan Tablets is selected for temporary relief of symptoms of colds, sinusitis, hay fever, or other upper respiratory allergies. Each tablet contains aspirin as an analgesic and antipyretic, an oral nasal decongestant to reduce swollen mucosa of the upper respiratory tract, and an antihistamine as a rhinitis suppressant.

Aspirin is both analgesic and antipyretic. Therapeutic doses of aspirin will effectively reduce an elevated body temperature. Also aspirin is effective in reducing the discomfort of pain associated with headache.

Phenylephrine HCl is an oral nasal decongestant (Sympathomimetic Amine), effective as a vasoconstrictor to help reduce nasal/sinus congestion.

Chlorpheniramine Maleate is an antihistamine effective in the control of rhinorrhea, sneezing and lacrimation in allergic and infectious disorders of the respiratory tract.

Warnings: May cause drowsiness. May cause excitability, especially in children. Do not take this product if you have asthma, glaucoma, difficulty in urination due to enlargement of prostate gland, high blood pressure, heart disease, diabetes, or thyroid disease except under advice and supervision of a physician. Do not exceed recommended dosage because at higher doses nervousness, dizziness, or sleeplessness may occur. If symptoms do not improve within seven days or are accompanied by a high fever, consult a physician before continuing use. This product contains aspirin. Do not take this product if you are allergic to aspirin.

Drug Interaction: Do not take this product if you are presently taking a prescription antihypertensive or antidepressant drug containing a monoamine oxidase inhibitor except under the advice and supervision of a physician.

Precaution: Do not give to children under six except under advice and supervision of physician. Avoid alcoholic beverages and driving a motor vehicle or operating heavy machinery while taking this product.

Dosage and Administration: Adults: Two tablets every four hours not to exceed 12 tablets in 24 hours. Children 6–12: One tablet every four hours not to exceed six tablets in 24 hours.

Professional Labeling: Same as those outlined under Indications.

How Supplied: Yellow/White uncoated tablets in bottles of 24, 50 and 100.
[*Shown in Product Identification Section*]

DRISTAN–AF®
Decongestant/Antihistamine/ Analgesic Tablets

Active Ingredients: Each Aspirin-Free Dristan-AF Tablet with Acetaminophen contains: Phenylephrine HCl 5 mg., Chlorpheniramine Maleate 2 mg., Acetaminophen 325 mg. and Caffeine 16.2 mg. to counteract possible drowsiness from the antihistamine.

Indications: Aspirin-Free Dristan-AF Decongestant/Antihistamine/Analgesic Tablets are indicated for temporary relief of concurrent symptoms of colds, sinusitis, hay fever, or other upper respiratory allergies: nasal congestion, sneezing, runny nose, fever, headache, and minor aches and pains.

Actions: Each ingredient in Aspirin-Free Dristan-AF Tablets is selected for temporary relief of symptoms of colds, sinusitis, hay fever, or other upper respiratory allergies. Each tablet contains Acetaminophen as an analgesic and antipyretic, an oral nasal decongestant to reduce swollen mucosa of the upper respiratory tract, and an antihistamine as a rhinitis suppressant.

Acetaminophen is both an analgesic and antipyretic. It is as rapidly absorbed and effective as aspirin, but will cause little or no gastric irritation. Therapeutic doses of acetaminophen will effectively reduce an elevated body temperature, and is effective in reducing the discomfort of pain associated with headache.

Phenylephrine HCl is an oral nasal decongestant, (Sympathomimetic Amine), effective as a vasoconstrictor to help reduce nasal/sinus congestion.

Chlorpheniramine Maleate is an antihistamine effective in the control of rhinorrhea, sneezing and lacrimation in allergic and infectious disorders of the respiratory tract.

Warnings: May cause drowsiness. May cause excitability, especially in children. Do not take this product if you have asthma, glaucoma, difficulty in urination due to enlargement of prostate gland, high blood pressure, heart disease, diabetes, or thyroid disease except under advice and supervision of a physician. Do not exceed recommended dosage because at higher doses nervousness, dizziness or sleeplessness may occur. If symptoms do not improve within seven days or are accompanied by a high fever, consult a physician before continuing use.

Drug Interaction: Do not take this product if you are presently taking a prescription antihypertensive or antidepressant drug containing a monoamine oxidase inhibitor except under the advice and supervision of a physician.

Precaution: Do not give to children under six except under advice or supervision of a physician. Avoid alcoholic beverages and driving a motor vehicle or operating heavy machinery while taking this product.

Dosage and Administration: Adults: Two tablets every four hours not to exceed twelve tablets in 24 hours. Children 6–12: One tablet every four hours not to exceed six tablets in 24 hours.

Professional Labeling: Same as those outlined under Indications.

How Supplied: Blue-green/white uncoated tablets in tins of 12 and bottles of 24, 50, and 100 tablets.

DRISTAN®
Nasal Mist
DRISTAN®
Menthol Nasal Mist

Active Ingredients: Phenylephrine HCl 0.5%, Pheniramine Maleate 0.2%
Other Ingredients: Dristan Nasal Mist: Benzalkonium Chloride 1:5000 in isotonic aqueous solution, Thimerosal preservative 0.002% (loss is unavoidable).

Dristan Menthol Nasal Mist: Benzalkonium Chloride 1:5000 in isotonic aqueous solution, Thimerosal preservative 0.002% (loss is unavoidable) with aromatics (Menthol, Eucalyptol, Camphor, Methyl Salicylate).

Indications: For temporary relief of nasal congestion, due to the common cold, sinusitis, hay fever or other upper respiratory allergies.

Warnings: Do not exceed recommended dosage because symptoms may occur such as burning, stinging, sneezing, or increase of nasal discharge. Do not use this product for more than 3 days. If symptoms persist, consult a physician. The use of this dispenser by more than one person may spread infection. For adult use only. Do not give this product to children under 12 years except under the advice and supervision of a physician. Keep this and all medicines out of the reach of children. In case of accidental ingestion, seek professional assistance or contact a poison control center immediately.

Dosage and Administration: With head upright, insert nozzle in nostril. Spray quickly, firmly and sniff deeply.

Adults: Spray 2 or 3 times into each nostril. Repeat every 4 hours as needed. Children under 12 years: As directed by a physician.

Professional Labeling: Same as those outlined under Indications.

How Supplied: 15 ml. and 30 ml. plastic squeeze bottles.
[*Shown in Product Identification Section*]

DRISTAN®
Long Lasting Nasal Mist
DRISTAN®
Long Lasting Menthol Nasal Mist

Active Ingredient: Xylometazoline HCl N.F. 0.1%.
Other Ingredients: Dristan Long Lasting Nasal Mist: Benzalkonium Chloride 1:5000 in isotonic aqueous solution, Thimerosal preservative 0.002% (loss is unavoidable).

Dristan Long Lasting Menthol Nasal Mist: Benzalkonium Chloride 1:5000 in isotonic aqueous solution, Thimerosal preservative 0.002% (loss is unavoidable) with aromatics (Menthol, Eucalyptol, Camphor, Methyl Salicylate).

Indications: Dristan Long Lasting Nasal Mist and Dristan Long Lasting Menthol Nasal Mist are indicated for temporary relief of nasal congestion due to the common cold, sinusitis, hay fever, or other upper respiratory allergies.

Actions: The sympathomimetic action of Dristan Long Lasting Nasal Mist and Dristan Long Lasting Menthol Nasal Mist constricts the smaller arterioles of the nasal passages, producing a prolonged gentle and predictable decongesting effect.

Warnings: Do not exceed recommended dosage because symptoms may occur such as burning, stinging, sneezing, or an increase of nasal discharge. Do not use for more than 3 days. If symptoms persist, consult a physician. The use of this dispenser by more than one person may spread infection. For adult use only. Do not give the product to children under 12 years except under the advice and supervision of a physician. Keep this and all medicines out of the reach of children. In case of accidental ingestion, seek professional assistance or contact a poison control center immediately.

Dosage and Administration: With head upright, insert nozzle in nostril. Spray quickly, firmly, and sniff deeply. Adults: Spray 2 or 3 times into each nostril. Repeat every 8 to 10 hours as needed. Children under 12 years: As directed by a physician.

Professional Labeling: Same as those outlined under Indications.

How Supplied: Dristan Long Lasting Nasal Mist: 15 ml. and 30 ml. plastic squeeze bottles.

Dristan Long Lasting Menthol Nasal Mist: 15 ml. plastic squeeze bottle.
[*Shown in Product Identification Section*]

Continued on next page

Whitehall—Cont.

DRY AND CLEAR®
Double Strength Cream
DRY AND CLEAR®
Acne Medication

Active Ingredients: Dry and Clear Double Strength Cream—10% Benzoyl Peroxide.
Dry and Clear Acne Medication Lotion—5% Benzoyl Peroxide.
Actions: Benzoyl Peroxide is a very effective antibacterial and drying agent. It speeds the flaking away of dead, blemished, upper skin layers, helping release trapped sebum and reveals a new skin layer underneath troubled skin. Also, the oxidizing action of Benzoyl Peroxide kills the acne-related bacteria P acnes.
Warnings: For external use only. Avoid contact with eyes, lips, and mouth. If undue skin irritation, excessive redness, peeling or any swelling occurs, discontinue use. If it persists, consult a physician. May bleach colored or dyed fabric. Keep out of reach of children.
Dosage and Administration: Clean affected areas thoroughly.
LOTION: Shake well. Apply a small amount with fingertips one to three times daily directly to the affected area. As excessive drying of the skin may occur, start with one application daily, then increase to two or three times daily.
CREAM: Start out by applying on only one or two blemished areas once during the first day; if no discomfort or reaction occurs, apply to the remainder of blemishes one to three times per day.
How Supplied: Dry and Clear Double Strength Cream is available in a 1.0 oz. tube. Dry and Clear Acne Medication —Lotion is a liquid dispersion available in 1.0 oz. and 2.0 oz. containers.

DRY AND CLEAR®
Medicated Acne Cleanser

Active Ingredients: Alcohol 50%, Salicylic Acid 0.5%, Benzoic Acid 0.5%, Benzethonium Chloride 0.1%.
Actions: Dry and Clear Medicated Acne Cleanser is specially formulated to combat the oil and dirt that attack a teenager's skin. Dry and Clear contains three effective germ killers which leave an invisible antibacterial barrier that works for hours. In addition, it has a special high concentration oil removing formula that penetrates surface oil, so that you can wipe away the oil and dirt that can cause problems to the skin.
Warnings: If skin becomes excessively dry, itchy or flaky, lessen the frequency of use. Avoid contact with eyes, lips and mouth. If severe skin irritation develops, discontinue use and consult a physician.
Dosage and Administration: Dry and Clear Medicated Cleanser should be used after washings to remove oil and dirt ordinary soap and water may leave behind. Moisten a cotton pad with cleanser and rub lightly over the entire face. Concentrate on oily areas, such as the forehead, cheeks and chin. Repeat the process if skin is excessively oily. Do not rinse after use. Dry and Clear leaves an invisible barrier of medication on the skin.
Professional Labeling: Same as those outlined above.
How Supplied: Dry and Clear Medicated Cleanser comes in a 4 oz. and 8 oz. bottle.

FREEZONE®
Solution

Active Ingredients: Zinc Chloride 2.18% w/w and Salicylic Acid 13.6% w/w in a collodion vehicle. Alcohol 20.5%, Ether 64.8% (some loss unavoidable).
Indications: For removal of corns and calluses.
Actions: Freezone penetrates corns and calluses painlessly, layer by layer, loosening and softening the corn or callus so that the whole corn or callus can be lifted off or peeled away in just a few days.
Warnings: Use only as directed. Do not use near fire or flame. Do not apply Freezone if corn or callus is infected. Diabetics and persons with impaired circulation should not use Freezone. For external use only. In case of accidental ingestion, contact a physician or a poison control center immediately. Keep all medication out of reach of children.
Precautions: Apply Freezone on corn or callus only. Avoid surrounding skin. In applying Freezone between the toes, hold toes apart until thoroughly dry.
Dosage and Administration: Using special glass applicator attached to cap, apply Freezone, drop by drop, directly onto the corn or callus. Avoid surrounding skin. Apply 2 coats daily. Repeat for 3 to 6 days. Then soak foot in warm water until corn or callus is easily removed. If condition persists, consult a physician. Replace cap securely.
Professional Labeling: Same as outlined under Indications.
How Supplied: Available in .31 Fl. Oz. glass bottle.

HEET®
Analgesic Liniment

Active Ingredients: Methyl Salicylate (15.0%), Camphor (3.6%), Oleoresin Capsicum (as Capsaicin 0.025%), Alcohol (70%).
Indications: For fast, temporary relief from minor aches and pains of arthritis, rheumatism, muscular low back pain, strains, muscle aches and pains, lumbago, neuralgia and neuritis.
Actions: Heet Liquid contains medications which penetrate into the skin and which act directly on nerves to replace pain arising from deep inside muscles with soothing warmth. The product increases blood flow to the affected area, thereby generating increased warmth to provide relief from minor pain and its stiffness. Helps tense aching muscles relax so mobility is increased.
Warnings: For external use only. Use Heet only as directed as it may be unsafe if directions are not followed. Do not use on irritated skin. Keep out of reach of children to avoid accidental poisoning. (If accidental ingestion occurs, contact a physician immediately.) If pain persists for more than 10 days or redness is present before Heet is applied or in conditions affecting children under 12 years of age, consult a physician immediately. Do not use near fire or flame. Do not get Heet in the eyes or on mucous membranes. If excessive irritation develops, discontinue use. If you have diabetes or impaired circulation, use Heet only upon the advice of a physician. Let Heet dry thoroughly before permitting contact with clothing.
Dosage and Administration: Using applicator attached to the bottle cap, brush Heet freely over and around sore areas. Do not bandage or apply external heat or hot water. If necessary, use Heet again in 15 minutes. When pain persists, Heet may be applied every two hours.
Professional Labeling: Same as stated under Indications.
How Supplied: Liquid: in 2.33 fl. oz. and 5 fl. oz. size bottles.

HEET®
Spray Analgesic

Active Ingredients: Methyl Salicylate (25%), Menthol (3.0%), Camphor (3.0%), Methyl Nicotinate (1.0%).
Indications: For fast, temporary relief from minor aches and pains of arthritis, rheumatism, muscular low back pain, strains, muscle aches and pains, lumbago, neuralgia and neuritis.
Actions: Heet Spray contains medications which penetrate into the skin and which act directly on nerves to replace pain arising from deep inside muscles with soothing warmth. The product increases blood flow to the affected area, thereby generating increased warmth to provide relief from minor pain and its stiffness. Helps tense aching muscles relax so mobility is increased.
Warnings: Avoid spraying in eyes. Contents under pressure. Do not puncture or incinerate. Keep away from fire or flame. Do not store at temperatures above 120°F. Keep out of reach of children. Use only as directed. Intentional misuse by deliberately concentrating and inhaling the contents can be harmful or fatal. For external use only. Do not use on broken or irritated skin. Keep out of reach of children to avoid accidental poisoning. (If swallowed accidentally, contact a physician immediately.) If pain persists for more than 10 days or redness is present before Heet is applied or in conditions affecting children under 12 years of age, consult a physician immediately. Do not get Heet in the eyes or on mucous membranes. If excessive irritation develops, discontinue use. If you have diabetes or impaired circulation, use Heet only upon the advice of a physician.
Dosage and Administration: Spray affected area once from a distance of 6 to 8 inches. Let dry. Spray again. May be reapplied every 2–3 hours for temporary relief. No rubbing is necessary. Do not bandage or apply external heat or hot water.

Professional Labeling: Same as stated under Indications.

How Supplied: In 5 fl. oz. non-fluoro-carbon aerosol spray cans.

INFRARUB®
Analgesic Cream

Description: InfraRub is a topical analgesic cream that is lightly and pleasantly scented.

Active Ingredients: Histamine Dihydrochloride 0.1% and Oleoresin Capsicum 0.4%.

Indications: An effective analgesic rub in a cream form for fast, soothing temporary relief of chronic minor pains of arthritis and rheumatism and the relief of muscular aches, minor aches and pains of lumbago, neuritis, neuralgia, sore joints and muscle sprains.

Actions: InfraRub increases the flow of blood and produces an analgesic action at the affected area. This action provides soothing warmth and temporary relief of pain.

Warnings: Use only as directed. For external use only. If pain persists more than seven days or redness is present or in conditions affecting children under 12 years of age, consult a physician immediately. If rash appears, discontinue use. Avoid contact with mouth, eyes, nostrils, sensitive or irritated skin. Keep out of reach of children.

Precautions: If patient has diabetes or impaired circulation, InfraRub should be used only upon the advice of a physician. Itching and hive-like elevations may develop in treated areas. These are temporary and should disappear quickly.

Dosage and Administration: Apply InfraRub freely to affected areas. Massage lightly until cream vanishes. Do not bandage or apply external heat or hot water. Repeat treatment 1–3 times daily and continue use as long as necessary. Wash hands after use. Do not apply to wounded or damaged skin. Allow to dry before putting on clothing.

Professional Labeling: Same as outlined under Indications.

How Supplied: Available in 1.5 and 3.5 oz. tubes.

MOMENTUM®
Muscular Backache Formula

Active Ingredients: Each Momentum Tablet contains Salsalate (Salicylsalicylic Acid) 5 gr., Microfined Aspirin 2½ gr., and Phenyltoloxamine Citrate 12.5 mg.

Indications: For the rapid symptomatic relief of the pain, inflammation and stiffness of muscular backache.

Actions: The action of the Microfined Aspirin starts to relieve pain of tense, knotted muscles in minutes. Relief is prolonged by the Salsalate with its longer duration of action. And the calmative action of the Phenyltoloxamine Citrate helps relax the tension that can cause muscles to tighten. As pain subsides, muscles loosen and become less stiff, more relaxed and mobility is increased.

Warnings: Do not drive a car or operate machinery while taking this medication as this preparation may cause drowsiness in some persons. Keep this and all medicines out of children's reach. In case of accidental overdose, contact a physician immediately.

Dosage and Administration: Adults: One or two tablets upon rising, then one or two tablets as needed at lunch, dinner, and bedtime. Dosage should not exceed 8 tablets in any 24-hour period. Not recommended for children.

Professional Labeling: Same as those outlined under Indications.

How Supplied: Bottles of 24 and 48 white, uncoated tablets.

OUTGRO®
Solution

Active Ingredients: Chlorobutanol 5%, Tannic Acid 25%, Isopropyl Alcohol 83% (by volume).

Indications: Provides fast, temporary relief of pain of ingrown toenails.

Actions: While Outgro temporarily decreases pain, reduces swelling and eases inflammation accompanying ingrown toenails, Outgro does not affect the growth, shape or position of the nail. Daily use of Outgro toughens tender skin—allowing the nail to be cut, and, thus preventing further pain and discomfort.

Warnings: Do not apply if toe is infected, but see a physician. Do not use if you are diabetic or have impaired circulation. Do not use near fire or flame. For external use only. In case of accidental ingestion, contact a physician or a poison control center immediately. Keep all medication out of reach of children.

Dosage and Administration: Use glass rod in bottle cap. Apply a few drops in the crevice where the nail grows into the flesh and along the entire margin of the nail. Work Outgro well under the nail. Let dry thoroughly. Don't rub off. Apply a few drops several times a day up to 10 days to toughen tender skin, allowing nail to be cut. If condition persists, consult a physician. Replace cap securely.

Professional Labeling: Same as those outlined under Indications.

How Supplied: Available in .31 Fl. Oz. glass bottles.

OXIPOR VHC®
Lotion for Psoriasis

Active Ingredients: Coal Tar Solution 48.5%, Salicylic Acid 1.0%, Benzocaine 2.0%, Alcohol 81% by volume.

Indications: Relieves itching, redness and helps dissolve and clear away the scales and crusts of psoriasis.

Actions: Coal tar solution helps control cell growth and therefore prevents formation of new scales. Salicylic acid has a keratolytic action which helps peel off and dissolve away scales. Benzocaine is a local anesthetic that gives prompt relief from pain and itching. Alcohol is the solvent vehicle.

Warnings: For external use only. Shake well before using. Avoid contact with eyes or mucous membranes and avoid unnecessary sunlight exposure after applying. Store at room temperature. Do not use near fire or flame and do not chill. Keep all medication out of reach of children.

Precaution: Not for prolonged use. If condition persists or if a rash or irritation develops, discontinue use and consult a physician.

Dosage and Administration: SKIN: Wash affected area before applying to remove loose scales. With a small wad of cotton, apply twice daily. Allow to air-dry before contact with clothing.
SCALP: Apply to scalp with fingertips making sure to get down to the skin itself. Shampoo. Then remove all loose scales with a fine comb.

Professional Labeling: Same as those outlined under Indications.

How Supplied: Available in 1.9 oz. and 4.0 oz. glass bottles.

PREDICTOR®
In-Home Early Pregnancy Test

Ingredients: Human Chorionic Gonadotropin (HCG) on sheep red blood cells, HCG Antiserum (rabbit) and special buffer solution.

Indications: PREDICTOR is used to determine pregnancy by the detection of HCG in the urine.

Actions: If, after following directions, (see dosage and administration), dark brown doughnut shaped ring appears in the test tube, the patient can assume she is pregnant. If no brown ring occurs, she is probably not pregnant.

Clinical studies have determined the Predictor Method to be 98% accurate. The Predictor Method has been used in thousands of hospitals and in over nine million laboratory tests.

Warnings: The test is completely safe. . . only a urine specimen is required. For In-Vitro Diagnostic Use, not for internal use.

Drug Interaction: Test results may be interfered with if urine contains a large quantity of protein or patient is taking medication.

Dosage and Administration: Predictor can be used as early as the 9th day after missed menstruation. Add a measured amount of first morning urine and the buffered solution to the chemical pellets in the test tube. Shake vigorously for 10 seconds. Place test tube in test stand and leave undisturbed for 2 hours. Test results must be read between 2 and 3 hours after starting test. If a dark brown doughnut shaped ring is visible the patient can assume she is pregnant. If no brown ring occurs, she is probably not pregnant. If test proves negative and menstruation does not occur within another 7 days, the test should be repeated.

Professional Labeling: Same as those outlined under Indications.

How Supplied: A kit containing test tube of reagents, vial of special buffer solution with press fit cap, dropper, lid and test stand in carton with package insert.

A refill kit containing test tube of reagents, vial of special buffer solution

Continued on next page

Whitehall—Cont.

with press fit cap, dropper, and package insert. (Note: Lid and test stand from complete Predictor Kit required for use.)

PREPARATION H®
Hemorrhoidal Ointment
PREPARATION H®
Hemorrhoidal Suppositories

Active Ingredients: Live Yeast Cell Derivative, supplying 2,000 units skin respiratory factor per ounce of ointment. Shark liver oil 3.0%; in a specially prepared rectal ointment base with Phenylmercuric Nitrate 1:10,000 (as a preservative).

Indications: To help shrink swelling of hemorrhoidal tissues caused by inflammation, and to give prompt, temporary relief in many cases from pain and itch in tissues.

Actions: Live Yeast Cell Derivative acts to: A) Increase the oxygen utilization of dermal tissue. B) Increases collagen formation. C) Increases the rate of wound healing. Shark liver oil has been incorporated to act as a protectant which softens and soothes the tissue. Preparation H also lubricates inflamed, irritated surfaces to help make bowel movements less painful.

Precaution: In case of bleeding, a physician should be consulted.

Dosage and Administration: Ointment: Apply freely night, morning, after each bowel movement and whenever symptoms occur. Lubricate applicator before each application and thoroughly cleanse after use.

Suppository: Insert one suppository night, morning, after each bowel movement and whenever symptoms occur. Store at controlled room temperature in cool place but not over 80° F.

Professional Labeling: Same as those outlined under Indications.

How Supplied: Ointment: Net wt. 1 oz. and 2 oz.

Suppository: 12's, 24's and 48's.

Reference: Goodson, W., Hohn, D., Hunt, T.K., Leung, D.Y.K.: Augmentation of Some Aspects of Wound Healing by a "Skin Respiratory Factor", J. Surg. Rsch. 21: 125-129, 1976.

[*Shown in Product Identification Section*]

PRIMATENE®
Mist
(Epinephrine)

Active Ingredients: Each spray delivers approximately 0.2 mg. Epinephrine. A 0.5% w/w (= 5.5 mg./cc.) solution of U.S.P. Epinephrine containing Ascorbic Acid as a preservative in an inert propellant. Alcohol 34%.

Indications: Provides temporary relief from acute paroxysms of bronchial asthma.

Warnings: For INHALATION ONLY. Contents under pressure. Do not puncture or throw container into incinerator. Using or storing near open flame or heating above 120° F may cause bursting.

Do not use unless a diagnosis of asthma has been established by a physician. Reduce dosage if bronchial irritation, nervousness, restlessness or sleeplessness occurs. Overdose may cause nervousness and rapid heartbeat. Use only on the advice of a physician if heart disease, high blood pressure, diabetes, or thyroid disease is present. If difficulty in breathing persists, or if relief does not occur within 20 minutes of inhalation, discontinue use and seek medical assistance immediately. Children under 6 years of age should use Primatene Mist only on the advice of a physician. KEEP THIS AND ALL MEDICINES OUT OF REACH OF CHILDREN.

Administration: Directions: 1. Take plastic cap off mouthpiece. (For refills, use mouthpiece from previous purchase.) 2. Take mouthpiece off bottle and fit other end of mouthpiece onto top of bottle. 3. Turn bottle upside down. Empty the lungs as completely as possible by exhaling. 4. Place mouthpiece in mouth with lips closed around opening. As you start to take a deep breath, squeeze mouthpiece and bottle together, releasing one full application. Complete taking the deep breath, drawing medication into your lungs. 5. Remove mouthpiece and hold breath for as long as comfortable. This distributes the medication in the lungs. Then exhale slowly, keeping the lips nearly closed.

Dosage: Start with one inhalation—then wait at least one minute; if not relieved, use Primatene Mist once more; do not repeat treatment for at least 4 hours.

Professional Labeling: Same as stated under Indications.

How Supplied: ½ fl. oz. (15 cc) with mouthpiece.

½ fl. oz. (15 cc) refill
¾ fl. oz. (22.5 cc) refill

[*Shown in Product Identification Section*]

PRIMATENE®
Mist Suspension
(Epinephrine Bitartrate)

Active Ingredients: Each spray delivers 0.3 mg. Epinephrine Bitartrate equivalent to 0.16 mg. Epinephrine base. Contains Epinephrine Bitartrate 7.0 mg. per cc. in an inert propellant.

Indications: Provides temporary relief from acute paroxysms of bronchial asthma.

Warnings: For INHALATION ONLY. Contents under pressure. Do not puncture or throw container into incinerator. Using or storing near open flame or heating above 120° F may cause bursting.

Do not use unless a diagnosis of asthma has been established by a physician. Reduce dosage if bronchial irritation, nervousness, restlessness or sleeplessness occurs. Overdose may cause nervousness and rapid heartbeat. Use only on the advice of a physician if heart disease, high blood pressure, diabetes, or thyroid disease is present. If difficulty in breathing persists, or if relief does not occur within 20 minutes of inhalation, discontinue use and seek medical assistance immediately. Children under 6 years of age should use Primatene Mist only on the

advice of a physician. KEEP THIS AND ALL MEDICINES OUT OF REACH OF CHILDREN.

Administration: Directions: 1. Shake well. 2. Hold inhaler with nozzle down while using. Empty the lungs as completely as possible by exhaling. 3. Purse the lips as in saying "o" and hold the nozzle up to the lips, keeping the tongue flat. As you start to take a deep breath, squeeze nozzle and can together, releasing one full application. Complete taking deep breath, drawing medication into your lungs. 4. Hold breath for as long as comfortable. This distributes the medication in the lungs. Then exhale slowly, keeping the lips nearly closed. 5. Rinse nozzle daily with soap and hot water after removing from vial. Dry with clean cloth.

Dosage: Start with one inhalation—then wait at least one minute; if not relieved, use Primatene Mist Suspension once more; do not repeat treatment for at least 4 hours.

Professional Labeling: Same as stated under Indications.

How Supplied: ⅓ fl. oz. (10 cc.) pocket-size aerosol inhaler.

PRIMATENE®
Tablets

Available in two formulas, "M" or "P", depending on state. See details below in section on "How Supplied".

Active Ingredients: Theophylline 130 mg., Ephedrine Hydrochloride 24 mg., Phenobarbital 8 mg. (⅛ gr.) per tablet. In those states where Phenobarbital is ℞ only, Pyrilamine Maleate 16.6 mg. is substituted for the Phenobarbital.

Indications: For relief and control of attacks of bronchial asthma and associated hay fever.

Actions: Experimental results[1] indicate the following: in inhibiting the release of bronchoconstricting mediators (histamine and slow-reacting substance of anaphylaxis), which is produced by antigen-antibody (IgE) interaction on sensitive cells, a combination of a sympathomimetic and methylxanthine is more effective than either drug alone.

Warning: If symptoms persist, consult your physician. Some people are sensitive to ephedrine and, in such cases, temporary sleeplessness and nervousness may occur. These reactions will disappear if the use of the medication is discontinued. Do not exceed recommended dosage.

People who have heart disease, high blood pressure, diabetes or thyroid trouble should take this preparation only on the advice of a physician. "M" Formula may cause drowsiness. People taking the "M" Formula should not drive or operate machinery. "P" Formula may be habit forming.

Dosage and Administration: Adults —1 or 2 tablets initially and then one every 4 hours, as needed, not to exceed 6 tablets in 24 hours. Children (6-12) One half adult dose. For children under 6, consult a physician.

Professional Labeling: Same as stated under Indications.

How Supplied: Available in two forms coded "M" or "P". "M" formula, containing pyrilamine maleate, is available in those states where phenobarbital is ℞ only. "P" formula, containing phenobarbital, is available in all other states. Both "M" and "P" formulas are supplied in glass bottles of 24 and 60 tablets.

---

1. Kooperman, W.J., Orange, R. P. and Austen, K.F.: J. Immunol. 105: 1906, Nov., 1970.
[*Shown in Product Identification Section*]

QUIET WORLD®
Analgesic/Sleeping Aid

Description: Occasionally people suffer from nighttime pain and have trouble falling asleep. Quiet World is specially formulated to provide relief of nighttime pain while it helps patients fall asleep.
Active Ingredients: Acetaminophen 2-½ gr. (162 mg.), Aspirin 3½ gr. (227 mg.), Pyrilamine Maleate (25 mg.) per tablet.
Indications: For occasional relief from nighttime pain while it helps one fall asleep.
Actions: Quiet World is for relief of occasional sleeplessness due to pain of headache, discomforts of colds or flu, sinus pain, muscle aches and menstrual discomfort.
Warnings: Keep this and all medicines out of children's reach. In case of accidental overdose, contact a physician immediately.
Precaution: Do not exceed 4 tablets in 24 hours. Do not drive a car or operate machinery after use. If pain persists for more than 10 days, or redness is present, or in conditions affecting children under 12 years of age, consult a physician immediately. Do not take without consulting a physician if under medical care.
Dosage and Administration: Take 2 tablets at bedtime to relieve pain and help fall asleep. If needed, may be repeated once after 4 hours.
Professional Labeling: Same as outlined under Indications.
How Supplied: Oblong Blue Tablets with "Q" imprinted. Tablets in bottles of 12's and 30's.

SEMICID®
Vaginal Contraceptive Suppositories

Description: Semicid is a contraceptive in vaginal suppository form.
Active Ingredient: Each slim, one-inch suppository contains 100 mg. of nonoxynol-9.
Actions: Semicid dissolves in the vagina and blends with natural vaginal lubrication to provide double birth control protection: a physical barrier, plus an effective sperm killing barrier that covers the cervical opening and adjoining vaginal walls. Each Semicid suppository contains the maximum allowable amount of nonoxynol-9, the most widely used non-prescription spermicide.
Semicid requires no applicator and has no unpleasant taste or odor. Nor does it drip or run like foams, creams and jellies. And it's not awkward to use like the diaphragm. As with all spermicides, some Semicid users experience irritation in using the product. However, since Semicid does not effervesce as some suppositories do, it is not as likely to cause a burning feeling.
Semicid is approximately as effective as vaginal foam contraceptives in actual use, but is not as effective as the pill or IUD.
Dosage and Administration: Insert one suppository into the vagina fifteen minutes before intercourse. Use the forefinger to position suppository as deeply as possible into the vagina. Proper positioning is key to Semicid's efficacy. If intercourse is delayed more than one hour, or repeated, another suppository must be inserted. Semicid can be used safely as frequently as needed and directions should be followed each time.
Precautions: If douching is desired, one should wait at least six hours after intercourse before douching.
If either partner experiences irritation, discontinue use. If irritation persists, consult a physician.
Do not insert in urethra.
Do not take orally.
If your doctor has told you that you should not become pregnant, ask your doctor if you can use Semicid.
If menstrual period is missed, a physician should be consulted.
If tray mold container has been damaged, do not use.
Keep out of reach of children.
How Supplied: Package of 10, in a partitioned tray mold container. Also available in a Double Pack containing 2 tray molds. Semicid Vaginal Contraceptive Suppositories should be stored at a temperature below 86°F (30°C).
Semicid is an effective contraceptive protection when properly used. However, no contraceptive method or product can provide an absolute guarantee against becoming pregnant.
It is essential that Semicid be inserted at least 15 minutes before intercourse.

SLEEP-EZE®
Tablets

Active Ingredient: Pyrilamine Maleate—25 mg. per tablet.
Indications: Nighttime sleeping aid.
Warnings: Do not give to children under 12 years of age. If sleeplessness persists continuously for more than 2 weeks, consult your physician. Insomnia may be a symptom of serious underlying illness. Take this product with caution if alcohol has been consumed. If you are pregnant or nursing a baby, consult your physician before using. Do not take this product if you have asthma, glaucoma, or enlargement of the prostate gland except under the advice and supervision of a physician. Keep all medicines out of the reach of children.
Drug Interaction: Take this product with caution if alcohol has been consumed.
Precaution: This product contains an antihistamine drug.
Dosage and Administration: Two tablets with water at bedtime.

Professional Labeling: Same as outlined under Indications.
How Supplied: Bottles of 12's, 26's, 52's and 100's.

TRENDAR®
Premenstrual Tablets

Active Ingredients: Acetaminophen 325 mg. (5 gr.) and Pamabrom 25 mg. per tablet.
Indications: Pre-period—for relief of puffiness and bloating due to water build-up, and symptoms of premenstrual discomfort such as headache, backache, pelvic discomfort, and painful breasts. During period—for relief of minor menstrual pain, cramps, headache, backache and other menstrual discomforts.
Warnings: Do not give to children under 12 or use for more than 10 days unless directed by a physician. Keep this and all medicines out of reach of children. In case of accidental overdose, contact a physician immediately.
Precautions: Do not take without consulting a physician if under medical care. Do not exceed recommended dosage because severe liver damage may occur.
Dosage and Administration: Start 4 to 7 days before period. Take 8 tablets daily—2 tablets after each meal, and at bedtime. Continue, if necessary, during period.
Professional Labeling: Same as those outlined under Indications.
How Supplied: Tablets in bottles of 24 and 50.

VIRO-MED®
Liquid

Active Ingredients: Each fluid ounce (2 tablespoonfuls) of Viro-Med Liquid contains Acetaminophen 10 gr., Pseudoephedrine HCl 30 mg., Dextromethorphan HBr 20 mg., Sodium Citrate 500 mg., and Alcohol 16.63%.
Indications: Viro-Med is indicated for the relief of all major virus cold and flu symptoms: Fever, nasal congestion, chills, headache, coughing, chest congestion, muscle aches, and scratchy throat.
Actions: The medications in this special Viro-Med formulation provide temporary relief of all major virus cold and flu symptoms.
Acetaminophen, both an analgesic and antipyretic, alleviates the pain and discomfort of headache and muscle aches, and reduces fever. It causes insignificant or no gastric irritation. And since acetaminophen is not a salicylate, Viro-Med can be taken by those who are sensitive to aspirin.
Pseudoephedrine HCl, a sympathomimetic amine, is an oral decongestant that vasoconstricts the nasopharyngeal mucosa thus reducing nasal/sinus congestion.
Dextromethorphan HBr, an antitussive, relieves or prevents cough.
Sodium Citrate provides an expectorant action that promotes the ejection of mucus or exudate from the lungs, bronchi, and trachea.

Continued on next page

Whitehall—Cont.

Precautions: If cough persists—which may indicate a serious condition—or in case of high fever—consult a physician. If relief does not occur within 10 days, discontinue use and consult a physician. **Warnings:** Individuals with high blood pressure, diabetes, heart or thyroid disease should use only as directed by physician. In case of accidental overdose, contact a physician immediately. Keep this and all medicines out of the reach of children.

Dosage and Administration: Adults: 2 tablespoonfuls (1 fl. oz.) every 3 or 4 hours, not to exceed 8 tablespoonfuls in 24 hours.

Children (6–12 years): 1 tablespoonful (½ fl. oz.) every 3 or 4 hours, not to exceed 4 tablespoonfuls in 24 hours. For children under six, consult a physician.

Professional Labeling: Same as outlined under Indications.

How Supplied: Viro-Med Liquid (dark amber) in 6 fl. oz. bottles.

VIRO-MED®
Tablets

Active Ingredients: Each Viro-Med Tablet contains Aspirin 5 gr., Chlorpheniramine Maleate 1 mg., Pseudoephedrine HCl 15 mg., Dextromethorphan HBr 7.5 mg., and Guaifenesin (Glyceral Guaiacolate) 50 mg.

Indications: Viro-Med is indicated for the relief of all major virus cold and flu symptoms: fever, nasal congestion, chills, headache, coughing, chest congestion, muscle aches, and scratchy throat.

Actions: The medications in this special Viro-Med formulation provide temporary relief of all major virus cold and flu symptoms.

Aspirin, both an analgesic and antipyretic, alleviates the pain and discomfort of headache and muscle aches, and reduces fever.

Chlorpheniramine Maleate, an antihistamine, acts to minimize tissue reaction to histamine. This relieves itching of the nasopharynx, eyes, and throat; sneezing; reduces nasal discharge; and shrinks and dries swollen membranes.

Pseudoephedrine HCl, a sympathomimetic amine, is an oral decongestant that vasoconstricts the nasopharyngeal mucosa thus reducing nasal/sinus congestion.

Dextromethorphan HBr, an antitussive, alleviates or prevents cough.

Guaifenesin is an expectorant that promotes the ejection of mucus or exudate from the lungs, bronchi, and trachea.

Precautions: If cough persists—which may indicate a serious condition—or in case of high fever—consult a physician. Do not drive or operate machinery while taking this medication as this preparation may cause drowsiness in some persons. If relief does not occur within 7 days, discontinue use and consult a physician.

Warnings: May cause drowsiness. May cause excitability, especially in children. Individuals with asthma, glaucoma, diffi-culty in urination due to enlargement of the prostate gland, high blood pressure, diabetes, heart or thyroid disease should use only as directed by a physician. Keep this and all medicines out of the reach of children. In case of accidental overdose, contact a physician immediately.

Dosage and Administration: Adults: 2 tablets every 4 hours. Do not exceed 12 tablets in 24 hours. Children (6–12): One half the adult dose. Do not give to children under 6 years of age or exceed the recommended dosage unless directed by a physician. Viro-Med Tablets contain no narcotics, barbiturates, or alcohol and may be taken day or night.

Professional Labeling: Same as outlined under Indications.

How Supplied: Orange/white uncoated tablets in bottles of 20 with a child-resistant safety closure, and bottles of 48 for households without young children.

The J.B. Williams Company, Inc.
767 FIFTH AVENUE
NEW YORK, NY 10153

ACU-TEST®
In-Home Pregnancy Test

Active Ingredient: hCG on sheep red blood cells, hCG antiserum from rabbits.
Indications: An *in vitro* pregnancy test for use in the home.
Actions: Indicates the presence of human chorionic gonadotropin, a hormone of pregnancy, in the urine.
Precautions: For use on or after the 9th day following the day when the menstrual period was due. The physician should be consulted if pregnancy is indicated.
Administration: Perform test exactly according to instructions, using the first morning urine.
How Supplied: Packages of one or two tests each with test tube, dropper and buffer solution.

DEEP-DOWN® Pain Relief Rub

Active Ingredients: Methyl salicylate 15%; menthol 5%; methyl nicotinate 0.7%; camphor 0.5%.
Indications: To relieve the pain of minor arthritis, sore joints, muscle aches and sprains, backache, lumbago.
Actions: Counterirritation: cutaneous stimulation for relief of pain in underlying structures.
Warnings: For external use only. Avoid getting in eyes or on mucous membranes, broken or irritated skin. Discontinue use if excessive skin irritation develops. If pain lasts more than 7 days, or redness is present, or in conditions affecting children under 12 years of age, consult a physician. Keep product out of children's reach. In case of accidental swallowing, call a physician or contact a poison control center immediately.
Dosage and Administration: Rub generously into painful area, then massage gently until ointment is absorbed and disappears. Reapply every 3 to 4 hours or as needed. Do not bandage.
How Supplied: Available in 1.25 and 3 oz collapsible tubes.

FEMIRON® Tablets

Active Ingredient: (Per Tablet) Iron (from ferrous fumarate) 20 mg.
Indications: For use as an iron supplement.
Actions: Supplements dietary iron intake; helps maintain iron stores.
Warnings: Keep out of reach of children.
Precaution: Alcoholics and individuals with chronic liver or pancreatic disease may have enhanced iron absorption with the potential for iron overload. NOTE: Unabsorbed iron may cause some darkening of the stool.
Drug Interaction Precaution: Taking with antacid or tetracycline may interfere with absorption.
Symptoms and Treatment of Oral Overdose: Toxicity and symptoms are primarily due to iron overdose. Abdominal pain, nausea, vomiting and diarrhea may occur, with possible subsequent acidosis and cardiovasular collapse with severe poisoning. **Treatment:** Induce vomiting immediately. Administer milk, eggs to reduce gastric irritation. Contact a physician immediately.
Dosage and Administration: Women: One tablet daily.
How Supplied: Bottles of 40 and 120 tablets.

FEMIRON® Multi-Vitamins and Iron

Active Ingredients: Iron (from ferrous fumarate) 20 mg; Vitamin A 5,000 I.U.; Vitamin D 400 I.U.; Thiamine (Vitamin B_1) 1.5 mg; Riboflavin (Vitamin B_2) 1.7 mg; Niacinamide 20 mg; Ascorbic Acid (Vitamin C) 60 mg; Pyridoxine (Vitamin B_6) 2 mg; Cyanocobalamin (Vitamin B_{12}) 6 mcg; Calcium Pantothenate 10 mg; Folic Acid .4 mg; and Tocopherol Acetate (Vitamin E) 15 I.U.
Indications: For use as an iron and vitamin supplement.
Actions: Helps insure adequate intake of iron and vitamins.
Warnings: Keep out of reach of children.
Precaution: Alcoholics and individuals with chronic liver or pancreatic disease may have enhanced iron absorption with the potential for iron overload. NOTE: Unabsorbed iron may cause some darkening of the stool.
Symptoms and Treatment of Oral Overdosage: Toxicity and symptoms are primarily due to iron overdose. Abdominal pain, nausea, vomiting and diarrhea may occur, with possible subsequent acidosis and cardiovascular collapse with severe poisoning. **Treatment:** Induce vomiting immediately. Administer milk, eggs to reduce gastric irritation. Contact a physician immediately.
Dosage and Administration: Women: One tablet daily.
How Supplied: Bottles of 35, 60, and 90 tablets.

GERITOL® Liquid
High Potency Iron & Vitamin Tonic

Active Ingredients: Per fluid ounce: Iron (from ferric ammonium citrate) 100 mg; Thiamine (B_1) 5 mg; Riboflavin (B_2) 5 mg; Niacinamide 100 mg; Panthenol 4 mg; Pyridoxine (B_6) 1 mg; Cyanocobalamin(B_{12}) 1.5 mcg; Methionine 50 mg; Choline Bitartrate 100 mg.

Indications: For iron or vitamin deficiency; for use as a dietary supplement.

Actions: Helps prevent deficiency in iron and specific vitamins.

Warnings: Keep out of reach of children.

Precaution: Alcohol accelerates absorption of ferric iron. Alcoholics and individuals with chronic liver or pancreatic disease may have enhanced iron absorption with the potential for iron overload. NOTE: Unabsorbed iron may cause some darkening of the stool.

Symptoms and Treatment of Oral Overdose: Toxicity and symptoms are primarily due to iron overdose. Abdominal pain, nausea, vomiting and diarrhea may occur, with possible subsequent acidosis and cardiovascular collapse with severe poisoning. **Treatment:** Induce vomiting immediately. Administer milk, eggs to reduce gastric irritation. Contact a physician immediately.

Dosage and Administration: For iron or vitamin deficiency, 3 tablespoonsful (1.5 fl. oz.) daily. As an iron and vitamin supplement, one tablespoon (0.5 fl. oz.) daily.

How Supplied: 4 ounce, 12 ounce, 24 ounce bottles.

GERITOL® Mega Vitamins

Active Ingredients: (per tablet) Vitamin A 10,000 I.U.; Vitamin C (Ascorbic Acid) 120 mg; Vitamin B_1 (Thiamine) 15 mg; Vitamin B_2 (Riboflavin) 15 mg; Vitamin B_6 (Pyridoxine) 10 mg; Vitamin B_{12} (Cyanocobalamin) 30 mcg; Niacin 100 mg; Calcium Pantothenate 20 mg; Iron (Ferrous Fumarate) 50 mg.

Indications: For use as a dietary supplement.

Actions: Supplements dietary intake of Vitamin A and C, the B-Complex Pantothenic acid, and iron.

Warnings: Keep out of reach of children.

Drug Interaction: Some interaction between therapeutic agents and micronutrients have been suggested. Individuals taking medications should consult the physician regarding vitamin supplementation.

Precaution: Alcoholics and individuals with chronic liver or pancreatic disease may have enhanced iron absorption with the potential for iron overload. NOTE: Unabsorbed iron may cause some darkening of the stool.

Symptoms and Treatment of Oral Overdose: Toxicity and symptoms are primarily due to iron overdose. Abdominal pain, nausea, vomiting and diarrhea may occur, with possible subsequent acidosis and cardiovascular collapse with severe poisoning. **Treatment:** Induce

vomiting immediately. Administer milk, eggs to reduce gastric irritation. Contact a physician immediately.

Dosage and Administration: As a dietary supplement: One tablet daily.

How Supplied: Bottles of 30, 60, and 100 tablets.

GERITOL® Tablets
High Potency Iron & Vitamin Tablets

Active Ingredients: (Per Tablet) Iron (as ferrous sulfate) 50 mg; Thiamine (Vitamin B_1) 5 mg; Riboflavin (Vitamin B_2) 5 mg; Vitamin C (as Sodium Ascorbate) 75 mg; Niacinamide 30 mg; Calcium Pantothenate 2 mg; Pyridoxine (Vitamin B_6) .5 mg; Cyanocobalamin (Vitamin B_{12}) 3 mcg

Indications: For iron or vitamin deficiency; for use as a dietary supplement.

Actions: Helps prevent deficiency in iron and specific vitamins.

Warnings: Keep out of reach of children.

Precaution: Alcoholics and individuals with chronic liver or pancreatic disease may have enhanced iron absorption with the potential for iron overload. NOTE: Unabsorbed iron may cause some darkening of the stool.

Symptoms and Treatment of Oral Overdose: Toxicity and symptoms are primarily due to iron overdose. Abdominal pain, nausea, vomiting and diarrhea may occur, with possible subsequent acidosis and cardiovascular collapse with severe poisoning. **Treatment:** Induce vomiting immediately. Administer milk, eggs to reduce gastric irritation. Contact a physician immediately.

Dosage and Administration: For iron or vitamin deficiency, 3 tablets daily or as directed by a physician. As a dietary supplement, 1 tablet daily.

How Supplied: Bottles of 14, 24, 40, 80, 100, 180 and 300.

P.V.M. Appetite Control Capsules

Active Ingredient: Each time-release capsule contains phenylpropanolamine hydrochloride, 75 mg.

Indications: For appetite control and weight reduction when used with a low calorie menu plan provided.

Actions: Phenylpropanolamine, a sympathomimetic amine, may act similarly to amphetamine.

Warnings: Do not exceed recommended dosage. Halt medication if nervousness, dizziness, or sleeplessness occur. If suffering from high blood pressure, depression, heart disease, diabetes, kidney disease, thyroid disease, if pregnant or nursing, do not take except under supervision of a physician. Do not take if already taking another medication containing phenylpropanolamine. Not for use by those under 18. Not to be used for periods exceeding 3 months.

Drug Interaction: Phenylpropanolamine may interact with monoamine oxidase inhibitors.

Symptoms and Treatment of Oral Overdosage: Sympathetic stimulation, nervousness, dizziness, elevated blood

pressure. Seek professional assistance, or contact a poison control center at once.

Dosage and Administration: Adults: One capsule at 10:00 a.m. each day.

How Supplied: Packages of 20 and 40 capsules, with nutritionally balanced diet plan.

P.V.M. Appetite Suppressant Tablets

Active Ingredients: Each tablet contains phenylpropanolamine hydrochloride, 25 mg.

Indications: For appetite control and weight reduction when used with a low calorie menu plan provided.

Actions: Phenylpropanolamine, a sympathomimetic amine, may act similarly to amphetamine.

Warnings: Do not exceed recommended dosage. Halt medication if nervousness, dizziness, or sleeplessness occur. If suffering from high blood pressure, depression, heart disease, diabetes, kidney disease, thyroid disease, if pregnant or nursing, do not take except under supervision of a physician. Do not take if already taking another medication containing phenylpropanolamine. Not for use by those under 18. Not to be used for periods exceeding 3 months. Keep out of reach of children.

Drug Interaction: Phenylpropanolamine may interact with monoamine oxidase inhibitors.

Symptoms and Treatment of Oral Overdosage: Sympathetic stimulation, nervousness, dizziness, elevated blood pressure. Seek professional assistance, or contact a poison control center at once.

Dosage and Administration: Adults: One tablet 3 times per day, 30 minutes before each meal.

How Supplied: Packages of 30 and 60 tablets, with nutritionally balanced diet plan.

SERUTAN® Concentrated Powder Laxative

Active Ingredient: Vegetable hemicellulose derived from Plantago Ovata 45%.

Indications: For aiding bowel regularity.

Actions: Softens stools, increases bulk volume and water content.

Warnings: Keep out of the reach of children.

Precaution: Patients with suspected intestinal disorders should consult a physician.

Dosage and Administration: Adults: Stir one heaping teaspoonful into a 6 oz. glass of water. Drink immediately. Take one to three times daily, preferably at mealtime.

How Supplied: $3\frac{1}{2}$ oz, 7 oz, 14 oz, and 21 oz bottles.

SERUTAN® Concentrated Powder —Fruit Flavored Laxative

Active Ingredient: Vegetable hemicellulose derived from Plantago Ovata 45%.

Continued on next page

Williams—Cont.

Indications: For aiding bowel regularity.
Actions: Softens stools, increases bulk volume and water content.
Warnings: Keep out of the reach of children.
Precaution: Patients with suspected intestinal disorders should consult a physician.
Dosage and Administration: Adults: Stir one heaping teaspoonful into a 6 oz. glass of water. Drink immediately. Take one to three times daily, preferably at mealtime.
How Supplied: 3 oz, 6 oz, 12 oz, and 18 oz bottles.

SERUTAN® Toasted Granules Laxative

Active Ingredients: Vegetable hemicellulose derived from Plantago Ovata 39%.
Indications: For aiding bowel regularity.
Actions: Softens stools, increases bulk volume and water content.
Warnings: Keep out of the reach of children.
Precaution: Patients with suspected intestinal disorders should consult a physician. Not to be taken directly by spoon.
Dosage and Administration: Adults: Sprinkle one heaping teaspoonful on cereal or other food, one to three times daily.
How Supplied: Available in 3½, 7, and 18 oz. plastic bottles.

SOMINEX® Sleep Aid

Active Ingredient: Pyrilamine maleate, 25 mg per tablet.
Indications: To induce drowsiness and assist in falling asleep.
Actions: An antihistamine with anticholinergic and sedative effects.
Warnings: Do not give to children under 12 years of age. Do not exceed recommended dosage unless directed by physician. Consult physician if sleeplessness persists continuously for more than 2 weeks. Take product with caution if alcohol has been consumed. Do not take if suffering from asthma, glaucoma, or enlargement of the prostate gland except under the advice and supervision of a physician. Keep product out of the reach of children. In case of accidental overdose, seek professional assistance or contact a poison control center immediately.
Drug Interaction Precaution: The CNS depressant effect of Sominex (pyrilamine maleate) is heightened by alcohol and other CNS depressant drugs.
Symptoms and Treatment of Oral Overdosage: Overdose may result in nausea, vomiting, feverishness, excitability, mydriasis, hallucinations and convulsions. Coma and cardiorespiratory collapse may ensue in severe cases. Approaches to treatment include halting absorption of the drug, inducing emesis, controlling convulsions and assisting ventilation.

Dosage and Administration: Take 2 tablets with water at bedtime.
How Supplied: Available in bottles of 8, 16, 32, 72, 124 tablets, blister packs of 10 capsules.

VIVARIN® Stimulant Tablets

Active Ingredient: 200 mg caffeine alkaloid per tablet. Compounded in a formula containing dextrose.
Indications: For use as a quick stimulant to combat drowsiness.
Actions: Stimulates cerebrocortical areas involved with active mental processes.
Warnings: Keep out of reach of children. For adult use only. Do not take more than 1 tablet in any 4 hour period. Product should not be substituted for normal sleep.
Drug Interaction: Use of caffeine should be lowered or avoided if drugs are being used to treat cardiovascular ailments, psychological problems, or kidney trouble.
Precaution: Higher blood glucose levels may result from caffeine use.
Symptoms and Treatment of Oral Overdosage: Convulsions may occur if caffeine is consumed in doses larger than 10 g. Emesis should be induced to empty the stomach.
Dosage and Administration: Adults: 1 tablet every 4 hours, as needed.
How Supplied: Available in packages of 16, 40 and 80 tablets.

Consumer Products Division
Winthrop Laboratories
Division of Sterling Drug Inc.
90 PARK AVENUE
NEW YORK, NY 10016

BRONKAID® Mist

Description: BRONKAID Mist, brand of epinephrine, USP, 0.5%, contains ascorbic acid as preservative in an inert propellant. Alcohol 33% (w/w). Each activation of the measured dose valve delivers 0.27 mg epinephrine.
Action: Epinephrine is a sympathomimetic amine which relaxes bronchial muscle spasm, as occurs in attacks of bronchial asthma.
Indication: For temporary relief of acute paroxysms of bronchial asthma
Warnings: FOR ORAL INHALATION ONLY. Reduce dosage if nervousness, restlessness, sleeplessness, or bronchial irritation occurs. Do not use if high blood pressure, heart disease, diabetes, or thyroid disease is present, unless directed by a physician. If prompt relief is not obtained, consult your physician.
Avoid spraying in eyes. Contents under pressure. Do not break or incinerate. Do not store at temperature above 120 F. Keep out of reach of children.
Precaution: Children under 6 years of age should use BRONKAID Mist only on the advice of a physician. Avoid indiscriminate use of BRONKAID Mist as many people do with similar medications. Use only when actually needed for relief.

Dosage and Administration: Start with one inhalation, then wait at least one minute. If not relieved, use BRONKAID Mist once more. Do not repeat treatment for at least 4 hours. If difficulty in breathing persists, consult your physician.
Directions for Use:
1. Remove cap and mouthpiece from bottle.
2. Remove cap from mouthpiece.
3. Turn mouthpiece sideways and fit metal stem of nebulizer into hole in flattened end of mouthpiece.
4. Exhale, as completely as possible. Now, hold bottle **upside down** between thumb and forefinger and close lips loosely around end of mouthpiece.
5. Inhale deeply while pressing down firmly on bottle, once only.
6. Remove mouthpiece and hold your breath a moment to allow for maximum absorption of medication. Then exhale slowly through nearly closed lips.
After use, remove mouthpiece from bottle and replace cap. Slide mouthpiece over bottle for protection. When possible, rinse mouthpiece with tap water immediately after use. Soap and water will not hurt it. A clean mouthpiece always works better.
How Supplied: Bottles of ½ fl oz (15 ml) NDC 0024-4082-15 with actuator. Also available—refills (no mouthpiece) in 15 ml (½ fl oz) NDC 0024-4083-16 and 22.5 ml (¾ fl oz) NDC 0024-4083-22

BRONKAID® Mist Suspension

Active Ingredients: Each spray delivers 0.3 mg epinephrine bitartrate equivalent to 0.16 mg epinephrine base. Contains epinephrine bitartrate 7.0 mg per cc in an inert propellant.
Indication: Provides temporary relief from acute paroxysms of bronchial asthma.
Warnings: For INHALATION ONLY. Contents under pressure. Do not puncture or throw container into incinerator. Using or storing near open flame or heating above 120°F may cause bursting. Do not use unless a diagnosis of asthma has been established by a physician. Reduce dosage if bronchial irritation, nervousness, restlessness, or sleeplessness occurs. Overdose may cause nervousness and rapid heartbeat. Use only on the advice of a physician if heart disease, high blood pressure, diabetes, or thyroid disease is present. If difficulty in breathing persists, or if relief does not occur within 20 minutes of inhalation, discontinue use and seek medical assistance immediately. Children under 6 years of age should use BRONKAID Mist Suspension only on the advice of a physician. Keep this and all medicines out of reach of children.
Administration: (1) SHAKE WELL. (2) HOLD INHALER WITH NOZZLE DOWN WHILE USING. Empty the lungs as completely as possible by exhaling. (3) Purse the lips as in saying the letter "O" and hold the nozzle up to the lips, keeping the tongue flat. As you start to

take a deep breath, squeeze nozzle and can together, releasing one full application. Complete taking deep breath, drawing medication into your lungs. (4) Hold breath for as long as comfortable. This distributes the medication in the lungs. Then exhale slowly keeping the lips nearly closed. (5) Rinse nozzle daily with soap and hot water after removing from vial. Dry with clean cloth.

Dosage: Start with one inhalation—then wait at least one minute; if not relieved, use BRONKAID Mist Suspension once more; do not repeat treatment for at least 4 hours.

Professional Labeling: Same as stated under Indication.

How Supplied: $\frac{1}{3}$ fl oz (10 cc) pocket-size aerosol inhaler (NDC 0024-4082-10)

BRONKAID® Tablets

Description: Each tablet contains ephedrine sulfate 24 mg, guaifenesin (glyceryl guaiacolate) 100 mg, and theophylline 100 mg.

Actions: Theophylline and ephedrine both produce bronchodilation through relaxation of bronchial muscle spasm, as occurs in attacks of bronchial asthma, although they do so through different mechanisms. Guaifenesin produces an expectorant action by increasing the water content of bronchial mucus, probably by way of a vagal reflex.

Indication: For symptomatic control of bronchial asthma

Precautions: The recommended dosage of BRONKAID tablets is appropriate for home medication for the symptoms of bronchial congestion and bronchial asthma. If this dosage does not afford relief, and symptoms persist or worsen, it is an indication that the nature of your illness requires the attention of a physician. Under these conditions, or if fever is present, do not experiment with home medications. Consult your physician. Individuals with persistent coughs, high blood pressure, diabetes, heart or thyroid disease should use only as directed by a physician. If dryness of throat, nervousness, restlessness or sleeplessness occurs, discontinue the dosage and consult your physician. Occasionally, in certain individuals, this preparation may cause urinary retention and, if so, discontinue medication. Do not exceed recommended dosage unless directed by a physician.

Dosage and Administration: *Adult Dosage:* 1 tablet every three or four hours. Do not take more than 5 tablets in a 24-hour period. Swallow tablets whole with water.

Children (6 to 12): $\frac{1}{2}$ tablet every three or four hours. Do not administer more than 5 times in a 24-hour period. Do not administer to children under 6 unless directed by a physician. Swallow whole with water.

Morning Dose: An early dose of 1 tablet (for adults) can relieve the coughing and wheezing caused by the night's accumulation of mucus, and can help you start the day with better breathing capacity.

Before an Attack: Many persons feel an attack of asthma coming on. One

BRONKAID tablet beforehand may stop the attack before it starts.

During the Day: The precise dose of BRONKAID tablets can be varied to meet your individual needs as you gain experience with this product. It is advisable to take 1 tablet before going to bed, for nighttime relief. However, be sure not to exceed recommended daily dosage.

How Supplied:
Boxes of 24 (NDC 0024-4081-02)
Boxes of 60 (NDC 0024-4081-06)

CAMPHO–PHENIQUE® Liquid

Description: Contains phenol 4.7% (w/w) and camphor 10.8% (w/w) in an aromatic oily solution.

Actions: Pain-relieving antiseptic for sores, cuts, burns, insect bites, fever blisters, and cold sores.

Indications: For relief of pain and to combat infection from minor injuries and skin lesions.

Warnings: Not for prolonged use. Not to be used on large areas or in or near the eyes. In case of deep or puncture wounds, serious burns, or persisting redness, swelling or pain, discontinue use and consult physician. If rash or infection develops, discontinue use and consult physician. Do not bandage if applied to fingers or toes.

Keep this and all medicines out of children's reach. In case of accidental ingestion, seek professional assistance or contact a poison control center immediately.

Directions for Use: For external use. Apply with cotton three or four times daily.

How Supplied:
Bottles of 1 fl oz (NDC 0024-5150-01)
           2 fl oz (NDC 0024-5150-02)
           4 fl oz (NDC 0024-5150-04)
Also available—*Gel*-in tubes of .23 oz (6.5 g) (NDC 0024-0212-01) and .50 oz (14 g) (NDC 0024-0212-02)

HALEY'S M-O®

Description: An emulsion of Phillips'® Milk of Magnesia with 25 per cent pure mineral oil.

Action: Laxative and lubricant preparation; the mineral oil acting as a lubricant and the Milk of Magnesia as a mild saline cathartic.

Indications: For the relief of constipation especially in patients with hemorrhoids, obstetric and cardiac patients, and in geriatric patients where straining at stool is contraindicated.

Contraindications: Abdominal pain, nausea, vomiting, or other symptoms of appendicitis.

Warnings: Not to be used when abdominal pain, nausea, vomiting, or other symptoms of appendicitis are present. Habitual use of laxatives may result in dependency upon them. When used daily or with frequent regularity, do not take within two hours of a meal because mineral oil may interfere with the absorption of pro-Vitamin A.

Dosage and Administration: *Adults,* 2 tablespoons on arising and at bedtime. *Children 3 to 6 years*—1 to 2 tea-

spoons; *7 to 12 years,* 2 to 4 teaspoons. *Under 3 years,* as directed by physician.

How Supplied: Haley's M-O is available as Regular and Flavored (sugar-free) in bottles of:
Regular— 8 fl oz (NDC 0024-3130-08)
           16 fl oz (NDC 0024-3130-16)
           32 fl oz (NDC 0024-3130-32)
Flavored— 8 fl oz (NDC 0024-3230-08)
            16 fl oz (NDC 0024-3230-16)
            32 fl oz (NDC 0024-3230-32)

Long Acting
NEO–SYNEPHRINE® II
brand of xylometazoline
hydrochloride
Nasal Spray 0.1%
Vapor Nasal Spray 0.1%
Nose Drops 0.1%
Children's Nose Drops 0.05%

Description: *Adult Strength Nasal Spray* and *Nose Drops* contain xylometazoline hydrochloride 0.1% with benzalkonium chloride and thimerosal 0.001% as preservatives. *Adult Strength Vapor Nasal Spray* contains xylometazoline hydrochloride 0.1% with aromatics (menthol, eucalyptol, camphor, methyl salicylate) and benzalkonium chloride and thimerosal 0.001% as preservatives. *Children's Nose Drops* contain xylometazoline hydrochloride 0.05% with benzalkonium chloride and thimerosal 0.001% as preservatives.

Action: Long-acting Nasal Decongestant

Indications: Provides long-lasting, 8 to 10 hour, temporary relief of nasal congestion due to common cold, sinusitis, hay fever, or other upper respiratory allergies, makes breathing through the nose easier, reduces swelling of nasal passages, and shrinks swollen membranes.

Warnings: Nasal Spray 0.1% and Nose Drops 0.1% should be administered only to adults. Do not give this product to children under 12 years. Children's Nose Drops 0.05% should be given only to children from 2 to 12 years of age. Do not give to children under 2 years of age unless under advice and supervision of a physician. Do not exceed recommended dosage because symptoms may occur such as burning, stinging, sneezing, or increase of nasal discharge. Do not use this product for more than three days. If symptoms persist, consult a physician. The use of this dispenser by more than one person may spread infection. Keep this and all drugs out of the reach of children. In case of accidental ingestion, seek professional assistance or contact a poison control center immediately. Do not use if allergic to xylometazoline.

Continued on next page

This product information was effective as of January 1, 1981. On these and other products of Consumer Products Division, Winthrop Laboratories, detailed information may be obtained on a current basis by direct inquiry to 90 Park Avenue, New York, NY 10016 (212) 972-4124.

Winthrop—Cont.

Dosage and Administration: *Spray 0.1% for adults*—Always hold head upright to spray. Insert nosepiece into nostril pointing it slightly backward. To spray, squeeze bottle quickly and firmly. Spray two or three times into each nostril every 8 to 10 hours. Do not use more than three times daily.

Solution 0.1% for adults and children over 12—two or three drops in each nostril every 8 to 10 hours. Do not use more than three times daily.

Solution 0.05% for children 2 through 12 years of age—two or three drops in each nostril every 8 to 10 hours. Do not use more than 3 times daily.

How Supplied: *Nasal Spray Adult Strength*—plastic squeeze bottles of 15 ml (½ fl oz) NDC 0024-1338-01; *Vapor Nasal Spray Adult Strength*—squeeze bottles of 15 ml (½ fl oz) NDC 0024-1339-01.

Nose Drops Adult Strength—bottles of 30 ml (1 fl oz) with dropper NDC 0024-1336-02; *Children's Strength 0.05%*—bottles of 30 ml (1 fl oz) with dropper NDC 0024-1337-02.

NEO-SYNEPHRINE® Hydrochloride brand of phenylephrine hydrochloride

Intranasal Preparations

Action: Rapid-acting nasal decongestant.

Indications: For temporary relief of nasal congestion due to common cold, hay fever or other upper respiratory allergies, or associated with sinusitis.

Precautions: Some hypersensitive individuals may experience a mild stinging sensation. This is usually transient and often disappears after a few applications. Do not exceed recommended dosage. Follow directions for use carefully. If symptoms are not relieved after several applications, a physician should be consulted. Frequent and continued usage of the higher concentrations (especially the 1% solution) occasionally may cause a rebound congestion of the nose. Therefore, long-term or frequent use of this solution is not recommended without the advice of a physician.

Prolonged exposure to air, metal, or strong light will cause oxidation and some loss of potency. Do not use if brown in color or contains a precipitate.

Adverse Reactions: Generally very well tolerated; systemic side effects such as tremor, insomnia, or palpitation rarely occur.

Dosage and Administration: *Topical*—dropper, spray, tampon, irrigation, or displacement. The *0.25% solution* is adequate in most cases (*0.125% for infants*). In resistant cases, or if more powerful decongestion is desired, the *0.5 or 1% solution* should be used. Also used as *0.5% jelly*.

How Supplied: Nasal spray 0.25%—15 ml (for children and for adults who prefer a mild nasal spray)—NDC 0024-1348-

03; nasal spray 0.5%—15 ml (for adults)—NDC 0024-1353-01; nasal solution 0.125% (for infants and small children), 1 fl oz bottles—NDC 0024-1345-02; nasal solution 0.25% (for children and adults who prefer a mild solution), 1 fl oz bottles—NDC 0024-1347-01 and 16 fl oz bottles—NDC 0024-1347-06; nasal solution 0.5% (for adults), 1 fl oz bottles—NDC 0024-1351-01; nasal solution 1% (extra strength for adults), 1 fl oz bottles—NDC 0024-1355-01 and 16 fl oz bottles—NDC 0024-1355-06; and water soluble nasal jelly 0.5%, ⅝ oz tubes—NDC 0024-1367-01.

Also available — NEO-SYNEPHRINE Mentholated Nasal Spray 0.5% (for adults), ½ fl oz bottles—NDC 0024-1364-01.

NTZ® Solution

Description: Contains phenylephrine hydrochloride 0.5%, thenyldiamine hydrochloride 0.1%, and benzalkonium chloride 1:5000 in a buffered solution.

Action: Decongestant nose drops. The antiseptic preservative and wetting agent, benzalkonium chloride, promotes spread and penetration of solution.

Indications: For relief of nasal congestion in the common cold, allergic rhinitis including hay fever, vasomotor rhinitis, acute and chronic sinusitis.

Precautions: Some hypersensitive individuals may experience a mild stinging sensation. The stinging sensation often disappears if the spray or solution is used as recommended.

Do not exceed recommended dosage. Follow directions for use carefully. If symptoms are not relieved after several applications, a physician should be consulted. Frequent and continued usage of NTZ solution occasionally may cause a rebound congestion of the nose. Therefore, long-term or frequent use of this solution is not recommended without the advice of a physician.

Prolonged exposure to air, metal, or strong light will cause oxidation and some loss of potency. Do not use if brown in color or contains a precipitate.

Adverse Reactions: NTZ is well tolerated, with only occasional mild transient stinging on instillation.

Dosage and Administration: Intranasally by spray, dropper, or tampon.

How Supplied: Bottles of 30 ml (1 fl oz) with dropper (NDC 0024-1375-01) Unbreakable plastic squeeze bottles of 22.5 ml (NDC 0024-1377-02) Ample air space above the liquid in the spray bottle assures most efficient operation.

pHisoDerm®

Description: pHisoDerm, sudsing emollient skin cleanser, is a unique liquid emulsion containing Sodium Octoxynol-3 Sulfonate, White Petrolatum, Water, Petrolatum and Lanolin and Lanolin Alcohol, Sodium Benzoate, Octoxynol-1, Methylcellulose, and Lactic Acid. pHisoDerm contains no perfumes and irritating alkali. Its pH value, unlike

that of soap, lies within the pH range of normal skin.

Actions: pHisoDerm is well tolerated and can be used frequently by those persons whose skin may be irritated by the use of soap or other alkaline cleansers, or by those who are sensitive to the fatty acids contained in soap. pHisoDerm contains an effective detergent for removing soil and acts as an active emulsifier of all types of oil—animal, vegetable, and mineral. It is a useful cleanser for the skin, hair, and scalp.

pHisoDerm produces suds when used with any kind of water—hard or soft, hot or cold (even cold sea water)—at any temperature and under acid, alkaline, or neutral conditions.

pHisoDerm deposits a fine film of lanolin cholesterols and petrolatum on the skin during the washing process and, thereby, helps protect against the dryness that soap can cause.

Indications: A sudsing emollient cleanser for use on skin, hair, and scalp of infants, children, and adults.

Useful for removal of ointments, cosmetics, and hair preparations from the skin and scalp.

Directions: For external use only. **HANDS.** Squeeze a few drops of pHisoDerm into the palm, add a little water, and work up a lather. Rinse thoroughly.

FACE. After washing your hands, squeeze a small amount of pHisoDerm into the palm or onto a small sponge or washcloth, and work up a lather by adding a little water. Massage the suds onto the face for approximately one minute. Rinse thoroughly. Avoid getting suds into the eyes.

BATHING. First wet the body. Work a small amount of pHisoDerm into a lather with hands or a soft wet sponge, gradually adding small amounts of water to make more lather. When using a washcloth use more pHisoDerm. Spread the lather over all parts of the body. Rinse thoroughly.

SHAMPOOING. First wet the hair. Apply a small amount of pHisoDerm (depending on the amount and length of hair) for the initial shampoo, rubbing thoroughly. Avoid getting suds into the eyes. Copious suds may not be produced by this preliminary washing. Rinse thoroughly. Repeat the process, using the same amount or an even smaller amount of pHisoDerm. This second shampoo will produce copious suds. Rinse thoroughly and dry.

BABY BATHING. First wet the baby's body. Work a small amount of pHisoDerm into a lather with hands or a soft wet sponge, gradually adding small amounts of water to make more lather. Spread the lather over all parts of the baby's body, including the head. Avoid getting suds into the baby's eyes. Wash the diaper area last. Be sure to carefully cleanse all folds and creases. Rinse thoroughly. Pat the baby dry with a soft towel.

Caution: pHisoDerm suds that get into the eyes accidentally during washing should be rinsed out promptly with a sufficient amount of water.

pHisoDerm is intended for external use only. pHisoDerm should not be poured into measuring cups, medicine bottles, or similar containers since it may be mistaken for baby formula or medications. If swallowed, pHisoDerm may cause gastrointestinal irritation.

pHisoDerm should not be used on persons with sensitivity to any of its components.

How Supplied: pHisoDerm is supplied in three formulations for regular, dry, and oily skin. It is packaged in sanitary squeeze bottles of 5 ounces and 1 pint. The regular formula is also available in squeeze bottles of 9 ounces and plastic bottles of 1 gallon.

Dry Skin Formula: A high emolliency cleansing formulation that is especially suitable for people with dry skin. It can also help prevent dry skin chapping. This formula can be used for bathing babies, children, and adults to keep skin naturally soft and supple.

Oily Skin Formula: A low emolliency cleansing formulation designed for skin that is especially oily. This formulation is not recommended for use in bathing babies.

WinGel®
Liquid and Tablets

Description: Each teaspoon (5 ml) of liquid and each tablet contain a specially processed, short polymer, hexitol stabilized aluminum-magnesium hydroxide equivalent to 180 mg of aluminum hydroxide and 160 mg of magnesium hydroxide. Mint flavored. Smooth, easy-to-chew tablets.

Action: Antacid.

Indications: An antacid for the relief of acid indigestion, heartburn, and sour stomach.

Warnings: *Adults and children over 6*—Patients should not take more than eight teaspoonfuls or eight tablets in a 24-hour period or use the maximum dosage of the product for more than 2 weeks, except under the advice and supervision of a physician.

Absorption of other drugs may be interfered with by the aluminum in the product.

Drug Interaction Precautions: This product should not be taken if the patient is presently taking a prescription antibiotic drug containing any form of tetracycline.

Dosage and Administration: *Adults and children over 6*—1 to 2 teaspoonfuls or 1 to 2 tablets up to four times daily, or as directed by a physician.

Professional Labeling: For the symptomatic relief of hyperacidity associated with the diagnosis of peptic ulcer, gastritis, peptic esophagitis, gastric hyperacidity, and hiatal hernia.

Acid Neutralization: WINGEL Liquid 23.2 mEq/2 teaspoons; WINGEL Tablets 24.6 mEq/2 tablets.

How Supplied: Liquid—bottles of 6 fl oz (NDC 0024-2247-03) and 12 fl oz (NDC 0024-2247-05).
Tablets—boxes of 50 (NDC 0024-2249-05) and 100 (NDC 0024-2249-06).

WYETH LABORATORIES
Division of American Home
Products Corporation
P.O. BOX 8299
PHILADELPHIA, PA 19101

ALUDROX®
Antacid
(alumina and magnesia)
ORAL SUSPENSION • TABLETS

Composition: Nonconstipating, noncathartic, effective and palatable antacid containing, in each 5 ml. teaspoonful of suspension, 307 mg. of aluminum hydroxide as a gel, and 103 mg. of magnesium hydroxide. Each tablet contains 233 mg. aluminum hydroxide as a dried gel and 83 mg. magnesium hydroxide. Sodium content is 0.07 mEq per tablet and 0.05 mEq per 5 ml suspension.

Indications: For the symptomatic relief of hyperacidity associated with the diagnosis of peptic ulcer, gastritis, peptic esophagitis, gastric hyperacidity, and hiatal hernia.

Dosage and Administration: Two tablets or 2 teaspoonfuls (10 ml.) of suspension every four hours, or as required. Suspension may be followed by a sip of water if desired. Tablets are designed to be chewed with or without water. Two ALUDROX tablets have the capacity to neutralize 23 mEq of acid; 10 ml. of ALUDROX suspension have the capacity to neutralize 28 mEq of acid.

Drug Interaction Precautions: This product must not be taken if the patient is presently taking a prescription antibiotic drug containing any form of tetracycline.

How Supplied: *Oral Suspension,* bottles of 12 fluidounces.
Tablets, boxes of 100; each tablet is sealed in cellophane so that a day's supply can be conveniently carried.

AMPHOJEL®
Antacid
(aluminum hydroxide gel)
SUSPENSION • TABLETS

Composition: *Suspension*—Each 5 ml. teaspoonful contains 320 mg. of aluminum hydroxide as a gel, and not more than 0.3 mEq of sodium. *Tablets* contain a dried gel. The 0.3 Gm. (5 grain) strength is equivalent to about 1 teaspoonful of the suspension and the 0.6 Gm. (10 grain) strength is equivalent to about 2 teaspoonfuls.

Indications: For the symptomatic relief of hyperacidity associated with the diagnosis of peptic ulcer, gastritis, peptic esophagitis, gastric hyperacidity, and hiatal hernia.

Dosage: *Suspension*—two teaspoonfuls followed by a sip of water if desired, five or six times daily, between meals and at bedtime. 2 teaspoonfuls have the capacity to neutralize 13 mEq of acid. *Tablets*—Two tablets of the 0.3 Gm. strength, or one tablet of the 0.6 Gm. strength, five or six times daily between meals and at bedtime. 2 tablets have the capacity to neutralize 18 mEq of acid.

Precaution: May cause constipation.

Drug Interaction Precautions: This

product must not be taken if the patient is presently taking a prescription antibiotic drug containing any form of tetracycline.

How Supplied: *Suspension*—Peppermint flavored; without flavor—bottles of 12 fluidounces. *Tablets*—a convenient auxiliary dosage form—0.3 Gm. (5 gr.), bottles of 100; 0.6 Gm. (10 gr.), boxes of 100.

COLLYRIUM
with ephedrine
SOOTHING EYE DROPS

Description: A neutral solution of boric acid and borax, containing 0.4% antipyrine, 0.1% ephedrine and not more than 0.002% thimerosal (mercury derivative).

Indications: Soothes, cleanses and refreshes tired or irritated eyes; eyes smarting from wind, sun glare, smog and minor irritants; eyes irritated by prolonged reading or television viewing or by allergies such as hay fever.

Dosage and Administration: Two or three drops in each eye as required.

Warning: If irritation persists or increases, patients are advised to discontinue use and consult physician. Dropper tip should not be allowed to touch any surface since this may contaminate solution. Do not use in conjunction with a wetting solution for contact lens or other eye lotions containing polyvinyl alcohol. Container should be kept tightly closed and stored at room temperature, approx. 77°F (25°C).

How Supplied: Bottles of ½ fl. oz. with built-in eye dropper.

COLLYRIUM
a neutral borate
solution with antipyrine
SOOTHING EYE LOTION

Description: Containing 0.4% antipyrine, boric acid, borax and not more than 0.002% thimerosal (mercury derivative).

Indications: Soothes, cleanses and refreshes tired or irritated eyes resulting from long use, as in reading or close work or due to exposure to sun, strong light, irritation from dust, wind, etc.

Dosage and Administration: Patients are advised to rinse cup with clean water immediately before and after each use, and avoid contamination of rim and interior surface of cup. The half-filled cup should be pressed tightly to the eye to prevent the escape of the liquid, and the head tilted well backward. Eyelids should be opened wide and eyeball rotated to insure thorough bathing with the lotion.

Warning: If irritation persists or increases, patients are advised to discontinue use and consult physician. Do not use in conjunction with a wetting solution for contact lens or other eye lotions containing polyvinyl alcohol. Container should be kept tightly closed and kept at room temperature, approx. 77°F.

How Supplied: Bottles of 6 fl. oz. with eyecup.

Continued on next page

Wyeth—Cont.

SMA®
Iron fortified
infant formula
READY–TO–FEED
CONCENTRATED LIQUID
POWDER

Breast milk is the preferred feeding for newborns. Infant formula is intended to replace or supplement breast milk when breast-feeding is not possible or is inadequate, or when mothers elect not to breast-feed.

SMA® is unique among prepared formulas for its fat blend, whey-dominated protein composition, amino acid pattern and mineral content. SMA®, utilizing a hybridized safflower (oleic) oil, became the first infant formula offering fat and calcium absorption equal to that of human milk, with a physiologic level of linoleic acid. Thus, the fat blend in SMA® provides a ready source of energy, helps protect infants against neonatal tetany and produces a ratio of Vitamin E to polyunsaturated fatty acids (linoleic acid) more than adequate to prevent hemolytic anemia.

By combining demineralized whey with skimmed cow's milk, SMA® adjusts the protein content to within the range of human milk, reverses the lactalbumin-casein ratio of cow's milk so that it is identical to that of human milk, and reduces the mineral content to a physiologic level.

The resultant 60:40 lactalbumin-casein ratio provides protein nutrition superior to a casein-dominated formula. In addition, the essential amino acids, including cystine, are present in amounts close to those of human milk. So the protein in SMA® is of high biologic value.

The physiologic mineral content makes possible a low renal solute load which helps protect the functionally immature infant kidney, increases expendable water reserves and helps protect against dehydration.

Use of lactose as the carbohydrate results in a physiologic stool flora and a low stool pH, decreasing the incidence of perianal dermatitis.

Ingredients: SMA® Concentrated Liquid or Ready-to-Feed. Water; nonfat milk; demineralized (electrodialyzed) whey; lactose; oleo, coconut, oleic (safflower), and soybean oils; soy lecithin; calcium carrageenan. *Minerals:* Potassium bicarbonate; calcium chloride and citrate; potassium chloride; sodium citrate; ferrous sulfate; sodium bicarbonate; zinc, cupric, and manganese sulfates. *Vitamins:* Ascorbic acid, d-alpha tocopheryl acetate, niacinamide, vitamin A palmitate, calcium pantothenate, thiamine hydrochloride, riboflavin, pyridoxine hydrochloride, beta-carotene, folic acid, phytonadione, activated 7-dehydrocholesterol, biotin, cyanocobalamin.

SMA® Powder. Nonfat milk; demineralized (electrodialyzed) whey; lactose; oleo, coconut, oleic (safflower), and soybean oils; soy lecithin.
Minerals: Calcium chloride; sodium bicarbonate; calcium citrate; ferrous sulfate; potassium hydroxide and bicarbonate; potassium chloride; zinc, cupric, and manganese sulfates. *Vitamins:* Ascorbic acid, d-alpha tocopheryl acetate, niacinamide, vitamin A palmitate, calcium pantothenate, thiamine hydrochloride, riboflavin, pyridoxine hydrochloride, riboflavin, pyridoxine hydrochloride, beta-carotene, folic acid, phytonadione, activated 7-dehydrocholesterol, biotin, cyanocobalamin.

PROXIMATE ANALYSIS
at 20 calories per fluidounce
READY-TO-FEED, POWDER, and
CONCENTRATED LIQUID:

	(w/v)
Fat	3.6%
Carbohydrate	7.2%
Protein	1.5%
60% Lactalbumin (whey protein)	0.9%
40% Casein	0.6%
Ash	0.25%
Crude Fiber	None
Total Solids	12.6%
Calories/fl. oz.	20

Vitamins, Minerals: In normal dilution, each quart contains 2500 I.U. vitamin A, 400 I.U. vitamin D$_3$, 9 I.U. vitamin E, 55 mcg. vitamin K$_1$, 0.67 mg. vitamin B$_1$ (thiamine), 1 mg. vitamin B$_2$ (riboflavin), 55 mg. vitamin C (ascorbic acid), 0.4 mg. vitamin B$_6$ (pyridoxine hydrochloride), 1 mcg. vitamin B$_{12}$, 9.5 mg. equivalents niacin, 2 mg. pantothenic acid, 50 mcg. folic acid, 14 mcg. biotin, 130 mg. choline, 420 mg. calcium, 312 mg. phosphorus, 50 mg. magnesium, 142 mg. sodium, 530 mg. potassium, 350 mg. chloride, 12 mg. iron, 0.45 mg. copper, 3.5 mg. zinc, 150 mcg. manganese, 65 mcg. iodine.

Preparation: *Ready-to-Feed* (8 and 32 fl. oz. cans of 20 calories per fluidounce formula)—shake can, open and pour into previously sterilized nursing bottle; attach nipple and feed. Cover opened can and store in refrigerator. Use contents of can within 48 hours of opening.
Powder—For normal dilution supplying 20 calories per fluidounce, use 1 scoop (or 1 standard tablespoonful) of powder, packed and leveled, to 2 fluidounces of water. For larger amount of formula, use ¼ standard measuring cup of powder, packed and leveled, to 8 fluidounces (1 cup) of water. Three of these portions make 26 fluidounces of formula.
Concentrated Liquid—For normal dilution supplying 20 calories per fluidounce, use equal amounts of SMA® liquid and water.

How Supplied: *Ready-to-Feed*—presterilized and premixed, 32 fluidounce (1 quart) cans, cases of 6; 8 fluidounce cans, case of 24 (4 carriers of 6 cans). *Powder*—1 pound cans with measuring scoop, cases of 12. *Concentrated Liquid*—13 fluidounce cans, cases of 24.

Also Available: NURSOY® (soy protein formula), for infants with special feeding needs, soy protein replaces the cow's milk protein in the formula. Does not contain corn syrup solids.
Concentrated Liquid, 13 fl. oz. cans, cases of 24. Ready-to-Feed, 32 fl. oz. cans, cases of 6.

Preparation of the standard 20 calories per fluidounce formula of NURSOY Ready-to-Feed and Concentrated Liquid is the same as for SMA® Ready-to-Feed and Concentrated Liquid respectively given above.

SIMECO®
Antacid—Antiflatulent
(aluminum hydroxide gel, magnesium hydroxide, simethicone)
SUSPENSION

Composition: Each teaspoonful (5 ml) contains aluminum hydroxide gel equivalent to 365 mg of dried gel, USP, 300 mg of magnesium hydroxide and 30 mg of simethicone. Sodium content is 0.3 mEq-0.6 mEq per teaspoonful. High potency and low dose are provided by high concentration of antacid per teaspoonful.

Indications: For the symptomatic relief of hyperacidity associated with the diagnosis of peptic ulcer, gastritis, peptic esophagitis, gastric hyperacidity and hiatal hernia. To relieve the symptoms of gas.

Dosage and Administration: Usually: 1 or 2 teaspoonfuls undiluted or with a little water to be taken 3 or 4 times daily between meals and at bedtime. 5 ml SIMECO suspension neutralizes 22 mEq of acid.

Drug Interaction Precautions: Alumina-containing antacids should not be used concomitantly with any form of tetracycline therapy.

How Supplied: Suspension—Cool mint flavor, available in 12 fl. oz. plastic bottles.

WYANOIDS®
Hemorrhoidal Suppositories

Description: Each suppository contains 15 mg extract belladonna (0.19 mg equiv. total alkaloids), 3 mg ephedrine sulfate, zinc oxide, boric acid, bismuth oxyiodide, bismuth subcarbonate, and peruvian balsam in cocoa butter and beeswax. Wyeth Wyanoids have an unusual "torpedo" design which facilitates insertion and insures retention.

Indications: For the temporary relief of pain and itching of hemorrhoidal tissue in many cases.

Warning: Not to be used by persons having glaucoma or excessive pressure within the eye, by elderly persons (where undiagnosed glaucoma or excessive pressure within the eye occurs most frequently), or by children under 6 years of age, unless directed by a physician. Discontinue use if blurring of vision, rapid pulse, or dizziness occurs. Do not exceed recommended dosage. Not for frequent or prolonged use. If dryness of the mouth occurs, decrease dosage. If eye pain occurs, discontinue use and see your physician immediately as this may indicate undiagnosed glaucoma. In case of rectal bleeding, consult physician promptly.

Usual Dosage: One suppository twice daily for six days.

Directions: Remove wrapper of suppository and insert suppository rectally with gentle pressure, pointed end first. Use preferably upon arising and at bedtime.

How Supplied: Boxes of 12.

Also Available: Wyanoid® Hemorrhoidal Ointment.
The ointment contains zinc oxide, boric acid, ephedrine sulfate, benzocaine and peruvian balsam in a soothing emollient base. Tubes of 1 ounce with applicator.

Minor Health Problems

A Guide to Self-Treatment

Of the many afflictions that humans are subjected to, most of them are more an inconvenience than a threat to everyday functioning. The common cold, athlete's foot, and many other ills can usually be self-treated with products obtainable without a prescription. If you follow the instructions that accompany these products, most will probably relieve the symptoms and cause no harmful effects. And as the instructions say, if the condition is not helped by the product being used, you should see your doctor.

The following descriptions of minor ailments you may wish to treat yourself were excerpted from the book, Consumer's Guide to OTC Remedies, written by Richard Harkness, a pharmacist who believes that the more you know about self-treatment products, the more wisely you will use them. In his book, he goes into greater detail about specific medications and how they work.

Acne

Acne is an inflammatory skin disease characterized by pimples, blackheads, and whiteheads. It is caused by increased activity of the sebaceous glands in the skin which normally produce the oils for the proper lubrication of the skin and hair. Teenagers are the most frequent victims of this condition because of the excess amounts of hormones their bodies produce during this period of growth which cause an excess production of oils that become blocked in the pores.

Except in cases of severe acne which should be treated by a dermatologist, most teenagers treat themselves with one or more of the many products available. These remedies fall into three classes: keratolytic drying and peeling preparations, plain skin cleansers, and vitamin A.

Allergy

The reason you feel so miserable when you have an allergy is that histamine is released in your body in response to the thing you are allergic to. The most common example of allergy is hay fever which is usually not caused by hay at all, but by pollens from many plants. Dusts, molds, and foods may also contribute to the symptoms—itchy nose, mouth, and throat, watery nose, sneezing, sensitivity to light, headache, irritability, insomnia, and lack of appetite. These symptoms are treated with some of the same preparations used to treat the common cold—decongestants and especially antihistamines.

Some allergies are so severe that they require treatment by a doctor who specializes in allergies. He builds up the patient's immunity to a particular allergy-causing substance by giving the patient a series of injections of small amounts of the substance.

Asthma, Bronchitis, and Emphysema

These three conditions are sometimes called wheeze diseases because of their effects on the lungs. They may be complicated by bacterial infection, but probably stem from more than one cause, including cigarette smoking and air pollution.

Bronchial asthma may have an allergic basis. The bronchial vessels in the lungs constrict when irritated and make breathing difficult. Bronchodilators, antihistamines, expectorants, and sedatives are some of the agents used to treat this condition.

Bronchitis is similar to asthma in that the bronchioles in the lungs are obstructed by mucus secretions and swollen membranes. Unlike asthma, however, bronchitis is not accompanied by spasm. The condition occurs mostly in middle-aged people, and is characterized by a cough that brings up thick yellow mucus. Cough medicine containing a decongestant to dilate bronchial passages, and an expectorant to loosen mucus is used for self treatment. Cough medicine containing a cough suppressant should generally be avoided because the cough is needed to bring up the mucus.

Emphysema is a lung condition in which the structures have deteriorated over the years, sometimes due to chronic bronchitis or bronchial asthma. It is often further aggravated by infections, air pollution, and cigarette smoking. Shortness of breath is the most common symptom. Cough medicine containing a decongestant and expectorant, but not a cough suppressant, helps expel mucus and phlegm from clogged bronchial passages. Bronchodilators may also be used.

Burns and Sunburn

A burn is the result of damage to the skin caused by heat from fire, electricity, chemicals, radioactivity, or friction. Sunburn results from over-exposure to ultraviolet light either from a sunlamp or the sun itself. The seriousness of a burn depends on the depth of damage to the skin and the extent of the area involved. A first degree burn is the least serious, resulting in pain and redness, but no blistering. A second-degree burn causes blisters. A third-degree burn is the most serious because it destroys skin and tissues, and, depending on the size of the area of skin burned, may cause shock and other serious problems.

You should limit yourself to treating only first and second degree heat burns, and milder forms of sunburn. Some products contain only a local anesthetic to relieve pain, and others contain an antiseptic which is useful for preventing blisters from becoming infected.

The best way to avoid sunburn is to use sunscreen products containing chemicals which filter out the burning rays of the sun, but allow the tanning rays to come through.

Take care to reapply them after swimming, or if you have been perspiring heavily.

The Common Cold

The most widespread single human illness is the common cold (coryza). Over 100 different viruses can cause this upper respiratory infection, and scientists for years have been trying to find a vaccine to protect against it—to no avail.

The cold virus is spread by coughing, sneezing, and direct contact. It is capable of living on inanimate objects such as handkerchiefs and eating utensils for hours. A cold usually lasts from two to seven days, but the symptoms—stuffy nose, sniffles, sneezing, and a general uncomfortable feeling—may make you want to seek some relief. There are many products on the market that will make these cold symptoms more tolerable—decongestants, antihistamines, pain relievers, and many others. Of course, if your cold is accompanied by fever, you will need rest, and advice from your doctor.

Constipation

Constipation is an abnormally slow movement of feces through the colon or large intestine. Most people are aware of what is abnormal for them, even though their habits may differ from another person's. Quite often constipation is caused by ignoring a natural urge to defecate because you are too busy doing something else like working or traveling. Any change in customary routine or diet, taking certain drugs, and stress or emotional upset can lead to constipation.

If you feel that your constipation must be treated, there are four basic types of laxatives to choose from; stimulants, salines, bulk formers, and lubricant-softeners. But remember—don't take a laxative if you have abdominal pain, nausea, or vomiting—symptoms which may indicate appendicitis. This calls for the advice of a doctor.

Cough

Coughs frequently accompany colds because of congestion in the lungs and throat. The cough is a natural reflex of the body in its efforts to get rid of phlegm from the air passages. Sometimes, however, coughing is dry and brings up no phlegm, which only irritates the air passages more. This kind of cough is the one most respon-sive to cough preparations which usually contain two basic types of drugs—cough suppressants and expectorants.

Another way to ease a cough is to use a vaporizer or humidifier which raises the moisture content in the sick room to help sooth and lubricate dried breathing passages.

Coughs that hang on for weeks need the attention of a doctor.

Dandruff

Dandruff is a common problem which is a result of oversecretion of the sebaceous glands. The scaling is sometimes accompanied by itching and inflammation. Severe cases require treatment by a dermatologist.

Products for treatment of dandruff contain one of these agents: keratolytic agents, tars, zinc pyrithione, or selenium sulfide. One of the milder medicated shampoos may be used regularly to keep dandruff under control.

Diaper rash and Prickly Heat

Diaper rash is an acute inflammtion of an infant's buttocks and groin caused by bacteria that decompose urine into ammonia. The ammonia breaks down the natural protective skin oils and irritation results.

Prickly heat, or heat rash is an acute irritation of the skin caused by blocked sweat ducts. This occurs mostly during hot, humid weather, or when too much clothing causes heavy sweating. This condition can occur in both infants and adults and is characterized by clusters of pinhead-size bumps that burn and itch.

These conditions are treated with one or more of the following agents; protectants which form a cover and/or absorb moisture, antiseptics to inhibit germ growth, healing agents, and antifungal agents.

Diarrhea

Diarrhea is the opposite of constipation. The symptoms are frequent passage of unformed and watery stools, sometimes accompanied by abdominal pain caused by the activity of the colon as it pushes waste matter along too fast. Diarrhea can be caused by bacterial or viral infection, eating spoiled food, or changes in the intestine caused by unfamiliar food and drink experienced while traveling. Some drugs, such as antibiotics, can also cause diarrhea.

Most products used to treat diarrhea contain an adsorbant which binds the bacteria or toxins causing the diarrhea and transports them through the intestines to be excreted. These products may also contain a substance which slows down the action of the intestine.

If diarrhea occurs in an on-again, off-again pattern over an extended period of time, it may be a sign that something is wrong and the help of a doctor is needed.

The Eyes

Redness, tearing or watering, stinging, itching, and swelling or congestion of the eyes when caused by allergy or minor irritation can often be treated with non-prescription products. However, if the condition lingers on, or you have any pain or blurring of vision, or an eye injury, you should promptly visit an eye doctor.

Eye preparations are of three basic types: decongestants—the only ones containing an active drug—artificial tears, and eye washes. People with glaucoma should avoid using any product containing a decongestant.

Feminine Hygiene

Deodorant sprays for application to the exterior vaginal area, and various types of douches for internal vaginal use are available.

Fungal Infections: Athlete's Foot, Jock Itch, Ringworm

Athlete's foot infection occurs between the toes and on the sole and heel of the foot. The skin may split and crack, and the primary discomfort is intense itching, often accompanied by burning and stinging. The disease is probably spread from one person to another through the use of common shower or dressing facilities that harbor the fungus. Excessive perspiration, heat, and shoes that give poor ventilation allow the condition to fester.

Jock itch infection is confined to the groin area where an athletic supporter (jock strap) is worn. This causes intense itching, and is aggravated by perspiration, heat, and poor ventilation.

Ringworm can occur anywhere on the body. It usually forms as a well-defined circular skin lesion about the size of a quarter, and it burns and itches.

All three of these conditions are treated with the same products, which contain antifungal agents and keratolytic agents.

Hemmorhoids

Hemmorhoids are small veins in or just on the outside of the rectum which have become swollen and inflamed because the flow of blood through them has become partially obstructed. This can be the result of straining at stool because of constipation, irritation from diarrhea, prolonged standing or sitting, or abdominal pressure caused by pregnancy. Bleeding, itching, burning, and soreness often are the uncomfortable result of hemmorhoids. Many people seek relief from non-prescription products they can purchase, however, if you suspect that you have hemmorhoids, you should confirm this with your doctor.

There are four basic types of agents used to alleviate hemmorhoid symptoms: anesthetics to relieve pain, astringents to constrict or draw together the swollen tissues, antiseptics to prevent infection, and lubricant-softeners for a soothing effect. Some products contain a combination of two or more of these agents, either in ointment or suppository form.

Indigestion

Everyone suffers from indigestion at one time or another. It can be caused by overindulgence in food or alcohol, poor chewing habits, swallowing air while eating, and certain drugs. Emotional upset can also cause indigestion, which complicates things even more.

The symptoms of indigestion include "heartburn," sour or acid stomach, cramps, nausea, and excessive gas. Fortunately most of these symptoms are not long-lasting, and easily respond to antacid products. Some products contain an extra ingredient to help with the gas problem.

If indigestion seems severe or occurs too frequently, it is advisable that you see a doctor.

Insomnia

Almost everyone experiences occasional sleeplessness. Lying awake, tossing and turning, is unpleasant, and can be harmful if too much sleep is lost. The principal ingredients used in non-prescription sleep aids are antihistamines because of their tendency to induce drowsiness.

If insomnia has become a constant problem for you, consult your doctor.

Liniments and Ointments for Arthritis

Besides the analgesics you take internally to treat arthritic pain, there are those that can be rubbed on the skin for relief of local pain. They are counterirritants that dilate the small blood vessels and bring blood closer to the skin's surface, producing increased circulation and warmth. Most of these compounds are "volatile oils" which have a familiar and pleasant odor. Oil of wintergreen, menthol, camphor, and turpentine oil are the most commonly used.

You must be careful when using these products not to cover them with bandages, because this may cause the skin to blister.

Menstrual Problems

The most common symptoms experienced before and during menstruation are irritability, bloating of the abdomen, and increased tenderness of the breasts. Sometimes there is also sharp, cramping pain in the pelvic region, and headache or upset stomach.

Most products used for this condition are pain relievers. Some have agents to decrease bloating, cramping, and tension.

Pain

Pain is nature's way of protecting you from the hazards of your environment. Without this warning signal, you wouldn't snatch you hand away from a hot stove, or know when you had torn a ligament in your ankle, or that you are developing an infection or disease. Fortunately, pain by its nature and severity will also tell you when to go to a doctor.

Sometimes pain comes from things that are not too serious, but are annoying. A headache, toothache, or minor arthritic or muscular ache will generally be temporarily relieved by an analgesic.

There are four basic analgesics available, either alone or in combination—aspirin, salicylamide, phenacetin, and acetaminophen. Some products also contain caffeine, which is not an analgesic. Caffeine is thought to be of value because it constricts dilated blood vessels which may be contributing to the headache.

Poison Ivy, Poison Oak, and Insect Bites and Stings

The reactions produced by contact with poison ivy, poison oak, poison sumac, and insect bites and stings are all the result of allergic reactions to substances foreign to the body. This results in inflammation and swelling of the skin, and intense itching. Treatment is needed to protect the injured skin, reduce itching, and reduce the chances of infection caused by scratching.

Some people are extremely sensitive to certain insect stings and may require emergency treatment at a hospital.

Five types of drugs are used to treat the symptoms of plant and insect-caused skin inflammation: local anesthetics, antihistamines, antiseptics, astringents, and hydrocortisone. Some products combine several of these drugs.

Psoriasis

Psoriasis is often confused with eczema, a term associated with many types of chronic skin disorders. Even dermatologists sometimes have difficulty differentiating between the two. Psoriasis is a chronic skin disease characterized by reddish patches covered with shiny, silvery scales. No one knows what causes it, and so far there is no certain cure. The lesions form, heal without scarring, and recur. They most commonly occur on the elbows and knees, the scalp, the back, and the buttocks. Psoriasis usually itches, but not as much as eczema.

The products used to treat psoriasis usually contain keratolytic agents or tars, or both.

Vitamins and Minerals

Vitamins are chemical compounds found in plants and animals which are necessary to maintain normal growth and metabolism of the body. Most vitamins cannot be manufactured by the body, so have to be gotten from the food you eat or from vitamin supplements. The same is true for minerals.

Most experts agree that the best way to get the proper vitamin and mineral intake is to eat a balanced diet. This is easier said than done, however. Some people do not or cannot plan and prepare a proper diet, either because they can't afford it, or they have developed poor eating habits. Foods that are cooked or processed often lose much of their vitamins. In addition, vitamin requirements increase during certain events in life such as pregnancy, illness, or dieting. However, when the diet is inadequate, necessary nutrients can be obtained from vitamin-mineral supplements.

Vitamins

Vitamin A is essential for healthy skin and hair, and necessary for adequate vision in dim light. It is found in milk, cream, butter, egg yolk, green leafy and yellow vegetables, and fish liver oils.

Vitamin B_1 (thiamine) is essential for normal digestion of food, because it helps digest carbohydrates into energy and fat. It is also essential for nerve cell and heart tissue function. It is found in dried yeast, fish, lean meat, liver, pork, poultry, milk, nuts, potatoes, and legumes (peas and beans).

Vitamin B_2 (riboflavin) helps maintain healthy skin, build and maintain body tissues, and use of oxygen by the cells. Milk, cheese, liver, lean meat, eggs, and leafy green vegetables provide this vitamin.

Vitamin B_3 (niacin) helps keep the body tissues in healthy condition, and the central nervous system functioning. Found in dried yeast, liver, lean meat, fish, eggs, whole-grains, and legumes.

Vitamin B_5 (pantothenic acid) is involved in the metabolism of carbohydrates, fats, and proteins. It also aids energy production, keeps the nervous system and gastrointestinal tract in healthy condition, and plays a role in immunity. Found in dried yeast, liver, eggs, nuts, kidney, and green leafy vegetables.

Vitamin B_6 (pyridoxine) aids the metabolism of proteins and fats, and is essential for proper cell function. Found in dried yeast, liver, organ meats, fish, vegetables, whole grain cereals, and legumes.

Vitamin B_{12} (cyanocobalamin) is needed to synthesize hemoglobin and the development of healthy red blood cells. It is also essential for nerve cell function and helps prevent certain forms of anemia. Sources are liver, kidney, lean meat, eggs, milk and milk products, salt-water fish, oysters, and meats in general.

Folic acid (B_9) helps in the manufacture of red blood cells and metabolism of food to energy. It's found in organ meats, liver, dried yeast, leafy green vegetables, and fruits.

Vitamin C (ascorbic acid) is essential for normal teeth, bones, blood vessels, formation of collagen (a protein that helps support body structures), wound healing, and is an antioxidant that helps the body absorb and use iron from food. It's found in citrus fruits, tomatoes, potatoes, cantaloupe, berries, cabbage, green pepper, and green leafy vegetables.

Vitamin D (calciferol) promotes absorption of calcium and phosphorus to make strong bones and teeth. From fish liver oils, salmon, tuna, egg yolk, butter, and ultra-violet light.

Vitamin E (alpha-tocopherol) is an antioxidant that helps prevent oxygen from destroying other substances in the body and is needed for stability of muscle, red blood cell tissue, and membranes. Vegetable oils, whole grain cereals, wheat germ, leafy vegetables, lettuce, egg yolk, and legumes contain this vitamin.

Vitamin K is essential for the formation of prothrombin, a substance necessary for normal blood clotting. This vitamin is available on prescription only for special conditions. It occurs naturally in leafy vegetables, pork liver, and vegetable oils. The body also makes its own.

Minerals

Minerals play an important role in fluid electrolyte balance, acid-base regulation, enzyme activation, blood clotting, and other areas such as potassium and calcium function in extracellular body fluids to ensure normal muscle activity. A proper proportion of calcium to phosphorus is necessary for good bone development. Iron is an important component of blood hemoglobin, as zinc is to insulin, and iodine is to thyroxin. Copper, magnesium, fluorine, chromium, and selenium are the other essential minerals.

Dosage Recommendations

A term you see on vitamin and mineral product labels is RDA (Recommended Daily Dietary Allowances). The RDA was established by the National Research Council as a guide to the amounts of vitamins needed for maintenance of good nutrition. Vitamin and mineral amounts are expressed as milligrams (mg.), micrograms (mcg.), or International Units (I.U.)

Vitamin and Mineral Interactions

● Iron absorption is decreased by antacids, and increased by vitamin C, when taken at the same time.

- Vitamin C effectiveness is reduced by aspirin.
- Vitamin B_{12} activity is reduced by vitamin C when they are taken together.
- Vitamin A activity is increased by vitamin C and vitamin E.
- Vitamin E activity is increased by vitamin C and reduced by iron when they are taken together.
- The absorption of fat-soluble vitamins (A, D, E, and K) is diminished by mineral oil laxative.
- The minerals, iron, calcium, and zinc, interfere with absorption of tetracycline antibiotic, so should not be taken within two hours of each other.

Warts and Corns

Warts and corns are both growths on the skin, but each has a different cause. Corns are caused by mechanical pressure and friction, usually from improperly fitted shoes or a foot deformity. Hard corns are found on the outer areas of the toes, while soft ones form between the toes. Warts are caused by a virus which can be passed by contact from one person to another. There are several different types of warts, but the common wart is sharply outlined, firm, rough, and light gray to grayish black in color. They grow most frequently on the back of the hands and fingers.

Keratolytic and caustic agents are used for treatment.

Weight Reduction

If you eat more food over an extended period of time than your body requires for producing energy it will be stored as fat and you will become overweight. To help curb the appetite or reduce the amount of food you eat, there are six different classes of products. Bulk formers make you feel full and thus you eat less. Glucose preparations raise your blood glucose levels and make you feel like you don't need as much to eat. Phenylpropanolamine is a vasoconstrictor that acts as an appetite suppressant. Benzocaine acts as a local anesthetic in your mouth and numbs your taste buds. Dietary or low-calorie food substitutes used in one meal a day cut down total calorie intake. And artificial sweeteners give you that sweet taste without the calories of sugar.

Worm Infestations

Worms are parasites that must have a host, human or animal, to remain alive. It is estimated that about one-third of the world's population harbors worms, especially in areas where health and sanitation conditions are poor.

Worm eggs or larvae are transmitted by contaminated hands or food to the mouth and are swallowed. They live and grow as parasites in the intestines, and their eggs are expelled in the stool to start the cycle all over again.

Symptoms of worm infestation are vague and may go unnoticed until an adult worm is discovered in the stool. Pinworm infestations can cause intense itching in the anal region. Roundworms may cause only vague abdominal pain, but can grow to several inches and are capable of using up significant amounts of the host's food.

Gentian violet is the only non-prescription agent available. It is used to eradicate pinworms. Other parasitic infections require prescription drugs for treatment. It's advisable to use a product prescribed by your physician in treating any worm infestation.

MEMORANDUM

Directory of Poison Control Centers

The Directory of Poison Control Centers has been compiled from information furnished by the National Clearinghouse for Poison Control Centers, Bureau of Drugs, 5600 Fishers Lane, Room 1347, Rockville, Md. 20857.
It includes those facilities which provide for the medical profession, on a 24-hour basis, information concerning the prevention and treatment of accidents involving ingestion of poisonous and potentially poisonous substances. Unless otherwise noted, inquiries should be addressed to: Poison Control Center

First Aid for Possible Poisoning

REMEMBER: ANY NON-FOOD SUBSTANCE MAY BE POISONOUS!

1. Keep all potential poisons—household products and medicines—out of the reach of small children.
2. Use "safety caps" (child-resistant containers) as intended to avoid accidents.
3. Have 1 oz. Syrup of Ipecac in your home and in your first aid kit for camping, travel, etc.
4. Keep your Poison Center's and your physician's phone number handy.

IF YOU THINK AN ACCIDENTAL INGESTION HAS OCCURRED:

1. Keep calm—do not wait for symptoms—call for help promptly!
2. Find out if the substance is toxic—Your Poison Control Center (listed by state and city on the following pages) or your physician can tell you if a risk exists and what you should do.
3. Have the product's container or label with you at the phone.

   A. IF A POISON IS ON THE SKIN:
   Immediately remove affected clothing.
   Flood involved parts of body with water, wash with soap or detergent and rinse thoroughly.

   B. IF A POISON IS IN THE EYE:
   Immediately flush the eye with water for 10 to 15 minutes.

   C. IF A POISON IS INHALED:
   Immediately get the person to fresh air. Give mouth to mouth resuscitation if necessary.

   D. IF VOMITING HAS BEEN RECOMMENDED:
   Give one tablespoon of Ipecac syrup followed by a glass (8 oz.) of clear liquid (water, juices, or pop). If the patient doesn't vomit within 15 to 20 minutes, give another tablespoon of Ipecac and more water. Do *not* use salt water. It can be dangerous.

NEVER INDUCE VOMITING IF:

1. The victim is in COMA (unconscious).
2. The victim is CONVULSING (having a fit or a seizure).
3. The victim has swallowed a CAUSTIC or CORROSIVE (e.g. LYE).

FOR REEMPHASIS:

1. Always call to be certain of possible toxicity before undertaking treatment.
2. Never induce vomiting until you are instructed to do so.
3. Do not rely on the label's antidote information—it may be out of date—call instead!
4. If you have to go to an Emergency Room, take the tablets, capsules, container, and/or label with you.
5. Don't hesitate to call your Poison Center or your doctor a second time if the victim seems to be getting worse.

Prepared by:
American Association of Poison Control Centers, William O. Robertson, M.D., Secretary

Directory of Poison Control Centers

ALABAMA

STATE COORDINATOR
Department of Public Health   832-3194
Montgomery 36117
Anniston
N.E. Alabama Regional Medical   237-5421
Center   Ext. 307
400 E. 10th St. 36201
Auburn
Auburn University   826-4037
School of Pharmacy 36830
Birmingham
Children's Hospital   933-4000
1601 6th Ave., S. 35233
Dothan
Southeast Alabama   794-3131
Medical Center 36301
Florence
Eliza Coffee Memorial Hospital   767-1111
P.O. Box 1079   Ext. 2046
600 W. Alabama St. 35630
Gadsden
Baptist Memorial Hospital   492-8111
1007 Goodyear Avenue 35903
Huntsville
Huntsville Hospital   539-6320
101 Sivley Road 35801
Mobile
University of So. Alabama   473-3325
Medical Center
2451 Fillingim St. 36617
Opelika
Lee County Hospital   749-3411
2000 Pepperill Parkway 36801
Tuskegee
John A. Andrews Hospital   727-8583
Tuskegee Institute 36088

ALASKA

STATE COORDINATOR
Department of Health &   465-3100
Social Services
Juneau 99811
Anchorage
Providence Hospital   274-6535
3200 Providence Dr. 99504

ARIZONA

STATE COORDINATOR
College of Pharmacy   626-6016
University of Arizona
Tucson 85724
Flagstaff
Flagstaff Hospital and   774-5233
Medical Center of Northern Arizona
1215 N. Beaver St. 86001
Phoenix
St. Luke's Hospital and Medical Center   253-3334
525 N. 18th St. 85006
Tucson
Arizona Hlth. Sciences Ctr.   626-6016
University of Arizona 85724
Yuma
Yuma Regional Med. Center   344-2000
Avenue A and 24th St. 85364   Ext. 321

ARKANSAS

STATE COORDINATOR
Department of Health   661-2397
Little Rock 72201
El Dorado
Warner Brown Hospital   863-2266
460 West Oak St. 71730
Fort Smith
St. Edward's Mercy Medical Center   452-5100
7301 Rogers Avenue 72903   Ext. 2043
Sparks Regional Med. Center   441-5011
1311 S. Eye St. 72901
Harrison
Boone County Hospital   741-6141
620 N. Willow St. 72601   Ext. 275, 276
Helena
Helena Hospital   338-6411
Newman Drive 72342   Ext. 340
Little Rock
Univ. of Arkansas Medical Center   661-6161
4301 W. Markham St. 72201
Osceola
Osceola Memorial Hospital   563-7180
611 Lee Ave. West 72370
Pine Bluff
Jefferson Hospital   535-6800
1515 W. 42nd Ave. 71601   Ext. 4706

CALIFORNIA

STATE COORDINATOR
Department of Health Services   322-2300
Sacramento 95814
Fresno
Central Valley Regional   445-1222
Poison Control Ctr.
Fresno Community Hospital and Medical Center
Fresno & R Sts.
P.O. Box 1232 93715
Los Angeles
Thos. J. Fleming Memorial Ctr.   664-2121
Children's Hosp. of Los Angeles   664-2121
P.O. Box 54700
4650 Sunset Blvd. 90054
Oakland
Children's Hosp. of The East Bay   654-5600
51st & Grove St. 94609
Orange
University of California   634-5988, 634-6011
Irvine Medical Center
101 City Drive South 92688
Sacramento
Sacramento Medical Center   453-3692
Univ. of California, Davis
2315 Stockton Blvd. 95817
San Diego
University Hospital   294-6000
San Diego Poison Information Ctr.
San Diego Medical Center
225 W. Dickinson St. 92103
San Francisco
San Francisco General Hosp.   666-2845
1001 Potrerro Ave. 94102
San Jose
Santa Clara Valley Medical Center   279-5112
751 S. Bascom Ave., 95128

COLORADO

STATE COORDINATOR
Department of Health; EMS Div.   320-8476
Denver 80220
Denver
Rocky Mountain Poison Center   629-1123
Denver General Hospital
W. 8th Ave. & Cherokee St. 80204

CONNECTICUT

STATE COORDINATOR
University of Connecticut   674-3456
Health Center
Farmington 06032
Bridgeport
Bridgeport Hospital   384-3566
267 Grant St. 06610
St. Vincent's Hospital   576-5178
2820 Main St. 06606
Danbury
Danbury Hospital   797-7300
95 Locust Ave. 06810
Farmington
Connecticut Poison Center   674-3456
University of Connecticut
Health Center 06032
Middletown
Middlesex Memorial Hospital   347-9471
28 Crescent St. 06457
New Haven
The Hosp. of St. Raphael   789-3464
1450 Chapel St. 06511
Drug Information Center
Dept. of Pharm. Ser.
Yale-New Haven Hospital   436-1960
789 Howard Ave. 06504
Norwalk
Norwalk Hospital   852-2160
24 Stevens St. 06852
Waterbury
St. Mary's Hospital   574-6011
56 Franklin St. 06702

DELAWARE

Wilmington
Wilmington Medical Center   655-3389
Delaware Division
501 W. 14th St. 19899

DISTRICT OF COLUMBIA

STATE COORDINATOR
Department of Human Resources   673-6694
Washington, D.C. 20009
Washington, D.C.
Children's Hospital National   745-2000
Medical Center
111 Michigan Ave., N.W. 20010

FLORIDA

STATE COORDINATOR
Department of Health and   487-1566
Rehabilitative Services
Tallahassee 32301
Apalachicola
George E. Weems Memorial   653-8853
Hospital P.O. Box 610
Franklin Square 32320

Bartow
Polk General Hospital   533-1111
2010 E. Georgia St.   Ext. 204-237
P.O. Box 81 33830
Bradenton
Manatee Memorial Hospital   746-5111
206 2nd St. E. 33505   Ext. 466
Daytona Beach
Halifax Hospital   258-1515
Dept. of Emerg. Ser.
Clyde Morris Blvd.
P.O. Box 1990 32014
Ft. Lauderdale
Broward General Medical Center   463-3131
1600 S. Andrews Ave. 33316   Ext. 1511
Fort Myers
Lee Memorial Hospital   332-1111
2776 Cleveland Ave.
P.O. Drawer 2218 33902
Ft. Walton Beach
General Hospital of   242-1111
Ft. Walton Beach   Ext. 106
1000 Mar-Walt Drive 32548
Gainesville
Shands Teaching Hosp.   392-3746
and Clinics
University of Florida 32610
Inverness
Citrus Memorial Hosp.   726-1551
502 Highland Blvd. 32650
Jacksonville
St. Vincent's Medical Center   389-7751
Barrs St. & St. Johns Ave. 32204   Ext. 8315
Key West
Florida Keys Mem. Hospital   294-5531
600 Junior College Rd.
Stock Island 33040
Lakeland
Lakeland General Hospital   686-4913
Lakeland Hills Blvd.
P.O. Box 480 33802
Leesburg
Leesburg General Hospital   787-7222
600 E. Dixie 32748   Ext.381
Melbourne
James E. Holmes Regional   727-7000
Medical Center   Ext. 675
1350 S. Hickory St. 32901
Miami
Jackson Memorial Hospital   325-6799
Attn: Pharmacy
1611 N.W. 12th Ave. 33136
Naples
Naples Community Hospital   262-3131
350 7th St. N. 33940   Ext. 2221
North Miami Beach
Parkway General Hosp., Inc.   651-1100
160 Northwest 170th St. 33169
Ocala
Munroe Memorial Hospital   732-1111
140 S.E. Orange St.   Ext. 187
P.O. Box 6000 32670
Orlando
Orlando Reg. Med. Ctr.   841-5222
Orange Memorial Hospital
1414 S. Kuhl Ave. 32806
Panama City
Bay Memorial Med. Ctr.   769-1511
600 N. MacArthur Ave. 32401   Ext. 415-416
Pensacola
Baptist Hospital   434-4811
1000 W. Moreno St. 32501

Punta Gorda
Medical Center Hospital 639-3131
809 E. Marion Ave. 33950
Rockledge
Wuesthoff Memorial Hospital 636-2211
110 Longwood Ave. 32955 Ext. 108
St. Petersburg
Bayfront Medical Center, Inc. 821-5858
701 6th St., S. 33701
Sarasota
Memorial Hospital 953-1332
1901 Arlington Ave. 33579
Tallahassee
Tallahassee Mem. Regional 599-5411
Medical Center
1300 Miccouskee Road 32304
Tampa
Tampa General Hospital 251-6995
Davis Islands 33606
Titusville
Jess Parrish Mem. Hospital 269-1100
951 N. Washington Ave. 32780 Ext. 194
West Palm Beach
Good Samaritan Hospital 655-5511
Flagler Dr. at Ext. 4250
Palm Beach Lakes Blvd. 33402
Winter Haven
Winter Haven Hospital, Inc. 299-9701
200 Avenue F., N.E. 33880

GEORGIA

STATE COORDINATOR
Department of Human Resources 894-5068
Atlanta 30308
Albany
Phoebe Putney Memorial Hosp. 883-1800
417 Third Avenue 31705 Ext. 4152
Athens
Athens General Hospital 543-5215
797 Cobb St. 30601
Atlanta
Grady Memorial Hospital 588-4400
80 Butler St., S.E. 30303 800 282-5846
(Deaf) 404 525-3323

Augusta
University Hospital 722-9011
1350 Walton Way 30902 Ext. 2440
Columbus
The Medical Center 324-4711
710 Center Street 31902 Ext. 6431
Macon
Medical Center of Central Georgia 742-1122
777 Hemlock St. 31201 Ext. 3144
Rome
Floyd Hospital 295-5500
P.O. Box 233 30161 Ext. 747
Savannah
Savannah Reg. Poison Ctr. 355-5228
Depart. of Emergency Med.
Memorial Medical Center
P.O. Box 23089 31403
Thomasville
John D. Archbold 226-4121
Memorial Hospital Ext. 169
900 Gordon Ave. 31792
Valdosta
S. Georgia Medical Center 242-3450
P.O. Box 1727 31601 Ext. 717
Waycross
Memorial Hospital 283-3030
410 Darling Ave. 31501 Ext. 170

GUAM

STATE COORDINATOR
Guam Memorial Hospital 646-5801
P.O. Box AX
Agana 96910
Agana
Pharmacy Service, Box 7696 344-9265
U.S. Naval Regional Medical 344-9354
Center (GUAM)
FPO San Francisco, CA 96630

HAWAII

STATE COORDINATOR
Department of Health 531-7776
Honolulu 96801
Honolulu
Kapiolani-Childrens Medical Center 941-4411
1319 Punahou St. 96826

IDAHO

STATE COORDINATOR
Department of Health and Welfare 334-2241
Boise 83701 1-800 632-8000
Boise
St. Alphonsus Hospital 376-1211
1055 N. Curtis Rd. 83704 Ext. 707
Idaho Falls
Idaho Falls Hospital 529-6111
Emergency Department
900 Memorial Dr. 83401
Pocatello
St. Anthony Hospital 232-2733
650 North 7th St. 83201 Ext. 244

ILLINOIS

STATE COORDINATOR
Division of Emergency Medical 785-2080
Services and Highway Safety
Springfield 62761
Chicago
Rush-Presbyterian-St. Lukes 942-5969
Medical Center
1753 W. Congress Parkway 60612
Peoria
St. Francis Hospital & 672-2334
Medical Center 1-800 322-5330
530 N.E. Glen Oak Avenue 61637
Springfield
St. John's Hospital 753-3330
800 East Carpenter 62702 1-800 252-2022

INDIANA

STATE COORDINATOR
State Board of Health 633-0332
Indianapolis 46206
Anderson
Community Hospital 646-5198
1515 N. Madison Ave. 46012

St. John's Hickey 646-8251
Memorial Hospital
2015 Jackson St. 46014
Angola
Cameron Memorial Hospital 665-2141
416 East Maumee St. 46703 Ext. 146
Columbus
Bartholomew County Hosp. 376-5277
2400 East 17th St., 47201
Crown Point
St. Anthony Medical Ctr. 738-2100
Main at Franciscan Rd. 46307

East Chicago
St. Catherine Hospital 392-1700
4321 Fir Street 46312 392-7203
Elkhart
Elkhart General Hospital 294-2621
600 East Blvd. 46514
Evansville
Deaconess Hospital 426-3405
600 Mary St. 47710

St. Mary's Hospital 477-6261
3700 Washington Ave. 47715

Welborn Memorial 426-8000
Baptist Hospital
401 S.E. 6th St. 47713
Fort Wayne
Lutheran Hospital 458-2211
3024 Fairfield Ave. 46807

Parkview Memorial Hospital 484-6636
220 Randalia Dr. 46805 Ext. 7800

St. Joseph's Hospital 423-2614
700 Boradway 46802
Frankfort
Clinton County Hospital 654-4451
1300 S. Jackson St. 46041
Gary
Methodist Hospital of Gary, Inc. 886-4710
600 Grant St. 46402
Goshen
Goshen General Hospital 533-2141
200 High Park Ave. 46526 Ext. 462
Hammond
St. Margaret Hospital 932-2300
25 Douglas St. 46320 Ext. 700
Huntington
Huntington Memorial Hospital 356-3000
1215 Etna Ave. 46750

Indianapolis
Methodist Hospital of Indiana, Inc. 927-3033
1604 N. Capitol Ave. 46202

Indiana Poison Center 630-7351
1001 West 10th St. 46202 800 382-9097
Kendallville
McCray Memorial Hospital 347-1100
Hospital Drive 46755
Kokomo
Howard Community Hospital 453-0702
3500 S. LaFountain St. 46901 Ext. 444
Lafayette
Lafayette Home Hospital 447-6811
2400 South Street 47902

St. Elizabeth Hospital 423-6271
1501 Hartfort St. 47904
LaGrange
LaGrange County Hospital 463-2144
Route #1 46761
LaPorte
LaPorte Hospital, Inc. 362-7541
1007 Lincolnway 46350 Ext. 212
Lebanon
Witham Memorial Hospital 482-2700
1124 N. Lebanon St. 46052 Ext. 44
Madison
King's Daughter's Hospital 265-5211
112 Presbyterian Ave. Ext. 109
P.O. Box 447 47250
Marion
Marion General Hospital 662-4694
Wabash & Euclid Ave. 46952
Mishawaka
St. Joseph's Hospital 259-2431
215 W. 4th St. 46544

Muncie
Ball Memorial Hospital 747-3241
2401 University Ave. 47303
Portland
Jay County Hospital 726-7131
505 W. Arch St. 47371 Ext. 159
Richmond
Reid Memorial Hospital 692-7010
1401 Chester Blvd. 47374 Ext. 622
Shelbyville
Wm. S. Major Hospital 392-3211
150 W. Washington St. 46176 Ext. 52
South Bend
St. Joseph's Hospital 234-2151
811 E. Madison St. 46622 Ext. 253
Ext. 264

Terre Haute
Union Hospital, Inc. 238-7000
1606 N. 7th St. 47804 Ext. 7523
Valparaiso
Porter Memorial Hosp. 464-8611
814 LaPorte Ave. 46383 Ext. 232, 312, 334
Vincennes
The Good Samaritan 885-3348
Hospital
520 S. 7th St. 47591

IOWA

STATE COORDINATOR
Department of Health 281-4964
Des Moines 50319
Des Moines
(Blank Mem. Hosp.)
Iowa Methodist Hospital 283-6212
1200 Pleasant St. 50308
Dubuque
Mercy Medical Center 588-8210
Mercy Drive 52001
Fort Dodge
Trinity Regional Hospital 573-3101
Poison Information Center
Kenyon Rd. 50501
Iowa City
Univ. of Iowa Hospital 356-1616
and Clinics 52240 800 272-6477
Waterloo
Allen Memorial Hospital 235-3941
1825 Logan Avenue 50703

KANSAS

STATE COORDINATOR
Department of Health & 862-9360
Environment Ext. 542
Topeka 66620
Atchison
Atchison Hospital 367-2131
1301 N. 2nd St. 66002
Dodge City
Dodge City Reg. Hosp. 225-2036
PO Box 1478
Ross & Ave. "A" 67801

Emporia
Newman Memorial Hospital 343-6800
12th & Chestnut Sts. 66801 Ext. 545
Fort Riley
Irwin Army Hospital 66442 239-7776
Fort Scott
Mercy Hospital 223-2200
821 Burke St. 66701 (Night: 223-0476)

Great Bend
Central Kansas Medical Center   793-3523
Night: 792-2511
3515 Broadway 67530
Hays
Hadley Regional Medical Center   628-8251
201 E. 7th St. 67601
Kansas City
University of Kansas   588-6633
Medical Center
39th & Rainbow Blvd. 66103

Bethany Medical Center   281-8880
51 N. 12th St. 66102
Lawrence
Lawrence Memorial Hospital   843-3680
325 Main St. 66044   Ext. 162, 163
Parsons
Labette County Medical   421-4880
Center   Ext. 320
S. 21st St. 67357
Salina
St. John's Hospital   827-5591
139 N. Penn St. 67401   Ext. 112
Topeka
Stormont-Vail Regional Med. Ctr.   354-6100
10th & Washburn Sts. 66606
Wichita
Wesley Medical Center   685-2151
550 N. Hillside Ave. 67214   Ext. 7515

KENTUCKY

STATE COORDINATOR
Department For Human   564-4935
Resources
Frankfort 40601
Ashland
King's Daughters Hospital   324-2222
2201 Lexington Ave. 41101
Berea
Porter Moore Drug, Inc.   986-3061
124 Main St. 40403
Fort Thomas
St. Lukes Hospital   292-3215
85 N. Grand Ave. 41075
Lexington
Central Baptist Hospital   278-3411
1740 S. Limestone St. 40503   Ext. 304

Drug Information Center   233-5320
University of Kentucky
Medical Center 40536
Louisville
Norton-Children's Hospital   589-8222
Pharmacy Dept.
200 E. Chestnut St. 40202
Murray
Murray-Calloway County   753-7588
Hospital
803 Popular 42071
Owensboro
Owensboro-Daviess County   926-3030
Hospital   Ext. 180
811 Hospital Court 42301   Night: Ext. 174
Paducah
Western Baptist Hospital   444-6361
2501 Kentucky Ave. 42001   Ext. 105
Night: Ext. 199

Prestonsburg
Poison Control Center   886-8511
Highlands Reg. Med. Ctr 41653   Ext. 160

South Williamson Appalachian   237-5686
Reg. Hosp.
Central Pharmaceutical Service
2000 Central Ave. 25661

LOUISIANA

STATE COORDINATOR
Emergency Medical Services   342-2600
of Louisiana
Baton Rouge 70801
Alexandria
Rapides General Hospital   487-8111
Emergency Dept.
P.O. Box 7146 71301
Baton Rouge
Doctors Hospital   927-9050
2414 Bunker Hill Dr. 70808
Lafayette
Our Lady of Lourdes Hosp.   234-7381
P.O. Box 3827
611 St. Landry St. 70501
Lake Charles
Lake Charles Memorial Hosp.   478-6800
P.O. Drawer M 70601
Monroe
Northeast University   342-2008
School of Pharmacy
700 University Ave. 71209

St. Francis Hospital   325-6454
P.O. Box 1901 71301
New Orleans
Charity Hospital   568-5222
1532 Tulane Ave. 70140
Shreveport
LSU Medical Center   425-1524
P.O. Box 33932 71130

MAINE

STATE COORDINATOR
Maine Poison Control Center   1-800 442-6305
Portland 04102
Portland
Maine Medical Center   871-2950
Emergency Division   1-800 442-6305
22 Bramhall St. 04102

MARYLAND

STATE COORDINATOR
Maryland Poison Information Center   528-7604
University of Maryland School of
Pharmacy
Baltimore 21201
Baltimore
Maryland Poison Information Center   528-7701
University of Maryland   800 492-2414
School of Pharmacy
636 W. Lombard St. 21201
Cumberland
Sacred Heart Hospital   722-6677
900 Seton Drive 21502

MASSACHUSETTS

STATE COORDINATOR
Department of Public Health   727-2670
Boston 02111
Boston
Massachusetts Poison Control System   232-2120
300 Longwood Ave. 02115   1-800 682-9211

MICHIGAN

STATE COORDINATOR
Department of Public Health　373-1406
Lansing 48909
Adrian
Emma L. Bixby Hospital　263-2412
818 Riverside Ave. 49221
Ann Arbor
University Hospital　764-5102
1405 E. Ann St. 48104
Battle Creek
Community Hospital　963-5521
183 West St. 49016
Bay City
Bay Medical Center　892-6589
100 15th St. 48706

Berrien Center
Berrien General Hospital　471-7761
Dean's Hill Rd. 49102
Coldwater
Community Health Center　278-7361
of Branch County
274 E. Chicago St. 49036
Detroit
Children's Hospital of Michigan　494-5711
Southeast Regional Poison Center
3901 Beaubien 48201

Mount Carmel Mercy Hosp.　864-5400
6071 W. Outer Dr. 48235　Ext. 416
Eloise
Wayne County General　Day: 722-3748
30712 Michigan Ave. 48132　Night: 274-3000
Flint
Hurley Hospital　766-0111
6th Ave. & Begole 48502
Grand Rapids
St. Mary's Hospital　774-6794
201 Lafayette, S.E. 49503

Western Michigan Regional Poison　442-4571
Center　800 632-2727
1840 Wealthy, S.E. 49506
Hancock
Portage View Hospital　482-1122
200-210 Michigan Ave. 49930　Ext. 209
Holland
Holland Community Hospital　396-4661
602 Michigan Ave. 49423

Jackson
W.A. Foote Memorial Hosp.　788-4816
205 N. East St. 49201
Kalamazoo
Midwest Poison Center
Borgess Medical Center　383-4815
1521 Gull Rd. 49001

Bronson Methodist Hospital　383-6409
252 E. Lovell St. 49006

Lansing
St. Lawrence Hospital　372-5112
1210 W. Saginaw St. 48914　372-5113

Marquette
Marquette General Hospital　562-9723
Upper Peninsula Regional Poison Center
420 W. Magnetic Dr. 49855

Midland
Midland Hospital　631-7700
4005 Orchard 48640　Ext. 304
Petoskey
Little Traverse Hospital　347-7373
416 Connable 49770

Pontiac
St. Joseph Mercy Hospital　858-7373
900 Woodward Ave. 48053　858-7374
Port Huron
Port Huron Hospital　987-5555
1001 Kearney St. 48060　987-5000
Saginaw
Saginaw General Hospital　755-1111
1447 N. Harrison 48602
Traverse City
Munson Medical Center　947-6140
Sixth St. 49684

MINNESOTA

STATE COORDINATOR
State Department of Health　296-5281
Minneapolis 55404
Bemidji
Bemidji Hospital 56601　751-5430
Brainerd
St. Joseph's Hospital 56401　829-2861
　Ext. 211

Crookston
Riverview Hospital　281-4682
320 S. Hubbard 56716
Duluth
St. Luke's Hospital　727-6636
Emergency Department
915 E. First St. 55805

St. Mary's Hospital　727-4551
407 E. 3rd St. 55805　Ext. 359
Edina
Fairview-Southdale Hospital　920-4400
6401 France Ave., S. 55435
Fergus Falls
Lake Region Hospital 56537　736-5475
Fridley
Unity Hospital　786-2200
550 Osborne Rd. 55432
Mankato
Immanual - St. Joseph's　387-4031
Hospital
325 Garden Blvd. 56001
Marshall
Louis Weiner Memorial　532-9661
Hospital 56258
Minneapolis
Fairview Hospital　371-6402
Outpatient Department
2312 S. 6th St. 55406

Hennepin Poison Ctr.　347-3141
Hennepin County Medical Center
701 Park Ave. 55415

North Memorial Hospital　588-0616
3220 Lowry North 55422

Northwestern Hospital　874-4233
810 E. 27th St. 55407
Morris
Stevens County Memorial　589-1313
Hospital 56267
Rochester
Southeastern Minn. Poison Control Ctr.　285-5123
St. Mary's Hospital
1216 Second St., S.W. 55901
St. Cloud
St. Cloud Hospital　251-2700
1406 6th Avenue, N. 56301　Ext. 221
St. Paul
Bethesda Lutheran Hospital　221-2301
559 Capitol Blvd. 55103

The Children's Hospital, Inc. — 227-6521
311 Pleasant Ave. 55102

St. John's Hospital — 228-3132
403 Maria Ave. 55106

St. Joseph's Hospital — 291-3348
69 W. Exchange 55102 — 291-3139

United Hospitals, Inc. — 298-8402
St. Luke's Division
300 Pleasant Ave. 55102

St. Paul-Ramsey Hospital — 221-2113
640 Jackson St. 55101

Willmar
Rice Memorial Hospital — 235-4543
402 W. 3rd St. 56201

Worthington
Worthington Regional Hosp. — 372-2941
1016 6th Ave. 56187

MISSISSIPPI

STATE COORDINATOR
State Board of Health — 354-6650
Jackson 39205

Biloxi
Gulf Coast Community Hospital — 388-1919
4642 West Beach Blvd. 39531

USAF Hospital Keesler — 377-2516
Keesler Air Force Base — 377-6555
39534 — 377-6556

Brandon
Rankin General Hospital — 825-2811
350 Crossgates Blvd. 39042 — Ext. 487
— Ext. 488

Columbia
Marion County General — 736-6303
Hospital 39429 — Ext. 217

Greenwood
Greenwood-LeFlore Hosp. — 453-9751
River Road 38930 — Ext. 2633

Hattiesburg
Forrest County General Hosp. — 264-4235
400 S. 28th Ave. 39401

Jackson
Mississippi Baptist Med. Ctr. — 968-1704
1225 N. State St. 39201

St. Dominic-Jackson Mem. Hosp. — 982-0121
969 Lakeland Dr. 39216 — Ext. 2345, 2346, 2347

State Board of Health — 354-6650
Bureau of Disease
Control 39205

University Medical Center — 354-7660
2500 N. State St. 39216

Laurel
Jones County Community Hospital — 649-4000
Jefferson St. at 13th Ave. 39440

Meridian
Meridian Regional Hosp. — 483-6211
Highway 39, North 39301 — Ext. 54

Pascagoula
Singing River Hospital — 938-5162
Highway 90 East 39567

University
School of Pharmacy — 234-1522
University of Mississippi
38677

Vicksburg
Mercy Regional Medical — 636-2131
Center — Ext. 250, 251
100 McAuley Dr. 39181 — Ext. 276

MISSOURI

STATE COORDINATOR
Missouri Division of Health — 751-2713
Jefferson City 65102

Cape Girardeau
St. Francis Medical Ctr. — 335-1251
St. Francis Drive 63701 — Ext. 217

Columbia
University of Missouri — 882-4141
Medical Center
807 Stadium Blvd. 65201

Hannibal
St. Elizabeth Hospital — 221-0414
109 Virginia St. 63401 — Ext. 101,183

Jefferson City
Charles E. Still — 635-7141
Osteopathic Hospital — Ext. 215
1125 S. Madison 65101

Joplin
St. John's Medical Center — 781-2727
2727 McClelland Blvd. 64801 — Ext. 393

Kansas City
Children's Mercy Hospital — 234-3000
24th & Gillham Rd. 64108

Kirksville
Kirksville Osteopathic — 626-2266
Hospital
800 W. Jefferson St. 63501

Poplar Bluff
Lucy Lee Hospital — 785-7721
330 N. 2nd St. 63901

Rolla
Phelps County Memorial Hosp. — 364-3100
1000 W. 10th St. 65401 — Ext. 136,137

St. Joseph
Methodist Medical Center — 271-7580
Seventh to Ninth on Faraon Sts. 64501 — 232-8481

Louis
Cardinal Glennon Memorial Hospital — 772-5200
for Children
1465 S. Grand Blvd. 63104

St. Louis Children's Hosp. — 367-2034
500 S. Kingshighway 63110

Springfield
Lester E. Cox Medical Center — 831-9746
1423 N. Jefferson St. 65802 — 1-800-492-4824

St. John's Hospital — 885-2115
1235 E. Cherokee 65802

West Plains
West Plains Memorial Hosp. — 256-9111
1103 Alaska Ave. 65775 — Ext. 258
— Ext. 259

MONTANA

STATE COORDINATOR
Department of Health and — 1-800-525-5042
Environmental Sciences
Helena 59601

Montana Poison Control System — 1-800-525-5042

NEBRASKA

STATE COORDINATOR
Department of Health — 471-2122
Lincoln 68502

Omaha
Children's Memorial Hospital — 553-5400
44th & Dewey Sts. 68105

Nebraska — 800-642-9999
Surrounding States — 800-228-9515

NEVADA

STATE COORDINATOR
Department of Human Resources   885-4750
Carson City 89710
Las Vegas
Southern Nevada Memorial Hosp.   385-1277
1800 W. Charleston Blvd. 89102

Sunrise Hospital Med. Ctr.   731-8000
3186 South Maryland Parkway 89109
Reno
St. Mary's Hospital   323-2041
235 W. 6th 89503

Washoe Medical Center   785-4129
77 Pringle Way 89502   Night: 785-4140

NEW HAMPSHIRE

Hanover
Mary Hitchcock Hospital   643-4000
2 Maynard St. 03755

NEW JERSEY

STATE COORDINATOR
Department of Health   292-5666
Trenton 08625
Atlantic City
Atlantic City Medical Center   344-4081
1925 Pacific Ave. 08401
Belleville
Clara Maass Memorial Hosp.   751-1000
1A Franklin Ave. 07109   Ext. 781
    Ext. 782
    Ext. 783

Boonton
Riverside Hospital   334-5000
Powerville Rd. 07055   Ext. 186,187
Bridgeton
Bridgeton Hospital   451-6600
Irving Ave. 08302
Camden
West Jersey Hospital   795-5554
Evesham Ave. and
Voorhees Tnpk. 08104
Denville
St. Clare's Hospital   627-3000
Pocono Rd. 07834   Ext. 6063
East Orange
East Orange General   672-8400
Hospital   Ext. 223
300 Central Ave. 07019
Elizabeth
St. Elizabeth Hospital   527-5059
225 Williamson St. 07207
Englewood
Englewood Hospital   894-3262
350 Engle St. 07631
Flemington
Hunterdon Medical Center   782-2121
Route #31 08822
Livingston
St. Barnabas Medical Center   992-5161
Old Short Hills Rd. 07039
Long Branch
Monmouth Medical Center   222-2210
Dunbar & 2nd Ave. 07740
Montclair
Mountainside Hospital   746-6000
Bay & Highland Ave. 07042
Mount Holly
Burlington County Memorial   267-7877
175 Madison Ave. 08060

Neptune
Jersey Shore Medical Center-
Fitkin Hospital   (800) 822-9761
1945 Corlies Ave. 07753
Newark
Newark Beth Israel   926-7240
Medical Center   926-7241
201 Lyons Ave. 07112   926-7242
    926-7243

New Brunswick
Middlesex General Hospital   828-3000
180 Somerset St. 08903   Ext. 425, 308
St. Peter's Medical Center   745-8527
254 Easton Ave. 08903
Newton
Newton Memorial Hospital   383-2121
175 High St. 07860   Ext.270, 1,2
    Ext. 273
Orange
Hospital Center at Orange   266-2120
188 S. Essex Ave. 07051
Passaic
St. Mary's Hospital   473-1000
211 Pennington Ave. 07055   (Ext. 441)
Perth Amboy
Perth Amboy General Hosp.   442-3700
530 New Brunswick Ave.   Ext. 2500
    08861
Phillipsburg
Warren Hospital   859-1500
185 Roseberry St. 08865   Ext. 280
Point Pleasant
Point Pleasant Hospital   892-1100
Osborn Ave. & River Front   Ext. 385
08742
Princeton
Medical Center at Princeton   734-4554
253 Witherspoon St. 08540
Saddle Brook
Saddle Brook General Hosp.   368-6026
300 Market St. 07662
Somers Point
Shore Memorial Hospital   653-3515
Brighton & Sunny Aves. 08244
Somerville
Somerset Medical Center   725-4000
Rehill Ave. 08876   Ext. 431, 432, 433
Summit
Overlook Hospital   522-2232
193 Morris Ave. 07901
Teaneck
Holy Name Hospital   833-3000
718 Teaneck Rd. 07666
Trenton
Helene Fuld Med. Ctr.   396-1077
750 Brunswick Ave. 08638
Union
Memorial General Hospital   687-1900
1000 Galloping Hill Rd. 07083   Ext. 237
Wayne
Greater Paterson General   942-6900
Hospital   Ext. 224
224 Hamburg Tnpk. 07470   Ext. 225
    Ext. 226

NEW MEXICO

STATE COORDINATOR
N.M. Poison, Drug Inf. & Med.   843-2551
Crisis Center   1-800-432-6866
University of New Mexico
Albuquerque 87131

NEW YORK

STATE COORDINATOR
Department of Health   474-3785
Albany 12210

Binghamton
Southern Tier Poison Center
Binghamton General Hospital   723-8929
Mitchell Avenue 13903

Our Lady of Lourdes   798-5231
Memorial Hospital
169 Riverside Drive 13905

Buffalo
Western N.Y. Poison Control Center   878-7000
Children's Hospital   878-7654
219 Bryant St. 14222   878-7655

Dunkirk
Brooks Memorial Hospital   366-1111
10 West 6th St. 14048   Ext. 414
                                        Ext. 415

East Meadow
Nassau County Medical Ctr.   542-2323
2201 Hempstead Tpk. 11554   542-2324
                                        542-2325

Elmira
Arnot Ogden Memorial Hosp.   737-4100
Roe Ave. & Grove 14901

St. Joseph's Hospital   734-2662
Health Center
555 E. Market St. 14901

Endicott
Ideal Hospital   754-7171
600 High Ave. 13760

Glens Falls
Glens Falls Hospital   792-3151
100 Park St. 12801   Ext. 456

Jamestown
W.C.A. Hospital   487-0141
207 Foote Ave. 14707   484-8648

Johnson City
Wilson Memorial Hospital   773-6611
33-57 Harrison St. 14707

Kingston
Kingston Hospital   331-3131
396 Broadway 12401

New York
N.Y. City, Dept. of Health   340-4494
Bureau of Laboratories   340-4495
455 First Ave. 10016

Nyack
Nyack Hospital (Pharmacy)
North Midland Ave.   358-6200
10960   Ext. 451
                                        Ext. 452

Rochester
Finger Lakes Poison   275-5151
Control Center
Life Line, Univ. of
Rochester Medical Center 14620

Schenectady
Ellis Hospital   382-4039
1101 Nott Street 12308   382-4121

Syracuse
Syracuse Poison Inf. Ctr.
Upstate Medical Center   476-7529
750 E. Adams St. 13210   473-5831

Troy
St. Mary's Hospital   272-5792
1300 Massachusetts Ave. 12180
Utica
St. Luke's Hospital Center   798-6200
P.O. Box 479 13502
Watertown
House of the Good   788-8700
Samaritan Hospital
Corner Washington &
Pratt Sts. 13602

NORTH CAROLINA

STATE COORDINATOR
Duke University Medical Center   684-8111
Durham 27710
Asheville
Western N.C. Poison Control Center
Memorial Mission Hospital   255-4660
509 Biltmore Ave. 28801
Charlotte
Mercy Hospital   379-5827
2001 Vail Ave. 28207

Durham
Duke University Medical Ctr.   684-8111
Box 3007 27710
Greensboro
Moses Cone Hospital   379-4105
1200 N. Elm St. 27420
Hendersonville
Margaret R. Pardee Memorial Hospital   693-6522
Fleming St. 28739   Ext.555, 556
Hickory
Catawba Memorial Hospital   322-6649
Fairgrove-Church Rd. 28601
Jacksonville
Onslow Memorial Hospital   353-7610
Western Blvd. 28540   Ext. 240
Wilmington
New Hanover Memorial Hosp.   343-7046
2131 S. 17th St. 28401

NORTH DAKOTA

STATE COORDINATOR
Department of Health   224-2388
Bismarck 58505
Bismarck
Bismarck Hospital   223-4357
300 N. 7th St. 58501
Fargo
St. Luke's Hospital   280-5575
Fifth St. at Mills Ave. 58122
Grand Forks
United Hospital   780-5000
1200 S. Columbia Rd. 58201
Minot
St. Joseph's Hospital   857-2553
Third St. & Fourth Ave., S.E. 58701
Williston
Mercy Hospital   572-7661
1301 15th Ave. W. 58801

OHIO

STATE COORDINATOR
Department of Health   466-2544
Columbus 43216
Akron
Children's Hospital   379-8562
281 Locust 44308

Canton
Aultman Hospital   452-9911
Emergency Room   Ext. 203
2600 Sixth St., S.W.
44710
Cincinnati
Drug & Poison Inf. Ctr.
Univ. of Cincinnati   872-5111
Medical Center, Rm. 7701
Bridge 45267
Cleveland
Academy of Medicine   231-8082
11001 Cedar Ave. 44106
Columbus
Children's Hospital   228-1323
700 Children's Dr. 43205
Dayton
Children's Medical Center   222-2227
One Children's Plaza 45404
Lorain
Lorain Community Hospital   282-2220
3700 Kolbe Rd. 44053
Mansfield
Mansfield General Hospital   522-3411
335 Glessner Ave. 44903   Ext. 545
Springfield
Community Hospital   325-1255
2615 E. High St. 44505
Toledo
Medical College Hospital   381-3897
P.O. Box 6190 43609
Youngstown
Mahoning Valley Poison
Control Center
St. Elizabeth Hospital & Med Ctr.   746-2222
1044 Belmont Ave. 44505
Zanesville
Bethesda Hospital   454-4221
Poison Information Center
2951 Maple Ave. 43701

OKLAHOMA

STATE COORDINATOR
Oklahoma Children's   271-5454
Memorial Hospital   800-522-4611
P.O. Box 26307
Oklahoma City 63126
Ada
Valley View Hospital   322-2323
1300 E. 6th St. 74820   Ext. 200
Ardmore
Memorial Hospital of   223-5400
Southern Oklahoma
1011-14th Ave. 73401
Lawton
Comanche County Memorial   355-8620
Hospital
3401 Gore Blvd. 73501
McAlester
McAlester General Hospital, West   426-1800
P.O. Box 669 74501   Ext. 240
Oklahoma City
Oklahoma Children's Memorial   271-5454
Hospital   800-522-4611
P.O. Box 26307
73126
Ponca City
St. Joseph Medical Center   765-3321
14th & Hartford 74601
Tulsa
Hillcrest Medical Center   584-1351
1653 East 12th 74104   Ext. 6165

OREGON

Portland
Oregon Poison Control and
Drug Info. Center
University of Oregon   225-8968
Health Sciences Center
3181 S.W. Sam Jackson   1-800-452-7165
Park Rd. 97201

PANAMA

ANCON
U.S.A. Meddac Panama   52-7500
Attn: Gorgas U.S. Army Hospital
APO Miami 34004

PENNSYLVANIA

STATE COORDINATOR
Department of Health   787-2307
Harrisburg 17120
Allentown
Lehigh Valley Poison Center   433-2311
17th & Chew St. 18103
Altoona
Altoona Region Poison Center   946-3711
Mercy Hospital
2500 Seventh Ave. 16603
Bethlehem
St. Luke's Hospital   691-4141
800 Ostrum St. 18015
Bloomsburg
The Bloomsburg Hospital   784-7121
549 E. Fair St. 17815
Bradford
Bradford Hospital   368-4143
Interstate Pkwy 16701
Bryn Mawr
The Bryn Mawr Hospital   527-0600
19010
Chambersburg
The Chambersburg Hospital   264-5171
7th and King St. 17201   Ext. 431
Chester
Sacred Heart General Hosp.   494-0721
9th and Wilson St. 19013   Ext. 232
Clearfield
Clearfield Hospital   765-5341
809 Turnpike Ave. 16830
Coaldale
Coaldale State General   645-2131
Hospital 18218
Coudersport
Charles Cole Memorial   274-9300
Hospital
RD #3, Route 6 16915

Danville
Susquehanna Poison Center   275-6116
Geisinger Medical Center
North Academy Ave. 17821
Doylestown
Doylestown Hospital   345-2281
595 W. State St. 18901
Drexel Hill
Delaware County Memorial   259-3800
Hospital
Lansdowne & Keystone Ave
19026
East Stroudsburg
Pocono Hospital   421-4000
206 E. Brown St. 18301

Easton
Easton Hospital   258-6221
21st & Lehigh St. 18042
Erie
Doctors Osteopathic   455-3961
252 W. 11th St. 16501

Erie Osteopathic Hospital   864-4031
5515 Peach St. 16509

Hamot Medical Center   455-6711
4 E. Second St. 16512   Ext. 521

Northwest Poison Center   452-3232
St. Vincent Health Center
P.O. Box 740 16512
Gettysburg
Annie M. Warner Hospital   334-2121
S. Washington St. 17325
Greensburg
Westmoreland Hosp. Assn.   837-0100
532 W. Pittsburgh St. 15601
Hanover
Hanover General Hospital   637-3711
300 Highland Ave. 17331
Harrisburg
Harrisburg Hospital   782-3639
S. Front & Mulberry St. 17101

Polyclinic Hospital   782-4141
3rd & Polyclinic Ave. 17105   Ext. 4132
Hershey
Milton S. Hershey Medical   534-6111
Center
University Dr. 17033
Jeannete
Jeannete District Memorial   527-3551
Hospital
600 Jefferson Ave. 15644
Jersey Shore
Jersey Shore Hospital   398-0100
Thompson St. 17740
Johnstown
Conemaugh Valley Memorial   535-5351
Hospital
1086 Franklin St. 15905

Lee Hospital   535-7541
320 Main St. 15901

Mercy Hospital   536-5353
1020 Franklin St. 15905
Lancaster
Lancaster General Hospital   299-5511
555 North Duke St. 17604

St. Joseph's Hospital   299-4546
250 College Ave. 17604
Lansdale
North Penn Hospital   368-2100
7th & Broad St. 19446
Lebanon
Good Samaritan Hospital   272-7611
4th & Walnut Sts. 17042
Lehighton
Gnaden-Huetten Memorial   377-1300
Hospital
11th & Hamilton St. 18235
Lewistown
Lewistown Hospital   248-5411
Highland Ave. 17044
Muncy
Muncy Valley Hospital   546-8282
P.O. Box 340 17756
Nanticoke
Nanticoke State Hospital   735-5000
W. Washington St. 18634

Paoli
Paoli Memorial Hospital 19301   647-2200
Philadelphia
Philadelphia Poison   922-5523
Information   922-5524
321 University Ave. 19104
Phillipsburg
Phillipsburg State General   342-3320
Hospital 16866
Pittsburgh
Children's Hospital   681-6669
125 DeSoto St. 15213
Pittston
Pittston Hospital   654-3341
Oregon Heights 18640
Pottstown
Pottstown Memorial Medical   327-1000
Center
High St. & Firestone Blvd.
19464
Pottsville
Good Samaritan Hospital   622-3400
E. Norwegian and
Tremont St. 17901
Reading
Community General Hospital   376-4881
145 N. 6th St. 19601

Reading Hospital and   378-6218
Medical Center 19603
Sayre
The Robert Packer Hospital   888-6666
Guthrie Square 18840
Sellersville
Grandview Hospital 18960   257-3611
Somerset
Somerset Community Hospital   443-2626
225 South Center Ave. 15501
State College
Centre Community Hospital   238-4351
16801
Titusville
Titusville Hospital   827-1851
406 W. Oak St. 16354
Tunkhannock
Tyler Memorial Hospital   836-2161
RD #1 18657
York
Memorial Osteopathic Hospital   843-8623
325 S. Belmont St. 17403

York Hospital   771-2311
1001 S. George St. 17405

PUERTO RICO

STATE COORDINATOR
University of Puerto Rico   765-4880
Rio Piedras   765-0615

Arecibo
District Hospital of   878-7272
Arecibo 00613   Ext. 7459
   7510
Fajardo
District Hospital of   863-3792
Fajardo 00649   863-0939
Mayaguez
Mayaguez Medical Center   832-8686
Department of Health   Ext. 1224
P.O. Box 1868 00709
Ponce
District Hospital of   842-8364
Ponce 00731

Rio Piedras
Medical Center of   764-3515
Puerto Rico 00936
San Juan
Pharmacy School   753-4849
Medical Sciences Campus
GPO Box 5067 00936
(Information only)

RHODE ISLAND

STATE COORDINATOR
Department of Health   ·   277-2401
Providence 02908
Providence
Rhode Island Hospital   277-4000
593 Eddy St. 02902

SOUTH CAROLINA

STATE COORDINATOR
Department of Health &   758-5625
Environmental Control
Columbia 29201
Charleston
Poison Information Serv.   792-4201
Medical University of
South Carolina
171 Ashley Ave. 29403
Columbia
Palmetto Poison Center   765-7359
College of Pharmacy   1-800-922-1117
University of S.C. 29208

SOUTH DAKOTA

STATE COORDINATOR
Department of Health   773-3361
Pierre 57501
Rapid City
West River Poison Ctr.   343-3333
Rapid City Regional   1-800-742-8925
Hospital East 57701
Sioux Falls
McKennan Hospital   336-3894
800 East 21st St. 57101   1-800-952-0123

TENNESSEE

STATE COORDINATOR
Department of Public Health   ·   741-2407
Nashville 37219
Chattanooga
T.C. Thompson Children's   755-6100
Hospital
910 Blackford St. 37403
Cookeville
Cookeville General Hospital   528-2541
142 W. 5th St. 38501
Jackson
Madison General Hospital   424-0424
708 W. Forest 38301
Johnson City
Memorial Hospital   926-1131
Boone & Fairview Ave. 37601
Knoxville
Memorial Research Center   971-3261
and Hospital
1924 Alcoa Highway 37920
Memphis
Southern Poison Center   528-6048
University of Tennessee
College of Pharmacy
874 Union Avenue 38163

Nashville
Vanderbilt University Hospital   322-3391
21st & Garland 37232

TEXAS

STATE COORDINATOR
Department of Health   458-7254
Austin 78756
Abilene
Hendrick Hospital   677-3551
19th & Hickory Sts. 79601   Ext. 266
                                     Ext. 267
Amarillo
Amarillo Hospital District   376-4431
Amarillo Emergency Receiving   Ext. 501
Center   Ext. 502
P.O. Box 1110   Ext. 503
2203 W. 6th St. 79175   Ext. 504
Austin
Brackenridge Hospital   478-4490
14th & Sabine Sts. 78701
Beaumont
Baptist Hospital of   833-7409
Southeast Texas
P.O. Box 1591
College & 11th St. 77701
Corpus Christi
Memorial Medical Center   884-4511
P.O. Box 5280   Ext. 556
2606 Hospital Blvd. 78405   Ext. 557
El Paso
R.E. Thomason General   544-1200
Hospital
P.O. Box 20009
4815 Alameda Ave. 79905
Fort Worth
W.I. Cook Children's   336-5521
Hospital   Ext. 17
1212 W. Lancaster 76102   336-6611
Galveston
Southeast Texas Poison   765-1420
Control Center
8th & Mechanic Sts. 77550
Houston
Southeast Texas Poison   654-1701
Control Center
8th and Mechanic St.
Galveston, Tex. 77550
Harlingen
Valley Baptist Hospital   423-1224
P.O. Box 2588   Ext. 283
2101 S. Commerce St. 78550
Laredo
Mercy Hospital   722-2431
1515 Logan St. 78040   Ext. 29
Lubbock
Methodist Hospital   792-1011
Pharmacy   Ext. 315
3615 19th St. 79410
Midland
Midland Memorial Hospital   684-8257
1908 W. Wall 79701
Odessa
Medical Center Hospital   337-7311
P.O. Box 633 79760   Ext. 250, 252
Plainview
Plainview Hospital   296-9601
2404 Yonkers St. 79072

San Angelo
Shannon West Texas 653-6741
Memorial Hospital Ext. 210
P.O. Box 1879
9 S. Magdalen St. 76901
San Antonio
Department of Pediatrics 223-1481
Univ. of Texas Health Science
Center at San Antonio
7703 Floyd Curl Dr. 78284
Tyler
Medical Center Hospital 597-0351
1000 S. Beckham St. 75701 Ext. 255
Waco
Hillcrest Baptist Hosp. 753-1412
3000 Herring Ave. 76708 756-6111
Wichita Falls
Wichita General Hospital 322-6771
Emergency Room
1600 8th St. 76301

UTAH

STATE COORDINATOR
Division of Health 533-6161
Salt Lake City 84113
Salt Lake City
Intermountain Regional 581-2151
Poison Control Center
50 N. Medical Drive 84132

VERMONT

STATE COORDINATOR
Department of Health 862-5701
Burlington 05401
Burlington
Vermont Poison Control 658-3456
Medical Center Hospital 05401

VIRGIN ISLANDS

STATE COORDINATOR
Department of Health 774-1321
St. Thomas 00801 Ext. 275
St. Croix
Charles Harwood Memorial 773-1212
Hospital 773-1311
Christiansted 00820 Ext. 221
Ingeborg Nesbitt Clinic 772-0260
Fredericksted 00840 772-0212
St. John
Morris F. DeCastro Clinic 776-1469
Cruz Bay 00830
St. Thomas
Knud-Hansen Memorial 774-1321
Hospital 00801 Ext. 224, 225

VIRGINIA

STATE COORDINATOR
Bureau of Emergency 786-5188
Medical Services
Richmond 23219
Alexandria
Alexandria Hospital 370-9000
4320 Seminary Rd. 22314 Ext. 555
Arlington
Arlington Hospital 558-6161
5129 N. 16th St. 22205
Blacksburg
Montgomery County 951-1111
Community Hospital
Rt. 460, S. 24060

Charlottesville
Blue Ridge Poison Center 924-5543
Univ. of Virginia Hospital 22908
Danville
Danville Memorial Hospital 799-2100
142 S. Main St. 22201 Ext. 3869
Falls Church
Fairfax Hospital 698-3600
3300 Gallows Rd. 22046 698-3111
Hampton
Hampton General Hospital 722-1131
3120 Victoria Blvd. 23661
Harrisonburg
Rockingham Memorial Hospital 434-4421
738 S. Mason St. 22801 Ext. 225
Lexington
Stonewall Jackson Hosp. 463-9141
22043
Lynchburg
Lynchburg Gen. Marshall 528-2066
Lodge Hosp., Inc.
Tate Springs Rd. 24504
Nassawadox
Northampton-Accomack 442-8000
Memorial Hospital 23413
Norfolk
DePaul Hospital 489-5111
Granby St. at Kingsley
Lane 23505
Petersburg
Petersburg General Hospital 861-2992
801 South Adams Street 23803
Portsmouth
U.S. Naval Hospital 397-6541
23708 Ext. 418
Richmond
Virginia Poison Center 786-9123
Virginia Commonwealth Univ.
Box 763 MCV Station 23298
Roanoke
Roanoke Memorial Hospital 981-7336
Belleview at Jefferson St.
P.O. Box 13367 24033
Staunton
King's Daughters' Hospital 885-0361
P.O. Box 2007 24401 Ext. 209
 Ext. 247
Waynesboro
Waynesboro Community 942-8355
Hospital Ext. 440
501 Oak Ave. 22980 Ext. 500
Williamsburg
Williamsburg Community Hosp. 229-1120
Mt. Vernon Ave. Ext. 65
Drawer H 23185

WASHINGTON

STATE COORDINATOR
Department of Social & 522-7478
Health Services
Seattle 98115
Aberdeen
St. Joseph's Hospital 533-0450
1006 North H. St. 98520 Ext. 277
Bellingham
St. Luke's General Hospital 676-8400
809 E. Chestnut St. 98225 676-8401
Longview
St. John's Hospital 636-5252
1614 E. Kessler 98632

Madigan
Madigan Army Medical   967-6972
Center Emergency Room 98431
Olympia
St. Peter's Hospital   491-0222
413 N. Lilly Rd. 98506
Seattle
Children's Orthopedic   634-5252
Hosp. & Med. Center
4800 Sandpoint Way, N.E.
98105
Spokane
Deaconess Hospital   747-1077
W. 800 5th Ave. 99210
Tacoma
Mary Bridge Children's   272-1281
Hospital   Ext. 259
311 S. L St. 98405
Vancouver
St. Joseph Community   256-2067
Hospital
600 N.E. 92nd St.
98664
Yakima
Yakima Valley Memorial   248-4400
Hospital
2811 Tieton Dr. 98902

WEST VIRGINIA

STATE COORDINATOR
Department of Health   348-2971
Charleston 25305
Charleston
West Virginia Poison System
3110 McCorkle Ave. SE 25304

Morgantown
Mountain State Poison Center   293-5341
Dept. of Pediatrics
West Virginia University
Medical Center 26506

WISCONSIN

STATE COORDINATOR
Department of Health & Social   267-7174
Services, Div. of Health
Madison 53701
Eau Claire
Luther Hospital   835-1511
1225 Whipple 54701
Green Bay
St. Vincent Hospital   433-8100
835 S. Van Buren St. 54305
LaCrosse
St. Francis Hospital   784-3971
700 West Ave. N 54601
Madison
University Hospitals   262-3702
and Clinics
600 Highland Ave. 53792
Milwaukee
Milwaukee Children's   931-4114
Hospital
1700 W. Wisconsin 53233

WYOMING

STATE COORDINATOR
Department of Health &   777-7955
Social Services
Cheyenne 82001
Cheyenne
Wyoming Poison Center   635-9256
De Paul Hospital
2600 East 18th St. 82001

Glossary

Terms commonly used in the health field

by Charlotte Isler, Clinical Editor, RN Magazine

A

Abdominal aneurysm - usually due to dilatation of the aorta, the largest abdominal blood vessel, into a protruding sac caused by a weakening of its wall. May also occasionally occur in other abdominal blood vessels.

Abortion - the loss of the fetus in the course of pregnancy. Abortion may be spontaneous, induced, or done for therapeutic reasons.

Abrasion - removal of a portion of skin due to injury or a surgical procedure.

Abruptio placentae - the premature detachment of an otherwise normal placenta, the organ through which the developing fetus obtains nourishment and oxygen.

Abscess - localized collection of pus under the skin or in another part of the body, such as the ear, tooth, lung, brain or the liver; usually due to infection.

Acidosis - a condition in which the acid/base balance of body fluids is disturbed, thereby decreasing the alkaline content.

Aciduria - acid condition of the urine.

Acupuncture - ancient oriental treatment method using long fine needles in various areas of the body to reduce pain and alleviate various other disease conditions.

Acute - the quick, sharp onset of a condition such as pain, usually of limited duration.

Adenoma - a benign growth that is generally well circumscribed. It exerts pressure against surrounding tissue instead of infiltrating it as do other tumors.

Adrenal glands - two glands, each located near one of the kidneys, that secrete the hormones adrenaline and cortisone.

Adsorbent - a substance that can suck other substances to its surface, without requiring a chemical agent.

Agoraphobia - the fear of being in an open space.

Airway - the respiratory tract, or any part of the respiratory tract that acts as a passage for air during the process of breathing.

Airway obstruction - any foreign body, or physical process that occludes the respiratory tract or any of its parts, making breathing difficult or impossible.

Albumin - a body protein present in tissue and body fluids.

Alcohol dependency - the inability to manage life's functions and responsibilities without consuming a given quantity of alcohol, or experiencing withdrawal symptoms if alcohol consumption is stopped. Alcoholism.

Alcohol poisoning - the toxic effects of excessive alcohol intake.

Alkaloid - a type of chemical contained in many drugs that is made from plants or manufactured synthetically.

Allergy - an abnormal bodily reaction due to an acquired hypersensitivity on exposure to environmental substances such as dust, pollen, foods, bacteria or physical agents (heat, cold, light) that may be slight or severe. Symptoms appear in the form of respiratory symptoms (tearing, wheezing, coughing, sneezing); skin conditions (rashes, wheals or hives); or such digestive tract symptoms as belching, flatus, nausea, vomiting, abdominal pain or diarrhea.

Amblyopia - impaired vision, due to hereditary, structural or dietary deficiency.

Amebiasis - an infection caused by one-celled microorganisms (amebae) that mainly involves the intestine but may spread to other body organs, especially the liver.

Amenorrhea - the absence, or sudden cessation of the menstrual blood flow.

Amino acid - a substance formed during the digestive breakdown of proteins.

Amniocentesis - the withdrawal, under sterile conditions, of a sample of fluid (amniotic fluid) from a thin, tough, transparent membranous sac (the amniotic sac) that surrounds, cushions and protects the developing fetus. Done to determine possible defects, and sometimes the sex of the unborn child.

Amniotic fluid - the protective fluid that is present in the amniotic sac during pregnancy to cushion the growing fetus against injury.

Amyotrophic lateral sclerosis (ALS) - a progressive disease of unknown cause of the nerves and muscles. It affects certain portions of the spinal cord with the muscles gradually wasting away (atrophy), which causes increasing weakness and eventual paralysis, especially in the muscles of the arms, shoulders, legs and those that control breathing.

Anabolism - the process of using energy to turn food taken into the body into living tissues.

Anaerobe - a microorganism that grows only when there is little, or no oxygen present.

Anal - the lowest portion of the intestinal tract.

Analgesic - a medication used to relieve pain.

Anaphylaxis - a severe form of allergic (hypersensitive) reaction to a substance that can be fatal if not treated immediately.

Androsterone - a male sex hormone.

Anemia - an abnormal condition of the blood in which there is a deficiency of red blood cells, and/or a deficiency of hemoglobin, the substance which carries oxygen from the lungs to the tissues.

Aneurysm - a condition in which the wall of an artery weakens, balloons out and may burst, causing severe, possibly fatal bleeding.

Angina - a choking or suffocative type of spasmodic pain.

Angina pectoris - a severe, paroxysmal pain in the chest with a feeling of oppression or suffocation, due to an insufficient supply of blood oxygen to the heart muscle. These symptoms are usually precipitated by exertion or excitement.

Angioedema - swelling of body tissues, usually as part of an allergic reaction.

Anomaly - an abnormality or defect of a body organ or structure.

Anorectal - referring to the lowest portion of the intestinal tract, the anal canal and the rectum.

Anorexia - a loss of appetite due to illness, emotional disturbance or ingestion of certain drugs.

Anorexia nervosa - a psychological illness, mostly in adolescent girls, in which the patient eats little or no food, resulting in severe weight loss and possible death if not treated.

Anorexics - a category of drugs that suppresses the appetite, taken to enable a person to lose weight.

Antacid - an alkaline drug that neutralizes excessive stomach acids.

Anthelmintics - drugs given to destroy and expel intestinal worms.

Antibacterial - a drug that counteracts, inhibits, or destroys bacteria.

Antibody - a constituent of blood and body fluids that acts to protect the body against infection.

Anticaries agent - a drug that protects teeth or bones against decay or destruction.

Anticholinergics - drugs that suppress secretions from the stomach and other internal organs such as glands, dilate the pupils of the eyes, and decrease the actions of the respiratory, gastrointestinal and urinary systems.

Anticoagulant - a drug given to slow the clotting action of blood.

Antidiarrheal - an agent or substance, usually a drug, that counteracts the effects of diarrhea.

Antidote - an agent or substance, usually a drug, that counteracts a poison applied to the body externally or via ingestion, either by accident or by intention.

Antiemetic - an agent or substance, usually a drug, that counteracts nausea and/or vomiting.

Antiflatulent - an agent or substance, usually a drug, that counteracts excessive gas in the intestinal tract.

Antifungal - an agent or substance, usually a drug, that counteracts the effects of fungal organisms that cause infections of the skin, nails, hair, and of the mucous membranes.

Antigen - a substance which causes the production of antibodies when it is absorbed by the body through ingestion of food, inhalation, or application to the skin.

Antihistamine - a drug that counteracts the action of histamine, an organic compound that acts as a powerful dilator of small blood vessels. Antihistamine drugs are used to relieve symptoms of allergy and those of the common cold.

Antimicrobial (antibacterial) - an agent, usually a drug, that acts to destroy or inhibit the actions of disease-causing microorganisms, such as bacteria.

Antipruritic - an agent, usually a drug, that decreases, stops or prevents itching.

Antipyretic - an agent, usually a drug, that reduces fever.

Antiseptic - an agent, usually a drug, that inhibits the growth and development of microorganisms, such as bacteria.

Antiserum - a specially prepared liquid portion of blood that contains antibodies against a specific disease.

Antispasmodic - an agent, usually a drug, that reduces or relieves spasms in certain body tissues such as the sphincter (muscular opening) of the stomach, gallbladder or the rectum. An antispasmodic can also relieve spasms in blood vessels, or in such body parts as the bronchi.

Antitussive - an agent, usually a drug, that relieves or stops spasms of coughing.

Anxiety - a psychological condition that causes fear, apprehension and feelings of imminent danger, with accompanying physical symptoms such as difficulty in breathing, restlessness and an increase in the rate of heart beats.

Aorta - the main artery (largest blood vessel in the body), that arises from the heart, arches through the chest down into the abdomen and carries oxygenated blood from the heart to smaller arteries, bringing oxygen to nourish the organs and tissues throughout the body.

Aphasia - the inability to speak, write or communicate via appropriate signs, or to understand the writing or speaking of others, usually as a result of brain damage.

Apoplexy (stroke) - a condition caused by hemorrhage, or bleeding in the brain from a ruptured blood vessel, due to weakness in the blood vessel's wall, or blockage of the vessel from a local clot, or one that traveled from another site (embolus) in the arterial system or the heart.

Aqueous humor - fluid produced in the front portion of the eyeball. This fluid bathes the anterior structures of the eyeball. If its normal outflow is blocked, painful, dangerous pressure develops inside the eye, a condition known as glaucoma.

Arrhythmia - irregularity in the pattern of the heart beat.

Arteriography - X-ray study of part of the arterial system to diagnose disturbance of the blood supply to any body part or area.

Arteriosclerosis - hardening of one or more arteries.

Arteritis - inflammation of one or more arteries.

Arthritis - a condition in which body joints and their supporting structures are inflamed and painful.

Ascites - an abnormal collection of fluid in the abdominal area due to disease conditions of one or more organs such as the liver, the heart or the kidneys.

Ascorbic acid (vitamin C) - a nutritional substance essential to normal body function. Deficiency causes scurvy, a condition in which the affected person suffers from bleeding and inflammation of the gums, loose teeth, and bleeding in other body areas.

Aseptic - a substance that kills microorganisms, and sterilizes the area to which it is applied; sterile.

Asphyxia - state of suffocation due to some form of interference with normal breathing.

Aspirate - fluid or tissue removed from the body via suction.

Asthma - a breathing disorder caused by infection or allergy in the bronchi.

Astringent - a medication that contracts blood vessels and other tissues, thereby reducing swelling, bleeding or secretions.

Atelectasis - collapse of a portion of a lung.

Athlete's foot - an infection of the foot caused by a fungal microorganism.

Atopic - a type of allergy that occurs only in humans.

Atrium - the upper, thin, muscular walled chamber of the right and left heart. The right atrium receives deoxygenated blood from the large veins before it courses through the lower right heart chamber (right ventricle) on its way to the lungs to be oxygenated. The left atrium receives oxygenated blood from lung vessels which then flows down into the lower left heart chamber (left ventricle), to be pumped out into the aorta and the arterial system to provide oxygen to the body tissues.

Atrophy - the wasting of tissue, muscles or any other body part or organ.

Auscultation - listening to various sounds, such as those produced by the heart or the lungs, with the ear or through a stethoscope.

Autism - a psychological disorder of children and some adults in which the person escapes real life by living in a world of fantasy, unable and unwilling to respond to ordinary human contact.

Autoantibody - an antibody produced by the body in reaction to its own tissues.

Autoantigen - a substance present in the body to which an individual is allergic.

Autogenous vaccine - a vaccine prepared from material taken from the body of a person who will subsequently receive the vaccine.

Autoimmune disease - a condition caused when the body produces antibodies against its own tissues.

Autoinfection - a condition in which a person becomes reinfected by microorganisms that had caused an earlier infection.

Autosomal inheritance - inherited traits passed on by genes located in 22 pairs of autosomes, which carry all characteristics other than those of sex.

Avitaminosis - a deficiency of essential vitamins.

B

Bacillary - referring to a bacillus, a rod-shaped type of microorganism occurring in some forms that are harmless, and in others that cause disease.

Bacteremia - blood poisoning caused by the presence of bacteria in the blood.

Barium enema - a diagnostic X-ray procedure done to examine the lower intestinal tract. Barium is given in the form of an enema to make the bowel visible on the X-ray film.

Beriberi - a disease involving the heart and the nervous system, caused by a deficiency of vitamin B_1 (thiamine).

Biliary - referring to the gallbladder or any portion of the gallbladder tract.

Biliary calculus - a stone in the gallbladder or in any part of the gallbladder tract.

Biopsy - the removal of a small portion of tissue from the body for diagnostic purposes.

Blackhead - fatty material that has hardened into a plug inside a skin pore.

Blepharitis - an inflammation of the eyelids.

Blister - a collection of fluid formed inside a sac on or in the skin, caused by irritation, fever, or one of various skin or infectious diseases.

Blood - the fluid that circulates through the arteries, veins and smaller blood vessels to bring nourishment to the tissues and remove wastes.

Blood brain barrier - a mechanism that prevents many substances that circulate in the blood, such as certain drugs, from getting into the circulation of the brain.

Blood component - any constituent of blood, such as red blood cells, white blood cells, platelets and others.

Blood gases - gases, such as oxygen and carbon dioxide that are dissolved in the blood.

Blood groups - also called blood types. There are four main blood groups (types) A, B, AB and O. There are also many sub-groups. Persons who have one type of blood can only receive a blood transfusion from another person who has the same blood type. The same is true for a blood donor, who can donate his blood only to a person of the same type. The exceptions are a donor of type O blood (universal donor), whose blood can be administered to any other person regardless of the other's blood type, and a person with type AB blood (universal recipient), who can receive blood from any other person, whatever his blood type. But the AB type donor can give blood only to another AB type recipient.

Blood pressure - the pressure exerted by the circulating blood against the walls of the blood vessels through which it flows.

Blood volume - the amount (volume) of blood in the body at any time, generally considered normal at 8 - 9% of body weight.

Boil - an area of skin filled with pus due to an infection.

Bone marrow - tissues that are contained in the cavities of bones. Red bone marrow contains developing red blood cells, white blood cells and platelets, while yellow bone marrow consists of a fatty substance.

Bowel - another term for the intestine, which consists of two parts: the small intestine and the large intestine (small bowel and large bowel).

Bowel incontinence - inability to retain or control bowel movements.

Bradycardia - a very slow heart beat, usually considered to be less than 60 beats per minute.

Breech presentation - a birth process in which the baby's buttocks present first in the mother's birth canal, in contrast to the more common head-first presentation. A breech birth process is more prone to complications, and more likely to require instrumentation or surgery during delivery than a normal, head-first presentation.

Bronchiectasis - a disease in which the bronchi (hollow tubular structures that carry inhaled air from the windpipe (trachea) to the lungs), and/or their smaller subdivisions (bronchioles) are widened due to repeated bouts of infection in the lungs. This disease is marked by foul-smelling breath and coughing spells, accompanied by spitting, and coughing up of mucous, pus-filled material from the bronchi.

Bronchitis - inflammation of the lining of the bronchi.

Bronchodilator - a drug given to dilate the bronchial tubes when they are shut down by spasms, such as occur in asthma.

Bronchogenic - any disease or other condition that arises in the bronchi.

Bronchopneumonia - inflammation, usually due to infection, of the lower portions of the bronchi (bronchioles) and the lungs.

Bronchoscopy - visualization of the windpipe (trachea) and the bronchial structures via an endoscope, a lighted instrument passed into these passages, for examination or treatment.

Bruxism - clenching or grinding of the teeth, usually done during sleep.

Bunion - a condition, usually due to wearing improperly fitting shoes, which causes a painful deformity of the big toe.

Bursitis - inflammation of a bursa, a sac-like cavity filled with a thick fluid that lubricates areas otherwise likely to sustain damage through friction; mainly affects bursae near joints, or those underneath the tendons that move the joints.

C

Calciferol (vitamin D) - an essential nutritional substance that affects the development of bone. With insufficient intake of this vitamin bone disease may occur.

Calcium - a vital element essential to the healthy composition of bones and teeth. Insufficient intake of calcium via foods may produce bone and teeth problems.

Callus - a hardened portion of skin, usually found on the palms of the hands or the soles, due to continual pressure and friction on these areas.

Caloric value - the measurement of heat produced by a food when it is burned (metabolized) in the body.

Calorie - a unit of heat content or energy.

Candida - a common type of yeastlike fungus. In man, Candida fungus is frequently found on the skin, in the throat, vagina, and in feces. Infection caused by this type of fungus is called candidiasis or moniliasis.

Canker sore - a small, usually ulcerated sore on the inside of the mouth, due to illness, irritation, or vitamin deficiency.

Capillary - relates to a tiny blood or lymph vessel.

Carbuncle - a skin condition caused by an infection, in which an area is filled with pus, enclosed by a hard covering that has a number of openings through which the pus may be discharged. It is bigger, and reaches down into the skin further than a boil.

Carcinogen - any substance in the environment or in food, or in some other agent, that may contribute to the development of cancer.

Cardiac - relating to the heart.

Cardiac arrest - a sudden stopping of the pumping of the heart that is fatal if not reversed within a few minutes.

Cardiac catheterization - the passing of a very fine tube into the chambers of the heart for diagnostic purposes.

Cardiovascular - relating to the heart or to the blood vessels.

Carditis - inflammation of the heart.

Caries - a condition that indicates decay of teeth or bones.

Cartilage - whitish, tough, flexible tissue situated around joints, in the spinal column, the ears, windpipe, voice box (larynx) and the tip of the nose.

Catabolism - the breakdown process of food during digestion into less complex substances.

Cataract - a condition in which the lens of the eye becomes cloudy, impairing vision. This process may be due to aging, disease, trauma, or may sometimes be found at birth as a congenital condition.

Catarrh - an inflammation of mucous membranes usually accompanied by a discharge. When it occurs only in the nose (as in the common cold), it is called rhinitis. If it affects both the nose and the throat, it is also called nasopharyngitis.

Catecholamines - chemical substances in the body that affect the actions of the involuntary nervous system.

Cathartic - a drug that speeds up the emptying action of the bowel.

Catheterization - a process in which a tube is passed into a body organ to empty it, as in urinary catheterization, or for diagnostic or treatment purposes.

CAT scan - a complex new X-ray procedure, whose full name is computerized axial tomography. It produces a reconstructed image of a transverse section of the body part being examined. It allows in-depth, accurate visualization that is helpful in diagnosing disease or injury, without the need to cut, or otherwise physically invade the body part.

Cat-scratch disease - a relatively mild infection believed to be transmitted via a virus that lives in cats, when a person is scratched by an otherwise healthy cat. Symptoms involve headache, fever and swelling of some lymph glands.

Cellulitis - inflammation of cellular or connective tissue in various parts of the body.

Centigrade - a measurement of heat used throughout the world based on a scale that is divided into 100 degrees. Normal body temperature on this scale is 37°C, which corresponds to the Fahrenheit scale at 98.6°F.

Central nervous system - that part of the nervous system that includes the brain and the spinal cord.

Cerebral hemorrhage - bleeding from an artery or other blood vessel in the brain, caused by weakness, injury, congenital abnormality or a disease such as high blood pressure.

Cerebral palsy - a condition of weakness, poor muscular coordination and spasm caused by damage to the brain that may occur before, during, or shortly after birth.

Cerebrospinal fluid - the fluid that bathes the brain and the spinal cord.

Cerebrovascular accident (CVA) - bleeding in the brain, the brain's coverings, or the formation of a blood clot that deprives a portion of the brain of oxygen which its tissues need to survive.

Cerumen - the wax in the ears.

Cerumenolytics - agents or drugs that dissolve ear wax.

Cervix - the neck of the womb, an important part of a woman's birth canal.

Cesarean section (C-section) - the surgical delivery of a baby through the abdomen, done when the baby is in distress during labor, when the mother is ill and not considered strong enough to cope with a normal vaginal delivery, or if the mother's birth canal is malformed, so that the baby cannot pass through safely.

Chalazion - a usually painless, slow-growing localized swelling in the margin of the eyelid due to a blockage of a small gland that is chronically inflamed.

Chancre - a symptom of syphilis, a venereal disease caused by spirochetal bacteria called treponema pallidum. The chancre is a hard skin lesion that occurs during the first stage of the disease, at the site where the spirochetes entered the body.

Chemotherapy - chemical agents or drugs used to treat various diseases, or to prevent them.

Chilblains - the swelling, reddening and itching of body parts such as the hands, fingers, nose and ears following prolonged exposure to cold.

Chloasma - brown pigmented spots or patches on the skin of the face and other parts of the body that occur with pregnancy, the menopause, or with the use of oral contraceptives.

Cholecystitis - inflammation of the gallbladder.

Cholecystokinetics - drugs that promote and affect the functioning of the gallbladder.

Cholera - an acute intestinal infection caused by bacteria that spread the disease via polluted water, food, insects and excrement.

Cholesterol - a white, crystalline substance that dissolves in fat and is present in all body tissues. It is a steroid made by the liver and the adrenal glands, and it is thought to contribute to the hardening of the arteries.

Cholinergics - drugs that act on the involuntary nervous system to increase the activity of internal organs such as the gastrointestinal tract, the heart, the lungs and produce expansion of the blood vessels.

Chorea - twitching, involuntary and irregular movement of the muscles that occurs in a number of nervous system diseases.

Chromosomes - the carriers of the genes that determine the sex and physical characteristics of each person.

Chronic - a state, or disease condition that lasts for a long period of time, without any appreciable change.

Ciliary body - a structure in the eye that holds and supports the iris (round colored portion of the eye) in place.

Circumcision - the removal of some or all of the foreskin (prepuce) of the penis, done in many infants shortly after birth, but also performed later in life if the foreskin interferes with normal function.

Cirrhosis - a degenerative disease of the liver in which liver cells are destroyed and replaced by useless fatty or fibrous tissue.

Citric acid - the acid found in citrus fruits. Useful as a scurvy preventive.

Claudication (intermittent) - lameness, limping and leg pain (chiefly in the calf muscles) on exertion. This happens when arteries narrowed by disease provide an insufficient blood supply to the muscles, often limiting the affected person to walking only a short distance at a time.

Claw toes - a deformity of the toes due to poorly fitting shoes.

Cleft lip (harelip) - a birth defect in which a baby is born with a split in the tissues below the nose extending down through the upper lip, or the lip may be absent entirely. This condition often occurs together with a cleft palate, causing feeding problems. Both conditions can be repaired by surgery.

Coagulation - the clotting of blood or other fluid into a gel or solid.

Coagulation time - a test to determine whether there is a deficiency in the blood that delays its ability to clot within a short time when it is exposed to air. The test is also done in persons who are taking certain drugs to lengthen the clotting time of the blood.

Cobalamin (vitamin B_{12}) - an essential nutritive substance required for the adequate development of the red blood cells, for normal functions of the nervous system, and for various other cellular functions.

Cobalt - an essential substance which is a component of vitamin B_{12}, normally present in green, leafy vegetables. Inadequate amounts in the diet may produce anemia in children.

Coitus - the act of sexual intercourse.

Colic - abdominal pain usually caused by cramps in the intestine or stomach.

Colitis - inflammation of the lower portion of the bowel called the colon.

Collagen - the predominant protein of the white fibers in connective tissue, cartilage and bone.

Colles fracture - a break in the wrist bone that causes the hand to be displaced backward and outward.

Colonoscopy - the visualization of the inside of the colon with a lighted tube called a colonoscope that is passed into the colon through the rectum.

Colostomy - an opening into the colon, created by abdominal surgery, to relieve an intestinal obstruction or other disease of the colon. This allows the discharge of feces through the opening instead of through the rectum.

Colostrum - the fluid expressed from a new mother's breast before her milk is formed in the breast glands, a process completed about three days after the baby's birth.

Colposcopy - an examination of the vagina and cervix with an instrument called a colposcope, that permits visualization of the internal portions of these body parts.

Coma - a level of unconsciousness from which a person cannot be aroused. Coma may be due to disease, drug abuse, other forms of poisoning or injury.

Comedone - blackhead.

Comminuted fracture - a break that occurs in such a way that the bone is broken into several pieces.

Communicable disease - a contagious disease that can be spread to other persons in a variety of ways.

Complete blood count - a laboratory examination done to determine whether a person has the normal quantity and appearance of blood constituents.

Compound fracture - a break in which the broken portion of the bone has penetrated the skin and created an open wound.

Compression fracture - a fracture in which one bony surface is driven towards another bony surface. Commonly found in fractures of the spine involving the bony segments of the spinal column.

Compulsive behavior - a psychological disturbance in which a person feels forced to behave in certain, often inappropriate ways.

Congenital - a condition, deformity or disease present at the time of birth.

Congestive heart failure - a condition in which the heart fails to provide sufficient pumping action to circulate blood adequately, resulting in congestion of the lungs and other vital organs due to the accumulation of blood.

Conjunctivitis - inflammation of the mucous membrane that lines the eye balls and the inner parts of the eyelids.

Contact dermatitis - irritation of the skin due to exposure to an irritating, or sensitizing substance such as poison ivy.

Contact lens - a very small lens made either of glass or plastic that is worn directly on the eye instead of eye glasses. It may also be worn by a person after a cataract operation, in which case the contact lens replaces the lens removed during surgery. A contact lens provides better vision for a person whose cataract has been removed because it permits peripheral vision, which eye glasses don't provide.

Contusion - a bruise; the swelling and discoloration that appear on the skin after an injury, or pressure has been applied to that area.

Convalescent serum - serum obtained from a person who has recovered from an infectious disease. It may be given to another person who is susceptible, to immunize him against the disease, or to modify its severity, if he develops it.

Conversion reaction - a psychiatric response to a stressful situation in which the affected individual suddenly cannot see, or becomes unable to walk, even though there is no physical basis for these symptoms.

Convulsion - seizure; the contraction of muscles in the entire body, or a body part, with resulting contortion of the affected parts. This condition may occur due to disturbances of the nervous system, as a symptom of epilepsy, during periods when an individual has a very high temperature, and in various other disease states.

Copper - an essential nutritive element present in such foods as organ meat, oysters, nuts and whole grain cereals. Its deficiency can cause anemia in children.

Corn - a thickened, often painful area on or between the toes. Usually caused by poorly fitting shoes.

Cornea - the clear, transparent portion of the eye that permits the entry of light, refracts light rays and helps focus the eye.

Coronary artery - the principal artery providing the blood supply to the heart via its right and left branches.

Coronary occlusion - the blockage or obstruction of the heart's blood flow; occurs as a result of heart disease in which the arteries of the heart narrow due to deposits that form on their walls, allowing formation of blood clots that cause the obstruction.

Corpus luteum - a small glandular structure in the egg-forming body (ovary) of a woman's reproductive tract, which secretes estrogen and progesterone hormones and plays an important part during pregnancy.

Coryza - nasal discharge and inflammation of the upper respiratory tract, as occurs during a cold, or in persons who have hay fever.

Counterirritant - a substance or medication applied to the skin to irritate and mildly inflame it, in order to produce a feeling of warmth and comfort; helpful when applied to painful muscle areas during a cold, or after exertion.

Cradle cap - a fatty type of skin condition in small infants who develop yellow scaly areas and skin cracks behind the ears, crusts on the scalp, and red pimples on the face. This condition is often worse during the winter than during other seasons.

Cranium - the bony structure of the skull that contains the brain.

Crepitus - a creaking, crackling or rattling noise heard and/or felt over broken bones or joints that are subject to wear and tear. The term is also used to describe a noisy discharge of gas from the intestine.

Crohn's disease - an inflammatory condition of a part of the intestine called the ileum. It may also affect the colon, and sometimes still other parts of the gastrointestinal tract. Also known as regional ileitis.

Croup - a respiratory condition in young children, often due to infection, featured by a harsh, brassy cough and crowing, difficult breathing. Commonly occurs at night. If unrelieved by exposure to a warm, moist environment produced by a steam inhalator, or bathroom filled with moisture by a hot, running shower, emergency treatment must be provided, preferably in a hospital.

Culture - a process in which microorganisms in a specimen such as blood, urine or a throat swab are placed in a nutrient broth and allowed to grow, so that they can be identified, and appropriate treatment given.

Cutaneous - pertaining to the skin.

Cyst - a sac of tissue anywhere in the body that contains fluid, gas, fatty or other matter.

Cystitis - inflammation of the urinary bladder, usually due to irritation or infection.

Cystoscopy - examination of the urinary bladder and the lower portion of the urinary tract with a lighted instrument called a cystoscope.

Cytology - the examination and study of cells.

Cytotoxic - any substance, drug, or other matter that is harmful to cells.

D

Debridement - removal of diseased, dirty or foreign matter from a wound.

Decongestant - a drug that relieves the discomfort and swelling caused by such conditions as hay fever or a cold, by shrinking the mucous membranes of the nose.

Decubitus (bed sore) - a condition caused by being bedfast, disabled, or having to lie in one position for a long time, allowing pressure on the area to break down the skin, and the underlying structures. It can be prevented by frequent change of position, exercise, good skin care and good nutrition.

Dehydration - great loss of body fluid due to vomiting, diarrhea, loss of blood and other disease conditions.

Delirium - a condition of confusion and restlessness, due to psychological or other causes, such as a high fever.

Delirium tremens - also known as the DT's; a condition of confusion and disorientation commonly associated with chronic alcoholism.

Delusion - a psychological disturbance in which a person has a false impression, belief or concept which he is convinced is true; reasonable discussion or argument will not change his belief.

Dementia - impairment of the mind; generally appears together with emotional and behavioral disturbances.

Demulcent - a substance or drug that soothes and relieves irritations of such body surfaces as the skin and mucous membranes. Internal mucous membranes, such as those lining the intestinal tract, are also relieved by demulcents when affected by certain irritating conditions.

Dengue - also known as dengue fever; an infectious disease that occurs commonly in the tropics, but may also be found in the southern U.S. It is a viral disease with symptoms that include joint pains, fever, rash, headache and weakness.

Depressant - a substance or drug that slows down excessive mental or physical activity. A tranquilizing drug, for instance, can be used to depress (reduce) excited behavior.

Depression - a state of mind in which a person feels low, has little or no hope, and may consider himself worthless. Counseling and/or treatment with an appropriate drug may relieve the condition.

Dermatitis - a skin condition caused by infection, irritation, or other disease.

Dermatologic - referring to skin, or the treatment of a skin condition.

Diabetes insipidus - a condition caused by a malfunctioning pituitary gland, which controls body fluids. Pituitary hormone replacement in the form of pituitary extract, or a synthetic substitute controls the disease.

Diabetes mellitus - a disease that can be inherited, in which the pancreas doesn't secrete sufficient insulin to properly utilize body carbohydrates. In milder, adult forms of the disease weight reduction, diet or oral medication may be sufficient for treatment. In more severe cases, and in the juvenile onset form of the disease, insulin must be injected at regular intervals, and a special diet followed to control the disease and to prevent complications.

Diabetic coma - a state of unconsciousness that results when blood sugar rises to a very high level and no effort is made to reduce it with an appropriate amount of insulin. When the blood sugar level is out of control, other metabolic disturbances follow that affect the nervous system and the level of consciousness. When this happens, treatment must be given immediately or death may result.

Diagnostic findings - findings that result from a careful physical examination, including the patient's history, laboratory tests and other special studies done to identify a condition or disease so that appropriate treatment may be started, if needed.

Diagnostic radiology - X-ray studies performed to study a complaint in order to contribute to the accurate identification of a condition or disease.

Diaper rash - reddened, irritated or sore skin in the diaper region. May be caused by insufficient exposure to air, infrequent diaper changes, the composition of the baby's urine, and other factors. Frequent diaper changes, skin exposure to air, careful rinsing of diapers during laundry to remove all traces of soap or bleach help to prevent this condition.

Diaphoresis - perspiration or sweat that is visible or perceptible.

Diaphoretic - a substance, drug or measure used to increase sweating.

Diarrhea - a condition in which a person has frequent watery bowel movements, with or without abdominal cramps, that may be caused as a result of eating certain foods, by intestinal infection or by a disease process.

Diastolic phase of blood pressure (diastole) - the lowest level noted during blood pressure measurement. It reflects the pressure within the artery and the heart's chambers as the heart muscles relax and the chambers fill with blood to prepare for the next contraction.

Dislocation - displacement of one or more bones of a joint, or other body part, from its original position. Commonly occurs during a traumatic event such as a fall.

Disorientation - a mental state in which a person is confused, may not recognize other persons he knows well, or know the time or place, or other facts he's normally well familiar with. May be due to a disease process, or to toxic states such as alcohol or drug abuse.

Diuretic - a substance or drug that causes increased urination.

Diverticulitis - a condition in which pouches (diverticula) in the colon (lower bowel) become filled with feces and other waste material, which in turn causes inflammation and frequently infection. Often accompanied by abdominal pain.

Diverticulum - one of a number of small pouches that develop inside the colon.

Dominant inheritance - some inherited traits are dominant over others. When a fetus receives two genetic traits, and one is stronger genetically than the other, he will be born exhibiting the dominant characteristic.

Dosage - the exact quantity of a drug that has been prescribed for a given time period.

Dropsy - a condition in which one or more body parts show swelling, usually due to a chronic disease; also called edema.

Dry socket - a condition that may follow tooth extraction. The blood clot formed after the extraction disintegrates prematurely, leaving the tooth socket empty and prone to infection. Generally occurs within two to three days after the extraction, and may last, causing considerable pain, for several weeks.

Ductus arteriosus - an opening between the artery that carries blood to the lungs (pulmonary artery) and the aorta, that closes shortly after birth under normal conditions.

Dumping syndrome - a condition that sometimes follows gastrointestinal surgery, particularly after removal, or partial removal of the stomach. Symptoms include sweating, dizziness, nausea, vomiting and palpitations (increased heart rate) after meals.

Duodenum - the first portion of the small intestine.

Duodenal ulcer - a lesion in the duodenum that results in the loss of tissue due to inflammation. The ulcer may penetrate the wall of the duodenum causing hemorrhage and other complications. It is caused by excessive secretion of stomach acid, intake of certain drugs, foods, or stress.

Dwarfism - a condition in which a person remains abnormally small.

Dysentery - a severe intestinal infection that produces diarrhea; it may be caused by a variety of microorganisms.

Dyskinesia - a condition in which a person has difficulty in carrying out voluntary movements.

Dysmenorrhea - pain during menstrual periods.

Dyspareunia - pain during sexual intercourse.

Dysphagia - difficulty in swallowing.

Dysphasia - difficulty in speaking, and in expressing oneself understandably to others, usually due to brain damage.

Dyspnea - difficulty in breathing; shortness of breath, usually due to disease of the heart or lungs.

Dystrophy, muscular - a disease of unknown origin in which muscles do not function normally, and eventually deteriorate.

Dysuria - difficulty or pain during urination.

E

Ecchymosis - an area of purplish discoloration on the skin, due to bleeding underneath that area.

Eclampsia - a condition in which a pregnant woman develops convulsions (seizures) shortly before, or during labor, as a result of having high blood pressure during the pregnancy, associated with kidney problems.

Ectopic pregnancy - a pregnancy which develops in one of the fallopian tubes (the tubes that conduct the fertilized egg from the ovary to the womb) instead of in the womb.

Eczematous - an acute or chronic inflammatory condition of the skin, due to allergy or other causes.

Edema - swelling in body tissues or in a body part, such as the legs.

Edentia - state of not having any teeth.

Electrocardiogram (ECG, EKG) - a record made by a machine called the electrocardiograph that traces the electrical activity of the heart, and indicates abnormalities if any are present.

Electroencephalogram (EEG) - a record made by a machine called an electroencephalograph that traces the electrical activity of the brain (brain waves).

Electrolyte - a substance capable of conducting an electric current when it is in solution.

Electromyogram (EMG) - a record made with a machine called an electromyograph that traces the electrical activity of muscles. It is used to diagnose muscle diseases.

Embolism - an obstruction in a blood vessel by a traveling blood clot or various other substances.

Emesis - the act of vomiting.

Emetic - a drug used to induce vomiting.

Emollient - a substance or drug that smoothes and softens irritated skin or mucous membranes.

Emphysema - a condition in which the lungs have enlarged air sacs which cause difficulty in breathing.

Empyema - the formation of pus in one of the body cavities, frequently the lung.

Encephalitis - inflammatory condition of the brain, usually due to infection.

Endocrine - refers to a gland, such as the pituitary, which secretes a hormone directly into the blood stream.

Endogenous - refers to a body process that begins, or is produced, in the body or in one of its parts.

Endometrium - the mucous membrane that lines the womb (uterus).

Endometriosis - a condition in which cells that normally line the walls of the womb begin to grow on the surfaces of other organs within the pelvic structure, and sometimes also in distant areas of the body.

Endotoxin - a toxic (poisonous) substance released by certain microorganisms inside the body when their cell walls are injured.

Enterocolitis - inflammation of the small and large intestines.

Enterovirus - a virus that lives in the intestinal tract.

Entropion - turning in of the eyelid toward the eye.

Enuresis - bedwetting during the night, a condition that occurs primarily in children. It is involuntary.

Enzyme - a body substance that reduces complex compounds such as food into simpler compounds so they can be absorbed by the body.

Epidemic - a contagious disease that spreads through a large area of a community, a country, and sometimes an entire continent.

Epidermis - the outermost portion of the skin.

Epididymitis - inflammation of the sperm duct in the testicles.

Epiglottis - a piece of cartilage behind and below the tongue that closes the top of the windpipe (trachea) when a person is about to swallow, so that the food will go down the gullet (esophagus) and not the windpipe.

Epilepsy - a disease of the nervous system in which the victim has convulsions (seizures) and lapses of unconsciousness at different intervals. Newer medications help to control this disorder.

Epiphysis - the end portion of long bone.

Epistaxis - nosebleed.

Erb's palsy - injury of the baby's upper arm muscles during birth which produces paralysis of the arm.

Eructation - the act of belching.

Erysipelas - a painful infection of the skin caused by streptococcus bacteria.

Erythema - a reddened condition of the skin, due to irritation or infection.

Erythema multiforme - a skin disease due to a variety of causes, which presents in the form of tiny elevations and small blisters.

Erythroblastosis fetalis - a blood disease of newborn infants caused by the interaction of blood factors between an Rh negative mother and a Rh positive father.

Erythrocyte - red blood cell.

Erythrocyte sedimentation rate (ESR) - a laboratory test that determines the presence of infection in the body.

Esophageal - referring to the esophagus (gullet).

Esophagoscopy - examination of the inside of the esophagus (gullet) with a lighted tube called an esophagoscope.

Essential fatty acids - fats ingested in foods that are broken down by the body into simpler fat compounds and absorbed.

Etiology - the study of the causes of disease.

Euphoria - a feeling of happiness and well being, not necessarily based on reality, that may be caused by a drug or illness.

Exocrine - a glandular secretion delivered directly, or through a duct to the linings of body parts or to the skin.

Exophthalmos - a condition in which the eyeballs protrude, present in certain diseases.

Exotoxin - toxic substances released by bacteria or other microorganisms in the body.

Expectorant - a medication that helps in getting rid of mucus and phlegm that has accumulated in the respiratory tract.

Extremity - an arm or a leg.

F

Fahrenheit - a scale for measuring temperature in which the freezing point is 32°F, normal body temperature is 98.6°F, and the boiling point is 212°F.

Fallopian tubes - the tubes that carry the egg from the ovary to the womb.

Fecal incontinence - inability to control bowel movements.

Feces - stool, bowel movement.

Fetal - pertaining to an unborn child in the mother's womb.

Fiberoptics - a process based on newer optical instruments that allows the visualization of many internal parts of the body.

Fibrillation - fast, purposeless twitching of muscles. An extremely dangerous condition when it happens to the heart muscle, and fatal if not reversed quickly.

Fibrin - a body protein essential in the clotting of blood when blood is exposed to air, such as during an injury.

Fibrosis - scar tissue that is formed after injury or surgery.

Fibrositis - an inflammation of fibrous tissue.

Fissure - a crack or fold in skin or underlying tissue.

Fistula - a passage or channel that is formed between two internal body parts, or between an interior part of the body and the surface.

Flatus - discharge of intestinal gas.

Fluorine - an element that helps to protect teeth when it is compounded with other substances and added to drinking water, or applied directly to teeth via toothpaste or a dental treatment.

Folacin (folic acid) - an essential nutritive substance required for the proper development of red blood cells. Deficiency causes various forms of anemia.

Foreign body - any substance or material embedded in a part of the body where it doesn't belong and where it may cause injury.

Foreskin - a fold of skin that covers the tip of the penis. Also known as the prepuce.

Fowler's position - a position in which a patient's head is elevated 18-20" and the knees are raised somewhat with a pillow or other support. Helpful in case of respiratory difficulties and various other conditions.

Fracture - a break in a bone, or other body part.

Fremitus - a thrill or noise perceived through vibrations when the hand is placed on a person's chest.

Frostbite - damage done to the skin and underlying tissues when exposed to cold.

Fumigation - disinfection of a contaminated area by means of antiseptic fumes.

Furuncle - same as a boil; an infected area of skin filled with pus.

G

Gallbladder series - X-ray examination of the gallbladder to determine whether it contains gallstones, or whether there are any other abnormalities in the gallbladder or related areas.

Gamma globulin - a body protein that contains antibodies against various infections. It may be injected into a person at danger of developing an infection, to confer temporary immunity.

Gangrene - tissue death that occurs if tissues freeze, are deprived of nourishment, after sustaining injury or with a severe infection.

Gastrectomy - the removal of the stomach by surgery.

Gastric aspiration - using suction to draw food or fluid from the stomach. Done for diagnostic purposes, after surgery of the abdomen, or in drug poisoning situations.

Gastric fluid - fluid secreted by, and present in the stomach. The stomach secretes several fluids, one of which is hydrochloric acid, which prevents the growth of bacteria and promotes digestion of food as it passes through.

Gastric lavage - a process of washing out the stomach, needed when a toxic substance has been ingested that must be removed as part of the treatment that helps the victim to survive. Lavage may also be done when a person is bleeding into the stomach. Iced fluid is injected via a tube into the stomach, removed, and new fluid is injected. The process is continued until the bleeding stops, or until a different treatment method is started.

Gastritis - inflammation of the stomach.

Gastrointestinal - refers to the stomach and the intestines.

Gastroscopy - an examination with a lighted tube called a gastroscope that enables the physician to inspect the inside of the stomach for any abnormalities or disease conditions.

Genetic disorder - a disease or abnormality that is passed on to a member of the next generation via heredity.

Genital wart - also known as venereal wart; caused by a virus, this type of wart is usually transmitted via sexual contact, and thrives in the warm moist areas of the genital and anal regions.

Genitourinary - refers to the genital and urinary tract areas.

Geriatric - refers to the elderly.

Germicide - any substance or drug that can kill germs.

Gestation - pregnancy.

Giardiasis - an intestinal infection caused by the organism Giardia lamblia.

Gigantism - a condition in which a person has an unusually large body, or body parts.

Gingivitis - inflammation of the gums. Symptoms include bleeding and discomfort. If untreated, infection and loss of teeth may result.

Glaucoma - an eye disease in which the fluid pressure within the eye rises, with or without accompanying pain. If the condition is not recognized, damage to eye structures and loss of vision may result.

Glucagon - a body hormone that activates sugar stored in the liver; it also affects various other body functions.

Glucose - body sugar.

Glycogen - the form in which glucose is stored in the liver.

Gonad - the sex gland; ovary in the female, and testicle in the male.

Gonococcus - the microorganism that causes gonorrhea.

Gout - a disease due to an unusually high amount of uric acid in the blood. Uric acid is deposited in the tissues, since the kidneys can't excrete the increased amount rapidly enough. Gout affects joints such as the big toe, which becomes inflamed, hot and painful.

Grand mal - the severe seizure of epilepsy.

Granulocyte - a white blood cell.

Granuloma - a nodular inflammatory lesion that contains areas of granulation. When found around the groin and genitals it is generally granuloma inguinale, a venereal dsease that requires specific medical treatment.

Gravid - pregnant.

Greenstick fracture - incomplete fracture of a long bone, usually seen in children, in which the bone is bent, but splintered only on its convex side.

Grippe - also called influenza. An acute infectious disease, caused by one of the various influenza viruses. Symptoms include chills, fever, elevated temperature, aches and pains all over the body, headache, weakness, loss of appetite and inflammation of the respiratory tract.

Growth retardation - a condition also known as "failure to thrive." It occurs as a result of genetic predisposition, certain diseases, endocrine disturbances, malnutrition and in cases where the infant does not receive enough attention and love.

Gynecologic - refers to any condition of the female, including the female anatomy and reproductive system.

H

Hallucinogen - a substance or drug that produces unrealistic perceptions in the individual who takes it.

Hammer toe - a congenital deformity, usually of the fourth or fifth toe at the joint that connects the toe to the foot bones (metatarsals).

Heimlich maneuver - a method used to quickly remove a chunk of food that has accidentally slipped into the respiratory tract of a person who will choke to death if the food is not recovered within a few minutes.

Hematemesis - vomiting blood.

Hematinic - an agent or drug that increases the number of red blood cells in the blood, as well as the concentration of hemoglobin.

Hematologic - referring to blood, or the study of blood.

Hematoma - a collection of blood, or of clotted blood somewhere in the body, usually caused by injury or following surgery.

Hematopoietic - the development of blood cells and other constituents.

Hematuria - blood in the urine.

Hemianopia - partial blindness, usually due to brain damage.

Hemiplegia - paralysis of one side of the body, frequently due to a stroke.

Hemodialysis - a process of removing impurities and waste from the blood with a machine when a person's kidneys are unable to perform this essential function.

Hemoglobin - the pigment in blood that carries oxygen to the tissues, carbon dioxide (a waste product) to the lungs, and colors the blood red.

Hemolysis - destruction of red blood cells; occurs in infection, due to a toxic substance or drug, or in the laboratory after freezing, thawing, or other activities or studies involving red blood cells.

Hemophilia - an inherited disorder in which the affected individual bleeds easily and may develop serious hemorrhage even after very minor injury, due to the presence of a clotting factor deficiency.

Hemoptysis - spitting up of blood that comes from a hemorrhage in the lungs, usually due to a disease such as tuberculosis.

Hemorrhage - severe bleeding in, or from any part of the body.

Hemorrhoid - an enlarged vein, or group of veins that develop this condition as a result of pressure, continual irritation or disease. Most frequently occurs in the veins of the rectum, but appears in other parts of the body as well.

Hemostasis - the process of stopping bleeding, either with drugs, or mechanically, with an instrument.

Hepatic - refers to the liver.

Hepatitis - inflammation of the liver, usually due to infection, or following ingestion of a toxic substance.

Hepatosplenomegaly - enlargement of the liver and spleen.

Hernia - a condition in which an organ inside one of the body's cavities protrudes from the cavity, usually due to a weakness of the muscles that surround it, or following disease or surgery.

Herpes simplex - a skin infection caused by the herpes simplex virus that may be triggered by many different events, such as exposure to sunlight, stress, pregnancy, or other infections. The virus appears in two forms: herpes simplex type I generally affects the face (mouth or lips); herpes simplex type II usually infects the genital area and is spread primarily through sexual contact.

Herpes zoster (shingles) - a viral infection whose configuration follows the pathways of certain nerves. It consists of crops of blisters that break and form crusted lesions. These may be preceded, accompanied, or followed by severe pain along the course of the affected nerve segment. The condition may be particularly serious and disabling in elderly and/or debilitated persons.

Hirsutism - a condition characterized by the growth of hair in unusual places and/or excessive amounts, especially in women.

Histoplasmosis - a fungus infection caused by an organism called Histoplasma capsulatum, found in the soil and in the excrement of a number of animals in various parts of the country. The infection affects the lungs when tiny particles of the fungus are inhaled.

Homeostasis - a balance within the body of its chemical and other functions and constituents, necessary for continued health.

Hormone - one of many body substances secreted by various glands, essential for normal body functioning.

Hospice - an institution which provides professional care to patients with chronic, irreversible or terminal diseases.

Humectant - an agent or substance that helps to preserve moisture in specific body areas such as the skin; or in a room, or in an oxygen tent.

Hydrocephalus - a condition which may be congenital or acquired, in which the head becomes abnormally large and there is increased pressure in the brain, due to excessive secretion and accumulation of cerebrospinal fluid in the ventricles (chambers in the brain).

Hyperalimentation - a process of providing food for a malnourished or debilitated person, or one unable to eat normally by infusing nourishing fluids directly into the bloodstream through a central vein.

Hyperglycemia - excessive amount of sugar in the blood, as happens in uncontrolled diabetes mellitus.

Hyperkalemia - excessive amount of potassium present in the blood.

Hyperplasia - an increase in tissue, or size of an organ.

Hyperpyrexia - excessively high fever.

Hypersensitivity - excessive sensitivity to an agent or stimulus, as happens when a person is allergic.

Hypersomnia - a condition in which a person sleeps excessively at intervals, but is normal during waking periods, in contrast to being inclined to sleep continuously, as happens during periods of somnolence.

Hyperthermia - an abnormally high body temperature that may be due to a heat stroke, or is brought on by the injection of foreign protein for treatment purposes, or by other physical agents, substances or equipment.

Hyperthyroidism - a condition in which the thyroid gland, situated at the front of the neck, is enlarged, swollen and produces an excessive amount of a thyroid hormone called thyroxine. This produces weight loss, nervousness, an increased heart beat and other symptoms. Treatment is aimed at counteracting the effects of the hormone.

Hypertonic - refers to a concentration of salt (sodium chloride) greater than that present in blood.

Hypertriglyceridemia - excessive amount of fatty substances in the blood.

Hypertrophic - excessive growth of an organ or body part.

Hyperventilation - overbreathing; an increase in the depth and/or rate of breathing that may cause dizziness and occasional fainting.

Hypervitaminosis - excessive intake of vitamins, with possible toxic reactions.

Hypnotic - an agent or drug given to induce sleep.

Hypocalcemia - an insufficient amount of calcium in the blood.

Hypoglycemia - an abnormally low blood sugar level.

Hypogonadism - inadequate functioning of the sex glands.

Hypokalemia - insufficient amount of potassium in the blood.

Hypotension - abnormally low blood pressure.

Hypothermia - abnormally low body temperature, due to accidental exposure to cold, immersion in cold water, or intentionally induced as a treatment, or during surgery by using an electrically controlled hypothermia mattress.

Hypotonic - refers to a concentration of salt lower than that present in blood.

Hypoventilation - reduced ventilation of the air sacs of the lungs (alveoli), due to inadequate breathing or blockage of the airways (bronchi). Prolonged hypoventilation may lead to respiratory depression and coma.

Hypovolemic shock - a state of shock caused by a greatly reduced volume of blood, generally due to hemorrhage.

Hypoxemia - inadequate oxygenation of blood.

Hysterectomy - the removal of the womb by surgery.

Hysteria - a psychological disturbance evidenced by inappropriate, excessively emotional behavior.

I

Iatrogenic - an effect upon the patient that results from the suggestions, treatment or prescribed activity by a doctor.

Icterus - jaundice; the yellow discoloration of the skin, due to an excess of bile in blood.

Idiopathic thrombocytopenic purpura (ITP) - a blood disease of unknown origin whose chief symptom is platelet destruction, which leaves the victim prone to bleed.

Idiosyncrasy (to drugs) - unusual sensitivity to certain drugs by some individuals.

Ileitis - inflammation of the part of the small intestine called the ileum.

Ileostomy - an opening created by surgery in the abdomen and the ileum (section of small intestine) to allow discharge of fecal material.

Ileus - acute intestinal obstruction due to various causes, accompanied by severe, colicky pain, vomiting and dehydration; a serious, potentially fatal condition, if not relieved by prompt, effective treatment.

Immune globulin - a pooled blood fraction that contains antibodies present in a large number of adults. When injected in an individual, it may confer temporary immunity against a number of infectious diseases.

Immunity, active - a person who has developed his own antibodies against a particular infectious disease is actively immune against that disease.

Immunity, passive - a person injected with immune globulin or some other type of inoculation is said to be passively (and usually only temporarily) immune against a particular infectious disease.

Immunization - the process of developing one's own antibodies against an infectious disease, or being inoculated with inactivated or killed microorganisms that cause a particular infectious disease, in order to develop antibodies and acquire protection against the infection.

Immunodeficient - every healthy individual has the capacity to fight infection with certain blood factors that fend off invading microorganisms, and prevent them from multiplying. Illness, disability and other factors may decrease a person's capacity to fend off harmful organisms, or the development of foreign cells, such as cancer cells, for instance. When that happens, the person is immunodeficient.

Immunodiffusion - a laboratory test in which the interactions of specific antigens and antibodies are observed.

Immunoglobulins - body proteins that function as antibodies to ward off infection.

Immunosuppression - suppression of the body's rejection mechanism by means of certain drugs.

Immunotherapy - treating the body in such a way as to bolster its capacity to ward off infection, or the invasion of harmful foreign cells such as cancer cells.

Impacted cerumen (ear wax) - ear wax that has hardened inside the ear, requiring special methods, such as softening and irrigation in order to remove it without damaging the delicate structures inside the ear.

Impacted feces - feces that have become too hard to leave the intestine in the process of normal elimination. Special softening agents or manual removal are required to remove the feces and prevent injury to the bowel.

Impaired consciousness - a state that occurs when a person is not fully alert, due to injury, drug abuse or for other reasons. He may be semiconscious, stuporous, or in coma.

Impetigo - an infection of the skin often seen in children, usually due to the staphylococcus bacterium. It is very contagious, and may spread all over the surface of the skin.

Impotence - the inability to complete the sex act.

Inadequate personality - a person who indicates by his behavior that he cannot cope with others, and with ordinary life responsibilities has an inadequate personality.

Inanition - a state of exhaustion due to lack of food, or the inability to assimilate (utilize) food properly.

Incontinence - the inability to control urination or the elimination of feces.

Incubation period - the period of time that elapses between exposure to an infectious disease, and showing symptoms of the disease.

Induced abortion - an abortion that is brought about by the use of drugs or other methods.

Infarction - tissue death due to deprivation of oxygen.

Infection - a disease process caused by the invasion and damaging action of microorganisms, such as bacteria or viruses.

Infectious mononucleosis - an infectious disease caused by a virus that is relatively mild and occurs mostly in young adults. Symptoms include headache, fever, sore throat, enlargd lymph glands and spleen. Also known as the "kissing disease."

Infertility - inability of an individual or a couple to have a child.

Infiltration - to pass, or inject fluid or any other material into the tissues.

Inflammation - the irritation, swelling and other harmful changes of tissue as a result of trauma, pressure, or other physical interference in some part of the body. May also be caused by illness, infection or drugs.

Influenza - an infectious disease caused by a variety of influenza viruses, some of which cause more severe illness than others. Symptoms include headache, fever, joint pains and cough.

Inguinal hernia - protrusion of a portion of intestine through a weakened muscular wall in the groin (inguinal region).

Injection - using a needle, attached to a syringe or other sterile container, to infuse liquid material into the skin, muscles or veins to administer drugs, feed, or hydrate an individual.

Inoculation - injection of a small quantity of inactivated or killed microorganisms, or toxin produced by the organisms, to challenge an individual's body to develop antibodies against these organisms.

Input and output (I & O) - measuring the amount of liquid a person consumes within a given period, such as 24 hours, against the amount of liquid (urine, wound drainage, vomitus, etc.) the person loses within that same time period. Done to determine whether the person receives enough liquid, and to calculate the amount of additional liquid that may need to be given to meet that person's fluid requirements.

Insomnia - inability to fall asleep, or to sleep long enough to meet the body's requirements for rest.

Insulin - a hormone produced by cell groups inside the pancreas (a gland lying across and behind the stomach) called the islets of Langerhans. Insulin converts blood sugar into body energy. When a person produces too little insulin, he develops diabetes mellitus.

Insulinoma - a tumor (growth) of the cell groups called islets of Langerhans in the pancreas, which may produce excessive amounts of insulin.

Insulin shock - a condition that results if a diabetic person takes too much insulin, if his body cannot utilize the amount of insulin injected, or if he doesn't eat enough food to balance the amount of insulin injected. Symptoms include a lowered blood sugar level, tremors, cold sweat, weakness, dizziness and coma, if the condition is not reversed quickly by eating or drinking carbohydrate-containing food such as a few pieces of sugar, or a glass of orange juice. If a person develops insulin coma, he must be given glucose by injection.

Intercurrent infection - a second infectious process that occurs in a person who already has an infectious disease.

Interferon - a natural body substance formed in response to infection that defends the body against further attack by the foreign cells, organisms or viruses.

Intermittent positive pressure breathing (IPPB) - artificial respiration via a breathing machine that intermittently inflates the lungs with air or oxygen under pressure in cases where a person is unwilling, as in a case of postoperative pain, or unable to breathe normally.

Interstitial - relating to a space between cells, or inside a body organ.

Intra-articular - inside a joint.

Intra-cranial - inside the skull.

Intramuscular injection - an injection of fluid or a drug into muscular tissue.

Intrauterine device (IUD) - a device inserted in the womb to prevent pregnancy.

Intravenous infusion - introducing fluid, nutritive substances or drugs into a vein with a sterile needle and syringe, or other sterile apparatus.

Intravenous pyelogram (IVP) - a diagnostic procedure in which the patient is given an intravenous injection of contrast agent, allowing diagnostic X-ray studies to be done of the kidneys and the urinary tract.

Intubation - insertion of a tube into a body opening or passage.

Iodine - a trace element essential to health in minute (trace) quantity. Also used externally as an antiseptic.

Iron - a trace element essential to certain body functions, such as the proper and adequate formation of hemoglobin. Iron deficiency results in anemia, "spoon nails," bowel disease and other symptoms.

Irrigation - bathing a body part or cavity with fluids or medicated fluids for cleansing, healing or antiseptic purposes.

Irritant - a drug or agent that irritates the skin or other body part, either accidentally or with intent to produce tissue stimulation.

Ischemic - a body part or area that has insufficient, or no blood supply.

Isolation - placement of a patient who has an infectious disease into a separate room or area, and using various other precautions to prevent the spread of the disease to others.

J

Jaundice - yellow discoloration of the skin and the whites of the eyes caused by the presence of too much bile in the blood, usually due to liver or gallbladder disease.

Jejunum - a portion of the small intestine.

K

Karyotype - a pattern of chromosomes, lettered and numbered in pairs to perform genetic study of an individual's hereditary characteristics.

Keratitis - inflammation of the cornea, the transparent structure located at the front of the eye.

Keratoconus - a condition of unknown origin in which the cornea becomes cone-shaped, which interferes with normal vision.

Keratolytic - refers to a drug or agent that loosens or separates the horny layer of skin.

Keratomalacia - a disease of the cornea (the transparent structure at the front of the eye) in which it becomes dry, ulcerated and may perforate. The cause is malnutrition or debilitating disease.

Kernicterus · a serious illness of the newborn in which the baby develops jaundice in certain portions of the brain.

Ketoacidosis - a state which results from the accumulation of incompletely metabolized fatty acids in the blood, upsetting the body's metabolic balance.

Kidney machine - a machine used to remove impurities and waste products from the blood of a person whose kidneys are unable to perform this vital function.

Knee-chest position - the patient is positioned by the doctor or an assistant so that he rests on his chest and knees, in order to facilitate certain examinations.

Koplik's spots - tiny blue-and-white spots surrounded by red rings that appear inside the mouth at the points where the upper and lower teeth meet. The spots appear during the first two or three days of the onset of measles, before the rash can be seen.

Korsakoff's psychosis - a condition in which a person's memory is impaired, and he is disoriented as to time and place. He may invent facts to cover up his inability to remember certain events. Usually caused by alcoholism.

Kwashiorkor - a condition of extreme malnutrition, especially of proteins. Occurs in children who live in poor countries, or in areas of deprivation. They develop anemia, swelling of body tissues, a pot belly and other physical characteristics.

L

Labyrinthitis - inflammation of the structures of the inner ear.

Laceration - a break or tear of skin or other body tissues, usually caused by injury.

Lacrimal apparatus - the tear glands, sacs, and ducts that produce tears, and carry them down through the eyes and into the nose.

Lactation - the process following childbirth during which milk is formed in the mother's breasts to enable her to nourish her infant through suckling.

Lactic dehydrogenase (LDH) - an enzyme in the blood that rises to higher levels within several days after a person has had a heart attack. Laboratory determination of this and other enzymes helps to make a diagnosis of heart attack, and to distinguish this condition from various other diagnoses.

Lactose - milk sugar.

Laparoscopy (abdominoscopy; peritoneoscopy; ventioscopy) - a surgical procedure in which an electrically lighted tubular instrument is passed through the abdominal wall to visualize the internal organs and structures for diagnostic or treatment purposes.

Laryngitis - inflammation of the voice box.

Laryngotracheobronchitis - a respiratory disease that occurs mostly in children as a result of infection of the respiratory tract.

Larynx - the voice box, which enables a person to speak.

Lavage - the washing out of an organ or body cavity, such as the stomach.

Legionnaire's disease - a pneumonia-like disease caused by the organism Legionella pneumophila, which infects persons who have been exposed to it in areas where the organisms live and have become activated.

Leprosy - an infectious disease, also known as Hansen's disease, caused by a mycobacterium that appears in various forms and affects nerves, the face, eyes or the extremities, depending on which type of the disease the patient has contracted. It may lead to destruction of tissue, causing various deformities in the affected body parts.

Leukapheresis - a process in which a certain amount of blood is removed from a donor, so that the white blood cells can be removed. The remaining blood is then returned to the donor. The separated white blood cells may be used to treat another person, or for various other purposes.

Leukemia - also known as cancer of the blood, leukemia is a disease of the blood-forming organs, which produces a large number of abnormal white blood cells. The disease occurs in acute and chronic form.

Leukocyte - a white blood cell.

Leukoplakia - small whitish, sometimes leathery patches on the skin that occur due to various causes.

Leukorrhea - a whitish vaginal discharge.

Levin tube - a tube that is passed into the stomach to aspirate fluid for examination, to drain fluid from the stomach postoperatively, or to perform certain treatments.

Lichen planus - a skin condition that may occur in many body areas, depending on the particular form of the disease affecting the patient.

Limbic system - that part of the nervous system that affects primarily the internal organs of the body.

Lipids - a collective term that includes body substances such as fatty acids, glycerides, and various others.

Lipoma - a benign growth composed of fatty tissues.

Lipoproteins - body compounds that contain both proteins and fatty substances.

Lithotomy position - a position in which the patient is placed on the back, with legs and knees raised for examination or treatment.

Lockjaw - a dangerous infectious disease caused by Clostridium tetani, an anaerobic bacterial organism. The disease is acquired when the organism invades the body through a dirty wound such as a nail puncture. The patient must be treated at once to prevent the disease, which produces spasms of all the voluntary muscles, including the jaw, which is clamped shut. Tetanus immunization, repeated at intervals, helps to protect people against this disease which may be fatal if treatment is delayed.

Lues - syphilis.

Lumbago - a general term for backache in the lower part of the spine: mid-or lower back, or the lumbar and/or lumbosacral area.

Lumbar puncture - the insertion of a sterile needle into the spinal canal to withdraw spinal fluid for examination, to administer spinal anesthesia during surgery, to instill medication and for various other purposes.

Lymph - a colorless fluid in the body that runs through the lymphatic channels and eventually joins the venous circulation. It consists of white blood cells and tissue fluid.

Lymphadenitis - inflammation of the lymph nodes, which are located throughout the body along the lymphatic channels.

Lymphangitis - inflammation of the lymphatic channels.

Lymphocyte - white blood cell made in lymph nodes.

M

Magnesium - an element present in the body that aids in muscle contraction, bone and tooth formation, nerve conduction and various other functions. Deficiency may produce irritability of muscles and nerves.

Malaise - a term that describes a general feeling of illness, headache, muscular, joint, and other pains that occur when a person has the flu or other febrile illness.

Malaria - an infectious, febrile disease transmitted (spread) through the bite of a mosquito that earlier sucked blood from another person infected by one of the several types of Plasmodium organisms that are capable of causing the disease.

Malignant - any condition that is resistant to treatment, is very severe, and may lead to death.

Mammography - X-ray examination of the breast.

Mania - a form of hyperactive behavior in which an individual becomes hyperexcitable; may be a phase of the mental disorder called manic-depressive psychosis.

Manic-depressive illness - a mental disease characterized by mood swings, in which the victim becomes alternately deeply depressed and highly excited.

Mantoux Test (PPD) - a test in which a small amount of a purified protein derivative (PPD) of tuberculin (the fluid containing the tubercle bacillus that causes tuberculosis) is injected into the skin, raising a small wheal. The area is inspected two days later to determine whether or not the person is susceptible to the disease.

Marasmus - extreme form of malnutrition.

Masochism - a psychologic condition in which a person derives sexual gratification while being abused or hurt.

Mastectomy - surgical removal of the breast.

Mastitis - inflammation of the breast.

Mastoiditis - inflammation of the mastoid, a bone located behind the ear.

Meconium - fecal material passed through the birth canal by the fetus if it is in distress, and by the newborn infant during the first few days of life. The stool is colored dark green, and its consistency is pasty.

Megacolon - a condition present at birth in some babies in which the nerves essential to elimination from the lower bowel are absent. This produces an accumulation of feces, and distention of the bowel and abdomen which requires surgical correction.

Melanoma - a tumor that appears on the skin. If malignant, it may spread to other parts of the body. The lesion is dark brown due to the pigment melanin.

Melasma (chloasma) - a patchy discoloration of the skin, often seen in pregnant women.

Melena - bowel movement that has a black, tar-like appearance, caused by bleeding somewhere in the intestinal tract. When such bowel movements are discovered, the individual should be promptly examined by a physician.

Menadione - a synthetic preparation of vitamin K, an essential nutrient which aids in the normal clotting process of blood. Deficiency may produce bleeding.

Menarche - the onset of the first menstrual period.

Meningitis - inflammation of the meninges, the covering membranes of the spinal cord and the brain.

Meningocele - a body defect in which a portion of the spinal cord membrane protrudes through the bones of the spinal column.

Menorrhagia - excessive bleeding during the menstrual period.

Metrorrhagia - irregular menses.

Micturition - urination.

Migraine - a severe headache that may appear on only one side of the head and cause other symptoms such as nausea, vomiting, and a special sensitivity to light and noise.

Miliary tuberculosis - a form of tuberculosis that spreads throughout the body into all tissues and organs.

Minimal brain dysfunction (MBD) - a developmental or learning disorder in children, more often in boys than in girls, for which no physical basis is found, although some have slight neurological symptoms. Among the symptoms these children show are hyperactivity, poor coordination of the muscles, impulsiveness and difficulty in perception. A child with such symptoms should be carefully examined by experts to help him overcome his problems.

Mitral valve - the valve that separates the upper left chamber of the heart from the lower left chamber.

Mononucleosis - same as infectious mononucleosis, or "kissing" disease; an infectious disease caused by a virus that occurs primarily in young adults, with symptoms such as fever, sore throat, enlarged lymph nodes and spleen, and an initial decrease of white blood cells that changes to an increase as the disease runs its course.

Morbidity - state of disease, or calculated ratio of a disease state to the normal state.

Moxibustion - a popular therapeutic process first used in the Orient that produces counter-irritation on some part of the skin; done by placing a cone-shaped container filled with cotton or similar material on the skin and setting the material on fire.

Mucosa - the smooth membranous lining of the interior organs of the body. It is present in the gastrointestinal tract, the respiratory tract, the urinary tract and the genitourinary tract of men and women.

Mucus - the material secreted by the mucous membranes.

Multipara - a woman who has given birth to two or more children.

Multiple sclerosis (MS) - a degenerative disease of portions of the nervous system that results in progressive disability of muscle functions. The affected person develops difficulty in walking, using his hands, or with his vision. The disease may show signs of improvement, then become worse again. It may progress to complete paralysis, or leave the victim partially disabled for many years without further progression of symptoms.

Munchausen's syndrome - describes the illness of a person who has the abnormal urge to manufacture signs of illness, such as an artificially elevated temperature, apparent blood in the urine or other body part or cavity where it is not normally found, and other symptoms or signs that have no physical basis. Psychiatric treatment must be obtained to discover the reasons for the person's need for forging the illness. Such persons often move from hospital to hospital to avoid being recognized, to gain admission and treatment for their often ingeniously produced "symptoms."

Muscular atrophy - weakness and wasting of muscles due to lack of use, illness that forces a person to remain in bed for long periods, and other conditions that result in the loss of muscle mass.

Muscular dystrophy - a disease that often starts during childhood, in which muscles begin to waste away and gradually become totally useless. The cause of this disease is not yet known; heredity appears to be a factor.

Musculoskeletal - refers to the muscles and the bones of the skeleton.

Myalgia - muscular pain.

Myasthenia gravis - a disease in which muscles are chronically weak and unable to function normally. The cause of this disease is not known. It occurs more frequently in women between the ages of 20-40, and requires symptomatic, supportive treatment.

Myeloma - a cancerous, progressive disease that involves the bloodforming organs of the bone marrow, causing plasma cell tumors, weakened bone structures, anemia and kidney damage.

Myocardial infarction - the sudden loss of blood supply to the heart muscle due to a dangerous narrowing of one of the blood vessels such as the coronary artery, or an obstruction such as a blood clot. Commonly called a heart attack.

Myoclonus - continuous rhythmic spasms of a muscle or a group of muscles.

Myoma - excessive growth of muscular tissue into a tumor.

Myositis - inflammation of a muscle, or a group of muscles.

Myringitis - inflammation of the ear drum.

Myxedema - a disease caused by insufficient secretion of the hormone thyroxine by the thyroid gland.

N

Narcotic - a medication given to relieve pain, that often also makes a patient sleepy or stuporous, or has still other side effects. Most of these drugs can lead to addiction if they are taken indiscriminately, or for long periods of time.

Narcotic antagonist - a drug that counteracts effects of a narcotic medication.

Nasal septum - the bone that separates the two sides of the nose.

Necrosis - death of cells, tissues or organs due to lack of oxygen, infection, injury, exposure to cold or burn.

Necrotizing enterocolitis - an extremely grave disease of the bowel that occurs in adults following certain types of abdominal surgery, and some other illnesses. It can also occur in newborns. The disease causes tissue death, abdominal pain, nausea, high fever and diarrhea that may be bloody. Treatment involves fluid replacement, relief of pain and antibiotics.

Neonatal - concerns the newborn period, generally the first four weeks after birth.

Neoplastic - refers to any abnormal growth in the body.

Nephritis - inflammation of the kidneys.

Nephropathy - disease state affecting the kidneys.

Neuralgia - pain that travels along peripheral nerve tracts.

Neuritis - inflammation of one or more nerves.

Neurologic - refers to an examination or study of the nervous system.

Neuroma - a tumor that arises from cells somewhere in the nervous system.

Neurosis - a behavioral disturbance with many symptoms; the most frequently apparent symptom is anxiety.

Neurosyphilis - the third stage of syphilis which includes involvement of the nervous system.

Nevus - a mole or birthmark.

Niacin (nicotinic acid, niacinamide) - an essential nutritive substance that aids metabolic functions. Deficiency causes pellagra, a disease that causes blisters, reddened areas and swelling of the skin, of the gastrointestinal system and the mucous membranes of the mouth; also affects the nervous system; alcoholics may have these symptoms because they frequently suffer from severe malnutrition and vitamin deficiencies.

Nightblindness - inability to see in the dark, or in poor light, due to vitamin A deficiency.

Nits - the eggs of a louse, found in the hair of persons with louse infestation.

Nocturia - frequent urination during the night, due to excessive fluid intake before going to bed at night, or to illness.

Nodule - a small swelling.

Nosocomial - refers to an infection, or other disorder picked up by a patient while he is hospitalized.

Nulliparous - refers to a woman who has never given birth.

Nystagmus - involuntary regular movements of the eyes, that may be due to congenital weakness or certain diseases.

O

Obstetric - refers to the care of the pregnant woman, including the prenatal period, labor, delivery and the period immediately following the delivery, as well as care in between pregnancies.

Occult blood - blood present in such small quantities and often altered in color or consistency that it can be detected only by chemical tests, or via microscopic or spectroscopic examination of the suspected material.

Ocular - refers to the eye.

Oligomenorrhea - abnormally infrequent or scanty menstruation.

Oligospermia - a low concentration of sperm in a man's ejaculate.

Oliguria - a small amount of urinary output in a given period of time.

Oncology - the study of cancerous diseases.

Ophthalmic - refers to the eye.

Opportunistic infection - an infection that occurs because an individual has lost his natural capacity to fight it, due to weakness and incompetence of his immune system, as a result of illness, malnutrition and other causes.

Optometry - a profession whose practitioners examine eyes, determine if a person has any eye problems or disease, and prescribe, and produce corrective lenses and other optical aids.

Oral cavity - the mouth.

Orthopedics - a medical specialty whose practitioners are experts in problems or diseases of bones, joints and related structures. Orthopedic surgeons are experts in setting fractured bones, performing bone and joint surgery, and in prescribing rehabilitative treatment for people who have bone and joint diseases, trauma, or deformities that require correction for adequate or improved functioning.

Orthopnea - inability to breathe except while sitting up.

Osmosis - a process in which fluid flows from one area where the liquid is of a lower concentration across a semi-permeable membrane to an area in which liquid is of a higher concentration.

Osteoarthritis - a degenerative disease that affects the joints, and often occurs as a person ages, or following injury.

Osteogenic sarcoma - a malignant bone tumor that most often occurs in the young, at ages 10-20.

Osteomalacia - a bone disease in which the bones soften and bend, with varying degrees of pain. May occur in pregnancy, metabolic disease or in vitamin D deficiency.

Osteomyelitis - inflammatory disease of the bone marrow, the surrounding bone and the end portions of bone (epiphyseal areas).

Osteoporosis - increasing weakness and fragility of the bones. Most frequently occurs in elderly, postmenopausal women and in elderly men.

OTC (over the counter, or nonprescription) drug - medicine that is available in the pharmacy or in other stores without a doctor's prescription. An OTC medication is safe and effective if the instructions on its label or box are carefully followed.

Otic - refers to the ear.

Otitis media - inflammation of the middle ear.

Otorhinolaryngologic - refers to the ear, nose and throat.

Ovary - the female sex gland, present on each side in a woman's lower abdomen. Inside, egg cells (ova) are formed. It also secretes sex hormones that help the development, growth and regulation of the female reproductive system.

Oxytocic - a drug or agent that speeds up the onset of strong uterine contractions during labor. It may also be given after delivery to cause the uterus to contract and prevent uterine bleeding.

P

Pacemaker - a built in mechanism that controls the heart's activity. When its mechanism doesn't function adequately, a mechanical pacemaker may be used, either temporarily or permanently. An artificial pacemaker may be external, or it may be inserted under the patient's skin. The latter technique is commonly used when the patient requires a permanent pacemaker.

Paget's disease - There are two unrelated diseases, both called by this name. One is a chronic bone disease, also known as osteitis deformans, the other is an unusual form of breast cancer.

Palpation - using the hands to touch, feel or lightly press a certain body area to determine if any abnormality is present.

Palpitation - a very rapid heart beat caused by exertion such as running, by excitement, nervousness, certain drugs and various disease conditions.

Pancreas - a glandular organ that lies across and behind the stomach. It produces pancreatic juice that aids in the digestion of food in the upper intestine. It also produces insulin.

Papanicolaou (Pap) smear - a reliable and simple test done on various body cells to determine abnormalities and detect the presence of cancer.

Papilledema - swelling inside the brain or nearby areas that affects the optic nerve and may compromise vision.

Paracentesis - a puncture of a body cavity for the purpose of removing fluid.

Paralysis - inability to move the extremities or a body part due to loss of muscular function.

Paranoid - a condition in which a person is abnormally suspicious of others, with feelings of delusion and of being persecuted by hostile people or forces.

Paraplegic - a condition in which both legs, and usually the lower portion of the trunk are paralyzed. This may happen after a stroke, an injury, and under certain other circumstances.

Parasite - an organism that lives on, and obtains its nourishment from, another organism called the host.

Parenteral drug administration - a method of administering a drug in some way other than through the gastrointestinal tract.

Parkinsonism - a disease in which the victim gradually loses control of his voluntary muscles. Also known as shaking palsy and paralysis agitans.

Paronychia - inflammation or infection in the tissue surrounding a finger or a toenail.

Parturition - childbirth.

Passive immunity - immunity temporarily conferred against a certain infectious disease by inoculating a person with a substance that contains antibodies against that disease.

Patch test - a skin test done to detect sensitivity of a person to certain substances to which he may be allergic, or to certain infections.

Pathogen - a disease-causing microorganism.

Pathologic - refers to disease, or to the study of disease.

Pediatric - refers to the medical specialty concerned with the care of children.

Pediculosis - infestation with lice.

Pellagra - a vitamin deficiency disease that occurs when a person doesn't eat enough foods containing niacin (nicotinic acid, nicotinamide). The vitamin is present in yeast, liver, meat and whole grain enriched cereals. Pellagra symptoms include blisters, reddened areas and swelling of the skin, the gastrointestinal system and the mucous membranes of the mouth. The nervous system may also be affected.

Peptic ulcer - an inflammatory injury in the lining of the stomach or the adjacent portion of small intestine, called the duodenum. Peptic ulcer is a disease that tends to occur in people who suffer from tension and anxiety. It is treated with drugs, diet, counseling, and may require blood replacement or surgery if the ulcer penetrates the wall of the stomach or intestine, causing hemorrhage and other complications.

Peristalsis - wavelike movements of the gastrointestinal tract to move its contents from one end to the other.

Peritonitis - inflammation of the lining of the abdominal cavity and its organs.

Pernicious anemia - a type of anemia that occurs mostly in elderly people when their bloodforming organs fail to develop red blood cells normally. The condition is treated by giving injections of vitamin B_{12}, a treatment that must be continued for the remainder of the person's life.

Pertussis - whooping cough.

Petit mal - a minor seizure in which the affected person may seem to be absent-minded, daydreaming, or twitching slightly for a few seconds, then return to his normal state.

Phenylketonuria (PKU) - inherited metabolic abnormality in which the affected individual is unable to process a certain constituent of protein foods called phenylalanine. A toxic side product is formed that accumulates first in the blood and urine, and subsequently affects the brain and nervous system, producing mental retardation if not recognized and treated early. The condition can be diagnosed in a newborn baby's urine or blood, and corrected by providing a diet free of foods containing phenylalanine. In many parts of the country a test for this condition is required by law, so that corrective action can be taken before symptoms appear.

Pheochromocytoma - a tumor in the adrenal gland that may cause high blood pressure and related symptoms, which disappear if the tumor is diagnosed and removed by surgery.

Phimosis - a condition in which the foreskin of the penis is narrowed so that it cannot be retracted over its tip.

Phlebitis - inflammation of a vein.

Phosphorus - an essential body element that aids in the formation of bones and teeth, the conduction of nervous impulses, in contraction of muscles and in enzyme activity.

Pituitary - an important endocrine gland, also called hypophysis, that is located at the base of the brain. It secretes a number of important hormones. These include an adrenal-stimulating hormone called ACTH, a growth-stimulating hormone, a thyroid-stimulating hormone, a gonadotropic hormone which stimulates the production of sex hormones in the ovaries and testicles, a hormone that stimulates milk production in mothers who are nursing, and a hormone that stimulates the production of the pigment called melanin.

Placenta - a structure that develops in the womb of a pregnant woman, which is attached to the umbilical cord, the organ through which the growing fetus obtains its food, oxygen, and discharges its wastes. The placenta also produces sex hormones that affect the course of pregnancy. After the birth of the baby, the placenta separates from its place of attachment in the womb, and is expelled a short while later.

Placenta previa - the premature separation of the placenta from the womb prior to the baby's birth, a serious complication of late pregnancy.

Plasma - the liquid portion of blood.

Plasmapheresis - a procedure in which blood is withdrawn from a donor, the red blood cells are removed, and are then retransfused into the donor; the remaining blood constituents are then separated and prepared for administration to patients who need the various blood fractions or plasma.

Platelets - tiny discs in the blood stream that aid in the clotting process also known as thrombocytes.

Pleural - refers to a thin membrane that covers the lungs and lines the inside of the chest wall.

Pleurisy - inflammation of the membrane covering the lungs and the inside of the chest wall. It usually causes pain on breathing and the development of fluid in the pleural cavity (space between the two layers of pleura).

Pneumoencephalogram (PEG) - X-ray studies of the brain following the injection of air or gas to make these structures visible.

Pneumonia - inflammation of the lungs.

Pneumothorax - a condition that occurs when air or gas gets into the pleural cavity and exerts pressure on the lung, causing it to collapse. When this happens as a result of trauma or rupture of a lung air sac, breathing problems develop requiring prompt treatment.

Polydipsia - increased amount of fluid intake due to excessive thirst.

Polyuria - excessive urination.

Porphyria - a metabolic defect that involves a group of body pigments called porphyrins. Depending on the type of illness, the affected person may have abdominal pain, the nervous system may be involved, and urine may turn dark brown on standing.

Postpartum - referring to the period that follows childbirth.

Postprandial - after a meal.

Potassium - an essential body element that aids in the contractions of muscles, in the transmission of nerve impulses, and in water, and acid-/base balance in the blood and tissues. Deficiency may produce disturbances of heart functions and interfere with other vital body activities.

Presbyopia - decreased elasticity of the lens of the eye that occurs in the elderly and impairs accommodation, thus interfering with accurate vision.

Preventive health care - a concept which provides for health examinations given at regular intervals to detect any beginning signs of illness, so that treatment can be provided to stop the illness before it can progress. Health counseling is also given, to help retain good health through appropriate diet, rest, exercise and other factors-that promote a healthy lifestyle.

Primigravida - a woman who is pregnant for the first time.

Proctitis - inflammation of the rectum.

Proctoscopy - examination of the rectal structures with a tubular instrument.

Prophylaxis - preventive treatment or health care.

Prostate - a gland present in men that surrounds the urethra (the passage through which urine flows from the bladder) at the point where it joins the urinary bladder.

Prostration - physical or mental exhaustion that may follow psychological stress, great physical exertion, exposure to very hot environmental temperatures, or severe illness.

Pruritus - itching.

Psoriasis - a skin disease that produces itchy reddened patches and scales. It is not a contagious disease, but tends to run in families.

Psychiatric - refers to an abnormal mental or emotional state.

Psychosis - severe emotional disturbance in which a person behaves irrationally, unpredictably, and may harm himself or others.

Pterygium - a disease of the eye in which a triangular piece of tissue grows out of the lining of the eyelid at its inner aspect (next to the nose) and extends toward the pupil of the eye.

Puerperium - the period of time between childbirth and the return of the womb to its normal, pre-pregnant size and shape.

Pulmonary - refers to the lungs.

Purpura - bleeding into the skin, as a result of injury or a blood disorder.

Pus - a thick, yellowish liquid produced by inflammation or infection. It consists of fluid (serum) and germ-destroying cells, other microorganisms and dead tissue.

Pyelonephritis - inflammation of the kidneys.

Pyloric stenosis - a narrowing of the muscular valve at the far end of the stomach called the pylorus.

Pyogenic - refers to an agent or organism that causes the formation of pus.

Pyorrhea - inflammation of the gums in the periodontal spaces (where the gums join the teeth), often accompanied by pus formation, and the loosening of teeth.

Pyridoxine (vitamin B_6) - an essential vitamin that aids the functions of body cells and the metabolism of amino and fatty acids. Deficiency of this vitamin may produce anemia, nervous system problems, skin lesions and seizures in small infants.

Pyuria - pus in the urine.

Q

Q fever - an infection caused by rickettsial microorganisms that occurs mainly on farms, and in slaughterhouse workers. It is acquired from animals such as goats and cows through contact with their urine and feces. Symptoms include headache, chills, fever and cough.

Quinsy - a sore throat, followed by an abscess in the tissues that surround the tonsils. This condition may occur together with tonsillitis. If the abscess becomes very large, it may need to be opened and drained.

R

Rabies - a virus infection transferred to man by an infected animal through a bite. The symptoms of the disease involve muscle spasms, paralysis, convulsions, excitement and rage, alternating with periods of calm. The virus moves along nerve channels and eventually enters the brain. Or, it may pass from an open skin surface into the body. Since the disease is potentially fatal, immunization must be provided when a person has been bitten by a rabid animal, or one suspected of having the disease.

Radiation therapy - the use of radioactive substances to treat a person for a variety of diseases, but especially those which produce large numbers of abnormal cells that have a destructive effect on human tissues, such as cancer. The effect of radiation therapy is to destroy the cancer cells. Measures are taken to protect healthy tissues.

Radionuclide - a radioactive substance that is used to perform diagnostic and treatment procedures in a field called nuclear medicine.

Refraction - an examination of the eyes by an eye doctor or an optometrist to determine the presence of nearsightedness, farsightedness or other vision abnormalities, prior to prescribing corrective lenses.

Regurgitation - vomiting.

Remission - a chronic disease whose symptoms have temporarily disappeared.

Renal failure - inability of the kidneys to perform their essential functions of removing waste products from the blood and excreting them in the urine.

Respiratory arrest - the sudden cessation of breathing.

Respiratory tract - the organs and passages concerned with breathing: the nose, pharynx, larynx, epiglottis, trachea, bronchi and the lungs.

Resuscitation - emergency procedures used to restart respiratory and heart functions that have stopped due to illness, trauma or for other reasons, to allow the victim to survive.

Retina - the light-sensitive inner layer of the eye that transmits nerve impulses to the optic nerve.

Retinol (vitamin A) - an essential vitamin that aids vision and certain cellular functions. Deficiency produces nightblindness, dry eyes and other eye problems.

Retrolental fibroplasia (RLF) - a disease of premature infants in which there is an abnormal growth of fibrous tissue behind the lens of the eye, causing blindness. The condition is caused by the excessive administration of oxygen after the birth of the premature infant, which is toxic to his eye structures.

Reverse isolation - isolation precautions used for the protection of the patient whose immune system is weak, so that he will not be exposed to any infectious organisms carried by people in his environment.

Reye's syndrome - a virus disease usually found in children that may follow an upper respiratory infection or other virus disease. It is a dangerous disease that affects the brain and nervous system, and produces fatty accumulations in various body organs. Special treatment procedures are now available in various medical centers to help victims to survive this illness.

Rheumatoid arthritis - an inflammatory disease of the joints of the fingers, wrists or feet, but it may also affect other joints. It produces pain and swelling, destroys surrounding cartilage and decreases motion in the affected joints. Rheumatoid arthritis is a chronic disease that may cripple the affected individual. Treatment includes heat, exercise, medication and rest, under the supervision of an experienced physician. The cause of the disease is not known. It may affect children as well as adults.

Riboflavin (vitamin B_2) - an essential vitamin that aids in protein metabolism, maintains healthy mucous membranes and helps the body convert food into energy. Deficiency may cause soreness and fissures of the lips.

Rickets - a disease of children caused by a deficiency of vitamin D, which prevents calcification (hardening) of the bones. As a result, the child develops bowlegs.

Roentgen - an international unit of X- and gamma radiation.

Rubefacient - a counterirritant which reddens the skin when applied.

Rubella - German measles.

Rubeola - measles.

S

Sadism - sexual gratification obtained by inflicting pain on another individual.

Salmonella infection - food poisoning caused by eating food contaminated by salmonella bacteria.

Salpingitis - inflammation of the fallopian tubes.

Scabies - a skin infection caused by a mite that burrows into the skin.

Scarlatina - also called scarlet fever. A skin disease that is highly contagious, caused by a streptococcal organism; symptoms include fever and a bright red rash over the body, followed later by peeling of the affected skin areas.

Scurvy - a disease caused by a deficiency of vitamin C; symptoms include a tendency to bleed into the gums, inflammation of the gums, and loose teeth.

Sedative - a drug given to reduce nervousness, abnormally great excitement or irritability.

Seminal fluid - the fluid that carries semen.

Sepsis - infection.

Septic abortion - an abortion performed under unsanitary conditions, with the result that the woman having the abortion develops an infection of her reproductive organs that may progress to blood poisoning.

Septicemia - blood poisoning. The presence of harmful organisms or their toxins in the blood stream.

Serum - the liquid portion of blood that is left after the clotting components have been removed.

Shock - a group of symptoms that occur when a person's circulatory system collapses. This may happen in a severe allergic response, when a person hemorrhages, after major surgery, serious burns, or following trauma.

Sigmoidoscopy - examination of the portion of colon (sigmoid colon) just above the rectum with a lighted tube.

Sims position - lying semi-prone.

Sinus - a small, hollow channel or passage inside the body, that may contain fluid or air.

Sodium - an essential element in the body that aids fluid and acid/base balance, nervous impulse transmission and muscle contractility. Deficiency may produce swelling of the tissues and other symptoms of fluid imbalance.

Staphylococcus - a bacterial organism that may cause different types of infections.

Stenosis - the narrowing of a channel, duct or passage in the body.

Sterile - an area that is free of germs.

Stimulant - a drug or other substance that increases mental or physical activity.

Stoma - an opening; a term used to describe an artificial opening made by a surgeon in a body part, such as a colostomy, an opening into the colon made through the abdominal wall.

Strabismus - an eye condition which makes it impossible for a person to focus both eyes on the same place. Treatment may include eye glasses, exercises, medication and surgery.

Streptococcus - a bacterial organism that causes a variety of infectious diseases.

Stroke - injury to the brain as a result of bleeding, or a blocked artery somewhere in the brain. Stroke may cause paralysis of one side of the body if the brain is damaged in an area that controls body movements. It is usually caused by chronic high blood pressure or hardening of the arteries (arteriosclerosis). Stroke is also called cerebral hemorrhage, or apoplexy. Expert rehabilitative treatment may restore most or all functions lost when the stroke first occurs.

Subcutaneous injection - an injection that is given under the skin.

Superinfection - a new infection of the same type a patient already has.

Supraventricular tachycardia - an increase in the heart rate caused by an electrical impulse in the heart that originates somewhere above the region of the ventricles (lower chambers of the heart).

Surfactant antiseptic - a specially prepared fluid that inactivates or kills certain bacteria, fungi and viruses when applied to the skin.

Sustained release dosage - a term that indicates that a drug has been manufactured so that tiny portions of each tablet or capsule are released over a period of hours at carefully calculated intervals.

Swimmer's ear - infection of the external ear caused by moisture, allergy, a disease-causing organism or a chemical irritant. More common during the summer season.

Symptom - some change in a body part, organ or function that indicates illness or a developing disorder.

Syncope - fainting.

Syndrome - a group of symptoms that occur together, suggesting the presence of a disorder or illness known to include this group of symptoms.

Synovial fluid - the fluid found in joints.

Synovitis - inflammation of the lining of a joint (synovial membrane).

Syringomyelia - a progressive disease that affects the nervous system by producing small cavities filled with fluid at the back of the spinal cord. Pain, weakness and loss of sensation occur in the victim's hand or arm, and the legs may become spastic.

Systemic - relating to the body as a whole.

Systemic lupus erythematosus - a disease that affects connective tissue (bone, tendons, cartilage) as well as other organs such as the heart, lungs and kidneys. The patient has pain in the muscles, joints, and in his abdomen. Various drugs are used to control the disease.

Systolic phase of blood pressure (systole) - the highest level noted during blood pressure measurement. It reflects the pressure within the artery and the heart's chambers as the heart muscles go into systole (contract), forcing blood to be pumped out of the heart, back into the arterial circulation.

T

Tachycardia - an abnormally fast heart rate.

Tachypnea - very rapid breathing.

Talipes - clubfoot; a congenital foot deformity in which the foot is twisted inward, outward or in several other abnormal positions so that normal use of the foot for standing and walking is not possible. May be corrected, or greatly improved by surgery.

Tamponade - compression of a body part as a result of an accumulation of fluid in a surrounding body area.

Tapeworm - one of a group of long worms that lives in the intestines of man as well as in animals; may grow as long as 30 feet.

Tendinitis - inflammation of a tendon, a tough and strong band of connective tissue that connects muscles to bones.

Tennis elbow - a condition in which there is pain either on the outer or inner portion of the elbow due to an inflammation in the surrounding structures. The outer (lateral epicondylitis) form is more common than the inner (medial epicondylitis). Pain is aggravated when the hand tries to grip or grasp an object.

Teratogen - any agent that may cause a growing fetus to be born with an abnormality.

Tetanus - lock jaw.

Tetany - a disorder caused by a calcium deficiency in the blood. Inadequate calcium levels produce irritability of the nerves, muscular cramps or spasms, and sometimes convulsions. There are several possible causes for the disease. Depending on the cause, treatment consists of calcium, vitamin D, or parathyroid hormone.

Tetrahydrocannabinol (THC) - marijuana.

Thalassemia - a particular type of anemia that occurs in areas that border on the Mediterranean, and in Southeast Asia.

Therapeutic abortion - an abortion performed on a woman likely to develop a serious mental or physical illness if she carries the pregnancy to term and gives birth to a child.

Therapeutic dosage - the quantity of a drug calculated to improve the condition for which it is being prescribed.

Thermography - a diagnostic device that uses the temperatures in various body parts to determine the presence of abnormal conditions in these areas.

Thiamine (vitamin B_1) - an essential vitamin that aids carbohydrate metabolism, and heart and nervous functions. Deficiency causes symptoms in the circulatory and nervous systems. Deficiency disease is called beriberi.

Thoracentesis - withdrawal of fluid from the pleural cavity (the cavity created by the membranes that line the lungs and the chest wall), to relieve pressure on the lungs.

Threatened abortion - signs and symptoms, such as spotting or vaginal bleeding, that are warning signals for a pregnant woman that she may not be able to continue to carry the pregnancy.

Thrombocytopenia - an abnormally small number of platelets in the blood.

Thrombophlebitis - inflammation of a vein, generally in the leg, that occurs along with the presence of thrombosis in that area.

Thrombosis - the presence of a blood clot inside a blood vessel, blocking the vessel.

Thrush - a fungal infection of the mouth.

Thyroidectomy - removal of the thyroid gland by surgery.

Thyroiditis - inflammation of the thyroid gland.

Tic douloureux - a condition that irritates the trigeminal nerve which branches out through the face, causing severe facial pain. Medication, dental therapy and neurosurgery can provide relief.

Tinnitus - a condition in which a person hears noises or ringing in his ears. May be caused by a problem of certain nerves, by inflammation and by certain drugs.

Tocopherol (vitamin E) - a vitamin that is believed to aid healing, and contribute to the stability of biologic membranes. Deficiency can produce destruction of red blood cells.

Topical anesthetic - an anesthetic agent directly applied to the area where pain relief is needed.

Topical medication - a medication directly applied to the area where it is needed, rather than being taken by mouth or in some other way.

Torticollis - a contraction, often occurring in spasms, of the muscles of the neck, which causes the head to be drawn to one side. May be a congenital condition, or acquired after birth.

Toxicologic - refers to the study of poisonous agents and how they affect the body.

Toxin - a poisonous substance. It may be a chemical agent, or a harmful substance secreted by a microorganism.

Trachea - the windpipe.

Tracheostomy - an incision made into the windpipe when a person is unable to breathe normally.

Transfusion - any fluid introduced into a vein, but generally refers to blood given as replacement for blood lost in hemorrhage due to injury, during surgery, or to increase an inadequate blood supply due to a blood disease.

Transient ischemic attack (TIA) - brief period during which an elderly person may be confused, feel dizzy, unable to remember certain events, experience weakness of the legs, tingling or burning of the arms or legs, or have slurred speech. This occurs because of a temporary spasm in one of the blood vessels of the brain that is narrowed by hardening of the arteries, or because of a temporary blockage in a blood vessel. Such attacks may be the warning signals of an impending stroke.

Transplant - the transfer of tissue or an organ from one body area to another, or from one person to another, to replace a missing, diseased, or non-functioning body part or organ.

Tremor - a state of trembling of one or more body parts, such as the hands or the head, due to illness or weakness.

Trendelenburg position - a position in which the patient's head is at an angle of 45° below his pelvis, while he is lying on the operating table, or in bed, if he is being treated for shock.

Trichinosis - a disease caused by a roundworm called Trichinella spiralis, that lives in pigs and is transmitted when a person eats infected pork that has not been adequately cooked. When the worms' larvae enter the bloodstream, they travel to all body tissues, where they cause an inflammatory response. As cysts they can survive in muscle fibers for years. Symptoms include fever, nausea, vomiting, diarrhea and abdominal pain in the first few weeks after infection. Muscle pains and swelling in the affected areas follow the initial symptoms.

Tube feeding - also known as gavage, this procedure is performed when a person is unable to take nourishment by eating and drinking normally. A tube is inserted through the nose or mouth and passed down into the stomach. It is anchored with adhesive tape so that it cannot move, and liquids or blended foods can then be given at prescribed intervals.

Tuberculosis - an infectious disease caused by the Mycobacterium tuberculosis. It affects primarily the lungs, but may also affect other organs, such as the stomach, skin, bones or lymph glands. A particularly severe type of the disease, called miliary tuberculosis, affects most body parts, including the brain. Infected sputum droplets passed through the air by coughing or sneezing transmit the disease to others. Treatment includes medication, adequate nourishment and sufficient rest.

Tularemia - an infectious disease acquired through bites from certain wild animals.

Turista - travelers' diarrhea; an intestinal infection caused by bacteria, viruses, and the toxins they secrete. It is acquired by eating contaminated food, or drinking contaminated water, usually while traveling in foreign areas.

Tympanic membrane - the eardrum; a structure that transmits sounds received from the outer ear by vibrating as the sound waves hit the membrane.

Type and crossmatch - a laboratory test done prior to giving a blood transfusion to make sure the donor's blood type and other blood characteristics match those of the recipient. If this is not done, the recipient may develop a serious, and possibly fatal reaction to the donor's blood.

Typhoid fever - an infectious disease caused by a salmonella bacillus. The disease is transmitted through food, water or milk contaminated by the organism. People who have the disease may continue to act as carriers after they recover by harboring the organisms in their urine and feces. Symptoms include headache, high fever, chills, and a rash on the chest and abdomen. Antibiotics, supportive measures and urine and stool precautions are used in the treatment.

U

Ultrasonography - a diagnostic technique that utilizes the reflection and transmission of ultrasonic waves to determine abnormality or disease of internal body structures.

Uremia - the presence of an abnormally high level of urea and other nitrogenous waste substances in the blood, caused by poorly or nonfunctioning kidneys.

Ureters - two tubes, each connecting a kidney to the bladder. Urine flows from the kidneys through the ureters into the bladder.

Ureteritis - inflammation of the ureters.

Urethra - the passageway through which urine flows from the bladder out of the body.

Urinary calculus - a stone in the urinary bladder; a hard, solid mass of varying size, formed somewhere in the urinary tract through an accumulation of body chemicals, that is lodged in the bladder. It may be very painful, and produce spasms and other urinary tract problems. A high fluid intake may help to pass the stone, and prevent future occurrences. Diet modifications may be prescribed.

Urinary incontinence - inability to retain or control urination.

Urinary urgency - frequency; a frequent urge to urinate; occurs with enlargement of the prostate that causes pressure on the bladder, with irritation, inflammation and infection of the bladder and the urethra.

Urine culture - a laboratory technique done to determine the presence and type of harmful microorganisms in the urinary tract, so that appropriate treatment can be prescribed.

Urolithiasis - the presence of a stone in the urinary tract.

Urologic - refers to the urinary tract.

Urticaria - hives; a rash usually due to an allergic reaction against food, a psychological event, a drug or some other environmental irritant.

Uterus - the womb.

V

Vaccine - a preparation that contains infectious organisms that are alive, or that have been inactivated or killed. When given to an individual in carefully prescribed amounts, his system is challenged to develop antibodies against these microorganisms and the disease they cause, so that he develops immunity against it.

Varices - varicose veins; a condition in which certain veins become dilated, knotted and weakened due to stress or disease.

Varicocele - enlarged scrotum due to a varicose enlargement of the veins of the spermatic duct, located inside the scrotum.

Varicose ulcer - an open, sore area on a varicose vein caused by erosion of the surface of the vein, or by infection.

Vascular - referring to the circulatory system.

Vascular fragility - a tendency of blood vessels to disintegrate due to brittleness, weakness, infection or disease.

Vasectomy - the process of cutting the vas deferens, which normally carries sperm from the testicles to the penis, for contraceptive purposes.

Vasoconstrictor - an agent or drug that causes blood vessels to constrict or narrow.

Vasodilator - an agent or drug that dilates blood vessels.

Venereal - refers to a disease, infection or other event affecting the genital area.

Ventricle - one of the two lower chambers of the heart. The left ventricle pumps oxygenated blood through the body to nourish the tissues; the right ventricle pumps blood to the lungs to be reoxygenated.

Ventricular failure - failure of the ventricles to pump blood adequately, due to injury, weakness or disease.

Vertigo - severe dizziness.

Vesicle - a bladder, or bladder-like structure, as in the case of a blister or sac-like cavity; caused by friction, inflammation or infection.

Virus - a small particle considered borderline between living and non-living matter. Viruses consist of molecules that are composed of proteins and nucleic acids. When they gain access to a living cell, they can change the cell's usual functions and reproductive capacity. Some viruses are useful, others cause disease.

Vitamin toxicity - a form of poisoning that occurs when a person ingests excessive amounts of vitamins.

Vitreous humor - the semifluid substance contained in the eyeball behind the lens.

Void - the process of urinating.

Vulva - the external female genitalia.

W

Wart - a benign hard growth on the skin caused by a virus; also known as verruca. May occur anywhere on the body, but appears most frequently on the sole of the foot, where it is called a plantar wart.

Wet lung - lung filled with fluid.

White blood cell- leukocyte; a constituent of blood, formed in the bone marrow and the lymph glands. White blood cells defend the body against infection.

Wound culture - a laboratory procedure done to determine whether a wound is infected, and to identify the microorganism that causes the infection.

X

X-chromosome - a sex chromosome; if a fetus has two X-chromosomes in its genetic make-up, it will develop as a female.

Xeroderma - a skin condition which produces excessively dry skin.

Y

Y-chromosome - a sex chromosome; if a fetus has a Y-chromosome in its genetic makeup, it will develop as a male.

Yellow fever - an infectious disease that is transmitted by various species of mosquitoes that carry the causative organism. High fever and jaundice are the main symptoms.

Z

Zinc - a trace element that aids wound healing, and acts as a component of several body enzymes.

Zoonosis - an infection or infestation present in animals as well as in man.

1981 PERSONAL HEALTH DIARY

Doctor's appointments

Date	Doctor	Checkup or Complaint	Treatment given or advice

Dental care

Date	Dentist	Checkup or Complaint	Cleaning, Prophylaxis Treatment given

Prescriptions filled

Drug dose; how often	Doctor who ordered it	Reason for taking it	Date of purchase or refill

Nonprescription drugs

Drug	Reason for purchase (complaint)	Date purchased	Effect